AIRCRAFT MAINTENANCE AND REPAIR

● FIFTH EDITION ●

FRANK DELP
RALPH D. BENT
JAMES L. McKINLEY

GREGG DIVISION
McGRAW-HILL BOOK COMPANY

New York Atlanta Dallas St. Louis San Francisco Auckland
Bogotá Guatemala Hamburg Lisbon London
Madrid Mexico Milan Montreal New Delhi Panama
Paris San Juan São Paulo Singapore Sydney Tokyo Toronto

AVIATION TECHNOLOGY SERIES

Aircraft Powerplants, Bent/McKinley
Aircraft Maintenance and Repair, Delp/Bent/McKinley
Aircraft Basic Science, Bent/McKinley
Aircraft Electricity and Electronics, Bent/McKinley

Sponsoring Editor: D. Eugene Gilmore
Editing Supervisor: Mitsy Kovacs
Design and Art Supervisor: Patricia Lowy
Production Supervisor: Priscilla Taguer

Text Designer: Phyllis Lerner
Cover Photograph: Michel Tcherevkoff/The Image Bank

Library of Congress Cataloging-in-Publication Data

Delp, Frank
  Aircraft maintenance and repair.
Bent's name appeared first on the earlier ed.

  Includes index.
  1. Airplanes—Maintenance and repair. I. Bent, Ralph D. II.
McKinley, James L.   III. Bent, Ralph D.   Aircraft maintenance
and repair. IV. Title.
TL671.9.D44   1986   629.134′6   86-21310
ISBN 0-07-004798-7

Aircraft Maintenance and Repair, Fifth Edition

  2 3 4 5 6 7 8 9 0   SEMSEM   8 9 3 2 1 0 9 8 7

ISBN 0-07-004798-7

CONTENTS

PREFACE

Aircraft Maintenance and Repair is designed to provide aviation students with the theoretical and practical knowledge required to qualify for certification as FAA airframe mechanics in accordance with Federal Aviation Regulations (FAR). This text covers the subjects categorized in the FAR under Airframe Structures and Airframe Systems and Components and should be used as a study text in connection with classroom discussions, demonstrations, and practical application in the shop and on aircraft.

Aircraft Maintenance and Repair is one of four textbooks in the McGraw-Hill Aviation Technology Series. The other books in the series are *Aircraft Powerplants, Aircraft Basic Science,* and *Aircraft Electricity and Electronics.* Used together, these texts provide information dealing with all prominent phases of aircraft maintenance technology.

In preparing this edition, the authors reviewed FAR Parts 65 and 147, Advisor Circular (AC) 65-2D, AC 65-15A, and AC 43.13-1A&2A to ensure that all required areas of study were included. Related Federal Aviation Regulations and the recommendations and suggestions of aviation maintenance instructors, aircraft manufacturers, aviation operators, and maintenance facilities were given full consideration in the revision of this text.

This revised edition retains all material from the previous edition relating to structures and systems that are employed on current operational aircraft. In addition, information dealing with expanding and emerging maintenance-related technologies has been incorporated to provide a comprehensive source of information for the aviation student, technician, mechanic, and instructor.

Each topic covered in this series of texts is explained in a logical sequence so students may advance step-by-step and build a solid foundation for performing aviation maintenance activities. Students' understanding of the explanations and descriptions given in the text should be enhanced by the use of numerous photographs, line drawings, and charts. Review questions at the end of each chapter will enable students to check their knowledge of the information presented.

In addition to being a classroom and shop instruction text, the book is valuable for home study and as an on-the-job reference for the mechanic. The materials in this text and in others in the series constitute a major source of technical knowledge for technical schools, vocational schools, high schools, industrial education divisions of colleges and universities, and training departments of aircraft factories and airlines.

Although this text is designed to provide information for the training of aviation personnel, the user must realize that each product and aircraft manufacturer establishes guidelines and procedures for the correct use and maintenance of their product or aircraft. Therefore, it is the responsibility of the user of the text to determine and follow the specific procedures recommended by the manufacturer when handling a specific product or when working on a specific aircraft or component.

Frank Delp
Ralph D. Bent
James L. McKinley

Acknowledgments

The authors wish to express appreciation to the following organizations for their generous assistance in providing illustrations and technical information for this text: Aeronetics, Division of AAR Corp., Elk Grove Village, IL; Aeroquip Corp., Jackson, MI; Air Transport Association of America, Washington, DC; Airbus Industries of North America, Inc., New York, NY; Aircraft Tools, Inc., Los Angeles, CA; AiResearch Manufacturing Co., Division of Garrett Corporation, Torrance, CA; Airpath Instrument Co., Kansas City, MO; Aluminum Company of America, Pittsburgh, PA; Anderson Equipment Co., Los Angeles, CA; Ayers Corporation, Albany, GA; Beech Aircraft Co., Wichita, KS; Bell Helicopter Textron Inc., Subsidiary of Textron Inc., Fort Worth, TX; Bendix Corp., Flight Systems Division, Teterboro, NJ; Boeing Co., Renton, WA; Boeing Commercial Airplane Co., Division of the Boeing Company, Seattle, WA; Boeing Vertol Company, Philadelphia, PA; British Aerospace, Civil Aircraft Division, London, England; Canadair Inc., Windsor Locks, CT; Ceconite, Inc., Los Angeles, CA; Cessna Aircraft Co., Wichita, KS; Chadwick-Helmuth Co., Inc., El Monte, CA; Cherry Aerospace Fasteners, Cherry Division of Textron, Inc., Santa Ana, CA; Christen Industries, Afton, WY; Cleveland Twist Drill, Cleveland, OH; Continental Airlines, Los Angeles, CA; DeVilbiss Co., Los Angeles, CA; DoAll Co., Des Plaines, IL; Douglas Aircraft Co., McDonnell Douglas Corp., Long Beach, CA; Edo Corp., College Point, NY; Embraer Aircraft Corporation, Ft. Lauderdale, FL; Embry-Riddle Aeronautical University, Daytona Beach, FL; Fairchild Industries, Germantown, MD; Federal Aviation Administration, Washington, DC; Fenwal, Inc., Ashland, MA; Fokker Aircraft U.S.A., Inc., Alexandria, VA; Flight Safety International, Flushing, NY; General Dynamics, San Diego, CA; Goodyear Aerospace Corp., Akron, OH; Grumman American Aviation, Savannah, GA; Hi-Shear Corporation, Torrance, CA; Houston Chemical Co., Houston, TX; Walter Kidde & Co., Wilson, NC; Kollsman Instrument Corp., Merrimac, NH; L-Tec Welding & Cutting Systems, Florence, SC; Lake Aircraft, Laconia, NH; Lincoln Electric Co., Cleveland, OH; Lockheed California Co., Division of Lockheed Corporation, Burbank, CA; McCreary Tire & Rubber Company, Indiana, PA; McDonnell Douglas Helicopter Company, Culver City, CA; Monogram/Aerospace Fasteners, Los Angeles, CA; Mooney Aircraft Corporation, Kerrville, TX; Nagel Aircraft Co., Torrance, CA; National Telephone and Supply Co., Cleveland, OH; Northrop Corp., Los Angeles, CA; Northrop University, Inglewood, CA; Olympic Fastening Systems, Inc., Downey, CA; Parker-Hannifan Corp., Cleveland, OH; Piper Aircraft Corp., Vero Beach, FL; Pyrotector, Inc., Hingham, MA; Randolph Products Co., Carlstadt, NJ; Razorback Fabrics, Inc., Manila, AR; Ren Plastics, East Lansing, MI; Robinson Helicopter Company, Torrance, CA; Rockwell Manufacturing Co., Power Tool Division, Pittsburgh, PA; Rohm and Haas Company, Philadelphia, PA; Schweizer Aircraft Corp., Elmira, NY; Scott Aviation, A Figgie International Company, Lancaster, NY; Sierra Engineering Co., Division of Cap Tech, Inc., Sierra Madre, CA; Sikorsky Aircraft, Division of United Technologies, Stratford, CT; Singer Company, Los Angeles, CA; Soaring Society of America, Hobbs, NM; Sperry Vickers Division, Sperry Rand Corp., Torrance, CA; Stanley Tools, New Britain, CT; Stits Poly-Fiber Aircraft Coatings, Riverside, CA; Systron-Donner Corp., Safety Systems Division, Concord, CA; Torrance Municipal Airport, Torrance, CA; U.M.A., Inc., Elkton, VA; United Air Lines, Los Angeles, CA; U.S. Industrial Tool & Supply Co., Plymouth, MI; U.S. Paint, Division of Grow Group, Inc., St. Louis, MO; Weatherhead Co., Cleveland, OH; Wedgelock Co., No. Hollywood, CA; Westland Inc., Arlington, VA; Wiss Manufacturing Co., Newark, NJ.

1 AIRCRAFT STRUCTURES

● INTRODUCTION

A thorough understanding of the structural components of aircraft and the stresses imposed on those components is essential for the certificated aircraft mechanic. Such understanding assures that the mechanic will be careful that repairs are designed and made in a manner which will restore the damaged part to its original strength. It is the purpose of this chapter to familiarize the mechanic with the principal structural components of various aircraft and to discuss the loads that are applied to these components during operation of the aircraft.

Principal Aircraft Structures

The principal aircraft load-carrying sections or components include the fuselage, lifting surfaces, control surfaces, stabilizers, and landing gear. The fuselage is the central aircraft component which has a cockpit or flight deck for the crew and a section for the passengers and cargo. The lifting surfaces include the wings on airplanes and gliders and the main rotors of helicopters. Control surfaces include ailerons, rudders, elevators, flaps, spoilers, and trim tabs. Stabilizers are used to improve the pitch and yaw stability of the aircraft. The landing gear may be fixed or retractable and may use skids, wheels, floats, or skis, depending on the type of aircraft and the operating terrain.

The **stresses** (effects of applied forces) to which structural members are subjected are **compression, tension, torsion, bending,** and **shear.** The following definitions will serve to aid the student in understanding the nature of each type of stress:

Compression is the stress that tends to crush or press together. The landing gear of an aircraft is subjected to compression when the aircraft is landing.

Tension is the stress in a member when a force tends to elongate or stretch it. A bolt tightened to hold parts firmly together is subjected to tension. A cable is in tension when it is used to lift an aircraft or engine.

Torsion is the stress of twisting. Rotating shafts under load are subjected to torsion.

Bending is actually a combination of compression and tension. When a bar is bent, the portion of the bar toward the outside of the bend is subjected to tension and the portion of the bar toward the inside of the bend is subjected to compression. The wings of an aircraft are subjected to bending stresses.

Shear is the stress developed when a force tends to cause a layer of material to slide along an adjacent layer. When two strips of metal are joined by means of rivets or bolts, a tensile force applied to the opposite ends of the assembled strips in a manner tending to pull them apart will produce shear stress in the rivets or bolts.

The effect of overstressing a part or assembly to the point where a permanent deformation takes place is called **strain.** If an aircraft part has become strained, the part very likely will no longer be airworthy.

When an airplane is designed, the loads which are likely to be applied to parts or assemblies of the airplane during operation are carefully computed and analyzed by engineers. This process is called **stress analysis.** The performance of the stress analysis ensures that the airplane will perform according to its approved specifications without danger of failure.

Nomenclature and Definitions

The drawings of Fig. 1-1 show a light airplane with the various components identified. Figure 1-2 shows photographs with additional labeling to identify parts of more modern and larger aircraft.

The definitions given below are provided as a convenient reference for the components of aircraft and some of the relationships between components. A detailed discussion of these definitions can be found in the companion text entitled *Aircraft Basic Science.*

Aileron One of a pair of movable control surfaces attached to the trailing edge of each wing tip. The purpose of the ailerons is to control the airplane in roll by creating unequal or opposing lifting forces on opposite sides of the airplane. Large jet airplanes often employ double sets of ailerons, a small inboard set for cruise speeds and a larger outboard set for approach and landing speeds.

Angle of incidence The angle between the chord of an airfoil and the longitudinal axis of an airplane.

Angle of stabilizer setting The angle of incidence of a vertical or horizontal stabilizer.

Angle of sweep The angle between a reference line in a swept or tapered airfoil and a given reference line established for the purpose. For fixed airfoils, the angle is measured between the lateral axis of the airplane and the reference line of the airfoil, usually the mean chord line.

Antidrag wire A wire in certain kinds of wing struc-

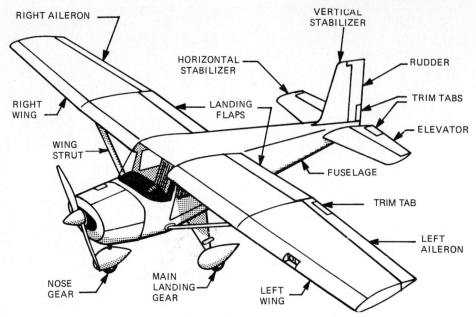

RIGHT AILERON

HORIZONTAL STABILIZER

VERTICAL STABILIZER

RUDDER

TRIM TABS

ELEVATOR

RIGHT WING

LANDING FLAPS

FUSELAGE

WING STRUT

TRIM TAB

LEFT AILERON

NOSE GEAR

MAIN LANDING GEAR

LEFT WING

FIG. 1-1 Light airplane with nomenclature.

tures, running from an inboard point near the trailing edge to an outboard point near the leading edge, designed to resist forces acting on the wing in the direction of flight.

Antilift wires Same as landing wires.

Balanced control surface A control surface that is in a desired condition of equilibrium about its hinge axis. Such a surface can be balanced for either static or aerodynamic conditions.

Balancing tab A tab so linked that when the control surface to which it is attached is deflected, the tab is deflected in an opposite direction, creating a force that aids in moving the larger surface.

Boom (also **Tailboom**) A tubular or truss structure extending aft from the aircraft fuselage. Normally found on helicopters to support the tail rotor and its systems or to support control surfaces on an aircraft having a pusher propeller installation.

Bulkhead A vertical structural member that, with other bulkheads, carries major structural loads in the fuselage. Bulkheads often include walls or partial walls which separate fuselage compartments from one another. Lighter frames or formers are used for support between bulkheads.

Cabane An arrangement of struts used to support a wing above the fuselage of an airplane.

Canard An aircraft or aircraft configuration having its horizontal stabilizing and control surfaces in front of the wing or wings.

Cantilever A beam or member supported at or near one end only, without external bracing.

Center section The middle or central section of an airplane wing to which the outer wing panels are attached.

Chord line A straight line connecting the leading edge and the trailing edge of an airfoil.

Cockpit On small aircraft, the area occupied by the pilot and passengers. On cabin airplanes, if the pilot's compartment is separated from the rest of the cabin, it is often called the cockpit.

Cockpit canopy A transparent cover for the cockpit.

Control cables Cables connecting the control levers with the control surfaces.

Control stick A vertical lever by means of which the pilot operates the longitudinal and lateral control surfaces of the airplane. The elevator is operated by a fore-and-aft movement of the stick, and the ailerons are moved by a sideways movement of the stick.

Control surface A movable airfoil or surface, such as an aileron, elevator, ruddervator, flap, trim tab, or rudder, used to control the attitude or motion of an aircraft in flight.

Control wheel A wheel or semiwheel used in connection with the control column in an airplane. Rotation of the wheel operates the ailerons for control about the roll axis. Fore-and-aft movement of the wheel operates the elevators to pitch the airplane about the lateral axis.

Cowling A removable cover or housing placed over or around an aircraft component or section, especially an engine.

Decalage The difference between the angles of incidence for two airfoils on the same airplane. It generally refers to the two wings of a biplane.

Dihedral angle The angle between the aircraft lateral axis and the projection of the wing axis of the airplane. If the tip of the wing is higher than the root section, the dihedral angle is positive; if lower, the dihedral angle is negative.

Drag strut Any strut used to resist drag or antidrag forces. In a wing it is a fore-and-aft compression member. In landing gear it is a strut that runs diagonally up into the airplane to resist drag forces.

Drag wire A wire in certain kinds of wing structures running from a forward inboard point to an aft outboard point to resist drag forces.

2

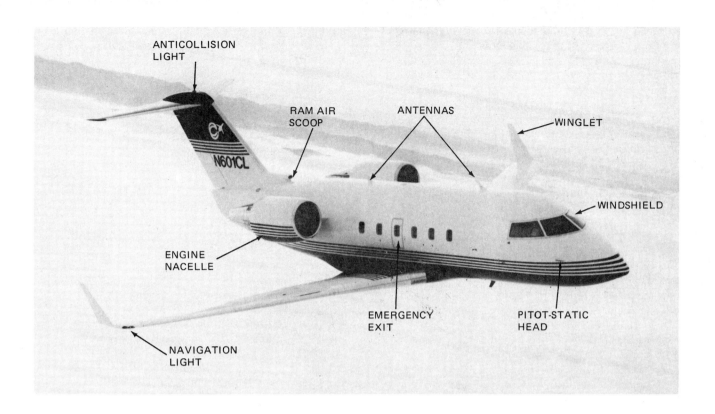

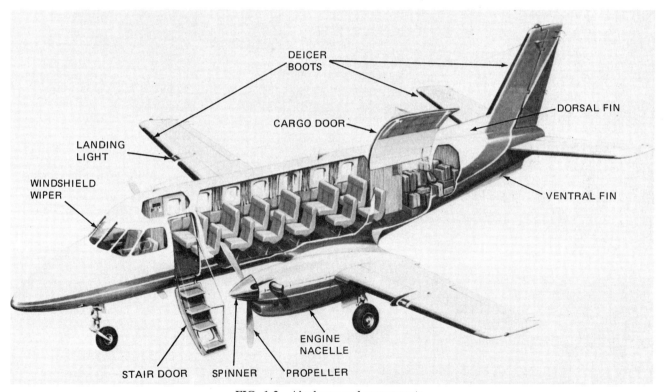

FIG. 1-2   Airplanes and components.

Elevator A movable auxiliary airfoil or control surface designed to control the pitch attitude of the aircraft and the angle of attack of the wing. It controls rotation about the lateral axis.

Elevons Control surfaces which serve the functions of both elevators and ailerons on all-wing and delta-wing aircraft.

Fairing A piece, part, or structure, having a smooth streamlined contour, used to cover a nonstreamlined object or to smooth a junction.

Fin A vertical stabilizer.

Firewall A fireproof or fire-resistant wall or bulkhead separating an engine from the rest of the aircraft structure to prevent the spreading of a fire from the engine compartment.

Flap A hinged, pivoted, or sliding airfoil or plate, normally located at the trailing edge of a wing, extended or deflected downward to increase the lift and/or drag. It is generally used for takeoff or landing.

Frame A vertical structural member which supports the stringers and skin of a wood or metal fuselage and gives the fuselage shape.

Fuselage The main or central structure of a heavier-than-air aircraft, typically elongated and approximately streamlined, which carries the crew and passengers and to which the wings are attached.

Gap The distance between the chords of two superposed airfoils.

Horizontal stabilizer A stabilizer mounted horizontally on an airplane affording longitudinal stability and to which elevators are attached.

Horn A short lever fastened to a control surface to which an operating cable or rod is attached.

Inspection door A small door used especially for inspection of the interior of an airplane.

Intercostal A rib or internal brace inside a box beam spar.

Interplane strut A strut between two wings or other surfaces.

Jury strut An auxiliary strut that braces a main strut or struts.

Landing gear The understructure that supports the weight of the airplane on the ground, also called **alighting gear.**

Landing wires Wires or cables that brace the wings against the forces that are opposite to the normal direction of lift. These wires attach to the upper wing above the fuselage and to the lower wing near the outboard end on a biplane.

Leading edge The foremost or front edge of an airfoil or a propeller blade. The rearmost edge is called the trailing edge.

Lift strut A structural member attached at one end to some midpoint of a wing or stabilizer and at the other end to the fuselage. This external structural member holds the wing or stabilizer in a fixed position relative to the fuselage and carries structural loads between the surface and the fuselage.

Lift wires Wires or cables that brace the wings against the forces of lift. They are also called **flying wires.**

Longeron A principal longitudinal (fore-and-aft) member of the framing of an aircraft fuselage, usually continuous across a number of points of support.

Main rotor The principal rotating airfoil used to generate lift and support the weight of a rotorcraft. A rotorcraft may have one or two main rotors. In a helicopter the main rotor generates propulsive thrust along with lift.

Nose wheel A wheel placed ahead of the main landing gear of an aircraft to support the weight of the forward portion of the airframe.

Plating The heavy metal skin, often tapered in thickness, used to cover the wings and other parts of large aircraft.

Rudder A hinged or movable airfoil used to control the yawing motion of an aircraft.

Rudder pedal Either one of a pair of cockpit pedals for operating a rudder or other directional-control device.

Ruddervator A control surface, set at a pronounced dihedral (forming a wide V), that serves as both a rudder and elevator.

Shock absorber A device built into the landing gear to reduce the shock during landing or taking off.

Skid A fixed type of landing gear made of tubular and/or flat structures, normally associated with helicopters.

Slat An auxiliary airfoil contoured to the leading edge of a wing when closed. When open, it forms the slot to improve airflow at high angles of attack.

Slot A fixed opening in the leading edge of an airfoil which is used to direct airflow over the surface at high angles of attack to improve control and lift at these attitudes.

Span The maximum distance, measured parallel to the lateral axis, from tip to tip of any surface such as a wing or stabilizer.

Spar A primary structural member of a wing, stabilizer, control surface, rotor, or other aerodynamic surface.

Spinner A fairing of approximately conic or paraboloidal shape, fitted coaxially with the propeller hub and spinning with the propeller.

Spoiler A device located on the top surface of a wing which can be extended to reduce or "spoil" the lift of the wing. This may be used to control the aircraft rate of descent, lateral movement (roll), or to increase braking effectiveness on landing.

Stabilator A horizontal control surface that is designed to serve as both a stabilizer and an elevator. It is moved about its hinge line by means of the pilot's control.

Stabilizer A fixed or adjustable airfoil or vane that provides stability for an aircraft.

Stagger With two or more superposed objects or objects fixed in a row, the advance or the amount of advance of one object ahead of another. The amount of advance of one wing of a biplane ahead of the other, of a compressor blade ahead of another, or of one rotor of tandem-rotor helicopter ahead of the other.

Stagger wire On a biplane, a diagonal wire, usually one of a pair forming an X, running fore and aft between the two wings and helping to maintain a constant stagger.

Stringer A longitudinal structural member installed between fuselage frames and formers to give support and strength to the skin.

Strut A supporting brace that bears compression loads, tension loads, or both, as in a fuselage between the longerons or in a landing gear to transmit the airplane loads.

Sweepback The backward slant from root to tip of an aerodynamic surface.

Tailboom See **Boom.**

Tail rotor The small rotor mounted on a shaft at the tail of a helicopter to counteract the torque of the main rotor and provide directional control for the helicopter. Sometimes it is referred to as an **antitorque rotor.**

Tail skid On certain older airplanes, a skid attached to the rear part of the airplane on the underside and supporting the tail.

Tail wheel A wheel at the tail of certain airplanes used to support the tail section on the ground. A tail wheel may be steerable, retractable, fixed, castering, etc.

Trailing edge The aft edge of an airfoil surface.

Trim tab A tab attached to the trailing edge of an airfoil, used to aid in control surface operation.

Wing rib A chordwise member used to give the wing its shape and to transmit the load from the surface covering to the spars.

Wing spar A principal spanwise member in the structure of a wing.

Wing tip The outer extremity of a wing.

Note: The following discussion focuses primarily on fixed-wing aircraft and is generally applicable to rotary-wing aircraft. A later section in this chapter addresses some of the structures unique to rotary-wing aircraft.

● FUSELAGES

The **fuselage** is the body to which the wings and the tail unit of an aircraft are attached and which provides space for the crew, passengers, cargo, controls, and other items, depending upon the size and design of the aircraft. It should have the smallest streamline form consistent with desired capacity and aerodynamic qualities of the aircraft. If an airplane is of the single-engine type, the engine is usually mounted in the nose of the fuselage, and the engine nacelle must be of such a construction that the engine accessories such as the carburetor, magnetos, ignition leads, strainers, fuel lines, and other parts are easily accessible for service and inspection.

The fuselage must have points of attachment for the wing or wings, tail surfaces, and landing gear so arranged and installed that they can be inspected, removed, repaired, and replaced easily. The fuselage must be strong enough at the points of attachment to withstand flying and landing loads. Finally it should be shaped to offer low resistance to the air and provide good vision for the pilot.

The design of many large aircraft is such that the wing structure extends through the fuselage, thus eliminating the necessity for the fuselage to carry strictly wing-generated loads and stresses. It is merely necessary for the fuselage attachment to have sufficient strength so there can be no failure under any condition which may occur in flight. A discussion of wing design is presented later in this chapter.

The structure of the fuselage should be strong enough to protect the passengers and crew in the event of a complete turnover. Emergency exits must be provided, the number being determined by the capacity of the cabin. The requirements for emergency exits are covered in Federal Aviation Regulations (FAR) Part 25.

Types of Fuselages

In general, we can say that fuselages are classified in three principal types, depending upon the method by which stresses are transmitted to the structure. The three types according to this classification are **truss, semimonocoque,** and **monocoque.**

A **truss** is an assemblage of members forming a rigid framework, which may consist of bars, beams, rods, tubes, wires, etc. The truss-type fuselage may be subclassified as the **Pratt truss** and the **Warren truss.** The primary strength members of both Pratt and Warren trusses are the four longerons. As defined previously, the longeron is a principal longitudinal member of the aircraft fuselage. In the truss-type fuselage, lateral bracing is placed at intervals. The lateral structures may be classed as bulkheads, although this is not strictly true from the technical standpoint; the spaces between the bulkheads are called **bays.**

A **Pratt truss** similar to the type used in present aircraft with tubular fuselage members is shown in Fig. 1-3. In the original Pratt truss the longerons were connected with rigid vertical and lateral members called struts, but the diagonal members were made of strong steel wire and were designed to carry tension only. In the Pratt truss shown in Fig. 1-3, the diagonal members are rigid and can carry either tension or compression.

A **Warren truss** is illustrated in Fig. 1-4. In this construction, the longerons are connected with only diagonal members. Normally, all members in the truss are capable of carrying both tension and compression. When the load is acting in one direction, compression loads are carried by every other member while the alternate members carry the tension loads. When the load is reserved, the members that are carrying tension previously now carry compression and those that were carrying compression now carry tension. This reversal of loading is shown in Fig. 1-5.

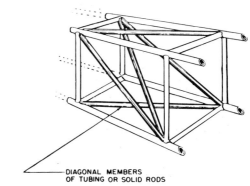

DIAGONAL MEMBERS OF TUBING OR SOLID RODS

FIG. 1-3 Pratt truss.

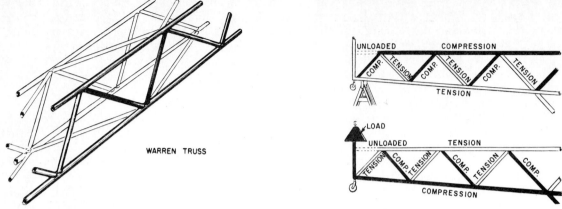

WARREN TRUSS

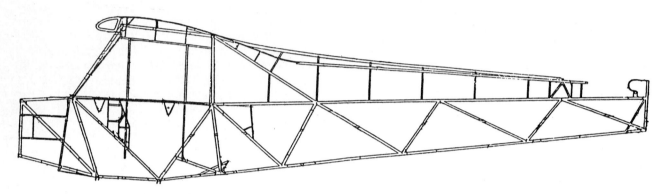

UNLOADED   COMPRESSION

COMP. TENSION COMP. TENSION COMP. TENSION

TENSION

LOAD

UNLOADED   TENSION

TENSION COMP. TENSION COMP. TENSION COMP.

COMPRESSION

FIG. 1-4 Warren truss.

FIG. 1-5 Reversal of loading on a truss.

FIG. 1-6 A steel tube fuselage using a Warren-type truss. *(Piper Aircraft Co.)*

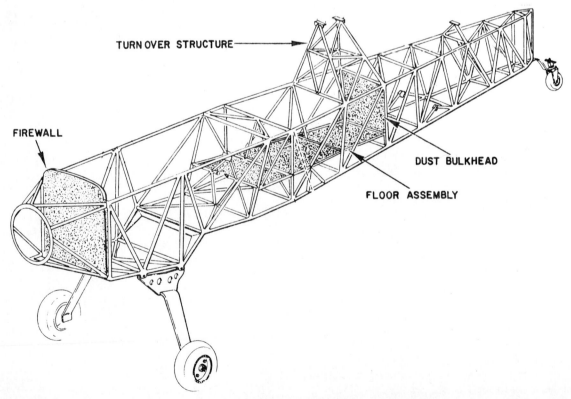

TURN OVER STRUCTURE

FIREWALL

DUST BULKHEAD

FLOOR ASSEMBLY

FIG. 1-7 A typical welded-steel fuselage. *(Schweizer)*

The determination as to the type of truss construction used in an aircraft may be academic in most cases, but if a modification to the aircraft truss structure is being considered, the type of construction can become important. In some aircraft it is very easy to identify the type of truss used, as shown in Fig. 1-6, which is clearly a Warren truss. Because of the location of structural attachments, the Pratt truss fuselage in Fig. 1-7 is somewhat disguised, but by careful examination the characteristic vertical and diagonal members can be identified. While these two fuselage structures are made of steel, it should be understood that a truss structure can be made of wood. aluminum, or any other structural material, according to the aircraft manufacturer's choice.

A **semimonocoque** structure consists of a framework of vertical and longitudinal members covered with a structural skin that carries a large percentage of the stresses imposed upon the structure. Figure 1-8 illustrates the construction of an all-metal semimonocoque tailboom. The vertical members of the tailboom are called **frames,** or **bulkheads.** Between the principal vertical members are lighter **formers,** or **rings,** to maintain the uniform shape of the structure. The longitudinal members are called **stringers,** and they serve to stiffen the metal skin and prevent it from bulging or buckling under severe stress.

The construction of a semimonocoque wood fuse-

FIG. 1-9 Semimonocoque wood fuselage.

lage is illustrated in Fig. 1-9. Although there are not many airplanes constructed in this manner, it is still important that the aircraft mechanic be aware of this type of construction and be prepared to make repairs if necessary. The bulkheads of the wooden semimonocoque fuselage are made of aircraft-quality plywood and are cut to a shape to fit the configuration of the fuselage. Between the bulkheads are longitudinal wooden stringers attached to the bulkheads by means of an approved glue. Small wooden corner blocks are often glued into the corners to provide reinforcement. Over the inner framework a strong skin of aircraft plywood is glued. A variety of manufacturing and repair techniques have been developed to hold the skin firmly in place while the glue sets (hardens). After such a fuselage is constructed, it is essential that the inside be thoroughly coated with spar varnish or some other waterproof protective material. One of the principal problems in the maintenance of wooden aircraft

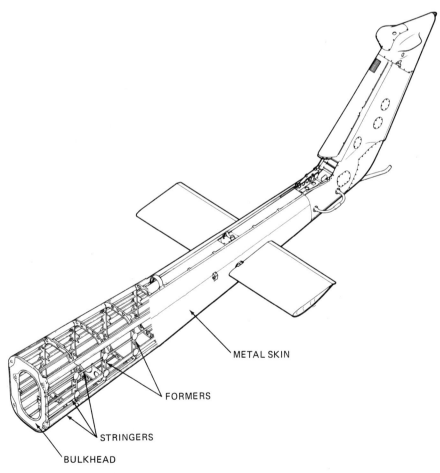

METAL SKIN

FORMERS

STRINGERS

BULKHEAD

FIG. 1-8 **Semimonocoque construction is employed in this helicopter tailboom.** *(Bell Textron)*

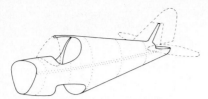

FIG. 1-10 Full monocoque metal fuselage.

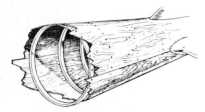

FIG. 1-11 A wooden monocoque structure.

structures is the slow deterioration resulting from the penetration of moisture through the protective coatings. Mechanics performing inspections on wood aircraft structures, particularly those which have not been kept in a dry hangar when not in use, must take great care to examine interior structures. Cases are on record where wings and control surfaces have failed in flight even though there was no evidence of deterioration on the outside. When moisture remains inside a wood structure for an appreciable length of time, the wood rots as a result of fungus which penetrates the wood cells.

A full monocoque fuselage, shown in Fig. 1-10, is one in which the fuselage skin carries all of the structural stresses. This construction merely involves the construction of a metal tube or cone without internal structural members. In some cases it is necessary to

have former rings to maintain the shape, but these do not carry the principal stresses imposed upon the structure. Very often this type of fuselage will be constructed by riveting two preformed halves together.

A wooden monocoque structure is illustrated in Fig. 1-11. It can be seen that this is merely a plywood shell with formers to hold the proper cylindrical or conical shape.

In many aircraft a mixture of construction types may be found. For example, an aircraft may have a steel tube cabin structure and a semimonocoque aft fuselage structure as in the Cessna Model 188 shown in Fig. 1-12.

General Construction of Fuselages

As explained previously, fuselages are designed with a variety of structural components. Truss-type fuselages consist of the rigid framework covered with fabric and dope, plywood, fiberglass, or metal. The aircraft shown in Fig. 1-13 have truss-type fuselages covered with fabric and dope.

The great majority of fuselages are all-metal and semimonocoque in construction. This applies to small, medium, and large aircraft. The interior structure to which the skin or plating is attached consists of longerons, frames, bulkheads, stringers, gussets, and possibly intercostal members riveted, bolted, or bonded together to form a rigid structure which shapes the fuselage. The skin or plating is riveted or bonded to the structure to form the complete unit. Views showing the construction of large aircraft fuselages are provided later in this chapter.

The types and thicknesses of materials used for covering the fuselage of a typical light airplane are shown in the drawings of Fig. 1-14. It will be noted that the thickness of the skin varies according to position on the fuselage. The required thickness of material for a given section of the fuselage is determined

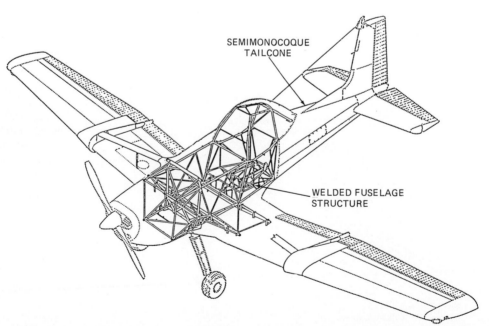

FIG. 1-12 Aircraft with a combination of steel tube and semimonocoque construction in its fuselage structure. (*Cessna Aircraft Co.*)

FIG. 1-13 Airplanes with truss-type fuselages.

by engineers during the design and stress analysis of the aircraft.

The number 2024 to describe the material refers to a particular aluminum alloy commonly used for aircraft structures. The letters and numbers following the initial numbers identify the condition of the material.

Fuselages for aircraft are designed with many similarities. The forward section of the fuselage usually contains the cockpit and passenger cabin. The shape of this section depends upon the passenger capacity and the performance specifications for the aircraft. The rear section, often referred to as the **tail cone,** is usually circular or rectangular in cross section and tapers toward the tail. Some aircraft are equipped with a sharp pointed fairing at the end of a tail cone called a "stinger." The function of the stinger is to reduce turbulence in airflow to the rear of the tail. This, in

turn, reduces drag. The drawings of Fig. 1-15 show the shapes of some fuselages for light aircraft.

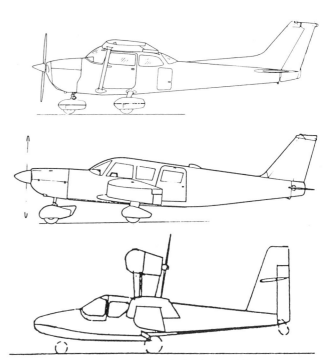

FIG. 1-15 Various light aircraft fuselage configurations. *(Cessna Aircraft Co., Piper Aircraft Co., Lake Aircraft Co.)*

Fuselage Components

Along with the bulkheads, formers, stringers, and skin, the aircraft fuselage incorporates many structurally reinforced areas to allow for the attachment of airframe components and to allow for openings in the fuselage for non-load-carrying items such as windows and doors. Components which are attached to the fuselage at reinforced areas include wings, landing gear, engines, stabilizers, jackpads, and antennas.

For the attachment of many components a simple doubler or gusset plate is used. This arrangement involves cutting sheet metal to the proper size for the required flight loads, shaping it to increase its rigidity, and attaching it to the fuselage in the area beneath the component being attached. An example of this type of reinforcement is a doubler placed between stringers to support the flight loads associated with the installation of a radio antenna as shown in Fig. 1-16.

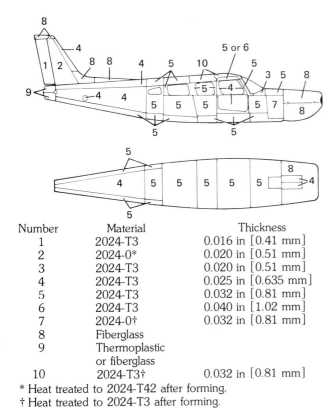

Number	Material	Thickness
1	2024-T3	0.016 in [0.41 mm]
2	2024-0*	0.020 in [0.51 mm]
3	2024-T3	0.020 in [0.51 mm]
4	2024-T3	0.025 in [0.635 mm]
5	2024-T3	0.032 in [0.81 mm]
6	2024-T3	0.040 in [1.02 mm]
7	2024-0†	0.032 in [0.81 mm]
8	Fiberglass	
9	Thermoplastic or fiberglass	
10	2024-T3†	0.032 in [0.81 mm]

* Heat treated to 2024-T42 after forming.
† Heat treated to 2024-T3 after forming.

FIG. 1-14 Materials and thicknesses for a light airplane fuselage. *(Piper Aircraft Corp.)*

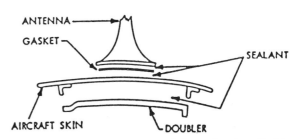

FIG. 1-16 A doubler is used to reinforce the aircraft skin where the antenna is installed.

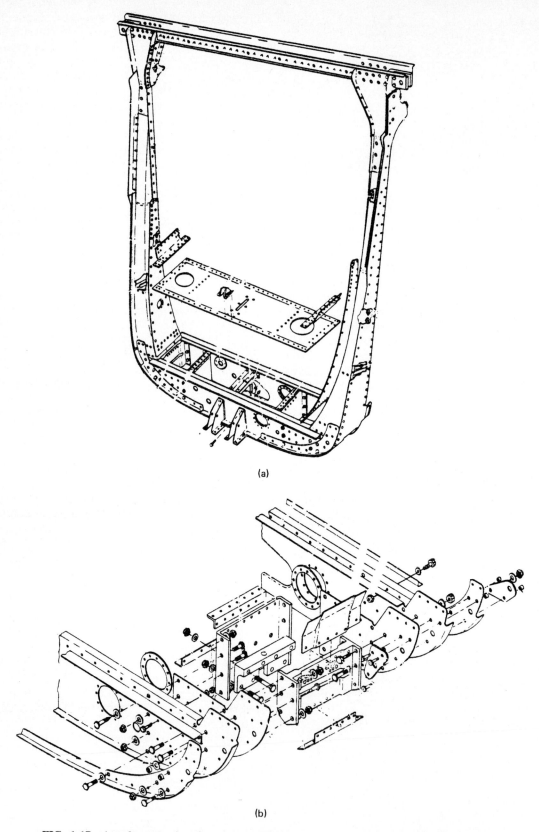

(a)

(b)

FIG. 1-17 Attachment points for wings and landing gear on a light aircraft fuselage structure. (a) Wing spar attachment. (b) Landing gear attachment area. Exploded view of landing gear attachment area. *(Cessna Aircraft Co.)*

Some attachment points require the use of special fittings such as forgings, castings, welded assemblies, or heavy sheet-metal structures to be able to withstand large loads such as occur through the wing and landing gear attachment points. An example of this type of arrangement is shown in Fig. 1-17. Note that the forgings are bolted to the surrounding bulkhead components and that the bulkhead components consist of several reinforcing layers of sheet-metal structure. The top portion of the bulkhead assembly includes the carry-through member for the aircraft front spar. This is a thick, formed sheet-metal member that is riveted to the bulkhead vertical members.

The aircraft fuselage structure must be designed to allow for openings for doors, windshields, and windows. This requires the use of thick sheet-metal structures or intricate steel tube structures in the area of these openings to allow the operational loads to flow around these openings. As a simple example of this redirection of loads, note in Fig. 1-18 how the Pratt truss design had to be changed to allow for the door opening. Another example is shown in Fig. 1-19 where a sheet-metal doubler is used around the window of a transport aircraft.

The structure of the aircraft vertical stabilizer may be an integral part of the aircraft fuselage as shown in Fig. 1-18, or the vertical and horizontal stabilizers may be attached to castings or reinforced bulkheads by some fastening means, such as bolts, so that they can be easily removed for replacement or repair operations.

Transport Aircraft Fuselages

Fuselages for transport aircraft generally include a section forward of the main cabin to provide a streamlined nose, a main cabin section which is almost uniformly cylindrical in shape, and a tail section which tapers to a minimal size at the extreme rear end. These shapes are illustrated in Fig. 1-20.

Many aircraft designs are now incorporating components which are termed "fail-safe." These major structural fittings are made in two parts and joined together by riveting or bonding. Each half of the two structural parts is capable of carrying the full required structural load of the assembly. With this design philosophy, the failure of one of the fitting components will not result in a structural failure of the attachment fitting which could result in separation of components in flight. This type of design is found on many

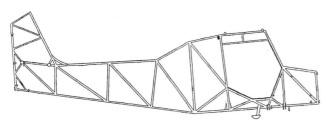

FIG. 1-18 In this aircraft the Pratt truss has been modified to allow a door to be placed on the side of the fuselage. *(Champion Aircraft Co.)*

corporate and transport aircraft and is illustrated in Fig. 1-21.

In some large aircraft, a fail-safe feature is also incorporated into the metal skin. For example, on a DC-8, titanium rip-stop doublers are used to reinforce the skin at strategic fuselage frames and at each door and window. In addition, beaded doublers are used in the window belt area forward of the front spar.

Because of their size, transport aircraft fuselages are commonly constructed by first building subassemblies of long panels several feet high as shown in Fig. 1-22. These panels are then joined on a mating jig to form the circular shape of a fuselage section as shown in Fig. 1-23. The fuselage is then assembled by connecting the forward, mid, and aft fuselage sections.

The forward section tapers the cross section of the fuselage to the front of the aircraft. This section has provisions for the flight crew stations.

The transport fuselage contains one or more midsection assemblies. These midsection assemblies are basically circular in shape with a constant cross-section size. The midsection contains structures to connect the fuselage to the wing and may include landing gear attachment points.

The aft section changes the cross-sectional shape of the fuselage into the size and shape necessary to join with the fuselage afterbody or tail cone. The afterbody or tail cone is the point of attachment for the aft flight control surfaces and, depending on the aircraft design, may also incorporate an engine installation area.

The fuselage sections are joined to complete the basic assembly of the fuselage. This assembly process for each of the sections and the mating of the sections is illustrated in Figs. 1-24 through 1-31.

Note from the illustrations of fuselage construction that a large number of special fixtures are used in the assembly of an aircraft fuselage. These fixtures allow for precision alignment of the structural components as each subassembly is put together. Various fixtures are also used to assure proper alignment of the subassemblies as they are joined to form the fuselage sections, and additional fixtures are used to join the sections into the completed fuselage.

The materials, type, and number of structural components used in the construction of transport aircraft fuselages vary throughout the structure according to the structural strength required and the thickness of material that is desired and acceptable. For example, the aft portion of a DC-8 fuselage skin is a 7075-T aluminum alloy, while the forward section is covered with 2014-T4 material. The skin thicknesses used typically vary from 0.05 in (inches) [1.27 mm (millimeters)] to 0.08 in [2.03 mm], depending on the type of aluminum alloy used and the stresses imposed on a particular area.

Prior to assembly, many of the fuselage components are treated to inhibit corrosion of the metal. These treatments may include the use of anodizing, sealants, and primer coatings. The selection of the metal alloys used in the construction is also a factor in control of corrosion. With proper selection of the metals that will be in contact with each other, dissimilar metal

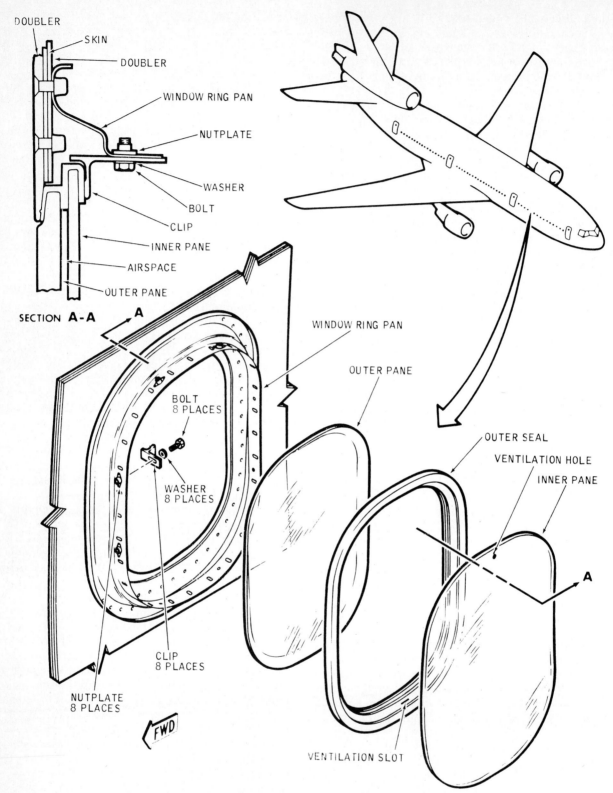

DOUBLER
SKIN
DOUBLER
WINDOW RING PAN
NUTPLATE
WASHER
BOLT
CLIP
INNER PANE
AIRSPACE
OUTER PANE

SECTION **A-A**

A

WINDOW RING PAN

OUTER PANE

BOLT
8 PLACES

WASHER
8 PLACES

OUTER SEAL

VENTILATION HOLE

INNER PANE

A

CLIP
8 PLACES

NUTPLATE
8 PLACES

FWD

VENTILATION SLOT

FIG. 1-19   Passenger compartment window.   (McDonnell Douglas Corp.)

FIG. 1-20   Fuselage shapes for large aircraft.

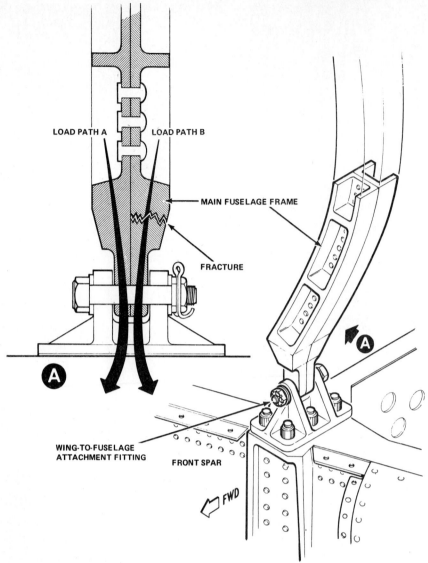

FIG. 1-21 A fall-safe design provides two load-carrying paths for operational loads. *(Canadair Inc.)*

corrosion can be reduced or eliminated. Also, by properly designing the fuselage component assemblies, areas which might trap moisture and other corrosive substances can be eliminated.

The assembly process for a fuselage may include the use of hand-operated tools, special power equipment, mechanical fasteners, and bonding materials. Many areas of the fuselage do not adapt well to the use of heavy stationary machinery, so hand-held tools must be used to connect various portions of the fuselage structure. These tools include drills, riveting guns, metal shavers, and tools for the installation of special fasteners.

Where possible, large stationary machines are used to assemble components. These machines can perform several operations in a rapid sequence. For example, the riveting of a fuselage section assembly is shown in Fig. 1-32. The large machine in the picture is a Manco-Crispin semiautomatic riveting machine by

which shaved riveting is accomplished. By means of these machines, a uniform fastening is made while a clamping action holds the members together under a pressure of 1720 psi (pounds per square inch) [11 859 kPa (kilopascals)]. On the external surface of the skin, the rivets are upset into countersunk cavities and then they are shaved smooth. This results in a very smooth, low-drag surface on the outside of the fuselage and is illustrated in Fig. 1-33. Sealing qualities and fatigue life are greatly improved by this method of riveting.

Bonding of structural components has been used for several years and has some unique advantages over conventional mechanical fasteners. First, it distributes the structural loads evenly over the full bonding area and does not require that the structures be disturbed by the drilling of holes. Second, the bonding agents can incorporate corrosion-inhibiting materials in their mixture and reduce or eliminate the possibility of corrosion occurring in the bonded seams. Last, by prop-

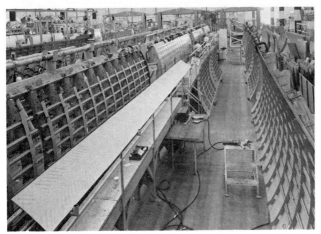

FIG. 1-22 Fabrication of fuselage panels. *(McDonnell Douglas Corp.)*

FIG. 1-23 Rear section of DC-8 fuselage. *(McDonnell Douglas Corp.)*

FIG. 1-24 Handling devices for large fuselage panels. *(Northrop Corp.)*

FIG. 1-25 Assembly of major fuselage section. *(Northrop Corp.)*

FIG. 1-26 Assembly of the Boeing 747 nose section. *(Northrop Corp.)*

15

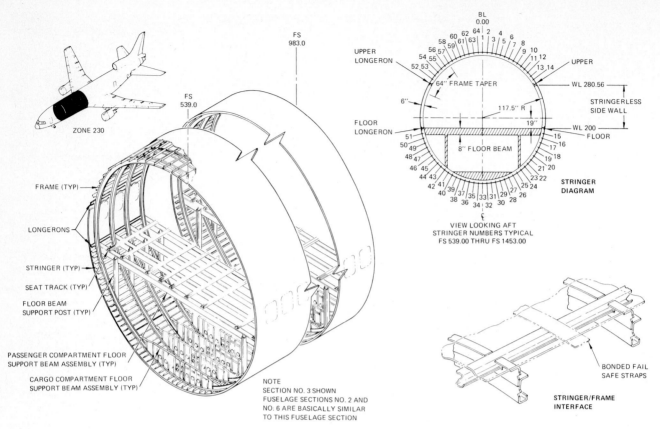

FIG. 1-27   No. 3 section of the L-1011.   *(Lockheed California Co.)*

FIG. 1-28   Structure of tail section.   *(McDonnell Douglas Corp.)*

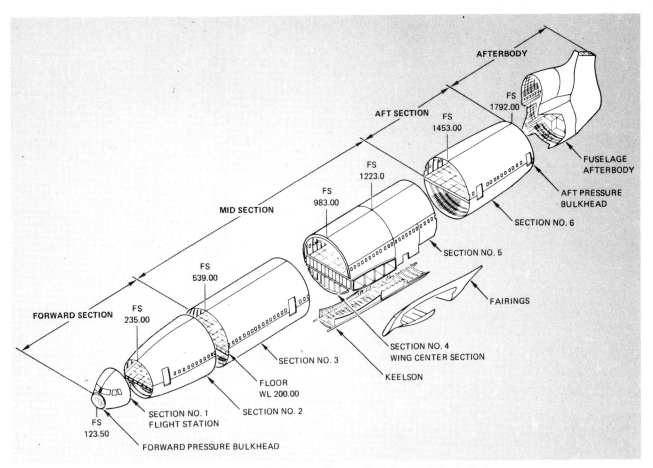

FIG. 1-29   L-1011 fuselage sections.   *(Lockheed California Co.)*

FIG. 1-30   Mating fuselage sections.   *(McDonnell Douglas Corp.)*

FIG. 1-31   Joining nose section to fuselage.   *(McDonnell Douglas Corp.)*

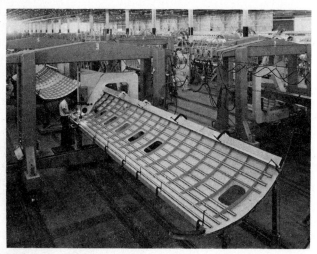

FIG. 1-32   Riveting a fuselage section.   *(McDonnell Douglas Corp.)*

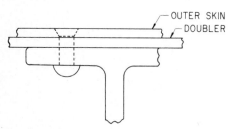

FIG. 1-33   Shaved-rivet installation.

erly designing the components, the slight amount of bonding agent that flows out from between components acts as a deflective barrier and prevents moisture or other substances from getting into the bonded seams and starting corrosion.

● WINGS

The purpose of this section is to identify the basic types of wing design and construction that can be found in most aircraft. Note that any wing requires spanwise members of great strength to withstand operational stresses, which are greatest during flight and upon landing.

Wing design can be divided into two types, cantilever and semicantilever (Fig. 1-34). A cantilever wing contains all of its structural strength inside the wing structure and requires no external bracing. This type of wing is normally found on high-performance aircraft and on transports. The semicantilever design obtains its strength both by internal wing design and external support and by bracing such as comes from struts and wires. This type of wing is usually found on light aircraft designs and relatively slow aircraft designed to carry heavy loads. All wings can be considered to

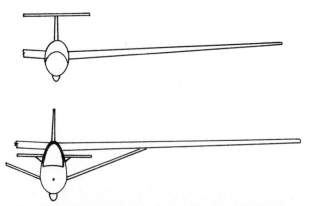

FIG. 1-34   The top aircraft has a cantilever wing attachment, and the bottom aircraft uses a semicantilever design.

be of semimonocoque construction as the internal structure carries the primary loads of the wing.

Basic Features of Wing Construction

Conventional wings are of three general types: **monospar, two-spar,** and **multispar.** True stressed-skin wings may have shear webs but no true "spars." The monospar wing has only one spar, the two-spar wing has two spars as the name indicates, and the multispar wing has more than two spars. A **wing spar,** sometimes called **wing beam,** is a principal spanwise member of the wing structure. The spars in the basic structure for the wings of a typical light, high-wing monoplane are shown in Fig. 1-35. The structure shown in the illustration would be similar in either a metal wing or a wood wing. In the metal wing all principal parts are made of aluminum alloy, and the tie rods or brace wires are made of steel. In the wood wing, the spars may be the only members made of wood or both the spars and the compression struts (ribs) may be made of wood. Observe the two names for the tie rods, or brace wires. The wires carrying drag loads are called **drag wires,** and those carrying the loads opposite drag are called **antidrag wires.**

The wing spars for a wood wing must be made of aircraft-quality solid wood and plywood. Wood spars

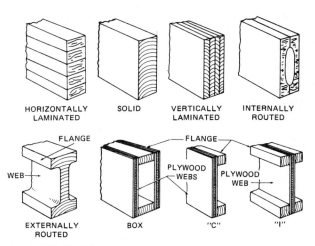

FIG. 1-36 Wood spar sections.

may be solid or may be built up as shown in Fig. 1-36.

Metal spars, like wood spars, may be made in a variety of designs. Examples of some metal spar types are shown in Fig. 1-37. These spar shapes may be achieved through an extrusion process or may be assembled by riveting and welding.

Figure 1-38 shows a general design for a light-aircraft wing to be covered with fabric. This type of structure may be made of wood or metal.

A **wing rib,** sometimes called a **plain rib,** is a chordwise member of the wing structure used to give the wing section its shape and also to transmit the air loads from the covering to the spars. The rib may extend from the leading edge of the wing to the trailing edge, or it may extend only to the rear spar, as in the area ahead of a flap or aileron. Ribs for wood wings are shown in Fig. 1-39. The rib shown in Fig. 1-39 (a) illustrates the use of compression ribs with heavy cap strips and solid plywood webs. While the rib shown only extends from the front spar to the rear spar, a compression rib may be full size. The rib in Fig. 1-39 (b) is a typical built-up or truss rib with cross bracing secured to the cap strips with plywood gussets. The cap strips are usually made of aircraft-grade spruce, which are first cut in straight strips and then bent to fit the rib configuration.

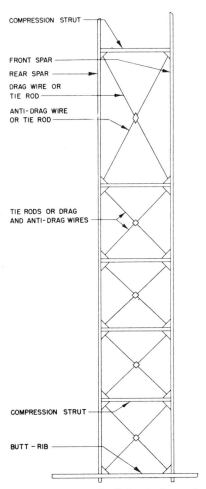

FIG. 1-35 Basic structure of a light-airplane wing.

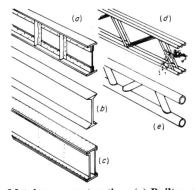

FIG. 1-37 Metal spar construction. (a) Built-up I-beam; (b) extruded I-beam; (c) built-up double-web spar; (d) welded-steel small-tubing structure; (e) welded-steel large-tubing structure.

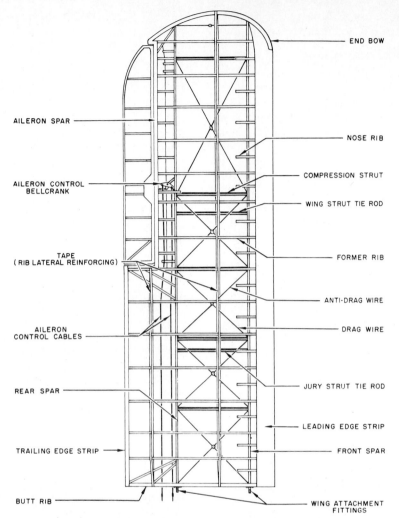

FIG. 1-38 General design of a light-airplane wing.

Labels in figure:

AILERON SPAR

AILERON CONTROL BELLCRANK

TAPE (RIB LATERAL REINFORCING)

AILERON CONTROL CABLES

REAR SPAR

TRAILING EDGE STRIP

BUTT RIB

END BOW

NOSE RIB

COMPRESSION STRUT

WING STRUT TIE ROD

FORMER RIB

ANTI-DRAG WIRE

DRAG WIRE

JURY STRUT TIE ROD

LEADING EDGE STRIP

FRONT SPAR

WING ATTACHMENT FITTINGS

Figure 1-39 (c) shows a built-up rib with a plywood web which has been lightened by cutting large holes in the portions having the least stress. The ribs shown in Fig. 1-39 (d) and (e) have continuous gussets which eliminate the need for leading-edge strips. The only

important difference between Fig. 1-39 (d) and (e) is the method of bracing.

Typical metal ribs are shown in Fig. 1-40. Starting at the top of the illustration, the built-up rib is used in conjunction with metal spars and is riveted to them. The stamped rib with lightening holes and the stamped rib with a truss-type cross section are used with either metal or wood spars. The rib at the bottom of the picture is stamped in three sections and is usually riveted to metal spars.

An assembled wood wing is shown in Fig. 1-41. Either a fabric or a plywood covering can be applied to this type of wing structure. Notice that wood compression ribs are used instead of the tubular members used in the illustration of Fig. 1-38.

Typical **stressed-skin** metal construction is shown in Fig. 1-42. The skin of the wing is riveted to the ribs and stringers. It serves not only as a covering but also as a part of the basic structure of the wing.

Light-Aircraft Wings

The wings of light aircraft include spars, ribs, and surface coverings. The spars are commonly wood or metal in older aircraft designs and metal in newer aircraft. Depending upon the airfoil used and the man-

FIG. 1-39 Ribs for wooden wings.

Labels in figure:

(a)

COMPRESSION RIB

LEADING EDGE STRIP — CAP STRIP

(b)

GUSSET

(c)

LIGHTENED PLYWOOD WEB

(d)

CONTINUOUS GUSSET

(e)

CONTINUOUS GUSSET

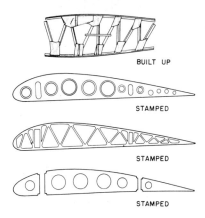

FIG. 1-40   Ribs for metal wings.

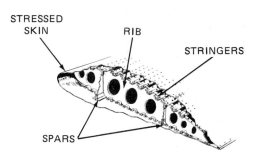

FIG. 1-42   Reinforced stressed-skin wing construction.

ufacturer's choice, one or two spars may be used to carry the flight loads. If a single spar is used, it is located near the midpoint of the airfoil chord line. If two spars are used, one is located near the leading edge and the other is located near the rear of the wing, usually just forward of the trailing-edge flight controls. Typical spar locations are shown in Fig. 1-43.

The spars include attachment points for connection to the fuselage, and, if the wings are of a semicantilever design, strut fittings located at a midpoint along the spar. If the landing gear or engine is mounted on the wing, the spars incorporate structural attachments for these components.

The wing structure includes compression members, either struts or ribs, and metal or wood ribs. Some wings make use of nose or false ribs which are located at the leading edge of the wing to maintain the proper shape of the leading-edge covering. The use of drag and antidrag wires are common on aircraft wings covered with fabric. Plywood- or metal-covered wings do not always make use of these internal wire components.

Fuel tanks are normally located in the inboard portion of the wing. The fuel tank may be a removable metal container, a bladder fuel cell located in a compartment, or an integral fuel tank. Figure 1-44 shows a removable tank which is made of metal and is held in a covered bay of the wing between the spars and ribs. Bladder fuel cells are rubberlike "bags" which

are placed in structurally reinforced wing areas, usually between the spars. These bladder tanks, illustrated in Fig. 1-45, eliminate the need for a large access opening in the wing for installation and removal of the fuel tank. The bladder tanks are normally installed and removed by rolling them up and working them through a small opening in the wing surface. Integral fuel tanks are built into the basic wing structure and cannot be removed.

An exterior view of the wing for a light, high-wing monoplane is provided in Fig. 1-46. This view shows many of the details of the wing other than purely structural ones. The wing is of all-metal construction with a single main spar, formed ribs, and stringers. An inboard section of the wing, forward of the main spar, is sealed to form an integral fuel bay area. Stressed skin is riveted to the spars, ribs, and stringers to complete the structure. Note that the wing skin has many plates and doors to provide access to the interior for inspection and required service.

Since the wing shown in Fig. 1-46 is fully cantilevered, the wing attachment fittings must be designed with adequate strength to carry the high stresses inherent in this type of construction. These attachment fittings are shown in details A and B in the illustration.

Transport Aircraft Wings

The **main frame** of a modern transport wing consists of the spars, ribs, bulkheads, and skin panels with spanwise stiffening members. The assembly of the structure may include the use of nonmetallic composite components and the bonding of metal structures as well as the use of conventional metal alloys and fasteners. The structural strength of the wing must be sufficient to carry its own weight along with the weight of the fuel in the wings, the weight of engines attached to the wings, and the forces imposed by the flight controls and landing gear. These stresses vary tremendously in direction and in magnitude during the aircraft's transitions from moving on the ground to flight operations to returning to the ground.

Figure 1-47 shows the basic structure of a typical modern transport wing. Transport wings consist of two or more main spars with intermediate spars used between the main spars in some designs. These intermediate spars assist the main spars in carrying the operational loads. The front and rear spars provide the main supporting structure for fittings attaching the fuselage, engine pylons, main landing gear, and flight

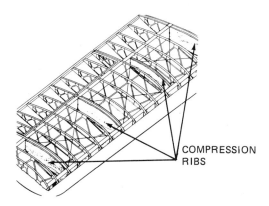

FIG. 1-41   Wooden-wing construction.

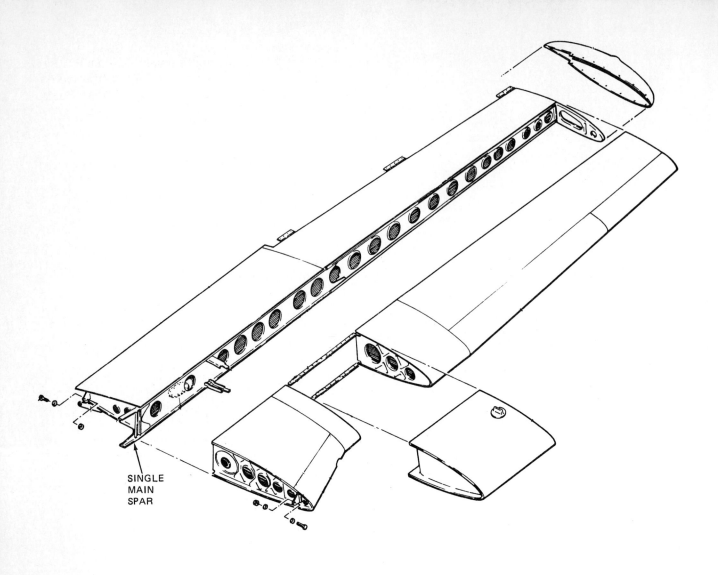

SINGLE
MAIN
SPAR

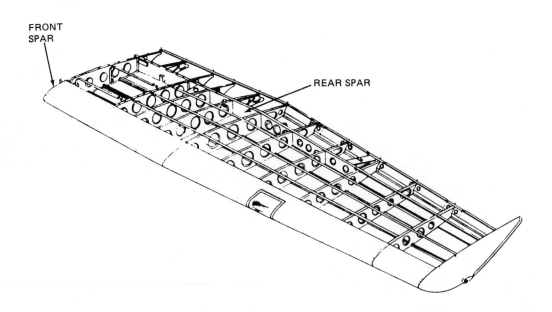

FRONT
SPAR

REAR SPAR

FIG. 1-43 Light-aircraft wings normally have one or two main spars. *(Piper Aircraft Co., Cessna Aircraft Co.)*

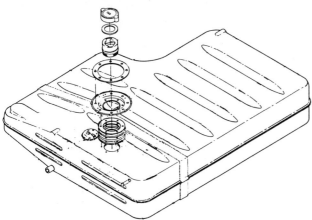

FIG. 1-44 A typical metal fuel tank. *(Cessna Aircraft Co.)*

surfaces to the wing. Between the spars are located ribs which, depending upon their design, may be used for purposes such as fuel bulkheads and the support of control surfaces along with providing the airfoil shape of the wing. Figures 1-48 and 1-49 show typical locations and uses for transport wing ribs.

The auxiliary structure of the wing includes the wing tips, leading edge, and trailing edge. The leading edge of the wing incorporates leading-edge ribs, structural reinforcement members, and attachment points for components such as slats and leading-edge flaps. The trailing edge also incorporates structural members

serving similar purposes to those of the leading edge. The trailing-edge structure normally incorporates an extensive structure to carry and transmit the loads imposed by the operation of the flight controls such as flaps and ailerons.

The wing internal structures are covered with large metal skin panels which have spanwise stringers attached to achieve the desired structural strength of the wings. The leading edge and trailing edge are attached with permanent-type fasteners. The wing tips are removable for inspection and maintenance.

In many transports, the wing is constructed in three or more major assemblies, such as the left- and right-wing panels and a center-wing section. These sections are joined with permanent fasteners to form a one-piece wing which is attached to the fuselage. Figure 1-50 shows wing sections being joined.

The fittings used to attach the fuselage, engine pylons, main landing gear, and flight control surfaces to the wing are secured with **interference-fit** and **close-tolerance** fasteners and are not considered removable except for structural repair. An "interference-fit" fastener is a bolt, pin, or rivet which is slightly larger than the hole in which it is installed. It must be pressed into place, and during this procedure it tends to stretch the metal into which it is installed. The result is that there can be no "play" or clearance between the fastener and the installation regardless of expansion or contraction due to temperature changes. The fastener and the fitting essentially become one unit.

Fuel tanks are included in the basic wing structure so that the wing serves as the fuel tank. This is known

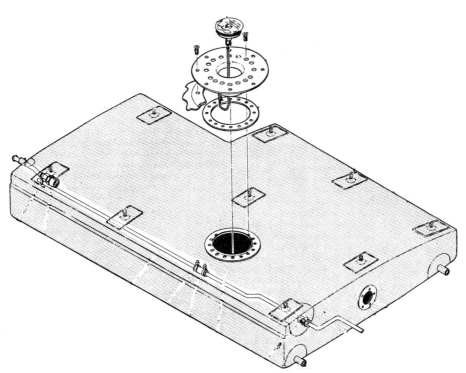

FIG. 1-45 A bladder-type fuel tank uses fasteners to hold the cell in position inside the supporting structure. *(Cessna Aircraft Co.)*

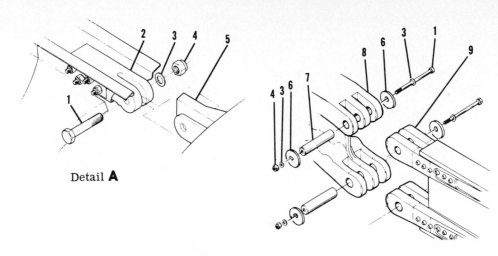

Detail **A**

Detail **B**

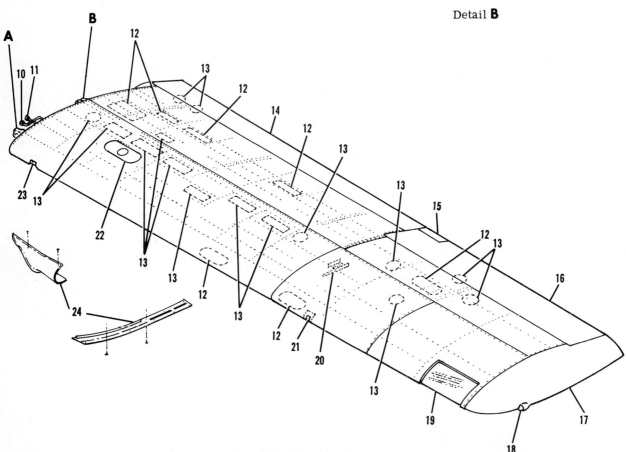

1. BOLT	13. PLATE
2. FWD FUSELAGE FITTING	14. FLAP
3. WASHER	15. AILERON TAB
4. NUT	16. AILERON
5. FWD WING FITTING	17. WING TIP
6. RETAINER	18. POSITION LIGHT
7. DOWEL PIN	19. LANDING AND TAXI LIGHTS
8. AFT FUSELAGE FITTING	20. PITOT TUBE
9. AFT WING FITTING	21. STALL WARNING UNIT
10. FUEL VENT LINE	22. FUEL FILLER DOOR
11. FUEL LINE	23. RAM AIR INLET
12. DOOR	24. FAIRING

FIG. 1-46 Exterior view of an all-metal wing for a light airplane. *(Cessna Aircraft Co.)*

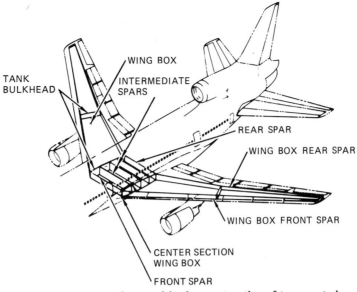

FIG. 1-47 Multiple spars are often used in the construction of transport aircraft wings. *(Lockheed California Co.)*

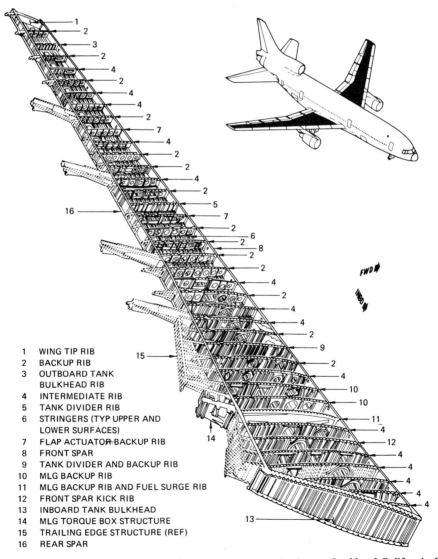

1	WING TIP RIB
2	BACKUP RIB
3	OUTBOARD TANK BULKHEAD RIB
4	INTERMEDIATE RIB
5	TANK DIVIDER RIB
6	STRINGERS (TYP UPPER AND LOWER SURFACES)
7	FLAP ACTUATOR BACKUP RIB
8	FRONT SPAR
9	TANK DIVIDER AND BACKUP RIB
10	MLG BACKUP RIB
11	MLG BACKUP RIB AND FUEL SURGE RIB
12	FRONT SPAR KICK RIB
13	INBOARD TANK BULKHEAD
14	MLG TORQUE BOX STRUCTURE
15	TRAILING EDGE STRUCTURE (REF)
16	REAR SPAR

FIG. 1-48 The internal structure of a modern transport wing. *(Lockheed California Co.)*

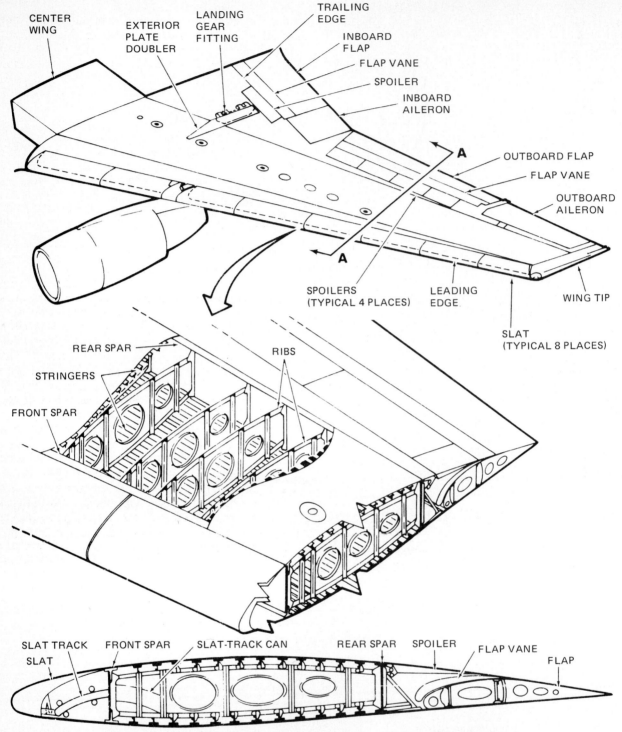

FIG. 1-49 Construction of the wing for the DC-10. *(McDonnell Douglas Corp.)*

as an **integral fuel tank design,** also referred to as a "wet wing." The integral tanks are sealed with special compounds applied to fasteners and between components during assembly. The inside of an integral tank is shown in Fig. 1-51. Areas of the wings that do not contain fuel are termed "dry bays."

Older transport aircraft wings are similar in construction to the modern jets with the exception that the use of bonded structures, composites, and integral fuel tanks are not commonly found. Older aircraft make use of metal fasteners such as rivets for assembly and use bladder or removable fuel tanks instead

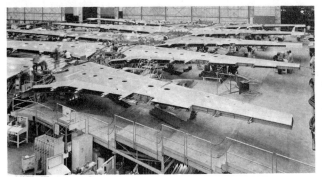

FIG. 1-50 Joining main wing sections. (McDonnell Douglas Corp.)

FIG. 1-51 Sealing of wing for the fuel tank. (McDonnell Douglas Corp.)

of integral tanks. The control system attachment is normally less complex than for modern transports because of the slower flight speeds and simpler control surface designs.

● TAIL AND CONTROL SURFACES

The stabilizers and the control surfaces of an airplane are constructed in a manner similar to the wings but on a much smaller scale. They usually include one or more primary members (spars) and ribs attached to the spars. The vertical stabilizer (fin) may be constructed as a part of the fuselage or may be a separate member that is both adjustable and removable. The tail section of an airplane, including the stabilizers, elevators, and rudder, is commonly called the **empennage.**

Horizontal Stabilizer

The horizontal stabilizer is used to provide longitudinal pitch stability to the aircraft and is usually attached to the aft portion of the fuselage. It may be located above or below the vertical stabilizer or at some midpoint on the vertical stabilizer.

The stabilizer may be constructed of wood, steel tubing, sheet metal, or composite materials. The method of construction is similar to that used for wings, with spars, ribs, stringers, and a surface skin being used. Examples of different types of horizontal stabilizers are shown in Figs. 1-52 through 1-54.

The horizontal stabilizer may be designed as a fixed surface attached to the tail cone or as a movable surface used to provide pitch trim.

If the stabilizer is designed to provide pitch trim, it normally is attached to the fuselage with a pivoting hinge as its rear spar. At the front spar is an attachment for a mechanical or hydraulic actuator which is controlled by the pilot to move the leading edge of the stabilizer up and down to change the trim of the aircraft (Fig. 1-55).

Vertical Stabilizers

The vertical stabilizer for an airplane is the airfoil section forward of the rudder and is used to provide longitudinal (yaw) stability for the aircraft. This unit is commonly called the **fin.** The construction of the vertical stabilizer is very much like that of the horizontal stabilizer, and, as mentioned previously, it may be constructed as an integral part of the fuselage. The rear structural member of the fin is provided with hinges for the support of the rudder. On many aircraft a **dorsal fin** is installed immediately forward of the vertical stabilizer. The function of the dorsal fin is to improve the yaw stability of the aircraft and to provide a streamline fairing between the vertical stabilizer and the fuselage. A dorsal fin is shown in Fig 1-56, item no. 2. The illustration also shows the swept-back vertical stabilizer with fittings and attachments.

Some aircraft, especially those equipped with floats or external cargo pods, may also require the addition of a ventral fin on the bottom of the fuselage in the area below the vertical stabilizer. Some aircraft also require the use of auxiliary vertical stabilizers,

FIG. 1-52 A welded-steel-tube horizontal stabilizer. (Schweizer)

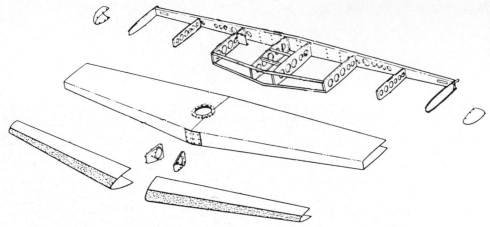

FIG. 1-53 A typical light-aircraft aluminum-structure horizontal stabilizer. *(Cessna Aircraft Co.)*

mounted on the horizontal stabilizer. Figures 1-57 and 1-58 illustrate these vertical surfaces.

Control Surfaces

The **primary control surfaces** of an airplane include the ailerons, rudder, and elevator. **Secondary control surfaces** include tabs, flaps, spoilers, and slats. The construction of the control surfaces is similar to that of the stabilizers; however, the movable surfaces usually are somewhat lighter in construction. They often have a spar at the forward edge to provide rigidity, and to this spar are attached the ribs and the covering. Hinges for attachment are also secured to the spar. Where it is necessary to attach tabs to the trailing edges of control surfaces, additional structure is added

to provide for transmission of the tab loads to the surface.

Control surfaces may be constructed of any combination of materials, with the more common combination being a sheet-metal structure (usually an aluminum alloy) covered with metal skins or fabric, a steel structure covered with fabric, or a wood structure covered with plywood or fabric. Each of these types of construction is treated by some method to inhibit the deterioration of the structure and the covering and includes drain holes to prevent water from becoming trapped inside the structure and causing the control surfaces to be thrown out of balance. Methods of joining the components may include metal fasteners as well as adhesives and bonding agents.

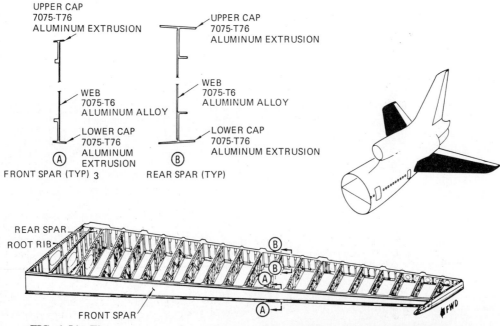

FIG. 1-54 Elevator construction components for an L-1011. *(Lockheed California Co.)*

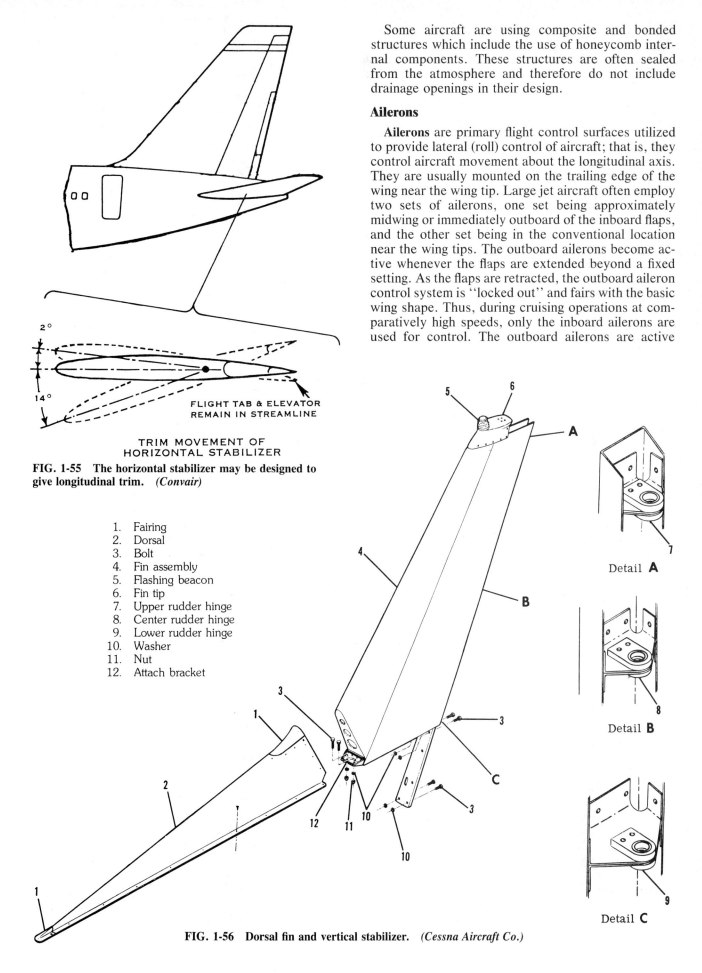

Some aircraft are using composite and bonded structures which include the use of honeycomb internal components. These structures are often sealed from the atmosphere and therefore do not include drainage openings in their design.

Ailerons

Ailerons are primary flight control surfaces utilized to provide lateral (roll) control of aircraft; that is, they control aircraft movement about the longitudinal axis. They are usually mounted on the trailing edge of the wing near the wing tip. Large jet aircraft often employ two sets of ailerons, one set being approximately midwing or immediately outboard of the inboard flaps, and the other set being in the conventional location near the wing tips. The outboard ailerons become active whenever the flaps are extended beyond a fixed setting. As the flaps are retracted, the outboard aileron control system is "locked out" and fairs with the basic wing shape. Thus, during cruising operations at comparatively high speeds, only the inboard ailerons are used for control. The outboard ailerons are active

2°

14°

FLIGHT TAB & ELEVATOR
REMAIN IN STREAMLINE

TRIM MOVEMENT OF
HORIZONTAL STABILIZER

FIG. 1-55   The horizontal stabilizer may be designed to give longitudinal trim.   *(Convair)*

1. Fairing
2. Dorsal
3. Bolt
4. Fin assembly
5. Flashing beacon
6. Fin tip
7. Upper rudder hinge
8. Center rudder hinge
9. Lower rudder hinge
10. Washer
11. Nut
12. Attach bracket

Detail **A**

Detail **B**

Detail **C**

FIG. 1-56   Dorsal fin and vertical stabilizer.   *(Cessna Aircraft Co.)*

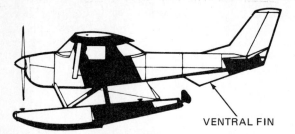

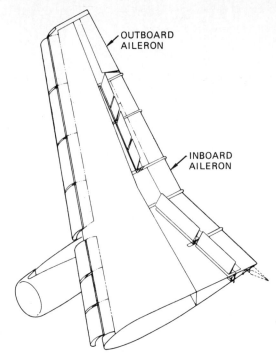

FIG. 1-57 A ventral fin is added to the bottom of a fuselage to improve the aircraft's longitudinal stability. *(Edo)*

during landing or other slow flight operations. Figure 1-59 shows a transport aircraft wing with this aileron configuration.

Ailerons for light aircraft are usually constructed with a single spar to which ribs are attached. Figure 1-60 illustrates this type of construction. The majority of currently manufactured aircraft are of all-metal construction with aluminum alloy skin riveted or bonded to the internal structure.

Aileron control systems operated by the pilot through mechanical connections require the use of balancing mechanisms so that the pilot can overcome the air loads imposed on the ailerons during flight. Balancing of the ailerons can be achieved by extending part of the aileron structure ahead of the hinge line and shaping this area so that the airstream strikes the extension and helps to move the surface. This is known as **aerodynamic balancing.** Another method which may be used is to place a weight ahead of the hinge line to counteract the flight loads. This is known as **static balancing.** Some aircraft may use a combination of these techniques. Figure 1-61 shows an aileron which uses the aerodynamic balance method, and Fig. 1-62 shows ailerons using the mass weight balance method.

FIG. 1-59 The L-1011 uses two ailerons on each wing. *(Lockheed California Co.)*

Aircraft such as jet transports use hydraulically operated ailerons and may not employ these forms of balancing. If the transport control system is designed to allow the pilot to operate the ailerons without hydraulic assistance, then some method of balancing or control by control tabs is used.

The geometry of the control system for the ailerons affects the amount that the ailerons move above or below the neutral setting. (The neutral setting fairs the ailerons with the wing contour.) Some aircraft have their ailerons operating symmetrically; that is, they move up the same amount that they move down. Other aircraft have the ailerons operating asymmetrically; that is, the upward-moving aileron moves further than the downward-moving aileron. This asymmetrical operation is used in some aircraft designs to reduce the amount of rudder pressure required when making turns. This reduces what is known as "adverse aileron yaw," which is caused by the downward-moving aileron creating an increase in aerodynamic drag, and results in the airplane yawing away from the direction of the desired turn. Aircraft having this arrangement are sometimes said to have differential ailerons. Figure 1-63 illustrates asymmetrical aileron movement.

Rudder

The rudder is the flight control surface that controls the aircraft movement about its vertical axis. The rudder is constructed very much like other flight control surfaces with spars, ribs, and skin.

Rudders are usually balanced both statically and aerodynamically to provide for greater ease of operation and to eliminate the possibility of flutter. It should be noted that some light-aircraft rudders do not

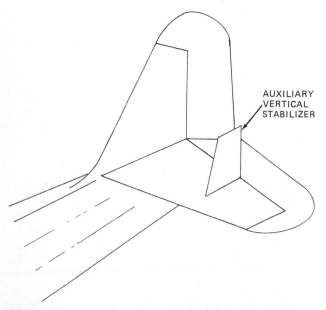

FIG. 1-58 Auxiliary fins may be added to the horizontal stabilizer to improve longitudinal stability.

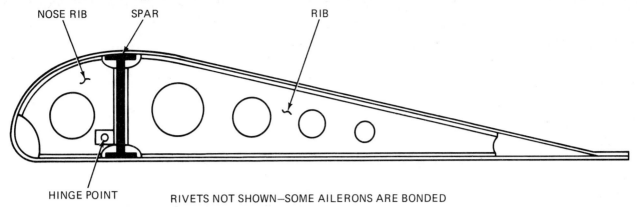

NOSE RIB   SPAR   RIB

HINGE POINT

RIVETS NOT SHOWN—SOME AILERONS ARE BONDED

FIG. 1-60   Aileron construction with a single spar.

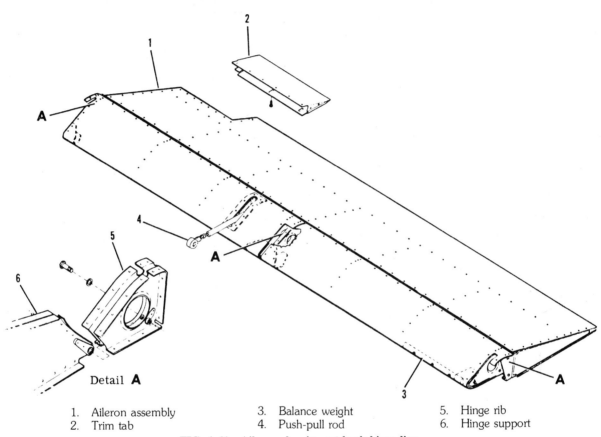

Detail **A**

1. Aileron assembly
2. Trim tab
3. Balance weight
4. Push-pull rod
5. Hinge rib
6. Hinge support

FIG. 1-61   Aileron showing set-back hinge line.

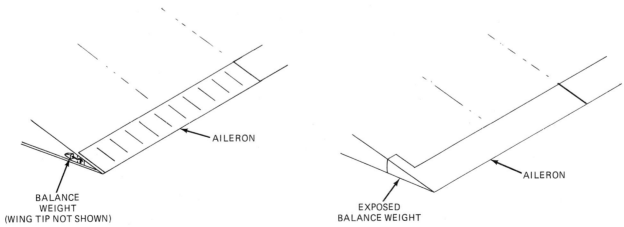

AILERON

BALANCE
WEIGHT
(WING TIP NOT SHOWN)

AILERON

EXPOSED
BALANCE WEIGHT

FIG. 1-62   Aileron balanced weights may be found inside the wing tip or exposed.

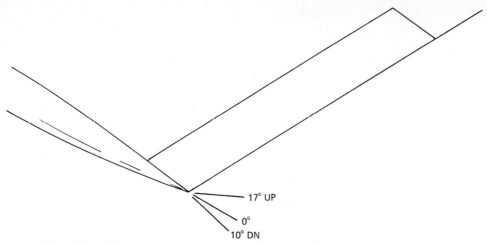

FIG. 1-63 Differential aileron movement allows each aileron to move up a greater amount than it can move down.

use any balancing method. Different rudders for light aircraft are shown in Fig. 1-64.

Rudders for transport aircraft vary in basic structural and operational design. Some are single structural units operated by one or more control systems. Others are designed with two operational segments which are controlled by different operating systems and provide a desired level of redundancy.

A single-unit rudder is shown in Fig. 1-65. This rudder is capable of being operated by three different hydraulic systems in the aircraft.

Figure 1-66 shows a rudder with an upper and a lower segment. Each segment is operated by a different hydraulic system.

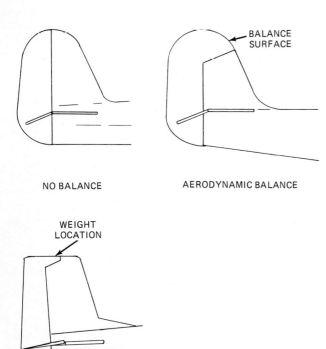

FIG. 1-64 Different rudder configurations.

The rudder shown in Figure 1-67 consists of two segments, upper and lower, and each segment consists of a forward and aft section. The forward rudder sections are attached to hinge brackets mounted on the rear spar of the vertical stabilizer. The aft rudder sections are supported by hinge brackets attached to the rear spar of the forward sections. The aft rudder sections are hinged to the forward sections and connected by pushrods to the vertical stabilizer structure. This provides aft-section displacement proportional to forward-section displacement, thus increasing the aerodynamic efficiency of the rudders. Trim and control tabs are not required with this type of rudder design because their functions are performed by the aft sections of the rudder.

Elevators

Elevators are the control surfaces which govern the movement (pitch) of the aircraft around the lateral axis. They are normally attached to hinges on the rear spar of the horizontal stabilizer. The construction of an elevator is similar to that of other control surfaces, and the design of the elevator may be unbalanced or balanced aerodynamically and/or statically. Typical elevator installations for light aircraft and transports are shown in Figs. 1-68 and 1-69.

Combination Control Surfaces

Some aircraft use combination control surfaces which combine the operation of at least two control and/or stabilizer surfaces into one component. By the use of combination surfaces, the construction of the aircraft can be simplified and the desired control response can be achieved. Examples of these types of control surfaces include **stabilators, ruddervators,** and **flaperons.**

A stabilator combines the function of a horizontal stabilizer and an elevator. This type of surface is used primarily on light-aircraft designs and on some high-performance military aircraft. The stabilator usually incorporates a static balance weight on an arm ahead of the main spar. This weight can project into the aircraft structure or be carried on the forward portion

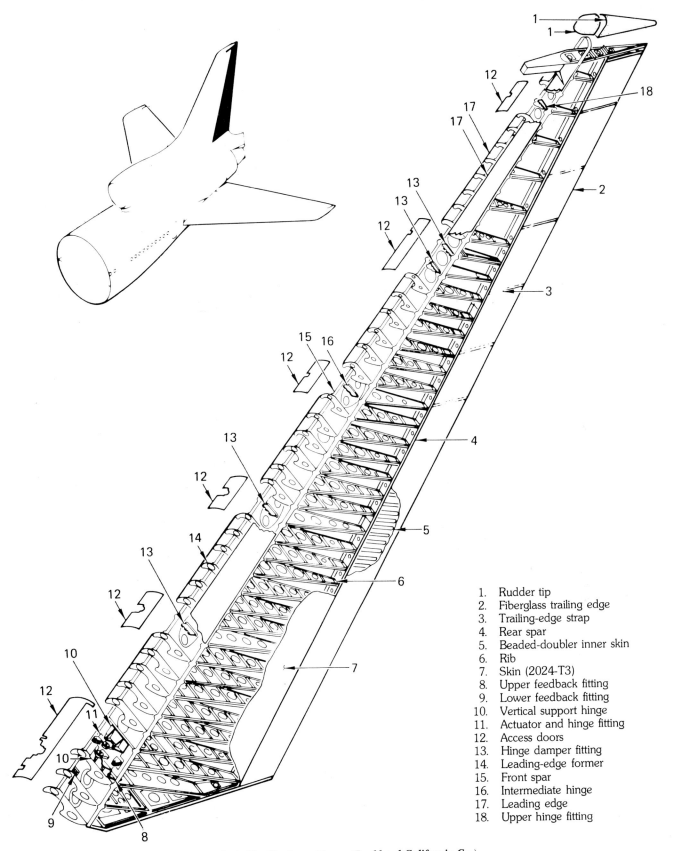

1. Rudder tip
2. Fiberglass trailing edge
3. Trailing-edge strap
4. Rear spar
5. Beaded-doubler inner skin
6. Rib
7. Skin (2024-T3)
8. Upper feedback fitting
9. Lower feedback fitting
10. Vertical support hinge
11. Actuator and hinge fitting
12. Access doors
13. Hinge damper fitting
14. Leading-edge former
15. Front spar
16. Intermediate hinge
17. Leading edge
18. Upper hinge fitting

FIG. 1-65 Single rudder. *(Lockheed California Co.)*

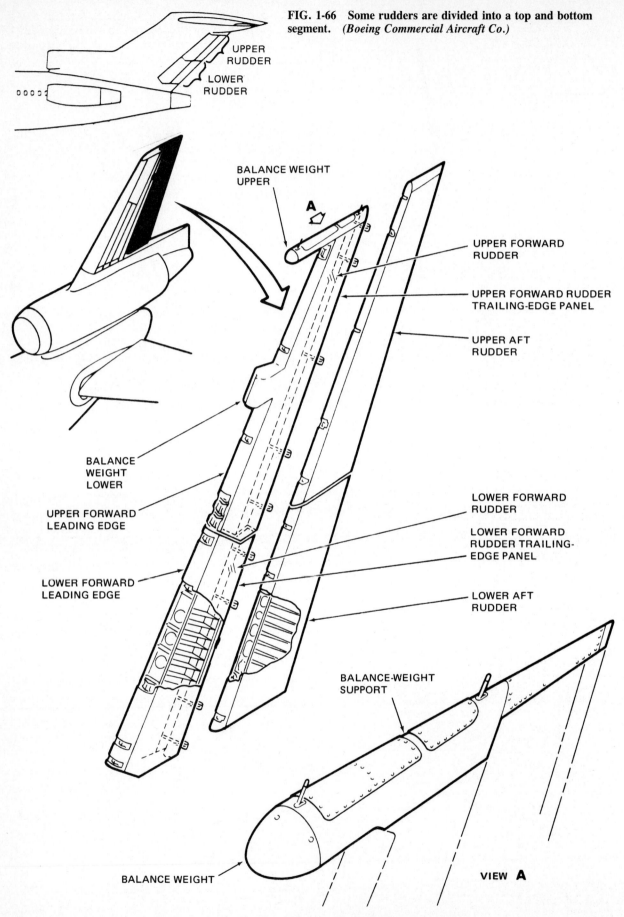

FIG. 1-66 Some rudders are divided into a top and bottom segment. *(Boeing Commercial Aircraft Co.)*

UPPER RUDDER

LOWER RUDDER

BALANCE WEIGHT UPPER

A

UPPER FORWARD RUDDER

UPPER FORWARD RUDDER TRAILING-EDGE PANEL

UPPER AFT RUDDER

BALANCE WEIGHT LOWER

UPPER FORWARD LEADING EDGE

LOWER FORWARD LEADING EDGE

LOWER FORWARD RUDDER

LOWER FORWARD RUDDER TRAILING-EDGE PANEL

LOWER AFT RUDDER

BALANCE-WEIGHT SUPPORT

BALANCE WEIGHT

VIEW **A**

FIG. 1-67 Four-section rudder. *(McDonnell Douglas Corp.)*

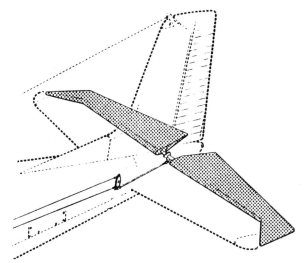

FIG. 1-68 The elevator of a light aircraft. (*Cessna Aircraft Co.*)

of the tips of the stabilator. A stabilator is normally equipped with an anti-servo tab which doubles as a trim tab. The anti-servo tab moves in the same direction as the control surface is moved to aid the pilot in returning the stabilator to the trimmed neutral position. A typical stabilator for a light aircraft is shown in Fig. 1-70.

Ruddervators are flight control surfaces which serve the functions of the rudder and elevators. This is accomplished by mounting the surfaces at an angle above horizontal as shown in the photograph of Fig. 1-71. When serving as elevators, the surface on each side of the tail move in the same direction, either up or down. When serving as a rudder, the surfaces move in opposite directions, one up and one down. When combined rudder and elevator control movements are made by the pilot, a control mixing mechanism moves each surface the appropriate amount to get the desired elevator and rudder effect.

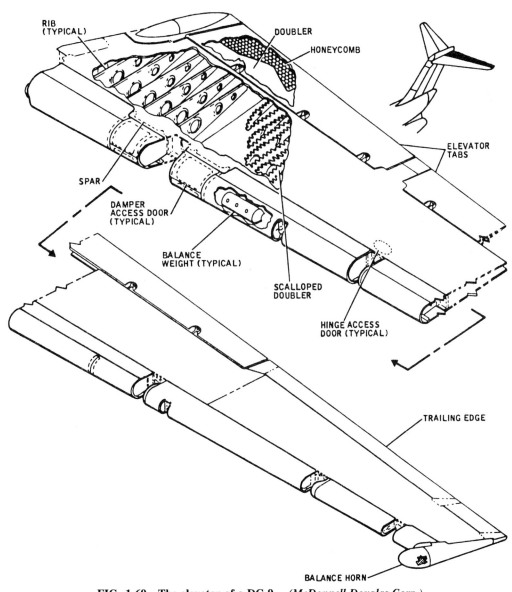

FIG. 1-69 The elevator of a DC-9. (*McDonnell Douglas Corp.*)

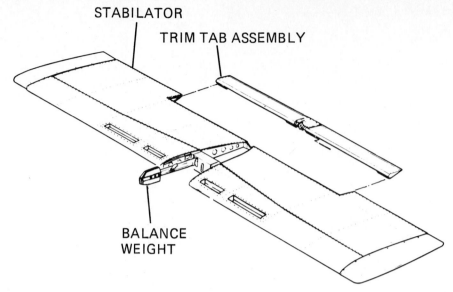

STABILATOR

TRIM TAB ASSEMBLY

BALANCE
WEIGHT

FIG. 1-70   Stabilator for a light airplane.   *(Piper Aircraft Corp.)*

Flaperons are surfaces which combine the operation of flaps and ailerons. These types of control surfaces are found on some aircraft designed to operate from short runways. The flaperon allows the area of the wing normally reserved for the aileron to be lowered and creates a full-span flap. From the lowered position the flaperon can move up or down to provide the desired amount of roll control while still contributing to the overall lift of the wing.

● SECONDARY FLIGHT CONTROL SURFACES

Because aircraft often are capable of operating over a wide speed range and with different weight distributions, secondary flight controls, also called auxiliary flight controls, have been developed. Some of these surfaces, called **tabs,** allow the flight crew to reduce or eliminate the pressure that they must apply to the flight controls. Other surfaces fall in a group termed **high-lift devices** which includes flaps, slats, and slots. These allow the lift and drag characteristics of the aircraft wing to be changed to allow slow-speed flight for takeoff and landing and high-speed flight for cruising. Still a third group of surfaces are used to reduce lift and generate drag. This group includes spoilers and speed brakes.

The number and complexity of the secondary control surfaces on a particular aircraft depends on the type of operation and flight speeds for which the aircraft is designed. Figure 1-72 shows the secondary flight control surfaces found on a typical jet transport aircraft.

Tabs

Tabs are small secondary flight control surfaces set into the trailing edges of the primary surfaces. These are used to reduce the pilot's work load required to hold the aircraft in some constant attitude by "loading" the control surface in a position to maintain the desired attitude. They may also be used to aid the pilot in returning a control surface to a neutral or trimmed-center position. Figure 1-73 demonstrates the tab action.

Tabs can be fixed or variable, and the variable tabs can be designed to operate in several different manners. While there are many different types of tabs and tab operating systems, we will look at the more common systems in use. Figure 1-74 shows different types of control tab configurations.

A fixed trim tab, shown in Fig. 1-75, is normally a piece of sheet metal attached to the trailing edge of a control surface. This fixed tab is adjusted on the ground by bending it in the appropriate direction to eliminate cabin flight control forces for a specific flight condition. The fixed tab is normally adjusted for zero control forces while in cruising flight. Adjustment of the tab is a trial-and-error process where the aircraft must be flown and the trim tab adjusted based on the

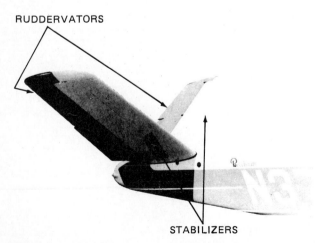

RUDDERVATORS

STABILIZERS

FIG. 1-71   Ruddervators on a Beechcraft Bonanza.

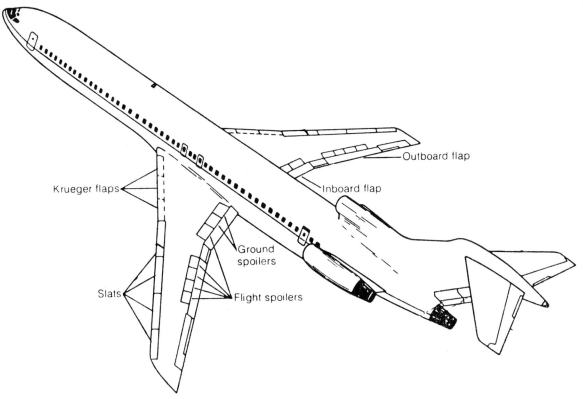

FIG. 1-72 The location of secondary flight controls on a Boeing 727. *(Boeing Commercial Aircraft Co.)*

pilot's report. The aircraft must then again be flown to see if further adjustment is necessary. Fixed tabs are normally found on light aircraft and are used to adjust rudders and ailerons.

Controllable trim tabs are found on most aircraft with at least the elevator tab being controlled. These tabs are normally operated mechanically by a cable and chain system, electrically by a screwjack mechanism or a motor to drive the cable and chain system, or hydraulically through actuators. When the pilot wishes to change the attitude of the aircraft with the trim system, he activates the trim control system and causes the trim tab to be deflected in the direction opposite to the desired movement of the control surface. When the trim tab is deflected into the airstream, the air tries to push the tab back flush with the control surface. Since the control mechanism prevents the tab from being pushed back flush, the whole control surface is moved.

Controllable trim tabs are adjusted by means of control wheels or cranks in the cockpit, and an indicator is supplied to denote the position of the trim tab. If the tabs can be operated electrically or hydraulically, they will incorporate some instrumentation to indicate tab position.

Servo tabs are used to aid the pilot in the operation of flight controls. When the pilot moves a primary flight control, a servo tab deflects in the proper direction to aid the pilot in moving the control surface. This reduces the force which the pilot must supply to the control system to maneuver the aircraft.

An anti-servo tab is used to aid the pilot in returning surface, such as a stabilator, to the neutral position

and prevent it from moving to a full deflection position due to aerodynamic forces. This type of tab has the opposite effect of a servo tab. The anti-servo tab often also serves as the pitch trim tab by allowing the pilot to adjust the neutral trim position.

A control tab is used on some transport aircraft as a manual backup to flight controls which are normally operated hydraulically. When in a manual reversion mode, the pilot can operate the control tabs, and by their tab action they will cause the flight controls to move in the appropriate direction.

Flaps

A wing flap is defined as a hinged, pivoted, or sliding airfoil, usually attached near the trailing edge of the wing. The purpose of wing flaps is to change the camber of the wing and in some cases to increase the area of the wing, thus permitting the aircraft to operate at lower flight speeds for landing and takeoff. The flaps

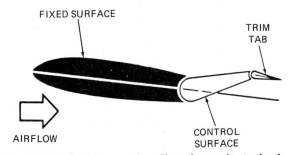

FIG. 1-73 Trim tabs must be adjusted opposite to the desired movement of the surface being controlled.

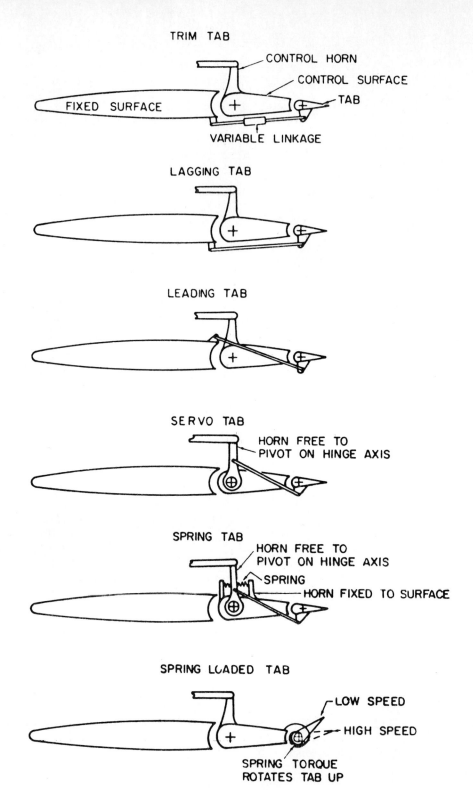

FIG. 1-74 Various types of trim tabs.

effectively increase the lift of the wings and, in some cases, greatly increase the drag, particularly when fully extended.

Various configurations for wing flaps are shown in Fig. 1-76. The **plain flap,** in effect, acts as if the trailing edge of the wing were deflected downward to change the camber of the wing, thus increasing both lift and drag. If the flap is moved downward sufficiently, it becomes an effective air brake. The plain flap may be hinged to the wing at the lower side, or it may have the hinge line midway between the lower and upper surfaces.

The **split flap,** when retracted, forms the lower surface of the wing trailing edge. When extended, the flap moves downward and provides an effect similar to that of the plain flap. Plain flaps and split flaps may

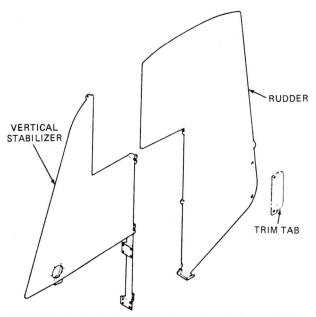

FIG. 1-75 A fixed trim tab is adjusted on the ground for the average flight condition. (Ayres Corp.)

be attached to a wing with three or more separate hinges, or they may be attached at the lower surface with a continuous piano hinge.

The **Fowler flap** and others with similar operation are designed to increase substantially the wing area as

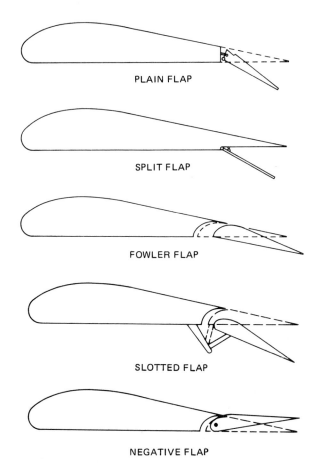

FIG. 1-76 Configurations for wing flaps.

the flap is extended. When retracted, the flap forms the trailing edge of the wing. As this type of flap is extended, it is moved rearward, often by means of a worm gear, and is supported in the correct position by means of curved tracks. The effect of the Fowler flap, when extended, is to greatly reduce the stalling speed of the aircraft by the increase in wing area and change in wing camber.

A slotted flap is similar to a plain flap except that as the flap is extended, a gap develops between the wing and the flap. The leading edge of the flap is designed so that air entering this gap flows smoothly through the gap and aids in holding the airflow on the surface. This increases the lift of the wing with the flap extended.

Some aircraft designs incorporate combinations of the Fowler and slotted flaps to greatly increase the lift and drag of the wing. When the flap is initially extended, it moves aft on its track. Once past a certain point on the track, further aft movement is accompanied by a downward deflection which opens up the slot between the flap and the wing. Many jet transport aircraft use this basic design with several slot openings being used to improve the airflow over the wing and flap surfaces. Figure 1-77 illustrates this type of flap combination.

A few aircraft, particularly sailplanes, incorporate a negative flap capability into the flap control design so that the flap can be raised above its neutral position. This changes the airfoil shape and allows the aircraft to fly at a higher speed with reduced drag.

Leading-Edge Flaps and Slats

Many airplanes are equipped with **leading-edge** flaps that are extended when the wing flaps are employed. The leading-edge flap, when retracted, forms the leading edge of the wing. When extended, the flap moves forward and down to increase the camber of the wing and provide greater lift at low flight speeds. The arrangement of a leading-edge flap is shown in Fig. 1-78.

Some aircraft have fixed slots built into the leading edge of the wings, usually only in the area of the ailerons. These slots allow airflow to be directed over the top of the wing at high angles of attack. This reduces the stalling speed of that portion of the wing and improves aileron control when flying at high angles of attack. When at normal flight attitudes, the slots have no significant effect on the flight characteristics of the aircraft. This type of design eliminates the mechanism required for the slats and eliminates the possibility of asymmetrical extension of the slats. A wing with a slot is shown in Fig. 1-79.

The use of **slats** on the leading edge of high-performance wings is a common method of reducing stalling speed and increasing lift at comparatively slow speeds. The slat forms the leading edge of the wing when not extended and creates a **slot** at the leading edge when extended. The slot permits air from the high-pressure area under the leading edge to flow up through the leading edge and to be directed along the top of the wing. This effectively reduces the possibility of stall at lower speeds. A drawing to illustrate the operation

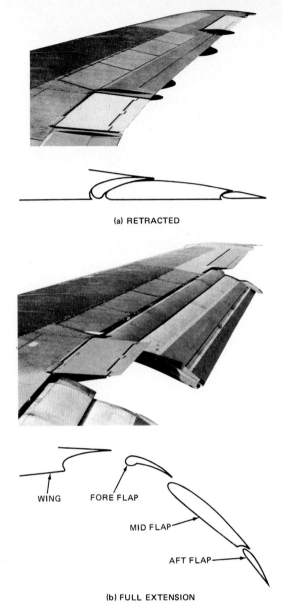

(a) RETRACTED

WING   FORE FLAP

MID FLAP

AFT FLAP

(b) FULL EXTENSION

FIG. 1-77   The retracted and extended position of the flap segments in a typical multiple-flap system.

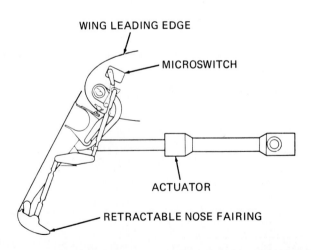

WING LEADING EDGE

MICROSWITCH

ACTUATOR

RETRACTABLE NOSE FAIRING

FIG. 1-78   Leading-edge flap.   *(Boeing Commercial Aircraft Co.)*

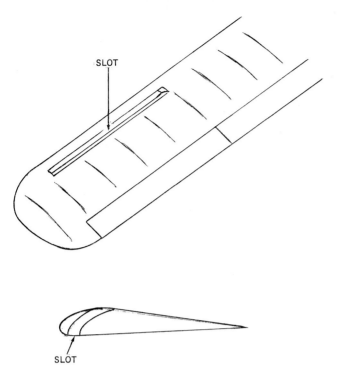

of slats is shown in Fig. 1-80. Slats which extend to form slots may be actuated aerodynamically or by mechanical controls.

Spoilers and Speed Brakes

Spoilers, also called "lift dumpers," are control surfaces which are used to reduce or "spoil" the lift on a wing. Spoilers are located on the upper surface of wings and are one of two basic configurations. The more common configuration on jet transports, shown in Fig. 1-81, is to have a flat panel spoiler laying flush with the surface of the wing and hinged at the forward edge. When the spoilers are deployed, the surface rises up and reduces the lift. The other configuration, shown in Fig. 1-82, is common among sailplanes and has the spoiler located inside the wing structure. When the spoilers are deployed, they rise vertically from the wing and spoil the lift.

Flight spoilers are used in flight to reduce the amount of lift that the wing is generating to allow controlled descents without gaining excessive air speed. Depending on the aircraft design, the spoilers may also be operated by the pilot's control wheel or stick. When the pilot moves the control left or right for a roll movement, the spoilers on the wing toward the center of the turn (upward-moving aileron) move upward and aid in rolling the aircraft into the turn. In

FIG. 1-79 Slots are fixed openings in the leading edge of the wing which improve aileron control at high angles of attack.

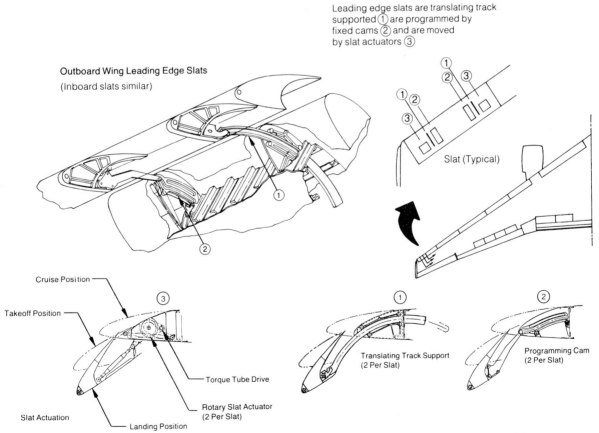

FIG. 1-80 The slats move forward and down as they are extended. *(Boeing Commercial Aircraft Co.)*

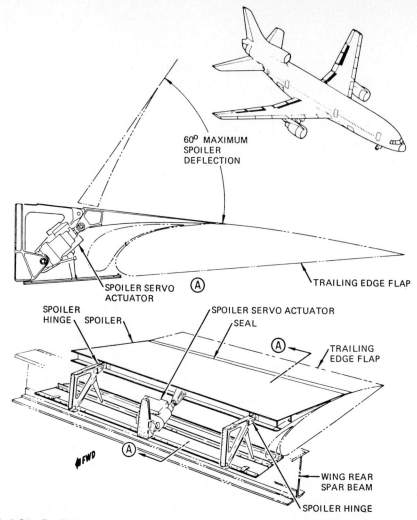

FIG. 1-81 Spoilers are commonly designed with a hinge at their leading edge. (*Lockheed California Co.*)

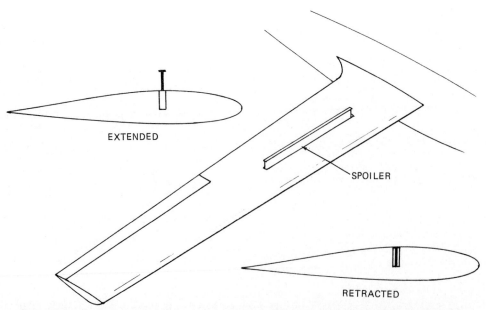

FIG. 1-82 Some aircraft, such as sailplanes, have the spoilers arranged so that they rise vertically out of the wing.

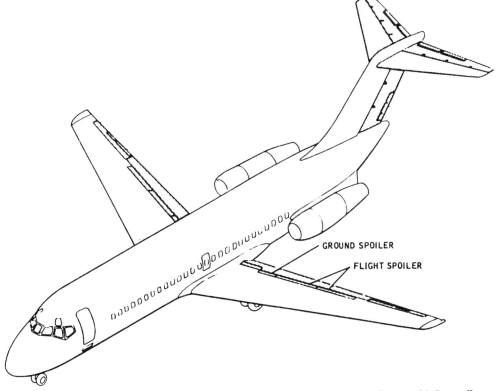

FIG. 1-83 Flight spoilers are normally located outboard of ground spoilers. *(McDonnell Douglas Corp.)*

some aircraft designs, the spoilers are the primary flight control for roll.

Ground spoilers are only used when the aircraft is on the ground and are used along with the flight spoilers to greatly reduce the wing's lift upon landing. They also increase the aerodynamic drag of the aircraft after landing to aid in slowing the aircraft.

Spoilers can be controlled by the pilot through a manual control lever, by an automatic flight control system, or by an automatic system activated upon landing. The typical relative location of flight and ground spoilers is shown in Fig. 1-83.

Speed brakes, also called **divebreaks,** are large drag panels used to aid in control of the speed of an aircraft. They may be located on the fuselage or on the wings. If on the fuselage, a speed brake is located on the top or the bottom of the structure. If speed brakes are deployed as a pair, one is on each side of the fuselage. If located on the wings, speed brakes are deployed symmetrically from the top and the bottom of the wing surface to control the speed of the aircraft as well as to act as spoilers to decrease the lift of the wings. See Fig. 1-84.

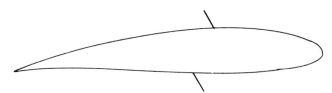

FIG. 1-84 Speed brakes on a wing open on the top and bottom of the wing.

On some aircraft designs, particularly gliders and sailplanes, there may not be any clear distinction between a spoiler and a divebrake because one control surface may serve the purpose of both actions, i.e., to decrease lift and increase drag.

● COCKPITS, CABINS, AND COMPARTMENTS

Cockpit, or Pilot's Compartment

The **cockpit** is that portion of the airplane occupied by the flight crew. From this cockpit radiate all controls used in flying the airplane. The word *controls* is a general term applied to the means provided to enable the pilot to control the speed, direction of flight, attitude, and power of an aircraft.

In designing an airplane, the engineers allow sufficient headroom, visibility, clearance for controls, and space for the movement of the hands and feet, keeping in mind the fact (for certain aircraft) that parachutes may be worn. These provisions are especially important in the case of airplanes designed for acrobatic use.

When the space occupied by the flight crew is completely enclosed, it may be referred to as a **cabin, flight deck,** or **crew compartment.**

The following information contains some of the guidelines that the manufacturers must take into account when designing the pilot's position in an aircraft. The cockpit or flight deck must be designed so that the required minimum flight crew can reach and operate all necessary controls and switches. Some du-

FIG. 1-85 The cabin of a modern high-performance light aircraft. *(Mooney Aircraft Co.)*

plication of controls and instruments may be required, depending upon the type of flight operations being carried out and the regulations under which the aircraft was certificated. The structure must be watertight to the extent that no leakage of water into the crew cabin occurs when flying through rain or snow. Noise and vibration must be within acceptable limits through design and proper insulation. For commercial transport aircraft, a lockable door must be used between the crew compartment and the passenger compartment.

For complete information concerning the requirements for the flight deck, refer to FAR Parts 23 and 25.

The arrangement of the cockpit, or pilot's compartment, for a modern light airplane is shown in Fig. 1-85. It can be seen that the cockpit is attractively and functionally designed to provide for safe and comfortable flight. The pilot's compartment of a jet airliner is shown in Fig. 1-86. Emphasized in this photograph are the many instruments and controls needed for the operation of the complex systems of a large jet transport aircraft.

Passenger Compartments

Passenger compartments must be designed and equipped to provide a maximum of comfort and safety for the passengers. This is particularly true for those aircraft certificated as air carriers for passenger service.

Passenger compartments must be adequately ventilated by means of a system that precludes the presence of fuel fumes and dangerous traces of carbon monoxide. The ventilation system is usually integrated with the heating system; and if the airplane needs to be pressurized, the pressurization system is also included in the design.

The seats in the passenger compartment of any aircraft must be securely fastened to the aircraft structure, regardless of whether or not the safety-belt load is transmitted through the seat. Each seat must be equipped with a safety belt that has been approved by the Federal Aviation Administration (FAA).

The windows for the passenger compartment of a large airplane must be designed and installed so there is no possibility that they will blow out when the compartment is pressurized. They must be able to withstand the continuous and cyclic pressurization loadings without undergoing a progressive loss of strength.

Figures 1-87 through 1-89 show typical jet transport passenger compartment features and dimension.

Doors

The doors for light aircraft are usually constructed of the same materials used for the other major components. Typically, the main framework of a door consists of a formed sheet-metal structure to provide rigidity and strength, and to this framework is riveted the sheet-metal outer skin. The metal used is aluminum alloy such as 2024-T4. The door frame is formed on a hydropress, stamp press, or drop hammer.

If the door is used for entrance to an upholstered cabin, the inside of the door will be covered with a matching upholstered panel. Inside the door structure will be located the door latching and locking mechanisms. The upper portion of the door will often contain a window made of a clear plastic similar to that used for the other cabin windows. The edge of the plastic sheet used for the window is protected with waterproof material and is held in the frame by means of one or more retainers designed to form a channel. The retainers are secured by means of rivets or screws. A door for a light airplane is shown in the drawing in Fig. 1-90.

Many modern aircraft are equipped with stair-type doors. These doors are designed as one-piece or two-piece doors. The one-piece door, shown in Fig. 1-91, is hinged at the bottom, and when the door is unlatched from the fuselage, it pivots outward and downward to become a stair for entering and leaving the aircraft. A two-piece version of this door, shown in Fig. 1-92, has a top half which is hinged at the top of the door frame. The top half is opened first and locked into position. The bottom half is then lowered and becomes the entrance stair. The stair-door is found on both pressurized and unpressurized aircraft.

The doors for a pressurized airliner must be much stronger and much more complex than the door for a light airplane. Typical of a door for the main cabin of a jet airliner is that shown in Fig. 1-93. As shown in the drawing, the door consists of a strong framework of aluminum alloy to which is riveted a heavy outer skin formed to the contour of the fuselage. At the top and the bottom edges of the door are hinged gates that make it possible, in effect, to decrease the height of the door so it can be swung outward through the door opening.

The hinging and controlling mechanism of the door is rather complex in order to provide for the necessary maneuvering to move the door outside the airplane when loading and unloading passengers. For safety in a pressurized airplane, the door is designed to act as

FIG. 1-86 The flight deck of one version of an L-1011. *(Lockheed California Co.)*

  1. External lighting controls
  2. Pilot's flight instruments
  3. Caution and warning panel
  4. Navigation radios and avionics flight system controls
  5. Engine instruments
  6. Copilot's flight instruments
  7. Pilot's control wheel
  8. Speed brake lever
  9. Throttles
10. Communication-navigation radio controls
11. Yaw trim wheel
12. Slat-flap control lever
13. Copilot's pitch trim wheel
14. Landing gear selector
15. Copilot's control wheel
16. Overhead circuit-breaker panel
17. Engine fire warning and extinguishing controls
18. Flight-control electronics system panel
19. Primary flight control system panel
20. Lighting control panels
21. Engine start panel
22. Anti-ice controls

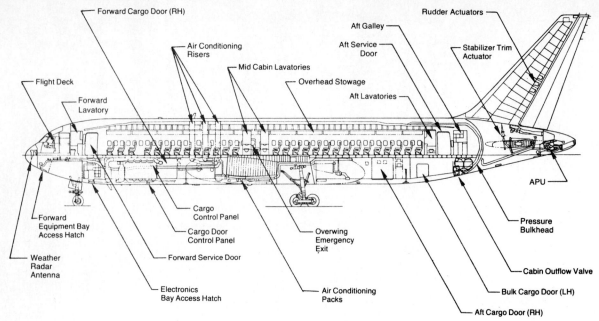

FIG. 1-87   Fuselage arrangement of a Boeing 767-200.   (*Boeing Commercial Aircraft Co.*)

a plug for the door opening, and the pressure in the cabin seats the door firmly in place. To accomplish this, the door must be larger than its opening and must be inside the airplane with pressure pushing outward. This prevents the rapid decompression of the cabin that could occur if the door should be closed from the outside and the securing mechanism should become unlatched.

Another type of entrance door being used in airliners is a vertical retracting door. This type of door stays inside the aircraft during operation and does not require the complex motions associated with the typical airliner hinged door. When being operated, the vertical door slides into the overhead area of the cabin, providing a clear door access opening for entering and leaving the aircraft. Figure 1-94 shows this type of door.

Requirements for Doors and Exits

The doors and special exits for passenger-carrying aircraft must conform to certain regulations designed to provide for the safety and well-being of passengers. These requirements are established by the FAA in FAR Parts 23 and 25. Some of these requirements include the following.

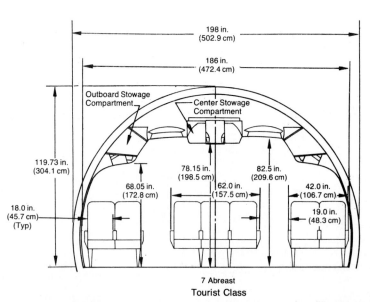

FIG. 1-88   Fuselage passenger compartment cross-section of a Boeing 767-200.   (*Boeing Commercial Aircraft Co.*)

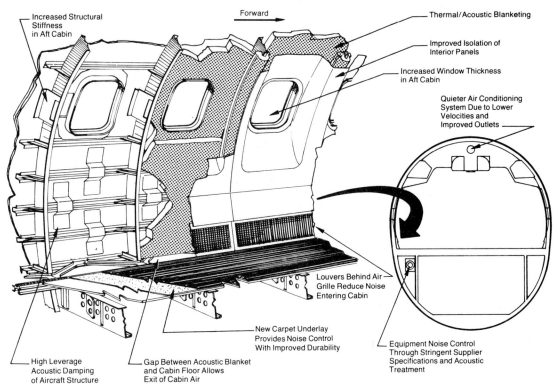

Passenger cabin soundproofing equivalent or better than current industry standard.

Increased Structural Stiffness in Aft Cabin

Forward

Thermal/Acoustic Blanketing

Improved Isolation of Interior Panels

Increased Window Thickness in Aft Cabin

Quieter Air Conditioning System Due to Lower Velocities and Improved Outlets

Louvers Behind Air Grille Reduce Noise Entering Cabin

New Carpet Underlay Provides Noise Control With Improved Durability

Equipment Noise Control Through Stringent Supplier Specifications and Acoustic Treatment

High Leverage Acoustic Damping of Aircraft Structure

Gap Between Acoustic Blanket and Cabin Floor Allows Exit of Cabin Air

FIG. 1-89 Acoustic control features of a Boeing 767-200. *(Boeing Commercial Aircraft Co.)*

Closed cabins on all aircraft carrying passengers must be provided with at least one adequate and easily accessible external door.

No passenger door may be located in the plane of rotation of an inboard propeller or within 5° thereof as measured from the propeller hub.

The external doors on transport aircraft must be equipped with devices for locking and for safeguarding against opening in flight either inadvertently by persons or as a result of mechanical failure. It must be possible to open external doors from either the inside or the outside even though persons may be crowding against the door from the inside. The use of inward-opening doors is not prohibited if sufficient measures are provided to prevent occupants from crowding against the door to an extent that would interfere with the opening of the door. The means of opening must be simple and obvious and must be so arranged and marked internally and externally that it can be readily located and operated even in darkness.

Reasonable provisions must be made to prevent the jamming of an external door as a result of fuselage deformation in a minor crash.

External doors for a transport airplane must be so located that persons using them will not be endangered by the propellers of a propeller-operated airplane when appropriate operating procedures are employed.

Means must be provided for a direct inspection of the door-locking mechanism by crew members to as-

certain whether all external doors for which the initial opening movement is outward, including passenger, crew, service, and cargo doors, are fully locked. In addition, visual means must be provided to signal to appropriate crew members that all normally used external doors are closed and in the fully locked position. This requirement is often met by placing indicator lights in the cockpit. These lights are operated by switches incorporated in the door-locking mechanisms.

All airplanes, except those with all engines mounted on the approximate center line of the fuselage and a seating capacity of five or fewer, must have at least one emergency exit on the opposite side of the cabin from the main door. If the pilot compartment is separated from the cabin by a door that is likely to block the pilot's escape in a minor crash, there must be an exit in the pilot's compartment.

The requirements for emergency exits are determined in accordance with seating capacity of the airplane and are also set forth in FAR Parts 23 and 25.

Figure 1-95 shows the location of doors on a jet airliner.

Cargo Compartments

Baggage and cargo compartments must be designed in such a manner that they will carry their approved capacity under all normal conditions of flight and landing without failure of any structural part. Each com-

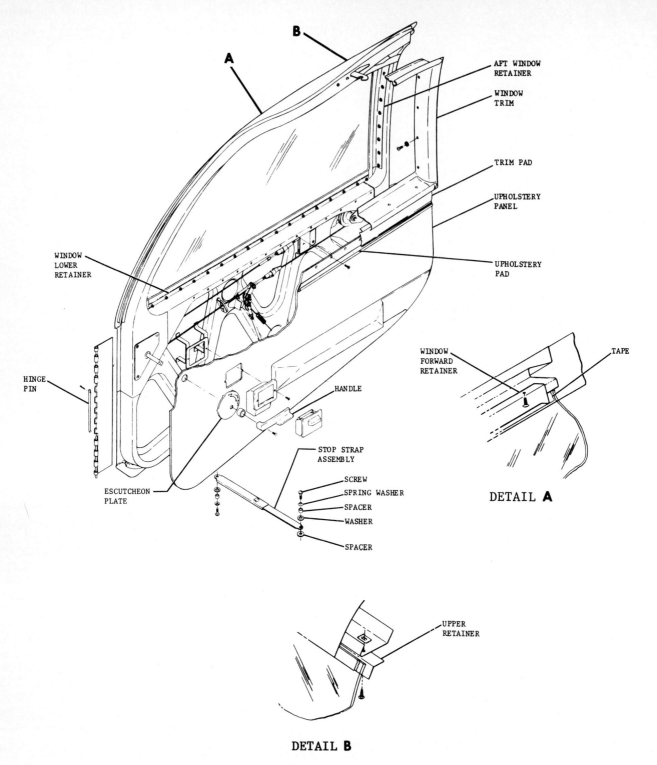

FIG. 1-90 Door for a light-airplane cabin. *(Cessna Aircraft Co.)*

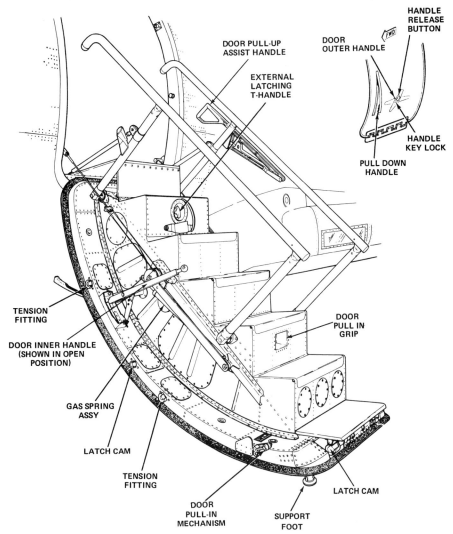

FIG. 1-91 A one-piece stair-door on a Canadair Challenger 601. *(Canadair Inc.)*

partment must bear a placard stating the maximum allowable weight of contents as determined by the structural strength of the compartment and the flight tests conducted for certification of the airplane. Suitable means must be provided to prevent the contents of baggage and cargo compartments from shifting.

Transport-type aircraft are provided with heavy decking and support structures which enable them to carry heavy freight in addition to baggage for the passengers. Freight is generally "containerized"; that is, the freight is packed in containers designed to fit the contour of the fuselage. Baggage is also containerized in many cases. Special loading equipment is employed to lift and roll cargo containers to move them into the airplane compartments. Powered rollers are built into the cargo decks to permit easy movement of the cargo containers. When the cargo containers are in position, they are secured so they cannot shift during flight or upon landing. A typical containerized cargo arrangement is shown in Fig. 1-96.

Cargo compartments must meet strict requirements for fire protection, as set forth in FAR Part 25. Mechanics making repairs and inspections in cargo compartments must ensure that all emergency and safety requirements are maintained.

● LANDING GEAR

In any study of aircraft structures it is necessary to consider the landing gear, its construction, its arrangement, and the methods by which it is attached to the aircraft structure. The method of attachment to the aircraft structure is important because of the need for transmitting landing loads to the aircraft without overstressing portions of the aircraft structure.

Types of Landing Gear

Landing gear must be classified as either **fixed** or **retractable,** and it may also be classified according to arrangement on the aircraft.

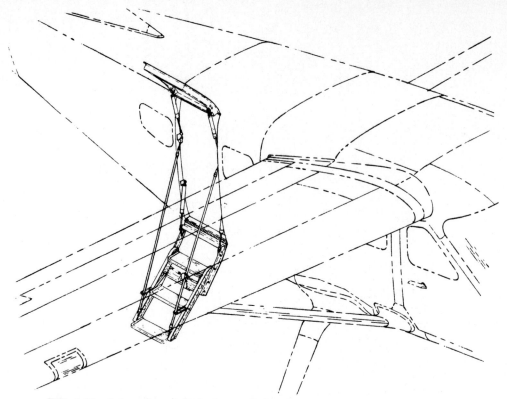

FIG. 1-92   A two-piece stair-door on a Cessna Caravan I.   *(Cessna Aircraft Co.)*

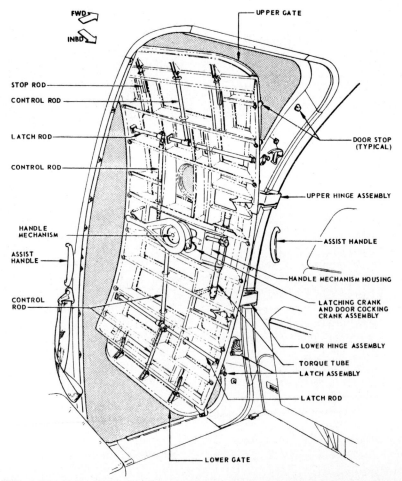

FIG. 1-93   Main cabin door for an airliner.   *(Boeing Commercial Aircraft Co.)*

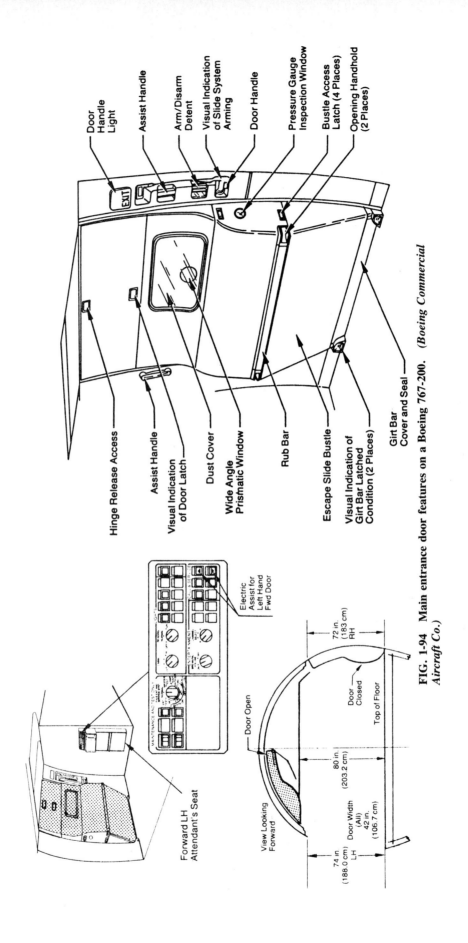

Door Handle Light

Assist Handle

Arm/Disarm Detent

Visual Indication of Slide System Arming

Door Handle

Pressure Gauge Inspection Window

Bustle Access Latch (4 Places)

Opening Handhold (2 Places)

Hinge Release Access

Assist Handle

Visual Indication of Door Latch

Dust Cover

Wide Angle Prismatic Window

Rub Bar

Escape Slide Bustle

Visual Indication of Girt Bar Latched Condition (2 Places)

Girt Bar Cover and Seal

Electric Assist for Left Hand Fwd Door

Forward LH Attendant's Seat

Door Open

Door Closed

Top of Floor

View Looking Forward

72 in. (183 cm) RH

80 in. (203.2 cm)

Door Width (All) 42 in. (106.7 cm)

74 in. (188.0 cm) LH

FIG. 1-94 Main entrance door features on a Boeing 767-200. *(Boeing Commercial Aircraft Co.)*

51

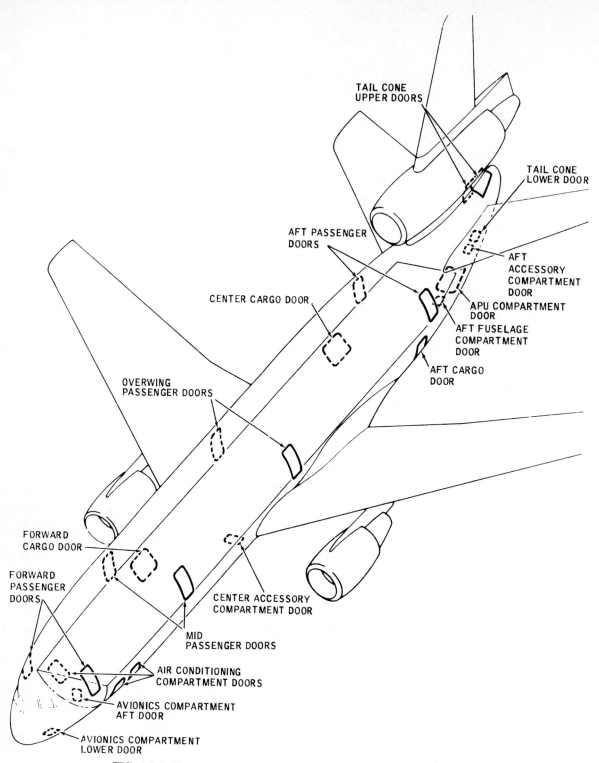

TAIL CONE
UPPER DOORS

TAIL CONE
LOWER DOOR

AFT PASSENGER
DOORS

AFT
ACCESSORY
COMPARTMENT
DOOR

CENTER CARGO DOOR

APU COMPARTMENT
DOOR

AFT FUSELAGE
COMPARTMENT
DOOR

AFT CARGO
DOOR

OVERWING
PASSENGER DOORS

FORWARD
CARGO DOOR

CENTER ACCESSORY
COMPARTMENT DOOR

FORWARD
PASSENGER
DOORS

MID
PASSENGER DOORS

AIR CONDITIONING
COMPARTMENT DOORS

AVIONICS COMPARTMENT
AFT DOOR

AVIONICS COMPARTMENT
LOWER DOOR

FIG. 1-95 Door placement for an airliner. *(McDonnell Douglas Corp.)*

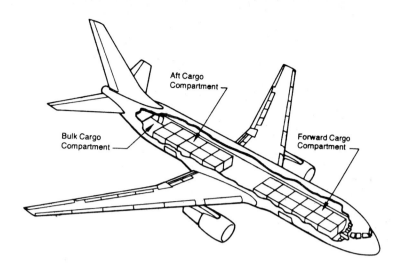

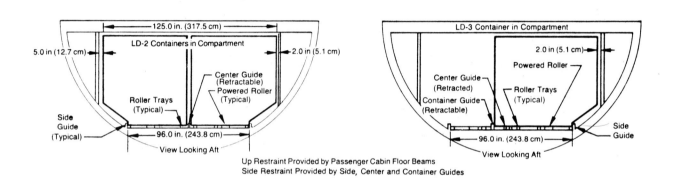

Up Restraint Provided by Passenger Cabin Floor Beams
Side Restraint Provided by Side, Center and Container Guides

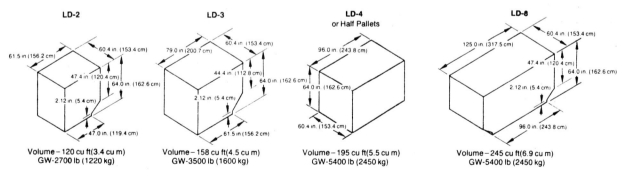

LD-2	LD-3	LD-4 or Half Pallets	LD-8
Volume – 120 cu ft(3.4 cu m)	Volume – 158 cu ft(4.5 cu m)	Volume – 195 cu ft(5.5 cu m)	Volume – 245 cu ft(6.9 cu m)
GW-2700 lb (1220 kg)	GW-3500 lb (1600 kg)	GW-5400 lb (2450 kg)	GW-5400 lb (2450 kg)

FIG. 1-96 Containerized cargo arrangement on a Boeing 767-200. *(Boeing Commercial Aircraft Co.)*

A fixed landing gear is attached to the airframe so that it is held in a fixed position. As it is always in the airstream, this type of landing gear generates a significant amount of aerodynamic drag. This arrangement is normally found on relatively low speed aircraft and aircraft designed for simplicity of operation.

A retractable landing gear is carried partially or completely inside the airframe structure to reduce drag. When necessary for landing, the gear is extended by some mechanism. The gear is retracted into the airframe after takeoff.

An aircraft can have a combination of fixed and retractable landing gear; an example is a floatplane which has wheels that retract into the floats. The floats are a fixed landing gear and the wheels are retractable.

The basic landing-gear configurations for aircraft operating on land includes conventional, tricycle, quadracycle, inline, and skids.

The two most common configurations are the conventional and tricycle arrangements. A conventional landing-gear configuration consist of two main landing gears located ahead of the aircraft center of gravity and a tailwheel located near the tail of the aircraft. With conventional landing gear the aircraft sits on the ground in a tail-low attitude. Tricycle landing gear consists of two main landing gears located aft of the center of gravity and a nose wheel located near the nose of the aircraft. With tricycle landing gear the aircraft sets in an approximately level flight attitude.

A quadracycle landing gear normally consists of two nose wheels and two main wheels. This configuration is found on some helicopters and on most float-equipped aircraft that incorporate retractable wheels in the float design.

Centerline landing gear is often found on aircraft such as sailplanes and gliders. This configuration has one main landing wheel mounted on the centerline of the fuselage and near the center of gravity of the aircraft. Small auxiliary wheels or skids may be located on the nose, tail, and wing tips of these types of aircraft.

Skid-type landing gear is usually reserved for use on helicopters as they normally take off and land vertically and do not require a landing or take-off run.

Two views of the main landing gear for the Boeing 747 airliner are shown in Fig. 1-97. Note that the main gear of this tricycle-gear-equipped aircraft includes two **body-gear struts** with four wheels each and two **wing-gear struts** with four wheels each. Thus there are 16 main wheels and two nose-gear wheels. Landing-gear units that incorporate four wheels with axles mounted on the ends of a main beam, as employed on the Boeing 747 and other large airplanes, are often referred to as "bogies." One of the main landing-gear struts and the four-wheel gear of a DC-8 airliner are shown in Fig. 1-98. This gear is designed to caster, or swivel, so that the airplane will turn more easily.

Shock-Absorbing Methods

Various methods are used to absorb the force of ground contact upon landing. These methods can be divided into two types of "shock-absorbing" pro-

FIG. 1-97 Multiple landing gear for the Boeing 747.

cesses: the energy-dissipating type and the energy-returning type. An energy-dissipating-type landing-gear cushions the contact with the ground and changes the energy of the contact into heat by causing a liquid to flow through a restricted orifice and/or heating air by compression. This heat is then radiated to the surrounding atmosphere. Examples of this type of landing gear include air-oleo and spring-oleo shock absorbers.

FIG. 1-98 Main gear unit for the DC-8 airliner.

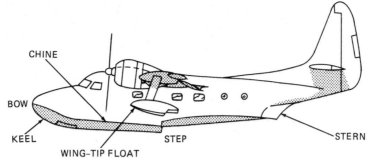

FIG. 1-99 Components and terms associated with a hull-type seaplane.

Energy-returning-type landing gear absorbs the shock of the aircraft contacting the ground and then returns the energy to the aircraft by exerting an upward force on the aircraft after a very short period of time. This type of landing gear includes the use of rigid gear legs, bungee cords, rubber disks, and spring-type landing gear.

In both types of shock-absorbing methods, some of the energy of ground contact is dissipated through the scrubbing of the tires and friction of motion between components and mounting structures.

Light aircraft may incorporate one or more of the types of landing gear. For example, most Cessna single-engine aircraft use a flexible steel tube or flat leaf spring for the main landing gear and an air-oleo shock absorber for the nose gear. Another common example is the use of bungee cords on the main landing gear and a spring-leaf tail wheel shock absorber on a Piper J-3 Cub. Most large aircraft use only air-oleo shock-absorbing landing gear.

A full discussion of landing-gear systems is provided in Chap. 10, "Landing-Gear Systems."

Retracting Systems

Retractable landing gear may be retracted manually, electrically, or hydraulically. The main struts of retractable landing gear are mounted on trunnions and bearings so that they can easily be swung upward into the fuselage or wing. The retracting mechanism may be a jackscrew arrangement, an electric-motor-operated screw or gear system, or a hydraulic actuating cylinder connected to suitable linking devices.

Hulls and Floats

Aircraft designed to operate from water make use of a hull-type fuselage structure or floats attached to the fuselage through a strut support system. These aircraft may be amphibious, incorporating a retractable wheel-type landing gear which allows the aircraft to operate from land or water. These aircraft normally use a fixed or retractable water rudder which improves the aircraft directional control when operating on the water.

The hull configuration shown in Fig. 1-99 uses the fuselage as the primary flotation component with sponsons extending outward from the fuselage or floats attached to the bottoms of the wings for lateral stability in the water. In some aircraft these stabilizing

floats retract into the wing and form the wing tip. If the hull-type seaplane is an amphibian, then the landing gear may be arranged in a conventional or tricycle configuration with the main gear extending and retracting into the fuselage or the wing. The nose wheel or tailwheel would retract into the fuselage.

Float-equipped aircraft normally use two floats attached to the fuselage through a series of struts, spreader bars, and brace wires as shown in Fig. 1-100. This arrangement allows aircraft designed for land op-

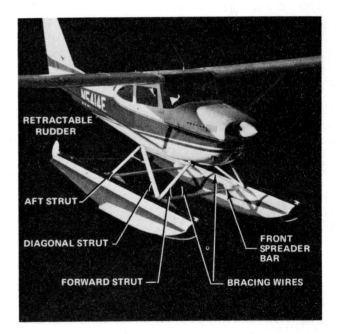

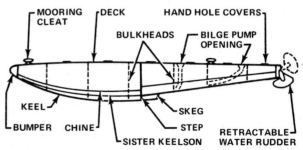

FIG. 1-100 Components and terms associated with a float-type seaplane. *(Edo)*

erations to be converted to water operations. The land operations capability can be retained by equipping the aircraft with wheels which can be retracted into and extended from the floats. Aircraft converted from landplanes to seaplanes by the addition of floats often require the addition of one or more auxiliary vertical fins to improve the yaw stability of the aircraft in flight.

Skis

Because of the many areas in which airplanes must operate in the winter without benefit of runways cleared of snow, it is necessary to equip airplanes to be used in these areas with **skis.**

Aircraft skis are similar in general appearance to snow or water skis with a turned-up toe at the front of the ski and a long ski body. These skis differ from water of snow skis in that they are relatively wide. The increase in width relative to length distributes the weight of the aircraft over a large area and reduces the chance of the aircraft sinking into the snow.

Skis may be used in place of wheels or in combination with wheels. The skis may be designed to allow the wheel to protrude below the ski just far enough so that the wheel will roll on a hard surface before the ski makes contact with the surface, but the wheel will not protrude so much as to cause excessive drag on the snow. The ski may also be designed to be ''retract-able'' in that the ski can be lowered below the wheel for landing on snow or raised well above the wheel for landing on a hard surface. The extension and retraction system is usually hydraulic.

Skis are held in the proper position relative to the landing attitude of the aircraft by the use of cables and a bungee cord as shown in Fig. 1-101.

Skis may be made of wood, metal, or composites and may be used on conventional or tricycle-geared aircraft. The attachment of the ski or the wheel-ski combination is at the standard axle used for the aircraft wheels.

● POWERPLANT STRUCTURES

The aircraft powerplant is usually enclosed in a housing, called a **nacelle,** and is attached to the aircraft by an engine mount. The engine must be isolated from the rest of the aircraft by a barrier known as a **firewall.**

Nacelles

An **engine nacelle** is used to enclose the engine in a streamlined housing to improve the aerodynamics of the aircraft, to support and protect the engine and its components, and to direct airflow into the engine for cooling and combustion and away from the engine for proper exhaust outflow.

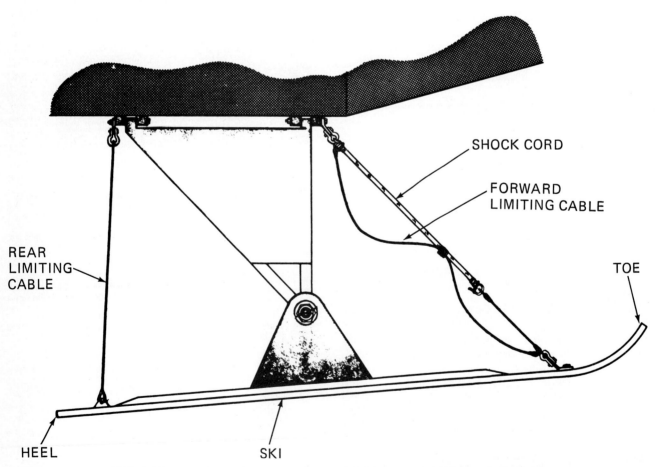

FIG. 1-101 A main landing-gear ski installation uses a forward and rear limiting cable and a shock cord to hold up the toe of the ski in flight.

FIG. 1-102 Engine nacelle for an all-metal light twin airplane.

The nacelle normally has removable segments which allow for access to the engine for maintenance. The nacelle may also incorporate cowl flaps for control of engine cooling in a reciprocating engine, thrust reversers or reverser support structures for jet engines, and auxiliary air doors for jet engine operation at low altitudes and slow speeds. The nacelle may also incorporate components of several engine monitoring systems such as fire detection and thrust indication.

The nacelle may be constructed of sheet metal and/or composite components assembled through a combination of removable fasteners, rivets, and bonding.

An engine nacelle for a light airplane is shown in Fig. 1-102. Note that this nacelle is securely attached to and streamlined with the wing. Here the wing structure is reinforced to carry the extra weight and thrust of the engine.

The structure employed to attach an engine nacelle or pod to a wing or fuselage may be referred to as a **strut** or a **pylon**. A nacelle for a Boeing 747 jet airliner

FIG. 1-103 Engine nacelle for a Boeing 747.

is shown in Fig. 1-103. This nacelle is also called a "pod," and, as can be seen in the photo, is mounted on a strut which extends into the wing. The wing is reinforced at the point where the engine struts are attached. The pylon used to support the engine nacelle on the rear portion of a Douglas DC-9 airplane is shown in Fig. 1-104.

Firewalls

All engines, auxiliary power units, fuel-burning heaters, and other combustion equipment which are intended for operation in flight as well as the combustion, turbine, and tail-pipe sections of turbine engines must be isolated from the remainder of the aircraft by means of firewalls, shrouds, or other equivalent means.

Firewalls and shrouds must be constructed in such a manner that no hazardous quantity of air, fluids, or flame can pass from the compartment to other portions of the aircraft. All openings in the firewall or shroud must be sealed with close-fittings fireproof grommets, bushings, or firewall fittings. Firewalls and shrouds must be constructed of fireproof materials such as stainless steel or titanium. These provide protection against both heat and corrosion.

Engine Mounts

An **engine mount** is a frame that supports the engine and holds it to the fuselage or nacelle. They vary widely in appearance and construction, although the basic features of construction are well standardized. Ideally, engine mounts are designed so that the engine and its accessories are accessible for inspection and maintenance.

Light-aircraft engine mounts may be of welded-steel tubing or aluminum alloy sheet metal. The construction will include some forged and metal plate components. Two types of light-aircraft engine mounts are shown in Fig. 1-105.

Reciprocating-engine-powered transport aircraft and many turbine-powered aircraft have the engine mounts made of steel tubing with some forgings and metal plates used in the designs. The engine mount for a DC-7B reciprocating-engine-powered aircraft is shown in Fig. 1-106.

Most modern jet-powered aircraft use forged metal mounts bolted to the airframe attachment points and to the engine similar to the mount shown in Fig. 1-107.

Many transport aircraft have the engine attachments designed to allow for a quick removal and installation of a complete engine and mount assembly. This requires that fluid lines, electrical cables, control linkages, and engine mount attachments to the airframe be designed for easy separation at or near the firewall. This type of arrangement is referred to as a QEC (Quick Engine Change) package.

The vibrations that originate in reciprocating engines are transmitted through the engine mount to the airplane structure; hence mounts for such engines must be arranged with some sort of rubber or synthetic

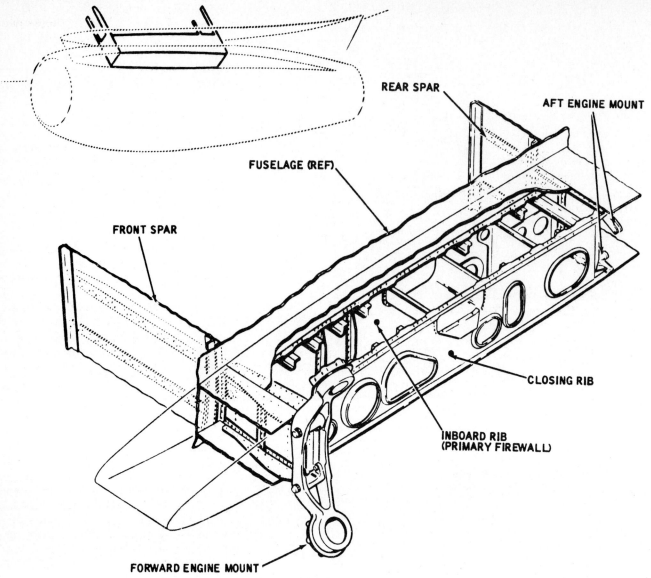

FIG. 1-104 Pylon for a fuselage-mounted engine. *(McDonnell Douglas Corp.)*

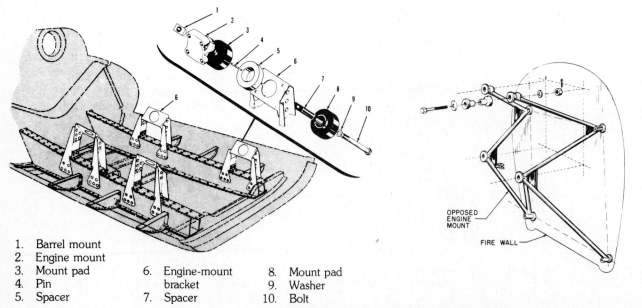

1. Barrel mount
2. Engine mount
3. Mount pad
4. Pin
5. Spacer
6. Engine-mount bracket
7. Spacer
8. Mount pad
9. Washer
10. Bolt

FIG. 1-105 Two types of light-aircraft engine mounts. *(Cessna Aircraft Co.)*

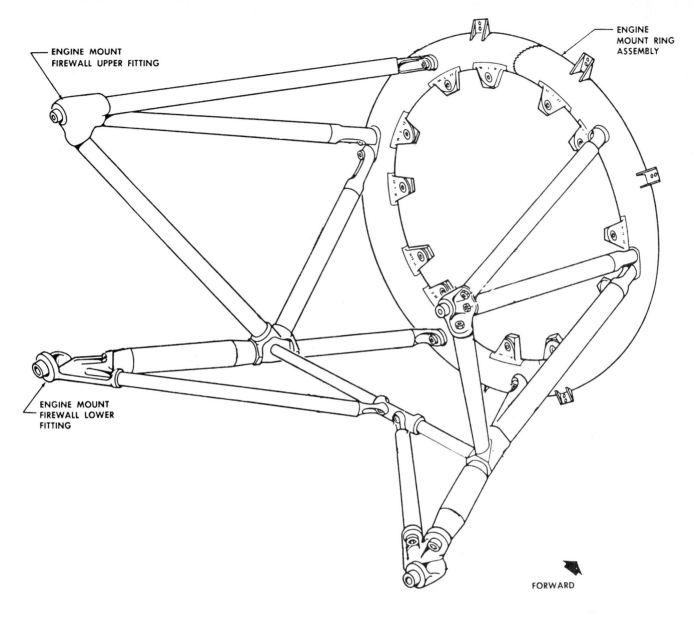

ENGINE MOUNT
FIREWALL UPPER FITTING

ENGINE
MOUNT RING
ASSEMBLY

ENGINE MOUNT
FIREWALL LOWER
FITTING

FORWARD

FIG. 1-106   Engine mount for a DC-7 reciprocating-engine-powered transport aircraft.
(McDonnell Douglas Corp.)

rubber bushings between the engine and mount attaching structure for damping these vibrations. These bushings are often a part of the engine-mounting bracket and may be installed on the engine at the factory. The maximum vibration absorption is obtained when the mounting bolts are tightened so that the engine can move within reasonable limits in a torsional (rotating) direction but is restrained from any fore-and-aft movement. The torsional motion is then damped by the restraining action of the pads or cushions and the friction of the metal surfaces held by the bolts. If these bolts are too tight, the mounting structure tends to vibrate with the engine, which is obviously undesirable. For this reason, mechanics should always consult the manufacturer's service manual when tightening such bolts.

Dynamic suspension is a method of mounting an engine so that the engine-propeller unit is effectively supported at its center of gravity (CG) by means of rubber-mounted links with pin ends that lie with their axes intersecting at the CG. The engine then acts as though it were supported on a universal joint at the CG. In the ordinary engine mount, many of the motions and forces are transmitted to the aircraft. With dynamic suspension, many of the vibrations and forces are stopped before they reach the fuselage.

Cowling and Fairings

Cowling and fairings are generally similar, but they differ in detail and to some extent in function. **Cowling** usually consists of detachable sections for covering portions of the airplane, such as engines, mounts, and

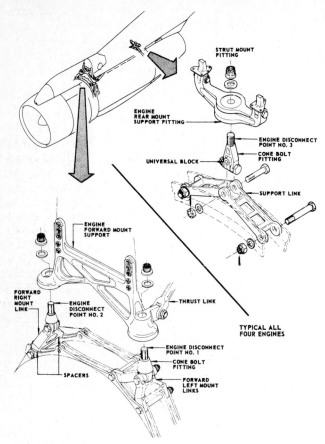

FIG. 1-107 Engine mounts for wing-mounted turbine engine.

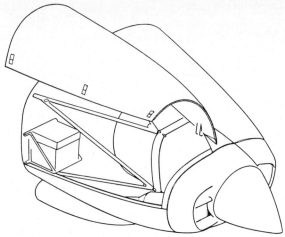

FIG. 1-108 Typical light-aircraft cowling equipped with hinged cowling doors. *(Cessna Aircraft Co.)*

other parts where ease of access is important. Cowling affords protection and also aids in streamlining the area covered.

Engine cowlings normally consist of formed sections, made of sheet metal, composite, or other fire-proof material, which are attached to each other and to the supporting structure with quick-disconnect fasteners and screws. The cowling area commonly encloses the engine completely except for the inlet and outlet areas which provide a path for engine cooling airflow. Cowlings often incorporate cowl flaps so that the pilot can control the size of these cooling openings, and, thus, the temperature of the engine.

Cowlings are designed to minimize the chance of liquids collecting in the cowling area by providing paths through which the liquids can flow to drain openings or to the airflow openings. This reduces the chance of fire by removing fuel and oil and reduces any weight problem that might develop from any liquid collecting in the cowl. These fluid paths are positioned so that the liquids will not come into contact with the engine exhaust system or exhaust gases downstream of the exhaust system. Figure 1-108 shows a typical light-aircraft cowling.

Cowling sections are normally of a size and weight convenient for one person to carry. When they are removed for inspection and maintenance work, they should be stored in numbered racks corresponding to numbers placed either temporarily or permanently on the cowling sections so that they can be replaced in the proper order.

A **fairing** is used principally to streamline a portion of an airplane, although it may protect some small piece of equipment or merely improve the appearance. Fairing units may be composed of several small sections or may be stamped or formed into one large section. The sections may be removable and attached in the same manner as cowling, or they may be permanently attached to the aircraft.

Cowling and fairing should be handled with care so that they are not bent or broken. Long strips of large sections are sometimes not rigid enough to support their own weight. Small parts made of light-gauge material are easily damaged during maintenance work. The finish must be unmarred; otherwise it should be refinished. Chafing strips, made of either fabric or fiber, may be used between pieces of installed cowling. These strips require renewing if they are worn to the point where metal parts rub together. Attachment devices are inspected to be sure that they function easily and securely. When they become badly worn or loose, they should be replaced.

● ROTORCRAFT STRUCTURES

The broad heading of **rotorcraft** includes both helicopters and gyroplanes. **Gyroplanes** differ from helicopters in that the rotor system is not driven by the engine in flight, but it may be prespun to an operating rpm prior to flight. During flight the gyroplane engine only provides forward thrust for the aircraft and the main rotor free-wheels or "autogyrates" by the air moving through the rotor. The gyroplane may have collective as well as cyclic controls, but the pedals operate a conventional rudder system. Other than this brief introduction to gyroplanes, all further references to rotorcraft will concern helicopters. Many of the aircraft components used on airplanes and helicopters are common to the gyroplane.

Helicopters have a rotor system which is driven by the aircraft engine, and through this rotor system the aircraft generates lift and propulsive thrust. Most helicopters have only one main rotor and rely on an auxiliary rotor to overcome the torque of the main rotor and maintain directional control.

Fuselage

The fuselage of a helicopter can be constructed of any combination of steel tubing, sheet metal, and composite materials. Each material is selected according to the structural shape and strength requirements and the familiarity of the manufacturer with the materials used. Most modern helicopters are constructed primarily of sheet aluminum with various structural components of steel and composites.

The two major assemblies of a single-rotor helicopter are the forward fuselage and the tailboom. Figure 1-109 shows a Bell 214ST fuselage assembly and identifies many of the major airframe components.

The forward fuselage contains the crew and passenger compartments and the engine, transmission, fuel tanks, electrical, and hydraulic systems. The main rotor system is driven by the transmission, and the transmission drives the tail rotor through a shaft extending through or mounted on the outside of the tailboom.

The primary purpose of the tailboom, called a "tailcone" in some helicopters, is to support the stabilizing surfaces and tail rotor of the helicopter. The tail rotor is used to control the yaw of the aircraft and to counteract the torque of the engine/transmission system. A vertical stabilizer provides stability in forward flight and relieves the tail rotor of some of its workload in forward flight. A tail skid projects below the tail rotor and vertical stabilizer and is used to protect the tail rotor from ground contact. A horizontal surface is found on most helicopters. This surface may be a fixed horizontal stabilizer, used to improve the pitch stability of the helicopter, or it may be a movable elevator, used to improve the pitch control of the craft.

Landing Gear

Helicopters can have landing gear that is either fixed or retractable. The fixed landing gear may consist of a pair of skids, wheels in a conventional or tricycle configuration, or floats. The retractable landing gear

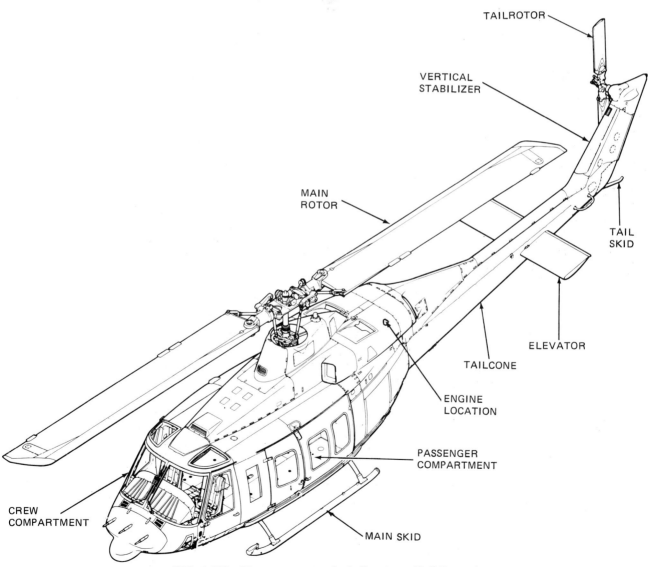

FIG. 1-109 The components of a helicopter. *(Bell Textron)*

consists of retractable wheels similar to fixed-wing aircraft.

The fixed-skid systems, shown in Fig. 1-109, may or may not incorporate a shock absorption system. If no shock absorber is used, then the skid structure is mounted directly on the bottom of the helicopter fuselage structure. If a shock absorber system is used, it usually includes an air-oleo cylinder near each end of each skid.

For the fixed-wheel-type landing gear, an air-oleo shock absorber is normally used. If a retractable landing gear is used, the gear normally incorporates an air-oleo shock absorber system.

Retractable landing gear on a helicopter are similar in basic design to the airplane retraction systems.

Helicopters can have floats installed in place of their normal landing gear. This type of conversion is most often found on helicopters equipped with skids due to the simplicity of the conversion. This allows the helicopters to operate equally well from land or water.

Helicopters that are not float-equipped but are used for extensive overwater operations to hard-surface landing areas often incorporate emergency floating devices attached to the landing gear or located in compartments on the lower sections of the fuselage. These flotation bags can be deployed by the pilot and are designed to keep the helicopter afloat after an emergency water landing. Figure 1-110 shows this type of flotation mechanism.

Rotor Systems

Helicopter rotor systems are major aircraft assemblies which are used to convert the engine power into lift, propulsive force, and directional control. Helicopters can have one or two main rotors. If the aircraft has one main rotor, it will have an auxiliary rotor system to counter the main rotor system torque.

The rotor blades may be constructed of wood, metal, composite materials, or some combination of these materials. Most modern rotor blades incorporate bonded metal components in combination with composite components for strength and fatigue resistance.

Rotor systems are driven by the aircraft powerplant through a transmission. The transmission is used to reduce the high engine rpm to a usable rotor rpm. The transmission also provides power to aircraft system components such as fluid pumps and electrical generators. Belts, hydraulic couplings, free turbine engines, and mechanical clutches are used on helicopters to connect the powerplant to the transmission.

A freewheeling unit is used to disconnect the engine from the rotor system any time that the engine power output is reduced to a point where it is no longer driving the rotor system. When the freewheeling unit disconnects the engine from the rotor system, the helicopter enters a type of flight known as "autorotation" where the air moving upward through the rotor system causes the rotors to turn. The aircraft can thereby descend to a landing with the rotor system providing lift, propulsion, and directional control, even though the engine may have failed.

Main Rotor Systems

There are three basic designs for the main rotor system. These are the **fully articulated, semirigid,** and **rigid** rotor systems.

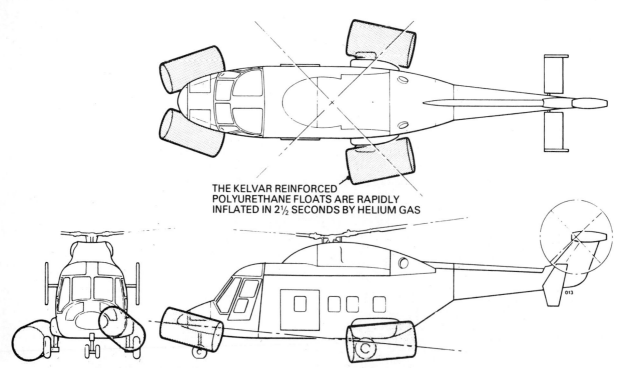

THE KELVAR REINFORCED POLYURETHANE FLOATS ARE RAPIDLY INFLATED IN 2½ SECONDS BY HELIUM GAS

FIG. 1-110 Flotation bags on a helicopter can be deployed if a water landing is necessary in an emergency. (Westland)

The fully articulated rotor system normally has three or more rotor blades and each blade can move by three different motions, independent of the other blades in the system. One motion, called **flapping,** is allowed through the rotor blade flap hinge, located near the rotor hub. This allows the blade to rise and fall as it rotates around the hub. The **lead-lag** motion is through the drag hinge. The drag hinge allows the blade to move ahead of (lead) or fall behind (lag) the normal axis of the hub extension. Each blade is also free to rotate about its central axis. This is called **feathering.** So, each blade can feather, lead or lag, and flap independently of the other blades. All of this motion is required so that the blades can change their angle of attack and speed through the air as the aircraft speed changes and different control inputs are fed to the rotor system from the pilot's controls. A fully articulated rotor head is shown in Fig. 1-111.

A semirigid rotor system, shown in Fig. 1-112, uses only two rotor blades. The blades are rigidly attached to the central hub. A teetering hinge is used to connect the hub to the rotor shaft. Through this teetering hinge the blades can flap, one up and one down, and feather, one increasing pitch and one decreasing pitch, as a unit. If the hub has the blades underslung, that is, the blades are on a lower rotational plane than the pivot point of the hub, a drag hinge may not be required.

Figure 1-113 is an illustration of a rigid rotor system. This type of rotor system does not allow the blades to flap or drag. They can only feather. This design can use any number of blades and has become very popular for use in many modern helicopter designs.

The rotor system contains mechanical adjustments which the mechanic can use to correct the track of the tip paths of the rotor blades. If the blades are not in track, that is, if each blade does not follow the same path as the other blades, then a low-frequency vibration will exist during flight.

Tail Rotor

The conventional tail rotor consists of a rotor of two or more blades located at the end of the tailboom. The tail rotor is used with single-rotor helicopters to counteract yawing movement resulting from the torque effect of the engine–transmission–main rotor system. It does this by generating a side thrust at the end of the tailboom which tries to rotate the helicopter about its vertical axis. This yawing thrust is varied to counter the yawing movement imposed by the main rotor torque. The tail rotor thrust is controlled by the pilot's foot pedal, called **antitorque pedals** or **rudder pedals.** As the pilot changes the power being delivered to the main rotor system or the amount of pitch in the main rotor blades, he also alters the angle of the tail rotor blades to maintain the heading of the aircraft. If no correction is made, the nose of the aircraft will swing to one side or the other, the direction being determined by the pilot's control inputs and the rotor system direction of rotation.

During cruising flight and hovering changes in altitude, the tail rotor corrects for torque. The tail rotor can also be used to change the heading of the helicopter when in a hover.

The Fenestron tail rotor system uses what might be called a ducted fan antitorque system. This system uses a multi-bladed fan mounted in the vertical fin on the end of the tailboom. This arrangement reduces aerodynamic losses due to blade tip vortices, reduces the blanking of the antitorque control system by the vertical stabilizer, and reduces the chance of people walking into the tail rotor.

The **ring guard** is a adaptation of the conventional

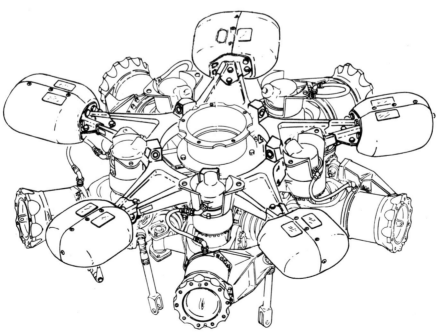

FIG. 1-111   A fully articulated rotor head.   *(Sikorsky)*

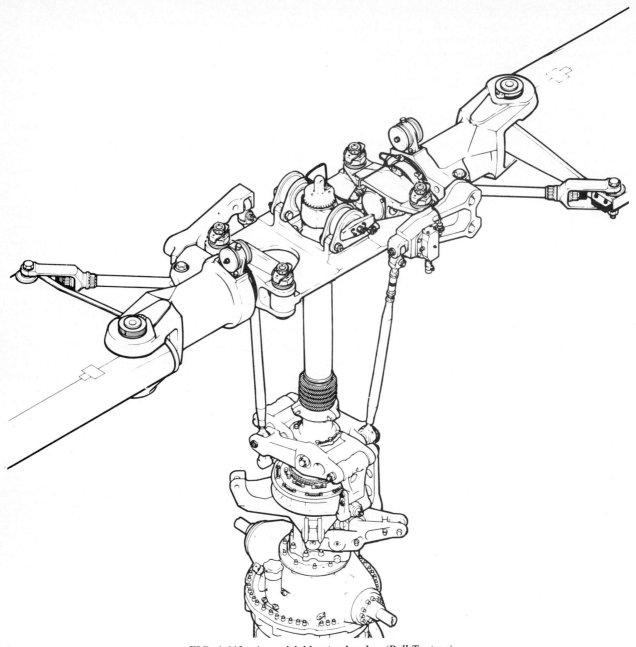

FIG. 1-112   A semirigid rotor head.   *(Bell Textron)*

tail rotor system which has a ring built around the tail rotor. This ring acts as a duct for the tail rotor, increases the safety of the tail rotor for ground personnel, and eliminates the vertical stabilizer blanking effect.

These three types of antitorque controls are shown in Fig. 1-114.

The NOTAR system (NO TAil Rotor), illustrated in Fig. 1-115, is under development by McDonnell Douglas Helicopter Company to eliminate the hazards, maintenance, and noise of the conventional tail rotor. This system uses a ducted airflow in a tail cone to generate a predetermined amount of lift on one side of the tail cone and a controllable rotating cold-air exhaust duct to counteract variations in the main rotor system torque.

Helicopter Flight Controls

The helicopter flight controls allow control of (1) movement about the three axes of the aircraft, (2) the engine power, and (3) the rotor system lift. The controls consist of the cyclic control, antitorque control, and throttle and collective control.

The cyclic control looks like a conventional stick control for an airplane. It allows the pilot to operate the main rotor system swash plate which tilts and causes the rotor blades to increase or decrease their blade angle at appropriate positions in the rotor plane of rotation. This causes the rotor to tilt and increase the rotor lift on one portion of the rotor disk and decrease the lift on the opposite portion of the disk. With this difference in lift across the disk the direction

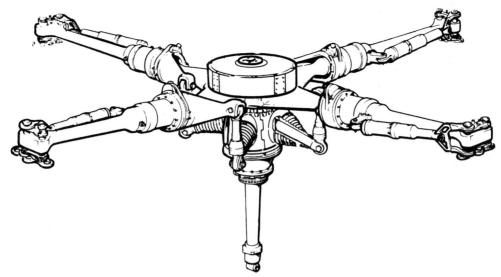

FIG. 1-113   A rigid rotor head. *(Westland)*

of lift of the rotor disk is changed, the rotor tilts and causes the helicopter to move in the appropriate direction, left or right laterally or forward or back longitudinally.

The antitorque control of the pilot's foot pedals have already been discussed in the section on the tail rotor.

The engine throttle control is usually incorporated in the twist grip located in the grip of the collective control. When the powerplant is under manual control of the pilot, he or she must twist the grip to increase

or decrease engine power as the situation requires. Most helicopters have a governor or coordinator mechanism which maintains an appropriate level of power output based on the rotor system load and the position of the collective control.

The collective control lever is located on the left side of the pilot's seat and moves up and down to control the amount of lift being generated by the main rotor system. This control causes all of the blades to increase their blade angle and lift when the control is

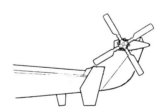

CONVENTIONAL TAIL ROTOR

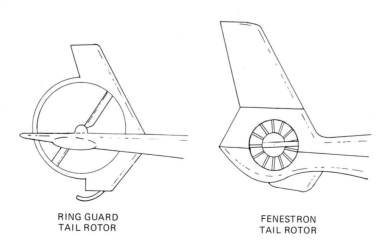

RING GUARD
TAIL ROTOR

FENESTRON
TAIL ROTOR

FIG. 1-114   Various types of tail rotors presently in use.

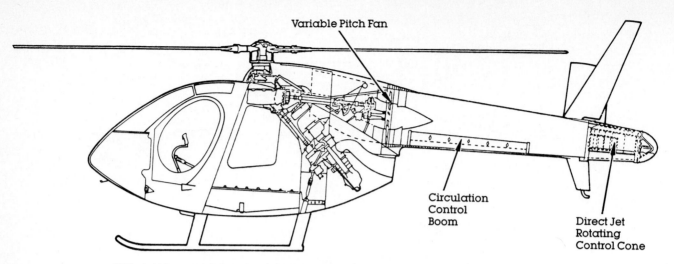

FIG. 1-115 A NOTAR helicopter uses a flow of air instead of a tail rotor to control the yawing motion. *(McDonnell Douglas Helicopter Co.)*

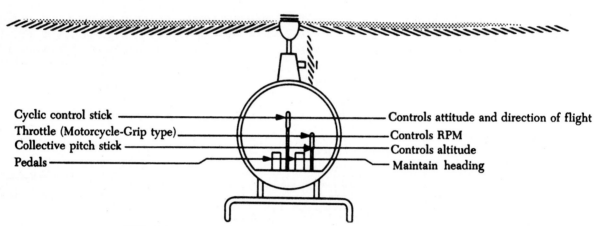

FIG. 1-116 The flight controls of a helicopter and their purpose.

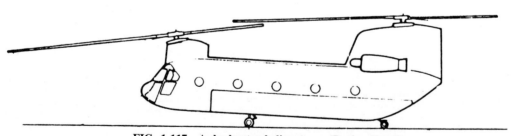

FIG. 1-117 A dual-rotor helicopter. *(Boeing Vertol)*

pulled up and decrease their blade angle and lift when it is moved down.

Pilot cockpit controls are shown in Fig. 1-116.

A few helicopter designs use a dual rotor system where two main rotors are attached at opposite ends of the aircraft and synchronized so that the rotor blades intermesh. These helicopters have the two rotors rotating in opposite directions, counteracting each other's torque, and do not require a tail rotor. The cockpit controls are the same as for a single-rotor helicopter. A dual-rotor helicopter is shown in Fig. 1-117.

● AIRCRAFT STATION NUMBERS

In the service, maintenance, and repair of aircraft, it is necessary to establish a method of locating components and reference points on the aircraft. This has been accomplished by establishing reference lines and **station numbers** for the fuselage, wings, nacelles, empennage, and landing gear. For large aircraft, the Air Transport Association of America (ATA) has set forth **zoning** specifications in ATA-100 *Specification for Manufacturers' Technical Data.* Zoning is discussed later in this section.

Fuselage Stations

Longitudinal points along the fuselage of an airplane are determined by reference to a zero **datum line** (F.S. [fuselage station] 0.00) usually at or near the forward portion of the fuselage. The position of the datum line is set forth in the Type Certificate Data Sheet or Aircraft Specification for the airplane and also in manufacturer's data. Fuselage stations for a light twin airplane are shown in Fig. 1-118. In this case, the datum line is located at the forward edge of the windshield. Station numbers are given in inches forward or aft of the datum line. Fuselage station numbers forward of the datum line are negative (−), and station numbers aft of the datum line are positive, but are not usually shown with a position (+) sign.

Wing Stations

To locate points on the wing of an airplane, the wing station (WS) numbers are measured from the center line of the fuselage. This line is also called the butt line (BL). Wing stations are indicated in inches either right or left of the fuselage centerline. Wing stations for the left wing of an airplane are also shown in Fig. 1-118.

Water Line

The water line (WL) is a line established for locating stations on a vertical line. The term "water line" originated with the design and building of ship hulls and was used as a vertical reference. Vertical measurements on an airplane may be either negative or

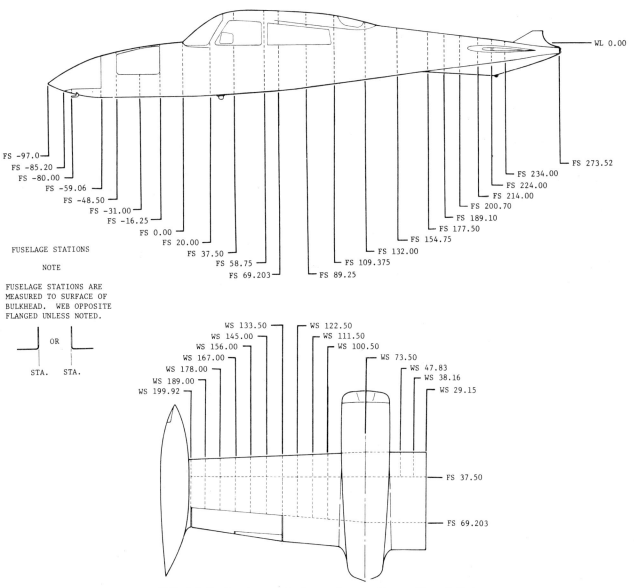

FIG. 1-118   Fuselage and wing stations.   *(Cessna Aircraft Co.)*

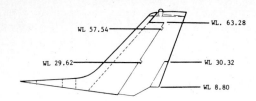

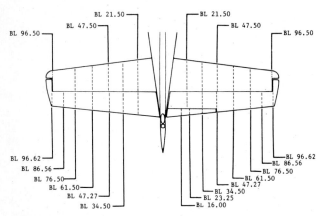

FIG. 1-119   Water-line stations and butt-line stations. *(Cessna Aircraft Co.)*

positive, depending upon whether the point is above or below the water line. WL stations are used to locate positions on the landing gear, vertical stabilizer, and at any other point where it is necessary to locate a vertical distance. Figure 1-119. shows how WL stations are used for locations on the vertical stabilizer of an airplane.

Butt Line

As mentioned previously, the butt line (BL) is the centerline of the fuselage. Positions on the horizontal stabilizer and elevator are given butt line stations numbers, as illustrated in Fig. 1-119.

Component Stations

Some aircraft components are given their own station reference lines. For example, an aileron may have aileron stations established across its span, starting with aileron station (AS), 0.00 being located at the inboard edge of the aileron. Positions outboard of the inboard station are indicated in inches. Other examples of component stations are shown in Fig. 1-120 and include winglet station, engine stations, and vertical stabilizer/rudder stations.

Summary

The two-view drawing of Fig. 1-121 shows how positions are located by means of fuselage stations, wing stations, water line, and butt line. It will be noted that a nacelle butt line (NBL) is established at the centerline of the nacelle for locating positions in the nacelle. In the drawing of Fig. 1-121, the NBL is at WS 71.52 which is 71.52 in [181.66 cm] from the fuselage centerline. Note that the center of the nose wheel is 4.34 in [11.02 cm] above the WL, thus placing the WL at the rim of the wheel.

● ZONING

As mentioned previously, **zoning** of large aircraft has been specified by the Air Transport Association of America in ATA-100. For complete details of the zoning specification, ATA-100 should be consulted; however, the basic zoning principle is explained here.

A zone is identified by one of three indicators, depending upon whether it is a major zone, major subzone, or simply a zone. Major zones are identified by three-digit numbers as follows:

Major Zone No.	Area
100	Lower half of the fuselage to the rear pressure bulkhead (below the main cabin deck)
200	Upper half of the fuselage to the rear pressure bulkhead
300	Empennage including fuselage aft of the rear pressure bulkhead
400	Powerplants and struts or pylons
500	Left wing
600	Right wing
700	Landing gear and landing gear doors
800	Doors
900	Reserved for uncommon differences between aircraft types not covered by standard series numbers

The standard series is from 100 to 800, and the special series numbers are in the 900 bracket.

Major Subzones

Major zones are divided into major subzones by the addition of a second digit to the major zone number. For example, the major zone 300 may be subzones as follows:

Major Subzone No.	Area
310	Fuselage aft of the pressure bulkhead
320	Vertical stabilizer and rudder
330	Left horizontal stabilizer and elevator
340	Right horizontal stabilizer and elevator

Zones

Subzones are divided by the use of a third digit in the three-digit number. The subzone 320 may, therefore, be divided into zones as follows:

Zone	Area
321	Vertical stabilizer leading edge
322	Vertical stabilizer auxiliary spar to front spar
323	Front spar to rear spar
324	Rear spar to trailing edge
325	Lower rudder
326	Upper rudder
327	Vertical stabilizer tip

From the foregoing it can be seen that the entire airplane can be divided into specific zones for the

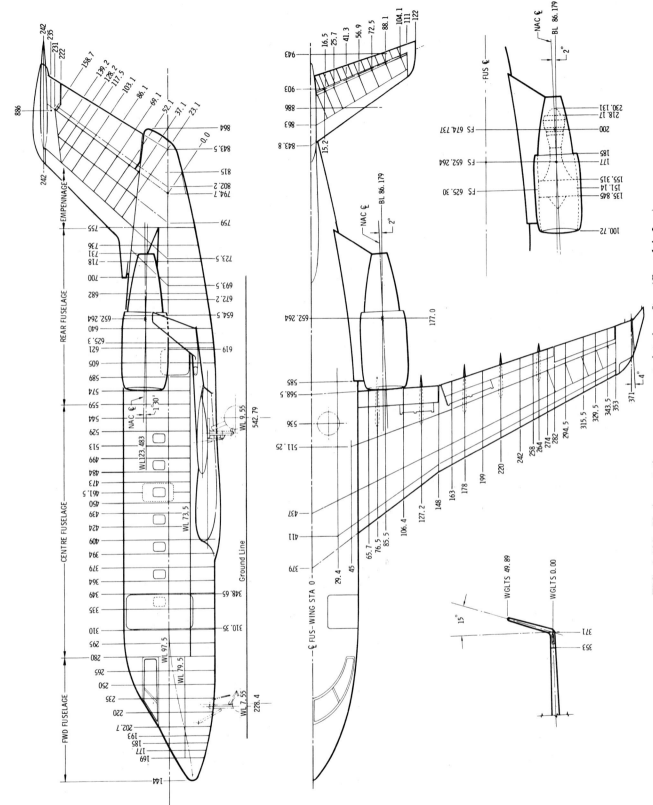

FIG. 1-120 Various stations on a corporate jet aircraft. *(Canadair Inc.)*

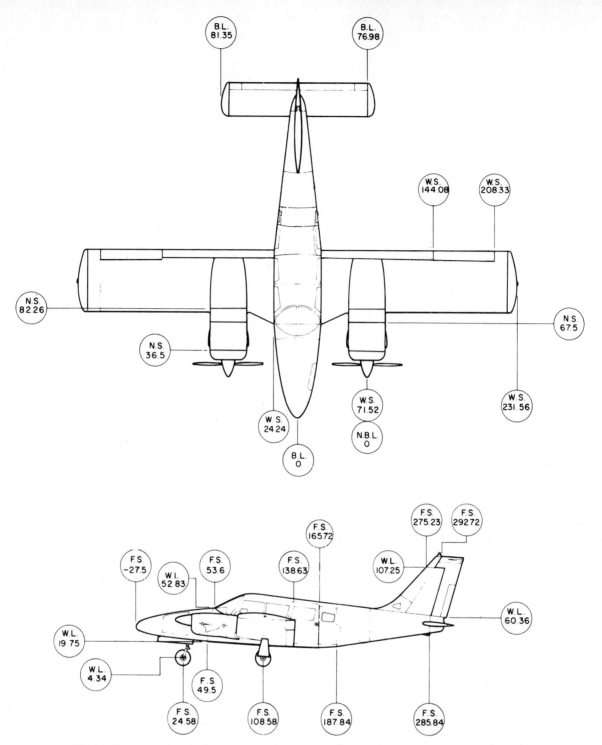

FIG. 1-121 Use of station numbers to establish positions on an airplane. *(Piper Aircraft Corp.)*

identification of any area which requires inspection, maintenance, or repair. The zone numbers can be utilized in computerized maintenance record systems to simplify the processing of records and instructions.

The application of zoning is illustrated in the draw-ing of Fig. 1-122. This drawing shows how major zone 100 is subdivided into zones on a Boeing 747 airplane. By reference to the zone numbers on the instructions, the mechanic can easily locate the area in which inspection or maintenance is to be done.

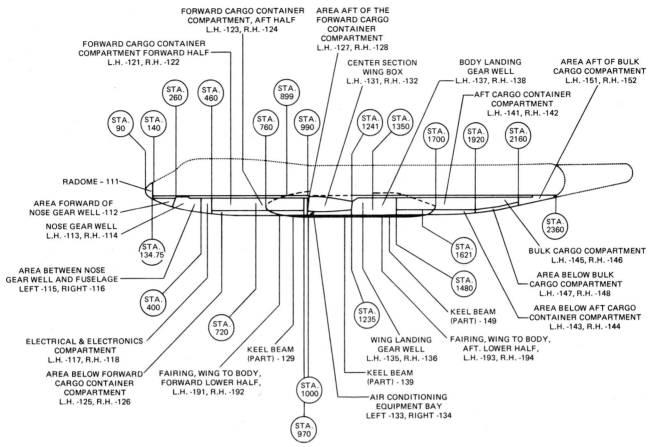

FIG. 1-122 Use of zoning to establish specific locations on a Boeing 747. *(ATA)*

● REVIEW QUESTIONS

1. What are the principal load-carrying structures of an airplane?
2. Name five *stresses*.
3. Compare *stress* and *strain*.
4. What is meant by *stress analysis?*
5. Define *angle of incidence*.
6. Define the term *chord line*.
7. Name three types of fuselages classified according to the method by which stresses are transmitted to the structure.
8. What is the load-carrying part of a *monocoque* fuselage?
9. Describe a *truss* structure.
10. What is the term for the longitudinal (fore-and-aft) structural members of a semimonocoque fuselage?
11. Describe the construction of a typical metal fuselage.
12. Why does the skin thickness on a metal fuselage vary at different locations?
13. What is a *fail-safe* feature in aircraft construction?
14. Discuss the construction of fuselages for large jet airplanes.
15. List the principle load-carrying structural components in a light-airplane wing.
16. What is the primary structural design difference between a cantilever wing and a semicantilever wing?
17. Discuss different types of construction for metal ribs in a light-airplane wing.
18. How is a metal wing sealed so it may be used as a fuel tank?
19. Discuss the construction of a large jet airplane wing.
20. What is the *main frame* of a large aircraft wing?
21. What is meant by *auxiliary structure* of a wing?
22. What *flight control surfaces* are generally attached to the wing of a large airplane?
23. Describe the construction of a typical stabilizer for a light airplane.
24. What is the purpose of a vertical stabilizer?
25. What is a *dorsal fin?*
26. Name the primary and secondary control surfaces of an airplane.
27. Discuss the need for drain holes in the bottom surfaces of ailerons and other control surfaces.
28. Why is the hinge line of an aileron usually set back from the leading edge?
29. Why are some ailerons rigged to provide differential control?
30. Why are rudders balanced both statically and aerodynamically?
31. How is aerodynamic balance accomplished on an elevator?
32. Describe a *stabilator*.
33. Why are *tabs* usually attached to the trailing edges of flight control surfaces?

34. What is a *trim* tab?
35. In which direction should an elevator trim tab be moved to cause the elevator to rise?
36. What is the purpose of a slat?
37. What are the requirements for seats in the passenger compartment?
38. Describe the design and construction of a typical window in the passenger compartment of a large airplane.
39. What type of landing gear is most commonly employed on aircraft?
40. What is the usual means for shock absorption in landing-gear struts?
41. Discuss the requirements for retractable landing gear.
42. What features of engine mounts provide for vibration dampening?
43. What is meant by *dynamic suspension?*
44. Of what materials should firewalls be constructed?
45. List some of the precautions advisable in the handling of cowling.
46. Name the principal structures of a helicopter.
47. Which helicopter control is used to control the vertical flight (lift) of the helicopter?
48. What is the purpose of a helicopter *tail rotor?*
49. Which helicopter flight control is used to control the direction of flight when the aircraft is in cruising flight?
50. Which helicopter flight control is used to control aircraft heading when hovering?
51. What is the purpose of the helicopter clutch?
52. Regarding a helicopter's main rotor system, what affects the amount of torque being generated?
53. Which helicopter control system is used to counteract the main rotor torque?
54. What is the purpose of a helicopter freewheeling unit?
55. What are the functions of the tailboom on a helicopter?
56. In what respect may the rotors be considered as structural members?
57. Explain the purpose of *station numbers* for an airplane.
58. List four types of station numbers.
59. Where is the butt line of an aircraft?
60. How are fuselage stations indicated as being ahead of or behind the datum line?
61. Explain the purpose and principle of *zoning* for large aircraft?
62. How are numbers used to identify the major zones?

2 AIRCRAFT WOOD STRUCTURES

Aircraft wood structures combine many of the attributes associated with metal and composite structures such as light weight, low cost, and high strength, while requiring only the minimum of special equipment for proper maintenance and repair. For this reason, many of the lighter aircraft that have been produced have made use of wood primary and secondary components such as wing spars, ribs, and control surfaces. A great many of these aircraft are still in operation, and a few designs are still in production using wooden structural components.

All aircraft having wood structures requires maintenance and repair from time to time; hence the aircraft mechanic must have knowledge of approved repairs and be able to accomplish such repairs. It is, therefore, the purpose of this chapter to provide enough information for mechanics to perform wood repairs as required in a general aviation shop and for enthusiasts of homebuilt airplanes to accomplish their objectives.

Figure 2-1 shows aircraft which incorporate wood in their structures.

FIG. 2-1 Airplanes having wood structures.

● AIRCRAFT WOODS

There are two principal types of wood, and all woods may be classed as one or the other. There are **softwoods** and **hardwoods.** The distinction between hardwoods and softwoods is not based on the "hardness" of the wood, but rather on the cellular structure of the wood.

Softwoods

Softwoods come from trees which have needlelike or scalelike leaves and are classified as evergreens or conifers. The wood of these trees is composed primarily of fibrous cells and has a smooth, even appearance when cut in cross section. Softwood has a high strength-to-weight ratio which makes it a very desirable structural material for use in aircraft construction. Softwood is usually used as a solid wood for spars, cap strips, and compression members and as a veneer for plywood cores.

Woods that are included in the softwoods used in aircraft are Sitka spruce, Douglas fir, Port Orford white cedar, and western hemlock. Sitka spruce is the wood used as a reference material to establish the suitability of other softwoods for use in aircraft construction and repair.

Hardwoods

Hardwoods come from trees which have broad leaves and are classified as deciduous because they lose their leaves each fall. The wood of these trees is composed of a mixture of large cells, causing pores in the wood, distributed among the smaller fibrous cells. These pores are often visible when the wood is cut smoothly. Hardwoods are generally heavier than softwoods and are used where their strength advantage makes the extra weight acceptable over the softwoods. Hardwoods are commonly used as solid wood for support blocks and tip bows and as veneers for the facing and core material of plywood.

Hardwoods commonly used in aircraft structures include mahogany, birch, and white ash.

Terminology for Woods

Even though the aircraft mechanic may not have occasion to use standard terminology for woods very often, it is considered desirable that the terms applied to woods be understood. The following definitions and the accompanying illustration of a wooden log, Fig. 2-2, should be studied and the meanings of the terms noted.

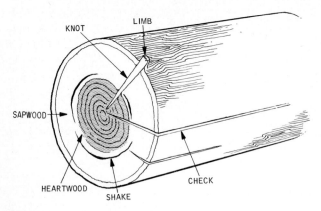

FIG. 2-2 Nomenclature for woods.

Annual rings Concentric layers of wood which can be seen at the end of a tree trunk which has been cut perpendicular to its length. The rings are caused by the different rates of growth during each year as the seasons change.

Bark The external covering of a tree trunk or branch.

Check A radial crack which cuts across the grain lines.

Compression failures Wrinkles or streaks across the grain line caused by mechanical stress on the wood after the annual rings had grown. For detection, compression failures may require close examination with a light source aimed almost parallel to the grain structure.

Compression wood Deformed grain structure in the wood caused by mechanical stress on the tree, such as supporting the weight of a heavy limb, during growth. It is characterized by wide annual rings when compared to the normal size of the tree's growth rings.

Decay A biological growth living off of the wood and causing a breakdown in the strength of the wood. Discoloration may also be present. Types of decay include dote, red heart, and purple heart.

Grain The lines in wood caused by the annual rings. Also, the direction of the wood fibers.

Hard knot A knot which is firmly embedded in the wood and shows no sign of coming loose.

Heartwood The center part of a tree trunk which is dead and carries no sap. This part of the tree serves only to support the tree.

Knot The base of a limb inside the tree. A knot will cause a deviation of the grain lines as they form around the knot.

Mineral streaks Coloring in the wood caused by minerals in the soil or other naturally occurring agents during the tree's growth.

Moisture content The weight of water contained in a wood sample compared to the weight of the wood sample if all the water was removed from the sample.

Pin knot A knot resulting from the growth of a twig.

Pitch pocket Voids between the annual rings which contain free resin. These pockets are usually relatively small in cross section and are not to be confused with shakes, which can be extensive.

Sapwood The part of a tree which is alive or partially alive and carries sap. Sapwood begins immediately under the bark and extends to the heartwood. The sapwood is often lighter in color than the heartwood.

Shake A separation between the annual ring layers.

Spike knot A knot that was cut through parallel to the limb during the sawing operation such that the knot runs across the board.

Split A crack in the wood resulting from rough handling.

Springwood The soft, light-colored part of the annual ring. This wood ring is normally wider than the summerwood ring because of the rapid tree growth during the spring season.

Summerwood The harder and usually darker part of each annual ring. This wood is formed during the slow summer season growth.

Evaluating Wood for Aircraft Use

The primary requirement for wood that is to be used in aircraft structures is that it be sufficiently sound and of such quality that it will provide the strength required for the structure. It has been determined through research that Sitka spruce is generally the best wood for use in aircraft structures because of its combination of lightness, strength, stiffness per unit weight, and toughness when compared to other species. Because of specific requirements, other species may be used due to unique qualities within the general evaluation criteria. The following information discusses the wood characteristics which the mechanic must consider when selecting wood of the desired species.

There are two classifications of water in wood, free water and cell water, as shown in Fig. 2-3. The free water is the water that flows up and down the tree carrying nutrients. Cell water is water trapped within the walls of the wood cells structure and is part of the structure of the tree. Aircraft woods are kiln-dried to remove all of the free water and a portion of the cell water so that the resulting moisture content is between 8 and 12 percent. A moisture content above or below this range is not considered acceptable.

Kiln-dried wood is dried by placing the boards of fresh-cut wood in a precisely controlled oven and raising the temperature to a specified level for a specified period of time. Not only does this process reduce the moisture content to the desired level, it also kills the

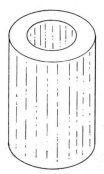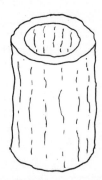

FIG. 2-3 A wood cell before *(left)* and after *(right)* drying. When the cell water is removed, the wood shrinks and becomes stronger.

74

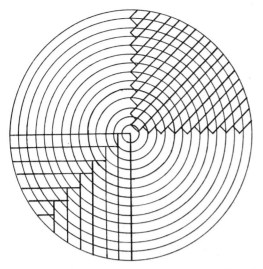

FIG. 2-4 This illustration shows two methods of cutting a log to obtain quarter-sawed wood.

insects and decay-producing organisms that may have infected the wood.

Specific Gravity. The specific gravity of aircraft woods should be from 0.34 to 0.40, depending upon the type of wood. Aircraft spruce should have a specific gravity of approximately 0.36.

The grain structure of the wood must be examined to determine if the wood has been properly cut, if the grain lines are sufficiently straight, and if there are a minimum number of annual rings per inch.

The way a board is cut is important as this affects the strength of the piece of wood and the shrinkage characteristics of the wood. Ideally, aircraft solid wood should be cut so that the annual rings are parallel to the narrow dimension of the board. This is known as **quarter-sawed** or **edge-sawed** and is illustrated in Fig. 2-4. For practical purposes a board is considered to be quarter-sawed if the annual rings are at an angle no greater than 45° to the narrow dimension.

The slope of a grain line is determined by looking at the side of a board and noting the angle that the grain line makes with the edge of the board. Ideally, the grain lines will be parallel to the edge of the board, but a deviation or slope of 1:15 is allowed. This means that a grain line starting at the edge of the board may not move more than 1 in [2.54 cm] from the edge of the board when it is 15 in [38.1 cm] from the starting point as shown in Fig. 2-5.

The number of annual rings per inch, or grain count, is another criterion which must be checked for aircraft-quality wood. The grain count is taken by counting the number of grain lines (annual rings) per inch on the sample. This is best done by looking at the end of a board and measuring a 1-in [2.54 cm] line perpendicular to the annual rings.

The minimum grain count for most softwoods is six rings per inch [2.54 cm], with the exception of Port Orford white cedar and Douglas fir which must have a minimum of eight rings per inch [2.54 cm].

When evaluating wood, the following defects are not acceptable: checks, shakes, splits, decay, compression wood, compression failure, and spike knots. Defects which might be acceptable, depending on their size, location, and condition, are hard knots, pin knot clusters, mineral streaks, and irregularities in grain direction. Evaluation criteria for these defects are given in Table 2-1.

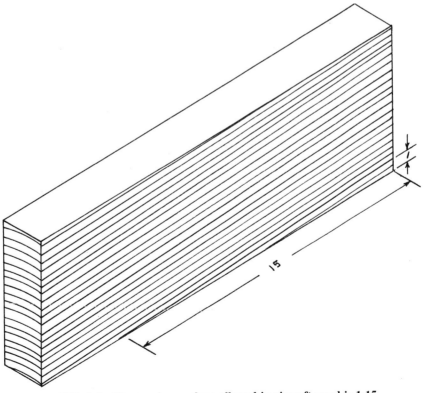

FIG. 2-5 The maximum slope allowed in aircraft wood is 1:15.

TABLE 2-1 Wood Defects

Defect	Acceptability
Checks	Not acceptable.
Compression failure	Not acceptable.
Compression wood	Not acceptable.
Cross grain	Spiral grain, diagonal grain, or a combination of the two is acceptable providing the grain does not diverge from the longitudinal axis of the material more than 1:15. A check of all four faces of the board is necessary to determine the amount of divergence. The direction of free-flowing ink will frequently assist in determining grain direction. If the deviation is greater than specified, the wood is not acceptable
Curly grain	Acceptable if local irregularities do not exceed limitations specified for cross grain.
Decay	Not acceptable.
Hard knots	Sound hard knots up to 3/8 in [9.5 mm] in maximum diameter are acceptable providing: (1) they are not in projecting portions of I-beams, along the edges of rectangular or beveled unrouted beams, or along the edges of flanges of box-beams (except in lowly stressed portions); (2) they do not cause grain divergence at the edges of the board or in the flanges of a beam more than 1:15; and (3) they are in the center third of the beam and are no closer than 20 in [50.8-cm] to another knot or other defect (pertains to 3/8 in [9.5-mm] knots—smaller knots may be proportionally closer). Knots greater than 1/4 in [5.7 mm] must be used with caution.
Interlocking grain	Acceptable if local irregularities do not exceed limitations specified for cross grain.
Mineral streaks	Acceptable, providing careful inspection fails to reveal any decay. Not acceptable if accompanied by decay.
Pin knot clusters	Small clusters are acceptable, providing they produce only a small effect on grain direction. Not acceptable if they produce a large effect on grain direction.
Pitch pockets	Acceptable in center portion of beam, providing they are at least 14 in [35.56 cm] apart when they lie in the same growth ring and do not exceed 1 1/2-in [3.81-cm] length by 1/8 in [3.18-mm] width by 1/8-in [3.18-mm] depth and providing they are not along the projecting portions of I-beams, along the edges of rectangular or beveled unrouted beams, along the edges of the flanges of box-beams. Otherwise, not acceptable.
Shakes	Not acceptable.
Spike knots	Not acceptable.
Splits	Not acceptable.
Wavy grain	Acceptable, if local irregularities do not exceed limitations specified for cross grain.

Practical Considerations. Specifications for aircraft woods as given in ANC-19 (government bulletin entitled *Wood Aircraft Inspection and Fabrication*) and in Federal Aviation Advisory Circular (AC) 43.13-1A provide that certain minor defects such as small solid knots and wavy grain may be permitted if such defects do not cause any appreciable weakening of the part in which they appear. As a practical rule, aircraft mechanics should not use any wood about which they have doubts. The safe policy is to use wood which is straight-grained, free from cracks, knots, or any other possible defect, and is guaranteed as aircraft quality.

Wood Substitutions

When repairing or rebuilding wood components, species substitution may be allowed if the structural strength of the component is not reduced. Table 2-2 shows types of wood that may be considered for substitution, with spruce being the reference wood. Note that the choice of a substitution may have to take into account changes in size, different gluing qualities, and different working qualities.

Plywood

Plywood is composed of an uneven number of layers (plies) of wood veneer assembled with the grain of each layer at an angle of 45 or 90° to the adjacent layers. The outside layers are called the **faces,** or the **face** and **back,** and the inner layers are called the **core** and **crossbands.** The core is the center ply, and the layers between the core and outer layers are the crossbands.

The layers of plywood are bonded with special glues of the synthetic resin type. Flat aircraft plywood is usually assembled with a thermosetting (hardened by heat) glue in a large, heated hydraulic press. It must be emphasized that aircraft plywood is of much higher quality than commercial grades. Every layer of wood in a sheet of aircraft plywood must be of excellent quality to provide for uniform strength throughout.

Plywood has a number of advantages over solid wood in that it is not likely to warp, it is highly resistant to cracking, and its strength is almost equal in any direction when stresses are applied along the length or width of a panel. Its change in dimensions is negligible with changes in moisture content.

The most commonly used types of plywood for aircraft manufacture are mahogany and birch. The core and crossbands may be made of basswood or a similar wood which provides adequate strength. Mahogany has a lustrous reddish-brown appearance, while birch is of a light yellow or cream color. Mahogany offers

TABLE 2-2 Aircraft Woods

Species of wood	Strength properties as compared to spruce	Maximum permissible grain deviation (slope of grain)	Remarks
Spruce (*Picea*): Sitka (*P. Sitchensis*), Red (*P. Rubra*), White (*P. Glauca*)	100%	1:15	Excellent for all uses. Considered as standard for this table.
Douglas Fir (*Pseudotsuga Taxifolia*)	Exceeds spruce	1:15	May be used as substitute for spruce in same sizes or in slightly reduced sizes providing reductions are substantiated. Difficult to work with hand tools. Some tendency to split and splinter during fabrication, and considerably more care in manufacture is necessary. Large solid pieces should be avoided due to inspection difficulties. Gluing satisfactory.
Noble Fir (*Abies Nobiles*)	Slightly exceeds spruce except 8% deficient in shear	1:15	Satisfactory characteristics with respect to workability, warping, and splitting. May be used as direct substitute for spruce in same sizes providing shear does not become critical. Hardness somewhat less than spruce. Gluing satisfactory.
Western Hemlock (*Tsuga Heterophylla*)	Slightly exceeds spruce	1:15	Less uniform in texture than spruce. May be used as direct substitute for spruce. Upland growth superior to lowland growth. Gluing satisfactory.
Pine, Northern White (*Pinus Strobus*)	Properties between 85 and 96% those of spruce	1:15	Excellent working qualities and uniform in properties but somewhat low in hardness and shock-resisting capacity. Cannot be used as substitute for spruce without increase in sizes to compensate for lesser strength. Gluing satisfactory.
White Cedar, Port Orford (*Charaecyparis Lawsoniana*)	Exceeds spruce	1:15	May be used as substitute for spruce in same sizes or in slightly reduced sizes providing reductions are substantiated. Easy to work with hand tools. Gluing difficult, but satisfactory joints can be obtained if suitable precautions are taken.
Poplar, Yellow (*Liriodendrow Tulipifera*)	Slightly less than spruce except in compression (crushing) and shear	1:15	Excellent working qualities. Should not be used as a direct substitute for spruce without carefully accounting for slightly reduced strength properties. Somewhat low in shock-resisting capacity. Gluing satisfactory.

a better gluing surface than birch because of its porosity.

When selecting or ordering plywood for aircraft use, the mechanic should make sure that the wood is of aircraft quality. Some commercial plywoods appear to be as good as aircraft plywood; however, it will be found that the quality is only on the surface and the strength does not compare with the aircraft-quality product.

Laminated Wood

Laminated wood is several layers of solid wood bonded together with an adhesive. Laminated wood differs from plywood in that each layer of wood has the grain running in the same direction where plywood has the grain direction of each layer at a large angle to the previous layer. Laminated wood tends to be more rigid than a piece of solid wood of the same size and is much more resistant to warpage. Laminated wood is used for components which require a curved shape, such as wing-tip bows and fuselage formers, and is used in place of solid wood, such as for solid-type wing spars.

● POWER TOOLS FOR WOODWORKING

Most of the machining required in making aircraft parts of wood or plywood can be carried out in an ordinary woodworking shop. Generally, standard woodworking machines can be used without change, but in some cases jigs and templates are provided for making parts such as spars, ribs, wing-tip bows, and similar framing parts. Woodworking tools suitable for making aircraft parts are described in the following paragraphs.

Circular Saws

The **circular saw** is employed principally for ripping, beveling, crosscutting, and mitering; however, other operations, such as dadoing, grooving, rabbeting, and molding, can be performed on this machine using special setups and attachments.

The saw blade for a circular saw is a disk of steel with teeth cut on the rim. The teeth are shaped and ground to provide the best cutting performance for the type of work to be done. The teeth of a ripsaw have the appearance of sharply angled chisels; the teeth of a crosscut saw are ground with a bevel on opposite sides of the alternate teeth, similar to a hand crosscut saw. **Combination saws** have both crosscut and rip teeth. These are arranged so there are four or five crosscut teeth to one rip tooth. This saw will do a reasonably good job for both crosscut and ripsawing.

Crosscut teeth are arranged so one tooth will cut one side of the groove and the next will cut the other side of the groove. The teeth are given a "set" (bent outward slightly) to make a cut a little wider than the saw blade. The teeth of crosscut and rip power saws are shown in Fig. 2-6.

A **bench saw** is illustrated in Fig. 2-7. This is a typical power tool for a woodshop which handles compara-

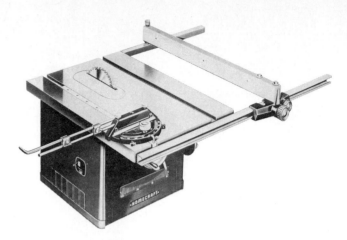

FIG. 2-7 A bench saw.

tively light woodwork such as that encountered in aircraft repair. As seen in the illustration, the saw bench is equipped with an adjustable fence and a protractor or miter guage to provide for a wide variety of sizes and angles. The fence, sometimes called a **rip fence,** is designed to guide the board being ripped. It assures that the cut will be uniform and the width of the cut board will be even throughout its length. The fence should never be used for crosscut work. During the ripping operation a slight pressure should be exerted against the fence. The miter gauge makes it possible to cut a board at any desired angle.

While using the bench saw for crosscutting or angle cutting, a rip fence should be moved as far from the saw as possible, or it should be removed entirely. The use of the bench saw is illustrated in Fig. 2-8. Note that the operator is standing to one side so as not to be struck by a piece of flying wood. Also, the operator does not place his hands on the work in such a position that the work could slip and cause him to move his hand into the saw. Where it is necessary to cut small pieces, the operator uses a pusher to move the work against the saw. The work is moved in a direction opposite the direction of saw rotation.

The height of the saw blade is adjustable to accommodate any thickness of wood up to the full capacity of the saw. The blade height should be adjusted so

RIP

CROSSCUT

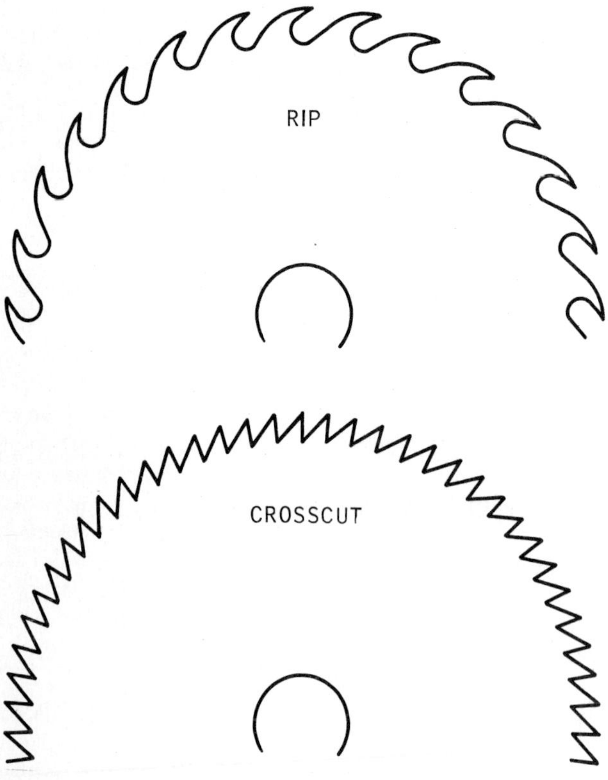

FIG. 2-6 Teeth of ripsaw and crosscut saw.

FIG. 2-8 Use of a bench saw.

that the saw teeth extend about ⅛ in [3 mm] above the work; thus the operator can see the tips of the teeth clearly. In using any high-speed rotating tool for shaping or cutting, the operator should wear a face shield or safety glasses to protect the eyes. Safety in all such operations is of primary importance because serious injury can be caused almost instantaneously.

Band Saw

A typical **band saw** is shown in Fig. 2-9. The band saw is used primarily for cutting curved outlines. Because of the narrow blade, it is easy to change the direction of a cut rapidly while the blade is cutting. The band saw is better suited for cutting very small pieces than is the bench saw, because the blade has much smaller teeth and it is both thinner and narrower.

In using the band saw, the **blade guide** should be adjusted so it is about ¼ in [6 mm] above the work. This steadies the blade and reduces blade breakage as well as the possibility of injury to the operator. Figure 2-10 shows a mechanic cutting a circular hole in a piece of plywood.

Satisfactory operation of a band saw requires regular maintenance and lubrication, as well as proper adjustment of the wheels, blade tension, and alignment. The blade should be inspected periodically to make sure that it has no cracks or broken teeth and that the teeth are sharp.

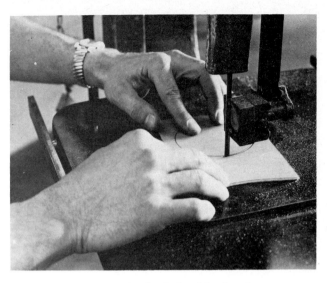

FIG. 2-10 Cutting a circular hole with a band saw.

Jigsaw

The **jigsaw** shown in Fig. 2-11 is used primarily for very fine and intricate work on comparatively small parts. It can be used for cutting very small curves and irregular outlines in sheets of wood without cutting through to the edge of the piece. This is accomplished by boring a small hole through the wood in the area to be cut, then inserting the jigsaw blade through the hole and installing the blade in the saw frame with the wood surrounding the blade. The wood is held steady in a position such that it will not bind the blade before the saw is started. It is then moved carefully against the teeth of the blade to make a cut following the outline which has been marked on the surface of the wood. Some saws have two fingers used to press down on both sides of the blade to keep the work from jumping up and down.

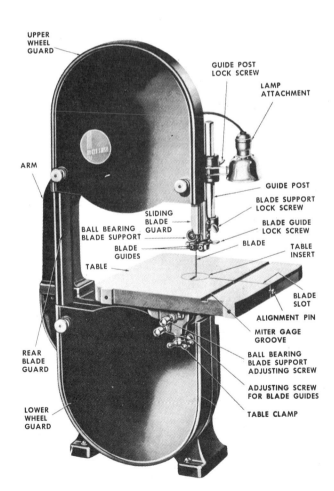

FIG. 2-9 A band saw.

FIG. 2-11 A jigsaw.

Jointer

A **jointer,** illustrated in Fig. 2-12, is used to cut smooth surface on wood which is to be joined by glue, or merely to smooth a rough surface. It is also used to provide a straight edge or to produce a plane surface, for squaring, tapering, rabbeting, and beveling.

The operator of a jointer must be very carefully in the use of the machine and the material to avoid being injured and damaging the work. The cutting blades of a jointer are very sharp and move at an extremely high speed [about 3400 rpm].

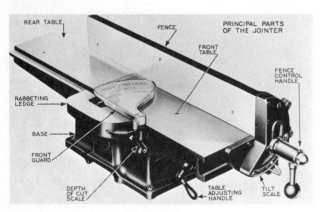

FIG. 2-12   A jointer.

In using the jointer, the operator must make certain that the tables are properly adjusted and that the cutters are set at the correct height. The fence must be at the proper position, and the angle of the tables must be checked. Because the use of a jointer may be somewhat awkward at first, it is good safe practice to pass the work through the machine while it is stopped to get the feel of the machine and to determine the best standing position.

When everything is in readiness, the jointer switch is turned on and the board is placed on the front table with the edge snugly against the fence. The operator stands at the side of the machine for proper balance. As the board is moved across the cutters, care must be taken to keep the hands clear. For working with comparatively small lengths of wood, a pusher should be used as a safety measure. The use of a jointer is shown in Fig. 2-13.

Disk Sander

The **disk sander,** illustrated in Fig. 2-14, is a valuable power tool for producing fine woodwork. It is generally used to smooth rough-cut surfaces and to aid in shaping small parts where other tools would be less effective. Sanders are also made in configurations other than that shown in the photograph. A belt sander utilizes an endless belt of heavy fabric coated with emery or other cutting granules on the outer surface. The belt is supported between two drums, one of which is driven by an electric motor. A smooth steel table supports the belt in the sanding area. Another type of sander is the **drum sander** which consists of a vertical drum around which is placed a cylinder of sanding cloth. The drum rotates at a high speed and also oscillates up and down.

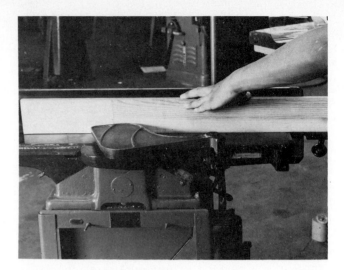

FIG. 2-13   Using the jointer.

Since the use of a sander is accompanied by hazards, the operator must exercise care as with the other power tools. The space between the table and the disk must be kept at a minimum (⅛ in [3.175 mm] or less), and very small or thin parts should not be sanded because of the danger that they may become wedged between the disk and the table. Such wedging can cause a very drastic reaction from the rapidly spinning disk. Bits of material may be thrown violently from the disk at a speed which could inflict severe injury to the operator or other person in the vicinity. In using the disk sander, the operator should apply pressure on the work down against the steady rest (table) and at the same time protect the hands by keeping them in such a position that they cannot inadvertently be brought into contact with the disk. The use of a disk sander is shown in Fig. 2-15.

Softwood joints to be glued should not be sanded because the pores of the wood become filled with fine sanding dust, thus reducing the glue penetration and weakening the glue joint.

FIG. 2-14   A disk sander.

FIG. 2-15 Using the disk sander.

● GLUES AND GLUING PROCEDURES

Glues are used almost exclusively for joining wood in aircraft construction and repair. A part is regarded as satisfactorily glued if the strength of the joint is equal to the strength of the wood. A strong joint has complete contact of glue and wood surfaces over the entire area of the joint and a thin, continuous film of glue between the wood layers unbroken by foreign particles or air bubbles.

To accomplish satisfactory glue work in aircraft wood structures, it is necessary that a number of exacting rules be observed and that all materials be of the high quality specified for aircraft woodwork. If either the glue or the wood is not of satisfactory quality, or if the techniques employed are not correct, the gluing job will be inferior and may result in failure.

Types of Glues

There are two broad categories of glue used in aircraft wood structure—**casein** and **synthetic resin.** The synthetic resin glues are commonly used in modern construction and repair operations.

Casein glues are manufactured from milk products, are highly water-resistant, and require the addition of sodium salts and lime to prevent attack by microorganisms.

Synthetic glues are of the urea formaldehyde, resorcinol formaldehyde, phenol formaldehyde, and epoxy types. Depending on the formulation of the glue, it may be water-resistant or waterproof and may be purchased in a liquid or powdered form. Synthetic glues are not attacked by microorganisms.

Mixing Glues

The mixing of glues must be done in accordance with the glue manufacturer's instructions to assure that the full strength of the glue will be available. The following discussion is meant to present guidelines for mixing glues so that the mechanic will have an idea of mixing requirements.

The container used for mixing glues must be of a material that will not react with the chemicals that make up the glue. The container and mixing tools must be clean and free of any contaminants or old glue.

In preparation for mixing, the ingredients are measured out in the proper proportions. These proportions may be either by weight or by volume. The ingredients may include powders and liquids, purchased as part of the glue, and water. The sequence of mixing may call for the powder to be added to water, water to be added to the powder, or two liquid components to be mixed in some specific sequence, such as adding a liquid catalyst to a liquid glue.

To properly mix glues, the room temperature generally must be at or above 70°F [21°C]. The process of mixing the glue requires that the speed of mixing be slow enough so that air is not whipped into the mixture. This would result in a weak glue joint. Once the glue is mixed, it may have to stand for some period of time to allow the components of the glue to interact before a proper glue joint can be formed.

Once the glue is ready to be used, it has a specific working life during which it can be applied with assurance that a proper glue bond will form. This time is influenced by the room temperature, with higher temperatures resulting in a shorter working life. If the ambient temperature is high, the working life of the glue can be extended by placing the glue container in a water bath of cool water (no lower than 70°F [21°C]). The average working life of glues is 4 to 5 hours at 70°F [21°C].

Surface Preparation for Gluing

To assure a sound glue bond the wood must be properly prepared to allow full surface contact between the components being joined. The condition of the wood must be such that the glue bonds properly with the surface of the wood. This includes being free of any surface contaminants and having the proper moisture content.

Wood surfaces to be glued should be smooth and true. Chapped or loosened grain, machine marks, and other surface irregularities are objectionable. Joints of maximum strength are made between two planed or smoothly sawed surfaces that are equally true.

While the wood surface must be true prior to gluing, the method of obtaining this trueness may affect the strength of the bond. For example, softwoods should not be sanded when preparing the surface for gluing. Sanding fills the wood pores with wood dust and prevents the glue from properly penetrating the surface. However, hardwoods can be sanded prior to gluing without any detrimental effects on the glue bond. With either type of wood, filing and planing are considered proper methods to prepare the surface for gluing. There should be no more than 8 h between the time that the surface is prepared for gluing and the gluing operation takes place.

The surface to be glued should be free of any paints, oils, waxes, marks, or particles that would interfere in any way with the proper bonding of the glue to the wood surface. The presence of wax on a surface can be detected by placing water drops on the surface. If they bead up, then wax is present and must be removed prior to gluing. This may be particularly useful in determining the surface condition of plywoods which may have been protected with a waxed paper.

The **moisture content** of wood when it is glued has a great effect on the warping of glued members, the development of checks in the wood, and the final strength of the joints. A moisture content at the time of gluing that is between 8 and 12 percent is generally regarded as satisfactory, but the higher the moisture content within this range the better will be the joint. If the moisture content is too low, the glue cannot wet the surface properly, and it sometimes produces what are called **starved joints,** that is, joints not adequately bonded. Gluing increases the moisture content of the wood; hence the moisture added in this manner must dry out or distribute itself in the wood before the part can be machined or finished. Other factors in establishing moisture content are the density and thickness of the wood, the number of plies, the glue mixture, and the quantity of glue used.

Proper Gluing Procedures

A strong joint in the wood is obtained from complete contact of glue and wood surfaces over the entire joint area and a continuous film of good glue between the wood layers that is unbroken by air bubbles or by foreign particles. Under these conditions, the glue penetrates the pores of the wood and forms a bond which is stronger than the bond between the original wood fibers. When broken, such a joint will not separate at the glue bond, but will fracture in the wood outside the bond.

Glue should be spread evenly over both surfaces forming the glue joint in the amount of no more than 1.5 oz/ft^2 (ounces per square foot). Either a brush or a soft-edged spreader may be used to apply the glue. If a brush is used, carefully inspect the surface after spreading the glue for any bristles that may have broken off.

Two different assembly methods may be employed in joining wood parts with glue. The **open assembly** method is often recommended because it reduces the time required for the glue to set up. In open assembly, the glue is applied to both surfaces to be joined, and the parts are not put together for a specified length of time. If pieces of wood are coated with glue and exposed to a free circulation of air, the glue thickens faster than when the pieces are laid together as soon as the glue is spread. This latter process is called **closed assembly.**

In gluing operations, the assembly time may be as little as 1 min or as long as 20 min, but the glue must remain at a satisfactory consistency throughout the period. Unless specifically stated to the contrary by the manufacturer of the glue, open assembly should not permit the glue to be exposed to the open air for more than 20 min.

Gluing Pressure

The functions of pressure on a glue joint are as follows: (1) to squeeze the glue into a thin, continuous film between the wood layers, (2) to force air from the joint, (3) to bring the wood surfaces into intimate contact with the glue, and (4) to hold them in intimate contact during the setting of the glue.

A light pressure is used with thin glue and a heavy pressure is used with thick glue. Corresponding variations in pressure are made with glues of intermediate consistencies. The pressure applied should be within the range approved for the types of wood being glued. For example, the gluing pressure should be between 125 and 150 psi [861.75 and 1034.25 kPa] for softwoods and between 150 and 200 psi [1034.25 and 1378.8 kPa] for hardwoods.

The method of applying pressure depends on the size, shape, and contour of the surface. Pressure can be applied by the use of clamps, nails, weights, nail strips, or screws.

Clamps are the preferred method of applying pressure as there is no damage to the wood being glued and they can be used in any position. Various types of clamps may be used as shown in Fig. 2-16, depending upon the size of the components being clamped. **Caul blocks,** shown in Fig. 2-17, are commonly used between the clamps and the wood to distribute the clamping force evenly over the entire glue joint. Caul blocks are wood blocks, usually twice as thick as the material being clamped with a maximum thickness of up to 1.5 in [3.81 cm].

For small pieces, such as gussets used on truss-type wing ribs, nails may be the only practical means of applying pressure. The length of the nails should be about four times the thickness of the gusset material and should be of aircraft quality and design. Aircraft nails have flat heads, barbed shanks, and a protective coating of cement or brass over the steel nail to inhibit corrosion. One advantage of the cement-coated nails over brass-plated ones is that they hold in the wood a little better. Nails should be spaced evenly on the centerline of the contact surfaces with a maximum spacing between nails of ¾ in [19 mm] and with a minimum of four nails per square inch of contact area. Nails may also be used to hold components in alignment prior to the application of pressure by some other

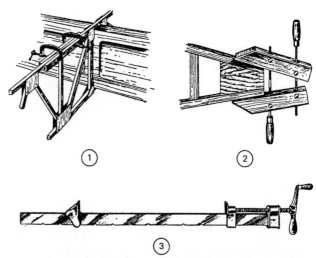

FIG. 2-16 Different types of clamps used in woodworking. (a) C-clamp, (b) hand screw clamp, (c) bar clamp.

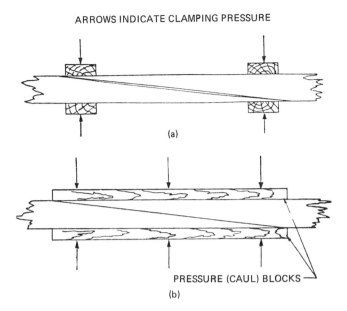

ARROWS INDICATE CLAMPING PRESSURE

(a)

PRESSURE (CAUL) BLOCKS

(b)

FIG. 2-17 Caul blocks (pressure blocks) are used to distribute the clamping pressure evenly over the entire splice area. (a) Wrong—concentrated pressure, (b) right—equalized pressure.

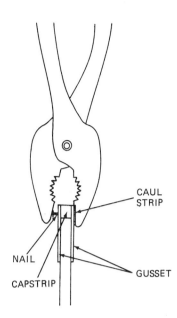

CAUL STRIP

NAIL

CAPSTRIP

GUSSET

FIG. 2-19 Pliers can be used to drive nails into ribs when making repairs on the aircraft.

means, such as clamps. In this case, the spacing would be several inches between nails.

Nails are not generally considered to be a required part of the finished assembly and are sometimes removed after the glue has dried in order to save weight. This is normally only done if weight is extremely critical as the amount of weight saved may only be a few pounds on an entire aircraft.

Nails may be installed with a tack hammer, as shown in Fig. 2-18, or by a pressing operation. When building components, the use of a hammer is convenient. However, when repairing components on the aircraft, the impact of a hammer on unsupported components may cause damage. In this case, the nails may be held in position and pressed into the structure with pliers as shown in Fig. 2-19. Regardless of the method

used to drive the nails, the nails should only go into the wood far enough for the head to rest on the surface of the wood. The head should not be driven into the wood as this causes damage to the wood.

For small surfaces which are horizontal, weights may be used to apply pressure. The weight can be in the form of shot bags or metal plates, with a caul block being used to assure that the weight is properly distributed as shown in Fig. 2-20.

Nail strips are usually associated with the installation of plywood panels onto a wood structure. Nail strips are made of thin strips of solid wood about ½-in [12.7-mm] wide with nails driven partially into the strip at intervals of about ½ in [12.7 mm]. The locations of the internal structural members are marked on the outside of the plywood panel to be installed, and glue is applied to the internal structure and to the plywood panel. The panel is then positioned on the structure, a few nails are driven through the panel into the structure to prevent movement, and then the nail strips are laid on the plywood at the markings for the internal structure and driven through

FIG. 2-18 Using a magnetic tack hammer.

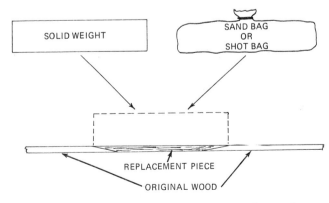

SOLID WEIGHT

SAND BAG OR SHOT BAG

REPLACEMENT PIECE

ORIGINAL WOOD

FIG. 2-20 Rigid or flexible weights can be used to apply pressure to small glue joints.

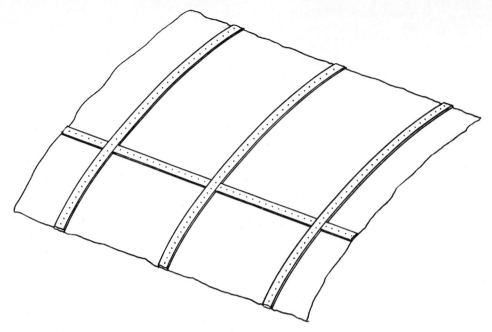

FIG. 2-21 Nail strips are used to apply pressure to plywood coverings and hold the cover to the internal structure while the glue dries.

the plywood to grip into the internal structure. Once the glue has set, the nail strips are split apart and the nails are removed from the structure. Figure 2-21 shows a structure being assembled by the use of nail strips.

In some assemblies, wood screws are used to apply pressure to a glue joint. Screws may be used in areas where there is sufficient material for the screw to bite into and where the screwhole will not result in a weakening of the structure. Screws are normally removed after the glue has set and the holes are filled with wood putty.

Pressure should be maintained on the glue joint for at least 7 h to assure that the glue has had time to set. Check the instructions for the glue being used to determine exact time requirements and any restrictions as to machining of the components prior to full curing of the glue.

Regardless of the method used to apply pressure to a glue joint, care should be taken to protect the clamps, caul blocks, and weights from coming into contact with the glue that is forced out of the joints. This can be done by using cellophane, waxed paper, or aluminum foil (if the glue will not react with the foil) between the structure and the pressure device.

Once the pressure has been applied, the assembly should be checked for any glue that has squeezed out from the joint. Remove as much of this glue as possible before it has a chance to set. Once all gluing operations are complete, the gluepot, brushes, and other gluing equipment should be cleaned with warm but not boiling water, because the latter will set the glue. All glue left over from a job should be discarded. Any glue spilled or dropped on tables or equipment should be removed before it sets.

CONSTRUCTION AND REPAIR OF WOOD STRUCTURES

In this section we provide basic information regarding wood aircraft construction and describe repairs for various parts of wooden structures commonly found in aircraft. Before attempting to repair a damaged wooden aircraft structure, the mechanic must understand the nature of the required repair and have the correct materials at hand to make the repair.

Nomenclature for Wooden Aircraft

The nomenclature for a wooden wing is shown in the illustration of Fig. 2-22. It will be observed that the parts are named according to standard practice for both metal and wooden wings. In the illustration, the **leading-edge strip,** the **plywood skin,** and the **corner block** are peculiar to wooden construction. Some of the nomenclature for a wooden fuselage is given in Fig. 2-23. Here again, the nomenclature is similar to that given for a metal fuselage of the semimonocoque type.

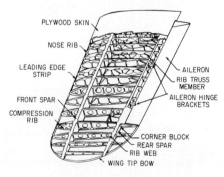

FIG. 2-22 Nomenclature for a wooden wing.

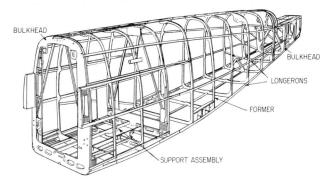

FIG. 2-23   Nomenclature for a wooden fuselage.

Bending and Forming Wood

The bending of wood is necessary to achieve the desired shape of components while maintaining the structural strength of a straight piece of wood. Any type of wood may be bent with a degree of shaping depending upon the size of the piece, the type of wood, and the technique used in preparing the wood for bending.

Solid wood is normally only bent over a very large radius and then only when the wood is of a small cross-sectional area. Only the best, clearest, straight-grained material should be considered for bending. Wood commonly used for bent components includes spruce, ash, and oak. Typical airframe components made of bent solid wood include wing-tip bows, rib cap strips, and fuselage stringers.

Laminated wood structures are commonly used to form any severely bent structure because of the ease with which the thin laminations can be formed and because of the high strength of the finished laminated structure. **Laminated wood** is a piece of wood built up of piles, or laminations, that have been joined (usually with glue) where the grain of all plies lies parallel. The plies are generally thicker than pieces of wood that could be called **veneer**. Laminated members, since they have a parallel grain construction, have about the same properties as solid wood, except that laminated members are usually more uniform in their strength properties and less prone to change shape with variations in moisture content. Curved laminated structures are used for items such as tip bows, formers, and bulkheads.

Plywood is formed to make leading-edge coverings and surface panels. Most curved plywood components start out as flat sheets and through various bending operations are formed to the desired shape. While solid and laminated structures are normally bent only in one direction, plywood is often bent in two planes by stretching it over formers, resulting in a double curvature. This double curvature is often found in areas such as fairings and wing tips.

Wood may be bent in a dry condition or after being soaked in water for some period of time. Dry bending allows the least amount of bending, while soaking the wood in cold water makes the wood more flexible. To increase the flexibility of the wood, it can be soaked in hot water or, for maximum flexibility, it can be heated in a steam chamber. A steam chamber, illus-

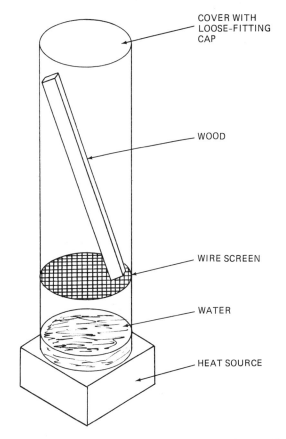

FIG. 2-24   A simple steam chamber for preparing wood to be bent.

trated in Fig. 2-24, does not need to be an elaborate affair, but it must be large enough to hold the wood and a quantity of water that will not boil away for several hours. The steam chamber should not be sealed so that any pressure will build up. This allows the steam to reach a temperature of no more than 212°F [100°C] and eliminates the chance of the chamber exploding from steam pressure. The wood should be exposed to the steam for 1 h per in [2.54 cm] of thickness with a maximum of 4 h exposure. Excessive heating causes the wood to break down structurally.

Immediately after steaming, the wooden part must be bent. If the curvature is slight, the part may be bent by hand over a form of the desired shape. If the curvature is pronounced, most of the deformation (change of shape) is accomplished by compression or shortening. This is done by using a forming die and holding strap, such as the one illustrated in Fig. 2-25. The wood to be bent is fitted snugly between the bulkheads shown in the picture and then bent over the forming die. In some cases, the type of clamp shown in the lower drawing of Fig. 2-25 does not hold. It is then necessary to use a vise-type clamp with outer and inner forming dies.

The wood, having been bent, should remain in the forms until it has cooled and dried enough to keep its shape. The forms are usually made with a slightly greater curvature than that required for the finished part to provide for the tendency of the wood to straighten out somewhat after it is taken out of the

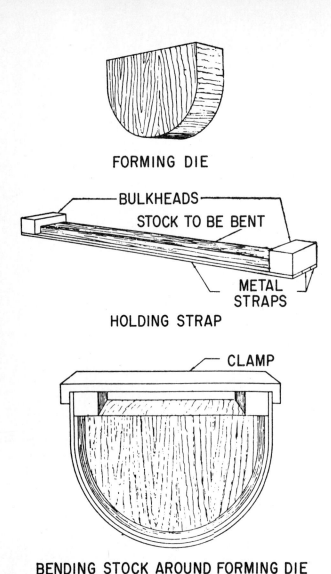

FORMING DIE

BULKHEADS

STOCK TO BE BENT

METAL STRAPS

HOLDING STRAP

CLAMP

BENDING STOCK AROUND FORMING DIE

FIG. 2-25   Using a forming die and holding strap.

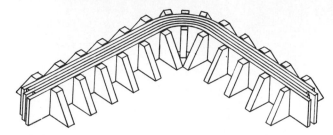

FIG. 2-26   A laminated wood structure is normally held in a jig until the glue dries.

is first slotted the length of the bend to be made, as shown in the upper drawing. A spline is inserted after applying glue to the surfaces, as shown in the middle drawing, and finally the part is bent to the necessary curvature, as shown in the bottom drawing of Fig. 2-27.

When curved plywood members are needed, several layers of veneer may be bent and glued in one operation, or the prepared plywood may simple be bent.

When built-up plywood members are desired, veneer strips or sheets are bent over a form after glue has been applied to their surfaces. The sheets or strips are held together, often with staples, while the glue sets, and then the member will retain its shape after it has been removed from the form. The grain of each successive layer of veneer should be perpendicular to that of the adjoining layer, but in some jobs the veneer is applied on the form with the grain running at an oblique angle of about 45° from the axis of the member. If the work is done carefully, a built-up plywood member should have about the same properties as a bent laminated member.

Parts such as the covering for the leading edge of a wing or a stabilizer may be formed of plywood which has been bonded with an adhesive that is subject to softening when heated. The plywood is soaked in hot water or steamed until it becomes soft. It is then bent over a form and clamped in place until dry. The curvature of the form must be a little sharper than the final curvature required to allow for a small amount of springback that will take place after a member has been taken off the form. Figure 2-28 shows the forming block, the plywood, and the clamps used in this method.

forms. In addition, the forms should be designed so that they expose as much as possible of the bent piece to the drying effect of the air.

Laminated wood members that do not require severe bending, such as wing-tip bows, may be formed without steaming or any other softening preparation. If the laminations are thin enough to take the necessary bend without splitting, they are cut to size and planed on both sides. Laminations sufficient in number to make up the required thickness are coated with glue and clamped in a form of the necessary shape. Time is allowed for the glue to set and for the wood to dry thoroughly, after which the wooden part will retain the shape of the form. If there is any springback, it will be very slight. In certain cases, where it is not desirable to use very thin laminations, or where the bending curvature is severe, the laminations may be steamed and bent to shape before being glued together. A laminated component in a jig is shown in Fig. 2-26.

Figure 2-27 illustrates the **spline method** of bending a solid member. This method is used where a bend is required in the end of a solid member, such as a stabilizer leading edge or a spar flange. The wooden part

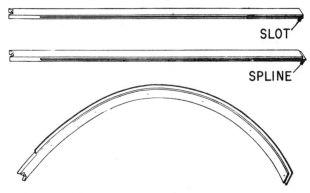

SLOT

SPLINE

FIG. 2-27   Spline method for bending a solid member.

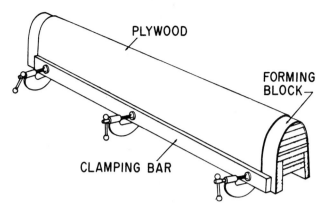

FIG. 2-28 Forming a leading edge over a forming block.

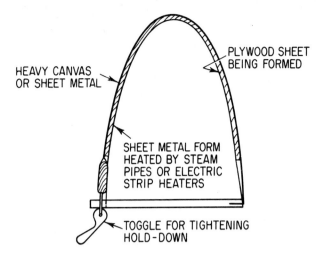

FIG. 2-29 A heated bending form.

In bending pieces of small radii or to hasten the bending of a great number of parts having the same curvature, it is sometimes necessary to use a heated bending form, such as that shown in Fig. 2-29. The surface temperature of this form may be as high as 149°C [300°F], if necessary, without damaging the plywood, but the plywood should be left on the form only long enough for it to dry to room conditions of temperature and humidity.

The degree to which plywood may be bent is illustrated in Table 2-3. Note that if plywood is selected with the grain lines 45° to the face grain rather than 90° to the grain line, then a sharper bend is possible. Also note that the greater the number of veneers in a plywood of a given thickness, the sharper the bend that is possible.

Wing Spar Construction

Wooden wing spars are constructed using several different techniques depending on the size of spar required and the structural strength requirements. Some aircraft may include several different construction techniques along the length of one spar as the required structural strength changes.

Based on the materials used in the structure, spars can be divided into two broad categories: **solid spars** and **built-up spars.**

Solid spars use solid wood as the primary components. These spars may be made of one piece of wood, rectangular in cross section, several pieces of solid

TABLE 2-3 Minimum Recommended Bend Radii for Aircraft Plywood

Plywood Thickness		10 Percent Moisture Content, Bent on Cold Mandrels		Thoroughly Soaked in Hot Water, Bent on Cold Mandrels	
		At 90° to Face Grain	At 0 or 45° to Face Grain	At 90° to Face Grain	At 0 or 45° to Face Grain
(1)	(2)	(3)	(4)	(5)	(6)
Inch	No. of plies	Inches	Inches	Inches	Inches
0.035	3	2.0	1.1	0.5	0.1
0.070	3	5.2	3.2	1.5	0.4
0.100	3	8.6	5.2	2.6	0.8
0.125	3	12	7.1	3.8	1.2
0.155	3	16	10	5.3	1.8
0.185	3	20	13	7.1	2.6
0.160	5	17	11	6	2
0.190	5	21	14	7	3
0.225	5	27	17	10	4
0.250	5	31	20	12	5
0.315	5	43	28	16	7
0.375	5	54	36	21	10

NOTE: Columns (1) and (3) may also be used for determining the maximum thickness of single laminations for curved members.

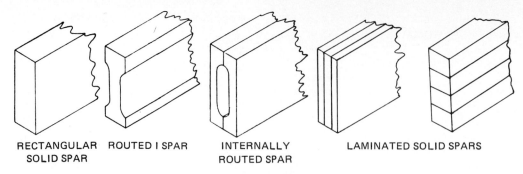

RECTANGULAR SOLID SPAR   ROUTED I SPAR   INTERNALLY ROUTED SPAR   LAMINATED SOLID SPARS

FIG. 2-30 Solid and laminated spars.

wood laminated together, an externally routed solid piece, or an internally routed spar formed by routing out portions of two boards and then joining the routed sides of the boards together to form a spar. Examples of these different types of solid spars are shown in Fig. 2-30. Solid spars may change in their external dimensions along their length, may have areas that are not routed, such as at fittings, and may include ply-wood plates attached to areas requiring reinforcements, such as at fitting attachments.

Built-up spars include a combination of solid wood and plywood components. Built-up spars can be divided into three basic types—**C-beam, I-beam,** and **box-beam** as illustrated in Fig. 2-31. C-beam and I-beam spars consist of a plywood web as the principal vertical member running the length of the spar. At the top and bottom of this web are located solid wood capstrips. For a C-beam the capstrips are only on one side of the spar, while an I-beam has capstrips on both sides of the web. Intercostals are located vertically between the capstrips at intervals to increase the strength and rigidity of the spar. Blocks are used between the capstrips to allow for the attachment of fittings.

A box-beam spar consists of a top and bottom solid-wood capstrip, plywood webs on the outside of the capstrips, with intercostals and blocks being used for strength, stiffness, and attachment of fittings.

Spar Repairs

When a spar is damaged, the damage must be evaluated to determine if the spar can be repaired or if it must be replaced and then what the economic factors are concerning the cost of a repair versus the cost of replacement. The economic factors must be decided between those doing the repair and the aircraft owner. Factors that determine the repairability of a spar include the existence of any previous repairs, the location of the damage, and the type of damage. If a spar has been repaired twice, it is generally considered to be unrepairable. If the damage is in such a location that a splice is not possible without interfering with wing fittings as discussed below, then it is unrepairable. If the damage is such that the integrity of the repair will be in doubt, such as the presence of extensive decay, then the spar is unrepairable. Keep in mind that each spar must be evaluated and no one set of rules can apply to all spars.

If a spar is determined to be repairable, the splice and the plates must be positioned so that the primary attachment fittings will not be in the area of the splice and so that minor fittings will not be repositioned by the reinforcement plates. In quoting from AC43.13-1A, paragraph 12:

A spar may be spliced at any point except under wing attachment fittings, landing-gear fittings, engine-mount fittings, or lift-and-inter-plane strut fittings. Splicing under minor fittings, such as drag wire, antidrag wire, or compression strut fittings is acceptable under the following conditions:

a. The reinforcement plates of the splice should not interfere with the proper attachment or alignment of the fittings. Do not alter the location of pulley support brackets, bellcrank support brackets, or control surface support brackets.

b. The reinforcement plates may overlap drag or antidrag wire or compression strut fittings, if the reinforcement plates are on the front-face of the front spar or on the rear-face of the rear spar. . . . The inside reinforcement plate should not overlap drag strut fittings, unless such overlapping does not require sufficient shortening of compression struts, or changes in drag-truss geometry to prevent adjustment for proper rigging.

On occasion, a solid or internally routed spar develops cracks in the grain line because of shrinkage in

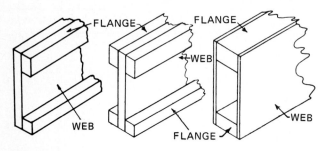

BUILT-UP C SPAR   BUILT-UP I SPAR   BOX SPAR

FIG. 2-31 Built-up spars.

the wood. If this occurs and it can be determined that the crack does not pose a major structural problem in the spar, the crack can be repaired by the application of surface plates. The dimensions and requirements for the repair are given in Fig. 2-32. Note that this illustration also deals with the repair of shallow edge defects on the top or bottom of a solid spar.

To properly attach the plates, the surface of the spar must be free of all finishing materials, such as varnish, and sufficient work space must be available to allow for clamps or other methods to be used to apply pressure to the plates. After the repair is completed, the surface is refinished with varnish.

If elongated bolt holes exist in a spar or cracks are found in the vicinity of bolt holes, a new section of spar should be spliced into place or the spar replaced entirely, unless some other method of repair has been specifically approved by competent authority. If the spar roots are being replaced, it may be advantageous to laminate the new section of the spar, using aircraft plywood for the outer faces.

Wooden wing spars are often repaired by splicing sections either on the ends or between the ends of the spar. The sections of the spar are spliced by use of a glued scarf joint and reinforcing plates. The scarf joint has proved to be the most satisfactory splice for solid wood, laminated wood, and plywood.

The desired slope for the scarf in softwoods is 12:1, but a slope of not less than 10:1 is acceptable. The scarf is cut to follow the grain of the wood and must be finished to a flat, smooth surface by use of a plane. The scarfed surface must not be sanded, since this will fill the pores of the wood with wood dust and tiny sand particles.

In making a spar splice, the mechanic must observe certain conditions and practice skills in a manner to produce a spliced joint as nearly perfect as possible. Among the conditions required are (1) a true and smooth surface on each member of the spliced joint, (2) a completed splice at least as strong as the original unspliced spar, (3) a thickness of the spar at the spliced joint which is the same as the original spar without regard to the splice plates, and (4) a glue joint which

is almost invisible when observed from the side of the finished splice.

To produce a satisfactory splice, the mechanic must employ a high degree of skill in planing the scarfed surfaces of the spar to be spliced. Note that the pressure applied to the plane as it moves over the surfaces of wood must be varied from A to B to C, as shown in Fig. 2-33. Periodically, the mechanic should check the trueness of the surface by means of a straightedge as shown in in Fig. 2-34. This will make it possible to observe high spots and then use a plane to remove such spots.

In starting to make a spar splice, the mechanic must plan the cut for both the original spar being spliced and for the new section to which it is to be joined. This requires careful measurement of the spar thickness and total length of the splice. Remember that the desired length of the splice should be 12 times the thickness of the spar. If the spar is ⅞ in [2.22 cm] thick, the splice should be 10½ in [26.67 cm] in length.

A

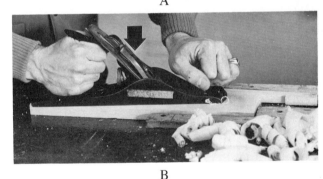

B

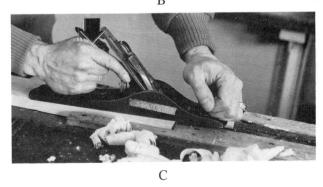

C

FIG. 2-33 Application of pressures at pressure points.

FIG. 2-32 Reinforcing a longitudinal crack in a solid or internally routed spar.

FIG. 2-34 Checking the trueness of a planed surface.

In any case, the length of the splice could not be less than 8¾ in [22.23 cm] in length for a ⅞ in thick spar.

After the damaged spar has been cut off to eliminate all cracked or otherwise damaged wood, the splice length is marked in the end of the cut spar and a diagonal line is drawn to indicate where the scarf cut is to be made. Since the spar will probably be in the wing, it will require a good measure of skill to cut the scarf with a dovetail or backsaw and then finish the scarfed surface to the required degree with a small hand plane. The new piece of spar stock to be installed can be scarfed and finished on the bench before it is joined to the section in the wing.

In cutting the scarf for a spar splice, the slope of the scarf should, as nearly as possible, be in the same direction as the slope of the grain in the wood. If the grain of the wood is parallel with the edges of the lumber, the scarf can be cut from either side. It will be found, however, that there is often a small degree of slope to the grain when one observes the edge of board. The mechanic will observe the slope of the edge grain and cut the scarf so it will slope in the same direction.

One method employed to ensure accuracy of the scarf faces for a splice is illustrated in Fig. 2-35. The first step is to cut the scarf faces as accurately as

possible with a dovetail saw, backsaw, or fine-toothed handsaw. The two faces are then placed together and clamped to a block as shown in the drawing. A fine-toothed saw is then used to recut the splice line. After the cut is made, the two parts are tapped together to close the space made by the saw cut. If the two faces are still not accurately matched, another saw cut is made. The process is continued until both scarf faces fit perfectly.

The techniques for gluing wood spar splices should follow those described earlier in this chapter. It must be remembered that the thickness of the glue will affect the thickness of the splice. For this reason, the two parts of the spar must be assembled to allow for the change as the joint is clamped and the glue squeezed out of the joint. The method for making this allowance is shown in Fig. 2-36. The completed splice will retain its full thickness if this operation is correctly performed.

The final operation in making the splice is to set the clamps with the correct pressure. The use of waxed paper to prevent adherence of the glue to the clamps and the use of caul blocks of adequate thickness must not be overlooked.

Upon completion of the basic splice operation, excess glue is removed and the surface is smoothed. Reinforcing plates of the correct dimensions are then glued on the sides of the splice according to the specifications indicated below.

Figure 2-37 shows a typical solid or laminated spar splice. The dimensions shown must be closely followed to produce an acceptable splice. Laminated spars may be replaced with solid spars or vice versa, provided the quality of the replacement is equal to or better than the original.

A splice for solid I-beam spars is shown in Fig. 2-38. The reinforcement plates are contoured to fit the routing of the spar in the web section. If the splice is made where the routing is feathered out to the full width of the spar, tapered plates conforming to the contour of the routing should be installed.

Figures 2-39 and 2-40 illustrate the methods for splicing built-up I-beam spars and box-beam spar flanges. The plywood webs and reinforcements used in these repairs must be of the same high-quality plywood as the original. Solid wood does not have the shear strength of plywood, since it does not have the variations of grain direction provided in plywood.

Box-beam spar webs are spliced as shown in Fig. 2-41. The face grain of the plywood replacement should be in the same direction as the original. The plywood replacement and reinforcements must be of the same type as the original. This is important, since the strength of the spar is calculated on the basis of the type of plywood used in the construction.

PARALLEL CLAMPS

FIG. 2-35 A method for obtaining true splice surfaces.

ALLOWANCE FOR GLUE SHRINKAGE

FIG. 2-36 Thickness allowance for a spar splice.

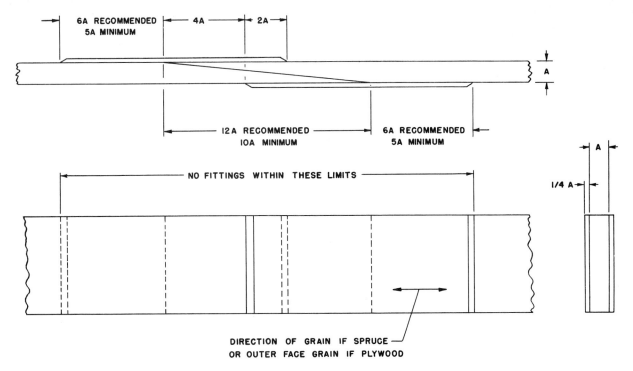

FIG. 2-37 Splicing solid or rectangular spars.

Rib Construction

Ribs give the wing and other airfoil sections the desired cross-sectional shape. In some wings, certain ribs take the compression load between the front and rear spars, in which case they replace the compression struts which would otherwise be used to separate members. A tapered wing may be tapered in width, tapered in thickness, or tapered in both thickness and width. Therefore, the ribs of tapered wings vary in size from wing tip to wing root, although the cross-sectional shape (airfoil section) of each rib is the same throughout in most designs.

Some ribs are built with the nose section, the center section between the spars, and the trailing-edge section as separate units, all being butted against the spar and fastened with glue and nails. Other ribs are constructed in one unit and slipped over the spar to their proper stations.

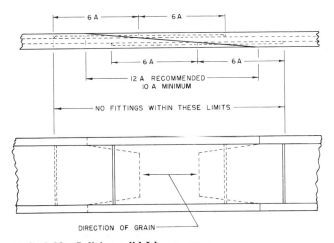

FIG. 2-38 Splicing solid I-beam spars.

The rib structure may consist of the truss type with plywood-gusseted joints, the lightened and reinforced plywood type, the full plywood-web type with stiffeners, or some other special design. It is very important that no change be made in the shape of an airfoil section during construction or repair.

When making replacement ribs, it is best if they are made from a drawing furnished by the manufacturer or from a drawing made by a repair agency and certified correct by the manufacturer. However, an original rib may be used as a pattern for making a new rib if it is not so badly damaged that comparison is inaccurate.

A wood rib is usually assembled in a **rib jig.** The rib jig is made by drawing a pattern of the rib on a smooth, flat plank and then nailing small blocks of wood to the plank so that they outline the rib pattern. During assembly, the capstrips are inserted between the blocks to hold them in the proper position for attachment of the vertical and diagonal members and the plywood gussets. Gussets are attached to the capstrips, verticals, and diagonals with nails and glue. Figure 2-42 shows a rib assembled in the jig and a completed rib.

The components of the rib are cut so that they are a "push" fit with perfect alignment between all contact surfaces. There should not be any visible gap between components, but none of the components should require more than a gentle push to position them onto the jig board.

Once all of the components are cut and their fit is checked by positioning them on the jig, glue is applied to all of the contact surfaces and the rib is assembled in the jig. Nails are used to apply pressure to the glue joints covered by the gussets. Once the glue has set, the rib is removed from the jig, excess glue is re-

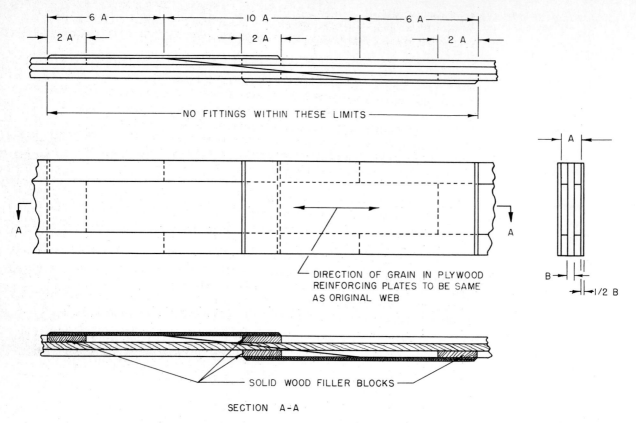

NO FITTINGS WITHIN THESE LIMITS

DIRECTION OF GRAIN IN PLYWOOD
REINFORCING PLATES TO BE SAME
AS ORIGINAL WEB

SOLID WOOD FILLER BLOCKS

SECTION A-A

FIG. 2-39 Splice for a built-up I-beam spar.

moved, and gussets are added to the opposite side of the rib. The rib is finished first by filing down any overhang of the gussets and then by varnishing the rib. Care must be exercised to prevent any varnish from getting on the wood in the areas where the rib will be glued to the spars.

When a rib must be repaired or installed on a wing which is already assembled, it is usually necessary to build the rib on the wing. This requires great precision to make sure that the rib is the same shape and size as the original. To do this a rib jig can be constructed, cut into sections to fit around the spars, and positioned on the wing to allow a rib to be built in place as shown in Fig. 2-43.

Wood ribs are commonly attached to the spar by the use of glue and then nailing the rib to the spar through the vertical members of the ribs. Ribs should not be attached by nailing through the rib cap strips (top and bottom pieces) as this will significantly weaken the ribs. Some rib installations make use of

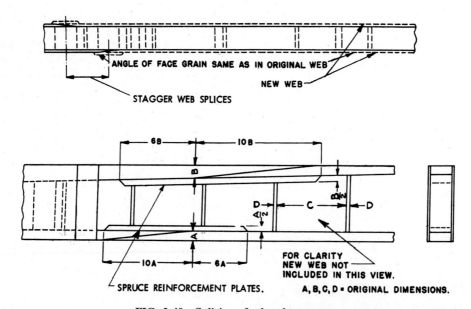

ANGLE OF FACE GRAIN SAME AS IN ORIGINAL WEB

NEW WEB

STAGGER WEB SPLICES

SPRUCE REINFORCEMENT PLATES.

FOR CLARITY
NEW WEB NOT
INCLUDED IN THIS VIEW.

A, B, C, D = ORIGINAL DIMENSIONS.

FIG. 2-40 Splicing of a box-beam spar.

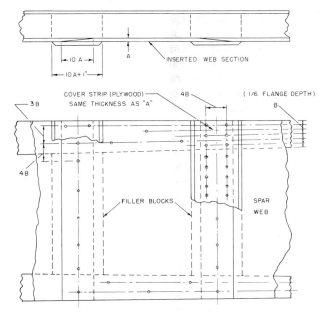

FIG. 2-41   Method of splicing a box-beam spar web.

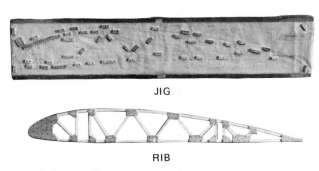

JIG

RIB

FIG. 2-42   Rib jig and completed rib.

corner blocks glued and nailed to the spars and the ribs to hold the ribs in position. After the ribs are attached to the spars, a cap strip may be placed on the top and bottom of the spars between the ribs to further stabilize the ribs on the spars.

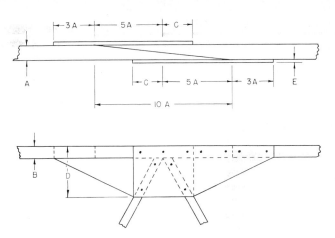

FIG. 2-44   Repair of a rib at truss member.

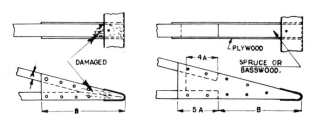

FIG. 2-45   Methods for repairing a damaged rib at the trailing edge.

Truss-Type Rib Repairs

Figures 2-44 to 2-48 show satisfactory methods of repairing damaged ribs. In Fig. 2-44, A, B, C, D, and E are the original dimensions. The reinforcement plates are plywood which are attached by glue and nails. The damaged web members are entirely replaced. This illustrates repair at a joint or between joints.

Figure 2-45 illustrates an acceptable method for repairing the trailing edge of a wood rib where the ends of the capstrips have been damaged by crushing or rotting. The damaged wood is entirely removed, and

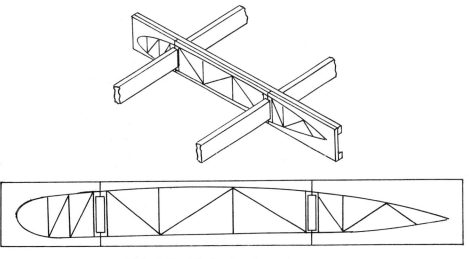

FIG. 2-43   Rib jig placed on wing spars.

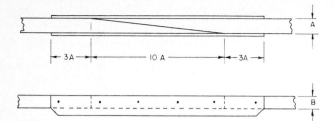

FIG. 2-46   Splice of a capstrip between joints.

a filler block is cut to fit the capstrips and re-form the end of the rib to the original dimensions. The filler block is so cut that the grain is in the same direction as that of the capstrips and is installed by gluing and nailing gussets to the sides. The joint between the filler block and the cut ends of the capstrip is also glued.

Figure 2-46 illustrates the proper method of making a splice in a capstrip between joints. The splice is made with at least a 10:1 scarf joint and glued. The reinforcement plates are plywood of the same thickness as the gussets used on the rib. They are glued and nailed, and the face grain is in the same direction as that of the gussets.

The illustration in Fig. 2-47 shows a rib capstrip splice at a spar. The original dimensions are shown by A, B, C, D, E, F, and G. The recommended scarf for the splice is 12:1, as shown in the figure. The gusset, or reinforcing plate, used is sometimes called a **saddle gusset** since it straddles the spar and extends down both sides. The gusset is so cut that the face grain is in the direction shown and the thickness is the same as for other gussets in the rib. As in the attachment of all gussets where glue and nails are used, the nails must not be driven so far that the heads are embedded in the wood. It should be remembered that *the strength of the wood splice is provided by the glue and not by the nails.*

Repairing Compression Ribs

Methods for repairing various types of wood compression ribs are shown in Fig. 2-48.

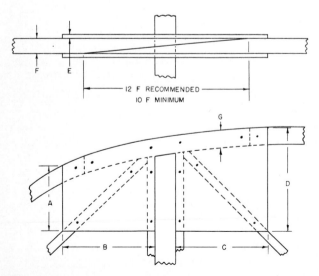

FIG. 2-47   Repair of a capstrip at a spar.

The first rib shown is the I-section type with wide, shallow capstrips and a plywood-center web with rectangular compression members on each side. This rib is indicated by A in the figure. It is assumed that the rib is cracked through the capstrips, web, and compression members. The capstrips of the rib are repaired according to methods shown in previous illustrations in this chapter. The compression members are cut and spliced as shown in D in the figure. Note that this splice is similiar to capstrip splices. To complete the repair, plywood reinforcing plates are glued to the sides of the rib. These plates restore the strength of the damaged web.

The rib shown in B of Fig. 2-48 is constructed like a standard rib except that it has a plywood web attached to one side and rectangular compression members on the other side. This rib is repaired in the same way as the rib in A, but the plywood reinforcement is extended for the full distance between the spars. See section B-B.

The illustration in C shows an I-section rib with a vertical stiffening member on each side of the plywood web. The cap strips are repaired as in A, and then plywood plates are installed on each side for the full distance between the spars. See section C-C.

Leading- and Trailing-Edge Strips

The leading edge of the wing, of an aileron, or of other airfoil surfaces may be provided with special nose ribs, stiffeners, and a covering of sheet metal or plywood to maintain its shape and carry local stresses. A metal or wooden strip is often used along the leading edge to secure the ribs against sidewise bending and to provide a surface for attaching the metal, fabric, or

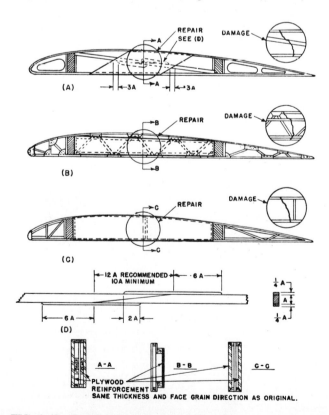

FIG. 2-48   Repair of wood compression ribs.

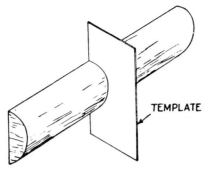

FIG. 2-49 A template used to shape the leading edge.

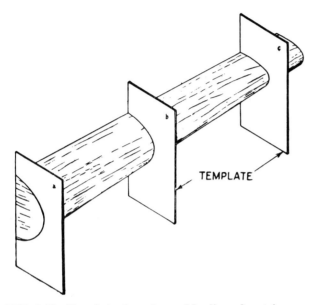

FIG. 2-50 Templates for a tapered leading-edge strip.

plywood covering. In some airplanes, the metal or plywood covering acts as the stiffener for the ribs instead of the leading-edge strip.

Figure 2-49 shows the use of a template in shaping the leading edge. The curved portion of the leading-edge strip completes the contour along the nose of the wing. It is important in forming the leading edge of the strip to use a template, corresponding to the curvature, for checking the work. Figure 2-50 shows that the templates for a tapered leading-edge strip vary in shape to correspond to sections along the strip. A drawing of the leading edge is used to obtain the dimensions required for laying out the template.

The trailing-edge strip of an airfoil surface may be of wood or metal. The wooden strip is made similar to the leading-edge strip. Templates may be used to indicate the camber of the rib.

The leading edges of wing and control surfaces are repaired by carefully made and reinforced splices, such as the one illustrated in Fig. 2-51, where a damaged leading-edge section of a horizontal or vertical stabilizer is repaired by splicing in a new section. To obtain additional gluing area, the skin is feathered into the strip. If this is done properly, only one reinforcing strip is required.

Wing-Tip Bow Construction and Repair

A wing tip may have any of several shapes. For example, it may be square, elliptical, or circular in plan form. If the wing tip is elliptical or circular, a wooden or metal wing-tip bow is required for attaching the plywood or fabric covering. A wooden bow for this purpose may be made of solid wood or laminations and bent to the required shape.

Figure 2-52 shows three types of wing-bow cross sections with the plywood surface and the tip bow indicated in each.

A wing-tip bow that has been badly damaged should be removed and replaced. A cracked or broken bow may be repaired by splicing in a new piece. The new piece may be spliced in at the spar. It should have the same contour as the original bow, and the splices should meet the requirements of a scarf joint, as explained elsewhere in this chapter.

Installation of Plywood Skin

Plywood for the skin of the airplane is cut and shaped to fit the surface to be covered, enough material being allowed to provide for scarfing where needed. Depending upon the design, it may be necessary to cut the skin larger than is needed and to trim it to size after it has been glued to the frame, particularly in the case of wing tips.

The next step is temporarily to nail the plywood to the frame in one corner, make any required adjustments, and then nail in the opposite corner. These temporary nails are driven through small strips of wood so that they can be pulled out easily. The corners having been secured, the plywood is then pressed down against the framework with the hands to be sure that it is in the exact position and that all supporting

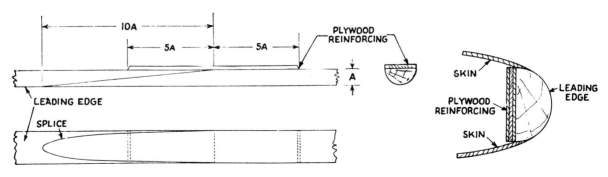

FIG. 2-51 Repair of a damaged leading-edge section.

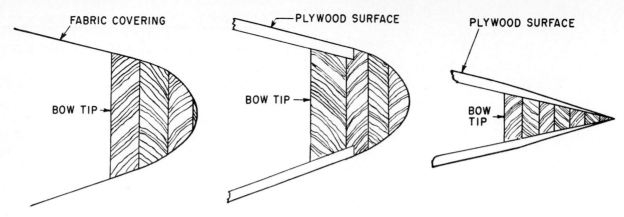

FIG. 2-52 Wing-bow cross-sections.

members, such as ribs and spars, are properly contacted.

If possible, the plywood is then marked on the inside so that the areas of contact with the internal structure are identified. The plywood is then removed and glue is applied to the contact area of the structure, which is indicated by the drawn lines on the plywood. The plywood is then carefully placed back on the structure and secured with nailing strips.

The nailing strips used to hold the plywood in place until the glue sets are strips of wood about 3/16 to 1/4 in [5 to 6 mm] thick and 1/2 in [12.7 mm] wide. The strips are first nailed near the center of the skin panel and then nailed outward in both directions. More nailing strips are applied, this time perpendicular to the first set, starting near the middle and working outward in whichever direction will avoid wrinkles and permit the plywood to lie smooth.

The nails are driven down tightly, and enough nailing strips are used to cover the entire surface of the supporting members. The width of the supporting member determines the number of nailing strips required. One nailing strip is used on surfaces 1/2 in [12.7 mm] wide. Several nailing strips, laid side by side, are used for covering wider surfaces.

The nails are driven so that those in one strip alternate with regard to those in an adjacent strip. If the plywood skin is from 1/16 to 3/32 in [1.59 to 2.38 mm] thick, 5/8-in [15.88-mm] nails spaced at 1 1/2-in [38.1-mm] intervals are used for holding the skin to the ribs. The object is to space the nails as close together as possible without splitting one of the parts being glued. Whenever nailing strips come into contact with the glue, waxed paper is placed under the strips to prevent them from being glued to the member.

When a leading edge is to be covered, the plywood is first cut to the approximate size of the section to be covered. The leading edge is then bent over a form or over the wing leading edge. It is often necessary to soften the wood by soaking or steaming prior to the bending operation. The plywood is held in place over the form or leading edge with shock cords, rubber straps, or any other apparatus that will provide an even pressure over the surface of the plywood without distorting the plywood or damaging the leading-edge structure.

When the plywood is thoroughly dry, the formed piece is fitted again and cut to the precise size. Glue is applied to the framework (nose ribs, spar, etc.) and the formed plywood. The plywood is placed on the frame and pressure is applied by means of nailing strips. These nailing strips may be started along one edge of the spar or along the leading-edge strip. More nailing strips are then laid over the nose ribs, starting with the center rib and working toward each end of the wing section. Soaking the nailing strips in warm water to make them bend more easily is a good treatment for those nailing strips laid over the curved portion of the leading edge.

Although nailing strips usually provide a satisfactory method for applying pressure to glue joints when installing plywood skins, other methods are also used, and some of these may be more effective than the nailing strips. One of these methods is to place a heavy piece of web strap around a wing immediately over a rib and the plywood after the glue has been applied. The strap is then tightened by small screw jacks, tapered blocks, or some other method, until the plywood skin is pressed firmly against the member to which it is being glued.

Another method which can be used is to apply pressure to the plywood over a glue joint by means of shot bags or sandbags. Great care must be exercised to make sure that the plywood is pressed against the structure to which it is being attached and that there is a good glue film in all joints.

Repair of Damaged Plywood Structures

When the stressed plywood skin on aircraft structures requires extensive repairs, it is essential that the manufacturer's instructions be followed carefully. When the repair is made according to manufacturer's specifications, the original strength of the structure is restored.

Before proceeding with any repair operations, the type and extent of damage to a plywood skin and the internal structure should be evaluated. Information that should be taken into account in determining whether repair or replacement is necessary and the type of repairs possible include the location of the damage, the size of the damaged area, the thickness of the plywood, whether the plywood has a single or

TABLE 2-4 Plywood Repair Selection

Repair	Limitation
Scarf patch	No restriction.
Surface patch	Must be entirely aft of 10% chord line or must wrap completely around leading edge and terminate aft of 10% chord line. Maximum perimeter of 50 in [127 cm] (subject to interpretation of AC43.13-1A).
Plug patch	Oval or circular in shape. Sizes permitted include 4- and 6-in [10.16- and 15.24-cm] diameter circles and 3 in by 4 1/2 in [7.62 by 11.43 cm] and 5 by 7 in [12.70 by 17.78 cm] ovals. Used to repair skin where no internal structure is involved.
Splayed patch	Maximum size of trimmed, round hole is 1 1/2 in [3.81 cm]. Maximum skin thickness is 1/10 in [2.54 mm].
Fabric patch	Maximum diameter of trimmed hole is 1 in [2.54 cm]. Edge of hole may be no closer than 1 in [2.54 cm] to any structural member. Not allowed on a leading edge or frontal area of a structure.

NOTE: This table is only intended to aid in the selection of a repair procedure. See AC43.13-1a, Chap. 1, for specific repair instructions.

double curvature, and the location of and damage to internal structural components.

If internal components are damaged then enough of the plywood covering must be removed to allow for access to and proper repair of these internal components. The repair of internal components should follow the guidelines established for spars and ribs—replacing or splicing in new sections by the use of scarf splices and reinforcement plates.

The curvature of the plywood must be determined if the damage area is of any significant size. If a piece of paper can be laid on the surface and smoothed out without wrinkling, then the plywood has a single curvature (bent in only one direction) and preparing a replacement panel will not require any special equipment. If the paper cannot be laid on the surface without wrinkling, then the plywood has a double curvature. If this is the case, a replacement panel must be obtained from the manufacturer or manufactured by the use of a mold or form and some sort of pressure mechanism to achieve the double curvature.

There are five repair procedures for plywood skin that can be used. They vary in complexity and their use may be restricted based on the location of the damage, size of the damaged area, and thickness of the plywood as shown in Table 2-4.

A **fabric patch** may be used on any plywood skin so long as the trimmed damage does not exceed 1 in [2.54 cm] in diameter and the hole is no closer than 1 in [2.54 cm] to any structural member. The wood around the hole is sealed and a fabric patch that extends beyond the hole by at least 1 in [2.54 cm] is then attached by the use of fabric dope. The patch is finished following the procedure for fabric dope application as covered in Chap. 3.

A **splayed patch** is a patch fitted into the plywood to provide a flush surface; it must not, however, be confused with a scarf patch. The splayed patch has tapered edges joined with glue to tapered edges cut on the hole in the plywood skin. The edge slope is cut at a 5:1 angle.

Splayed patches may be used where the largest dimension of the hole to be repaired is not more than 15 times the skin thickness and the skin thickness is not more than $\frac{1}{10}$ in [2.54 mm].

A splayed patch is applied as shown in Fig. 2-53. Two concentric circles are drawn around the damaged area with a pair of dividers. The difference between the radii of the circles is five times the skin thickness. The inner circle is cut out and a smooth bevel is made from the outer circle to the inner circle. A patch is cut and tapered to fit the hole and is beveled to match the bevel of the hole. Glue is applied to the beveled surfaces, and the patch is placed in the hold. The patch is the same type and thickness as the plywood being repaired. The patch is installed with the face grain in the same direction as that of the skin.

After the patch is in place, a pressure plate cut to the exact size of the patch is centered over the patch, with waxed paper between the two, and pressed firmly against the patch with a weight, such as a sandbag, or clamp. Since there is no reinforcing behind the splayed patch, care must be used to avoid excess pressure.

Plug patches may be used where only the skin has been damaged and where no internal structures will interfere with the installation of the doubler. Plug patches come in two shapes, oval and round, and in two sizes as shown in Figs. 2-54 and 2-55.

The procedures for making both types of plug patches are the same. The hole is trimmed to the exact dimensions of the plug with the edges at right angles to the surface. A doubler made of ¼-in [6.35-mm] plywood is cut. If a round patch is being made and there is no access to the inner surface of the skin being repaired, a cut is made across the doubler as shown in Fig. 2-54 so that it can be worked into the hole. The plug is then made from the same thickness and type of plywood as the original skin covering. The grain of the plug should align with the grain of the original skin. Screw holes are drilled in the plug as shown in the illustrations.

Next, the inside of the original skin is scraped to remove varnish and glue residue and the doubler is glued in place in the inner side of the skin. Gluing pressure can be applied by the use of clamps or nail strips. If clamps are used, the glue must be allowed to set before proceeding with the repair. Glue is applied to the doubler and the plug, the plug is positioned on the doubler, and screws are used to attach a pressure plate to the top of the plug and to hold the plug

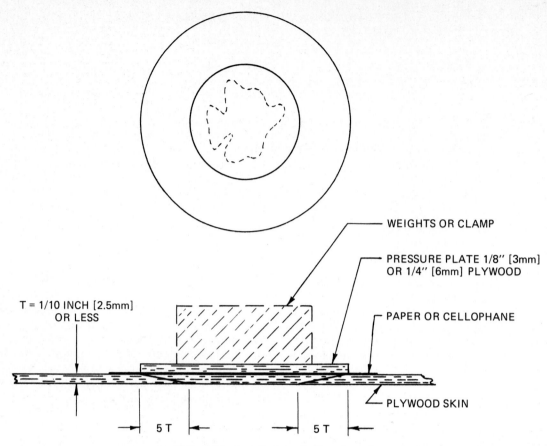

WEIGHTS OR CLAMP

PRESSURE PLATE 1/8" [3mm]
OR 1/4" [6mm] PLYWOOD

PAPER OR CELLOPHANE

T = 1/10 INCH [2.5mm]
OR LESS

PLYWOOD SKIN

5 T   5 T

FIG. 2-53   Installation of splayed patch.

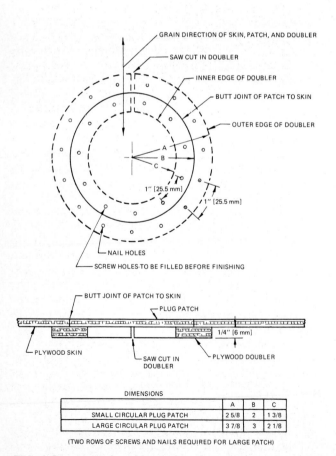

GRAIN DIRECTION OF SKIN, PATCH, AND DOUBLER

SAW CUT IN DOUBLER

INNER EDGE OF DOUBLER

BUTT JOINT OF PATCH TO SKIN

OUTER EDGE OF DOUBLER

A
B
C

1" [25.5 mm]

1" [25.5 mm]

NAIL HOLES

SCREW HOLES-TO BE FILLED BEFORE FINISHING

BUTT JOINT OF PATCH TO SKIN

PLUG PATCH

1/4" [6 mm]

PLYWOOD SKIN

SAW CUT IN
DOUBLER

PLYWOOD DOUBLER

DIMENSIONS

	A	B	C
SMALL CIRCULAR PLUG PATCH	2 5/8	2	1 3/8
LARGE CIRCULAR PLUG PATCH	3 7/8	3	2 1/8

(TWO ROWS OF SCREWS AND NAILS REQUIRED FOR LARGE PATCH)

FIG. 2-54   A circular plug patch.

tightly against the doubler. Be sure to use wax paper or cellophane between the plate and the plug to prevent the plate from bonding to the surface. Once the glue has dried, the screws, pressure plate, and nail strips (if used) are removed, the screw holes are filled with wood putty, and the surface is smoothed and refinished.

A **surface patch** is a type which is applied to the outer surface of a plywood skin. It is sometimes called a "scab" patch. Surface patches may be applied where damage has occurred to a skin between or along framing members. The damaged skin should be trimmed to a triangular- or rectangular-shaped opening, depending upon the exact location of the damage relative to the framing members. Where the framing members form a square corner and the damage does not extend to the next parallel member, a triangular opening should be made. The angles of the triangle should be rounded with a radius of at least five times the thickness of the skin. Doublers made of plywood at least as thick as the skin are applied on the undersurface of the patch seams to provide additional strength. These doublers are extended from one framing member to another and are strengthened at the ends by saddle gussets attached to the framing members. Figure 2-56 illustrates methods for making approved surface patches.

After a surface patch has been applied and the glue has set, the patch should be covered with fabric. The fabric strengthens and protects the patch and reduces

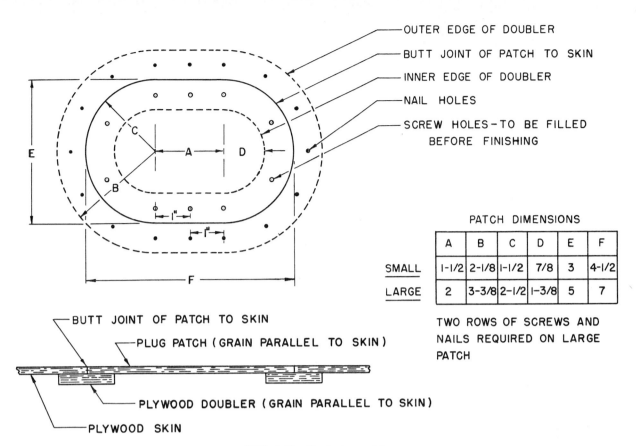

Labels on figure:
- OUTER EDGE OF DOUBLER
- BUTT JOINT OF PATCH TO SKIN
- INNER EDGE OF DOUBLER
- NAIL HOLES
- SCREW HOLES—TO BE FILLED BEFORE FINISHING

PATCH DIMENSIONS

	A	B	C	D	E	F
SMALL	1-1/2	2-1/8	1-1/2	7/8	3	4-1/2
LARGE	2	3-3/8	2-1/2	1-3/8	5	7

TWO ROWS OF SCREWS AND NAILS REQUIRED ON LARGE PATCH

- BUTT JOINT OF PATCH TO SKIN
- PLUG PATCH (GRAIN PARALLEL TO SKIN)
- PLYWOOD DOUBLER (GRAIN PARALLEL TO SKIN)
- PLYWOOD SKIN

FIG. 2-55   Oval plug patch.

the drag a raised patch would cause. The fabric should overlap the original plywood skin by at least 2 in [5.08 cm].

Surface patches are not permitted when the edges of the patch are forward of the 10 percent chord line. A patch which extends entirely around the leading edge so that the edges are aft of the 10 percent chord line is permissible. The leading edge of a surface patch should be beveled with an angle of at least 4:1. Surface patches may have a perimeter of as much as 50 in [127 cm] and may extend from one rib to the next.

A **scarf patch** is preferred for most plywood skin repairs. The scarf patch is flush with the edges beveled to a 12:1 slope. The scarf patch also employs reinforcements under the patch where the glue joints occur. Scarf patches may be employed wherever the damaged plywood skin has a curvature with a radius of more than 100 times the thickness of the skin.

Figure 2-57 illustrates methods for making scarfed flush patches. A study of the illustration will aid in understanding the general principles involved in the installation of scarf patches.

When the back of the skin is accessible, temporary backing blocks are often used to give additional support until the glue joint has set. The backing blocks are shaped to fit the curvature of the skin and are used to hold the nails. After the patch is completed and the glue has set, the nails and backing blocks are removed.

When the damage to the skin is not greater in dimension than 25 times the skin thickness and the back side of the skin is accessible, a round scarf patch may

be installed. A solid block of wood is shaped to fit the curvature of the skin and is cut to the same size as the outer dimension of the patch. After it has been trimmed to a circular shape, the center of the block is cut out to the same size as the hole in the skin. The block is installed on the back of the skin with waxed paper between the block and the skin. Nails are driven through nailing strips, through the scarf patch, and into the block. After the glue has set, the temporary backing block is removed along with the nailing strips and nails. This produces a patch which is flush on both sides. The patch is filled and finished to match the original skin.

In all types of large scarf patches, it is necessary to support the glued joints with backing. If the scarf is at a spar where the width of the spar exceeds the width of the scarf, it is not necessary to provide additional backing. When the scarf joint is along a rib, it is necessary to add plywood backing so that the widths of the backing and the rib together are equal to the width of the scarf. The thickness of the backing is three times the thickness of the skin, with a minimum thickness of ¼ in [6.35 mm]. Where the ends of backing strips join the framing members such as ribs, the ends of the backing strips are supported by means of saddle gussets which are glued and nailed to the framing member. The saddle gussets are made of plywood and have a depth of at least 1 in [2.54 cm]. The length of the saddle gusset is 30 times the thickness of the skin, and the thickness is the same as that of the skin.

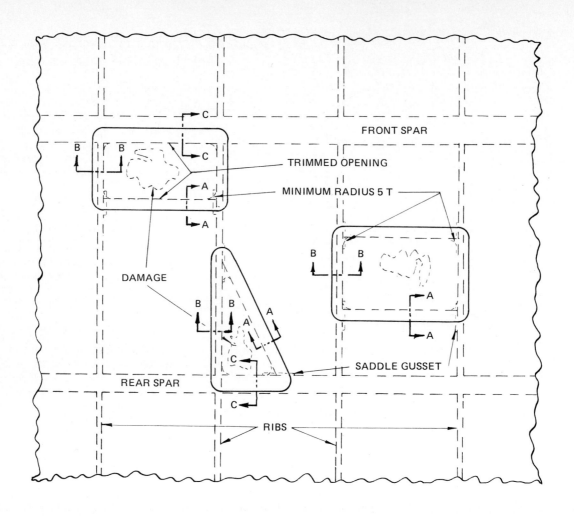

FRONT SPAR

TRIMMED OPENING

MINIMUM RADIUS 5 T

DAMAGE

SADDLE GUSSET

REAR SPAR

RIBS

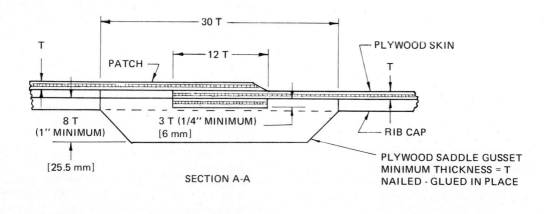

30 T

12 T

PLYWOOD SKIN

T

PATCH

T

8 T
(1" MINIMUM)

3 T (1/4" MINIMUM)
[6 mm]

RIB CAP

[25.5 mm]

SECTION A-A

PLYWOOD SADDLE GUSSET
MINIMUM THICKNESS = T
NAILED - GLUED IN PLACE

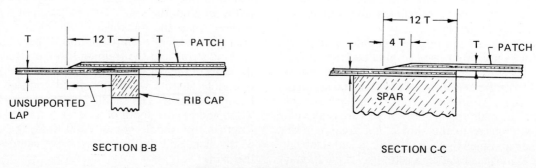

T

12 T

T

PATCH

UNSUPPORTED
LAP

RIB CAP

SECTION B-B

12 T

4 T

T

T

PATCH

SPAR

SECTION C-C

FIG. 2-56 Surface patches.

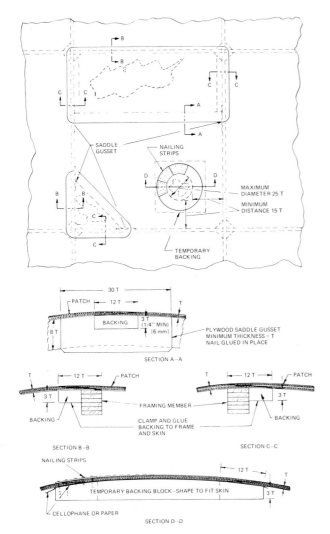

FIG. 2-57 Scarf patches.

It is recommended that soft-textured plywood such as poplar or spruce be used for backing strips for scarfed flush patches in order to avoid warping of the patch and adjoining skin.

Fiber Insert Nut Plates

Fiber insert nut plates are installed at various locations in the wings and fuselage for the attachment of inspection doors, fuel-tank cap covers, and other parts. If one of these nuts is damaged, or if a machine screw breaks off in it, the portion of the wooden strip carrying the nut and extending about 1 in [2.54 cm] on each side should be sawed out and replaced by a new section that is glued and nailed in place. These nut strips are ⅜-in [9.53-mm] plywood strips with the nuts embedded at regular intervals. Finally, a ¹⁄₁₆-in [1.59-mm] thick plywood strip is glued and nailed over the nuts and drilled on correct centers to allow the passage of the machine screws. This is a better method of attaching nut plates than the use of wood screws.

Skis

Wooden ski runners which are fractured are usually replaced, but a split at the rear end of the runner having a length not more than 10 percent of the ski length may be repaired by attaching, with glue and bolts, one or more wooden crosspieces across the top of the runner.

Finishing Repaired Wood Surfaces

Wood surfaces of an airplane structure which have been repaired must be finished to prevent the absorption of moisture, oil, or other contaminants and to prevent deterioration. In every case the proper finish must be selected and the surface prepared in accordance with approved practice.

The interior surfaces of wooden structures such as wings and control surfaces should be thoroughly coated with spar varnish or lion oil. Two coats of either finish brushed onto the clean surface will usually be sufficient. Before the finish is applied, it is important to see that all excess glue, grease, oil, crayon marks, and similar contaminants are removed. Sawdust, shavings, loose wood particles, and similar material should also be removed from the inside of the structure.

When a structure is designed so that it is not possible to reach the interior after the outer skin is installed, it is necessary to finish the interior before the last pieces are fixed in place. In such cases, care must be taken to see that areas to be glued are not coated. After assembly, it is sometimes possible to reach through inspection holes with a small "touch-up" spray gun and apply finish to small areas.

Exterior surfaces, whether plywood or solid wood, are comparatively easy to finish. Such surfaces must be clean; that is, excess glue, grease, oil, etc., must be removed. Oil and grease spots can be removed with naphtha or a similar petroleum solvent. Small nail holes, scratches, or depressions in the wood surface should be filled with plastic wood or a similar compound, and the surface should be sanded smooth after the material has dried. Two coats of spar varnish, wood sealer, or MIL-V-6894 varnish should be applied as a base. MIL-V-6894 varnish is dopeproof and should be used when the final finish is to be lacquer or dope.

After the sealer or base varnish is applied to a wood surface and the varnish has dried, it may be necessary to sand the surface lightly to remove rough spots. The final finish can then be applied in as many coats as required. This is usually done with a spray gun. The operation of spray equipment is discussed in Chap. 4.

End-grain wood surfaces require more finish than side-grain surfaces because of the tendency of the grain to absorb the finish. It is good practice to use a wood filler before applying the varnish. The wood filler is applied after the end grain has been smoothed with sandpaper. After the wood filler has dried, a clear or pigmented sealer may be used in two or more coats. The surface can then be finished as previously described.

● CARE OF AIRCRAFT WITH WOOD STRUCTURES

The earliest models of successful aircraft were constructed largely with wood structures. Fuselages were then changed to welded steel structures, while the airplane was still equipped with wood-structured wings and control surfaces. The maintenance and care of these airplanes were handled remarkably well by the mechanics in both civil and military areas. The key to success in the maintenance of the wood structures was the selection of the best woods for aircraft structures and the proper finishing of the woods to prevent the absorption of moisture.

Control of Moisture

Moisture is the deadliest enemy of wood. Wood that is kept dry will seldom, if ever, deteriorate over a period of many years. Dry, in this sense, means that it holds no more moisture than its natural content under dry-air conditions. On the other hand, when unprotected wood is exposed to water for an appreciable length of time, fungus begins to grow and penetrate the wood cells. This is the cause of decay, dry rot, or whatever term may be used to describe deterioration due to fungus.

Moisture also has the effect of causing wood to swell. If wood is alternately wet and dry over a period of time, it will crack and warp; this will reduce its structural strength and cause stresses of various kinds.

It is apparent from the above that one of the primary considerations in the care of airplanes with wood structures is to ensure that the wood is finished with an effective, water-resistant coating. **Spar varnishes** of the phenol formaldehyde type (MIL-V-6893) of glyceryl phthalate type (MIL-V-6894) are commonly employed for the finishing of wood structures. Another synthetic finish with a polyurethane base is becoming increasingly popular for finishing purposes.

An important factor in preventing moisture from affecting wood structures is to ensure that drain holes are provided in all low points and that the holes are kept open. The drain holes will permit collected water to drain out and the area to dry. It is important to consider drain holes when repairing or recovering an airplane. Sometimes a mechanic may fail to take note of the position of all drain holes, with the result that some critical areas may not have drain holes.

One of the best methods for extending the service life of an airplane with wood structures is to store it in a dry, well-ventilated hangar when it is not in use. This, of course, is not always possible; however, the practice may well pay for itself in reduced maintenance costs.

Effects of Temperature

Temperature changes, although not as critical as moisture, cause stresses and dimensional changes which can lead to cracks, looseness of fittings, and deterioration of finishes. Desert conditions, with extremes of temperature and low humidity, can cause a maximum of shrinkage in wood structures. This can lead to loose fittings and separation of some glued joints. It is incumbent upon mechanics, under these circumstances, to be particularly alert to detect these conditions.

High temperatures also lead to deterioration of finishes. High temperatures lead to the evaporation of plasticizers in coatings, and this causes brittleness and cracking. In such cases, it is necessary to remove or rejuvenate finishes and restore them to optimum condition.

Low temperatures are likely to cause damage if moisture is present. Freezing of wet structures can cause rupture of fibers and cells, thus weakening the parts affected.

Operation and Handling

As with any type of airplane, one having wood structures can be damaged by improper operation and handling. Pilots must not exceed flight limits set forth for the aircraft and should use great care in landing and taxiing. Careless operation can lead to broken or cracked spars and other wood structures.

Moving an aircraft on the ground must be done with care to avoid cracking or breaking ribs and other structures in the wings and control surfaces. **Note:** Approved walkways and steps must be utilized when it is necessary to climb upon the aircraft. Lifting and pushing must be accomplished by applying pressure or force only to solid structures which can withstand the forces applied.

● INSPECTION OF AIRPLANES HAVING WOOD STRUCTURES

The inspection of wood structures requires a great amount of care on the part of the mechanic. Because of the nature of wood, it tends to hide the beginnings of deterioration and cracks. The following discussion is designed to make the mechanic aware of some of the problems that may be encountered when inspecting wood structures and some methods that can be used to detect these problems.

Defects in Wood Structures

During the inspection of an airplane with wood structures, the mechanic must know what to look for that will indicate a defective or weak structure and the necessity for repair. The following are defects most commonly found when performing a complete inspection:

Dry Rot and Decay. These conditions are essentially the same and are caused by fungus in damp or wet wood. The appearance may be black, brown, gray, or some combination of the three colors. The wood may be breaking down into particles, or there may be a softening of the surface. Dry rot and decay can also be detected by pressing a sharp-pointed instrument such as a scribe into the wood to determine the force necessary to penetrate the wood. If the force required is less than that required for the same depth of penetration in sound wood, it is a sign that deterioration has taken place. These conditions require replacement of the defective part.

Separated Glue Joints. Wherever a glue joint is found open or separated, the structure must be rebuilt.

Deteriorated Glue Joints. This condition is caused by aging and deterioration of the glue. Casein glue which was not treated to prevent fungus will deteriorate in the presence of moisture. Synthetic resin glues are not generally subject to this type of deterioration. Deteriorated glue joints require rebuilding of the structure affected.

Cracks. Shrinkage of the wood or stress applied to it can cause cracks. Whatever the cause, the cracked member must be replaced.

Compression Failure. This type of failure is caused by a compressive force acting essentially parallel to the grain of the wood. Compression failure is indicated by a line or lines extending across the grain where the wood fibers have been crushed. A test for a compression failure is to apply a small amount of free-running ink to the wood near the suspected break. The ink will flow along the normal grain until it reaches a compression failure. At this point it will flow cross-grain along the failure.

Surface Crushing. This defect is caused when the wood is struck by a hard object. This produces indentation, abrasion, and rupture of the wood fibers. Damaged parts should be replaced or repaired.

Staining. Stains that are caused by moisture indicate that a glue joint has failed or that the protective coating is deteriorating. This type of stain is usually dark in color and tends to expand along the grain of the wood. When water stains are found, the cause must be corrected and the affected parts replaced or repaired. Surface stains that are easily removed without removing wood do not usually require replacement of affected parts. The protective coating on such parts must be restored.

Corrosion. Corrosion of attachment bolts, screws, nails, and fittings in or on wood structures indicates the presence of moisture. Corroded parts should be replaced, and the cause of moisture intrusion eliminated.

Inspection Procedures

Before a major inspection is started on an aircraft with wood structures, the aircraft should be perfectly dry. In a warm, dry climate, this presents no problem; however, in other areas it is well to have the aircraft stored in a dry, well-ventilated hangar for a few days prior to the inspection. Humidity (moisture in the air) causes wood to swell, thus closing cracks and open glue joints so they are not easily detected.

In cases where maintenance manuals are available for an aircraft, the manufacturer's instructions should be followed. In other cases, the inspection should be carried out with a checklist and in a sequence that will ensure a thorough examination of every structural part of the aircraft.

At the start of the inspection, it is a good plan to examine the complete exterior surface of the aircraft for condition and contour. If the aircraft is covered with plywood, a noticeable defect on the surface can indicate damage inside. If the plywood is covered with fabric and a crack or split appears in the fabric, the fabric must be removed so the plywood underneath can be examined for damage.

If the surface of the plywood is warped or wavy, defects are indicated inside the structure. Access through an inspection hole or by removal of a section of plywood skin is necessary in order to examine the interior. If the plywood is not stressed, i.e., does not carry a structural load, a small amount of undulation (waviness) can be permitted.

Where openings are not already provided in the plywood cover for access to the interior or wings, it is often necessary to provide cutouts, and they should be made adjacent to members of the wing frame. The cutaway section should be made as small as possible and closed after the work is completed. Closing is accomplished by the same method as previously described for making repairs. A triangular cutout section is easiest to make, and it presents a small area of opening; however, the oval cutout has a better appearance, provided that time and space permit this type of repair.

To examine the inside of areas where direct visual inspection is not possible, it is necessary to employ aids such as a flashlight, mirror, magnifying glass, and possibly a borescope or similar instrument. The interior areas should appear clean, unstained, and solid. Glue seams or joints should show no cracks or separations. Glue joints can be checked by attempting to insert one of the thinnest leaves of a feeler gauge into the joint. If the feeler gauge can penetrate the joint, the joint must be disassembled and repaired.

The finish inside the wood structure should indicate no deterioration. If it has become opaque or has a rough milky appearance, it should be removed to reveal the condition of the wood underneath. If the wood is clean, solid, and unstained, it can be refinished with approved varnish.

Wood wings which are covered with fabric are somewhat easier to examine than those covered with plywood. In all cases they should be inspected for all the defects listed previously. If the wing is to be recovered with new fabric, a very thorough examination can be made of the glue joints and wood condition.

The quality of wood wing structures covered with fabric can be checked by applying moderate pressure in various areas. Grasping a rib tip at the trailing edge and attempting to move it up and down will reveal damage and failure of glue joints. If there is noticeable movement, the condition must be repaired after removing fabric as necessary.

Aileron attachment fittings, usually on the rear spar, are checked by the application of pressure. If they are loose or move too easily, repair or replacement is required.

The ribs on a fabric-covered wing can be checked by examination and feel. Those which can be moved or are out of shape require opening of the fabric for further examination and repair.

Elevators, rudders, stabilizers, and fittings can be inspected in the same manner as that employed for wings. Fittings which are loose or corroded may require replacement, and it may be necessary to repair enlarged or elongated bolt holes. Bolts must fit snugly in bolt holes.

In cases where a spar is laminated and bolts pass

through the laminated section to attach a fitting, the bolts should be loosened to take the pressure off the area. This will allow any separations between the layers of wood to be revealed. Care must be taken to retighten the bolts to the correct torque after the inspection. All bolted areas should be checked for cracks, loose bolts, crushed wood, and corrosion. Defects must be repaired.

If, during inspection, glue deterioration is found, a major rebuilding job may be required to restore the structure to its original strength. Glue deterioration is indicated when a joint has separated and the glue surface shows only the imprint of the wood with no wood fibers clinging to the glue. If the glue is in good condition, any separation will occur in the wood and not in the glue. This type of separation is usually caused by excessive stress due to a hard landing or other improper operation of the airplane.

Regardless of the type of wood structure, a thorough visual inspection should be performed with and without stress being placed on the structure. The stress inspection usually requires at least two people, one to do the inspecting and one to apply stress to the structure. The stress is applied by pushing up, pulling down, and twisting the structure by applying pressure at the primary structures such as the end of the wing spars. Do not apply so much stress as to damage the structure!

While the stress is being applied and released, examine the external surfaces for any unusual wrinkles that may appear. Inside the structure, listen for unusual noises and check for unusual movement between parts and cracks that open up under stress. Also look for any powder flow from joints, indicating abrasion and breakdown of glue joints. If anything irregular is noted, investigate the area further until a defect is found or until the movement or sound is determined to be normal.

● REVIEW QUESTIONS

1. What types of trees produce *softwoods? Hardwoods?*
2. What are some uses of hardwoods in aircraft structures?
3. What is considered to be the best type of wood for aircraft structures?
4. How does *laminated* wood differ from *plywood?*
5. What are *annual rings* in wood?
6. What is the difference between checks and shakes?
7. What is meant by *compression* wood?
8. What is the maximum grain deviation or slope allowed for structural aircraft wood?
9. What is meant by the term *quarter-sawed?*
10. What is the minimum number of annual rings allowable per inch in aircraft structural woods?
11. What are the two classifications of water found in wood?
12. What should be the moisture content for aircraft woods?
13. Explain the term *kiln-dried.*

14. Describe aircraft plywood.
15. What are the advantages of plywood?
16. What are the most common types of plywood for aircraft use?
17. What types of glues are most satisfactory for aircraft wood assembly?
18. Which type of glue requires additives to inhibit the growth of microorganisms?
19. From what source should information be obtained regarding the use of a particular glue?
20. What is meant by the *working life* of a glue?
21. Describe a wood surface that is properly conditioned for gluing.
22. What is the effect of sanding on a wood surface to be glued?
23. What is the glue pressure recommended for use with softwoods?
24. How is gluing pressure applied?
25. What is the purpose of *caul blocks?*
26. What is a good average pressing time for a glue joint?
27. Explain *open assembly* of a glue joint.
28. In general, what is the maximum time that glue should be exposed to the air in the open-assembly process?
29. How are aircraft nails treated to prevent corrosion?
30. What is the purpose of a nailing strip?
31. Explain how wood can be formed to produce curved shapes.
32. What is the desired slope for the scarf in a spar splice?
33. Explain how reinforcement plates are applied to a spar splice.
34. How should the scarf cut be made in a piece of spar stock with respect to the slope of the grain in the wood?
35. What methods can be used to apply pressure when making a spar splice to a solid spar?
36. What method is used to prevent glue from sticking to caul blocks and clamps?
37. Discuss the construction of I-beam spars and box-beam spars.
38. Describe an approved repair for elongated bolt holes in the end of a spar.
39. Explain how a duplicate rib can be constructed.
40. If the trailing edge of a wing rib is broken, how should the repair be made?
41. Describe a rib capstrip splice.
42. Discuss the use of nails in the installation and construction of ribs.
43. What precaution must be taken when driving aircraft nails into gussets on a wood rib?
44. How is a template used in the repair of leading edges?
45. Describe the construction of a wing-tip bow.
46. Explain how plywood is applied to a wing.
47. Why is a nailing strip used in the installation of plywood?
48. How is plywood held tightly in place while the glue is drying? Give three methods.
49. Describe the installation of a surface patch in a plywood repair.

50. What is the difference between a *splayed* patch and a *scarfed* patch?
51. Describe the installation of a *plug* patch in plywood.
52. What is the maximum diameter allowed for a circular plug patch?
53. Under what condition may a wooden ski be repaired with wooden crosspieces across the top of the runner?
54. Describe the finishing of a wooden surface.
55. What is the most important consideration in the preservation of wood aircraft structures?
56. By what methods is a wood aircraft structure protected against moisture?
57. Discuss the effects of temperatures on wood.
58. Name the principal defects which may be found in wood aircraft structures.
59. Why should an aircraft be thoroughly dry before an inspection of wood structures is started?
60. How may inspection access be provided for a closed compartment in a plywood-covered wing?
61. Discuss methods for determining whether a glue joint is separated.
62. What inspections should be made with respect to bolts and fittings attached to the wood spar of a wing or control surface?
63. How can you tell whether a separation is caused by glue deterioration or by excessive stress?

3 FABRIC COVERINGS

Although the majority of modern aircraft are constructed of metal, there are still many requirements for aircraft fabrics of various types, and there are many fabric-covered aircraft certificated for operation. It is, therefore, essential that the aircraft mechanic be familiar with approved fabric materials and processes.

Fabric covering for aircraft has been in use for many years because of its low cost, ease of installation, ease of repair, light weight, strength, and durability. In addition, the design and construction of a fabric-covered airplane is such that it does not require the special manufacturing and repair equipment associated with metal aircraft.

Aircraft-covering fabrics are made of cotton, polyester fiber, glass fiber, and linen. Approved methods for the application of cotton are set forth in the FAA publication AC43.13-1A and are also covered in this text. Because of the durability and strength of polyester fabrics, many aircraft owners are recovering their aircraft with this material. Two such processes are sold under the names Poly-Fiber and Ceconite. Covering an airplane under these processes must be accomplished according to the instructions provided by the fabric manufacturer.

To add to the variety of processes used for aircraft covering, some aircraft manufacturers have devised their own processes for covering aircraft. These often combine the cotton and polyester processes. When recovering modern fabric-covered aircraft, consult the aircraft manufacturer's service manuals for specific information about their processes.

Nomenclature for Fabrics

To be able to properly handle, inspect, and install fabrics requires that the mechanic be familiar with some of the basic terminology used with woven fabrics. While this list is not complete, it will serve as a basis for terms presented in later portions of this chapter. Referring to Figs. 3-1 and 3-2 will be helpful in understanding some of the following terms.

Bias A cut, fold, or seam made diagonally across the warp and fill fibers of a piece of cloth. Bias-cut fabric allows the materials to be stretched slightly for better forming to structural contours.

Bleaching A chemical process used to whiten textile materials. Grade A airplane fabric is not bleached and is usually a light cream color. Bleaching, if not properly done, can weaken a material and make it unfit for use.

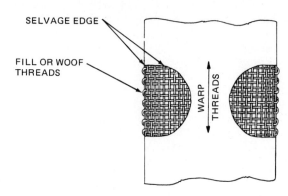

FIG. 3-1 Warp and fill, or woof.

Calendering A process of ironing fabric by threading it wet between a series of heated and cold rollers to produce a smooth finish. That is, it causes the **nap** to lay close to the surface. The nap is the "fuzzy" surface caused by the thousands of ends of individual fibers.

Fill The fibers of a piece of fabric that are woven into the warp fabric. These fibers run perpendicular to the length of the fabric as it comes off of a roll of material.

Mercerizing A chemical process in which cotton is exposed to the action of a strong caustic solution

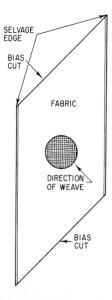

FIG. 3-2 Bias-cut fabric.

which tends to shrink the material and give it a silky appearance.

Selvage edge The naturally bound edge of a length of fabric. The selvage edge is where the fill fibers turn around and go back through the warp fibers during the weaving process.

Sizing A textile glue used to stiffen and protect fabrics and threads. It gives "body" to a material.

Thread count The number of thread, either warp or fill, on the edge of a piece of fabric. The thread count uses a unit of measurement of "threads per inch."

Warp The threads in a woven fabric that run the length of the fabric.

Weight Fabric weight indicates the weight of the fabric per unit of area. The weight is commonly stated as ounces per square yard.

Woof Same as Fill.

Organic Fabrics

Organic fabrics are those made from plant materials. These include two grades of cotton fabrics and linen.

The standard approved aircraft covering has been, for many years, **grade A mercerized cotton cloth.** This material is identified by the SAE number AMS 3806, and the specifications are set forth in FAA Technical Standard Order (TSO) C15. Approved fabric predoped with cellulose nitrate dope is numbered MIL-C-5643, and fabric predoped with cellulose acetate butyrate dope is numbered MIL-C-5642. The minimum tensile strength of approved grade A fabric in the new, undoped condition is 80 lb/in [140 N/cm (newtons per centimeter)]. This means that a strip of the fabric 1 in [2.54 cm] in width must be able to support a weight of 80 lb [355.84 N] in tension without breaking. The fabric can be tested with a pull-test machine or by securing a known width to the material in a suitably designed clamp and then suspending a weight from it. If the test strip is 2 in [5.08 cm] wide, it should be able to support a weight of 160 lb [72.58 kg (kilograms)]. After fabric has been used on an airplane, its minimum permissible strength is 70 percent of new strength, or 56 lb/in [98 N/cm] for grade A fabric undoped. This means that when the fabric on an airplane has deteriorated to the point where the strength is less than 56 lb/in [98 N/cm], the fabric must be replaced. Fabric may be tested with approved testing machines while still on the airplane, or a piece may be cut from the airplane and given a pull test after the dope has been removed. Testing of fabric will be discussed later in this chapter.

The military specification for grade A fabric is MIL-C-5646. A fabric having this number or the number AMS 3806 (TSO C15) has, in the past, been considered acceptable for all aircraft. However, with the advent of inorganic covering materials, grade A cotton may not be used on an aircraft originally covered with an inorganic fabric unless approval is obtained from the aircraft manufacturer or the FAA. To determine the original fabric covering material used on an aircraft, check the aircraft service manual.

Grade A fabric must have a thread count of 80 to 84 threads per inch in both length and width. The weight of the fabric must be not less than 4 oz/yd^2 (ounces per square yard) [135.6 g/m^2 (grams per square meter)]. The fabric is calendered after weaving to lay the nap and make the finished material smooth.

For aircraft having a wing loading of no greater than 9 lb/ft^2 [43.94 kg/m^2] and a placarded never-exceed speed no greater than 160 mph [257.5 km/h (kilometers per hour)], a lighter-weight fabric may be used (Wing loading can be determined by dividing the maximum allowed gross weight of the aircraft by the wing area.) This fabric is designated as **intermediate-grade aircraft fabric** and carries the number AMS 3804 (TSO C14). The minimum tensile strength of this fabric in the new, undoped condition is 65 lb/in [113.75 N/cm]. Remember that "pounds per inch" does not have the same meaning as "pounds per square inch." The thread count for intermediate fabric is 80 minimum to 94 maximum threads per inch [32 to 37 threads per centimeter] for both warp and woof (fill).

With intermediate-grade cotton, observe the same precaution concerning aircraft originally covered with an inorganic fabric. Also, intermediate-grade fabric is no longer commonly available. Its only value is as a reference material to determine the minimum strength to which fabric can be allowed to deteriorate before the fabric must be replaced. This will be discussed in detail in a later section of this chapter.

For many years early in the history of aviation, linen was commonly used for the covering of aircraft. Linen, being woven from flax fiber, is strong, light, and durable. Aircraft linen is an especially fine grade of linen cloth, and if it complies with the requirements of TSO C15, it is suitable for use on certificated aircraft originally covered with organic fabric. The British specification 7F1 meets all the requirements of TSO C15.

Inorganic Fabrics

An **inorganic fabric** (synthetic fabric) is one which requires chemical processing to create the fiber. Once the fiber is created, it is woven in the same manner as used for organic material. The inorganic fabrics have two advantages over organic fabrics in that they resist deterioration by the ultraviolet rays of the sun and they resist attack by microorganisms. The only significant disadvantage associated with inorganic fabrics is the care required to assure proper bonding of the dopes and finishing products to the fabric as will be explained later in this chapter.

There are two types of inorganic fabrics used to cover aircraft: **polyesters** (Dacron-type materials) and **fiberglass.**

The polyester fabrics are manufactured under the trade names of Stits Poly-Fiber and Ceconite. These materials come in a variety of weights, thread counts, and tensile strengths. These fabrics have become very popular as replacements for the organic materials due to their ease of installation and resistance to deterioration when compared to organic materials.

Razorback is the most widely used type of fiberglass material for covering aircraft. It has an advantage over all other types of materials in that is impervious to deterioration, heat, and most chemicals. As a result it is often the fabric of choice for aircraft subject to exposure to chemical environments such as agricultural operations.

Surface Tape

Surface tape, also called **finishing tape,** is usually cut from the same material that is being used to cover the airplane. The edges are **pinked** (cut with a saw-toothed edge) to provide better adhesion when doped to the surface and to reduce the tendency to ravel. The edges of surface tape made from synthetic materials are often cut in a straight line with the edges being sealed by heat to prevent raveling. Surface tape material is used to reinforce the fabric covering at openings and fittings, protect and seal rib attachment processes, and streamline surface irregularities.

A roll of surface tape is shown in Fig. 3-3. This tape should have the same fiber, yarn size, tensile strength, and number of threads per inch as the fabric upon which it is applied. The sizing must not exceed 2.5 percent; however, approved tape will usually fulfill this requirement.

FIG. 3-3   A roll of surface tape.

Surface tape is available as straight-cut, where the edges of the tape are parallel to the warp threads, and as bias-cut, for use on surfaces with compound curvatures such as at wing tips and curved trailing edges. The tape is supplied in standard-length rolls (such as 100 yd [91.44 m]) and can be ordered in various widths ranging from about 1 in [2.54 cm] to 6 in [15.24 cm] or more.

Reinforcing Tape

Reinforcing tape is a special product that has a much larger warp thread than fill thread. It is used over ribs between the lacing cord and fabric covering to prevent the cord from cutting or wearing through the fabric and to help distribute the air loads. Reinforcing tape is also often used for inter-rib bracing of wing structures prior to installation of the fabric covering.

Reinforcing tape bearing the specification number MIL-T-5661, or equivalent, is approved for aircraft use. It is ordinarily obtainable in several widths that conform to the different widths of ribs or rib capstrips. This tape is of a material similar to the fabric covering used on the airplane. The tensile strength is at least 150 lb per ½ in [525.35 N or 53.6 kg/cm]. If a synthetic fabric or fiberglass covering is being installed, the reinforcing tape may be the standard cotton type, or it may be a special tape designed and manufactured for use with the covering being applied. In all cases, it is wise to consult the specifications applicable to the job or process concerned. A roll of reinforcing tape is shown in Fig. 3-4.

FIG. 3-4   A roll of reinforcing tape.

Sewing Threads and Lacing Cords

Sewing thread, for either machine sewing or hand sewing, is used to join two fabric edges together during the installation or repair of fabric covering materials. Cords are normally heavy threads used where a significant amount of strength is required of each stitch, such as when attaching a fabric covering to wing ribs or fuselage stringers.

Machine thread, also called **machine-sewing thread,** is used in all machine sewing. For use with organic fabrics it is made of cotton, carries a specification number V-T-276b, and is described as 20/4 ply to indicate the size. It has a tensile strength of 5 lb [22.25 N] per single strand, and a nominal weight of 1 lb [0.4536 kg] for 5000 yd [4572 m]. It is sometimes described as a white, silk-finish, no. 16, four-cord cotton thread with a Z twist. This thread provides durable seams when used with a sewing machine.

Hand-sewing thread for organic fabrics carries the specification number V-T-276b, Type III B, and is used for all hand sewing. It is an unbleached, cotton, silk-finish thread, no. 8, four-cord, with a tensile strength of 14 lb [62.27 N or 6.35 kg] for a single strand, and a normal weight of 1 lb [0.4536 kg] for 1650 yd [1508.76 m].

The **twist** of a thread or cord may be either right or left. The term **S twist** designates a right-twist thread. The words **machine, machine twist, Z twist,** and **left twist** all refer to a left-twist thread. Figure 3-5 shows a left-twist cord. The importance of the twist of hand-sewing thread is based on the direction in which the hand-sewn seam is installed. Right-handed people should make seams from right to left using a left-twist thread held taught with the left hand while each stitch

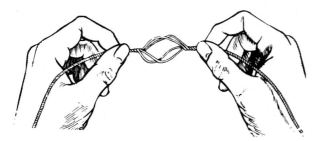

FIG. 3-5   A left-twist cord.

is being made. Left-handed people should work in the opposite direction. In this manner, the thread will not untwist while hand sewing and the resulting seam will be strong and tight.

A thread or cord which has been sized to produce a hard, glazed surface to prevent the thread from fraying or weakening is known as a **silk finish** thread or cord.

When an airplane is covered with a synthetic fabric under a Supplemental Type Certificate or a Parts Manufacturer's Approval, special cords and threads made of the same material as the fabric are often recommended. For example, in the Poly-Fiber covering process, polyester fabric is used and polyester lacing cord and sewing threads are required.

Lacing cord, as mentioned previously, is used for lacing fabric to the structure, and is often referred to as **rib-stitching cord** or **rib-lacing cord.** This is because it is commonly used for stitching or lacing the fabric to the wings of an airplane. Acceptable lacing cords carry the specification numbers MIL-T-6779 or MIL-C-2520A for a linen cord and MIL-T-5660 for a cotton cord. The cord must have a minimum tensile strength of 40 lb [18.14 kg] single or 80 lb [36.29 kg] double.

Lacing cord is often waxed when received. If it is not, it should be waxed lightly before use. Beeswax is suitable for this purpose. Waxing is accomplished by drawing the cord under tension across a piece of the wax.

A **braided cord,** illustrated in Fig. 3-6, is made by

FIG. 3-6   A braided cord.

weaving strands of thread together to form either a solidly woven cord or one with a hollow-channel center, such as that illustrated in Fig. 3-7. Some cords have a channel made with a hollow center which con-

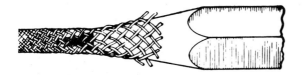

FIG. 3-7   Braided cord with a hollow center.

tains one or more straight, individual threads called a **core,** the purpose of which is to increase the strength of the cord and to hold the outer braided cover to a rounded contour. Figure 3-8 shows a braided cord with a core.

FIG. 3-8   Braided cord with a core.

In the covering of aircraft, the braided cords are not commonly used; however, the mechanic should be aware of such materials because they are encountered occasionally. Braided cords meeting the specifications MIL-C-5649 and MIL-C-5648 are approved for use in lacing fabric to aircraft structures.

Waxed cords are used for attaching **chafing strips.** These cotton or synthetic cords may be either four-ply or five-ply, but they must be double-twist and waxed. The chafing strips are sometimes hand-sewn russet-leather reinforcing strips that are placed on movable brace wires or rods at their points of intersection and on places where chafing may occur on control cables and the tubing of the structure. In place of leather, it is common practice to use synthetic or plastic materials such as neoprene, Corprene, Teflon, and polyethylene formed as sheet or tubing, to provide resistance to wear and abrasion.

Grommets

Grommets are installed where it is necessary to reinforce holes in textile materials used for drainage, lacing, or inspection. A grommet consists of one or two parts, depending upon the type. A **metal grommet,** used for lacing eyes, consists of two parts as shown in Fig. 3-9. These parts may be made of either brass or aluminum.

The smallest metal grommet generally used is No. 00 ($\frac{5}{32}$ in [3.97 mm]). It is used for lacing holes in an

FIG. 3-9   A metal grommet.

opening made for inspection purposes. This particular type of inspection opening is not generally found on modern airplanes because different types of inspection openings have been designed.

Plastic grommets are used for drainage and ventilation purposes. Plain grommets are simply thin plastic washers which are doped directly on the fabric after the first coat of dope has dried. This installation is shown in Fig. 3-10. Grommets are placed on the bot-

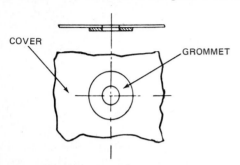

FIG. 3-10 **Installation of a plastic grommet.**

tom of the trailing edges of horizontal flight surfaces, the bottom of vertical surfaces, and the low points of fuselage structures. For horizontal surfaces with a positive dihedral, the grommets are on the outboard side of the ribs. For a negative dihedral, the grommets are on the inboard side of the ribs. A neutral dihedral requires a grommet on each side of a rib. These configurations are shown in Fig. 3-11. These drain grommets allow any moisture inside the structure to drain out when on the ground and in flight.

Where exceptionally good drainage and ventilation

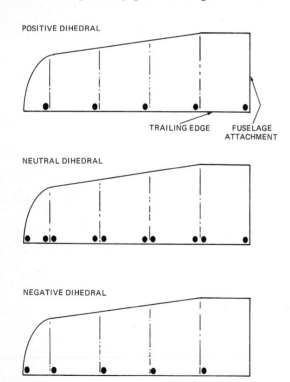

FIG. 3-11 **The bottom view of a horizontal stabilizer showing desired drain grommet locations for different dihedral angles.**

is desired, as with seaplanes, **marine** or **seaplane grommets** are installed. A grommet of this type is shown in Fig. 3-12. This grommet is constructed with a streamlined aperture which creates a suction and causes increased air circulation in the part to which it is applied.

After the installation of plain plastic grommets or seaplane grommets, the fabric in the grommet opening should be cut out with a sharp knife or similar instrument. The opening should not be punched out because this does not remove the fabric and the opening is likely to close and prevent proper drainage and ventilation.

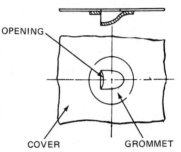

FIG. 3-12 **A seaplane grommet.**

Inspection Rings

Inspection rings are installed on the fabric of the fuselage or wings where it is necessary to examine fittings, internal bracing, cables, and similar items inside the covered structure. The plastic rings, about 4 in [10.16 cm] in diameter, are often doped onto the fabric in the proper location. Except when necessary for installation or adjustment, the center is not cut out until the first annual or 100-h inspection is made. After the inspection is made, a metal inspection cover or plate is installed in the hole. the plastic ring provides support for the inspection plate, which is held in place by spring clips attached to the inside surface. An inspection ring is shown in Fig. 3-13.

Use of Leather

Russet strap leather is sometimes used in the fabrication of reinforcing patches on doped fabric surfaces where heavy wear is caused by control cables and rods, and it can also be used for making chafing strips which are used anywhere on the structure where friction is encountered by the fabric covering. This leather has a hard, glazed surface that makes it resistant to the usual deteriorating influences.

Horsehide leather is thinner than russet strap leather and does not wear as well. The finish is soft, and the color is usually brown or black. It can be used for the same purposes as russet strap leather where the wear is less, and it can also be used to a certain extent for making reinforcing patches which are placed around flanges which protrude through the fabric covering. Figure 3-14 shows a sewed leather reinforcing patch applied where a control cable passes through a fabric cover.

Special Fasteners

While the use of rib-lacing cord is the classic method of attaching fabric to wing, stabilizer and control sur-

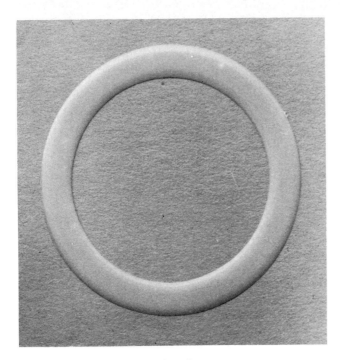

FIG. 3-13 A plastic inspection ring.

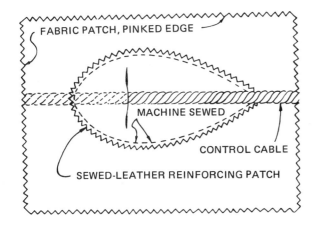

FIG. 3-14 A sewn leather reinforcing patch.

face ribs, several other methods are employed. Some of these are associated with particular aircraft designs, and some are approved through the use of Supplemental Type Certificates (STCs) or field approvals. It should be noted that each of the methods to be discussed is used on metal ribs. Only rib lacing is used with wood ribs.

Self-tapping screws are used by some manufacturers as the standard method of attaching fabric to ribs. A plastic washer is used under the screw head to distribute the load onto the fabric surface. The screws used should be long enough to allow at least two threads of the grip (threaded part) to extend beyond the metal inside the structure. The use of screws for fabric attachment is shown in Fig. 3-15.

Pull-type rivets with large heads, shown in Fig. 3-16, are employed in some aircraft designs. These rivets require that a small hole be opened in the reinforcing tape and the fabric. The rivet is inserted through the reinforcing tape, fabric covering, and metal rib. A

pulling tool is then used to expand the tail of the rivet and the fabric attachment is complete.

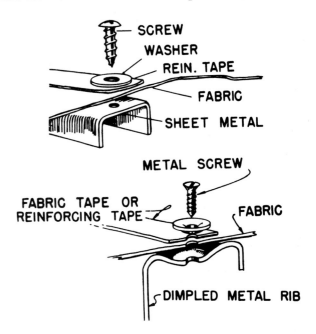

FIG. 3-15 Use of self-taping screws to hold fabric.

FIG. 3-16 A fabric rivet.

Various types of metal clips have been used on aircraft as original installation methods and as approved replacement processes for original attachment methods. Fabric clips like the one shown in Fig. 3-17

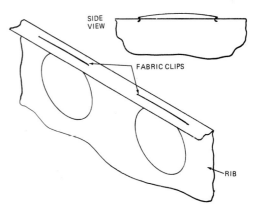

FIG. 3-17 Fabric clips are used to hold the fabric onto the ribs in some aircraft. In this illustration the fabric has been eliminated to show how the clips are positioned on a rib.

have been used by aircraft manufacturers as original attachment methods. The clips are flexed and slipped through small holes in the reinforcing tape and fabric. Through the shape of the clip, they lock into position in the metal rib.

Martin clips, made by the Arbor Company, are used in place of other types of attachment methods because of their simplicity and quick installation. These clips require a hole in the fabric and the rib. The clips are flexed to reduce the size of the tooth in the wire and inserted through the opening in the structure as shown in Fig. 3-18. The tooth then expands and locks the fabric into position on the rib. The clips are supplied in a wire roll and are cut to the lengths required for each rib.

Miscellaneous Materials

Beeswax is used to coat hand-sewing threads and rib-lacing cord prior to installation. This wax provides a coating on the thread or cord which protects it from deterioration and provides lubrication as it is pulled through the fabric. Beeswax is purchased in block form or as small disks as shown in Fig. 3-19.

Blued carpet tacks are sometimes used to hold the fabric covering in place on a wooden structure temporarily while the permanent hand sewing or tacking is being done. The finish protects the tacks from rust to some extent in the same manner that a blued finish protects a firearm. However, these tacks are solely used for *temporary* use. If driven in for permanent use, they may split, crack, and otherwise weaken the wood in which they are placed, and they eventually work loose from the vibration of the airplane. Care

DISC

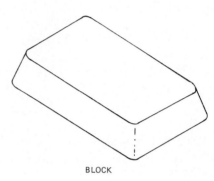

BLOCK

FIG. 3-19 Beeswax can be purchased as a block or as small disks.

must be taken that large tacks are not used with small wood structures because of the danger of splitting the wood.

Brass, tinned iron, or **Monel metal tacks** are rust-proof, and they do not cause the damage that results from the use of blued carpet tacks. These tacks are

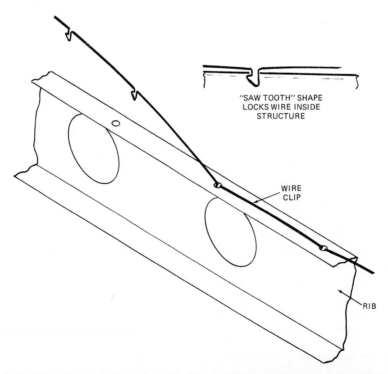

"SAW TOOTH" SHAPE
LOCKS WIRE INSIDE
STRUCTURE

WIRE
CLIP

RIB

FIG. 3-18 Martin clips are used to hold fabric to the structure in a manner similar to fabric clips. The fabric has been eliminated in this illustration for clarity.

sometimes used for permanently tacking the covering on wooden structures.

Pins are used for holding the edges of the covering temporarily while the cover is being shaped to the structure before the hand sewing begins. A **T pin,** such as the one illustrated in Fig. 3-20, is desirable because it can be inserted and removed easily while the fabric is under tension.

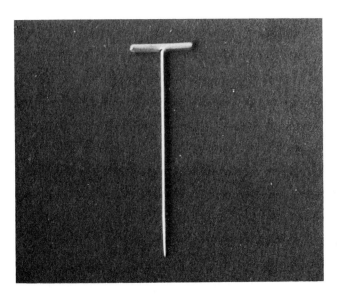

FIG. 3-20 A T pin.

● DOPES AND FINISHING MATERIALS

The word **dope** has many meanings, and in aircraft use it does not have a precise definition. **Aircraft dope** has been defined as a colloidal solution of cellulose acetate butyrate or cellulose nitrate; however, other solutions have been developed which serve the function of dope for sealing, tautening, and protecting airplane fabric coverings, and these can also properly be called dopes. It is incumbent upon the aircraft mechanic to make sure of the type of dope being used and to understand its characteristics.

Because of this generalization of the term, all references to dope in this text indicate any one of several different finishing products.

Dopes are supplied as a clear coating material and as a pigmented material. Pigmented dopes have particles added which give a color to the dope. The most prominent pigment material associated with aircraft is aluminum oxide, which gives the dope a silver color and is used to reflect the sun's ultraviolet rays. Other pigmenting materials include chemical compounds of titanium, chromium, and iron.

Some pigments arc prone to "bleeding" through subsequent layers of dope. That is, the pigment of the dope will move up into the next layer of paint and cause a change in the color. Red is notorious for bleeding, and if covered with a color such as while, the result will be a pink surface. Because of this problem, nonbleeding pigments have been developed and should be used when a background color, such as red, is to be trimmed with some other color.

Aircraft nitrate and butyrate dopes shrink as they dry. This feature is used in organic and fiberglass covering operations to aid in creating a taught fabric finish. This taughtening feature is not desired when covering an aircraft with polyester material. As a result, nontautening nitrate and butyrate dopes and special dopes for polyester materials have been developed. These dopes should be used whenever the taughtening action of the dope is to be kept to a minimum.

Nitrate and Butyrate Dopes

Nitrate dope is composed of nitrocellulose (similar to celluloid and gun cotton) combined with plasticizers and thinners. The plasticizers are needed to provide flexibility and resistance to cracking after the dope has cured. Nitrate dope is highly flammable in both liquid and dry states. Its principal advantages over butyrate dope are low cost, ease of application, and better adhesion.

Butyrate dope is composed of cellulose acetate butyrate with suitable plasticizers and thinners added. Butyrate dope is more fire resistant than nitrate dope and provides greater shrinkage of fabric. Care must be taken not to apply too many coats of butyrate dope because the fabric may become too tight and warp the structure over which the covering is applied. Some processes use a combination of a few coats of nitrate dope finished with several coats of butyrate dope.

Synthetic dopes under proprietary trade names have been developed for polyester materials and are being utilized successfully. When using such a dope, the mechanic must follow exactly the manufacturer's instructions.

A **quick-building** (QB) **dope** is designed to make an extra-heavy layer for each coat, thus making fewer coats necessary than would be the case for ordinary nitrate dope. This type of dope contains an extra-large percentage of materials which form solids upon drying.

Fungicidal Additives

Cotton and linen fabrics are subject to attacks by fungus with the result that their strength is reduced, even though they were originally finished properly. To combat this situation, fungicides were developed for addition to the dope employed for the first coat.

A military specification, MIL-D-7850, requires that the first coat of a covering process with acetate butyrate dope be treated with the fungicide zinc dimethyldithiocarbonate. This is a powder which forms a suspension with the dope when properly mixed. The specified amount of the powder is first mixed with a small amount of dope to form a paste. Additional dope is then added and mixed with the paste. This thinned paste is then mixed with the proper amount of dope to meet the manufacturer's specifications.

Another fungicide, copper naphthonate, is also used, but it has a tendency to bleed out onto light-colored fabrics.

Fungicidal dope is applied in a very thin consistency to ensure saturation of the fabric. When this has been accomplished, the other coats can be applied in the most suitable consistency.

Aluminum Powders and Pastes

Aluminum-pigmented dope, also referred to as **silver dope,** is applied to the fabric after all of the necessary components of the cover (surface tapes, inspection rings, drain grommets, etc.) have been installed. The aluminum dope contains particles of aluminum oxide which form an aluminum layer on the surface of the fabric to reflect the ultraviolet rays of the sun. Without this aluminum pigment, the fabric would deteriorate quickly.

Aluminum-pigmented dope is made merely by adding aluminum powder or paste to the dope. For clear nitrate dope, 8 to 16 oz [226.8 to 453.6 g] of aluminum paste or 5 to 8 oz [142 to 227 g] of aluminum powder is added to 1 gal (gallon) [3.79 L (liters)] of the dope and mixed thoroughly to give the proper concentration of aluminum in the dope. To mix aluminum paste with dope, a small amount of the clear dope or dope thinner is mixed with the paste and the mixture is worked until all lumps are completely removed. Sufficient dope should be added so the mixture will flow easily, and after mixing completely the mixture is added to the clear dope and the entire amount is then stirred until the aluminum is evenly distributed. To obtain the best finish, a small amount of dope thinner should be added. This will help the minute flakes of aluminum to come to the surface and form a solid, light-tight layer.

Dope is available with the aluminum oxide premixed in the dope. Do not confuse this dope with pigmented dopes that may only be giving a silver color to the dope and do not provide the ultraviolet protection for the fabric.

Rejuvenators

A **fabric rejuvenator** is a thin, dopelike finish to which powerful solvents have been added. Its purpose is to soften and penetrate old dope finishes, thus replacing some of the solvents and plasticizers which have been lost by evaporation and oxidation over a period of years. If a dope finish is not badly cracked and if the fabric under the dope is still in good condition, rejuvenation can add considerable time to the life of the covering. On the other hand, if the fabric is weak, it is likely that the rejuvenation will further weaken it and hasten the need for a recover job. A material specifically manufactured as a rejuvenator should be used generally for the rejuvenation of nitrate dope finishes. Thinned acetate butyrate dope can be used for rejuvenating either nitrate dope or butyrate dope finishes. This product will have more shrinking effect than nitrate rejuvenator. This makes it essential that the fabric under the dope be in very good condition.

Special Finishing Products

The use of synthetic fabrics has brought about the development of finishing products designed to be more compatible with these materials than are the conventional nitrate and butyrate products. These newer products have been developed by both the finish manufacturers and the synthetic material manufacturers as part of a covering "system."

Adhesives are often used to attach fabric to airframe structures. This has proved to be an easier method than hand-sewing operations with no reduction in the security of attachment. Two products that are widely used for this purpose are Poly-Tak for the Stits Poly-Fiber covering process and Super Seam Cement for use with Ceconite and Razorback glass cloth (fiberglass).

WARNING: Be aware that any product used with a covering system must be approved by the manufacturer of the covering process and the FAA. Some products are advertised as performing as well as approved products but have not been approved for use through the FAA/PMA approval procedure. Only use quality products that carry an FAA/PMA approval on their label.

The Stits Poly-Fiber covering process makes use of several proprietary products in its covering process. These include Poly-Tak for attaching the fabric to the structure, Poly-Brush for initial bonding of the finishing material to the fabric, Poly-Spray for ultraviolet protection and build-up, and Poly-Tone or Aero-Thane for a durable clear or pigmented finish.

Cooper Aviation Supply Company produces several products for use with the Ceconite covering processes. These include Super Seam Cement for bonding fabric to the structure, Dac-Proofer as a first coat, and Spra-Fill as a built-up ultraviolet protective coat.

Again, care must be exercised in the selection of products for use with inorganic materials. To vary the process from what is approved by the manufacturer for that material may render the aircraft unairworthy.

Solvents and Thinners

Solvents and thinners are used in the fabric covering finishing process to clean the material prior to the application of dopes and finishing products and to reduce the viscosity of liquids so that they can be properly applied. Each type of finishing product may require the use of a specific thinner (reducer), and the product manufacturer's instructions should be consulted prior to the use of any thinners or solvents. The wrong type of thinner will usually make the coating unfit for use. When the special dopes and finishes marketed under proprietary trade names are used, it is vital that the thinner or reducer supplied or recommended by the manufacturer be employed. The following discussion deals with some of the more common solvents and thinners used with fabric covering processes.

Nitrate dope and lacquers are thinned by means of a thinner called **nitrate dope and lacquer thinner.** Specifications TT-T-266a or MIL-T-6094A meet the requirements for this product. Butyrate dope must be thinned with **cellulose acetate butyrate dope thinner,** MIL-T-6096A or equivalent. The mechanic must always be certain to use the correct thinner for the particular coating material being mixed.

Acetone is a colorless liquid which boils at 56.5°C

and freezes at −94.3°C. It is suitable for removing grease from fabric before doping and is very useful in cleaning dope and lacquer from suction-feed cups and spray guns. It is widely used as an ingredient in paint and varnish removers but should not be used as a thinner in dope because it dries so rapidly that the doped area cools quickly and collects moisture. The absorbed moisture in the fabric then prevents uniform drying and results in **blushing,** which is moisture contamination of the dope.

Retarders

Retarder, or **retarder thinner,** is a special slow-drying thinner used to slow the drying time of dope and other finishing products. When humidity is comparatively high, rapid drying of dope causes blushing. Retarder is mixed with the dope to reduce the tendency to blush. Blushing is caused by the condensation of moisture in the surface of the dope and results in a weak and useless finish. The condition is explained more fully in a later section. Retarder for nitrate dope carries the specification MIL-T-6095A. For butyrate dope, MIL-T-6097A is used.

Consult the manufacturer's literature for approved retarders for proprietary finishing products.

● FACILITIES AND EQUIPMENT FOR AIRCRAFT COVERING

The fabric covering of aircraft requires a work area specially configured for the handling of large airframe structures in a controlled and fire-safe environment and a collection of quality tools and equipment that are unique to the fabric covering operations.

The Fabric Shop

The room or section of a building utilized for the preparation and installation of fabric covering is often called the **fabric shop.** This shop should be well-lighted, clean, well-ventilated, and of sufficient size to accommodate any size of aircraft upon which fabric is to be installed. It would be well to have the fabric shop air-conditioned or temperature-controlled, if possible, for two principal reasons: (1) the comfort of the workers, and (2) the proper temperature and humidity for best results in covering.

The fabric shop should be capable of being sealed off from the general aircraft maintenance area, especially when the dopes and finishing products are being applied. Because of the fire hazard associated with the use of finishing products, the work area should be configured to minimize any fire hazard and adequate fire-fighting equipment should be on hand.

Tools and Equipment for Covering

The degree of success the mechanic will have in producing a first-class covering job often depends upon the availability of suitable tools and equipment. The tools described here are generally considered necessary in addition to the standard hand tools usually available in an aircraft repair shop. A covering job can be accomplished without all the tools and equipment mentioned; however, the need sometimes exists for every one of the items.

The small **harness awl** is useful for making small holes in fabric or other similar materials.

The **magnetic tack hammer** is most useful for picking up and holding tacks which are too small to be held in the fingers while driving.

The common **pocket knife** is always useful for cutting textile materials and wood.

A variety of **needles** are required for rib lacing and hand sewing. Straight upholsterer's needles up to 16 in [40.64 cm] in length and 12-gauge diameter are needed for rib lacing thick wings. Smaller needles of the same type are used for the thinner wings. For hand sewing, both straight and curved needles are needed. Typical upholster's needles are shown in Fig. 3-21.

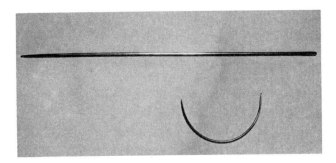

FIG. 3-21   Upholsterer's needles.

Because temporary tacks are often used to hold fabric in place on wooden structures, it is often necessary to pull such tacks. The **claw tack puller** is the best tool for this purpose.

A pair of **bent-handle trimmer's shears,** 10 or 12 in [25 or 30 cm] in length, is an absolute must for cutting fabric, tapes, etc. The shears must be handled carefully to avoid damaging the cutting edges and should be used only for cutting comparatively soft materials. Trimmer's shears are shown in Fig. 3-22.

FIG. 3-22   Trimmer's shears.

Pinking shears are needed to produce the pinked edge that is required for tape, patches, and other fabric pieces which are to be cemented or doped to another surface. The cutting edges of pinking shears must be protected when not in use and must be kept sharp. The sharpening of pinking shears must be done by an

..pert who has the proper grinding equipment available. Pinking shears are shown in Fig. 3-23.

FIG. 3-23 Pinking shears.

A metal or wooden **straightedge** or **yardstick** is used for measuring and marking straight lines.

A steel **measuring tape** at least 50 ft [15.24 m] in length is necessary for measuring wings, fuselages, and lengths of fabric. The tape should be kept clean and dry.

A **sewing thimble** is useful for pushing a needle through thick seams where extra pressure is necessary.

A large **cutting table** is needed for laying out and cutting the aircraft fabric covering. The height should be convenient for the operator, but usually about 31 in [78.74 cm] is approximately correct for the average person. The table should be 7 ft [2.13 m] wide and 25 ft [7.62 m] long. The top should be hard, smooth, and free of splinters. The edges of the table are usually marked off in feet and inches by means of brass tacks, or a rule may be fastened to the edge of the table. The table should be kept free from dust and polished frequently; care should be taken not to leave any wax or oil that will damage the fabric.

In shops doing fabric work on a regular basis, rolls of the covering material are mounted on rollers inside a storage cabinet placed near the cutting table so that, while the fabric can be unrolled as needed, only that which is about to be used is outside the cabinet. this installation makes it possible to avoid soiling or wrinkling the fabric.

A **surface-tape cutter** is used for cutting surface tape and also for making patches having pinked edges. this tool is also called a **pinking machine.** There are several types of these machines, one of which is illustrated in Fig. 3-24.

The smaller pinking machines can be operated either by a hand lever or by a motor. They may have one or two cutters for cutting various shapes of patches and various widths of tape.

The larger pinking machines have several cutters. These cutters can be adjusted to various widths for cutting a roll of airplane fabric into different widths of surface tape simultaneously.

All surface-tape cutters should be provided with safety guards to protect the operator's hands, especially since the machine's appearance is deceptive and may cause the operator to become careless.

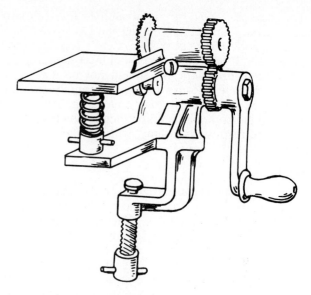

FIG. 3-24 A pinking machine.

Easels and Trestles

An **easel,** such as the one illustrated in Fig. 3-25, may be used to support the airfoil in a nearly vertical position while the fabric covering is being rib-laced to

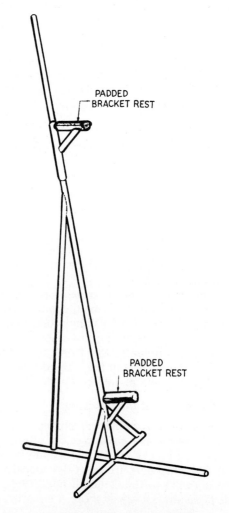

FIG. 3-25 An easel for supporting an airfoil.

the structure. An easel is usually made of metal tubing with welded joints and is supplied with two padded bracket rests, as shown in the illustration. In Fig. 3-26 two easels are being used to support a wing in a vertical position for rib lacing.

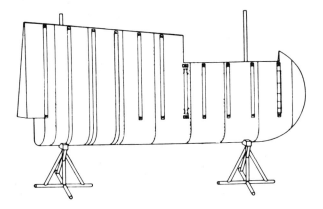

FIG. 3-26   Two easels used to support a wing.

Trestles, or "saw horses," are needed to support wing panels in the horizontal or flat position. The trestles must be adequately padded to prevent damage to the wing structure and fabric. Wing panels are placed on the trestles while measuring, fitting, and installing the fabric covering. Care must be taken to see that the wing panel is supported at points where the structure is of sufficient strength to prevent damage.

Sewing Machines

A **sewing machine** is basically a mechanism designed to join textiles or similar materials by means of a seam or seams consisting of a series of interlocked stitches. The sewing machine used for sewing aircraft fabric is a heavy-duty, industrial-type machine larger and more durable than the family sewing machine. This type machine is shown in Fig. 3-27.

FIG. 3-27   An industrial-type sewing machine. (*Singer Co.*)

● SELECTION OF FABRIC COVERING MATERIAL

The selection of the type material to be used on an aircraft and the covering system to be used must be determined by the mechanic and the aircraft owner. General factors which will influence this decision include the mechanic's familiarity with the different systems, the operational characteristics of the aircraft, the desires of the owner, and the cost of the processes. When considering the cost of a process, take into account the initial cost of the covering operation and the life expectancy of the covering material. A system for which the price is 25 percent higher than another system, but lasts twice as long, may be a desirable choice. For specific costs, contact suppliers of the materials required.

Minimum Fabric Requirements

The minimum strength of a fabric used to recover an aircraft must meet the minimum strength requirements of the covering material originally used on the aircraft. When dealing with aircraft originally covered with organic materials, this evaluation can be made by determining the aircraft V_{ne} (red-line airspeed) and wing loading.

The V_{ne} is found by looking at the aircraft operating limitations found in the aircraft specification, type certificate data sheet, or approved operator's handbook. If the V_{ne} is greater than 160 mph [257.5 k/h], then grade A cotton is the minimum fabric type that can be used on the aircraft.

The wing loading is found by dividing the maximum gross weight of the aircraft by the wing area. The maximum gross weight allowed can be found in the same documents used to determine the V_{ne}. The wing area might be found in the aircraft documents, or it may have to be determined by measurement of the aircraft. The wing area is the surface area of the wing as viewed from directly over the aircraft and ignores any curvature on the surface due to airfoil shape.

If the wing loading is found to be greater than 9 lb 1 ft^2 (pounds per square foot) [4.39 g/cm^2] then grade A cotton must be used to cover the aircraft.

If the wing loading is no greater than 9 lb/ft^2 [4.39 g/cm^2] and the V_{ne} is no greater than 160 mph [257.5 k/h] and the aircraft was not originally covered with some stronger fabric, then the fabric used on the aircraft must meet the standards of intermediate-grade cotton.

It should be noted that intermediate-grade cotton is no longer commonly available, but applicants for mechanic's certificates are still being asked by examiners to evaluate aircraft for the minimum grade of fabric required. The minimum grade of fabric required will be useful information when evaluating fabric that is installed on an aircraft to determine when it must be replaced. This aspect of fabric evaluation is covered in a later section of this chapter.

If an aircraft was originally covered with an inorganic material, the original type of covering material is considered the minimum required for that aircraft.

STCs and Other Approvals

With the various inorganic processes presently available for covering an aircraft, it is often found desirable to abandon the organic fabrics in favor of these more modern materials.

Stits Poly-Fiber products and Ceconite products are approved for use on most, if not all, production aircraft having fabric coverings through STCs. If covering with these products is desired, contact the manufacturer or one of their dealers for full details of material selection. Be sure to check any material used to verify that it is the correct, approved material by examining the markings on the material. Ceconite can be identified by the word "CECONITE" and the type number of the fabric (101, 102, 103, etc.) stamped on the selvage edge of the fabric at 1-yd [0.91 m] intervals. Poly-Fiber materials can be identified by the stamping "POLY-FIBER D-101A (or D-103 or D-104), FAA PMA, STITS AIRCRAFT" on the selvage edge at 1-yd [0.91-m] intervals or two rows of three-line or six-line stamps spaced 24 in [0.61 m] apart in the center area, alternating each 18 in [0.46 m]. Examples of the Poly-Fiber stamps are shown in Fig. 3-28.

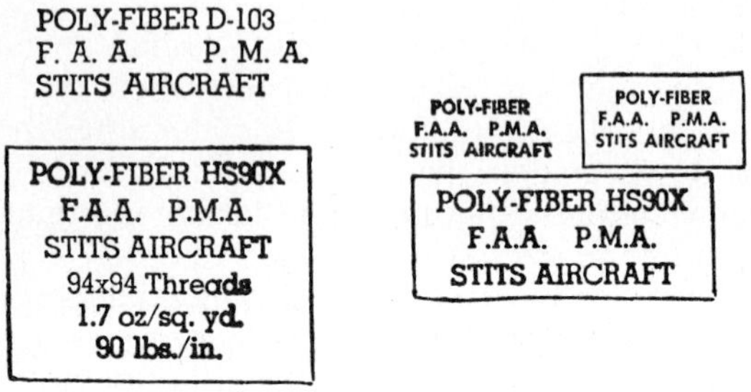

POLY-FIBER D-103
F. A. A.   P. M. A.
STITS AIRCRAFT

POLY-FIBER HS90X
F.A.A. P.M.A.
STITS AIRCRAFT
94x94 Threads
1.7 oz/sq. yd.
90 lbs./in.

POLY-FIBER
F.A.A. P.M.A.
STITS AIRCRAFT

POLY-FIBER
F.A.A. P.M.A.
STITS AIRCRAFT

POLY-FIBER HS90X
F.A.A. P.M.A.
STITS AIRCRAFT

FIG. 3-28   Examples of the Stits Poly-Fiber logo used to mark Poly-Fiber fabrics.   *(Stits Aircraft)*

Razorback Fabric is a fiberglass material that is approved as replacement fabric for all aircraft, regardless of the type of fabric originally used. This material does not make use of an STC, but it is approved based on the requirements of FAA Advisory Circular No. 20-44. Razorback fabric can be identified by stamping along the selvage edge at regular intervals.

● APPLICATION OF FABRIC COVERS FOR AIRCRAFT

Fabric covers are manufactured and applied to various aircraft structural units, such as control surfaces, fuselages, and wings. Even airplanes that are generally classified as "all metal" will sometimes have fabric-covered control surfaces. The instructions given here are general enough to meet the usual requirements, and at the same time specific techniques are explained in enough detail so that mechanics should not encounter any serious difficulty in applying their knowledge.

Preparing the Structure

Prior to the installation of fabric on an aircraft structure, the structural integrity should be checked and all necessary repairs made. All wires and cables should be in place or "fish wires" should be in position so that after the cover is installed, the cables and wires

can be pulled through the structure using the fish wires. All protrusions should be covered or cushioned so that they will not puncture the fabric covering. Any coating or finish such as zinc chromate or spar varnish should be covered with dope-proof paint, aluminum foil, cellophane tape, or masking tape. This prevents the cements, dopes, and other finishing products used on the fabric from attacking the protective coatings.

When covering a fuselage it is often desirable to install the headliner and all internal systems and components prior to covering it with fabric. Wings should have all of the ribs braced in position by installing inter-rib bracing to prevent the ribs from twisting and shifting when the fabric is installed and tightened. Reinforcing tape is often used for this purpose as shown in Fig. 3-29.

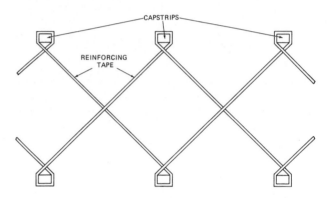

FIG. 3-29   Application of inter-rib bracing.

The required and desired location of inspection openings should be determined. Factory drawings can be used for this purpose, as can the old cover that was removed from the structure. If no information is available as to the proper location of these openings, make a sketch of the structure and note the locations necessary to install, adjust, and inspect the structure.

Complete all rigging and safety operations necessary.

Fabric Seams

Fabric seams are used to join pieces of fabric together and to attach fabric to the aircraft structure.

Machine-sewn seams are used to join large pieces of fabric together to form blankets or envelopes by using a sewing machine. There are four types of machine-sewn seams: the **plain overlap,** the **folded fell,** the **French fell,** and the **modified French fell.** The French fell and folded fell are the strongest of these seams. The modified French-fell seam is often used because of its ease of sewing. A plain overlap seam is sometimes used where selvage or pinked edges are joined. Examples of each of these seams are shown in Fig. 3-30.

Hand sewing is used to close fabric edges after the material is positioned on the structure. Before starting the hand-sewing operation, the fabric is straightened on the structure and tack stitches are placed about

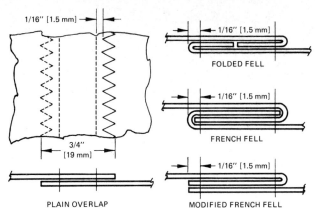

FIG. 3-30 Types of seams.

every 6 to 12 in [15.24 to 30.48 cm] along the opening to be sewed. Tack stitches are simply stitches through the two pieces of fabric being joined that hold the fabric in position while the hand-sewing operation is performed.

Hand sewing is performed by starting at one end of the opening, folding the fabric edges under until the edges of the fabric just touch. There should be at least ½ in [12.7 mm] of material folded under with any excessive amount of material being cut off. The needle is pushed through the fabric no more than ¼ in [6.4 mm] from the edge of the fold, through the other fold, and tied in a square knot locked with a half hitch on each side. A baseball stitch is then used, as shown in Fig. 3-31, until the opening is closed. The baseball stitches should be no more than ¼ in [6.4 mm] back from the edge of the fold and should be spaced no more than ¼ in [6.4 mm] apart along the opening. A lockstitch should be included in the hand sewing at 6-in [15.24 cm] intervals. This will prevent the whole seam from opening if a thread should break. A lockstitch is a modified seine knot, which will be discussed later in this chapter. At the end of the sewing, the seam is finished with a lockstitch and a half hitch. If the original thread is not long enough to completely close the seam, the stitching should be tied off with a

modified seine knot and half hitch and a new thread started at the next stitch spacing.

Doped seams are formed by using approved adhesives to attach the fabric to the structure and to attach the fabric to another piece of fabric. To attach the fabric to the structure, a strip of adhesive is brushed onto the structure and the fabric is immediately placed on the adhesive and pressed into it. Fabric is bonded to fabric in a similar manner with a coat of adhesive being applied to the fabric and the other piece of fabric being pressed into the first coat. The amount of minimum overlap of the fabric onto the structure or another piece of fabric varies depending upon the materials and adhesives being used, but it is in the range of 2 to 4 in [5.08 to 10.16 cm]. Consult the instructions for the adhesive and fabric being used for specific information.

Most covering operations require the use of machine-sewn seams, but machine sewing by the mechanic has been all but eliminated because of the availability of envelopes. In most covering processes, doped seams have eliminated the need for hand-sewing operations.

Covering Methods

There are two methods which can be used to cover a structure, the **envelope method** and the **blanket method**. Each method has its own advantages. It is up to the mechanic to determine which best fits the project at hand.

The envelope method involves making or buying a sleeve which can slide over the prepared structure. The sleeve has been sewed together on a sewing machine so that only a small portion of the material must be closed by hand sewing or a doped seam.

If an envelope must be made, the component to be covered should be measured to determine the size of the envelope. When laying out the fabric, special consideration is given to the width of the fabric (selvage edge to selvage edge) and the spacing between the ribs or stringers. The machine-sewn seams should be located so that no seam is positioned where any rib-lacing or other attachment mechanism will penetrate the seam.

Once the dimensions are available and the position of the seams is determined, the fabric strips are sewed together. In most instances the seams run longitudinally on the fuselage and chordwise on wings and other surfaces. Seams perpendicular to the direction of flight are acceptable if they do not disrupt the airflow. Once the fabric strips are sewed together, the fabric is folded over and sewed to form a tube. One end of the tube is normally closed to complete the sleeve. This envelope construction process is shown in Fig. 3-32. The envelope is now ready to install on the structure.

The blanket method of covering involves the use of fabric as it comes off the roll. It is cut to size and folded over the structure to be covered as shown in Fig. 3-33. If the structure is too large to be covered by the material as it comes off the roll, strips of the material are sewed together as done in the first step

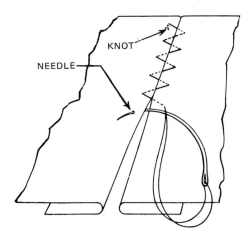

FIG. 3-31 Baseball stitch.

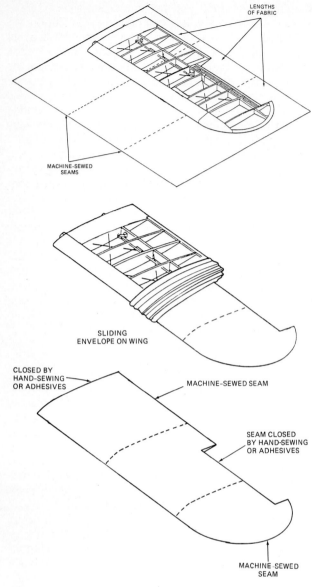

FIG. 3-32 Prominent steps in making and installing an envelope cover. *(Christen Industries Inc.)*

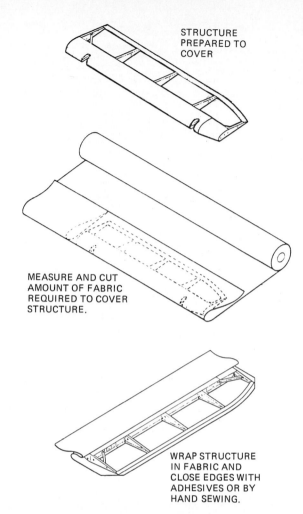

FIG. 3-33 Covering an aileron by the blanket method. *(Christen Industries Inc.)*

of making an envelope. The fabric is then wrapped around the structure and closed along the open edge by hand sewing or using a doped seam.

Installation of Fabric

Once the method of covering is determined and the structure is prepared to receive the cover, the fabric is positioned on the structure. If the covering material is organic or fiberglass, sliding an envelope onto the structure will require some care as the envelope will be a snug fit onto the structure. Polyester envelopes are loose-fitting and slide on easily. Regardless of the type of material, care will be required to prevent snagging or tearing of the fabric as it is positioned on the structure.

Once in position, all seams are closed by hand sewing, mechanical attachments, or doped seams. The only restriction placed on the use of doped seams concerns organic fabrics. Unless the adhesive being

used is approved for higher speed, doped seams may not be used with organic fabrics when the V_{ne} is greater than 150 mph [241.4 km/h] when using the blanket covering method. Also, unless otherwise approved by the manufacturer of a covering system, all doped seams should overlap the fabric by at least 4 in [10.16 cm]. Seams of this type commonly have a 4 in [10.16 cm] wide piece of surface tape placed over the seam if the seam is at the leading edge of a surface. 3 in [7.62 cm] wide surface tape is used if the seam is at the trailing edge. A typical mechanical attachment method is shown in Fig. 3-34.

With the fabric in position, organic and polyester materials can be shrunk to some extent. Organic fabrics are preshrunk prior to the application of dopes by saturating the fabric with water. This is done by wiping down the fabric with a wet sponge and allowing the fabric to dry. Polyester fabrics are shrunk by the use of an electric iron. With the iron set for the temperature recommended by the fabric manufacturer (generally around 250°F [121.1°C]), the fabric is shrunk by moving the iron smoothly over the surface to remove all of the sag and wrinkles from the fabric. Care must be taken during this process to keep the sewn seams straight and away from areas where stitching or mechanical attachment of the fabric would penetrate the

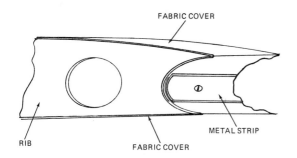

FABRIC COVER

RIB

FABRIC COVER

METAL STRIP

FIG. 3-34 Metal strip used to attach fabric to a structure.

seam. Complete details and steps to be followed for specific polyester products can be found in the fabric manufacturer's literature.

To give the details of each finishing process established by the inorganic fabric manufacturers at this point would be very confusing as the processes are quite varied. Therefore, the remaining discussion will deal with the organic process. A summary of current inorganic processes is given in Table 3-1. This table is for general reference only, as the processes are subject to change as the products continue their evolution.

Once the fabric is smooth and tautened the proper amount, the first coat of clear dope is applied. This should be a thin coat of nitrate dope containing a fungicide and applied with a brush to assure proper penetration of the fabric.

With the second coat of clear dope, install the antitear tape, reinforcing tape, drain grommets, inspection rings, and reinforcing patches.

Antitear tape is surface tape, wide enough to extend beyond the reinforcing tape, that is placed over the top of all ribs on aircraft with a V_{ne} of more than 250 mph [402.3 km/h]. For these aircraft, tapes are also placed on the bottom of all ribs within the propeller slipstream. The **slipstream** is defined as the propeller diameter plus one extra rib space.

Reinforcing tape is placed on the top and bottom of all ribs and on all stringers which are to be fastened to the fabric covering by rib lacing or mechanical fasteners. This tape should be the same width as that of the rib or stringer.

Drain grommets, inspection rings, and reinforcing

TABLE 3-1 Summary of Fabric Covering Processes

Operation	Organic	Razorback	Poly-Fiber	Ceconite
Shrinking prior to doping.	Soak with water.	None.	Electric iron.	Electric iron.
Initial coat.	Brush on nitrate dope with fungicide added.	One coat of nitrate dope sprayed on.	Poly-Brush applied by brush or spray gun (with some limitations on the use of the gun).	Thinned nitrate dope mixed with Super Seam Cement and brushed on.
Build up coats.	Nitrate and butyrate dope. Minimum of two buildup coats, brushed or sprayed.	Spray on two to five coats of butyrate dope until fabric is tautened.	N/A.	Two brushed on coats of nitrate dope.
Installation of grommets, rib stitching, fasteners, and surface tapes.	Install with second coat of dope.	Perform after fabric has tautened.	Attach with local coat of Poly-Brush.	Accomplish after third brush coat of nitrate dope. Use Super Seam Cement with nitrate dope for proper adhesion of tapes.
Build up coats.	One coat of clear dope, brushed or sprayed.	Apply two coats of butyrate dope by brush.	Second coat of Poly-Brush applied with spray gun.	Brush or spray on three coats of dope.
Ultraviolet protection.	Minimum of two coats of aluminum-pigmented dope.	Apply 1 coat of aluminum dope as a filler coat and undercoat for light pigmented finish coats.	Minimum of three coats of Poly-Spray for buildup and ultraviolet protection, applied with a spray gun.	Apply two coats of aluminum dope.
Finishing coats (pigmented).	Minimum of three coats.	Spray on two coats of pigmented dope.	Poly-Tone or Aero-Thane applied by spray gun.	Apply three coats of pigmented dope.

NOTE: Poly-Fiber, Poly-Brush, Poly-Spray, Poly-Tone, and Aero-Thane are registered trademarks of Stits Aircraft.
Super Seam Cement and Ceconite are trademarks of Ceconite, Inc.
Razorback is a trademark of Razorback Fabrics, Inc.
Contact the fabric manufacturer for full details on approved covering processes.

121

patches are placed on the surface at the locations described previously in this chapter.

Rib Lacing and Other Attachment Methods

Following the application of the initial coats of dope or finishing products, the fabric covering must be attached to internal structural components by the **rib-stitching process** or mechanical processes. These processes are commonly required on wings, stabilizers, and control surfaces. Their use on fuselages is often limited to stabilizer surfaces incorporated in the fuselage basic structure.

The mechanical processes have been discussed in an early part of this chapter and include the use of screws, rivets, and metal clips. The following discussion covers the rib-stitching process as it is the more complex of the operations. The only part of the rib-stitching process applicable to the other processes involves the determination of attachment spacing and layout procedures. For this discussion the structure will be considered to be a wing.

Rib-lacing, or rib-stitching, must be accomplished in accordance with the aircraft manufacturer's instructions. The spacing between the stitches can be determined from the covering removed from the aircraft or from the aircraft manufacturer's maintenance information. If this information is not available, the chart shown in Fig. 3-35 may be used to establish an acceptable maximum rib-stitch spacing. Note that the spacing is based on the aircraft V_{ne} and the location of the ribs in relation to the propeller slipstream. The maximum spacing allowed for aircraft with speeds just below 250 mph [402.3 km/h] and all higher airspeed values is 1 in [2.54 cm]. Some manufacturers have determined that the spacing on their aircraft can be greater than that indicated on this chart. In those cases, the manufacturer's information should be followed. Be aware that these spacing values are maximums—spacing may be closer as required, but it may not be greater.

The top of one rib should be marked with the proper stitch spacing. Start at the forward area of the rib, just

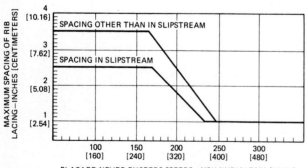

NOTES
1. IF ORIGINAL RIB STITCH SPACING CANNOT BE DETERMINED, USE SPACING INDICATED IN THESE CURVES.
2. LACING TO BE CARRIED TO LEADING EDGE WHEN VELOCITY EXCEEDS 275 MPH [440 KM/H]

FIG. 3-35 Chart to show spacing of rib stitches.

aft of the leading-edge material, and mark the first stitch. The second stitch is marked at one-half of the required spacing. The rest of the stitches are marked at the maximum allowed distance or some closer spacing. The distance between the last two is half-spaced. If the use of the maximum allowed spacing does not match the length of the rib, the spacing can be decreased evenly along the length of the rib or a short stitch spacing may be used near the front or rear area of the rib. Examples of stitch spacing are shown in Fig. 3-36.

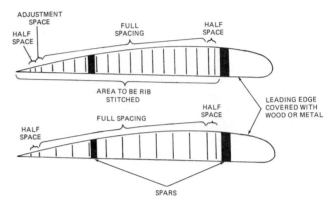

FIG. 3-36 Rib stitching requires that the first and last stitches be half-spaced.

With one rib laid out, the same pattern can be repeated on the top and bottom of all ribs. On many aircraft, the spacing between each stitch on the bottom of the rib must be reduced slightly due to the shorter rib length resulting from the difference in curvature between the top and bottom of the rib. The rib stitching should pass through the wing as perpendicular to the wing chord line as possible.

Some mechanics find it desirable to prepunch the stitching holes with a needle before starting the operation.

The wing is normally placed vertically on easels with the leading edge down when performing the rib-stitching operation. Plan the operation so that the lacing knots are on top surfaces of high-wing aircraft and on the bottom of low-wing aircraft. The stitching can be started at either end of the rib but is commonly started near the leading edge. The properly waxed rib-stitching cord is used for this operation.

The starting stitch is a double loop and is performed as shown in Fig. 3-37. This stitch involves the use of square knots and half hitches. The remaining stitches are a modified seine knot which is tied as shown in Fig. 3-38. This is different from the seine knot. Some aircraft require that all rib stitching use a double loop for strength. Each loop involves tying the modified seine knot. The knots are to remain on the surface of the fabric, not pulled back inside the structure unless this is approved by the aircraft manufacturer or the STC's process. The last stitch is a modified seine knot, secured with a half hitch.

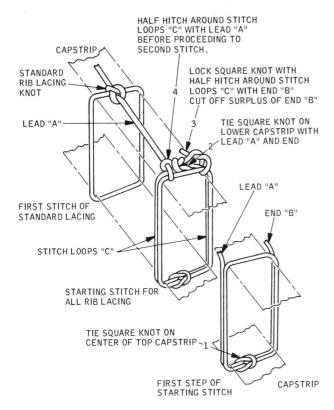

FIG. 3-37 How a double-loop starting stitch is made.

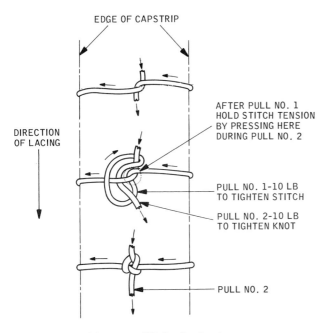

FIG. 3-38 Making a modified seine knot.

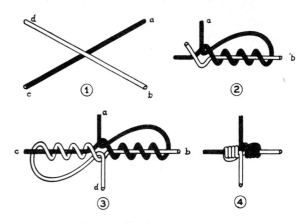

FIG. 3-39 Making a splice knot.

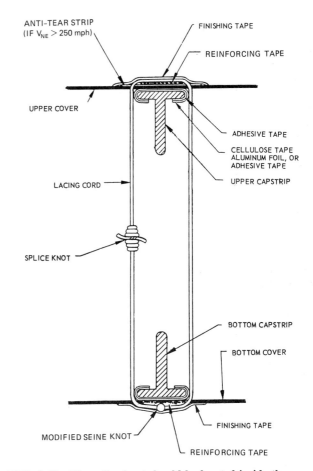

FIG. 3-40 The splice knot should be located inside the structure, not on the surface of the fabric.

If the cord should break or be too short to complete the stitching of a rib with one piece of cord, a second piece can be attached. This is done by the use of the splice knot as shown in Fig. 3-39. This knot should be positioned on the length of cord so that it is located inside the structure as in Fig. 3-40. The splice knot should not be located on the surface of the fabric.

When all of the rib stitching is completed, the remainder of the covering process can be performed.

Application of Surface Tape

Upon completion of rib lacing, the fabric cover should be ready for the **application of surface** (finishing) **tape.**

Surface tape should be applied over all rib lacing, seams, leading and trailing edges, and other points where reinforcement is necessary. A coat of dope is brushed on the areas where the tape is to be applied

123

and then the tape is immediately placed on the wet dope. Another coat of dope is brushed over the tape and care is taken to see that all air bubbles are worked out from under the tape. An excess of dope will cause runs and sags and may drip through the fabric to the inside of the wing; hence the mechanic must use only the amount of dope required to fill the tape and bond it securely to the surface.

If the aircraft has a V_{ne} greater than 200 mph [321.8 kph], all surface tape placed on trailing edges should be notched at 18 in [45.72 cm] intervals. If the tape begins to separate from the trailing edge, it will tear loose at a notch and prevent the loss of the entire strip. If the entire strip were lost, the controllability of the aircraft could be affected.

Finishing Process

When the fabric is properly attached to the structure and all of the surface tapes, grommets, and inspection rings are in place, the remaining coats of dope or finishing material can be applied. The application may be by brushing or spraying, depending on the process being used.

Using the organic process, one coat of clear dope is applied, followed by at least two coats of dope containing the aluminum pigment previously discussed. There should be enough aluminum-pigmented dope on the fabric so that light will not pass through the coating. Light blocking can be determined by placing a fire-safe light source on one side of the fabric and looking through the other side of the fabric. If light is visible, then the coating is not yet sufficient. When making this determination, all surrounding light should be blocked out on the viewing side. When the aluminum coating is sufficient, at least three coats of pigmented dope should be applied. These are normally sprayed on.

Between each coat of dope, the surface can be sanded lightly to remove any irregularities. Care must be taken when sanding around any protrusions such as rib-stitch knots so that the sandpaper does not cut through the dope and into the fabric.

A thorough discussion of painting equipment, techniques, and problems can be found in Chap. 4.

Fabric Inspection

The testing of fabric is used to determine if the fabric has sufficient strength to assure safe operation of the aircraft. The fabric should be tested at regular intervals, normally each annual inspection.

The portion of the fabric to be tested should be in an area where deterioration would be the most rapid. This includes surfaces which receive the most sunlight, such as the top of the wing and the top of the fuselage. Areas painted with dark colors absorb the most ultraviolet rays from the sun. Additionally, areas which are subject to collecting moisture or exposure to chemical should be inspected. Chemical exposure areas include the area around the battery box and aft of the battery drain tube.

The strength of the fabric is based on its tensile strength. Normal testing techniques involve the use of a Seyboth or Maule "punch" tester. The Seyboth

tester penetrates the fabric and indicates the strength of the fabric by a scale on the top of the tester. The Maule tester applies pressure to the fabric and is not normally used with enough force to penetrate airworthy fabric. A scale on the side of the Maule tester indicates the force that is being applied in pounds per inch of tensile strength. Both of these testers are shown in Fig. 3-41.

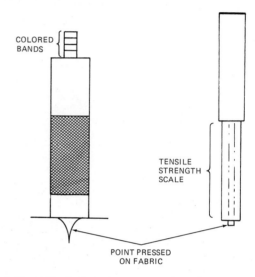

FIG. 3-41 A Seyboth-type tester, on the left, uses colored bands to indicate the fabric strength. A Maule-type tester has a scale to indicate the fabric strength.

The minimum strength for an aircraft requiring grade A cotton is 56 lb/in [10 kg/cm]. For an aircraft requiring intermediate-grade cotton, the minimum strength is 46 lb/in [8.21 kg/cm]. Polyester fabrics should be tested to the minimum value required of the original fabric covering—this may be a higher value than for the organic materials. Razorback glass fabric does not have to be tested for tensile strength.

Referring back to the discussion of the selection of fabric for use on an aircraft, the fabric that is installed only has to meet the requirements of the minimum-grade fabric required on that aircraft. For example, if an aircraft only required intermediate-grade cotton and was covered with grade A cotton, the grade A cotton can deteriorate to the minimum values allowed for intermediate-grade material before it must be replaced. This is where all of the calculations to determine the minimum required grade of fabric are useful.

To perform a classic test of fabric, a strip of fabric 1 in [2.54 cm] wide and several inches long is cut from the installed material. All of the dope is removed from the fabric. The fabric is then clamped at one end to a supporting fixture, and a clamp on the other end is attached to a load. The load is increased until the minimum standards are met or until the fabric breaks. Figure 3-42 shows one method of performing this test.

When the inspection is completed and if the fabric is airworthy, the holes created by the fabric testing must be repaired before returning the aircraft to service. Indentations left by the Maule tester often return to a smooth surface on their own accord.

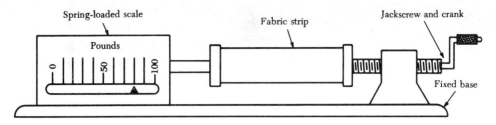

FIG. 3-42 One method of testing the tensile strength of a fabric sample.

● REPAIR OF FABRIC COVERINGS

When fabric is damaged, the mechanic must consider several factors to determine the method of repair. First, is the damage repairable or should the entire covering be replaced? While the damage may be repairable, if the remainder of the original fabric is only marginal in strength, it may be advisable to replace the entire covering. Next, because this will affect the type of repair that can be performed, what is the V_{ne} of the aircraft? Last, where are the internal structural members in relation to the damaged area? These factors influence the selection of the type of repair to be performed.

Tears in Fabric

Tears in a fabric covering can usually be repaired by sewing and doping on a fabric patch. The objective is to restore the original strength and finish to the repaired area.

A single tear should be repaired by removing all of the pigmented and aluminized dope around the area to be covered with the patch and then sewing the tear using a baseball stitch as shown in Fig. 3-43. The dope can be removed by softening and scraping or by sanding. The most satisfactory method is to apply a heavy coat of dope to the area and allow it to soften the old surface dope, which can then be removed by scraping. Strong solvents such as acetone can be used to soften the old dope, but care must be taken to see that the solvent does not drip through the opening to the lower surface of the fabric where it will cause blisters. When the cleaned surface around the tear has been sewed and the stitches locked every 8 to 10 stitches, a piece of pinked-edge surface tape or fabric is doped over the seam. The tape or fabric patch should extend at least 1½ in [3.81 cm] beyond the tear in all directions. Additional coats of dope are applied to the patch, sanding between coats to produce a smooth finish. The final coats of pigmented dope are applied and finished according to procedures explained previously. The dope used must be compatible with the original.

If a tear is of the V type, the procedure is the same as that described above; however, the sewing should start at the apex of the V in order to hold the fabric in place while the seams are completed. This is illustrated in Fig. 3-44.

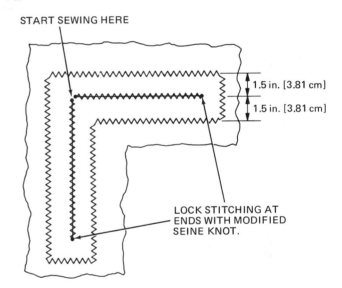

FIG. 3-44 Method of sewing a V-type tear.

Doped Repairs

Doped-on repair patches can be employed on all fabric-covered aircraft which have a never-exceed speed not greater than 150 mph [241.35 km/h]. A doped-on patch can be used for a damaged area which does not exceed 16 in [40.64 cm] in any direction. A repair of this type is made by trimming the damaged area and then removing the old dope in the area where the patch is to be applied. The patch is cut to a size which will overlap the old fabric at least 2 in [5.08 cm] for any patch not over 8 in [20.32 cm] across. For holes between 8 and 16 in [40.64 cm], the patch should overlap the original fabric by one-quarter the distance of the major dimension of the repair.

Where doped-on patches extend over a rib, the patch must be cut to extend at least 3 in [7.62 cm]

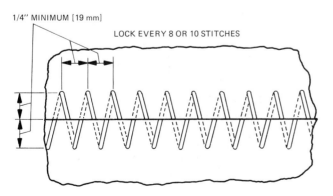

FIG. 3-43 Sewing a tear with a baseball stitch.

beyond the rib. The patch is then laced to the rib over a new piece of reinforcing tape. The original lacing and reinforcing tape should not be removed. A piece of surface tape is placed over the new lacing on the top and bottom of the structure and the dope is built up using the sequence for a new fabric cover—clear coats, aluminum coats, and pigmented coats.

Sewn-in Patch

If the V_{ne} of the aircraft is greater than 150 mph [241.4 k/h] and the damage does not exceed 16 in [40.64 cm] in any direction, a sewn-in patch can be used. The first step is to trim out the damage in a rectangular or circular shape. The dope is then removed for at least 1½ in [3.81 cm] from the edge of the fabric in the same manner as previously discussed. A patch of material of the same type as being repaired is then cut to be sewed into the opening. This patch should be cut so that there will be at least ½ in [12.7 mm] of extra material on all sides. The patch is then marked for the size of the opening. Tack stitches are used to hold the patch in position with the marked edge just touching the edges of the cut opening. The patch is then sewed in using a baseball stitch with lockstitches every 8 to 10 stitches. The ½-in [12.7-mm] extra material is folded inside the structure during the sewing operation, as shown in Fig. 3-45, and prevents the threads of the patch from being pulled out of the fabric.

A surface patch is now cut to cover the sewn-in patch. This patch should extend beyond the cut edge of the fabric by at least 1½ in [3.81 cm]. If the cut edge is within 1 in [2.54 cm] of a structural member, the surface patch must extend at least 3 in [7.62 cm] beyond the members. The surface patch is attached by dope. Rib stitching is performed over new reinforcing tape if either the sewn-in or surface patch covers a structural member. Surface tape is placed over the rib stitching, and the patched area is finished with dope. Figure 3-46 shows a sewn-in patch repair.

Doped-on Panel Repair

When the damage to an aircraft fabric surface is greater than 16 in [40.64 cm], a panel should be doped on. In this type of repair, the old fabric is cut out along

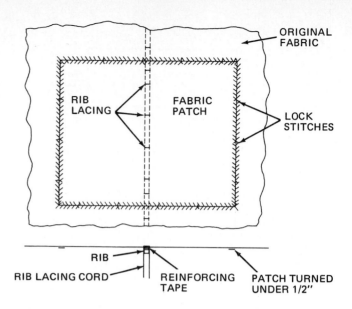

FIG. 3-46 A sewn-in patch.

a line approximately 1 in [2.54 cm] from the ribs nearest the repair. The fabric on the leading and trailing edges is not removed unless both the top and bottom of the wing are to be repaired. The surface tape is removed from the ribs adjacent to the repair, but the lacing and reinforcing tape are left intact. The patch panel is cut to a size which will overlap the trailing edge by at least 1 in [2.54 cm], extend around the leading edge and back to the forward spar, and extend at least 3 in [7.62 cm] beyond the ribs on each side of the repair.

If the leading edge of a wing is either metal- or wood-covered, the patch may be lapped over the old fabric at least 4 in [10 cm] at the nose of the leading edge.

The area of the old fabric that is to be covered by the patch must be thoroughly cleaned and a generous coat of new dope applied. The new panel is then put in place and pulled as taut as possible. A coat of dope is applied to the patch where it overlaps the old fabric. After this coat has dried, a second coat of dope is applied to the overlapped area.

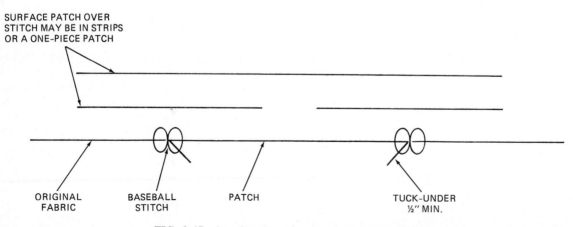

FIG. 3-45 An edge view of a sewn-in patch repair.

Reinforcing tape is placed over the ribs under moderate tension and is laced to the ribs in the usual manner. The rib stitches are placed between the original rib stitches. The new patch panel is then given a coat of dope and allowed to dry. Surface tape is applied with a second coat of dope over the reinforcing tape and edges of the panel. Finishing of the panel is then accomplished in the normal manner.

Sewed-in Panel Repair

If a panel repair cannot give the proper tautness by using the doped-on panel repair, a sewed-in panel repair can be performed. As with the doped-on panel, this repair is for damage exceeding 16 in [40.64 cm] in any one direction.

To perform the repair, remove the surface tape from the ribs, the leading edge, and the trailing edge adjacent to the damaged panel. Trim back the damaged fabric to within 1 in [2.54 cm] of the center line of the adjacent ribs. Fabric should not be removed from the leading and trailing edges unless the repair involves both the top and bottom fabric surfaces. Do not remove the reinforcing tape and rib-stitching at the ribs.

A patch should be cut that will extend 3 in [7.62 cm] beyond the ribs, to the trailing edge, and around the leading edge to the front spar on the opposite side of the wing.

Clean the area of the original fabric to be covered by the patch and pin or tack-stitch the patch in place. Take care to pull the patch tight and eliminate any wrinkles. The patch is now attached to the original fabric by hand sewing with the edge of the patch tucked under 1/2 in [1.27 cm]. After the patch is attached, new reinforcing tape is laid over the ribs and the patch is rib-stitched to the ribs.

A coat of clear dope is now applied. Surface tapes are then laid along the sewed seam, over the rib-stitching, and at other areas appropriate for the aircraft area repaired. The surface is now finished following the regular doping procedures.

This type of repair can be used to cover both the top and bottom surfaces of one or more adjacent rib bays.

Fabric Rejuvenation

In some cases it is possible to rejuvenate or restore the condition of dope coatings on an aircraft. When the dope has hardened to the extent that it is beginning to crack, it should be rejuvenated, provided that the fabric underneath is still strong enough to meet FAA-specified requirements. If the fabric is at or near minimum strength, no attempt should be made to rejuvenate it.

Fabric rejuvenator is a specially prepared solution containing strong solvents and plasticizers designed to penetrate age-hardened dope and restore its flexibility. The fabric surfaces to be rejuvenated should be thoroughly cleaned to remove wax, oil, and any other contaminating material. Rejuvenator is then applied to the dry dope surface in accordance with the manufacturer's directions. The application is usually performed with a spray gun.

After the application of rejuvenator, the old dope should soften through to the fabric. Cracks may then be sealed and the surface allowed to set. Finishing coats of clear and pigmented dopes can then be applied in the normal manner.

There are several rejuvenator products on the market, and the manufacturer's instructions for each should be followed. Be aware that in some cases, the rejuvenator will cause the fabric to sag and not retauten as the solvents evaporate. This may require that the surface being treated be recovered. For this reason it is advisable to test the effect of a rejuvenator on a small surface before attempting rejuvenation of any large surfaces.

● REVIEW QUESTIONS

1. Name types of fabric suitable for covering an airplane.
2. What is the difference between *warp* and *fill*?
3. What is the *selvage* edge of fabric?
4. What is meant by *bias-cut* fabric?
5. Give the TSO number and MIL specification number for grade A fabric.
6. What is the minimum tensile strength for new grade A fabric?
7. To what extent may the tensile strength of grade A fabric decrease while it is on the airplane before it must be replaced?
8. Give the conditions which make mandatory the use of grade A fabric or the equivalent.
9. Under what conditions may *intermediate-grade* fabric be installed on an airplane?
10. Describe *surface or finishing tape*. For what purpose is it used?
11. What is the purpose of *reinforcing tape?*
12. Why is *Dacron polyester fiber* more desirable as a covering than grade A fabric?
13. What is the difference between *S-twist* and *Z-twist* threads?
14. Give the specifications for a typical *machine-sewing thread*.
15. What is the minimum tensile strength for *rib-lacing cord?*
16. What is the purpose of using beeswax when hand sewing?
17. Under what conditions should *seaplane grommets* be installed?
18. Describe the installation of a *plastic inspection ring*.
19. What methods may be used to attach fabric to wing ribs?
20. Why should the fabric in the center of a drain grommet be cut out rather than punched out?
21. What is the purpose of using *aluminum-pigmented dope* on aircraft fabric?
22. Compare *acetate butyrate* dope and *cellulose nitrate* dope.
23. Describe the preparation of aluminum-pigmented dope.
24. What thinner should be used for nitrate dope?

25. What is the purpose of a *retarder?*
26. What is the cause of *blushing?*
27. At what point in a doping operation should fungicidal dope be applied?
28. What conditions should exist in a good fabric shop?
29. List the tools and equipment needed in a fabric shop.
30. What types of needles are required for aircraft fabric work?
31. Describe *pinking shears.*
32. Why is it necessary to notch the edges of surface tape at the trailing edge of a wing?
33. At what intervals should hand-sewed seams be locked with a lock stitch?
34. What types of stitches are usually employed in hand sewing?
35. Name the types of machine seams used with aircraft fabric.
36. Under what conditions can doped seams be used?
37. What width of lap is required for a lapped and doped seam at the trailing edge of a wing or control surface?
38. Describe the envelope and blanket methods for covering a wing.
39. Why is it a good practice to save the old fabric in large sections when recovering an airplane?
40. Describe the purpose and installation of inter-rib bracing.
41. What materials are used for dopeproofing?
42. How is damage to the fabric prevented at chafe points?

43. What is the purpose of *reinforcing tape* used over ribs?
44. Describe the function and installation of *antitear strips.*
45. What determines the spacing between rib stitches?
46. How is the first loop of rib lacing or stitching secured?
47. What type of knot is used to lock each rib-stitch?
48. At what locations must surface tape be installed?
49. At what point in the sequence of covering operations are inspection rings and drain grommets installed?
50. What method is used to tighten polyester fabric?
51. What is used to preshrink organic fabrics?
52. Under what conditions is a sewed-in patch required for damaged fabric?
53. Explain the requirements for a sewed-in panel repair.
54. Under what conditions is a doped-on patch allowed?
55. When a repair patch or panel extends over a rib, what must be done with respect to the rib?
56. What precaution must be taken when applying dope to a previously doped surface after a repair?
57. What precautions must be taken with respect to fabric rejuvenation?
58. Describe various methods for testing fabric to determine the extent of deterioration.
59. Which fabric covering material does not have to be punch-tested?

4 AIRCRAFT PAINTING AND MARKING

Aircraft are normally painted to provide both protection for the aircraft surfaces and a pleasing appearance. Many different types of finishing materials, generally called ''paints,'' are used on aircraft. Each type serves one or more purposes, and each must be applied in some specific manner to assure proper adhesion and an acceptable durability.

This chapter examines the equipment used to apply paints and the different paints that are commonly used for aircraft. In addition this chapter discusses the application of paint trim and the application of aircraft registration numbers. Keep in mind that the information in this chapter is general in nature and the manufacturers of specific painting equipment and finishing products should be consulted concerning the proper use and application of their individual products.

The three methods of applying paint are by brushing, by dipping, and by spraying. Using a paint brush is understood by most people and is not discussed here. Dipping involves no more than submersing prepared objects in a container of paint. Spray paint is the commonly used method of applying paint over large surfaces. The majority of this chapter deals with the spray painting process.

● AIRCRAFT FINISHING MATERIALS

Various coatings or finishes are employed for the finishing of fabric, wood, plastics, fiberglass, and metals. Included among finishing materials are primers, wash primers, metal treatments, varnishes, lacquers, enamels, and other coatings. It is the responsibility of the mechanic to be sure he understands the nature of the materials and procedures used in applying a finish to a particular part of an airplane. The finish manufacturer provides detailed instructions for the proper methods of application of approved finishes.

Primers

Primers and wash primers are undercoats applied to a metal to inhibit corrosion and to provide a good base for the application of paint, lacquer, or enamel. The wash primer is applied directly to the bare, clean metal, and this is followed by one or two coats of primer.

A **wash primer** is a priming agent which has been thinned to a very light consistency so it will leave an extremely thin layer on the bare metal surface. This layer will be approximately 0.5 mil [0.0005 in or 0.013 mm] or less in thickness. Some wash primers include etching or metal conditioning agents such as phosphoric acid so they treat the metal for better adhesion while protecting the metal from corrosion. One such wash primer is described as a two-part butyral–phosphoric acid resin containing corrosion-inhibiting pigments. It conforms to MIL P-15328C and MIL C-8514(ASG). It is recommended for use on all clean metal surfaces as a pretreatment before primer coating.

Another wash primer designed for use on Al-Clad aluminum is a zinc chromate wash primer. This product is formulated for use with a urethane primer and urethane enamel.

There are a number of primers and surfacers available for aircraft use. Among these are **zinc chromate primer, red iron oxide, gray enamel undercoat, urethane,** and **epoxy types.**

An approved zinc chromate primer is manufactured under specification MIL-P-6889A, Types I and II. Type I is used under normal atmospheric conditions; Type II is used under conditions of high humidity. This primer is best applied by spraying and is available in either a yellow or dark green color. The surface to which the primer is applied must be completely dry and clean.

Zinc chromate primer is commonly used on aluminum, aluminum-alloy, and magnesium surfaces and is also suitable for iron or steel. It is thinned with toluene to the proper consistency for spraying or brushing. Toluene has a characteristic odor and can be identified easily by any person who had had experience with it.

Red iron oxide primer is normally thinned with a petroleum thinner such as naphtha or mineral spirits. It can be sprayed or brushed on a surface; however, a better finish is obtained by spraying. After one coat of red iron oxide primer is applied to a surface, an additional coat which has been mixed with clear enamel or varnish can be applied as a final coating. This practice is employed where it is necessary to use a special color coating over the primer for the sake of appearance. Red iron oxide primer is commonly used for iron or steel surfaces.

Gray enamel undercoat is a lacquer-type primer and surfacer used under colored lacquer, synthetic enamel, or acrylic lacquer. It is thinned with nitrate lacquer thinner. This type of undercoat is particularly suitable for fine sanding to provide a perfectly smooth base for the finish coats.

An epoxy-type chromate primer developed and produced by Stits Aircraft Coatings Company is called Stits Epoxy Chromate Primer EP-420. This is described as a corrosion-inhibiting, fast-drying, heavy duty, chemical- and solvent-resistant, amine-cured primer. This primer requires the addition of a catalyst in a ratio of one part catalyst to two parts primer before it is put into use. After 30 min or more, the primer is ready to spray. It is important to remember that this type of product has a limited pot life. That is, it will start to set up after 7 or 8 h and can no longer be sprayed. Spray guns, paint pots, paint hoses, and brushes must be cleaned with methyl ethyl ketone (MEK) or an approved reducer before the material has hardened.

A urethane primer developed and produced by the U.S. Paint, Lacquer and Chemical Company is designated AA-92 Alumigrip Urethane Primer. This is a two-part primer requiring the addition of a catalyst in a ratio of one part catalyst to two parts primer. This primer is designed for use with the urethane enamel produced by the same company for Al-Clad aluminum applications.

It is emphasized that in the use of any coating process, the mechanic must follow the directions of the manufacturer of the product being used.

Lacquers

Lacquers were originally finishes developed in the Orient to produce a high gloss on wood products. In general, a lacquer is a good finishing material for metal or wood. Lacquers may be pigmented to provide a desired color, and they may produce either a gloss finish or a flat finish.

Lacquers are one of the easiest types of finishing materials to apply. Once applied, the coating may have to be buffed to reach its maximum gloss. Any damage to a lacquer finish is generally easy to repair.

Lacquers are manufactured for special purposes such as fuel resistance and hydraulic-fluid resistance. The following specification numbers denote special-purpose lacquers:

MIL-L-6047	Fuel resistant
MIL-L-7146	Hydraulic-fluid resistant
MIL-L-6806	Clear coating for aluminum
MIL-L-006805	Dull black instrument lacquer
MIL-L-19537	Acrylic nitrocelluose lacquer

Enamels

Enamels originally came out as alkyd enamels and have evolved into the present acrylic enamels. This paint finish provides a glossy, hard surface which has good resistance to scratching and abrasion. Their disadvantages include the requirement of more care during application, a longer drying time, and special precautions when repairing any damage to the surface.

Various finish manufacturers supply enamels in both one-and two-part preparations with various characteristics of durability, heat, and weather resistance to match the needs of different aircraft operations.

Polyurethane

Polyurethane finishing materials provide a very high gloss surface with excellent durability, weathering resistance, and abrasion resistance. Due to their resistance to chemical attack, they are often used by aircraft manufacturers in places subject to exposure to strong chemical agents, such as areas containing Skydrol-type hydraulic fluids.

These finishes normally are a two-part mixture with a catalyst added to activate the drying or "hardening" process. Once the catalyst is added, the material has a specific working life, after which it may not be used. These finishes are often part of a finishing "process" where the finish material provides the best life and durability when used in conjunction with a specific surface cleaning operation, a surface priming coat, a corrosion inhibitor, and a finish topcoat, as shown in Fig. 4-1.

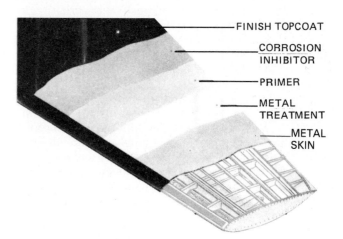

FINISH TOPCOAT
CORROSION INHIBITOR
PRIMER
METAL TREATMENT
METAL SKIN

FIG. 4-1 Sequence of finishing products for a metal aircraft. *(U.S. Paint)*

Polyurethane finishes should not be waxed. Wax tends to "yellow" the finish, and it collects dirt, reducing the cleanliness of the aircraft surface. Mild soap and water are recommended for cleaning and solvents are applied with a soft cloth to remove oil and grease.

One problem that is found with polyurethanes is the difficulty in removing or "stripping" large areas with solvents and chemicals. This type of finish resists most stripping materials. Consult the finish manufacturer for specific information about removing old polyurethane coatings

Thinners

Thinners, also called **reducers,** are used to reduce the viscosity of finishing products so that they will flow properly through the spray gun and onto the surface being painted. Each finish product may require a specific reducing liquid. While some thinners may indicate that they are compatible with all types of finishing products or with a specific group of products, such as all enamels, it is best to only use the reducer recommended by the finish manufacturer. If the wrong thinner is used, the paint may not mix with the thinner, the thinner might prevent the paint from drying, or the thinner may attack the coats of paint beneath the coat being applied. If you must determine if a thinner can be used with a product and cannot contact the finish manufacturer, try out the reducer with a sample of the paint and use the sample on a test panel. Be aware that there may be long-term problems with a suspect thinner that cannot be determined by this test method.

New Types of Materials

It must be emphasized that the materials described in this section are not the only ones approved for aircraft use. We have given information on the products that are the most commonly used; however, new materials and processes may be approved at any time. Since the industry has developed many types of new fabrics and finishes, the mechanic is likely to encounter unfamiliar ones and in such a case should study carefully the instructions provided by the manufacturer. All approved materials are required to be accompanied by complete instructions. The word of caution we must offer is that the user of any product should make sure that anything used on an aircraft is tested and approved.

● PAINT SPRAY EQUIPMENT

Spray painting equipment represents a significant investment for any company. If the equipment is properly maintained and used, it will more than pay for itself. If the equipment is misused or not properly maintained, it can cost quite a bit more for a company in damage to aircraft finishes and poor customer relations. Therefore, it is important that all aircraft mechanics have a basic understanding of the proper operation, use, and maintenance of aircraft spray equipment.

The Spray Gun

In almost all paint and dope finishing work on aircraft, the finish is applied with a spray gun. The principal advantages of the spray gun are the speed with which paint or dope may be applied and the smooth finish of the sprayed surface.

Spray guns are manufactured in a number of different types and sizes. Sizes vary from the small airbrush guns to the heavy-duty production guns used with pressure tanks. Guns are made to spray all types of fluids including heavy, sticky compounds such as automobile undercoat. Spray guns are manufactured for both *conventional* spraying and *airless* spraying. The nozzle and aircap of the conventional spray gun are designed to mix air with the paint stream to aid in atomization of the liquid. Airstreams are also utilized to shape the pattern which the gun will deposit. Various patterns for a spray gun are shown in Fig. 4-2. Airless spray guns such as the Binks Model No. 43 gun do not mix air with the paint before it leaves the nozzle. This results in reduced overspray, less paint "fog" in the air, and a saving of paint. Regardless of the type of spray gun being used, the mechanic must be certain to adjust it correctly for the type of paint being applied.

One of the popular spray guns for general use in conventional spraying is the type of MBC gun manufactured by the DeVilbiss Company. A gun of this type is shown in Fig. 4-3. The important parts are labeled in the drawing. Figure 4-4 shows the same spray gun used with a liquid container, also called a **cup.** The spray gun also can be used with a pressure tank (pressure pot), in which case the liquid is fed under pressure from the tank through a hose to the gun. Spray guns manufactured by the Binks Manufacturing Company are also extensively employed for the application of all types of finishes. The choice, in any case, depends upon the preference of the operator.

As shown in the illustration of Fig. 4-3, a spray gun includes a **fluid adjustment** which controls the **fluid valve,** a **spreader adjustment valve,** an **air-valve assembly,** an **air cap,** a **fluid inlet,** and an **air inlet.** The balance among air pressure, airflow, fluid pressure, and fluid flow is controlled by adjusting the valves concerned to provide the desired spray quality and pattern. Air flowing through the center area of the air cap and through holes near the center mixes with fluid from the fluid tip and produces an atomized spray. Air flowing from the openings in the horns of the air cap impinges on each side of the fluid spray to produce an elongated spray pattern. This pattern may be adjusted for a wide or narrow area by changing the setting of the spreader adjustment valve. The pattern can be made vertical or horizontal by turning the air cap.

If the spray gun is used with a pressure tank, the fluid is fed under pressure to the fluid inlet of the gun. The fluid pressure must be correct to obtain the proper fluid flow. The pressure is controlled by means of a regulator on the pressure tank.

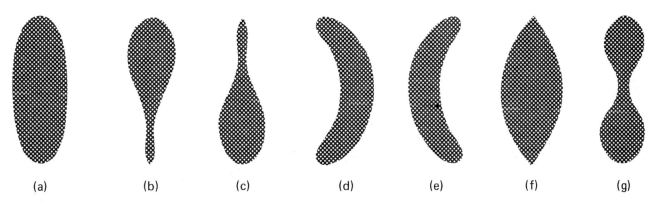

(a) (b) (c) (d) (e) (f) (g)

FIG. 4-2 Correct and distorted spray-gun patterns.

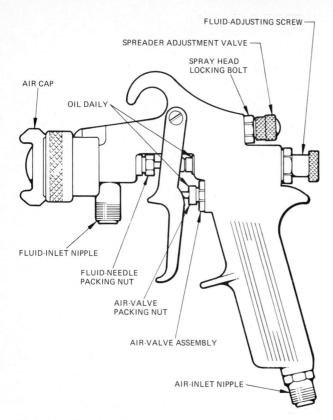

FIG. 4-3 **Drawing of a typical spray gun.** *(DeVilbiss Co.)*

FIG. 4-4 **Spray gun with paint cup.** *(DeVilbiss Co.)*

The air pressure, fluid pressure, airflow, and fluid flow are adjusted to provide the best spray quality for the material being sprayed. Manufacturers often give the most satisfactory settings for the application of each product and also specify the viscosity for best results.

The best results in the use of a spray gun are obtained when the gun is properly maintained and serviced. Bearing surfaces and moving parts should be lubricated daily with a light oil. The lubrication of the gun should be done according to the manufacturer's instructions.

After each use of the gun, it is necessary that it be cleaned thoroughly to prevent the accumulation of dried paint in the nozzle and paint passages. It is not usually necessary to take the spray gun apart to clean it, because paint solvent sprayed through the gun will ordinarily clean out the paint. The outside of the gun should be thoroughly washed with solvent.

It is desirable to disassemble the gun periodically and inspect it for wear and accumulation of paint and dirt. Worn parts should be replaced.

The packing nuts around the fluid-needle and air-valve stem should be kept tight, but not so tight that parts cannot move freely.

It is not wise to allow the gun to become so dirty that soaking of the complete gun becomes necessary. Also, the gun should not be left immersed in solvent or thinner. It is especially important to avoid the use of caustic alkaline solutions for cleaning because alkalis destroy aluminum alloy components of the gun.

An unbalanced or distorted spray pattern indicates a dirty air cap. The air cap should be removed and washed thoroughly in clean thinner. If reaming of the air-cap holes is necessary, a matchstick, broom bristle, or some other soft material should be used. Do not use a hard or sharp instrument because it may permanently damage the cap.

Spray-gun parts are not ordinarily removed, except for the air cap. When replacing the air-valve assembly, the air-valve spring should be properly seated in the recess in the body of the gun. When removing any parts which seal on a gasket, the condition of the gasket should be examined. When the fluid tip is replaced, it must be tightened carefully.

Using the Spray Gun

The difference between a first-class finishing job and a poor job is often detemined by the use of the spray gun. An experienced mechanic who has mastered the techniques in handling a spray gun usually has no difficulty in producing a good finishing job.

The first requirement is to have the gun properly adjusted for the type of finishing material being applied. The operator may test the gun by trying it against a test surface. When the desired pattern is obtained, the operator may start applying the finish.

The air pressure for the gun must be correctly adjusted. This pressure is normally controlled by an **air transformer.** The device acts as a pressure regulator to provide the correct pressure as adjusted by the knob on the top. This unit has fittings for the incoming air from a standard air-pressure line and one or more outlet fittings for the attachment of the air hose to the gun.

Among the conditions which the operator of a spray gun must observe are the following:

1. The gun must be held at the correct distance from the surface being sprayed (6 to 10 in [15 to 25 cm]). If the gun is held too close, it is likely to cause runs or sagging.

2. Air pressure should be correctly adjusted.

3. The trigger must be released at the end of each pass; otherwise, excessive paint buildup occurs when the direction of spray gun movement is reversed.

4. The gun must be moved in a straight line, parallel to the surface being sprayed. Moving the gun in an arc causes heavy paint buildup and runs in the center portion of the pass.

5. The paint must be strained before use. This is to remove large particles which may clog the spray nozzle and cause a rough painted surface.

6. The correct type of air cap and spray nozzle must be used. Consult the appropriate instructions for the material being sprayed.

7. The paint must be thinned to the correct consistency (vicosity). Manufacturers of aircraft finishes often recommend testing the viscosity with a Zahn viscosity cup. This is accomplished by placing the required amount of finish in the specified cup and noting the time required in seconds for the finish to drain from the cup.

8. See that the surface to be sprayed is clean. A **tack cloth** may be used to wipe away dust or other particles. A tack cloth is a specially treated soft cloth which can be used to wipe a surface and remove all dust but leaves no wax, oil or other material on the surface that would interfere with the adhesion of coatings.

9. The temperature and humidity must be within the proper range for satisfactory results; otherwise a variety of problems may occur.

A normal spray pattern for a spray gun forms an elongated oval having a length 2 1/2 to 3 times the width. This is shown in Fig. 4–2 (a). This pattern indicates that the spray gun is clean and properly adjusted for the liquid being sprayed. The pattern at (b) is top-heavy and indicates that the horn holes are partially plugged, there is an obstruction on top of the fluid tip, or there is dirt on the air cap seat or fluid tip seat. Causes for the bottom-heavy patterns at (c) are the same as for the top-heavy pattern except that the obstruction is on the bottom side of the fluid tip. Heavy right or left patterns shown at (d) and (e) indicate that one or the other of the horn holes is partially clogged or that there is dirt on either the right or left side of the fluid tip. The heavy center pattern shown at (f) indicates that the spreader adjustment valve is set for too low an airflow, or, for a pressure feed, the fluid pressure is too high for the atomization air being used, or the material flow is in excess of the cap's normal capacity. The condition can also be caused by too large or too small a nozzle. A split spray pattern (g) is due to air and fluid flows not being

properly balanced. Increasing fluid pressure or decreasing spreader air should correct the condition.

Air Transformer

An air transformer, shown in Fig. 4–5, is a device that removes oil, dirt, and moisture from compressed air; regulates the air pressure; indicates the regulated air pressure by means of gauges; and provides outlets for spray guns and other air tools.

The air transformer removes entrained dirt, oil, and moisture by baffles, centrifugal force, expansion chambers, impingement plates, and filters, thus allowing only clean, dry air to emerge from the outlets. The air-regulating valve provides positive control, ensuring uniform, regulated pressure. The pressure gauges indicate regulated pressure and, in some cases, main line air pressure. Valves control air outlets for hose lines to spray guns and other air-operated equipment. The drain valve provides for elimination of accumulated sludge which consists of oil, dirt, and moisture.

The air transformer should be installed at least 25 ft [8 m] from the compressor and should have its air take-off from the main line rising from the top of the

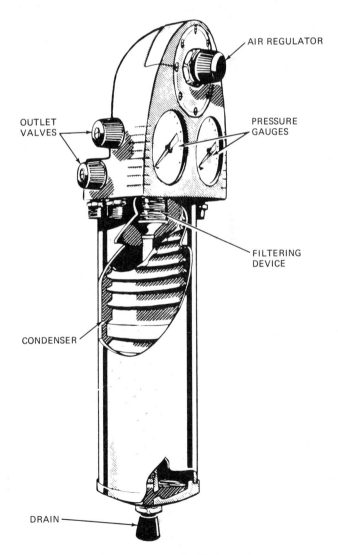

FIG. 4-5 An air transformer. *(DeVilbiss Co.)*

133

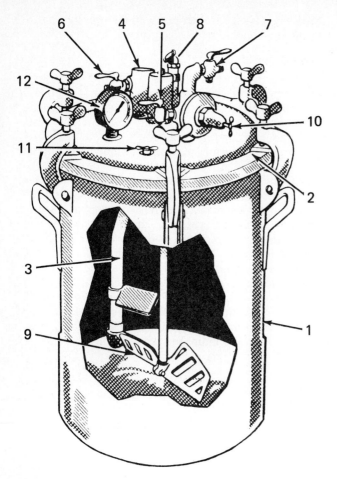

FIG. 4-6   A pressure tank. *(DeVilbiss Co.)*

line. This is to prevent liquid water from entering the transformer air inlet. The main line should be equipped with a water trap or drains to prevent the accumulation of water. The drain at the bottom of the air transformer should be opened at least once a day to remove moisture and sludge.

Pressure Tank

The pressure tank, also called a "pressure pot" or "pressure-feed tank," is a closed metal container that provides a constant flow of paint or other material to the spray gun at a uniform pressure. These tanks range in size from 2 to 120 gal [7.57 to 454.2 L]. A pressure feed tank is illustrated in the drawing of Fig. 4-6.

Fluid is forced out of the tank by the compressed air in the tank. To change the rate of fluid flow from the tank, the air pressure is adjusted by means of the pressure regulator. If the tank is the type without a regulator, the air pressure is controlled by the air transformer. Pressure tanks are designed for working pressures up to 110 psi [759 kPa].

As can be seen in the illustration of Fig. 4-6, a typical pressure feed tank consists of a shell (1), clamp-on lid (2), fluid tube (3), fluid header (4), air-outlet valve (5), fluid-outlet valve (6), air-inlet valve (7), safety relief valve (8), agitator (9), pressure regulator (10), release valve (11), and a pressure gauge (12).

The agitator is an essential mechanism for a pressure tank. Its purpose is to ensure that the finishing materials being sprayed are kept in a thoroughly mixed condition. The most convenient type of agitator is driven by an air motor.

Pressure tanks are often utilized with a separate fluid container set inside the tank. This reduces the cleanup problems and makes it possible to change rapidly from one material to another.

The following instructions are typical for the cleaning of a pressure feed system:

1. Back out the air pressure regulator adjusting screw and release the pressure from the tank by means of the relief valve or safety valve.

2. Loosen the spray-gun air-cap ring three turns, hold a cloth over the air cap, and pull the trigger to force fluid from the hose back into the tank.

3. Remove the fluid hose from the spray gun and attach it to a **hose cleaner.** The hose cleaner is a pressurized tank containing the appropriate solvent. Run air and solvent through the fluid hose and the fluid tube on the tank until the solvent runs clear.

4. Dry the hose with compressed air.

5. Clean the air cap and fluid tip on the spray gun.

6. Clean the tank and reassemble.

The success of any spray painting operation depends upon the care and attention of those operating the equipment. When equipment is properly operated and maintained, it produces the desired results. The mechanic should consult the manufacturer's information regarding the materials to be used in the equipment to be sure of using the correct spray tips and the correct air and fluid pressures.

● FINISHING OF METAL AIRCRAFT AND PARTS

Since all aircraft contain metal parts and most aircraft are of all-metal construction, it is important that the mechanic be familiar with certain principles involved in metal finishing. In this section we do not discuss the processes of plating or the special chemical finishes because they are not usually in the realm of general airframe maintenance. If such a process is required by the manufacturer, the work can be done by an organization which specializes in this type of work.

Corrosion Protection

A metal fuselage is usually painted for two principal reasons: corrosion prevention and appearance. **Corrosion** is an electrochemical process in which oxygen or other elements combine with metals to form various compounds such as rust, aluminum oxide, metal chlorides, and other metal salts. The first requirement for corrosion is the presence of moisture; the other is a combination of dissimilar metals or metals and chemicals. If a metal is kept dry and clean, it will not corrode; however, a little moisture in the presence of other elements can cause severe corrosion.

In the design and manufacture of aircraft structures, engineers are careful to avoid a design of any assembly of parts which requires the contact of dissimilar metals. If two dissimilar metals must be joined, the surfaces are usually insulated from each other by means of special coatings, treated tapes, or other means.

When preparing a metal structure for refinishing, the mechanic must be careful to avoid any condition which can cause corrosion and must remove any corrosion-causing condition which may be found. When in continuous contact with metals, hygroscopic materials (those which absorb and hold moisture), such as leather or canvas, are very likely to cause corrosion. Such materials should be waterproofed before installation.

The improper application of aircraft finishes can lead to **filiform corrosion** (so named because it forms in fine filaments). If phosphoric acid from an etching solution or wash primer is trapped under subsequent coatings before complete conversion to the phosphate film, filiform corrosion will develop under the finish coating, damaging both the metal and the finish. To avoid this condition, it is necessary that there be adequate moisture in the air or in the wash primer to complete the conversion of the phosphoric acid to phosphate. Humidity should be such that a minimum of 0.09 lb of water is present in each pound of air [90 g per kilogram of air]. This would be accomplished with a relative humidity of 57 percent at 70°F [21.1°C] or a relative humidity of 49 percent at 75°F [23.9°C]. If the humidity is not great enough to provide the required moisture, a small amount of distilled water may be added to the wash primer. Since a typical wash primer thinner is alcohol, water can be mixed with it.

Another important consideration in the conversion of the phosphoric acid in the wash primer is to allow sufficient time for the conversion to take place before applying the next coating. This is normally 30 to 40 min.

If filiform corrosion starts, it will continue until removed. If it is discovered, the finish in the affected area and possibly the entire finish of the airplane will have to be removed and all traces of the corrosion eliminated.

Surface Preparation

The preparation of a metal surface for finishing depends upon the type of paint job required. Three general situations are considered here. The first situation is the painting of a new airplane having a bare, polished Al-Clad finish. The preparation of a new aluminum surface involves only thorough cleaning and treating with a phosphoric acid etch and/or a wash primer. The phosphoric acid etch is also referred to as a **conversion coating.**

Another condition involves refinishing an airplane over an old finish. In this case, the mechanic must determine what type of finish was previously applied to the airplane and then make sure that the material for the new finish is compatible with the old finish. Preparation of an old finish for refinishing usually requires sanding to remove the oxidized outer layer of finish. Any additional treatment required before application of the new finish will be described in the finish manufacturer's instructions.

The third situation which the mechanic may encounter is the complete stripping of the old finish and treatment of the metal surface prior to the application of the new finish.

Stripping

Several paint-stripping products are available, and these usually fall into two categories. **Wax-free paint remover** is a highly volatile liquid and evaporates rapidly after it is applied. For this reason, stripping large areas of an airplane surface with this material is a slow and arduous process. **Wax-type stripper** has the consistency of thick cream because of the wax which holds the solvent in contact with the paint surface long enough to lift or dissolve the old coatings. Wax-type stripper is applied with a brush in a thick layer and is allowed to remain on the surface until the coating lifts or dissolves. Some manufacturers recommend laying a polyethylene drop cloth over the stripper-coated surface to slow the drying of the solvents. The stripper should not be removed from the surface until all the paint has lifted or softened. If an area dries before this happens, additional stripper should be applied to the dried area. When all the old finish has softened or lifted, the stripper and finish can be flushed off with water.

Acrylic lacquer will not lift and wrinkle when stripper is applied, but it will soften. When acrylic lacquer has softened, it should be scraped off with a nonmetallic scraper, and then the area should be washed with MEK, acetone, or similar solvent. A powerful spray gun should be used to spray the solvent into cracks, crevasses, and metal joints or seams. The purpose of the solvent is to remove all traces of wax which would otherwise be left by the stripper.

Polyurethane coatings are not easily removed with paint stripper; however, if the stripper is retained on the surface for sufficient time, the bond between the coating and primer is loosened and the coating can be removed. The surface should then be scrubbed with MEK, acetone, toluol (toluene), or xylol.

Paint stripper should not be allowed to come into contact with Plexiglas windows, fiberglass parts, fabric, or other plastic or porous materials. The active agents in the stripper damages some materials and is absorbed by others, neither of which is acceptable.

The principal consideration in the stripping of an airplane is to see that all wax and other residues are completely removed from the surface. This is accomplished by proper solvents as mentioned and by washing with approved cleaners.

Paint stripping agents must not be used on metal aircraft which employ adhesive-bonded seams rather than riveted seams. Stripping material is likely to penetrate the bonded seams and render the entire structure unairworthy. Manufacturers specify methods by which seams can be masked and protected if stripping operations are necessary.

For specific stripping procedures consult the manufacturer of the finish being removed or the stripper's manufacturer.

Conversion Coatings

Conversion coatings are applied to fresh, clean metal to aid in preventing corrosion and to microscopically roughen the surface for better adhesion of additional coatings. A conversion coating for aluminum or steel can be phosphoric acid etch which leaves a tough, inorganic phosphate film on the metal.

The treatment of a magnesium surface requires a chromic acid etch. This solution can be prepared by mixing approximately 1 percent chromic anhydride (CrO_3), 0.78 percent calcium sulfate ($CaSO_4$), and 98.22 percent water. This solution should be brushed on the bare magnesium and allowed to remain for 1 to 3 min. It should then be washed off with water and the surface dried. After drying, the surface is suitable for the application of a wash primer.

Wash Primers

A typical wash primer is described as a two-part butyral–phosphoric acid resin containing corrosion-inhibiting pigments. Other wash primers contain chromic acid as the etching agent. Wash primer may be applied directly to clean, bare metal, or it may be applied over the conversion coating described previously. For best results, it is recommended that the wash primer be applied over the conversion coating.

The wash primer developed by the Stits Aircraft Coatings Company utilizes as many as four types of liquids. These are the pretreatment wash primer and metal conditioner, wash primer reducer, wash primer acid component, and wash primer retarder. To prepare the wash primer for use, the base component of the wash primer is shaken and mixed thoroughly. Then equal parts of the acid and base components are mixed and stirred thoroughly. The reducer is used to thin the mixture if necessary to reduce the viscosity which should be such that the flow from a No. 2 Zahn viscosity cup requires 15 to 18 s. In warm, humid weather when it is desired to slow the drying time, the wash primer retarder is added to the mixture.

Wash primers should be applied in one very thin wash coat, not more than 0.5 mil [0.013 mm] in thickness. The wet, thin coat will penetrate the microscopic craters on the metal surface and any corrosion pits that exist.

Wash primers are manufactured in a variety of formulas by different companies, and it is essential that the mechanic follow carefully the directions on the container or in the manufacturer's instruction manual. An important point to observe is the pot life of the primer. After the components of the wash primer are mixed, the pot life is usually from 6 to 8 h. All material should be used during the pot life period; unused material should be discarded.

Application of Primers

A primer serves two principal purposes: improved bonding and corrosion protection. It provides a bonding layer for the finish coatings in that the primer makes a good bond with the metal and the finish coating makes a good bond with the primer. The primer usually contains zinc chromate or some other corrosion-inhibiting material, thus providing corrosion protection. To ensure that a primer serves its functions adequately, it is most essential that it is applied as specified and that the other materials with which it is used are compatible.

Zinc chromate primer has been a standard for years in the finishing of metal aircraft and parts. It is an effective primer when properly applied over clean aluminum or steel. Zinc chromate primer complies with MIL-P-8585A specification and is either yellow or green in color. It should be thinned to the proper consistency with toluol and applied with a spray gun on metal surfaces which have been etched with a phosphoric acid solution or other conversion coating. Application over a wash primer is not recommended unless all the chemical action of the wash primer is known to have been completed so that no phosphoric acid will be trapped against the metal. Zinc chromate primer provides a coating that will not permit water vapor to penetrate to the wash primer to aid in completing the chemical conversion to the phosphate film.

Two-part **epoxy primers** are popular for use under the urethane and polyurethane coatings. The primer is prepared for use by mixing the required quantity of catalyst with the base component. There is a waiting period (induction time) of 30 to 40 min before the mixture is ready for spraying. This time is necessary to allow the catalytic action to progress to a point where the primer is satisfactory for spraying.

Epoxy primers may be used on steel, aluminum, magnesium, or fiberglass. For the most complete protection against corrosion, the epoxy primer is applied over a wash primer.

Finish coatings should be sprayed over the epoxy primer within 24 h of primer application. Otherwise, the primer forms a hard surface to which the finish coating will not adhere properly. If more than 24 h has elapsed since the application of epoxy primer, the surface can be roughened with 400-grit wet-or-dry sandpaper, Scotch Brite pads, or other recommended material before the application of finish coats.

Acrylic lacquers and enamels should not be applied over an epoxy primer for at least 5 h and preferably overnight. Acrylics have a tendency to penetrate epoxy primer if it is not fully cured, and this results in a poor surface appearance. Urethane and polyurethane coatings can be sprayed on epoxy primers after 1 h curing time. These coatings soften the surface of the epoxy and form a chemical bond with the primer.

When epoxy primer materials are handled, it is important that the catalyst container be kept tightly closed except when the material is poured. The catalyst is reactive to moisture and will absorb it from the air if the container is not closed. If the catalyst has absorbed considerable moisture and the container is resealed, a chemical action can take place which will cause the container to burst.

Typical instructions for the application of an epoxy primer are as follows:

1. See that the surface is thoroughly cleaned and dust free.

2. Add exactly one part catalyst to two parts of the

primer base component. Stir thoroughly and allow 30-min induction time before application. In high humidity allow 1-h induction time to avoid curing agent "bloom."

3. After the two components are mixed, reduce with epoxy reducer to attain a viscosity of 19 to 21 s with a No. 2 Zahn viscosity cup. Additional thinning is required in hot weather.

4. Apply spray coats at 30-min intervals.

Instructions for the application of epoxy primer will vary for different manufacturers. For example, one instruction for a particular product requires a mixture of one-to-one catalyst and base component. This same instruction requires the application of only one coat of primer to a thickness of approximately 0.0005 in [0.013 mm]. It is most important, therefore, that the mechanic pay strict attention to the appropriate instructions.

Another primer specifically designed for use under urethane coatings is urethane primer. This is a two-part primer which must be mixed a short time before use and must be used within 6 to 8 h after mixing.

Typical instructions for the application of urethane primer on Al-Clad aluminum are as follows:

1. Mix two parts urethane primer with one part urethane primer catalyst. Add urethane reducer as needed to obtain a viscosity of 18 to 22 s with a No. 2 Zahn viscosity cup.

2. Allow the catalyzed material to stand for an induction period of 30 min.

3. Spray one coat of the urethane primer on the Al-Clad aluminum surface which has been previously coated with chromate wash primer. Allow to air dry at 77°F [25°C] for at least 4 h before applying urethane finish coats. Urethane enamel must be applied within 48 h; otherwise the primer will need a light sanding before the enamel is applied.

In some cases, primer or enamel will **crater** or **crawl** as soon as it is sprayed on the surface. This means that it does not remain flat and smooth but forms small craters and ridges as if being repelled from areas of the surface. This is usually caused by oil or some other contaminant on the surface. It is usually necessary to remove the fresh coating and thoroughly clean the area with an approved solvent. In some cases, anticrater solutions are available to reduce or eliminate cratering. Such solutions must be used only as directed.

After the application of a primer, the spray equipment should be cleaned thoroughly and immediately. Some primers, such as epoxy primer, will set up hard within a short time and ruin the equipment. Spray guns, paint cups, pressure pots, and paint hoses must be disassembled to the extent possible, and every trace of the primer should be removed. Reducer or MEK is suitable for this purpose.

Finishes

We have mentioned a number of finishes in the discussions on surface preparation and priming. A wide variety of finish coatings are available, each with its special characteristics. A number of these finish coatings have been described earlier in this chapter.

Lacquers, both nitrate and acrylic, are quick-drying and easily applied with a spray gun, provided that they are properly thinned with the correct reducer to meet the conditions of temperature and humidity at the time they are applied. Because of their fast-drying characteristics, they soon dry dust-free. Care must be taken to assure that lacquers are not sprayed over coatings which they will cause to lift and wrinkle.

Enamels do not dry as fast as lacquers and should, therefore, be applied in a dust-free spray booth. Some enamels are designed for air drying, and others should be baked to cure the finish. In any event, the surface of the enamel should be dry before being exposed to conditions where dust may settle and mar the finish.

As mentioned previously, urethane and polyurethane products are being used extensively for finishing aircraft. When properly applied, they provide a high gloss ("wet look"), durability, and ease of maintenance. Typical instructions for a urethane coating are as follows:

1. Prepare the surface to be coated as previously explained with wash primer and epoxy primer. The primer should have been applied not more than 36 h before the finishing is begun.

2. Mix catalyst in proportions given by the manufacturer. Stir thoroughly and add reducer to lower to a spray viscosity of 17 to 19 s with a No. 2 Zahn viscosity cup. Filter through a 60 × 48 mesh (or finer) cone filter. Allow 20-min induction time before spraying.

3. Apply a light, wet tack coat with a spray gun and follow with two medium cross coats at 10- to 20-min intervals. The dry film thickness should be approximately 1.7 mils [0.0017 in or 0.041 mm]. A DeVilbiss model MBC-510 or JGA-502 spray gun with a No. 30 air cap and EX tip and needle at 45 lb [310 kPa] pressure has been tested and found satisfactory.

High-Visibility Finishes

It is often necessary or desirable to make certain aircraft more visible than usual, and for this purpose manufacturers have developed finishes which reflect more light than the conventional finishes. These coatings are not used over the entire airplane but on wing tips, for fuselage striping, cowlings and/or empennage. The finishes are made in two general types; those which are temporary and may be removed easily after the need has passed and those which will last for up to 9 months.

High-visibility (fluorescent) finishes consist of a transparent coat of pigmented finish applied over a white, reflective base coat. A clear, ultraviolet-absorbing topcoat helps retard fading of the brilliant, transparent pigments. The high visibility of the finish results from light reflecting off the white base coat.

The application of high-visibility finishes is the same as for other type coatings. The mechanic should make certain that the materials used are compatible and that the instructions of the manufacturer are being followed. The materials are often sold in complete kits which include everything required plus instructions.

It is not usually possible to restore faded and weathered high-visibilitycoatings. The transparent pigment coating should, therefore, be stripped off down to the white base coat and a new coating of finish applied.

Identification of Finish Coatings

When it becomes necessary to repair or touch up an airplane finish, the nature of the previous coating must be determined in order to ensure that the new coating will adhere to the old coating without lifting or otherwise damaging it.

Various methods and techniques for identification of finishes are employed. To begin, it is a good plan to examine the airplane logbook to see if the finish is identified. If the airplane has not been refinished since new, the type of finish can be identified by the manufacturer.

Cellulose nitrate dope and lacquer dissolve when wiped with a cloth saturated with nitrate thinner or reducer. The distinct odor of cellulose nitrate also aids in making an identification. Synthetic engine oil, MIL-L-7808 or equivalent, softens cellulose nitrate finishes within a few minutes after application but has no effect on epoxy, urethane, or acrylic finishes.

MEK wiped onto acrylic finishes picks up pigment but does not affect epoxy, or urethane finishes unless rubbed into the surface.

In all cases where a product is to be used for refinishing, the manufacturer's instructions should be consulted. Often the instructions provide information regarding the compatibility of other finishes with that which is to be applied.

Touchup of Finishes

Airplane finishes which have become scratched, scraped, cracked, or peeled should be repaired as quickly as possible in order to prevent the onset of corrosion. Any of the old finish that is loose or deteriorated should be removed. It is best to confine the operation to as small an area as possible; however, if the finish is badly deteriorated, it is best to strip an entire panel or refinish the entire airplane.

The old finish can be removed by the careful use of abrasive paper to take off the damaged coating and "feather" in the edges of the damaged area with the original coat. The surface should then be cleaned and all traces of dirt, wax, oil, and other contaminates removed. If the old finish is removed down to bare metal, the same sequence of primers and coatings should be followed as has been previously described. The same type materials as originally used on the aircraft should be used for the repair so that any interaction of products is avoided. If the original type of paint used cannot be located, select a product that will not interact with the coating being repaired.

Spray application of finishes is desirable, and the use of an air brush rather than a large spray gun may be appropriate, depending on the area being repaired. Be sure to protect the surrounding parts of the aircraft and work area from overspray.

Good-quality acrylic finishes are available in aerosol containers, and these may be used for a finish coat provided that the undercoat material is compatible. Acrylic finish can be applied over epoxy primer if done within about 6 h of the epoxy application. If acrylic lacquer is applied over an old acrylic finish, it is considered good practice to soften the old finish with the application of acrylic thinner, either by wiping or spraying, immediately prior to applying the finish coat. The thinner must be dried before the finish is applied.

Urethane enamel can be applied over an old epoxy or urethane coating but should not be applied over an old alkyd enamel surface. The surface should be thoroughly washed with an emulsion cleaner and then steam-cleaned. The surface is then sanded with 280- to 320-grit aluminum oxide or silicon carbide paper and wiped down with MEK or toluol. Urethane enamel can then be sprayed on the surface as previously explained.

Safety

All those involved with the finishing of airplanes must keep in mind that many solvents, lacquers, and other materials used are highly flammable. Great care must be taken to assure that ignition of flammable materials cannot take place.

Dry sanding of cellulose nitrate finishes can create static charges which can ignite nitrate fumes. The interior of a freshly painted wing or fuselage contains vaporized solvents. If a static discharge should take place in this atmosphere, it is most likely that there will be an explosion and fire. It is recommended that wet sanding be performed in every case possible because the water is effective in dissipating static charges.

Finishing materials should be stored in closed, metal containers in a fireproof building. The building should be well ventilated to prevent the accumulation of flammable vapors.

The floor of a dope room or paint booth should be kept free of spray dust and sanding residue. These can be ignited by static discharges or by a person walking over them. It is recommended that the floors be washed down with water frequently to prevent the buildup of flammable residues.

The use of a drill motor to drive a paint-mixing tool should be avoided. Arcing at the motor brushes can ignite flammable fumes.

Solvents and other solutions are often injurious if they should splash on the skin or in the eyes. Mechanics using the materials should be protected with clothing which covers the body, goggles for the eyes, and an air filter for the nose and mouth.

The use of respirators when spraying finishes is highly recommended and with some finishing products it is mandatory. Some finishing materials will coat the inside of the lungs and cause health problems. Always check the product manufacturer's safety recommendations and then follow these.

Common Painting Problems

If the conditions for the application of an aircraft finish are not correct, one or more irregularities in the paint surface may show up. These irregularities are addressed here as they relate to spray painting, but most of them are also applicable to brushing and dipping operations.

Blisters or bubbles are small raised circular areas with a layer of paint over them. These may be caused by oil or water in the air line of the spray gun. These may also be caused by applying a second coat of paint too soon over a fresh first coat that is still giving off large quantities of thinner.

Blushing is when the paint appears to be cloudy or milky. This is caused by the vehicle in the paint evaporating so fast that the surface temperature of the paint is reduced to the point where the moisture in the air condenses and mixes with the paint.

Orange peel is the term for paint that creates an irregular surface like the surface of an orange peel. The paint is of varying thickness on the surface and does not flow out properly. This may be caused by improper air pressure at the gun, the gun being held too far away from the surface, or insufficient thinning of the paint.

Pinholes are small holes or depressions in the paint. These are caused by insufficient drying time between coats or paint that has not been thinned enough.

Runs and sags are usually found on vertical or sloping surfaces and are the result of a heavy coat of paint being applied in an area. The heavy coat has such a buildup that gravity takes over and the paint runs down the surface before it can properly set. This can be caused by an improperly adjusted spray gun or by moving the gun too slowly.

The correction for each of these problems involves eliminating the stated cause. In some cases, depending on the finishing product being used, the paint may have to be completely removed. In other cases it may be allowed to dry for some period of time and then sanded lightly before continuing with the process. Still another solution may be to apply a corrective coat to the surface, normally consisting of a combination of paint, thinners, and retarders. In each case, follow the product manufacturer's recommendations.

Masking and Decorative Trim

Aircraft are not painted only one color. Most aircraft contain at least a line or two of decorative trim, with some even being painted in two-tone or multitone color combinations. Even if the aircraft does not have any decorative trim, registration numbers must be applied. The techniques for the application of trim are not complicated, but they do require some care on the part of the painter.

Templates and chalk lines are normally used in laying out the trim lines. The lines should not be laid out with a pencil or pen that can damage the surface or leave permanent marks. The surface of the finish must be hard enough (dry enough) so that this work will not damage the finish. For many finishing materials the paint must not have been on the aircraft more than a few hours or a few days when the trim color is applied. If the paint has been on too long and has cured, the trim color may not properly adhere to the surface coat.

Once the trim lines are laid out, masking tape is laid along the lines. The masking tape used should be of a type whose adhesive will not be attacked by the solvents in the trim paint. Propylene masking tape is a type that is commonly used. This tape also has a smoother edge than conventional crepe paper masking tape and gives a sharp trim line. Paper or plastic is then taped onto the trim tape so that a protective cover is placed over the surface areas next to the trim areas. This protects these surfaces from overspray.

When all of the masking and protective covers are in place, the area to be painted is wiped with a clean cloth containing solvent, and after this is dry, the paint is applied.

● REGISTRATION MARKS FOR AIRCRAFT

The finishing of certificated aircraft involves the application of required identification marks as set forth in FAR Part 45. This section gives the general requirements for such markings; however, the mechanic should consult the latest regulations when applying the markings to an aircraft.

All aircraft registered in the United States must be marked with nationality and registration marks for easy identification. The marks must be painted on the aircraft or otherwise affixed so they are as permanent as the finish. the marks must contrast with the background and be easily legible. The letters and numbers must be made without ornamentation and must not have other markings or insignia adjacent to them which could cause confusion in identification.

Required Markings

The registration and nationality markings for United States registered aircraft consists of the Roman capital letter N followed by the registration number of the aircraft. The registration number is issued by the FAA when the aircraft is first registered.

When marks that include only the Roman capital letter N and the registration number are displayed on **limited, restricted,** or **experimental aircraft,** or on aircraft which have **provisional certification,** the words "limited," "restricted," "experimental," or "provisional airworthiness" must be displayed near each entrance to the cockpit or cabin. The letters must be not less than 2 in [5.08 cm] or more than 6 in [15.24 cm] in height.

Location of Marks for Fixed-Wing Aircraft

Registration marks for fixed-wing aircraft must be displayed on both sides of the vertical tail surface or on both sides of the fuselage between the trailing edge of the wing and the leading edge of the horizontal stabilizer. If the marks are on the tail of a multi-vertical-tail aircraft, the marks must be on the outer surfaces of the vertical sections.

If the aircraft has engine pods or components which tend to obscure the sides of the fuselage, the marks can be placed on the pods or other components.

Location of Marks for Non-Fixed-Wing Aircraft

Helicopters or other rotorcraft must have nationality and registration markings displayed on the bottom surface of the fuselage or cabin with the top of the marks toward the left side of the fuselage and on the side surfaces of the fuselage below the window lines as near the cockpit as possible.

Airships (dirigibles and blimps) must have markings displayed on the upper surface of the right horizontal stabilizer and on the undersurface of the left horizontal stabilizer, with the top of the marks toward the leading edge, and on each side of the bottom half of the vertical stabilizer.

Spherical balloons must display markings in two places diametrically opposite each other and near the maximum horizontal circumference of the balloon.

Nonspherical balloons must have markings displayed on each side of the balloon near the maximum cross section and immediately above either the rigging band or the points of attachment of the basket or cabin suspension cables.

Sizes of Nationality and Registration Marks

Except for special cases discussed in FAR Part 45, the height of letters and numbers for fixed-wing air-craft must be equal and at least 12 in [30.48 cm] high.

Marks for airships and balloons must be at least 20 in [50.8 cm] in height. The marks on the bottom of the fuselage or cabin of a rotorcraft must be four-fifths as high as the fuselage is wide or 20 in [50.8 cm] in height, whichever is less. The marks on the sides of the rotorcraft cabin must be a minimum of 2 in [5.08 cm] but need not be more than 6 in [15.24 cm] in height.

The width of the characters in the markings must be two-thirds the height of the characters except for the number 1 and the letters M and W. The number 1 must have a width one-sixth the height and the letters M and W may be as wide as they are high. The thickness of the strokes or lines in the letters and numbers must be one-sixth the height of the characters. The spaces between the characters must not be less than one-fourth the width of the characters. For 12-in-[30.48-cm-] high letters, this equals a width of 8 in [20.32 cm] for all letters except W and M, which are 12 in [30.48 cm] wide, and a 1, which is 2 in [5.08 cm] wide. The space between characters is 2 in [5.08 cm].

Laying Out Letters and numbers

Letters and numerals for the markings on aircraft are formed as shown in Fig. 4-7. The illustration is

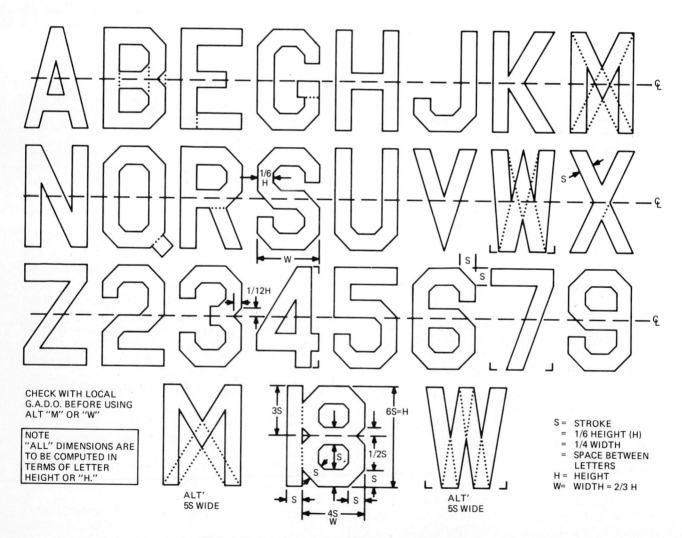

FIG. 4-7 Letters and numerals for aircraft marking.

not intended to show the correct interval or spacing between the characters but merely to indicate the type and proportions of approved characters.

To lay out numerals or letters, a master template, such as the one shown in Fig. 4-8, can be constructed. With this device it is possible to lay out any letter or numeral. For some letters or numerals it is necessary to do a small amount of additional construction, but the template will provide the principal guidelines. Some people find that an additional template measuring 2 by 12 in [5.08 by 30.48 cm] aids in making the diagonal lines of the characters. This guide can be made of Plexiglas or sheet metal.

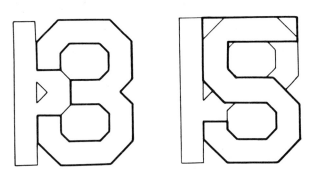

FIG. 4-8   Template for laying out letters and numerals.

When laying out the registration letters and numbers on the side of the aircraft, light guide lines are drawn with chalk, and after the letters are outlined properly, paint trim tape is laid along the lines and masking and covers are placed over the rest of the aircraft to protect it from overspray. The masked-off characters are wiped with a soft cloth containing solvent to remove chalk marks and any oil or other contaminants. The surface is then sprayed with the appropriate color.

Stencils for laying out registration numbers are available as are decals. The stencils are faster than laying out the number by hand, but additional expense is involved. The use of decals may be warranted if spraying is not practical or if the numbers are only temporary. Decals also result in additional expense.

● REVIEW QUESTIONS

1. Describe the operation of a spray gun.
2. What are the adjustments on a spray gun?
3. What type of devices should be used to clean the holes in the air cap of a spray gun?
4. How is the shape of the spray pattern adjusted?
5. What will happen if the spray gun is moved in an arc when spraying instead of parallel to the surface?
6. How is the viscosity (consistency) of the sprayed material checked?
7. Give causes of distorted spray patterns.
8. What are the functions of an *air transformer*?
9. How often should the air transformer be drained?
10. Describe a paint *pressure tank*.
11. What cleaning procedures should be followed after completing a finishing job with pressure tank equipment?
12. Describe a *wash primer*.
13. Why is an epoxy-type primer supplied in two parts?
14. What are the advantages of urethane and polyurethane enamels?
15. For what reasons are finishing coats applied to metal surfaces?
16. Why is it necessary to avoid contact between dissimilar metals in an aircraft structure?
17. What condition can lead to *filliform corrosion*?
18. Why should relative humidity be comparatively high when wash primers are applied?
19. What is meant by a *conversion coating*?
20. What is the value of an etch for a metal surface before finishing?
21. What preparation should be made before finishing new aluminum?
22. Explain and describe paint-stripping procedures and precautions.
23. Why should a metal surface be thoroughly cleaned with solvent after stripping?
24. What precaution must be taken when stripping an airplane with bonded metal seams?
25. Describe the preparation of a two-part wash primer.
26. What are the principal reasons for applying a primer before finishing a metal surface?
27. What precaution must be taken with respect to time when using two-part primers or finishes?
28. Describe the preparation and application of a two-part epoxy primer.
29. What precautions must be taken in the application of a lacquer finish over other finishes?
30. How is restoration of a high-visibility finish accomplished?
31. Describe a procedure for the touchup of damaged finishes.
32. List safety precautions for the operation of an aircraft finishing facility.
33. What markings are required on any aircraft registered in the United States?
34. Describe the form and size of the characters used for official aircraft markings.
35. Where are markings required on different types of aircraft?
36. What devices may be used to assist in the laying out of aircraft markings?
37. What causes runs or sags to appear when using a spray gun?
38. What type of tape should be used when laying out aircraft paint trim lines?
39. What is the total length of the area on which the N-number N1234M is installed if 12-in [30.48-cm] letters are used?

5 WELDING EQUIPMENT AND TECHNIQUES

The aircraft mechanic, particularly in the general aviation field, in some cases is called upon to repair important aircraft parts by welding. If one is ignorant or careless, the weld may fail and cause the destruction of an airplane and everyone aboard. It is, therefore, essential to be well acquainted with the approved welded repairs, techniques for welding, and the operation of welding equipment. The mechanic who is not sufficiently skilled to perform an airworthy welded repair should call upon a qualified welder to do the work. In any event, the mechanic must be able to inspect and evaluate the quality of any welded structure or welded repair.

Welding Processes

Welding is a process used for joining metal parts by either fusion or forging. **Forge welding** is the process used by a blacksmith when heating the ends of wrought iron or steel parts in a forge fire until the ends are in a plastic state and then uniting them by the application of mechanical pressure or blows. **Fusion welding** is the process used by welders in the aircraft and other industries whereby enough heat is applied to melt the edges or surfaces of the metal so that the molten (melted) parts flow together, leaving a single, solid piece of metal when it cools. In both forge and fusion welding, the process is described as a **thermal metal-joining process** because heat is required. Only the fusion type of welding is used in aircraft work.

The principal types of aircraft fusion welding are **oxyacetylene (or oxy-fuel) welding,** commonly called **gas welding, electric-arc welding,** and **inert-gas arc welding.** A variety of special welding processes and techniques have been developed, but these are generally employed only in the manufacturing of parts.

Gas welding and **inert-gas arc welding** are the most frequently used of all welding processes in aviation. Gas welding produces heat by burning a properly balanced mixture of oxygen and acetylene or other fuel as it flows from the tip of a welding torch. Since the temperature of an oxyacetylene flame at the tip point of the torch may be from 5700°F [3149°C] to 6000°F [3316°C], it is apparent that it is hot enough to melt any of the common metals.

Another gaseous fuel that produces almost as much heat as acetylene is a mixture of methylacetylene and propadiene stabilized. This fuel is safer than acetylene because it does not become unstable at any operating pressure. It is sold under the trade name of MAPP by Airco Welding Products.

The heat required for the fusion of metal parts can be produced by an electrical current. Electric welding includes **electric-arc welding, electric-resistance welding** and inert-gas arc welding. In **electric-arc welding,** the heat of an electric arc is used to produce fusion of the parts by melting the edges of the parts being joined and the end of the welding electrode and then allowing the molten metal to solidify in a welded joint. The arc is formed by bringing together two conductors of electricity, the edges being joined, and the electrode, and then separating them slightly. **Electric-resistance welding** is a process whereby a low-voltage high-amperage current is brought to the work through a heavy copper conductor offering very little resistance to its flow. The parts are placed in the path of the current flow where they set up a great resistance to it. The heat generated by the current flow through this resistance is great enough to fuse the parts at their point of contact. **Spot welding** is a commonly used version of electric-resistance welding.

Inert-gas arc welding is a process in which an inert gas such as helium or argon blankets the weld area to prevent oxidation of the heated metal. This is particularly important in welding titanium, magnesium, stainless steels, and other metals that are easily oxidized when subjected to melting temperatures. Tungsten inert-gas (TIG) welding and metal inert-gas (MIG) welding are commonly used forms of inert-gas welding. The names **Heliarc** and **Heliweld** are trade names that have been used to designate tungsten inert-gas welding when helium is used as the inert gas.

Oxyacetylene-Welding Equipment

The oxyacetylene-welding equipment may be either portable or stationary. A **portable apparatus** can be fastened on a hand truck or cart and pushed around from job to job. It consists of one cylinder containing oxygen; one cylinder containing acetylene; acetylene and oxygen pressure regulators complete with pressure gauges and connections; a welding torch with a mixing head, tips, and connections; two lengths of colored hose, with adapter connections for the torch and regulators; a special wrench; a pair of welding goggles; a safety flint and file gas lighter; and a fire extinguisher. Figure 5-1 shows a portable welding outfit.

Stationary equipment, as shown in Fig. 5-2, is used where several welding stations are located close to each other and the stations can be supplied with gases through a manifold system. The oxygen and acetylene

142

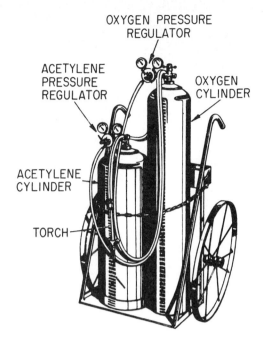

FIG. 5-1 A portable welding outfit.

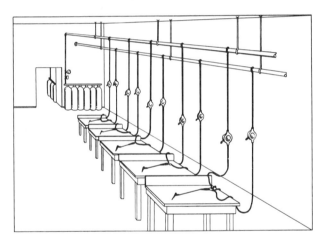

FIG. 5-2 A stationary welding system with manifolds.

cylinders, located in areas separate from each other for safety, feed into the appropriate manifold through a master regulator. The master regulator sets the maximum pressure for the manifold. Each work station has a line regulator so that the welder can set the pressure as necessary for the particular task. In some shops, the acetylene does not come from cylinders. Instead, it is piped directly from an acetylene generator, an apparatus used for producing acetylene gas by the reaction of water upon calcium carbide.

When an acetylene manifold is used, flashback protection is required between the manifold and the acetylene bottles to prevent a flashback flame from reaching the bottles. This flashback protection can be provided by a hydraulic (water) protective device or by a dry-type device. The hydraulic device feeds acetylene into a water tank below the surface of the water, and the acetylene must bubble up through the water to enter the manifold system. Any flashback would be blocked by the water. The dry-type device uses the pressure generated by the flashback to press a sleeve over ridge on a mandrel, as shown in Fig. 5-3. This

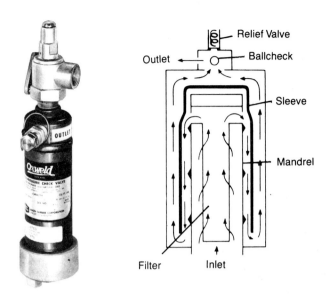

FIG. 5-3 A dry-type flashback protection device. (*Linde Div., Union Carbide Corp.*)

blocks the flow of gas from the inlet. Excess pressure is vented out through the relief valve.

Acetylene

Acetylene is a flammable, colorless gas with a distinctive odor that is easily detected, even when strongly diluted with air. It is a compound of carbon and hydrogen having the chemical symbol C_2H_2, which means that two atoms of carbon are combined with two atoms of hydrogen.

When acetylene is mixed with air or oxygen, it forms a highly combustible gas. Since the range of explosive mixtures is very wide (from 97 percent air with 3 percent acetylene to 18 percent air with 82 percent acetylene), it can be very dangerous unless carefully handled. It has a flame spread of 330 ft/s [99 m/s]. To prevent it from burning back to the source of supply during welding, the acetylene, when mixed with air or oxygen, must flow from the torch at a velocity greater than the flame spread, or the absorption of heat by the torch tip must be sufficient to prevent the flame from entering the tip.

Under low pressure at normal temperature, when free from air, acetylene is a stable compound; however, when it is compressed in an empty container to a pressure greater than 15 psi [103 kPa], it becomes unstable, and at 29.4 psi [202.74 kPa] pressure it becomes self-explosive, and only a slight shock is required to cause it to explode even when it is not mixed with air or oxygen.

Although this gas is highly explosive, it is shipped in cylinders under high pressure with a high degree of safety. This is possible because the manufacturers place a porous substance inside the acetylene cylinder and then saturate this substance with **acetone**, which

143

is a flammable liquid chemical that absorbs many times its own volume of acetylene. A cylinder containing a correct amount of acetone can be charged to a pressure of more than 250 psi [1724 kPa] with safety, under normal conditions of handling and temperature.

Acetylene is a manufactured gas. An **acetylene generator** is a device in which acetylene is produced by the direct combination of carbon and hydrogen, resulting from the reaction of water upon calcium carbide.

Calcium carbide is a compound of carbon and calcium (CaC_2), which is prepared by fusing limestone and coal in an electric furnace. When calcium carbide comes into contact with water, it absorbs the water rapidly and decomposes. The carbon combines with the hydrogen to form acetylene, and the calcium combines with the oxygen to form calcium hydrate (slacked lime). One pound [0.4536 kg] of pure, clean carbide will supply about 5 ft^3 [141 L] of acetylene, but it is customary to figure only 4½ ft^3/lb [127.35 L per 0.454 kg] to allow for impurities. Acetylene gas is sold by weight and contains 14.5 ft^3/lb [411 L per 0.454 kg].

An acetylene cylinder is a welded steel tank provided with a valve in the neck for attaching the pressure regulator and drawing off the acetylene. The cylinder is filled with a porous material saturated with acetone. Safety-fuse plugs, which release the gas from the cylinder in case of fire, are provided. Since the escaping gas is flammable, the holes in the plug are made so small that they will not allow the flame to burn back into the cylinder.

Acetylene cylinders are available in several sizes, holding up to 300 ft^3 [8.5 m^3] of gas at a maximum pressure of 250 psi [1724 kPa]. The cubic feet of acetylene gas in a cylinder may be found by weighing the cylinder and subtracting the tare weight stamped on the cylinder from the gross weight; that is, the weight of an empty cylinder is subtracted from the weight of a charged cylinder. The difference is in pounds; hence this figure is multiplied by 14.5 to obtain the number of cubic feet in the cylinders. Figure 5-4 is an exterior view of an acetylene cylinder.

Oxygen

Oxygen is a tasteless, colorless, odorless gas that forms about 23 percent by weight and about 21 percent of volume of the atmosphere.

Oxygen is an extremely active element. It combines with almost all materials under suitable conditions, sometimes with disastrous results. For example, grease and oil are highly combustible in the presence of pure oxygen; hence it is important to avoid bringing pure oxygen into contact with oil or grease. Such a mixture of oxygen and oil can produce a violent explosion. There are recorded cases of welders being killed by turning a stream of pure oxygen into a can of grease. Even grease spots on clothing may lead to explosions if they are struck by a stream of oxygen.

Oxygen is necessary to make acetylene burn at a temperature high enough to melt metal in welding. In technical language, oxygen supports the combustion of the gas used in producing the welding flame.

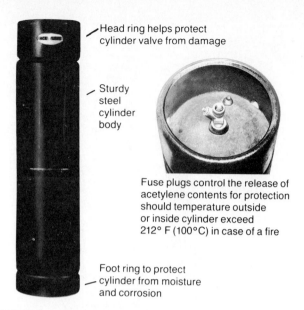

Head ring helps protect cylinder valve from damage

Sturdy steel cylinder body

Fuse plugs control the release of acetylene contents for protection should temperature outside or inside cylinder exceed 212° F (100°C) in case of a fire

Foot ring to protect cylinder from moisture and corrosion

FIG. 5-4   An acetylene cylinder. (*Linde Div., Union Carbide Corp.*)

The standard cylinder for storing and shipping oxygen gas for welding and cutting purposes is a seamless, steel, bottle-shaped container like the one shown in Fig. 5-5. It is made to withstand exceedingly high pressures. Although an acetylene cylinder is normally charged at a pressure of 250 psi [1724 kPa] at a temperature of 70°F [21.1°C], an oxygen cylinder is initially charged at the plant to a pressure of 2200 psi [15,171 kPa] at a temperature of 70°F [21.1°C].

Two sizes of oxygen tanks are generally available. The standard size is a cylinder having a capacity of 220 ft^3 [6.23 m^3] and the small cylinder has a capacity of 110 ft^3 [3.11 m^3]. Since the weight of oxygen is 0.08926 lb/ft^3 [1.43 kg/m^3], 11.203 ft^3 [0.32 m^3] equal 1

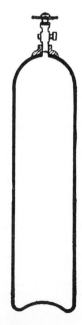

FIG. 5-5   An oxygen cylinder.

lb [0.4536 kg]. To find the quantity of oxygen in a cylinder, simply subtract the weight of an empty cylinder from the weight of a charged cylinder, and multiply the number of pounds by 11.203 to obtain the cubic feet of oxygen in the cylinder.

Figure 5-6 shows the construction of an oxygen-cylinder valve assembly. A safety device (bursting disk) is contained in the nipple at the rear of the valve and consists of a thin copper-alloy diaphragm.

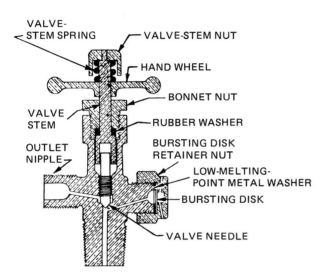

FIG. 5-6   An oxygen cylinder valve.

The valve in Fig. 5-6 is a needle type. The valve stem is in two parts, and the two sections are connected by a slide joint that allows the lower section to move up and down in opening and closing the valve. The lower section is threaded and contains a valve-seat needle made of Monel metal. Connected to the upper section of the stem is a hand wheel that is used for operating the valve. A rubber or synthetic compression washer around the valve stem provides a gastight seal, and is held in place with a bonnet nut. When the valve is completely open, the lower section exerts pressure against the upper section of the stem and compresses the gasket, thus preventing leakage.

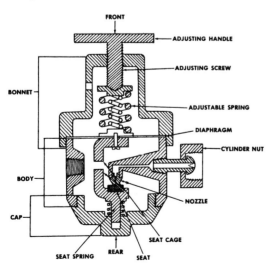

FIG. 5-7   A single-stage pressure regulator.

When the cylinder is not in use, the valve is covered with a protector cap. This is an important feature in preventing the valve from being broken in handling.

Acetylene and Oxygen Regulators

Acetylene and **oxygen regulators** are mechanical instruments used to reduce the high pressure of the gases flowing from their containers and to supply the gases to the torch at a constant pressure and volume as required by the torch tip or nozzle.

Almost all regulators are either of the nozzle or the stem type and are available for either single-stage or two-stage pressure reduction. Figure 5-7 is a sectional drawing of a single-stage pressure regular. Figure 5-8 shows how a single-stage pressure regulator works. Figure 5-9 is a sectional drawing of a two-stage pres-

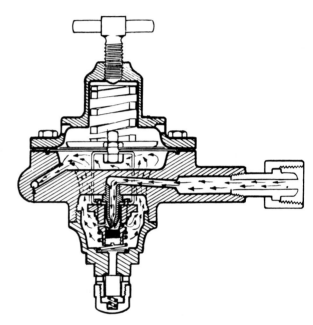

FIG. 5-8   Operation of a single-stage pressure regulator.

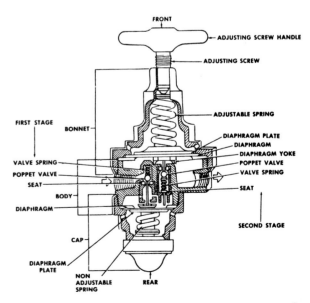

FIG. 5-9   Cutaway drawing of a two-stage pressure regulator.

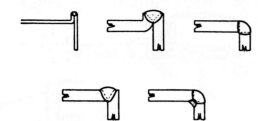

FIG. 5-27 Good corner joints.

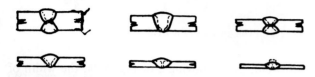

FIG. 5-28 Properly formed butt joints.

experience, poor technique, or carelessness. Figure 5-29 shows a large number of faults commonly found in the weld-metal formation of various joints. Any weld which has an appearance similar to one of the drawings in this illustration should be rejected.

Chemical Changes Produced by Welding

A **chemical change** occurs when a substance is added to the metal or taken away. The great heat of the oxyacetylene flame will cause the loss of one or more of the chemical constituents of a piece of metal if the flame is turned on the metal for any length of time; this loss usually will result in a reduction of such physical properties of the metal as tensile strength, ductility, and yield point. Also, if some element is added to the metal by the welding process, or if there is some material change in one or more of the chemical constituents, the change will usually lower the strength of the metal.

Physical Changes Produced by Welding

A **physical change** is a change of any kind that takes place without affecting the chemical structure of a metal. Some of the physical changes most important in welding are changes in the melting point, heat conductivity, and rate of expansion and contraction.

The melting point is the degree of temperature at which a solid substance becomes liquid. Pure metals have a melting point, but alloys have a **melting range**. Welders should know the approximate melting points

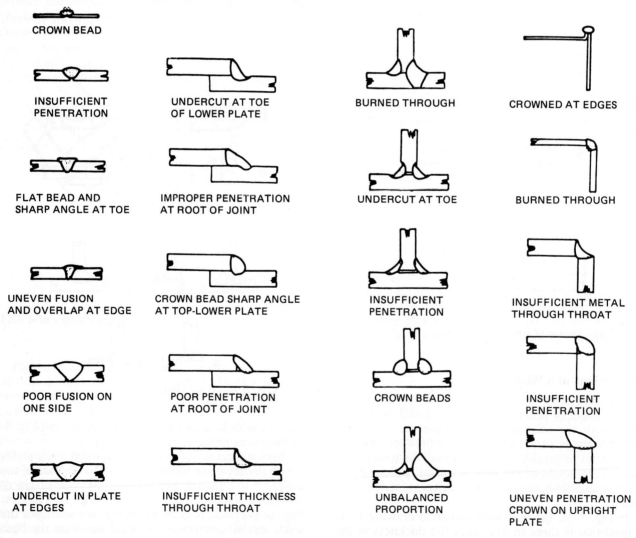

CROWN BEAD

INSUFFICIENT PENETRATION

UNDERCUT AT TOE OF LOWER PLATE

BURNED THROUGH

CROWNED AT EDGES

FLAT BEAD AND SHARP ANGLE AT TOE

IMPROPER PENETRATION AT ROOT OF JOINT

UNDERCUT AT TOE

BURNED THROUGH

UNEVEN FUSION AND OVERLAP AT EDGE

CROWN BEAD SHARP ANGLE AT TOP-LOWER PLATE

INSUFFICIENT PENETRATION

INSUFFICIENT METAL THROUGH THROAT

POOR FUSION ON ONE SIDE

POOR PENETRATION AT ROOT OF JOINT

CROWN BEADS

INSUFFICIENT PENETRATION

UNDERCUT IN PLATE AT EDGES

INSUFFICIENT THICKNESS THROUGH THROAT

UNBALANCED PROPORTION

UNEVEN PENETRATION CROWN ON UPRIGHT PLATE

FIG. 5-29 Common faults in welding.

of the various metals with which they work because they must often weld together metals which have widely different melting points. If a metal includes an alloyed element, the melting point is lowered; hence the melting points given in tables for alloyed metals vary according to the proportion of alloying elements present, and should be considered with this fact in mind.

Expansion is an increase in dimensions (length, width, thickness) of a substance under the action of heat. If a metal structure is unevenly heated, there will be an uneven expansion, and this will produce distortion (warping) and possibly breakage. On the other hand, if the temperature is raised progressively throughout the whole mass of the object, the action is uniform and there is no distortion or breakage.

Applying this to welding, it can be understood that if the heat from the welding flame is concentrated at one point on a metal object, the metal in the heated area tends to expand where the heat is applied, and the portion which opposes this expansion may be distorted, cracked, or severely strained.

Tables giving the properties of metals usually include the coefficients of expansion. A **coefficient of expansion** of any metal is the amount that the metal will expand per inch for each degree rise in temperature. For example, aluminum has a coefficient of expansion of 0.00001234 while steel has a coefficient of expansion of 0.00000636. This shows that aluminum expands more than steel for each degree rise in temperature. In both these cases, the coefficient refers to a rise of 1°F [0.5556°C].

To apply this knowledge, a simple formula can be used. Let A represent the length in inches of the piece of metal, B the temperature in degrees Fahrenheit, and C the coefficient of expansion. Then, expansion in inches = $A \times B \times C$. Thus, if a piece of aluminum is 1 in [2.54 cm] long and is raised in temperature 1°F [0.5556°C], and its coefficient of expansion is 0.00001234, then the expansion is $1 \times 1 \times 0.00001234$, or 0.00001234 in [0.0000312 cm].

Contraction is the shrinking of a substance when cooled from a high temperature. It is the reverse of expansion. Unless there is some restraint, materials contract as much when cooled as they expanded when they were heated, assuming that the temperature is uniform throughout.

In a trussed frame, whether it is in an airplane or a bridge, there is a restriction of the free movement of the metal parts. When such restrictions are present and the metal is malleable (capable of being worked into shape by hammering, rolling, or pressing), warping will take place. If the metal is brittle, it will usually crack.

If the piece of metal is "open," that is, if no obstructions or restrictions hinder its free expansion and contraction, there is no danger of its being damaged from expansion and contraction. An example of open metal occurs in the case of an ordinary bar of metal, a length of unattached tubing, or some similar detached piece of metal.

If the metal is "closed," as in Fig. 5-30, there is danger from expansion and contraction. The bar that

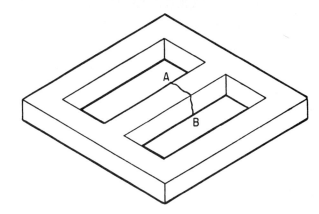

FIG. 5-30 Welding a closed section required heating of the entire closed area.

was formerly free and unattached is now the center section in Fig. 5-30, and it is fastened rigidly to a solid frame. If the break marked with the letters A and B in Fig. 5-30 is welded, provision must be made for expansion and contraction. Since the crosswise and lengthwise members of the frame are rigid, they do not permit the ends of the bar in the center to expand; hence the only place where expansion can take place while the metal is heated during the welding process is at the point of the weld. When this portion begins to cool, the center bar contracts and shortens, while the frame in which it is placed refuses to surrender to the inward pull of the ends of the center bar. Warping occurs along the line of weld, or possibly a break occurs.

To avoid this damage, a trained welder heats the whole object before attempting to weld the break in the center piece. The whole object expands equally, pulling apart the edges of the break. The welder makes the weld and allows the object to cool. All of it cools to the same extent, contracts equally, and suffers neither warpage nor breakage. Figure 5-31 shows examples of shrinkage in welded metal objects.

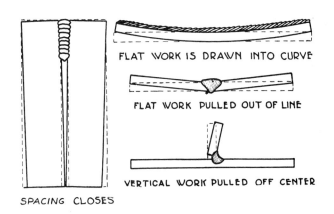

FIG. 5-31 Shrinkage of metal caused by welding.

Conductivity

Conductivity is the physical property of a metal that permits the transmission of either an electric current or heat through its mass. The **rate of conductivity** is the speed at which a metal body will transmit either an electric current or heat through its mass. The rate of conductivity varies among metals. Radiation (heat loss) influences both the rate and the distance of heat conductivity. Thus, metals which are good heat conductors may be poor radiators, and those which are good radiators may be poor conductors.

In welding, it should be understood that a considerable amount of heat is carried away from the point of application and is lost to the surrounding atmosphere. For this reason, metals which have a high conductivity require more heat in welding that those with a low conductivity, other things being equal.

Another thing to remember in welding is that the higher the conductivity, the more extensive and the hotter will become the heated area around the weld. Therefore more expansion can be expected with metals of high conductivity, other things being equal.

Effect of High Temperatures on Strength of Metals

Some metals have absolutely no strength, or almost no strength, when they are raised to extremely high temperatures. In some cases, this temperature may be far below the melting point of the metal. For example, aluminum alloys, brass, bronze, copper, cast iron, and certain alloy steels become very brittle at high temperatures near their melting points. If such metals are strained while at these high temperatures, they will break, or check, in the area that has been heated.

For example, the melting point of aluminum is 1218°F [659°C]. At 210°F [99°C], it has 90 percent of its maximum strength; at 400°F [204°C], it has 75 percent; at 750°F [399°C], it has 50 percent; at 850°F [454°C], it has 20 percent; and at 930°F [499°C], it has only 8 percent of its maximum strength. Yet at 930° [499°C] it is still far below the melting point.

● SETTING UP THE WELDING EQUIPMENT

In order for efficient welding to take place, the equipment must be set up properly. This will allow a proper torch flame to be created, afford the maximum safety for the operator, and prevent unnecessary wear or damage to the equipment. In this discussion, the general procedures used for a portable system are addressed, but the basic procedures discussed are also applicable to a stationary system. When working with specific welding equipment, always follow the equipment manufacturer's procedures and recommendations.

Assembling the System

The first step in setting up portable welding apparatus is to fasten the cylinders to the cart, or hand truck. The purpose of this step is to prevent the cylinders from being accidentally pulled or knocked over. The protecting cap that covers the valve on the top of the cylinder is not removed until the welder is ready to make a connection to the cylinder.

The second step in setting up the apparatus is to "crack" the cylinder valves. The welder stands at the

side of, or behind, the cylinder outlet, as shown in Fig. 5-32, and opens the cylinder valve slightly for a moment and then quickly closes it. The purpose of this step is to clear the valve of dust or dirt that may have settled in the valve during shipment or storage. Dirt will cause leakage if it gets into the regulator, and it will mar the seat of the regulator inlet nipple even if it does not actually reach the regulator.

FIG. 5-32 Correct position for the operator when opening the cylinder valve.

The third step is to connect the regulators to the cylinders. The welder uses a tight-fitting wrench to turn the union nut as shown in Fig. 5-33 and makes certain that the nut is tight so that the gas will not leak.

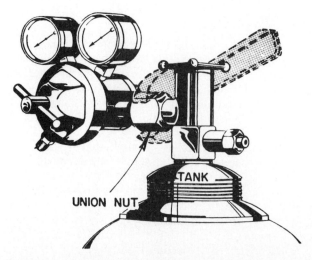

FIG. 5-33 Wrench in position for tightening the union nut.

154

The fourth step is to connect the hoses to their respective regulators. The green hose is connected to the oxygen regulator and the red hose is connected to the acetylene regulator. With the cylinder valves open, the regulator adjustment handles should be turned clockwise a sufficient amount to blow gas through the hoses and clear any dust or dirt. The handles are then turned counterclockwise until there is no pressure on the diaphragm spring and the cylinder valves are closed.

The fifth step is to connect the hoses to the torch, as shown in Fig. 5-34. The acetylene fitting, identified by the groove around the nut, has a left-hand thread and, therefore, will fit only the acetylene fitting on the torch. A tight-fitting wrench should be used to avoid damage to the nuts.

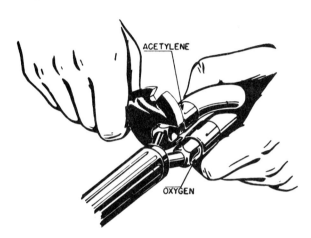

FIG. 5-34 Connecting the gas hose to a torch.

The sixth step in setting up the welding equipment is to test for leaks. This should not be done by using a lighted match at the joints. No open flame should be allowed in the vicinity of welding equipment except for the flame of the torch. There are several ways to test for leaks, but the best method is to apply soapy water to the joints with a brush. Before making this test, the oxygen and acetylene needle valves on the torch are closed. The cylinder valves are opened, and then the regulator adjusting screws are turned to the right (clockwise) until the working gauges show only a low pressure. The brush is dipped in the soap solution, and the solution is spread evenly over the connections. If there is a leak, it is betrayed by a soap bubble.

When finding a leak, the welder should close the cylinder valves and search for the source of trouble. It is generally sufficient to tighten the connecting unit slightly in order to stop the leak. Less common sources of trouble are dirt in the connection, which must be cleaned out, or marred seats or threads in the connection. If the seats or threads are damaged, the connections should be replaced. Having removed the trouble causing a leak, the welder must again test for leaks to be absolutely certain that none exist.

Ordinarily, the welder knows the correct tip size for the work to be done, a small opening for thin metal or a larger opening for thick metal being provided. On the assumption that the apparatus is set up, the next job is to adjust the working pressure of the gases.

Setting the Pressure

Figure 5-32 shows a welder in the correct position for opening the cylinder valve, regardless of whether the cylinder has a regulator attached or not. When a regulator is installed on the cylinder, the operator stands behind or to the side of the regulator and opens the valve slowly. If the regulator is defective, pressure may build up behind the glass and cause it to burst. This would be likely to inflict injury on anyone standing in the area immediately in front of the regulator.

When ready to open the cylinder valves, the welder should open the acetylene cylinder valve about one complete turn and open the oxygen valve all the way, slowly in both cases. If a valve wrench is used on the acetylene valve, this should be left on the valve so that the acetylene flow can be turned off quickly if a flame appears at a fitting or at a hose rupture. Then the welder sets the working pressure for the oxygen and the acetylene by turning the adjusting screw on the regulator to the right (clockwise) until the desired pressure reading is obtained on the gauge. As mentioned before, the exact pressure required for any job primarily depends upon the thickness of the metal, and this determines the size of the welding tip used. Remember, do not allow the acetylene pressure in the hose to exceed 15 psi.

Lighting the Torch

To light the torch, the welder opens the acetylene needle valve on the torch three-quarters of a turn, and then uses the spark lighter to light the acetylene as it leaves the tip. The welder should do this as quickly as possible in order to prevent a large cloud of gas from developing. The flame should be large, very white, and smoky on the outer edges. If the flame produces much smoke, the welder "cracks" the oxygen needle valve very slightly and as soon as the flame appears to be under control, continues slowly to open the oxygen needle valve until a well-shaped bluish-white inner cone appears near the tip of the torch. This cone is surrounded by a second outer cone or envelope which varies in length, depending upon the size of the welding tip being used. This is known as a **neutral flame** and is represented by the upper drawing in Fig. 5-35.

Oxyacetylene Flames

A welding flame is called **neutral** when the gas quantities are adjusted so all the oxygen and acetylene are burned together. Theoretically, 2½ volumes of oxygen are required to burn 1 volume of acetylene in order to produce this neutral flame, but actually it is only necessary to provide 1 volume of oxygen through the torch for 1 volume of acetylene consumed, because the remainder of the required oxygen is taken from the atmosphere. The carbon monoxide and hydrogen gas that come out of the first zone of combustion combine with oxygen from the air to complete the combustion, thus forming carbon dioxide and water vapor.

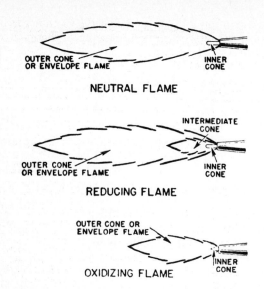

FIG. 5-35 Neutral, reducing, and oxidizing flames.

The neutral flame produced by burning approximately equal volumes of acetylene and oxygen oxidizes all particles of carbon and hydrogen in the acetylene, and it has a temperature of about 6300°F [3482°C]. This neutral flame should have a well-rounded, smooth, clearly defined, blue-white central cone. The outer cone, or envelope, flame should be blue with a purple tinge at the point and edges.

A neutral flame melts metal without changing its properties and leaves the metal clear and clean. If the mixture of acetylene and oxygen is correct, the neutral flame allows the molten metal to flow smoothly, and few sparks are produced. If there is too much acetylene, the carbon content of the metal increases, the molten metal boils and loses its clearness, and the resulting weld is hard and brittle. If too much oxygen is used, the metal is burned, there is a great deal of foaming and sparking, and the weld is porous and brittle.

A neutral flame is best for most metals. However, a slight excess of one of the gases may be better for welding certain types of metal under certain conditions. For example, an excess of acetylene is commonly used with the nickel alloys, Monel and Inconel. On the other hand, an excess of oxygen is commonly used in welding brass.

A **carburizing,** or **reducing,** flame is represented by the middle drawing of Fig. 5-35. This occurs when there is more acetylene than oxygen feeding into the flame. Since the oxygen furnished through the torch is not sufficient to complete the combustion of the carbon, carbon escapes without being burned. There are three flame zones instead of the two found in the neutral flame. The end of the brilliant white inner core is not as well defined as it was in the neutral flame. Surrounding the inner cone is an intermediate white cone with a feathery edge, sometimes described as greenish-white and brushlike. The outer cone, or envelope, flame is bluish and similar to the outer cone, or envelope, flame of the neutral flame.

An **oxidizing flame** is represented by the lower drawing of Fig. 5-35. It is caused by an excess of oxygen flowing through the torch. There are only two cones; but the inner cone is shorter and more pointed than the inner cone of the neutral flame, and it is almost purple. The outer cone, or envelope, flame is shorter than the corresponding portion of either the neutral flame or of the reducing flame, and is of a much lighter blue color than the neutral flame. In addition to the size, shape, and color, the oxidizing flame can be recognized by a harsh, hissing sound, similar to the noise of air under high pressure escaping through a very small nozzle.

The **oxidizing flame** is well-named. It oxidizes, or burns, most metals, and it should not be used unless its use is definitely specified for some particular purpose. Since an oxidizing flame is generally objectionable, the welder must examine the flame every few minutes to be sure of not getting an oxidizing flame. The welder does this by slowly closing the torch oxygen valve until a second cone or feathery edge appears at the end of the white central cone, then opening the oxygen valve very slightly until the second cone disappears.

Figure 5-36 shows a neutral or oxidizing flame with an irregular-shaped outer cone, or envelope, flame produced by an **obstructed tip.** When this flame is discovered, the welder should immediately shut down the welding apparatus and either clean the tip or replace it.

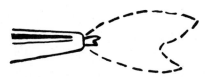

FIG. 5-36 Flame produced by an obstructed tip.

After learning to adjust the flame so that the proportions of oxygen and acetylene are correct, the welder must then learn how to obtain a **soft flame.** This is a flame produced when the gases flow to the welding tip at a comparatively low speed. If the gases flow to the welding tip at a comparatively high speed, under too much pressure, they produce a **harsh flame** that is easily recognized because it is noisy. A harsh flame destroys the weld puddle and causes the metal to splash around the edges of the puddle. It is very difficult to get the metal parts to fuse properly with a flame of this kind.

If the mixture of acetylene and oxygen, and the pressure, are correct, the welder may still fail to obtain a soft neutral flame if the welding tip is dirty or obstructed in any manner. An obstructed welding tip does not permit the gas mixture to flow evenly, and it restricts the source of heat required to melt the metal; therefore, a good weld is very difficult to produce.

If there is any fluctuation in the flow of the gases from the regulators, the mixture will change, regardless of other conditions; hence a good welder watches the flame constantly and makes any necessary adjustments to keep it neutral and soft.

Cleaning the Tip

Small particles of carbon, oxides, and metal can be removed from the tip of a welding torch with a soft copper wire, a drill of the correct size, a tip cleaner manufactured for the purpose, shown in Fig. 5-37, or any other suitably shaped device which will not damage the tip. Care must be taken to maintain a smooth, round orifice through which the gases can emerge.

If the tip becomes worn to the extent that the opening of the orifice flares out or is bell-shaped, the end of the tip should be ground square on a piece of fine emery cloth held flat against a smooth surface. The tip should be held perpendicular to the surface of the emery cloth and moved back and forth with straight strokes.

FIG. 5-37 Tip cleaners. (Linde Div., Union Carbide Corp.)

The outside surface of the tip can be cleaned with fine steel wool to remove carbon, oxides, and particles of metal. After the outside is cleaned, the orifice should be cleaned to remove any material which may have entered.

Backfire and Flashback

A **backfire** is a momentary backward flow of gases at the torch tip, causing the flame to go out and then immediately to come on again. A backfire is always accompanied by a snapping or popping noise. Sometimes the word *backfire* is used loosely to mean a **flashback,** but a true backfire is not as dangerous as a flashback because the flame does not burn back into the torch head and does not require turning off the gases.

There are five common causes of backfires: (1) there may be dirt or some other obstruction in the end of the welding tip; (2) the gas pressures may be incorrect; (3) the tip may be loose; (4) the tip may be overheated; or (5) the welder may have touched the work with the tip of the torch.

If the tip is dirty or obstructed, it is removed and cleaned or replaced. If the gas pressures are wrong, they are adjusted. If the tip is loose, the torch is turned off and the tip tightened. If the tip is overheated, the torch is turned off and allowed to cool. If the tip touches the work, the welder merely avoids repeating the error.

Flashback is the burning back of the flame into or behind the mixing chamber of the torch. Where flashback occurs, the flame disappears entirely from the tip of the torch and does not return. In some instances, unless either the oxygen or the acetylene, or both, are turned off, the flame may burn back through the hose and pressure regulator into the gas supply (the manifold or the cylinder) causing great damage. Flashback should not be confused with **backfire,** as explained before. The welder must always remember that if a flashback occurs, there will be a shrill hissing or squealing, and the flame will burn back into the torch. The welder must quickly close the acetylene and oxygen needle valves to confine the flash to the torch and let the torch cool off before lighting it again. Since a flashback extending back through the hoses into the regulators is a symptom of something radically wrong, either with the torch or with the manner of its operation, the welder must find the cause of the trouble and remedy it before proceeding.

How to Shut Down the Welding Apparatus

The procedure for shutting down the welding apparatus is as follows:

1. Close the acetylene needle valve on the torch to shut off the flame immediately.
2. Close the oxygen needle valve on the torch.
3. Close the acetylene cylinder valve.
4. Close the oxygen cylinder valve.
5. Remove the pressure on the regulators' working-pressure gauges by opening the acetylene valve on the torch to drain the acetylene hose and regulator.
6. Turn the acetylene-regulator adjusting screw counterclockwise (to the left) to relieve the pressure on the diaphragm, and then close the torch acetylene valve.
7. Open the torch oxygen valve, and drain the oxygen hose and regulator.
8. Turn the oxygen-regulator adjusting screw counterclockwise to relieve the pressure on the diaphragm; then close the torch oxygen valve.
9. Hang the torch and hose up properly to prevent any kinking of the hose or damage to the torch.

● GAS WELDING TECHNIQUES

Welding may be considered as both a skill and an art. Expert welders need technical understanding of the processes with which they are working and many hours of practice to develop the manual dexterity necessary to produce a quality weld. Although certificated aircraft mechanics are not always expected to be expert welders, they still need to know a good weld when they see one, and they should be able to perform a satisfactory welding job when it becomes necessary. Furthermore, they should know their own abilities and whether a welding specialist should be called in to do a particular repair job.

Identification of Metals

The mechanic must be able to identify various metals before attempting to weld them so that the proper torch tip, filler rod, and technique required can be determined. In some organizations, metals may be marked with painted bands of different colors on tubes and bars or by means of numbers on sheet stock. Where there are no colored bands or numbers on the metal, three types of tests are commonly used: (1) the **spark test,** (2) **chemical tests,** and (3) the **flame test.**

In the identification of metals by means of the spark test, **ferrous metals** may be recognized by the characteristics of the spark stream generated by grinding with a high-speed grinding wheel. A ferrous metal is one that contains a high percentage of iron. In general, nonferrous metals cannot be identified by a spark test because they do not produce a large shower of sparks and may produce almost none.

In applying the spark test, the most sensible procedure is to obtain samples of various metals and to grind these samples to compare them with the piece of metal being identified. When a known sample produces the same spark characteristics as the unknown piece of metal, identification is accomplished. The characteristics to be observed are (1) the volume of the spark stream, (2) the relative length of the spark stream (in inches), (3) the color of the spark stream close to the grinding wheel, (4) the color of the spark streaks near the end of the stream, (5) the quantity of the sparks, and (6) the nature of the sparks.

In volume, the stream is described as extremely small, very small, moderate, moderately large, and large. The relative length may vary from 2 to 70 in [5 to 177 cm], depending upon the metal. For example, cemented tungsten carbide produces an extremely small volume of sparks and the stream is usually only about 2 in [5.08 cm] long. On the other hand, machine steel produces a large volume and may be about 70 in [180 cm] long. These particular figures apply when a 12-in [30.48-cm] wheel is used on a bench stand. The actual length in each case depends upon the size and nature of the grinding wheel, the pressure applied, and other factors.

In color, the stream of sparks may be described as red, white, orange, light orange, or straw-colored. The quantity of sparks may be described as none, extremely few, very few, few, moderate, many, or very many. The nature of the sparks may be described as forked or fine-and-repeating (exploding sparks). In some cases, the sparks are described as curved, wavy, or blue-white, but in most instances the terms previously given apply.

Some handbooks for welders include tables showing these characteristics of the sparks, but all the terms used to describe the spark stream are only comparative. One person will describe the color as orange, while another person will refer to the same stream of sparks as light orange or even straw-colored. Because of this situation, the use of the known samples saves time and promotes accuracy.

A chemical test for distinguishing between **chrome-nickel corrosion-resisting steel (18-8 alloy)** and **nickel-chromium-iron alloy (Inconel)** should be known by welders. A solution consisting of 10 g cupric chloride dissolved in 100 cm³ hydrochloric acid is used. One drop is applied to the unknown metal sample and allowed to remain on the metal for about 2 min. At the end of this time, three or four drops of water are slowly added with a medicine dropper. The sample is then washed and dried. If the metal is stainless steel, the copper in the cupric chloride solution has been

deposited on the metal, leaving a copper-colored spot. If the sample is Inconel, the spot left is white.

A **flame test** is used to identify **magnesium alloys.** The welding flame is directed on a small sample until the metal is brought to the melting point. If the metal sample is magnesium alloy, it will ignite at once and burn with a bright glow.

Preparation of the Metal

The elements to be welded should be properly held in place by welding jigs, or fixtures, that are sufficiently rigid to prevent misalignment due to expansion and contraction of the heated material. These jigs, or fixtures, must also positively locate the relative positions of the pieces to be welded.

The parts to be welded should be cleaned before welding by sandpapering or brushing with a wire brush or by some similar method. If the members to be welded have been metallized, the surface metal should be removed by careful sandblasting.

All mill scale, rust, oxides, and other impurities must be removed from the joint edges or surfaces to prevent them from being included in the weld metal. The edges, or ends, to be welded must be prepared so that fusion can be accomplished without the use of an excessive amount of heat.

In addition to cleaning the surfaces, the edges may need to be **beveled** down with a grinding wheel or a file so that they will fuse with the smallest possible amount of heat. Whether or not a welder must bevel the edges is determined by the thickness of the metal. For example, if two pieces of steel 1-in [2.54-cm] thick are to be welded, the welder should **bevel,** or "V out," the joint in order to prepare the metal so that the weld will extend all the way through.

It is apparent that the use of too much heat will burn the metal. In addition, an excessive amount of heat will radiate from the weld into the base metal and will cause it to expand at first and to contract later; this will result in warping if the metal is "soft" or in cracking if the metal is brittle.

Holding the Torch

Figure 5-38 shows one method for holding the torch when welding light-gauge metal. In this method, the

FIG. 5-38   Holding the torch for welding light metal.

torch is held as one might hold a pencil. The hose drops over the outside of the wrist, and the torch is held as though the welder were trying to write on the metal.

Figure 5-39 shows how the torch can be held for welding heavier work. In this method, the torch is held as one would hold a hammer; the fingers are curled underneath and the torch balanced easily in the hand so that there is no strain on the muscles of the hand. A good way to describe the grip of the torch is to say that it should be held like a bird, tight enough so that it cannot get away but loose enough so it will not be crushed.

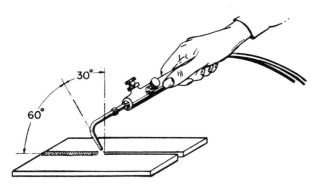

FIG. 5-39 Holding the torch for welding heavy metal.

Forehand Welding

Forehand welding, sometimes called **forward welding,** is a welding technique in which the torch flame is pointed forward in the direction the weld is progressing. In other words, it is pointed toward the unwelded portion of the joint, and the **rod** is fed in from the front of the torch, or flame. Figure 5-40 shows how this is done.

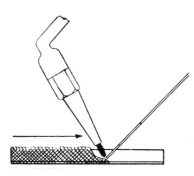

FIG. 5-40 Forehand welding.

The torch head is tilted back from the flame to allow it to point in the direction that the weld is progressing. The angle at which the flame should contact the metal depends upon the type of joint, the position of the work, and the kind of metal being welded, but the usual angle is from 30 to 60°.

This forehand, or forward, technique must not be confused with the backhand, or backward, technique shown in Fig. 5-41 and explained in detail later in this chapter. The two techniques are distinctly different.

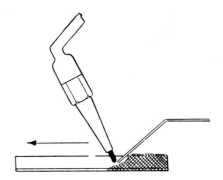

FIG. 5-41 Backhand welding.

When forehand welding, filler rod is added to the pool of melting metal in front of the torch flame. The angle of the rod in relation to the torch must vary for different operations, but it is always necessary to add it to the weld by holding the end of the rod down into the molten pool of base metal formed by the fusing of the joint edges. If the rod is held above the pool and permitted to melt and drop into the weld, impurities floating on the surface of the molten metal will be trapped and a poor joint will be produced.

When the rod is used, it can be kept straight, or it can be bent to form a right angle near the end, as shown in Fig. 5-42.

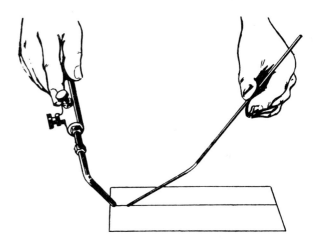

FIG. 5-42 Welding rod bent to facilitate application.

The welding torch is brought down until the white cone of the flame is about ⅜ in [3.175 mm] from the surface of the base metal. It is held there until the flame melts a small puddle of metal. The tip of the rod is then inserted in this puddle, and as the rod melts the molten pool is gradually worked forward.

Backhand Welding

Backhand welding, sometimes called **backward welding,** is a technique in which the flame is directed back toward the finished weld, away from the direction the weld is progressing, and the rod is fed in from the back of the torch, or the flame. This is the method illustrated in Fig. 5-41. Figure 5-43 also illustrates this

159

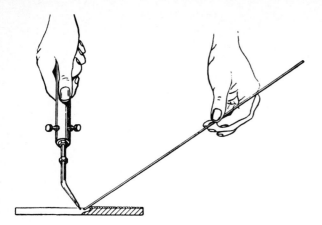

FIG. 5-43   Backhand welding technique.

technique and shows that the torch flame is pointed toward the finished weld (the shaded part of the bar) at an angle of about 60° to the surface of the work. The welding rod is added *between* the flame and the finished weld. The flame is moved back and forth across the seam with a semicircular motion, thus breaking down the edges and the side walls of the base metal in order to fuse them to the necessary depth. In this backhand technique, the semicircular motion is directed so that the base of the arc falls toward the finished weld. Thus, in welding a seam like that in Fig. 5-43, the welder uses a right-to-left, or counter-clockwise, motion.

Whether the forehand or the backhand technique is used, the end of the filler rod is always held in the pool and given a slight alternating or back-and-forth rocking movement as metal is added from the rod to the pool. This movement of the rod must not be made too energetically. It must be controlled so that the melted metal from the pool is not shoved over onto the metal which is not yet hot enough to receive it.

The backhand technique is preferred by most welders for metals having a heavy cross section. The metal being welded may be held in any position except for welding seams that run vertically. By using the backhand technique, the large pool of melting metal that must be kept up at all times is more easily controlled, and the required depth of fusion in the base metal is easier to obtain.

Torch Motions

The welder may use either the **semicircular motion** shown in Fig. 5-44 or the continuous **circular motion** shown in Fig. 5-45. Regardless of the motion, the welder keeps the motion of the torch as uniform as possible in order to make smooth even-spaced ripples.

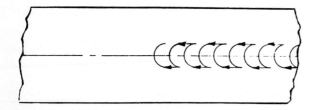

FIG. 5-44   Semicircular welding motion.

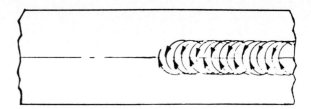

FIG. 5-45   Circular welding motion.

These **ripples** are the small, wavelike marks left on the surface of the completed weld by the action of the torch and welding rod.

A very slight circular motion of the torch is preferred in welding very thin material because the thin metal heats rapidly. Using a slight circular motion of the torch allows the welder to travel along the work faster and avoid burning holes in the metal.

Figure 5-46 shows the use of the forward, or forehand, technique in welding thin-walled tubing or light-gauge metal. The torch is held so that it is inclined at an angle of from 50 to 60° to the surface of the work. Notice that the filler rod is being held so that it is added to the little pool of molten metal in front of the torch flame.

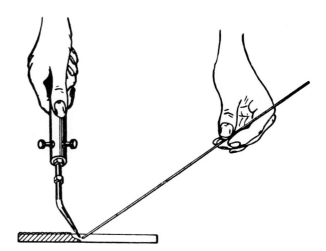

FIG. 5-46   Forehand technique used in welding thin-walled metal.

● WELDING POSITIONS

The four **welding positions** are **flat-position welding, vertical-position welding, horizontal-position welding,** and **overhead-position welding.** The welder must be able to make a good weld in any one of these four positions. A **welding position** refers to the plane (position) in which the work is placed for welding.

Two of the terms refer to welding the top or bottom surface of a work in a horizontal plane (flat work); overhead position is used when the underside of work is welded and flat position when the topside of work is welded. The other two refer to welding work in a vertical plane but make a distinction according to the direction of the line of weld. Thus horizontal position is used when the line runs across from side to side; vertical position when the line runs up and down. The

line of weld is simply the path along which the weld is laid.

Figures 5-47 to 5-49 illustrate the four positions as seen from different viewpoints.

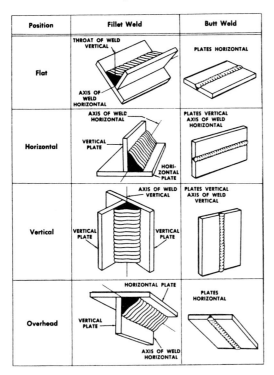

FIG. 5-47   The four positions for welding.

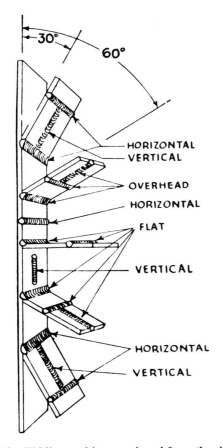

FIG. 5-48   Welding positions as viewed from the side.

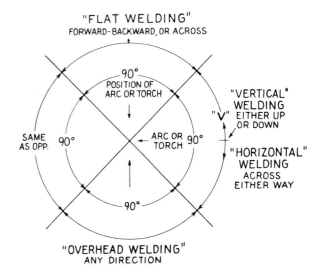

FIG. 5-49   Torch directions for different welding positions.

Flat-Position Welding

The **flat position** is the position used when the work is laid flat or almost flat and welded on the topside with the welding torch pointed downward toward the work. Thus, if a weld is made with the parts to be welded laid flat on the table, or inclined at an angle less than 45°, it is designated as being flat. The weld may be made in this position by the forehand or by the backhand technique, depending upon the thickness of the metal. The seam runs horizontally.

Vertical-Position Welding

The **vertical position** is the position used when the line of the weld runs up and down (vertically) on a piece of work laid in a vertical, or nearly vertical, position. The welding torch is held in a horizontal, or almost horizontal, position. Thus, when the parts are inclined at an angle of more than 45°, with the weld running vertically, it is described as a vertical weld. The weld should be made from the bottom with the flame pointed upward at an angle of from 45 to 60° to the seam for welding in this position. The rod is added to the weld in front of the flame as it is in ordinary forehand welding. Figure 5-50 shows how the filler rod is added to the weld in front of the flame while making a weld in the vertical position.

Horizontal-Position Welding

The **horizontal position** is the position used when the line of weld runs across (horizontally) on a piece of work placed in a vertical, or almost vertical, position; the welding torch is held in a horizontal, or almost horizontal, position. Thus, when a weld is made with the parts in a vertical position, or inclined at an angle of more than 45° with the seam running horizontally, it is called a **horizontal** weld. The seams in this horizontal position may be welded by either the forehand or the backhand technique; in either case, the flame should point slightly upward in order to aid in keeping the melting metal from running to the lower side of the seam. The welding rod should be added to the weld at the upper edge of the zone of fusion, since it

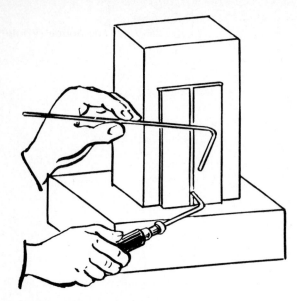

FIG. 5-50   Adding rod when making a vertical weld.

dissipates some of the heat and lowers the temperature enough to help in holding the melting metal in the proper place. Figure 5-51 shows the hands of the welder holding the torch and the rod in this position.

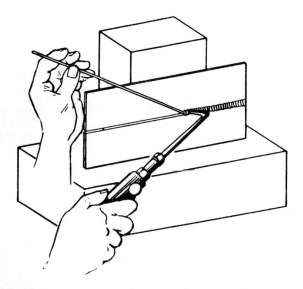

FIG. 5-51   Positions of hand and torch for a horizontal weld.

Overhead-Position Welding

The **overhead position** is the position used when work is flat (horizontal), or almost flat, and is welded on the lower side with the welding torch pointed in an upward direction toward the work. Thus, when a weld is made on the underside of the work with the seam running horizontally, or in a plane that requires a flame to point upward from below, it is described as an overhead weld.

Either the forehand or the backhand technique can be used in welding seams in an overhead position. In either case, the flame must be pointed upward and

held at about the same angle as it is for welding in a flat position. The volume of flame used for overhead welding should not be permitted to exceed that required to obtain a good fusion of the base metal with the filler rod. Unless the welder avoids creating a large pool of melting metal, the metal will drip or run out of the joint, thus spoiling the weld. Figure 5-52 shows a welder's hands holding the rod and torch correctly for this type of weld.

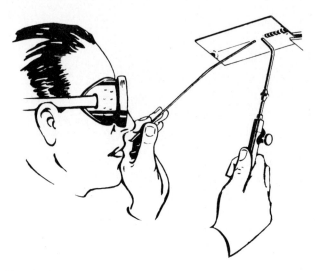

FIG. 5-52   Positions of hands and torch for an overhead weld.

● TYPES OF JOINTS

A **joint** is that portion of a structure where separate base-metal parts are united by welding. The word **weld** is often used to refer to a **joint**. For example, a **butt weld** is a welded butt joint. The word **seam** is often used to refer to a welded joint, especially in a case of tanks and containers.

Five different types of joints are used to weld the various forms of metal. These are (1) butt joints, (2) tee joints, (3) lap joints, (4) corner joints, and (5) edge joints.

Butt Joints

A **butt joint** is a joint made by placing two pieces of material edge to edge in the same plane so that there is no overlappng. It is called a **butt joint** because the two edges, when joined, are abutted together.

Butt joints are used in welding to join all kinds of metal forms, such as sheet, bar, plate, tube, and pipe; in aircraft welding, however, butt joints are not generally used for joining tubing, because such joints are not strong enough for aircraft purposes.

Figure 5-53 shows **flange butt joints.** These can be used for sheet metal up to 0.0625 in [1.59 mm] thick. The edges to be welded are turned up to 80 or 90°, from one to three times the thickness of the metal, and the flanges are melted down and fused together to form the weld. Since the flanges supply enough metal to fill the seam, a filler rod is not used.

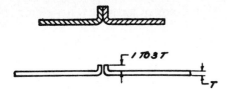

FIG. 5-53 Flange butt joints.

Figure 5-54 shows two drawings of a **plain butt joint.** This joint can be used for thicknesses up to ⅛ in [3.175 mm] when the weld is made with the oxyacetylene flame. Where the thickness is greater, other types of welding are used. It is necessary to use a filler rod when a plain butt joint is formed by gas welding in order to obtain a sufficiently strong weld.

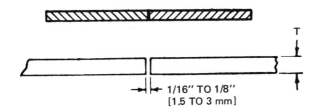

FIG. 5-54 A plain butt joint.

Figure 5-55 includes four drawings that show how the edges of metals with heavy cross sections should be prepared. The four types are the single V, the double V, the single U, and the double U.

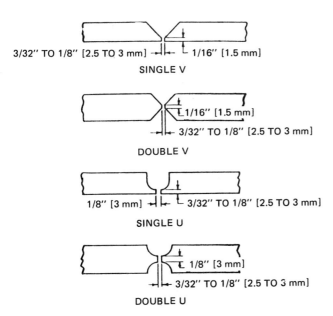

FIG. 5-55 Four ways in which edges of metal can be prepared for welding.

The joint with a single-V bevel is known as a **single-V butt joint.** It is used for metal ⅛ to ½ in [3.175 to 12.70 mm] thick where the joint can be welded from one side only. The joint with a double-V bevel is used for solid shapes that can be welded from both sides.

The angle of bevel for both of these joints should be 45° for the oxyacetylene process. The double-V joint requires about one-half the amount of welding rod required for the single V, but it is more expensive to prepare.

The single-U butt joint and the double-U butt joint are widely used for solid shapes of great thickness because they require less welding rod than the V-type joints.

All butt joints are suitable for any kind of load stresses if they are made so that there is full penetration, good fusion, and proper reinforcement.

Tee Joints

Figure 5-56 shows how the metal is prepared for various types of tee joints. A **tee joint** is a form of joint made by placing the edge of one base part on the surface of the other base part so that the surface of the second part extends on either side of the joint in the form of a T. Filler rod is used with tee joints.

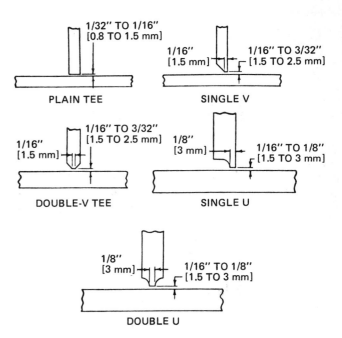

FIG. 5-56 Preparation of metal for welded tee joints.

The **plain tee joint** is acceptable for most metal thickness in aircraft work and also may be used for heavier metals where the weld can be located so that the load stresses will be transverse (perpendicular) to the longitudinal dimensions of the weld. The only preparation required is cleaning the surface of the horizontal member and the end of the vertical member. The weld is then made from each side with penetration into the intersection. This results in a **fillet weld** having a general triangular cross-sectional shape. (Any weld which joins two parts which are at right angles to each other may be called a **fillet weld.** Corner joints, lap joints, and edge joints also require fillet welds.)

The **single-V tee joint** is widely used for plates and shapes where the joint can be welded from only one side and where the thickness is ½ in [12.70 mm] or less. This joint is acceptable for normal loading if there is full penetration with fusion into both members.

The **double-V tee joint** is used for welding heavy plates and shapes where the joint can be welded from both sides. It is suitable for all types of loading if the weld metal is fused together at the end of the branch member and if the penetration exists in both members.

The single-U joint is used for plates 1 in [2.54 cm] thick or thicker, where the weld can be made from only one side. The double-U joint is suitable for all plates and other solid shapes of heavy cross section where the joint can be welded from both sides. Generally, the mechanic will not be required to use the single-U and double-U joints because most aircraft welding is done on plates thin enough for the other types of joints.

Lap Joints

Figure 5-57 shows three types of **lap joints.** A weld securing a lap joint is called a **lap weld.** The lap joint is a joint made by lapping one base over the other, and is used in plate, bar, tubing, and pipe. These joints are widely used in the construction of articles fabricated from plate and sheet metal (flat, wrought metals), but a lap joint is not as efficient as a butt joint for distributing load stresses. The lap joint is commonly used where the primary load stress will be transverse (perpendicular) to the line of weld.

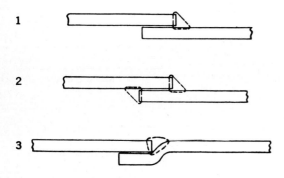

FIG. 5-57   Three types of lap joints.

The **single-welded lap joint,** shown in drawing 1 of Fig. 5-57, is used for sheet, plate, and structural shapes where the loading is not severe. The same type of joint can be used for telescope splices in steel tubing, and in that application it is better than a butt joint.

The **double-welded lap joint,** shown in drawing 2 of Fig. 5-57, is used for sheet and plate where the strength required is greater than that which can be obtained when a single weld is used. This type of joint provides for great strength, when properly made, in all ordinary thicknesses of sheet and plate.

The **offset,** or **joggled, lap joint,** shown in drawing 3 of Fig. 5-57 is used for sheet and plate where it is necessary to have a lap joint with one side of both plates or sheets in the same plane; that is, on one side the surface is flush. This type of joint provides for a more even distribution of load stresses than either the single or double lap joint, but it is more difficult to prepare.

In all three types of lap joints, a welding rod must be used.

Edge Joints

Figure 5-58 shows types of edge joints for plate and sheet. An **edge joint** is a form of joint made by placing a surface of one base part on a surface of the other base part in such a manner that the weld will be on the outer surface planes of both parts joined. This type of joint is not used where a high joint strength is required, but it is widely used for fittings composed of two or more pieces of sheet stock where the edges must be fastened together. This use is acceptable because the joint is not subjected to high stresses. Edge joints can be used also for tanks that are not subjected to high pressures. In Fig. 5-58, drawing 1 shows a joint used for thin sheets, and drawing 2 shows a joint adaptable to thick sheets.

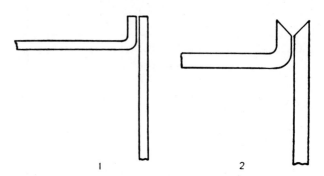

FIG. 5-58   Edge joints for plate and sheet.

Edge joints are usually made by bending the edges of one or both parts upward at a 90° angle, placing the two bent ends parallel to each other, or placing one bent end parallel to the upright unbent end, and welding along the outside of the seam formed by the two joined edges.

Corner Joints

A **corner joint** is made by placing the edge of one part at an angle on an edge or a surface of another part so that neither part extends beyond the outer surface of the other, the structure resembling the corner of a rectangle.

Figure 5-59 shows three types of corner joints for plate and sheet. The **closed type of corner joint,** shown in drawing 1 of Fig. 5-59, is used on the lighter-gauge metals, where the joint is subjected to moderate stresses only. It is made without adding much, if any, filler rod because the edge of the overlapping sheet is melted and fused to form the bead.

The **open type of corner joint,** shown in drawing 2 of Fig. 5-59, is used on heavier sheet for the same

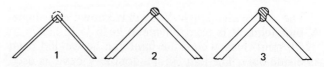

FIG. 5-59   Three types of corner joints.

purpose as a closed type of corner joint. It is made by fusing the two edges at the inside corner and adding enough welding rod to give a well-rounded bead of weld metal on the outside. If such an open joint is required to bear a fairly heavy load, an additional weld must be made on the inside corner to provide the necessary strength, as shown in drawing 3 of Fig. 5-59, where a light concave bead has been laid on the inside.

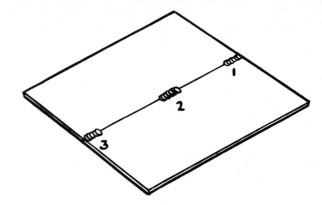

FIG. 5-60   Stagger, or skip, welding.

● WELD QUALITY

The properly completed weld should have the following characteristics:

1. The seam should be smooth and of a uniform thickness.

2. The weld should be built up to provide extra thickness at the seam.

3. The weld metal should taper off smoothly into the base metal.

4. No oxide should be formed on the base metal at a distance of more than ½ in [12.7 mm] from the weld.

5. The weld should show no signs of blowholes, porosity, or projecting globules.

6. The base metal should show no sign of pitting, burning, cracking, or distortion.

How to Reduce Distortion and Residual Stress

To reduce distortion and residual stress produced by welding, the expansion and contraction of the metal should be controlled. The distortion is especially noticeable in welding long sections of thin sheet metal because the thinner the metal being welded, the greater the distortion.

Four things a welder can do to control the action of those forces which adversely affect the finished weld are the following: (1) Distribute the heat more evenly; (2) put a smaller amount of heat into the weld; (3) use special jigs to hold the metal rigidly in place while it is being welded; and (4) provide a space between the edges of the joint. The nature of each welding job determines whether only one or all four of these methods should be used.

In discussing expansion and contraction, the even distribution of heat was explained. Preheating the entire metal object before welding sets free the stored-up forces and permits a more uniform contraction when the welding job is completed.

Putting a smaller amount of heat into a weld is difficult for a beginner, although an experienced welder can estimate accurately the amount of heat required. This is an example of the skill that comes from experience. One of the "tricks of the trade" is to use a method called **stagger welding**, shown in Fig. 5-60. The operator welds briefly at the beginning of the seam, skips to the center, then jumps to the end, comes back to where the first weld ended, and repeats this staggered process until the weld is finished.

Another term for stagger welding is **skip welding**, which is defined as a welding technique in which al-

ternate intervals are skipped in the welding of a joint on the first pass and completed on the second pass or successive passes. The purpose is to prevent any one area of the metal from absorbing a great deal of heat, thus avoiding buckling and the tendency toward cracking.

When a welder uses special jigs to hold the metal rigidly in place while it is being welded, excessive movements of the metal are hindered and the severe distortion resulting from expansion and contraction is prevented.

A **jig** is a rigid structure or mechanism, either wood or metal, which holds parts while they are being worked on (drilled, sawed, welded, etc.) before assembly, or which holds the component parts while they are being assembled or disassembled. Therefore, a welding jig is simply a contrivance that holds the metal sections rigidly in place while a seam is welded. Jigs are fastened tightly, but not so tightly that they will hinder the normal expansion and contraction of the metal at the ends of the joints. If a jig is fastened too tightly, it causes internal stresses in the metal that lower its ability to carry heavy loads.

The fourth method for reducing distortion and residual stresses is the **careful spacing** of the pieces to be welded. Figure 5-61 shows how a **tapering space** is allowed between the pieces that are to be welded together. This tapering space is a distance equal to the thickness of the metal for every foot of seam length. For example, if a welder is to make a joint between two pieces of metal which are both ½ in [12.7 mm] thick and 1 ft [30.45 cm] long, the space between them should be ½ in at the ends opposite the starting point. If these same two pieces were 2 ft [60.96 cm] long, then the space at the wider ends would be twice as much, or 1 in [2.54 cm].

Figure 5-62 shows a method of providing for con-

FIG. 5-61   Tapering space to allow for metal contraction.

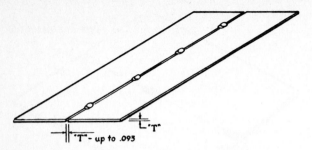

FIG. 5-62　Tack welding to hold metal in position.

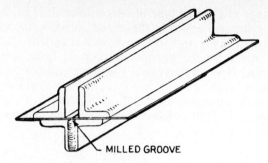

FIG. 5-65　Use of a welding jig.

traction in butt joints. The edges are set parallel and tack-welded. A **tack weld** is one of a series of small welds laid at intervals along a joint to hold the parts in position while they are being welded. This method is used for making short, straight seams or the curved seams on tubing, cylinders, tanks, etc.

Figure 5-63 shows how the edges for butt joints may be set and spaced, the amount of spacing depending upon the kind of metal being welded, usually ranging from ⅛ to ⅜ in [3.18 to 9.53 mm] for each foot [30.48 cm] of the seam length. This method is better for flat sheets and longitudinal seams of cylindrical shapes.

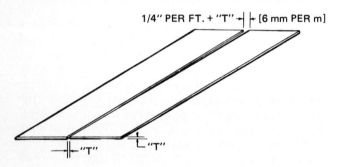

FIG. 5-63　Spacing of metal parts for welding.

Figure 5-64 is a welding jig for sheet-metal butt joints. It is useful for both flat sheets and longitudinal seams of cylindrical shapes.

Figure 5-65 shows a jig consisting of four pieces of angle iron, used for welding butt joints in sheet metal. The angles for supporting the work on the lower side

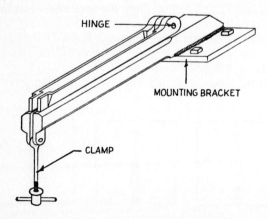

FIG. 5-64　A welding jig for sheet-metal butt joints.

may be bolted or welded together. A recess of ⅟₃₂ to ³⁄₆₄ in [0.794 to 1.191 mm] deep and from ½ to ¾ in [12.7 to 19.05 mm] wide is machined in the center. This is labeled "milled groove" in the illustration.

The jig shown in Fig. 5-66 is used for welding corner joints. It consists of three pieces of angle iron. The edge of the piece used to support the work on the lower side is ground- or machined-off to provide about ⅟₁₆-in [1.59-mm] clearance for the joint. This enables the fusion to penetrate the base metal all the way through at this point. These jigs are held in place on the metal by means of C-clamps.

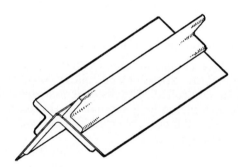

FIG. 5-66　Welding jig for corner joints.

In welding plate stock where the shape of the part permits, the butt joints may be set up as illustrated in Fig. 5-63 but if the shape of the work is such that the joint edges must be parallel, either the skip-welding procedure, previously explained, or the **step-back method** should be used for welding the joint. Either of these methods will lower the heat strains because the heat is more evenly distributed over the whole length of the seam, thus causing the expansion and contraction to be uniform.

The **step-back method,** also called the **back-step method,** is a welding technique in which the welder welds and skips intervals between tack welds with each successive pass until the joint is completely welded. As each pass is completed, the welding is "back-stepped" or "stepped-back" to the next unwelded interval near the beginning of the weld. Figure 5-67 illustrates the step-back method. This should be studied and compared with the stagger welding shown in Fig. 5-60 and a more detailed drawing of this same "skip" method shown in Fig. 5-68.

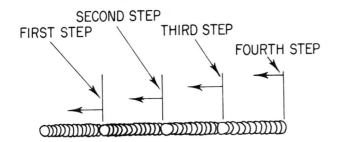

FIG. 5-67   The step-back method of welding.

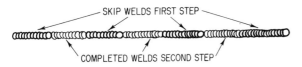

FIG. 5-68   Details of skip welding.

Figure 5-69 shows that when it is not possible to design a jig for the work, and the metal is held in such a manner that normal expansion and contraction are restrained, the edges of the sheet may be bent up at the joint, as shown in the upper drawing, or a bead may be formed in each sheet parallel to the seam, ⅝ to 1 in [1.59 to 2.54 cm] from the joint, as shown in the lower drawing of Fig. 5-69. Normally, either of these forms will straighten sufficiently on cooling to relieve the strain of the weld. However, if for any reason bends of this type are not practical, the welder may place chill plates or a cold pack of wet nonflammable material on the metal near the joint and parallel to the seam to reduce the flow of heat and the expansion that follows.

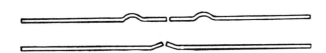

FIG. 5-69   Use of bend or bead to restrain distortion.

Figure 5-70 shows the welding procedure for reducing stresses in tee joints. The welding in this case alternates from one side of the vertical member to the other. If the plate is heavy, the tee joints are heated to a dull red on the opposite side from the side on which the weld is being made. A separate torch is used for this purpose. If done carefully, this heating causes a uniform expansion on both sides of the plate and produces an even contraction that prevents the parts from being pulled out of their correct alignment.

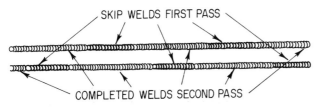

FIG. 5-70   Reducing stresses in welding a tee joint.

There are several methods for providing for the expansion in the welding of castings. The one selected in each case depends upon the type, kind, and shape of the casting and also on the nature of the break being welded. The welder who has mastered the principles and techniques already described should have no trouble in selecting the correct procedure for each job. For example, the entire casting might require preheating to a temperature that will prevent expansion strains on one job, while on another job it might be enough to apply local preheating, that is, heat applied only in the vicinity of the welding zone.

When preheating is applied, the parts preheated must be cooled evenly and slowly. Depending upon the design and other factors, the opposing parts or sections may be preheated to relieve the strains that come from welding. Mechanical devices, such as screw jacks, may be used as an additional precautionary measure. Figure 5-71 shows the application of methods of providing for expansion in the welding of rectangular castings, and Fig. 5-72 shows the method of providing for expansion in the welding of circular castings.

When parts are fabricated or repaired by welding, there is usually some stress which remains. This stress should be relieved to obtain the full strength of the

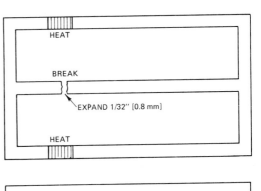

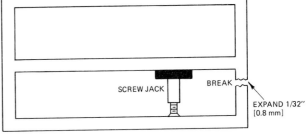

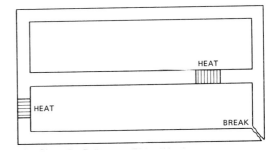

FIG. 5-71   Providing for expansion in welding rectangular castings.

167

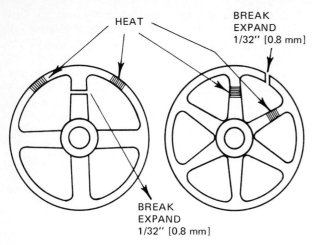

FIG. 5-72 Providing for expansion in welding circular castings.

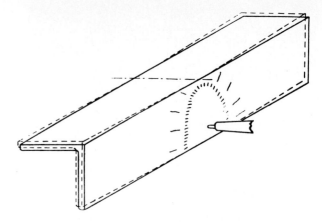

FIG. 5-74 Use of heat to straighten an angle section.

weld and the base metal. **Heat treatment,** which is discussed in considerable detail in *Aircraft Basic Science,* is the most reliable method of relieving stress, provided that the part can be heated in a furnace to the stress-relieving temperatures and then cooled slowly and evenly. For example, aluminum and aluminum alloys require a temperature of from 700 to 800°F [371 to 427°C]; gray cast iron, 900 to 1000°F [482 to 538°C]; nickel-chromium-iron alloy (Inconel), 1400°F [760°C]; carbon steels up to 0.45 percent carbon, 1000 to 1200°F [538 to 649°C]; chrome-molybdenum-alloy steel, 1150 to 1200°F [621 to 649°C]; and chrome-nickel stainless steel (18-8), from 1150 to 1200°F [621 to 649°C].

Local heating with the welding flame may be used to relieve or eliminate distortion in structures fabricated of steel tubing, angle iron, and similar materials by bringing the metal to a red heat at the proper locations. Figure 5-73 shows a tube pulled out of alignment by weld shrinkage being given this treatment, and Fig. 5-74 shows an angle iron pulled out of alignment by weld shrinkage being given a similar application of local heat.

Practices to Avoid

Welds should not be filed to present a smooth appearance. Filing will usually weaken the weld.

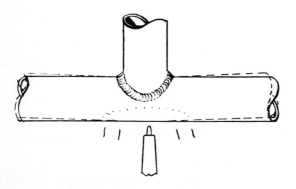

FIG. 5-73 Application of heat to straighten a tube.

Welds must not be filled with solder, brazing metal, or any other filler.

When it is necessary to reweld a joint, all the old weld metal must be removed before proceeding with the new weld.

A new weld should never be made over an old weld if it can be avoided. The heat of rewelding increases the brittleness of the weld material and causes it to lose strength.

A weld should never be made over a joint that was previously brazed. Brazing metal (brazing filler rod) penetrates and weakens the steel.

Simple Tests for Welds

There are many reliable tests for welds, but at this stage of training, the mechanic should be able to apply one or two very simple tests to judge progress. One of these is usually called the **bend test.** The welder allows the metal to cool slowly, and then picks it up with a pair of pliers and clamps the metal in a vise with the weld parallel to the top of the jaws of the vise and slightly above the top of the vise, as shown in Fig. 5-75. The welder strikes the top of the metal with a hammer so that the metal is bent along the line of the weld. The weld should be bent in on itself, that is, bent so the bottom of the weld is in tension and the top is in compression. If the weld breaks off very sharply and shows a dull, dirty break and the presence of blowholes, the weld is unsatisfactory. If the weld has been made properly, the metal will not break off short. Instead, it is distorted under the blows of the hammer until it forms an angle of at least 90° without cracking under repeated hammering.

A **visual inspection** is another simple test. The welder examines the smoothness of the bead, the amount of reinforcement (making certain that the seam is at least 25 to 50 percent thicker than the base metal), and the cleanliness of the completed weld. The contour should be even. It should extend in a straight line, and its width and height should be consistent. No pits should be present.

It should be understood that a clean, smooth, fine-appearing weld is not necessarily a good weld, because it may be dangerously weak inside. However, the opposite is true; that is, if the weld is rough pitted,

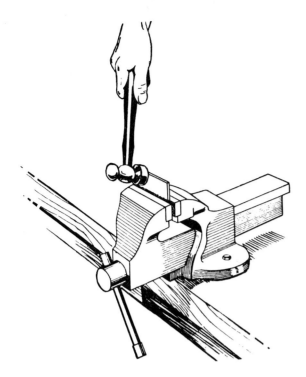

FIG. 5-75 Bend test for a weld.

uneven, and dirty looking, the weld is almost always unsatisfactory inside.

Gas-Welding Aluminum, Magnesium, and Titanium

It is strongly recommended that the appropriate type of inert-gas welding be employed when aluminum, magnesium, or titanium parts must be joined by welding. These metals and their alloys oxidize very rapidly when heated, and it is difficult to protect the surfaces from oxidation in gas welding even though flux is liberally applied.

When magnesium reaches a sufficiently high temperature, it burns with a very bright flame. Care must, therefore, be taken to avoid a situation where magnesium shavings, particles, or scraps can be ignited.

Titanium, in the molten state, reacts rapidly with oxides and oxygen. When being welded, it must be completely protected from oxygen.

Pure aluminum and some of its alloys can be gas welded. Designations for weldable aluminum and alloys are 1100, 3003, 4043, and 5052. Alloys 6053, 6061, and 6151 can be welded if provision is made for heat treating after welding.

Aluminum should be welded with a soft neutral flame or a slightly reducing flame when either acetylene or hydrogen is used for the welding gas. This assures that there will be no oxygen in the flame to combine with the aluminum.

Before starting to weld aluminum, the edges to be welded must be thoroughly cleaned. Solvents can be used to remove grease, oils, or paint. The solvent must be such that it evaporates completely dry and leaves no residue. Oxides can be removed from the areas to be welded with fine emery paper. Care must be taken not to scratch the aluminum outside the weld areas because this will cause corrosion.

The preparation of the edges of aluminum sheet or plate which is to be gas welded depends upon the thickness of the material. For thicknesses of 0.060 in [1.52 mm] or less, a 90° flange can be formed on the edges. The height of the flange should be about the same as the thickness of the metal. A cross-section drawing of flange edges is shown in Fig. 5-76 (a). If the metal is between 0.060 and 0.190 in [1.52 and 4.83 mm], the penetration of the weld is improved by notching the metal as shown in Fig. 5-76 (b). This practice also aids in preventing distortion of the metal due to expansion. If the metal thickness is greater than 0.190 in [4.83 mm], it should be beveled and notched as shown in Fig. 5-76 (c).

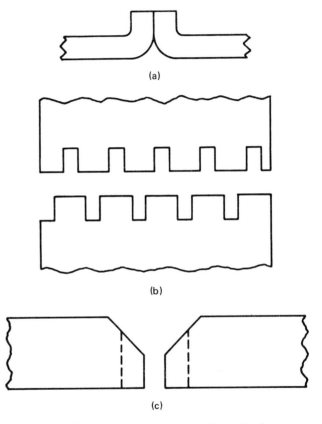

FIG. 5-76 Edge preparation for gas-welding aluminum sheet and plate.

When the metal edges have been cleaned and prepared as explained, aluminum welding flux should be applied. If possible, the flux should be brushed on both the flame side and the opposite side of the metal. The welding rod should also be dipped in the flux. After completion of the weld the flux should be removed completely by washing. If flux remains, it will cause corrosion.

As mentioned previously, the flame used for aluminum welding should be soft (mild). This type of flame is produced by adjusting the torch as low as possible without causing the tip to pop. The flame is applied to the edges of the work at an angle of approximately 45° until the aluminum begins to melt. It is difficult to tell when the aluminum has reached melting temperature because its appearance does not change appreciably. Touching the tip of the welding rod to the heated area will reveal when the aluminum is beginning to soften. If the aluminum becomes too hot, it will drop away and form a hole in the material. If the flame is too harsh, this condition will be aggravated. In any case, only an experienced welder should attempt to perform this type of work.

If possible, the material to be welded should be supported in a jig or fixture which will reduce distortion as much as possible. The material should be preheated before starting the weld by passing the torch over the entire area surrounding the weld. Care must be taken not to overheat the material because doing so will change the structure of the metal and reduce its strength.

The welding of magnesium with butt joints is accomplished in a manner similar to the welding of aluminum. (The butt weld is generally the only type of weld made with magnesium when using oxyacetylene equipment.) The edges to be welded should be cleaned and the oxides removed. Solvents are used to remove oil or grease, and fine emery cloth or paper can be used to remove the oxides.

Edge preparation of sheet magnesium differs from that of aluminum because magnesium alloys cannot be bent sharply without cracking. For sheet magnesium alloy with thickness of 0.040 in [1.02 mm] or less, the edges should be bent up in a curve as shown in Fig. 5-77 (a). For sheet thicknesses from 0.040 to 0.125 in [1.02 to 3.18 mm], the edges of the metal are left square with a space of 0.0625 in [1.59 mm] between the edges of the sheets to be welded. For magnesium plate with thicknesses between 0.125 and 0.250 in [3.18 and 6.35 mm], the edges should be beveled as shown in Fig. 5-77 (c). The bevel on each edge is approximately 45°, making an included angle of 90°. A space is allowed between the sheets as shown. for magnesium plate more than 0.250 in [6.35 mm] in thickness, the edges are beveled as for the thinner plate; however, the space between the edges is increased to 0.125 in [3.18 mm].

The welding rod used with magnesium alloys must be of the same alloy as the material being welded and should be available from the manufacturer of the alloy. A protective coating is applied to the magnesium alloy welding rod to protect it from corrosion. This coating must be removed before the rod is used in welding.

The experienced welder will usually develop the most satisfactory techniques for welding magnesium, based on experience. The weld may be made in much the same way as for aluminum, or the tip of the welding rod may be kept in the center of the molten pool as the weld continues. It is recommended that the weld be made in one continuous pass unless oxidation takes place. In this case, the welding must be stopped and all the oxide removed before continuing.

To prevent distortion, the edges of the joint should be tack welded at intervals of 0.5 to 3 in [12.7 to 76.2 mm], depending upon the shape and thickness of the metal. Distortion which does occur can be straightened with a soft face mallet while the metal is still hot.

Completed welds should be allowed to cool slowly to the level where the material can be handled. Then the weld should be scrubbed clean with a stiff brush and water to remove the flux. After this the part should be soaked in hot water to dissolve and remove any traces of flux not removed by brushing. After soaking, the part should be treated by immersion in an approved acid bath to neutralize alkalinity, then rinsed in fresh water and dried as quickly as possible. Clean, bare magnesium will corrode rapidly unless given a treatment to provide a corrosion-resistant chemical coating. One such treatment is accomplished with an approved chromic-acid solution. Another treatment that is suitable for many magnesium alloys is the dichromate treatment. This involves boiling the magnesium in a solution of sodium dichromate after an acid pickle bath. This treatment is effective for corrosion prevention and provides a good base for primers and finishes. It can be used for all magnesium alloys except those containing thorium.

● ELECTRIC-ARC WELDING

The term **electric-arc welding,** also referred to as **stick-electrode** welding, is used here to denote the standard arc process which utilizes an electrode filler rod and is generally employed for welding heavy steel. This method requires a special generator to produce a low-voltage, high-amperage current for the arc. The power supply may be an electric, motor-driven generator, an engine-driven generator, or a special transformer.

The electric arc is made between the tip end of a small metal wire, called the **electrode,** which is clamped in a holder held in the hand, and the metal being welded. A gap is made in the welding circuit by holding the tip of the electrode 1/16 to 1/8 in [1.59 to 3.18 mm] away from the work. The electric current jumps the gap and makes an arc which is held and moved along the joint to be welded. The heat of the arc melts the metal. The arc is first caused ("struck") by touching the electrode to the metal, and then the electrode is withdrawn slightly to establish the correct gap across which the arc flows.

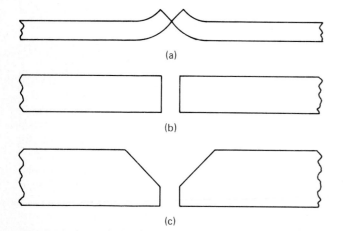

(a)

(b)

(c)

FIG. 5-77 Edge preparation for gas-welding magnesium sheet and plate.

Good welders do more than simply hold the arc. They must, first of all, be able to select the correct size and type of electrode for each job. They must know which machine to use for the job and be able to set the current and voltage controls properly. They must be able to manipulate the electrode and arc to make a satisfactory weld under varying conditions. In addition, welders must have a knowledge of joint preparation, positioning the work, distortion, and many other factors which enter into the final result of a good weld. They must be skilled in both the mechanics and craft of welding. Nearly anyone can "stick two pieces of metal together," but becoming a good welder requires study, training, and practice.

The Welding Circuit

The operator's knowledge of arc welding must go beyond the arc itself to include how to control the arc, and this requires a knowledge of the welding circuit and the equipment which provides the electric current used in the arc. Figure 5-78 is a diagram of the welding circuit. The external circuit begins where the electrode cable is attached to the welding machine and ends where the ground cable is attached to the welding machine. When direct-current, straight-polarity power, is used, the current flows through the electrode cable to the electrode holder, through the holder to the electrode, and across the arc. From the work side of the arc, the current flows through the base metal to the ground cable and back to the welding machine. The circuit must be complete for the current to flow, which means that it is impossible to weld if the cables are not connected to the machine or to either the electrode or the work. All connections must be firm so the current can flow easily through the entire circuit.

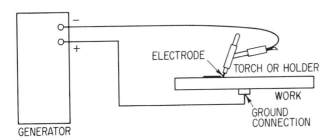

FIG. 5-78 An arc-welding circuit.

The several types of welding machines include motor generators, engine-driven generators, transformers, rectifiers, and combination transformers and rectifiers. Figure 5-79 illustrates a typical arc-welding power supply. Each type has its place and purpose, but the basic function of each is the same, that is, to provide a source of controlled electric power for welding. This controlled electric power has the characteristic of high amperage at low voltage. The high amperage is required to provide sufficient heat at the arc to melt the metal being welded. The voltage must be low enough to be safe for handling and yet high enough to maintain the arc. The welding machine permits the operator to control the amount of current used. This, in turn, controls the amount of heat at the arc. Some welding machines permit the operator to select either a forceful or soft arc and to control its characteristics to suit the job.

Welding Arc

The action which takes place in the arc during the welding process is illustrated in Fig. 5-80. The "arc stream" is seen in the middle of the picture. This is the electric arc created by the current flowing through air between the end of the electrode and the work. The temperature of this arc is from 6000 to 11 000°F [3315° to 6090°C] which is more than enough to melt the metal. The arc is very bright, as well as hot, and cannot be looked at with the naked eye without risking painful, though temporary, injury. It is, therefore, essential that the operator wear a suitable protective hood like the one shown in Fig. 5-81.

The arc melts the plate, or base, metal and actually digs into it, even as the water flowing through a nozzle on a garden hose digs into the earth. The molten metal forms a pool or "crater" and tends to flow away from the arc. As it moves away from the arc, it cools and solidifies. A slag forms on top of the weld to protect it during cooling. The slag comes from the flux coating on the electrode.

Arcs for welding are produced by different kinds of power supplies and the various types of power produce arcs with different characteristics. The power supply may be designated dcsp, dcrp, or ac. Dcsp means **direct current, straight polarity.** Straight polarity is the condition when the electrode is negative and the base metal or work is positive. Dcrp means **direct current, reverse polarity,** where the electrode is positive. The direction of current will have a pronounced effect on the depth and penetration of the weld.

Ac power, of course, means alternating current. With ac power the order in which the leads from the power source are connected will make no difference.

Electrode or Rod

In preparing to perform arc welding, the operator should seek to determine the best power source and type of welding rod for the welding being done. Very often, however, only one source of power is available, and the only choices the operator has are the direction of welding current and type of rod.

The function of the electrode is much more than simply to carry current to the arc. The electrode is composed of a core of metal rod or wire material around which a chemical coating has been extruded and baked. The core material melts in the arc, and tiny droplets of molten metal shoot across the arc into the pool. The electrode provides filler metal for the joint to occupy the space or gap between the two pieces of the base metal. The coating also melts or burns in the arc and serves several functions. It makes the arc steadier, increases the arc force, provides a shield of smokelike gas around the arc to keep oxygen and nitrogen in the air away from the molten metal, and provides a flux for the molten pool, which picks up impurities and forms the protective slag. The elec-

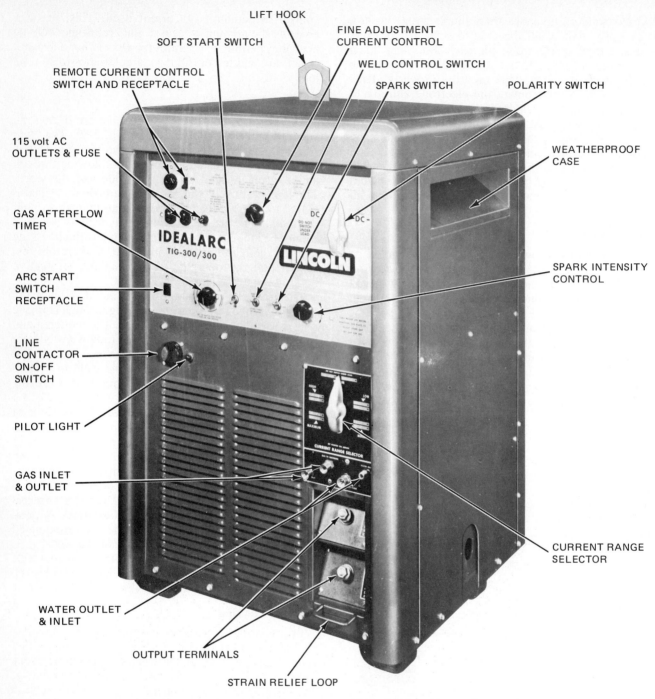

LIFT HOOK

SOFT START SWITCH

FINE ADJUSTMENT
CURRENT CONTROL

WELD CONTROL SWITCH

REMOTE CURRENT CONTROL
SWITCH AND RECEPTACLE

SPARK SWITCH

POLARITY SWITCH

115 volt AC
OUTLETS & FUSE

WEATHERPROOF
CASE

GAS AFTERFLOW
TIMER

ARC START
SWITCH
RECEPTACLE

SPARK INTENSITY
CONTROL

LINE
CONTACTOR
ON-OFF
SWITCH

PILOT LIGHT

GAS INLET
& OUTLET

CURRENT RANGE
SELECTOR

WATER OUTLET
& INLET

OUTPUT TERMINALS

STRAIN RELIEF LOOP

IDEALARC
TIG-300/300

LINCOLN

FIG. 5-79 Power supply unit for arc welding. *(Lincoln Electric Company.)*

trodes to be used in any arc-welding operation depends upon the material being welded, the type of power being used, and the type of weld. The operator must make certain that the rod chosen will supply the strength required of the weld.

● INERT-GAS WELDING

The term **inert-gas welding** describes an electric-arc welding process in which an inert gas is used to shield the arc and molten metal to prevent oxidation and

burning. The process originally employed helium for the gas shield, and the name **Heliarc** was given the process by L-TEC Welding & Cutting Systems. Many improvements have been made in the original process and techniques, and new names have been assigned.

Tungsten inert-gas (TIG) welding is accomplished by means of a torch with an unconsumable tungsten electrode. The electrode is used to sustain the arc and the molten pool of metal. Filler rod is added to the pool to develop the desired thickness of bead. Inert gas, usually argon, is fed to the weld area through the gas cup on the torch. The gas cup surrounds the elec-

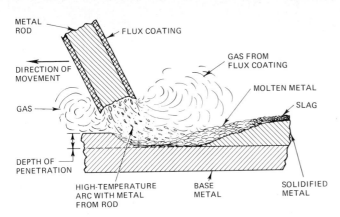

FIG. 5-80   The action in a welding arc.

FIG. 5-81   A welding helmet. *(Linde Div., Union Carbide Corp.)*

trode and directs the gas in a pattern to prevent the intrusion of oxygen and nitrogen from the air. Because the gases used with TIG welding are not now limited to inert types, this type of welding has been designated gas tungsten arc (GTA) welding. In some cases it has been found beneficial to mix small amounts of oxygen and other gases with the inert gas to gain the best results.

Another type of inert-gas welding utilizes a metal electrode which melts and is carried into the weld pool to provide the extra thickness desired. This type of weld has been called metal inert-gas (MIG) welding and is also called gas metal arc (GMA) welding. In this type of welding, the metal electrode must be of the same material as the base metal being welded. Since the electrode is consumed in this process, the electrode wire is automatically fed through the torch so that the torch is held a constant distance from the work surface. Carbon dioxide is a commonly used gas for the MIG process.

Advantages of Inert-Gas Welding

Inert-gas welds, because of 100 percent protection from the atmosphere, are stronger, more ductile, and more corrosion-resistant than welds made with ordinary metal-arc processes. In addition, the fact that no flux is required makes welding applicable to a wider variety of joint types. Corrosion due to flux entrapment cannot occur, and expensive postwelding cleaning operations are eliminated. The entire welding action takes place without spatter, sparks, or fumes. Fusion welds can be made in nearly all metals used industrially. These include aluminum alloys, stainless steels, magnesium alloys, titanium, and numerous

other metals and alloys. The inert gas process is also widely used for welding various combinations of dissimilar metals, and for applying hard-facing and surfacing materials to steel.

Equipment for Gas-Arc Welding

The equipment used for inert-gas welding consists primarily of the power supply, the torch, and the gas supply, together with connecting hoses and cables. For torches which require cooling, a water system must be included.

A typical torch for inert-gas welding is illustrated in Fig. 5-82. This is the Linde HW-17 torch, suitable for thin-to-medium metal thicknesses. The torch consists of the collet and collet body to hold the tungsten electrode, the gas lens for controlling and directing the gas flow, the gas cup, the handle through which current and gas flow, and supporting structures.

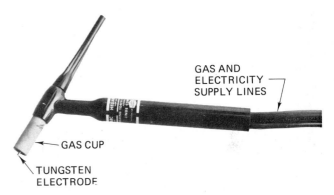

FIG. 5-82   A torch for inert-gas welding. *(Linde Div., Union Carbide Corp.)*

The power supply for inert-gas welding can be the same as that employed for standard arc (stick-electrode) welding, or it may be especially designed for inert-gas welding. A portable power-supply unit for Heliarc welding is shown in Fig. 5-83. This is the Linde HDA 300 welder which can supply 300 A for a 60 percent duty cycle. The unit also includes the argon cylinder, argon regulator, and tow cart. When purchased as a complete welding unit, the torch, connecting lines and other accessories are included.

Type of Power for Gas-Arc Welding

As mentioned previously, inert-gas welding can be accomplished with direct current, straight polarity (dcsp); direct current, reverse polarity (dcrp); or with alternating current, high-frequency stabilized (achf). Achf or dcrp power is generally recommended for magnesium and aluminum alloys and castings while dcsp power is recommended for stainless steel, copper alloys, nickel alloys, titanium, low-carbon steel, and high-carbon steel. Achf or dcrp provides the best results with beryllium-copper alloys or copper alloys less than 0.040 in [1.102 cm] thick.

The effects of different types of current may be understood by studying the diagrams of Fig. 5-84. In direct-current welding, the welding current may be hooked up as either sp or rp. As previously explained,

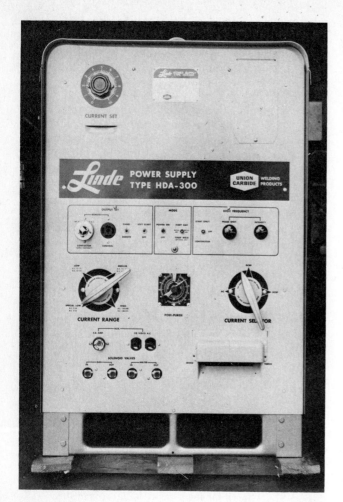

FIG. 5-83 A portable power-supply unit. (*Anderson Equipment Company.*)

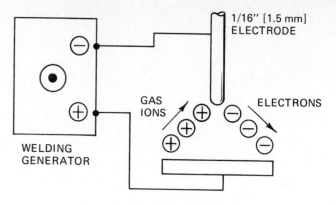

STRAIGHT POLARITY

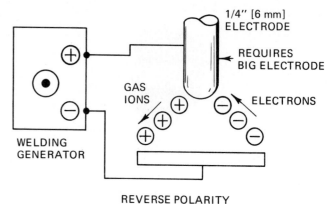

REVERSE POLARITY

FIG. 5-84 Action of different types of welding current.

the machine connection for dcsp welding is with the electrode negative and the work positive. The electrons will then flow from the electrode to the work as shown in the illustration. For dcrp welding, the connections are reversed and the electrons flow from the work to the electrode. The following explains why dcrp or achf power is required for aluminum welding. The oxide coating on aluminum has a much higher melting point than aluminum and interferes with the fusion of the metal. With dcrp power, the electrons leaving the surface of the base metal break up the oxides as they flow to the electrode. This same effect takes place during one-half of each ac cycle when achf power is used.

In straight-polarity welding, the electrons hitting the plate at a high velocity exert a considerable heating effect on the plate. In reverse-polarity welding, just the opposite occurs; the electrode acquires this extra heat which then tends to melt the end. Thus, for any given welding current, dcrp requires a larger-diameter electrode than dcsp. For example, a ¹⁄₁₆-in [1.59-mm]-diameter pure-tungsten electrode can handle 125 A of welding current under straight-polarity conditions. If the polarity were reversed, however, this amount of current would melt off the electrode and contaminate the weld metal. Hence, a ¼-in [6.35-mm]-diameter

pure-tungsten electrode is required to handle 125 A dcrp satisfactorily and safely.

These opposite heating effects influence not only the welding action but also the shape of the weld obtained. Dcsp welding will produce a narrow, deep weld; dcrp welding, because of the larger electrode diameter and lower currents generally employed, gives a wide, relatively shallow weld. The difference is illustrated in Fig. 5-85.

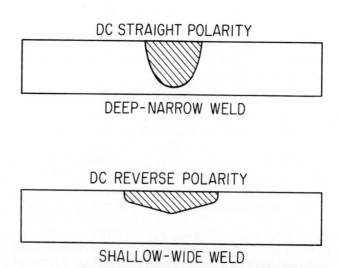

FIG. 5-85 Effects of different polarities on the weld.

One other effect of dcrp welding should be considered here, namely, the so-called **cleaning effect.** The electrons leaving the plate or the gas ions striking the plate tend to break up the surface oxides, scale, and dirt usually present.

Theoretically, straight ac welding is a combination of dcsp and dcrp welding. This can be explained by showing the three current waves visually. As illustrated in Fig. 5-86, half of each complete ac cycle is

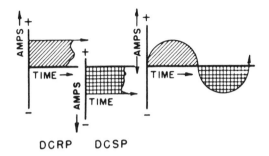

FIG. 5-86 **Illustration of ac wave through one cycle.** (*Linde Div., Union Carbide Corp.*)

dcsp and the other half is dcrp. Actually, however, moisture, oxides, scale, and other materials on the surface of the work tend to prevent the flow of current in the reverse-polarity direction. This effect is called **rectification.** For example, if no current at all flows in the reverse-polarity direction, the current wave will look something like the curve in Fig. 5-87.

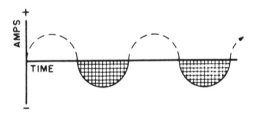

FIG. 5-87 **Rectified wave through two cycles with reverse polarity completely rectified.** (Linde Division, Union Carbide Corp.)

To prevent the effects of rectification, it is common practice to introduce into the welding current a high-voltage, high-frequency, low-power additional current. This high-frequency current jumps the gap between the electrode and the workpiece and pierces the oxide film, thereby forming a path for the welding current to follow. Superimposing this high-voltage, high-frequency current on the welding current provides the following advantages:

1. The arc may be started without touching the electrode to the workpiece.
2. Better stability of the arc is obtained.
3. A longer arc is possible. This is particularly useful in surfacing and hard-facing operations.
4. Welding electrodes have a longer life.

5. The use of wider current ranges for a specific diameter electrode is possible.

A typical weld contour produced with high-frequency stabilized alternating current is shown in Fig. 5-88, together with both dcsp and dcrp welds for comparison.

FIG. 5-88 **Comparison of dcsp and dcrp welds with achf weld.** (*Linde Div., Union Carbide Corp.*)

● INERT-GAS WELDING TECHNIQUES

Many of the preparation and welding techniques are the same or similar for inert-gas welding as for oxyacetylene welding. In this section we address the methods and procedures that are different for inert-gas welding when compared to oxyacetylene welding operations.

Welding Joint Design

Although there are innumerable welding joint designs possible, the basic types are **butt joint, lap joint, corner joint, edge joint,** and **tee joint.** Almost any TIG or MIG weld will be one or a combination of two or more of these basic types. Selection of the proper design for a particular application depends primarily on the following factors:

1. Physical properties desired in the weld
2. Cost of preparing the joint and making the weld
3. Type of metal being welded
4. Size, shape, and appearance of the part to be welded

Filler metal in the form of welding rod need not be used if proper reinforcement and complete fusion of the edges can be obtained without it. The joint designs described in this section are but a few of the many that can be successfully welded with the inert-gas method.

No matter what type of joint is used, proper cleaning of the work prior to welding is essential if welds of good appearance and physical properties are to be obtained. On small assemblies, manual cleaning with a wire brush, steel wool, or a chemical solvent is usually sufficient. For large assemblies, or for cleaning on a production basis, vapor degreasing or tank cleaning may be more economical. In any case, it is necessary to remove completely all oxide, scale, oil, grease, dirt, rust, and other foreign matter from the work surfaces.

Precautions should be taken when using certain chemical solvents such as carbon tetrachloride, trichlorethylene, and tetrachlorethylene, which break down in the heat of an electric arc and form a toxic gas. Welding should not be done when these gases are present, and the solvents should not be exposed to the heat of the welding torch. Inhalation of the fumes can be dangerous; hence proper ventilation equipment should be provided to remove fumes and vapors from the work area.

The square-edge **butt joint** shown in Fig. 5-89 is the easiest to prepare, and it can be welded with or without filler metal, depending on the thickness of the pieces being welded. Joint fit for a square-edge butt joint should always be true enough to assure 100 percent penetration with good fusion. When welding light-gauge material without adding filler metal, extreme care should be taken to avoid low spots and burn-through. The heavier thickness generally requires filler metal to provide adequate reinforcement.

FIG. 5-89   Square-edge butt joint.

The single-V butt joint, shown in Fig. 5-90, is used where complete penetration is required on material thicknesses ranging between ⅜ and 1 in [9.5 and 25.4 mm]. Filler rod must be used to fill in the V. The included angle of the V should be approximately 60°; the root face will measure from ⅛ to ¼ in [3.18 to 6.35 mm], depending on the composition and thickness of the pieces being welded.

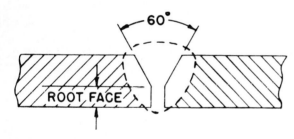

FIG. 5-90   Single-V butt joint.

The double-V butt joint of Fig. 5-91 is generally used on stock thicker than ½ in [12.7 mm], where the design of the assembly being welded permits access to the back of the joint for a second pass. With this type of

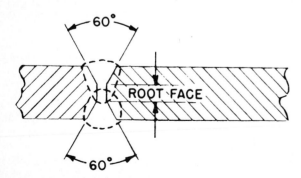

FIG. 5-91   Double-V butt joint.

joint, proper welding techniques assure a sound weld with 100 percent fusion.

A flange-type butt joint such as that illustrated in Fig. 5-92 should be used in place of the square-edge butt joint where some reinforcement is desired. This joint is practical only on relatively thin material, about 0.065 to 0.085 in [1.65 to 2.16 mm].

FIG. 5-92   Flange joint.

A **lap joint** has the advantage of eliminating entirely the necessity for edge preparation. Such a joint is shown in Fig. 5-93. The only requirement for making a good lap weld is that the plates be in close contact along the entire length of the joint and that the work be thoroughly cleaned as explained previously. On material ¼ in [6.35 mm] thick or less, lap joints can be made with or without filler rod. When no filler metal is used, care must be taken to avoid low spots or burn-through. The lap-type joint is not usually recommended on material thicker than ¼ in [6.35 mm] except for rough fitup. When so used, filler rod must always be added to assure good fusion and buildup. The number of passes required depends on the thickness of the pieces being joined.

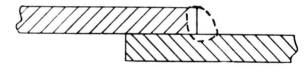

FIG. 5-93   Lap joint.

Corner joints are frequently used in the fabrication of pans, boxes, and all types of containers as well as for other heavier purposes. The type A corner joint, shown in Fig. 5-94, is used on material thicknesses up to ⅛ in [3.18 mm]. No filler metal is required, as the amount of base metal fused is sufficient to assure a sound, high-strength weld. Type B, as shown in the illustration, is used on heavier material that requires filler rod to provide adequate reinforcement. Type C is used on very heavy material where 100 percent penetration is impossible without the beveled-edge preparation. The nose should be thick enough to prevent burn-through on the first pass. The number of passes required depends on the size of the V and thickness of the members being welded. On all corner joints, the pieces must be in good contact along the entire seam.

All **tee joints** require the addition of filler rod to provide the necessary buildup. Such a joint is shown in Fig. 5-95. The number of passes on each side of the joint depends upon the thickness of the material and the size of the weld desired. When 100 percent pene-

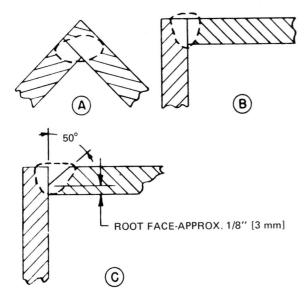

FIG. 5-94 Corner joints.

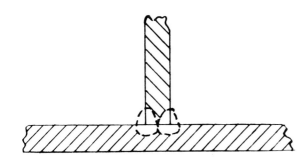

ROOT FACE-APPROX. 1/8" [3 mm]

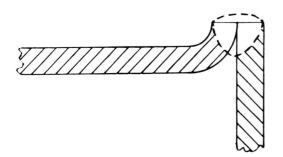

FIG. 5-95 Tee joint.

protect the underside of the weld from atmospheric contamination resulting in possible weld porosity or poor surface appearance. In addition to these functions, weld backup prevents the weld puddle from dropping through by acting as a **heat sink** and drawing away some of the heat generated by the intense arc. The backup also can physically support the weld puddle. A heliarc weld can be backed up by (1) metal backup bars, (2) introducing an inert-gas atmosphere on the weld underside, (3) a combination of the first two methods, or (4) use of flux backing, painted on the weld underside.

Flat, metal backup bars are generally used on joints where the bar does not actually touch the weld zone. If the bar comes in contact with the underside of the weld, nonuniform penetration may occur and the weld underside may be rough and uneven.

A type of backup bar more commonly used is that shown in Fig. 5-97, where the surface is cut or machined out directly below the joint. On square-edge butt joints, for example, where fitup is not too accurate and filler rod is required, a bar of this sort will protect the bottom of the weld from excessive contamination by the atmosphere and will draw the heat away from the weld zone.

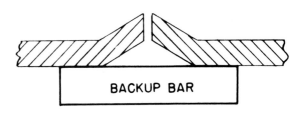

BACKUP BAR

BACKUP BAR

FIG. 5-97 Use of a backup bar with a cutout.

tration is required, the welding current must be adequate for the thickness of the web material.

A typical **edge joint** is shown in Fig. 5-96. Such joints are used solely on light-gauge material and require no filler rod. Preparation is simple, and the joint is economical to weld. This type of joint should not be used, however, where direct tension or bending stresses will be applied to the finished joint because it will fail at the root under relatively low stress loads.

Weld Backup

On many heliarc welding applications, the joint should be backed up. This is done for several reasons. On light-gauge material, backing is usually used to

Apparatus Check

Before starting to weld, the entire welding setup should be thoroughly checked. It is most important to use the proper-size electrode, gas cup, etc. All components must be functioning properly to realize the full advantage of this type of welding. The following instructions can be used as a guide:

1. Check all connections in the gas supply line for tightness. Be sure that good seals are obtained between the torch body, the cap, and the gas cap, because any air leakage into the gas stream will contaminate both the weld and the electrode. Be sure any gaskets required are in good condition and firmly in place. After welding, the electrode should have a clean, silvery appearance upon cooling. A dirty, rough electrode surface usually signifies air leakage in the torch or gas supply system.

FIG. 5-96 Edge joint at a corner.

2. Check the welding current and gas-flow settings. They should be preset to the approximate values recommended for the material being welded.

3. Select the proper gas cup and electrode size.

4. Check the rate of water flow through the torch if it is the water-cooled type. Flow rates lower than those recommended decrease torch efficiency and may result in damage to the torch, particularly if the torch is being used at or near its maximum capacity.

5. Check the ground connection to be sure it is securely clamped to the workpiece. The workpiece should be cleaned at the point of contact, preferably by grinding, to assure good contact.

Starting an Arc

There is nothing difficult about starting an arc in the proper manner. The procedure explained in this section should ensure a good start and maximum protection of the work from atmospheric contamination at the start of the welding operation.

In arc welding with a tungsten electrode (TIG), the electrode does not have to touch the work to start the arc. The superimposed high-frequency current jumps the gap between the welding electrode and the work, thus establishing a path for the welding current to follow. To strike an arc, the torch is held in a horizontal position about 2 in [5.08 cm] above the work or starting block, as shown in Fig. 5-98. The end of

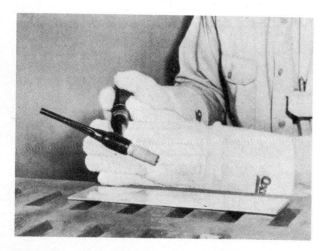

FIG. 5-98 Torch in position ready to strike an arc.

the torch is then swung quickly down toward the work so the end of the electrode is about ⅛ in [3.18 mm] above the metal. The arc strikes at this distance. The downward motion should be made rapidly to provide the maximum amount of gas protection to the weld zone. The position of the torch when the arc strikes is shown in Fig. 5-99.

In dc welding, the same motion is used for striking the arc. In this case, however, the electrode must actually touch the work in order to start the arc. As soon as the arc is struck, the torch is withdrawn so the electrode is about ⅛ in [3.18 mm] from the work. This prevents contamination of the electrode in the molten pool. High frequency is sometimes used to

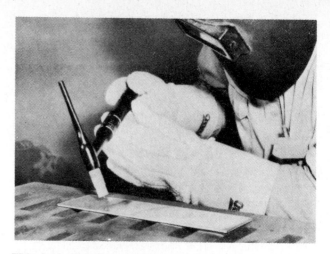

FIG. 5-99 Torch in position when arc is struck.

start a dc arc. This eliminates the need for touching the workpiece. The high-frequency current is automatically turned off by means of a current relay when the arc is started.

The arc can be struck on the workpiece itself or on a heavy piece of copper or scrap steel, and then carried to the starting point of the weld. A carbon block should not be used for striking the arc because it is likely to contaminate the electrode and cause the arc to wander. When welding with a hot electrode is commenced, the action must be very rapid because the arc tends to strike before the torch is in the proper position.

To stop an arc, the torch is merely snapped quickly back to the horizontal position. This motion must be made rapidly so the arc will not mar or damage the weld surface or work.

Arc Wandering

With the torch held stationary, the points at which an arc leaves the electrode and impinges upon the work may often shift and waver without apparent reason. This is known as **arc wandering** and is generally attributed to one of the following causes: (1) low-electrode-current density, (2) carbon contamination of the electrode, (3) magnetic effects, and (4) air drafts. The first two causes are indicated by a very rapid movement of the arc from side to side, generally resulting in a zigzag weld pattern. The third cause, magnetic effect, usually displaces the arc to one side or the other along the entire length of the weld. The fourth causes varying amounts of arc wandering, depending upon the amount of air draft present.

When current density of the electrode is at a sufficiently high level, the entire end of the electrode will be in a molten state and completely covered by the arc. When too low a current density is used, only a small area of the electrode becomes molten, resulting in an unstable arc which has poor directional characteristics and is difficult for the operator to control. Too high a current density results in excessive melting of the electrode.

When a carbon block is used to strike the arc, electrode contamination often results. As the electrode touches the carbon, the molten tungsten on the tip of the electrode forms tungsten carbide. This has a lower melting point than pure tungsten and forms a larger molten ball on the end of the electrode. This, in effect, reduces the current density at the electrode end and arc wandering occurs. The electrode can also be contaminated by touching it to the workpiece or filler rod. When electrode contamination occurs in any form, it is best to clean the electrode by grinding, breaking off the end, or using a new electrode.

Magnetic effects are not generally encountered and are too complex to be discussed fully in this text. The most common magnetic action on the arc, however, results from the magnetic field set up by the current flowing in the work. This field may tend to attract or repel the arc from the normal path. One method for remedying this condition is to alter the position of the ground connection on the work until the effects are no longer noticed.

Making a Butt Weld

After the arc has been struck with a TIG torch, as previously explained, the torch should be held at about a 75° angle to the surface of the work. The starting point of the weld is first preheated by moving the torch in small circles, as shown in Fig. 5-100, until a small molten pool is formed. The end of the electrode should be held approximately ⅛ in [3 mm] above the work. When the puddle becomes bright and fluid, the torch is moved slowly and steadily along the joint at a speed that will produce a bead of uniform width. No oscillating or other movement of the torch, except for the steady forward motion, is required.

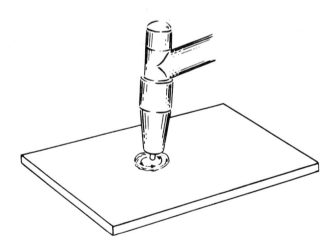

FIG. 5-100 Forming the molten puddle.

When filler metal is required to provide adequate reinforcement, the welding rod is held at about 15° to the work and about 1 in [2.5 cm] away from the starting point. The starting point is then preheated as explained previously to develop the molten pool. When the puddle becomes bright and fluid, the arc is moved quickly to the rear of the puddle, and filler rod is added by quickly touching the leading edge of the puddle. The rod is removed and the arc is brought back to the leading edge of the puddle. As soon as the puddle becomes bright again, the steps are repeated. This sequence is continued for the entire length of the weld. Figure 5-101 illustrates the steps as described. The rate of forward speed and the amount of filler rod added depend on the desired width and height of the bead.

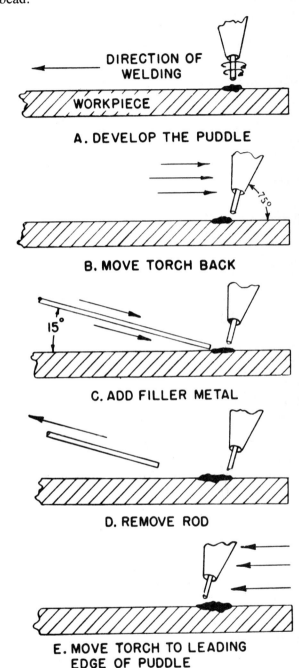

FIG. 5-101 Steps in starting an inert-gas weld.

For making **butt joints** on a vertical surface, the torch is held perpendicular to the work and the weld is usually made from top to bottom. When filler rod is used, it is added from the bottom or leading edge of the puddle in the manner described previously. Figure 5-102 shows correct positioning of the rod and torch relative to the work.

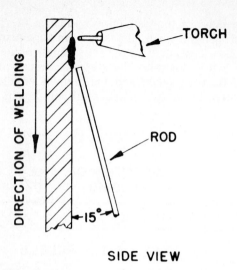

FIG. 5-102 Position of torch and filler for vertical TIG weld.

Making a Lap Weld

A **lap weld,** or **joint,** is started by first developing a puddle on the bottom sheet. When the puddle becomes bright and fluid, the arc is shortened to about $\frac{1}{16}$ in [2 mm]. The torch is then oscillated directly over the joint until the sheets are firmly joined. Once the weld is started, the oscillating movement is no longer required. The torch is merely moved along the seam with the electrode held just above the edge of the top sheet.

In lap welding, the puddle developed will be boomerang- or V-shaped as shown in Fig. 5-103. The center of the puddle is called the **notch,** and the speed at which this notch travels will determine how fast the torch can be moved forward. Care must be taken to see that the notch is completely filled for the entire length of the seam. Otherwise, it is impossible to get 100 percent fusion and good penetration.

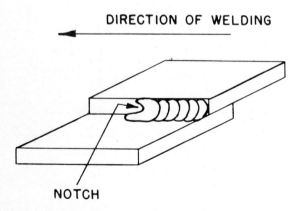

FIG. 5-103 Shape of puddle in lap welding.

When filler metal is used, faster welding speeds are possible because the rod helps to fill the notch. Complete fusion must be obtained rather than allowing bits of filler rod to be laid into the cold, unfused base metal. The rod should be alternately dipped into the puddle

and withdrawn $\frac{1}{4}$ in [6.35 mm], as illustrated in Fig. 5-104. By carefully controlling the melting rate of the top edge, and by adding just enough filler metal where needed, a good uniform bead of correct proportions can be obtained.

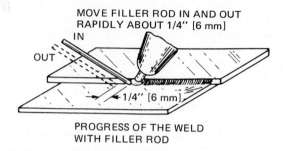

FIG. 5-104 Procedure for lap welding with TIG.

Making a Corner or Edge Weld

The **corner** or **edge weld** is the easiest type to make. A puddle is developed at the starting point, and the torch is then moved straight along the joint. Rate of travel is regulated to produce a uniform bead. Too slow a welding speed will cause molten metal to roll off the edges. Irregular or too-high speeds will produce a rough, uneven surface. No filler metal is required.

Multipass Welding

Multipass welding is generally required for welding material over $\frac{1}{4}$ in [6.35 mm] thick. The number of passes required depends upon the thickness of the material, the current-carrying capacity of the equipment involved, and the assembly being fabricated. The first pass should be a **root weld** and provide complete fusion at the bottom of the joint. Subsequent passes can be made at higher currents owing to the backup effect of the root weld. Care should be taken to prevent inclusions between weld layers. On heavy work, it is sometimes advantageous to carry all the beads along simultaneously in a staggered arrangement to utilize the residual heat of preceding passes.

Techniques with MIG Welding

Two general techniques or processes are employed when welding with MIG (GMA). These are called **spray-arc transfer** and **short-circuit transfer.**

In spray-arc transfer the metal from the electrode is carried to the molten pool in fine droplets by the force of the arc and by gravity. The power source for this process is constant-voltage direct current, reverse polarity. For best results with this process, the work should be level or nearly so. The shielding gas employed with spray-arc transfer is usually argon with 1 or 2 percent oxygen for stabilization of the puddle and arc.

When short-circuit transfer is used, the tip of the metal electrode is touched to the metal to provide a short circuit. This results in a high amperage which melts the end of the electrode into the pool. The electrode is constantly fed into the pool to maintain the arc and transfer the metal. When steel is welded with short-circuit transfer, the shielding gas can be pure CO_2 or a mixture of CO_2 and argon. For stainless steel, the mixture of gases is helium, argon, and CO_2.

In welding with any particular type of equipment, the mechanic should consult the manual supplied with the equipment to ensure that the most effective gases and techniques are employed.

● CONCLUSION

In this section we have explained common types of gas and electric-arc welding. Oxyacetylene is the most common form of welding used in the aviation maintenance field. The plain electric-arc (stick-electrode) system is commonly used for heavy industrial construction in steel. Inert-gas welding, on the other hand, is used in a wide variety of precision welding on many different types of metals and alloys. For this reason it is particularly well adapted for welding structures and parts for aerospace vehicles.

There are many other types of welding, some of which are **submerged-arc, plasma,** and **electron-beam welding.** These are specialties and are usually practiced by highly skilled welders. They are not usually done by the average airframe and powerplant mechanic; hence, detailed descriptions of these processes are considered beyond the scope of this text.

● REVIEW QUESTIONS

1. What is meant by *fusion welding?*
2. Why is it usually necessary to add metal in the form of a welding rod while making a weld?
3. List the items necessary for a complete portable welding outfit.
4. Briefly describe *acetylene gas* and explain why it is used in gas welding.
5. At what pressures does acetylene gas become unstable and in danger of exploding?
6. What material is placed inside an acetylene cylinder to absorb the gas and thus assure safe handling?
7. What is the maximum pressure of the gas in an acetylene cylinder?
8. Why is it necessary to keep oxygen equipment free from oil or grease?
9. To what pressure is an oxygen cylinder charged?
10. How can you determine the volume of gas in an oxygen cylinder?
11. Discuss the importance of a protector cap over the valve on an oxygen cylinder.
12. Describe a gas pressure regulator and explain its function.
13. Why are two pressure gauges used on a cylinder gas regulator?
14. List the main differences between an oxygen pressure regulator and an acetylene pressure regulator.
15. How does a welder adjust the gas regulator to increase pressure?
16. Name the two principal types of welding torches.
17. Which type is generally preferred for aircraft welding? Why?
18. Explain the function of the *mixing head.*
19. What determines the size of tip to be used in a welding torch?
20. How are oxygen and acetylene torch hoses identified?
21. How is the danger of connecting the hoses incorrectly avoided?
22. What are the two principal functions of welding goggles?
23. Why should a friction lighter be used to ignite the gas at the tip of an oxyacetylene welding torch?
24. Briefly describe the steps for setting up oxyacetylene welding apparatus.
25. What method should be used in testing for oxyacetylene leaks?
26. In lighting an oxyacetylene welding torch, what gas should be turned on first?
27. Explain how to adjust the oxyacetylene torch for a *neutral flame.*
28. Why is the neutral flame best for welding steel?
29. Describe the appearance of a neutral oxyacetylene flame.
30. What is the effect of using an oxidizing oxyacetylene flame?
31. Compare the carbonizing (carburizing) flame with the oxidizing flame.
32. What is the effect of a damaged or obstructed oxyacetylene welding torch tip orifice?
33. Explain how a gas welding torch tip can be cleaned properly.
34. Why is a *soft flame* better than a *harsh flame* for welding?
35. What are some of the causes for popping at the welding tip?
36. Give the procedure for shutting down the oxyacetylene welding apparatus.
37. Discuss the knowledge of welding necessary for the aircraft mechanic.
38. How should the welding torch be held for heavy welding?
39. Explain the difference between *forehand* and *backhand* welding.
40. Explain the purpose of the *filler rod.*
41. Approximately how far should the oxyacetylene welding flame cone be held from the base metal?
42. Describe the application of welding rod to the weld.
43. Explain *circular* and *semicircular* motion of the torch.
44. At what angle is the oxyacetylene torch flame applied to the metal?
45. Name the four common positions of a weld.
46. Describe how metal is prepared for welding.
47. Why are the edges of the metal beveled in many cases?
48. Describe a *butt joint* in welding.
49. Why is it not necessary to use filler rod for a flange butt joint?
50. Under what conditions is a *double-V tee joint* used?
51. Describe a *single-welded lap joint.*
52. Name the various parts of a weld.

53. What are the three most important proportions of a weld?
54. What should be the width of the welding bead?
55. What should be the depth of penetration in welding?
56. What are the usual causes of improperly formed weak welds?
57. Describe the chemical changes which may take place during gas welding.
58. What is the effect of expansion in welding?
59. Explain *coefficient of expansion*.
60. What precautions must be taken in welding a *closed* metal assembly?
61. Discuss the effect of high temperatures on the strength of metals.
62. What actions can a welder take to reduce the effects of distortion and residual stresses?
63. Explain *stagger* welding and *skip* welding.
64. What is the purpose of a welding jig?
65. When welding heavy plate, how may welding stresses be reduced?·
66. How is *preheating* accomplished?
67. Explain *stress relieving*.
68. What is meant by the *spark test* for the identification of metals?
69. Describe a good quality completed weld.
70. What is meant by the *bend test* for a weld?
71. What type of flame should be used for aluminum and magnesium welding?
72. How are the edges of thin aluminum sheet prepared for gas welding? Aluminum plate over 0.25 in [6.35 mm] thick?
73. Describe procedures for making magnesium butt welds with a gas-welding process.
74. Describe the process of *electric-arc* welding.
75. Describe the *electrode* for arc welding.
76. What are two functions of the electrode?
77. What is the purpose of the coating on the electrode?
78. Describe the *welding circuit*.
79. What is the nature of the power used for electric-arc welding with respect to voltage and amperage?
80. What type of devices supply the power for arc welding?
81. Describe what takes place in the welding arc.
82. What temperature is developed in the arc?
83. Explain the three types of current which may be used for arc welding.
84. Describe *inert-gas* or *gas arc* welding.
85. What is the nature of the electrode used with inert-gas welding?
86. Explain the difference between TIG and MIG welding.
87. Give the advantages of inert-gas welding.
88. What equipment is necessary for doing inert-gas welding?
89. What types of electrical power are used with inert-gas welding?
90. What is the difference in the effects of *dcsp* and *dcrp* current?
91. Why is dcrp or achf power required for welding aluminum and magnesium?
92. Why is a larger electrode required for dcrp welding power?
93. What are the advantages of *achf* power?
94. Describe two techniques which may be used with MIG welding.
95. Name five basic joints for inert-gas welding.
96. How should metal be prepared before inert-gas welding is started?
97. Why is a weld backup used with some welds?
98. List the checks that should be made before inert-gas welding is started.
99. Describe the process of striking an arc.
100. Why is it undesirable to strike the arc on a carbon block?
101. What is meant by *arc wandering?*
102. What are the principal causes of arc wandering?
103. Describe the process of starting an inert-gas weld.
104. What is meant by a *multipass weld?*

6 CONSTRUCTION AND REPAIR OF WELDED AIRCRAFT STRUCTURES

WELDING OF AIRCRAFT METAL PARTS

As mentioned in other sections of this text, a rather wide variety of welding processes have been developed for joining various types of metals for aircraft. Oxy-fuel welding is still practiced extensively for the manufacture and repair of steel aircraft structures; however, inert-gas welding (Heliarc or TIG and MIG) is more commonly used for the welding of aluminum, stainless steels, titanium, and magnesium alloys.

This chapter deals with the conventional methods used for the repair of steel structures which are easily performed by the mechanic either in the shop or in the field with portable equipment.

Modern metal airplanes are designed so that the skin of the airplane, rather than the interior structures of steel tubing, carries a large part of the loads and stresses during flight. As a result, there is a smaller amount of steel structures in the newer airplanes, but there are still many parts of structures built with steel.

CONSTRUCTION OF STEEL-TUBE ASSEMBLIES BY WELDING

In dealing with aircraft steel tubing the aircraft mechanic is generally concerned with repairs rather than building a complete structure. It should be understood, however, that extensive repairs require that portions of the structure be removed and replaced with new structures. For this reason, some of the general considerations given to building structures are addressed in this section. Be aware that for any repair, the aircraft manufacturer or the FAA should be consulted to identify specific repair techniques that are acceptable for a particular aircraft.

Types of Steel Tubing

The steel tubing used most extensively for aircraft structures, engine mounts, and similar parts, is **chromium-molybdenum,** also called **chrome-molybdenum** or **chrome-moly.** It is usually designated by the SAE number 4130. The above descriptive terms refer to a group of steels included under the general classification of molybdenum steels that contain chromium as well as molybdenum. The principal properties of these steels are resistance to impact, fatigue, abrasion, and high-temperature stress. They are capable of deep-hardening when given a suitable heat treatment, they

have good machinability, and they are easily welded by gas and electric-arc methods.

Aircraft steel tubing is sized according to its outside diameter and wall thickness. Tubing with an outside diameter from $\frac{3}{16}$ to $2\frac{1}{2}$ in [4.76 mm to 6.35 cm] is available and wall thickness may run from 0.035 in [0.89 mm] for the $\frac{3}{16}$ in to 0.120 [3.05 mm] for the $2\frac{1}{2}$ in. Most diameter tubing sizes are available in various wall thicknesses. For example, $\frac{7}{8}$ in [2.22 cm] diameter tubing is available with several wall thicknesses from 0.035 to 0.120 in [0.89 to 3.05 mm].

When selecting the size of tubing to use for a project, determine the type of material originally used along with the original outside diameter and wall thickness. Material that does not meet the minimum specifications of the original tubing should not be used.

While tubing is generally thought of as being circular in cross section, steel tubing may be purchased in streamline (teardrop), oval, square, and rectangular cross section.

Joint Designs

The location where two or more pieces of tubing come together is known as a **joint.** If the pieces radiate out from the joint, this is called a **cluster.** When reconstructing a structure, the joint design should match that of the original.

Tubing running lengthwise in a fuselage is normally of one piece or several pieces telescoped together with larger pieces at the front of the aircraft and smaller pieces toward the rear of the aircraft. The smaller pieces are slipped inside of the larger pieces and are welded in position, normally by the use of a scarf or fishmouth weld, to be discussed later. Short tubing pieces are used for the vertical, lateral, and diagonal pieces that make up the truss structure. These types of structures were discussed in Chap. 1 of this book.

Steel-tube control surfaces normally have a continuous piece of tubing making up the leading and trailing edges with short pieces used for the ribs and diagonal members.

Before short pieces of material are joined to larger pieces to form clusters or joints, they are contoured to fit the joint as if they were going to be glued in place. At a cluster, as shown in Fig. 6-1, the perpendicular piece is cut to fit the longitudinal piece and then the diagonals are cut to fit the other pieces. Because of the thin wall thickness normally used, the pieces should be a close fit with no allowance purposely made for expansion.

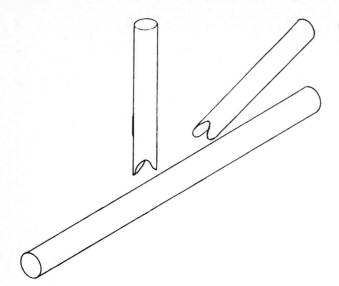

FIG. 6-1 Tubing shapes to form a good welded joint.

Alignment Jigs

A suitable jig must be used in the construction of aircraft steel-tube assemblies by welding. This jig is used to support and to hold the various members of the assembly in their proper positions until they are permanently fastened. Jigs should be rigid enough to withstand the usual strains without losing their shape when the parts are being assembled.

In some factories, the jigs for welding flat assemblies are made of boiler plate ⅜ to ½ in [9.53 to 12.7 mm] thick. These plates are fitted with suitable clamps, or blocks, to receive and hold the members of the assembly.

In a case where only one unit is to be built, the jig for the construction of flat assemblies may be entirely made of wood on the same general plan as a mass-production jig made of metal. A flat-top table may be used as the base, and wood blocks grooved to receive the members fastened to this base with nails, or screws. A piece of reasonably heavy iron or steel plate, or thick nonflammable material, is placed under the joint to protect the wood during welding.

If the tubular structure is not flat, such as a steel-tube engine mount, a more complicated jig is required. It may have a heavy steel-base plate and a top plate of a lighter gauge, supported with angle-iron vertical members that are welded to plates to obtain the greatest amount of rigidity. Holes and clamps are provided for holding the members to be welded, and the assembly is left in the jig after welding until it has cooled.

Welding Procedure

Oxyacetylene welding equipment is normally used to weld steel tubing. However, many people prefer to use inert-gas welding. While there is no requirement for any specific process to be used, the mechanic should choose the process that he or she is most comfortable using and that will produce an airworthy repair. If an inert-gas process is used, check the completed structure for any residual magnetism that might affect the aircraft magnetic compass. Any residual magnetism should be removed by the use of a degausser.

When welding an assembly, it is desirable to tack-weld the components before completing any one weld. Tack welding involves making three or four small equally spaced welds between each of the components. These welds help to prevent the components from shifting during the welding process.

When you are ready to weld the structure, weld each joint in turn. A joint should be welded in quarters, alternating across the weld as shown in Fig. 6-2. This reduces the chance of the tubing warping out of alignment.

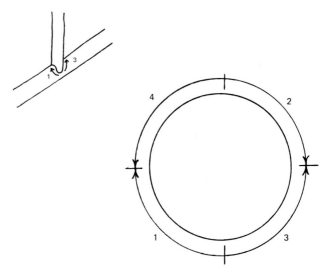

FIG. 6-2 Sequence of welding a joint.

Attachment of Welded Fittings

Aircraft fittings of interest to welders are principally small attachments or connections that are fastened to tubing members. They may be built up of one or more thicknesses of sheet metal, or they may be forged or machined from bars or billets. The method of welding fittings to tubular members depends upon the load stress they will carry in operating conditions.

Moderately stressed fittings that are not subjected to vibrating stresses are generally made of a single-thickness of sheet steel and are welded to only one wall of the tube as shown in Fig. 6-3.

Fittings or lugs for transmitting high stresses are

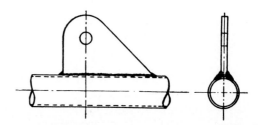

FIG. 6-3 Simple fitting where the stress is moderate.

welded to the supporting members at more than one point. High-stressed fittings attached to the main member of a structural unit halfway between station points are welded to both walls of the tube as shown in Fig. 6-4, where the tube is slotted and the fitting is inserted.

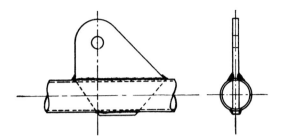

FIG. 6-4   Inserted fitting where stresses are high.

Fittings attached to the main members of tubular structures where brace members terminate are also welded to the brace members in most cases. The main members and ends of the brace members may be slotted and the fitting welded in, as shown in Fig. 6-5, or the fitting may be built up of two or three sections with fingers, extending to the brace members, as shown in Fig. 6-6.

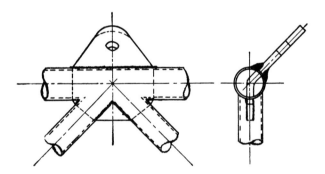

FIG. 6-5   Inserted fitting at a station.

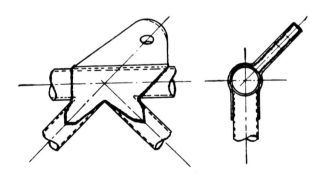

FIG. 6-6   Fitting reinforced with welded fingers.

Figure 6-7 shows a representative male fitting for round struts. It consists of a bearing sleeve or bushing welded to the strut end, which is reinforced with a

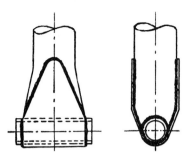

FIG. 6-7   Fitting for the end of a round strut.

steel plate formed around the bearing. The plate is welded to the bearing sleeve and strut with a fillet weld.

The fitting in Fig. 6-8 is a typical female strut-end connection used for round struts. This is forged and machined to fit into the strut end and is attached to the strut with a combination riveted and welded joint.

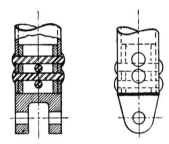

FIG. 6-8   Female fitting for the end of a round strut.

The fitting illustrated in Fig. 6-9 is a forged and machined male fitting for elliptical or streamlined struts. This fitting is inserted by slotting the strut end to receive its tang, and the attachment is made by means of a fillet weld.

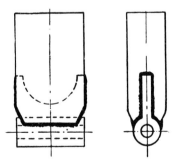

FIG. 6-9   Forged and machined fitting for the end of a streamline strut.

The fitting shown in Fig. 6-10 is a typical female fitting for streamlined or elliptical struts, and it also may be used for round sections. It is built up of sheet steel and bearing sleeves. The strut end is slotted and formed to receive the fitting.

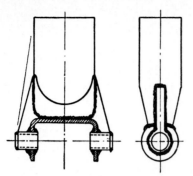

FIG. 6-10 Female end fitting for streamline strut.

Corrosion Protection

After welding, hollow steel structures may be filled with hot linseed oil or petroleum-base oils, under pressure, in order to coat the inside surface and discourage corrosion. This also helps to detect weld cracks because the hot oil will seep through cracks that are not otherwise visible to the eye. This is not applicable in all cases, but it is recommended where a large portion of the structure has been rewelded. Carefully examining all joints with a medium-power magnifying glass, at least 10 power, after first removing all scale, is an acceptable method of inspection for repaired structures.

Corrosionproofing the interior steel-tube structures can also be done satisfactorily by filling the structures with an epoxy primer or tube sealing solutions and draining before sealing. Sealing the members only, without the use of a preservative, by permanently closing all openings to prevent air from circulating through them is also considered an acceptable method for protecting the interior of repaired structures, provided that the interior of the tubing is thoroughly dried.

Finishing of Welded Structures

Once the structure has been welded, a protective coating should be applied. Prior to the application of the protective coating, all oil, grease, dirt, and welding residue should be removed. This involves the use of a wire wheel, abrasive paper, or sandblasting to remove particles and the use of a solvent to remove any grease or oil. As soon as the metal has been cleaned, it should be finished immediately and not touched by ungloved hands until at least a priming coat has been applied. If this precaution is not observed, corrosion will set in later.

A very satisfactory protection for finishing the exterior of tubing is obtained by spraying or brushing two coats of zinc chromate primer with 4 oz [113.4 g] of aluminum-bronze powder per unthinned gallon [3.785 L] in the second coat of primer. This finish provides excellent protection against corrosion and is very dopeproof. Any equivalent finish using oil-base primers and enamels is acceptable. Excellent epoxy primers are now available; they should be used as directed by the manufacturer. The portions of the structure coming in contact with doped fabric should

be given a protecting strip of tape or a coat of dopeproof paint if the base finish is not already dopeproof.

● INSPECTION OF STEEL-TUBE STRUCTURES

A visual inspection is the primary means of examining a welded steel structure. The structure is checked for proper alignment, evidence of deformation, and any indication of cracking. Alignment and deformation can be verified by a symmetry check, as is discussed in Chap. 15, and by placing a straightedge along the tubing. Cracks in the tubing and weld defects can be checked with a magnifying glass.

If bent or cracked structures are found, check around the damaged area for secondary damage. Secondary damage may be created in some areas away from the primary damage because of the transmission of loads through the structure from the primary area.

A check for internal corrosion in tubing can be made by tapping on the tubing with a small hammer. Any dull sounds or sudden changes in sound when compared to the surrounding tubing may indicate a weak structure. A center punch and hammer can be used to check if suspect tubing is corroding internally. When the center punch is held against the tubing and tapped with a hammer, badly corroded tubing will give way. In the same manner a Maule fabric tester can be used to apply pressure on the tubing. The bottom of the tubing in the lower portions of the structure are the most likely to corrode internally.

More detailed inspections of an area may be performed by dye-penetrant inspection, magnetic-particle inspection, x-ray inspection, ultrasonic inspection, and eddy-current inspection.

Inspection of a welded structure is easily accomplished by means of **dye-penetrant** inspection. In this process, the dye penetrates any small cracks or fissures and then seeps out when a developer is applied to the joint. Thus the crack is revealed as a bright red line.

Fluorescent-penetrant inspection can be used for detecting cracks or other flaws in a welded structure. A liquid containing a fluorescent material is applied to the part to be inspected and is allowed to penetrate cracks, laps, and other discontinuities. The part is then washed with a suitable solvent and dried, after which a developing powder is applied to draw the penetrant to the surface. Excess powder is brushed off, and the part is examined under ultraviolet light (black light). Cracks and other flaws are revealed as fluorescent markings.

Magnetic-particle inspection (Magnaflux) by means of magnetic powder applied to a magnetized part is an efficient, practical, and nondestructive method that will reveal the presence of tiny cracks and other flaws in a welded part. The surface to be examined should be reasonably smooth and free from scale because it is difficult to find cracks in the irregular surface of the weld metal. Sandblasting is a suitable method for cleaning the surface in preparation for the magnetic-particle inspection.

Magnetization of tubular clusters and other welded joints in tubular structures usually is accomplished by means of cables wrapped in coils around the area to be inspected. The mechanic must follow the appropriate instructions to ensure that the magnetization is produced in the correct direction. After the inspection the magnetization must be neutralized with an alternating-current field coil.

X-ray inspection was limited in value in the past because of the inaccessibility of many joints and the necessity of taking exposures from several angles to make certain that all defects were found. However, the results are very satisfactory and the recent developments in this field have reduced the cost and time. The use of radioactive cobalt "bombs" has made it possible to x-ray joints at almost any location.

Two other suitable inspection processes are useful for detecting the presence of cracks, inclusions, and other defects not noticeable on the surface. These are **ultrasonic** inspection and **eddy-current** inspection. With ultrasonic inspection, high-frequency sound waves are applied to the part being inspected. These sound waves are reflected from the opposite side of the material or from any flaw which they encounter. Wave signals from the flaw are compared with the normal wave to determine the location and size of the flaw. In an eddy-current inspection, eddy currents are generated in the part by means of electromagnetic waves. If a flaw exists, the indicator will show a value different from the normal response. A well-qualified operator can diagnose the response to determine the nature of the flaw.

● AIRCRAFT TUBING REPAIR

Steel tubing is adaptive to aircraft construction because it is strong for its weight and can be repaired easily. In making repairs, either steel tubing or sheet stock having code numbers 1025 (carbon steel), 4130 (chrome-moly), or 4330 (nickel-chromium-molybdenum) might be used. In any case, if replacements are being made, the replacement material should be the same as the original. Repairs can be made with little equipment. All that is required is a welding apparatus, a short section of steel to replace the damaged section, and the tools to cut and prepare the metal for welding.

Procedures for Weld Repairs

The parts to be welded should be cut to the proper dimensions and secured in place with clamps or jigs to assure correct alignment. In the case of a major rework of a fuselage, it is likely that the entire fuselage must be placed in a jig to keep it properly aligned while the repair is being made.

The areas to be welded must be thoroughly cleaned by wire brushing, filing, or by some other method to assure a weld free of such defects as inclusions or contamination. Only a steel wire brush should be used because any small amount of other metals left on the surface will weaken the weld.

The torch flame should be adjusted for a reasonably soft condition; that is, the force of the flame should not be such that it will blow the molten pool of metal away from the weld. For comparatively thin tubing, the inner cone would not be more than $\frac{1}{8}$ in [3.18 mm] long.

The size of the welding torch tip is primarily governed by the thickness of the metal. Table 5-1 in Chap. 5 gives typical tip sizes.

The tip should be large enough to permit rapid welding but small enough to avoid overheating and burning the metal. Burning weakens the metal and causes it to crack when it contracts because of cooling. Rewelding is objectionable for the same reason; that is, it tends to overheat the metal, and thus might lead to structural failure in flight. In preheating metal, the flame is pointed in the direction of welding.

The **welding (filler) rod** usually is made of mild steel for welding chrome-moly steel because it flows smoothly and contributes to a uniform, sound weld. Flux is not required. Some welders recommend the use of a welding rod made of alloy steel, but the disadvantages of alloy steels sometimes appear to outweigh the advantages. In any event, if the repaired part requires heat treating, it is necessary that the welder use heat-treatable filler rod.

All steels tend to be weak when very hot but strong and tough when cold. This is especially true in the case of chrome-moly steel; hence it may crack if placed under a comparatively light stress while it is still very hot. One way to avoid trouble is to use **welding jigs** that will not restrict the expansion and contraction of the welded members. Another precaution is to avoid overheating the metal while it is being welded at or near an edge. The reason for this is that an edge gets hot very fast and may crack before the welder realizes the condition. The welder can reduce losses from this source by drawing the welding flame away slightly whenever it approaches an edge.

Welders are cautioned against filing welds in an effort to make a smooth-appearing job, because such treatment reduces the strength of the part. Likewise, it is forbidden to fill a weld with solder, brazing metal, or any other filler. When it becomes necessary to reweld a joint that was previously welded, all the old weld material is thoroughly removed before rewelding. A weld should not be made over an old weld because the repeated heating weakens the material and makes it brittle.

Welding should never be done over a brazed area or where the brazing has been removed. If a repaired area were covered with a corrosion-resistant material before the repair were made, this material should be replaced after the repair is completed.

For standard steel-tubing repairs, it is good practice to sandblast the welded area after welding to provide a good clean metal base for the application of primer. The weld should be primed before corrosion has had a chance to start, and the clear surface should be protected from any contamination before it is primed.

Controlling Distortion

When steel-tube structural units and steel fittings are constructed or repaired, welders can expect the usual expansion, contraction, and shrinkage of the weld metal. In addition, they must prevent any extraordinary loss of metal thickness from excess scaling during welding. If they apply the correct procedure, these factors may be controlled within satisfactory limits.

Cracking can be prevented by reducing the strains on the weld and hot-base metal caused by weight or restriction of the normal processes of expansion and contraction. For example, one end of a web member may be welded to the flange member of a truss and permitted to cool before the opposite end of the web member is welded. Also, joints of a tubular assembly in which several members terminate should be welded first and allowed to cool before the opposite ends are welded. This is done because the additional time required to weld such joints permits the heat to flow from the weld into the members, and this heat flow causes them to expand. If the members are connected to similar joints at the opposite end, it is advisable to apply heavy clamps, chill plates, or wet nonflammable material to the members, close to the weld, in order to restrict this heat flow and thus reduce the expansion.

When fittings are welded, shrinkage strains and their accompanying tendency to cause cracking can be reduced greatly by beginning the weld at the fixed end and working toward the free end of the opening or seam. Cold-rolled alloy-steel forms or heat-treated forms are annealed before welding to reduce the brittleness. Another practice is to relieve the stresses of alloy-steel parts after welding by heating the whole part uniformly to a temperature between 1150 and 1200°F [621 to 649°C] and then allowing the part to cool very slowly.

If a joint is held together by both riveting and welding, the rivet holes are lined up and the welding is completed before the rivets are driven. This procedure prevents the shearing stress on the rivets and the elongation of the holes caused by the expansion and contraction of the metal.

Warpage is controlled by using enough clamps and correctly constructed jigs. **Progressive welding,** which is welding progressively along the joint from the beginning to the end, either continuously from start to finish, or in sections with each section tied in or joined to the next, is another method for reducing strains. A third method is to heat the member on the opposite side from which the weld is made.

Shrinkage is provided for by making the required allowance for normal shrinkage as indicated by a trial weld under similar conditions. An allowance of $^1/_{32}$ in [0.794 mm] at each end of a truss or web member is often enough. This allowance is a rough, general one for both steel-tube structural units and fittings built up of sheet metal, but it is not a substitute for careful work.

Devices for Holding Tubular Structures in Alignment

Figure 6-11 is a drawing of a jack and a tube. Figure 6-12 is a drawing of a fixture for holding tubular structures in alignment during repair, showing the jack set up between struts and the clamp on the outside of the struts. This clamp is adjustable and is placed on the

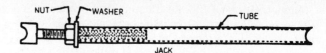

FIG. 6-11 Jack and tube used for alignment.

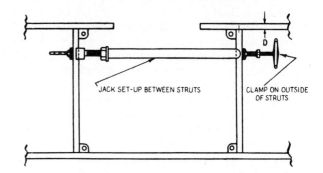

FIG. 6-12 Fixture with jack and tube holding structure in alignment.

outside of the members directly over and parallel to the jack to prevent the assembly from spreading apart.

The original dimensions are obtained from drawings or by measuring the corresponding member of the airplane that is not distorted. If the latter method is followed, the main member is lightly prick-punched, in line with the center of the brace member intersections, and the dimensions are then taken with trammel points and a bar. These measurements are applied to the structure being repaired and the clamps are used to bring the members into the correct position.

Repairs to Fittings

When the fitting welded to a structural member is discovered to be broken or worn, it is removed and a new fitting installed. The new fitting must have physical properties at least equal to those of the original part or unit. In removing the damaged fitting, care must be taken that the tube to which it is attached is not damaged, and the new fitting must be installed in the same manner as the original. If a damaged fitting attached to a main member, where truss members terminate, cannot be removed without weakening the structural members, the part of the tubing having the damaged fitting attached to it should be removed, and a new section and fitting should then be installed.

Repairing Bends and Dents

Most repairs on aircraft tubing require the cutting out and welding in of a partial replacement tube, or the replacement of a whole section of tubing, but some repairs are relatively minor. An example is the straightening of a piece of fuselage tubing which has become slightly bent or buckled. If the bent or buckled part is not made of a heat-treated steel, it should be stronger after straightening because the cold working which the metal receives in the straightening process adds to its strength.

One device useful for straightening bent or buckled tubing is a heavy-duty C-clamp as shown in Fig. 6-13.

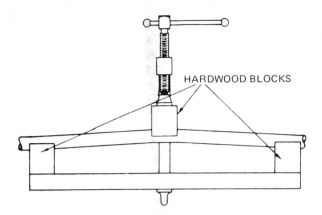

FIG. 6-13　C-clamp used to straighten bent tubing.

Three blocks of hardwood are required for use with the C-clamp. These blocks are cut to fit the shape of the tubing, and the tubing grooves are lined with a soft material such as leather or heavy cloth. Another unit of required equipment is a steel bar, sufficiently strong to withstand the bending stress applied when the tubing is straightened. One of the grooved blocks is placed at each end of the bent section of tubing and the blocks are held in place by the C-clamp and bar, the latter spanning the bent area and backing up the wooden blocks as shown in the illustration. The third block is placed under the jaw of the clamp to bear against the tubing at the point of greatest bend. Since the C-clamp jaws apply pressure to force the tubing toward the steel bar, the tubing is straightened as the clamp is tightened. The handle of the C-clamp should be turned until the tubing is bent slightly past the straight position to allow for spring-back. The clamp and blocks are removed and the tubing is tested by placing a straightedge on both the side and the top of the tube. If the tube is straight, the job is completed. However, if a bend is still apparent, the operation must be repeated until the desired result is obtained.

Whenever a bent tube is straightened, the adjoining welded joints must be examined for cracks. If cracks are found, they must be repaired. They usually occur at the point where the maximum bend was corrected. Briefly, the repair is made by drilling a hole at each end of the crack and welding a split steel sleeve over the crack. The details of such a repair are given later in this chapter. Remember that the tube straightening procedure illustrated and described above is done only if the tube is not dented, crushed, or kinked.

Another minor local defect in tubing is one in which a section of tubing has been slightly flattened; that is, it has become slightly oval-shaped or out-of-round. This defect is remedied by first drilling a steel block to the diameter of the tube to be re-formed. This block, which is usually about 4 in [10 cm] square, is sawed in half lengthwise through the center of the hole, and the two sections are separated. A small quantity of cup grease or oil may be applied to the blocks on the surfaces that will come into contact with the tube. The two grooved steel blocks, obtained by sawing through the original block, are clamped into position over the out-of-round portion of the tube. The clamp is grad-

ually tightened and pressure is applied, as shown in Fig. 6-14 and the assembly is rotated around the tube until it assumes its original, normal shape. Heating the tubing to a dull red makes this procedure easier. If the out-of-round portion of the tube is longer than the length of the two steel blocks, the procedure is repeated throughout the length of the out-of-round area until the whole length has resumed its original round shape.

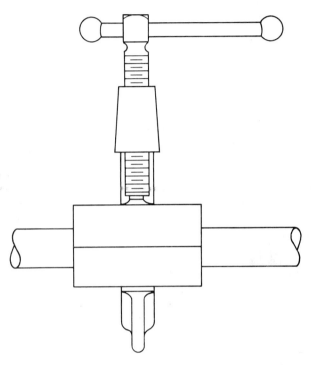

FIG. 6-14　Use of a grooved steel block to re-form steel tubing.

If the defect is a minor, smooth dent in the tubing, not deeper than one-twentieth the tube diameter, and is clear of the middle third of the tube section, it may be disregarded. If the dent is large enough to require removal, and the tubing is not out-of-round for any considerable distance, the dent may be pushed out by air pressure. An air fitting is placed in the tube at one of the self-tapping screws provided at the ends of the main steel tubes, found in some aircraft, so that an air pressure of about 75 psi [520 kPa] or more can be applied inside the tubing. It may be necessary to drill a hole for the installation of a temporary fitting. The hole is welded closed after the dent is removed. The dented area is heated with the welding torch until it is dull red, and the air pressure is maintained until it forces out the dent and restores the tubing to its original shape.

In some cases the combination of heat and air pressure is not sufficient to straighten the tube. Under these conditions, a welding rod is tack-welded to the center of the dented area and pulled while the area is pressurized and heated. When the dent has been pulled out in this manner, the welding rod is removed,

189

the heated area is allowed to cool, and then the air pressure is released. The air-pressure fitting is then removed and the opening is closed.

Surface Patches

If a crack, hole, or significant dent is found in a tube, it may be repaired by one of the following methods.

When a crack is located, all finish must be removed with a wire brush, steel wool, or by sandblasting. If the crack is in an original weld bead, the existing bead is carefully removed by chipping, filing, or grinding. When this has been done, the crack is welded over along the original welded line. A common error in following this procedure is to remove some of the tubing material while taking off the weld bead.

If a small crack is near a cluster joint but not on the weld bead, the finish is removed and a No. 40 (0.098-in [2.49-mm]) hole is drilled at each end of the crack to prevent the crack from spreading. A split reinforcement tube is welded in place completely around the tubing over the cracked area. The repair tubing in this case should have an inside diameter approximately the same as the outside diameter of the tubing being repaired. The repair section is cut at an angle of 30° as shown in Fig. 6-15 before being split so it will fit over the repaired section. The repair tubing should extend a distance of at least 1½ times the diameter of the tubing being repaired beyond each end of the crack. This is shown in the illustration. When the weld is completed and cooled, a coat of zinc chromate or other primer is applied to the area where the finish was removed. Finally, the area is given finishing coats to match the adjoining surfaces.

Under certain conditions, a dent or hole in tubing can be repaired by an external patch which does not completely surround the tubing. If a dent is not deeper than one-tenth the tube diameter and does not encompass more than one-quarter the tube circumference; if

it is free from cracks, abrasions, and sharp corners; and if the tube can be substantially re-formed without cracking before the application of the patch, then a patch such as that shown in Fig. 6-16 can be used. A hole in tubing which is not longer than the tube diameter and does not involve more than one-quarter the tube circumference can be patched in this same manner. Such a patch is not permitted in the middle third of the tube section and must not overlap a tube joint.

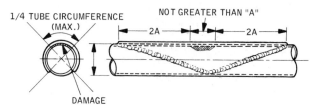

FIG. 6-16 Welded patch repair for dent or hole.

Heat-treated compression members can be returned to their original strength, if the dents are minor, by means of a split tube clamped in place over the damaged section, as shown in Fig. 6-17, where the split tube is called a **splint tube** because it serves as a splint for an injured section. This type of repair should be considered only for temporary purposes, and a suitable permanent repair should be made as soon as possible. For this temporary repair, the split tube should have a wall thickness equal to that of the tube being repaired, and it must be clamped tight enough to prevent both the split tube and the clamps from becoming loose in service. Such a repair should be inspected frequently until the time it is replaced.

If the dents occur in tubular members which are not heat-treated, such dents may be reinforced by welding repairs illustrated in Fig. 6-15. The reinforcement tube is clamped in place and welded along two sides and at the ends as explained previously. This method of repair is satisfactory for short struts or dents in long members near the center of the span because such members are under greater bending stress near the center of the span and their full strength must be retained.

The **split sleeve** reinforcement illustrated in Fig. 6-15 is suitable for repairing cracks, dents, gouges, and other types of damage in structural tubing. In many cases it is necessary to straighten the member because of the bend that occurred at the time of the damage. After the member has been straightened it is necessary that the structure, especially at the welded joints, be thoroughly inspected to detect any possible secondary

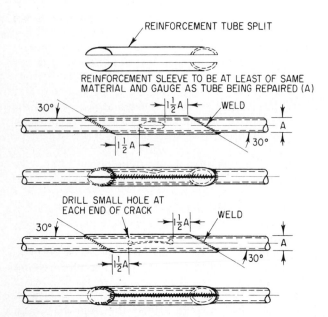

FIG. 6-15 Split-sleeve reinforcement.

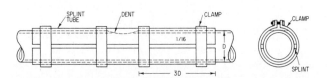

FIG. 6-17 Clamped-tube reinforcement for heat-treated tube.

190

damage which may have occurred. The dye-penetrant method of inspection lends itself well to this inspection. Cracks in welds must be repaired by removing the old weld and rewelding the joint.

Where damage has occurred at a cluster, a patch repair is often desirable. If tubular members, such as fuselage longerons, have sustained local damage at a cluster, they are repaired by welding on a **patch plate,** also called a **finger plate.** Such a repair is illustrated in Fig. 6-18. The patch must be of the same material and thickness as the injured tube and of a size sufficient to cover the damage. The fingers that extend onto the truss members should have a width equal to the diameter of the brace tube and a length equal to at least 1½ times that of the diameter. The ends of the fingers should be rounded or pointed to prevent heating the tube to an annealing temperature in a direct cross section at these spots. Rounding the ends of the fingers also helps to distribute the load, thus reducing stress concentration. Figure 6-19 shows additional details of finger plate repairs.

To prepare a patch for the repair of damage at a cluster, it is best to make a template by cutting a piece of heavy paper in the shape of the required patch. The paper is fitted around the cluster to be repaired and marked for correct size. It is then cut out and tested

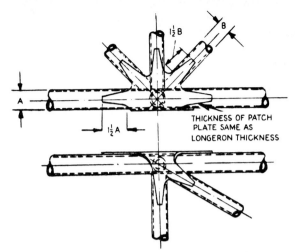

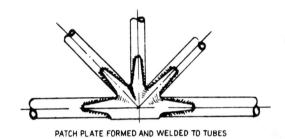

PATCH PLATE BEFORE FORMING AND WELDING

PATCH PLATE FORMED AND WELDED TO TUBES

FIG. 6-19   Details of finger patch repair.

by placing it in the position of the patch. When correctly shaped, paper template is placed on a piece of sheet steel of the correct type and thickness and the steel is marked for cutting.

The patch should be trimmed so that it will extend past the dent in both directions and have fingers as wide as the brace members. All the existing finish on the part to be repaired must be removed. The patch is clamped into position and tack-welded in several places where its edges touch the tubing. It is heated, and light hammer blows with the ball end of a ball peen hammer are applied to form the patch around the repair area. The patch should not be overheated, but it must be softened enough so it can be formed to the tubing with a gap of not more than $\frac{1}{16}$ in [1.59 mm] between the tubing and the patch. The patch is then fused to all the tubes involved by welding around all the edges. When the weld is completed and cooled, the surface around the joint is refinished.

Major Welded Repairs

Unless the damage to the member of a steel-tube structure is comparatively slight, it is usually better to remove the injured section and to weld in either a partial replacement tube or an entirely new section of tubing. Any tube cutting is done with a hacksaw and not by the oxyacetylene-flame cutting process. The manner of removing tubes and the number to be removed are determined by the location and extent of the damage. Any tubes inserted as replacements are joined at their ends by means of a splice.

Splicing in the case of partial tube replacements may

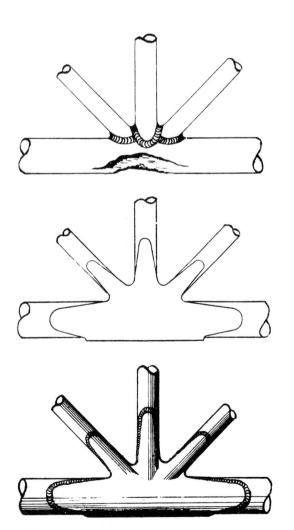

FIG. 6-18   Patch plate repair for damage at a cluster.

191

be done by using an external replacement tube of the next larger diameter, in which case the replacement tube is spliced to the stub ends of the original tubing, or it may be done by using a replacement tube of the same diameter together with either internal or external reinforcing sleeves.

If the original damaged tube includes fittings or castings that have been made especially to fit the tube, the spliced replacement tube must be of the same diameter as the original tubing, and this calls for either internal or external **reinforcing sleeves** under or over the splices.

If no fittings or castings are attached to the original tubing, it is possible to use an **external replacement tube.**

The two principal types of splice welds permitted in the repair of aircraft tubing are the **diagonal (scarf) weld** and the **fishmouth weld.** A splice is never made by butt welding. The best form is the **fishmouth weld,** sometimes called a **fishmouth joint.** It is a tubular joint used in joining two pieces of tubing end to end, which in the edges are cut to resemble a fish's mouth. For pieces of equal diameter, a butt joint with the joining ends of both pieces cut in matching fishmouths is used in conjunction with an inner sleeve; while for pieces of unequal diameter, a reduction joint with only the end of the larger piece cut in a fishmouth. A **scarf joint** is a joint between two members in line with each other, in which the joining ends of one or both pieces are cut diagonally at an angle of about 30° from a center line (scarf cut). In welding aircraft tubing, for example, scarf joints are used both as butt joints and reduction joints.

A **reduction joint** is the joint made between two members of unequal diameter or width, both members being on the same general plane, that is, not at an angle to each other. Reduction joints are used, for example, in the welding of aircraft tubing for joining tubes end to end for greater length, as in the construction of longerons, to repair defective sections of tubing, or to brace a section of a piece of tubing. When additional length is the main purpose, the end of the smaller tube is telescoped into the end of the larger tube, far enough for adequate bracing. A welded joint of this nature is sometimes called a **telescope joint.** When repair or bracing of a central section is the main purpose, a short section of larger tubing is slipped over the smaller tube like a sleeve. Scarf joints and fishmouth joints are usually used in welding reduction joints on aircraft tubing, but occasionally a plain reduction joint with unshaped edges is used.

Figure 6-20 shows a **scarf-butt joint.** Figure 6-21 shows a **scarf-butt splice** reinforced with a steel gusset plate. This splice is sometimes used to join the ends of the circular member of a radial engine mount. The

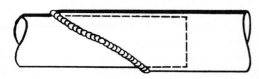

FIG. 6-20   A scarf-butt joint.

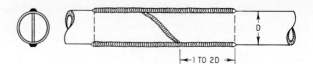

FIG. 6-21   A scarf-butt splice with reinforcing plate.

ends of the tube are prepared with a slot to receive the gusset plate which extends from one to two diameters on each side of the weld between the tube ends. The gusset plate should be ¼ in [6.35 mm] wider than the exterior diameter of the tube and the cut for the scarf splice should be made at an angle of 30°.

Figure 6-22 is a **fishmouth reduction splice** having the end of the telescoping tube cut to give a fishmouth shape. The length of the cut on the outside measurement of the tube is from one to two diameters of the smaller tube. This joint has a greater length of welded seam than a butt or scarf splice and does away with heating the tube to a welding temperature in a direct cross section. It is used for splicing continuous members of steel-tube fuselages and members of other units where tube splices of different diameters are required by the construction.

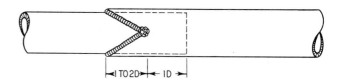

FIG. 6-22   A fishmouth reduction splice.

Figure 6-23 is a **scarf reduction splice** having the end of the telescoping tube cut diagonally at an angle of 30°. This joint is used for splicing members of different diameters and resembles the fishmouth splice to the extent that the tube is not heated to a welding temperature in a direct cross section.

The fishmouth weld is stronger than the scarf (diagonal) joint because of its resistance to bending stresses. There is no single straight line of weld through the structure where a fishmouth weld is used; hence a straight-line break cannot occur if the part is subjected to vibration or shock. However, in some aircraft repairs it will be found that the location of the damage and its extent are such that a diagonal type of weld must be used to the exclusion of the fishmouth type.

The following precautions must be observed in splicing:

1. A cut for splicing purposes must not be made in the middle third of a section of tubing because aircraft tubing must withstand high bending stresses.

2. Only one partial replacement tube can be inserted in any one section of a structural member, because more than one would weaken the member too much. If more than one tube in a joint is injured, the entire joint must be removed and a new, preassem-

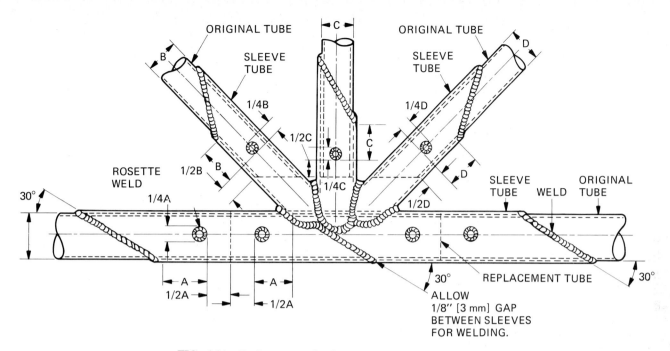

FIG. 6-31 Replacement of a damaged cluster weld at a station.

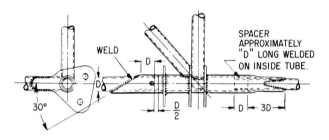

FIG. 6-32 Repair of station with fittings using repair sleeve of larger diameter than original.

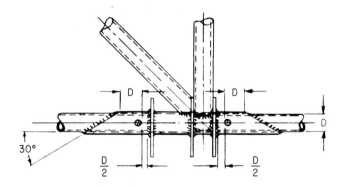

FIG. 6-33 A simple sleeve repair at a station with fittings.

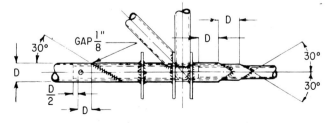

FIG. 6-34 Repair where there is a large difference in diameter of the longeron on each side of the station.

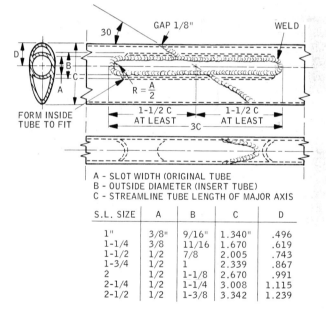

A - SLOT WIDTH (ORIGINAL TUBE
B - OUTSIDE DIAMETER (INSERT TUBE)
C - STREAMLINE TUBE LENGTH OF MAJOR AXIS

S.L. SIZE	A	B	C	D
1"	3/8"	9/16"	1.340"	.496
1-1/4	3/8	11/16	1.670	.619
1-1/2	1/2	7/8	2.005	.743
1-3/4	1/2	1	2.339	.867
2	1/2	1-1/8	2.670	.991
2-1/4	1/2	1-1/4	3.008	1.115
2-1/2	1/2	1-3/8	3.342	1.239

FIG. 6-35 A streamline tube splice using an inner round tube.

tubes to provide for full penetration of the weld. The round tubing section is fitted in the slots as shown and welded in place.

Figure 6-36 illustrates the accepted splice for streamline tubing where a split sleeve is welded over the original tube to reinforce the splice. This repair is applicable to wing-and-tail surface brace struts and similar members. In this method the original tubing is cut squarely across and the split sleeve is scarfed at 30°. The outer sleeve is cut along the trailing edge and then opened up to fit over the original tubing. It is then welded at the trailing edge to the inside tubing

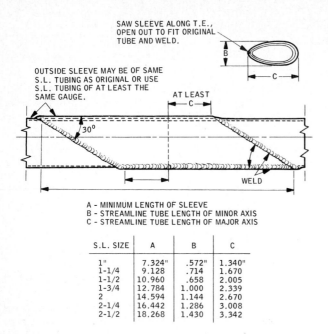

FIG. 6-36 Streamline tube splice using a split sleeve.

A - MINIMUM LENGTH OF SLEEVE
B - STREAMLINE TUBE LENGTH OF MINOR AXIS
C - STREAMLINE TUBE LENGTH OF MAJOR AXIS

S.L. SIZE	A	B	C
1"	7.324"	.572"	1.340"
1-1/4	9.128	.714	1.670
1-1/2	10.960	.658	2.005
1-3/4	12.784	1.000	2.339
2	14.594	1.144	2.670
2-1/4	16.442	1.286	3.008
2-1/2	18.268	1.430	3.342

and along the end scarfs. The dimensions are given in the table.

The splice shown in Fig. 6-37 utilizes an inside sleeve of streamline tubing as a reinforcement. This tubing is the same as the original; however, the size is reduced by cutting off the trailing edge and rewelding. The reinforcing tube is inserted in the ends of the original tubing which has been cut with a 45° scarf. A gap of 1/8 in [3.18 mm] is allowed for welding the two ends together and to the inner sleeve. Rosette welds are used as shown to secure the inner sleeve.

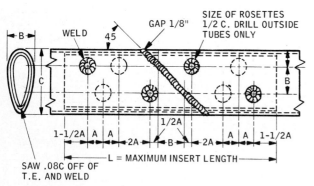

SIZE OF ROSETTES 1/2 C. DRILL OUTSIDE TUBES ONLY

L = MAXIMUM INSERT LENGTH

SAW .08C OFF OF T.E. AND WELD

A IS $\frac{2}{3}$ B

B IS MINOR AXIS LENGTH OF ORIGINAL STREAMLINE TUBE
C IS MAJOR AXIS LENGTH OF ORIGINAL STREAMLINE TUBE

S.L. SIZE	A	B	C	L
1"	.382	.572	1.340	5.16
1-1/4	.476	.714	1.670	6.43
1-1/2	.572	.858	2.005	7.72
1-3/4	.667	1.000	2.339	9.00
2	.763	1.144	2.670	10.30
2-1/4	.858	1.286	3.008	11.58
2-1/2	.954	1.430	3.342	12.88

FIG. 6-37 Streamline tube splice using an inside streamline tube reinforcement.

Figure 6-38 illustrates the splicing method where steel plates are used to reinforce the splice. The steel plates are twice the thickness of the tubing wall. Slots are cut in the streamline tubing according to the dimensions given in the table and the plates are welded into the slots. The ends of the streamline tubing are scarfed at 30° and welded together. A gap of 1/8 in [3.18 mm] is allowed to facilitate the weld.

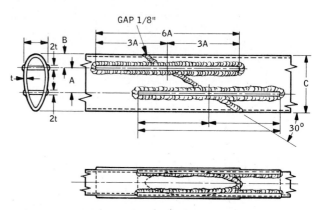

A - STREAMLINE TUBE LENGTH OF MINOR AXIS, PLATE WIDTHS.
B - DISTANCE OF FIRST PLATE FROM LEADING EDGE, 2/3A.
C - STREAMLINE TUBE LENGTH OF MAJOR AXIS.

S.L. SIZE	A	B	C	6A
1"	.572	.382	1.340	3.43
1-1/4	.714	.476	1.670	4.28
1-1/2	.858	.572	2.005	5.15
1-3/4	1.000	.667	2.339	6.00
2	1.144	.762	2.670	6.86
2-1/4	1.286	.858	3.008	7.72
2-1/2	1.430	.954	3.342	8.58

FIG. 6-38 Streamline tube splice using steel-plate inserts.

Repair of Engine Mounts

Welded engine mounts are particularly vulnerable to damage by cracking, largely because of the vibration to which they are subjected. Landing loads on such mounts are also particularly severe because the weight effect of the engine is multiplied several times during a hard landing. For these reasons the materials used in the manufacture of engine mounts should be of high quality, and the welded joints must be uniform and strong. Engine-mount repairs are accomplished in the same manner as other tubular-steel repairs; however, replacement tubes should be large enough to slip over the original tubing. A fishmouth joint is recommended although a 30° scarf may be used if necessary. Rosette welds are used to assure a completely rigid joint.

Repairs to engine mounts must be governed by accurate means of checking the alignment. When new tubes are used to replace bent or damaged tubes, the original alignment of the structure must be maintained. This is done by measuring the distance between points of corresponding members that have not been distorted and by reference to the drawings furnished by the manufacturer.

If all members are out of alignment, the engine mount must be replaced by one supplied by the manufacturer; the method of checking the alignment of the fuselage or nacelle points should be requested from the manufacturer.

Minor damage, such as a crack adjacent to an engine attachment lug, may be repaired by rewelding the ring and extending a gusset or a mounting lug past the damaged area. Engine-mount rings that have been extensively damaged should not be repaired, but should be replaced unless the method of repair is approved by an authorized agency.

Wing- and Tail-Surface Repairs

Built-up tubular wing- or tail-surface spars may be repaired by using any of the standard splices and methods of repair described in this chapter if the spars are not heat-treated. If they are heat-treated, the entire spar assembly must be re-heat-treated to the manufacturer's specifications after the repair is completed. This is usually less practicable than replacing the spar with one furnished by the manufacturer of the airplane.

Damaged wing brace struts made from either round or streamlined tubing are usually replaced by new members bought from the original manufacturer. There is no objection from an airworthiness viewpoint to repairing such members in any correct manner. Brace struts must be spliced only adjacent to the end fittings. When making repairs to wing- and tail-surface brace members, particular attention must be paid to the proper fit and alignment.

Welded Repair of Fabric-Covered Steel Fuselage

When it is necessary to make a repair of a fabric-covered, steel-tubing fuselage without the removal of large sections of fabric, care must be taken to see that the fabric is not damaged by heat or set afire. Fabric covering is often very flammable; hence it should not be exposed to the sparks from welding, and heat conducted through the tubing should be stopped before it reaches the fabric.

To protect the fabric, it is cut and laid back away from the area to be welded. This usually requires a cut along the longeron and perpendicular to the longeron on each side. When the fabric is rolled back, it should not be creased or folded because this will crack the dope and possibly weaken the fabric. Wet cloths are then wrapped around the tubing on all sides of the area to be repaired. These cloths will prevent the heat from being conducted to the fabric. Additional wet cloth is placed over the fabric where sparks from the welding process could reach to the fabric.

After the welding is completed and the tubing refinished, the fabric is sewed, reinforced, and doped as has been described earlier in this text.

● SPECIAL WELDING REPAIRS

Certain aircraft components require special handling when being repaired by welding. This special handling may be necessary for proper restoration of component strength or for the safety of the mechanic when performing the repair operation.

Steel Parts Which Must Not Be Welded

Airplane parts that depend for their proper functioning on strength properties developed by cold working must not be welded. These parts include (1) streamlined wires and cables; (2) brazed or soldered parts (the brazing mixture or solder will penetrate hot steel and weaken it); (3) steel parts, mostly of nickel-alloy steels, which have been heat-treated to improve their physical properties, particularly aircraft bolts, turnbuckle ends, axles, and other heat-treated steel-alloy parts.

Figure 6-39 shows landing gear assemblies that are not generally regarded as repairable for the following reasons: (1) The axle stub is usually made from a highly heat-treated nickel-alloy steel and carefully machined to close tolerances; hence such stubs are generally replaceable and should be replaced if damaged; (2) the oleo portion of the structure is usually heat-treated after welding and is precisely machined to make certain that the shock absorber will function properly. These parts would be distorted by welding after machining.

The spring steel strut, also shown in Fig. 6-39 and installed on a number of Cessna airplanes, cannot be welded without severely reducing its strength. If a strut of this type is damaged or found to be cracked, it should be replaced with an airworthy part.

Repairable Axle Assemblies

Figure 6-40 shows three types of landing-gear and axle assemblies formed from steel tubing. These may be repaired by any standard method shown in the previous sections of this chapter. However, it is always necessary to find out whether or not the members are heat-treated. It must be remembered that all members which depend on heat treatment for their original physical properties should be re-heat-treated after the welding operation. If it happens that the heat-treat value cannot be obtained from the manufacturer, some test must be made, such as the Brinell or Rockwell hardness tests applied in several places of the member being tested. Welding must be done with a rod which can be heat-treated.

Damaged ski pedestals which are constructed of welded tubular steel can be repaired according to the methods described previously in this chapter. Care should be taken to note whether the pedestals are heat-treated; and if they are, they should be welded with a heat-treatable rod and re-heat-treated after the repair is made.

Repair of Engine Exhaust Units

Exhaust manifolds for reciprocating engines and exhaust cones and noise suppressors for turbine engines are usually constructed of stainless steel, Inconel, or other high-temperature alloy. Welding of cracks in these parts is most satisfactorily accomplished by means of inert-gas welding. It is is important for the mechanic to determine what the alloy is and to use the correct type of filler rod for the weld.

A strong jig is required for holding the parts of an exhaust manifold in position during construction and

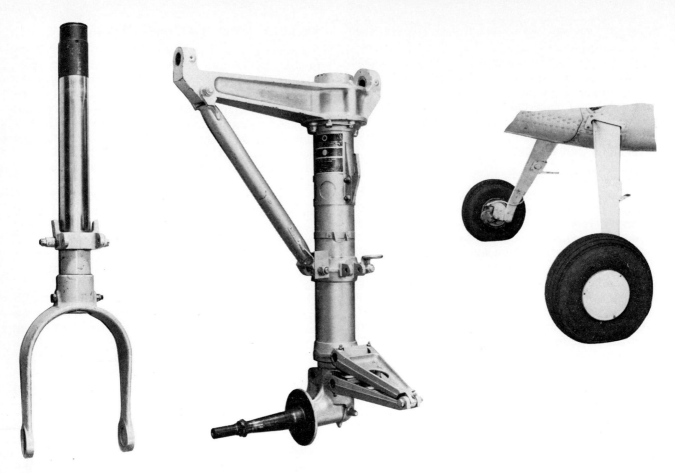

FIG. 6-39   Landing gear assemblies which cannot be repaired by welding.

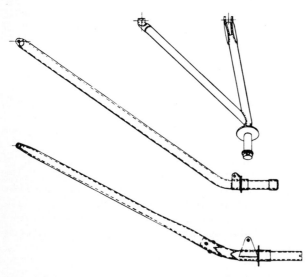

FIG. 6-40   Three types of landing gear and axle assemblies that can be repaired by welding.

for maintaining the correct alignment during assembly and repair. The typical unit may have a heavy bedplate with fittings for locating and holding the parts in position while welding is done, making allowance for the expansion and contraction of the parts in a longitudinal direction without permitting them to get out of line.

The repair of exhaust manifolds usually consists of welding cracks or breaks, patching worn parts, and replacing broken or worn fittings.

Before repairing a crack or break, the metal on the inside and outside must be clean and bright, and there must be a $\frac{1}{16}$- to $\frac{3}{32}$-in [1.59- to 2.38-mm] hole drilled at each end of the crack to prevent it from spreading. If the crack is more than 2 in [5.08 cm] long, the break is tacked at 2-in intervals. When gas welding is used for the repair of exhaust units, distortion and cracking on cooling are reduced by heating the part to between 400 and 600°F [204 and 316°C]. In repairing stainless-steel exhaust units, if much welding has been done, the units are preheated to between 1900 and 2000°F [1038 and 1093°C]; they are then cooled slowly and evenly to relieve the residual stresses caused by welding and to restore the metal to its original condition.

When a damaged fitting is replaced, the old fitting, including the weld-metal deposit, must be ground off and the section cleaned inside before the new fitting is made and welded in place.

It is often necessary to repair sections of the exhaust manifold that telescope together because they are subjected to considerable wear. The worn portion is removed and replaced with a new section made of sheet stock of the same gauge and kind of metal as the original portion. In gas welding, a heavy coat of flux is applied to the edges on the lower side to prevent oxidation of the weld metal and the base metal.

Repair of Fuel and Oil Tanks

When fuel and oil tanks are repaired, either by inert-gas or oxy-fuel welding, it is most important that the tank be thoroughly purged of any fuel or oil fumes before the welding is begun. Even if a fuel tank has been empty for a long time and appears to be dry inside, it is still likely that enough fumes can be released by the heat of welding to create an explosive mixture. The correct procedure in such cases is to wash the tank with hot water and a detergent and then allow live steam to flow through the tank for about 3 min. This treatment will vaporize and remove any residual fuel or oil that may be in the tank.

The welding of tanks, whether they be constructed of aluminum, stainless steel, or titanium should be done by inert-gas if possible. As previously explained, this method produces a smooth weld with a minimum of distortion due to heat and also eliminates oxidation and burning of the metal.

There are several types of welded seams used in the construction of aluminum tanks for aircraft. These include butt joints, corner joints, edge joints, and lap joints. When baffle plates are riveted to the shell, the rivets are headed by welding to make them liquid-tight.

Corrugated beads, formed into the sheet, adjacent and parallel to the seams, provide for expansion and contraction. These beads, acting as expansion joints, close up slightly when the metal expands under the heat of welding and straighten out on cooling enough to relieve the strains of contraction. In addition, they add stiffness to the metal and help to prevent buckling.

Figure 6-41 shows a riveted joint between the shell and baffle plate with a rivet headed to the shell by welding.

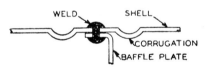

FIG. 6-41 Welded joint with rivets to secure baffle plates.

Figure 6-42 shows a joint used to secure the baffle plates to the shell in some types of tank construction. The plates either extend through a slot and are welded to the shell, or they are located at the seams in the shell and are welded to the shell when the seams are made.

Figure 6-43 shows a mechanical lock seam sealed by welding in the construction of some types of shells.

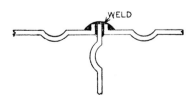

FIG. 6-42 Welded joint to secure baffle plate in a tank.

FIG. 6-43 A welded lock seam.

Figure 6-44 shows a joint adaptable for small seams. The turned edges provide stiffness to the sheet at the joint, tend to maintain alignment during welding, and supply additional metal for the weld.

FIG. 6-44 Welded seam with turned-up edges.

Figure 6-45 shows how edge joints may be used for corner seams in making a tank and for welding hand-hole cover plates into the shell.

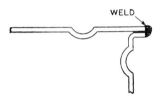

FIG. 6-45 Corner-seam edge joint.

Figure 6-46 shows a corner seam widely used in tank construction. It is welded like a flanged butt joint.

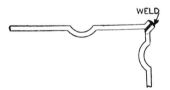

FIG. 6-46 Flanged corner-seam joint.

Figure 6-47 shows a butt-type joint with a stiffener strip between the butt ends that is extended above the plates. Fillet welds are used to secure the whole assembly.

If a tank is repaired by gas welding, it is extremely important to remove all welding flux after a repair in order to prevent corrosion. As soon as welding is completed, a tank is washed inside and outside with great quantities of hot water and is then drained. It is then either immersed in 5% nitric or sulfuric acid or filled with this solution and also washed on the outside with the same solution. The acid is left in contact with the weld about 1 h and then rinsed carefully with

FIG. 6-47 A butt-type joint with stiffener strip.

clean, fresh water. The efficiency of the cleaning process is tested by applying some acidified 5% silver nitrate solution to a small quantity of rinse water that has been used for the last washing of the weld. If a white precipitate is formed, the cleaning has not been done thoroughly, and the washing must be repeated.

Cowlings

Aluminum and aluminum-alloy **cowlings** are usually repaired by patching worn spots; welding cracks, or breaks, caused by vibration; and replacing worn or broken fittings.

A crack, or break, is repaired by welding the fracture. Inert-gas welding should be used if possible, but a skilled operator can make suitable repairs by gas welding. All welds must have enough penetration to provide a small bead on the lower side. In repairing cracks that extend into the sheet from a hole in the cowl or from the edge, the cracks are lined up, tacked, and welded progressively, starting from the end of the crack toward the edge or opening. A cowling having been repaired by welding must be finished on the outside to provide a smooth surface.

Worn spots may be repaired by removing the worn section and replacing it with a new piece that is cut to fit the removed portion and then formed to the required shape before installation. It is then placed in position and tack-welded at intervals of 1 to 2 in [2.5 to 5 cm] around the edges before the actual welding is performed.

● SOLDERING AND BRAZING

In general, soldering may be described as either **soft** or **hard,** depending upon the type of material used for the soldering bond, which determines the temperature required in the process. In **soft soldering,** the sealing and securing of a joint between two metal pieces is accomplished with solder that consists of an alloy of tin and lead. The percentages of the two metals vary according to the particular type of solder and the strength required. Common solders are referred to as 40-60, 50-50, and 60-40, the first number being the percentage of tin and the second number being the percentage of lead. The percentages of the two metals have a substantial effect on the melting point of the solder. Pure lead melts at 621.5°F [327.5°C] and pure tin melts at 449.38°F [231.88°C], but an alloy of 63 percent tin and 37 percent lead melts at 361°F [182.78°C]. Solder designated 50-50 has a melting point of approximately 420°F [215 to 256°C].

It must be pointed out that special solders may contain metals other than tin, for example, silver, antimony, or bismuth. Special solders are required for best results in certain soldering processes.

The difference between soft soldering and **brazing,** or **hard soldering,** is in the temperature. By definition, if the filler metal has a melting point of more than 800°F [426.67°C], the process is called brazing or hard soldering.

In soft soldering, the melted solder is spread over the adjoining surfaces with a soldering ''iron'' (copper) or a jet of flame. The solder does not actually fuse with the metals being joined but bonds to them on the surface; that is, the base metal does not melt. Soldering produces a relatively weak joint but is satisfactory for many purposes. It is especially useful in making airtight joints of sheet metal that do not have to withstand much pull or vibration, and it is also used to seal electrical connections. Where soldering is attempted, it is necessary to employ flux such as rosin, zinc chloride, or sal ammoniac to clean the surfaces to be soldered and prevent the formation of oxides so the solder can adhere to the metal.

The metals commonly soldered are iron, tin, copper, brass, galvanized iron, and terneplate. Aluminum, stainless steel, titanium, and other metals can be soldered under the proper conditions and with the right materials. Ordinary lead-tin solder cannot be used for all soldering. Special fluxes are available, however, which make possible a broad application of such solder.

The use of soft or hard soldering for the repair of aircraft parts is strictly limited. Generally these processes should not be employed for any stressed (load-bearing) part. In certain instances, silver soldering or brazing may be employed, but the repair must be approved and passed by proper government authority if it is used on a certificated aircraft.

Soldering Copper

The **soldering copper** is the solid, pointed block of copper alloy forming the head (tip) of a soldering tool (soldering iron or soldering copper). It is attached to the handle by means of an iron shank with a tang. The copper is heated, usually in a flame, and then used to melt and spread the solder on the surfaces to be joined. It must be emphasized that the soldering copper must be clean and well-tinned and the correct flux must be applied.

Soldering coppers are manufactured in many sizes and shapes. Figure 6-48 shows four common shapes used in commercial sheet-metal work.

It is common practice to employ electric soldering irons because of their convenience where electric power is available. The electric tool contains a resistance heating element inside the hollow copper head. An electric soldering iron is shown in Fig. 6-49.

As explained previously, a soldering copper (either flame-heated or electrically-heated) must be tinned before it can be used. If the copper is not tinned, the solder will not adhere to it and the heat will not be conducted in sufficient quantity to melt the solder and heat the joint. To tin the copper, the tip is first filed clean and in the correct shape. After being filed to shape, the copper is heated and then filed again slightly to remove any oxide which has formed. When bright and clean the tip is dipped into a flux before solder is applied. If rosin-core solder is used, it is not necessary to dip the tip in flux. When the entire point is covered with melted solder, the copper is ready for use.

Flux

Flux is, in general, any chemical compound, such as borax, ammonium chloride, sodium carbonate, zinc chloride, rosin, or stearic acid, which unites with ox-

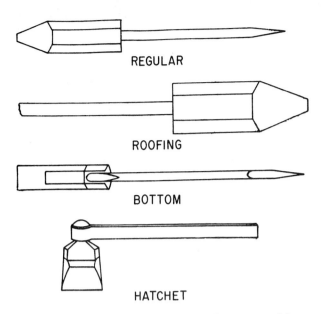

FIG. 6-48 Common soldering coppers for commercial work.

FIG. 6-49 An electric soldering iron.

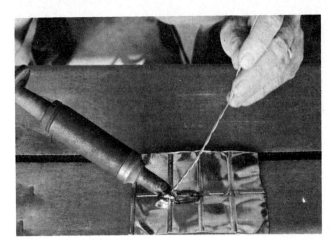

FIG. 6-50 Soldering a seam.

ides and other impurities in molten metal and floats them to the surface. In soldering, the most common fluxes are acid (hydrochloric acid in which zinc has been dissolved), rosin, and paste fluxes. The use of acid fluxes is not approved for aircraft work because of the corrosive effects of such fluxes. The fluxes recommended for aircraft work are rosin and nonacid paste flux. Excess paste flux should be wiped off after the soldering is completed.

Fluxes for hard soldering (silver soldering, brazing, and eutectic welding) are (1) powdered borax, (2) powdered borax and carbonate of soda, and (3) special patented fluxes designed for specific types of hard soldering.

Soft Soldering

The technique for **soft soldering** involves clean parts, proper fit, and correct flux. Scraping, filing, or wire brushing are the usual cleaning methods. Scale, dirt, and oxides are thoroughly removed. The cleaned surfaces are then fitted in place, coated with the proper flux, and the hot soldering copper applied with the solder to the adjoining parts. A small additional amount of flux is often necessary to remove any oxides that may form and to help the melting of the solder that is already applied. It is essential that the soldering copper be kept in contact with the work until the solder is thoroughly sweated into the joint. Poor solder joints are often the result of insufficient heat.

When soldering a seam such as that shown in Fig. 6-50, the parts to be soldered should be tacked with drops of solder unless they are otherwise fastened together. The solder is picked up with the soldering copper and transferred to the metal where it is deposited along the seam. Flux should be used as required to cause the solder to adhere to the metal.

To finish the seam, a hot, well-tinned soldering copper is applied with the point extending over the seam on the single thickness of metal; the heel or back of the copper is over the seam itself, at an angle of about 45°. The bar of solder or wire solder is touched to the copper while in this position. As it melts, the copper is drawn slowly along the work, keeping it at an angle and permitting it to sweat the solder into the entire width of the seam.

Hard Soldering

Silver soldering is a process of hard soldering with a composition of copper, zinc, silver, and tin. Since soft-soldered gasoline- and oil-pipe joints, and similar joints, fracture with repeated vibration, this type of solder is used. It is suitable for bronze parts, copper, stainless steel, and brass. Since the solder cannot be melted with a soldering copper, it is necessary to use a neutral torch flame for heating the solder and the joint. It is usually necessary to heat the parts and the solder to a red heat in order to melt the solder and cause it to flow into the joint. The correct type of flux must be used for the materials being soldered.

The process called **brazing,** in which a brass-type rod is used for "soldering" the joint, is also a form of hard soldering. Still another process is called **eutectic welding.** The term **eutectic** describes low-melting-point metals. Eutectic welding is a form of welding akin to hard soldering in which the welding material has a lower melting point than the metal being welded; thus this type of welding can be classed as hard soldering and is similar to brazing or silver soldering.

Sweat Soldering

Sweat soldering, also called **sweating,** is a method of soldering in which the parts to be soldered are first tinned (coated with solder), and then the melted solder is drawn between the surfaces to be soldered by capillary attraction with the application of heat. Sometimes a soldering iron is used and sometimes a neutral gas flame (torch) is used to melt and flow the solder in the joint. The torch is required in hard soldering or brazing.

● REVIEW QUESTIONS

1. What type of steel is commonly used for tubular steel structures in aircraft?
2. If major repair work is done on a welded steel tubular fuselage, what precautions must be taken?
3. What principal factor governs the size of a welding tip?
4. When welding a structure which will require heat treating, what type of filler rod must be used?
5. When welding a section of tubing into a structure, why is it a good practice to allow one end to cool after welding before welding the other end?
6. Describe a method for straightening a bent section of tubing in a fuselage.
7. Under what conditions is it permissible to ignore a dent in structural tubing?
8. Describe a method for removing a dent from steel tubing.
9. Describe a method that may be employed to detect small cracks in a welded joint.
10. Before welding a reinforcing sleeve or patch over a crack in tubing, what should be done with respect to the crack?
11. Describe the installation of a *finger plate patch*.
12. At what angle is the scarf for a repair sleeve cut?
13. Describe a *fishmouth* cut for a sleeve.
14. Why is a fishmouth joint stronger than a scarf joint?
15. When cutting a length of replacement tubing which is to be spliced with inner sleeve reinforcements, how much clearance must be allowed for each end of tubing?
16. How are inner splice sleeves placed into position for welding a replacement tube between stations?
17. What are the lengths of the original tube stubs required when splicing in a new replacement section between stations and the replacement section is telescoped over the original stubs?
18. Describe a *rosette weld*.
19. What is the maximum clearance between an outer reinforcement sleeve and the tube inside it?
20. Describe the replacement of a cluster weld with the use of outside reinforcement sleeves.
21. What precautions must be taken when making a welded repair on a fabric-covered fuselage?
22. What special care must be taken with the inspection and repair of welded engine mounts?
23. Describe three methods for welding steel-attachment fittings to tubular structures.
24. Explain how a fuselage structure can be held in alignment while making welded repairs.
25. Describe three methods for splicing streamline tubing.
26. What type of landing gear axle structures are not repairable by welding?
27. Why is it not permissible to weld a steel structure which has been brazed?
28. What types of nondestructive inspections can be performed to assure that welds have been made properly?
29. How can the interior of welded steel tubing be protected against corrosion?
30. Discuss the weld repair for exhaust parts.
31. What precaution must be taken before welding fuel and oil tanks?
32. What should be done to welds that are made on the outside surface of cowlings?
33. What is meant by *soldering?*
34. What is the effect of alloying tin and lead to produce material for soft soldering?
35. What is the difference between *soft soldering* and *hard soldering?*
36. What are the three hard soldering processes?
37. How would you *tin* a soldering copper?
38. What is the function of a *flux* in soldering?
39. Describe the procedure for soft soldering.
40. Why is a torch needed for hard soldering or for brazing?
41. What would be the best type of soldering to join two pieces of stainless steel?
42. Discuss the limitations on soldering as a method for aircraft repair.

7 SHEET METAL CONSTRUCTION AND REPAIRS

For a number of years after the first operation of airplanes, and during World War I, the structural repair of aircraft involved woodwork, dope and fabric, and welding. After all-metal airplanes were developed, before and after World War II, structural assembly and repair of aircraft involved a much greater proportion of sheet-metal work and a declining amount of wood, fabric, and welding. Today's metal aircraft utilize aluminum alloy, magnesium, titanium, stainless steel, aluminum alloy bonded sandwich (honeycomb), glass fiber, and other materials. The thicknesses are from thin sheet (up to 0.080 in [2.03 mm]) to heavy plate (0.080 in [2.03 mm] and above), sometimes an inch or more in thickness, depending on the stresses to be carried by the section of skin involved.

The construction of aircraft components from sheet metal may be necessary when performing modifications to aircraft or as part of a repair operation. The basic standards and techniques presented in this chapter that deal with repair procedures are directly applicable to the assembly of new aircraft and components. It is important that the mechanic realize that the information presented here is of a general nature. For specific information about repairs to a particular model aircraft, consult the manufacturer's maintenance manual and structural repair manual.

Damage to an aircraft structure may be caused by corrosion, vibration, impact of rocks or other objects, hard landings, excessive loads in flight, collision, and crash damage. In every case of such damage it is the duty of the mechanic to make a very careful inspection of all affected parts and assess the degree of damage. The mechanic must then determine the type of repair required and design the repair so that the strength of the structure will be returned to its original value or greater. This process requires a thorough knowledge of the structure, the materials of which it is constructed, and the processes employed in the manufacture.

Fasteners for metal structural assemblies once consisted largely of aluminum alloy rivets and plated steel bolts. As the performance of aircraft was increased, strength requirements for certain structures necessitated the use of such fasteners as Hi-Shear rivets, Huck Lockbolts, close-tolerance bolts, and other high-strength fasteners. For assemblies where it was not possible to work on both sides to install rivets, a number of different types of blind rivets were developed. The use and installation of special fasteners are discussed later in this chapter and in the companion text *Aircraft Basic Science*.

● HAND TOOLS FOR SHEET-METAL WORK

Most common hand tools are used at one time or another when working with sheet-metal structures. In this section we will look at those tools which are principally associated only with sheet-metal construction and repair operations. A discussion of general-use hand tools can be found in the companion text *Aircraft Basic Science*.

Hammers

Figure 7-1 shows two types of hammers often used by aircraft mechanics in the repair and forming of sheet-metal aircraft parts. The hammers shown are used for smoothing and forming sheet metal and are commonly called **planishing hammers.** The hammer with the square face is used for working in corners. When it is necessary to work in the radius of a bend, a hammer with a cross peen is used.

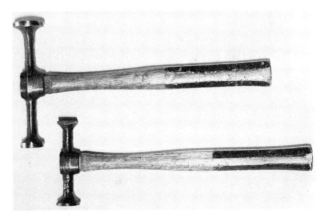

FIG. 7-1 Planishing hammers.

Hand Snips and Shears

Several types of **hand snips** and **shears** are shown in Fig. 7-2. These are named as follows: (1) right-hand straight snips, (2) left-hand straight snips, (3) double-cutting shears, (4) circular-cutting shears, (5) bench shears, and (6) aviation snips. The latter are especially made for cutting heat-treated aluminum alloy, stainless steel, and titanium. The blades have small teeth on their cutting edges and the handles are made to give great leverage. Aviation snips are shown in Fig. 7-3.

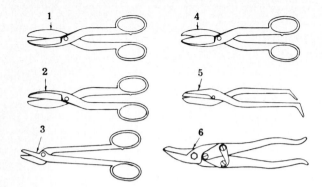

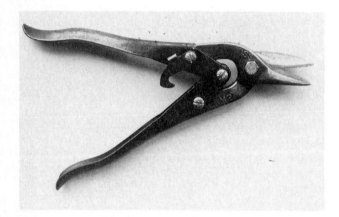

FIG. 7-2 Hand snips and shears.

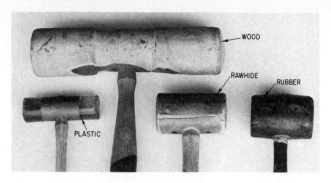

FIG. 7-5 Soft mallets for working metal.

shrinking metal when forming a curved flange is shown in Fig. 7-6. This mallet is made from a hardwood such as maple and is called a **shrinking mallet** or **hammer.** Its use in forming a curved metal flange is discussed later in this chapter.

FIG. 7-3 Aviation snips.

Hand Nibbling Tool

A **hand nibbling tool** is used to remove metal from small areas by cutting out small pieces of metal with each "nibble." This tool is most useful in confined areas where using snips is not possible and where a minimum amount of metal distortion is desired. A hand nibbling tool is shown in Fig. 7-4.

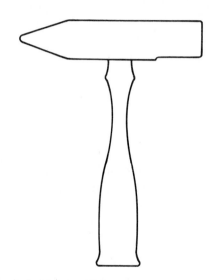

FIG. 7-6 A shrinking mallet.

FIG. 7-4 Hand nibbling tool. *(U.S. Ind. Tool & Supply)*

Punches

Hand punches, usually called simply **punches,** are shown in Fig. 7-7. The **center punch** is used to produce a small conical indentation in metal to help center a drill and hold it in position while starting a hole. It is also used to mark a point on metal for reference in measuring. The **solid punch** is for general use wherever such a tool is appropriate. A **transfer punch** provides

Mallets

Soft mallets (see Fig. 7-5) are of particular importance in the forming of sheet-metal parts to prevent damage to the metal. The mallet may be made of wood, rawhide, rubber, or plastic and is used in forming sheet metal over stakes or forms. Soft hammers or mallets should be used in any case where there is a possibility of causing damage by the use of a steel hammer.

A special type of mallet or hammer used to aid in

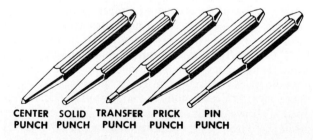

CENTER PUNCH SOLID PUNCH TRANSFER PUNCH PRICK PUNCH PIN PUNCH

FIG. 7-7 Hand punches.

a means for transferring the position of a drilled hole from one part to another. When using the transfer punch, the size of the shank must be the same as that of the hole being transferred. The **prick punch** is used primarily for marking a point in metal. The **pin punch** is useful for installing or removing metal pins from cylindrical shafts or other parts. The punch diameter must be slightly less than the diameter of the pin.

Figure 7-8 is one type of **hand lever punch.** This

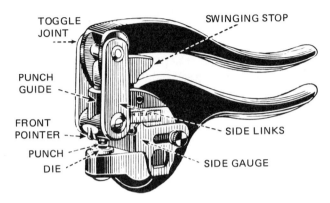

FIG. 7-8 A hand lever punch.

punch is designed to produce great force such that a hole may easily be punched through aluminum or other soft metal. A **rotary lever punch** is shown in Fig. 7-9.

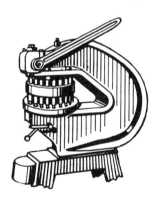

FIG. 7-9 A rotary lever punch.

Hand Rivet Set

A **hand rivet set** is shown in Fig. 7-10. This type of set is used in commercial sheet-metal work and is also used for some hand-riveting operations in aircraft work. The holes in the hand-rivet set are for the purpose of drawing rivets through the metal before riveting. A rivet is inserted through a drilled hole in the metal, and the hole in the set is placed over the protruding shank of the rivet. With the head of the rivet held against a suitable backing block, the set is struck lightly with a hammer. This draws the sheets of metal together and causes them to fit snugly against the inside of the head of the rivet. The shank of the rivet may then be headed with the hammer.

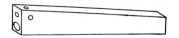

FIG. 7-10 A hand rivet set.

Wire and Sheet-Metal Gauges

Wire and sheet-metal gauges are used for measuring the diameter of wire and the thickness of sheet metal. Figure 7-11 shows one form of this type of gauge. It is simply a circular disk with slots cut around its circumference and numbered to indicate dimensions and measurements obtained by inserting the wire or sheet metal into the slot.

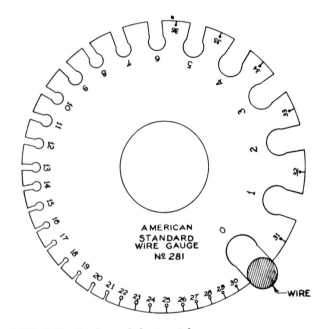

FIG. 7-11 A wire and sheet-metal gauge.

Rivet Gun and Set

The **rivet gun,** or **riveting hammer,** is the device most commonly used by the mechanic for driving rivets. The rivet gun is equipped with a **rivet set** designed to fit the head of the rivet being driven. The set is inserted into the **set sleeve** of the gun and is held in place by means of a **retaining spring.** The retaining spring must always be in place to prevent the set from flying out and causing injury to anyone who may be in the vicinity. During operation a piston in the gun is driven rapidly back and forth by compressed air which is alternately directed to one side of the piston and then the other. This causes the piston to strike the set rapidly, driving the rivet against the bucking bar and forming the bucked head. The cut-away drawing in Fig. 7-12 illustrates the construction and operating mechanism of a typical rivet gun. Various other designs for rivet guns are also shown in Fig. 7-12.

Rivet guns are available in various sizes, starting with 1X, the smallest, which is used for rivets of $\frac{1}{16}$- and $\frac{3}{32}$-in [1.59- and 2.38-mm] diameter. The size of rivet guns increases progressively for rivets of larger diameter, the most commonly used size being the 3X,

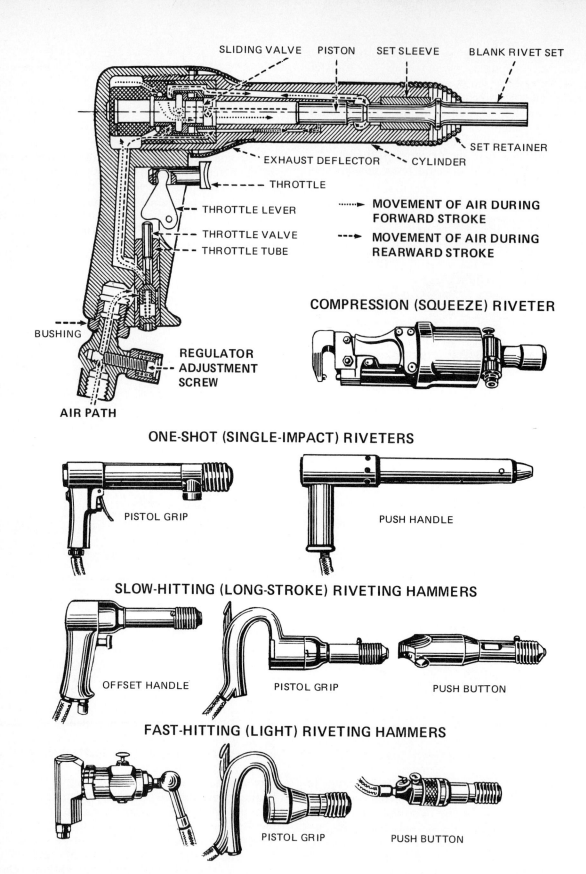

SLIDING VALVE · PISTON · SET SLEEVE · BLANK RIVET SET

SET RETAINER

EXHAUST DEFLECTOR · CYLINDER

THROTTLE

THROTTLE LEVER

THROTTLE VALVE

THROTTLE TUBE

·······▶ MOVEMENT OF AIR DURING FORWARD STROKE

---▶ MOVEMENT OF AIR DURING REARWARD STROKE

BUSHING

REGULATOR ADJUSTMENT SCREW

AIR PATH

COMPRESSION (SQUEEZE) RIVETER

ONE-SHOT (SINGLE-IMPACT) RIVETERS

PISTOL GRIP

PUSH HANDLE

SLOW-HITTING (LONG-STROKE) RIVETING HAMMERS

OFFSET HANDLE

PISTOL GRIP

PUSH BUTTON

FAST-HITTING (LIGHT) RIVETING HAMMERS

PISTOL GRIP

PUSH BUTTON

FIG. 7-12 Construction and types of rivet guns.

which is used for rivets of from ³⁄₃₂- to ⁵⁄₃₂-in [2.38- to 3.97-mm] diameter. For larger-size rivets, 4X and 5X rivet guns may be used. There are several larger sizes of rivet guns used for even larger rivets than the ones we have mentioned.

Rivet sets are made in many sizes and shapes to meet different requirements for riveting and to provide for the different types of rivets. The **shank** of a rivet set is the part inserted into the rivet gun. Shanks are made in uniform standard sizes to fit standard rivet guns. Figure 7-13 illustrates typical rivet sets for use with a rivet gun.

Rivet sets designed for use with universal- or brazier-head rivets have a cupped head to fit over the rivet head. The cup is curved with a slightly larger radius than that of the rivet head to assure that the maximum force of the gun is applied to the center of the rivet head, causing the rivet to draw the riveted materials together as the bucked head is being formed.

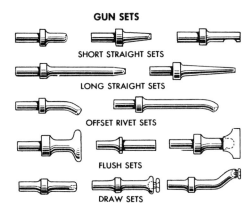

FIG. 7-13 Rivets sets.

Rivet guns and rivet sets perform better work and will last longer if they are properly handled and serviced, the latter meaning ordinary good care, including lubricating, cleaning, etc.

A rivet set should not be placed against steel or other hard metal when the air power is on; this practice will ruin the rivet set.

A rivet set can be a deadly weapon. If a rivet set is placed in a rivet gun without a set retainer and the throttle of the gun is open, the rivet set may be projected like a bullet out of the gun and cause either a severe injury to a person or the destruction of equipment.

A few drops of light machine oil should be placed daily in the air intake of the rivet gun. Depending upon use, the rivet gun should be disassembled and cleaned, worn parts replaced, and then reassembled and lubricated.

Bucking Bars

A **bucking bar** is a smooth steel bar made up in a variety of special shapes and sizes and used to form a head on the shank of a rivet while it is being driven by a rivet gun. The edges are slightly rounded to prevent marring the material, and the surface is perfectly smooth. The face of the bar, placed against the

shank of the rivet, is flat. Bucking bars are sometimes called **dollies, bucking irons,** or **bucking blocks.**

For best results, the mechanic should choose a bucking bar of the proper weight and shape for a particular application. A common rule of thumb is that the bucking bar should weigh approximately 1 lb [450 g] less than the number of the rivet gun with which it is being used. For example, the bucking bar to be used with a 3X gun should weigh about 2 lb [900 g]. Figure 7-14 illustrates a group of bucking bars.

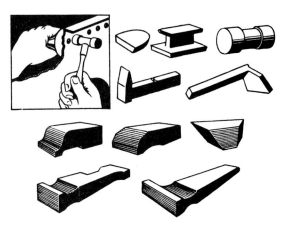

FIG. 7-14 Bucking bars.

Expanding bucking bars, shown in Fig. 7-15, are steel blocks whose diameters or widths can be adjusted. A bucking bar of this type is attached to the end of a hollow steel shaft which contains a bar that can be twisted to expand or reduce the width of the block. It is used to buck (upset) rivets on the inside of tubular structures or in similar spaces that cannot be reached by regular bucking bars. The space must be small enough for one side of the partly expanded block to press against the tip of the rivet's shank and for the other side to press against a strong supporting surface. Expanding bucking bars speed up the process of riveting the skin on the wing section.

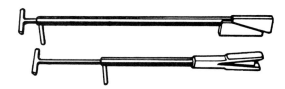

FIG. 7-15 Expanding bucking bars.

Sheet Fasteners

Because of the necessity for holding sheets of metal close together during the riveting process, a fastener of some type is essential. Otherwise the rivet will tend to expand between the sheets and leave a gap which reduces the strength of the joint and promotes the accumulation of moisture between the sheets. This, of course, leads to corrosion. The tool designed to meet the need is called a **sheet fastener** and is quickly and easily installed. Sheet fasteners are commonly called "Clecos," a trade name applied by an early developer and manufacturer of sheet fasteners.

Sheet fasteners have been designed and used in many styles and shapes; however, they are presently limited to relatively few designs. One of the popular sheet fasteners, manufactured by the Wedgelock Company, is illustrated in Fig. 7-16. Figure 7-17 shows the internal construction of the fastener.

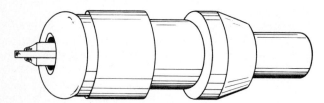

FIG. 7-16   A sheet fastener.

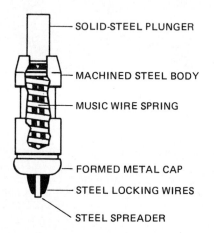

SOLID-STEEL PLUNGER

MACHINED STEEL BODY

MUSIC WIRE SPRING

FORMED METAL CAP

STEEL LOCKING WIRES

STEEL SPREADER

FIG. 7-17   Construction of a sheet fastener.

The fastener consists of a machined steel body in which is installed a plunger, coil spring, locking wires, and a spreader. When the plunger is depressed with the fastener pliers, the locking wires extend beyond the spreader and "toe in," reducing the diameter. The locking wires can then be inserted in a drilled hole of the proper size as shown in Fig. 7-18. When the pliers are released, the locking wires are drawn back over the spreader. This causes the wires to separate and grip the sides of the drilled hole as in Fig. 7-19. Removal of the fastener is accomplished by reversing the process of installation.

Hole Finder

A **hole finder** is a tool used to transfer existing holes in aircraft structures or skin to replacement skin or patches. The tool has two leaves parallel to each other and fastened together at one end. The bottom leaf of the hole finder has a pin installed near the end which is aligned with a bushing on the top leaf as shown in Fig. 7-20. The desired hole to be transferred is located by fitting the pin on the bottom leaf of the hole finder into the existing rivet hole. The hole in the new part

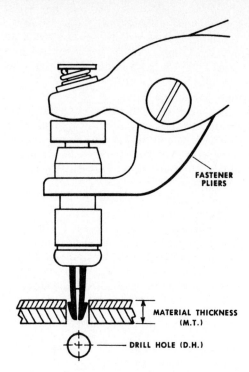

FASTENER PLIERS

MATERIAL THICKNESS (M.T.)

DRILL HOLE (D.H.)

FIG. 7-18   Inserting a sheet fastener in a drilled hole.

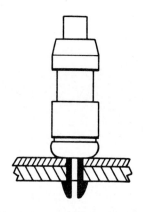

FIG. 7-19   Locking wires gripping sheet metal.

is made by drilling through the bushing on the top leaf. If the hole finder is properly made, holes drilled in this manner will be perfectly aligned. A separate hole finder must be used for each diameter of rivet.

Rivet Cutter

A **rivet cutter,** shown in Fig. 7-21, is used to cut rivets to the proper length for a particular installation. The cutter is hand-operated, has sized holes so that the rivets are not distorted when cut, and has a gauge which can be set to the desired length of the cut rivet.

● FLOOR AND BENCH TOOLS FOR SHEET-METAL WORK

There are many sheet-metal tools that are large enough in size that they are mounted on work benches or are free-standing. Most shops only have a few of the large tools, such as a drill press, shear, and brake. The purpose of discussing the various large tools is to

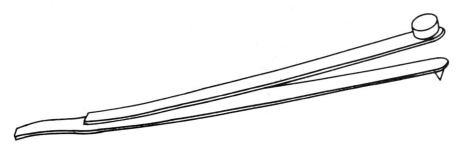

FIG. 7-20 A hole finder.

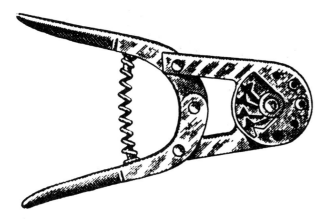

FIG. 7-21 Rivet cutter.

make mechanics aware of the large variety of tools that may be of use to them when working with sheet-metal structures. Access to many of these tools may be available for short-term use by renting the use of the tools from companies heavily involved in sheet-metal structures. When renting the use of these tools, the work is normally taken to the tool since the size and weight of the equipment may prevent transport and setup of the tools at the mechanic's work site.

Squaring Shears

Squaring shears, shown in Fig. 7-22, are used to cut and square sheet metal. The mechanism consists of two blades operated either by foot or motor power. The lower blade is attached securely to the bed which has a scale graduated in fractions of an inch for measuring the sheet being cut. The other blade is mounted on the upper crosshead and is moved up and down to cut the metal stock. The upper blade is set at angle to the lower blade so the cut will take place at only one point on the metal at a time. The cut then takes place progressively across the width of the sheet.

Foot-power squaring shears usually can cut mild-carbon steel up to 22 gauge. Aluminum alloys up to 0.050 in [1.27 mm] and above can be cut without difficulty. To operate, the long bed gauge is set parallel to or at an angle with the blades according to the shape desired. The metal is placed on the bed of the machine and is trimmed off from ¼ to ½ in [6.35 to 12.7 mm] to make a straight edge on the sheet. The trimmed edge is held against the gauge, and the sheet is sheared to size. To square the sheet, the end that has been cut last is held against the side gauge, and from ¼ to ½ in [6.35 to 12.7 mm] is trimmed off. The sheet is turned over, with the straightedge held against the long gauge that has been set to the required distance, and then the other edge is sheared.

The parts numbered in Fig. 7-22 are as follows: (1) housing and leg, (2) lower crosshead, (3) foot treadle, (4) turnbuckle for adjusting blade, (5) T slot for gauge bolt, (6) upper crosshead, (7) upper blade, (8) bed, (9) side gauge, and (10) bolt for extension arm.

Gap-Squaring Shears

Gap-squaring shears, shown in Fig. 7-23, resemble the regular squaring shears except that the housing is constructed so that the sheet may pass completely

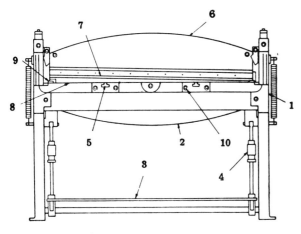

FIG. 7-22 Squaring shear.

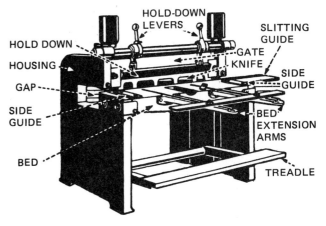

FIG. 7-23 Gap-squaring shear.

through the machine, thus making possible the cutting of any desired length. The gap-squaring shears are used where the regular squaring shears are too narrow to split long sheets.

Slitting Shears

Slitting shears, shown in Fig. 7-24, are used to slit sheets in lengths where the squaring shears are too narrow to accommodate the work. Slitting shears of the lever type, for cutting heavier grades of sheet metal, are commonly used and are known as lever shears. The parts numbered in Fig. 7-24 are (1) base, (2) lower blade, (3) upper blade, (4) die, (5) punch, and (6) handle. Such shears should not be used to cut rods or bolts unless fitted with a special attachment. Some lever shears have a punching attachment on the end (opposite the blades) for punching heavy sheets, as shown in Fig. 7-25.

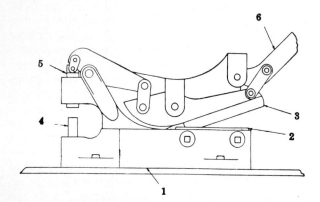

FIG. 7-24   Slitting shears.

PUNCH - - - -

FIG. 7-25   Lever shears with punching attachment.

Throatless Shears

Throatless shears are shown in Fig. 7-26. They are usually made to cut sheet metal as thick as 10 gauge in mild-carbon steel and 12 gauge in stainless steel. For aluminum-alloy stock they can cut much heavier sheets. The frame of the throatless shear is made so that sheets of any length may be cut and the metal may be turned in any direction, allowing irregular lines to be followed or notches to be made without distorting the metal.

FIG. 7-26   Throatless shears.

Rotary Slitting Shears

Rotary slitting shears are shown in Fig. 7-27. The numbered parts of the drawing are (1) shank for bench standard, (2) frame, (3) back gear, (4) hand crank, (5) adjustable gauge, (6) lower rotary cutter, (7) upper rotary cutter, and (8) cutter adjusting screw.

Rotary slitting shears consist of a frame with a deep throat fitted with circular, disk-shaped cutters fastened to parallel shafts and connected with gears. The cutting wheels are operated by a crank or by a power-driven wheel. Such shears are used for slitting sheet metal and cutting irregular curves and circles. The edge of the sheet is held against the gauge, and the

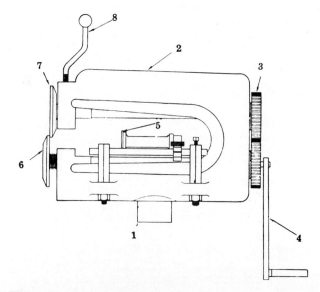

FIG. 7-27   Rotary slitting shears.

end of the sheet is pressed against the cutting wheel. The handle is turned until the full length of the strip has been cut. For irregular curves, the gauge is slid back out of the way and the handle turned slowly; and at the same time the operator keeps the cutting wheels on the line to be cut.

Scroll Shear

A **scroll shear,** shown in Fig. 7-28, is used to cut short, straight lines on the inside of a sheet without cutting through the edge. The upper cutting blade is stationary, while the lower blade is movable. The tool is operated by a handle connected to the lower blade.

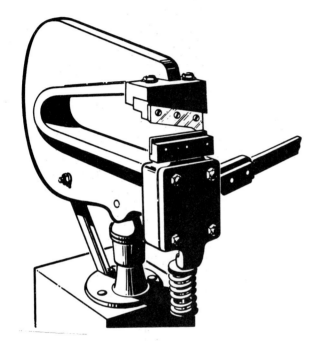

FIG. 7-28 Scorll shears.

Unishears

A portable **Unishear** is shown in Fig. 7-29. Unishear is merely a trade name for a type of power shear similar to a nibbling machine. It has a high-speed, narrow, reciprocating shearing blade and adjustments of vertical and horizontal clearances, depending on the thickness of the metal to be cut. It is especially

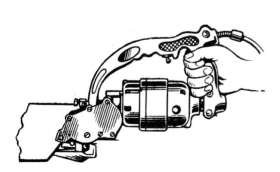

FIG. 7-29 A portable Unishear.

useful in cutting internal curved patterns where the radius is small. A machine for the same purpose is also made in the stationary form.

Nibbling Machine (Nibbler)

A **nibbling machine (nibbler),** shown in Fig. 7-30, is a machine with a die and a vertical cutting blade that travels up and down at a relatively high speed. The stroke is longer than that of the Unishear, and it is adjustable. This machine is used for cutting mild steel up to a thickness of ½ in [12.7 mm] and to cut circles and curves of complex shapes in heavy sheets. The machine operates on the shearing principle and leaves rough edges.

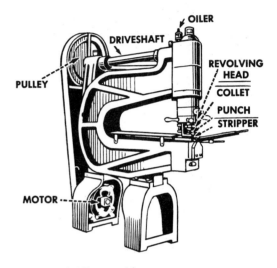

FIG. 7-30 A nibbling machine.

Folding Machines

A **bar-folding machine,** or **bar folder,** is a tool commonly used to turn (bend over) narrow edges and to turn rounded locks on flat sheets of metal to receive stiffening wires. A stop gauge is set to the width of the fold desired, the sheet metal is held against the stop, and the bending leaf of the machine is turned over by lifting the bending handle. As the bending leaf swings over, it folds the sheet. The bar-folding machine is shown in Fig. 7-31.

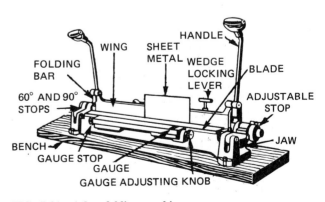

FIG. 7-31 A bar-folding machine.

A **pipe-folding machine** is illustrated in Fig. 7-32. This is a machine designed to bend flanges either on flat sheets or on stock that has previously been formed into a cylindrical shape. Bar-folding and pipe-folding machines are not commonly used in aircraft sheet-metal repair.

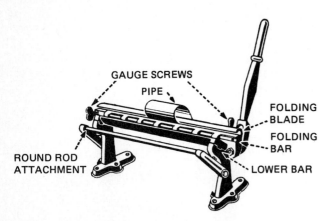

FIG. 7-32   A pipe-folding machine.

Cornice Brake

The **cornice brake,** also called a **leaf brake,** is a machine used to make simple bends in flat sheet-metal stock. A drawing illustrating this type of brake is shown in Fig. 7-33. The cornice brake can form locks

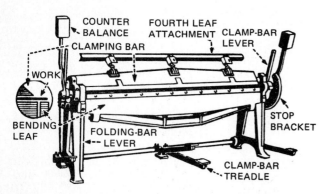

FIG. 7-33   A cornice brake.

and seams, turn edges, and make bends through a wide range of angles. It operates like a bar-folding machine except that a clamping bar takes the place of the stationary jaw of the latter. The bar is raised so that the sheet of metal can be pushed in to any desired distance and the clamping bar is then lowered to hold the metal in place. A stop gauge is set at the angle or amount of bend to be made, and then the bending leaf is raised until it strikes the stop. When it is desired to make a bend having a given radius, a **radius bar** having the correct radius for the bend is secured to the clamping bar. Figure 7-34 shows the relative positions of the parts when making the bend.

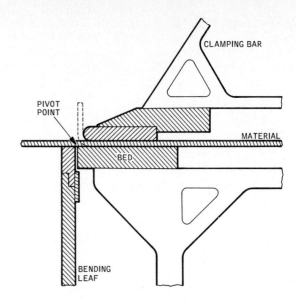

FIG. 7-34   Positions of parts in making a bend.

Box and Pan Brake

The **box and pan brake,** also called a finger brake, is shown in Fig. 7-35. This brake differs from the cornice brake in that it does not have a solid upper

FIG. 7-35   A box and pan brake.

jaw. The upper jaw is composed of fingers which can be positioned or removed from the upper leaf of the brake. This allows the forming of boxes, pans, and similar shapes without having to distort existing sides to make the final bend. By using different combinations of fingers, the width of the upper jaw can be changed to fit specific needs. The jaws are held on the upper leaf by a thumbscrew as shown in Fig. 7-36.

Forming Roll

The **forming roll,** shown in Fig. 7-37, is used to form sheet metal into cylinders of various diameters. It consists of right-end and left-end frames, between which are mounted three solid-steel rolls which are connected with gears and operated either by means of

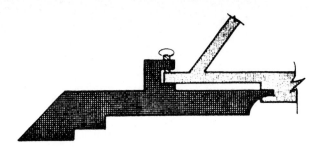

FIG. 7-36 Upper jaw can be repositioned by loosening the thumbscrew.

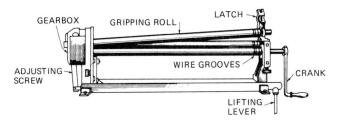

FIG. 7-37 A forming roll.

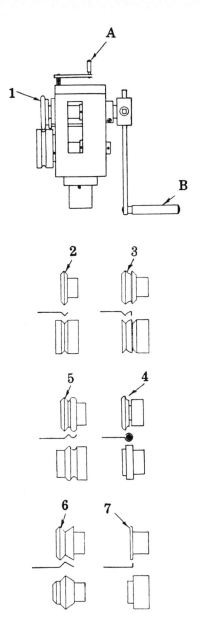

FIG. 7-38 A turning machine.

a power drive or a hand crank. The front rolls can be adjusted to the thickness of the metal by two thumbscrews located either on the bottom or the top of each end frame. These rolls grip the metal when it is started in the machine, and carry it to the rear, or forming, roll, which is adjusted in the same manner as the front pair. The forming roll is called a **slip-roll** former. The top roll in this type is so arranged that one end can be loosened and raised, permitting the work to be slipped out at the end to prevent distortion of the metal. Small cylinders and pipes can be formed on the slip-roll former.

Turning Machine

A **turning machine** is a short-throated rotary device used on circular work to turn a narrow edge (flange) or to score a crease. The upper roll die is disk-shaped with a round edge. The lower roll is cylindrically shaped with a semicircular groove running around its side near the outer end. This machine is sometimes referred to as a **burring, turning,** or **wiring machine,** since it performs all these functions, provided the correct attachments are available.

A turning machine with a variety of attachments is shown in Fig. 7-38. In this drawing the parts are (1) turning rolls, (2) elbow-edging rolls, (3) burring rolls, (4) wiring rolls, (5) elbow-edging rolls, (6) elbow-edging rolls, and (7) burring rolls. The letter A refers to a small crank screw, and the letter B refers to the crank that controls the rolls.

Beading Machines

The **beading machine,** shown in Fig. 7-39, is used to turn beads on pipes, cans, buckets, etc., both for stiffening and for ornamental purposes. It is also used on sheet-metal stock that is to be welded to prevent buckling and breaking of the metal. The numbers in the drawing refer to (1) single-beading roll, (2) triple-

beading roll, (3) double-beading roll, and (4) ogee-beading roll. This machine was used extensively for aluminum oil lines on early aircraft to provide beads for holding clamped rubber tubing.

Crimping Machine

The **crimping machine,** shown in Fig. 7-40, is used to make one end of a pipe joint smaller so that several sections may be slipped together. The mechanism is similar to that of the beading machine but the rolls are corrugated longitudinally. The parts numbered in the drawing are (1) vertical adjustment handle, (2) crank, (3) crimping rolls, and (4) adjustable gauge.

Combination Rotary Machine

The **combination rotary machine** is a three-speed, motor-driven combination of the burring, turning, wiring, elbow-edging, beading, crimping, and slitting ma-

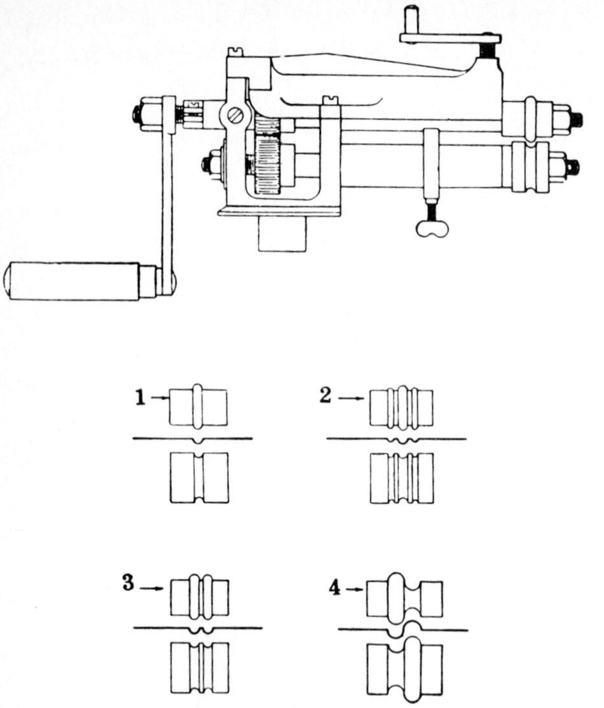
1
2
3
4

FIG. 7-39 A beading machine.

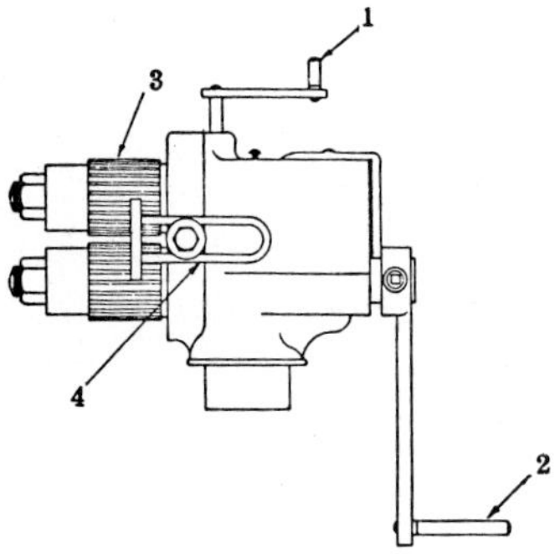
1
3
4
2

FIG. 7-40 A crimping machine.

chines. This machine is illustrated in Fig. 7-41 with numbers indicating the following types of rollers: (1) thin forming rolls, (2) thick forming rolls, (3) burring rolls, (4) wiring rolls, and (5) elbow-edging rolls. This machine is supplied with a spanner wrench for quickly changing the different rolls. It is most useful where a variety of operations are to be performed.

Drop Hammer

Drop hammers are used to form sheet-metal parts between a punch and die which have previously been constructed to provide the required shape. Since expensive matching dies are required, the drop hammer is economical only for large quantities of standard production parts. The weighted hammer is generally the male portion of a forming die that is raised and then allowed to drop freely between vertical guides onto the stock, which forces it into the matching portion of the die. The hammer may be raised by a rope running over a drum, by a vertical board running be-

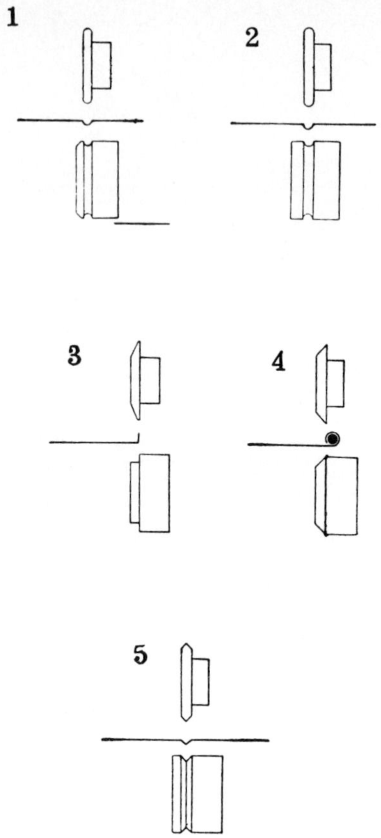
1
2
3
4
5

FIG. 7-41 Combintion rotary machine.

tween two opposed cylinders, or by air, steam, or hydraulic mechanism. The drop hammer is illustrated in Fig. 7-42.

Metal-Cutting Band Saw

The **metal-cutting band saw** is similar to a wood-cutting band saw in construction. Because of the different properties of metals which may be cut, the saw

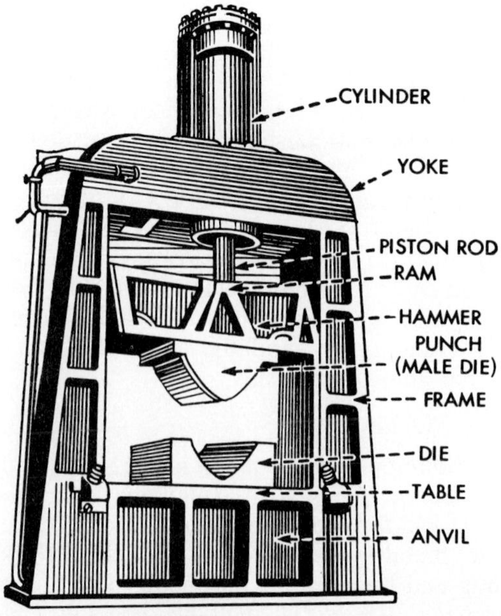
CYLINDER
YOKE
PISTON ROD
RAM
HAMMER
PUNCH (MALE DIE)
FRAME
DIE
TABLE
ANVIL

FIG. 7-42 A drop hammer.

must be adjustable in speed. The metal-cutting blades must have hard-tempered teeth which will cut through hard metal without excessive wear or breakage. A metal-cutting band saw is shown in Fig. 7-43.

In using a band saw to cut metal, the operator

FIG. 7-44 Stakes.

plate and used to bend and shape sheet metal to the desired form by hand or by hammering. Its variety of shapes provides a convenient means for backing up or supporting otherwise inaccessible portions of intricately shaped pieces. Stakes are not machines, but they are usually classed with bench machines and tools. In order to hold these stakes, a flat, iron plate with square, tapered holes is fastened to the bench, and the stakes are set in these holes so as to be held securely while the work is being done.

Metal-Spinning Lathes

A **metal-spinning lathe,** shown in Fig. 7-45, is used to form sheet metal into shapes which have a circular cross section, such as spinners for propellers. The machine differs from other metal lathes in that it has

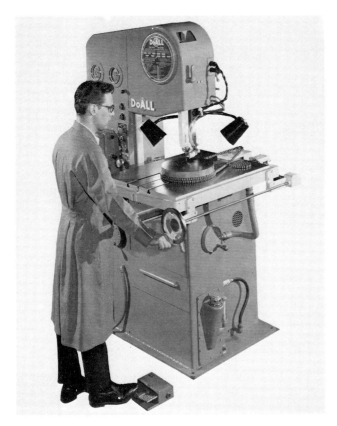

FIG. 7-43 Metal-cutting band saw. *(DoAll Co.)*

should refer to a chart to determine the type of blade and the blade speed for any particular metal. Table 7-1 gives blade speeds.

Stakes

A **stake** is a type of small anvil having a variety of forms, as shown in Fig. 7-44. It can be set in a bench

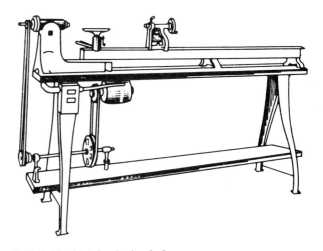

FIG. 7-45 Metal-spinning lathe.

TABLE 7-1 Pitch and Velocity Settings for Carbon-Steel Saw Blades

Material	Blade Pitch, Teeth, per in			Blade Velocity, ft/min		
	½ in Thick	1 in Thick	3 in Thick	½ in Thick	1 in Thick	3 in Thick
Carbon steels	10	8	4	175	175	150
Manganese steels	10	8	4	125	100	80
Nickel steels	10	10	4	100	90	80
Nickel-chrome steels	10	8	4	100	90	75
Molybdenum steels:						
4017–4042	10	4	4	135	125	110
4047–4068	10	8	4	125	100	75
Chrome-molybdenum steels	10	8	4	100	75	50
Corrosion-resistant steels, 303, 416	10	8	4	100	80	60

Note: For complete information on the operation of a power saw for metal cutting, the manufacturer's chart should be consulted.
For some types of materials a high-speed steel blade or a tungsten-carbide blade should be used.
When cutting many types of materials, cutting fluids or lubricants should be used.
To prevent tooth stripping and breaking of teeth, at least two teeth should be in contact with the work.

no back gears, carriage, or lead screws. It is rigid, and the spindle is usually driven by a step-cone pulley. Speed is important; hence the machine is adjustable over a wide range. In general, the thicker the metal, the slower must be the speed. Forms are constructed to provide the shape required for the finished product, and the metal is shaped by spinning over these forms.

Drill Press

A drill press is a bench- or floor-mounted machine designed to rotate a drill bit and press the sharpened point of the bit against metal in order to drill a hole. The drill press is driven by an electric motor through a speed-changing mechanism, either a belt transmission or a gear transmission. A drill press is shown in Fig. 7-46.

The belt transmission consists of two stacks of V-belt pulleys which may vary progressively in size from 2 to 6 in [50.8 to 101.6 cm]. The pulleys are arranged so that one set decreases in size as the belt is moved up the stack and the other decreases as the belt is moved down the stack. Thus, as the belt is moved up or down the pulleys, the ratio of the motor speed to the spindle speed is changed. This is an important feature because the speed of rotation for the drill bit

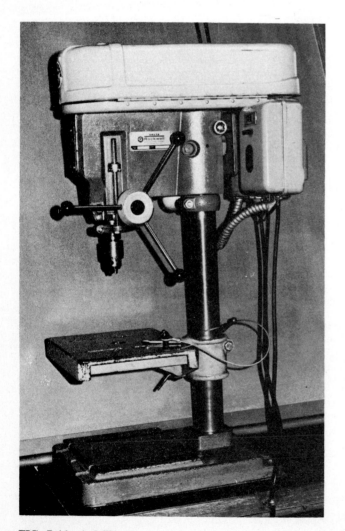

FIG. 7-46   A drill press.

should vary in accordance with the type of material being drilled and the size of the hole being drilled.

The drill press spindle is either fitted with a standard chuck or provision is made for the insertion of drill bits with tapered shanks. Many drill presses are arranged so that a drill chuck with a tapered shank can be installed when the machine is driving small drills and, when large drills are used, the chuck can be removed and a drill with a tapered shank inserted directly into the hole in the spindle.

When used correctly, the drill press makes it possible to do precision drill work. There should be no play in the spindle, spindle bearings, or chuck, and all should be in perfect alignment. The drill point should be properly sharpened and should indicate no wobble when the machine is turned on.

The work being drilled must be securely clamped to the drill press table so it cannot move during the operation. If it is not clamped to the table, it can catch in the flutes of the drill bit and spin around. Many operators have severely injured their hands and fingers by such a spinning part.

The operator of a drill press should make certain that the machine speed is adjusted correctly for the work being performed, that the drill point has the angle most suitable for the material, and that the correct drilling pressure is applied with the feed lever.

Other Power Tools

In addition to the tools mentioned in the foregoing, the mechanic will encounter others from time to time. Some of these are **stretchers, shrinkers,** and the **hydroform.**

A metal stretcher is a machine having two pairs of jaws spaced closely to each other. When a flange of sheet metal is placed between the jaws, the metal is first clamped tightly and then a strong force is applied automatically to increase the distance between the pairs of jaws. This stretches the metal slightly. The jaws then release, the metal is moved a short distance sideways, and the cycle is repeated. Thus, the metal is stretched in small increments along the full length to be stretched until the desired amount of stretch is attained.

A **metal shrinker** operates on the same principle as the stretcher except that when the jaws grip the metal, they move toward each other, thus compressing and shrinking the metal.

A **hydroform** is similar to a hydraulic press. A form in the shape and contours of the sheet-metal part to be formed is made from hardwood or other durable material. The metal to be formed is placed over the form (die) and pressed into shape with a thick rubber blanket or similar device. Pressure is applied hydraulically.

● PREPARATION FOR LAYOUT WORK

Working Surface

Before beginning aircraft layout work, the mechanic should find a good working surface, such as a smooth, flat bench or table. A good surface plate is ideal if a small sheet of material is to be used for the layout. In working with a large sheet of material, it is important to avoid bending it; hence it is a good practice to have a helper to assist in laying the sheet on the working surface. To protect the under surface of the material from any possible damage, it is often advisable to place a piece of heavy paper, felt, or plywood between the material and the working surface.

Layout Fluids

Layout fluids of various kinds are applied to a metal surface for layout work so that the pattern will stand out clearly while the mechanic is cutting along the drawn or scribed lines. Among the fluids or coatings used are **zinc chromate, bluing fluid, flat white paint, and copper sulfate solution.** The coatings used should be easily scratched away with a scriber or other marking instrument so the mark will show clearly.

Zinc chromate is a metal primer which can be sprayed on a metal surface in a thin coat. It serves not only as a good background color for the pattern used in layout work but also acts as a protection for the surface during the layout work. It tends to prevent corrosion and helps to prevent scratches. Zinc chromate need not be removed from a part after the layout and forming are completed.

Bluing fluid, also called **Dykem blue,** is brushed on the metal surface. Although both scribed lines and pencil work show up clearly on a metal surface coated with zinc chromate, this is not the case with bluing fluid. The scribed lines will be clearly visible against the dark background, but pencil work is difficult to see. Chemically, bluing fluid is merely a blue or purple dye dissolved in alcohol or a similar solvent. It does not protect metal against corrosion or serve as a binder for paint; hence it must be removed from the part with alcohol or other suitable solvent.

Flat white paint, soluble in water, can be used for some types of layout work. To be sure that it will come off when water is applied, a small sample area can be painted on a piece of scrap metal.

Another layout fluid is a **copper sulfate solution.** Scribed lines on iron or steel stand out clearly when this solution is brushed on the surface. Through a chemical action, a coating of copper is deposited on the iron or steel. The scribed lines show as a bright steel color through the copper-colored coating. Copper sulfate solution must not be used on aluminum or aluminum-alloy surfaces. Field use of commercial felt markers that will not damage the metal provide a "no-mess" pocketable layout dye that is removable with acetone.

Planning the Work

Having examined a blueprint from which a design is to be transferred to material, the mechanic should plan the job carefully. If the part to be made is small, it may be possible to make it from scrap metal that is found to be sound after having been examined carefully to make sure it has no scratches or nicks. If there is no suitable scrap available, it may be advisable to cut the part from a corner of a large sheet of metal,

thereby avoiding the waste that would occur if it were cut from the center.

In many cases it may be advisable to do the layout on a piece of cardboard or stiff paper before marking the metal for cutting. This is particularly true where the shape is complex and there is considerable danger of mistakes. This technique is particularly adaptable to field use where the repair is being made in or on the aircraft. It is a show of poor workmanship to produce a good repair with all the layout lines and mistakes showing. The mechanic may attach the paper layout to the aircraft with rubber cement or other suitable, temporary adhesive when checking for proper size and shape.

Reference Edges and Reference Lines

When a mechanic "trues up" one edge of a sheet of metal on a squaring shear, or if the sheet is received with one edge already straight, that edge can be used as a **reference edge.** A reference edge provides a line from which various measurements can be made, thus increasing the uniformity and accuracy of the work. If there are two such reference edges at right angles to each other, it is even better, for then the operator can obtain a much greater degree of accuracy in layout. When possible, these reference edges should be edges of the finished part; however, if the finished part is to have an irregular outline, it may be advisable to prepare one or two reference edges even though they will disappear when that portion of the material is cut away in finishing the part.

When cutting tools are not available, or when it is not practical to establish a reference edge, **reference lines** should be drawn or scribed, preferably two lines at right angles. These may be established only temporarily and have no relation to other lines except as reference lines, or they may be center lines for holes. In a like manner, the center line for the completed part may serve as one of the reference lines. In this case, the mechanic merely erects a perpendicular to the center line of the part, thus obtaining the two desired lines.

Reference edges and reference lines may be better understood if they are regarded as **base lines** used in the construction of angles, parallel lines, and intersecting lines required in the layout. However, in the strict sense of the term, a base line is the horizontal reference line, as viewed by the observer; hence it is technically correct to speak of reference lines and edges as previously explained.

Care of Material During Layout

We have already mentioned the importance of not wasting material by cutting a part from the center of the sheet. It is likewise a matter of good judgment to avoid making cuts that extend into the center. A good mechanic tries to do layout work along existing edges, leaving as much material intact and usable as possible.

The mechanic who wears a wristwatch or rings should be careful to see that these do not scratch the material. Leaving tools and instruments on the material is another source of damage. When weights are used to hold a pattern, or template, on the material, they should be smooth on their lower surface or be padded with felt. They should also be free from sharp corners or projections that might accidentally injure the material. Manufacturers of aircraft and sheet-metal parts may spray a thin coat of polyvinyl alcohol (PVA) or polyvinyl chloride (PVC) on new sheet metal to help prevent "handling rash." These green-gold coatings are water-soluble and are washed off as necessary for fabrication and painting.

When a scriber is used in layout work, the lines are sharper, cleaner, and more accurate than they are when made with a pencil, but there is always a danger that the mechanic will make an unnecessary scratch, especially on aluminum sheet. When a scratch is left on Al-Clad or any other similar corrosion-resisting sheet, trouble is likely to occur. Since Al-Clad is made up of two layers of pure aluminum and a harder aluminum-alloy core, scratching the surface permits any exposed aluminum alloy to corrode. For this reason, the finished part should have no scratches or nicks whatsoever. "Scratched Al-Clad is scrap Al-Clad."

Since there are conditions of stress and vibration present in the operation of an airplane, any scratched metal surface, whether it is aluminum or some other metal, may develop cracks from the scratches. This, of course, would result in failure of the part and the possible loss of an airplane. This does not mean that the scriber should not be used in layout work. It means simply that scratched layout marks should be cut away from the finished part.

Templates or patterns are made of sheet metal which has been coated with layout fluid. Scribe marks on these make clean, accurate lines and are not detrimental since the pieces are not going to be installed on aircraft.

The use of a black lead (graphite) pencil for marking on sheet metal should be done carefully so that no pencil lines are made on the metal that makes up the finished part. The graphite pencil will cause some stress concentration on the surface of the metal as a result of the pressure on the pencil point used to make the mark. Additionally, any graphite remaining on the metal surface will cause corrosion. Black lead pencil lines should only be made on edges that are to be cut away and to indicate the centers of holes. No marks should be made on the metal that will make up the finished component.

● BEND ALLOWANCE AND SETBACK

Mechanics generally encounter a curve where there is a bend line on a blueprint. Unless they know how to handle curves in bending metals, they cannot succeed with layout work. They must realize that a curved corner requires less metal than a square corner and that they must decide how to cut the stock correctly before bending it.

Factors in Bending

Bending is a forming operation extensively used in aircraft work. The **bend allowance,** abbreviated BA, is the length of sheet metal required to make a bend over a given inside radius (that is, it is the distance from the beginning to the end of the bend), measured perpendicular to the axis of the bend and along the neutral axis. The distance of the bend allowance depends upon the thickness of the metal, the type of metal, the radius of the bend, and the degree of the bend.

Characteristics of a Bend

When a piece of sheet metal is bent, the material on the outside of the bend is in **tension** and stretches; the material on the inside of the bend is in **compression** and shrinks. Where the two forces of tension and compression meet within the metal, there is a plane that neither stretches nor compresses. This plane remains the same length after bending as its length before bending and is called the **neutral axis.** It is approximately 44.5 percent through the thickness of the metal, measuring from the inside of the bend.

A drawing giving the nomenclature of a bend is shown in Fig. 7-47. As shown in the drawing, the bend begins and ends at the **bend tangent lines,** and the length of the neutral axis between the two lines is the **bend allowance.** Since the neutral axis does not change in length, the BA can be measured on the flat part before the metal is bent.

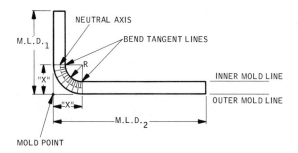

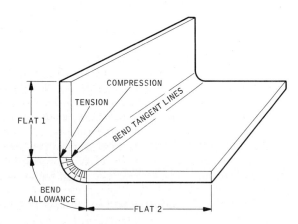

FIG. 7-47 Nomenclature of a bend.

The **mold-line dimensions** of a part are given from the end of the metal part to the outer mold point. The **outer mold point** is the intersection of the outer mold lines after the part is bent. This point is shown in the drawing of Fig. 7-47. When the part is bent around a given radius, the metal will not extend to the mold point, and the material required to make the part will be smaller in length than the sum of the mold-line dimensions. The amount of material saved by bending around a given radius is called **setback**.

To find the setback, both the BA and the *X* **distance** must be known. The *X* distance is shown in Fig. 7-47. For a 90°-angle bend the *X* distance is equal to the **bend radius** R plus the thickness T of the metal. As shown in the drawing, the *X* distance is the distance from the **bend tangent line** to the mold point and is measured on either side of the bend.

The *X* distance may be found by using a *K* chart, which is shown in Table 7-2. *K* is the tangent of one-half the bend angle (α or *alpha*). and the *K* chart will give the value of *K* for any angle of bend from 1 to 180°.

The formula for finding the *X* distance is:

$$K \times (R + T)$$

where K = tan ½ bend angle = tan $\frac{\alpha}{2}$
R = inside bend radius
T = thickness of the metal.

For the student who would like to understand how the *K*-value is derived, the following explanation is offered. Referring to Fig. 7-48, the tangent of an angle is determined by using one-half the angle of the bend as one of the acute angles in a right triangle and then finding the ratio of the length of the side opposite the

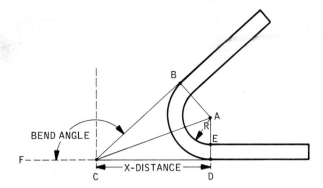

FIG. 7-48 How the *K* value is determined.

angle to the length of the side adjacent to the angle. For example, in the triangle of Fig. 7-49 *a/b* is the tangent of the angle *A*. This is also expressed

$$\tan A = \frac{a}{b}$$

If $a = 2$ and $b = 1$, $a/b = 2/1$ and the tangent of angle *A* is therefore 2. From a table of tangents we find that the angle *A* is then equal to about 64°.

In the diagram of Fig. 7-48, the angle *CAD* is equal to one-half the angle *BAD*. The tangent of angle *CAD*

TABLE 7-2 K Chart

Deg.	K	Deg.	K	Deg.	K	Deg.	K	Deg.	K
1	0.0087	37	0.3346	73	0.7399	109	1.401	145	3.171
2	0.0174	38	0.3443	74	0.7535	110	1.428	146	3.270
3	0.0261	39	0.3541	75	0.7673	111	1.455	147	3.375
4	0.0349	40	0.3639	76	0.7812	112	1.482	148	3.487
5	0.0436	41	0.3738	77	0.7954	113	1.510	149	3.605
6	0.0524	42	0.3838	78	0.8097	114	1.539	150	3.732
7	0.0611	43	0.3939	79	0.8243	115	1.569	151	3.866
8	0.0699	44	0.4040	80	0.8391	116	1.600	152	4.010
9	0.0787	45	0.4142	81	0.8540	117	1.631	153	4.165
10	0.0874	46	0.4244	82	0.8692	118	1.664	154	4.331
11	0.0963	47	0.4348	83	0.8847	119	1.697	155	4.510
12	0.1051	48	0.4452	84	0.9004	120	1.732	156	4.704
13	0.1139	49	0.4557	85	0.9163	121	1.767	157	4.915
14	0.1228	50	0.4663	86	0.9324	122	1.804	158	5.144
15	0.1316	51	0.4769	87	0.9489	123	1.841	159	5.399
16	0.1405	52	0.4877	88	0.9656	124	1.880	160	5.671
17	0.1494	53	0.4985	89	0.9827	125	1.921	161	5.975
18	0.1583	54	0.5095	90	1.000	126	1.962	162	6.313
19	0.1673	55	0.5205	91	1.017	127	2.005	163	6.691
20	0.1763	56	0.5317	92	1.035	128	2.050	164	7.115
21	0.1853	57	0.5429	93	1.053	129	2.096	165	7.595
22	0.1943	58	0.5543	94	1.072	130	2.144	166	8.144
23	0.2034	59	0.5657	95	1.091	131	2.194	167	8.776
24	0.2125	60	0.5773	96	1.110	132	2.246	168	9.514
25	0.2216	61	0.5890	97	1.130	133	2.299	169	10.38
26	0.2308	62	0.6008	98	1.150	134	2.355	170	11.43
27	0.2400	63	0.6128	99	1.170	135	2.414	171	12.70
28	0.2493	64	0.6248	100	1.191	136	2.475	172	14.30
29	0.2586	65	0.6370	101	1.213	137	2.538	173	16.35
30	0.2679	66	0.6494	102	1.234	138	2.605	174	19.08
31	0.2773	67	0.6618	103	1.257	139	2.674	175	22.90
32	0.2867	68	0.6745	104	1.279	140	2.747	176	26.63
33	0.2962	69	0.6872	105	1.303	141	2.823	177	38.18
34	0.3057	70	0.7002	106	1.327	142	2.904	178	57.29
35	0.3153	71	0.7132	107	1.351	143	2.988	179	114.59
36	0.3249	72	0.7265	108	1.376	144	3.077	180	Inf.

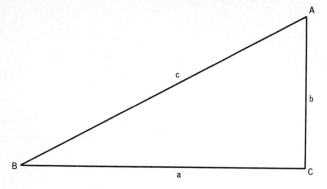

FIG. 7-49 Triangle to illustrate the tangent of an angle.

is CD/AD. This can also be given $CD = \tan CAD \times AD$, which is merely another form of the same equation.

$$AD = AE + ED \quad \text{or} \quad R + T$$

Therefore,

$$\tan CAD = \frac{CD}{R + T}$$

or

$$CD = \tan CAD \times (R + T)$$

By former definition and demonstration it is known that CD is the X distance, and we therefore conclude that

$$X \text{ distance} = \tan CAD \times (R + T)$$

The angle BAD can be proved by geometry to be equal to the bend angle FCB, and the angle CAD is equal to ½ BAD or ½ FCB. It is clear then that

$$X \text{ distance} = \tan ½ FCB \times (R + T)$$

or

$$X \text{ distance} = K \times (R + T)$$

Bend Allowance

An empirical formula has been derived which is suitable for determining **bend allowance.** Remember that bend allowance is the distance between tangent lines before a bend is made, or we may say it is the amount of material needed for the bend. The empirical formula for bend allowance is

$$\text{Bend allowance} = [(0.01743R) + (0.0078T)]\alpha$$

When X distance and bend allowance are known, the **setback** is the difference between the sum of the two X distances and the bend allowance. That is,

$$\text{Setback} = 2X - \text{bend allowance}$$

The amount of material required to make the part is called the **developed width** (DW). Since material is saved by bending around a radius, the amount of metal required to make the bent part will be the difference between the sum of the mold-line dimensions and the amount saved at the bend. That is,

$$DW = MLD_t - SB_t$$

where DW = developed width
MLD_t = total mold-line distance (sum of mold lines)
SB_t = sum of setbacks

As an example problem, consider the diagram of Fig. 7-50. We proceed with the problem as follows:

Since the bend (α angle) is a 90° angle, the K value is 1.000 as determined from the chart.

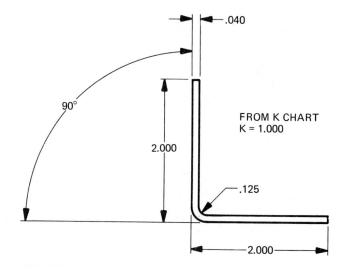

FIG. 7-50 Determining the values of a bend.

1. Find the X distance:

$$\begin{aligned} X &= K \times (R + T) \\ &= 1.000 \times (0.125 + 0.040) \\ &= 1.000 \times 0.0.165 \\ &= 0.165 \text{ in } [4.191 \text{ mm}] \end{aligned}$$

2. Find bend allowance:

$$\begin{aligned} BA &= [(0.01743R) + (0.0078T)]\,\alpha \\ &= [(0.01743 \times 0.125) + (0.0078 \times 0.040)] \times 90 \\ &= (0.00217875 + 0.0003120) \times 90 \\ &= (0.00249075) \times 90 \\ &= 0.22416750 \\ &= 0.224 \text{ in } [5.69 \text{ mm}] \end{aligned}$$

3. Find setback:

$$\begin{aligned} SB &= 2X - BA \\ &= 2(0.165) - 0.224 \\ &= 0.330 - 0.224 \\ &= 0.106 \text{ in } [2.69 \text{ mm}] \end{aligned}$$

4. Find developed width:

$$DW = MLD_t - SB_t$$
$$= 2.000 + 2.000 - 0.106$$
$$= 4.000 - 0.106$$
$$= 3.894 \text{ in } [98.91 \text{ mm}]$$

The flat layout of the foregoing problem is developed from left to right on the material as illustrated in Fig. 7-51. To locate the bend tangent lines on the flat stock, we must find the length of the unbent portion of each leg or flange and add the bend allowance between the flat sections. To find the length of one **flat**, or **flange**, we subtract one X distance from one mold-line distance. That is,

$$2.000 - 0.165 = 1.835 \text{ in } [46.61 \text{ mm}]$$

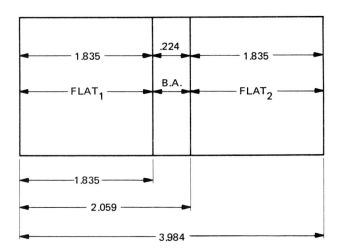

FIG. 7-51 **Developing the flat layout for a bend.**

The foregoing equation locates the first bend tangent line from the left edge. We add the bend allowance to find the second bend tangent line; that is,

$$1.835 + 0.224 = 2.059 \text{ in } [52.30 \text{ mm}]$$

This equation locates the second bend target line from the left edge of the metal. Now we find the length of the second flat section or flange by subtracting one X distance from the second mold-line distance.

$$2.000 - 0.165 = 1.835 \text{ in } [46.61 \text{ mm}]$$

We add this result to the former quantity, 2.059, to find the total developed width of the flat stock.

$$2.059 + 1.835 = 3.894 \text{ in } [98.91 \text{ mm}]$$

This is the developed width as shown in the drawing of Fig. 7-51.

When a part has more than one bend, the length of the flat section between the bends is found by subtracting the X distance of each bend from the mold-line distance. This is illustrated in Fig. 7-52, and the

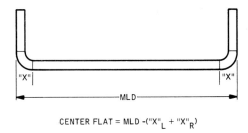

CENTER FLAT = MLD - ("X"$_L$ + "X"$_R$)

FIG. 7-52 **A part with two bends.**

equation may be shown as

$$\text{Center flat} = MLD - (X_l + X_r)$$

where MLD = mold-line distance
X_l = X distance, left
X_r = X distance, right

Bend-Allowance Tables

When **bend-allowance tables** are available for the type of metal being used, it is possible to save calculation time. The values shown in Table 7-3 are suitable for nonferrous sheet metal such as aluminum alloy and are derived from the empirical formula mentioned earlier. Common alloys are designated 2024-T3, 2024-T4, 7075-T3, etc. These numbers indicate type of alloy and temper of aluminum alloy materials.

If we desire to form a 60° bend in a sheet of aluminum alloy where the thickness of the metal is 0.040 in [0.102 mm] and the radius of the bend is ³⁄₁₆ in [4.76 mm], we locate the thickness of the metal from the row of figures at the top of Table 7-3. Under 0.040 we locate the value in the line opposite ³⁄₁₆ which is the radius dimension. In this case we find the value to be 0.00358. To find the bend allowance, we multiply 0.00358 (the bend allowance for 1°) by 60 to determine the bend allowance for 60°. Hence, the bend allowance that we are calculating is 60 × 0.00358 or 0.21480 in [5.46 mm]. This is the amount of material required to make the bend desired.

Geometrical Method

Another method for finding the bend allowance for a given bend is to solve the problem with **geometrical processes**. That is, we compute the length of the material in the bend by finding the circumference of a circle having the same radius as the bend neutral axis, and from this we find the length of the material represented by the bend as a part of the circle.

Refer to Fig. 7-53. The bend angle is 110° and the bend radius is 0.50 in [12.7 mm]. The thickness of the material is ³⁄₁₆ in [4.76 mm]. As mentioned previously, the neutral axis of the material is 0.445T from the inside of the bend. Since T is ³⁄₁₆ in, the neutral axis is 0.445 × ³⁄₁₆ or 0.0834 in [2.12 mm] from the inside of the bend. Then, we compute the circumference of the circle where the dimensions given are

$$R = 0.50 + 0.0834 = 0.5834 \text{ in } [14.82 \text{ mm}]$$
$$\text{Cir} = 2\pi R$$
$$= 2 \times 3.1416 \times 0.5834$$
$$= 3.666 \text{ in } [93.12 \text{ mm}]$$

223

TABLE 7-3 Nonferrous Sheet-Metal Bend Allowances for 1° (Thickness and Radius in Inches)

Thickness→ Radius	.016	.020	.022	.025	.028	.032	.040	.045	.051	.064	.072	.081	.091	.128	5/32	3/16	
1/32	.00067	.00070	.00072	.00074	.00077	.00079											
1/16	.00121	.00125	.00126	.00129	.00131	.00135	.00140	.00144	.00149	.00159	.00165						
3/32	.00176	.00179	.00180	.00183	.00186	.00188	.00195	.00199	.00203	.00213	.00220	.00226	.00234				
1/8	.00230	.00234	.00235	.00238	.00240	.00243	.00249	.00253	.00258	.00268	.00274	.00281	.00289	.00317			
5/32	.00285	.00288	.00290	.00292	.00295	.00297	.00304	.00308	.00312	.00322	.00328	.00335	.00343	.00372	.00394		
3/16	.00339	.00342	.00344	.00347	.00349	.00352	.00358	.00362	.00367	.00377	.00383	.00390	.00398	.00426	.00449	.00473	
7/32	.00394	.00397	.00398	.00401	.00403	.00406	.00412	.00417	.00421	.00431	.00437	.00444	.00452	.00481	.00503	.00528	
1/4	.00448	.00451	.00454	.00456	.00458	.00461	.00467	.00471	.00476	.00486	.00492	.00499	.00507	.00535	.00558	.00582	
9/32	.00503	.00506	.00507	.00510	.00512	.00515	.00521	.00526	.00530	.00540	.00546	.00553	.00561	.00590	.00612	.00636	
5/16	.00557	.00560	.00562	.00564	.00567	.00570	.00576	.00580	.00584	.00595	.00601	.00608	.00616	.00644	.00667	.00691	
11/32	.00612	.00615	.00616	.00619	.00621	.00624	.00630	.00634	.00639	.00649	.00655	.00662	.00670	.00699	.00721	.00745	2024-O
3/8	.00666	.00669	.00671	.00673	.00676	.00679	.00685	.00689	.00693	.00704	.00710	.00717	.00725	.00753	.00776	.00800	
13/32	.00721	.00724	.00725	.00728	.00730	.00733	.00739	.00743	.00748	.00758	.00764	.00771	.00779	.00808	.00830	.00854	
7/16	.00775	.00778	.00780	.00782.	.00785	.00787	.00794	.00798	.00802	.00812	.00819	.00826	.00834	.00862	.00884	.00909	
15/32	.00829	.00833	.00834	.00837	.00839	.00842	.00848	.00852	.00857	.00867	.00873	.00880	.00888	.00917	.00939	.00963	
1/2	.00884	.00887	.00889	.00891	.00894	.00896	.00903	.00907	.00911	.00921	.00928	.00935	.00943	.00971	.00993	.01018	
17/32	.00938	.00942	.00943	.00946	.00948	.00951	.00957	.00961	.00966	.00976	.00982	.00989	.00997	.01025	.01048	.01072	
9/16	.00993	.00996	.00998	.01000	.01002	.01005	.01012	.01016	.01020	.01030	.01037	.01043	.01051	,01080	.01102	.01127	
19/32	.01047	.01051	.01051	.01055	.01057	.01058	.01065	.01070	.01073	.01083	.01091	.01098	.01105	.01133	.01157	.01181	2017-T3
5/8	.01102	.01105	.01107	.01109	.01112	.01114	.01121	.01125	.01129	.01139	.01146	.01152	.01160	.01189	.01211	.01236	
21/32	.01156	.01160	.01161	.01164	.01166	.01170	.01175	.01179	.01183	.01193	.01200	.01207	.01214	.01245	.01266	.01290	
11/16	.01211	.01214	.01216	.01218	.01220	.01223	.01230	.01234	.01238	.01248	.01254	.01261	.01269	.01298	.01320	.01345	
23/32	.01265	.01268	.01269	.01273	.01275	.01276	.01283	.01288	.01291	.01301	.01309	.01316	.01322	.01351	.01374	.01399	
3/4	.01320	.01323	.01324	.01327	.01329	.01332	.01338	.01343	.01347	.01357	.01363	.01370	.01378	.01407	.01429	.01454	
25/32	.01374	.01378	.01378	.01381	.01384	.01386	.01392	.01397	.01401	.01411	.01418	.01425	.01432	.01461	.01484	.01508	
13/16	.01429	.01432	.01433	.01436	.01438	.01441	.01447	.01451	.01456	.01466	.01472	.01479	.01487	.01516	.01538	.01562	2024/T3
27/32	.01483	.01496	.01487	.01490	.01493	.01494	.01501	.01506	.01509	.01519	.01527	.01534	.01540	.01569	.01593	.01617	
7/8	.01538	.01541	.01542	.01545	.01547	.01550	.01556	.01560	.01565	.01575	.01581	.01588	.01596	.01625	.01647	.01671	
29/32	.01592	.01595	.01596	.01599	.01602	.01604	.01616	.01615	.01619	.01629	.01636	.01643	.01650	.01679	.01701	.01726	2024/T6
15/16	.01646	.01650	.01651	.01654	.01656	.01659	.01665	.01669	.01674	.01684	.01690	.10697	.01705	.01734	.01756	.01780	
31/32	.01701	.01704	.01705	.01708	.01711	.01712	.01718	.01724	.01727	.01737	.01745	.01752	.01758	.01787	.01810	.01835	
1	.01755	.01759	.01760	.01763	.01765	.01768	.01774	.01778	.01783	.01793	.01799	.01806	.01814	.01843	.01865	.01889	

The distance for 1° on the circumference of the circle is 3.66 ÷ 360 (number of degrees in a circle) or 0.01018 in [0.26 mm]. When we multiply this by 110, the number of degrees in the bend we obtain 1.1198 in [28.44 mm], the bend allowance. If we compare this with the figures in Table 7-3, we find that we have obtained the same value for the bend allowance that would have been obtained if we had used the table.

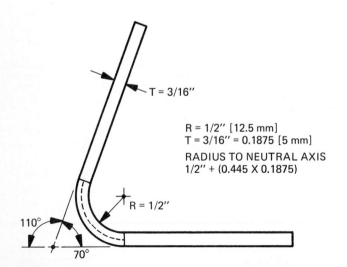

FIG. 7-53 Determining bend allowances by geometrical computation.

R = 1/2″ [12.5 mm]
T = 3/16″ = 0.1875 [5 mm]
RADIUS TO NEUTRAL AXIS
1/2″ + (0.445 X 0.1875)

Open and Closed Angles

Figure 7-54 shows two interior angles. The interior angle on the left is 65° and is called a **closed angle** because it is less than 90°. The interior angle on the right is 140° and is called an **open angle** because it is greater than 90°. These terms are used in problems for determining setback. A 90° interior angle is neither open nor closed. In Fig. 7-54, notice that the closed-angle flange leans toward the leg. The angle is 65°, which is 25° less than 90°; hence it is said to be closed 25° or have a 25° closed bevel. The open-angle flange leans away from the leg. The angle in the illustration is 140°, which is 50° more than 90°; hence it is said to be open 50° or have a 50° open bevel.

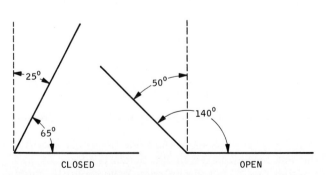

FIG. 7-54 Closed and open angles.

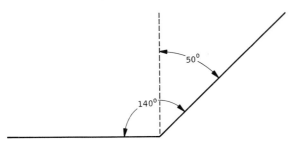

FIG. 7-55 Example for determining setback.

Setback Development Chart

Figure 7-55 shows a bend that has an angle of 140°. This is greater than 90° by 50°; hence the angle is described as being 50° open. The thickness of the material used for the bend is shown to be 0.064 in [1.63 mm]. The radius of the bend is ⅛ in [3.18 mm], which is equivalent to 0.125 in [152.4 mm]. The leg is 6 in [3.175 mm] long and the flange is 4 in [101.6 mm] long. The problem is to find the length of stock to be cut.

Refer to Fig. 7-56. This is called a **setback development chart,** and it is also referred to as a **J chart.** To solve the problem stated in the previous paragraph, place a ruler or straightedge on the chart so that it lines up with a bend radius of 0.125 in the scale at the top of the chart and a thickness of 0.064 on the scale at the bottom of the chart. The heavy, horizontal line represents an angle of 90°. Everything above the line is for closed angles and everything below the line is for open angles. The degrees indicated on the scale at the right of the chart show the amount of closed bevel and open bevel for the various angles.

Since the angle we are using is 140°, it is an open angle and has an open bevel of 50°. Therefore we locate the horizontal line for this bevel and follow it across the chart until it hits the ruler connecting the bend radius with the stock thickness value at a point on a curve. In this case we find that the intersection of the 50° bevel line and the ruler occurs near the curve for 0.030 in [0.76 mm]; hence the setback is 0.030 in. If the intersection of the 50° bevel line and the ruler occurred between the curves, we could estimate the position and interpolate the setback. For example, if the thickness of the material were 0.075 in [1.91 mm], we would find that the intersection of the 50° line and the ruler would be about halfway between the 0.030 and the 0.040 curves. We would then call the setback 0.035 in [0.89 mm].

In the problem illustrated in Fig. 7-55, the length of the leg has been given as 6 in [152.4 mm] and the length of the flange as 4 in [101.6 mm]. These lengths add to a total of 10 in [254 mm]. To obtain the length of the stock to be cut, we subtract the setback of 0.030 (½₂) in from the 10 in and obtain 9.97 in [253.2 mm]. This is the length to which the stock should be cut.

Note: The setback development chart should be used only for open bevels up to 60° and closed bevels up to 60°. Furthermore, the chart is subject to greater error than would be likely when using the other meth-

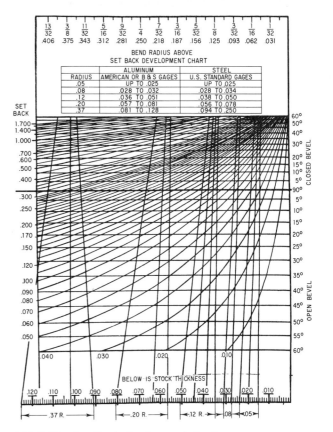

FIG. 7-56 A setback development chart.

ods described; hence when great accuracy is required, it is best practice to avoid the use of the chart.

Bending the Part

In bending a sheet-metal section to produce a required bend accurately, reference lines must be used. The type and location of the reference lines depend upon the type of bending machine employed. The most common type of bending machine for aircraft sheet-metal work is the cornice brake, which was described earlier in this chapter.

Since a bend begins at the bend tangent line, this line will be positioned directly below the center of the radius bar on the brake as shown in Fig. 7-57. In this position the bend tangent line will be out of sight; hence another reference line must be established for visual reference. This is called the **sight line,** and its position is located the distance of the radius from the bend tangent line. This is shown in Fig. 7-57. When the part is placed in the brake, the sight line is directly below the nose of the radius bar. This, of course, will position the bend tangent line (BTL) directly below the center of the radius bar, and the bend will be formed between the bend tangent lines.

The sight line is the only line required on the flat layout and may be used with a cornice brake, bar folder, or finger (box) brake, since they all bend metal in the same manner.

If a production machine, such as a press brake, is used, the reference line used to position the part is called a **bend line** and is located between the two bend

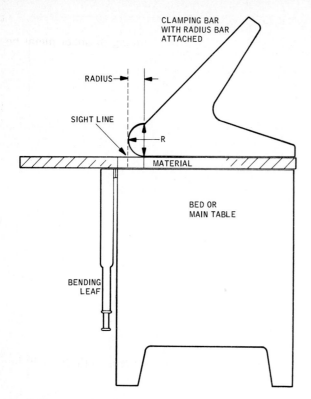

FIG. 7-57 Locating sheet metal in the brake.

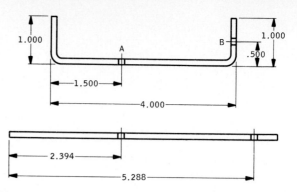

FIG. 7-59 Locating the positions of holes with reference to bends.

tangent lines. The positioning of metal on a press brake is shown in Fig. 7-58.

It must be emphasized that great care is needed to produce an accurate bend. The placing of the metal, the setting of the brake, and the actual bending operation all require precision to assure that the bend will meet the specifications required.

Once the metal is in the correct position in the brake, the bending leaf is raised until the desired angle is formed. The metal will have to be bent slightly more than the desired angle since the metal will spring back

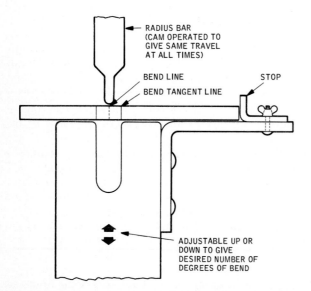

FIG. 7-58 Bending with a press or vertical brake.

slightly when the bending leaf is lowered. The exact amount of overbending required depends on the type of metal being worked and its thickness.

When holes are to be drilled in any of the legs or flanges of a part before the part is bent, the hole centerline dimensions are treated the same as mold-line dimensions. This is illustrated in Fig. 7-59. To find the exact location of a hole center from the left edge of the part, the mold-line dimensions and the hole-center dimensions are added and then the setback of all bends between the left edge and the hole center are subtracted. In Fig. 7-59, it is necessary to determine the developed width of the metal to form the part illustrated.

To locate the center of hole A from the left edge, the mold-line dimension of the left leg is added to the mold-line dimension from the left leg to the center of the hole and the setback of the left bend is then subtracted.

$$1.000 + 1.500 - 0.106 = 2.394 \text{ in } [60.8 \text{ mm}]$$

Next, to locate the center of hole B, all the mold-line dimensions from the left edge of the part to the center of hole B are added and the setback distances of both bends are subtracted.

$$1.000 + 4.000 + 0.500 - 0.212 = 5.288 \text{ in } [134.32 \text{ mm}]$$

The setback distance 0.212 is the sum of the setback distances for both bends.

● FABRICATION OF SHEET-METAL PARTS

Although not often called upon to make complex parts for an aircraft, the aircraft mechanic should have some knowledge of the techniques employed. The making of parts from sheet metal involves cutting to correct dimensions, bending, stretching, and shrinking.

Prior to making a part, the mechanic must determine the dimensions of the part to be made, either from a blueprint or from the part to be duplicated. This requires the use of layout techniques described previously.

Templates

A template is a pattern from which the shape and dimensions of a part may be duplicated. A template may be made from galvanized iron sheet, steel sheet, aluminum sheet, or other metal. The metal is coated with layout fluid, zinc chromate primer, copper plating (for bare iron or steel), or some other material which can be scratched or marked to provide accurate dimension lines. After all dimension lines are accurately marked on the template, it is cut to the required shape.

If only one part is to be made, making a template is usually not necessary. Instead, the time otherwise used to make a template is used to make the actual part. Where several parts are to be made, using a template ensures accuracy and uniformity in the parts.

Cutting Sheet Metal

A previous section of this chapter discussed the various tools that are used to cut sheet metal. The selection of the proper tool is dictated by the size of the metal to be cut, both thickness and surface dimensions, by the length and shape of the cut, and by the accessibility of the material to be cut.

If the mechanic is working with new metal and cutting it to be shaped and prepared for installation, the large tools are normally used at least until the piece is down to a size where finishing contours are being made. If the mechanic is working on or in the aircraft, light air-powered tools and hand tools are commonly used. This often involves the use of snips, nibblers, and saws to trim out damaged areas and files and drills to prepare the area for the installation of the new components.

When cutting metal, it is important for the mechanic to understand not only how to properly use each tool, but the damage that can result from improper use of the tool. For example, when using some types of shears, the starting or finishing edge of the shear tears the metal before starting to cut properly. On these tools, the metal cut should be started in from the end of the cutting blade and the cut should be stopped before running off of the other end of the shear blade. The metal can be repositioned and the cut continued, section by section, until the whole length of the piece is cut. If the mechanic is not sure how a tool will perform, he or she should use it on a scrap piece of metal before cutting on a piece to be used in a repair.

When using aviation snips, note that some snips are designed to cut arcs to the left, some to the right, and some straight. Be sure to use the proper type of snip required for the job.

When cutting metal, wear the clothing and protective gear appropriate to the type of cutting being performed. Special consideration should be given to eye protection when cutting with power tools and when working with hand tools above eye level. Metal shavings and file particles can result in eye damage. The handling of cut sheet metal can result in cuts on the mechanic's skin if proper gloves and protective clothing are not worn. If possible, remove sharp edges from metal immediately after it is cut.

Bending Sheet Metal

We have discussed the bending of sheet metal before; however, certain practices should be reemphasized. If possible, a bend in sheet metal should be made across the grain. This will reduce the tendency of the metal to crack. On bare aluminum sheet, the grain can be seen; however, on clad sheet aluminum, the grain is not readily apparent. Normally, the grain of clad aluminum sheet runs lengthwise with a full sheet. Furthermore, the manufacturer's identification letters and numbers are aligned with the grain.

The procedure in making a simple bend is as follows:

1. Cut the required metal sheet to the dimensions required for the part, deburr, and smooth the edges.
2. Determine the correct radius for the bend.
3. See that the correct radius bar is installed on the break.
4. See that the break is clean and free of metal particles and scraps.
5. See that the sight line is correctly marked on the metal to be bent.
6. Install the metal in the break with the sight line correctly positioned under the radius bar.
7. Clamp the metal in place with the clamping bar.
8. Set the stop on the break for the required bend angle, making allowance for springback.
9. Rotate the bending leaf to the stop.
10. Remove the bend part and check the bend for accuracy.

If the bend radius is too large to be made on a standard leaf break, it may be possible to accomplish it on a vertical brake equipped with the correct radius bar. If a still larger bend radius is required, a metal roller can be used.

Joggle

When a reinforcing angle is attached to metal sheet across a splice, it is usually necessary to **joggle** the angle. This is accomplished with joggle bars of the correct dimension or with a shop-made device. Joggle bars or dies can be made of either metal or hardwood. If a large number of parts are to be joggled, metal should be used to make the joggling tool.

A joggled part is shown in Fig. 7-60. The principle involved in the making of a joggle is illustrated in Fig. 7-61.

Curved Flanges

Making **curved flanges** involves the stretching or shrinking of the flange. Figure 7-62 shows examples of each.

To make a curved inside flange, it is necessary to shrink the flange metal. This can be accomplished in several ways. One method for shrinking the flange is to use a V-block which is made either of hardwood or metal. If the block is made of metal, it is necessary that the edges of the V be rounded off to avoid damaging the part.

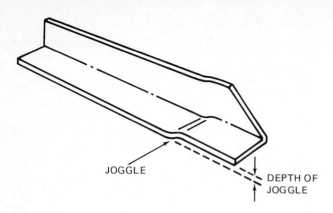

FIG. 7-60   A joggled part.

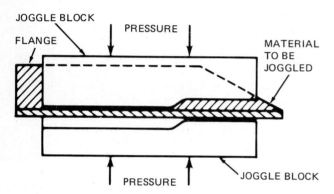

FIG. 7-61   How a joggle is made.

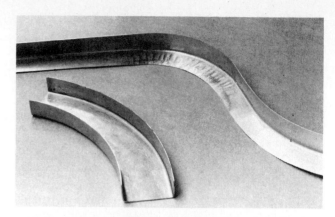

FIG. 7-62   Different types of curved flanges.

To shrink the flange, the angle is placed on the V-block as shown in Fig. 7-63, and the flange is struck on the edge with moderate blows from a soft hammer. The blows are directed slightly toward the inside of the angle to prevent the flange from bending outward. The part is moved continuously back and forth across the V as the blows are struck to provide a uniform bend. If bends occur in the flange, they are removed by lightly planishing against a flat wooden block. If a **metal shrinker** is available, the curved flange can be made more easily than by use of the hand method.

To make a part with an external curved flange, the flange must be stretched. Usually this is done by using a power-driven hammer or a metal stretcher. The flange is placed flat against the bed of the hammer and moved continually back and forth under the hammer blows until the desired curve is obtained. If the metal work hardens too much, annealing it is necessary before continuing the stretching process. If a power hammer is not available, the flange can be hammered by hand to stretch the metal. Shrinking and stretching of metal flanges can be done most effectively and easily by means of shrinking or stretching machines, described earlier.

To form a curved part with a flange as shown in Fig. 7-64, a flat layout is made and the metal is cut to the required dimensions as shown in Fig. 7-65. Form-blocks are made of hardwood or metal with a size and shape to match the part. The metal is clamped between the formblocks in a vise as shown, and the flange is

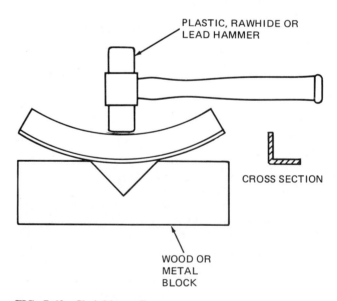

FIG. 7-63   Shrinking a flange.

formed with a shrinking mallet. A hardwood wedge block is held against the metal on the side opposite the mallet strokes to prevent the metal from buckling. Mallet strokes are applied evenly along the flange curve, gradually shrinking the metal until the flange is formed.

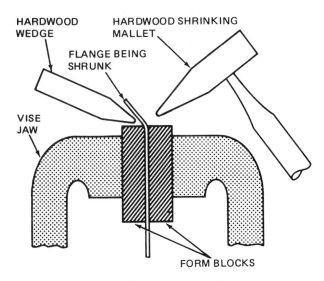

FIG. 7-64 Forming a flange on a curved part.

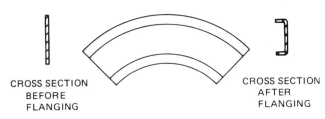

CROSS SECTION
BEFORE
FLANGING

CROSS SECTION
AFTER
FLANGING

FIG. 7-65 Flat layout for curved part to be flanged.

Metal Bumping

The fabrication of parts involving compound curves, when done by hand, is accomplished by **bumping.** This process requires the use of a rounded wooden mallet and either a sandbag or a die. Parts such as fairings are usually formed on the sandbag.

A typical sandbag for metal bumping is a leather pouch about 18 in [45 cm] square filled with sand and securely sewed to prevent leakage of the sand. Before being filled with sand, the bag is coated on the inside with a plastic material to prevent the sand from working into the pores of the leather.

To form a part, the mechanic selects a piece of soft aluminum alloy of the correct size and thickness for the part. After the metal is trimmed, the edges should be smoothed. With the metal against the sandbag, the mechanic carefully applies blows with the bumping mallet until the desired shape is attained. Templates are used to check the progress of the forming and the final shape. Upon completion of the forming, the part is trimmed to final dimensions and the edges are smoothed with a file. Irregularities caused by bumping the formed surface may be removed with **hand metal rollers.** A set of these metal rollers consists of two oval-shaped rollers held against each other by means of a spring steel frame. An adjustment is provided to increase or decrease the pressure of the rollers against the surface of the formed metal. The rollers may be made of steel or hardwood.

Small parts with compound curves are usually made

with a die, or formblock. The die can be made of hardwood or metal, depending upon the number of parts to be made. It consists of a block into which a cavity of the correct shape has been cut. A holddown plate of a size and shape to fit the die is required to hold the metal while it is being shaped. The shape of the cavity in the die is checked with templates to assure that it is correct.

To form a part, the metal is clamped between the holddown plate and die as shown in Fig. 7-66. The metal is then slowly forced into the cavity with a correctly shaped hammer or other forming tool.

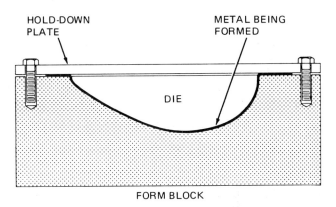

FIG. 7-66 Use of a formblock and holddown plate in forming a small part with compound curves.

Relief Holes

When two sheet metal bends intersect, it is necessary to provide relief holes in the metal at the intersection of the bends to allow space for the metal in the flanges. If relief holes are not provided, the metal crowds together in the corners and sets up stresses which would lead to cracks.

Figure 7-67 shows how the metal should be laid out and drilled to provide relief holes. The size of the holes is a minimum of ⅛ in [3.18 mm] for metal thicknesses of 0.064 in [1.63 mm] or less and greater for thicker metals. As shown in the drawing, the holes are drilled with centers at the intersections of the inside-bend tangent lines. This position provides maximum relief or clearance.

● RIVETING

A **rivet** is a metal pin or bar with a cylindrical shank, used for fastening two or more pieces of metal together. The metal pieces to be joined have holes of the proper size drilled through them. The shank of the rivet is inserted through one of these holes. One end of the rivet has a head formed previously by the manufacturer. The size and shape of the head are chosen to fit the requirements of the application. After the rivet is inserted through the holes in the metal, a **bucked head** is formed on the end opposite the manufactured head. This bucked head is formed by any of

229

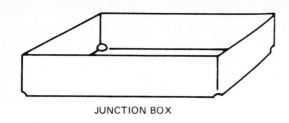

JUNCTION BOX

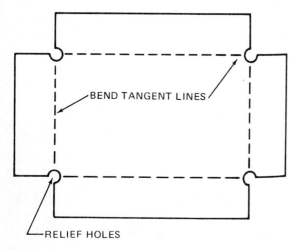

BEND TANGENT LINES

RELIEF HOLES

FIG. 7-67 Flat layout showing location of relief holes.

the various methods described in this chapter. Figure 7-68 illustrates popular head styles and standard head markings for aircraft rivets.

Types of Solid Rivets

In the past there have been many different types of solid rivets for aircraft construction. Because of standardization in the industry, two principal types have evolved. These are the **universal-head rivet** (MS20470 or AN470) and the **countersunk-head rivet** (MS20426 or AN426). There are other types in use, and these are described briefly in this text. In addition to the common types, there are special types of rivets which are used where the standard types cannot be used because of design or where special strength characteristics are required. A careful study of Fig. 7-68 makes it possible to identify the various common types of aircraft rivets.

The **universal-head rivet** (MS20470 or AN470) is used throughout the interior aircraft structure where special rivets are not required and in the exterior surfaces where skin friction is not critical. The head of the universal rivet is designed to combine the strength features of the old brazier-head, roundheaded, and flatheaded rivets. The head of the universal rivet is about twice the diameter of the shank and is slightly flattened on the top.

A **countersunk-head rivet** (MS20426 or AN426) is one which has a head flat on the top and beveled toward the shank so that it may fit in either a countersunk or a dimpled hole. When it has been driven, the top of the head is flush with the surface of the skin. The bevel, or slope, of the underside of the head forms an angle of 100°. Countersunk-head rivets are

used where it is necessary to provide a smooth surface. This may be where it is necessary to install other material over the heads of the rivets or on the outer skin of the airplane in order to reduce drag.

The mechanic will encounter some aircraft structures where some of the older-type rivets have been used; hence it is deemed wise to discuss them here briefly.

The **brazier-head rivet** (MS20455 or AN455) is similar in appearance to the universal-head rivet, but the head has a greater diameter and is thinner near the edges, as shown in Fig. 7-68.

A **flatheaded rivet** (MS20442) has a head which is flattened on both the top and the bottom. This rivet is normally used for internal structure where it does not affect the drag of the airplane.

A **roundheaded rivet** (MS20430) has a head which includes approximately 144° of a sphere. This rivet is used internally and sometimes externally, where it is desired that the rivet absorb some tensile stress.

Aluminum-alloy rivets can be made from any available aluminum alloy, but the strength requirements for various types of rivet joints and alloys have been satisfactorily met with the rivet alloys now in use. These are 1100, 2117T, 2017T, 2024T, 5053T, 5056T, and 6061T. The alloys most commonly used for aircraft structures are 2117T, 2017T, and 2024T. 2117T rivets may be driven in the condition in which they are received from the manufacturer. 2017T and 2024T rivets are usually heat-treated and driven immediately, or they may be heat-treated and stored at subzero temperatures to prevent age-hardening. Rivets which must be refrigerated in order to remain soft are called **icebox rivets** and must be driven within 5 to 10 min after removal from the icebox.

Icebox rivets will age-harden very quickly at ordinary temperatures but at $-50°F$ they will remain soft enough for driving for several weeks. At 32°F, they will remain soft for only about 24 h.

The aluminum-alloy and temper designation of a rivet or any aluminum alloy includes the alloy number, a letter, and usually a one- or two-digit number. The letter following the alloy number indicates condition of the alloy. The meanings of the letters are as follows:

—F   As fabricated (for wrought products)
—O   Annealed (for wrought products)
—H   Strain-hardened
—W   Solution heat-treated and aged at room temperature (used only with those alloys which are also furnished in the artificially aged temper)
—T   Heat-treated temper

The number following the letter indicates the type of heat treatment and other processes which have been applied to the alloy.

Commonly used aluminum-alloy aircraft rivets are designated 2017-T4, 2117-T4, and 2024-T4. The T4 following the alloy number indicates that the rivets are solution heat-treated only. After the rivet is driven, it is in the T3 condition because it has been cold-worked as well as heat-treated.

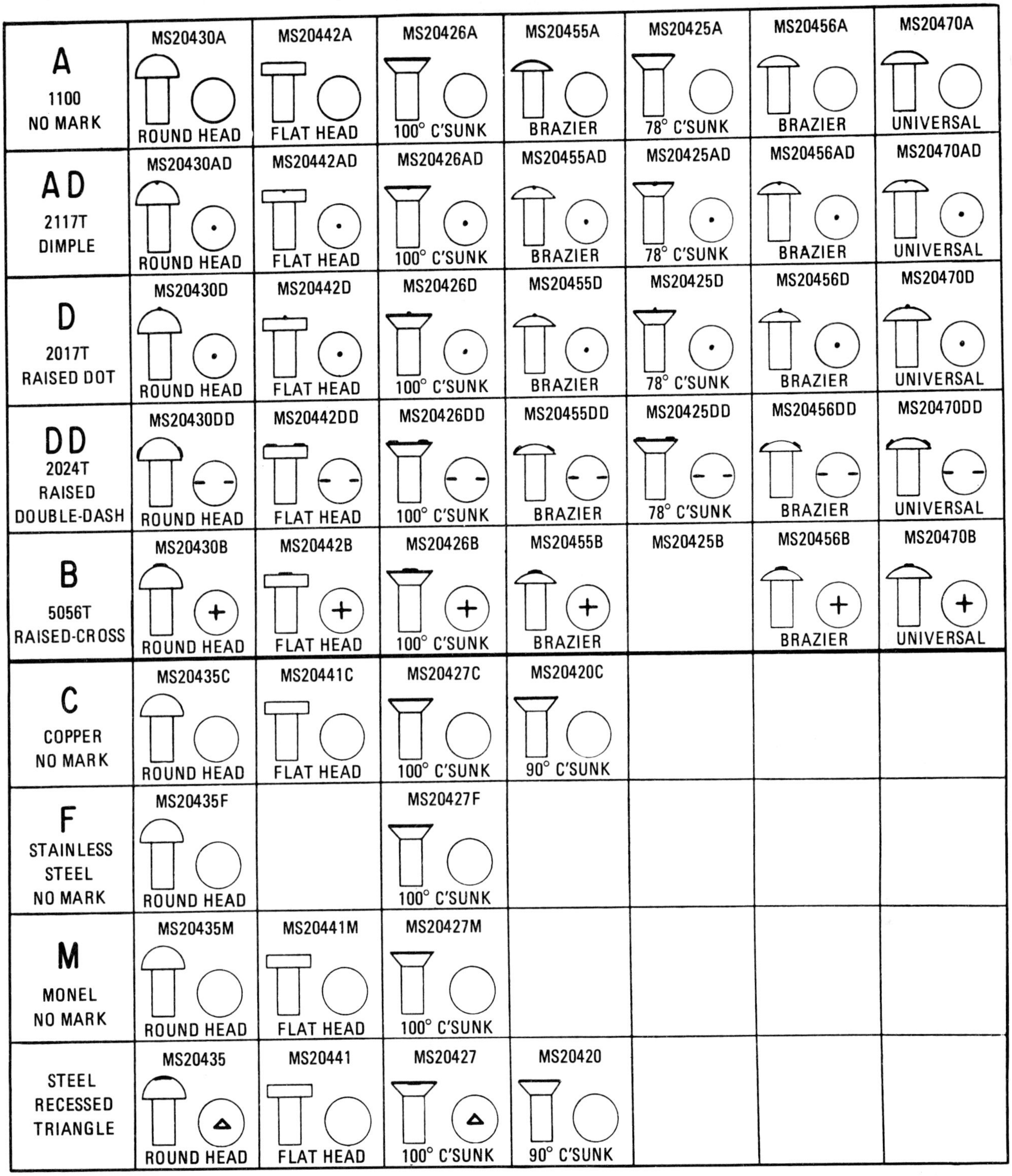

Material	Round Head	Flat Head	100° C'SUNK	Brazier	78° C'SUNK	Brazier	Universal
A 1100 NO MARK	MS20430A ROUND HEAD	MS20442A FLAT HEAD	MS20426A 100° C'SUNK	MS20455A BRAZIER	MS20425A 78° C'SUNK	MS20456A BRAZIER	MS20470A UNIVERSAL
A D 2117T DIMPLE	MS20430AD ROUND HEAD	MS20442AD FLAT HEAD	MS20426AD 100° C'SUNK	MS20455AD BRAZIER	MS20425AD 78° C'SUNK	MS20456AD BRAZIER	MS20470AD UNIVERSAL
D 2017T RAISED DOT	MS20430D ROUND HEAD	MS20442D FLAT HEAD	MS20426D 100° C'SUNK	MS20455D BRAZIER	MS20425D 78° C'SUNK	MS20456D BRAZIER	MS20470D UNIVERSAL
D D 2024T RAISED DOUBLE-DASH	MS20430DD ROUND HEAD	MS20442DD FLAT HEAD	MS20426DD 100° C'SUNK	MS20455DD BRAZIER	MS20425DD 78° C'SUNK	MS20456DD BRAZIER	MS20470DD UNIVERSAL
B 5056T RAISED-CROSS	MS20430B ROUND HEAD	MS20442B FLAT HEAD	MS20426B 100° C'SUNK	MS20455B BRAZIER	MS20425B	MS20456B BRAZIER	MS20470B UNIVERSAL
C COPPER NO MARK	MS20435C ROUND HEAD	MS20441C FLAT HEAD	MS20427C 100° C'SUNK	MS20420C 90° C'SUNK			
F STAINLESS STEEL NO MARK	MS20435F ROUND HEAD		MS20427F 100° C'SUNK				
M MONEL NO MARK	MS20435M ROUND HEAD	MS20441M FLAT HEAD	MS20427M 100° C'SUNK				
STEEL RECESSED TRIANGLE	MS20435 ROUND HEAD	MS20441 FLAT HEAD	MS20427 100° C'SUNK	MS20420 90° C'SUNK			

FIG. 7-68 Head styles and markings for aircraft rivets.

Rivet Codes

To identify rivets correctly and to identify the material from which they are made, certain code systems have been developed. The two methods used in the aircraft industry are (1) a number system and (2) a symbol system.

The letters and numbers which identify a rivet indicate the type, material, and size. For example, MS20470AD-3-4 is interpreted as follows: MS (Military Standard) denotes that the rivet meets the specifications set forth by the military services; 20470 indicates a universal head; AD shows that the material is 2117T aluminum alloy; the figure 3 gives the diameter in thirty-seconds of an inch; and the figure 4 gives the length of the shank in sixteenths of an inch.

The following breakdown explains the meaning of each portion of the MS number:

MS	MS standard part (indicates Military Standard)
20426	Type (countersunk head in this example)
DD	Alloy (2024T in this example)
5	Diameter in thirty-seconds of an inch
5	Length in sixteenths of an inch

In the case of the countersunk-head rivets, the length is given to include the head of the rivet. This is done because the top of the rivet head is flush with the skin when the rivet is driven.

The symbol code for the material of a rivet is also illustrated in Fig. 7-68. Mechanics who use aircraft rivets should memorize this code, and they should check the symbol on each rivet that they use. By so doing, they will avoid the possibility of rivet failure in the aircraft structure.

The AN rivet designation system is basically the same as the MS designation system. If the "MS20" is removed from the MS designation and "AN" is substituted, the AN designation will be given. For example, MS20426AD-5-8 designates the same rivet as AN426AD-5-8. Both of the designation systems are found in current use.

In addition to the MS and AN codes, mechanics working on large aircraft will encounter National Aerospace Standard (NAS) codes on aircraft blueprints and assembly drawings. The NAS-523 rivet code is illustrated in Fig. 7-69 and is used to describe rivet and installation specifications for a particular assembly. Mechanics will find instructions for the rivets to be used in a particular repair setup with coding in four quadrants designated NW (upper left), NE (upper right), SW (lower left), and SE (lower right).

The upper right (NE) quadrant designates the rivet part number, either AN or MS, and the material of which it is made. In the NW section of the chart, note that the code letters BJ identify an MS20470AD (AN470AD) rivet which is a universal-head rivet made of aluminum alloy 2117-T3. Only a few codes are shown in this chart owing to lack of space. For a complete listing, the mechanic should consult NAS-523.

The upper right (NE) quadrant specifies the diam-

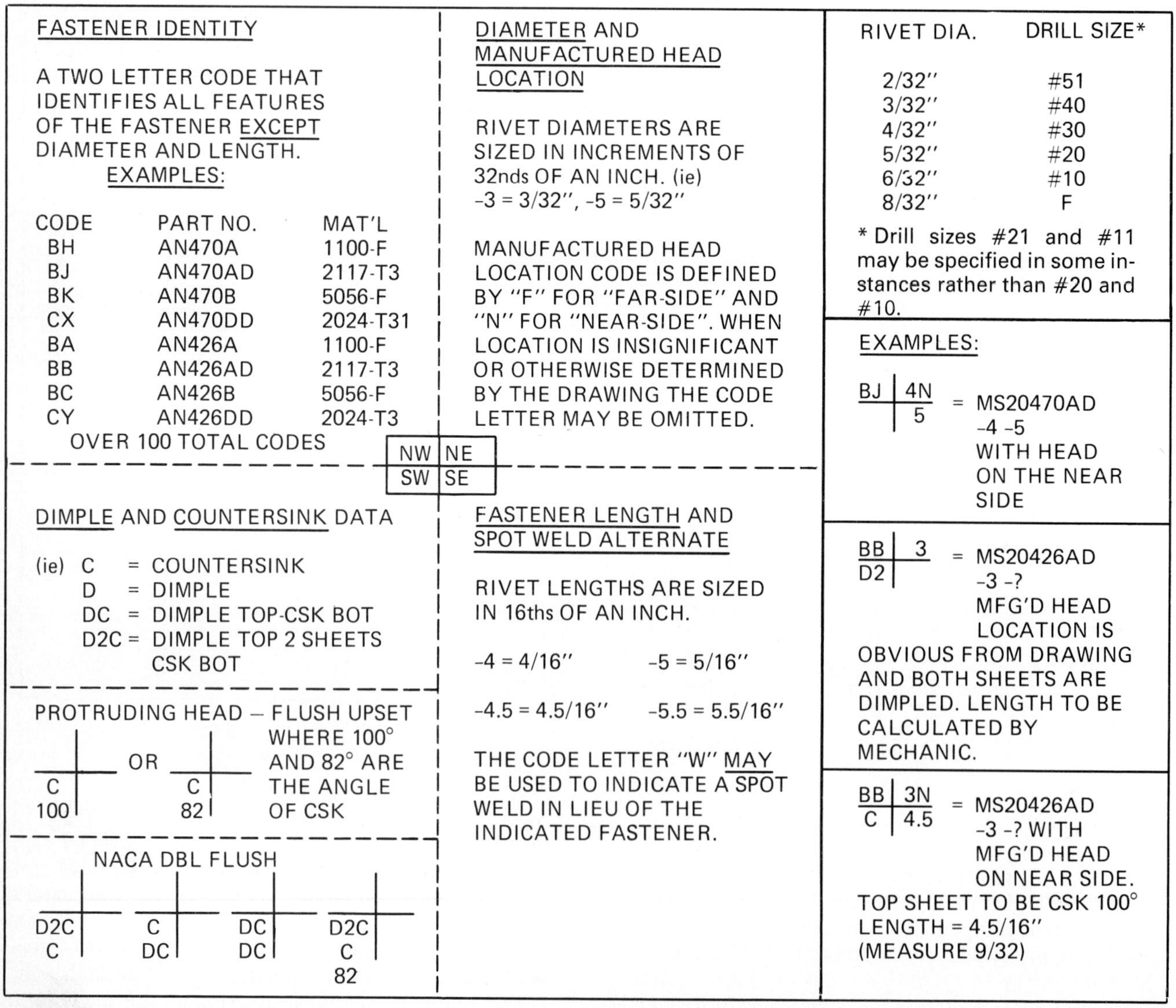

FASTENER IDENTITY

A TWO LETTER CODE THAT IDENTIFIES ALL FEATURES OF THE FASTENER EXCEPT DIAMETER AND LENGTH.
EXAMPLES:

CODE	PART NO.	MAT'L
BH	AN470A	1100-F
BJ	AN470AD	2117-T3
BK	AN470B	5056-F
CX	AN470DD	2024-T31
BA	AN426A	1100-F
BB	AN426AD	2117-T3
BC	AN426B	5056-F
CY	AN426DD	2024-T3

OVER 100 TOTAL CODES

NW	NE
SW	SE

DIMPLE AND COUNTERSINK DATA

(ie) C = COUNTERSINK
D = DIMPLE
DC = DIMPLE TOP-CSK BOT
D2C = DIMPLE TOP 2 SHEETS CSK BOT

PROTRUDING HEAD — FLUSH UPSET

```
        OR         WHERE 100°
                   AND 82° ARE
 C          C      THE ANGLE
100        82      OF CSK
```

NACA DBL FLUSH

```
D2C    C    DC    D2C
 C    DC    DC     C
                  82
```

DIAMETER AND MANUFACTURED HEAD LOCATION

RIVET DIAMETERS ARE SIZED IN INCREMENTS OF 32nds OF AN INCH. (ie) -3 = 3/32", -5 = 5/32"

MANUFACTURED HEAD LOCATION CODE IS DEFINED BY "F" FOR "FAR-SIDE" AND "N" FOR "NEAR-SIDE". WHEN LOCATION IS INSIGNIFICANT OR OTHERWISE DETERMINED BY THE DRAWING THE CODE LETTER MAY BE OMITTED.

FASTENER LENGTH AND SPOT WELD ALTERNATE

RIVET LENGTHS ARE SIZED IN 16ths OF AN INCH.

-4 = 4/16"   -5 = 5/16"

-4.5 = 4.5/16"   -5.5 = 5.5/16"

THE CODE LETTER "W" MAY BE USED TO INDICATE A SPOT WELD IN LIEU OF THE INDICATED FASTENER.

RIVET DIA.	DRILL SIZE*
2/32"	#51
3/32"	#40
4/32"	#30
5/32"	#20
6/32"	#10
8/32"	F

* Drill sizes #21 and #11 may be specified in some instances rather than #20 and #10.

EXAMPLES:

```
BJ | 4N
   |       = MS20470AD
   5        -4 -5
            WITH HEAD
            ON THE NEAR
            SIDE
```

```
BB | 3
D2 |       = MS20426AD
            -3 -?
            MFG'D HEAD
            LOCATION IS
```
OBVIOUS FROM DRAWING AND BOTH SHEETS ARE DIMPLED. LENGTH TO BE CALCULATED BY MECHANIC.

```
BB | 3N
C  | 4.5   = MS20426AD
            -3 -? WITH
            MFG'D HEAD
            ON NEAR SIDE.
```
TOP SHEET TO BE CSK 100° LENGTH = 4.5/16" (MEASURE 9/32)

FIG. 7-69 The NAS-523 rivet code.

eter of the rivet and the required positioning of the manufactured head of the rivet. The letters N and F are used to indicate that the manufactured head be placed on the near or far side of the repair, respectively.

The lower left (SW) quadrant provides dimple and countersink information. Letters and numbers as shown are placed in the SW quadrant to show the mechanic exactly what type of installation is to be made.

The lower right (SE) quadrant of the symbol gives the fastener length and indicates whether a spot weld may be used as an alternate method.

The column on the right of the quadrant shown in Fig. 7-69 is included here to provide additional information and examples for the student.

In addition to standard code numbers for fasteners and fittings, manufacturers often design their own items of hardware and apply their own part numbers. The mechanic must use the manufacturer's structural repair manual and be sure to employ the parts specified.

● RIVETING PRACTICES

The use of the proper size and spacing of rivets and their proper installation determines whether a riveted assembly will hold up to operational stresses. If any of these items is insufficient, the structure may fail, resulting in damage to the structure and injury to the aircraft occupants.

The use of specific rivet sizes and placements is dictated by the type and amount of stress placed on a structure and the size of the material being used. The following information is based on standard industry practices. For specific rivet selection and repair procedures, consult the aircraft manufacturer's manuals.

Rivet Sizes

In replacing rivets, the original size should be used if this size will fit and fill the holes. If not, the holes should be drilled or reamed for the next larger rivet. The rivet diameter for a sheet-metal joint should be approximately three times the thickness of the heavier sheet, or somewhat larger for thin sheets.

In determining the size of rivets to be used in any repair of aircraft, the mechanic must comply with the provisions of FAA publications. These set forth the policies and regulations of the FAA relative to the repair, maintenance, and overhaul of aircraft and engines. In the repair of military aircraft, the mechanic should follow military standards as set forth in technical orders and handbooks.

Rivet Spacing

The spacing of rivets in a replacement or a repair of stressed sheet metal may be determined by observing the spacing in adjacent parts of the same aircraft. The minimum spacing for aircraft rivets is three times the diameter of the rivet shank. The minimum edge distance is two times the diameter of the rivet shank, as shown in Fig. 7-70. Although the minimum edge distance for rivets is given as two times the diameter

of the rivet shank, it is recommended that the edge distance be not less than 2½ times the rivet shank diameter when the rivet is of the countersunk type. This will assure adequate strength of material along the edge of the sheet.

The space between rivets in a single row is called **pitch,** and the distance between rows of rivets is called **gauge.** These terms are illustrated in Fig. 7-71. The spacing between any two rivets is measured from the center of the shank of one to the center of the shank of the other.

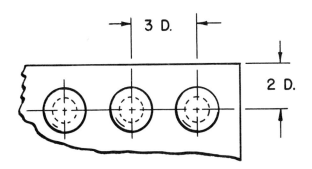

FIG. 7-70 Minimum rivet spacing.

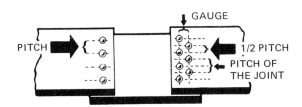

FIG. 7-71 Rivet pitch and gauge.

It is general practice to limit the maximum pitch (space between rivets in a single row) to 24 times the thickness of the sheet metal. For example, if the thickness of the sheet metal is 0.083 in [2.11 mm], 24 × 0.083 in = 1.992 in, or 2 in [50.8 mm] for practical purposes.

Rivets Required for a Repair

The number of rivets required in any repair is determined by the strength necessary for the riveted joints. This strength is based upon two considerations. First, we must determine the **shear strength** of the rivets. The shear on a rivet is the load that tends to cut the rivet in two parts as shown in Fig. 7-72. Second, the **tensile strength** of the sheet metal must be determined. These two forms of strength, considered together, constitute the basis for determining how many rivets are needed.

The shear strength of rivets and the tensile strength of materials may be determined from engineering tables. When these values are known, it is possible to determine the number of rivets required in a repair by dividing the shear strength of one rivet into the required tensile strength of the joint. For example, if the shear strength of a ⅛-in [3.175-mm] 2117-T3(AD) rivet is 344 lb [1530.8 N] and it is necessary to provide a

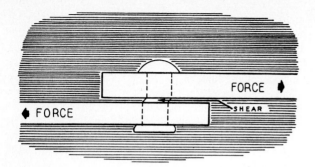

FIG. 7-72 Shear on a rivet.

tensile strength of 5600 lb [24 920 N] to a joint, the number of rivets required would be 5600/344 = 16.03. To make sure that the strength is adequate, it would be best to use 17 rivets.

In making a riveted seam, both the shear strength of the rivet and the **bearing strength** of the metal sheet must be taken into consideration. The bearing strength is the amount of force applied to a rivet installed in metal sheet which will cause the rivet to elongate the rivet hole in the sheet. If the bearing strength is greater than the shear strength of the rivet, the rivet will shear before the hole is elongated. If the shear strength of the rivet is greater than the bearing strength of the metal, the metal will yield and the rivet will pull through the metal.

Tables have been prepared to designate the number or rivets necessary to restore the strength to a given section of sheet aluminum alloy when using 2117-T3 rivets. Table 7-4 is an example for rivets from ³⁄₃₂ to ¼ in [2.38 to 6.35 mm] in diameter and aluminum-alloy sheet thicknesses from 0.016 to 0.128 in [0.406 to 3.25 mm]. When such tables are available, it is a simple matter to determine the number of rivets necessary for any particular repair.

If it is desired to repair a 2-in [50.8-mm] break in a sheet of 0.025-in [0.635-mm] aluminum-alloy skin on an airplane, the number of rivets would be determined as follows:

1. Select the size of rivet. Since the riveted sheet is 0.025 in [0.635 mm] thick, the rivet diameter must be at least three times this amount. This requires a rivet of at least 0.075 in [1.91 mm] in diameter. The next larger standard rivet is ³⁄₃₂ in [2.38 mm]; hence this is the size to be used.

2. Refer to Table 7-4 and note that when the thickness *T* of the sheet is 0.025 in [0.635 mm], the number of ³⁄₃₂-in [2.38-mm] rivets should be at least 8.6 per inch of width *W* of the repair. The break to be repaired is 2 in [50.8 mm] long; hence 17.2 rivets are required. We therefore use 18 rivets on each of the repair to restore the required strength.

The layout for the repair discussed above could appear as shown in Fig. 7-73. There can be variations in the design of a layout, provided the basic requirements of edge distance, rivet size, and rivet spacing are met. It will be observed in the illustration that rivets are spaced at a greater distance than the minimum.

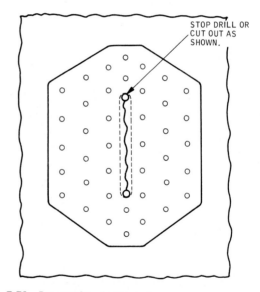

STOP DRILL OR CUT OUT AS SHOWN.

FIG. 7-73 Layout for rivet repair.

TABLE 7-4 Number of 2117-T3 Protruding-Head Rivets Required Per Inch of Width *W*

Aluminum Alloy Sheet Thickness *T*, in	Rivet Diameter, in					No. of AN-3 Bolts
	³⁄₃₂	⅛	⁵⁄₃₂	³⁄₁₆	¼	
0.016	6.5	4.9				
0.020	6.9	4.9	3.9			
0.025	8.6	4.9	3.9			
0.032	11.1	6.2	3.9	3.3		
0.036	12.5	7.0	4.5	3.3	2.4	
0.040	13.8	7.7	5.0	3.5	2.4	3.3
0.051		9.8	6.4	4.5	2.5	3.3
0.064		12.3	8.1	5.6	3.1	3.3
0.081			10.2	7.1	3.9	3.3
0.091			11.4	7.9	4.4	3.3
0.102			12.8	8.9	4.9	3.4
0.128				11.2	6.2	4.2

If a rivet table is not available when a repair is to be made, the number of rivets can be determined by considering the strength of the rivets and metal in accordance with a standard formula, as follows:

$$\text{No. of rivets} = \frac{\text{length of break} \times \text{thickness} \times 75\,000}{\text{shear strength or bearing strength}}$$

In the formula, the figure 75 000 is based upon the tensile strength of aluminum alloy and is an indication of the strength to be restored. The **shear** or **bearing-strength value** must be that which is the lowest of the two values. For example, the shear strength of an MS20470-AD-4 (⅛-in [3.175-mm]) rivet is given as 388 lb [1726 N] in the ANC-5 manual, a government manual specifying standards for aircraft metals. The bearing strength for a ⅛-in [3.175-mm] rivet in sheet aluminum alloy having a thickness of 0.040 in [1.8 mm] is given as 308.4 lb [1372 N] for metal having a tensile strength of 60 000 psi [414 000 kPa]. Since this is less than 388 lb [1726 N], we would use 308.4 lb [1372 N] for the value in the formula.

Drilling Holes for Rivets

To make a good riveted joint, it is essential that the rivet hole be drilled properly. The first requirement for a perfectly drilled hole is the use of a drill that is ground accurately. New drills usually have a satisfactory point, but after they are worn they should be sharpened or discarded. The dimensions for a correctly ground point are shown in Fig. 7-74. Observe the **drill-point angle** (118°) and the **drill-rake angle** (12°). For materials which are soft, for example, soft aluminum, lead, wood, and plastics, it is better to have the drill sharpened with a smaller drill-point angle such as 90° for medium soft materials and 45° for very soft materials. For very hard and tough materials such as steel, stainless steel, and titanium, a larger drill-point angle (125 to 150°) and a smaller drill-rake angle (10°) are recommended. The dimensions suggested here are for guidance and are not meant to indicate an absolute requirement. The experienced mechanic will adjust the dimensions to get the best results for the job at hand.

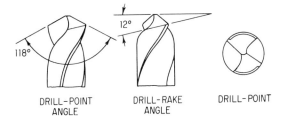

FIG. 7-74 Dimensions for a correctly ground drill point.

Drill speed is also an important factor in getting good results. The proper speed for aluminum alloy will not produce the best results with stainless steel or titanium. Drill speed determines the rate at which the outer cutting edge of the drill is moving across the material being cut. For example, a ⅛-in [3.18-mm] drill having a circumference of 0.3927 in [9.97 mm] turning at the rate of 1222 rpm will have a cutting speed of 40 ft/min [1219.2 cm/min]. When harder materials are drilled, slower speeds are required. In addition, a cutting and cooling lubricant is needed. Lubricating oil, lard oil, water-soluble oil, and others are used. Table 7-5 shows drill and cutting speeds for various sized drills. This table provides information for commonly used drill sizes at variously recommended cutting speeds. For values not shown on the chart, it is merely necessary to compute or extrapolate from the ones shown.

It must be explained that the values given in Table 7-5 are not required but are recommended for optimum

TABLE 7-5 Drill and Cutting Speeds

Cutting Speed, ft/min [cm/min]	30 [914]	40 [1219]	50 [1524]	60 [1829]	70 [2134]	80 [2438]	90 [2743]	100 [3048]
Diameter, in [mm]				rpm				
¹⁄₁₆ [1.59]	1833	2445	3056	3667	4278	4889	5500	6111
³⁄₃₂ [2.38]	1222	1630	2038	2445	2853	3260	3667	4074
⅛ [3.18]	917	1222	1528	1833	2139	2445	2750	3056
³⁄₁₆ [4.76]	611	815	1019	1222	1426	1630	1833	2037
¼ [6.35]	458	611	764	917	1070	1222	1375	1528
⁵⁄₁₆ [7.95]	367	489	611	733	856	978	1100	1222
⅜ [9.33]	306	407	509	611	713	815	917	1019
⁷⁄₁₆ [11.13]	262	349	437	524	611	698	786	873
½ [12.7]	229	306	383	458	535	611	688	764

results. A cutting speed of 100 ft/min [3048 cm/min] is recommended for aluminum alloys; however, lower speeds can be used very satisfactorily. For stainless steel and titanium, a cutting speed of 30 ft/min [914.4 cm/min] is recommended, but a lower or higher speed can be used. Care must be taken with the harder and tougher materials to avoid too much speed and pressure which will result in overheating the drill and rendering it useless.

In drilling larger holes of ³⁄₁₆ in [4.76 mm] or more, it is wise to drill a pilot hole first. The pilot drill should not be more than one-half the diameter of the final hole. This is particularly true when drilling harder materials.

Before using a drill bit, the mechanic should examine it to see that it is straight, that the point conforms to required standards, and that the shank is not scored or otherwise damaged.

The location of a hole to be drilled may be indicated by marking with a pencil or, in the case of heavy sheet stock, by making a slight indentation with a center punch. For holes which must be held within extremely close tolerances, a **drill jig** is normally used. This device holds the drill accurately in position while the hole is being drilled.

When beginning to drill a hole, the mechanic must be very careful to hold the drill perpendicular to the material being drilled and must also steady the drill and motor so that the drill will not move away from the correct position and damage the adjacent material. It is common practice to start the drill by placing it in position and turning it by hand before turning on the electric or air power to operate the motor. By this method the hole will be started, and the drill will usually remain in the proper position. Figure 7-75 shows a mechanic holding the drill properly for starting to drill a hole.

Figure 7-76 illustrates properly and improperly drilled holes. The left and middle drawings show holes that are clean and in good alignment. The right drawing shows two holes which were drilled at an angle and would not be suitable for riveting.

A hole is not complete until it is both drilled and burred. **Burring** is the process of removing rough edges and chips from a newly drilled hole. It is usually

FIG. 7-75 Proper method for starting a drill.

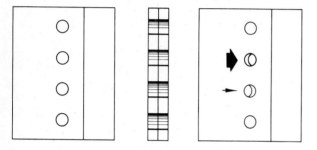

FIG. 7-76 Properly and improperly drilled holes.

done by hand with a drill larger than the hole, or it can be done with a special burring tool which is merely a piece of metal with sharp edges. When two or more sheets are drilled at the same time, it is necessary to remove chips and burrs from between the sheets. Figure 7-77 illustrates the results of leaving material between drilled sheets. Removal of burrs from drilled holes (deburring) may be accomplished with a manufactured **deburring tool,** a countersink using a very light cut, or other tool which will clear the edges of a drill or punched hole. Care must be taken to remove only the rough edges and chips from the hole.

FIG. 7-77 Material between sheets of metal.

Installing Rivets

The installation of common rivets consists of drilling holes slightly larger (0.001 to 0.003 in [0.025 to 0.076 mm]) than the rivet shank in the parts to be joined, removing the burrs from the edges of the holes, inserting the rivet, and driving the rivet. A No. 40 drill is used for a $\frac{3}{32}$-in [2.382-mm] rivet, a No. 30 drill is used for a $\frac{1}{8}$-in [3.175-mm] rivet, and a No. 21 drill is used for a $\frac{5}{32}$-in [3.97-mm] rivet. Note that the first dash number of a rivet (dia.) when added to the first

number of the drill size will equal 7. A -2 rivet requires a No. 51 drill; a -3 rivet, a 40 drill; a -4 rivet, a 30 drill; a -5 rivet, a 21 drill; and a -6 rivet, an 11 drill. This is referred to as the 7-rule and is coincidental. It gives the mechanic a method which helps to remember drill sizes, but is applies only to rivet sizes -2 through -6. The rivet is usually driven by means of a pneumatic hammer and a bucking bar to "back-up" the rivet.

To install countersunk rivets, it is necessary to provide a conical depression in the surface of the skin so that the head of the rivet is flush with the surface. This depression is made by means of a **countersink** when the skin is sufficiently thick and by **dimpling** when the skin is thin. The use of a machine countersink is limited by the size of the rivet and the thickness of the skin. Generally, sheet metal should not be machine-countersunk entirely through the sheet. For sheet metal of 0.040- to 0.051-in [1.02- to 1.28-mm] thickness it is common practice to countersink not more than three-fourths the thickness of the sheet. For repairs on an airplane the specifications for use of machine countersinking usually may be determined from the rivets installed by the manufacturer.

A countersink for use in a drill press or drill motor is shown in Fig. 7-78. The pilot of the countersink assures that the countersunk portion of the hole will be properly centered. It is good practice to use an adjustable stop on the drill motor or drill press to ensure that the depth of the countersink will be accurate. A sheet of metal should never be countersunk through more than 99 percent of its thickness.

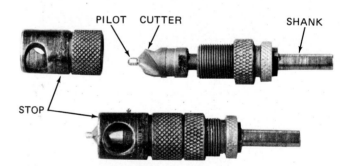

FIG. 7-78 A countersink.

Dimpling for countersunk rivets is a common practice when using a relatively thin skin such as 0.016 to 0.025 in [0.41 to 0.64 mm] in thickness. **Dimpling** can be accomplished with a dimpling bar and flush set as shown in Fig. 7-79. The rivet head is the die which forms the dimple. When thin skin is attached to a heavier structural member, the heavy member is sub-countersunk and the skin is dimpled into the countersunk depression, as illustrated in Fig. 7-80. For production work in a factory, dimpling often is accomplished with dimpling dies used in a pneumatic squeeze riveter.

It is sometimes necessary to dimple heavy sheet in a highly stressed part of the airplane in order to retain the maximum strength of the sheet. A process called **hot dimpling** has been developed for this purpose. Hot

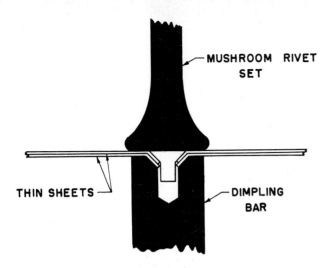

FIG. 7-79 Use of a dimpling bar for dimpling.

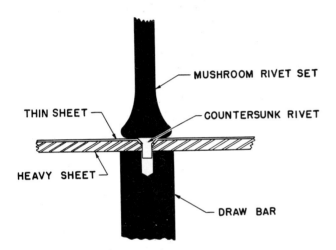

FIG. 7-80 Dimpling thin skin into countersunk sheet.

dimpling is performed with a special hot-dimpling machine consisting of heated dies which can be pressed together pneumatically to form a dimple as shown in Fig. 7-81. A process wherein the sheet metal is caused to *flow* to the shape of dies is called **coin dimpling**.

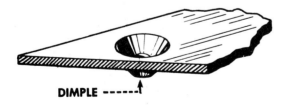

FIG. 7-81 Dimple formed with heat.

Figure 7-82 shows an automatic hot-dimpling machine manufactured by Aircraft Tools, Inc. The operator sets the controls of the machine according to charts supplied by the manufacturer, which set forth the temperatures and pressures required for various types and thicknesses of materials.

The material, having been previously drilled, is

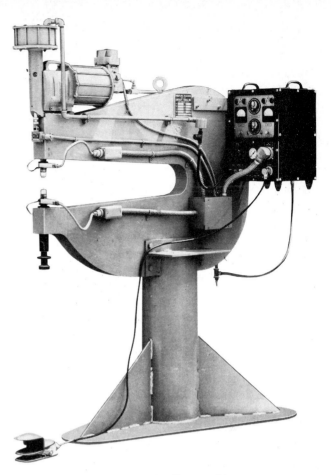

FIG. 7-82 Automatic hot-dimpling machine.

placed over the stationary die with the pilot of the die projecting through the hole in the material. The operator then presses on the foot control of the machine. This brings upper and lower dies toward each other; thus they press on the material and their heat is transferred to the material. As the material becomes heated sufficiently, the pressure of the dies causes it to be formed. This pressure comes from a compressed-air system. The initial pressure on the dies is limited to prevent the material from being deformed before it has been heated sufficiently. After the material reaches the forming temperature, additional pressure is applied automatically to the dies to complete the forming operation. This pressure is maintained for a predetermined number of seconds, and then it is automatically released.

Another method for hot dimpling employs a resistance-heating machine. The dies of the machine are electrodes which pass a current through the metal to be riveted and cause it to heat. When the metal has been heated sufficiently, full pressure is applied to the dies to form the dimple.

The rivets are installed by the use of a rivet gun and a bucking bar. The size of the rivet gun and bucking bar are selected to match the size of the rivet.

The various rivet guns can be adjusted to deliver the required blow for each size of rivet. The most desirable practice is to adjust the gun so that the bucked head of the rivet will be properly shaped, using as few blows of the rivet gun as possible. When the rivet gun is adjusted with too light a blow, the rivet may be work-hardened to such a degree that the head will not be formed properly without cracking the rivet.

A bucking bar is used as shown in Fig. 7-83. The bar is held firmly against the shank of the rivet while the rivet gun with the correct set is applied to the manufactured head. It is essential that the bucking bar be placed against the shank of the rivet before the rivet is driven. If the operator of the rivet gun starts to drive the rivet before the bucking bar is in place, the sheet in which the rivet is being installed will be damaged.

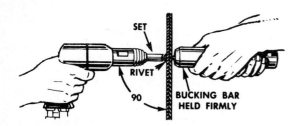

FIG. 7-83 Bucking a rivet.

The correct installation of a rivet is dependent upon the proper use of the bucking bar as well as the rivet gun. The face of the bucking bar must be held square with the rivet, or the rivet may "clinch"; that is, the bucked head will be driven off center. Sometimes the operator can control the formation of the bucked head by carefully tilting the bucking bar. Both the rivet gun and the bucking bar must be firmly in place against the rivet before the throttle of the gun is opened to drive the rivet. Figure 7-84 illustrates rivets improperly installed.

It should be noted that there are several names used to identify the head formed on the shank of the rivet during the bucking operation. These include: bucked head, formed head, shop head, and buck tail.

Dimensions of Installed Rivets

When rivets are installed in a standard repair, it is necessary that certain minimum dimensions be observed. Figure 7-85 shows the minimum dimensions for bucked rivet heads and length of rivet. Although the drawing shows 0.65D as the desired height of the bucked head, a minimum height of 0.50D will be accepted.

With experience, a visual inspection will tell the mechanic if the rivet has been upset properly. A gauge, such as that shown in Fig. 7-86, can also be used. One gauge like this is needed for each diameter rivet. The hole in the gauge is the diameter of the bucked head, and the thickness of the gauge corresponds to proper head height. The gauge is placed over the bucked head and irregularities are immediately apparent.

Shaved Rivets

On modern, high-speed aircraft, it is necessary to remove every possible cause of drag from the outer

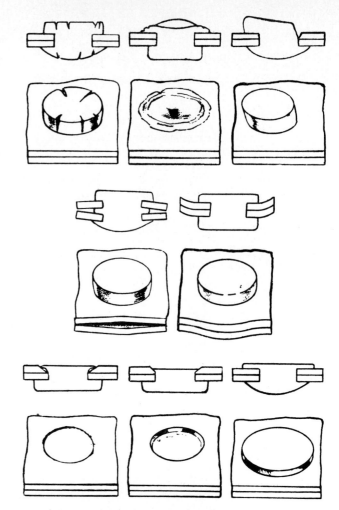

FIG. 7-84 Improperly installed rivets.

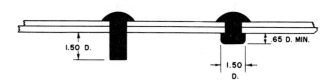

FIG. 7-85 Minimum dimensions for a rivet.

FIG. 7-86 A rivet gauge.

surface of the airplane skin. For years flush (counter-sunk-type) rivets were installed in skin and other structural sections exposed to airflow. To obtain the most nearly perfect surface, shaved-riveting techniques were developed.

In preparation for shaved riveting, standard rivet holes are drilled in the metal to be riveted. This may be done by the manual method or by automatically programmed machines. On the outer surface of the metal the holes are countersunk with a 60° tool instead of the conventional 100° countersink.

Standard rivets are installed with the rivet head inside the metal skin, and the shank of the rivet is driven to form a head in the conical depression on the outer surface. The forming of the rivet shank to fill the depression can be done with a standard rivet gun and smooth-faced bucking bar, but, during production, it is often done with automatic machines.

After the rivet is driven sufficiently to fill the countersunk hole completely, the excess of rivet material projecting above the surface of the skin is shaved with a small rotary mill called a **rivet shaver,** shown in Fig. 7-87. With this tool, the surface of the skin and rivet is made extremely smooth so drag will be reduced to the minimum. For the manual process, the rivet shaver is held in the hand as one would hold a drill motor. It is prevented from cutting too deeply by means of a carefully adjusted stop.

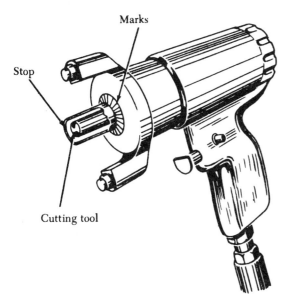

FIG. 7-87   A rivet shaver.

Removing Rivets

In the repair of sheet-metal aircraft is is often necessary to remove rivets. However, great care must be used, or damage may be done to the metal from which the rivets are removed. Rivets are removed by drilling through the manufactured head with a drill one size smaller than the shank of the rivet. The mechanic must make sure that the drill is started and held in the exact center of the rivet head. The drill should penetrate no further than the base of the rivet head, or the rivet hole may be enlarged by the drill. Usually the rivet head will come off as soon as the drill has penetrated the proper distance. If the rivet head does not come off, a pin punch the same diameter as the hole may be used to snap the head off as shown in Fig. 7-88. After the head of the rivet is removed, the shank may be pushed or driven out with the pin punch.

When replacing rivets in a hole where a rivet pre-

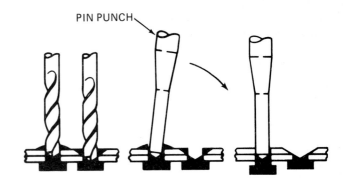

FIG. 7-88   Removing a rivet.

viously has been installed, it is necessary to ascertain that the hole has not been enlarged beyond the correct tolerance for the rivet being installed. If the hole is too large, it should be drilled to the correct size for the next larger rivet to be used.

● TYPICAL REPAIRS

The number of different types of repairs for damaged sheet-metal structures is almost endless; hence we can provide only a few typical examples in this text and explain the requirements for repairs. The primary objective of a sheet-metal repair is to restore the original strength of the structure without increasing the weight of the vehicle any more than necessary. The mechanic or superior must usually decide whether to replace a damaged structure or make a repair. In any event, the repair must be made in accordance with the manufacturer's instruction or the methods set forth in FAA Advisory Circular 43.13-1A. In some cases it may be necessary to design a special repair and have it analyzed by engineers to assure that it will accomplish its purpose. This is especially true for high-stressed structures and pressurized structures.

Classifications of Sheet-Metal Damage

Several aircraft manufacturers have developed classifications of damage that are used to determine the corrective action necessary to return an aircraft to an airworthy condition. Each manufacturer establishes the damage level based on the aircraft and the area of the aircraft involved. The classifications of damage are **negligible, repairable,** and **replacement.**

Negligible damage is that damage which does not affect the airworthiness of the aircraft. This level of damage may be allowed to exist or can be repaired by minor patching operations. Typical of this type of damage are dents in the skin that are not cracking, cracks in areas of low stress that can be covered by a 2-in [5.08-cm] circle, and surface scratches in low-stress areas.

Repairable damage is damage which might affect the airworthiness of the aircraft and could result in a loss of function of a component or system if not repaired. Repairable damage can be repaired by the use of a patch or by the insertion of a replacement component. This might include holes in the skin and cracked or broken formers and stringers which are not significantly deformed.

Replacement damage is damage which cannot be practically repaired and where repairing is specifically prohibited. This type of damage includes extensive corrosion, parts that are twisted or warped beyond usable limits, and components requiring alignments jigs for proper repair.

Repairs for Small Holes

Small holes in sheet-metal skin may be repaired by means of a patch plate or a flush patch if the damage does not affect ribs or other structural members. The rough edges of the hole may be smoothed with a file or cut away with a **hole saw.** A hole saw is a small, circular saw, the shank of which can be inserted in the chuck of a drill motor or drill press. Several hole saws are shown in Fig. 7-89.

FIG. 7-89 Hole saws.

During use of a hole saw with a drill motor, it is usually necessary to drill a pilot hole and use a hole-saw pilot or a hole-saw guide with a pilot. This keeps the saw in place while cutting the metal.

Small holes may be punched in sheet metal with a **chassis punch.** The chassis punch includes a punch-and-die assembly with a screw device for pulling the punch through the metal. The punch has sharp edges which enable it to cut progressively as the screw is turned.

The patch for a small hole can be riveted to the outer surface of the skin, or it may be made flush as shown in Fig. 7-90. In either type of patch the number of rivets should conform to the patterns shown in Fig. 7-90 which illustrates patches for 1-, 2-, and 3-in [2.54-, 5.08-, and 7.62-cm] round holes.

Where a flush patch is used, the patch is placed on the inner side of the skin. A plug is cut to fit the hole and is riveted to the patch. The rivets should be of the flush type as previously described in this chapter.

Replacement of Skin Panels

In cases where damage to stressed skin has occurred over an extensive area, it is often necessary to replace an entire panel. The original panel is removed by carefully drilling out the rivets at the seams. A new panel of the same material and thickness is cut to the same size as the original. The rivet pattern at the seams must conform to the original pattern. In cases where a portion of a panel is replaced and different rivet patterns are used on the opposite edges of panels, it is best to copy the pattern of the stronger seam. Before a damaged panel is replaced, the interior of the struc-

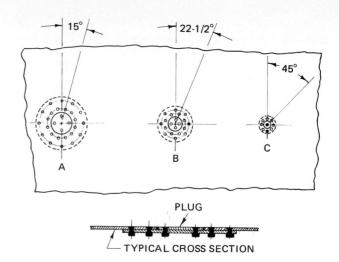

DIMENSIONS OF CIR. PATCH PLATES

DESIGNATION	A	B	C
DIAMETER (OUTSIDE)	7 1/2" [19 cm]	5" [13 cm]	2 1/2" [6 cm]
DIA. INNER RIVET CIRCLE	4" [10 cm]	3" [8 cm]	1 3/4" 4.5 cm]
DIA. OUTER RIVET CIRCLE	6 1/2" [16.5 cm]	4" [10 cm]	–
DIAMETER (INSIDE)	3" [8 cm]	2" [5 cm]	1" [2.5 cm]
NO. OF RIVETS (A-17ST-5/32)	24	16	8
PLUG RIVETS TO BE USED AS REQUIRED			

FIG. 7-90 Flush patch for a small hole.

ture must be inspected carefully. All damaged ribs, bulkhead, or other damaged structures must be repaired before replacing the skin panel.

Repairs of Sheet-Metal Ribs

Typical repairs for formed sheet-metal and built-up ribs are shown in Fig. 7-91. In making repairs of the

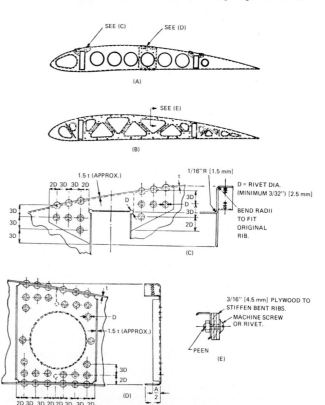

FIG. 7-91 Repairs for sheet-metal ribs.

type shown, the mechanic must use the correct number of rivets of the proper size and material. The replacement material and material used in making reinforcements must be of the same type as that used in the original structure. Furthermore, the material must have the same heat treatment as the original. The thickness of the repair material must be the same or greater than that of the original.

Repairs for formed sheet-metal rib cap strips are illustrated in Fig. 7-92. The repairs shown are indicative of the types of repairs required; however, many different types of repairs can be made as long as the strength and durability are adequately restored.

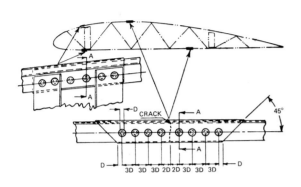

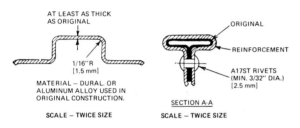

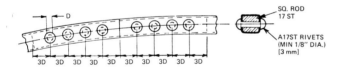

FIG. 7-92   Repairs for metal rib cap strips.

Splicing of Sheets

Splicing of sheet metal should be accomplished as shown in Fig. 7-93. A double row of rivets in a splice, as shown in the upper part of the drawing, will give a seam strength which is 75 percent of the sheet strength without holes. The pattern shown in the lower part of the drawing will give a seam strength of 83 percent of the sheet without holes.

When splicing sheets, the splice should be designed as illustrated in the following examples:

Material: 2024-T3 A1-Clad sheet, 0.032-in [0.813-mm] thickness
Width of sheet (length of splice) W = 12 in [30.48 cm]

1. Select the rivet diameter approximately three times the sheet thickness. Thus, 3 × 0.32 = 0.096 in [2.44 mm]. Use ⅛-in [3.175-mm] 2117-T4 (AD) rivets.

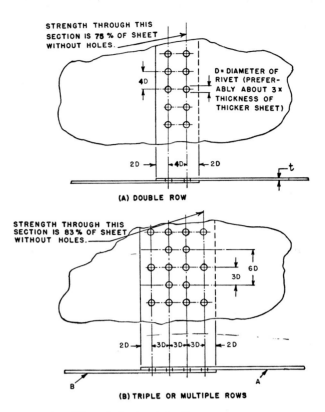

FIG. 7-93   Riveted sheet-metal splices.

2. Determine the number of rivets required per inch of width W from Table 7-4. The number of rivets per inch equals 6.2, hence the total number of rivets required is 12 × 6.2 = 74.4, or 75 rivets.

3. Lay out the rivet pattern with spacings not less than those shown in Fig. 7-93. With the rivet pattern shown in Fig. 9-32(b), 75 rivets can be installed in the 12-in [30.48-cm] width. This will make a satisfactory splice for the material used.

In the splice example above, if flush rivets are used, it is recommended that an edge distance of 2½D (rivet diameter) be used. For universal-head rivets an edge distance of not less than 2D is satisfactory.

Stringer and Flange Splices

Splices for stringers and flanges are shown in Fig. 7-94. The original material is shown unshaded, the reinforcing material shaded. Remember that **stringers** are the longitudinal supporting members to which the skin of the fuselage or wing is attached. The stringers are attached to the bulkheads or beltframes (formers) which are principal structural members of the assembly and are designed to take both compression and tension loads. Therefore, these riveting principles must be followed.

1. To avoid eccentric loading and buckling in compression, splicing or reinforcing parts are placed as symmetrically as possible about the centerline of the member. Attachment is made to as many elements as necessary to prevent bending in any direction.

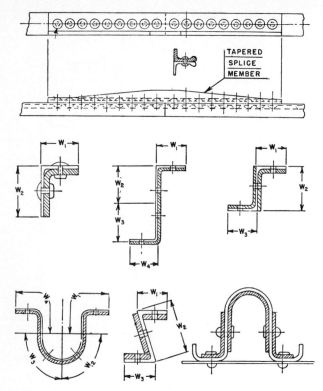

FIG. 7-94 Splices for stringers and flanges.

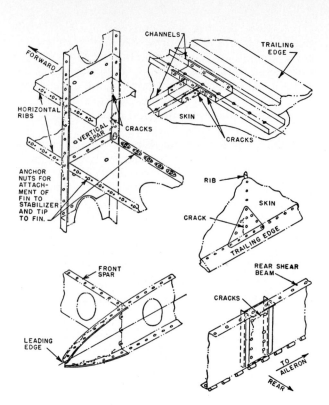

FIG. 7-95 Repairs for cracked structures.

2. So that reduction of strength under tension of the original member is avoided, the rivet holes at the end of the splice are made small, that is, not larger than the original skin-attaching rivets, and the second row of rivets is staggered back from the ends.

3. To prevent concentrating the loads on the end rivet and the consequent tendency toward progressive rivet failure, the splice member is tapered at the ends. This also has the effect of reducing the stress concentration at the ends of the splice.

4. When several adjacent stringers are spliced, the splices should be staggered if possible.

5. The diameter of rivets in stringers should be between two and three times the thickness of the leg but should not be more than one-quarter its width.

Repairing Cracked Structures

Methods for repairing cracked structures are shown in Fig. 7-95. This illustration shows repairs at the intersection of ribs and spars at both the leading edge and the trailing edge of a wing or other airfoil. Reinforcing plates must be of the same alloy and approximately 1½ times the thickness of the original material. In every case where cracks are repaired, the cracks should be stop-drilled before installing any reinforcements. **Stop drilling** can be defined as the process of drilling a small hole at the extreme end of a crack to prevent the crack from progressing farther into the material. The hole at the end of the crack removes the sharp stress-concentration area.

The condition causing cracks to develop at a particular point is stress concentration at the point combined with the repetition of the stress, as would occur with vibration. Stress concentrations are caused by nicks,

scratches, or incorrect design factors. Complete failure of wing structures has been caused by stress concentrations where material has been cut to form a notch. In all repairs, the mechanic must make sure that material is not cut to form a sharp angle between two edges and that where two edges come together to form an angle, the material is rounded ("radiused") to a radius sufficient to prevent stress concentrations. The radius should be made as smooth as possible.

Members of aircraft structures which have developed cracks at fittings can be repaired as shown in Fig. 7-96. The treatment of cracks in these repairs is the same as described previously.

Special Repairs

Where specific instructions for sheet-metal structural repairs are not available in publications such as Advisory Circular 43.13-1A and 2 published by the FAA, they are usually shown in the manufacturer's manuals. For example, Fig. 7-97 is an illustration of a fuselage stringer repair provided in the service manual for a Cessna aircraft. Although a repair similar to this could be designed without the manual, it is good practice to use the manufacturer's design when available.

Another repair illustrated in the manufacturer's manual is shown in Fig. 7-98. In this case the repair illustrated is for a cracked channel member. Note that the crack is stop-drilled as described previously.

The mechanic may encounter bonded metal structures from time to time. In such cases the mechanic should consult the manufacturer's maintenance manuals to ensure that repairs are made in accordance with specifications.

An airplane utilizing bonded metal construction is

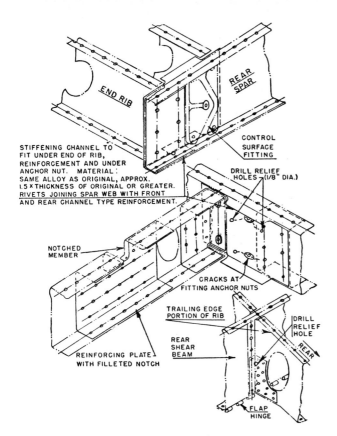

FIG. 7-96 Repairs for cracks at fittings.

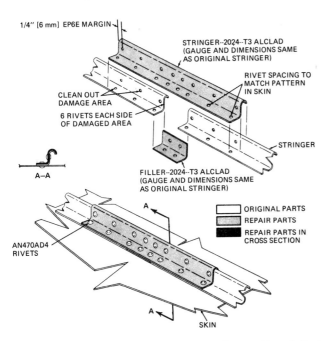

FIG. 7-97 Repair of fuselage stringer. (*Cessna Aircraft Co.*)

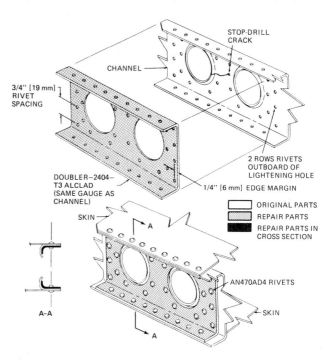

FIG. 7-98 Repair of cracked channel member. (*Cessna Aircraft Co.*)

FIG. 7-99 Airplane with bonded metal structure. (*Grumman American Aviation*)

shown in Fig. 7-99. As mentioned earlier, the bonded metal seams provide for a uniform distribution of stresses, thus making possible a structure with an improved strength-to-weight ratio.

Bonded metal skin is repaired in accordance with the standard practices set forth in FAA Advisory Circular AC 43.13-1A and 2 describing riveted repairs.

The rivets are countersunk and then smoothed over with an epoxy filler which is sanded smooth. The final finish is urethane enamel.

A typical repair for the wing leading edge of a bonded metal airplane is shown in Fig. 7-100. Repair instructions are as follows:

1. Trim out the damaged area in a rectangular pattern and deburr.

2. Place the repair doubler beneath the wing skin as shown in Fig. 7-100. Note that the doubler is 2024-T3 A1-Clad aluminum. (Note: Dimensions given are typical.)

3. Holding the repair doubler in place, drill ⅛-in [3.18-mm] dimple holes through the wing skin, spacing the holes ⅝ in [15.88 mm] apart, center to center. (Note: This repair can be completed in the area of wing ribs by installing the doubler in two places, one on each side of the rib flange.)

4. Secure the doubler to the wing leading edge with ⅛-in [3.18-mm] diameter countersunk Cherry rivets (CR162) or equivalent. If bucked rivets are used, exercise caution to prevent nearby bond damage. (Cherry rivets are blind rivets and will be described later in this section.)

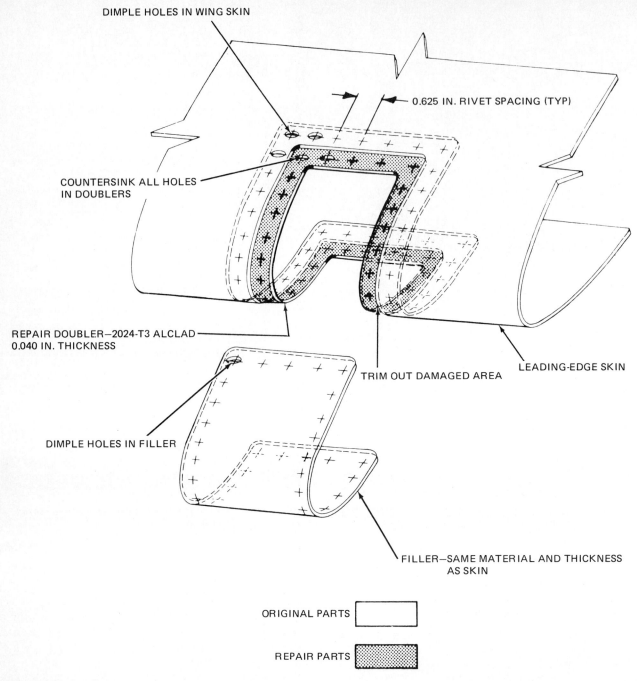

DIMPLE HOLES IN WING SKIN

0.625 IN. RIVET SPACING (TYP)

COUNTERSINK ALL HOLES
IN DOUBLERS

REPAIR DOUBLER—2024-T3 ALCLAD
0.040 IN. THICKNESS

TRIM OUT DAMAGED AREA

LEADING-EDGE SKIN

DIMPLE HOLES IN FILLER

FILLER—SAME MATERIAL AND THICKNESS
AS SKIN

ORIGINAL PARTS

REPAIR PARTS

FIG. 7-100 Leading-edge repair. *(Grumman American Aviation)*

5. Place the preformed filler flush with the skin over the doubler. The filler must be the same material and thickness as the skin.

6. Hold the filler in place, drill dimple holes through filler, spacing holes ⅝ in [15.88 mm] apart, center to center.

7. Secure the filler to the doubler as directed in step 4.

8. Use an epoxy filler and sand smooth. Finish to match aircraft.

A wing rib repair as specified in a manufacturer's manual is shown in Fig. 7-101. This may be compared with the repairs shown in Fig. 7-91.

In cases where ribs are damaged extensively, it is usually best to replace the entire rib. The mechanic must exercise judgment in determining whether a repair can be made satisfactorily and economically.

Instructions for the repair shown in Fig. 7-101 are as follows:

1. If the rib damage consists of a crack, stop-drill the crack if it does not extend to the edge of the part and add a reinforcement plate to carry the stress across the damaged portion and to stiffen the joints

2. If the area is to be repaired is damaged extensively, trim out the damaged area and deburr.

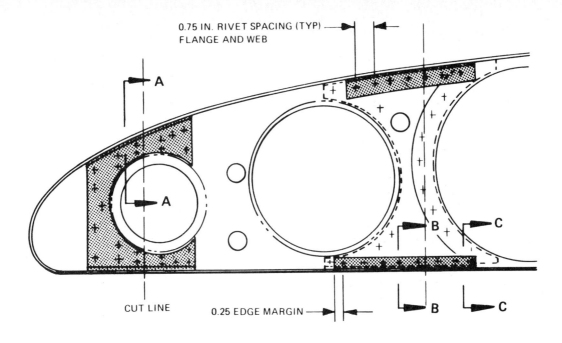

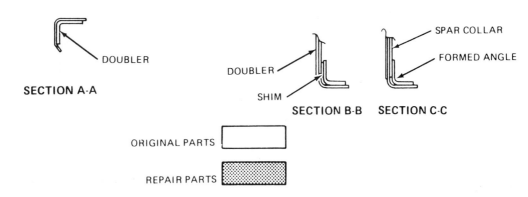

FIG. 7-101 Wing rib repair. *(Grumman American Aviation)*

3. Make repair parts from 6061-T6 aluminum alloy or equivalent.

4. Hold the doubler, 0.032 in [0.81 mm] thick, in place against the damaged area on the rib structure. If extra support is needed, place a formed angle against the inside portion of the rib nested under the flange; place a doubler on the opposite side of the rib against the damaged area.

5. With repair parts held in place, drill ⅛-in [3.18-mm] diameter holes through repair parts and rib structure, spacing holes ¾ in [19.05 mm] apart, center to center. Holes drilled at the ends of the formed angle should be placed ¼ in [6.35 mm] from the edge.

6. Install all rivets, ⅛-in [3.18-mm] diameter Cherry rivets CR162, CR163 or equivalent, with wet zinc chromate primer. If bucked rivets are used, exercise caution to prevent nearby bond damage.

7. After the repair is completed, the repaired area should be coated with zinc chromate primer.

It should be understood that the repairs just covered for bonded repairs are not the same as repairs for composite or honeycomb structures. Bonded structures, as used here, only refers to sheet-metal structures bonded together by an adhesive. The repair of composites and honeycomb structures is covered in Chap. 8.

● SPECIAL RIVETS AND FASTENERS

Standard rivets cannot meet all the requirements of fabrication and strength in the construction of aircraft; hence it becomes necessary to use a wide variety of special rivets which are designed for specific purposes. This need for special rivets is so pronounced that some manufacturers have built large organizations devoted entirely to the design and production of special rivets and fasteners.

Space does not permit descriptions of all the special rivets and fasteners available; however, we shall describe a few typical fasteners so the student will understand the principles involved in their design and application. In all cases, when a fastener is to be used, it must be specified in the repair or installation instructions, and the manufacturer's instructions must be followed.

Blind Rivets

Blind rivets are rivets designed to be installed in places where it is impossible to use a bucking bar to form the bucked head. These rivets are so designed and constructed that they can be installed and expanded from one side of the material. Their use is generally confined to locations such as the trailing edges of airfoils (rudder, ailerons, flaps, etc.) and other places where one side of the material is inaccessible for riveting.

Cherry rivets are blind rivets which are manufactured by Cherry Fasteners, Townsend Division, Textron, Inc. A Cherry rivet is a hollow rivet with an expanding stem inserted through the center, as illustrated in Fig. 7-102. The rivet is inserted in a carefully driven rivet hole, and the stem is pulled into the rivet, causing it to expand and grip the material firmly.

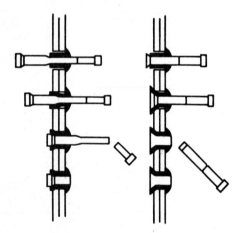

FIG. 7-102   Installation of Cherry rivets.

There are two general types of Cherry rivets: the self-plugging and the pull-through hollow type. When the self-plugging type is installed, the stem breaks off when sufficient pressure has been exerted to expand the rivet completely. The remaining stub of the stem is then cut off and filed smooth. In the installation of the pull-through hollow rivet, the stem is completely pulled through the rivet. This type of rivet does not have the shear strength of the self-plugging type.

Cherry rivets must be installed according to the manufacturer's specifications and in accordance with pertinent government regulations.

The **standard Cherrylock rivet** is installed as shown in Fig. 7-103. The rivet is inserted into the correctly drilled hole as shown in view *a*. View *b* shows the action as the pulling head (not shown in the drawing) begins to pull the stem and form a blind head adjacent to the blind sheet. At this time the two sheets of metal are being drawn together. In view *c* the two sheets are firmly clamped together and the rivet head is seated. As the stem pulls into the hollow rivet, as shown in view *d,* the drilled hole is filled; when the breaknotch is flush with the rivet head and the hole is filled, view

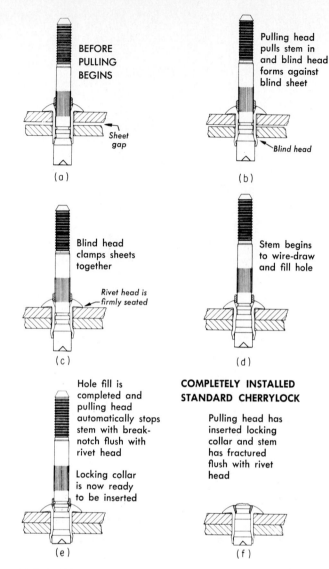

FIG. 7-103   Installation of Cherrylock rivet. (*Cherry Fasteners, Townsend Division, Textron, Inc.*)

e, the locking collar is inserted by the installing tool and the stem breaks off flush with the top of the rivet head. The installed rivet is shown in view *f.*

The **bulbed Cherrylock rivet** installation is shown in Fig. 7-104. The action is similar to that described for the standard Cherrylock rivet; however, a different type head is formed.

The installation of Cherrylock rivets is accomplished with either hand guns or pneumatic power guns. The guns are manufactured with a provision for changing pulling heads to accommodate different styles and sizes of rivets. The mechanic must follow the specifications given by the manufacturer for the installation of the rivets. The *Cherry Rivet Process Manual* provides information on installation and the proper types of gun and pulling heads.

Cherry rivets are identified by numbers to indicate type, grip length, and shank diameter. For example, CR2163-6-4 indicates a 2017T aluminum-alloy rivet with a universal head. ⁵⁄₃₂ in [4.76 mm] in diameter

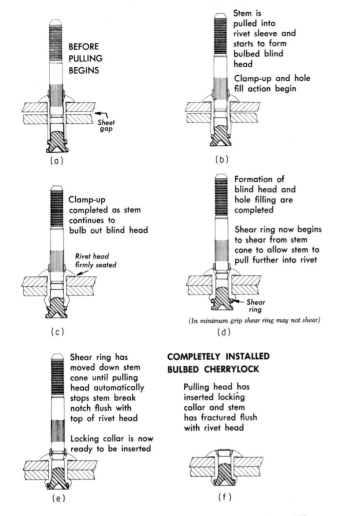

FIG. 7-104 Installation of bulbed Cherrylock rivet. (*Cherry Fasteners, Townsend Division, Textron, Inc.*)

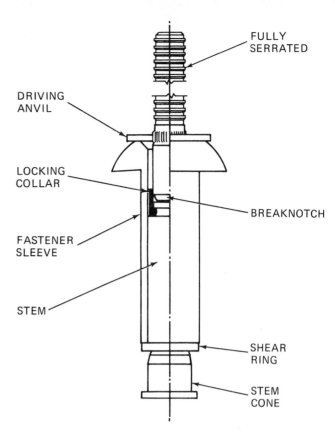

FIG. 7-105 A Cherrymax rivet. (*Cherry Fasteners, Townsend Division, Textron, Inc.*)

(the -6) and having a maximum grip length of ⁴/₁₆ in [5.36 mm] (the -4).

An improved blind rivet system called the **Cherrymax fastening system** features an improved rivet and simplified installation tooling. The rivet and installation are designed to meet or exceed the requirements of National Aerospace Standards (NAS) for blind rivets.

A drawing of a Cherrymax rivet is shown in Fig. 7-105. The complete rivet, before installation, consists of the serrated fastener stem with a break notch, shear ring, and plug section; a locking collar that provides a mechanical lock to the stem; the fastening sleeve with a locking-collar dimple to receive the locking collar; and the driving anvil which ensures flush stem breaks and a flushed installed collar.

The sequence of events that occur during installation of a Cherrymax rivet are illustrated in the cross-sectional views of Fig. 7-106. In view 1, the rivet has been installed in a properly drilled hole as set forth in NAS standards. The pulling head of the installing tool has been placed over and is gripping the serrations on the stem. The nose assembly of the pulling head is in contact with the driving anvil on the rivet head. View 2 shows the action that takes place when the tool is

actuated. The rivet stem is pulled into the rivet sleeve. The shear ring forms a large, bulbed blind head; seats the manufactured head; clamps the sheets tightly together; and expands the rivet sleeve by compressing the sleeve between the shear ring and driving anvil. View 3 shows that continued pulling of the rivet stem shears the shear ring which slides down the smooth stem cone to accommodate the ¹/₁₆-in [1.59-mm] grip range. The location of the shear ring on the stem will vary from minimum to maximum grip within the grip range. Further stem pulling causes the locking collar to engage the driving anvil. View 4 shows what happens when the locking collar engages the driving anvil and the stem continues to be pulled. The pressure of the driving anvil forms the locking collar into the locking void in the rivet head, locking the two components together. Continued pulling fractures the stem at the breaknotch, providing a flush, burr-free installation. The driving anvil and the pulling portion of the stem are discarded.

Cherrymax rivets are available in aluminum alloy, Monel, and stainless steel. Specifications for their use will note the type, size, and materials to be used for any particular installation.

Another blind rivet which meets the requirements of National Aerospace Standard 1400 (NAS 1400) is shown in Fig. 7-107. This rivet is known by the trade name **Olympic-Lok** and has some features similar to the Cherry rivet described earlier. The Olympic-Lok rivet is designed to provide high performance in both tensile and shear strength.

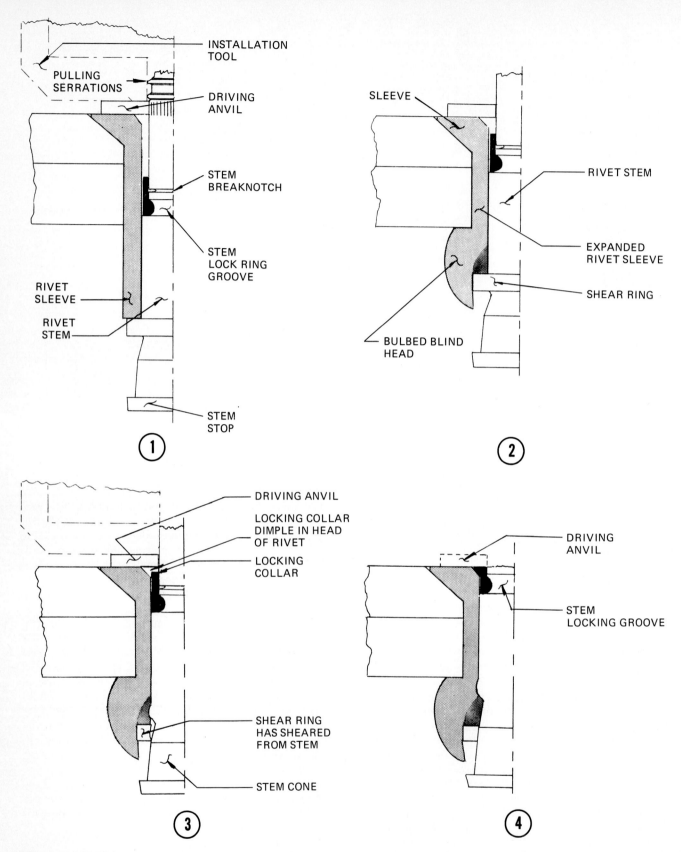

FIG. 7-106 Installation sequence of a Cherrymax rivet. *(Cherry Fasteners, Townsend Division, Textron, Inc.)*

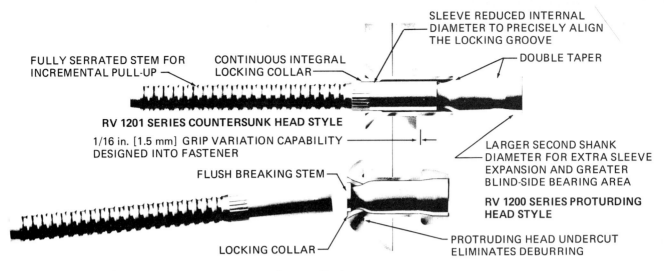

FULLY SERRATED STEM FOR
INCREMENTAL PULL-UP

CONTINUOUS INTEGRAL
LOCKING COLLAR

SLEEVE REDUCED INTERNAL
DIAMETER TO PRECISELY ALIGN
THE LOCKING GROOVE

DOUBLE TAPER

RV 1201 SERIES COUNTERSUNK HEAD STYLE

1/16 in. [1.5 mm] GRIP VARIATION CAPABILITY
DESIGNED INTO FASTENER

LARGER SECOND SHANK
DIAMETER FOR EXTRA SLEEVE
EXPANSION AND GREATER
BLIND-SIDE BEARING AREA

RV 1200 SERIES PROTURDING
HEAD STYLE

FLUSH BREAKING STEM

LOCKING COLLAR

PROTRUDING HEAD UNDERCUT
ELIMINATES DEBURRING

FIG. 7-107   Olympic-Lok rivet. *(Olympic Fastening Systems, Inc.)*

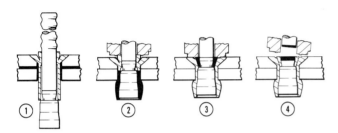
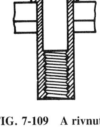

FIG. 7-108   Installation sequence for an Olympic-Lok rivet. *(Olympic Fasteners, Inc.)*

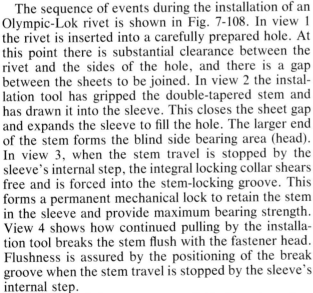

FIG. 7-109   A rivnut.

The sequence of events during the installation of an Olympic-Lok rivet is shown in Fig. 7-108. In view 1 the rivet is inserted into a carefully prepared hole. At this point there is substantial clearance between the rivet and the sides of the hole, and there is a gap between the sheets to be joined. In view 2 the installation tool has gripped the double-tapered stem and has drawn it into the sleeve. This closes the sheet gap and expands the sleeve to fill the hole. The larger end of the stem forms the blind side bearing area (head). In view 3, when the stem travel is stopped by the sleeve's internal step, the integral locking collar shears free and is forced into the stem-locking groove. This forms a permanent mechanical lock to retain the stem in the sleeve and provide maximum bearing strength. View 4 shows how continued pulling by the installation tool breaks the stem flush with the fastener head. Flushness is assured by the positioning of the break groove when the stem travel is stopped by the sleeve's internal step.

Olympic-Lok fasteners are available in various sizes and materials. Materials include aluminum alloy, stainless steel, and Monel metal.

Rivnuts

A **rivnut** is a specialized type of blind rivet which also can be used as a nut because it is threaded inside to fit the threaded shank of a screw or a bolt, as illustrated in Fig. 7-109. Rivnuts are manufactured by the B. F. Goodrich Company and used for both aircraft and general commercial purposes. The rivnut is installed with a rivet gun containing a mandrel which is screwed into the threads of the rivnut. The rivnut is expanded by tension on the mandrel which causes the shank to expand as shown in the figure.

Hi-Shear Rivets

Hi-Shear rivets are a specialized type of rivet manufactured by the Hi-Shear Corporation, designed to provide exceptional resistance to shear loads in a riveted joint.

The Hi-Shear rivet is a two-piece rivet. The pin is generally made of alloy steel, although some are stainless steel and others are 7075T aluminum alloy. Most collars are made from 2117T or 2024T aluminum alloy, although some are of heat-resistant mild steel.

The hole into which the rivet is inserted must be drilled to extremely close tolerances as specified by the manufacturer. The rivet may be installed with a rivet gun and bucking bar, as illustrated in Fig. 7-110. The sequence of drawings in the illustration shows the action taking place during the installation process.

Hi-Shear rivets can be removed easily by cutting the aluminum collar off the shank of the rivet. This can be accomplished with the cape chisel. The point of the chisel is applied to the collar on one side of the shank, and a bucking bar is held against the opposite side. The chisel is then struck with a medium-weight hammer. Care must be taken to see that the chisel is

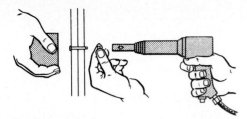

PREPARING TO INSTALL A HI-SHEAR RIVET
WITH A RIVET GUN AND BUCKING BAR

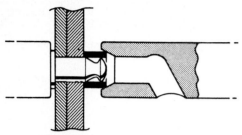

RIVET GUN AND COLLAR IN PLACE

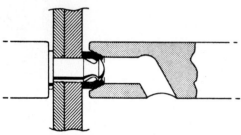

COLLAR BEING DRIVEN INTO GROOVE

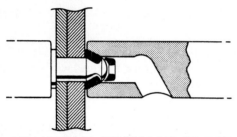

COLLAR BEING FINISHED AND TRIMMED

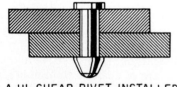

A HI-SHEAR RIVET INSTALLED

FIG. 7-110   Installation of a Hi-Shear rivet.

not touching the sheet metal in which the rivet is installed.

Cherry Lockbolts

Cherry lockbolts serve a purpose similar to the Hi-Shear rivet and are manufactured in both the **pull type** and the **stump type.** The pull type is shown in Fig. 7-111. These fasteners are approved under Na-

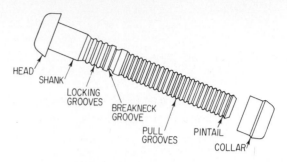

FIG. 7-111   A pull-type Cherry lockbolt. *(Cherry Fasteners, Townsend Division, Textron, Inc.)*

tional Aerospace Standard specifications and can be used for both aircraft and space vehicles.

The Cherry lockbolt consists of a steel or aluminum-alloy pin with various head designs, and grooves around the pin into which is swaged a collar which may be made of aluminum-alloy (2024-T4), steel, or Monel metal.

The pull-type lockbolt is installed as indicated by the drawings of Fig. 7-112. The pin is inserted from one side of the work, the locking collar is placed over the projecting lockbolt pin tail, the gun is applied, and the chuck jaws automatically engage the pull groove of the projecting pin tail. (See view 1.)

Depressing the gun trigger causes a pull to be exerted on the pin, as shown in view 2. The reaction of the pull is taken against the collar by the swaging anvil which draws the work tightly together as in a fitting-up operation, and the pin is pulled into the hole. As the pull on the pin increases, the anvil of the tool is drawn over the locking grooves of the pin to form a rigid, permanent lock. (See view 3.)

Continued buildup of force automatically breaks the lockbolt pin in tension at the breakneck groove, and the pin tail is automatically ejected. (See view 4.) View 5 shows the completed installation of the lockbolt.

The installation of the stump-type lockbolt is shown in Fig. 7-113. The stump bolt is inserted in the precision drilled hole and the collar is placed over the grooved end. The driving gun is fitted with a swaging set, and a bucking bar is used against the head of the lockbolt. The air hammer can be applied to the swaging set or to the bucking bar, depending upon the rigidity of the work.

In view 3 of Fig. 7-113, the gun has swaged the collar over the locking grooves of the stump bolt to provide a positive lock. The swaging set is designed so it does not touch the stump because this would cause the installation to be loose.

Jo-Bolts

A particular fastener described as a **self-locking, external-sleeve, internally threaded, blind fastener** is also referred to as a **Jo-Bolt.** Figure 7-114 (a) is a photograph of several Jo-Bolts sold under the trade name Visu-Lock, together with a pneumatic installation tool. The drawings in Fig. 7-114 (b) illustrate the installation of the fastener.

The Visu-Lock Jo-Bolt consists of three components. These are the nut, screw, and sleeve. The nut

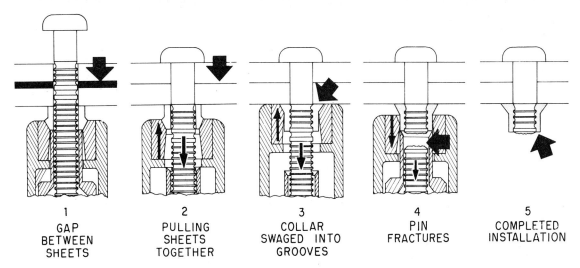

1
GAP
BETWEEN
SHEETS

2
PULLING
SHEETS
TOGETHER

3
COLLAR
SWAGED INTO
GROOVES

4
PIN
FRACTURES

5
COMPLETED
INSTALLATION

FIG. 7-112   Installation of a pull-type lockbolt.

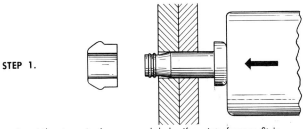

STEP 1.

Insert the stump in the prepared hole. If an interference fit is required drive the stump into the hole with a hammer or air hammer.

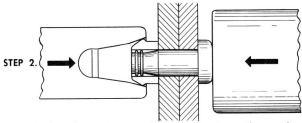

STEP 2.

Apply the collar to the grooved end of the stump. Then apply the swaging set to the collar. Use bucking bar against the head. The air hammer can be applied to the swaging set or to the bucking bar depending upon the rigidity of the work.

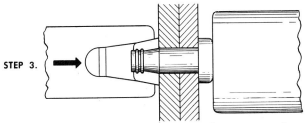

STEP 3.

The swaging set is forced down over the collar, swaging collar material into the locking grooves providing a positive lock. Note that the swaging set DOES NOT touch the stump which would cause looseness.

FIG. 7-113   Installation of stump-type lockbolt.

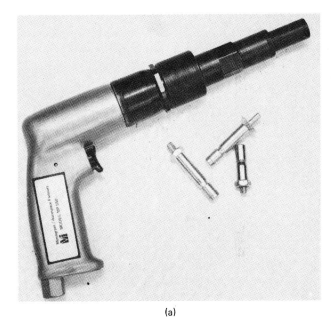

(a)

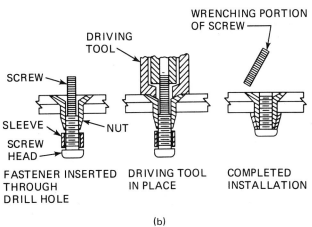

SCREW

SLEEVE

SCREW
HEAD

NUT

FASTENER INSERTED
THROUGH
DRILL HOLE

DRIVING
TOOL

DRIVING TOOL
IN PLACE

WRENCHING PORTION
OF SCREW

COMPLETED
INSTALLATION

(b)

FIG. 7-114   Jo-Bolts and installation. *(Monogram/Aerospace Fasteners)*

is the threaded outer body in which the left-hand-threaded screw is inserted. The nut may have a hexagonal head, a countersunk head, or a millable head. The screw is manufactured with a head on the blind end. This head serves to pull the sleeve over the nose of the nut, thus causing the sleeve to expand and form a grip to hold the metal between the head of the nut and the sleeve.

The screw is flattened on both sides at the outer end to provide a grip for the installing tool. During installation, the installing tool holds the head of the nut stationary and rotates the screw in a clockwise direction. This moves the screw into the nut and expands the sleeve, thus forming the blind head. When the predetermined pressure is applied to the structure, the wrenching portion of the screw breaks off and the installation is complete.

When installing a blind fastener of the type described, the mechanic must consult appropriate specifications to be sure of using a fastener of the correct material, design, and size. The installing tool must be provided with the correct adapters to fit the fasteners being installed. The installing tool may be either pneumatic or manually operated.

● REVIEW QUESTIONS

1. What precautions must be used in handling sheet metal during layout?
2. What precautions should be observed when marking sheet metal with a black lead pencil?
3. What precaution must be observed with reference to scribed lines on sheet-metal parts?
4. Define *bend allowance*.
5. With reference to a bend, define *mold line, setback,* and *bend tangent line*.
6. What is meant by *X distance?*
7. How would you find *X* distance using the *K* chart?
8. Give the *empirical formula* for bend allowance.
9. Compute the bend allowance for a 60° bend with a ¼-in [6.35-mm] radius when the thickness is 0.050 in [1.27 mm].
10. Compute the developed width of a piece of aluminum-alloy sheet which is to be formed into a Z section with two bends of 110° each around a radius of ⅜ in [9.33 mm], when the thickness of the metal is 0.060 in [1.52 mm], the mold-line distance for each flange is 2 in [50.8 mm], and the mold-line distance for the inside flat section is 3 in [76.2 mm].
11. In bending a part on a cornice brake, discuss the importance of *bend tangent line* and *sight line*.
12. Explain *closed* and *open* angles.
13. Describe *squaring shears* and explain their use.
14. For what purpose is the *gap-squaring shear* used?
15. Explain the use of *slitting shears*.
16. What is the advantage of *throatless shears?*
17. For what type of work would *rotary slitting shears* be used?
18. What is a *Unishear? A nibbling machine?*
19. Compare a *bar-folding machine* and a *cornice brake*.

20. What is the purpose of the *radius bar* on a cornice brake?
21. How does a *box* and *pan brake* differ from a *cornice brake?*
22. For what special purpose is the *forming roll* or *slip-roll former* designed?
23. Explain the use of a *drop hammer*.
24. In operating a metal-cutting band saw, what determines blade pitch and speed to be used?
25. Describe a *drill press* and its use.
26. Explain how a *hand planishing hammer* is used.
27. What features of *aviation snips* make them useful for cutting tough metal?
28. For what purposes are *soft mallets* employed?
29. Describe two common types of chisels used in metal work.
30. What is the purpose of a hand nibbler?
31. Describe a router.
32. How is a router cut controlled in depth? Laterally?
33. Describe a wire and sheet-metal gauge.
34. Explain how a *hole finder* is constructed and how it works.
35. What is the purpose of a *rivet cutter?*
36. When is a *rivet shaver* used?
37. What determines the size of *rivet gun* and *bucking bar* used?
38. Describe a *rivet*.
39. How are rivets for aircraft use identified?
40. Explain the meaning of MS20470AD-4-5.
41. Compare a *universal-head* rivet with a *countersunk* rivet.
42. What is an *icebox* rivet?
43. Explain how the *rivet gun, rivet set,* and *bucking bar* are used in installing rivets.
44. What preparation is necessary for installing flush rivets?
45. Describe the process known as *hot dimpling*.
46. Give the minimums for spacing between rivets and *edge distance*.
47. Define *pitch* and *gauge* with reference to rivet installation.
48. How is the number of rivets for a given repair determined?
49. Explain the significance of *shear strength* and *bearing strength* in determining the number of rivets for a repair.
50. Explain the meaning of *bearing strength*.
51. Give the minimum dimensions for a driven rivet.
52. Explain the importance of a properly sharpened drill point.
53. What is the importance of drill speed with respect to materials being drilled?
54. What is the purpose of a *drill jig?*
55. Why is *burring* important in preparing rivet holes?
56. How is the size of a rivet gun related to rivet size?
57. Describe the care and service of a rivet gun.
58. Describe a *bucking bar* and what determines the weight of the bucking bar to be used for a particular job.
59. Describe the purpose and construction of a *sheet fastener*.

60. What is meant by a *shaved rivet,* and how is rivet shaving accomplished?
61. Explain how a rivet should be removed from an assembly.
62. What are the general classifications of sheet-metal damage?
63. Describe the flush patch for a hole in sheet metal of less than 3 in [7.62 cm] in diameter.
64. What should be done when extensive damage has occurred to a panel in a sheet-metal structure?
65. When replacing a panel in a sheet-metal structure, what determines the rivet pattern at the seams?
66. What determines the type of material to be used in the repair of a sheet-metal rib?
67. Give the general principles applicable to stringer splices.
68. What is the purpose of *stop-drilling* cracks?
69. Explain some of the causes of cracks in sheet-metal structures.
70. Wherever cuts are made which form a sharp angle between two edges of sheet metal, what should be done to prevent stress concentration?
71. Where can the mechanic obtain information regarding special repairs applicable to particular aircraft?
72. What type of repairs may be used for the sheet-metal structures of a light airplane which employs metal-bonded construction?
73. What is meant by the term *blind rivet?*
74. Explain the use and installation of Cherry rivets.
75. What is the difference between a *bulbed* Cherrylock rivet and a standard Cherrylock rivet?
76. What are the advantages of a Cherrymax rivet?
77. Describe the installation of a Cherrymax rivet.
78. Describe the parts of a Cherrymax rivet.
79. Describe the sequence of events during the installation of an Olympic-Lok rivet.
80. Explain the use and installation of a *rivnut.*
81. Discuss the value of fasteners such as the Hi-Shear rivet and the Cherry lockbolt.
82. What is an important characteristic of the hole into which a Hi-Shear rivet is to be installed?
83. How is a Hi-Shear rivet removed?
84. Describe installing a pull-type Cherry lockbolt.
85. Describe the installation of a Jo-Bolt.
86. Explain the construction of a *template.*
87. Discuss the bending of sheet metal.
88. How can very large-radius bends be made?
89. What is the purpose of a *joggle?*
90. How is a joggle made?
91. Describe how a curved inside flange is made.
92. How is an external or outside curved flange made?
93. How is a flange made on a curved edge?
94. Describe two *metal-bumping* processes.
95. Why are relief holes required at the corners in a box structure?

8 PLASTICS AND COMPOSITES

The use of modern materials in aircraft has reduced the weight and construction costs of aircraft and increased the performance and strength. Due to their unique characteristics, these materials have generally been applied to specific areas of aircraft. These materials include transparent and opaque plastics and bonded structural components of metallic and nonmetallic composition.

The use of many of the materials discussed in this chapter is rapidly increasing, and the mechanic must realize that the information presented here is general in nature. Consult the aircraft or material manufacturer for specific information about the proper handling of their products. Keep in mind that the proper equipment, solvents, and adhesives that work well on one type of material may not work at all on another material that appears to be of a similar type.

● AIRCRAFT PLASTICS

Plastics have been used for windshields, windows, landing light covers, and interior furnishing of aircraft for many years. These materials will continue to be used because of their low cost and ease of maintenance.

Characteristics of Plastics

Plastics can be classified by many methods. One generally accepted method of classification is by their response to heat.

Thermosetting plastics are plastic compounds or solutions that require the application of heat to set up properly or "harden." Once these materials have set, further application of heat does not allow them to be formed in a controllable manner. Any further addition of heat normally results in deformation or structural weakening. Thermosetting materials include many bonding materials that fall under the broad plastic classifications and many materials that can also be called resinous.

Thermoplastic materials are those which soften with the application of heat. When softened, these materials can be shaped as required and retain their structural strength when cooled. This characteristic allows this type material to be used to form items such as windshields and landing light covers. This type of material includes transparent plastics such as Plexiglas.

The thermoplastic materials are those which the mechanic is most likely to be called upon to handle and repair; therefore, the remainder of this section deals with these types of materials.

The basic characteristics of clear plastic materials such as Plexiglas must be understood by the mechanic so that the material is handled properly. (Plexiglas is a registered trademark of the Rohm and Haas Company.)

Plastics are used in place of glass for windows because they are lower in weight and there is no reduction in clarity. Plastic is much more resistant to breaking than glass, and when it does break the edges are dull, reducing the chance of injury to personnel. Plastic is a poor conductor of heat and thus provides some level of thermal insulation. Plastic has the disadvantage of readily accepting a static charge and thus attracting dust and dirt particles. Also, being softer than glass, plastic is more easily damaged by surface abrasion than glass. This sensitivity is substantially reduced in some types of hardened plastics.

Types of Clear Plastics

There are two general classifications of clear plastics used in aircraft: **acrylics** and **cellulose acetates.** The mechanic needs to be able to distinguish between these two materials in order to properly install and repair them. Acrylic materials, such as Plexiglas, are the more modern materials and have replaced acetate materials in most usages. While these materials have been described here as clear, they are available in tints to reduce light penetration. This is most evident when a green- or gray-tinted plastic is used for aircraft windshields. This tinting performs the same purpose as the pilot wearing sunglasses; that is, it reduces the level of light intensity entering the cockpit.

The two materials can be identified by their visual and burning characteristics and by their reaction to certain chemicals and solvents.

When viewed edge-on, acrylic material appears clear or the color of the tinting if the material is tinted. Some clear pieces of acrylic material appear slightly green or blue-green. Acetate material appears yellow when viewed edge-on. When burned, acrylic burns with a clear flame and gives off an aroma described as fairly pleasant or fruitlike. Acetate burns with a heavy black smoke and a strong, pungent odor. If a sample of acrylic material is rubbed with a cloth moistened in acetone, the plastic turns white. Acetone softens acetate but does not affect its clarity. If zinc chloride is placed on acetate, it turns the material milky, but has no effect on acrylic.

Storage and Protection

Plastics are normally supplied in sheets measuring up to 4 by 8 ft [1.22 by 2.44 m]. To protect the surface of the sheet, it is covered with a masking paper. The masking paper can be peeled back to inspect the plastic as necessary and then replaced without difficulty. If the masking is to be reused, do not allow the adhesive side of the paper to touch another area of the paper where the adhesive is present. These two adhesive sides are very difficult to separate. If the masking paper adhesive has dried out and will not peel off of the surface easily, aliphatic naphtha can be used to moisten the paper. This will soften the adhesive and allow it to be removed. Once the masking is off, wash the area with clean water to remove any residue of the naphtha.

Parts that have been formed are often coated with a masking material that is sprayed on to the surface. When dry, this material has the feel and elasticity similar to rubber cement. This material can be removed by peeling up a corner and then using an air gun to lift the masking off of the part.

When working with plastic material that is protected by masking, it is advisable to only remove as much material as necessary to prepare and mount the component. When the component is installed and all handling is completed, remove the remainder of the masking material. This provides the maximum of surface protection.

Plastic sheets should be stored in racks or on flats. When stored in racks, the sheets should be stored on edge at a 10° angle from the vertical, as shown in Fig. 8-1. The bottom edges should rest on blocks about 3 in [7.62 cm] wide, no more than 42 in [1.07 m] apart. If stored flat, plastics should be fully supported underneath, thinner and smaller sized pieces placed on top of thicker and larger sized pieces as shown in Fig. 8-2.

Formed pieces should be stored in individual racks. If formed pieces are to be stacked, be sure that there is no possibility of damage resulting from the stacking process. Use padding as necessary to prevent damage.

Any plastic that is stored should have a spray-type or paper masking installed. Care should be taken to remove rough edges from plastics that have been cut before placing them in a storage rack or stack. Do not allow any dirt, plastic, metal, or other particles to get between pieces of plastic as this can damage the plastic surface even with a masking installed.

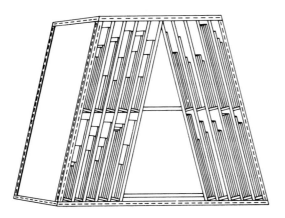

FIG. 8-1 **Plastic sheets stored on edge in racks.** *(Rohm and Haas Company)*

STACKING PLEXIGLAS SHEETS

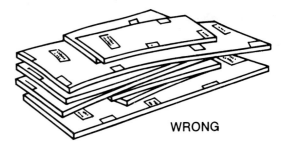

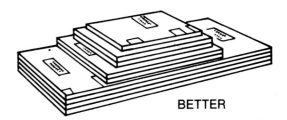

FIG. 8-2 **The correct and incorrect way to store plastic sheets on the flat.** *(Rohm and Haas Company)*

Cleaning Plastics

The best way to clean plastic surfaces is by flowing fresh water across the surface and then using your hand to gently remove any particles adhering to the surface. A mild soap and water solution can be used if required. The use of a cloth when cleaning plastics should be done with care to prevent trapping particles in the cloth which can damage the surface as the cloth is moved over the surface. When using a cloth, always use a clean soft cloth, not a shop rag, even if it is clean. Shop rags often contain small metal particles even after having been cleaned. These metal particles will damage the surface.

There are several commercial cleaners available that can be used to clean plastics. These commercial materials often include a wax and an antistatic component which reduces the static buildup on the plastic. Commercial waxes that do not contain cleaning grit can be used to polish clean plastics surfaces. These waxes will fill in some of the fine scratches that appear on plastic and improve the visual clarity to some degree. Machines should not be used when polishing as their high speed of operation may heat the plastic and cause distortion.

Plastic should not be rubbed with a dry cloth since this is likely to scratch the surface and can cause a buildup of static electricity.

Solvents such as lacquer thinner, benzine, carbon tetrachloride, acetone, and other similar materials should never be used on plastic sheet because they will penetrate the surface and cause **crazing**. Crazing is the formation of a network of fine cracks in the surface of the material. The effect of crazing is to destroy the clarity of vision through the material and to weaken the structural strength.

Manufacturer's manuals usually specify the types of cleaning agents suitable for the plastic windshields and windows for specific aircraft. Certain neutral petroleum solvents such as kerosene or aliphatic naphtha cleaning fluid are sometimes specified for the removal of oil or grease. If these are used, the surface should be dried as quickly as possible and then washed with water and a mild detergent. A detergent conforming to MIL-C-18687 is recommended. Aromatic naphtha should never be used.

Cutting Plastics

When cutting plastics the mechanic must keep in mind that excessive stress on an area will cause the plastic to crack. Also, when using some types of power tools for cutting, chipping will occur along the edge of the cut. For these instances, the guidelines drawn on the plastic should be far enough from the finish edge so that the chipping will not be on the finished edge. Chipping can be avoided somewhat by feeding the plastic slowly through the cutting blade.

One of the characteristics of plastic is that it is an insulator. Therefore, any heat buildup in the cutting area does not dissipate into the surrounding material but is held in the cutting area. This causes the plastic to melt and flow onto the cutting blade, preventing further cutting of the material. To counteract this quality, some sort of cooling may have to be used when cutting plastics, especially when cutting thick pieces. Cooling can be achieved by the use of an air stream aimed at the cutting area or by a cutting fluid if the operation allows the use of a fluid without electrical or other dangers existing.

Any of the following power tools can be used to cut plastic if proper care is taken: radial arm saws, table saws, band saws, jig saws, and scroll saws. Obviously, the smoother the cutting operation, the less chance there is of chipping or cracking the plastic. For this reason, circular saws are preferred for straight cuts and band saws are preferred for curved cuts. All saw teeth should have a uniform rake and height.

Short, straight cuts can be made in plastics such as Plexiglas by using a straightedge and a scribe. Scribe a deep line across the material to be cut. Place a rod or some type of edge directly under the scribe line. Press evenly and quickly down on both sides of the scribe line and the plastic will break along the scribe line.

When cutting plastics, especially with power tools, wear eye protection. When working around power tools, avoid loose clothing which could be entangled in the tools.

Forming Plastics

Thermoplastic materials can be shaped with or without the use of heat, depending on the severity of the forming required. When cold-forming material, the plastic can be bent if the radius of the bend is at least 180 times the thickness of the material. This only allows a slight shaping to the plastic. For most applications heat is used to soften the material and form it to the desired shape.

Plastic may be formed by the use of a hot oil bath, a heater strip, a hot air chamber, or a heat gun. The particular device used is dictated by the type and amount of forming necessary.

An oil bath is convenient to use when a small piece of plastic must be formed, such as when making a surface or plug patch for a contoured surface. The oil bath is heated to the proper forming temperature for the plastic being used in an appropriate sized container. The oil should be in the range of 250 to 350°F [121 to 177°C]. Water cannot be used as it boils away at 212°F [100°C]. The plastic piece is placed in the bath, and after it softens it is placed on a form to achieve the desired shape.

A heater strip is used to heat a straight line on the plastic so that it can be bent along that line. These heaters work well for thinner plastics as the width of the heated area is fairly small.

For forming large pieces, a heated air chamber can be used. This chamber must be large enough to accommodate the plastic piece being formed and the forming structure. The chamber is heated, and the plastic is formed on the forming structure. The structure may be in the form of a mold or the components may be free-blown by the use of air pressure. Once the plastic is shaped, it is allowed to cool gradually and then trimmed to the proper size.

This hot-air chamber method is used in shops for one-time forming operations. The mechanisms used for production forming of plastics are beyond the scope of this text.

A heat gun is used to soften small areas of a plastic piece so that it can be shaped to fit a particular installation. For example, when installing a plastic windshield, the shapes of the corners do not always align properly with the aircraft structure. A heat gun can be used to soften the corners and allow the windshield to be fitted to the airframe.

When forming any plastic, keep in mind that the material must be heated to approximately 300°F [149°C]. If this material is touched when heated, bare skin will be burned. This is especially a problem when working with an oil bath as the hot oil will stay on the skin. Wear the appropriate protective clothing and eye protection when forming plastics.

Drilling Plastics

When drilling plastics a modified high-speed drill bit is recommended. For drilling completely through plastic materials, the bit should be reprofiled to have an included angle of 60° and the rake angle should be cut to zero. This allows the bit to scrape the plastic rather than cut the plastic. If the bit cuts into the plastic, it can grab and break the surface being drilled. For drilling partway through plastic, shallow holes with depth-to-diameter ratios of 3:1 or less should be drilled with a bit having a tip angle of 90°. If the ratio is 3:1 or greater the tip angle should be 118°.

Most drilling operations do not require the use of a coolant. If deep holes are being drilled, a coolant may be required. The plastic can be cooled by the use of an air jet, water, or a water-soluble oil mixed with water. If a pilot hole is used to guide the full-size bit, the pilot hole can be filled with a coolant. The pilot hole helps guide the full-size bit along with providing the coolant supply. Masking paper around a hole drilled using a liquid coolant should be removed immediately after drilling the hole to prevent a residue from being left on the surface.

When drilling thin plastic, it should be backed up with a wood block to prevent chipping or breaking of the plastic as the drill bit exits the plastic.

When drilling plastic, use only light to moderate pressure on the bit and use a slow rate of feed. When appropriate, the plastic being drilled should be clamped in a fixture for safety. Always wear proper eye protection when drilling and observe safety rules concerning the use of liquid coolants around electrically operated drills and equipment.

Cementing of Plastics

Cementing of aircraft plastics, in particular aircraft windshields and windows, is required for repairs and for the attachment of certain components such as vent windows. If a plastic joint is properly shaped and the adhesive is properly applied, a strong joint is formed.

When preparing the surfaces to be joined, they must be cut to the proper shape, formed as necessary, and checked to be sure that all surfaces and edges to be joined are in full contact. The edges do not need to be roughed as the bonding is caused by actually melting the pieces together chemically.

The adhesive commonly used for plastic windows and windshields is methylene chloride alone or in combination with other chemicals. The specific cement used with a plastic varies depending on the specific type of plastic. A cement syrup can be made by mixing plastic shavings with the cement. The syrup is sometimes desirable as it is easier to handle than the liquid cement, especially when working on vertical surfaces and on the bottom of surfaces.

Cement is applied on the full mating surface, and the two parts are then held in contact until the cement has set. The pressure used should be just enough to assure full contact, about 1 psi [6.9 kPa]. Excessive pressure could result in distortion as the cement works by softening the materials and allowing the surfaces to intermingle.

Once the cement has dried, the strength of the joint can be increased by applying heat to the joint area. The cementing of the joint introduces the solvent cement into the material and leaves a softened area at the joint. By heating the joint, the solvents in the plastic move outward into the surrounding material, causing the joint to harden. This action is shown in Fig. 8-3.

Installation of Plastic Windows and Windshields

The first step when the replacement of a windshield or window is necessary is the removal of the mechanism holding in the old component. This structure may be a panel or retainer strip that is riveted or held in by bolts or screws. Remove the old component as carefully as possible so that it is not damaged and can be used for a reference as to the location of holes and contour when installing the replacement piece.

The replacement piece should have the masking peeled back from the edges about 1 in [2.5 cm] and

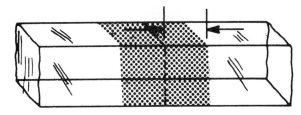

(a) ROOM TEMPERATURE EQUILIBRIUM

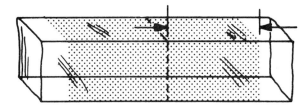

(b) EQUILIBRIUM AFTER HEAT TREATMENT

FIG. 8-3 Effect of heat treatment on a plastic joint.

then the piece is placed in the installation to determine if trimming is necessary. If the component fits into the structure, then proceed with the mounting. If the component does not fit properly into the structure, mark the edges that need to be trimmed. The edge should then be trimmed with a band saw, hand file, or belt sander to within about ¼ in [6.35 mm] of the trim line and then the fit should be rechecked. After the fit check, continue the trimming until the new piece fits properly into the structure channels. It may be necessary to fit and trim the new windshield or window several times in order to achieve a proper fit. It is better to do this in small steps rather than rush the job and remove too much material. After the material is fitted, a heat gun may have to be used to heat local areas and adjust the contour slightly to reduce any installation stresses caused by the flexing required to fit properly.

The fitted piece should fit a minimum of 1⅛ in [2.86 cm] into the channel, but it must be at least ⅛ in [3.18 mm] from the bottom of the channel to allow for expansion and contraction of the plastic material. The exact dimensions vary from one aircraft to another. When fitting the piece, do not force the panel into position as this may cause the plastic to crack or craze. Once the new windshield or window is fitted, it should be removed and a padding of rubber or felt should be attached to the edges that will be in the channel.

Holes for the installation of bolts, screws, and fittings should be drilled through the plastic. These holes should be ⅛ in [3.18 mm] larger in diameter than the bolt or screw to be installed to allow for expansion and contraction of the plastic panel. The panel is then positioned in the structure, and the bolts and screws are installed. The bolts and nuts are tightened until just snug and then backed off one full turn to allow for expansion and contraction.

Once the panel is in position, the required retainer strips are installed by rivets, screws, and/or bolts. The remainder of the masking is removed and the panel is cleaned.

Each aircraft service manual should address the removal and installation of plastic windshields and windows. The specific instructions for a particular aircraft should be followed.

Inspection of Plastic Components

The inspection of windshields and windows is visual. The surfaces should be checked for cracks and surface damage. Surface abrasion should be checked, and, if not deep, this abrasion can be removed by an abrasion removal process such as the Micro-Mesh process. Any crazing (small fissures in the plastic) should be evaluated as to structural weakening of the plastic and interference with pilot vision. If excessive crazing is found, the windshield or window should be replaced. Any damage that is in the pilot's normal area of vision and that cannot be restored to a clear vision area is cause for replacement of the plastic component.

Repair of Cracks

Cracks commonly appear on the edges of a piece of plastic radiating out from a pressure point or a mounting hole. If the crack is in the pilot's normal vision area, the panel should be replaced. If the crack is not in the normal vision area, the crack should be stop-drilled, as shown in Fig. 8-4, and a patch installed, as in Fig. 8-5.

The surface patch of the same thickness as the original material should be cut to extend beyond the edges of the crack at least ¾ in [1.91 cm] and formed to lay fully on the surface contour. The edges of the patch should be tapered as shown and the patch is spread with adhesive and positioned on the surface of the panel being repaired. Pressure is then applied to the patch for several hours. After 24 h, the patch can be polished to achieve clear edges.

Repair of Holes

When a hole is found in a plastic windshield or window, any cracks radiating from the holes should be stop-drilled. The hole is then dressed with a file and abrasive paper to remove rough edges. If a surface patch is to be installed, this completes the hole preparation. If a plug patch is to be installed, the hole should be trimmed out to a circle or oval that tapers outward as shown in Fig. 8-7.

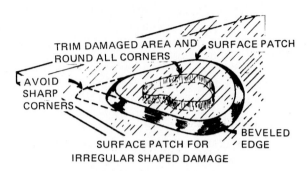

FIG. 8-6 A surface patch for a hole in plastic.

For a surface patch, a patch is prepared in the same manner as for a patch over a crack. The patch is shaped and extends beyond the edge of the damage at least ¾ in [1.91 cm]. The patch is then attached with adhesive in the same manner as used for the patch over a crack.

For the plug patch, a plug is cut from material thicker than the original material. The plug is cut to the proper size as shown in Fig. 8-7, and the taper is more severe than that of the prepared hole. The plug is heated and pressed into the hole to allow the plug to match the edges of the hole. After the plug has

FIG. 8-4 Stop-drill cracks in plastic.

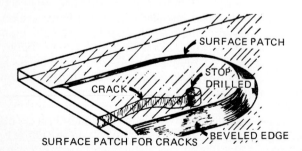

FIG. 8-5 A surface patch for a crack in plastic.

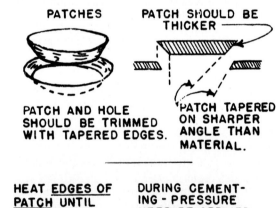

FIG. 8-7 The plug patch repair process.

cooled, it is removed, adhesive is applied, and the plug is installed in the hole. Apply pressure until the adhesive has dried. The plug can then be trimmed down by filing and sanding so that it is flush with the original panel on both sides. The patched area is then buffed and polished to a clear surface.

COMPOSITES

Composite structures are those aircraft structural and nonstructural components that are assembled from metal and fibers and are joined by the use of adhesives. The use of these materials has developed over a long period of time, and the expansion of their use has required the development of materials, adhesives, and processes that are both economical and structurally sound in an aircraft operational environment.

Bonded and composite structures have found uses in all segments of aircraft design from fuselage and landing gear structures to propellers, helicopter rotor blades, and flight control surfaces. The advantages are the high strength-to-weight ratio when compared to conventional sheet-metal and steel structures, a low sensitivity to sonic vibration, reduced assembly costs because of the reduction in the number of fasteners required, and smooth surfaces reducing aircraft drag. A bonded honeycomb section is shown in Fig. 8-8. The specific material used for the face, honeycomb core, and backplate material varies and can include any combination of metal, natural fibers such as wood, and synthetic materials.

On occasion, references are made to **fiber reinforced plastics,** also called FRPs. This simply refers to a composite structure using a fiber or fabric embedded in an epoxy material. The term **advanced composite** is also used in some manuals. This generally refers to any composite structure using a fiber or fabric material stronger than fiberglass.

This section deals with some of the general inspection and repair techniques associated with composite and bonded structures. For specific instructions on recommended inspection and repair techniques, consult the aircraft manufacturer's maintenance manual.

Sheet-Metal Bonding

The bonding of sheet metal has been used to produce a smooth surface free of irregularities caused by rivets and other metal fasteners. This type of structure requires an internal structure similar to conventional metal aircraft assemblies except that the components may be joined by a bonding adhesive.

The advantages of this type construction are primarily in the improved aerodynamic efficiency of the surface because of the undisturbed airflow over the surfaces. This type of construction often requires special assembly processes to apply heat and pressure to the components in order for the adhesive to bond properly. While constructing an aircraft completely by the bonding process has occurred, the primary application is in the bonding of structural support members to skin structures. An example of this type structure is the bonding of stringers to a wing panel for a transport aircraft.

The inspections used with this type of structure are discussed along with the inspection procedures used with other bonded structures in a later section. Repairs to this type of structure are covered in the chapter on sheet-metal structures.

Composite Materials

A variety of materials have been used in composite structures. While only the more common materials used will be discussed here, the mechanic should be aware that composite technology is evolving at a rapid rate and the aircraft manufacturer should be contacted for specific information concerning the types of material used in a structure and the type of materials recommended for use in the repair of structures. Also, be aware that some of the materials used can be toxic and irritation or injury may result from the handling of some composite fabrics.

The more common types of fibers used in composite structures include: fiberglass, Kevlar, graphite, carbon, and boron. These materials may be supplied in woven fabrics or as unidirectional materials. Woven fabric is available with various types of weaves, various fiber counts per thread, and various thread counts per inch, depending on the specific purpose of the fabric. Unidirectional material has all of the structural fibers lying in the same direction and only a few fibers or an adhesive being used to keep the fabric in a flat shape.

Some fabric materials are available with a metal coating. Each fiber is coated with a thin metal covering to provide lightning protection for the structure. This type of fabric is normally used on the outer layer of a structure.

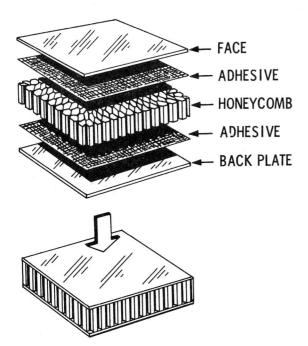

FACE
ADHESIVE
HONEYCOMB
ADHESIVE
BACK PLATE

FIG. 8-8   Honeycomb sandwich construction.

Composite Adhesives

Composite adhesives are often refered to as epoxies, but a more proper term is a **plastic resin matrix**. Matrix is used in this sense to mean a material which encases or surrounds a fiber.

Matrices are generally two part resins which must be mixed in proper proportions to achieve the required hardening of the resin. These are quite similar in operation to household epoxies in that neither of the matrix components will harden, or "set," until they are mixed together. Some matrices require a high level of heat to set properly while other will cure at room temperatures of at least 70° F [21° C]. Room-temperature-curing matrices can be heated to some extent to reduce their curing time.

A special type of matrix is a **synthetic foam**. This is a matrix which contains microscopic air bubbles or "microballoons." This material is provided as a two-part matrix which must be mixed; then it can be used to fill voids and small openings in honeycomb or foam structures in accordance with the aircraft manufacturer's instructions. This material is not generally recommended for use in areas where the material could enter an engine inlet if it becomes loose and separates from the damaged area.

Matrix materials can be purchased in premeasured packets containing enough resin to complete one average size repair. The material can also be purchased in bulk units by weight or by volume, depending on the source. Bulk purchases are generally more economical for shops requiring large volumes or doing frequent repairs. When purchased in bulk, it is the mechanic's responsibility to measure out the exact quantity of each part of the mixture to assure proper curing and bonding. This will require the use of an accurate scale which can measure weights as low as one gram. Matrices are commonly mixed according to the weight of each matrix component and not by volume. Matrix materials should be stored in a refrigerator or freezer to assure an adequate shelf life.

Machining of Composites

The machining of non-metallic composite materials requires some special techniques. Composite components may be rough-trimmed with tin snips or metal shears. Close trimming may be performed with a cutting wheel. Honeycomb structures are best cut with a cutting wheel or a saw tipped with carbide or diamond materials, depending on the specific composite being cut. Edges of composites can be finished with sanding disks, sandpaper, or files.

When drilling holes in composites, special care may be required for different materials. For example, Kevlar should be drilled with a bit one size larger than the desired hole size due to the thermal expansion of the hole as the material is drilled. Additionally, Kevlar will cut cleaner if water is used at the drill site. The Kevlar fiber will absorb the water and be stiffer, allowing a cleaner cut with the bit. On the other hand, graphite should be drilled with a bit one size smaller than the desired hole size as the dust from the drilling will wear the hole slightly larger than the drill bit. Drill

bits for composites are often ground with an included angle of 135 degrees to reduce the chance of the bit pulling through the material and separating the laminations. When possible, drilling should be backed with wood and the rate of feed should be slow enough to prevent bursting through the back side of the material.

When machining composites, the work should be performed on a vacuum table or a vacuum line at the work site and should be used to draw away as much of the dust and particles as possible. This will reduce the chance of personal contact with the material and keep the aircraft and shop area free of contaminents.

Composite Safety

When working with any composite materials, proper safety precautions must be observed to prevent long-term personal injury and damage by fire.

Many of the composite fabrics and fibers are made of very fine tow fibers. These fibers may be stiff and brittle. As a result, the tow fibers are rigid enough to penetrate unprotected skin and are brittle enough that they easily break off at the skin surface. These fibers may be very difficult to remove from the skin and may cause a toxic reaction or infection. Some materials, especially matrix components, can cause alergic-like or toxic reactions when in contact with the skin. For this reason, always wear protective clothing and gloves when handling fabrics and matrix materials.

When sanding fiber and fabric surfaces, as must be done when repairing structures, a fine powder or dust is generated. To prevent this powder or dust from entering his or her respiratory system, the mechanic should wear an approved respiratory filter when working with these materials.

Eye protection in the form of goggles or a faceshield should be worn to keep the dust and powder particles out of the eyes. Furthermore, when working with matrix materials and solvents, eye protection must be worn. Some of the solvents and matrix components can cause permanent blindness within a few seconds of contact with the eye.

Because of the unknown long-term affect of many of the composite materials, the mechanic should be fully clothed to minimize the possibility of particles entering the pores of the skin. This includes the wearing of a long sleeve shirt or laboratory-type coat. After working with composite materials, the mechanic should bathe at the end of the day to flush particles from the skin and hair.

Standard fire precautions should be observed when working with composites. This includes working in well ventilated areas and having the appropriate type of fire extinguisher at hand.

Composite Structures

Composite structures are made from a combination of materials in the form of sheets, fibers, foams, and honeycomb material joined by adhesives. The most common structural arrangement is similar to that shown in Fig. 8-8, with a sheet or fiber covering making up the face and back plate and a foam or honeycomb material making up the core. Other structural arrangements use a hollow or solid tube made of metal or composite material wrapped by fibers in specific directions. These materials are saturated with an adhesive to form a structural member. This assembly is then joined to foam, honeycomb, or web components to give the desired structural shape, and the shaped assembly is then wrapped with and bonded to a surface material. This type of structure is shown in cross section in Fig. 8-9.

A basic composite structure is composed of several layers of one type of fiber or fabric material bonded with an epoxy material. If more than one type of fiber or fabric material is bonded with an epoxy, the result is termed a **hybrid** composite structure.

Inspection of Composite Structures

The specific inspection method used for a composite structure varies with the composite material used and the manufacturer's experience with inspection methods. The information presented here is a summary of the methods commonly used.

A **ring test** can be used to detect voids and separations between the surface layer and underlying layers. A 1-oz [28.4-g] brass hammer or a quarter is used to tap on the bonded areas. If the bonding is intact, the tapping gives a solid "ring." If there is a void under the surface, the tapping gives a dull sound. If a separation is located, the extent of the separation has to be evaluated by other inspection methods, by internal inspection, or by opening the structure.

When performing the ring test, the component structure may change in sound due to a transition to a different internal structure rather than because of a damaged structure. An example of this type of internal configuration would be where only a part of the internal structure contains a honeycomb core with other areas made of only fabric sheet materials. The honeycomb area will give a different sound than the fabric sheet areas and a change in sound would be expected when crossing the boundary between these areas.

An **ultrasonic analyzer** can be used to transmit a signal into the panel. The sensors of the analyzer receive the signal as a vibration and display the signal on a cathode-ray tube. A trained operator can evaluate the display and determine the location and extent of damage as the unit is positioned on different parts of the structure.

X-ray can be used to locate separation in open struc-

tures as well as corrosion and water inside of enclosed structures. The use of x-ray is an involved operation that requires the services of specially trained technicians to operate the equipment and interpret the x-ray films.

Fiberglass or other transparent materials can be examined for entrapped water by **backlighting.** This requires that any surface covering, such as paint, be removed. A strong light is placed on one side of the panel, and the other side of the panel is examined for any dark areas indicating water or corrosion.

Acoustic emission monitoring can be performed to detect corrosion and disbonding of the adhesive bond. This inspection method employs a very sensitive microphone and amplifier. The microphone is placed on the surface of a bonded structure. If active corrosion is present, the noise associated with the bubbles generated by the corrosion activity can be detected as a hissing sound. If the panel being inspected is heated to about 150°F [74.5°C] disbonding of the adhesive will be indicated by a crackling sound.

Composite Repair Techniques

The classification of damage and the repair methods have not been standardized in the aviation industry. Each manufacturer has developed a method of classifying damage and an appropriate repair procedure. The repair procedures presented here are intended to give the mechanic some background as to commonly used procedures.

Damage to only one skin surface with no damage to the core can be repaired by the installation of a surface patch. Prior to the installation of the surface patch, the surface material is cleaned of paint and finishing material several inches out from the damaged area.

The damaged area is tapered back using a small disk sander. Each layer of the material is tapered between 0.5 and 1 in [1.27 and 2.54 cm] until all of the damage has been removed and a set of concentric circles is created by the tapering back of the material layers. Patches of the appropriate repair material, such as structural fiberglass, are cut. If three layers of the fabric have to be cut back, then four patches are cut. The first patch is the size of the material removed from the innermost portion of the tapered area. The next two patches are the size of the next two layers that were cut back. The fourth patch is large enough to extend beyond the damaged area by 1 in [2.54 cm] on all sides. The adhesive is mixed, the time is noted so that the matrix will not be worked past its working life, and a thin coat of adhesive is placed over the prepared area. Each patch is saturated with adhesive in turn and placed on the repair, taking care to line up the fabric weave with the weave of the layers being repaired.

Some curing processes make use of a heat tent or heat blanket. These may require that a thermocouple probe be placed about 1 in [2.54 cm] from the edge of the patch to monitor the surface temperatue of the repair area and control the operation of the heating equipment.

Once the patches are in place, the patch area for a distance of several inches beyond the patch is covered

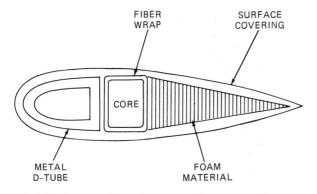

FIG. 8-9 An assembly using composite components.

with a **peel ply** layer. This nylon fabric will allow the excess matrix to flow through to its upper surface; the peel ply and excess matrix can then be peeled off of the patch when the matrix is cured. If a vacuum bag is to be used to apply pressure to the patch during curing a **breather-bleeder material,** such as felt, is place around the edges of the peel ply. This will provide a path for the air to flow through during the vacuum bagging process and it will also absorb matrix that has been worked to the edges.

Once the peel ply and breather-bleeder are in position, a vacuum port is placed on one corner of the surface with a piece of breather-bleeder material under it. The patch area is then covered with a heavy piece of film plastic and sealed airtight around all of the edges. If a vacuum is to be used, a hole is cut for the vacuum attachment and the fitting is installed. The area around the vacuum port is then sealed airtight. The vacuum source is now connected and turned on. The source should create a vacuum of at least 23 inHg [584 mmHg] and the plastic over the patch should be free of wrinkles. The complete repair arrangement is shown in Fig. 8-10.

The excess matrix in the patch can now be worked out with a plastic squeegee. The squeegee should be flexible and have no sharp edges that could cut the plastic film. All of the air bubbles in the patch are worked toward the edge of the patch and excess matrix is worked toward the breather-bleeder material. The squeegee is used until no more matrix can easily be moved away from the patch. Care must be taken not to remove too much matrix as this will render the patch "unairworthy." The time should be checked when working the matrix so that the pot life of the matrix is not exceeded. The matrix should not be worked past its pot life.

If a vacuum system was not being applied to the patch, the patch should now have pressure applied by the use of weights of spring clamps. C-clamps should not be used as these will lose their clamping pressure when some of the matrix flows out of the patch, reducing the thickness of the patch.

Heat can now be applied if appropriate. This can be in the form of a heat blanket in full contact with the patch surface or a heat tent supplied with hot air from a heat gun. In either case, the amount of heat applied should be held constant by monitoring the surface temperature of the repair with the thermocouple. Special heat monitoring unit are available which will automatically turn the heat source on and off to keep the temperature of the patch at the desired value. Care should be taken not to apply too much heat initially

as the initial "out-gassing" of the matrix may cause air bubbles to appear in the patch if it is curing too quickly.

Heat lamps and hand-held guns are not recommended because of the difficulty in maintaining a constant and controlled level of heat on the patch for the required curing period. The use of oven is not recommended unless the complete part can be placed in the oven and there is no chance of causing any damage to the component by the oven heat.

In some aircraft a surface patch can be riveted on by the use of blind rivets, as shown in Fig. 8-11. Still other aircraft may allow the use of a potting compound to repair small defects in one skin surface. The use of a potting compound is discussed shortly.

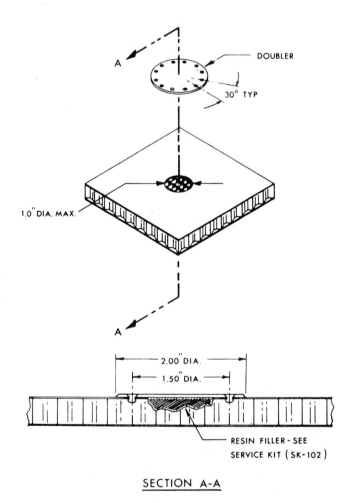

SECTION A-A

FIG. 8-11 A riveted surface patch repair. (*Grumman American Aviation*)

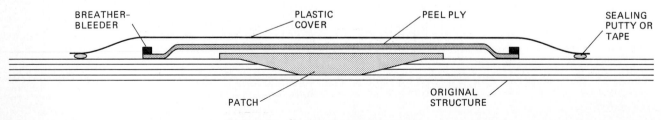

FIG. 8-10 Vacuum bag arrangement.

If damage penetrates the skin surface and involves the core material, the damaged material must be removed. This can be done by the use of a router and template, as shown in Fig. 8-12, a hole saw, or a fly cutter. The router cuts out the damaged core, while the template is used to guide the movement of the router. The shape of the cleaned-out area is circular, oval, or rectangular. The depth of the routing operation is determined by the depth of the damage penetration, as shown in Fig. 8-13. If the damage is on a sloping surface, bridges can be used to allow the router to cut parallel with the undamaged surface as shown in Fig. 8-14.

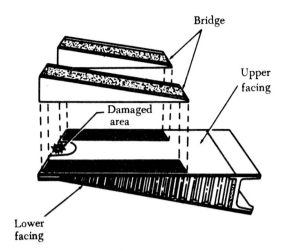

FIG. 8-14 Bridges used for router support.

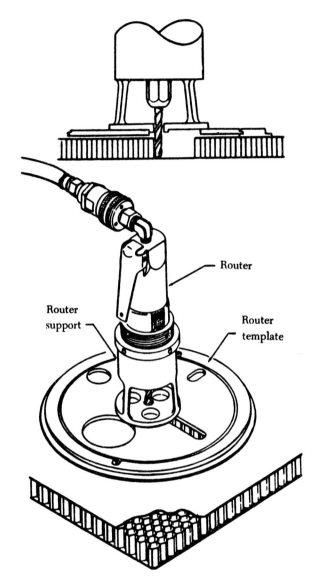

FIG. 8-12 Router, support assembly, and template.

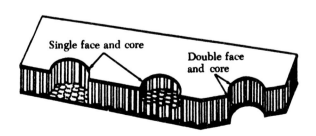

FIG. 8-13 Areas routed out prior to repair.

After the routing has been completed, the bent edges of the core material should be straightened by the use of a knife blade or pick if a core replacement is to be used. This aids in assuring bonding contact between the existing core material and the plug core material. If a syntactic foam is to be used, the core material should be undercut beyond the edges of the surface opening to anchor the foam within the structure. The routed-out area should be cleaned with a solvent, taking care not to leave any solvent in the area after the cleaning is completed. This could cause the existing adhesive to break down.

One of four techniques might be used to repair this type of core damage. The first technique involves the use of a **syntactic foam** and is often used if the damage is no more than 1 in [2.54 cm] in diameter. A piece of plastic is laid down around the repair opening as shown in Fig. 8-15. A Duxseal tube is formed around the opening. Instead of syntactic foam, some repairs may require that a similar compound be mixed. This requires that a potting compound be mixed, and a material such as **microballoons** added to reduce the density of the potting compound and improve its flexibility. Microballoons are tiny hollow spheres that act like very small bubbles in the mixture. In either case the material is worked into the damage by the use of a wooden dowel or toothpick until the damaged area is full and no air pockets remain inside the repair. Sufficient material should be used so that it is above the surface of the skin. Once the mixture has cured, the Duxseal and the plastic are removed. The excess mixture is trimmed off and the surface is finished. If the repair is to be vacuum bagged, a thin coat of matrix should be placed over the trimmed foam and allowed to cure before applying the surface patch and vacuum. This prevents air from being drawn up through the foam material and into the patch, rendering the patch "unairworthy."

A second type of repair involves the use of a piece

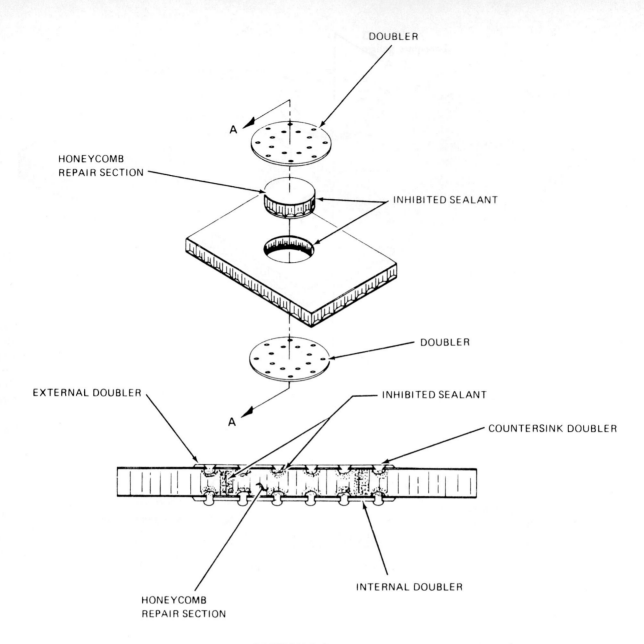

SECTION A-A

FIG. 8-19 A core replacement by riveting.

core material in the original structure has been re-moved. The plug patch being used has both surface plates still attached for increased riveting area.

If damage penetrates both skins, a hole is routed out through the entire panel. Plug and surface patches are prepared, and the pieces are assembled as shown in Fig. 8-18. A similar riveted repair is shown in Fig. 8-19.

While some of the repairs illustrated show the trimmed surface opening without any tapering, many manufacturers now require that the surface material be tapered back and the surface patch be composed of several layers as discussed for surface repairs.

The Warp Clock

The warp of a fabric is the fibers which run the length of the fabric, parallel to the manufactured (sel-vage) edge, as discussed in the chapter on aircraft fabrics. The warp fibers of a composite material are considered to be stronger than the fill fibers and are used as a reference to properly align patches. The warp clock is used to indicate fiber directions different from a reference direction.

For composite repairs the surface layer of original material is considered to be the reference material and the zero warp angle aligns with the warp of this fabric. The warp direction of some materials can be deter-mined by tracer threads. The warp direction of uni-directional fabrics is readily apparent as there are few, if any, fill fibers used. If no tracer threads are used or if the damaged structure cannot be disected, the main-tenance manual or the manufacturer can provide the warp directions referenced to a warp clock. The warp clock is shown in Fig. 8-20.

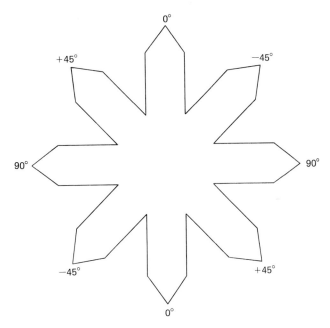

FIG. 8-20 Warp clock.

For example, four layers of a structure may have a warp orientation of 0, +45, 90, -45. This gives the outer layer as the reference direction (0), the second layer of fabric is laid at an angle 45 degrees to the left of the first layer (+45), the third layer is 45 degrees to the right of the first layer (-45), and the last layer is perpendicular to the surface layer (90). With this information the mechanic would lay the innermost patch with its warp perpendicular to the surface warp direction. The next patch would be laid 45 degrees to the right of the zero direction, the next layer 45 degrees to the left and the top layer in alignment with the 0 direction.

● REVIEW QUESTIONS

1. What is the principal difference between *thermoplastic* and *thermosetting* plastics?
2. What types of plastic materials are most commonly used for aircraft windshields and windows?
3. How can you tell the difference between *acrylic* and *acetate* plastic sheet?
4. How should plastic windows and windshields be cleaned?
5. Discuss the handling and storage of plastic sheet.
6. What precautions should be taken when handling unprotected plastic sheet?
7. Describe the cutting and drilling of plastic sheet.
8. Describe the process for cementing plastic sheet.
9. Describe the repair of a small hole in plastic sheet.
10. What must be done when applying a patch to a curved plastic surface?
11. What precautions must be taken when installing plastic sheet with bolts or rivets?
12. Compare the thermal expansion characteristics of plastic sheet with those of aluminum.
13. How are edges of plastic panels protected when installed in window frames or windshield channels?
14. What may be used to remove masking paper that has dried on a plastic sheet?
15. What is *crazing* and what may cause it to occur?
16. What are the methods that may be used to heat plastic prior to forming it?
17. What are the advantages of *composite construction* when compared to conventional sheet-metal construction?
18. Describe *honeycomb sandwich* material.
19. Describe a satisfactory repair for a small cut in a fiberglass structure where only the outer layer is affected.
20. Describe a repair for damage where the core material in a honeycomb structure has been cut or crushed.
21. Describe the use of a router in cutting out a damaged section of facing and core.
22. What is the purpose of adding *microballoons* to the resin for a potted repair?
23. When a sheet-metal patch is used to repair a metal-faced honeycomb structure, what should be done with respect to the edges of the patch?
24. Describe a riveted repair for a honeycomb structure.
25. Explain the *ring test* for inspection of bonded laminates and seams.
26. What methods are employed for the inspection of laminates and seams?

9 AIRCRAFT HYDRAULIC AND PNEUMATIC SYSTEMS

Hydraulic and pneumatic systems in aircraft provide a means for the operation of large aircraft components which could not be operated satisfactorily with human power alone. The operation of landing gear, flaps, control boost systems, and other components is largely accomplished with hydraulic power systems. Pneumatic systems are used in some aircraft designs to perform the same type of operations performed by hydraulic systems. However, the majority of aircraft that have pneumatic systems use them only as backup systems for the operation of hydraulic components when the hydraulic system has failed.

● PRINCIPLES OF HYDRAULICS

Hydraulics is a division of the science of fluid mechanics which includes the study of liquids and their physical characteristics, both at rest and in motion. The type of hydraulics applied to aircraft and other aerospace-vehicle systems is called **power hydraulics** because it involves the application of power through the medium of hydraulics. Among the uses of hydraulic systems in aerospace-vehicle systems are the operation of landing gear and gear doors, flight controls, brakes, and a wide variety of other devices requiring high power, quick action, and/or accurate control.

Characteristics of Liquids

In general, and for practical purposes, liquids are regarded as being incompressible. This means that the volume of a given quantity of a liquid will remain constant even though it is subjected to high pressure. Because of this characteristic, it is easy to determine the volume of hydraulic fluid required to move a piston through its operating range. For example, if a piston is 4 in [10.16 cm] in diameter and its stroke is 10 in [25.4 cm], the volume of liquid necessary to move the piston through its full stroke is 125.67 in³ [2.06 L]. This is determined as follows:

The volume of the cylinder through which the piston moves is equal to the area of the pistonhead multiplied by the length of the cylinder. The area of the pistonhead is determined by the formula $A = \pi r^2$; hence for the piston in the example, $A = 3.1416 \times 2^2 = 12.567$. Multiplying this value by 10, we obtain the volume 125.67 in³ [2.06 L]. We know then that it will require 125.67 in³ hydraulic fluid to move the piston through its 10-in [25.4-cm] stroke.

Because of the relative incompressibility of a liquid, we know that a given output volume from a hydraulic pump will provide an equal volume of fluid at the operating unit. For example, if a hydraulic pump discharges 100 in³ [1.639 L] of fluid through a filled connecting line between the pump and an actuating cylinder, the piston in the cylinder will have to move through sufficient distance to provide a volume of 100 in³ [1.639 L] to accommodate the fluid.

Hydraulic fluids and other liquids expand as temperature increases; hence, safeguards must be provided in hydraulic systems to allow for the expansion and contraction of fluid as temperature changes. Devices to provide the necessary protection are called **thermal relief valves.**

A liquid which is confined will seek its own level as shown in Fig. 9-1. Here the liquid is in a container open at the top and is subjected only to the force of gravity. Assuming that the container shown in the illustration is level, the pressure is the same at all points on the bottom of the container. The liquid surfaces at *A, B, C,* and *D* are all equidistant from the bottom of the container.

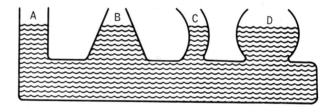

FIG. 9-1   Liquid seeks its own level.

A basic principle of hydraulics is expressed in Pascal's law formulated by Blaise Pascal in the seventeenth century. This law states that a confined hydraulic fluid exerts equal pressure at every point and in every direction in the fluid. This is true under static conditions and when the force of gravity is not taken into consideration. In Fig. 9-2 if the piston *P* has a face area of 1 in² [6.45 cm²] and a force of 10 lb [44.48 N] is applied to it, the fluid in the container will exert 10 psi [68.95 kPa] in all directions on all surfaces within the container. In actual practice the weight of the fluid would cause a small increase in the pressure on the bottom and lower sides of the container.

When liquids are in motion, certain *dynamic* characteristics must be taken into consideration. One of the principal factors in liquid motion is **friction.** Friction exists between the molecules of the liquid and

268

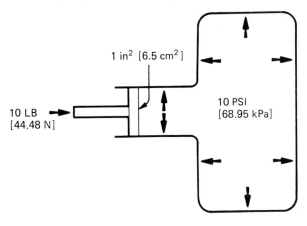

FIG. 9-2 Fluid pressure is the same in all directions.

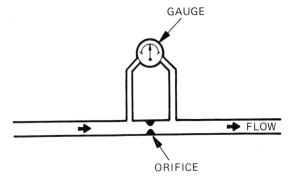

FIG. 9-4 Differential pressure across an orifice.

between the liquid and the pipe through which it is flowing. The effects of friction increase as the velocity of liquid flow increases. The result of friction can be seen in the simple experiment illustrated in Fig. 9-3.

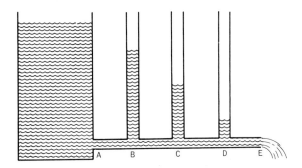

FIG. 9-3 Reduction of pressure because of friction.

As the liquid flows from the container through a pipe which is open at the end, the pressure of the liquid decreases progressively until it becomes 0 psi at the open end of the pipe. If the pressure at A is 4 psi [27.58 kPa], then it will be 3 psi [20.69 kPa], 2 psi [13.79 kPa], 1 psi [6.895 kPa], and 0 psi at B, C, D, and E, respectively. As liquid velocity increases through a given length of pipe, the pressure differential between the ends of the pipe will increase. The same is true when a liquid is flowing through a restriction in a pipe. For this reason, the rate of fluid flow can be determined by measuring the pressure differential on opposite sides of a given restrictor. This is illustrated in Fig. 9-4. The differential pressure reading on the gauge will increase as liquid velocity through the restrictor increases, and the reading of the gauge can be converted to gallons per minute or some other rate measurement.

Friction in a moving liquid produces heat, and this heat represents a loss of energy in a hydraulic system. According to the **law of conservation of energy**, which states that energy can neither be created nor destroyed, energy converted to heat must be subtracted from the total energy of the moving liquid. Hence, if a hydraulic pump is discharging hydraulic fluid at a

rate and pressure equivalent to 3 hp [2.24 kW], and in the system the equivalent of 0.2 hp [0.149 kW] is converted to heat, the power available for useful work is reduced to 2.8 hp [2.09 kW].

Performing Work with a Liquid

Power is the product of force and distance divided by time. **Work** is force times distance; hence, power can be defined as work divided by time.

Force may be considered as a ''push'' or ''pull'' or any cause which tends to produce or change motion. In the English system, force is measured in pounds; in the metric system, it is measured in grams, kilograms, or newtons (N). To measure the force of hydraulics, we must be table to determine **force per unit area.** This is called **pressure** and is measured in pounds per square inch (psi) or kilopascals (kPa).

Power can be measured in **horsepower** (hp) or **watts** (W). One horsepower is the power required when 550 lb of force is exerted through a distance of 1 ft in 1 s. This power can also be expressed as 550 ft · lb/s. To determine the amount of power required to do a given amount of work in a given time, divide the work by the time. For example, if a hydraulic actuating cylinder lifts a weight of 11 000 lb a distance of 2 ft in 5 s, we find the power as follows:

$$P \text{ (ft-lb/s)} = \frac{11\ 000 \times 2}{5}$$

$$= 4400 \text{ ft-lb/s } [607.2 \text{ kg-m/s}]$$

To convert this to horsepower, we divide by 550 and obtain the value of 8 hp. To obtain horsepower directly from the first computation, we merely include the horsepower factor, 550, in the equation; thus

$$P \text{ (hp)} = \frac{11\ 000 \times 2}{5 \times 550} = 8 \text{ hp } [5.97 \text{ kW}]$$

One of the principal advantages of hydraulics is the fact that force can be multiplied to almost any degree by the proper application of hydraulic pressure. In the diagram of Fig. 9-5 a piston and cylinder with a diameter of 2 in [5.08 cm] is used to develop a force of 2500 lb [11 125 N] by acting through a cylinder with a diameter of 10 in [25.4 cm]. The area of the 2-in [5.08-cm] piston is 3.1416 in² [20.27 cm²]. (The area of a

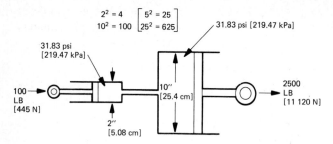

FIG. 9-5 Multiplication of force by means of hydraulics.

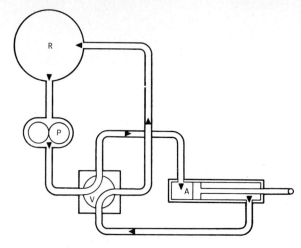

FIG. 9-6 A simple hydraulic system.

circle is $r^2 \times \pi$.) The area of the 10-in piston is then $5^2 \times 3.1416$, or 78.54 in² [506.71 cm²]. When a force of 100 lb [444.8 N] is applied to the small piston, a pressure of 100/3.1416 is developed in the system. This pressure is 31.83 psi [219.47 kPa]. The force exerted by the large piston is then 31.83×78.54, or approximately 2500 lb [11 120 N]. It will be noted that the areas of circles are proportional to the squares of the diameters; hence the force developed by one piston driving another is also proportional to the squares of the diameters. In the foregoing problem, the square of the diameter of the smaller piston is 2×2 or 4, and the square of the larger piston is 10×10 or 100. The ratio is then 4:100 or 1:25. Since the force applied to the small piston is 100 psi [689.5 kPa], the force delivered by the large piston is 100×25, or 2500 lb [11 125 N].

Since energy cannot be created or destroyed, the multiplication of force is accomplished at the expense of distance. In the foregoing problem, the ratio of force multiplication is 25:1. The distance through which the pistons move must then be in an inverse ratio, or 1:25. That is, the large piston will move one twenty-fifth the distance the small piston moves. If the small piston is connected to a fluid input with check valves so it can act as a pump, it can be moved back and forth, and during each forward stroke it will move the large piston a short distance. This action can be observed in the hydraulic jacks which are used to raise automobiles or airplanes.

In some aircraft hydraulic systems, fluid pressures of as much as 5000 psi [34 475 kPa] are employed. With a pressure of this level, a very small actuating cylinder can exert tremendous force. For example, a cylinder having a cross-sectional area of 2 in² [12.9 cm²] can exert a force of 10 000 lb [44 480 N].

A Simple Hydraulic System

Basically, a hydraulic system requires a source of hydraulic power (the pump); pipes or hoses to carry the hydraulic fluid from one point to another; a valve mechanism to control the flow and direction of the hydraulic fluid; a device for converting the fluid power to movement (actuating cylinder or hydraulic motor); and a reservoir to store the hydraulic fluid.

A **simple hydraulic system** is shown in the diagram of Fig. 9-6. The pump (P) draws hydraulic fluid from the reservoir (R) and directs it under pressure to the four-way valve (V). When the valve is in the position shown, the fluid will flow into the left end of the

actuating cylinder (A) and force the piston to the right. This moves the piston rod and any device to which it is connected.

As the piston moves to the right, the fluid to the right of the piston is displaced and flows out the port at the right end of the cylinder, through the tubing to the valve, and from the valve to the reservoir. When the valve is rotating one-quarter turn, the reverse action will take place.

It must be emphasized that the diagram shown is not intended to illustrate an actual system but only to illustrate the principle of a hydraulic system. In an actual system, a pressure regulator or relief valve is necessary between the pump and the valve in order to relieve the pressure when the cylinder reaches the end of its travel. Otherwise, the pump would be damaged or the tubing would burst.

Another simple system is illustrated in Fig. 9-7. This system is similar to a hydraulic brake system. Hy-

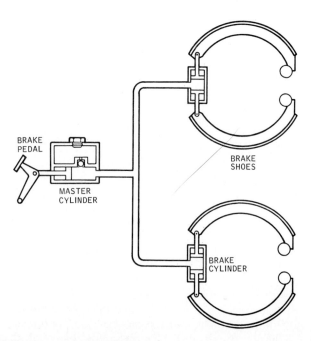

FIG. 9-7 Hydraulic brake system.

270

draulic fluid is stored in the cylinder and is directed through a valve into the master cylinder as it is needed. When the brake pedal is depressed, the fluid is directed to the brake cylinders; these cylinders push the shoes apart, thus causing them to bear against the brake drum and provide brake action. When the pedal is released, springs attached to the brake shoes cause the shoes to contract and push inward on the brake cylinders, thus causing some of the fluid to return to the master cylinder.

● HYDRAULIC FLUIDS

Purposes of Hydraulic Fluids

Hydraulic fluids make possible the transmission of pressure and energy. They also act as a lubricating medium, thereby reducing the friction between moving parts and carrying away some of the heat.

Hydraulic-Fluid Types

There are three principal types of hydraulic fluids: **vegetable-base fluids, mineral-base fluids,** and **fire-resistant fluids.**

Vegetable-base fluids are usually mixtures containing castor oil and alcohol and are colored blue, blue-green, or almost clear. They are still used in some brake systems but are not generally found in hydraulic-power systems.

Mineral-base fluids consist of a high-quality petroleum oil and are usually colored red. They are used in many systems, especially where the fire hazard is comparatively low. Small aircraft which have hydraulic power systems for operating wheel brakes, flaps, and landing gear usually use mineral-base fluids conforming to MIL-O-5606. Mineral-base fluids are less corrosive and less damaging to certain parts than other types of fluid.

A mineral-base, synthetic hydrocarbon fluid called Braco 882 has been developed by the Bray Oil Company and is used extensively by the military services in place of MIL-O-5606. The fluid is red in color and meets the specifications of MIL-O-83282. This fluid has the advantage of increased fire resistance, and it can be used in systems having the same types of seals, gaskets, hoses, etc., that are used with petroleum base MIL-0-5606.

Fire-resistant fluids used in transport aircraft are usually of the phosphate ester type. Typical of such fluids are Skydrol 7000, 500, 500A, and 500B. These fluids are colored light green, blue, and purple (500A and 500B), respectively. Seals, gaskets, and hoses used with the fluid are made of butyl synthetic rubber or Teflon fluorocarbon resin. Great care must be taken to see that the units installed in the hydraulic system are of the type designed for fire-resistant fluid. When gaskets, seals, and hoses are replaced, positive identification must be made to assure that they are made of butyl rubber or an approved equivalent material such as Teflon fluorocarbon resin.

Fire-resistant hydraulic fluid will soften or dissolve many types of paints, lacquers, and enamels. For this reason, areas which may be contaminated with this type of fluid must be finished with special coatings. When any of the fluid is spilled, it should immediately be removed and the area washed.

Handling Hydraulic Fluids

In addition to any other instructions given in the airplane manufacturer's manual, the following should be observed in the use of hydraulic fluids.

1. Mark each airplane hydraulic system to show the type of fluid to be used in the system. The filler cap or filler valve should be marked so that it is immediately apparent to a mechanic what type of fluid should be added to the system.

2. Never under any circumstances service an airplane system with a type of fluid different from that shown on the instruction plate.

3. Make certain that hydraulic fluids and fluid containers are protected from contamination of any kind. Dirt particles quickly cause many hydraulic units to become inoperative and may cause severe damage. If there is any question regarding the cleanliness of the fluid, it should be filtered through a filter paper into a dustfree container. Containers for hydraulic fluid should never be left open to the air for longer than necessary.

4. Never allow hydraulic fluids of different types to become mixed. Mixed fluid will render a hydraulic system useless.

5. Do not expose fluids to high heat or open flames. Vegetable- and mineral-base fluids are highly flammable. Phosphate ester fluids are considered fire-resistant and will not support combustion in the absence of extremely high heat.

6. Avoid contact with the fluids. While the vegetable- and mineral-based fluids do not cause any irritation for most people when in contact with skin, the phosphate ester fluids can cause skin irritation and pain. If skin contact occurs, wash the fluid off with soap and water. Consult a physician if irritation persists. Take precautions to prevent any hydraulic fluid from getting in the eyes or from being inhaled as a mist or vapor. The phosphate ester fluids cause the greatest amount of irritation in these areas. For eye contact, flush well with water and, if a phosphate ester fluid is involved, apply an anesthetic eye solution. Reaction to inhaled vapors (coughing and sneezing) stops after the vapor or mist is eliminated. For all cases of eye contact and inhalation of hydraulic fluids, consult a physician.

7. Wear protective gloves and a face shield whenever handling phosphate ester fluids and whenever working around any hydraulic lines that are under pressure.

● HYDRAULIC RESERVOIRS

A hydraulic reservoir is a tank or container designed to store sufficient hydraulic fluid for all conditions of operation. Usually the hydraulic reservoir must have the capability of containing extra fluid not being circulated in the system during certain modes of operation. When accumulators, actuating cylinders, and other units are not containing their maximum quantities of fluid, the unused fluid must be stored in the reservoir. On the other hand, when a maximum amount of fluid is being used in the system, the reservoir must still have a reserve adequate to meet all requirements. Reservoirs in hydraulic systems which require a reserve of fluid for the emergency operation of landing gear, flaps, etc., are equipped with **standpipes,** flaps, etc. During normal operation, fluid is drawn through the standpipe. When system fluid is lost, emergency fluid is drawn from the bottom of the tank.

Hydraulic reservoirs vary in complexity from nothing but a can with a vent hose on top of the cap and an outlet at the bottom to sophisticated designs incorporating filters, quantity indicators, and pressure relief systems. Reservoirs can be broken down into two basic types, **in-line** and **integral,** and these can be further classified as **pressurized** and **unpressurized.**

Hydraulic fluid reservoirs provide a compartment to store hydraulic fluid when it is not in use in a system and they also provide sufficient fluid to make up for normal losses of fluid by seepage past seals. Reservoirs are not designed to be completely filled, but they do have an air space above the fluid level to allow for expansion of the fluid when it is heated during system operation.

A reservoir provides some means of checking the fluid level and of being replenished. The quantity-indicating method may be nothing more than a dipstick on the filler cap, or it may have a remote indicating system to display the quantity on the aircraft flight deck. Replenishment is normally by adding fluid directly to the reservoir through a filler opening. When multiple reservoirs are used in an aircraft for independent or redundant hydraulic systems, one reservoir may be filled by the overflow from another reservoir.

In-Line Reservoirs

In-line reservoirs are those which are separate components in the hydraulic system. This is the most common type of reservoir. These can be pressurized or unpressurized.

Unpressurized reservoirs are normally used in aircraft flying at lower altitudes, such as below 15 000 ft [4583 m], or whose hydraulic systems are limited to those associated with ground operations, such as brakes.

Pressurized reservoirs are commonly found in aircraft designed for high-altitude flight and those which require a pressure feed to the hydraulic pumps. Along with providing a positive feed to the hydraulic pumps, a pressurized reservoir reduces or eliminates the foaming of the fluid when it returns to the reservoir. The reservoir may be pressurized by spring pressure, air pressure, or hydraulic pressure.

A simplified drawing of a spring pressurized reservoir is shown in Fig. 9-8. The compression spring on top of the reservoir piston pressurizes the fluid in the reservoir and provides a positive pump inlet pressure for initial start-up of the pump. When the pump is

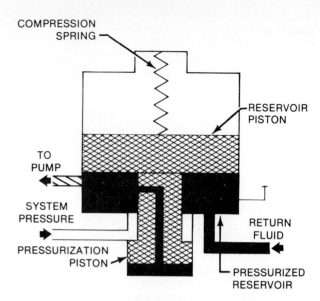

FIG. 9-8 A reservoir pressurized by spring and hydraulic pressure. (Bell Helicopter Textron)

running, system pressure (3000 psi [20 685 kPa] in this case) is applied to the small area on top of the pressurization piston and increases the pressure inside the reservoir to 75 psi [517.13 kPa]. This assists the spring in providing a positive pressure to the pump inlet and also prevents cavitation of the pump.

Turbine engine bleed air or a venturi-type aspirator can be used to pressurize a reservoir with air. Bleed air can be fed through a pressure regulator to establish the proper pressure and then into the top of the reservoir. When using a venturi-type aspirator, the low-pressure section of the venturi draws air into the reservoir and increases the pressure. The use of air pressure does not require any elaborate chambering of the reservoir as is required by the other methods; the reservoir is simply pressurized with air.

Hydraulic pressure can be used to pressurize the reservoir in a manner similar to that used to assist the spring in pressurizing the reservoir. Figure 9-9 shows the reservoir from a Lockheed L-1011 airliner. Hydraulic pressure entering the pressure port flows through the depressurization valve and into the area just above the pressurization piston. The force on this piston causes the reservoir piston to try to move downward, which pressurizes the reservoir. The high pressure used is 3000 psi [20 685 kPa], which gives a reservoir pressure of 85 psi [586 kPa]. The depressurization valve is used to equalize the pressure in the two piston areas during servicing. An electric pump is used to pressurize the system before engine start so that the engine-driven pumps inlet lines are under positive pressure, which reduces pump wear.

Integral Reservoirs

Integral reservoirs are integral with the hydraulic pump. These types of reservoirs are often found in small aircraft where the compact arrangement of this type of mechanism is desirable. An example of this is the brake master cylinder used with many light aircraft systems. As shown in Fig. 9-10, the upper portion of

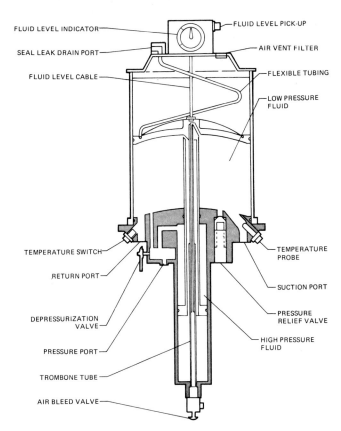

FIG. 9-9 A reservoir pressurized by hydraulic pressure. *(Lockheed-California Co.)*

Labels on figure 9-9:
- FLUID LEVEL INDICATOR
- SEAL LEAK DRAIN PORT
- FLUID LEVEL CABLE
- FLUID LEVEL PICK-UP
- AIR VENT FILTER
- FLEXIBLE TUBING
- LOW PRESSURE FLUID
- TEMPERATURE SWITCH
- RETURN PORT
- DEPRESSURIZATION VALVE
- PRESSURE PORT
- TROMBONE TUBE
- AIR BLEED VALVE
- TEMPERATURE PROBE
- SUCTION PORT
- PRESSURE RELIEF VALVE
- HIGH PRESSURE FLUID

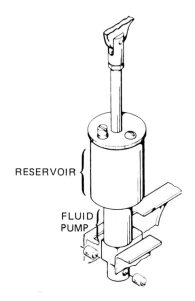

FIG. 9-10 A reservoir in the same assembly as the fluid pump. *(Cessna Aircraft Company)*

Labels on figure 9-10:
- RESERVOIR
- FLUID PUMP

the assembly serves as the reservoir and the lower portion serves as the pump to operate the brake.

Reservoir for Large Aircraft

As an example of a hydraulic reservoir for a large, transport category airplane, Fig. 9-11 shows a drawing of one of the reservoirs for a DC-10 airplane. This reservoir weighs 53 lb [24.04 kg], is cylindrical in shape and protected by a perforated shield around the shell, and has an internal volume (including expansion space) of 12 US gal [45.425 L]. The bottom of the reservoir is provided with six large ports for suction and return lines, and five small ports. The small center port is for pressurizing the reservoir. Any two of the remaining small ports are for the reservoir temperature sensor and drain valves. When installed, all ports not used are plugged.

A fluid quantity transmitter and actuating links are located on top of the reservoir cover. The lower end of the linkage is attached to the transmitter rotor shaft, while the upper end is attached to the fluid-level pointer at the top of the relief and sampling valve. Fluid-level changes in the reservoir raise or lower the pointer by extending or retracting the linkage and cause the transmitter rotor to change position. The transmitter delivers an electrical signal to the remote quantity indicator located in the flight compartment.

A calibrated fill level instruction plate, mounted adjacent to the reservoir sight glass, provides instructions for determining fluid levels within the pressurized system.

Reservoir for a Helicopter

A hydraulic reservoir for one model of a Sikorsky helicopter is shown in Fig. 9-12. This reservoir, referred to by the manufacturer as a **hydraulic fluid tank,** consists of an upper housing and a lower housing. The upper housing consists of a filler neck, an adapter, and a window sight gauge. The filler neck consists of a cap which screws onto the neck, a scupper with an overboard drain, and a strainer which is secured to the inside of the filler neck. The adapter, on top of the upper housing, consists of an adapter housing with a micronic filter element and a vent line which runs from the adapter fitting to the scupper. The lower housing incorporates a baffle plate, micronic filter element, drain plug, and relief valve with a differential cracking pressure of 6 to 8 psi [41.37 to 55.16 kPa]. Fluid returning to the tank circulates around the baffle plate and passes through the micronic filter element to the supply portion of the tank. If the filter element becomes clogged to the extent that a 6- to 8-psi [41.37- to 55.16-kPa] pressure builds up in the return portion of the tank, the relief valve opens to allow fluid to bypass the filter element and flow directly from the return portion of the tank to the supply portion. The tank (reservoir) may be drained by connecting a coupling and hose to the external supply coupling.

● HYDRAULIC PUMPS

Hydraulic pumps are designed to cause fluid flow and are made in hundreds of different designs from simple hand pumps to very complex, multiple-piston, variable-displacement pumps. We shall examine a few pumps which could be used for aircraft or space vehicles.

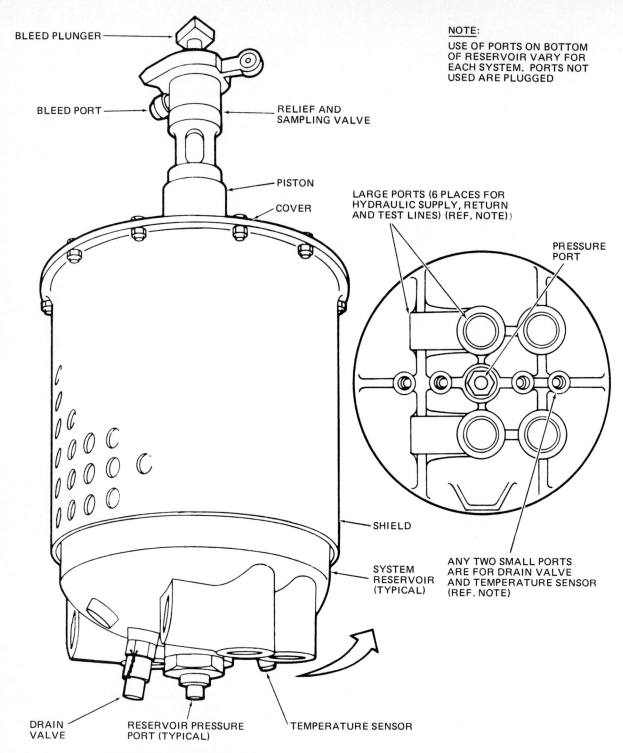

BLEED PLUNGER

BLEED PORT

RELIEF AND
SAMPLING VALVE

PISTON

COVER

LARGE PORTS (6 PLACES FOR
HYDRAULIC SUPPLY, RETURN
AND TEST LINES) (REF. NOTE))

PRESSURE
PORT

SHIELD

SYSTEM
RESERVOIR
(TYPICAL)

ANY TWO SMALL PORTS
ARE FOR DRAIN VALVE
AND TEMPERATURE SENSOR
(REF. NOTE)

DRAIN
VALVE

RESERVOIR PRESSURE
PORT (TYPICAL)

TEMPERATURE SENSOR

FIG. 9-11 Hydraulic reservoir for the DC-10 airplane. *(Douglas Aircraft Division, McDonnell Douglas Corp.)*

Hand Pumps

A diagram of a **single-acting hand pump** is shown in Fig. 9-13. This diagram illustrates the basic principle of a piston pump. When the handle is moved toward the left, the piston movement creates a low-pressure condition and draws fluid from the reservoir through the check valve and into the cylinder. Then when the handle is moved toward the right, the piston forces the fluid out through the discharge check valve. The check valves allow the fluid to flow only in one direction, as shown by the arrows.

A **double-acting piston-displacement type** of hand pump is shown in the drawing of Fig. 9-14. The IN port from the reservoir is connected to the center of the cylinder where there is a space between the two pistons and surrounding the shaft connecting the pis-

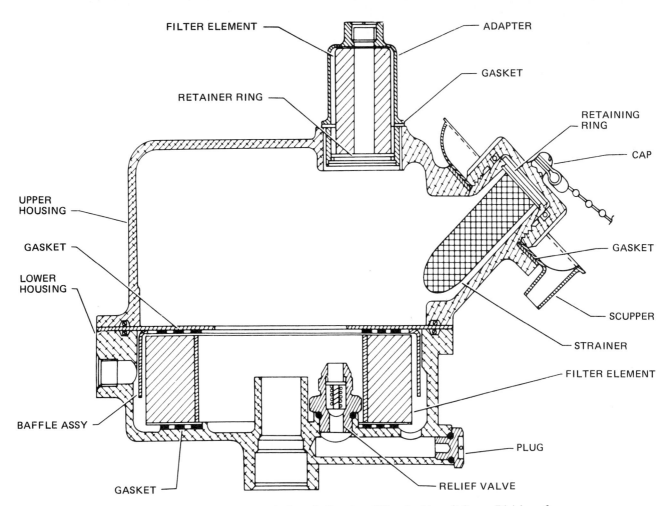

FIG. 9-12   **Hydraulic reservoir for a helicopter.** *(Sikorsky Aircraft Corp., Division of United Technologies Corp.)*

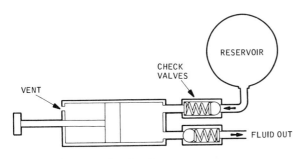

FIG. 9-13   **Single-acting hand pump.**

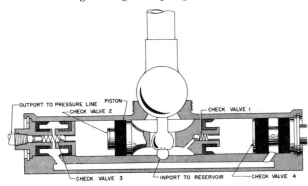

FIG. 9-14   **A double-acting, piston-displacement pump.**

tons. In each piston is a check valve (Nos. 1 and 2) and a passage which allows fluid to flow from the center chamber to the spaces at each end of the dual piston assembly. When the pump handle is moved to the right, the piston assembly moves to the left forcing fluid out through check valve 3 into the system. The check valve in the left-hand piston is held closed by fluid and spring pressures. As the piston assembly moves to the left, a low-pressure area is created in the chamber in the right end of the cylinder, and this causes fluid to flow through check valve 1 into the chamber. Check valve 4 is held in the closed position by spring and fluid pressure. When the pump handle is moved to the left, the piston assembly moves to the right and the fluid is forced out of the right-hand chamber through check valve 4 into the system. Note that a fluid passage connects the outlet chambers at each end of the cylinder.

Gear-type Pump

A **gear-type pump** is shown in the drawing of Fig. 9-15. This pump is classed as a **positive-displacement pump** because each revolution of the pump will deliver a given volume of fluid, provided the pump is not worn and no leakage occurs. One of the two gears is driven

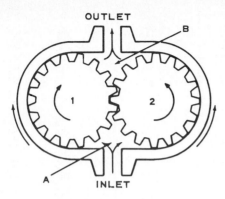

FIG. 9-15 A gear-type pump.

by the power source which could be an engine drive or an electric-motor drive. The other gear is meshed with and driven by the first gear. As the gears rotate in the direction shown, fluid enters the IN port to the gears where it is trapped between the gear teeth and carried around the pump case to the OUT port. The fluid cannot flow between the gears because of their closely meshed design; hence it is forced out through the OUT port.

Vane-type Pump

The **vane-type pump** is also classed as a positive-displacement pump because of its positive action in moving fluid. This pump is illustrated in the drawing of Fig. 9-16 and consists of a slotted rotor located off-center within the cylinder of the pump body with rectangular vanes free to move radially in each slot. As the rotor turns, the vanes are caused to move outward by centrifugal force and contact the smooth inner surface of the casing. Since the rotor is eccentric with respect to the casing, the vanes form chambers which increase and decrease in volume as the rotor turns. The inlet side of the pump is integral with the side of the casing in which the chambers are increasing in volume. Thus the fluid is caused to enter the chambers because of the low-pressure area created by the expanding chambers. The fluid is carried around the

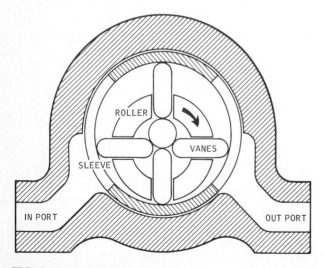

FIG. 9-16 A vane-type pump.

casing to the point where the chambers begin to contract, and this section of the casing is connected to the output port of the pump. The contraction of the chambers forces the fluid into the outlet port and system.

Gerotor Pump

A **gerotor pump,** shown in Fig. 9-17, consists of a housing containing an excentric-shaped stationary liner, an internal gear rotor having five wide teeth of short height, a spur driving gear having four narrow teeth, and a pump cover which contains two crescent-shaped openings. One opening extends into an inlet port and the other connects to an outlet port. In Fig. 9-17 the pump cover is shown with the inner surface visible to display the inlet and outlet openings inside the pump. When the cover is turned over, the inlet is on the left and the outlet on the right.

During operation, the gears turn clockwise. As the cavities move from the bottom of the gear to the top of the gear, they increase in volume, resulting in a vacuum being created in this area. As this cavity passes the inlet port, fluid is drawn into the cavity. As this cavity moves to the right side of the pump, the size of the cavity is decreased and fluid is forced out of the pump via the outlet port.

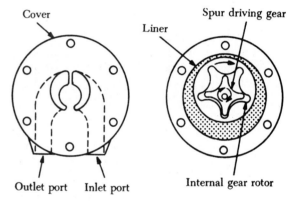

FIG. 9-17 Gerotor-type power pump.

Multiple-Piston Pumps

One of the most widely used hydraulic pumps for modern aircraft is the **axial multiple-piston pump.** A drawing to illustrate this type of pump is shown in Fig. 9-18. The pump consists of a drive shaft to which the pistons are attached by means of ball sockets, a cylinder block into which the pistons are inserted, and a stationary valving surface which fits closely against one end of the cylinder block. The drive shaft is connected to the cylinder block by means of a universal link to rotate the cylinder block with the drive shaft. The axis of rotation for the cylinder block is at an angle to the axis of rotation of the drive shaft; hence the pistons are caused to move in and out of the cylinders as rotation occurs. The pistons on one side of the cylinder block are moving outward, thus increasing the volume of the cylinder spaces; on the other side of the cylinder block, the pistons are moving

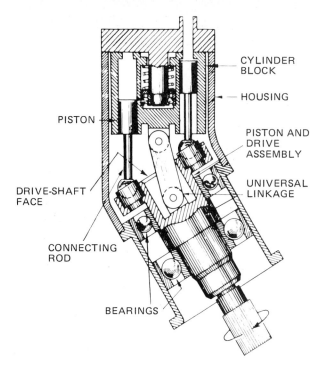

FIG. 9-18   Cutaway drawing of an axial piston pump.

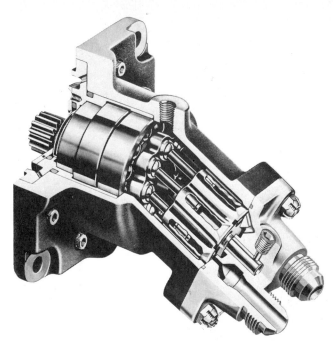

FIG. 9-19   A fixed-delivery piston pump. (*Sperry Vickers Div., Sperry Rand Corp.*)

inward. The valve plate is made with two slots such that one slot is bearing against the side of the cylinder block on which the pistons are moving away from the valving surface; the other slot is bearing against the side on which the pistons are moving toward the valving surface. The slots in the valving surface are connected to inlet and outlet chambers to provide fluid feed to the pistons on the inlet side and an outlet for the pressure fluid on the other side. As the drive shaft rotates, the pistons on one side of the cylinder block draw fluid through the valving surface slot, and the pistons on the other side force the fluid through the outlet slot.

A cutaway illustration of a **fixed-delivery pump** manufactured by Sperry Vickers, Division of Sperry Rand Corp., is shown in Fig. 9-19. **Fixed delivery** means that the pump will normally deliver a fixed amount of fluid at a given number of revolutions per minute. A **variable-delivery pump** is shown in Fig. 9-20. This pump is designed so the alignment of the rotational axis of the cylinder block can be changed as desired to vary the volume of fluid being delivered at a given rpm. By changing the angle of the rotational axis, the stroke of the pistons is decreased or increased; hence the volume of fluid pumped during each stroke of the pistons is reduced or increased. If the axis of the cylinder block is parallel to the axis of the drive shaft, no fluid will be delivered because there will be no movement of the pistons within their respective cylinders.

Cam-type, Variable-Delivery Pump

A cam-type piston pump operates on the principle of the multiple-piston pumps described in the foregoing section; however, the drive shaft axis is parallel with the pistons. The movement of the pistons necessary to create a pumping action is caused by a cam

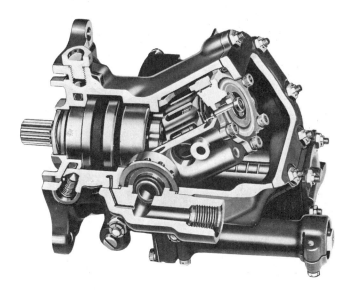

FIG. 9-20   A variable-delivery pump. (*Sperry Vickers Div., Sperry Rand Corp.*)

or wobble plate. As the cam rotates, the elevated portion pushes the pistons into the cylinders, causing them to eject the fluid into the OUT port. The pistons on the descending portion of the cam draw fluid from the IN port of the pump. The angle of the cam or wobble plate, as established by the pressure-controlling device, determines the amount of fluid expelled during each stroke of the pistons, thus providing the variable delivery required. Check valves are located at the outlet of each piston to prevent pressurized fluid from flowing back into the cylinders as the pistons move back in the cylinders. The operation of the cam-type piston pump is illustrated in Fig. 9-21. (See also Figs. 9-78 and 9-79.)

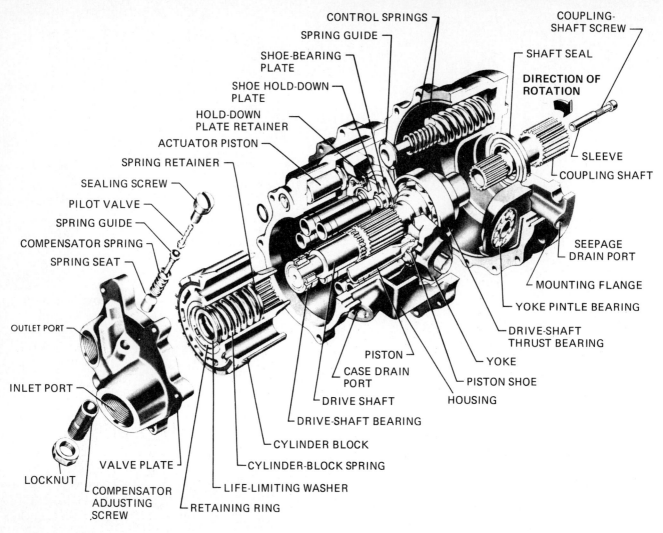

FIG. 9-21   A cam-type piston pump. *(Sperry Vickers Div., Sperry Rand Corp.)*

To protect the engine-driven pump and hydraulic system, pumps are provided with a **shear section** on the drive shaft. If the pump seizes or is prevented from rotating, the shaft will shear and prevent further damage.

● PRESSURE-CONTROL DEVICES

Numerous devices have been designed to control pressure in hydraulic systems; however, we shall attempt to describe but a few of the most important. Among these are **relief valves, pressure regulators,** and **deboosters.**

Relief Valve

A **relief valve** is comparatively simple in construction, and its function is to limit the maximum pressure which can be developed in a hydraulic system. Thus it acts as a safety valve similar in function to one which would be found in an air- or steam-pressure system. During operation, the relief valve remains closed unless the system pressure exceeds that for which the valve is adjusted. At this time the valve

opens and allows the fluid to flow through a return line to the reservoir.

A drawing to illustrate the construction of a relief valve is shown in Fig. 9-22. During normal operation, the valve is on its seat and fluid flows from the IN port to the OUT port without restriction. As the pressure on the line increases to a level above that for which the valve spring is adjusted, the valve lifts off its seat and the fluid then flows through the valve and out the return line. The pressure at which the relief valve lifts is called the "cracking pressure." The design of the valve must be such that it will not rapidly open and close and cause chattering, since this would damage the system. Relief valves are used to control maximum system pressure and to control pressure in various parts of the subsystems. For example, a relief valve, called a **wing-flap overload valve,** is often placed in the DOWN line of the wing-flap subsystem to prevent lowering of the flaps at too high an airspeed. The pressure in the DOWN line will rise above a specified level because of air pressure against the wing flaps if the airspeed is too great. The wing-flap overload valve will then open and allow excess pressure to be re-

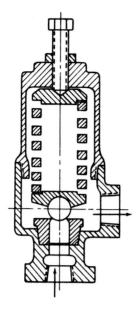

FIG. 9-22 Construction of a relief valve.

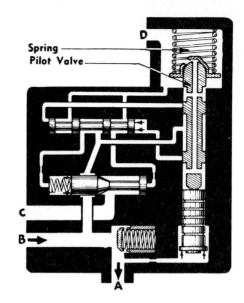

FIG. 9-23 An unloading-type pressure regulator.

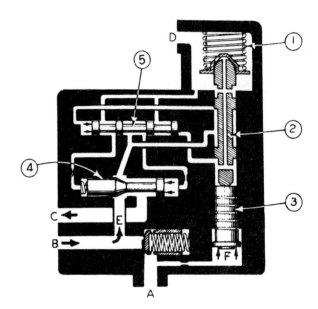

FIG. 9-24 Unloading valve in the "kicked-out" position.

lieved, thus causing the down movement of the flaps to stop.

When several relief valves are incorporated in a hydraulic system, they should be adjusted in a sequence which will permit each valve to reach its operating pressure. Thus, the highest-pressure valves should be adjusted first, the others in the order of descending pressure values.

Pressure Regulators

A **pressure regulator** is designed to maintain a certain range of pressures within a hydraulic system. Usually the pressure regulator is designed to relieve the pressure on the pressure pump when it is not needed for operating a unit in the system. Some pressure regulators are also called **unloading valves,** because they *unload* the pump when hydraulic pressure is not required for operation of landing gear, flaps, or other subsystems. Continuous pressure on the pump increases wear and the possibility of failure.

A pressure regulator which is also an unloading valve is illustrated in Fig. 9-23. In this view, the unit is operating to supply fluid for charging an accumulator (hydraulic-pressure storage chamber) and to supply fluid pressure for operating units in the system. Fluid flows into port *B* and out of port *A* to the system. The check valve is off its seat because of the fluid pressure being exerted by the pressure pump. When the pressure in the accumulator builds up to the maximum level for the system, the same pressure is exerted in chamber *F*, Fig. 9-24. This pressure moves the plunger (piston) (3) upward to raise the **pilot valve** (2) against the pressure of the spring (1). In Fig. 9-23, observe that fluid pressure is applied to one of the pilot-valve chambers through a passage from the inlet line, around an annular groove surrounding the unloading valve [(4) in Fig. 9-24], and to the pilot valve. As the pilot valve is raised, this pressure is ported and

directed through a passage to the left end of the **directional spool** (5). This spool moves to the right and causes hydraulic pressure to be directed against the right end of the unloading spool, thus moving it to the left. This permits the main flow of fluid to go from port *B*, through passage *E*, and out the return port *C*. Under this condition the power pump is unloaded because the fluid has free flow back to the reservoir. The regulator is said to be "kicked-out" in this position. The check valve has seated because of spring pressure and holds the pressure locked in the system. In the drawings, port *D* is the "bleed-off" port which permits fluid from the chambers at the ends of the directional spool and unloading spool escape and allow movement of the spools as required.

When a subsystem is operated and fluid pressure in the pressurized part of the system drops to a predetermined level, the pilot valve and plunger will move back to the lower position, directing pressure against the right end of the directional spool as shown in Fig. 9-25. The directional spool moves to the left and causes fluid pressure to be directed to the left end of the unloading spool, moving it to the right and blocking the return line. Pump pressure then builds up and opens the check valve (bullet valve) to allow fluid flow to the operating system through port A. This position is often referred to as "kicked-in."

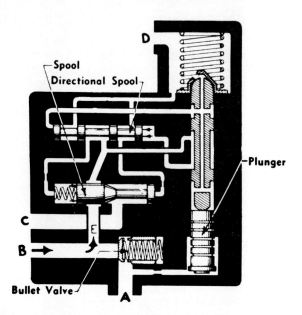

FIG. 9-25 Moving to the "kicked-in" position.

Another type of pressure regulator which serves a purpose similar to the one just described is the Bendix balanced type. A drawing of this regulator in the "kicked-in" position is shown in Fig. 9-26. In this drawing, the bypass valve E is held closed by spring pressure and system pressure. Fluid from the power pump enters at port F, and the pressure forces the check valve G off its seat and allows the fluid to flow out port H to the accumulator and the system. When the system operating requirements are met, the pressure continues to build up from the pump and throughout the area in operation. This pressure bears against the poppet valve I and also increases above the piston N because of the sensing line O. The piston N has greater area than the poppet valve I; hence the force downward increases faster than the force upward. At a certain point the force downward becomes equal to the force upward and the valve is then said to be in the **balanced** condition. As pressure continues to increase, the downward force becomes greater than the upward force and the rod M moves downward against the force of the spring L. The hollow piston rod M moves downward and contacts the poppet valve, thus forcing it off its seat. Pressure fluid then can flow through the passage K to act against the directional valve C which pushes the bypass valve E off its seat. When this occurs, pressure fluid entering port F can flow out through port D to the reservoir and the pressure entering the port F drops to the free-flow level. Check valve G is then immediately seated by spring pressure to trap the high pressure in the system. This is the "kicked-out" position, and it is illustrated in Fig. 9-27.

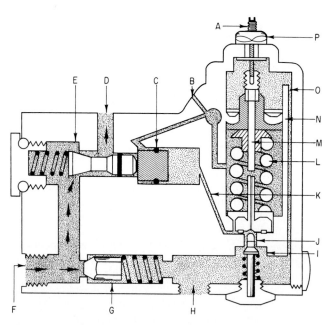

FIG. 9-27 Bendix pressure regulator in the "kicked-out" position.

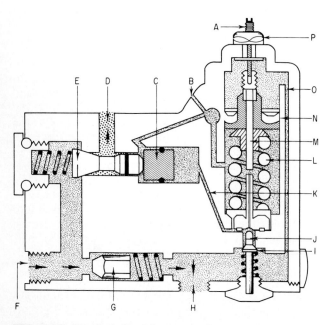

FIG. 9-26 Bendix balanced-type regulator.

For proper operation, the regulator should remain in the kicked-out position until the pressure in the system has dropped to the lower operating level. This it will do, because the pressure for the initial kick-out was great enough to overcome the force of the spring L and the pressure against the poppet I. Since the poppet has been lifted from its seat, the only force necessary to keep the valve in the kicked-out position is that on the piston N acting against the spring L. Therefore, the pressure in the system will drop substantially before the valve kicks in again.

The kick-out pressure of the valve is adjusted by turning the adjusting screw A. This changes the effect length of the rod below the piston and changes the amount of force necessary to bring about the kicked-out condition.

Thermal Relief Valves

A **thermal relief valve** is similar to a regular system relief valve; however, such valves are installed in parts of the hydraulic system where fluid pressure is trapped and may need to be relieved because of the increase caused by higher temperatures. During the flight of an airplane, it is quite likely that fluid in many of the hydraulic lines will be at a low temperature. When the airplane lands, this cold fluid will be trapped in the landing-gear system, the flap system, and other systems, because selector valves are in the neutral or OFF position. The fluid-temperature increase owing to warm air on the ground results in fluid expansion and could cause damage unless thermal relief valves are incorporated in the systems. Thermal relief valves are adjusted to pressures which are above those required for the operation of the systems; hence they do not interfere with normal operation.

Debooster Valve

In some hydraulic systems, it is desired to reduce system pressure to some lower pressure for operation of a particular unit. Typical of such pressure-reduction devices is the **debooster** employed in some brake systems. Such a valve operates by the differential area of two pistons. If a small-area piston is connected by a rod to a large-area piston, the two pistons will be capable of developing pressure in inverse proportion to their areas. Figure 9-28 illustrates the debooster principle. If the area of the small piston is 1 in² [6.45 cm²] and the area of the large piston is 4 in² [25.8 cm²], the large piston can transmit a pressure of only one-quarter that of the small piston. When 1000 psi [6895 kPa] is applied to the small piston, a force of 1000 lb [4448 N] will be exerted through the rod to the large piston. Since the large piston has a 4-in² [25.8-cm²] area, a force of 1000 lb [4448 N] will develop a pressure of only 250 psi [1723.8 kPa] in the large cylinder. In actual practice the construction of the debooster valve is more complex than that shown in the drawing; however, the principle of operation is as explained.

Other types of pressure reducers employ springs and pistons to cause a reduction in pressure. Such pressure-reducing valves utilize springs to create the pressure differential required. For example, if a spring-controlled valve is adjusted to open and relieve all pressure above a given level, the pressure transmitted to an actuating cylinder will be effectively reduced.

● ACCUMULATORS

An **accumulator** is basically a chamber for storing hydraulic fluid under pressure. It can serve one or more purposes. It dampens pressure surges caused by the operation of an actuator. It can aid or supplement the system pump when several units are operating at the same time and the demand is beyond the pump's capacity. An accumulator can also store power for limited operation of a component if the pump is not operating. Finally, it can supply fluid under pressure to make up for small system leaks that would cause the system to cycle continuously between high and low pressure. In this section we shall discuss three types of accumulators.

Diaphragm-type Accumulator

Since hydraulic fluid is incompressible, practically speaking, some means is necessary to provide sustained pressure on the fluid if effective energy storage is to be attained. For this purpose compressed air or an inert gas is used. The usual construction of the accumulator is such that a volume of compressed air is applied to a volume of fluid so the fluid will continue to be under pressure. The fluid and air are separated by a diaphragm so air cannot enter the hydraulic system.

The **diaphragm-type accumulator** consists of a sphere separated by a synthetic-rubber diaphragm as shown in Fig. 9-29. The sphere is constructed in two parts which are joined by means of screw threads. At the bottom of the sphere is an air valve, such as a Schrader valve, and at the top is a fitting for the hydraulic line. A screen is placed at the fluid outlet inside the sphere to prevent the diaphragm from being pressed into the fluid outlet.

During operation of the accumulator, the air chamber is **preloaded** or **charged** with air pressure approximately one-third maximum system pressure. As soon as a very small amount of fluid is forced into the fluid side of the accumulator, the system pressure gauge will show the pressure in the air chamber. This provides a means for checking the **air charge** (pressure) in the accumulator. If the system is inactive and the main pressure gauge shows zero pressure, a few strokes of the hand pump will cause the pressure gauge to rise suddenly to the charge pressure in the accumulator. The accumulator charge can also be checked by the reverse method. For example, if the system gauge shows a pressure of 1500 psi [10 342.5 kPa] when the system pump is not operating and the brakes are depressed and released a number of times, the pressure will decrease to the accumulator charge pressure and then will suddenly fall to zero.

It should be noted that some aircraft hydraulic systems monitor the hydraulic pressure by indicating the

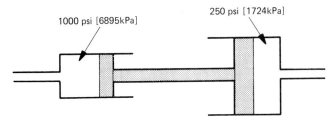

1000 psi [6895kPa]

250 psi [1724kPa]

FIG. 9-28 Principle of the debooster.

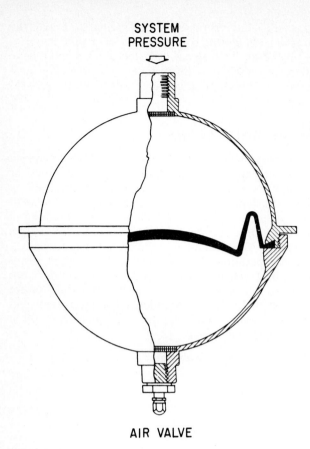

AIR VALVE

FIG. 9-29   A diaphragm-type accumulator.

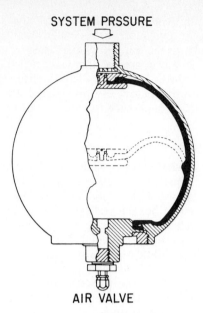

SYSTEM PRSSURE

AIR VALVE

FIG. 9-30   A bladder-type accumulator.

pressure on the air side of the accumulator. When the system has no hydraulic pressure, the gauge for the system indicates the accumulator air pressure. As soon as the hydraulic pressure is greater than the air charge, the air is compressed to the value of the hydraulic system.

Bladder-type Accumulator

The **bladder-type accumulator** usually consists of a metal sphere in which a bladder is installed to separate the air and the hydraulic fluid. The bladder serves as the air chamber, and the space outside the bladder contains the hydraulic fluid. The construction of a bladder-type accumulator is shown in Fig. 9-30. The air valve is at the bottom of the sphere, the fluid port is at the top. Initially, the bladder is charged with air pressure as specified in the aircraft manual. When fluid is forced into the accumulator, the bladder collapses to the extent necessary to make space for the fluid, depending upon the fluid pressure. As long as fluid is in the accumulator, the air pressure is at the same level as the fluid pressure.

Piston-type Accumulator

Many modern hydraulic systems employ **piston-type accumulators** because they require less space than an equivalent spherical accumulator. A piston-type accumulator is shown in Fig. 9-31. Note that this unit consists of a cylinder with a free piston inside to separate the air from the hydraulic fluid. The piston is

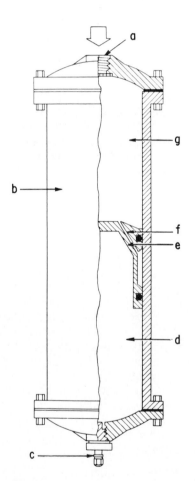

a. Fluid port	d. Air chamber
b. Cylinder	e. Piston assembly
c. High-pressure air valve	f. Drilled passage
g. Fluid chamber	

FIG. 9-31   A piston-type accumulator.

equipped with seals which effectively prevent the air from leaking into the fluid chamber and vice versa.

Servicing Accumulators

Accumulators should be checked for proper air charge at regular intervals. With no hydraulic pressure on the system the accumulator should have a charge of between one-third and one-half of the system's operating hydraulic pressure. Specific values are given by the aircraft manufacturer. Many accumulators are equipped with permanent pressure gauges, while some require the use of a hand-held gauge.

If the accumulator must be charged, hydraulic pressure is removed from the system and the accumulator is charged. Nitrogen is the gas commonly used, but dry air may be used in some cases.

Removal and Installation of Accumulators

Great care must be exercised in the servicing and repair of hydraulic systems. This is particularly true of the high-pressure systems which operate at pressures in excess of 3000 psi [20 685 kPa]. Before an accumulator or any other unit is removed, the mechanic must make certain that all the pressure in the system has been relieved. This is accomplished by operating one of the subsystems until all pressure is gone, and the main pressure gauge reads zero pressure. The air pressure in the accumulator is reduced to zero by opening the air valve in accordance with the manufacturer's instructions. The accumulator can then be disconnected; however, provision should be made for fluid drainage. If the system contains a synthetic, fire-resistant fluid, such as Skydrol 500, the fluid must not be permitted to drain onto painted areas or other parts where the fluid can cause damage.

The installation of an accumulator is usually the reverse of removal. The air chamber of the accumulator is downward when the accumulator is installed. Sometimes the air charge is placed in the accumulator before installation. In any event, the manufacturer's instructions should be followed. Particular care must be taken to see that all seals, valves, and fittings are of the proper type for the fluid being used in the system.

If hydraulic fluid is found in the air chamber of an accumulator, there is a leak between the two chambers. In such cases, the accumulator must be removed and repaired.

● SELECTOR VALVES

Selector valves are used to direct the flow of hydraulic fluid to or from a component and achieve the desired operation. These valves fall into one of four general types: rotary, poppet, spool or piston, and open-center-system selector valves. The valves may be positioned by the pilot directly, by an electrical or electronic control, by hydraulic pressure, or by pneumatic pressure.

Rotary Valve

When a **rotary four-way valve** is in the position shown in Fig. 9-32 (a), the fluid will be flowing from the valve at the top port and will cause the actuating cylinder to be extended. When the valve is rotated 90° as in Fig. 9-32 (b), the fluid to and from the actuating cylinder will be in the opposite direction, and the cylinder will retract.

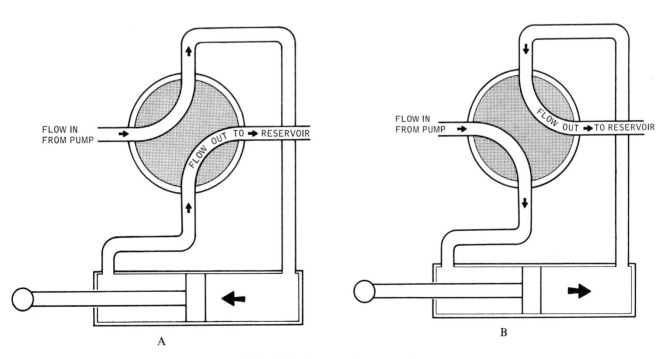

FIG. 9-32 A rotary four-way valve.

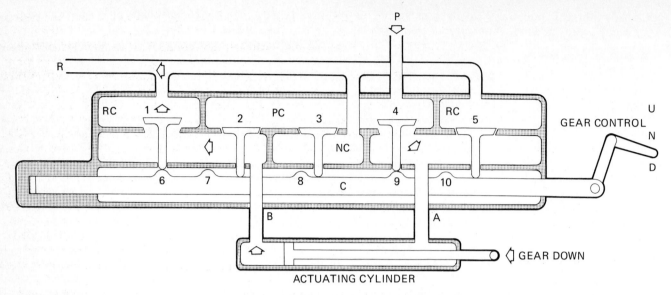

FIG. 9-33 Poppet-type four-way valve.

Poppet Valve

Another type of flow-control valve is shown in Fig. 9-33. The valve is shown operating a landing gear system. This type of valve can be used to operate an actuator for any aircraft system. In this valve assembly, individual **poppet valves** are used to open and close the ports to change the direction of fluid flow. The valves are operated by cam lobes on cam rod C. Fluid enters the valve through line P from the pressure pump, and with the gear control in the DOWN position, it passes through open valve 4 and on to the actuating cylinder. As the piston moves to the left, fluid from the left end of the actuating cylinder flows through passage B and open valve 1 to the return chamber and back to the reservoir through the return line R.

If the gear-control handle is placed in the neutral position, cam lobe 8 will open poppet valve 3, and cam lobes 6 and 9 will close poppet valves 1 and 4, assuming, of course, that the poppets are equipped with springs which keep them closed unless they are lifted by a cam lobe. When poppet valve 3 is open, fluid flow will pass from the pressure chamber PC to the neutral chamber NC and from thence to the return manifold, thus permitting the fluid to flow freely and thereby reducing the load on the pressure pump. In the neutral position, valves 2 and 5 are closed because cam lobes 7 and 10 are not yet in position to open them.

When the gear control handle is placed in the UP position, valves 2 and 5 will be open and the others will be closed. Fluid will therefore flow through poppet valve 2 and out the passage B to the left end of the actuating cylinder. The piston will move to the right and force fluid through passage A and poppet valve 5 to the return chamber and return line to the reservoir.

Some poppet valve assemblies are arranged with valves in a radial position, and they are opened and closed by means of a rotary cam unit. The results are the same in any case. Poppet valves are also manu-factured with electric controls, and the individual valves are opened and closed by means of solenoids.

Spool or Piston Selector Valves

A schematic drawing of a typical **spool-type selector valve** is shown in Fig. 9-34. The three positions of the

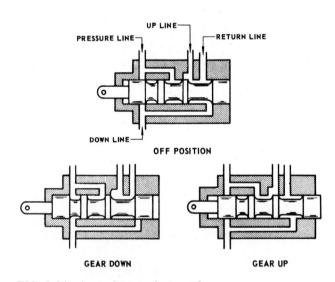

FIG. 9-34 A spool-type selector valve.

valve are shown to illustrate the passages for fluid in the OFF, DOWN, and UP positions. Note that there is no fluid flow when the valve is in the OFF position; hence the valve must be used in a system where a pressure regulator or variable delivery pump is employed. Otherwise a high pressure would build up and cause excessive wear or other damage to the pressure pump. The use of this valve is not restricted to landing gear systems.

A simple **piston-type selector valve** is illustrated in the drawing of Fig. 9-35. In the first drawing, the valve

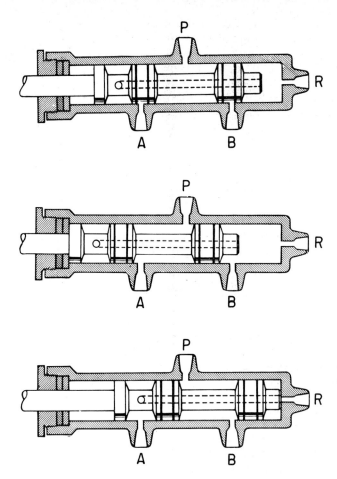

FIG. 9-35 A piston-type selector valve.

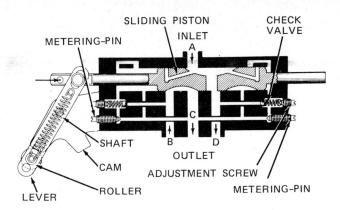

FIG. 9-36 An open-center system selector valve.

The valve illustrated in Fig. 9-36 consists of a housing which has four ports, a piston, two metering pins, two relief valves, and a spring-loaded roller and cam-arrangement which is attached to the end of the piston. The roller and cam arrangement is designed to hold the piston in either the operating position after it has been engaged or the neutral position.

In the illustration the sliding piston is in one of the two operating positions. The sliding piston has been moved manually to the right and is held in position by the spring-loaded cam mechanism. Fluid under pressure flows from the inlet port A through port D to one side of the hydraulic actuating piston, moving the actuating piston to its fully extended or retracted position. Fluid returning from the opposite side of the piston enters the selector valve at B and discharges through the return port C to the reservoir.

Figure 9-37 shows the same valve in the neutral position where it is held by the lever and cam arrange-

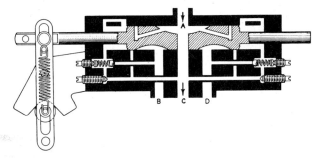

FIG. 9-37 Open-center selector valve in the neutral position.

is in the OFF position, and fluid flow is blocked because both port A and port B are blocked by the piston. In the second view, port A is open to allow fluid to flow out to an actuating cylinder; the return flow from the cylinder enters port B and flows out port R to the reservoir. The third view shows the reverse position where fluid flows out port B and back through port A. The center of the piston rod is provided with a drilled passage which allows the return fluid to flow to the right and out through the return port R.

Open-Center-System Selector Valve

The details of an open-center hydraulic system are given later in this chapter; however, it is important to understand that in this type of system all selector valves are connected in series to a common fluid supply and return line. The valve shown in Fig. 9-33 is suitable for an open-center system.

Like other forms of selector valves, the **open-center selector valve** provides a means of directing hydraulic fluid under pressure to one end of an actuating cylinder and of simultaneously directing fluid from the opposite end of the actuating cylinder to the return line. The advantage is that the valve automatically returns to neutral when the actuating cylinder reaches the end of its stroke. The fluid output of the power pump is directed through this valve to the reservoir when the valve is in neutral position.

ment. The position of the lever, which rotates about the shaft, is determined by the position of the roller which rolls on the cam. In the neutral position, the inlet port A is connected directly to the return port C, thus allowing the fluid to flow freely through the valve.

The valve is automatically returned to the neutral position by action of fluid pressure which opens the relief valve and admits fluid pressure to the end of the piston. This pressure forces the valve piston back to the neutral position. The action takes place for either position of the valve.

● AUTOMATIC-OPERATING CONTROL VALVES

An automatic-operating control valve is one that is designed to operate without being positioned or activated by any force outside of the hydraulic fluid pressure or flow. These valves are located in line with the system flow and function to perform operations such as prevent or restrict flow in a line, allow flow at the proper time, and change control of components between independent pressure systems.

Orifice or Restrictor Valves

An **orifice** is merely an aperture, opening, perforation, passage, or hole. A **restrictor** can be described as an orifice or similar to an orifice. A **variable restrictor** is an orifice which can be changed in size so its effect can be altered. The size of a fixed orifice must remain constant, whereas a variable restrictor permits adjustment to meet changing requirements.

The purpose of an orifice, or a variable restrictor, is to limit the rate of flow of the fluid in a hydraulic line. In limiting the rate of flow, the orifice causes the mechanism being operated by the system to move more slowly.

Figure 9-38 is a drawing of an orifice. This form of the device is merely a fitting which contains a small passage and which has threaded ends. When fluid enters the IN port, which is the larger of the two ports, the fluid flows through the central passage and out through the OUT port, which is the smaller of the two ports, thus limiting the rate of flow. An orifice of this construction may be placed in a hydraulic line between a selector valve and an actuating cylinder to slow the rate of movement of the actuating cylinder.

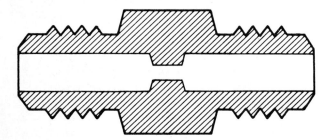

FIG. 9-38   Drawing of an orifice.

Figure 9-39 is a drawing of a **variable restrictor.** In this drawing, there are two horizontal ports and a vertical, adjustable needle valve. The size of the passage through which the hydraulic fluid must flow may be adjusted by screwing the needle valve in or out. The fact that the passage can be varied in size is the feature that distinguishes the variable restrictor from the simple fixed orifice.

Check Valves

It is often necessary to prevent hydraulic-fluid flow in one direction while permitting free flow in the opposite direction. The **check valve** is designed to accom-

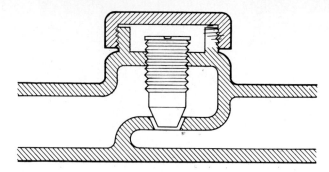

FIG. 9-39   A variable restrictor.

plish this purpose. The construction of a simple ball check valve is shown in Fig. 9-40. Fluid pressure at port A will tend to push the ball off its seat and allow the fluid to flow through the valve. When the pressure is applied at port B, the ball will hold firmly on its seat and prevent the flow of fluid. Check valves are used as individual units in hydraulic systems and they are also used as components of more complex valves and devices to control the flow of fluid in a given direction.

During the installation of a check valve, the mechanic must observe the direction of flow indicated on the body of the valve. Usually there is an arrow on the body or case of the valve to show the direction of the free fluid flow.

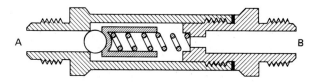

FIG. 9-40   A ball check valve.

Orifice Check Valve

An **orifice check valve** is designed to provide free flow of hydraulic fluid in one direction and restricted flow in the opposite direction. One of the most common applications of this device is in the UP line of a landing-gear system. Since landing gear is usually quite heavy, it tends to fall too rapidly upon lowering, unless some means of restricting its movement is utilized. Since the UP line of a landing-gear actuating cylinder is the return line for hydraulic fluid from the actuating cylinder to the reservoir, any restriction in this line will limit the movement of the gear. That is, the gear movement must await the flow of the return fluid as it moves toward the down position. An orifice check valve is also used for certain flap control systems. Because of the air pressure on the flaps during flight, there is a continuous force tending to raise the flaps to a streamline position. It is therefore advisable in some systems to restrict the UP movement by placing an orifice check valve in the DOWN line of the flap system.

The construction of an orifice check valve is illustrated in Fig. 9-41. When the valve is on its seat, fluid flow can occur only through the center orifice, but

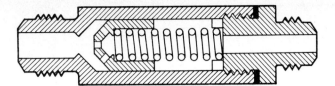

FIG. 9-41 Construction of an orifice check valve.

when the fluid flow is in the opposite direction, the valve moves off its seat and there is free flow of the hydraulic fluid through multiple openings.

The improper installation of an orifice check valve in a landing-gear system can cause serious problems. If the valve is installed in the reverse position, the movement of the landing gear is restricted as the gear is raised, but there is free flow as it is lowered. The hydraulic pressure in the system plus the force of gravity causes the gear to lower with excessive speed; when it reaches the end of its travel, the inertial forces are likely to damage the aircraft structure because of the sudden stop.

Metering Check Valve

A **metering check valve,** sometimes called a **one-way restrictor,** serves the same purpose as an orifice check valve. However, the metering check valve is adjustable while an orifice check valve is not.

A drawing of a metering check valve is shown in Fig. 9-42. This unit has a housing, a metering pin, and

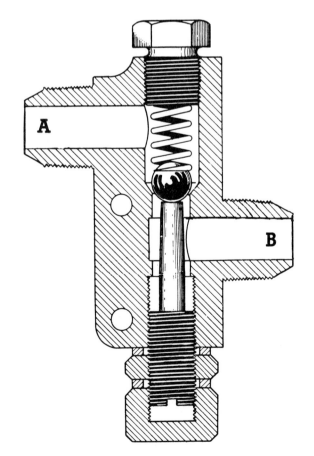

FIG. 9-42 A metering check valve.

a check-valve assembly. The pin is adjusted to hold the ball slightly off its seat. When fluid enters port *B*, it forces the ball away from its seat and then flows out through port *A* to the actuating cylinder. When the flow of fluid is reversed, the fluid entering from the actuating cylinder flows through the tiny opening between the ball and its seat, thus restricting the flow. By adjusting the metering pin in or out with a screwdriver, the rate at which the fluid can return from the actuating cylinder is controlled because the position of the metering pin changes the width of the opening between the ball and its seat.

Hydraulic Fuse

The **hydraulic fuse** shown in Fig. 9-43 is a device designed to seal off a broken hydraulic line and prevent excessive loss of fluid. It permits normal flow in a line; but if the flow increases above an established level, the valve in the fuse closes the line and prevents further flow.

In reference to the figure, fluid enters the fuse through the passage at the right and flows between the outer case and the inner cylinder. It then passes through cutouts in the left end of the inner cylinder and out through the center opening. At the right end of the inner cylinder is a metering orifice, which permits a small amount of fluid to enter the cylinder behind the poppet valve. During normal operation the pressure of this fluid is approximately the same as the pressure on the opposite side of this poppet; hence there is no movement of the poppet. As fluid flow increases, the pressure differential across the poppet also increases. If this differential becomes excessive, the poppet moves to the left and closes the exit port of the fuse, thus stopping the fluid flow. The fuse remains closed only as long as a substantial pressure differential exists. If the pressure differential decreases to a certain predetermined level, the spring unseats the poppet and permits normal flow to resume.

Sequence Valve

A **sequence valve** is sometimes called a **timing valve** because it times certain hydraulic operations in proper sequence. This unit has been called a "load-and-fire" check valve, although **sequence valve** is the correct term. A common example of the use of this valve is in a landing-gear system where the landing-gear doors must be opened before the gear is extended, and the gear must be retracted before the doors are closed.

Figure 9-44 is a drawing of a sequence valve. It is essentially a bypass check valve that is automatically operated. There is a free flow of hydraulic fluid from port *A* to port *B,* but the flow from *B* to *A* is prevented unless the ball is unseated by depressing the plunger.

Figure 9-45 is a schematic diagram of a landing-gear system with sequence valves. During the retraction of the landing gear, the fluid flows under pump pressure from the selector valve to the landing-gear cylinder and to the sequence valve *A*. In this position, sequence valve *A* is closed, thus preventing the fluid from entering the door cylinder. As the landing-gear actuating-cylinder piston approaches the end of its travel, either the piston rod or some other part of the landing-gear

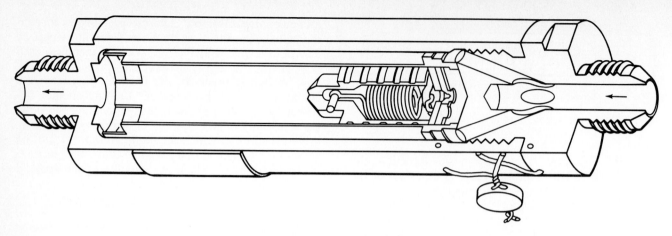

FIG. 9-43   A hydraulic fuse.

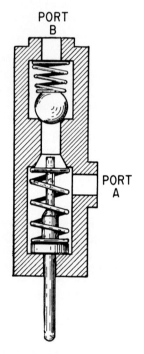

FIG. 9-44   A sequence valve.

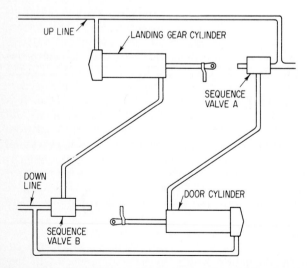

FIG. 9-45   Landing-gear system with sequence valves.

mechanism depresses the plunger of the sequence valve, thereby permitting the fluid to flow to the door actuating cylinder and to close the doors. The fluid displaced at the other end of the landing-gear actuating cylinder by the motion of the piston passes to the DOWN line through sequence valve *B*. The flow is not restricted, because it is flowing directly from port *A* to port *B* in the sequence valve illustrated in Fig. 9-44.

During the extension of the landing gear, the fluid under system pressure flows through the DOWN line and enters the door-actuating cylinder, but it is prevented from moving the landing-gear actuating-cylinder piston because sequence valve *B* is closed. However, when the door actuating-cylinder piston reaches the limit of its travel, the plunger on sequence valve *B* is depressed, and a passage is opened for the fluid to enter the landing-gear actuating cylinder and extend the gear. The fluid displaced by the motion of the door actuating-cylinder piston flows to the UP line through sequence valve *A* without restriction.

Sequence valves are sometimes used in conjunction with hydraulically operated landing-gear UP locks and DOWN locks. In such instances, the sequence valve either blocks the fluid from the landing-gear actuating cylinder until the unlocking cylinder (sometimes called the **unlatching jack**) has released the lock or prevents the fluid from entering the locking jack until the landing gear has reached its fully retracted or extended position. Sometimes the sequence valve and the unlocking jack are manufactured as one unit.

To illustrate the operation of a sequence valve in a landing-gear system, the drawing of Fig. 9-46 is provided. This drawing shows a view of the sequence valve in the open position. If the valve is installed with port *B* connected to the landing gear UP line and port *A* connected to the gear door actuating cylinder, fluid entering at port *B* cannot pass through to the actuating cylinder until the landing gear has been retracted and the valve plunger pressed in as shown in the drawing. Hence, the gear doors cannot be closed until the gear is retracted.

For the part of the system extending the landing gear, the sequence valve is installed with port *B* con-

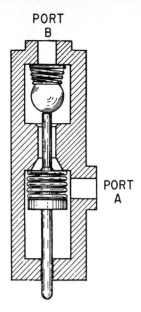

FIG. 9-46 Sequence valve in open position.

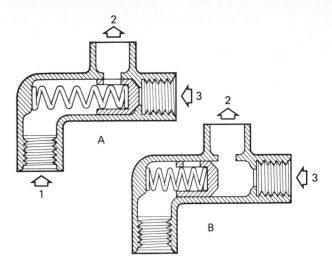

FIG. 9-47 Operation of a shuttle valve.

nected to the DOWN line of the landing-gear actuating cylinder. The plunger of the valve is not depressed until the gear doors are open; hence the gear cannot be extended until the door operation is nearly complete.

If, in the installation and adjustment of the landing-gear system, the sequence valves are not set correctly, it is possible for the landing gear to strike the gear doors. If the landing-gear mechanism hits the doors on either the up or down operation, it is quite likely that the sequence valve in one or the other lines is not adjusted correctly.

Shuttle Valves

Quite frequently in hydraulic systems it is necessary to provide alternate or emergency sources of power with which to operate critical parts of the system. This is particularly true of landing-gear systems in the case of hydraulic-pump failure. Sometimes the landing gear is operated by an emergency hand pump and sometimes by a volume of compressed air or gas stored in a high-pressure air bottle. In either case it is necessary to have a means of disconnecting the normal source of hydraulic power and connecting the emergency source of power. This is the function of the **shuttle valve.**

The operation of a shuttle valve is shown in the drawings of Fig. 9-47. Port 1 of the valve is the normal entrance for hydraulic fluid from the pressure system. Port 2 is the outlet leading to the DOWN line of the landing-gear actuating cylinder. In view A the valve is in the normal position with free passage of fluid from port 1 to port 2. If main system pressure fails and it is desired to lower the landing gear, the landing-gear selector valve is placed in the DOWN position and emergency pressure is applied to port 3. As explained previously, this pressure can come from an emergency pump or from a high-pressure air bottle. The emer-

gency pressure forces the shuttle valve to the left as in view B and opens port 2 to port 3; thus fluid or air is permitted to flow through the valve to the DOWN line of the actuating cylinder. Return fluid from the cylinder will flow through the normal UP line, back through the main selector valve, and to the reservoir.

The installation of a shuttle valve in the landing-gear system is shown in the schematic drawing of Fig. 9-48. The DOWN line is blocked when emergency pressure is applied, and emergency fluid or air enters the cylinder, flowing from port 3 to port 2 and into the actuating cylinder.

Priority Valve

A **priority valve** is a sequence valve that is operated by hydraulic pressure rather than by a mechanical means. This valve is used to allow one actuator to operate and complete its operation before allowing a second component to operate. This gives the first component a priority over the second, thus the name "priority valve." A priority valve is represented in Fig. 9-49, and a simplified system using a priority valve is shown in Fig. 9-50. When actuators A and B are both selected at the same time, pressure is available at the intersection of the lines. The priority valve in actuator B's line requires that full-system pressure be applied to it to overcome the spring that is holding the spool closed. Since fluid is flowing to actuator A, the pressure is below the operating value of the valve. Once actuator A has stopped moving and the hydraulic pressure is up to near full value, the poppet has enough pressure applied to it to offseat the spool valve and allow fluid to flow to actuator B. When fluid flows in the opposite direction, the seat shifts to the left and a free flow of fluid occurs.

While this has shown a priority valve used for sequencing, these valves are also used to give one component priority over another component in unrelated operations. For example, in some aircraft a priority valve is used to give the flight control actuators priority to system pressure over the landing gear and flap systems.

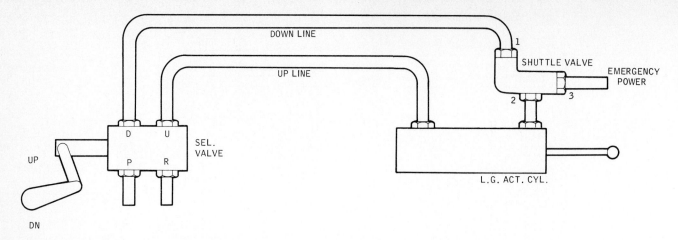

FIG. 9-48 Location of a shuttle valve in a landing-gear system.

(A) INSUFFICIENT PRESSURE

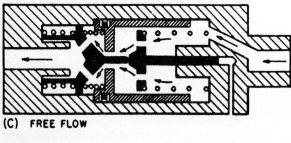

(B) FULL PRESSURE

(C) FREE FLOW

FIG. 9-49 A priority valve.

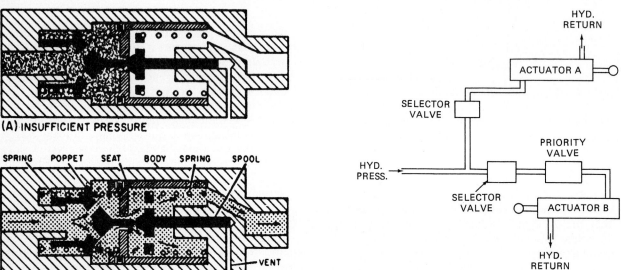

FIG. 9-50 Location of priority valve in a system.

FIG. 9-51 Hydraulic actuating cylinders.

HYDRAULIC ACTUATORS

Hydraulic actuators are devices for converting hydraulic pressure to mechanical motion (work) or power. The most commonly utilized actuator is the **actuating cylinder;** however, **servo actuators** and **hy-**

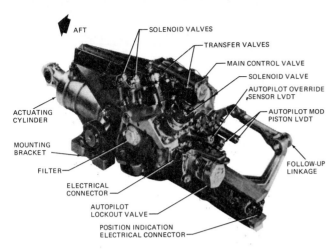

FIG. 9-52 A servo actuator.

draulic motors are also employed for special applications where modified motion is required. Actuating cylinders, sometimes called "jacks," are used for direct and positive movement such as retracting and extending landing gear and the extension and retraction of wing flaps, spoilers, and slats. Servo actuators are employed in situations where accurately controlled intermediate positions of units are required. The servo unit feeds back position information to the pilot's control, thus making it possible for the pilot to select any control position required. The servo actuator is used to move large control surfaces such as the rudder,

elevator, and ailerons. Servo units are also used to aid the pilot in the operation of cyclic and collective pitch controls in a helicopter.

Actuating Cylinders

The design of actuating cylinders is determined by the functions which they are to perform. Different types of actuating cylinders are shown in Fig. 9-51. The cylinder shown in Fig. 9-51 (a) is a **single-acting** cylinder. Hydraulic pressure is applied to one side of the piston to provide force in one direction only. When hydraulic pressure is removed from the piston, a return spring moves the piston to its start position.

A **double-acting** actuating cylinder is designed so hydraulic pressure can be applied to both sides of the piston. Thus, the cylinder can provide force in either direction. A double-acting cylinder is shown in Fig. 9-51 (b). This type of cylinder is used for the operation of retractable landing gear, wing flaps, spoilers, etc.

Many variations of the basic actuator cylinder have been designed, usually for special applications. The mechanic will find information on these in the applicable manufacturer's maintenance manuals.

Servo Actuators

A servo actuator is designed to provide hydraulic power to aid the pilot in the movement of various aircraft controls. Such actuators usually include an actuating cylinder, a multiport flow control valve, check valves, and relief valves together with connecting linkages. Figures 9-52 and 9-53 show the compo-

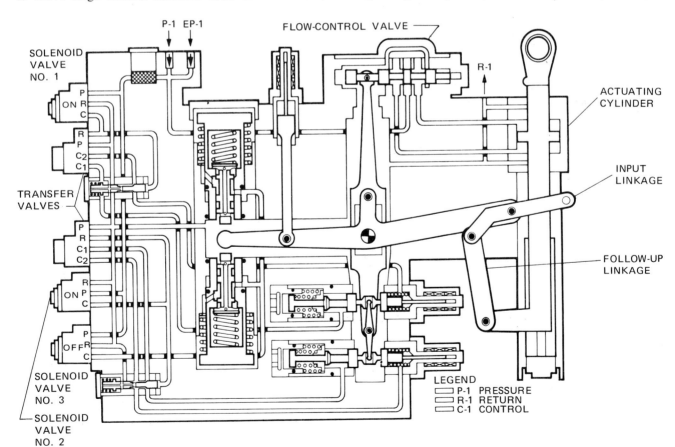

FIG. 9-53 A servo actuator.

nents of a servo actuator. When the pilot moves a cockpit control in a particular direction, force is applied to the flow control valve in the actuator, causing it to direct fluid pressure to the actuating cylinder. The piston in the actuating cylinder moves in a direction to assist the pilot in moving the flight control. As the piston moves to the position called for by the pilot's control, the linkage between the piston and the flow control valve moves the flow control valve back to a neutral position and stops the flow of hydraulic fluid and hence the movement of the piston. The reverse action takes place when the pilot moves the cockpit control in the opposite direction.

Hydraulic Motors

A hydraulic motor is illustrated in Fig. 9-54. Note that the motor is almost identical to the multiple-piston

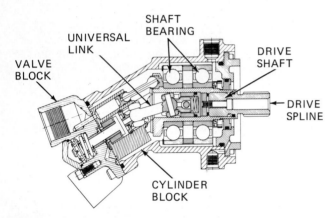

FIG. 9-54   A hydraulic motor.

hydraulic pump described previously. When hydraulic fluid pressure is applied to the input port, it forces the pistons downward in the cylinders. Since the cylinder block axis is at an angle to the axis of the output shaft, the extension of the piston rods causes both the cylinder block and the output shaft to rotate. The two assemblies are connected by a universal linkage at the center. As each piston reaches its fullest extension, the cylinder is rotated past the input slot in the valve plate and on to the return slot. The piston is then moved inward in the cylinder, and the hydraulic fluid is discharged to the return line. The hydraulic motor's rpm depends upon hydraulic fluid pressure and the load on the motor.

A hydraulic motor has the advantage over an electric motor of being able to operate through a wide range of speeds from 0 rpm to the maximum for the particular motor. Variable-speed electric motors can provide some flexibility in the rate of actuation; however, they lose efficiency as speed decreases.

● HYDRAULIC FILTERS

Hydraulic filters are required to filter out any particles which may enter the hydraulic fluid. These particles may enter the system when it is being serviced or during wear of operating components. If these con-

taminants were allowed to remain in the circulating fluid, they could damage the seals and cylinder walls, causing internal leakage and prevent components such as check valves from seating properly. The number and location of filters in a hydraulic system depend on the model aircraft, but they are normally found at the inlet and outlet of the reservoir and the pump outlet. Commonly used filters are of the micronic type and porous metal type.

A **micronic filter** contains a treated paper element to trap particles in the fluid as the fluid flows through the element. The micron filters can be designed to filter out particles as small as 3 micrometers (μm). (A micrometer is equal to 0.0000394 in or 0.0001 mm.) A micron filter assembly is shown in cutaway in Fig. 9-55.

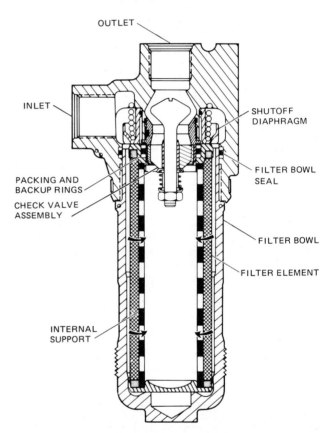

FIG. 9-55   A cutaway of a micron filter. (*Lockheed-California Co.*)

Porous metal filters are composed of metal particles joined together by a sintering process. These filters can trap particles as small as 5 μm in size.

Most modern filter assemblies are placed in line. They consist of a head assembly, a bowl assembly, and a filter element. The head assembly contains the fluid line connections, a bypass valve in case the filter becomes clogged, and, in some systems, a "pop-out" indicator to allow ready identification of a clogged filter. The bowl assembly is mounted on the bottom of the head assembly. This is the housing that contains the filter element. An exploded view of a filter is shown in Fig. 9-56.

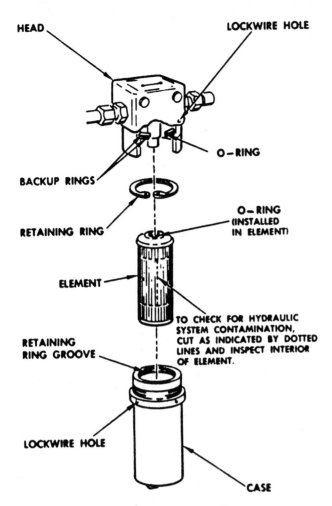

FIG. 9-56   Exploded view of a micron filter.

When filters are serviced, all pressure should be removed from the hydraulic system. When removing the bowl and element, care should be taken to prevent prolonged contact of the fluid with the aircraft, clothing, or skin—especially if a phosphate ester fluid is being used. If a micronic element is used, this is replaced with a new element and the old element can be opened to check for contamination. If a porous metal element is used, this should be cleaned or replaced in accordance with the appropriate service manual.

● HYDRAULIC PLUMBING COMPONENTS

As indicated previously, the various operating devices of a hydraulic system require tubing, fittings, seals, couplings, and hoses to transmit fluid pressure from unit to unit. To prevent leakage and ensure effective operation, various types of seals are employed. These are described in this section; however, there are so many different types that this section is limited to those that are likely to be encountered by the aircraft mechanic.

Seals and Packings

The purpose of hydraulic packing rings and seals is to prevent leakage of the hydraulic fluid and thereby preserve the pressure in the aircraft hydraulic system. Seals are installed in most of the units that contain moving parts, such as actuating cylinders, valves, and pumps. Packing rings, seals, or gaskets are made in a variety of shapes and sizes.

The handling, installation, and inspection of rings, seals, and gaskets in an aircraft hydraulic system are extremely important because a scratched or nicked packing ring may cause the failure of a unit in the system at a critical time.

Typical shapes for hydraulic packing rings, seals, and gaskets are shown in Fig. 9-57. These drawings show the standard O-ring seal, chevron seal, universal gasket, and crush washer.

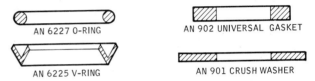

FIG. 9-57   Shapes for packing rings, seals, and gaskets.

The **O-ring** seal is probably the most common type used for sealing pistons and rods because it is effective in both directions. The O ring is easy to install and does not need to be adjusted. Care must be taken to see that the ring is the correct size in both ring diameter and cross-sectional diameter and that it is of the correct type of material. It should be examined to be sure that there are no cuts, nicks, or scratches on the surface which could permit leakage of fluid. When the ring is installed, it should be lubricated with hydraulic fluid of the type with which it is to be used. It should not be twisted or distorted after installation, or it will not seal effectively.

The O-ring seal should not be used alone in a system where the pressure is greater than 1500 psi [10 342.5 kPa]. If the hydraulic pressure is too great, the ring can become pinched between the moving part and stationary part of the unit, thus damaging the ring and destroying the seal. When the O ring is used in higher-pressure systems, **backup rings** (nonextrusion devices) are installed. Where the pressure is exerted alternately in each direction, these backup rings are installed on both sides of the O ring. They are usually made of Teflon.

The V-shaped (chevron) seal and the U-shaped seal must be installed with the same care as that used for other types of seals. The size of the seal must be correct and there must be no nicks, scratches, or other damage on the seals. When high pressure is exerted in only one direction, one set of seals is sufficient, but when the pressure is alternately applied, first in one direction and then in the other, two sets of seals are required because this type of seal works effectively in only one direction. The installation of a dual set of chevron seals is shown in Fig. 9-58.

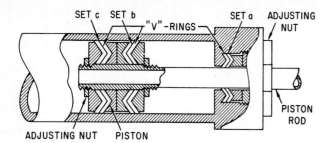

FIG. 9-58 Installation of a dual set of chevron seals.

The general procedure to follow in installing V-shaped or U-shaped seals is as follows:

1. Install one ring at a time, being sure that it is seated properly. Never install such rings in sets.

2. Use shim stock (very thin metal sheet) to protect the packing rings if the packing crosses sharp edges or threads. The shim stock should be from 0.003 to 0.010 in [0.076 to 0.254 mm] thick. It is rolled and then placed over the threads or sharp edges. After the packing is installed, the shim stock is removed.

3. If the unit in which the packing is being installed does not have an adjustable packing gland nut, insert metal shims of graduated thickness behind the adapters to hold the packing securely in place.

4. If the unit in which the packing is being installed has an adjustable packing gland, adjust the gland nut until the V-ring stack is held together firmly but not squeezed. The gland nut is then loosened to the first lock point.

5. Whenever possible, the mechanic should check the unit by hand for free operation after installation before the hydraulic pressure is applied.

6. In all cases, the mechanic should consult the manufacturer's instructions regarding the installation of seals.

Hydraulic Tubing

The metal tubing used in hydraulic systems must be of sufficient strength to withstand the pressures to which it may be subjected. For hydraulic systems in which a pressure of 1500 psi [10 342.5 kPa] will be exceeded, corrosion-resistant (stainless-steel) or titanium tubing is often used for the high-pressure sections of the system. In other parts of the system, such as the return lines and the pump suction lines, aluminum-alloy tubing is satisfactory. A generally suitable alloy is 5052, hardened in accordance with manufacturer's requirements.

Metal tubing installed in aircraft hydraulic systems should be free from scratches, dents, nicks, wrinkles, or any other defect which will either limit the flow of fluid or lead eventually to tube failure. It must be remembered that hydraulic fluid under high pressure contains great energy and can cause considerable injury or damage if suddenly released through the failure of a tube or fitting. This is particularly true of high-pressure systems where the pressure is often higher than 3000 psi [20 685 kPa].

Certain tolerances are permitted to allow for very minor defects in tubing. For example, a small amount of flattening in bends is acceptable, provided the smaller diameter of the tube is not less than 75 percent of the original outside diameter. A smooth dent is allowable if it is not in the heel of a bend and if it is not deeper than 20 percent of the diameter of the tube.

Aluminum-alloy tubing which has nicks or scratches no deeper than 10 percent of the wall thickness of the tube and not in the heel of a bend, may be repaired by burnishing out the nick or scratch with hand tools. If tubing has severe die marks, seams, or splits, it should be replaced. Cracks or other defects in the flared end of tubing are also cause for rejection.

Where the damage of a section of tubing is severe and it is not economical to replace the entire section of tubing, a repair may be effected by cutting out the damaged section of tubing and replacing it with a new section made up to fit the space where the damaged tubing was removed. The new section is installed by means of standard tubing fittings of the type approved for the system. Where the section removed is very short, the space may be filled by means of the fittings only. In any case where a section of tube is cut out and a new section is inserted, care must be taken to see that no metal chips or particles get into the system. The cut ends of the tube should be smooth and clean before flaring or before installing flareless fittings. The inside of the tubing should be cleaned by drawing a piece of soft cloth through the tube with soft safety wire or a strong piece of string.

Except for very small diameter tubing, it is necessary to use a suitable bending tool for making bends in the tubing. Otherwise the tubing will flatten or wrinkle at the bend.

Tube Fittings

Tube fittings are assemblies for joining sections of tubing in a system and to hydraulic accessories. The most commonly used fittings are the standard **AN-type fittings,** examples of which are shown in Fig. 9-59, and **flareless fittings,** illustrated in Fig. 9-60.

An AN fitting is used for flared tubing and must include a body, sleeve, and nut for the complete assembly. The fitting itself is designed in a number of different shapes to provide for a variety of installations. For example, we may find straight fittings, T fittings, elbow fittings, and cross fittings, all in the

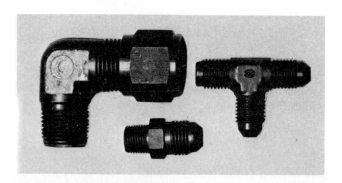

FIG. 9-59 Flare-type fittings.

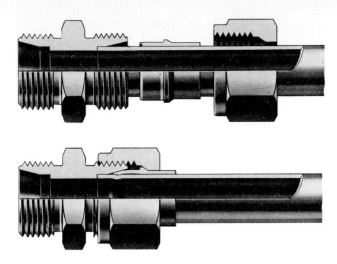

FIG. 9-60 Flareless fittings.

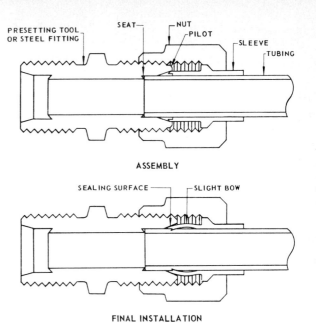

FIG. 9-62 Installation of flareless fittings.

same system. The hydraulic seal for a flared-tube fitting is formed between the flare cone on or within the fitting and the flare at the end of the tubing. The tube flare is pressed tightly against the flare cone by means of the sleeve and the nut.

When flare fittings are to be used, the tubing should be flared with a tool designed for the purpose. The standard angle for the flare is 37° as shown in Fig. 9-61. Care must be taken to avoid using tubing with the 45° automotive-type flare. To make a double flare, which is required for some installations, a special double-flaring tool is required.

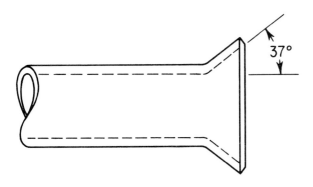

FIG. 9-61 Tubing correctly flared.

Flareless fittings are installed as shown in Fig. 9-62. The installation of this type of fitting is very critical because too much torque will cut the tubing and cause it to fail, and too little torque will permit the fitting to slip or leak. If specific instructions for the installation of a particular flareless fitting are not available, a general rule for the installation may be used. The fitting is installed with the sleeve, and the end of the tubing is seated firmly against the counterbored shoulder in the body of the fitting. The nut is turned to pull the sleeve into the body until strong resistance to turning is encountered. At this time, the sleeve should be in solid contact with the taper inside the body. The nut is then turned one-sixth to one-third turn so that the

inner edge of the sleeve will indent the tube and form a seat. Flareless tube fittings are assigned standard specification numbers from MS 21900 upward to MS 21918.

The flareless fitting described in the foregoing is only one of a number of different types. Figure 9-63 shows another type of single-ferrule flareless fitting and two types of double-ferrule flareless fittings. In addition to those shown, the mechanic is likely to encounter other designs. In all cases, the installation of any particular fitting must be done according to the instructions provided by the manufacturer.

Installation of Hydraulic Tubing

When a section of hydraulic tubing is installed, the fittings at each end should come together in good alignment and without the application of any force. The fitting nuts should be easily tightened, usually by hand, before the final torque is applied with a suitable torque wrench.

Before the tubing is installed, the fittings at the ends of the tubing sections should be examined closely to make sure that there is no dirt, lint, or other substance in the fittings or threads. Extreme cleanliness must be practiced at all times.

A straight section of tubing should never be installed between two fixed points on the structure of the airplane. Changes in temperature will cause contraction and expansion, which are likely to cause failure of the connections. Wherever tubing must be installed between rigid or fixed points, a bend is made in the tubing to allow for contraction and expansion.

Flexible Hydraulic Hose

For portions of a hydraulic system between parts of the airplane where there is relative movement and possible vibration, flexible hose is required. In the replacement of hose sections, the mechanic must observe several precautions. The hose replacement must

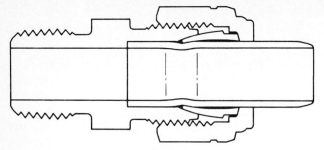

SINGLE - FERRULE FITTING

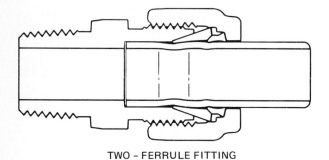

TWO - FERRULE FITTING

TWO - FERRULE FITTING

FIG. 9-63 Single- and double-ferrule flareless fittings.

TABLE 9-1 Ball diameters for testing hose restrictions or kinking

Hose Size	Ball Size
-4	5/64
-5	9/64
-6	13/64
-8	9/32
-10	3/8
-12	1/2
-16	47/64
-20	61/64

pected that a Teflon hose has been bent or twisted out of shape, a steel ball of the proper size can be used to check for interwall separation. If the ball passes through the hose, the hose is not damaged. Table 9-1 shows the different balls to use with different hose sizes.

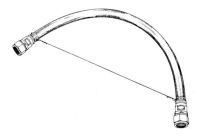

FIG. 9-64 Wire can be used to hold tubing in its installed shape. *(Aeroquip Corp.)*

be of the same type and material as the original part. The replaced section must not be twisted or stretched. Twisting can be detected by the painted or woven **layline** which should be straight along the axis of the hose and not spiraling around it. The hose should have a small amount of slack to allow for movement and vibration. It is particularly important that high-pressure hose be installed in high-pressure sections of the system and that the material of the hose be correct for the type of fluid in the system.

Teflon hose has come into wide usage in aircraft because of its ideal temperature operating range (-65 to $400°F$ [-54 to $204°C$]) and its resistance to attack by hydraulic fluids. While this type of hose is considered superior to the rubber-type hoses, Teflon hoses have certain characteristics which must be taken into account when handling them. When exposed to high pressure and temperature, Teflon takes a "set" and no attempt should be made to straighten the hose or bend it out of this "set" position. When a Teflon hose is removed with the intention of reinstalling it, support the hose in its installed shape. This may require using a support wire as shown in Fig. 9-62 (a). If it is sus-

Hydraulic hoses are often made with reusable end fittings so that a hose can be replaced without the need for a complete assembly. When a new hose section is cut and the original fittings are to be used, the mechanic must be sure to follow the manufacturer's instructions regarding the installation of the fittings, and he or she must make certain to use the proper type and size of hose for the installation. A hose with reusable fittings is shown in Fig. 9-65. Used fittings should be very carefully inspected before installation on a new section of hose. The inner sleeve, threads, nut, etc., must be checked for cracks, nicks, or scratches which could cause failure. This is particularly important for the high-pressure section of a system.

Another type of reusable fitting, designed particularly for high-pressure hose, is shown in Fig. 9-66. This is the Aeroquip "little gem" fitting designed for use with high-pressure hose. The carefully trimmed, metal-sheathed hose is inserted into the socket until the end is even with the back of the socket threads. The nipple is then inserted into the socket and screwed into place while the hose is held to ensure that it does not back out of the socket.

The nipple spur cuts an annular lip in the tube stock of the hose, thus forming an effective fluid seal. The hose reinforcement is separated from the annular lip

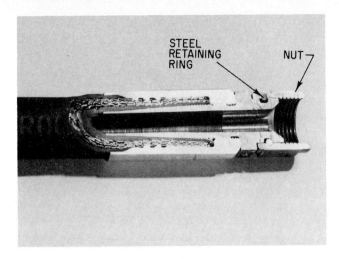

FIG. 9-65 Hose with reusable fittings.

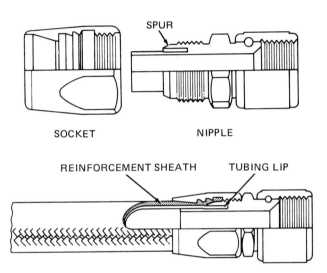

FIG. 9-66 Reusable fittings for high-pressure hose. *(Aeroquip Corp.)*

and is gripped firmly between the outside of the nipple and the serrations inside the socket.

Installation of Flexible Hose

When installing hydraulic hoses, the following guidelines should be followed:

1. Route hoses so that they do not pass through high-temperature areas without proper protection.

2. The lay lines should be used to avoid twisting the hose during installation.

3. The hose should be supported at intervals no greater than 24 in [60.96 cm] apart.

4. A hose should be 5 to 8 percent longer than that required to reach between two fittings. This slack allows for expansion, contraction, and flexing of the hose and airframe without damaging the hose or fittings.

5. Hoses should not be bent sharper than the recommended bend radius for a specific hose type, size, and operating pressure. Consult the hose manufacturer for specific bend radius limitations for specific hoses and uses.

Quick-Disconnect Couplings

Where it is necessary to disconnect hydraulic lines frequently, such as at the firewall of an engine nacelle, **seal couplings** or "quick-disconnect" fittings are often employed. A simplified drawing to illustrate the construction of such a coupling is shown in Fig. 9-67. As shown in the drawing, each end of the coupling contains a check valve. When the coupling is loosened, the check valves close and prevent the escape of fluid. When the coupling is assembled, the valves are opened by a pin or other mechanism to provide free flow for the fluid. If a seal coupling is found to be leaking, the coupling should be replaced.

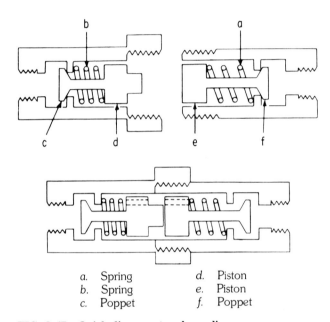

a. Spring	*d.* Piston
b. Spring	*e.* Piston
c. Poppet	*f.* Poppet

FIG. 9-67 Quick-disconnect seal couplings.

● HYDRAULIC SYSTEMS FOR AIRCRAFT

Aircraft hydraulic systems have been designed in many configurations for a wide variety of aircraft. Some very simple systems are used for light aircraft, while extremely complex systems have been designed for operating large jet aircraft, both military and commercial. On a light airplane, a power hydraulic system may be used only for landing gear and flaps. On a large transport aircraft the system is used for landing gear, flaps, spoilers, control-surface boost, retractable-stair operation, brakes, leading-edge slats, and other devices. In this section we shall examine a variety of aircraft hydraulic systems.

System with Pressure Regulator or Unloading Valve

Figure 9-68 is a schematic drawing of a direct pressure system that has its pressure regulated by an unloading valve (pressure regulator) operating in conjunction with an accumulator. This system is also termed a **closed-center system.**

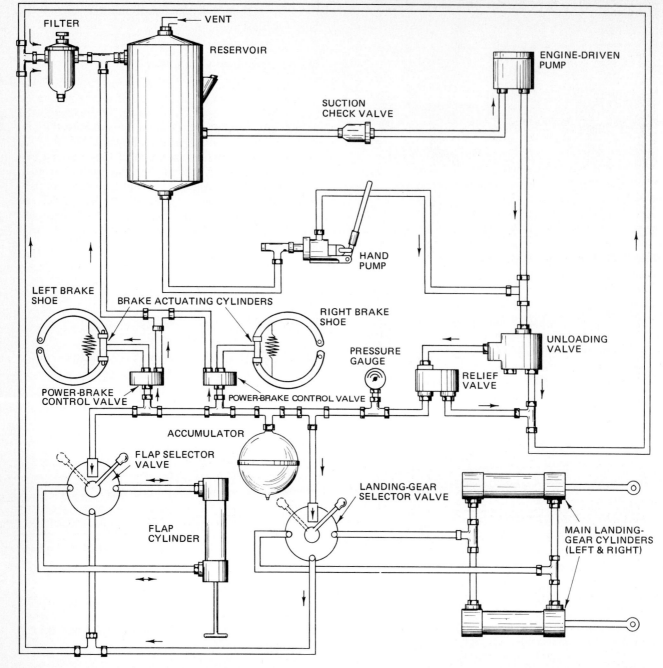

FIG. 9-68 Hydraulic system with a pressure regulator.

When the actuating equipment is not in use, pressure is relieved from the continuously operating engine-driven pump by means of the unloading valve after the accumulator is charged to the correct level. As soon as a subsystem is operated, pressure first comes from the accumulator for operation; when accumulator pressure has dropped to a predetermined level, the unloading valve "kicks-in" and directs pump flow to the operating system. A study of the diagram shows that the pump output flows directly through the unloading valve and back to the reservoir when no pressure is required. When a subsystem (brakes, landing gear, or flaps) is operated, pump pressure flows through the subsystem and back to the reservoir through the subsystem return line.

The main relief valve in the system is located between the unloading valve and the return line. If the unloading valve should become stuck in the kicked-in position, the excess pressure would be bypassed through the relief valve to the reservoir. The pressure gauge would show higher than normal pressure, and the system would probably be making noise because of the operation of the relief valve. The relief valve is usually set at least 100 psi [689.5 kPa] above the normal operating pressure.

Open-Center System

An **open-center hydraulic system** consists basically of a fluid reservoir, filter, check valve, pump, relief valve, selector valves, actuating units, and tubing to

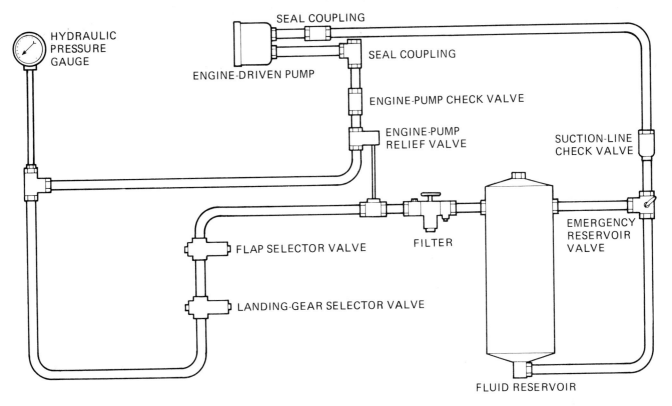

FIG. 9-69   A simple, open-center system.

connect the units. As shown in the diagram of Fig. 9-69, the system consists of a single circuit for fluid flow with selector valves in series. The fluid flows continuously through the system under low pressure except when a subsystem is operated. For example, if the landing gear is to be raised, the gear selector valve is moved to the UP position and the main flow of fluid is rerouted to the gear selector valve. The return fluid from the actuator flows back through the selector-valve passage and then continues on to the next selector valve in the system. As soon as the actuator reaches the end of its operation, the valve automatically "kicks-out" and allows free flow of fluid through the system. One of the advantages of the open-center system is that it does not require expensive and complicated pressure regulators; the power pump can be a simple gear pump, although a fixed-displacement piston pump is likely to be used.

A disadvantage of the open-center system is that the operation of only one subsystem at a time is possible without interference from other systems. For example, if the flap subsystem precedes the landing-gear subsystem, and the two systems are operated at the same time, the speed of gear operation will be limited by the amount of fluid returning from the flap actuating cylinder. As soon as the flap operation is complete and the flap selector valve kicks out, the landing-gear operation proceeds at its normal rate.

Light-Plane Hydraulic System

A schematic diagram of a hydraulic system for a light multiengine airplane is shown in Fig. 9-70. This system is installed in the Piper Apache PA-23 airplane to operate the wing flaps and landing gear.

From the diagram it is seen that the engine-driven hydraulic pump (10) draws hydraulic fluid from the reservoir (15) and pumps it through the pressure port of the "Powerpak" assembly into the landing-gear-selector pressure chamber. When the two selector valves are in the neutral position, the fluid travels from the landing-gear selector valve (1) through the flap selector valve (2) and back to the reservoir.

The Powerpak assembly is a modular unit which includes the reservoir, relief valve, hand pump, landing-gear selector valve, wing-flap selector valve, filters, and numerous other small parts essential to the operation. When both selector valves are in the neutral position, the system acts as an open-center system in that the fluid flows first through one selector valve and then through the other before returning to the reservoir. During this time the fluid flows freely at a reduced pressure. Since the fluid supply line runs first through the landing-gear selector valve, the flaps cannot be operated while the landing-gear subsystem is in operation. Each selector valve has a separate return line to allow fluid from the actuating cylinder or cylinders to flow back to the reservoir.

The diagram of Fig. 9-71 shows the fluid flow when the landing-gear selector is placed in the UP position. When the selector valve is placed in either operating position, it is held in the position by a detent which consists of a ball, O ring, plunger, and spring. The ball snaps into a groove in the spool which operates the poppet valves and prevents the spool from moving

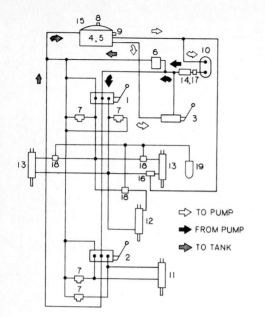

1. Landing-gear selector
2. Flap selector
3. Hand pump
4. Emergency fluid-trap stand pipe
5. Emergency hand-pump check filter
6. Main relief valve
7. Thermal relief valve
8. Atmospheric vent
9. Filter and filtering port
10. Pump
11. Flap-actuating cylinder
12. Nose-gear actuating cylinder
13. Main-gear actuating cylinder
14. System check
15. Reservoir
16. Antiretraction valve
17. Hydraulic filter
18. Shuttle valves
19. CO₂ bottle

▷ TO PUMP

▶ FROM PUMP

▷ TO TANK

FIG. 9-70 Schematic diagram of the hydraulic system for a light twin-engined airplane. *(Piper Aircraft Corp.)*

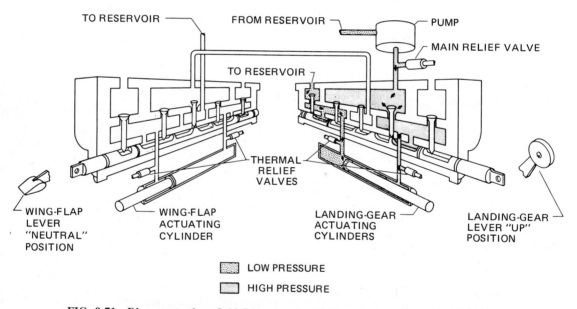

LOW PRESSURE

HIGH PRESSURE

FIG. 9-71 Diagram to show fluid flow when the landing-gear selector valve is in the UP position. *(Piper Aircraft Corp.)*

linearly until the operation is complete. When the actuating cylinder reaches the end of its movement, pressure builds up to approximately 1150 psi [7829 kPa]. This pressure acts against the plunger of the detent mechanism and relieves the pressure of the spring, thus allowing the ball to pop out of the groove. A spring then causes the spool and selector lever to return to the neutral position.

Figure 9-72 shows the fluid flow in the system when the wing-flap selector valve is placed in the DOWN position. The action is generally the same as that described in the foregoing paragraph. It should be noted that the fluid to the flap selector valve has passed through the landing-gear selector valve first, and that the landing-gear valve is in the neutral position.

The fluid used in the above-described system is petroleum-type, MIL-O-5606. The operating pressure is 1150 psi [7829 kPa], and the main relief valve "cracking" pressure is 1250 to 1300 psi [8618.8 to 8963.5 kPa]. Thermal relief valves are set to open at 2000 to

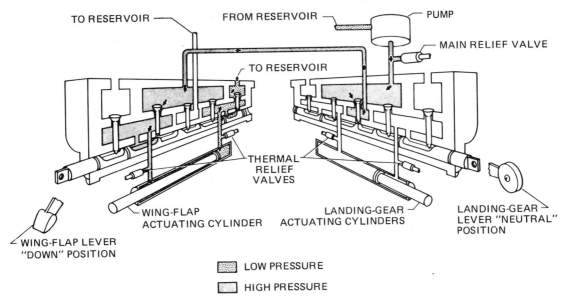

FIG. 9-72 Fluid flow when the wing-flap selector valve is in the DOWN position. *(Piper Aircraft Corp.)*

2050 psi [13 790 kPa to 14 134.8 kPa] or 1850 to 1900 psi [12 755.8 to 13 100.5 kPa], depending upon the particular model of Powerpak. The main reservoir capacity is approximately 4.5 pints [2.13 L] with an emergency supply of 0.95 pint [0.45 L].

Troubleshooting and servicing of the hydraulic system should be accomplished in accordance with the instructions given in the *Piper Apache Service Manual.* General inspection can be performed as with any other system and includes checking for leaks, loose tubing or fittings, loose attachments, damaged tubing, and other common discrepancies. Operational checks can be made only with the airplane on jacks.

A comparatively simple hydraulic system is illustrated in Fig. 9-73. Since this system serves one function only, raising and lowering the landing gear, it requires no selector valves. Direction of fluid flow is controlled by the reversible, electrically driven pump.

The reservoir, gear pump, relief valves, reversible motor, filter, and shuttle valve are all integrated into one assembly. A pressure switch is installed on a cross fitting connected to the pump mount assembly. This switch opens the electrical circuit to the pump solenoid when the gear fully retracts and the pressure in the system increases to approximately 1800 psi [12 400 kPa]. The switch continues to hold the circuit open until the system pressure drops to approximately 1500 psi [10 340 kPa], when it again operates to build up pressure as long as the gear selector handle is in the UP position. The DOWN position of the selector does not affect the pressure switch.

The pump is a gear-type unit driven by a 14-V reversible motor designed to operate in a pressure range of 2000 to 2500 psi [13 790 to 17 237 kPa]. A **thermal relief valve** is connected to the gear-up pressure line to prevent excessive pressure due to thermal expansion of the fluid. This valve maintains pressure in the system up to 2350 ± 50 psi [16 230 ± 345 kPa]. An additional relief valve is incorporated in the system to return hydraulic fluid to the reservoir if pressure should exceed 4000 psi [27 436 kPa]. The **shuttle valve,** located in the base of the pump, allows fluid displaced by the actuating cylinder pistons to return to the reservoir without back pressure.

The system includes a **free-fall valve** that allows the landing gear to drop in the event of a system malfunction. The valve is controlled manually or by a gear backup extension device that is operated by a pressure-sensing chamber. This chamber moves the free-fall valve to lower the gear, regardless of gear selector handle position, depending upon engine power (propeller slipstream) and airspeed. Landing-gear extension occurs even if the selector is in the UP position at airspeeds below approximately 118 mph [190 km/h] with engine power off. The device also prevents the gear from retracting at airspeeds below approximately 93 mph [150 km/h] at sea level with full power, even though the selector switch may be in the UP position. The sensing device operation is controlled by a differential air pressure across a flexible diaphragm which is mechanically linked to the hydraulic free-fall valve and an electric switch which control the pump motor. A high-pressure and static air source for actuating the diaphragm is provided in a mast mounted on the left side of the fuselage above the wing. Manual override of the device is provided by an emergency gear lever located between the front seats to the right of the flap handle. The emergency free-fall lever must be held in the UP position to retract the gear and in the DOWN position to extend the gear.

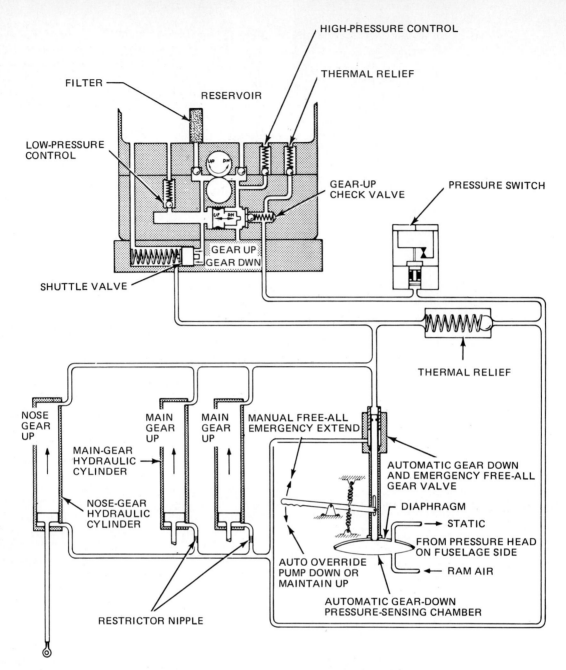

FIG. 9-73 Hydraulic system for landing-gear operation. *(Piper Aircraft Corp.)*

● HYDRAULIC SYSTEM FOR BOEING 727 AIRLINER

The hydraulic system described here represents the installation in one particular model of the Boeing 727 airplane. It must be emphasized that modifications are made from time to time and the information given here may not apply to other models of the same airplane. The student is reminded that maintenance and repair work on any hydraulic system must be done in accordance with the manufacturer's instructions for the particular airplane on which the work is to be performed.

The hydraulic power system for the Boeing 727 airliner is typical of those employed for modern jet-trans-

port-type aircraft. These systems are of the high-pressure type, utilizing pressures more than 3000 psi [20 685 kPa]. The advantage of high-pressure systems is that they can deliver more power for a given weight of fluid and system components than can the lower-pressure systems.

The Boeing 727 incorporates three separate and independent hydraulic power systems. These are designated "hydraulic system A," "hydraulic system B," and "standby hydraulic system." Hydraulic fluid is supplied from two pressurized reservoirs and one unpressurized reservoir, each system being supplied by one of the reservoirs. System A receives fluid under pressure from two engine-driven pumps installed on engines Nos. 1 and 2. System B receives fluid under pressure from two electric, motor-driven pumps installed in the left fairing adjacent to the rear of the left-wing root.

The standby system receives fluid pressure from one electric-motor-driven pump installed in the left sidewall of the aft stairwell. This system operates only on demand and supplies hydraulic power for the leading-edge devices and the lower-rudder operation.

Figure 9-74 is a schematic diagram to show the interconnections between units in each system and between the systems. Note that system A supplies hydraulic power for the outboard flight spoilers,

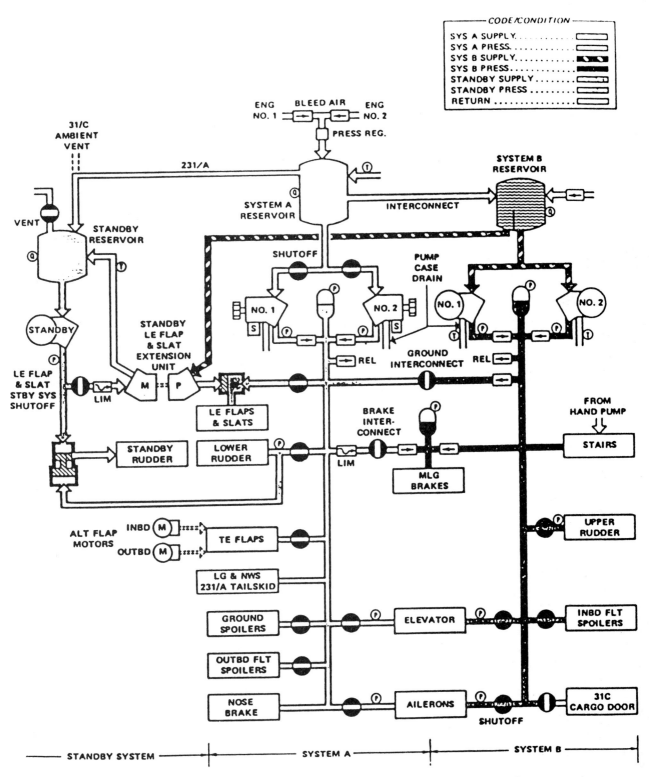

FIG. 9-74 Schematic diagram of hydraulic power system for a Boeing 727 airplane. *(Boeing Commercial Aircraft Co.)*

ground spoilers, ailerons, leading-edge flaps, landing gear, nose-wheel steering and brakes, elevators, lower rudder, and main-wheel brakes, when the brake interconnect valve is open.

System B supplies power to the ailerons, elevators, inboard flight spoilers, aft airstairs, upper rudder, and main-wheel brakes. The interconnections between system B and system A are shown in the schematic drawing of Fig. 9-74. Note that certain operating components are provided with power by both systems.

A **modular unit** is used in each of the systems combining a number of the smaller system components in one case to simplify maintenance. The modular units serve as manifolds directing hydraulic fluid to the various easily replaceable cartridge-type components. This allows component removal without disrupting tube connections. As an example of the function of a modular unit, the one installed in system A contains a pressure filter, two check valves, two pressure warning switches, a pressure-relief valve, and a bypass valve.

The **hydraulic fluid** used for the Boeing 727 systems is Skydrol 500B, a fire-resistant, phosphate ester–base, synthetic fluid. This purple fluid has an operating temperature range of -65 to $+225°F$ [-53.9 to $107.2°C$], with a pour point below $-90°F$ [$-67.8°C$]. With this fluid, the seals, gaskets, and hoses must be made of either butyl rubber or Teflon fluorocarbon resin. Other materials will soften, swell, or deteriorate. As previously explained, Skydrol fluid can cause damage to ordinary paints and enamels; therefore, precautions must be taken to prevent spillage. Where spillage is likely, special protective materials are used. Mechanics servicing systems using Skydrol should take every precaution to prevent the fluid from coming in contact with their skin or getting it in their eyes. Protective clothing and goggles or a face shield are recommended.

Since the hydraulic power system employs pressure up to and more than 3000 psi [20 685 kPa], the tubing carrying the high pressures must be of a material which will withstand all pressure to which they may be subjected. All pressure lines in the systems subject to more than 1500 psi [10 342.5 kPa] are made of seamless, corrosion-resistant (stainless-) steel tubing. This tubing is used in class 1 fire zones and on the landing-gear structure, regardless of pressure. All other lines are made of seamless aluminum-alloy tubing. Tubing of ¾-in [1.91-cm] outside diameter or less requires flareless-type fittings. For pressures under 1500 psi [10 342.5 kPa] aluminum-alloy fittings are used; for greater pressures, titanium and steel fittings are used. Tubing of 1-in [2.54-cm] outside diameter and larger requires flared-type fittings. On this tubing size, aluminum fittings are used, except in class 1 fire zones and on the landing-gear structure where titanium or steel fittings are used. The mechanic who repairs or services the systems must make sure that all replacement tubes and fittings are of the correct type and material for the section of the system in which they are located.

When it is necessary to replace a tubing assembly, the mechanic should obtain a new tube assembly hav-

ing the same part number as the existing assembly. However, tube assemblies whose dash numbers have an "X" suffix are not stocked as spares; they can be replaced only by bending another tube assembly to the same contour from the same material as the existing tube assembly.

Flexible hose used in the hydraulic systems is made of Teflon fluorocarbon resin and designed for high pressure or medium pressure. High-pressure hoses are used in the pressure lines and medium-pressure hoses are used in supply lines, return lines, and brake lines.

Servicing of any particular airplane hydraulic system must be accomplished according to the specific instructions issued by the manufacturer for the particular airplane. On the Boeing 727, the servicing station is located in the aft left-wing fairing area and is accessible through an access door. The filling equipment consists of a manually operated hand pump, reservoir selector valve, system A and standby-system fluid-quantity indicators, service connection for external fluid servicing, and the necessary tubing and hydraulic lines. The arrangement of the equipment in the filling area is shown in Fig. 9-75.

Hydraulic Power System A

Hydraulic system A, illustrated in the schematic drawing of Fig. 9-76, is powered by engine-driven hydraulic pumps mounted on engines Nos. 1 and 2. Engine No. 1 is mounted in the pod on the left rear portion of the fuselage; engine No. 2 is in the center of the fuselage near the tail of the airplane.

System A includes the equipment necessary to store, pressurize, deliver, control, monitor, and filter the hydraulic fluid to operate the systems previously noted. Hydraulic fluid for the system is stored in a reservoir which is pressurized by engine bleed air routed through a filter and a pressure regulator to ensure a positive supply of hydraulic fluid to the pumps. Two supply shutoff valves controlled by either separate engine fire switches or separate hydraulic shutoff switches are installed downstream of the reservoir to stop the flow of hydraulic fluid to the engine area in case of an engine failure or fire.

Two **variable-displacement** engine-driven pumps supply fluid to the various systems upon demand. Each pump is equipped with an electrically controlled depressurizing valve to depressurize the pump when output is not required. As explained previously, a variable-displacement pump is provided with an automatic control such that it will deliver fluid under pressure as needed for operation but will not be pumping fluid when there is no need for it.

A filter in the pressure line from each pump filters the fluid before it enters the various subsystems. A pressure switch in the pressure line from each pump is connected to a pump low-pressure warning light on the third crew member's panel to provide an indication of low hydraulic pressure. A piston-type accumulator is provided in the system to absorb sudden pressure surges. Pressure gauges in the control cabin and accumulator servicing station are connected to the gas side of the accumulator to monitor hydraulic pressure when the system is pressurized and accumulator pre-

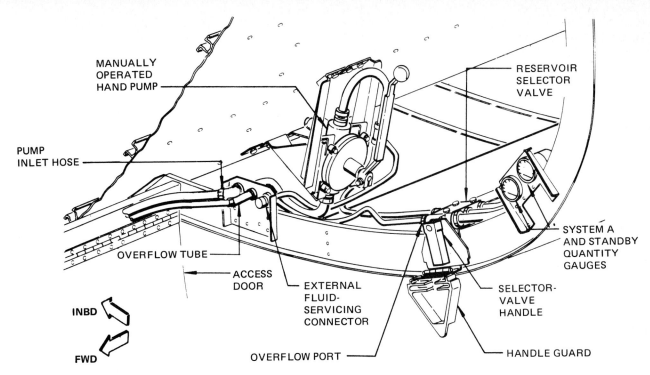

FIG. 9-75 Hydraulic equipment in the filling area. *(Boeing Co.)*

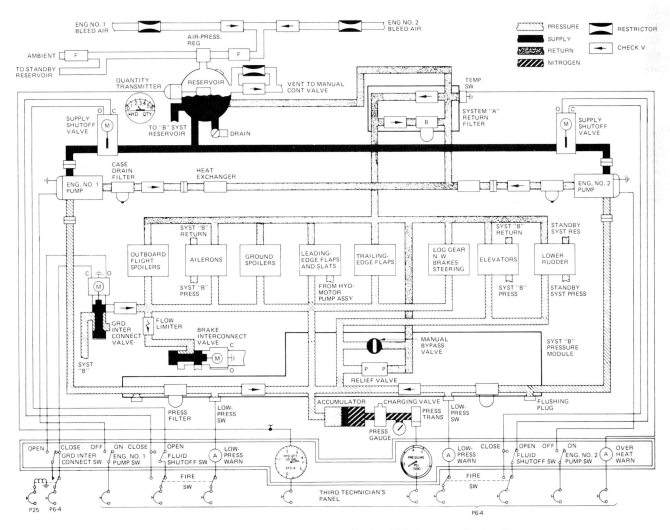

FIG. 9-76 Diagram of system A on a Boeing 727 airplane. *(Boeing Co.)*

load when the system is not pressurized. The accumulator preload consists of nitrogen gas under pressure (approximately 2000 psi [13 790 kPa] when the system is depressurized).

A pressure-relief valve protects the system against damage in case a malfunction permits the pressure to rise to an abnormally high level. A pump-case drain filter in each pump return line is provided to detect incipient pump failures and to filter return-line fluid before it enters the reservoir. A hydraulic fluid heat exchanger in the pump return line is provided to cool the hydraulic fluid by transferring heat from the fluid to a cooling airflow. A system return filter just ahead of the reservoir filters returns fluid from the subsystems supplied by system A. Hydraulic-fluid overheat is sensed by a switch installed in the system return filter assembly and indicated by a warning light in the control cabin.

A brake interconnect valve is installed to supply hydraulic power to the brakes from system A whenever system B is inoperative and the brake system is intact.

When the airplane is on the ground, system A can be depressurized through a manual bypass valve. Placing the bypass valve handle in the OPEN position connects the pressure and return lines, thus permitting pressurized fluid to return to the reservoir. For ground operation, system A can be pressurized to supply normal pressure without engine operation by attaching an external hydraulic pressure source to the airplane at the engine hydraulic self-sealing disconnect fittings. System A can also be pressurized without engine operation by attaching an external electrical ground power supply to the airplane electrical system, opening the ground interconnect valve and operating system B pumps. System B pumps are then feeding pressure into system A.

Hydraulic Reservoir

System A on the Boeing 727 airplane is supplied with fluid from a 5.4-gal [20.44-L] reservoir which is pressurized to approximately 45 psi [310 kPa] by bleed air from engines Nos. 1 and 2. Pressurization of the reservoir assures a positive fluid supply to engine-driven pumps.

Air from the engine bleed is fed through check valves, a filter, and a pressure regulator. The regulator is designed to admit air to the reservoir if the pressure is below the required amount, and it will relieve air from the reservoir if pressure rises above the correct level. It also acts as a vacuum relief valve when the reservoir pressure drops below 0.50 psi [3.45 kPa] under ambient pressure. In this case, air entering the reservoir is filtered by the vent filter. A schematic drawing of the reservoir pressurization system is shown in Fig. 9-77.

Engine-Driven Pumps

As explained previously, the engine-driven hydraulic pumps are of the variable-displacement or variable-delivery (VD) type. Each pump has a maximum displacement of 1.77 in^3 [29 cm^3] per revolution and at 3000 rpm delivers approximately 22½ gal/min [85.17

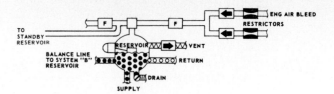

FIG. 9-77 Reservoir pressurization system.

L/min] at 2850 psi [19 651 kPa]. Pump discharge pressure is limited by a **pressure compensator,** and each pump may be depressurized by an electrically controlled **depressurizing valve.**

The control mechanism for the variable-displacement pump is shown in Fig. 9-78. Remember that the output of this type of pump is determined by the angle of a **cam plate** which rotates to produce a reciprocating action of the pump pistons. The cam-plate angle is changed by varying the position of the **hanger** upon which it is mounted. Figure 9-78 shows schematically how the hanger position is changed as required by the output pressure of the pump.

In the top drawing, the pump pressure is high (3000 psi [20 685 kPa]) and the cam plate is level; hence there is no reciprocating motion of the pump pistons and no fluid output. Observe that the high pressure is acting against the **high-pressure compensator spool valve,** thus moving the valve against a spring and allowing fluid to be directed around the **low-pressure**

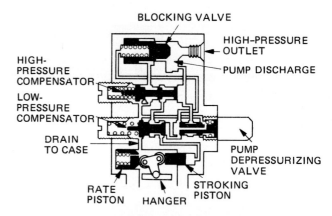

FULL PRESSURE, NO-FLOW CONDITION

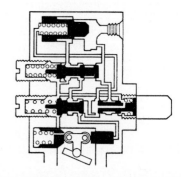

FULL PRESSURE, FULL-FLOW CONDITION

FIG. 9-78 Control system for a variable-displacement hydraulic pump.

compensator spool and on to the end of the **stroking piston.** The stroking piston forces the hanger to the left against the rate piston spring, thus bringing the cam plate to the NO-FLOW position.

The lower drawing shows the position of controlling elements when the system is using fluid and the cam is in the FULL-FLOW position. Since system pressure then drops, the spring has pushed the high-pressure compensator spool to the right, thus opening passages

so the fluid pressure against the stroking piston is released. The rate piston spring has moved the hanger to the right against the stroking piston and changed the angle of the cam. The cam can be seen clearly in the drawing of the pump in Fig. 9-79.

Modular Unit

The modular unit for system A is shown in the drawing of Fig. 9-80. As shown in the drawing, this

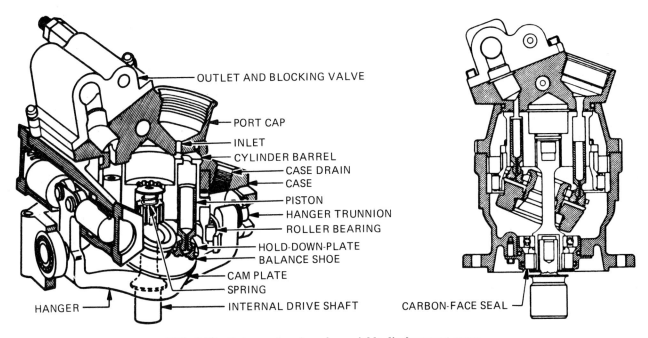

FIG. 9-79 Cutaway drawing of a variable-displacement pump.

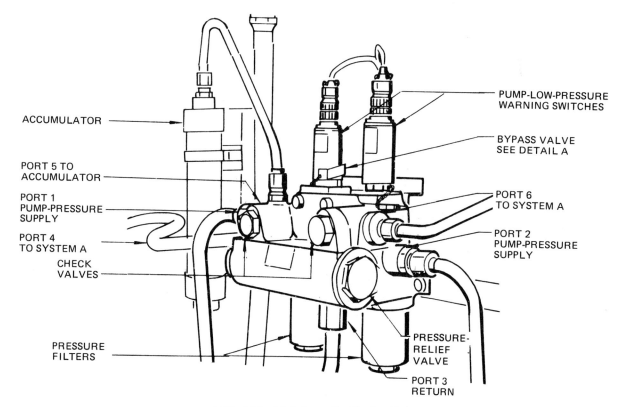

FIG. 9-80 Modular unit. (*Boeing Co.*)

unit contains filters, check valves, a relief valve, a bypass valve, and pressure-warning switches. By bringing these units together in one case, the maintenance of the system is simplified. A schematic flow diagram of the modular unit is shown in Fig. 9-81.

Heat Exchanger

Because of the high pressures involved in the system and the high rates of fluid flow, the hydraulic fluid becomes heated as the subsystems are operated. For this reason it is necessary to provide cooling for the fluid. The **heat exchanger,** shown in Fig. 9-82, is a heat radiator similar in design and construction to an oil cooler for an engine. Note that the heat exchanger is equipped with a temperature-operated bypass valve to increase the fluid flow through the cooling element as temperature rises.

One heat exchanger is installed in each engine-driven pump-case drain return line. Each heat-exchanger unit consists of an inlet scoop, oil cooler, ejector duct, exhaust outlet, engine bleed-air ejector nozzle, and an air-ejector shutoff valve. The heat exchanger for the No. 1 engine pump is in the No. 1 engine strut, and the heat exchanger for the No. 2 engine pump is in the tail section of the airplane on the right side. Cooling is provided by ram air in flight and by engine bleed-air ejection when the airplane is on the ground.

The temperature-operated bypass valve in the oil-cooler fluid inlet controls the volume of return fluid circulating through the oil cooler. At fluid temperatures above 100°F [37.78°C] the bypass valve starts to close, porting return fluid through the oil cooler. At a fluid temperature of 155°F ± 5° [68.33°C ± 2.78°] the bypass valve will be fully closed, porting all return fluid through the oil cooler.

Accumulator

The **accumulator** for system A is a cylindrical, free-floating piston-type unit, precharged with nitrogen gas. As explained previously, the purpose of the unit is to store fluid under pressure and to protect the system against sudden pressure surges. A fluid line is con-

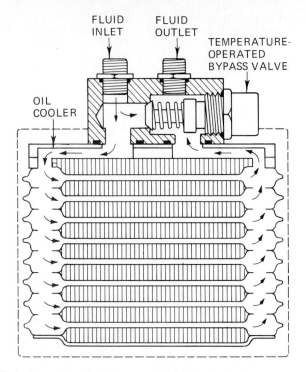

FIG. 9-82 Heat-exchanger cooling unit.

nected to the fluid end of the accumulator, and a nitrogen line is connected to the opposite end. The accumulator is mounted vertically in the airplane with the fluid end at the top. On the nitrogen end is connected a direct-pressure gauge, a pressure transmitter, and a nitrogen charging valve. The pressure transmitter is connected electrically to the pressure gauge on the third crew member's panel in the cabin.

The preload gas pressure placed in the accumulator is approximately 2000 psi [13 790 kPa] when the ambient temperature is 65 to 70°F [18.33 to 21.11°C]; hence the pressure gauges indicate 2000 psi when the system is not in operation and is depressurized. When hydraulic pressure is applied above 2000 psi, the accumulator begins to charge, and the nitrogen is com-

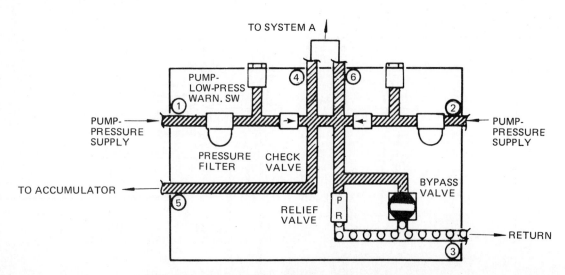

FIG. 9-81 Schematic flow diagram of the modular unit.

pressed to a pressure equal to the hydraulic pressure. The pressure gauges then show system pressure.

The accumulator is installed in the aft-stairwell left sidewall. The accumulator charging valve and direct-reading gauge are located aft of the left-wing fairing area and are accessible through an access door.

Valves

The valves incorporated in system A are the **relief valve, hydraulic supply shutoff valve, ground interconnect valve, brake interconnect valve,** and **bypass valve.**

The purpose of the relief valve, discussed previously, is to protect the system against excessive pressure. It is set to relieve at 3500 ± 50 psi [24 132.5 ± 344.75 kPa] and reset at 3100 psi [21 374.5 kPa] minimum.

The **hydraulic supply shutoff valves** are provided to stop the flow of hydraulic fluid to the engine area. These valves are electrically operated and are automatically shut off when the engine fire switch is operated. The valves are also operated from switches on the third crew member's panel.

The **ground interconnect valve** is provided so system A can be pressurized for ground operation and testing through system B. System B is pressurized by electrically driven pumps; hence it can be operated without running the engines.

The **brake interconnect valve** connects system A to the brake system when system B is inoperative and the brake system is intact. This allows brake operation and brake-accumulator charging using system A pressure. The valve is electrically operated by a switch on the third crewman's panel.

The **bypass valve** is installed in the modulator unit to provide for depressurization of the system during ground maintenance operations. The valve provides a flow of only 5 gal/min [18.95 L/min]; hence the system will operate when the engines are running, even if the valve is open. Remember that the engine-driven pumps furnish 22½ gal/min [85.28 L/min] each at full-flow position. During flight, the bypass valve is lock-wired in the CLOSED position.

System B and Standby System

The system B and standby systems were discussed earlier in this chapter; since their operation is similar to that explained for system A (except for specific function and source of hydraulic power), it is not deemed essential that their details be described further. Servicing and repair of any of the systems must be done in accordance with the maintenance practices given in the manufacturer's manual or in the maintenance orders provided by the air carrier; hence further discussion here is not necessary.

● HYDRAULIC SYSTEM FOR A LOCKHEED L-1011

The Lockheed L-1011 hydraulic system is presented as a representation of a modern transport aircraft with multiple redundant systems for the supply of hydraulic power and the operation of controls. Many modern transport and corporate aircraft have systems which are similar with the same philosophy of multiple redundancy.

General Description

The L-1011 hydraulics are arranged in four separate, parallel, continuously operating systems, identified as A, B, C, and D. All power systems utilize a low-density phosphate ester hydraulic fluid pressurized to a standard 3000 psi [20 685 kPa]. The low-density hydraulic fluid provides a weight savings over conventional phosphate ester fluid.

The four independent systems are designed for maximum flight control safety and performance and have the following capabilities:

1. If one hydraulic system is inoperative, the aircraft control capability and rate of control is not reduced.

2. If two hydraulic systems are inoperative, the aircraft can complete any planned flight.

3. If three systems are inoperative, the aircraft can maintain safe flight control throughout the normal operational range of the aircraft. One hydraulic system is sufficient to operate all flight controls.

A schematic diagram of the hydraulic system is shown in Fig. 9-83.

Hydraulic Pumps

There are 11 hydraulic pumps in the design of the hydraulic systems, including engine-driven pumps, **air turbine motor**-driven pumps, **power transfer units,** a **ram air turbine,** and electrically operated pumps.

The primary hydraulic power source for each of the four systems is the engine-driven variable displacement pump. Engine Nos. 1 and 3 drive one pump each and engine No. 2 drives two pumps. The engine-driven pumps are identical and interchangeable with the air turbine motor (ATM) pumps. Each of these pumps is capable of pressurizing the hydraulic system to 3000 psi [20 685 kPa] and provides a flow of up to 38.8 gal [146.86 L] per minute. The engine-driven pumps are constantly operating during engine operation. Pump switches on the flight engineer's panel allow each pump to be depressurized. This reduces pump internal pressure and simultaneously shuts off flow to the system. Indicator lights on these control switches show the mode of operation of the pumps. A cutaway of an engine-driven pump is shown in Fig. 9-84.

The secondary hydraulic power sources for the hydraulic systems are the two ATM-driven pumps. An ATM, shown in Fig. 9-85, is located on each side of the aircraft in the unpressurized wing-to-fuselage fairing. One is connected to system B and the other to system C. Pneumatic power for ATM operation is supplied by bleed air from any one or more engines, from the aircraft auxiliary power unit compressor, or from a ground source.

The ATM pumps are normally used for inflight backup in the event of depressurization of engine pumps in system B or C to supply added flow during peak demands. These pumps can supply full power to systems A and D through the power transfer units

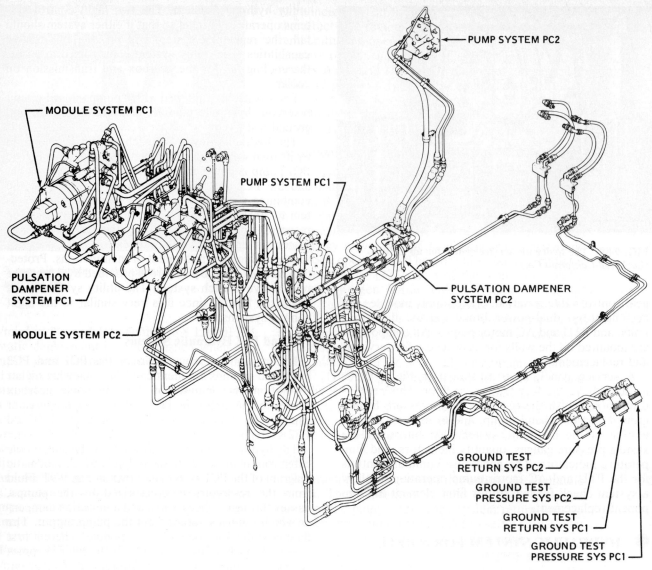

FIG. 9-90 The hydraulic system for a helicopter—actuators not shown. *(Bell Helicopter Textron)*

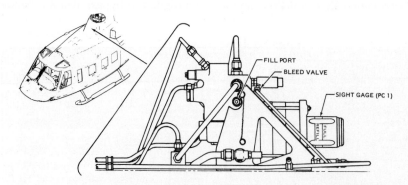

FIG. 9-91 Hydraulic reservoir and filter assembly for a helicopter. *(Bell Helicopter Textron)*

From the filter, fluid flows to a shutoff valve and a solenoid pilot valve. The pilot can shut down either system by opening the solenoid valve with a cockpit toggle switch. When the solenoid is energized, pressure is directed to the shutoff valve and system pressure is routed to the return line, depressurizing the

system downstream of these control valves. If power to the solenoid is interrupted, the shutoff valve is closed and full system pressure is restored. Electric interlocks prevent both PC1 and PC2 from being shut down in this manner at the same time.

Excess pressure in the system is released by the

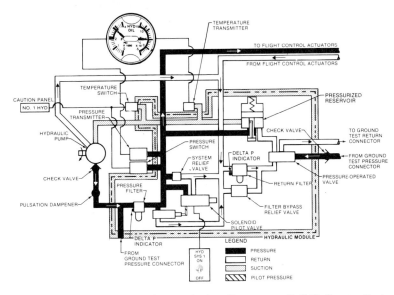

FIG. 9-92 Schematic of a helicopter hydraulic system. *(Bell Helicopter Textron)*

system relief valve, and the relieved fluid returns to the reservoir. The relief valve begins to open at 3500 psi [24 132 kPa] and is fully open at 3850 psi [26 345.8 kPa]. The valve reseats when pressure drops to 3250 psi [22 408.8 kPa].

Downstream of the relief valve the pressure is applied to a pressure switch, a pressure transmitter, and the reservoir pressurization line. The pressure switch operates a cockpit annunciator when pressure is lost and disables the solenoid switch for the opposite system. The pressure transmitter drives a pressure gauge in the cockpit. The reservoir pressure is maintained at 75 psi [517 kPa] by the system pressurization piston.

After passing the reservoir pressurization line, the fluid exits the module and flows to the flight control actuators. Return fluid from the actuators is routed back to the module, through the return filter in the module, and into the reservoir. The return filter has a red button to indicate when the filter is clogged, but, unlike the pressure filter, the return filter can be bypassed.

From the reservoirs the fluid is fed back to the pumps. A temperature switch and a temperature transmitter in the line between the reservoirs and the pumps send signals to cockpit displays. The transmitter allows the pilot to monitor the fluid temperature, and the switch activates an annunciator light to warn of excessive heat in the fluid.

The system can be operated by a ground cart through the ground test connection. The quantity of fluid in the reservoirs is indicated at the sight gauge on the module as shown in Fig. 9-89.

● PNEUMATIC SYSTEMS FOR AIRCRAFT

The principle of operation for a pneumatic power system is the same, with one important exception, as that of a hydraulic power system. The air in a pneumatic system is compressible; hence the pressure in the system can reduce gradually from the maximum

system pressure to zero pressure. In the hydraulic system, as soon as the accumulator fluid has been used and the pump is not operating, the fluid pressure immediately drops from accumulator pressure to zero pressure. The entire pneumatic system, including the air-storage bottles, can act to store air pressure. In the hydraulic system, the only pressure-fluid storage in the accumulators, and the pressure is supplied by compressed air or gas in the air chamber of the accumulator.

The air in a pneumatic system must be kept clean by means of filters and also be kept free from moisture and oil droplets or vapor. For this reason, liquid separators and chemical air driers are incorporated in the systems.

Another important feature of a pneumatic system is that there is no need for return lines. After the compressed air has served its purpose, it can be dumped overboard which saves tubing, fittings, and valves.

Pneumatic-System Description

The pneumatic system described in this section is utilized in the Fairchild F-27 Friendship airliner. It provides power for operation of the landing-gear retraction and extension, nose-wheel centering, propeller brakes, main-wheel brakes, and passenger-entrance-door retraction. The system description includes only the development and delivery of compressed air to each component or subsystem, not to the actual *operation* of the component or subsystem. The pneumatic power in the airplane is delivered by one of two systems: the primary system and the emergency system.

The power section of the primary pneumatic system is that portion which is located in each engine nacelle, shown in Fig. 9-93. It consists of a **gearbox-driven compressor, bleed valve, unloading valve, moisture separator, chemical drier, back-pressure valve** (right nacelle only), and a **filter.** In addition, each nacelle contains a **shuttle valve, disk-type relief valve,** and a **ground charging connection** to aid in ground maintenance or

315

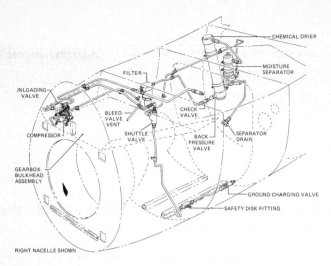

FIG. 9-93 Pneumatic system in engine nacelle. (*Fairchild Industries, Inc.*)

initial filling. Each power section independently supplies compressed air to the primary and emergency systems. The air in the primary system is stored in two storage bottles, and the system delivers the air for normal operation components as required by directional valves. A schematic diagram of the pneumatic power system is shown in Fig. 9-94.

A 100-in³ [1.64-L] bottle is used for the main-wheel brakes, and a 750-in³ [12.3-L] bottle is used for gear operation, nose-wheel centering, propeller brakes, and passenger-door retraction. A pressure-relief valve is installed to protect the system from excessive pressure buildup. In the air-supply tube from the large primary bottle, an air filter is installed to filter the air for the primary system. An **isolation valve,** which is in the tube between the large primary bottle and the smaller brake bottle, permits maintenance to be performed downstream of the valve without discharging the large bottle. On the downstream side of the isolation valve, a pressure reducing valve is used to reduce system pressure from 3300 to 1000 psi [22 753 to 6895 kPa]. All components except the pressure gauges and the power-section components are located in the fuselage pneumatic compartment.

Air Pressure Sources

Two views of the **compressor** for the pneumatic system are shown in Fig. 9-95. One compressor is located in each engine nacelle. The compressors are of four-stage, radial design, providing a delivery pressure of 3300 psi [22 753 kPa] and 2 ft³/min [5.66 m³/min] at sea-level intake pressure on a standard day. As shown in the drawings, the cylinders and pistons of the compressor diminish in size from No. 1 to No. 4. The cylinders are caused to reciprocate in the proper sequence by a cam-assembly mechanism which rotates with the crankshaft.

The arrangement of the crankshaft and cam in the four-stage compressor is such that when the No. 1 cylinder is on the compression stroke, the No. 2 cylinder is on the intake stroke and the compressed air enters the No. 2 cylinder. When No. 2 cylinder com-

presses, the air enters No. 3 cylinder which is on the intake stroke. When No. 3 cylinder compresses, the air is delivered to the No. 4 cylinder which is on the intake stroke. The No. 4 cylinder then compresses, and the air is delivered to the system. Thus the air has been moved from the No. 1 cylinder through the four stages to be further compressed in each stage. The interstage lines are finned to provide cooling and reduce the heat of compression.

Ducted ram air is provided for cooling of the finned cylinders and the finned interstage lines. Oil pressure from the gearbox provides lubrication for the compressor through a drilled passage in the mounting flange. Air is compressed by stages 1 through 4 of the compressor, while overpressure protection is provided by means of relief valves between stages 1 and 2, and 2 and 3. Compressed air from stage 4 is then routed by an intercooler line to the bleed valve mounted on the compressor.

While the version of the F-27 being discussed makes use of an engine-driven air compressor to power the pneumatic system, other aircraft commonly make use of other power sources. Air for the pneumatic operation of controls can be provided by the engine compressor bleed air. Some aircraft use this medium-pressure air (100 to 150 psi [689 to 1034 kPa]) for operation after passing it through a pressure regulator and conditioners such as filters and driers. Other aircraft use this air to operate air turbine motors which allows an increase in operation pressure on the pump side of the air turbine motor. Still other aircraft make use of a hydraulic motor or an electric motor to operate a high-pressure pneumatic pump. This high-pressure air is then regulated, conditioned, and allowed to flow on to the systems to be operated.

Air-storage bottles are used for emergency operations when hydraulic or pneumatic pressure sources have been lost. The bottles are normally pressurized with nitrogen, but some aircraft require the use of carbon dioxide. These bottles will power a system, normally a landing-gear extension system or a brake system, for only a brief period of time. The bottles must be recharged on the ground.

Storage Bottle

The primary air-storage bottle for the F-27 is constructed of steel with a plastic coating on the inner surface to provide a longer service life. The bottle is mounted above the fuselage pneumatic panel and is fitted with three ports. It has a volume of 750 in³ [12 290.3 cm³] and stores air at 3300 psi [22 753.5 kPa] for operating landing-gear, propeller-brake, nose-steering, and rear-door-retracting subsystems. The air pressure is reduced to 1000 psi [6895 kPa] before being routed to subsystems other than brakes. The bottle is provided with a standpipe which permits the withdrawal of air without the danger of allowing any accumulated moisture to enter the operating systems. Accumulated moisture can be drained from the bottle by means of a drain valve located on the bottom. Access is gained to the air bottle through the fuselage pneumatic power panel door.

Aircraft which use the pneumatic system only for

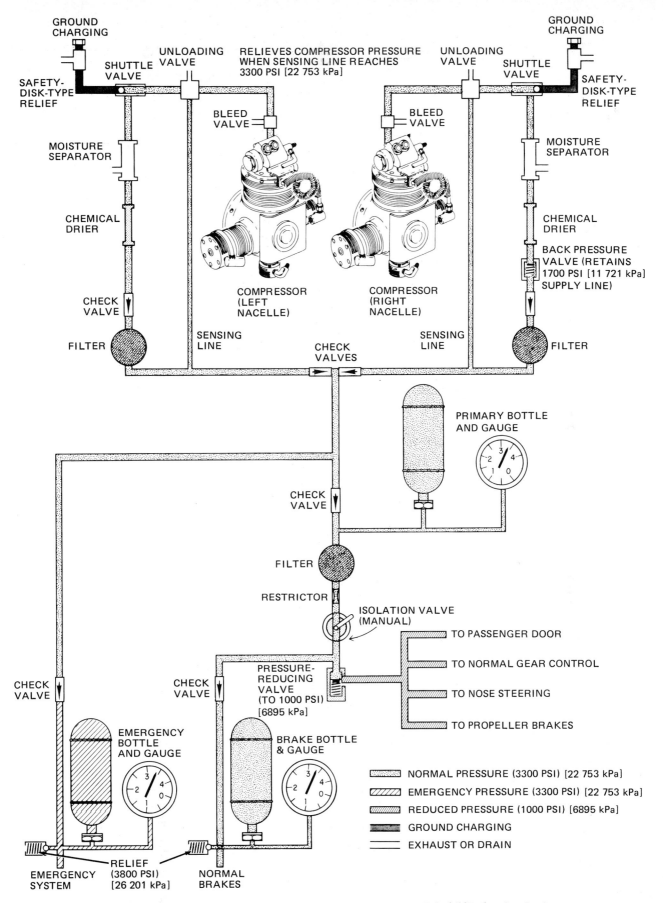

FIG. 9-94 Schematic diagram of pneumatic power system. *(Fairchild Industries, Inc.)*

Labels within the figure:

GROUND CHARGING

SHUTTLE VALVE

UNLOADING VALVE

RELIEVES COMPRESSOR PRESSURE WHEN SENSING LINE REACHES 3300 PSI [22 753 kPa]

UNLOADING VALVE

SHUTTLE VALVE

GROUND CHARGING

SAFETY-DISK-TYPE RELIEF

BLEED VALVE

BLEED VALVE

SAFETY-DISK-TYPE RELIEF

MOISTURE SEPARATOR

MOISTURE SEPARATOR

CHEMICAL DRIER

CHEMICAL DRIER

BACK PRESSURE VALVE (RETAINS 1700 PSI [11 721 kPa] SUPPLY LINE)

COMPRESSOR (LEFT NACELLE)

COMPRESSOR (RIGHT NACELLE)

CHECK VALVE

CHECK VALVES

SENSING LINE

SENSING LINE

FILTER

FILTER

PRIMARY BOTTLE AND GAUGE

CHECK VALVE

FILTER

RESTRICTOR

ISOLATION VALVE (MANUAL)

TO PASSENGER DOOR

TO NORMAL GEAR CONTROL

TO NOSE STEERING

TO PROPELLER BRAKES

CHECK VALVE

CHECK VALVE

PRESSURE-REDUCING VALVE (TO 1000 PSI) [6895 kPa]

EMERGENCY BOTTLE AND GAUGE

BRAKE BOTTLE & GAUGE

NORMAL PRESSURE (3300 PSI) [22 753 kPa]

EMERGENCY PRESSURE (3300 PSI) [22 753 kPa]

REDUCED PRESSURE (1000 PSI) [6895 kPa]

GROUND CHARGING

EXHAUST OR DRAIN

EMERGENCY SYSTEM

RELIEF (3800 PSI) [26 201 kPa]

NORMAL BRAKES

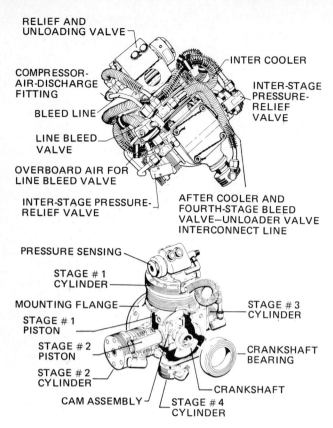

FIG. 9-95 Four-stage pneumatic compressor.

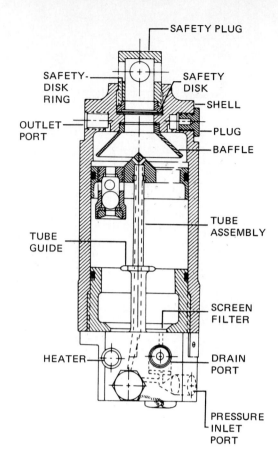

FIG. 9-96 Moisture separator.

emergency purposes have the storage bottles equipped with a charging valve for ground servicing and a control valve to release pressure into the system being controlled. The control valve may be an on-off type valve where all of the bottle's contents is released at one time, or it may be such that the pilot can control the amount of pressure being applied to a system. The on-off control is found on landing "blow-down" systems, while the controllable valve is typically used for brake systems.

Moisture Control

In a pneumatic system it is of the utmost importance that the air in the system be completely dry. Moisture in the system can cause freezing of operating units; interfere with the normal operation of valves, pumps, etc., and cause corrosion. It is for this reason that moisture separators and chemical driers are used in pneumatic systems.

In each compressor pressure line, a mechanical **moisture separator,** shown in the drawing of Fig. 9-96, is installed to remove approximately 98 percent of any moisture and/or oil that may pass from the compressor. The separator is an aluminum tubular chamber, mounted vertically on the outboard side of the right nacelle and on the inboard side of the left nacelle.

Two valves are installed in the bottom of the separator. An inlet air pressure of 750 psi [5171 kPa] maximum closes the drain valve, while the inlet valve remains closed, thus preventing air from entering the separator. When pressure reaches 900 ± 150 psi [6205.5 ± 1034 kPa], the inlet valve opens and allows

air to flow. The inlet valve stays open as long as inlet pressure is above 1050 psi [7240 kPa]. The air entering the inlet port flows through the inlet valve seat, guide, and tube assembly, and through the orifices in the retainer assembly onto the baffle. The moisture droplets are deflected by the baffle, separated from the air stream, and caused to settle at the bottom of the air chamber against the closed drain valve.

As long as the inlet air pressure remains above 400 ± 150 psi [2758 ± 1034 kPa], the flow of air is through the inlet port, guide, tube assembly, and outlet port. When inlet air is reduced to 0 psi, the residual air flows through the ball check of the retainer assembly and out the open drain valve, pushing the collected moisture ahead of it. The separator is equipped with a safety disk which will burst at 5800 to 6200 psi [39 991 to 42 749 kPa] as a safety measure against overpressurization.

In the unit base is a small thermostatically controlled heater which prevents freezing of any moisture in the bottom of the air chamber. The heater is automatically operated by a hermetically sealed thermostat, located in the moisture separator body. The thermostat closes the electrical circuit at 35°F [1.67°C] to provide heating and opens the contacts at 85°F [29.44°C] maximum. With the primary bus switch ON and either the master or external power switch ON, 28-V dc power is available to the separator from the dc primary bus. To function properly, the moisture separator must be mounted vertically with the overboard drain at the bottom.

A tubular, **chemical-drier** housing is installed in each nacelle downstream of the mechanical moisture separator. The driers are mounted on brackets, one is located in the upper, inboard side of the left nacelle, the other on the upper, outboard side of the right nacelle. Each drier has an inlet and outlet port and contains a desiccant cartridge. Air is directed through this replaceable cartridge, and any moisture which the mechanical moisture separator has failed to remove will be absorbed by the dehydrating agent in the cartridge. The cartridge with dehydrating agent specification MIL-D-3716 incorporates two bronze filters, one at each end, which allows a 0.001-in [0.03-mm] maximum-size particle to pass through.

Filters

Three sintered pneumatic filters are used, one in each compressor circuit and one in the primary circuit. The **filter** is a vertically mounted unit, containing a replaceable filter element of stainless steel which removes foreign matter of 10μm or larger from the compressor output air. Two of the filters are mounted, one on the inboard side of the left nacelle on the forward side of the station 101 bulkhead and the other on the outboard side of the right nacelle on the aft side of the station 101 bulkhead. The filters are accessible for inspection when the main landing gear is in the extended position. The other filter is located on the top of the fuselage pneumatic panel and filters air as it comes from the primary storage bottle.

Other types of filters commonly found in pneumatic systems include micronic and wire screen filters. The micronic filter has a replaceable cartridge, while the wire screen filter can be cleaned and reused. The basic construction of these filters is the same as the micronic filter units used in hydraulic systems.

Pressure Control Valves

The **bleed valve,** controlled by compressor lubricating oil pressure, directs the compressed air to the compressor circuit relief valve and unloading valve. In the event the compressor oil pressure drops below 40 psi [275.8 kPa], the bleed valve will direct compressed air from the fourth stage overboard.

Pressure output from the bleed valve is routed to a **relief valve** in the unloading valve. The relief valve protects all components of the compressor circuit from excessive pressure buildup in the event any component downstream of the compressor malfunctions. The relief valve is set to open at 3800 psi [26 201 kPa].

The **unloading valve** contains a sensing valve and a directional control valve, and it directs compressor output through dehydration equipment to the system or vents the output overboard. The directional control valve, controlled by the sensing valve, opens and vents overboard when system pressure reaches 3300 psi [22 753.5 kPa], and closes when system pressure is less than 2900 psi [19 955.5 kPa].

A **back-pressure valve,** illustrated in Fig. 9-97, is installed in the pressure tube of the right nacelle only, to ensure that the engine-driven air compressor output is kept at a predetermined value of 1700 ± 150 psi [11 721.5 ± 1034 kPa]. This is to provide and maintain a

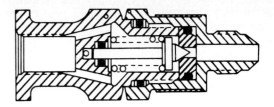

FIG. 9-97   Back-pressure valve.

fixed back pressure of approximately 1700 psi upstream of the air-drying equipment. The back-pressure valve is similar in construction and operation to a check valve and consists of a valve seat, piston, and spring. It is installed in the outlet port of the chemical drier and is directly connected to the inlet port of a check valve. The right engine compressor, or a ground charging unit, must be used for normal charging of the pneumatic system.

Poppet-type, spring-loaded, line-check valves are installed in the primary system, and each is identified by part number according to tube size. The construction of such a valve is shown in Fig. 9-98. One valve

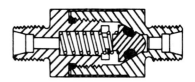

FIG. 9-98   Check valve.

is located in the inlet tube just before the point where the tube enters the primary bottle inlet port. This is a No. 3 check valve and is used with 3/16-in [4.76-mm] tubing. Note that the No. 3 designation for the check valve is an indication that the valve is to be used with 3/16-in tubing.

Another check valve is installed in the supply tube leading to the brake storage and is located on the left center edge of the fuselage pneumatic panel. This is a No. 6 valve and is used with 3/8-in [9.33-mm] tubing. Two spring-loaded, poppet-type, line-check valves are installed in each pneumatic power system in each nacelle. One No. 4 valve is installed in the outlet end of the back pressure valve; the other valve, a No. 3 size, is installed in the upper outlet port of the "T" fitting at approximate nacelle station 98.

A spring-loaded, piston **relief valve** is installed in the primary system and is located halfway up the fuselage pneumatic panel on the left side. The valve is preset, safetied, and tagged by the manufacturer for a cracking pressure of 3800 ± 50 psi [26 201 ± 345 kPa]. It protects the primary system from excessive pressure buildup in the event of thermal expansion or compressor power system malfunction.

This relief valve is designed to relieve pressure as a metering device instead of an instantaneous on-off valve. Its rate of relief automatically increases in direct proportion to the amount of overpressure. It reseats when the pressure decreases to approximately 3400 psi [23 400 kPa].

As mentioned previously, the air pressure employed for the operation of the landing-gear, propeller-braking, nose-wheel-steering, and passenger-door-retraction subsystems is reduced from 3300 [22 753.5] to 1000 psi [6895 kPa]. This is accomplished by means of the **pressure-reducing valve** installed in the primary pressure supply line. This valve is mounted on the pneumatic power panel just below the isolation valve as shown in the drawing of Fig. 9-99. The pressure-

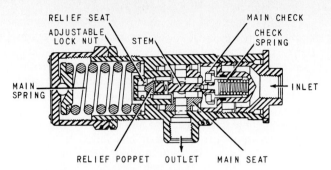

FIG. 9-100 Pressure-reducing valve.

thus work on the subsystems may be performed without discharging the entire system. The isolation valve is a two-position (open-close) type installed on the top right side of the pneumatic panel. The valve contains a spring-loaded, poppet-type plunger which is cam- and lever-operated. The location of the valve in the system is shown in Fig. 9-94. Connected to the valve lever is a push-pull rod-and-latch assembly which prevents closing the pneumatic panel door while the valve is in the closed position. This arrangement eliminates the possibility of operating the airplane while the air pressure is shut off.

Selector valves for pneumatic systems are similar in construction and operation to those used for hydraulic systems.

Miscellaneous System Components

The tubing used for the pneumatic system follows the pattern described for hydraulic systems. For the high-pressure sections of the system, stainless-steel tubing is employed. This type of tubing is used where the pressures reach or exceed 3000 psi [20 685 kPa]. The steel tubing conforms to specification MIL-T-8504 and varies in size from 3/16 to 3/8 in [4.76 to 9.33 mm] outside diameter (OD). Steel tubing is used to carry pressurized air from the compressor to the three storage bottles, pressure gauges, emergency brakes, and brake valve, and to the emergency landing-gear selector valve. Each end of the tubing is connected by the use of MS flareless fittings. Aluminum tubing is used to carry reduced pressurized air throughout the remainder of the system and conforms to specification MIL-T-7081. The aluminum tubing also uses MS flareless fittings and varies in size from 3/16 to 3/8 in [4.76 to 9.53 mm] OD. The network of tubing is stabilized by the use of clamps, clamp blocks, T fittings, unions, and elbows. Bonding strips are used as necessary to reduce static buildup and interference.

Pneumatic Manifold

An aluminum manifold having seven ports is mounted just below and to the left of the pressure-reducing valve on the pneumatic panel. As shown in the drawing of Fig. 9-99, the manifold is connected directly to the pressure-reducing valve. The manifold receives 1000 psi [6895 kPa] air pressure and passes this air to the nose-steering, propeller-brake, landing-gear, and passenger-door subsystems through a network of aluminum tubing. The lower end port of the manifold is sealed by a threaded plug.

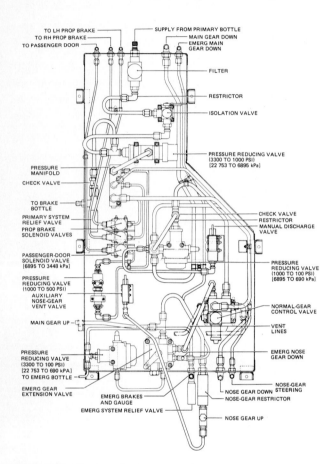

FIG. 9-99 Pneumatic power panel.

reducing valve contains dual springs and poppets which not only reduce pressure but also provide for pressure relief of the reduced pressure should the valve fail. A cross-section of the valve is shown in Fig. 9-100.

Additional protection is afforded the reducer relief valve by a restrictor elbow upstream of the isolation valve. The restrictor prevents excessive flow to the reducer and reducer relief valve.

Flow Control Valves

Installed in both the right and left nacelles is a two-position, three-port **shuttle valve.** The valve functions to direct air to the primary system from the compressor or the ground charging valve while preventing air flow from escaping through the lines not being used for supplying air.

The pneumatic power system is provided with an **isolation valve** so that the air-pressure storage section of the system can be isolated from the subsystems;

Primary Pressure Gauge

A direct-reading pressure gauge is connected to the primary air-storage bottle and is mounted in the pneumatic instrument panel on the right side of the crew compartment to provide a visual indication of the pressure in the primary bottle. The gauge is mounted adjacent to the emergency pressure gauge and is illuminated with two post lights. The dial of the gauge is calibrated from 0 to 4 × 1000 psi [6895 kPa] and should read 3300 psi [22 753.5 kPa] when the system is fully charged.

Ground Charging Valve

A **ground charging valve** is installed in both the left and right nacelles to provide a means of initial filling or ground charging the entire pneumatic system during the period when the engines are not operating. Normal ground charging is accomplished by using the right nacelle charging valve. If the system pressure is below 1000 psi [6895 kPa], the isolation valve should be closed before charging. The left nacelle charging valve should be used only during maintenance pressure checking of nacelle components or servicing the system with a dry-air source of supply.

The charging valve also acts as a protective device against an excessive rate of inlet airflow. The valve serves as a restrictor by providing a fixed orifice through which all ground-supplied compressed air must pass.

Safety-Disk Fitting

Just upstream of the ground-charging valve in each nacelle is a two-port safety-disk fitting incorporating a disk-type pressure relief assembly. The disk will rupture at approximately 4300 to 4950 psi [29 650 to 34 000 kPa], allowing air to escape through drilled passages in the retainer.

● SUMMARY OF MAINTENANCE PRACTICES

The maintenance of hydraulic and pneumatic systems should be performed in accordance with the aircraft manufacturer's instructions. The following is a summary of general practices followed when dealing with hydraulic and pneumatic systems.

Service

The servicing of hydraulic and pneumatic systems should be performed at the intervals specified by the manufacturer. Some components, such as hydraulic reservoirs, have servicing information adjacent to the component.

When servicing a hydraulic reservoir the mechanic must make certain to use the correct type of fluid. Hydraulic fluid type can be identified by color and smell; however, it is good practice to take fluid from an original marked container, then to check the fluid by color and smell for verification. Fluid containers should always be closed except when fluid is being removed. This practice reduces the possibility of contamination. Funnels and containers employed in filling the hydraulic reservoir must be clean and free of dust and lint.

When a system has lost a substantial amount of fluid and air has entered the system, it is necessary to fill the reservoir, purge the system of air, then add fluid to the FULL mark on the reservoir. Air is purged from the system by operating all subsystems through several cycles until all sounds of air in the system are eliminated. Air in a system causes a variety of sounds including banging, squealing, and chattering. The reservoir should be filled before the air is purged.

When cleaning filters or replacing filter elements, be sure there is no pressure on the filter. When changing hydraulic filters, wear the appropriate protective clothing and use a face shield as necessary to prevent fluid from contacting the eye. After filters have been cleaned or replaced, the system may have to be pressure-checked to locate any leaks in the filter assembly. Hydraulic fluid leaks are readily apparent because of the appearance of fluid. Large pneumatic leaks are indicated by the sound of escaping air and the feel of an airflow. Small pneumatic leaks should be located by the use of a soap and water solution.

Flushing a Hydraulic System

When inspection of hydraulic filters indicates that the fluid is contaminated, flushing the system is necessary. This should be done according to the manufacturer's instructions; however, a typical procedure for flushing the system is as follows:

1. Connect a ground hydraulic test stand to the inlet and outlet test posts of the system.
2. See that the fluid in the test unit is the same type as that used in the aircraft.
3. Pump clean, filtered fluid through the system and operate all subsystems until no further signs of contamination are found upon inspection of the filters. The airplane must be raised on jacks so the landing gear can be operated.
4. Disconnect the test stand and cap the ports.
5. See that the reservoir is filled to the FULL line.

Inspections

Hydraulic and pneumatic systems are inspected for leakage, worn or damaged tubing, worn or damaged hoses, wear of moving parts, security of mounting for all units, safetying, and any other condition specified by the maintenance manual. A complete inspection includes an operational check of all subsystems.

Leakage from any stationary connection in a system is not permitted, and if any such leak is found, it must be repaired. A small amount of fluid seepage may be permitted on actuator piston rods and rotating shafts. In a hydraulic system a thin film of fluid in these areas indicates that the seals are being properly lubricated. When a limited amount of leakage is allowed at any point, it is usually specified in the appropriate manual.

Tubing must not be nicked, cut, dented, collapsed, or twisted beyond approved limits as explained previously. The identification markings or lines on flexible hose will show whether the hose has been twisted.

All connections and fittings associated with moving

units should be examined for play evidencing wear. Such units should be in an unloaded condition when they are checked for wear.

Accumulators should be checked for leakage, air or gas preload, and position. If the accumulator is equipped with a pressure gauge, the preload can be read directly. Otherwise, the system pressure gauge can be used as explained previously. The accumulators should be mounted with the air chamber upward.

An operational check of the system can be performed using the engine-driven pump, an electrically operated auxiliary pump if such a pump is included in the system, or a ground test unit. The entire system and each subsystem should be checked for smooth operation, unusual noises, and speed of operation for each unit. The pressure section of the system should be checked with no subsystems to see that pressure holds for the required time without the pump supplying the system. System pressure should be observed during operation of each subsystem to see that the engine-driven pump will maintain required pressure.

Troubleshooting and Maintenance Practices

The troubleshooting of hydraulic and pneumatic systems varies according to the complexity of the system concerned and the components in the system. It is, therefore, important that the mechanic refer to the troubleshooting information furnished by the manufacturer.

Lack of pressure in a system can be caused by a sheared pump shaft, defective relief valve, pressure regulator or unloading valve stuck in the "kicked out" position, lack of fluid in a hydraulic system, check valve installed backward, or any condition which permits free flow back to the reservoir or overboard. If a system operates satisfactorily with a ground test unit but not with the system pump, the pump should be examined.

If a system fails to hold pressure in the pressure section, the likely cause is the pressure regulator or unloading valve, a leaking relief valve, or a leaking check valve.

If the pump fails to keep pressure up during operation of the subsystem, the pump may be worn, or one of the pressure-control units may be leaking.

High pressure in a system may be caused by a defective or improperly adjusted pressure regulator or unloading valve or by an obstruction in a line or control unit.

Unusual noise in a hydraulic system, such as banging and chattering, may be caused by air or contamination in the system. Such noises can also be caused by a faulty pressure regulator, another pressure control unit, or a lack of proper accumulator action.

An example of a troubleshooting chart for a hydraulic system is shown in Fig. 9-101. This chart is for one particular system and does not necessarily apply to other systems.

Maintenance of hydraulic and pneumatic systems involves a number of standard practices together with specialized procedures set forth by manufacturers. The mechanic may be called upon to replace valves,

actuators, and other units including tubing and hoses. In every case, the mechanic must exercise care to prevent system contamination; avoid damage to seals, packings, and other parts; and apply proper torque in connecting fittings.

Flexible hose, particularly the type with a Teflon fluorocarbon resin tubing, tends to take a set after a period of time. During the process of removing and reinstalling such hose sections, the mechanic should make no effort to straighten or change the shape of the hose. It is recommended that the hose be tied with a piece of cord or safety wire to hold its shape. When flexible hose is installed, the metal sleeve of the hose fitting should be held with a wrench while the nut is tightened to the fitting. Otherwise, the hose may be twisted and damaged. Twisted hose can be detected by observing the woven wire braiding or the painted lines on the outside of the hose.

Overhaul of hydraulic and pneumatic units is usually accomplished in approved repair facilities; however, replacement of seals and packings may be done from time to time by mechanics in the field. When a unit is disassembled, all O-ring and chevron seals should be removed and replaced with new seals. The new seals must be of the same material as the original and should carry the correct manufacturer's part number. No seal should be installed unless it is positively identified as the correct part and its shelf life has not expired.

When installing seals, the mechanic must exercise care to assure that the seal is not scratched, cut, or otherwise damaged. When it is necessary to install a seal over sharp edges, the edges should be covered with shim stock, plastic sheet, or masking tape. Sharp-edged metal tools should not be used to stretch the seals and force them into place.

When it is necessary to replace metal tubing, the old section of tubing can be used as a template or pattern for forming the new part. In many cases, the tubing section can be procured from stock or from a parts dealer by specifying the correct part number.

The replacement of hydraulic units and tubing always involves the spillage of some hydraulic fluid. The mechanic should take care to see that the spillage of fluid is kept to a minimum by closing valves, if available, and by plugging lines immediately after they are disconnected. All openings in hydraulic and pneumatic systems should be capped or plugged to prevent contamination of the system. It is particularly important to see that fire-resistant hydraulic fluid is not allowed to get on painted surfaces or other material which would be damaged. Fire-resistant fluids (phosphate ester type) have a powerful solvent characteristic and should be immediately removed from any surface which may be damaged including the skin.

The importance of the proper torque applied to all nuts and fittings in a system cannot be overemphasized. Too much torque will damage metal and seals, and too little torque will result in leaks and loose parts. In every case, the mechanic should procure torque wrenches with the proper range before assembling units of a system.

Additional information regarding aircraft plumbing,

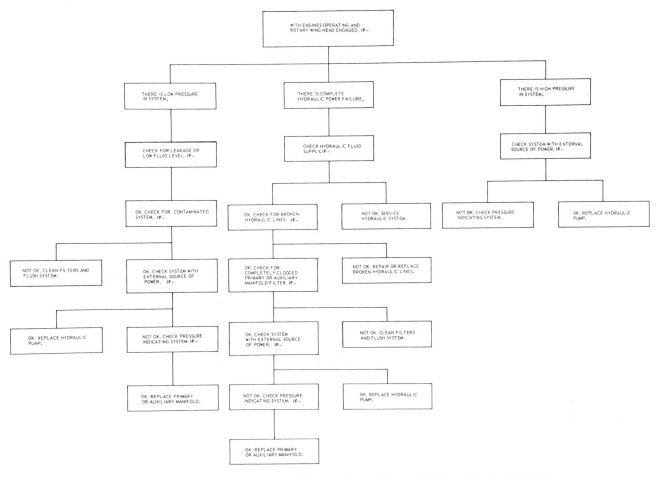

FIG. 9-101 Troubleshooting chart. *(Sikorsky Aircraft Corp., Division of United Technologies Corp.)*

including plumbing for hydraulic and pneumatic systems, is provided in the associated text on aircraft basic science.

● REVIEW QUESTIONS

1. What is the principal difference between a hydraulic power system and a pneumatic power system?
2. Explain how force and power are developed through the use of hydraulic fluids.
3. What principle is expressed in Pascal's law?
4. Discuss the effects of friction in moving liquids.
5. Explain the multiplication of force by means of hydraulics.
6. Why is a gear-type pump described as a *positive displacement pump*?
7. In an axial multipiston pump, what causes the reciprocating motion of the pistons?
8. Describe two types of *variable delivery* pumps and explain the operation of each.
9. Describe a *rotary, four-way valve*.
10. Explain how *poppet valves* control fluid flow.
11. Explain the operation of *spool-type valves*.
12. How are the selector valves in an *open-center system* connected with respect to one another?
13. Describe an *orifice check* valve. For what purpose would such a valve be used?
14. Explain a *sequence valve* operation and purpose.
15. What can occur if a sequence valve is not properly adjusted?
16. Under what conditions is a *shuttle valve* required?
17. Explain the operation and use of a *hydraulic fuse*.
18. Explain the operation and use of a *priority valve*.
19. Describe the operation of a *relief valve*.
20. What determines the *cracking pressure* of a relief valve?
21. Why is a *wing-flap overload valve* installed in the down line of a flap-actuating system?
22. Describe a *pressure regulator*. An *unloading valve*.
23. How does a pressure regulator or unloading valve serve to prolong the life of the system pump?
24. Why are *thermal-relief valves* needed in certain sections of a hydraulic system?
25. Explain the *debooster* principle.
26. What are the two functions of an *accumulator*?
27. Describe a piston-type accumulator.
28. In what position should an accumulator be installed?
29. What precautions should be taken before removing an accumulator from a hydraulic system?
30. What is a *hydraulic actuator*?

31. Describe a *double-acting hydraulic actuating* cylinder.
32. How does a *servo actuator* differ from an actuating cylinder?
33. Compare a hydraulic motor with a piston-type pump.
34. Discuss the installation of *O-ring seals*.
35. When O-ring seals are used in high-pressure systems, what devices are often necessary?
36. What are different filter elements that may be found in hydraulic systems?
37. What precautions should be followed when installing hydraulic hoses?
38. When removing *Teflon* hoses that are to be reused, what precautions should be followed?
39. How does a *gerotor pump* work?
40. What are the two basic styles of reservoirs?
41. List the different types of hydraulic pumps used on an L-1011.
42. What gases may be used to charge the pneumatic bottles?
43. What are uses for pneumatic bottles in a hydraulic system?
44. How should a *chevron seal* be installed with respect to fluid pressure?
45. What should be done to protect seals from damage during installation?
46. What materials are used for hydraulic tubing in high-pressure systems?
47. To what extent can a bend in hydraulic tubing be straightened without making it unacceptable?
48. To what extent may nicks or scratches in aluminum be repaired by burnishing?
49. Describe two types of tubing fittings.
50. Describe the installation of *flareless fittings*.
51. What will occur if a flareless fitting is over-torqued?
52. Where in a hydraulic system is flexible hose used?
53. Describe the installation of hydraulic tubing and the conditions which must be observed.
54. How do you install reusable fittings to flexible hose?
55. Describe a quick-disconnect *seal coupling*.
56. Describe a hydraulic reservoir.
57. What is the purpose of a *standpipe* in a reservoir?
58. Why is it necessary to pressurize some reservoirs?
59. Give three methods by which a hydraulic reservoir may be pressurized.
60. Where would the mechanic look for information regarding the servicing of a hydraulic reservoir?
61. Name three types of hydraulic fluids and describe their basic characteristics.
62. What precaution must be taken with a phosphate ester fluid such as Skydrol?
63. Compare a *direct-pressure* hydraulic system with an *open-center* system.
64. Describe the Powerpak in the hydraulic system for the Piper Apache airplane.
65. Why cannot the landing gear and flaps be used at the same time in a Piper Apache hydraulic system?
66. Describe the operation of a light airplane hydraulic system designed for operation of landing gear only.
67. What is the purpose of the *free-fall* valve?
68. What is the principal advantage of a high-pressure hydraulic system?
69. Name the three principal hydraulic systems for the Boeing 727 airplane.
70. What types of pumps are employed in the hydraulic power systems for the Boeing 727 airplane?
71. What materials are used for tubing, gaskets, and seals in a system operated with Skydrol hydraulic fluid?
72. What systems are served by system A in the Boeing 727?
73. Describe the heat exchange and why it is needed.
74. What type of accumulator is used in the Boeing 727 and what is the gas preload?
75. What is the purpose of the *ground interconnect valve*?
76. For what functions is the pneumatic power system on the Fairchild F-27 airplane used?
77. How is the high-pressure air stored in the Fairchild F-27 pneumatic system?
78. Describe the operation of the four-stage compressor.
79. What is the purpose of the *isolation valve* in the F-27 pneumatic system?
80. Explain the need for dry air in a pneumatic system.
81. Describe the operation of the *moisture separator*.
82. What is a *desiccant*?
83. What is the function of the *back-pressure valve*?
84. What air pressure is actually used for the operation of the landing-gear, propeller-braking, nose-wheel-steering, and passenger-door subsystems?
85. How is lowered pressure obtained from the high-pressure air source?
86. Explain the use of the ground-charging valve.
87. What tubing is used in the F-27 pneumatic system?
88. List the principal considerations necessary when servicing a hydraulic reservoir.
89. How may a hydraulic system be purged of air?
90. How may a hydraulic system be flushed to eliminate contamination?
91. List inspections which should be made to assure the airworthiness of a hydraulic system.
92. What conditions may cause lack of pressure in a hydraulic system?
93. What may cause the pressurized section of a hydraulic system to lose pressure?
94. How may a removed section of tubing be useful in the manufacture of a new section?

10 AIRCRAFT LANDING GEAR SYSTEMS

Landing-gear designs for aircraft vary from simple, fixed arrangements to very complex retractable systems involving many hundreds of parts. In this section we shall deal with typical examples of landing gear and the systems by which they are operated. Because of the many different designs in use, we cannot cover specific details of many systems; however, we shall describe some of the types in common use and the standard practices followed in maintenance, repair, and service. In all cases, the mechanic should refer to the appropriate maintenance manual when servicing particular aircraft.

● TIRES AND WHEELS

The tires and wheels of an airplane are subject to severe stresses during landing and in taxiing over rough ground. Failure of a tire or wheel can lead to extremely serious accidents, often resulting in the complete destruction of the aircraft and injury or death to the crew and passengers. For these reasons, the mechanic must make certain the wheels and tires of the aircraft are in good condition for all environments under which the aircraft may operate.

Aircraft Tires

Aircraft tires are manufactured in a variety of sizes and strengths, and the correct types are specified by the manufacturers according to the size and landing speed of the aircraft involved. Construction is similar to that of automobile and truck tires. The number of fabric plies in the tires varies from 2 to 16 or more. The majority of tires in use today on light aircraft are of the tube-type, while most transport aircraft tires are of the tubeless type. Tube-type tires make use of inner tubes to hold the air charge. **Balance marks** are placed on tires in the form of a red dot on the side of the tire at the lightest point.

Aircraft tires are classified by type numbers according to performance as shown in the following table:

Type	Design and Rating
I	Smooth contour
II	High pressure
III	Low pressure
IV	Extra low pressure
V	Not applicable
VI	Low profile
VII	Extra high pressure, low speed
	Extra high pressure, high speed
VIII	Extra high pressure, low profile, low speed
	Extra high pressure, low profile, high speed

Tires classified as Types I, II, IV, and VI are phasing out because these classifications are inactive for new design. Tires classified as Types III, VII, and VIII are manufactured under the provisions of FAR 37.167 and are approved under Technical Standard Order (TSO) No. C62b. Such tires are required to be permanently marked with the brand name or name of the manufacturer responsible for compliance and the country of manufacture if manufactured outside the United States; the size, ply rating, and serial number; the qualification test speed and skid depth when the test speed is greater than 160 mph [257.6 km/h], also the word *reinforced* if applicable; and the applicable TSO number. Type III tires and those specified as low-speed tires are approved for ground speeds of less than 160 mph [257.6 km/h].

In all cases of tire replacement, the mechanic must determine that the type of tire specified for the aircraft is installed.

Aircraft tires may be **recapped** (have new tread added) by FAA-approved repair stations. When a tire is recapped, the tire structure is checked for soundness and then a new layer of tread is attached to the original carcass. The use of recapped tires is not an acceptable practice on all aircraft. This is not as a result of any decrease in strength, but the fact that recapped tires may be slightly larger than new tires. If recapped tires are used on retractable-gear aircraft, the slightly oversize tire may jam in the wheel well. This could result in the aircraft having to make a gear-up landing. Check with the aircraft manufacturer's manual when determining if recapped tires may be used on a specific model aircraft.

Tire Structure

A **tire** is a layered structure designed to withstand the shock and sudden acceleration of landing, the heat of brake applications, and the abrasion of landing and turning. As shown in Fig. 10-1, there are many different components of a tire.

The **steel wire beads** serve as the foundation for the attachment of the fabric plies and provide firm mounting surfaces on the wheel. The **plies** are diagonal layers of rubber-coated nylon cord fabric, laid in alternating directions, that provide the strength of the tire. The ply material wraps around the wire beads. The apex strips and flippers prevent the bead from abrading the plies. **Chafers** are used to protect the tire during mounting and demounting, to insulate the carcass from brake heat, and to provide a good seal between the

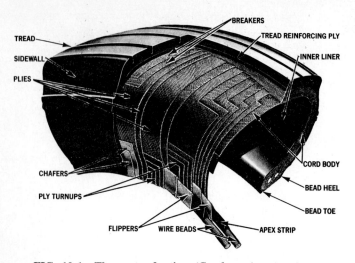

TREAD
SIDEWALL
PLIES
BREAKERS
TREAD REINFORCING PLY
INNER LINER
CHAFERS
PLY TURNUPS
CORD BODY
BEAD HEEL
BEAD TOE
FLIPPERS
WIRE BEADS
APEX STRIP

FIG. 10-1 The parts of a tire. *(Goodyear Aerospace)*

tire and wheel. An inner layer of rubber is used to form an air seal on tubeless tires and to prevent tube chafing on tube-type tires. **Breakers** and the tread reinforcing plies are used to increase the structural strength on some tires. All of the parts of the tire except the tread make up the tire carcass.

The **tread** is the rubber compound on the surface of the tire which is designed for runway contact. The pattern, or grooves, in the tread are designed for maximum traction in widely varying runway conditions.

The terms **sidewall, bead toe,** and **bead heel** are used to designate the areas indicated in Fig. 10-1.

Tire Storage

Tires should be stored in areas that are cool, dry, and dark. Moisture causes the rubber and ply material to deteriorate. Exposure to ozone, such as from electric motors, battery chargers, and other electrical equipment, can cause the rubber to age rapidly. Petroleum products, such as oil, grease, hydraulic fluid, and gasoline, and solvents attack the rubber.

To prevent distortion, tires should be stored vertically in racks. If they must be stacked on their sides, the stacks should be no more than four high.

Tubes

Tire tubes are made of rubber sections that are vulcanized together. Ribs on the tube are designed to provide traction between the tire liner and the tube so that the tire will not rotate in relation to the tube,

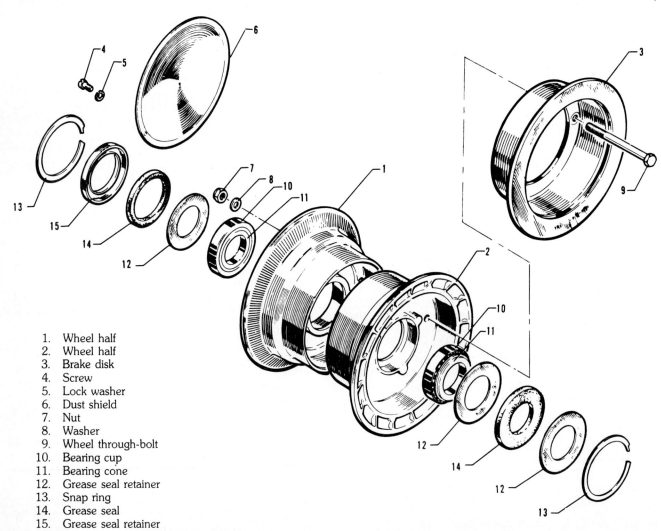

1. Wheel half
2. Wheel half
3. Brake disk
4. Screw
5. Lock washer
6. Dust shield
7. Nut
8. Washer
9. Wheel through-bolt
10. Bearing cup
11. Bearing cone
12. Grease seal retainer
13. Snap ring
14. Grease seal
15. Grease seal retainer

FIG. 10-2 Main wheel assembly for a light airplane. *(Piper Aircraft Corp.)*

causing abrasion damage. An **air valve** is vulcanized to the tube to allow inflation and deflation.

Wheel Construction

Airplane wheels are constructed by a number of methods. Among these are (1) forming of heavy-sheet aluminum alloy, (2) casting of aluminum or magnesium alloy, and (3) forging of aluminum or magnesium alloy.

One type of wheel assembly is shown in the exploded drawing of Fig. 10-2. This is a two-piece, cast-alloy wheel designed for a light airplane. The two wheel halves are joined together with the brake disk by means of the wheel through-bolts. Bearing cups are pressed into recesses in each wheel half. Grease seals and grease-seal retainers are installed outside each bearing to prevent the escape of grease.

Another type of wheel for a light aircraft is shown in Fig. 10-3. This wheel is composed of a hub with a flange on each side. The bearings and grease-seal arrangement are similar to those in Fig. 10-2.

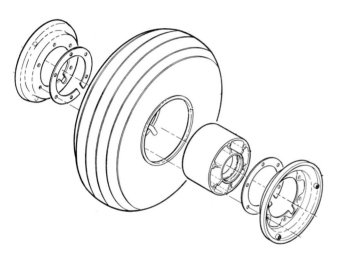

FIG. 10-3 A hub-and-flange wheel assembly. (Cessna Aircraft Co.)

A main wheel assembly for a small jet airplane is shown in the drawing of Fig. 10-4. This assembly is designed for use with tubeless tires. Note that the wheel is composed of a flange which bolts to the hub.

The hub and flange are held together with 15 high-strength bolts and self-locking nuts. A packing is installed between the two wheel parts to provide an air seal. The wheel hub contains an inflation valve for inflating and deflating the tire.

The hub also has five keys that engage and drive the tangs of the rotating brake disks. Three **fusible plugs** mounted in the wheel hub are designed to release air from the tire in the event that the temperature of the wheel reaches the point where the wheel and/or tire may be damaged.

The wheel rotates on two tapered roller bearings, the cups of which are shrink-fitted into the hub of each wheel half. The bearing cones are retained in the wheel halves and protected from dirt and moisture by bearing seals.

As discussed in previous wheel descriptions, aircraft wheels are commonly made in two pieces, inboard and outboard, to facilitate the changing of tires. Typical of such a wheel for a jet airliner is that shown in the drawing of Fig. 10-5. This is a cutaway drawing of the main landing-gear wheel for the Douglas DC-9 airplane and is described as a Goodyear 40 × 14, type VII, forged-aluminum, split-type wheel. The wheel halves are joined by 12 high-tensile steel bolts with self-locking nuts. An air seal is provided by an O-ring installed in a groove in the outer wheel half to prevent loss of air from the tubeless tire. Standard, tapered roller bearings are installed in each wheel half. The inner bearings are protected against loss of lubricant and the entrance of dirt by moisture-resistant seals. The tires are protected against blowouts resulting from excessive pressure created by heat by three fusible plugs equally spaced around the wheel. The plugs are installed in an accessible location to allow replacement without removing the tire.

On the inside half of the wheel are installed the steel keys which hold the brake rotor disks. These are secured to the wheel forging by means of screws.

The main wheels for wide-bodied transports are of the same basic design as the DC-9 example. Wheel design features may include a pressure-release plug to release excessive pressure and a deflector over the fusible plug and release plug to prevent them from causing damage to the aircraft when they are forced out of the wheel assembly.

Nosewheels for aircraft are constructed and serviced in a manner similar to main wheels. Nosewheels are often smaller in diameter and width than main wheels, and only a few aircraft use brakes on the nosewheel. If a nosewheel is not designed to accept a brake assembly, a fusible plug is not used. A pressure release device may still be used. A cross-sectional drawing of a nosewheel for a large airplane is shown in Fig. 10-6.

Demounting and Mounting Tires

Regardless of the type or size of tire involved, the same basic procedures and the exercise of certain precautions will assure that the tire will continue to hold air. The general procedures are not difficult, and it is only necessary that the mechanic use good judgment and follow the instructions provided by both the manufacturer of the airplane and the manufacturer of the tire.

Before a wheel is removed from the airplane, the tire should be deflated. This is an important safety procedure. Deflation is accomplished by removing the core from the air valve or as specified in service instructions. The wheel is then removed according to instructions, the mechanic being careful to see that the bearings are protected from damage and dirt.

With the wheel lying flat, the tire beads are broken away from the rims by applying pressure in even increments around the entire sidewall as close to the tire beads as possible. Sharp tools should not be used to pry the tire loose because the tire air seal will likely be damaged and the wheel can be nicked or scratched. It is recommended that an approved demounting machine be used to free tire beads from wheel rims.

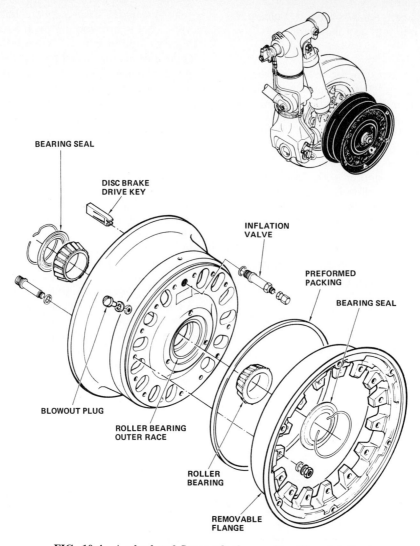

FIG. 10-4   A wheel-and-flange wheel assembly. *(Canadair Inc.)*

Labels in figure: BEARING SEAL, DISC BRAKE DRIVE KEY, INFLATION VALVE, PREFORMED PACKING, BEARING SEAL, BLOWOUT PLUG, ROLLER BEARING OUTER RACE, ROLLER BEARING, REMOVABLE FLANGE

The nuts and bolts holding the wheel halves together should then be removed and the wheel halves separated from the tire. The O-ring air seal or packing found in tubeless tire installations should be carefully removed and placed in a protected area where it will not be damaged or contaminated with dirt.

The wheel, tire, and tube (if used) should be inspected in accordance with the manufacturer's guidelines. After the components are determined to be airworthy, the tire can be mounted on the wheel.

If a tube-type wheel and tire are being assembled, the following general procedure is used. Before placing the tube in the tire, the tube should be lightly dusted with tire talc. This is to prevent the tube from sticking to the inside of the tire. An excessive amount of talc should not be applied. To obtain the proper balance of the tire and tube, the inner tube should be placed in the tire so that the yellow strip is located at the red dot in the tire. Mating of the tire and tube in this manner will bring the unit into the balance tolerance required. Before the tube is placed in the tire, the tube should be inflated sufficiently to give it shape but not so much that the rubber is stretched.

If a tubeless wheel and tire are being assembled, the following general procedure is used. The tire should be examined to make sure the word "tubeless" is molded on the sidewall. The beads of the tire must be inspected to see that there are no nicks, cuts, or other conditions which can cause air leaks between the tire and the wheel rim.

The air-seal mating surface of the wheel should be cleaned with denatured alcohol. Small particles of sand or dirt in this area can cause leakage of air. The air valve in the rim should be examined to make sure that the seal between the valve stem and the wheel rim is intact.

The wheel air seal (O-ring) should be lubricated with a light coat of grease, preferably of the type conforming to MIL-L-7711. This permits the seal to slide easily into the seal seat when the two halves of the wheel are joined. The seal should be equalized on the wheel and not twisted. If the seal is reused, it should be installed as nearly as possible in the position originally placed.

With only a few exceptions, the remainder of the installation is the same for both types of assemblies.

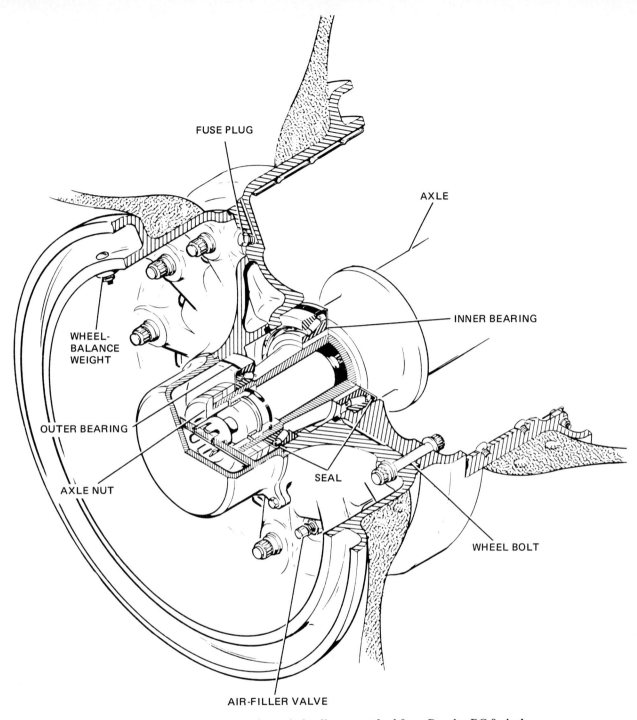

FUSE PLUG

AXLE

INNER BEARING

WHEEL-
BALANCE
WEIGHT

OUTER BEARING

AXLE NUT

SEAL

WHEEL BOLT

AIR-FILLER VALVE

FIG. 10-5   Cutaway drawing of a main landing-gear wheel for a Douglas DC-9 airplane.

The wheel hub and flanges are now assembled on the tire. On the tube-type tire, the side of the hub with the air valve is placed in the tire first, the valve is pulled into position on the wheel half, and the second half of the wheel is inserted into the tire. For a tubeless tire, the wheel halves are placed on the tire, taking care to align the tire balance mark (red dot) with the air valve in the wheel. In both cases check inside the center of the wheel (where the axle goes through) to be sure that the tube or the packing seal is not pinched between the wheel halves.

Bolts are now installed, taking care that the bolts

and nuts are on the appropriate side. In some installations the use of an antiseize may be required—check the aircraft maintenance manual. If countersunk washers are used under the bolt heads, they are usually positioned with the countersink toward the bolt head. The bolts are now brought down flush with the wheel using an alternating tightening sequence. Once all of the bolts are flush, an alternating torque sequence is used to tighten the bolts. They are first torqued to about 25 percent of final torque, and then torque is brought up to installation torque in increments of 20 to 25 percent, using an alternating torque sequence.

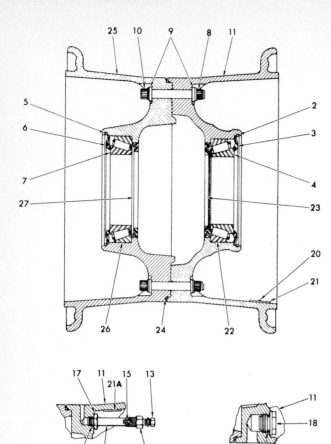

1. Tire bead seat
2. Retaining ring
3. Outboard bearing seal
4. Outboard bearing cone
5. Retaining ring
6. Inboard bearing seal
7. Inboard bearing cone
8. Self-locking nut
9. Countersunk washer
10. Wheel bolt
11. Wheel subassembly, outer half
12. Valve subassembly
13. Valve cap
14. Adapter
15. Valve core
16. O-ring packing
17. Valve stem
18. Pressure-release plug
19. O-ring packing
20. Drive screw
21. Data plate
21A. Instruction plate
22. Bearing cup
23. Grease baffle
24. O-ring packing
25. Wheel subassembly, inboard half
26. Bearing cup
27. Grease baffle

FIG. 10-6 Cutaway drawing of a nosewheel for a large airplane. *(Goodyear Aerospace)*

The tire is now placed in an inflation cage before being inflated. This prevents damage and injury if the wheel or tire is defective and ruptures during inflation. With the valve core removed, a tube-type tire is inflated slightly and then allowed to deflate. This allows any wrinkles in the tube to straighten out. The valve core is then installed and the tire is inflated to operational pressure. A tubeless tire is first inflated to partial pressure to seat the tire bead to the wheel. It may be necessary to use a strap around the surface of the tread to prevent the tire from expanding radially. This aids smaller tires in seating properly against the wheel. Once the bead is seated, the strap is removed and the

tire is inflated to operating pressure. Nitrogen is the preferred gas for tire inflation.

Tires should be allowed to set, fully inflated, for 12 to 24 h before being installed on an aircraft. This allows any small leaks to become evident and allows the tire to "grow." Because of this growth the larger size causes the pressure to drop slightly. The tire is brought back up to pressure, removed from the cage, and installed on the aircraft.

If the tires are to be installed on an aircraft with retractable gear, a retraction check should be performed if there is any doubt as to proper clearance between the tire and the wheel well structure when the wheel is retracted.

During the installation of tires on automobile wheels, a soap solution is sometimes used to make the bead of the tire slip more easily over the rim. This should not be done with airplane tires because it may cause slippage of the tire on the rim, particularly upon landing. If the tire slips on the rim, the valve stem will be pulled out of the tube and the tire will deflate. If tubeless tires slip on the rim, the air seal will be broken and the tire will deflate.

Tire and Wheel Inspection

The inspection of tires and wheels should be performed periodically to assure that they are not damaged or worn excessively. The frequency and extent of inspections depends on the type of aircraft and flying activity involved.

The surface condition of a tire can be inspected with the tire on the aircraft. The tread should be checked for abnormal wear. If the tread is worn in the center of the tire, but not on the edges, this indicates that the tire is overinflated and the operational air pressure should be reduced. On the other hand, if the tire is worn on the edges, but not in the center, this indicated underinflation. These situations are shown in Fig. 10-7.

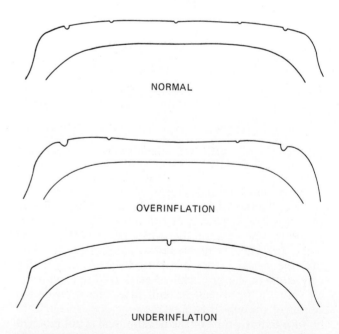

FIG. 10-7 Examples of tread wear indicating overinflation and underinflation.

Certain aircraft normally wear the tread unevenly due to the type of landing gear used. For example, aircraft with spring-steel landing gear have the main wheels suspended out from the side of the fuselage on a spring-steel gear leg. When the aircraft is in flight the wheel hangs down with the outer edge of the tire below the inside edge of the tire. When the aircraft is on the ground, the two edges are perpendicular to the ground. When the aircraft lands, the tires slide outward in transition from the hanging position, thus wearing off the tread on the outside of the tire faster than on the inside of the tire. This wear is normal.

The tread is normally allowed to wear down until the groove pattern is on the verge of being completely removed. The minimum amount of tread that is acceptable varies with the tire and the aircraft manufacturer.

The following are different types of tire damage and some guidelines to follow in determining airworthiness. Consult the tire or aircraft manufacturer's manuals for specific information. Any damage which does not penetrate through the tread and into the carcass plies is generally acceptable. However, if the tread damage involves peeling tread, thrown tread, or deep damage across the tread that could lead to peeling or throwing, the tire should be removed from service. Blister and bulges indicate a separation within the tread or between ply layers. These tires should be removed from service.

Flat spots indicate excessive use of brakes for deceleration and when turning. If sufficient tread remains and the tire does not cause an out-of-balance condition, this is generally acceptable. If plies are showing, insufficient tread remains, or the tire is out of balance, then the tire should be replaced.

Damage to the sidewalls that is acceptable includes cuts, small cracks, and weather checking (a random pattern of shallow cracks), provided that the cord is not exposed or damaged.

Damage that is visible when the tire is removed from the wheel includes bead damage and inner liner damage. Damage in these areas is more critical for tubeless tires than for tube-type tires because of the air sealing requirements. Check with the manufacturer for specific information as to airworthiness standards.

The recapping of tires is a standard industry practice. To be recapped, the tire carcass must be in airworthy condition. Some ply damage may be acceptable, depending on the type of tire and the number of plies involved. Tires can be recapped as often as five times, but most are not recapped more than three times because of carcass deterioration.

Tires that are recapped must be permanently marked to provide required information. Whenever it is necessary to replace the area containing the original markings, such markings must be replaced. In addition, each retreaded tire must display the letter R followed by a number such as 1, 2, or 3 to signify the sequential number of recaps which have been applied. A marking must be applied to display the speed category increase if the tire is qualified for increased speed in accordance with the requirements of FAR 37.167 (TSO-C62). The month and year of recapping must be shown together with the name of the person or agency that applied the recap. Each repaired or recapped tire should not exceed the static unbalance limits as set forth in TSO-C62.

Operators such as airlines, through experience with the operating characteristics of tires, establish criteria for the recapping of tires. For example, an airline may find that a particular tire can make approximately 200 landings for each time it is recapped and that it can be recapped at least 10 times before the carcass becomes unairworthy. Some airlines buy tires from tire manufacturers and pay for the tires in accordance with the number of landings the tire can make during its life.

Tubes should be inspected for chaffing, thinning, and elasticity. The valve stem should be checked for flexibility where it attaches to the tube. The tube can be checked for leaks by inflating slightly and then placing it in a water tank.

Inner tubes can usually be repaired in the same manner as those used for automobiles. It is recommended that the repair patches be vulcanized and that an excessive number of patches be avoided. This is because the weight of the patching material can affect the balance of the wheel-and-tire assembly.

Airplane wheels receive very severe stresses at times; hence it is of the utmost importance that they be kept in airworthy condition. Unsatisfactory conditions for aircraft wheels include cracks, dents, abrasion, corrosion, distortion, looseness of assembly bolts, and worn or loose bearings. The degree of any such condition should be checked to determine whether the wheel should be repaired or replaced.

Cracks in wheels usually require replacement of the wheel; however, if it is believed that a crack can be repaired, the repair should be approved by an inspector of the FAA.

Small dents in formed sheet-metal wheels do not necessarily impair the strength of the wheel. However, if the wheel is dented or distorted to the extent that it wobbles, it should be repaired or replaced.

To thoroughly inspect a wheel, the wheel must first be disassembled, and then cleaned of all paint, grease, dirt, and corrosion.

Inspection of large cast or forged wheel parts is accomplished with fluorescent penetrant, dye penetrant, eddy-current, and ultrasonic methods. All parts are examined for cracks, nicks, cuts, corrosion, damaged threads, and any other damage including excessive wear. Damage which exceeds the manufacturer's limits requires replacement of the part involved. Cracked wheel forgings or castings must be replaced. Particular attention is given to tire bead seats to assure that they are smooth and will not allow leakage of air.

In the inspection and repair of any aircraft wheel, the mechanic must determine whether the wheel is made from aluminum, magnesium, or some other metal because the treatment varies in some respects with different metals. The manufacturer's maintenance manual sets forth procedures and processes that are correct for a particular model of wheel.

Split-type wheels must be examined to determine the amount of wear in the assembly bolt holes. If the bolts have loosened during operation, they can very quickly enlarge the holes in the wheels. Sometimes enlarged or elongated holes can be repaired with inserts; however, the repair must have the approval of the manufacturer or an FAA representative.

Wheel bearings are inspected by removing the wheels and examining the bearings and bearing cups (races). The bearings should be washed in a suitable petroleum solvent and then dried. The rollers should show no signs of wear, discoloration, or roughness and should rotate freely in their cages. The bearing cups should be smooth with no signs of ripple, cracks, scoring, galling, corrosion, discoloration, or any other damage. If the bearings are in good condition, they can be reinstalled in accordance with the manufacturer's instructions.

Bearing cups are pressed into the wheel assembly. If they are damaged, they must be pressed out and replaced. If the bearing cup is loose in the wheel, the bearing recess in the wheel is oversize and the wheel must be replaced.

During inspection of the wheel bearings, the felt grease retainers should be examined for effectiveness. If they are hardened or glazed, they should be reconditioned or replaced with new ones.

Wheel Installation

There are various procedures used for the installation of wheel assemblies on an aircraft. The following provides some general guidelines.

The axle is cleaned and inspected. Surface damage and any damage to the axle threads are standard inspection items along with the condition and security of bolts holding the axle onto the landing-gear leg. The wheel bearings are cleaned and packed with approved grease. The wheel and tire are inspected and assembled. The wheel assembly and bearings are carefully slid onto the axle and back against a rear collar or stop on the axle. The retaining nut is next installed and safetied.

Great care must be exercised to see that the wheel-retaining nuts are not overtightened. In the absence of specific instructions, the wheel-retaining nut is tightened snug but not tight. The nut is then backed off about one serration (castellation) or one-sixth turn before bending up the tab on the tab-lock washer or installing the cotter pin.

The grease cover or wheel cover, if used, is then installed. During this installation any required brake, air pressure sensors, and speed sensor components are installed and connected as appropriate for the specific aircraft.

● LANDING-GEAR CONFIGURATIONS

The majority of aircraft are equipped with landing gear that can be classified as **tricycle** or **conventional.**

Tricycle landing gear is characterized by having a nosewheel assembly and two main gear assemblies, one on each side of the aircraft as shown in Fig. 10-8. This arrangement places the aircraft fuselage in a level attitude when on the ground. In this attitude the pilot has good forward visibility and the cabin area is level for the ease of movement of passengers inside the aircraft on the ground. This configuration also makes the aircraft stable during ground operations and easy to control. This is especially important during takeoff and landing.

Conventional-geared aircraft, illustrated in Fig. 10-9, have two main wheel assemblies, one on each side of the aircraft, and a tail wheel. This arrangement is normally associated with older aircraft and those designed for rough field operations. This arrangement has the advantage of reduced drag in the air and reduced landing-gear weight. There is some loss of forward visibility for the pilot when maneuvering on the ground due to the aircraft nose-high attitude. This configuration requires more skill when taxiing and during takeoff and landing when compared to a tricycle-geared aircraft.

● CLASSIFICATION OF LANDING GEAR

The **landing gear** of an airplane serves a number of very important functions. It supports the airplane during ground operations, dampens vibrations when the airplane is being taxied or towed, and cushions the landing impact. The landing of an airplane often in-

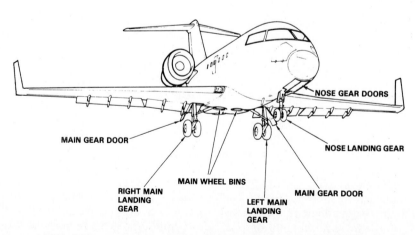

FIG. 10-8   A tricycle landing-gear arrangement. *(Canadair Inc.)*

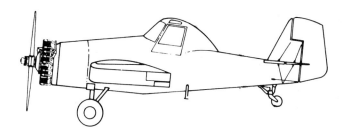

FIG. 10-9 An aircraft with a conventional landing-gear configuration. *(Ayres Corp.)*

volves stresses far in excess of what may be considered normal; hence the landing gear must be constructed and maintained in a manner which provides the strength and reliability to meet all probable landing conditions.

The landing gear of an airplane consists of main and auxiliary units, either of which may be fixed (nonretractable) or retractable. The **main landing gear** provides the main support of the airplane on land or water. It may include a combination of wheels, floats, skis, shock-absorbing equipment, brakes, retracting mechanism, controls, warning devices, cowling, fairing, and structural members needed for attachment to the primary structure of the airplane.

The **auxiliary landing gear** consists of tail or nose landing-wheel installations, skids, outboard pontoons, etc., with the necessary cowling and reinforcements.

Nonabsorbing Landing Gear

Nonabsorbing landing gear includes those types of landing gear that do not dissipate the energy of the aircraft contacting the ground during landing. They only store the energy to return it to the aircraft at a later time. These types of gear include **rigid landing gear**, **shock-cord landing gear**, and **spring-type gear.**

A rigid landing gear is commonly found on helicopters and sailplanes. This gear is rigidly mounted to the aircraft with no specific component to cushion the ground contact other than through the flexing of the landing gear or airframe structure. An example of this type of gear is the landing-gear skid of the helicopter shown in Fig. 10-10. The landing gear of a sailplane is often no more than a wheel and tire mounted directly on the airframe. The tire provides some cushioning effect, but no mechanism is designed specifically to soften the ground contact. Both of these types of aircraft rely on pilot skill for a soft ground contact.

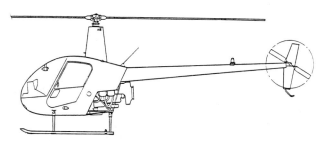

FIG. 10-10 A skid-equipped helicopter. *(Robinson Helicopter Company, Inc.)*

When rubber **shock cord** is used, the landing-gear struts are usually made of steel tubing mounted in such a manner that a stretching action is applied to tightly wound rubber cord. When landing shock occurs, the cord is stretched, thus storing the impact energy of landing. The stored energy is gradually returned to the aircraft during the landing roll.

Shock cord must be replaced periodically because of rubber deterioration. The cord is color-coded to indicate when it was manufactured, thus giving the mechanic the information needed to determine the life of the cord. According to MIL-C-5651A, the color code for the year of manufacture is repeated in cycles of 5 years. Table 10-1 shows the colors of the code threads for each year and quarter of year.

TABLE 10-1 Cord Color Codes

Year	Color	Quarter	Color
1975 and 1980	Black	1st	Red
1976 and 1981	Green	2d	Blue
1977 and 1982	Red	3d	Green
1978 and 1983	Blue	4th	Yellow
1979 and 1984	Yellow		
1980 and 1985	Black		

The color coding is composed of threads interwoven in the cotton sheath which binds the strands of rubber cord together. Two spiral threads are used for the year coding and one thread for the quarter of the year. If the mechanic inspected a shock-cord installation in 1986 and found that the cord had two yellow threads and one blue thread spiraling around the sheath, this would indicate that the cord was manufactured in 1984 during April, May, or June.

Shock cord should be replaced when it shows any sign of deterioration, especially if it is over 5 years in age. Deterioration is indicated by "necking" (narrowing) of the cord and by breaks or worn spots in the sheath. The necking of the cord is caused by individual strands in the cord being broken.

The landing-gear struts for some aircraft consist of single, tapered strips or tubes of strong, spring steel or composite material. The one end of the strut is bolted to the heavy structure of the aircraft under the cabin area, and the axles are bolted to the opposite ends. A landing gear of this type is shown in Fig. 10-11.

On ground contact during landings, the gear flexes and stores the impact energy. As with the shock-cord gear, the stored energy is returned to the aircraft during the landing roll.

Shock-Absorbing Landing Gear

Shock-absorbing landing gear dissipates the impact energy of landing through some means. Most of these types of landing gear do this by forcing a fluid through a restriction. The movement of this fluid generates heat, and the heat is radiated into the surrounding atmosphere, thus dissipating the landing energy.

There are two types of shock-absorbing landing gear

FIG. 10-11 Spring-type landing gear.

commonly used, the spring-oleo and the air-oleo types.

Spring-oleo struts, not usually found in modern aircraft, consist of a piston-type structure and a heavy, coiled spring. The piston-and-cylinder arrangement provides an oil chamber and an orifice through which oil is forced during landing. When the airplane is airborne, the strut is extended, and the oil flows by gravity to the lower chamber. When the plane lands, the piston with the orifice is forced downward into the cylinder and the oil is forced through the orifice into the upper chamber. This action provides a cushioning effect to absorb the primary shock of landing. As the strut collapses, the coil spring is compressed, thus providing additional cushioning. Thus the spring supports the aircraft weight on the ground and during taxiing, and the oleo strut absorbs the shock of landing.

The **air-oil,** or **air-oleo, shock strut** can be used for either nonretractable or retractable landing gear. This type of gear is generally constructed as shown in Fig. 10-12, although there are many variations of the design. See also Figs. 10-14 and 10-42.

In the strut shown in Fig. 10-12, the ring-seal nut (1), the compressing-ring seal (2), and the ring seal (3) form the group which seals the air pressure in the upper part of the strut. The upper bearing (4) keeps the inner cylinder (11) aligned with the outer cylinder (10). The snubber valve (5) releases when the weight is off the landing-gear strut to allow the strut to extend. The outer torque collar is (6). The lower bearing (7) helps keep the inner cylinder aligned inside the outer cylinder. The filler plug (8) is used to plug the hole through which the cylinder is filled with hydraulic fluid. The bearing lock screw (9) is used to maintain the position of the upper bearing on the inner cylinder.

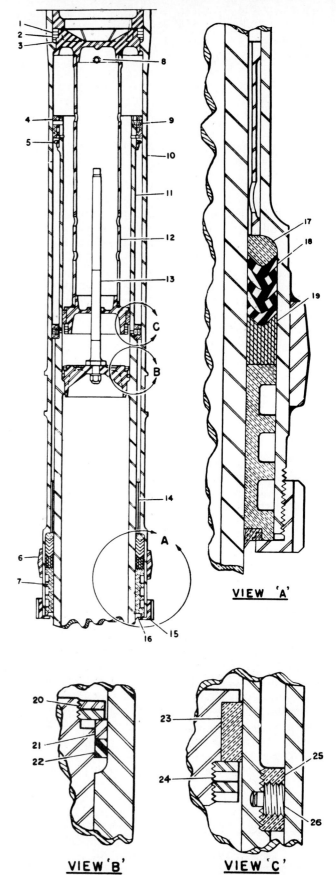

VIEW 'A'

VIEW 'B'

VIEW 'C'

FIG. 10-12 Air-oil shock strut.

The metering pin (13), extending into the piston tube (12), restricts the flow of fluid from the lower part of the cylinder to the upper part when the cylinder is being compressed during landing or taxiing. The metering pin varies in cross section to provide different rates of fluid flow during the compression stroke of the strut. Thus the movement of the strut in compressing is restricted to the rate determined to be most effective throughout the compression stroke.

The bearing spacer ring (14) is located between the lower part of the outer cylinder and the inner cylinder. The bearing (packing) nut (15), at the bottom of the cylinder, holds the lower bearing and the packing ring seals in position. The bearing nut may also be referred to as a gland nut. The wiper ring (16) prevents dirt or other foreign material from being drawn into the cylinder as the piston moves into the cylinder during compression. Some struts include a scraper ring below the wiper ring to provide greater protection.

View A of Fig. 10-12 is an enlarged drawing of the seals and bearing at the lower end of the shock strut, marked A in the first drawing. The upper packing spacer (17), the neoprene packing (18), and the lower packing spacer (19) are compressed together to form a tight seal between the inner and outer cylinders.

View B is an enlarged drawing of the seal nut (20), compressing ring seal (21), and the ring seal (22), which are shown within the circular arrow marked B in the first drawing.

View C is an enlarged drawing of the piston bearing (23), piston-bearing lock nuts (24), the stop nut (25), and the nut lock screw (26), shown within the circular arrow marked C in the first drawing.

As mentioned previously, the shock struts absorb the shocks of landing and taxiing. The initial shock of landing is cushioned by the hydraulic fluid being forced through the small aperture at the metering pin. As the strut is further compressed by the weight of the airplane, the pressure on the air in the upper part of the strut is increased until the air pressure is capable of sustaining the weight of the entire airplane. As the airplane rolls along the ground, the compressed air in the strut acts as a spring to reduce shocks.

Air-oleo struts are also designed to utilize an **orifice tube** rather than an orifice and metering pin to provide a restriction for the flowing from the lower chamber to the upper chamber of the strut upon compression. A cutaway and exploded view of such a strut is shown in Fig. 10-13. Note that the strut has an **orifice plate** at the bottom of the orifice tube. Some air-oleo struts include both a metering pin and an orifice tube (metering tube) in addition to the orifice tube.

The principle of operation of an air-oleo strut is the same for all struts, regardless of the type of fluid metering employed. During compression of the strut at landing, the orifice provides a restriction of fluid flow, and this reduces the rate at which the piston (inner cylinder) can move into the outer cylinder. This provides a cushioning effect to reduce the shock of landing. As the fluid flows through the orifice into the upper chamber, the air in the upper chamber is compressed to the point that the entire weight of the air-

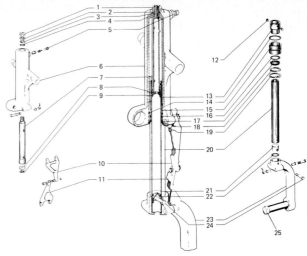

1. Nut	14. Outer O ring
2. Washer	15. Lower bearing
3. Retainer	16. Inner O ring
4. O ring	17. Wiper strip
5. Valve assembly	18. Washer
6. Oleo strut housing	19. Snap ring
7. Orifice tube	20. Piston tube
8. Orifice plate	21. Piston plug
9. Snap ring	22. O ring
10. Upper torque link	23. Fork assembly
11. Lower torque link	24. Bolt assembly
12. Bearing retainer pin	25. Axle nut
13. Upper bearing	

FIG. 10-13   Construction of an air-oleo strut. *(Piper Aircraft Corp.)*

craft is supported by the air in the landing-gear struts. The compressed air then acts as a shock absorber during the time that the aircraft is taxiing.

The **snubber** device is designed to prevent the strut from extending too rapidly on takeoff or during a bad landing. If the rate of strut extension is too great, the shock which occurs due to the impact at the end of the stroke can cause damage to the landing gear and the supporting structure in the aircraft.

The main-gear shock strut for a transport aircraft, illustrated in Fig. 10-14, is made of steel, and consists of an **outer and inner cylinder,** a **piston** attached to the upper inner side of the outer cylinder, and an **orifice rod** attached to the inner cylinder. This construction varies from others; however, the functional principle is the same as that for other air-oil-type shock struts.

The shock strut is filled with hydraulic fluid (MIL-O-5606) and charged with dry compressed air or nitrogen to absorb landing and taxi shock loads. Landing shock absorption is accomplished by the flow of hydraulic fluid through a variable orifice formed by the tapered orifice rod through an opening in the piston and by the flow of hydraulic fluid through openings in the **piston rod.** As the shock strut is compressed, the tapered orifice rod permits a diminishing rate of hydraulic-fluid flow from the inner-cylinder chamber to the upper side of the piston. Landing and taxi shocks are also cushioned by the increasing volume of hy-

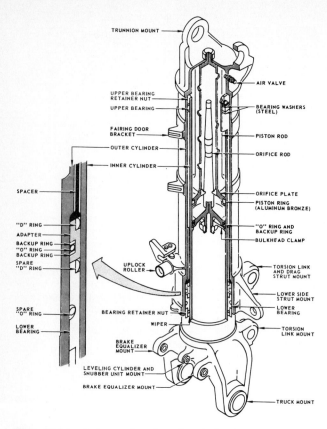

FIG. 10-14 Cutaway drawing of main landing-gear shock strut.

draulic fluid above the piston which further compresses a volume of gas in the upper end of the outer cylinder. The shock strut is serviced with hydraulic fluid through an air valve in the upper inboard side of the outer cylinder. The shock strut is serviced with dry, clean air or nitrogen through the air valve to the specified shock-strut extension given on a servicing chart on the keel beam of the fuselage in the left wheel well.

Upper and lower bearings in the shock strut provide sliding surfaces and an air-oil seal between the inner and outer cylinders. Between the lower bearing and the spacer, a **seal adapter** with annular grooves is installed. A D-ring and an O-ring seal with backup rings are inserted in the grooves to provide the air-oil seal between the cylinders. The shock struts have annular grooves in the lower bearing for storage of spare D and O rings. The spare seals can be used to replace the working seals without complete disassembly of the shock strut.

The oleo struts for the main gear and the nose gear are usually similar in function. However, since the nosewheel must be able to swivel as the airplane turns on the ground, the mounting of the nose gear differs from that of the main gear. To provide for this requirement, the nose gear strut is mounted in an outside tube or other structure. The strut is supported by bearings mounted in the top and bottom of the structure. The bearings and seals are held in place by means of gland nuts and/or snap rings.

Since the nose gear can swivel, provision must be

made to establish the wheel alignment straight ahead when the gear is retracted and when landing. This is accomplished by means of external, mechanical centering devices such as springs or by **centering cams** inside the strut. When cams are employed, a cam ring is mounted around the top of the piston to form the upper cam and another cam ring is mounted inside the bottom of the outer cylinder. When the strut is fully extended, the cam faces mate and hold the nosewheel in the centered position.

Oleo struts are provided with high-pressure **air valves** mounted in the top of the strut. The valve may contain a high-pressure core similar in appearance to the core found in a tire valve but specially constructed for high pressure, or it may be the type without a core. In any case, the use of the valve in servicing the strut is set forth in the manufacturer's instructions. **A tire valve core must never be used.**

Air-oleo struts always have an instruction plate permanently attached to the outside of the strut or nearby. This plate specifies the type of hydraulic fluid to be used in the strut and gives instructions for inflation, deflation, and filling with fluid. Typical instruction plates are shown in Fig. 10-15.

An important feature of an air-oleo strut, either for the nose gear or the main gear, is the use of **torque links,** sometimes referred to as "scissors," to maintain the alignment of the wheel.

The axle and wheel may be attached to the piston by means of a bolted forging or by means of a **fork.** The fork may straddle the wheel or may be one-sided. Both types are shown in the illustrations of this chapter. The axle and mounting structure, whether a fork or an attaching fitting at the base of the piston, must be designed to withstand severe shock loads, and therefore are made of high-strength material such as forged alloy steel.

Another type of arrangement has appeared which is called an **oil snubber gear,** shown in Fig. 10-16. This design is used on the Cessna Caravan and consists of an oleo strut with an air chamber that is not pressurized above atmospheric pressure. The oleo mechanism, called an **oil snubber shock strut,** absorbs the landing energy. A large tubular drag link spring provides cushioning during taxi operations and fore- and aft-stability for the nose gear.

Fixed Gear

Nonretractable (fixed) landing gear is generally attached to structural members of the airplane with bolts, but it is not actually "fixed" because it must absorb stresses; hence the wheels must move up and down while landing or taxiing in order to absorb shocks. The landing gear is often equipped with a fairing where it joins the fuselage or wing to reduce the drag (air resistance), and such a fairing may be assembled in sections. Chafing strips are used to prevent excessive wear between the sections of the fairing because there is usually some motion between these sections. **Wheel pants** are often used to cover the wheel and tire to reduce their drag. Nonretractable landing gear may have bracing, or it may be of the cantilever type without bracing.

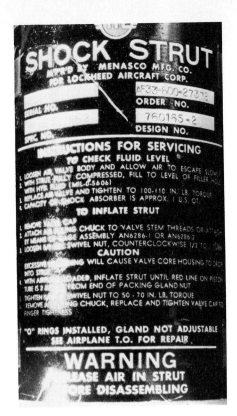

FIG. 10-15   Instruction plates for landing gear.

Fixed landing gear are usually found on small aircraft and aircraft where aerodynamic cleanliness is not a factor.

Retractable Gear

Retractable landing gear was developed to eliminate as much as possible the drag caused by the exposure of the landing gear to airflow during flight. Usually the landing gear is completely retractable (that is, it can be drawn entirely into the wing or fuselage); however, there are aircraft in which a portion of the gear wheels is still exposed after the gear is retracted. The direction of retraction varies. On some airplanes, the retraction is toward the rear; on others the landing gear folds inward toward the fuselage; and on still others it folds outward toward the wing tips. The method of retraction also varies, although modern aircraft usually have gear which is power operated. The retraction is normally accomplished with hydraulic, electric, or pneumatic power. In addition to the normal operating system, emergency systems are usually provided to ensure that the landing gear can be lowered in case of main system failure. Emergency systems consist of stored air or gas which can be directed into actuating cylinders or mechanical systems that can be operated manually.

It must be emphasized that the landing gear of an airplane is of primary importance in the safe operation of the aircraft and because of this, the mechanic must be especially careful in the inspection and maintenance of landing-gear systems. Since retractable-type landing gear is much more complex than fixed gear, it is essential that each operating component of the gear be carefully examined at frequent intervals to assure that there will be no chance of failure.

During the operation of an airplane with retractable landing gear, the system which raises and lowers the gear must operate without fail, and the gear must remain in the down-and-locked position after it is lowered. Periodically the airplane should be placed on jacks and the gear operated to assure that the oper-

1. Nose Wheel
2. Drag Link Spring
3. Shimmy Dampener
4. Shock Strut
5. Trunnion
6. Forward Support
7. Aft Support

FIG. 10-16   Oil snubber nose-gear assembly. (*Cessna Aircraft Co.*)

ating system and the **down** and **up locks** function effectively.

Another important feature of retractable landing gear is the safety mechanism which prevents gear retraction while the airplane is on the ground. This safety system often consists of an electric circuit which includes switches, sometimes called "squat switches," operated by the extension and compression of the landing-gear struts. As long as the gear struts are compressed, the switches are open and an electrically operated lock prevents the raising of the gear. When the airplane leaves the ground, the gear struts extend and the switches are closed. This permits operation of the landing-gear control lever to raise the gear.

Another safety feature included with retractable landing-gear systems is the **warning horn.** If the gear is in the retracted position and the throttle is retarded to a below-cruise power setting, as is done when landing, the warning horn sounds and warns the pilot that the landing gear is not in the down position.

There are various types of landing-gear **position indicators.** These show whether the landing gear is up or down and whether it is locked. One type of indicator has a needle or a miniature wheel for each unit. The indicator is built into a single instrument on the instrument panel and arranged so that the needle or wheel moves along with the actual movement of the landing gear from the DOWN to the UP position (and in the same direction), thus simplifying its reading by the pilot. Many airplanes have indicator lights, such as a green light that glows when the gear is down and locked, a red light to indicate that the gear is not fully up or down, and an amber light to indicate that the gear is fully retracted and locked. If lights are used, green lights will always be used, but only the red or the amber light may be used.

Hulls and Floats

Airplanes operated from water may be provided with either a **single float** or a **double float,** depending upon the design and construction; however, if an airplane is actually a flying boat, it has a **hull** for flotation and then may need only wing-tip floats. **Amphibious** airplanes have floats or a hull for operating on water and retractable wheels for land operation.

Skis

Skis are used for operating on snow and ice. The skis may be made of wood, metal, or composite materials. There are three basic styles of skis. A conventional ski, shown in Fig. 10-17, replaces the wheel on the axle. The shock cord is used to hold the toe of the ski up when landing. The safety cable and check cable prevent the ski from pivoting through too great an angle during flight.

The wheel-ski is designed to mount on the aircraft along with the tire. The ski has a portion cut out that

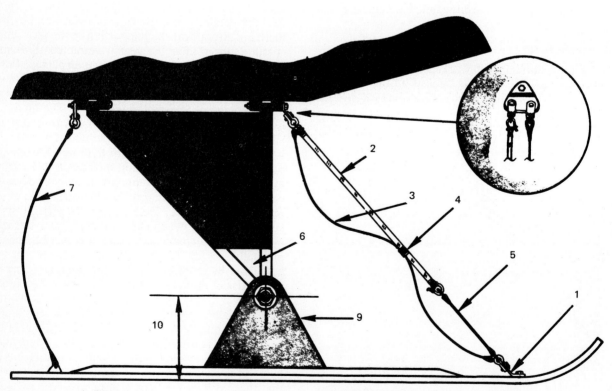

1. Fitting
2. Shock Cord
3. Safety Cable
4. Tape
5. Crust-cutter Cable
6. Fabric removed to facilitate inspection
7. Check Cable
8. Clevis
9. Ski Pedestal
10. Pedestal Height

FIG. 10-17   A typical ski installation.

allows the tire to extend slightly below the ski so that the aircraft can be operated from conventional runways with the wheels or from snow or ice surfaces using the ski. This arrangement has a small wheel mounted on the heel of the ski so that it does not drag on conventional runways.

Retractable wheel-ski arrangements have the ski mounted on a common axle with the wheel. In this arrangement the ski can be extended below the level of the wheel for landing on snow or ice. The ski can be retracted above the bottom of the wheel for operations from conventional runways. A hydraulic system is commonly used for the retraction system operation.

● SHIMMY DAMPERS

The **shimmy damper** is a hydraulic snubbing unit which reduces the tendency of the nose wheel to oscillate from side to side. Shimmy dampers (dampeners) are usually constructed in one of two general designs, **piston-type** and **vane-type,** both of which might be modified to provide power steering as well as shimmy damper action.

Piston-Type Dampers

A piston-type shimmy damper is simply a hydraulic cylinder containing a piston rod and piston and filled with hydraulic fluid. Figure 10-18 illustrates the principle of operation. The piston has an orifice which restricts the speed at which the piston can be moved in the cylinder. When the damper piston rod is connected to a stationary structure of the nose gear (air-oleo cylinder) and the damper cylinder is attached to the rotating part (air-oleo piston) of the gear, any movement of the nosewheel alignment to the right or left causes the piston in the shimmy dampener to be moved inside the cylinder. If the movement is relatively slow, there will be little resistance from the shimmy damper; however, if the movement is rapid, there is strong resistance because of the time it takes to cause the fluid in the cylinder to flow through the orifice from one side of the piston to the other. Shimmy dampers are usually provided with an overload feature, such as some type of relief valve, to release pressure if a turning load becomes great enough to cause structural damage.

Large shimmy dampers may incorporate a temperature compensating system which allows the fluid in the damper to expand and contract with changes in temperature without overpressurizing the system. The hollow piston rod is vented to the oil chamber with one end of the rod sealed and a compensating piston, spring, and plug being installed in the other end. When servicing the damper, the piston is inserted a specified distance into the rod. With the unit full of fluid, the spring and plug are then installed. This places a slight pressure load on the system. If the ambient temperature increases, the fluid expands and pushes the piston against the spring. If the ambient temperature decreases, the fluid reduces in volume and the spring pushes the piston further into the rod to prevent the formation of a vacuum or an air pocket in the damper.

Vane-Type Dampers

Vane-type dampers are designed with a set of moving vanes and a set of stationary vanes as shown in the drawing of Fig. 10-19. The moving vanes are mounted on a shaft which extends outside the housing. When the shaft is turned, the chambers between the vanes change in size, thus forcing hydraulic fluid from one to the other. The fluid must flow through restricting orifices, providing a dampening effect to any rapid movement of the vanes in the housing. The body or housing of the vane-type damper is usually mounted on a stationary part of the nose landing gear, and the shaft lever is connected to the turning part. Thus any movement of the wheel alignment to the right or left causes a movement of the vanes in the shimmy damper.

Damper Inspections

Shimmy dampers do not require extensive maintenance; however, the mechanic should check them for leakage and effectiveness of operation. If the damper has a fluid replenishment reservoir, the fluid quantity should be checked periodically and fluid of the specified type added if necessary.

When inspecting shimmy dampers, the mount bolts and fittings should be checked closely for any evidence of wear. Many aircraft use bushings in the fittings so that the fit of the bolts in the fittings can be renewed by replacing the bolts and bushings. If these mountings

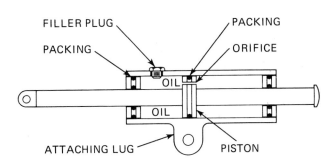

FIG. 10-18 Drawing of a piston-type shimmy damper.

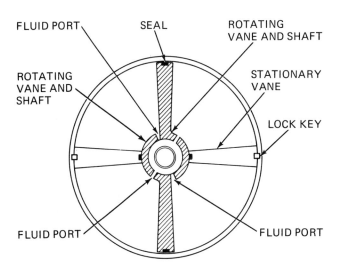

FIG. 10-19 Principle of a vane-type shimmy damper.

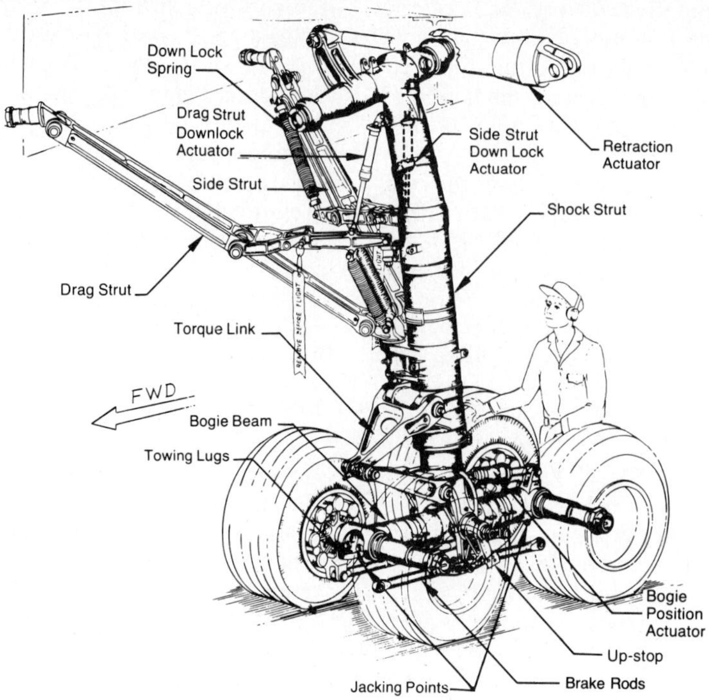
Down Lock
Spring
Drag Strut
Downlock
Actuator
Side Strut
Side Strut
Down Lock
Actuator
Retraction
Actuator
Shock Strut
Drag Strut
Torque Link
FWD
Bogie Beam
Towing Lugs
Bogie
Position
Actuator
Up-stop
Jacking Points
Brake Rods

FIG. 10-20 The main landing gear for a Boeing 767. ***(Boeing Commercial Aircraft Company)***

are allowed to become worn, the damper will be loose on the nosewheel and will allow shimmying to occur.

LANDING-GEAR COMPONENTS

Landing-gear assemblies are made up of various components designed to support and stabilize the assembly. The following terms identify many of these components. It will be helpful to refer to Figs. 10-20 and 10-21 when discussing the definitions. The terms are presented here as they relate to retractable landing-gear systems. When the terms are used with fixed landing gear, the exact use of the components may vary. Be aware that different manufacturers will occasionally use different terms for the same basic components.

Trunnion

The **trunnion,** shown in Fig. 10-22, is the portion of the landing-gear assembly which is attached to the airframe. The trunnion is supported at its ends by bearing assemblies which allow the gear to pivot during retraction and extension. The landing-gear strut extends down from the approximate center of the trunnion.

Strut

The **strut** is the vertical member of the landing-gear assembly that contains the shock-absorbing mechanism. The top of the strut is attached to, or is an integral part of, the trunnion. The strut forms the cylinder for the air-oleo shock absorber. The strut is also called the **outer cylinder.**

Piston

The **piston** is the moving portion of the air-oleo shock absorber. This unit fits inside of the strut, and the bottom of the piston is attached to the axle or other component on which the axle is mounted. Other terms used for the piston are **piston rod, piston tube,** and **inner cylinder.**

Torque Links

The **torque links** are two A-frame-type members, as shown in Fig. 10-23, used to connect the strut cylinder to the piston and axle. The torque links restrict the extension of the piston during gear retraction and hold the wheels and axle in a correctly aligned position in relation to the strut.

The upper torque link is connected to a clevis fitting on the lower forward side of the shock strut. The lower torque link is connected to a clevis fitting on the axle. The upper and lower torque links are joined together, as shown in the drawing, by a bolt and nut spaced with washers. Each link is fitted with flanged bushings. The gap between the flanged ends of the bushings is taken up by a washer.

Truck

The **truck** is located on the bottom of the piston and has the axles attached to it. A truck is used when wheels are to be placed in tandem (one behind the other) or in a dual-tandem arrangement. The truck can tilt fore and aft at the piston connection to allow for changes in aircraft attitude during takeoff and landing and during taxiing. The truck is also called a **bogie.**

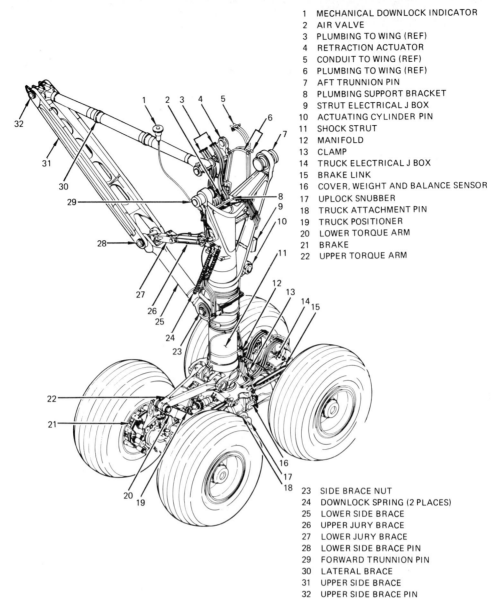

1	MECHANICAL DOWNLOCK INDICATOR
2	AIR VALVE
3	PLUMBING TO WING (REF)
4	RETRACTION ACTUATOR
5	CONDUIT TO WING (REF)
6	PLUMBING TO WING (REF)
7	AFT TRUNNION PIN
8	PLUMBING SUPPORT BRACKET
9	STRUT ELECTRICAL J BOX
10	ACTUATING CYLINDER PIN
11	SHOCK STRUT
12	MANIFOLD
13	CLAMP
14	TRUCK ELECTRICAL J BOX
15	BRAKE LINK
16	COVER, WEIGHT AND BALANCE SENSOR
17	UPLOCK SNUBBER
18	TRUCK ATTACHMENT PIN
19	TRUCK POSITIONER
20	LOWER TORQUE ARM
21	BRAKE
22	UPPER TORQUE ARM

23	SIDE BRACE NUT
24	DOWNLOCK SPRING (2 PLACES)
25	LOWER SIDE BRACE
26	UPPER JURY BRACE
27	LOWER JURY BRACE
28	LOWER SIDE BRACE PIN
29	FORWARD TRUNNION PIN
30	LATERAL BRACE
31	UPPER SIDE BRACE
32	UPPER SIDE BRACE PIN

FIG. 10-21   The main landing gear for a Lockheed L-1011. *(Lockheed-California Company)*

Drag Link

The **drag link** is designed to stabilize the landing-gear assembly longitudinally. If the gear retracts forward or aft, the drag link will be hinged in the middle to allow the gear to retract. This is also called a **drag strut**.

Side Brace Link

The **side brace link** is designed to stabilize the landing-gear assembly laterally. If the gear retracts sideways, the side brace link is hinged in the middle to allow the gear to retract. This is also called a **side strut**.

Overcenter Link

An **overcenter link** is used to apply pressure to the center pivot joint in a drag or side brace link. This prevents the link from pivoting at this joint except when retracting the gear, thus preventing collapse of the gear during ground operation. The overcenter link is hydraulically retracted to allow gear retraction. This component is also called a **downlock** and a **jury strut**.

Swivel Gland

A **swivel gland** is a flexible joint with internal passages which route hydraulic fluid to the wheel brakes and the bungee cylinder of a landing gear. Swivel glands are used where the bend radius is too small or space limitations prevent the use of coiled, hydraulic lines.

A swivel gland, which is illustrated in Fig. 10-24, may be mounted on a bracket secured to the main-gear trunnion fitting. The gland remains stationary and is the terminus of the stationary hydraulic lines. The movable portion of a swivel gland is connected to the

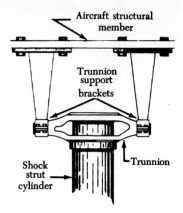

FIG. 10-22 Trunnion and bracket assembly.

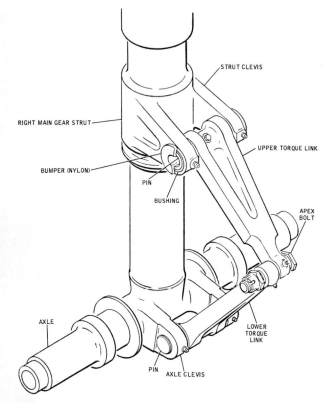

FIG. 10-23 Torque links.

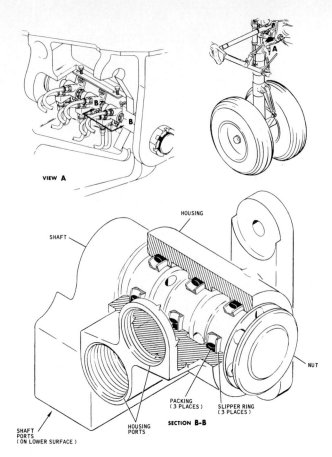

FIG. 10-24 Swivel glands for the transfer of fluid pressure. (*McDonnell Douglas Corp.*)

hydraulic lines that are routed down the strut to the bungee cylinder and the wheel brakes.

In Fig. 10-24, it can be seen that the gland consists of annular grooves separated from one another by means of slipper rings and packings to isolate the pressure fluid from the return fluid. Thus the gear can be raised and lowered without disturbing the fluid passage to and from the brakes and bungee cylinder.

Main Landing Gear

The variety of designs for the main landing gear for aircraft makes it impractical to do more than discuss typical examples and to examine features common to the majority of types. The important consideration for the mechanic is to understand the type at hand and to follow the appropriate instructions for service, inspection, maintenance, and repair.

A main-landing-gear unit of an airplane includes a shock-absorbing device such as an air-oleo strut, axle or axles, mount for the axles, a wheel or wheels, brakes, tire or tires (with or without tubes), torque links, an upper mounting trunnion to provide for retraction, and assembly hardware.

One type of retractable main landing gear is illustrated in Fig. 10-25. The assembly consists principally of the shock strut; the wheel; the brake assembly; the trunnion and side brace; the torque link, or "scissors"; the actuating cylinder, the down and up locks; and the bungee system.

To retract the gear, the actuating cylinder is extended by hydraulic pressure. Since the actuating cylinder can provide greater force during extension of the cylinder than it can during retraction because of the greater piston area exposed to fluid pressure, the extension movement of the actuating cylinder is used to retract the gear. Retraction of the gear requires the greater force because of gravity. Extension of the actuating cylinder causes the gear to rotate on the trunnion pin until the gear is approximately in a horizontal position. When the gear reaches the full UP position, a pin on the strut engages the up latch and locks the gear in the UP position.

When the gear is extended, the first movement of the actuating cylinder releases the UP lock. This per-

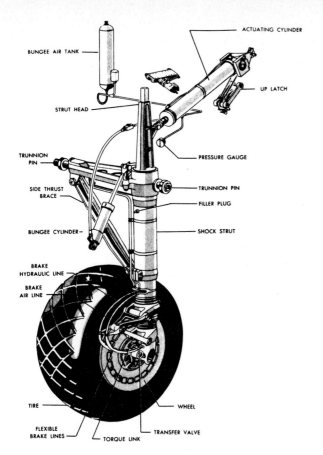

Labels in figure:
BUNGEE AIR TANK
STRUT HEAD
TRUNNION PIN
SIDE THRUST BRACE
BUNGEE CYLINDER
BRAKE HYDRAULIC LINE
BRAKE AIR LINE
TIRE
FLEXIBLE BRAKE LINES
TORQUE LINK
ACTUATING CYLINDER
UP LATCH
PRESSURE GAUGE
TRUNNION PIN
FILLER PLUG
SHOCK STRUT
WHEEL
TRANSFER VALVE

FIG. 10-25 Retractable main landing gear.

mits the gear to fall of its own weight, and the actuating cylinder acts to snub the rate of fall. Usually there is an **orifice check valve** in the UP line of the landing-gear hydraulic system; this restricts the fluid flow from the actuating cylinder to the return line, thus slowing the rate of gear descent. As the gear approaches the DOWN position, the actuating cylinder moves it to the full DOWN position. In the DOWN position, a blade engages the DOWN-lock track and slides into the DOWN-lock latch as shown in Fig. 10-26. The DOWN lock prevents the gear from retracting after it has been lowered.

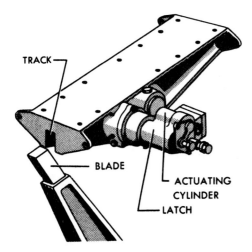

Labels in figure:
TRACK
BLADE
ACTUATING CYLINDER
LATCH

FIG. 10-26 A down-lock mechanism.

The landing gear shown in Fig. 10-25 is equipped with a pneumatic **bungee** system for emergency operation. The purpose of the system is to provide air or gas pressure to lower the gear in the event of hydraulic power failure. The bungee tank is charged with air or gas at a high pressure, and when it becomes necessary to lower the gear in an emergency, the air or gas is released from the tank by means of a valve and is carried through tubing to a special bungee cylinder. This cylinder provides enough force to lock the gear in the DOWN position. In many systems, the air or gas is directed to a **shuttle valve** which blocks off the hydraulic system and opens the down line to the main-landing-gear actuating cylinder which then lowers and locks the gear. In any case, the landing-gear control handle must be placed in the DOWN position.

When the operation of a retractable gear system includes the opening and closing of gear doors, an associated system controlled by **sequence valves** is often used to operate the doors. The sequence of operation is (1) opening of doors and (2) lowering of gear. During retraction, the gear retracts and then the doors close. The doors can be operated through the hydraulic system or by a mechanical linkage in connection with the movement of the landing gear mechanism.

In many designs, the landing-gear doors are closed when the gear is extended or retracted. In such cases, the doors must operate twice for either retraction or extension of the gear.

Another example of a main-landing-gear unit is shown in Fig. 10-27. Observe that this gear assembly includes all the features already discussed in this section. Note particularly the torque links and the spacer installed between the links. This spacer establishes the alignment of the wheel. When main wheel alignment is checked and is found to be incorrect, the correction is made by installing a spacer of different thickness.

The strut housing is also the cylinder for the oleo strut and incorporates the trunnion upon which the gear rotates during extension and retraction. The air valve and hydraulic fluid plug are on the side of the housing near the top.

When the gear is down and locked, it is held in this position by means of the DOWN-lock assembly, the overcenter upper and lower side braces, and the DOWN-lock spring.

Nose Landing Gear

One type of retractable nose gear is illustrated in Fig. 10-28. The operation of this gear is similar to that of the main gear, and the movement of the gear is in a straight fore-and-aft direction. Note the inclusion of a shimmy damper to control oscillations and a static ground wire to discharge any static buildup on the aircraft when the plane lands.

The nose gear for a single-engine light airplane with retractable gear is shown in Fig. 10-29. This drawing is of particular interest in that it shows one method by which the steering mechanism is engaged with the nosewheel strut when the gear is extended and how it will disengage when the gear is retracted. The steering bellcrank is connected to the steering rods and through

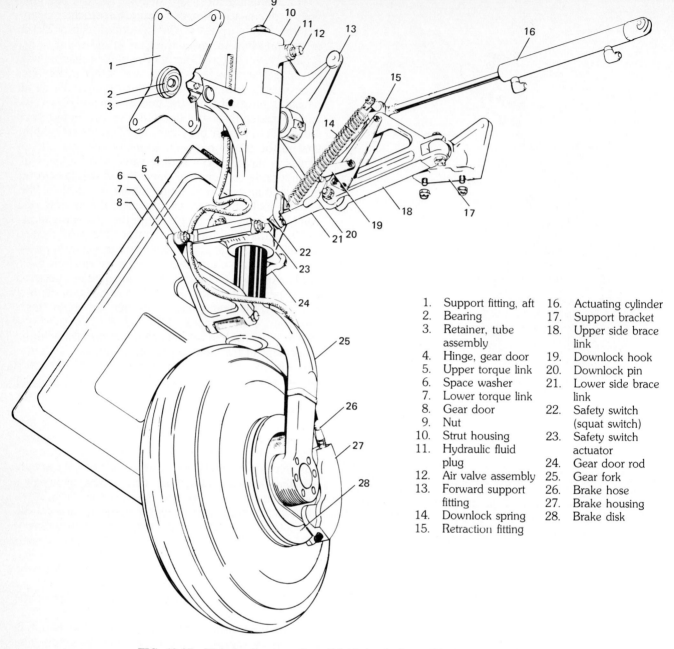

1. Support fitting, aft	16. Actuating cylinder
2. Bearing	17. Support bracket
3. Retainer, tube assembly	18. Upper side brace link
4. Hinge, gear door	19. Downlock hook
5. Upper torque link	20. Downlock pin
6. Space washer	21. Lower side brace link
7. Lower torque link	
8. Gear door	22. Safety switch (squat switch)
9. Nut	
10. Strut housing	23. Safety switch actuator
11. Hydraulic fluid plug	24. Gear door rod
12. Air valve assembly	25. Gear fork
13. Forward support fitting	26. Brake hose
14. Downlock spring	27. Brake housing
15. Retraction fitting	28. Brake disk

FIG. 10-27   Main landing gear for a light twin airplane. *(Piper Aircraft Corp.)*

the rods to the rudder pedals. When the gear is extended, the steering bellcrank engages the steering arm which is attached to the upper part of the strut. Moving the steering arm will turn the nosewheel strut and the nosewheel for steering.

Tail Wheel

Many older aircraft and some special-use aircraft have a conventional landing-gear configuration. This configuration requires the use of a **tail wheel.** The tail wheel is mounted on a short spring, oleo, or other assembly on the bottom of the fuselage near the rudder. The tail wheel may be fixed in alignment with the fuselage longitudinal axis, or it may be designed to rotate, allowing the aircraft to turn easily.

Fixed-alignment tail wheels are found only on aircraft such as gliders which are not normally taxied. A tail wheel that can rotate may be steerable, full-swiveling, and lockable. A steerable tail wheel responds to cabin rudder controls to aid in controlling aircraft direction of movement on the ground. A full-swiveling tail wheel is not controllable and pivots freely on its mounting. Most steerable tail wheels incorporate a free-swivel capability which automatically disengages the steering capability when the pilot makes very tight turns using the main wheel brakes. A lockable mechanism is used with some tail wheels to aid in directional control during takeoff and landing. This mechanism locks the tail wheel in alignment with the aircraft longitudinal axis. When the lock is disengaged,

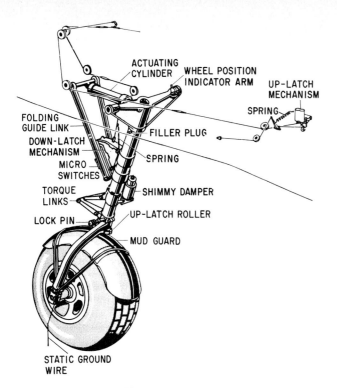

FIG. 10-28 Retractable nose gear.

the tail wheel returns to its full-swivel or steerable operation. A steerable tail wheel with a full-swivel capability is shown in Fig. 10-30.

● RETRACTION SYSTEMS

The purpose of retractable landing gear is to reduce the drag of the aircraft or to adapt the aircraft for landing on different surfaces, as with retractable wheels used with floats. Various systems have been designed to retract the gear. These include mechanical systems, hydraulic systems, and electric systems.

Mechanical System

Some older aircraft use a **mechanical retractable landing-gear system** and many current-production light aircraft make use of a mechanical emergency extension system. A mechanical system is powered by the pilot moving a lever or operating a crank mechanism.

The lever arrangement is found on many older Mooney aircraft and involves the use of a lever, approximately 2 ft [0.61 m] long, located in the cabin, which moves through an arc of 90° to retract or extend the gear. When the lever is moved from the vertical to the horizontal position, the lever unlocks the gear, and, through the use of overcenter springs, torque tubes, and bellcranks, retracts the gear. The gear is locked up by securing the cabin lever in a locking device on the cabin floor. The opposite operation extends the gear. The lever locks in the vertical position to lock the gear down. The lever serves as the gear position indicator. This system does not require an emergency extension system.

Current-production aircraft make use of mechanical

gear extension systems as emergency systems. These systems are most easily adapted to electrically operated landing gear. A ratcheting control or a crank mechanism is engaged by properly positioning the manual control. This engages the mechanical system with the gear system normally operated by the electric motor. As the ratchet or crank is operated, the gear mechanism rotates until the gear is fully extended. The standard gear indicating system is used in most systems to indicate when the gear is down and locked.

Electrical Retraction System

An electrically operated gear system is shown in Fig. 10-31. This type of system is often used on light aircraft where the weight of the landing gear is not so great as to require large operating motors. When the gear selector is positioned, an electric motor is energized and operates a gear which rotates a cam plate or spider that opens the doors, positions the gear, and closes the doors. Once the gear is in the selected position, a microswitch breaks the circuit to the motor and causes the appropriate gear indication to be displayed.

The throttle has a microswitch that sounds a warning horn if the gear is in the retracted position and the throttle is moved to a low power setting.

Hydraulic Retraction System

A **hydraulic retractable landing gear** makes use of hydraulic pressure to move the gear between the retracted and extended positions. While this system is commonly used for all sizes of aircraft, it is used exclusively where the landing gear is large and could not economically be operated by any other method.

The power for the operation of the system may be generated by engine-driven pumps, electrically operated pumps, or, for emergency operation, hand pumps. Electrically operated pumps are often found on light aircraft while transport aircraft rely primarily on engine-driven pumps.

A basic hydraulic retraction system is shown in Fig. 10-32. This system uses a reversible electric motor to generate the hydraulic pressure. The direction of pump operation is dictated by whether the gear selector is positioned to retract or extend the gear.

When retracting the gear, the gear selector is positioned by the pilot and the pump begins operation. Pressure exits the pump on the right, passes through the gear-up check valve, and flows to the actuators, raising the gear. Fluid on the opposite side of the actuators is forced back into the reservoir at the shuttle valve.

The pump continues to operate until the pressure switch senses approximately 1800 psi [12 411 kPa]. The pump then shuts down, and pressure is held in the system by the actuator seals and the gear-up check valve, which prevents reverse flow back through the pump. The gear is held up by this hydraulic pressure and does not make use of any up-lock devices. If the pressure should drop below about 1500 psi [10 343 kPa], the pressure switch turns the pump back on and repressurizes the system.

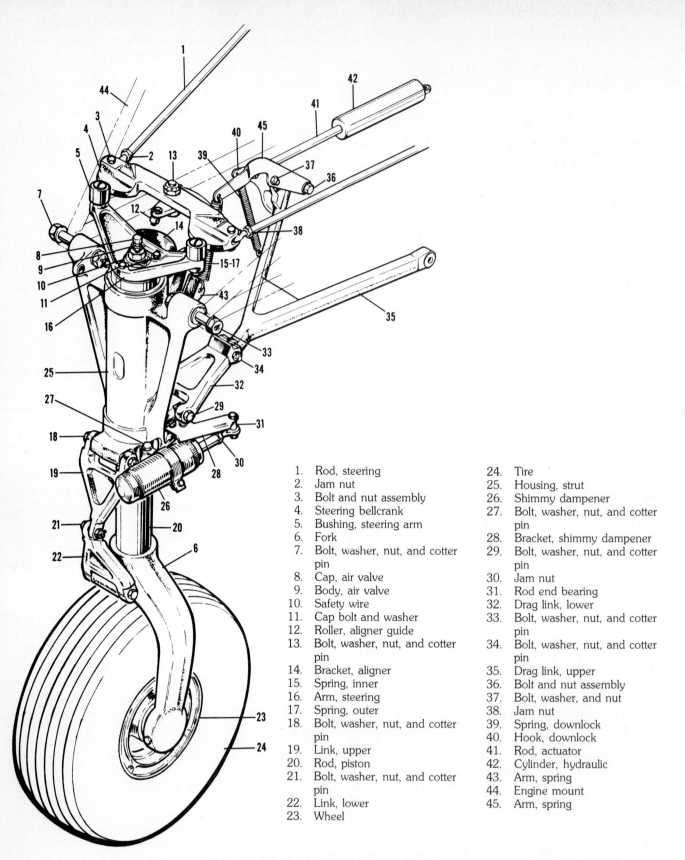

1. Rod, steering
2. Jam nut
3. Bolt and nut assembly
4. Steering bellcrank
5. Bushing, steering arm
6. Fork
7. Bolt, washer, nut, and cotter pin
8. Cap, air valve
9. Body, air valve
10. Safety wire
11. Cap bolt and washer
12. Roller, aligner guide
13. Bolt, washer, nut, and cotter pin
14. Bracket, aligner
15. Spring, inner
16. Arm, steering
17. Spring, outer
18. Bolt, washer, nut, and cotter pin
19. Link, upper
20. Rod, piston
21. Bolt, washer, nut, and cotter pin
22. Link, lower
23. Wheel
24. Tire
25. Housing, strut
26. Shimmy dampener
27. Bolt, washer, nut, and cotter pin
28. Bracket, shimmy dampener
29. Bolt, washer, nut, and cotter pin
30. Jam nut
31. Rod end bearing
32. Drag link, lower
33. Bolt, washer, nut, and cotter pin
34. Bolt, washer, nut, and cotter pin
35. Drag link, upper
36. Bolt and nut assembly
37. Bolt, washer, and nut
38. Jam nut
39. Spring, downlock
40. Hook, downlock
41. Rod, actuator
42. Cylinder, hydraulic
43. Arm, spring
44. Engine mount
45. Arm, spring

FIG. 10-29 Nose gear for a light airplane showing the steering mechanism. *(Piper Aircraft Corp.)*

FIG. 10-30　A steerable tail wheel. *(Scott Aviation)*

When the gear is retracted, the system is prevented from overpressurization caused by an increase in ambient temperature by the thermal relief valve in the pump-reservoir assembly.

To extend the gear normally, the gear selector is positioned down, the pump starts to operate to send pressurized fluid to the shuttle valve. The shuttle valve shifts to the left, and pressure is applied to the actuators. (This pressure is less than retraction pressure because the weight of the gear helps in the extension operation.) Fluid on the other side of the actuators flows back to the gear-up check valve, which has been pushed off its seat by pressure shifting the center spool valve to the right. The fluid then moves to the reservoir inlet to the pump. When the gear is fully extended, the pump is shut off by a gear microswitch.

The restricted elbow in the nose gear line is used to slow the nose gear extension and prevent damage. If the hydraulic system should fail, the landing gear free-falls into position. With the hydraulic system intact, free-fall extension occurs if the free-fall control is pulled. This equalizes pressure on both sides of the actuators and the gear falls to the extended position.

● **STEERING SYSTEMS**

Steering systems are used to control the direction of movement of an aircraft while taxiing. While a few aircraft have castering nosewheels, the vast majority of aircraft are equipped with some sort of steering system.

Mechanical Steering Systems

Mechanical steering systems are found on small aircraft where the pilot can press on the rudder pedal and cause the nosewheel or tail wheel to turn without any form of powered assistance. Some aircraft have the rudder pedals directly linked to the nosewheel steering arm, while others use a spring interconnect. An example of a system using a spring-operated bungee rod is shown in Fig. 10-33. When the pilot pushes on the rudder pedal, the spring inside the rod is compressed and applies pressure to the ears on the steering collar. As the aircraft rolls forward, the spring pressure causes the nose gear to turn.

For tail-wheel aircraft, the rudder control cables are connected to the tail-wheel steering arms through springs. When the rudder is deflected, one spring is stretched and the aircraft begins to turn as it rolls forward. Most tail wheels are equipped with a full-swivel capability that disengages the steering control when the wheel pivots through more than about 45° from the aircraft centerline. This allows tight turns to be completed. The tail wheel is re-engaged by returning the aircraft to a straight line of taxi with differential braking. A tail-wheel system is shown in Fig. 10-34.

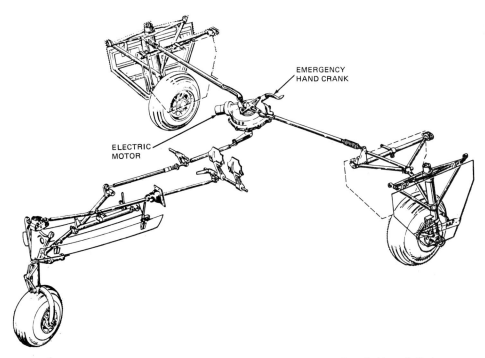

EMERGENCY
HAND CRANK

ELECTRIC
MOTOR

FIG. 10-31　Electrically operated landing-gear system. *(Beech Aircraft Co.)*

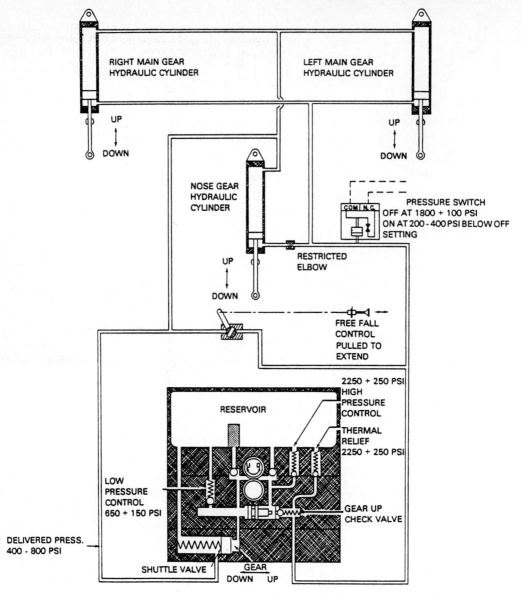

FIG. 10-32 Retraction system for a light twin-engine airplane. *(Piper Aircraft Corp.)*

Power Steering Systems

Power steering systems are used for aircraft which require large amounts of force to be applied to the nosewheel to achieve efficient steering control. This includes all large aircraft.

Power steering systems can be controlled by the pilot's rudder pedals, by a steering wheel in the cockpit, or by a combination system allowing full system travel with a steering wheel and a small degree of directional control with the pedals. Operation of either of the controls causes an actuator on the nosewheel to turn the nosewheel and change the direction of movement. A follow-up system is used to provide only as much nosewheel deflection as the pilot requires based on the amount the pedal or steering wheel is deflected.

Referring to Fig. 10-35, when the pilot operates the wheel or pedal, the balance of the follow-up differ-

ential mechanism is upset and this unit pivots and actuates the steering control valve. The steering control valve directs hydraulic pressure to the appropriate steering cylinder and releases pressure for the other cylinder. When the nosewheel starts to rotate, the cable around the steering collar on top of the nosewheel strut moves and returns the follow-up differential mechanism to a neutral position. This centers the steering control valve and stops rotation of the nosewheel. If the pilot's control is moved a large amount, the follow-up differential mechanism is deflected a large amount, requiring that the cylinders turn the nosewheel a large amount to return the follow-up unit and steering control valve to a neutral position. A similar operation would occur if the control were moved a small amount. The nosewheel would only move a small amount before the follow-up differential mechanism returned to the neutral position.

In the system shown in Fig. 10-35, the towing by-

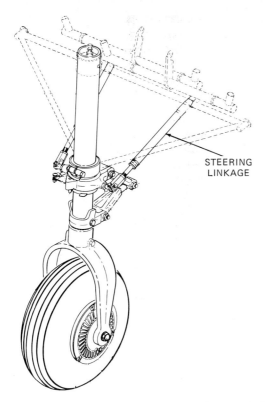

STEERING
LINKAGE

FIG. 10-33 Steering links for a light-aircraft nosewheel. *(Cessna Aircraft Co.)*

pass valve is used by maintenance personnel to bypass the steering commands so that the aircraft can be towed without damaging the operating mechanism.

● TRANSPORT AIRCRAFT LANDING-GEAR SYSTEMS

Transport aircraft, both corporate jets and airliners, have similar hydraulic landing-gear systems. The following discussions will acquaint the mechanic with typical landing-gear systems for these large aircraft.

Corporate Jets and Dual-Wheeled Transports

Corporate jet aircraft and many airliners, such as the Douglas DC-9, have a tricycle, fully retractable landing gear mounting two wheels on each gear. The nose gear is a dual-wheel, steerable type with the oleo strut mounted in the forward, lower section of the fuselage. The main gear consists of two pairs of wheels and brakes on oleo struts mounted in the wing-root area aft of the right- and left-wing rear spar.

The main-gear inboard doors, when used on the aircraft, and the nose-gear compartment doors are connected to their respective gear assemblies through linkages which sequence the doors to the open position during gear travel and to the closed position at the end of each cycle. The nose-gear attached doors

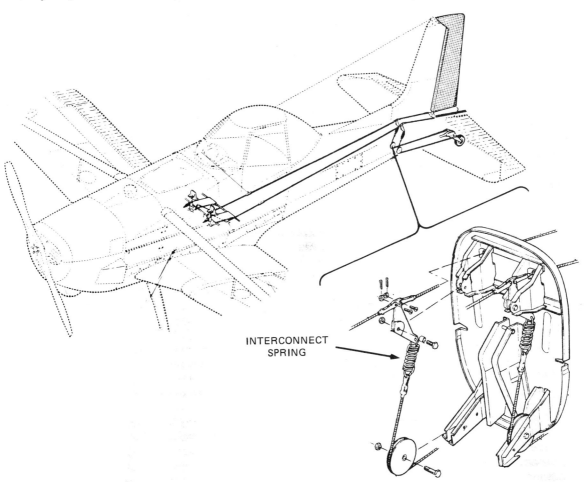

INTERCONNECT
SPRING

FIG. 10-34 Tail wheel steering arrangement. *(Cessna Aircraft Co.)*

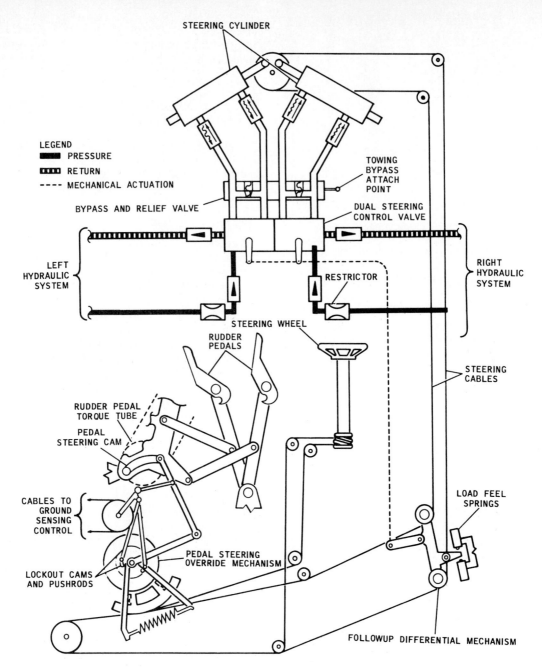

FIG. 10-35 Nosewheel steering arrangement for a transport aircraft. (*McDonnell Douglas Corp.*)

and the main-gear outboard doors move with the gear. Each wheel well is completely enclosed by doors when the gear is retracted, and the major portion of each wheel well is enclosed after the gear is extended.

Some aircraft do not use main inboard doors but retract the main gear so that it is flush with the underside of the wing. A **brush seal,** shown in Fig. 10-36, or an inflatable pneumatic seal is used to seal the edges of the wheel flush with the bottom of the wheel well.

Gear retraction and extension and the mechanical release of the door latches are controlled by the landing-gear control lever. The hydraulic power system

actuates the gear, door latches, bungee cylinders, brakes, and the nosewheel steering system.

One of four methods is used to extend the landing gear if hydraulic power is lost, preventing hydraulic extension of the landing gear. (1) Some aircraft make use of an air bottle to "blow" the gear down, substituting air pressure for hydraulic pressure. This pneumatic extension has the disadvantage that the system must be bled of all air before being returned to service. (2) Some aircraft make use of a mechanical system where the operation of a hand crank or ratchet performs the extension operation. (3) Other aircraft have a separate hydraulic system, powered by a hand

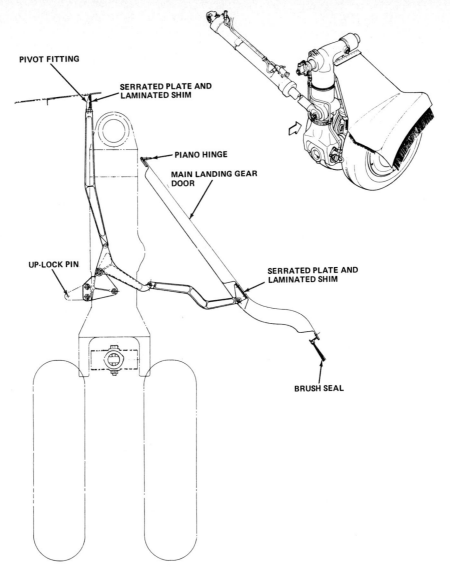

FIG. 10-36 Brush seals used to seal gap between retracted wheel and gear door. *(Canadair Inc.)*

pump, to extend the gear. (4) The fourth method of emergency extension that appears to be becoming very popular for aircraft is the use of a mechanical system to release the up locks and allowing the gear to free fall into the down-and-locked position.

The nosewheel steering system is hydraulically controlled through its full range of travel by a steering wheel located on the captain's left console. The rudder pedals can be used for limited steering control to either side of the neutral position for directional control during takeoff and landing. When the steering cylinders are in the neutral position, they act as shimmy dampers.

Each main-gear wheel is fitted with a hydraulic power disk brake. The brakes are controlled by the brake control valves which are operated by a cable system connected to the brake pedals. An electrically controlled **antiskid system** provides a locked-wheel protection feature and affords maximum efficiency to the brake system. The antiskid-system dual–servo

valves meter applied pressure to the brakes as required to provide maximum braking effect without skidding.

An electrically monitored indicating-and-warning system provides the flight crew with all the necessary gear- and gear-door position indications. These indications are visible in the cockpit.

Each main gear consists of two wheels and brakes attached to an oleo (air-oil) strut which is mounted on a support fitting on the rear spar in each wing-root area. Typical main-gear assemblies are shown in Figs. 10-37 and 10-38.

The main gear in Fig. 10-37 is supported laterally by the **side brace links.** These are locked in the DOWN position by **overcenter links** which are driven hydraulically by a **bungee cylinder** and mechanically by the **bungee springs.** The side brace links and the overcenter links fold up along the rear strut during gear retraction. The main gear is hydraulically raised to the UP position by a main-gear actuating cylinder and is

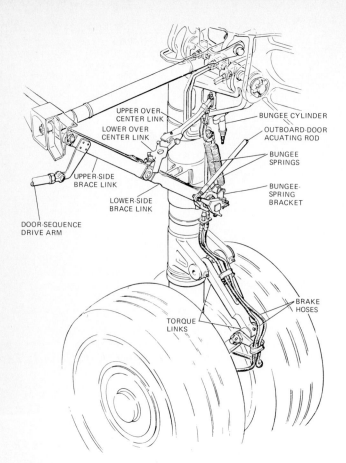

FIG. 10-37 Main landing gear for a DC-9 airplane.
(McDonnell Douglas Corp.)

held in the UP position by the main-gear doors and latches during flight.

The main gear in Fig. 10-38 uses the actuator to extend and retract the gear. An internal lock mechanism in the actuator locks the gear in the extended position. An external mechanical up-lock is used to hold the gear in the retracted position.

A typical **main-gear** door arrangement and the doors' position in relation to the landing gear are shown in Fig. 10-39. The doors enclose the main-gear wheel wells and a section of the wing-root area when the gear is retracted. There are two doors for each gear, designated as the **inboard door** and the **outboard door.**

The inboard door, the larger of the two, is square, with the outboard portion curved upward to conform to the shape of the adjoining fuselage structure. The core of the door is honeycomb construction strengthened by heavy frames. The door is exceptionally sturdy because it must support the weight of the main-gear assembly in the retracted position. A single hook-and-roller-type latch assembly holds the door in the CLOSED position. The door is actuated by a single hydraulic cylinder that attaches to a clevis on the forward frame and to the bracket attached to the shear web.

The outboard door is a smaller, irregular-shaped, honeycomb-core-type assembly attached to the lower wing section by a standard piano-type hinge. The door is linked directly to the gear strut by a pushrod and follows the gear strut during the gear extension and retraction operations.

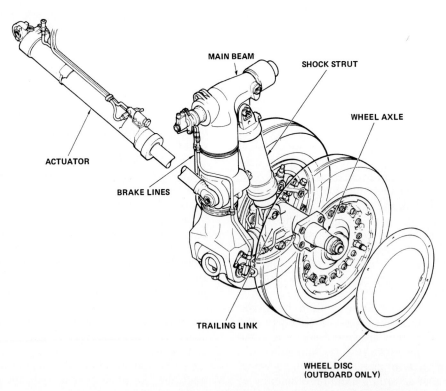

FIG. 10-38 Main landing gear for a Canadair Challenger 601. *(Canadair Inc.)*

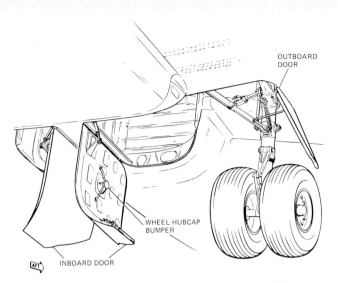

FIG. 10-39 **Transport aircraft main-gear doors.** *(Mc-Donnell Douglas Corp.)*

The **nose gear** is typically a dual-wheel, steerable, oleo shock-strut unit which retracts forward and up into the fuselage during flight and is completely enclosed by doors when retracted. An example of the unit and its associated parts is shown in Fig. 10-40.

The nose-gear strut is supported by the side braces and the cross arm, which form an integral part of the strut casting, and by the drag links. The wheels are mounted on an axle that is attached to the lower end of the strut piston. Overcenter linkage, which is attached between the drag links and the fuselage structure, locks the drag links and strut in the DOWN position. The nose-gear actuating cylinder is attached to a cross-arm crank and to the fuselage structure on the left side of the assembly. The cylinder is compressed when the gear is extended.

The nosewheel steering cylinders are mounted on the upper forward side of the strut cylinder body, and the pistons are attached to the piston and axle by the torque links.

The nose-gear doors may be mechanically operated by the nosewheel extension and retraction or, as shown in Fig. 10-41, some doors may be operated hydraulically while others move with the gear. In this example, the forward doors are opened hydraulically. The gear then extends or retracts and moves the mechanically linked aft door with it. The forward doors then close once the nose gear is fully extended or retracted. The sequence of operation of the forward doors and the landing-gear movement is controlled by the sequencing operation of the electrically operated selector valve. The selector valve receives door and gear position signals from the microswitches and proximity switches and, according to these signals, directs hydraulic pressure to the actuators in the proper sequence.

The nose-gear strut supports the forward portion of the airplane, absorbs landing shock, and steers the airplane through ground maneuvers.

The strut is supported by the side braces and cross

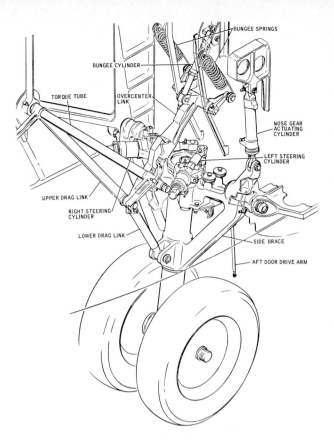

FIG. 10-40 **Nose gear for a DC-9.**

arm, which are part of the strut casting, and by the drag links. The major components of the strut are the **cylinder body,** the **steering cylinder,** and the **piston.** The cylinder body is the major support for the strut with the side braces and cross arm as an integral part of the body. The steering cylinder is installed inside the body between the body and the piston and mounts the steering bosses on the top side. The piston is inside the steering cylinder and is the shock absorber and support for the axle and wheels. Torque links are attached to the steering cylinder and to the axle boss. They transfer steering motion from the steering cylinder to the wheels and limit the extension length of the piston during gear retraction. The *main* steering cylinder described here must not be confused with the two cylinders called the **right steering cylinder** and the **left steering cylinder** shown in Fig. 10-40. These two units are *actuating cylinders.*

The side braces and cross arm support the nose-gear strut vertically and laterally. A torque arm extension on the left side brace is the attach point for the nose-gear actuating cylinder. The drag link is attached to the forward side of the strut body and supports the strut longitudinally. The gear is locked in the DOWN or UP position by the overcenter linkage. Internally, the nose-gear strut contains a metering-pin and strap assembly, a metering-plate and plate support, a piston seal adapter with static and dynamic O rings and D rings, and a piston guide. The internal construction of the strut is illustrated in Fig. 10-42. Observe that the

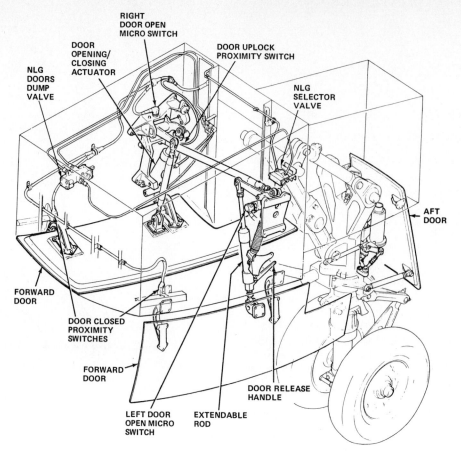

FIG. 10-41 Nose-gear doors and operating mechanism for a Canadair Challenger 601. (*Canadair Inc.*)

strut resembles others which have been described previously.

As shown in the drawing, the metering-pin, plate, and centering assemblies are installed inside the piston assembly. The piston assembly is installed inside the steering-cylinder assembly, and the steering assembly is installed inside the cylinder body. The cylinder body is the main support for all nose-gear-strut components. The steering cylinder is free to rotate within the body and rides on a pair of bushings on the body. It is secured within the body by a jam nut at the top of the cylinder. The piston is free to rotate, compress, or extend within the steering cylinder. It is retained by a gland nut at the bottom of the steering cylinder and by the nose-gear torque links. The metering-plate support assembly is held in position by the same jam nut that retains the steering cylinder. The metering pin is attached directly to the piston assembly and moves with the piston.

The **nose-gear linkage** consists of the **drag links, overcenter linkage,** and **torque-tube assembly.** These are illustrated in Fig. 10-43. The drag links are the longitudinal-axis support members for the nose-gear strut in the DOWN position. They consist of three tubular links. The upper two links are connected to the nose-gear support structure by a torque tube that acts as a pivot point. The lower drag link attaches to the upper two links at the midway point and connects to

the nose-gear-strut clevis on the lower forward side of the cylinder body. The junction point of the three drag-link members is also the connecting point for the lower **overcenter link.** The overcenter links hold the drag links and the nose-gear strut in the downlocked position. The links lock over center when the gear is fully extended and when the gear is fully retracted. When in the down-and-locked position and it is desired to retract the gear, the overcenter links are released by the hydraulically actuated **bungee cylinder** to permit gear retraction. The bungee cylinder, which is attached to the upper overcenter link, can be seen in Fig. 10-40.

When the gear is in the UP position, the overcenter links are normally released by the same bungee cylinder but, in the absence of hydraulic power, they can be released by a manually operated trip lever and roller that is connected to the alternate extension control lever mechanism. The two bungee springs are a mechanical backup for the hydraulically operated bungee cylinder.

The upper two nose-gear drag links are fitted with cranks at the pivot axis points. These cranks are the connecting points for the nose-gear forward-door drive linkage. The forward doors are cycled to the open position during gear travel and are closed at the end of each cycle of gear travel.

The **ground-sensing control mechanism** provides a

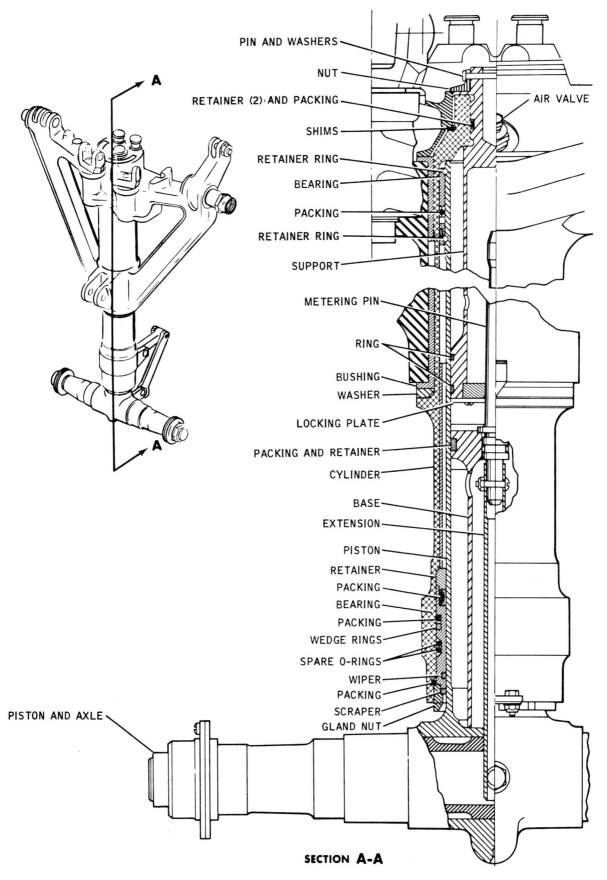

SECTION A-A

FIG. 10-42 Cross section of a nose-gear strut.

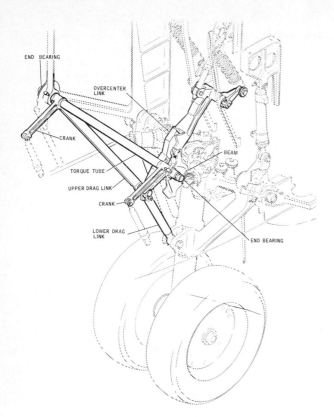

FIG. 10-43   Nose-gear actuating linkage.

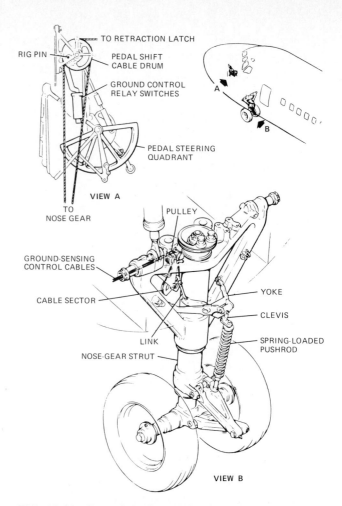

FIG. 10-44   Ground-sensing mechanism on a DC-9.

mechanical means of establishing a ground or flight mode with the functions of various systems differing as the mode changes.

The mechanism, shown in the drawings of Fig. 10-44, consists of a few simple linkages and a two-way, closed cable circuit actuated by the nose-gear links during gear-strut extension and compression. When the airplane takes off, the strut extends and establishes the flight mode. When the airplane is on the ground, the strut is compressed and the ground-operation mode is established.

The linkage for the ground-sensing control mechanism on the nose gear consists of a lever, a spring-loaded rod, and a cable sector. The linkages in the flight compartment consist of a cable drum and shaft that drives the pedal steering override mechanism, and a striker that actuates the ground control relays. The two-way, closed-circuit cable system runs from the sector on the nose gear to the cable drum on the rudder pedal-override mechanism. The **antiretraction latch cable** takes off from the same cable drum.

When the nose-gear strut extends, the nose-gear upper torque link draws the linkage downward, pulling the spring-loaded rod assembly down, and rotates the cable sector clockwise. The cable drives the pedal-override cable drum and shaft, which disengages the pedal steering mechanism. At the same time, the ground-control relays are actuated, causing various electrical circuits to assume the flight mode.

When the nose-gear strut is compressed, a ground mode is established. The pedal steering system is actuated to permit rudder-pedal steering, the antiretrac-

tion latch is engaged to prevent inadvertent operation of the landing-gear control lever, and the ground-control relays assume the ground operations mode. The feature which prevents retraction of the gear while the airplane is on the ground is required on all aircraft having retractable landing gear. The design of these systems varies widely although they all serve the same function.

Some aircraft rely on electrical position sensing systems rather than mechanical systems to determine if the aircraft is on the ground or in flight. The sensors in these systems are commonly called **squat** or **WOW switches** (WOW meaning Weight On Wheels). If the aircraft weight is on the landing gear, the squat switch will not allow the gear to be retracted by maintaining an open electrical path to the retraction system. The squat-switch system may use one or more sensors on one or more of the landing-gear legs, depending on the particular model aircraft.

The landing-gear extension-and-retraction system is composed of two major systems designated as the **mechanical control system** and the **hydraulic control system.** These are illustrated in Fig. 10-45.

In the more complex systems the mechanical control system is divided into four sections. These are (1) the landing-gear control valve cable system; (2) the main-gear inboard door-sequence follow-up valve sys-

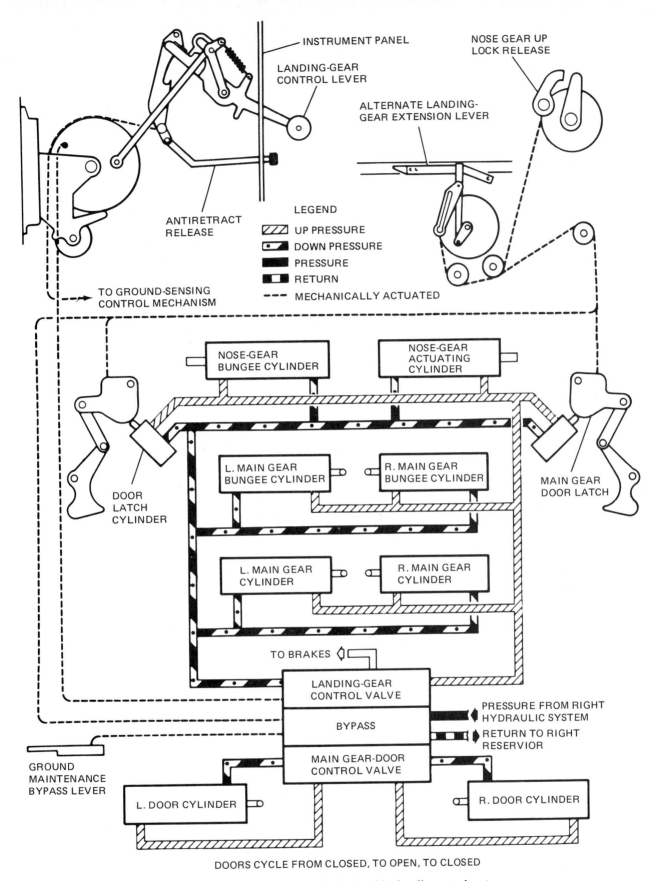

FIG. 10-45 Landing-gear mechanical and hydraulic control systems.

tem; (3) the alternate, or bypass, valve system; and (4) the subsystems.

The **landing-gear control-valve cable system** is a dual-cable system that runs from the landing-gear control-lever cable drums in the flight compartment to the landing-gear control-valve cable drums in the right wheel well. This cable system operates the landing-gear control valve during normal operation.

The **main-gear door-sequence valve follow-up system** is made up of two push-pull cables and associated linkages on the main-gear side braces to drive the main-gear inboard doors open and closed. The sequence valves are also linked to the landing-gear control-valve cable drums for initial motivation.

The **alternate, or bypass valve, system** is a dual-cable system. One cable drives the bypass valve cable drum, which actuates the bypass valve, the door-latch releases, and the door skids. The other cable actuates the nose-gear overcenter release mechanism. The alternate system (bypass valve) is used as a backup system to free-fall the gear in case of hydraulic power failure.

The hydraulic control system is divided into two sections. The landing-gear control valve and the door-sequence valves compose the basic system. The second section is the alternate, or bypass, system mentioned above. The bypass valve is used on the ground to relieve door-cylinder pressure and permit the doors to be opened manually for ground-maintenance access.

The landing-gear control valve ports hydraulic pressure to the main- and nose-gear actuating cylinders, the bungee cylinders, and the main-gear door-latch cylinders. The door-sequence valves port pressure to the door-actuating cylinders.

When the landing-gear control lever is placed in the GEAR UP position, the cable system positions the landing-gear control valve to port *up* pressure to the main- and nose-gear actuating cylinders, *unlock* pressure to the bungee cylinders, and *unlock* pressure to the door-latch cylinders. At the same time the cable-drum linkages position the door-sequence valves in the door-open position. As the gear travels toward the UP position, the side braces fold up, driving the door follow-up mechanism toward the door-closed position. As the gear nears the end of upward travel, the follow-up mechanism positions the door-sequence valves to the door-closed position, and the doors close. The door-latch cylinders lock the latches to secure the doors which, in turn, support the gear.

The nose-gear linkage will move to the overcenter position when the gear is up, and the bungee springs

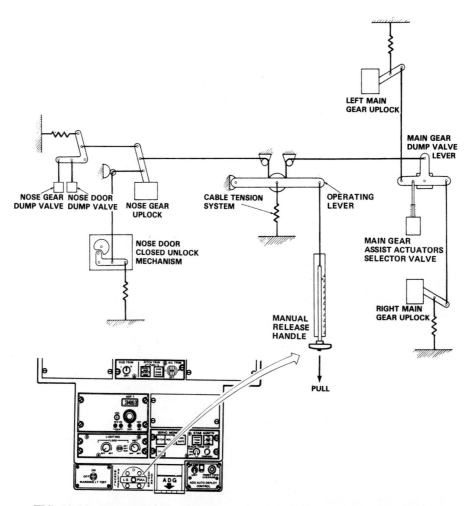

FIG. 10-46 Schematic of an emergency gear extension system. *(Canadair Inc.)*

will hold the overcenter locked condition. To extend the gear, the landing-gear control lever is placed in the GEAR DOWN position. The cable system positions the landing-gear control valve and the door-sequence valves to port (direct) hydraulic fluid to the door-actuating cylinders and the gear-actuating cylinders. The fluid pressure moves the gear-actuating cylinders in the *down* direction and causes the door-latch cylinders and the bungee cylinders to unlock. As the gear moves down, the door follow-up mechanism begins to drive the door-sequence valves toward the *up* position. By the time the gear is down and locked, the door-sequence valves have reached the closed position and the inboard doors close. The nose-gear doors are actuated mechanically through linkage with the gear; they are sequenced to the open position during gear travel and to the closed position at the end of each travel cycle.

In the event of hydraulic power failure or a jammed control valve, the gear can be extended by free-fall. When the alternate landing-gear control lever (located in a floor well to the right of the center pedestal) is pulled up, two backup systems are actuated. One cable system operates the nose-gear mechanical release to free the nose gear, and the other system operates the bypass valve, the door latches, and the door skids. The gear will then free-fall and lock in the down position. The bungee springs assure the locked condition of the gear in the down position.

A schematic for a manual release system is shown in Fig. 10-46. In the example shown, when the release handle is operated, the up locks are released, dump valves remove hydraulic pressure from the actuators, and the gear free-falls by gravity into the down-and-locked position. Before operating this type of extension mechanism, system control must be properly positioned to assure correct operation and prevent damage to system components.

Smaller and less complicated aircraft may use a system that does not rely on mechanical operation of the control valves, but on electrical control. When the gear selector control is positioned to retract or extend the gear, electrical power is supplied to hydraulic control selector valves which direct hydraulic pressure in the proper sequence to the landing-gear door actuators and the landing-gear actuators.

Large Transport Aircraft

Because of the complexity of the landing-gear systems for a large jet airliner, no attempt will be made in this text to describe such gear in detail. The principles of operation are similar to those previously discussed; however, the mechanic desiring detailed design, construction, and assembly information should consult the manufacturer's maintenance manual. It is our purpose here to give a brief description of the landing gear for a typical large transport airplane, primarily so comparisons can be made with those pre-

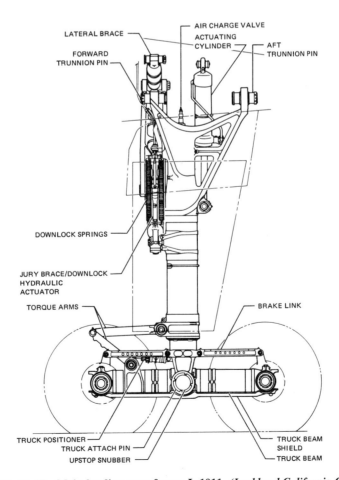

FIG. 10-47 Main landing gear for an L-1011. (*Lockheed California Co.*)

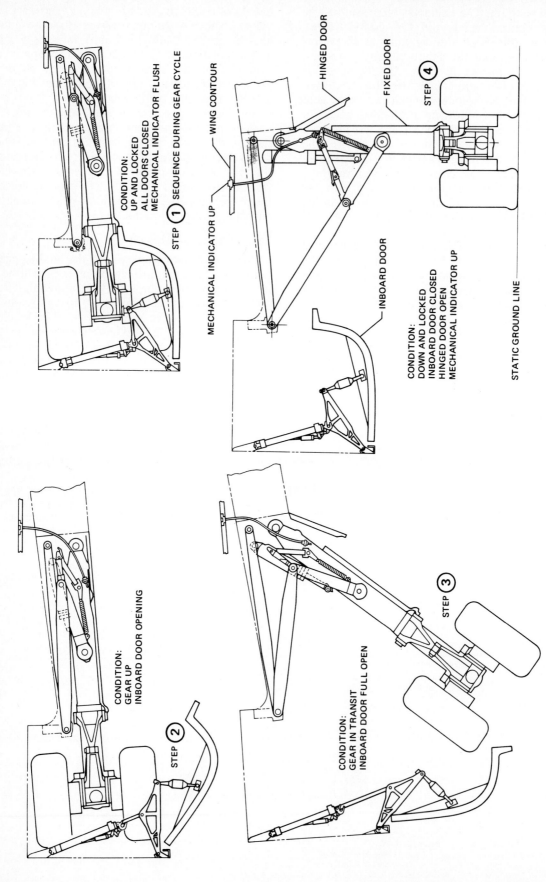

CONDITION:
UP AND LOCKED
ALL DOORS CLOSED
MECHANICAL INDICATOR FLUSH

STEP ① SEQUENCE DURING GEAR CYCLE

CONDITION:
GEAR UP
INBOARD DOOR OPENING

STEP ②

MECHANICAL INDICATOR UP

WING CONTOUR

HINGED DOOR

FIXED DOOR

STEP ④

INBOARD DOOR

CONDITION:
DOWN AND LOCKED
INBOARD DOOR CLOSED
HINGED DOOR OPEN
MECHANICAL INDICATOR UP

STATIC GROUND LINE

CONDITION:
GEAR IN TRANSIT
INBOARD DOOR FULL OPEN

STEP ③

FIG. 10-48 Sequence of landing-gear and door operations. (*Lockheed California Co.*)

viously discussed and so the student will have an appreciation of the magnitude of the engineering involved and the great skill and precision necessary to produce systems and mechanisms which perform their functions so effectively.

Figure 10-47 illustrates the arrangement of the main landing gear on the Lockheed L-1011. Observe that the main gear has many of the same components and features of the gear mechanisms described previously in this chapter. One of the principal differences is that this particular gear has four wheels mounted on a truck assembly at the bottom of the oleo shock strut. The arrangement of four wheels on a truck and beam assembly is referred to as "bogie" landing gear. Bogie landing gear is used on very large aircraft to provide a wide distribution of the load.

Each main-gear unit retracts into a wheel well in the fuselage, and gear doors close over the gear to provide a completely smooth wing-root and fuselage surface. The extension sequence is shown in Fig. 10-48. As with other systems for large aircraft, the gear actuation for retraction and extension is accomplished by means of hydraulic power. Because of the four wheels on each main gear, a smaller wheel can be used than would otherwise be required. An emergency extension system is provided for the gear in case of hydraulic power failure.

In a landing gear of this type a **trunnion,** pivoting on an axis parallel to the airplane centerline, provides the main attachment for each main landing gear. Trunnion support bearings are carried in a **torsion box** attached to the wing rear spar. Drag and side loads are transmitted from the oleo strut to the structure through brace struts as shown in Fig. 10-49.

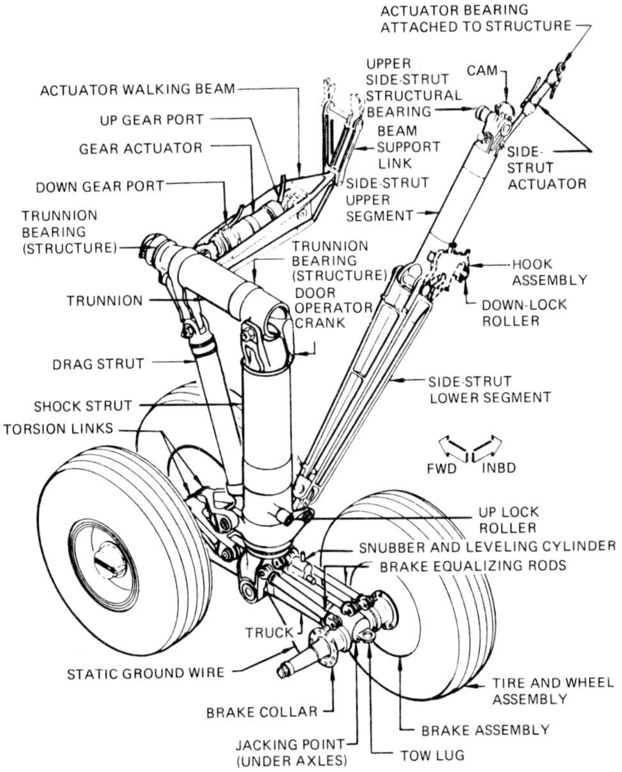

Figure 10-49 illustrates the principal components of the main-gear structure. The drawing should be studied carefully to note the similarities and differences when comparing the gear with those previously described. Observe particularly the **snubber-and-leveling cylinder** necessary to afford smooth operation of the truck-type wheel-and-axle supporting structure. Note also the **side-strut actuator** and the main-gear actuator with the **actuator walking beam.** Also note that the truck is attached to the strut piston by a hinge arrangement.

Lugs are provided on the forward side of the outer and inner cylinders for attachment of the **torsion (torque) links** to keep the inner cylinder, which is attached to the main-gear wheel truck, from turning within the outer cylinder. The lugs on the forward side of the outer cylinder are also used for drag-strut attachment. Three lugs on the lower terminal of the inner cylinder provide attachment points for the brake equalizer rods and the snubber and leveling cylinder. Lugs on the lower inboard side of the outer cylinder furnish an attachment for the lower side-strut segment universal fitting. Shock-strut doors are attached to the outer cylinder.

A **lock roller** on the lower aft side of the shock-strut outer cylinder contacts a **rabbit-ear crank** on main-gear retraction. Movement of the crank actuates the main-gear position switch and the door-control valve. The lock roller simultaneously engages a power-operated lock hook. This holds the landing gear securely in the up-and-locked position. Rotation of the lock crank to the GEAR-LOCKED position also actuates a lock switch in the circuit with the position switch to illuminate green, down-and-locked indicating lights or a red, gear-unlocked, warning light.

The majority of fuselage and wing loads, with the airplane on the ground, are transmitted through the main-gear support trunnion, drag strut, and side strut into the main-gear shock strut. In turn, the loads in the main-gear shock strut are transmitted through the main-gear trucks into the four wheels of each main gear. The main-gear truck is a T-shaped, tubular steel beam to which the forward and aft axles are attached. These are shown in Fig. 10-49. A jacking pad and a towing eye are formed on the front and aft ends of the truck beam. The forward horizontal arms of the truck beam carry the two-piece forward axle. One axle stub is secured in each horizontal arm. Integral flanges on the truck-beam arms carry the forward brake assemblies. The one-piece aft axle is installed through the aft end of the truck beam and locked in position through the truck beam and axle. The aft axle is machined on each side of the truck beam to support movable collars. Each movable collar carries an aft-brake assembly and provides an attachment lug for a brake equalizing rod. The **brake equalizing rods** link the movable collars with the lugs on the lower terminal shock-strut inner cylinder above the truck beams. The brake equalizing rods prevent "porpoising" (raising of rear-gear wheels) when the brakes are applied on landing or during the taxi roll. The center portion of the truck beam is machined and drilled to mate with the yoke at the lower end of the shock-strut inner

ACTUATOR BEARING ATTACHED TO STRUCTURE

UPPER SIDE-STRUT STRUCTURAL BEARING CAM

ACTUATOR WALKING BEAM

UP GEAR PORT

GEAR ACTUATOR

STRUCTURAL BEAM SUPPORT LINK

SIDE-STRUT UPPER SEGMENT

SIDE-STRUT ACTUATOR

DOWN GEAR PORT

TRUNNION BEARING (STRUCTURE)

TRUNNION BEARING (STRUCTURE)

HOOK ASSEMBLY

DOOR OPERATOR CRANK

DOWN-LOCK ROLLER

TRUNNION

DRAG STRUT

SIDE-STRUT LOWER SEGMENT

SHOCK STRUT

TORSION LINKS

FWD INBD

UP LOCK ROLLER

SNUBBER AND LEVELING CYLINDER

BRAKE EQUALIZING RODS

TRUCK

STATIC GROUND WIRE

TIRE AND WHEEL ASSEMBLY

BRAKE COLLAR

BRAKE ASSEMBLY

JACKING POINT (UNDER AXLES)

TOW LUG

FIG. 10-49 Main landing-gear components.

361

cylinder. A lug is formed on the truck beam directly above the rear axle for the attachment of the snubber-and-leveling cylinder. One large bolt attaches the truck to the shock strut. Hydraulic and pneumatic tubing, electric wiring, and a truck leveling switch are attached or bracketed to the truck. A static ground wire is attached to a lug on the underside of the truck between the forward wheels and the shock strut. This wire discharges the static electrical charge which often builds up on the aircraft during flight.

● INSPECTION AND MAINTENANCE OF LANDING GEAR

A thorough inspection of landing gear involves the careful examination of the entire structure of the gear including the attachments to the fuselage or wings, struts, wheels, brakes, actuating mechanisms for retractable gear, gear hydraulic system and valves, gear doors, and all associated parts. It is recommended that the mechanic follow the instructions given in the manufacturer's manual for the aircraft being inspected. This is particularly important for the more complex types installed on aircraft with retractable gear.

Fixed-Gear Inspection

Fixed landing gear should be examined regularly for wear, deterioration, corrosion, alignment, and other factors which may cause failure or unsatisfactory operation.

During a 100-h period or annual inspection of fixed gear, the airplane should be jacked up so the gear does not bear the weight of the aircraft. The mechanic should then attempt to move the gear struts and wheels to test for play in the mounting. If any looseness is found, the cause should be determined and corrected.

When landing gear which employs rubber shock (bungee) cord for shock absorption is inspected, the shock cord should be inspected for age, fraying of the braided sheath, narrowing (necking) of the cord, and wear at points of contact with the structure. If the age of the shock cord is near 5 years or more, it is advisable to replace it with new cord, regardless of other factors. Cord which shows other defects should be replaced, regardless of age.

Shock struts of the spring-oleo type should be examined for leakage, smoothness of operation, looseness between the moving parts, and play at the attaching points. The extension of the struts should be checked to make sure that the springs are not worn or broken. The piston section of the strut must be free of nicks, cuts, and corrosion.

Air-oil struts should undergo an inspection similar to that recommended for spring-oleo struts. In addition, the extension of the strut should be checked to see that it conforms to the distance specified by the manufacturer. If an air-oil strut "bottoms," that is, is collapsed, obviously the air has been lost from the air chamber. This is probably due to a loose or defective air valve or defective O-ring seals. Before an air-oil strut is removed or disassembled, the air valve should be opened to make sure that all air pressure is re-

moved. Severe injury and/or damage can occur as the result of disassembling a strut when even a small amount of air pressure is still in the air chamber.

The method for checking the fluid level of an air-oil strut is given in the manufacturer's maintenance manual. Usually the fluid level is checked with the strut collapsed and all air removed from the strut. With the strut collapsed, the fluid level should be even with the filler opening unless other instructions are given by the manufacturer. In all cases, the mechanic must use the correct fluid when refilling or replenishing the fluid in a strut. Most airplanes with oleo struts use MIL-O-5606 fluid.

The entire structure of the landing gear should be closely examined for cracks, nicks, cuts, corrosion damage, or any other condition which can cause stress concentrations and eventual failure. The exposed lower end of the air-oleo piston is especially susceptible to damage and corrosion which can lead to seal damage as the strut is compressed and the piston moves past the strut lower seal, causing the seal to leak fluid and air. Small nicks or cuts can be filed and burnished to a smooth contour, eliminating the point of stress concentration. If a crack is found in a landing-gear member, the member should be replaced.

All bolts and fittings should be checked for security and condition. Bolts in the torque links and shimmy damper tend to wear and become loose due to the operational loads placed on them. The nosewheel shimmy damper should be checked for proper operation and any evidence of leaking. All required lubrication should be performed in accordance with the aircraft service manual.

Inspection of Retractable Landing Gear

Inspection of retractable landing gear should include all applicable items mentioned in the foregoing discussion of inspection for fixed gear. In addition, the actuating mechanisms must be inspected for wear; looseness in any joint, trunnion, or bearing; leakage of fluid from any hydraulic line or unit; and smoothness of operation. The operational check is performed by jacking the airplane according to manufacturer's instructions and then operating the gear retracting-and-extending system. Particular attention must be given to the location of the approved **jacking points.** The jacking points (pads) are placed in locations where the strength of the structure is adequate to withstand the concentrated stress applied by the jack.

During the operational test, the smoothness of the operation, effectiveness of up and down locks, operation of the warning horn, operation of indicating systems, clearance of tires in wheel wells, and operation of landing-gear doors should be checked. Improper adjustment of sequence valves may cause doors to rub against gear structures or wheels. The manufacturer's checklist should be followed to assure that critical items are checked. While the airplane is still jacked up, the gear can be tested for looseness of mounting points, play in torque links, condition of the inner strut cylinder, play in wheel bearings, and play in actuating linkages.

The proper operation of the antiretraction system

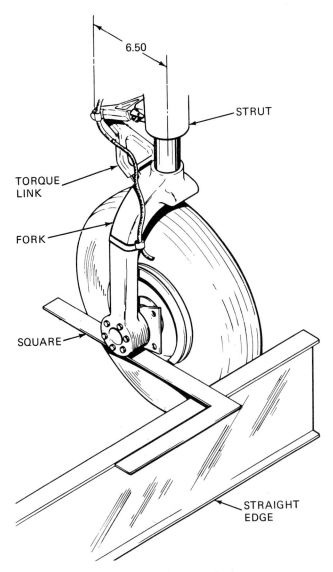

6.50

STRUT

TORQUE
LINK

FORK

SQUARE

STRAIGHT
EDGE

FIG. 10-50 Alignment of main-gear wheels.

should be checked in accordance with manufacturer's instructions. Where safety switches are actuated by the torque links, the actual time of switch closing or opening can be checked by removing all air from the strut and then collapsing the strut. In every case, the adjustment should be such that the gear control cannot be placed in the UP position or that the system cannot operate until the shock strut is very near the fully extended position.

Alignment of Main-Gear Wheels

The alignment of main-gear wheels should be checked periodically to assure proper handling characteristics during landing, taxiing, and takeoff and to reduce tire wear. Wheel alignment of oleo-equipped landing gear is adjusted by means of shim washers installed between the torque links at the joint between the upper and lower links. For spring steel landing gear, alignment is adjusted by the use of shim plates between the gear leg and the axle mount.

The following is a typical alignment check procedure for a light airplane:

Place a straightedge of sufficient length to reach across the front of both main landing-gear wheels. Butt the straightedge against the tire at the hub level of the wheels. Jack the airplane up just high enough to obtain a dimension of 6.5 in [16.51 cm] between the centerline of the strut piston and the centerline of the centerpivot bolt of the gear torque links. See Fig. 10-50. Devise a support to hold the straightedge in the location described above.

Set a square against the straightedge and check whether its outstanding leg bears on the front and rear side of the brake disk. If it touches both the forward and rear flange, the landing gear is correctly aligned with 0° toe-in. The toe-in for this particular gear is 0 ± ½°.

If the square contacts the rear side of the disk, leaving a gap between it and the front flange, the wheel is toed out. If a gap appears at the rear flange, the wheel is toed in.

To rectify the toe-in and toe-out condition, remove the bolt connecting the upper and lower torque links and remove or add spacer washers to move the wheel in the desired direction. Should a condition exist where all spacer washers have been removed and moving the wheel in or out is still necessary, then the torque link assembly must be turned over. This will put the link connection on the opposite side, allowing the use of spacers to go in the same direction.

Some aircraft landing gear is checked for alignment with the full weight of the aircraft on the gear. The gear is placed on greased plates, as shown in Fig. 10-51, to eliminate any ground friction affecting the alignment check. A straightedge and square are used as described previously. In this instance the gear is checked for both toe-in and toe-out as well as camber, as shown in Fig. 10-52. Some aircraft use tapered shin plates between the landing gear leg and the axle to adjust toe-in/toe-out and camber.

Inspection and Repair of Floats and Skis

Inspection of floats and skis involves examination for damage due to corrosion, collision with other objects, hard landings, and other conditions which may lead to failure. Tubular structures for such gear may be repaired as described in the section covering welded repairs of tubular structures.

Floats should be carefully inspected for corrosion damage at periodic intervals, especially if the airplane is flown from salt water. If small blisters are noticed on the paint, either inside or outside the float, the paint should be removed and the area examined. If corrosion is found to exist, the area should be cleaned thoroughly, and a coat of corrosion-inhibiting material applied. If the corrosion penetrates the metal to an appreciable depth, it is advisable that a patch be applied in accordance with approved practice. Special attention should be given to brace wire fittings and water rudder control systems.

If the floats or hull has retractable landing gear, a retraction check should be performed along with the other recommendations mentioned for retractable landing-gear systems. Sheet-metal floats should be repaired using approved practices described elsewhere

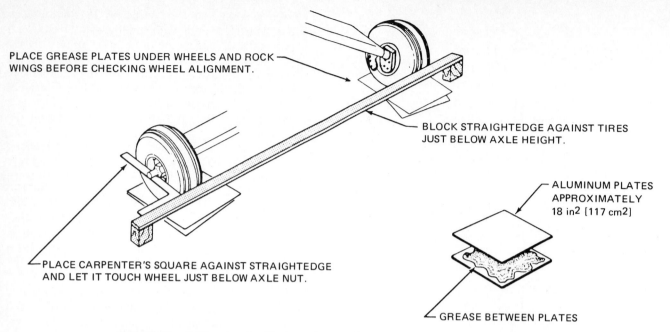

PLACE GREASE PLATES UNDER WHEELS AND ROCK WINGS BEFORE CHECKING WHEEL ALIGNMENT.

BLOCK STRAIGHTEDGE AGAINST TIRES JUST BELOW AXLE HEIGHT.

ALUMINUM PLATES APPROXIMATELY 18 in2 [117 cm2]

PLACE CARPENTER'S SQUARE AGAINST STRAIGHTEDGE AND LET IT TOUCH WHEEL JUST BELOW AXLE NUT.

GREASE BETWEEN PLATES

FIG. 10-51   Setting up a landing gear for an alignment check. *(Cessna Aircraft Co.)*

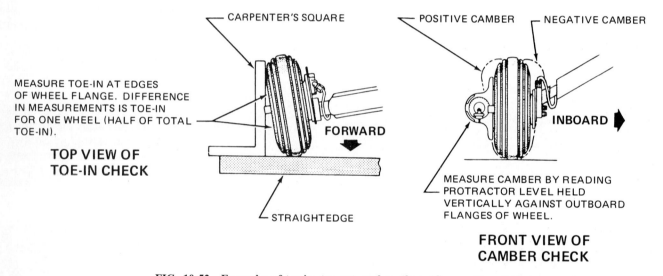

CARPENTER'S SQUARE

POSITIVE CAMBER   NEGATIVE CAMBER

MEASURE TOE-IN AT EDGES OF WHEEL FLANGE. DIFFERENCE IN MEASUREMENTS IS TOE-IN FOR ONE WHEEL (HALF OF TOTAL TOE-IN).

FORWARD

INBOARD

TOP VIEW OF TOE-IN CHECK

STRAIGHTEDGE

MEASURE CAMBER BY READING PROTRACTOR LEVEL HELD VERTICALLY AGAINST OUTBOARD FLANGES OF WHEEL.

FRONT VIEW OF CAMBER CHECK

FIG. 10-52   Examples of toe-in, toe-out, and camber. *(Cessna Aircraft Co.)*

in this text; however, the seams between sections of sheet metal should be waterproofed with suitable fabric and sealing compound. A float which has undergone repairs should be tested by filling it with water and allowing it to stand for at least 24 h to see if any leaks develop.

Skis should be inspected for general condition of the ski, cables, bungees, and fuselage attachments. If retractable skis are used, checks in accordance with the general practices for retractable gear should be followed. For repair of skis, the manufacturers furnish approved repair instructions.

Jacking Aircraft

When working on the aircraft landing gear, it is often necessary to raise a landing gear or the complete air-

craft off of its landing gear and support it on jacks or other supports. When raising the aircraft, care must be taken to use the proper mechanisms to raise the aircraft so that it can be done safely and without damaging the aircraft. Each manufacturer should provide specific jacking instructions in the aircraft maintenance manual. The following information illustrates some common methods. Figure 10-53 (a) and (b) shows some of the components and methods discussed below.

When lifting a single-wheel landing gear off of the ground, a mechanical or hydraulic jack is used. Special jack points may be built into the fuselage for this purpose or special jacking fittings may have to be installed on the airframe. Jack points are found on the wings and fuselage. Some landing gear can be jacked up using fittings or surfaces on the gear structure or by the attachment of special adapters.

The type of jack used depends on the height of the jack point above the ground and the weight of the aircraft. For many light aircraft, automotive floor jacks may be sufficient. Large aircraft and aircraft with jack points high above the ground may require the use of special aircraft jacks. Always use a jack of the size and stability appropriate to the task being performed.

When replacing a tire or working on the brake of a landing gear with a dual or dual-tandem arrangement, the manufacturer may allow the use of a gear ramp. The aircraft is moved onto a support ramp using only one of the dual wheels. This frees one wheel assembly from the ground and allows the wheel, tire, or brake to be serviced.

Some light aircraft can have their nosewheels raised off of the ground by placing weights on the horizontal stabilizer or by pulling down on the tie-down ring. This should be done only if the manufacturer has ap-

proved the procedure. Some aircraft can be damaged structurally using this procedure.

Any time that an aircraft is to be placed on jacks, make sure that it is stable and do not allow people in or under the aircraft if there is a chance of injury or the aircraft slipping off of the jacks. When performing gear retraction checks, it may be necessary to enter or leave the aircraft while it is on the jacks. This should be done carefully to avoid a sudden shift in weight that will cause the aircraft to come off the jacks. It may be necessary in some aircraft to have someone in the aircraft before it is jacked up and only allow them to leave the aircraft after the checks are complete and the aircraft is back on its own gear.

The following are some guidelines that should be followed when jacking aircraft:

1. Perform jacking in a hangar free of air currents.
2. Use equipment that is in good condition.
3. Make use of locking devices once the aircraft is

A

FIG. 10-53   (a) Methods of raising a landing gear with a jack or a ramp. *(Canadair Inc.)*

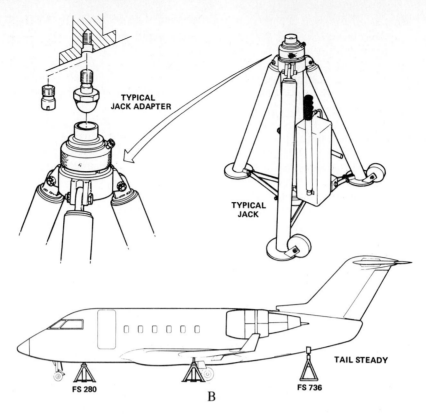

FIG. 10-53 (b) An aircraft jack adapter and typical jack locations. *(Canadair Inc.)*

raised to the desired height. Do not rely on the jack hydraulic system to support the aircraft. These locking devices mechanically lock the jack piston in position.

4. Keep equipment and people from under the aircraft unless necessary to perform a maintenance operation and then only when the aircraft is stable and on locked jacks.

5. Use supports whenever necessary to stabilize an aircraft that is on jacks.

6. When lowering the aircraft, retract the jack piston well below the jack point before removing the jack from under the aircraft. Some oleo landing-gear struts may bind in the extended position and may suddenly lower the airframe as the weight of the aircraft overcomes the binding force.

● DESIGN AND OPERATION OF BRAKE ASSEMBLIES

The various brake designs discussed here reflect the variety of braking capabilities required for different size aircraft. Light aircraft can rely on a simple shoe brake or single disk brake because the landing speeds are slow and the aircraft is light in weight. Large aircraft, such as transports, land at high speeds and weigh several tons. These aircraft require very powerful multisurfaced brakes in order for the brakes to be effective at slowing the aircraft.

Internal Expanding-Shoe Brakes

The types of internal expanding-shoe brakes are (1) the **one-way** or **single-servo,** and (2) the **two-way** or **dual-servo type. Servo action** in a brake of this type means that the rotation of the brake drum adds braking energy to the brake shoes and makes them operate more effectively and with less effort by the pilot.

In single-servo brakes, the servo action is effective for one direction of the wheel only, as contrasted with a **dual-servo** or **reversible type,** which operates, and may be adjusted, to give servo action in either direction. Both types are supplied with either single-shoe or two-shoe construction. Brake shoe assemblies are attached to the landing-gear strut flange by means of bolts through the torque plate on the axle, which has as many as 12 equally spaced holes, with bolts in only one-half of the holes. The alternate holes are used to

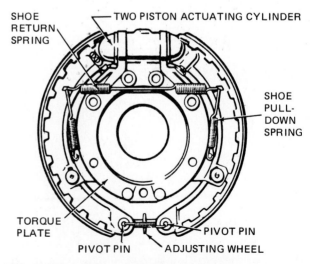

FIG. 10-54 A dual-servo-type brake assembly.

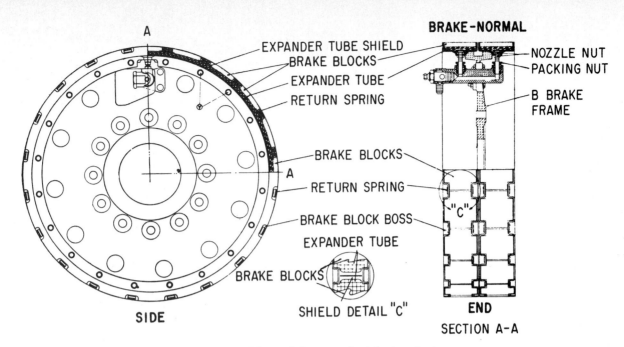

FIG. 10-55 Views of the expander-tube-type brake.

permit a variation of the position of the brake assembly to assure that the brake cylinder is at the top or highest position on the assembly. The brake drum is attached to the wheel and rotates with it.

A dual-servo brake assembly is shown in the drawing of Fig. 10-54. As explained previously, dual-servo brakes are effective for either direction of wheel rotation; hence they are interchangeable between the left and right wheels of the airplane and are effective for both forward and backward motion of the airplane. These brakes may be operated hydraulically, mechanically, or pneumatically.

Expander-Tube Brakes

Side and end views of an **expander-tube type of brake** are shown in Fig. 10-55, and Fig. 10-56 illustrates the principle of operation. Each expander-tube brake consists of four main parts: (1) **brake frame,** (2) **expander tube,** (3) **return springs,** and (4) the **brake blocks.** The single-type brake has one row of blocks around the circumference and is used on small aircraft. The duplex-type, expander-tube brake has two rows of brake blocks and is designed for larger aircraft. An inner fairing, or shield, fits between the **torque flange** on the axle and the brake frame to protect the frame against water.

FIG. 10-56 Principle of operation of the expander-tube brake.

The brake expander tube is a flat tube made of synthetic-rubber compound and fabric. It is stretched over the circular brake frame between the side flanges, and it has a nozzle that is connected with the hydraulic-fluid line by means of suitable fittings.

The brake blocks are made of a material which is similar to that used for molded brake linings. The blocks have notches at each corner to engage with lugs on the brake frame and to prevent movement with the brake drum as it rotates. There are grooves across the ends of each block, and the flat return springs are inserted in these grooves. The ends of the springs fit into slots in the side flanges of the brake frame, holding the blocks firmly against the expander tube and keeping them from dragging when the brake is released.

The expander-tube brake is hydraulically operated and can be used with any conventional hydraulic brake system. When the brake pedal is pressed, the fluid is forced into the expander tube. The frame prevents any expansion either inward or to the sides. The pressure of the fluid in the tube forces the blocks radially outward against the brake drum. When the pressure is released, the springs in the ends of the blocks tend to force the fluid out of the expander tube and to pull the blocks away from contact with the brake drum. This action is increased by the tube itself, since it is molded slightly smaller in diameter than the brake frame and tends to contract without the help of the springs. Each block is independent in its action; hence there is no buildup of servo action and no tendency to grab.

During the inspection and servicing of expander-tube brakes, the mechanic must make sure that no hydraulic pressure is applied to the brakes when a brake is not enclosed in its drum. If the brake blocks are not restrained by the drum when hydraulic power is applied, the retaining grooves at the ends of the blocks will be broken and the blocks will pop out.

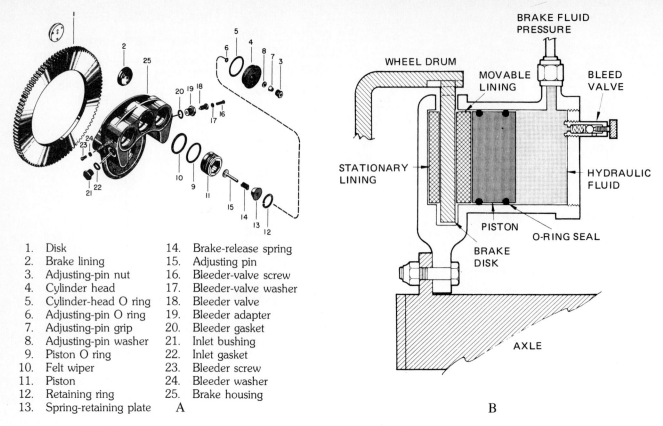

1. Disk
2. Brake lining
3. Adjusting-pin nut
4. Cylinder head
5. Cylinder-head O ring
6. Adjusting-pin O ring
7. Adjusting-pin grip
8. Adjusting-pin washer
9. Piston O ring
10. Felt wiper
11. Piston
12. Retaining ring
13. Spring-retaining plate
14. Brake-release spring
15. Adjusting pin
16. Bleeder-valve screw
17. Bleeder-valve washer
18. Bleeder valve
19. Bleeder adapter
20. Bleeder gasket
21. Inlet bushing
22. Inlet gasket
23. Bleeder screw
24. Bleeder washer
25. Brake housing

A

B

FIG. 10-57 (a) Exploded view of a single-disk-type brake. (b) Cutaway of the single-disk brake.

When the brake blocks are worn to their allowable limits, they are easily replaced. The return springs which retain the blocks are removed by pressing down on one end clip with a screwdriver or other tool and sliding the springs out of the rectangular holes in which they are held. When all the blocks have been removed, the entire assembly is cleaned and inspected before installing new blocks. The new blocks are installed one at a time with the return springs to hold them in place.

If the expander tube is found to be damaged upon removal of the brake blocks, the tube must be replaced.

Single-Disk Brakes

One of the most popular types of brakes, especially for smaller aircraft, is the **single-disk brake.** An exploded view of such a brake is shown in Fig. 10-57 a and a cutaway is shown in 10-57 b. This brake is manufactured by the Goodyear Aerospace Company.

The main disk (1) of the brake shown in Fig. 10-57 a is locked into the wheel by means of teeth or keys around the outer rim of the disk, causing it to turn with the wheel. On each side of the disk are located the linings (2) which bear against the disk when the brakes are applied, causing the wheel to slow down or stop.

One lining of the brake is mounted in a recess in the plate attached to the main axle structure. The other lining (2) is mounted against the piston (11) and moves according to the amount of hydraulic pressure applied

to the piston. In Fig. 10-57 a, three pistons are incorporated in the brake housing (25), hence three linings must be mounted on the opposite side of the disk to back up the movable linings. Single-disk brakes may be constructed with as many separate pistons and linings as deemed advisable for the airplane for which they are designed. Each, piston is equipped with separate sets of linings which bear against the brake disk (1) when the brakes are applied.

Another type of single-disk brake is illustrated in the exploded view of Fig. 10-58. This view does not show the disk, which is located between the two linings, but illustrates the braking components. This brake utilizes contoured brake blocks as linings for both the pressure plate and back plate, sometimes called the **anvil.** Pressure is applied to the pressure plate by means of two round pistons mounted in the brake cylinder. When the brake is assembled, the linings are riveted to the pressure plate and back plate. They are replaced when one segment becomes worn to a thickness of below 0.099 in [2.51 mm] or if signs of uneven wear are evident.

Most hydraulic brake systems require a method for the removal of air from the system. In Figs. 10-57 a and 10-58, items 16 to 20 and 15 to 17, respectively, compose the **brake bleeder valve** assembly. In order to bleed the air from the brakes, the valve is opened slightly and hydraulic fluid under pressure is applied to the piston. A complete discussion of brake bleeding is found at the end of this chapter.

Although modern aircraft operate the single-disk

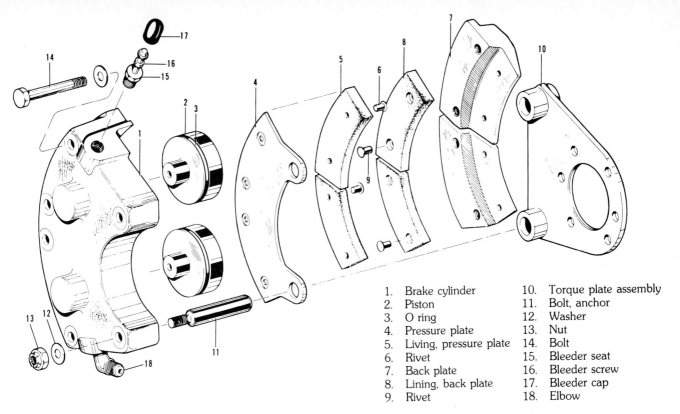

1. Brake cylinder	10. Torque plate assembly
2. Piston	11. Bolt, anchor
3. O ring	12. Washer
4. Pressure plate	13. Nut
5. Living, pressure plate	14. Bolt
6. Rivet	15. Bleeder seat
7. Back plate	16. Bleeder screw
8. Lining, back plate	17. Bleeder cap
9. Rivet	18. Elbow

FIG. 10-58   Brake components for a single-disk brake. *(Piper Aircraft Corp.)*

brake by hydraulic power, some older aircraft are designed with mechanically operated single-disk brakes.

Multiple-Disk Brakes

Multiple-disk brakes are used on large aircraft where a substantial amount of braking force is required. They are operated by hydraulic pressure.

The construction of a typical **multiple-disk brake** assembly is shown in Fig. 10-59. This brake assembly is used on the Douglas DC-9 airplane.

The brake assembly in Fig. 10-59 is described as a **dual-system, five-rotor, disk-type power brake.** Each brake contains two independent cylinder and passageway systems; and each system contains seven brake pistons, two **bleed valves,** one **hydraulic pressure port,** and its associated passageways. Each brake also contains one **carrier,** four **stator plates,** one **pressure plate,** one **back plate,** five **rotor plates,** and one **torque tube.**

The carrier houses the two independent internally drilled, hydraulic passageway systems; 14 hydraulic pistons, seven for each system; the **brake return assemblies;** four bleed valves; and two pressure ports, one for each system.

The four stator plates and the pressure plate are keyed to the torque tube of the brake. The stator plates consist of a steel heat-sink-type core with 14 stainless-steel pads riveted onto both outer surfaces. The pads are comparable with brake linings on conventional disk-type brakes but resist wear more effectively. The heat-sink feature helps to absorb and carry the heat away from the stainless-steel brake pads.

The five rotor plates are keyed to the wheel and rotate with the wheel. Each rotor plate consists of a steel heat-sink-type core with each outer surface faced with a bronze sheet. The bronze sheet takes the wear, while the stainless-steel **wear pads** on the stator plates remain comparatively stable.

The **torque tube** is the structural drum-type member that links the carrier with the back plate. It provides the keys for the stator plates and ties the brake assembly to the axle flange. The torque tube is the structural backbone of the brake assembly and transfers brake moment to the axle and gear strut.

Braking action is produced by hydraulic pressure forcing the pistons against the pressure plate which, in turn, forces the disk stack together and creates friction between the rotating and stationary disks. Each piston is fitted with an organic insulator to prevent brake heat transfer to the pistons and carrier. When hydraulic-fluid pressure is released from the brake pistons, the return springs and pins pull the pressure place and the pistons to the full OFF position, thus allowing the disks to release and the wheel to rotate.

A self-adjusting mechanism on the return pins maintains a constant running clearance throughout the life of the brake. No adjustment is necessary.

While not shown in the DC-9 multiple-disk brake, **wear indicators** are often included in the brake design. These are rods that are extension of the return pins. As the brake linings wear and the adjuster operates, the wear indicator moves into the assembly. When the exposed length of the rod has decreased to a predetermined minimum length, the brakes must be serviced to maintain full braking capability.

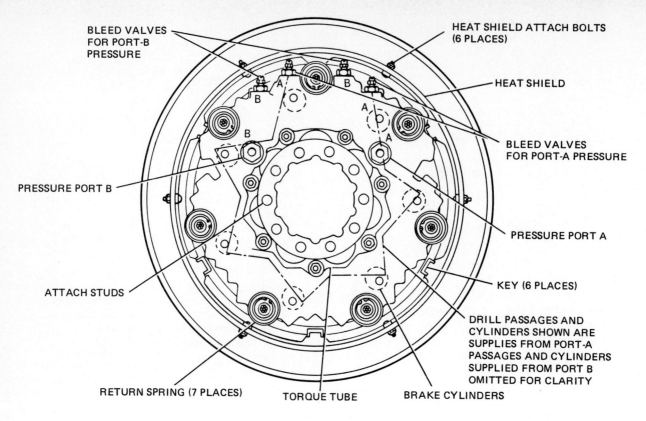

BLEED VALVES FOR PORT-B PRESSURE

HEAT SHIELD ATTACH BOLTS (6 PLACES)

HEAT SHIELD

BLEED VALVES FOR PORT-A PRESSURE

PRESSURE PORT B

PRESSURE PORT A

ATTACH STUDS

KEY (6 PLACES)

DRILL PASSAGES AND CYLINDERS SHOWN ARE SUPPLIES FROM PORT-A PASSAGES AND CYLINDERS SUPPLIED FROM PORT B OMITTED FOR CLARITY

RETURN SPRING (7 PLACES)

TORQUE TUBE

BRAKE CYLINDERS

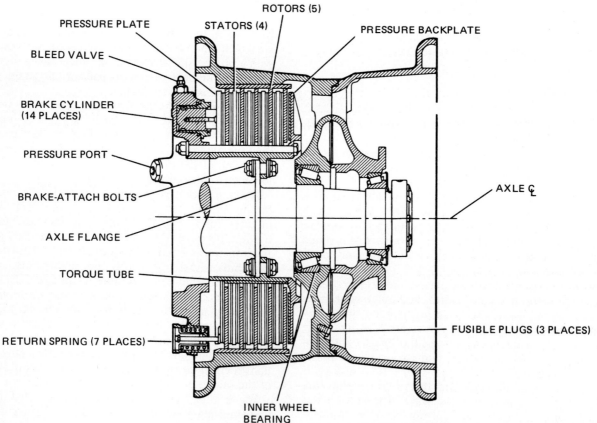

ROTORS (5)

PRESSURE PLATE

STATORS (4)

PRESSURE BACKPLATE

BLEED VALVE

BRAKE CYLINDER (14 PLACES)

PRESSURE PORT

BRAKE-ATTACH BOLTS

AXLE ₵

AXLE FLANGE

TORQUE TUBE

FUSIBLE PLUGS (3 PLACES)

RETURN SPRING (7 PLACES)

INNER WHEEL BEARING

FIG. 10-59   Multiple-disk-type brake for the Douglas DC-9.

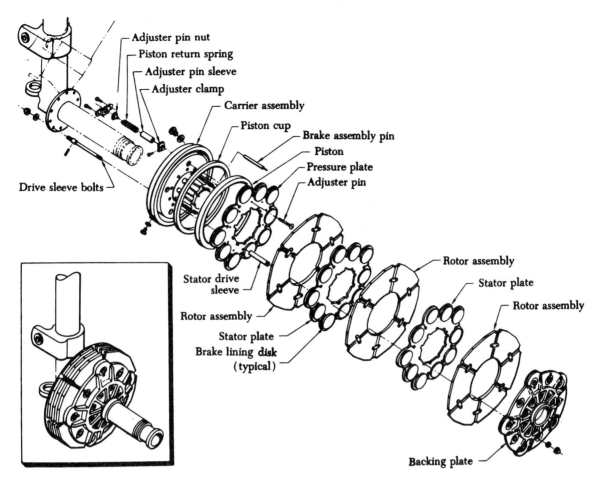

FIG. 10-60   Exploded view of a segmented rotor brake.

Segmented Rotor-Disk Brakes

Segmented rotor-disk brakes are heavy-duty brakes designed for use with high-pressure hydraulic systems using power brake control valves or power boost master cylinders. Braking action results from several sets of stationary, high-friction-type brake linings making contact with rotating (rotor) segments. This action is the same as occurs with multiple-disk brakes. An exploded view of this type brake is shown in Fig. 10-60, and a cross section of the brake is shown in Fig. 10-61.

A carrier assembly is the brake component which is attached to the landing-gear shock strut flange and on which all of the other components are mounted. The piston cups and pistons are placed in two grooves, which act as cylinders, in the carrier assembly. The automatic adjusters, which compensate for lining wear, are threaded into holes equally spaced around the face of the carrier. Each adjuster is composed of an adjuster pin, adjuster clamp, return spring, sleeve, nut, and clamp hold-down assembly.

The pressure plate is notched to fit over the stator drive sleeve. This component is stationary on the sleeve. An auxiliary stator plate fits next to the pressure plate and has brake lining material attached to the side away from the pressure plate.

The rotor segment plate is installed next. This part

is notched on the outside to mate with the wheel and rotate with it. The plate is made up of several segments as shown. Alternating stator plates, with brake lining material on both sides, and rotor assemblies are installed until the proper number of each is in place. After the last rotor segment plate is in position, a compensating shim is installed to space the backplate out from the carrier, and then the backplate is installed. The backplate contains brake lining on the side

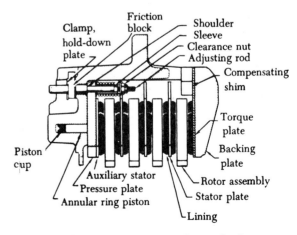

FIG. 10-61   Cutaway of a segmented rotor brake.

toward the rotors. The compensating shims allow the brake linings to wear down until the piston is out of travel. The shims are then removed, causing the pistons to be moved back into the cylinder and more of the available brake lining can now be used.

Because of the gap between the rotor segments and the space between the lining sections, more brake cooling can be achieved than is possible with the multiple-disk brake, allowing more braking action to be achieved before a limiting temperature is reached.

Braking Heat Energy

Stopping a high-speed aircraft, either upon landing or as required for an aborted takeoff, involves the conversion of a great amount of kinetic energy to heat at the brakes and main wheels. This energy may be specified in foot-pounds or joules.

Brake limitation charts have been prepared for some airplanes to give crew members and maintenance personnel a means of determining how to deal with hot brake situations safely and effectively. One such chart for a comparatively small jet airplane is shown in Fig. 10-62. The specified purpose of the chart is to avoid in-flight fires and to ensure adequate brake capacity at all times for a rejected takeoff.

Note in the chart of Fig. 10-62 that the factors used in determining the amount of energy absorbed by the brakes in a given situation are (1) the indicated airspeed in knots at the time the brakes are applied, (2) the gross weight of the airplane, and (3) the density altitude at the airport where the braking occurs. The proper use of the chart will establish a condition zone for any particular braking event. For each zone, a particular set of requirements is set forth. These are as follows:

Zone I. Normal zone: Below 1.0 Million ft·lb [138 000 kg·m]

1. No special requirement under normal operations.

Zone II. Normal zone: 1.0 to 2.05 million ft·lb [138 000 to 282 900 kg·m]

1. Delay subsequent takeoff as indicated by chart.

Zone III. Caution zone: 2.05 to 4.0 million ft·lb [282 900 to 552 000 kg·m]

1. Move airplane to clear active runway as uneven braking could cause one or more tires to deflate if energy was in the upper range.
2. Use brakes sparingly to maneuver.
3. Do not set parking brake.
4. Allow to cool for the time indicated by chart.
5. After cooling, make a visual check of brakes.

Zone IV. Danger zone: Over 4.0 million ft·lb [552 000 kg·m]

1. Clear runway immediately as fusible plugs will blow 2 to 30 min after stop.
2. Do not apply dry chemical or quench until fusible plugs have released tire pressure.
3. Do not approach for ½ h or until fusible plugs have blown.
4. Two to three hours are required for brakes to cool enough for safe removal when artificial cooling is not used.
5. Tires, wheels, and brakes must be replaced.

The dotted lines in the chart of Fig. 10-62 are to show how a particular braking event can be evaluated and the appropriate zone located. The steps are as follows:

1. Locate aircraft gross weight on the chart.
2. Project vertically to indicated airspeed line.
3. Project from the airspeed line horizontally to intersect the zero altitude line.
4. Project parallel to the nearest density line to intersect the correct altitude vertical line.
5. Project horizontally to give correct zone, kinetic energy, and ground cooling time.

The example demonstrated on the chart is for an airplane with a gross weight of 15 000 lb [6804 kg]. The indicated airspeed at the time the brakes were applied was 110 kn. The density altitude was 5000 ft [1524 m]. When these values are applied to the chart it is revealed that the kinetic energy is 2 350 000 ft·lb (3 186 172 J) in the caution zone and the cooling time is 28 min.

If an airplane is equipped with thrust reversers, the energy absorbed by the brakes is reduced from the

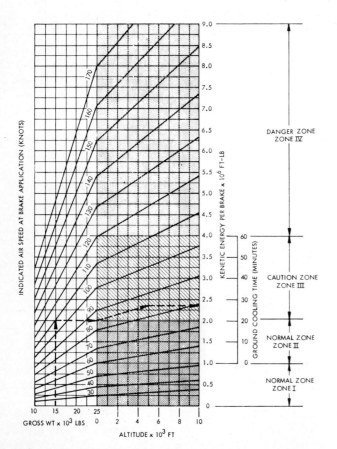

FIG. 10-62 Brake limitation chart. *(Goodyear Aerospace)*

values shown above. The amount of reduction depends upon the time that the thrust reversers are operated.

● AIRCRAFT BRAKE SYSTEMS

Brake-actuating systems for aircraft can be classified as mechanically operated, hydraulically operated, or pneumatically operated. All brake-actuating systems provide for applying brakes on one side of the aircraft or all aircraft brakes by operating foot pedals or hand levers.

Mechanical brakes are found on only a few of the older, small airplanes. A mechanical brake-actuating system includes pulleys, cables, and bell cranks for connecting the foot pedals to the brake-shoe operating mechanism.

In some airplanes, the hydraulic brake system is a subsystem of the main hydraulic system. In other airplanes, there is an entirely independent brake system. Many of the large airplanes have a power-brake system which is a subsystem of the main system. The smaller airplanes usually have an independent, master brake-cylinder system.

Pneumatic brake systems utilize air pressure instead of fluid pressure to operate the brakes. Some hydraulic brake systems are arranged with a pneumatic backup system for operation in case of hydraulic-fluid loss or failure of hydraulic pressure.

For the purposes of this discussion, we will concentrate on hydraulically operated brake systems.

Independent Brake Systems

An *independent brake system*, shown in Fig. 10-63, is usually found on small aircraft. This system is self-contained and independent of the aircraft main hydraulic system. The basic components of this type of system are a reservoir, a master cylinder operated by the brake control pedal or handle, a brake assembly on the wheel, and necessary lines, hoses, and fittings. Expander-tube, shoe, or disk-brake assemblies may be used with this type of system.

The **reservoir** is a storage tank that supplies the fluid to compensate for small leaks in the connecting lines or cylinders. The reservoir may be a part of the master cylinder or it may be a separate unit as shown in the drawing. It is vented to the atmosphere to provide for feeding the fluid to the master cylinders under the force of gravity; hence the fluid must be kept at the correct level, or air will enter the system and reduce its effectiveness.

The **master cylinder** is the energizing unit. There is one for each main landing-gear wheel. The master cylinder is actually a foot-operated, single-action reciprocating pump, the purpose of which is to build up hydraulic-fluid pressure in the brake system.

One type of master cylinder for light aircraft is illustrated in Fig. 10-64. This master cylinder is a type designed and built by the Goodyear Tire and Rubber Company and is used in some models of older aircraft. It is a simple but effective unit, normally connected by a linkage to the brake pedal mounted on the rudder pedal. The hydraulic fluid enters the master cylinder

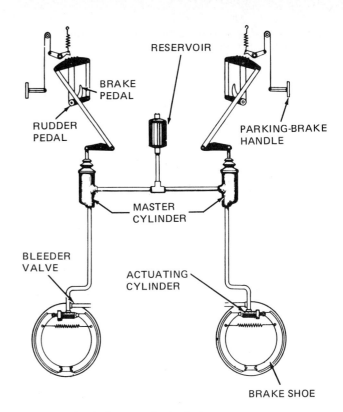

FIG. 10-63 A shoe-type brake system.

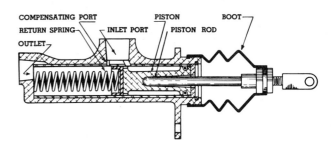

FIG. 10-64 A master cylinder.

through the **inlet port** and **compensating port** from the external reservoir which supplies the master cylinders for both the right and left brake systems. The application of the brake forces the **piston** into the cylinder and causes hydraulic fluid to flow toward the brake-actuating cylinder in the wheel. The illustration shows the cylinder in the horizontal position, but when it is installed in the aircraft, it is in a vertical position with the eye of the piston rod downward. When the piston moves against the **return spring** the compensating port is closed and the fluid in the cylinder is trapped under pressure. Continued pressure applied through the brake pedal forces the fluid pressure to the brake-actuating cylinder and applies the brake. When the force is removed from the brake pedal, the piston is returned to the OFF position by means of the return spring, and the compensating port is again open to the reservoir. The compensating port permits the fluid to flow toward or away from the reservoir as temperature changes, thus preventing a buildup of pressure when the brake is off.

With this type of master cylinder, the brakes are locked in the ON position for parking by means of a ratchet-type lock that is constructed as part of the mechanical linkage between the foot pedal and master cylinder. If an increase of temperature occurs, expansion increases the volume of fluid. This is compensated for by means of a spring built into the linkage. To unlock the brakes the pilot applies enough force to the brake pedals to unload the ratchet-type lock.

Another Goodyear master cylinder is used on a number of modern, light aircraft. This cylinder is illustrated in Fig. 10-65. These cylinders are mounted on the rudder pedals as shown in the drawing of Fig. 10-66. In the illustration of Fig. 10-65, this type of master cylinder incorporates a fluid reservoir (8) on the top of the cylinder (11) within the same body (7). A plastic filler plug (18) is used to close the opening in the cover (4), which is threaded into the body. The filler plug is not vented because sufficient ventilation

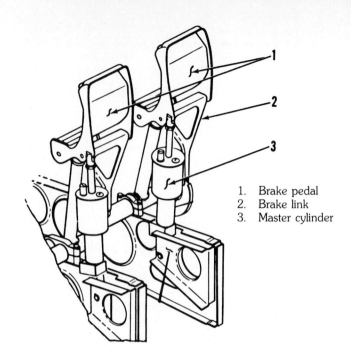

1. Brake pedal
2. Brake link
3. Master cylinder

FIG. 10-66   Master cylinders mounted on brake pedals.

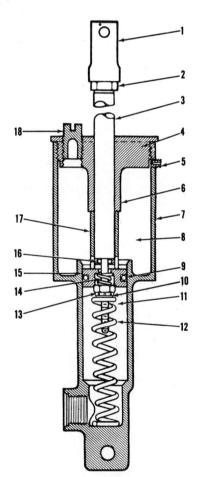

1.	Clevis	10.	Washer
2.	Jamb nut	11.	Cylinder
3.	Piston rod	12.	Piston return spring
4.	Cover	13.	Nut
5.	Setscrew	14.	Piston spring
6.	Cover boss	15.	Piston
7.	Body	16.	Lock-o-seal
8.	Reservoir	17.	Compensating sleeve
9.	O ring	18.	Filler plug

FIG. 10-65   A Goodyear master cylinder.

is provided by clearance between the piston rod (3) and the piston-rod opening through the cover boss (6).

With the exception of the piston return spring (12), all internal operating parts are assembled onto the piston rod. These parts are the piston (15), piston spring (14), "lock-o-seal" (16), and compensating sleeve (17). A seal between the piston and the cylinder walls is provided by the O-ring (9) installed in a groove around the piston. As pressure is applied to advance the piston rod into the cylinder, the piston remains stationary until the lock-o-seal is seated on the piston which requires a 0.040-in [1.016-mm] movement of the piston rod. Proper operation of the master cylinder depends upon this seating action. When the lock-o-seal is seated, fluid cannot pass the piston, and with continued movement of the piston rod forcing the piston into the cylinder, pressure in the cylinder is increased. At any time during the stroke that force on the piston is eased, the piston return spring will tend to keep the piston seated against the lock-o-seal, maintaining pressure in the cylinder. As the force is further eased, allowing the piston return spring to force the piston to retreat, the upper end of the compensating sleeve will contact the cover boss; thus the piston is forced to unseat itself from the lock-o-seal. This allows additional fluid from the reservoir to enter the cylinder. This positive unseating also allows unrestricted passage of fluid from the cylinder to the reservoir while the piston is in the static position. This is to compensate for any excess fluid which may be present in the system due to pumping or from thermal expansion.

Mechanical linkages are required to transmit the energy of the foot to the master cylinder. Some airplanes have the master cylinders mounted on the rudder pedals, and others have the master cylinders mounted at a distance from the pedals. A system of rods, levers, bell cranks, and cables is often employed to carry the mechanical energy to the master cylinders. In Fig. 10-63, the **brake pedals** are toe brakes mounted on the rudder pedals. When the brake pedals are pressed, the linkage causes the master cylinder piston to move into the cylinder and force fluid into the brake lines. When brakes of this type are pressed, it is necessary for the pilot to balance the force on one pedal with equal force on the other pedal unless he wishes to turn the airplane. The brakes and rudder control are operated independently; however, since the brake pedals are on the rudder pedals, the pilot should be practiced in their use. Other control arrangements make use of **heel brakes,** operated by the pilot pressing his or her heel on the brake pedal, and a **central hand brake lever,** which operates all brakes at the same time.

The **fluid lines** may consist of flexible or rigid tubing or a combination of both. Usually flexible tubing is employed with retractable gear systems and between the movable parts of the shock strut.

The **brake-actuating** mechanism of the brake assembly causes braking action to occur when pressure from the master cylinders is transmitted to them.

The **parking-brake mechanism** is a subassembly of the usual hydraulic brake system. The control for the mechanism is in the pilot's compartment and usually consists of a pull handle or lever. When the brake pedals are depressed and the parking-brake lever is pulled back by hand, the brakes are locked in the ON position. Depressing the brake pedals or releasing a parking-brake handle, depending on the system, again releases the brakes. Depending upon the type of master cylinder used, depressing the pedals will either build up enough pressure to unseat the parking valve, or it will unload a ratchet-type parking lock.

With respect to parking brakes, the setting of these brakes when the main brakes are hot may cause serious damage. Hot brakes should be allowed to cool before the parking brakes are applied.

Power Boost Systems

Power boost systems are used on aircraft that land too fast or are too heavy for an independent brake system to operate efficiently but that do not require the power of a power-brake system. This system, shown in schematic form in Fig. 10-67, uses hydraulic system pressure to operate the brakes.

When the pilot depresses the brake pedal, the power boost master cylinder opens a metered line to allow hydraulic system pressure to flow to the brakes. The metering mechanism is either a tapered pin or variable-size orifice. The further the pedal is depressed, the more fluid flows through the metering device with the resulting increase in braking action. When the pedal is released, the pressure inlet line is blocked and the master cylinder ports the pressure in the brake line to a hydraulic system return line.

This system receives pressure from the main hydraulic system through a check valve which prevents loss of fluid and pressure if the main hydraulic system should fail. Between the check valve and the master cylinder is an accumulator that stores fluid under pressure to operate the brakes for a few braking cycles if hydraulic system pressure is lost. The accumulator also assures adequate brake response if at the time of application the main hydraulic system has other demands placed upon it.

A shuttle valve is normally installed in the brake line with a pneumatic bottle available for emergency operation of the brakes if all hydraulic power is lost.

Power-Brake System

A power-brake system is used to operate the brakes of large aircraft where the independent and power boost systems are not adequate. The pilot operates the system by depressing the brake pedal. This causes a power-brake control valve to direct system hydraulic pressure to the brakes and operate the brake assembly. The brake pedal is connected to the power-brake control valve through an arrangement of cables, pulleys, bell cranks, and linkages.

The power-brake control valve for a transport aircraft is illustrated in Fig. 10-68. These are also called **brake metering valves.** One metering-valve assembly is used for each main landing-gear brake.

In a typical system four hydraulic lines are attached to each valve. These are for pressure, return, brakes, and automatic braking. Valve ports are opened or closed by operating a circular grooved, sliding **valve rod** (spool). The linkage end of the valve rod projects beyond the valve body while the opposite end is supported in a sealed **compensating chamber.**

When the brake pedals are depressed, an inward movement is imparted to the metering valve rod through the mechanical linkage and cables. As the rod moves in, the return port is closed, and the pressure port is opened to direct hydraulic fluid pressure to the brakes. A passage through the valve rod permits the hydraulic fluid under pressure to enter a compensating chamber enclosing the inner end of the valve rod. Pressure acting on the end of the rod creates a return force tending to close the valve. This return force varies with the intensity of braking force and provides *feel* at the pedals. The desired braking effort is obtained by depressing the pedals a greater or lesser distance. Cable stretch and adjustment of pedal position permits the valve rod to move back until both pressure and return ports are closed. At this point the braking effort remains constant. This condition is shown schematically in Fig. 10-68. Releasing the brake pedals allows the pressure in the compensating chamber to move the valve rod out and open the brake line to the return line. As pressure in the brake line falls, the brakes are released, and return force on the valve rod is relieved.

Automatic braking to stop the rotation of the wheels before retraction is provided by a small-diameter piston-actuating cylinder attached to the meeting valve. The cylinder is connected to the landing-gear retract hydraulic line. When the landing-gear control is placed to UP, hydraulic pressure is directed to the automatic cylinder and the piston extends. One end of the piston rod rests on the valve rod; hence extension of the piston opens the metering valve and applies the brakes.

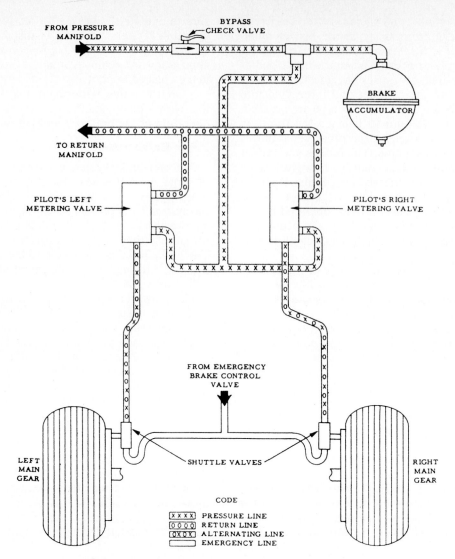

FIG. 10-67 Schematic of a power boost brake system.

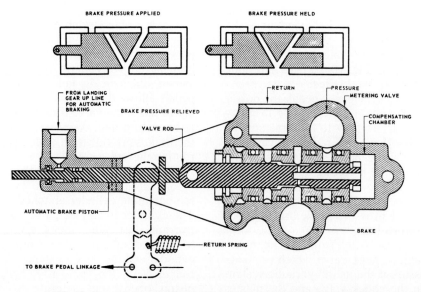

FIG. 10-68 A power-brake control valve for a transport aircraft.

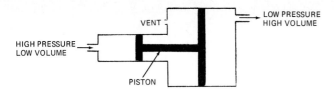

FIG. 10-69 Debooster valve.

Debooster Valve

A **brake debooster valve** is used in systems where the high pressure of the hydraulic system is used to operate brakes that are designed for use with lower pressure. This valve is positioned in the hydraulic line between the power-brake control valve and the brake assembly. High pressure from the power-brake control valve is applied to the small piston of the debooster valve, as shown in the schematic drawing in Fig. 10-69. This exerts a force on the large piston in the low-pressure chamber. The pressure in the large chamber is reduced in proportion to the difference in sizes of the small and large pistons. If the hydraulic system operates at 3000 psi [20 685 kPa] and the small piston has an area of 1 in^2 [6.45 cm^2], 3000 lb [1360.8 kg] of force are applied to the small piston and, through the solid linkage, to the large piston. If the large piston has an area of 3 in^2 [19.35 cm^2] the 3000 lb [1360.8 kg] of force on 3 in^2 [19.35 cm^2] results in a fluid pressure of 1000 psi [6895 kPa].

In reducing the pressure in the system, the debooster valve also increases the volume of flow in the low-pressure chamber. In the example above, if the piston assembly moves 1 in [2.54 cm], the high-pressure system changes volume 1 in^3 [16.39 cm^3], while the 1-in [2.54-cm] movement of the low-pressure piston causes a change in volume of 3 in^3 [49.16 cm^3]. This increase in volume is used to obtain the desired amount of brake cylinder travel without exerting a high pressure on the system.

Multiple Power-Brake Actuating System

The brake-actuating system for a large commercial airplane involves many components and a number of subsystems and is described briefly here to provide the student with a general understanding of how such a system operates. This information also emphasizes the need for careful work on the part of the mechanic while servicing, maintaining, and repairing such a system.

The schematic diagram of Fig. 10-70 shows the operating components and subsystems of the DC-10 brake system. As can be seen in the drawing, the brake pedals of the airplane are mechanically connected to the brake valves which control hydraulic pressure to the brakes. Each brake pedal controls two cable systems. These cable systems operate a pair of corresponding dual brake control valves that are located in the right and left main-gear wheel wells.

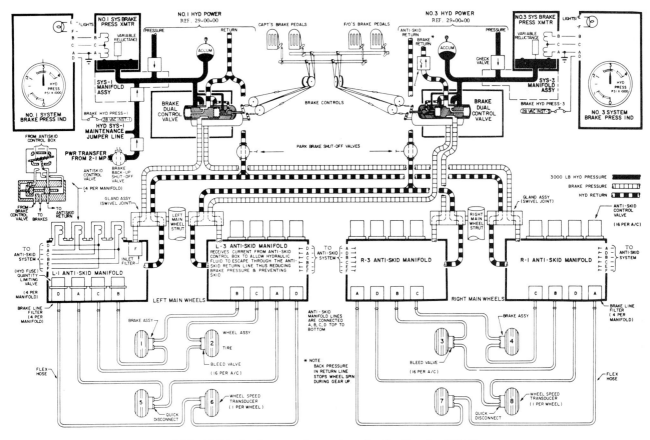

FIG. 10-70 Brake-operating systems for the Douglas DC-10.

The brakes are operated by two completely independent hydraulic power systems. The No. 1 hydraulic system supplies pressure to No. 1 brake system, and the No. 3 hydraulic system supplies pressure for the No. 2 brake system. Each wheel brake is actuated by power from both systems through independent pressure-metering valves. Each brake system consists of a dual brake control valve, pressure accumulator, brake pressure transmitter and indicator, brake system manifold, eight skid-control valves, eight fluid quantity limiter valves, a skid-control manifold for each gear, and a parking brake valve, all of which contribute to the actuation of the independent cylinders in the eight main wheel brakes. Although both brake pressure systems are normally used at all times, either system is capable of stopping the airplane on a maximum-gross-weight landing.

● ANTISKID SYSTEMS

Jet-transport aircraft are usually equipped with **antiskid systems** to prevent loss of airplane control on the ground which would be caused by skidding of the wheels. The system installed on the Douglas DC-9 airplane provides a good example of the operation of an antiskid system.

The system for the DC-9 airplane is a completely automatic, electrically controlled means of preventing each individual main-gear wheel from skidding during brake operation. The system consists of a solid-state circuitry **control box,** four **wheel-speed sensor transducers,** four **dual-servo valves,** four **failure-indicating lights,** and one **system arming switch.** (Note: *Solid-state* refers to electronic systems which utilize transistors, microprocessors, and similar devices in place of electronic vacuum tubes.) The antiskid system has a locked-wheel protection feature which prevents braking action prior to wheel rotation. The system is controlled by a two-position, three-pole switch that will arm or deactivate the system and reset the indicating lights. When the antiskid system is deactivated, the wheel-brake system is controlled directly through the brake control valves by means of the brake pedals. When the antiskid system is armed, the brakes are controlled by the dual-servo valves which meter the hydraulic-fluid pressure supplied by the brake-control valves through the pilot's applicating the brake pedals.

Antiskid protection is accomplished through the control of wheel torque at the point of maximum braking effectiveness, just before an impending skid. This point, however, changes continuously as the airplane travels down the runway, because there is a greater weight down on the landing-gear and larger-tire-footprint area, as well as changing environmental conditions on the runway itself. Yet, whatever the airplane or runway conditions are, the antiskid system's self-adaptive modulation continuously determines the maximum pressure at which braking can be utilized and automatically applies that pressure.

Basically, there are three elements to the antiskid system: (1) the frequency-modulated wheel-speed sensor transducers that sense speed change; (2) the control-box circuitry, which computes on the basis of

speed change information; and (3) the servo valves which meter the appropriate brake pressure to prevent stoppage of wheel rotation. A schematic diagram of the antiskid control circuit is shown in Fig. 10-71.

The control box contains a solid-state printed circuit card for each wheel brake and two self-test cards. Each wheel card is divided into two basic circuits: (1) a control circuit and (2) a memory circuit. The control circuit senses the rate of wheel departure from free-rolling wheel speed, while at the same time rejecting false skid signals generated by mechanical noise or normal wheel deceleration of the slowing airplane. The sensing of rate-of-change of wheel speed, rather than wheel speed itself, creates an anticipatory feature which provides the high response necessary for wheel torque control. The memory circuit provides the delineation or reference curve to which the sensor information is compared to produce this anticipation.

The two self-test cards provide a means for checking the components of the antiskid system. If any component is inoperative, the failure-indicating light comes on. The test card does not single out the component but does indicate the section of the system involved. The brake in that section reverts to nonautomatic operation.

The dual-servo valves are two-stage, pressure-modulating, control valves which provide a ratio of brake pressure to pilot's metered pressure, proportional to the signal from the control unit. The servo valves modulate the brake pressure in both an increasing and decreasing direction to produce more effective braking.

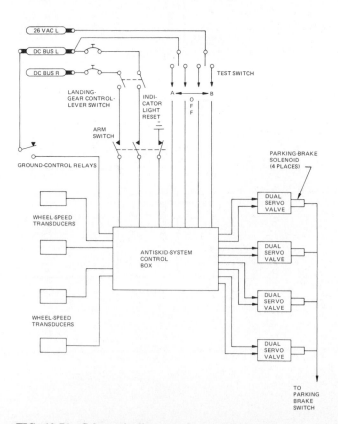

FIG. 10-71 Schematic diagram of an antiskid system.

The wheel-speed transducers are the detecting elements of the antiskid system. They are variable-reluctance, frequency-modulating, sine-wave generators driven by each main-gear wheel. These transducers provide a sinusoidal (sine-wave-shaped) signal whose frequency is proportional to wheel speed; they are unaffected by changes in signal amplitude.

In flight, during letdown procedure, the antiskid system is armed by placing the arming control switch in the ARMED position. At this time a small voltage is applied to the memory circuit in the control box, and the locked-wheel protection becomes effective. The wheel brakes will be released; that is, no hydraulic pressure will be allowed beyond the dual-servo valves with the brake pedals depressed. While it is not advisable to do so as a general policy, a pilot could land the airplane with both feet solidly on the brake pedals. The airplane would land with brakes off, and then the system would automatically and rapidly apply brake pressure compatible with airplane and runway conditions. The pilot's function is to select and hold a steady brake pressure high enough to skid a tire under normal conditions. The antiskid system's function is to adjust the pressure selected by the pilot to give the best stopping performance under existing airplane and runway conditions.

During ground roll, with the brakes fully applied, the pressure bias modulation provides the mean pressure level usable by each wheel brake and permits wheel skid control to operate about this mean. This results in fast, efficient control of brake torque since only small pressure changes are necessary. The pressure bias-modulation circuit achieves its mean level by integrating the amplitude and duration of the control signal. Thus, as a wheel recovers from a skid and the rate control signal ends, a bias voltage remains on the valve proportional to the time integral of the amplitude and duration of the last signal added to the bias generated by the preceding skids. The bias results in a pressure from the servo valve such that as bias voltage increases, pressure decreases. This bias will decrease in the absence of a skid signal according to a time characteristic determined for the airplane. Thus, at recovery of a wheel to normal speed, brake pressure will come on at a slightly lower level than that at which the skid occurred. This sampling of skid pressure and corresponding correction of bias level occur constantly throughout the ground roll because skid pressure levels are constantly changing.

For operation of the locked-wheel control circuit, the wheel-speed transducer frequency pulses are converted into a dc voltage constant over the airplane speed range from maximum to 10 kn. A comparator amplifier measures a voltage for all other wheels. Should this voltage drop while any other wheel is rolling and delivering a voltage, an overdriving signal is sent to the servo valve driver effecting full pressure release at the locked wheel. On wet runways with the very small coefficient friction, a skidding or stopped wheel could take longer to recover to synchronous speed. Normal reapplication of pressure would be too fast. The control-box memory circuits remember what the wheel speed was before skidding and allow the

wheel to recover to very near that speed before reapplication of pressure. However, as the pressure returns, it does not do so to the former level, but to a lower level, and it is slowly allowed to increase as the pressure bias-modulation circuit discharges.

The antiskid-system wheel-speed transducers are variable-reluctance, sine-wave generators used to detect a skid condition in each of the four main-gear wheels. The transducers are installed in the axle of each main-gear wheel and are coupled to the wheel hubcap. A transducer is bidirectional; that is, its output is the same in either direction of rotation. A fixed, wound coil provides the magnetic field for the transducers, and wheel rotation produces variations in the magnetic air gap at 50 cycles per revolution. This is accomplished by rotation of a toothed rotor inside a mating toothed-stator segment. The flux changes thus produced induce an ac component on the dc input line. The frequency of this ac component is sensed as wheel speed by the control-unit circuits.

The transducer envelope contains two independent sensor units. One unit serves the antiskid system, and the other unit serves the spoiler automatic control system. Although both sensor units are housed in a common body, their functions in their respective systems differ. Throughout this discussion relative to the antiskid system, reference to the transducers deals only with that part of the transducer that affects the antiskid system. Figure 10-72 shows both sections of the transducer because the parts affecting the antiskid system and the spoiler system are inseparable.

During the landing approach, with the arming switch in the ARMED position, the antiskid system is activated when the landing-gear safety switches open. At this

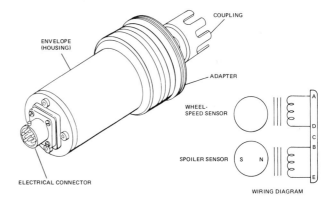

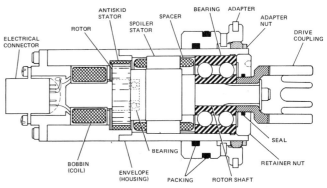

FIG. 10-72 Drawing of a wheel-speed transducer.

time, the control circuit will have a small voltage imposed on the memory portion of the circuit. Prior to landing, the wheel-speed transducers have no direct effect on the system because the wheels are not turning and the system is under locked-wheel protection. Immediately upon touchdown, the wheels begin to spin and the transducers supply a voltage to the control circuit. From this point to the cutoff point, which is approximately 15 mph [24 km/h] the wheel-speed transducers sense any variation in wheel rotation speed. Since each wheel transducer controls an individual wheel brake, a variation at the individual level will cause a brake-pressure release for a brief time at the wheel involved. If an individual wheel-speed transducer should fail, the corresponding brake servo valve reverts that brake to nonautomatic operation.

When wheel speed decreases to approximately 15 mph [24 km/h], the voltage produced by the transducers will be at a level to deactivate the antiskid system and revert the braking system to nonautomatic operation.

A schematic diagram of one of the antiskid system dual-servo valves is shown in Fig. 10-73. These are electrically operated, slave-metering, hydraulic valves used in the antiskid system to prevent skidding of the wheels during brake application. Each dual-servo valve has a single inlet pressure port and a single return port. There are two pressure outlet ports that direct hydraulic fluid to the inboard and outboard brake of the corresponding gear served by the valve. A small, normally closed, solenoid-operated shutoff valve is incorporated into each dual-servo valve to shut off the flow of hydraulic fluid through the servo pilot section of the valve whenever the parking brakes are required.

During normal brake operation, with the antiskid system deactivated, the dual-servo valves are ported to permit the brake-control valves to meter pressure directly to the brakes. When the antiskid system is armed and brake pressure is applied to the dual-servo valves, the servo valves act to reduce braking-fluid pressure whenever a wheel starts to skid. A force balance is set up between the inlet pressure and the outlet pressure by means of **feedback pistons** in the ends of the valve slide (spool). As long as no differential pressure is applied by the flapper-nozzle valve (first-stage valve), the slide forces are balanced and the slide is held open by a spring. When a skid signal is applied, the servo pilot stage applies a differential pressure to the slide ends and unbalances the slide toward the return port. Brake pressure is then metered down until the differential force between the feedback pistons equals the differential force created across the spool. At this point, the spool is again balanced and centered with both inlet and return closed to the brake. When the skid signal is removed or reduced, the reverse action occurs.

The spool spring force adds about 50 psi [345 kPa] bias in the open direction. The pilot's metered brake pressure is fed directly to the brakes as long as no electrical skid signal is applied. When a skid control signal is applied, the ratio of brake pressure to pilot's metered pressure is reduced in proportion to the signal strength.

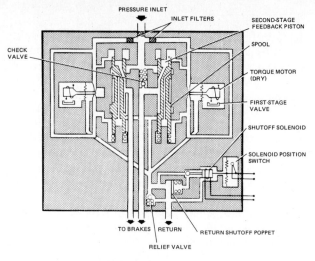

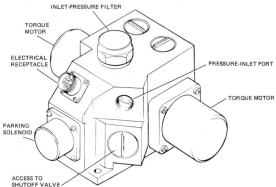

FIG. 10-73 Antiskid system dual-servo valve.

An electrical switch is coupled to the shutoff solenoid valve plunger and is actuated when the plunger is moved from the OPEN position to the BYPASS position. The switch completes a circuit to the antiskid indicating light to notify the pilot that one or more dual-servo valves are inoperative and the corresponding brakes have reverted to nonautomatic operation.

● BRAKE MAINTENANCE

The proper inspection and maintenance of the brake system is vital to the safe operation of the aircraft. Without proper brake operation the aircraft may not be able to stop in the runway length available. On the other hand, if the brakes lock up, a tire may blow out and cause loss of control of the aircraft with resulting damage and injury.

Always refer to the aircraft manufacturer's instructions when inspecting and maintaining brake systems. The information presented here is meant as an introduction to brake maintenance tasks.

WARNING: Brake systems may include compounds using asbestos in the construction of the brake lining material. Use appropriate respiratory and other health protective measures when working with these systems.

Inspection of Brakes

Brake inspection is accomplished at the same time that wheels are removed for other inspections. Shoe-type brakes are inspected for wear of the lining and security of the shoes on the axle mounting. The brake drum in the wheel is inspected for smoothness and freedom from cracks. Small, circumferential marks or grooves are not cause for rejection; however, they can be smoothed by the use of proper grinding equipment if desired.

The amount of wear permissible for the lining is usually specified in the manufacturer's manual. In case of doubt, the brake shoes should be relined.

Some aircraft employ the expander-tube-type brake, which should be examined for lining wear, condition of expander tube, condition of lining blocks (linings) with respect to cracked or broken grooves, condition of the leaf springs which hold the linings in place, and condition of the brake drum. *During the inspection procedure while the wheel is removed, the brake pedals must not be depressed.* When the wheel is removed, there is nothing to restrain the outward movement of the linings except the small leaf springs which pass through the grooves in the ends of the linings and engage the slots in the mounting flanges. Pressure applied to the expander tube at this time will break the linings at the grooved ends and render them useless.

The linings for single-disk-type brakes consist of flat cylinders or thick disks made of a tough abrasion-resistant material similar to that used for the linings of brake shoes. The manufacturer specifies the amount of wear which may be permitted for these linings before it is necessary to replace them. It is usually possible to inspect these linings without removing the wheel.

Some brake linings cannot be fully cured during manufacture, and the curing operation must be completed after the linings are installed on the aircraft. The curing process involves accelerating the aircraft to a moderate speed and then applying moderate to heavy braking force to heat up the linings. This situation is commonly found on certain models of single-disk brakes. If this curing operation is not performed, the linings will not provide maximum performance. Consult the brake manufacturer's information to determine if this process is required for specific brake models and for specific curing procedures.

The brake disks should be inspected for pitting and grooving. If these surface defects exceed the manufacturer's limits, the disk must be resurfaced or replaced.

During inspection of single-disk-type brakes, the mechanic should check the retaining clips which hold the brake disk in the wheel on some types of disks. If the disk is distorted or the clips are broken, the brake disk will not stay in the correct position and brake failure will result.

Multiple-disk brakes are manufactured in a number of configurations, generally for use on large aircraft. It is therefore necessary that the mechanic follow the specifications given in the manufacturer's maintenance manual when inspecting and servicing such brakes. Wear of multiple-disk brakes is determined by noting the extension of the **wear indicator pin.** When the pin has reached the minimum allowable dimension, maintenance action is required. During major inspec-

tions brakes are disassembled and disks examined for wear and for damage resulting from heat. The lugs or keys holding the rotor disks in the wheels are examined for wear and security.

The actuating parts such as the pistons, pressure plates, and similar parts must also be examined for condition. Leaking pistons must be repaired as directed.

The hydraulic systems which actuate brakes should be inspected for the same defects which may be found in any other hydraulic system. Aluminum-alloy and steel tubing should be examined for wear at contact points and for security of the mounting attachments. Fittings should be checked for leakage of fluid. If it is necessary to replace a fitting or a section of tubing, the mechanic must make certain to install the correct part and should check the part number and then compare the part with the one removed. It must be remembered that fittings are made of steel or aluminum alloy, that they may be flare-type or flareless fittings, and that the threads may be for pipe fittings, flare-type fittings, or flareless fittings. Proper identification is, therefore, extremely important.

Brake systems may be serviced with different types of fluid, and the mechanic must be sure to use the correct type. Large aircraft often have power brakes supplied with the same fluid in the main hydraulic system. It is therefore likely that the brake hydraulic system will employ Skydrol or an equivalent fire-resistant fluid. On the same airplane, it will be found that the landing-gear struts are serviced with MIL-O-5606 petroleum-base fluid.

Flexible hoses used in the brake system must be examined for swelling, sponginess, leakage, and wear of the outer covering. A brake hose which has become soft or swollen is likely to cause "spongy" brakes because the hose will expand and take up some of the fluid volume. The effect is similar to the presence of air in the system.

During the inspection of brakes and brake systems, the mechanic should follow up on any discrepancies, defects, and malfunctions reported by the pilot or other crew member. Among items which may be reported are dragging brakes, grabbing brakes, fading brakes, excessive pedal travel, and the brake pedal slowly moving down when brakes are applied. The causes of these malfunctions vary to some extent, depending upon whether the brakes are of the drum, expander-tube, single-disk, or multiple-disk types. The causes also vary according to the method by which hydraulic pressure is applied to the brakes.

Dragging brakes can be caused by air in the brake hydraulic system, broken down or weak return springs, sticking return pins, or defective valves. When brakes are released, all hydraulic pressure should be released from the brake cylinders; however, if a valve sticks closed or is plugged, the pressure may not be released and the brakes will drag.

Grabbing brakes are usually caused by oil or some other foreign matter on the drums and linings or disks and linings. In addition, worn disks and drums can cause grabbing.

Fading brakes are usually caused by the condition of a the lining. If the brakes have been overheated and

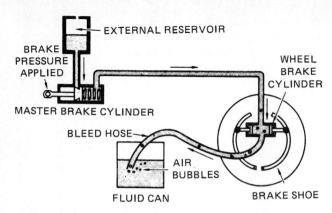

FIG. 10-74   Gravity method of bleeding brakes.

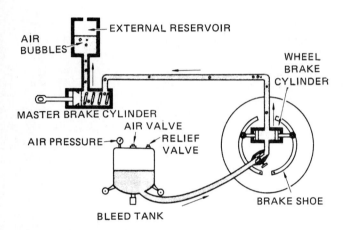

FIG. 10-75   Pressure method of bleeding brakes.

the linings burned, glazing is likely to take place on the surface of the linings, and this condition can result in brake fade.

Excessive brake pedal travel can be caused by worn brakes, lack of fluid in the brake system, air in the system, and improperly adjusted mechanical linkages. In some very large aircraft, the brake control cylinders are located in the wheel wells in the wings. The control cylinders are connected to the brake pedals through a system of levers, cables, and pulleys. If this system is worn or not adjusted properly, excessive pedal travel will result.

A leaking piston seal in a brake master cylinder will cause the pedal to slowly creep down while pedal pressure is applied. In such a case, the master cylinder should be overhauled.

Bleeding of Brakes

When a brake line has been disconnected for any reason, or after overhaul or replacement of any part of the brake hydraulic system, it is usually necessary to bleed the system to remove air from lines, valves, and cylinders. This is accomplished by flowing brake fluid through the system. Air in the brake hydraulic system causes spongy brakes and may cause the brakes to drag. This is because the air contracts and expands as pressure is applied or released, thus creating the spongy feeling and reducing the positive

pressure which should be available for brake operation.

Aircraft brake systems usually incorporate bleeder fittings for the attachment of bleeder hoses. The fittings are installed at the brake assembly.

To bleed the brakes, a clear plastic tube is connected to the brake bleeder fitting, and the free end of the tube is submerged in a container of clean brake fluid. The reservoir for the system is filled with the correct type of fluid, and the brakes are operated to pump fluid through the lines, valves, and cylinders. Air bubbles are seen through the clear plastic tube as the fluid passes out and into the container. When the fluid flows with no air bubbles passing through the line, the bleeder valve is closed and the bleeder tube disconnected. The reservoir is then refilled to the proper level with the correct type of fluid. This is known as **gravity bleed** and is illustrated in Fig. 10-74. For any type of brake system, the manufacturer's instructions should be followed to ensure that the bleeding procedure is correct.

For some aircraft, a **pressure bleeding system** is employed. For this type of bleeding, brake fluid is forced through the system by means of a pressurized reservoir connected to the system brake bleed fitting. Fluid is forced through the system, back to the reservoir, until no bubbles appear in the fluid outflow. This is illustrated in Fig. 10-75.

● REVIEW QUESTIONS

1. What are the parts of a *tire structure*?
2. How should tires be stored?
3. What is the purpose of an *inflation cage*?
4. Why should newly mounted tires be allowed to set for several hours before being installed on an aircraft?
5. How are overinflation and underinflation indicated in the tread wear pattern?
6. Describe the different types of ski arrangements used on aircraft.
7. Of what materials are airplane wheels usually constructed?
8. Describe the construction of a wheel for a light airplane.
9. What is the advantage of having wheels constructed in two parts?
10. What means is employed to prevent air from leaking through the joint between tubeless wheel halves?
11. Describe the bearings used with airplane wheels.
12. What is the purpose of *fusible plugs* in aircraft wheels?
13. What is the purpose of a *pressure-release plug*?
14. Compare the construction of main wheels with nosewheels.
15. Discuss the heat energy involved with braking a high-speed airplane and how various levels of heat may be dealt with.
16. How are aircraft tires classified?
17. What markings are required on aircraft tires?
18. What are the important points in the mounting of tires with inner tubes?

19. How can one determine whether a tire can be retreaded?
20. What markings are required on a retreaded tire?
21. Give the procedure for removing and replacing a tubeless tire on an aircraft wheel.
22. How can the age of rubber shock cord be determined?
23. Under what conditions should rubber shock cord be replaced?
24. Describe a steel spring landing gear.
25. What is the difference between *spring-oleo* struts and *air-oleo* shock struts?
26. What is the purpose of the *metering pin* in an air-oleo shock strut?
27. What provision is made in the design of an air-oleo strut to prevent sand and dirt on the piston from being drawn into the cylinder?
28. Does fluid or air support the weight of the aircraft with air-oleo struts during taxiing?
29. What is done to prevent an oleo strut from extending too rapidly and causing impact damage?
30. What power sources are employed for the operation of retractable landing gear?
31. What locks are incorporated in retractable landing-gear systems and what are their functions?
32. What device is used to warn a pilot that the landing gear has not been extended prior to landing?
33. What is meant by *auxiliary landing gear*?
34. What type of warning signal is often used in an airplane in addition to position indicators?
35. Describe the *antishimmy device* used with tail wheels.
36. What is the function of a *shimmy damper* installed with a nose gear?
37. Describe the construction of a *shimmy damper*.
38. Describe a typical main landing-gear strut.
39. What features must a nose gear assembly have that are not required for main gear?
40. What is the function of *torque links*?
41. What is a *squat switch*?
42. List and describe the basic parts of a transport aircraft landing-gear assembly.
43. What different operational capabilities may be incorporated in a tail-wheel installation?
44. What are the four methods that may be used for the emergency extension of the landing gear?
45. What is the purpose of a *WOW switch*?
46. What is the purpose of the *follow-up differential mechanism* in a nosewheel steering system?
47. What is the function of the main-gear swivel glands?
48. Give two important purposes for torque links, or "scissors."
49. Explain the purpose of the *overcenter linkage* in the nose-gear mechanism.
50. What is the purpose of the *ground-sensing control mechanism*?
51. What cushions the shock of landing when an air-oil strut is installed in the landing gear?
52. Name four types of brakes used on aircraft.
53. Describe the principle of operation for the expander-tube brake.
54. How is braking action developed with the single-disk-type brake?
55. Describe a multiple-disk brake.
56. Name three ways to supply brake-actuating power.
57. Under what condition is a pneumatic system used with a hydraulic brake system?
58. Describe a master cylinder.
59. Where in a brake system is flexible tubing used?
60. Describe the operation of a parking brake.
61. What is a *power boost master cylinder*?
62. When should a parking brake not be applied?
63. Describe *expanding-shoe* brakes.
64. What will happen if brake pressure is applied to expander-tube brakes when the brake drum is not installed?
65. How are brake blocks replaced in an expander-tube brake?
66. Describe a *multiple-disk* brake for a large airplane.
67. How is the wear of large multiple-disk brakes indicated?
68. Briefly describe the operation of an *antiskid system*.
69. Why is it not possible to land an airplane with wheels locked if the antiskid system is armed?
70. Describe a *wheel-speed transducer*.
71. List precautions to be observed when *jacking* an aircraft.
72. How does a *segmented rotor-disk brake* differ from a *multiple-disk brake*?
73. Describe the operation of a *debooster valve*.
74. What may be necessary to properly complete the curing of some brake linings after they are installed?
75. List conditions to be checked when inspecting landing gear.
76. What is the cause of an air-oil strut "*bottoming*?"
77. What is important in the jacking of an airplane?
78. Describe an operational test of landing gear.
79. How is alignment of the main gear wheels checked?
80. What conditions should be checked in the inspection of airplane wheels?
81. How would you inspect airplane wheels?
82. What should be done if cracks are found in a wheel?
83. Explain how bolts should be tightened in the assembly of an aircraft wheel.
84. Why is it not necessary to adjust disk brakes?
85. What may be the cause of dragging brakes, grabbing brakes, and fading brakes?
86. What may be the cause of excessive brake travel?
87. What would be the effect of a leaking seal in a master cylinder?
88. Why is it necessary to *bleed* brakes?
89. Describe a process for bleeding brakes.
90. What conditions should be checked in the inspection of aircraft floats?
91. Describe an operational check of retractable landing gear.

11 AIRCRAFT FUEL SYSTEMS

The aircraft fuel system is used to deliver fuel to the engines safely under a wide range of operational conditions. The system must have a means of safely holding the fuel, allow filling and draining of the tanks, prevent unwanted pressure buildups in the system, protect the system from contamination, and assure a steady supply of fuel to the engine when it is located some distance from the tank.

The system must also provide a means of monitoring the quantity of fuel on the aircraft during flight and, in some aircraft, a means of checking fuel pressures, temperatures, and flow rates.

All of these capabilities must be carried out without compromising the safety of the aircraft or its occupants. This chapter discusses methods used to meet these requirements.

For a full discussion of the characteristics of fuels and fuel additives, refer to the companion text *Aircraft Basic Science*.

TYPES OF FUEL SYSTEMS

All fuel systems can be classified in one of two broad categories: **gravity feed** and **pressure feed.**

Gravity-Feed Fuel Systems

A gravity-feed fuel system uses the force of gravity to cause fuel to flow to the engine fuel-control mechanism. For this to occur, the bottom of the fuel tank must be high enough to assure a proper fuel pressure head at the inlet to the fuel control component (i.e., carburetor) on the engine. In high-wing aircraft this is accomplished by placing the fuel tanks in the wings. An example of this type of system is shown in Fig. 11-1. Some aircraft designs achieve the proper pressure head by placing the fuel tank in the fuselage.

Pressure-Feed Fuel Systems

A pressure-feed fuel system, a simple version of which is shown in Fig. 11-2, uses a pump to move fuel from the fuel tank to the engine fuel-control component. This arrangement is required because the fuel must be at high pressure when delivered to the fuel-control component of the engine, because the fuel tanks are located too low for sufficient pressure head to be generated, or because the tanks are some distance from the engine. The system in Fig. 11-2 is for a low-wing aircraft where the wing tanks are on the same approximate level as the carburetor.

Most large aircraft and aircraft with medium to high-powered engines require a pressure-feed system, re-gardless of fuel tank location, because of the large volume of fuel that must be delivered to the engines at a high pressure.

Understand that when reference is made to high pressure in the fuel feed system, the value is on the order of 20, 30, or 40 psi [13.9, 206.9, or 275.8 kPa], not in the thousands of pounds per square inch as in hydraulic systems.

REQUIREMENTS FOR FUEL SYSTEMS

The purpose of a fuel system is to deliver a uniform flow of clean fuel under constant pressure to the carburetor or other fuel-control unit. This supply must be adequate to meet all engine demands at various altitudes and attitudes of flight. Recommended installations employ gravity-feed or mechanical pumping systems.

The location of the various units in the fuel system

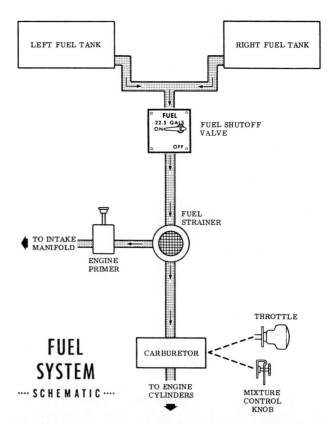

FUEL SYSTEM
···· SCHEMATIC ····

FIG. 11-1 A light aircraft gravity-feed fuel system. (*Cessna Aircraft Co.*)

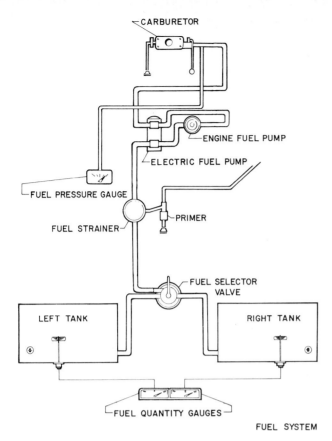

FIG. 11-2 A light aircraft pressure-feed fuel system. *(Piper Aircraft Co.)*

must be such that the entire fuel supply, except that which is designated as **unusable fuel,** is available for use when the airplane is in the steepest climb, in the best angle of glide, or in any reasonable maneuver.

Reliability

Each fuel system must be constructed and arranged to ensure a flow of fuel at a rate and pressure established for proper engine and auxiliary power unit functioning under each likely operating condition. Auxiliary power units are usually installed in large transport-type aircraft only. In case the certification of the aircraft involves unusual maneuver approval, the fuel system must perform satisfactorily during these maneuvers.

Each fuel system must be arranged so that any air which may be introduced into the system as a result of fuel depletion in a tank will not result in power interruption for more than 20 s for a reciprocating engine and will not cause the flameout of a turbine engine.

Each fuel system for a turbine engine must be capable of sustained operation throughout its flow and pressure range with fuel initially saturated with water at 80°F [27°C] and having 0.75 cm³ of free water per gallon [3.79 L] added and cooled to the most critical condition for icing likely to be encountered in operation.

To assure that fuel systems and components meet the requirements of applicable Federal Aviation Reg-

ulations, systems are tested under actual or simulated operating conditions. These tests involve the individual components as well as the complete system.

Fuel-System Independence

Each fuel system must meet engine operation requirements by allowing the supply of fuel to each engine through a system independent of each part of the system supplying fuel to any other engine. That is, the fuel system must be designed so any one engine can operate without being affected by fuel-system problems for another engine.

Fuel-system independence for a multiengine airplane is further assured by the requirement that each fuel system be arranged so that, in at least one configuration, the failure of any one component (other than a fuel tank) will not result in the loss of power of more than one engine or require immediate action by the pilot to prevent the loss of power of more than one engine. If a single fuel tank or a series of tanks interconnected to function as a single tank is used on a multiengine airplane, there shall be a separate tank outlet for each engine, and each outlet shall be equipped with a **shutoff valve.** The shutoff valve may also serve as the firewall shutoff valve if the line between the valve and the engine compartment does not contain more than 1 qt [0.94 L] of fuel, or any greater amount shown to be safe, that can drain into the engine compartment. The tank or series of tanks shall have at least two vents arranged to minimize the probability of both vents becoming obstructed simultaneously.

Filler Caps

Filler caps must be designed to minimize the probability of incorrect installation or loss of the caps in flight. Some fuel caps incorporate vents which keep the fuel tank at atmospheric pressure. The filler cap or the area immediately next to the cap should be placarded to indicate the proper type of fuel and quantity of fuel for the tank.

Lightning Protection

The fuel system must be designed and arranged to prevent the ignition of fuel vapor within the system by direct or swept lightning strikes to areas where these are likely to occur. In addition, the design must be such that fuel vapor cannot be ignited by corona or streamering at fuel vent outlets.

Fuel Flow

The fuel flow for a **gravity-fed system** must be at least 150 percent of the takeoff fuel consumption of the engine. For pressure pump systems, the fuel flow for each reciprocating engine must be at least 125 percent of takeoff fuel flow. These quantities are established by appropriate tests.

For transport category airplanes, each fuel system must provide at least 100 percent of the fuel flow required under each intended operating condition and maneuver. The systems are tested under established conditions to assure that the flow rate is adequate. If a flowmeter is in the system, it is blocked off to see if the full flow requirements are met when fuel is by-passing the flowmeter.

If an engine can be supplied with fuel from more than one tank, the fuel system for each reciprocating engine must supply the full fuel pressure to that engine in not more than 20 s after switching to any other tank containing usable fuel. This would occur when engine malfunction becomes apparent due to the depletion of the fuel supply in any tank from which the engine fuel can be fed. In the case of a turbine engine which can be supplied from more than one tank, in addition to having appropriate manual switching capability, the system must provide an automatic switching capability. This must be designed to prevent interruption of fuel flow to an engine without attention by the flight crew when any tank supplying fuel to that engine is depleted of usable fuel during normal operation. This requires, of course, that another tank contains usable fuel for the engine in question.

If fuel can be pumped from one fuel tank to another in flight, the fuel tank vents and the fuel transfer system must be designed so that no structural damage to the tanks can occur because of overfilling.

The **unusable fuel** quantity for each fuel tank and its fuel-system components must be established at not less than the quantity at which the first evidence of engine malfunction occurs under the most adverse fuel feed condition for all intended operations and flight maneuvers involving fuel feed from that tank.

It must be impossible, in a gravity-feed system with interconnected tank outlets, for enough fuel to flow between the tanks to cause an overflow from any tank vent under any condition of intended operation or flight maneuver. The system is tested with full tanks to assure that this requirement is met.

Hot-Weather Performance

Fuel systems must perform satisfactorily in hot weather operation. Systems must be free of **vapor lock** when operating with fuel at 110°F [43°C] under critical conditions. The tanks of transport-type aircraft should be pressurized to prevent vapor lock under all operating conditions. Tests are made under takeoff and climb conditions to assure that the system meets all requirements. Fuel boost pumps installed in the bottom of a fuel tank are an effective method to reduce the possibility of vapor lock.

● FUEL TANKS

Fuel tanks are used to store the fuel for the aircraft until it is used by the engines. The following section discusses the requirements and components associated with fuel tanks to assure a proper supply of fuel for the engines.

Fuel-Tank Requirements

Fuel tanks for aircraft may be constructed of aluminum alloy, terneplate, fuel-resistant synthetic rubber, plastics, or stainless steel. Tanks that are an integral part of the wing are of the same material as the wing and have the seams sealed with fuelproof sealing compound.

The material selected for the construction of a particular fuel tank depends upon the type of airplane in which the tank will be installed and the service for which the airplane is designed. Fuel tanks and the fuel system, in general, must be made of materials that will not react chemically with any fuels that may be used. Aluminum alloy, because of its light weight, strength, and ease with which it can be shaped and welded, is widely used in fuel-tank construction. Many aircraft now use synthetic-rubber bladders for fuel cells. These cells are light in weight and give excellent service if maintained according to the manufacturer's instructions.

Metal fuel tanks generally are required to withstand an internal test pressure of 3½ psi [24.13 kPa] without failure or leakage and at least 125 percent of pressure developed in the tank from ram effect. Furthermore, they must withstand without failure any vibration, inertia loads, and fluid and structural loads to which they may be subjected during operation of the aircraft. Fuel-tank strength and durability are proven by means of extensive pressure and vibration tests prescribed in FAR Parts 23 and 25.

Integral fuel tanks, such as those in the wings of jet airliners, must be provided with facilities for the inspection and repair of the tank interiors. This requirement is met by installing access panels in the skin on the bottom side of the wings.

Fuel tanks located within the fuselage of a transport aircraft must be capable of withstanding rupture and retaining the fuel underneath the inertia forces that may be encountered in an emergency landing. These forces are specified as 4.5 *g* (gravity) downward, 2.0 *g* upward, 9.0 *g* forward, and 1.5 *g* sideward. Such tanks must be located in a protected position so that exposure to scraping action with the ground will be unlikely. For pressurized fuel tanks, a means with fail-safe features must be provided to prevent buildup of an excessive pressure differential between the inside and outside of the tank.

Fuel tanks must be equipped with sumps to collect sediment and water. On transport-type aircraft the sump capacity must be at least 0.10 percent of the total tank capacity or 1/16 gal [0.24 L], whichever is greater; and on other types of aircraft the sump capacity must be 0.25 percent of the tank capacity or 1/16 gal [0.24 L], whichever is greater. The construction of the tank must be such that any hazardous quantity of water in the tank will drain to the sump when the airplane is in the ground attitude. If the fuel system for small aircraft is supplied with a sediment bowl that permits ground inspection, the sump in the tank is not required. Fuel sumps and sediment bowls must be equipped with an accessible drain to permit complete drainage of all the sump or sediment bowl. The drain must discharge clear of all portions of the airplane and must be provided with means for positive locking of the drain in the closed position, either manually or automatically.

Fuel tanks are required to have an expansion space of not less than 2 percent of the tank capacity. In the case of nontransport aircraft, if the tank vent discharges clear of the aircraft, no expansion space is required. The construction of the tank must be such that filling the tank expansion space is not possible when the airplane is on the ground. Fuel tanks that may be filled through a pressure fitting under the wing are equipped with automatic shutoff devices to prevent overfilling the tank.

The fuel-tank filler connection must be designed in such a manner that any spilled fuel will drain clear of the airplane and will not enter the wing or any portion of the fuselage. This is usually accomplished by means of a fuel-tight scupper and overboard drain. The filler cap must provide a tight seal and be designed so that it cannot come off in flight. The filler connection must be marked with the word *Fuel,* the minimum grade of fuel, and the capacity of the tank. Each fuel filling point, except pressure-fueling connection points, must have a provision for electrically bonding the airplane to ground fueling equipment.

The total usable capacity of the fuel tanks for non-transport aircraft must be sufficient for not less than ½-h operation at rated maximum continuous power. Fuel tanks having a capacity of 0.15 gal [0.569 L] for each maximum (except takeoff) horsepower are considered suitable. Fuel quantity indicators must be calibrated to show zero gallons when the usable fuel supply is exhausted.

The fuel capacity for transport-type aircraft is determined by the manufacturer in accordance with the intended use of the aircraft. Provision is made for the maximum range of the aircraft plus more fuel for conditions where the aircraft is diverted to an alternate field.

A number of special requirements are provided for the installation of fuel tanks in aircraft. These requirements are established principally to provide for safety, reliability, and durability of the fuel tank.

The method for supporting tanks must be such that the fuel loads are not concentrated at any particular point of the tank. Nonabsorbent padding must be provided to prevent chafing and wear between the tank and its supports. Synthetic-rubber bladders or flexible fuel-tank liners must be supported by the structure so that they are not required to withstand the fuel load. The interior surface of the tank compartment must be smooth and free of any projections that might damage the liner unless the liner is provided with suitable protection at possible points of wear. A **positive pressure** must be maintained within the vapor space of all bladder cells under all conditions of operation, including the critical condition of low airspeed and rate of descent likely to be encountered in normal operation. Pressure is maintained by means of a tank vent tube, the open end of which is faced into the wind to provide continuous ram air pressure.

Fuel-tank compartments must be ventilated and drained to prevent the accumulation of flammable fluids or vapors. The compartments adjacent to tanks that are an integral part of the airplane structure must also be ventilated and drained.

Fuel tanks must not be installed on the engine side of the fire wall or in any fire zone unless the construction and arrangement are such that the zone can be proved to be as safe as it would be if the tank were not in the zone. Not less than ½ in [12.7 mm] of clear air space must be provided between the fuel tank and the fire wall and between the tank and any fire zone. No portion of the engine nacelle skin that lies immediately behind a major air egress opening from the engine compartment may act as the wall of an integral tank. This requirement is to prevent the spread of fire from the engine compartment to the fuel tanks.

Fuel tanks must not be installed in compartments that are occupied by passengers or crew except in the case of single-engine airplanes. In this case a fuel tank that does not have a capacity of more than 25 gal [94.75 L] may be located in personnel compartments if adequate drainage and ventilation are provided. In all other cases, the fuel tank must be isolated from personnel compartments by means of fumeproof and fuelproof enclosures.

Spaces adjacent to tank surfaces must be ventilated to avoid fume accumulation due to minor leakage. If the tank is in a sealed compartment, ventilation may be limited to drain holes large enough to prevent excessive pressure resulting from altitude changes.

No engine nacelle skin immediately behind a major air outlet from the engine compartment may act as the wall of an integral fuel tank.

Each fuel tank must be vented from the top part of the expansion space. Each vent outlet must be located and constructed to minimize the possibility of its being obstructed by ice or other foreign matter and to prevent the siphoning of fuel during normal operation.

The venting capacity must allow the rapid relief of excess pressure differences between the interior and exterior of the tank. Air spaces of tanks with interconnected outlets must be interconnected to maintain equal pressure in all interconnected tanks.

Vent lines must be installed in such a manner that there are no undrainable points in any line where moisture can accumulate with the airplane in either the ground or level-flight attitude. No vent may terminate at a point where the discharge of fuel from the vent outlet will constitute a fire hazard or from which fumes may enter personnel compartments. The vents must be arranged to prevent the loss of fuel, except fuel discharged because of thermal expansion, when the airplane is parked in any direction on a ramp having a 1 percent slope.

Carburetors with **vapor elimination** connections must have vent lines to lead vapors back to one of the fuel tanks. If there is more than one tank and if it is necessary to use these tanks in a definite sequence for any reason, the vapor vent return line must lead back to the fuel tank to be used first unless the relative capacities of the tanks are such that return to another tank is preferable.

For acrobatic-category airplanes, excessive loss of fuel during acrobatics, including short periods of inverted flight, must be prevented. Fuel must not siphon from the vent when normal flight has been resumed after any acrobatic maneuver for which the airplane is approved.

Fuel tank outlets must be provided with **fuel screens.** If a fuel booster pump is installed in the tank, the pump inlet must be provided with a screen. The screen

Vane-type Fuel Pump

One of the most satisfactory pumps for positive delivery of fuel is the **vane pump.** This is similar to the hydraulic vane pump described in Chap. 9. A schematic diagram of such a pump is shown in Fig. 11-6. The rotor holds the sliding vanes and is installed in the liner with its axis of rotation eccentric to the axis of the liner. When the rotor is turning, the vanes maintain a constant contact with the surface of the liner. Fuel enters the inlet port and is forced by sliding vanes through the outlet port. The floating pin aligns the sliding vanes against the surface of the liner. In one position the two lower vanes extend from the rotor, while the two upper vanes are forced into the rotor by the surface of the liner.

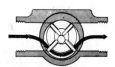

FIG. 11-6   Vane-type fuel pump.

Variable-Volume Pumps

The pump shown in Fig. 11-7 is known as a **variable-volume vane-type pump.** This pump delivers varying amounts of fuel under constant pressure to the carburetor. The amount of fuel is regulated to meet the demands of the carburetor.

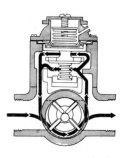

FIG. 11-7   Variable-volume vane-type pump.

This type of pump is designed to deliver much more fuel than the amount normally needed by the engine. Fuel enters the pump at the inlet side and is forced around the housing to the outlet side by the action of the sliding vanes. The spring-loaded relief valve is adjusted so that it releases at a specific pressure. When the pump pressure is above the predetermined setting, the relief valve is forced up from its seat and the excess fuel is relieved to the inlet side of the pump.

This relief valve has a diaphragm, which has two functions: (1) It provides venting to the atmosphere or to supercharger pressure, and, by means of a balancing action, (2) it helps to maintain a constant discharge pressure no matter how much the pressure on the suction side of the pump may vary. When the diaphragm-type relief valve is used in a pressure-type

fuel system, the pilot may complain that the fuel pressure is normal on the ground but increases with altitude. This may occur when the air vent on the fuel pump is partly clogged.

The **bypass valve,** shown in the pump diagram of Fig. 11-8, provides a means for the boost pump to force fuel around the vanes and rotor of the main pump for starting the engine or for emergency operation if the main pump fails. The bypass valve is held in the closed position by a spring when the pump rotor is turning.

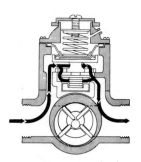

FIG. 11-8   Fuel bypassing the fuel pump.

The relief-valve spring in some pumps is located within a metal bellows to compensate for variations in atmospheric pressure. Other types use a fuel-resistant synthetic-rubber diaphragm instead of bellows. **When relief valves are designed to compensate for atmospheric pressure variations, they are known as balanced relief valves.**

The chamber housing the diaphragm of the fuel pump incorporates a tapped hole to which a vent line is attached. As the airplane climbs to higher altitudes, the atmospheric pressure on the fuel in the tank decreases, resulting in a lowered fuel-pump inlet pressure. To compensate for this lower pressure, the relief-valve diaphragm is vented to the atmosphere or to the fuel tanks. Thus, the decrease in atmospheric pressure in the tanks is compensated for by the pressure-relief valve. Sometimes the diaphragm is vented to the carburetor deck or to the carburetor air scoop. This subjects the diaphragm to atmospheric pressure plus ram pressure. **Ram pressure is pressure that is developed in the carburetor air scoop by the forward speed of the airplane.** The vent has a restrictor fitting in the line. If a diaphragm is ruptured, the restrictor limits the loss of fuel through the vent when the pump inlet pressure is greater than atmospheric pressure or restricts the amount of air entering the pump inlet when the pump inlet pressure is less than that of the atmosphere.

To adjust the pressure setting on a fuel pump, the adjusting-screw locknut is loosened and the adjusting screw is turned clockwise to increase pressure or counterclockwise to decrease pressure. Usually, markings on the pump body show the correct direction to turn the adjusting screw to increase or decrease pressure. If no markings are visible, turn the screw very slightly in one direction while noting the effect on the pressure gauge. When the pressure has been set, the locknut should be tightened and safetied with the proper gauge safety wire.

Fuel pumps vary in general design. There may be from two to six sliding vanes; sometimes the aligning pin, which holds the vanes against the liner surface, is omitted and other means are used to accomplish the same result. Some pumps use the syphon (metal bellows) type of balanced relief valve, while others use the diaphragm type. Regardless of the variations in design, the operating principle of all vane-type engine-driven fuel pumps remains the same.

Centrifugal Pumps

Centrifugal pumps are used to move fuel from fuel tanks to engines and other tanks. These pumps are electrically operated and may be designed to operate at one speed or may be designed for the crew member to select one of several speeds, depending on the operational situation. A centrifugal pump is shown in Fig. 11-9.

The centrifugal pump pressurizes the fuel by drawing fuel into the center inlet of a centrifugal impeller and expelling it at the outer edge of the impeller as shown in Fig. 11-10. This type pump may be designed to be mounted with the electric motor on the outside of the fuel tank or for the entire pump and motor to be located inside the fuel tank in which case it is referred to as a **submerged pump.** Because a centrifugal impeller is used, when the pump is not in operation, fuel can flow through the pump. This eliminates the need for any bypass mechanism.

For ease of pump maintenance, most pumps are installed in or on the fuel tank with a mechanism that allows the pump to be removed and installed without draining the fuel tank. The mechanisms that close off the fuel lines and allow pump removal may be auto-

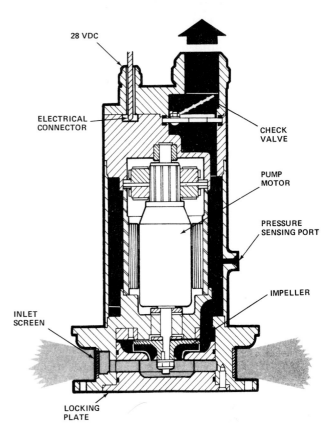

FIG. 11-10   Cutaway of a centrifugal fuel pump.

matically operated as the pump is removed or may have to be activated by the mechanic prior to pump removal.

Ejector Pump

An **ejector pump** is used to scavenge fuel from remote areas of fuel tanks and to provide fuel under pressure to an operating engine fuel-control unit. This type of pump has no moving parts but relies on the flow of returned fuel from the engine-driven pump to pump fuel. Figure 11-11 is an illustration of an ejector pump.

The ejector pump works on the venturi principle. Engine-driven fuel pumps supply the engine fuel-control unit with more volume than is necessary for operation in order to be sure that the engine is never starved for fuel. Excess fuel from this pump is routed back to the motive flow inlet of the ejector pump. This returned fuel is at a high pressure, on the order of 300 psi [2068.5 kPa], but at a low volume. As the motive flow fuel exits the ejector nozzle in the venturi area, a pressure drop is created and fuel from the inlet screen is drawn into the low-pressure area. The motive flow continues on through the venturi and draws the fuel from the tank with it. This induced flow of fuel is at a pressure on the order of 30 psi [206.8 kPa], but is of great enough volume to supply the engine-driven fuel pump.

If the ejector pump is used as a fuel scavenge pump, the induced flow is delivered to an area of the fuel tank next to the tank outlet.

Since ejector pumps require a motive flow for op-

FIG. 11-9   An electrically operated centrifugal fuel pump.

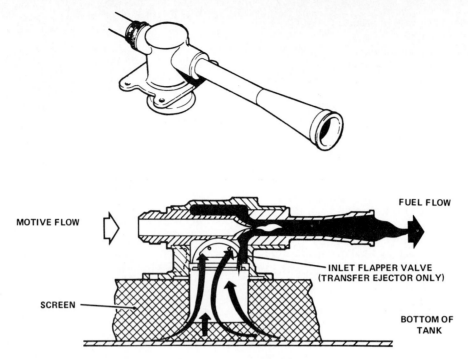

FIG. 11-11   Operation of an ejector pump.

eration, they do not begin operating until the engines are running. Centrifugal pumps are used in conjunction with ejector pumps to start the engine. After the engines are started, the centrifugal pumps are turned off and the ejectors maintain the required flow.

● FUEL SYSTEM COMPONENTS

The fuel system consists of many components which are used to clean the fuel and control the direction of flow after it leaves the tank. The number and types of these units varies among aircraft, but the basic purpose of these items must be understood by the mechanic to properly inspect and maintain a fuel system.

Fuel Strainers and Filters

Because of the ever-present possibility of fuel contamination by various types of foreign matter, aircraft fuel systems are required to include **fuel strainers** and **filters.** The fuel is usually strained at three points in the system: first, through a finger strainer or boost-pump strainer in the bottom of the fuel tank; second, through a master strainer, which is usually located at the lowest point in the fuel system; and third, through a strainer in the carburetor or near the fuel-control unit.

A fuel strainer or filter is required between the fuel tank outlet and the inlet of either the fuel-metering device (carburetor or other fuel-control unit) or an engine-driven positive-displacement pump, whichever is nearer the fuel tank outlet. The strainer or filter must be accessible for draining and cleaning and must incorporate a screen or element which is easily removable.

The strainer or filter must have a sediment trap and adequate provision for easy drainage. It must be mounted in such a manner that its weight is not supported by the connecting lines or by the inlet or outlet connections of the strainer or filter. The fuel-flow capacity of the strainer or filter must be such that fuel-system functioning is not impaired with the fuel contaminated to a degree greater than that established for the particular engine. The mesh size and the flow ports must be adequate to filter the fuel properly and also allow adequate fuel flow for the engine.

The tank strainer keeps larger particles of foreign matter in the tank from entering the system lines. The main strainer, located at the lowest point in the system, collects foreign matter from the line between the tank and the strainer and also serves as a water trap. The filter, or screen, in the carburetor or near the fuel control in a jet-engine system removes the extremely fine particles that may interfere with the operation of the sensitive valves and other operating mechanisms. Some filters are so fine that they remove all particles larger than 40 microns (μm) in diameter. (A **micron** is one-thousandth of a millimeter.)

A main fuel screen for a light airplane is shown in Fig. 11-12. This unit includes a glass sediment bowl and a screen and is called a **gascolator.** It consists of a cast-metal top, or cover, the screen, and the glass bowl, together with the necessary assembling parts. The bowl is attached to the cover by a clamp and thumbnut. Fuel enters the unit through the inlet on the top, filters through the screen, and exits through a connection to the carburetor inlet. At designated periods the glass bowl is drained and the screen is removed for inspection and cleaning. The tank and carburetor screens are also cleaned periodically, depending upon the installation, type of strainer, and inspection procedure established for the system.

An exploded view of one of the fuel-strainer assem-

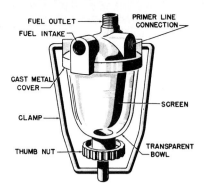

FIG. 11-12 Main fuel screen for a light aircraft.

blies for a light twin-engine airplane is shown in Fig. 11-13. This fuel strainer is located in the nacelle of each engine and is attached to the lower-center part of the fire wall. A quick drain valve is incorporated at the bottom of the unit to permit the drainage of a small amount of fuel during the preflight inspection. This is to ensure that no water will reach the carburetor.

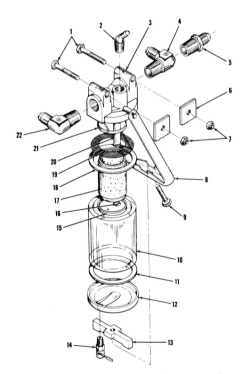

1. Bolt	11. Lower gasket
2. Elbow	12. Cap
3. Body assembly	13. Stiffener
4. Fitting for left engine installation	14. Drain valve
5. Fitting for right engine installation	15. Lid assembly
6. Mounting bracket	16. Retainer spring
7. Nut	17. Filter
8. Arm assembly	18. Upper gasket
9. Bolt	19. Flat screen
10. Glass bowl	20. Standpipe
	21. Filter ring
	22. Elbow

FIG. 11-13 Fuel-strainer assembly for a light twin-engine airplane. (Cessna Aircraft Co.)

Fuel filters for turbine-engine systems include by-pass valves which allow fuel to flow even though the filter is clogged. **Bypass warning system** switches are included in the filter assembly to provide a signal to the cockpit notifying the pilot or other crew member that a particular filter is bypassing fuel or is nearing a condition where it will bypass fuel. A bypass warning switch in some filters is operated by the movement of the bypass valve as it opens. In other filters, the warning switch is operated by the pressure differential developed as pressure on the input side of the filter increases owing to filter clogging. Figure 11-14 is an installation drawing of a micronic filter assembly for a turbine-engine system showing the filter bowl, filter element, filter drain tube, bowl packing, filter head, and electrical connections for the bypass warning switch.

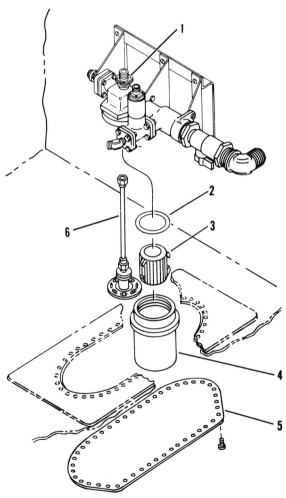

1. Electrical connection for fuel pressure indicator on filter head
2. Packing
3. Filter element
4. Filter bowl
5. Access cover
6. Filter drain hose

FIG. 11-14 Fuel filter assembly for a turbine-engine aircraft. (Sikorsky Aircraft Corp., Division of United Technologies Corp.)

Drains

Aircraft fuel systems must be provided with **drains** such that the entire system can be drained with the airplane in its normal ground attitude. Drains are available at fuel strainers and at sumps as well as at other locations.

Each drain must be located so that it will discharge clear of all parts of the airplane. The drains must have manual or automatic means for positive locking in the closed position. Each drain must have a drain valve that is readily accessible and can be opened and closed easily. The drains must be located or protected to prevent fuel spillage in the event of a landing with landing gear retracted.

Fuel Selector Valves

Fuel selector valves, sometimes called **fuel cocks,** provide a means of shutting off the fuel flow, selecting the tank in a multiple-tank installation, transferring fuel from one tank to another, and directing the fuel to one or more engines in a multiengine airplane. One or more of these valves are used to shut off all fuel to each engine. Such a valve must be positive and quick-acting, and the valve controls should be located within easy reach of the pilot (or pilots) or the flight engineer. In multiple-tank installation, the valve arrangement should be so arranged that each tank can be used separately. No shutoff valve may be on the engine side of any firewall. There must be means to guard against inadvertent operation of each shutoff valve and to allow flight crew members to reopen each valve rapidly after it has been closed.

Each shutoff valve and fuel system control must be supported so that loads resulting from its operation or from accelerated flight conditions are not transmitted to the lines connected to the valve. Each valve and fuel system control must be installed so that gravity and vibration will not affect the selected position.

Each fuel valve handle and its connections to the valve mechanism must have design features that minimize the possibility of incorrect installation. Each check valve must be constructed, or otherwise incorporate provisions, to prevent incorrect assembly or connection of the valve.

Fuel-shutoff valves for large aircraft are interconnected with fire protection systems so fuel may be shut off automatically if there is an overheat or fire situation in any engine nacelle. These arrangements must comply with the regulations covering fire suppression systems.

Fuel selector valves for light airplanes are usually simple in design, construction, and operation. The selector valve shown in Fig. 11-15 consists of a cylindrical aluminum housing with several fuel inlet ports around its circumference. The outlet port is located on the end. A center shaft, or plug, directs fuel from one of the inlet ports to the outlet connection. This center shaft is connected by linkage to the cockpit control. When the control is in the OFF position, the center shaft in the valve does not line up with any fuel connections around the circumference of the selector casing.

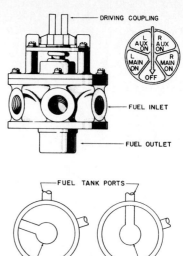
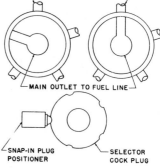

FIG. 11-15 Fuel selector valve for a light airplane.

An exploded view of a cam-operated ball-type valve for light aircraft is shown in Fig. 11-16. As the cam is rotated, it is possible to turn on one or both of the tanks to which the valve is connected. This type of valve is usually employed where a main tank and an auxiliary tank are connected to the system.

Fuel-control valves in large transport aircraft are usually operated by electric motors. Switches to control the motors are located on the flight engineer's fuel-control panel in the aircraft immediately aft of the pilot's compartment. An electrically operated valve assembly of this type includes a reversible electric motor linked to a sliding valve assembly. The motor

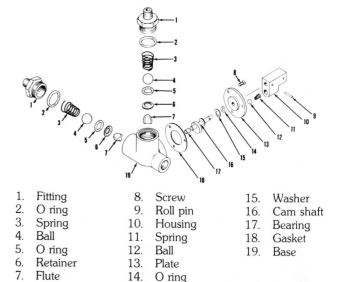

1. Fitting	8. Screw	15. Washer
2. O ring	9. Roll pin	16. Cam shaft
3. Spring	10. Housing	17. Bearing
4. Ball	11. Spring	18. Gasket
5. O ring	12. Ball	19. Base
6. Retainer	13. Plate	
7. Flute	14. O ring	

FIG. 11-16 Cam-operated ball-type valve. (*Cessna Aircraft Co.*)

moves the valve **gate** in and out of the passage through which the fuel flows, thus shutting the fuel off or turning it on. The valves are usually placed near the tanks with which they are associated.

Combination Fuel Unit

A fuel unit that combines the functions of the fuel valve, fuel strainer, and booster pump is shown in the exploded view of Fig. 11-17. This unit is employed on certain early models of the Beechcraft Bonanza and Debonair airplanes. An examination of this illustration will reveal the conical valve (2), which is operated by the handle (14). The spring (15) exerts pressure on the valve to hold it snugly in the valve seat, thus preventing leakage. Two pump check valves (7) are required at each end of the pump cylinder in order to provide opening and closing of the fuel passages as the pump is operated. One valve at each end is in the inlet passage, and the other valve is in the outlet. The pressure-relief valve is also shown (16). The pump handle (17) is hinged to the bracket (18) and linked to the piston (19). The fuel strainer (20) fits into a chamber adjacent to the pump cylinder. When the unit is assembled, the drain valve (21) is at the bottom of the strainer chamber.

Fuel Heaters

Fuel heaters are used with fuel systems for turbine engines to prevent ice crystals in the fuel from clogging

system filters. Water in turbine fuel does not settle out quickly as it does in gasoline. If the temperature of the fuel in the tanks is below the freezing point of water, these water particles will freeze. As the fuel with these ice particles tries to pass through the fuel filters, they filter out the ice and become clogged. This causes the filter bypass to open and allows unfiltered fuel to flow to the engine.

To prevent these filters from being clogged, the fuel is passed through a fuel heater prior to entering the filter. The fuel heater is a heat exchanger which uses engine compressor bleed air, engine oil, or, if the hydraulic system generates sufficient heat, hydraulic fluid to heat the fuel above freezing and melt the ice crystals. The fuel and water mixture can then flow to the engine and be burned. The ratio of water to fuel is very slight and does not affect the operation of the engine.

Fuel Lines and Fittings

In an aircraft fuel system, the various components are connected by means of aluminum alloy, copper, or other types of tubing and flexible hose assemblies with approved connecting fittings. A typical fuel hose assembly is shown in Fig. 11-18. This hose is made of

FIG. 11-18 Fuel hose cutaway. *(The Weatherhead Company)*

synthetic rubber and is reinforced with fiber braid embedded in bonding material. The hose conforms to MIL-H-5593A and is connected with an AN-773 hose-end assembly. Another hose assembly suitable for fuel systems is shown in Fig. 11-19. This is the Weather-

FIG. 11-19 Hose assembly with reusable fittings.

head 3H-241 hose assembly equipped with reusable type end fittings. This hose has a working temperature range of −40 to +300°F [−40 to +149°C] when used with fuel. The hose is covered with stainless-steel braid. Fuel lines must be of a size that will provide the required fuel-flow rate under all conditions of operation.

The installation of the fuel lines must be such that there are no sharp bends, that is, bends with a radius of less than three diameters. Fuel lines must be routed so that there are no vertical bends where water or vapor can collect. A bend downward and then upward

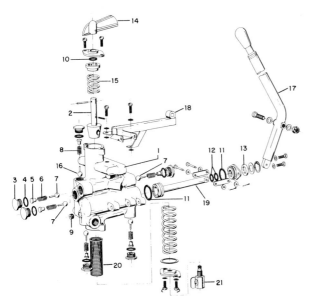

1. Housing
2. Fuel selector valve
3. Plug
4. O ring (AN629D-6)
5. Guide
6. Check valve spring
7. Valve
8. Pressure-relief valve spring
9. Plug (AN932-2)
10. O ring, selector valve
11. O ring, piston head and cylinder head
12. O ring, piston rod
13. Felt washer
14. Valve handle
15. Valve spring
16. Pressure-relief valve
17. Pump handle
18. Bracket
19. Pump piston
20. Fuel strainer
21. Drain valve

FIG. 11-17 Combination fuel unit. *(Beech Aircraft Co.)*

will permit water to collect, and a bend upward and then downward will permit vapor to collect.

If a copper line is used in a fuel system, it should be annealed after bending and at overhaul periods; however, aluminum lines should not be annealed.

Parts of the fuel system attached to the engine and to the primary structure of the airplane must be connected by means of flexible hose assemblies. Flexible hose assemblies should also be used to connect a stationary unit with a unit under vibration.

Fuel lines must be securely anchored to prevent vibration during operation of the engine. Usually the mountings and clamps installed by the manufacturer will be adequate. Metal lines should be bonded to prevent radio interference. All fuel lines and fittings must be of an approved type.

● FUEL SUBSYSTEMS

Fuel subsystems are not involved in the direct flow of fuel from the tank to the engine but are used to prevent damage to the system, improve the operational capability of the aircraft, and eliminate hazardous conditions. All of the systems discussed here are not used on all aircraft, but some, such as vent systems, are required on all aircraft fuel systems.

Primers and Priming Systems

Unlike an automobile engine, non-fuel-injected, reciprocating aircraft engines must often be primed before starting because the carburetor does not function properly until the engine is running. For this reason, it is necessary to have a separate system to charge, or prime, the cylinders with raw fuel for starting. This is accomplished by the **priming system.** The usual arrangement is to have the primer draw fuel from the carburetor inlet bowl or fuel strainer and direct it to a distributor valve, which, in turn, distributes the fuel to the various cylinders. Figure 11-20 illustrates the action of a typical priming system used on a small aircraft engine. Other priming systems, used on internally geared supercharged engines, discharge the fuel into the supercharger diffuser section through a jet located on the carburetor or in the diffuser section.

The priming system shown in Fig. 11-20 has an undesirable feature in that the pump-body assembly is located in the pilot's cockpit. This causes the addition of fuel lines in the pilot's compartment and presents

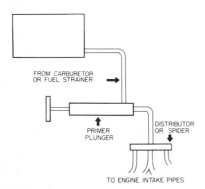

FROM CARBURETOR
OR FUEL STRAINER →

PRIMER
PLUNGER

DISTRIBUTOR
OR SPIDER

TO ENGINE INTAKE PIPES

FIG. 11-20 Priming system for a light aircraft engine.

a fire hazard. For this reason, remote-control electric-solenoid primer valves have been developed. The solenoid valve is usually located on or near the carburetor and is wired to a control switch in the cockpit. When the switch is engaged, the solenoid-actuated valve opens and allows fuel, under booster-pump pressure, to enter the priming system. The valve is returned to the closed position by means of a spring. **Engines equipped with fuel-injection systems do not require separate priming systems because the injection system pumps fuel directly into the intake ports of the engine.**

Vent Systems

Fuel **vent systems** are designed to prevent the buildup of pressure in the fuel tanks and allow proper flow of fuel from the tanks. The expansion of fuel in the tanks when they are full could pressurize the tank sufficiently to cause structural damage if the tank were not vented. Also, without a vent, as fuel is used from the tank, a vacuum would build up in the tank and fuel would not be able to leave the tank.

The vent system for a light aircraft may be as simple as a hole drilled in the fuel cap or a tube running from the top portion of the fuel tank to the outside of the aircraft. Some vent systems for these aircraft have t heir openings pointing in the direction of flight to supply a slight pressure to the tank and aid the fuel flow to the engine.

Large aircraft have a vent system which allows each tank to vent to a high point in the system once tank pressure has exceeded some specified valve (normally in the 2- to 6-psi [13.8- to 41.4-kPa] range). If tank pressure exceeds the predetermined value, a tank vent valve opens and vents the tank to a special vent compartment called a **surge tank, vent compartment,** or **vent box.** This compartment allows fuel to vent from the tanks, which prevents pressure buildup as well as fuel spilling overboard. The compartment is vented through a standpipe which extends to the top of the tank as shown in Fig. 11-21. The compartment cannot fill under any normal conditions. Some aircraft have their vent systems configured so that the fuel tanks on the right side must vent through the left vent compartment and vice versa.

Pressure Fueling Systems

A **pressure fueling system** is also referred to as a **single-point fueling system.** There is a difference between these terms in that a single-point fueling system for a large aircraft uses only one fueling connection to fill all of the fuel tanks. A pressure fueling system may use the same equipment to fuel the aircraft, but the aircraft have separate fueling connections for each fuel tank. For the purpose of further discussion here, a pressure fueling system is considered the same as a single-point fueling system.

A pressure fueling system uses pressure from the fueling station or truck to force fuel into the aircraft tanks. This is done through a fueling fitting on the side of the aircraft or under the wing. A fueling control panel is located next to the fitting. The control panel allows the operator to monitor the fuel quantity in

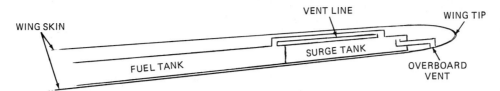

FIG. 11-21 Typical arrangement of a surge tank.

each tank and control the fuel valves for each tank. Through this panel the operator can fill each tank to the desired quantity. A fueling panel is shown in Fig. 11-22.

When the fueling connection is made at the fueling panel and the valve on the fuel hose is opened, the fueling manifold is pressurized with fuel. The operator can then select which tanks are to be filled by opening electrically operated fill valves.

When a tank becomes full, a float-operated shutoff valve is closed by the rising fuel level in the tank and prevents any more fuel from entering a tank. The operation of these valves not only prevents overfilling any tank, but it also allows all tanks to be filled from one position with a minimum of operator activity. The person doing the fueling can close the fill valve for any tank when the desired quantity is indicated or can allow all tanks to be filled and only terminate the fueling operation when all tanks indicate full and no more fuel is flowing into the aircraft.

Fuel-Jettisoning Requirements

For transport-type aircraft, if the maximum takeoff weight for which the aircraft is certified is greater than 105 percent of the certified landing weight, provision must be made to **jettison** enough fuel to bring the weight of the airplane down to the certified landing weight. The average rate of fuel jettisoning must be 1 percent of the maximum takeoff weight per minute, except that the time required to jettison the fuel need not be less than 10 min.

The fuel-jettisoning system and its operation must be free of fire hazards, and the fuel must discharge clear of any part of the airplane. Fuel fumes must not

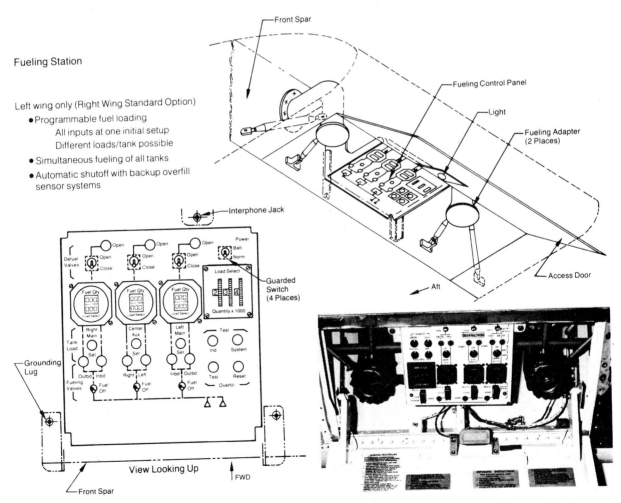

FIG. 11-22 Underwing fuel station on a Boeing 767. (*Boeing Commercial Aircraft Company*)

enter the airplane during operation of the jettisoning system. During operation of the system, the controllability of the airplane must not be adversely affected. Additional detailed requirements of the jettisoning system are specified in Federal Aviation Regulations.

Depending on the aircraft design, the force for fuel jettison is by gravity or by centrifugal pumps in the fuel tanks. Control valves have to be positioned to configure the fuel manifolds for dumping. Most aircraft dump the fuel from openings at the wing tips, but some aircraft make use of a dump chute which extends down from the wing.

Oil-Dilution Systems

It is a well-known fact that oil congeals in cold weather, and such oil in the working parts of an engine makes the engine difficult to turn and, therefore, hard to start. To end this trouble, motorists in cold climates sometimes dilute the crankcase oil of their automobile engines with kerosene. Similarly, a rather ingenious method, known as **oil dilution,** is employed to facilitate starting aircraft engines when the temperature is very low. With this method, a length of tubing connects the carburetor or other fuel pressure source through a solenoid valve to the oil Y drain or elsewhere to the oil system.

The oil is diluted after the engine has been operated and is fully warmed up, for example, at the end of a flight before shutting down the engine. With the engine running at a fast idle, the oil-dilution-valve switch is turned on and held in the ON position for the time specified in the operator's manual. After dilution the engine is immediately shut down with the dilution valve open so that the fuel will remain in the oil. The next time the engine is started, the diluted oil flows freely to all bearing surfaces, and the engine turns easily.

Figure 11-23 is a simplified schematic diagram showing the arrangement of an oil-dilution system. When the oil-dilution switch in the cockpit is closed, the valve is lifted from its seat by the solenoid. Fuel then flows through the inlet port and valve. It exits through the outlet port and is directed to the oil-system connection.

Students usually raise the question of the disposal of the fuel in the oil when the engine is running. The explanation is simple. Gasoline has a lower vaporization point than oil. The heat of the engine, after a

few minutes of operation, vaporizes the fuel, and the fuel vapors pass out through the oil-system breathers.

A fuel system that has an oil-dilution system must be checked regularly to ascertain that the valve is operating properly. On occasions, oil-dilution valves have become inoperative through sticking or some mechanical failure, with consequent damage resulting from excessive gasoline in the fuel supply. A sticking oil-dilution valve may, in some systems, be detected by checking the fuel pressure. A drop in fuel pressure can indicate a sticking valve. Excessive vapors coming from the engine breathers may also indicate this condition, and since it constitutes a fire hazard, it must be corrected immediately.

A **hopper-type oil tank** is important for large aircraft that utilize dry sump engines and carry a substantial supply of oil in the oil tank. The hopper in the tank segregates the oil that has been diluted from the large supply in the tank. This separation is not complete, but it is sufficient to reduce substantially the amount of fuel required for dilution.

It must be noted that aircraft powered by piston engines and designed for long-distance flight actually carry oil considerably in excess of what is required for the flight. The extra oil provides for good temperature control of the engine, and it also makes available a reserve in case of leakage or excessive oil consumption by the engine.

Requirements for Fuel-System Indicators, Warning Lights, and Controls

As explained in other sections of this chapter, fuel systems for aircraft require a number of indicators, depending upon the type and design of the system involved. Indicators which are or may be required are fuel-quantity indicators, fuel-pressure indicators, fuel-temperature indicators, fuel-flow indicators, and others. The indicators must be located at points where they are readily available to the appropriate member or members of the flight crew.

If the unusable fuel supply for any fuel tank exceeds 1 gal [3.79 L] or 5 percent of the tank capacity, whichever is greater, a red arc must be marked on the fuel-quantity indicator for that tank extending from the calibrated zero reading to the lowest reading obtainable in level flight.

Indicators, either gauges or warning lights, must be provided at pressure fueling stations to indicate failure of the automatic shutoff means to stop fuel flow at the desired level.

Fuel tanks with interconnected outlets and airspaces may be treated as one tank and need not have separate fuel-quantity indicators. Each exposed sight gauge used as a fuel-quantity indicator must be protected against damage.

If a fuel-flowmeter system is installed in a fuel system, each metering component (fuel-flow transmitter) must have a means of bypassing the fuel flow if malfunction of the metering component severely restricts fuel flow.

There must be means to measure fuel pressure in each system supplying reciprocating engines at a point downstream of any fuel pump except fuel injection

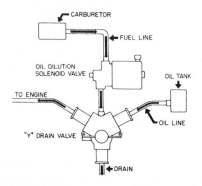

FIG. 11-23 Arrangement for an oil-dilution system.

pumps. If necessary for the proper fuel-delivery pressure, there must be a connection to transmit the carburetor air intake static pressure to the proper fuel pump relief valve connection. If this connection is required, the gauge balance lines must be independently connected to the carburetor inlet pressure to avoid erroneous readings.

Fuel-pressure warning lights are installed in appropriate locations to inform members of the flight crew that fuel pressure has dropped below a safe level as the result of depletion, fuel-pump failure, ice in the system, or a clogged fuel filter. In some cases an aural warning system is provided in connection with the warning light.

Each fuel-tank selector control must be marked to indicate the position corresponding to each tank and to each cross-feed position. If safe operation requires a specific sequence for the use of any tanks, that sequence must be marked on or adjacent to the selector for those tanks. Each valve control for each engine must be marked to indicate the position corresponding to each engine controlled.

Each **emergency control,** including each fuel-jettisoning and fluid-shutoff control, must be colored red.

Fuel System Instruments

A discussion of fuel quantity indicating systems, along with pressure, flow rate, and temperature monitoring instruments, is covered in Chap. 13.

● TYPICAL AIRCRAFT FUEL SYSTEMS

Light Airplane Gravity-Feed System

The simple fuel system for a light single-engine airplane is shown in Fig. 11-24. The fuel tanks for this system are mounted in the wing roots and are constructed of welded aluminum alloy. The fuel tanks are held securely in place by means of padded steel straps attached to the wing spars. The padding is treated to make it nonabsorbent. The fuel filler caps are on the top of the wing, and the fuel outlets for the tanks are at the lowest point in the inboard end of the tanks. Fuel flow is by gravity to the fuel valve located forward of the fire wall. From the valve the fuel flows to the "gascolator" (sump and screen assembly) in the lowest point of the system. From the sump the fuel

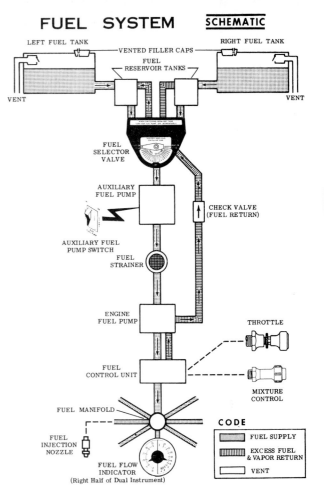

FIG. 11-25 Fuel system for a high-performance single-engine aircraft. *(Cessna Aircraft Co.)*

lines lead to the carburetor and to the primer pump which is located on the instrument panel.

Light Airplane Pressure-Feed System

The pressure-feed fuel system for a typical light airplane is shown in Fig. 11-25. This fuel system has two fuel cells made of fuel-resistant synthetic rubber. The cells are held in place in the wing compartments by means of snap fasteners. The fuel cells are vented to the atmosphere through vents in the fuel caps and vent lines. Metal fuel lines run from the fuel cells to the reservoir tanks which are mounted in the side walls of the fuselage, just behind the firewall.

From the reservoir tanks, fuel flows to the selector valve. The selector valve has four positions: right, left, both, and off. These four positions allow the pilot to select the fuel tanks used to supply the engine. Off is used to shut off fuel flow to the area forward of the firewall when the aircraft is parked and when servicing the system.

From the fuel selector the fuel flows to the electric fuel pump. When the fuel pump is operated by the rocker switch in the cabin, the fuel system downstream of the pump is pressurized. This pump is used as a backup for the engine pump if it should fail and for starting the engine. The pump does not restrict

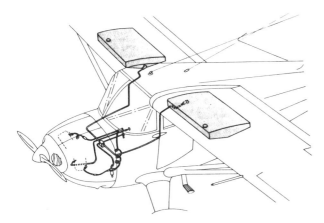

FIG. 11-24 Fuel system for a light single-engine airplane.

flow when it is not running, which allows the engine-driven pump to draw fuel from the tanks.

The fuel next flows through a strainer to remove any contamination. From there it moves through flexible lines to the engine-driven fuel pump which boosts the pressure up to the value needed by the fuel control unit. Excess fuel volume generated by the pump is returned through a check valve to the fuel selector. The fuel-control unit is controlled by the throttle and mixture controls in the cabin.

Fuel from the fuel-control unit is delivered to the engine cylinders and to a pressure-operated fuel flow indicator in the cabin area.

Fuel System for a Light Twin Airplane

A schematic diagram of the fuel system for a light twin airplane is shown in Fig. 11-26. The fuel system shown is employed with models of the airplane that utilize direct fuel injection for the engines.

The fuel supply is contained in two fuel bladders, one located in each wing-tip tank. The bladders are made of fuel-resistant synthetic rubber with fabric reinforcement. The total fuel capacity of each bladder

is 51 gal [193.3 L], of which 50.5 gal [191.4 L] is usable. The wing-tip tanks are streamlined aluminum alloy shells designed to give adequate structural support to the fuel bladders. The tanks are easily removed from the wing tips to which they are secured by means of bolts through the attaching fittings. An electrically operated boost pump is incorporated in each fuel tank to furnish fuel pressure for priming, starting, and emergency use in case the engine-driven pump should fail. From the boost pumps, fuel is fed to the selector valves located in the wings and then through the fuel strainers and engine-driven pumps to the fuel-injection unit. The engine-driven fuel-injection-pump assembly includes a vapor separator and a pressure-regulating valve.

A **vapor-return line** is provided between the fuel-injection pumps and the fuel tanks. This eliminates the collection of vapor and resulting vapor lock in the pump or fuel-injection unit. The vapor-return lines carry some fuel in addition to the vapor back to the fuel tanks. Quick drain valves are provided in each wing-tip tank and in each fuel strainer to facilitate draining of water or sediment. These are used to drain

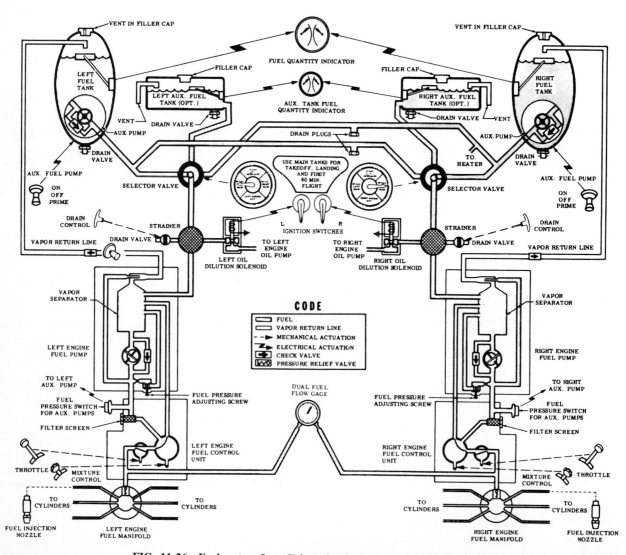

FIG. 11-26 Fuel system for a light twin airplane. (*Cessna Aircraft Co.*)

a small amount of fuel during each preflight inspection to ensure that all water and sediment are removed before the airplane is flown.

The fuel-system diagram of Fig. 11-26 should be studied carefully to observe the relative positions of all the units of the system. The fuel-quantity gauge units can be seen in each tank, and these are electrically connected to the **fuel-quantity indicators** located on the instrument panel of the airplane. It can be noted also that the fuel booster pumps in the tanks are electrically operated through switches that are located in the cockpit. The booster pumps are provided with bypass arrangements so that there will be a free flow of fuel when the pumps are not operating. The oil-dilution solenoid valves receive fuel from the main fuel-strainer cases. These valves are also operated by switches in the cockpit.

Since this system is designed for operation with direct fuel-injection units, the fuel-pressure gauges are connected between the fuel controls and the fuel manifolds. This is to give an indication of the pressure actually applied to the injection nozzles, thus providing the pilot with an accurate measure of engine power.

Fuel System For A Turboprop Airplane

The fuel system shown in Fig. 11-27 is for a small turboprop aircraft. The center tank is an integral one having three compartments. Fuel in the two outboard main tanks flows by gravity through flapper valves into the center main tank. Fuel in the outer tanks must be transferred to the main tank before it can be used by the engines. This transfer is achieved by a submerged centrifugal pump in each outer tank. Fuel in the tip tanks is transferred to the main tank by pressurizing the tip tank with engine bleed air. All tanks are vented through valves to vent exits on the underside of each wing.

Two submerged centrifugal boost pumps are located in the main center fuel tank. Fuel from these pumps is fed to a fuel manifold, through a shutoff valve for each engine, through fuel filters, and then to the engine pumps and the engine fuel-control units.

Three fuel quantity indicators are provided, one for the main tank, one dual-needle gauge for the outer tanks and a dual-needle gauge for the tip tanks. A fuel flow indicator is provided for each engine.

A sniffle valve in each tip tank prevents over- or

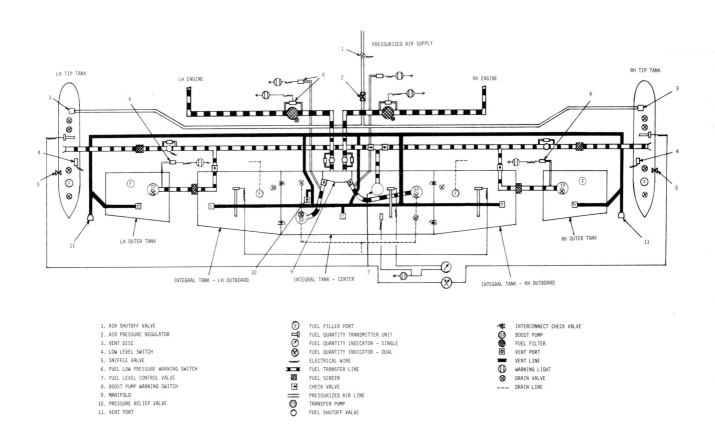

FIG. 11-27   Fuel system for a turboprop aircraft. (*Flight Safety International, Inc.*)

underpressurization and is used to depressurize the tank before fueling.

Fuel Systems for Jet Airliners

Although it is not possible in a standard textbook to provide a detailed description of the fuel system for a modern jet airliner, we shall give a brief description of such systems so that the student will have a concept of their size and complexity.

Figure 11-28 is a schematic diagram of the fuel system in one wing of a jet-transport aircraft. The fuel system is an arrangement of fuel tanks and component systems which ensure that the engines are supplied with fuel in the proper amount at all times. The fuel is distributed in four main tanks, two outboard reserve tanks, and a center-wing tank. The fuel tanks and all system components are suitable for use with any acceptable fuel that conforms to the engine manufacturer's specifications. This fuel tank arrangement is shown in Fig. 11-29 and the configuration of a twin-engine transport is shown in Fig. 11-30.

All the fuel tanks are located in the interspar area

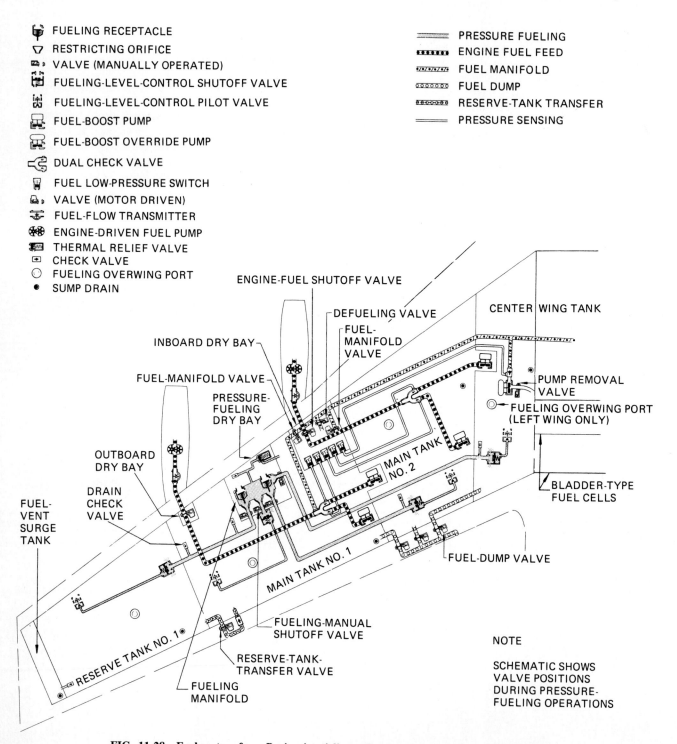

FIG. 11-28 Fuel system for a Boeing jet airliner. (*Boeing Commercial Aircraft Company*)

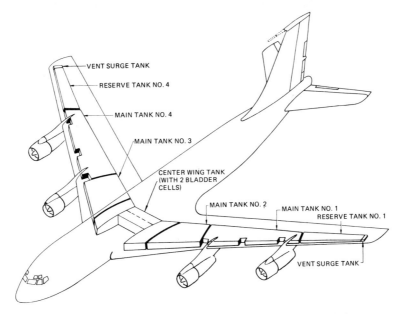

FIG. 11-29 Fuel tank arrangement for a four-engine jet airliner.

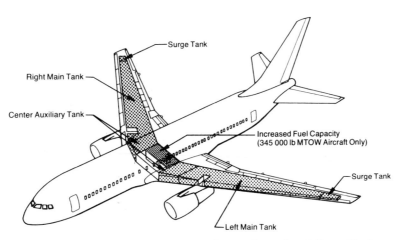

FIG. 11-30 Fuel tank arrangement for a twin-engine airliner. *(Boeing Commercial Aircraft Company)*

of the wing structure between the front and rear spars. The wing skin and ribs form the walls of the tanks, and the intermediate ribs serve as baffle plates to prevent excessive sloshing and rapid weight-shifting of the fuel. The four main tanks and two reserve tanks are completely integral with the wing structure. The center-wing tank consists of two integral sections at the wing roots and a center-wing cavity containing bladder-type fuel cells. All fuel tanks are made fuel-tight by the use of sealing compound and sealed fasteners.

A **fuel-vent system** provides positive venting to the atmosphere of all fuel tanks, fuel cells, and cavities, thereby preventing excessive internal or external pressures across the tank walls during all flight maneuvers. Venting of the four main tanks, two reserve tanks, and integral sections of the center-wing tank is accomplished with sealed spanwise upper-wing skin-stiffener ducts, interconnected with appropriate drains and vent tubing that connect to vent ports located in critical

areas of the tanks. The vent system is connected to a surge tank at the wing tip that is vented overboard through a vent scoop. The center-wing cavity is vented overboard through a separate vent and drain system. The cavity vent system maintains atmospheric pressure on the outside of the bladder-type fuel cells. The fuel cells are vented into the integral sections of the center-wing fuel tank.

The **engine fuel-feed system** consists of fuel lines, pumps, and valves, which distribute the fuel to the engines. This system includes four tank-to-engine fuel-feed systems that are interconnected by a fuel manifold such that fuel may be delivered from any main tank or the center-wing tank to any or all engines. The two reserve tanks store fuel and supply the fuel by gravity flow to main tanks Nos. 1 and 4 through electrically operated transfer valves. The fuel-feed line from each main tank is pressurized by two boost pumps that are controlled by separate switches and independent circuits so that engine operation will not

403

be affected by power failure to any single boost pump. The center-wing-tank boost pumps, known as the **fuel-boost-override** pumps, will override the main-tank boost pumps to supply fuel through the manifold to the engines. The distribution of fuel to the engines is controlled by electric-motor-driven slide valves in the fuel lines. The valves are classified into three groups: (1) **engine fuel-shutoff valves,** which shut off fuel to the engines; (2) **fuel-manifold valves,** which control manifold distribution; and (3) **reserve-tank-transfer valves,** which control fuel from the reserve tanks to main tanks Nos. 1 and 4. All these valves are controlled by manually operated switches located on the flight engineer's panel in the cabin.

Pressure fueling is accomplished from a station located on the lower surface of each wing between the inboard and outboard engine nacelles. Each pressure-fueling station consists of two fueling-nozzle-ground connectors, two fueling receptacles, and a fueling manifold. Four fueling manual shutoff valves at each fueling station permit the fuel tanks to be serviced individually. Each station services the main and reserve tanks on its respective side of the airplane. The center-wing tank is serviced from either wing station. The maximum fuel-delivery pressure is 50 psi [344.75 kPa]. A **restricting orifice plate** at each fueling manual shutoff valve limits the flow rate for the tank serviced. The approximate flow rates for the various tanks are as follows: main tanks Nos. 1 and 4, 234 gal/h [16 025 L/h]; main tanks Nos. 2 and 3, 227 gal/h [12 214 L/h]; and reserve tanks Nos. 1 and 4, 65 gal/h [1760 L/h]. The center-wing tank rate is 250 gal/h [946 L/h] per side except on certain airplanes.

Each tank has a **fueling-level-control pilot valve** (see Fig. 11-31) that actuates a **fueling-level-control shutoff valve** to shut off the fuel flow automatically when the maximum tank capacity has been reached. A **fueling preset system** permits the tanks to be fueled to a pre-

determined level without constant observation of the fuel-quantity indicators. The fueling-preset-system controls are located on the flight engineer's panel. Preset switches and potentiometers are actuated in conjunction with fuel-quantity indicators. The preset system incorporates signal lights at the fueling station to inform the refueling operator that the desired quantity of fuel has been pumped into the various tanks.

The **fuel-dump system,** consisting of lines, valves, dump chutes, and chute-operating mechanism, provides the means whereby fuel can be dumped in flight. Each wing contains an extendable dump chute, which must be fully extended before fuel can be dumped. Each chute is fed fuel by dump lines from the main and center-wing tanks on their respective sides of the airplane. The reserve tank fuel is transferred to and dumped with the main outboard tank fuel. The controls are located on the flight engineer's auxiliary panel. When all dump valves are open, the system will dump all fuel in excess of 10 848 lb [4921 kg] at an average rate of approximately 2500 lb [1134 kg] per min. The 10 848 lb of fuel remaining in the fuel tanks is required as a safety measure to allow the airplane adequate flight time to reach a suitable airport and make a safe landing. The principal reason for dumping fuel is to reduce the landing weight of the airplane prior to making an emergency landing.

The **fuel-quantity-indicating system** incorporates electric capacitance tank probes mounted internally in each fuel tank. The probes have a compensator for fuel-density variations. The probes feed signals to the fuel-quantity indicators on the flight engineer's lower panel. These indicators are calibrated to show the weight of fuel remaining in each tank.

In addition to the fuel-quantity-indicating system, provisions are made to determine the quantity of fuel in each tank with the airplane in the taxi attitude by calibrated **drip sticks** located in the wing's lower surface. When the cap and hollow drip-stick assembly is drawn out from the wing's lower surface, fuel enters the open top of the stick when it reaches the fuel level and can be observed at a small drip hole near the cap base. The drip-stick reading in inches when fuel first appears at the drip hole is compared with a special chart to give a reading of fuel quantity in gallons or kilograms.

The **fuel-indicating system** utilizes a **fuel-flow transmitter** to send electrical signals to the fuel-flow indicators at the pilot's station. The fuel-flow indication makes it possible for the pilot to determine individual engine power output and also the flight time remaining before the airplane must land and refuel.

The **fuel-temperature-indicating system** is required to tell when there may be danger of ice crystals forming in the fuel. It must be remembered that jet airliners fly regularly at altitudes of over 30 000 ft [9144 m] and the fuel, therefore, reaches temperatures well below the freezing point of water. The fuel-temperature-indicating system provides a means for checking the temperature of fuel in main tank No. 1 and in the fuel line at each engine. The system consists of an **indicator** and a **five-position selector switch** on the flight engineer's lower panel. A temperature bulb is located in

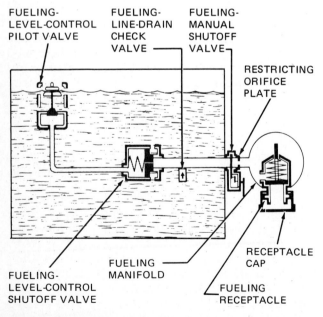

FUELING-LEVEL-CONTROL PILOT VALVE

FUELING-LINE-DRAIN CHECK VALVE

FUELING-MANUAL SHUTOFF VALVE

RESTRICTING ORIFICE PLATE

FUELING-LEVEL-CONTROL SHUTOFF VALVE

FUELING MANIFOLD

RECEPTACLE CAP

FUELING RECEPTACLE

FIG. 11-31 Fuel-level-control system.

main tank No. 1 and in the outlet side of the fuel filter at each engine.

Each engine has a manually controlled engine fuel-deicing system, which removes any ice formed in the fuel before it reaches the fuel-control unit. The principal components of each deicing system are a **fuel filter,** an **air-control valve,** and **fuel-deicing heater.** The control switches are located on the flight engineer's lower panel.

The **fuel filter** is fitted with a pressure warning switch that detects filter icing and then turns on the fuel-icing-indicator light on the flight engineer's lower panel. The **air-control valve** controls the flow of high-pressure discharge air from the engine compressor to the heater through which all the fuel passes. A fuel-temperature bulb is located on the outlet side of the filter to monitor the exit temperature.

All fuel tanks have an exterior filler cap for individual tank servicing. The caps are located on the top of the wings, as shown in Fig. 11-28, thus making it possible to fill the tanks when pressure fueling is not available. Some aircraft cannot be completely filled through the overwing filler caps.

The main tanks have baffle check valves installed in the bottom of the inboard ribs to allow fuel to flow inboard toward the boost pumps during normal flight attitude and to prevent fuel flow away from the pump area during turbulence or airplane maneuvers. This provision ensures that engine stoppage will not be caused by a momentary cutoff of fuel flow.

Pressure defueling of the main tanks or center-wing tank is accomplished through a defueling valve located in the inboard dry bay of each wing. The fuel boost pumps in the main tanks or the override pumps in the center-wing tank deliver fuel to the defueling valves through their respective fuel-manifold valves. The defueling rate is approximately 50 gal/min [189.5 L/min] for each tank. Alternatively, fuel can be drawn from the tanks through the defueling valve by means of the truck defueling pump. The reserve tanks are defueled through the reserve-tank-transfer valve to the adjacent main tanks. Residual fuel in each tank can be drained through fuel-sump drain cocks located in the bottom of each tank.

The following components of the fuel system should be located in Fig. 11-28 and the purpose of each unit determined:

Fueling receptacle. The attachment for the pressure fueling hose. The receptacle is fitted with a valve that is automatically closed when the fueling hose is disconnected.

Restricting orifice. A flow-limiting device to prevent excessive fuel flow during pressure fueling.

Manually operated shutoff valves. These valves are provided at the pressure-fueling station to permit a positive closing of fuel lines.

Fueling-level-control shutoff valve. This valve automatically closes the fueling line to a tank when that tank is filled to its maximum level.

Fueling-level-control pilot valve. During pressure fueling, this valve closes when the full fuel level is reached. The closing of this valve causes pressure to be applied to the fueling-level-control shutoff valve, thus causing it to close (see Fig. 11-31).

Motor-driven valve. These are slide valves operated by electric motors. They are used for fuel control throughout the system.

Fuel-flow transmitter. The electrically operated unit that senses the rate of fuel flow to each engine.

Another fuel-system layout for a large jet airplane is shown in Fig. 11-32. This drawing shows the center and left-wing portions of the fuel system for the DC-10, wide-bodied jet airplane. The right-wing arrangement is essentially the same as that of the left wing. The DC-10 fuel system consists of four subsystems. These are the **storage, fuel-distribution, dump,** and **indicating systems.** The storage system includes the **integral tanks, sumping, vent system,** and **continuous scavenging.** The fuel-distribution system includes **tank refueling/defueling, engine and auxiliary power unit (APU) fuel supply,** and a **manifold fuel drain.** The dump system provides a means for dumping fuel overboard. The indicating system includes **fuel-quantity indicating lights, fuel-schedule light system, tank boost pump** and **low-pressure lights,** and **tank fuel temperature.**

Fuel is stored in three integral tanks in the wing. The tanks are numbered from left to right and correspond with the engine designation. That is, the left wing tank is No. 1, the inboard tank is No. 2, and the right wing tank is No. 3. The inboard section of each wing, outboard of the fuselage, is interconnected by large-diameter lines to form the No. 2 tank.

Sumping of the tanks is accomplished by means of manually operated sump drain valves located in the low point of each tank. A **continuous-scavenging system** prevents water from accumulating in tank low points where it could support the growth of microorganisms and cause a corrosion problem.

The fuel-vent system permits equalization of pressure differential in the tanks that is created during refueling/defueling or maneuvering of the airplane. The system is designed to prevent siphoning or spilling of fuel during normal flight or ground maneuvers.

Refueling/defueling is accomplished through four pressure refueling adapters, two located in each wing leading edge outboard of the engine nacelles. A refueling control panel is located between the two adapters in the right wing. Defueling is accomplished through the refueling adapters by means of ground suction equipment or by using the airplane boost pumps to move fuel through the lines.

Engine fuel is delivered from the tanks directly to the engines by means of fuel boost pumps as shown in the drawing of Fig. 11-32. The refueling manifold is also used as a **cross-feed manifold** to permit cross-feeding for engines and intertank fuel transfer. The cross-feed system makes it possible to supply any engine with fuel from any tank. It also makes it possible to transfer fuel from any tank to any other tank for the purpose of balancing the weight distribution and to maintain an acceptable position for the airplane CG.

As shown in Fig. 11-32, the APU is supplied with fuel from the line that supplies the No. 2 engine. Note

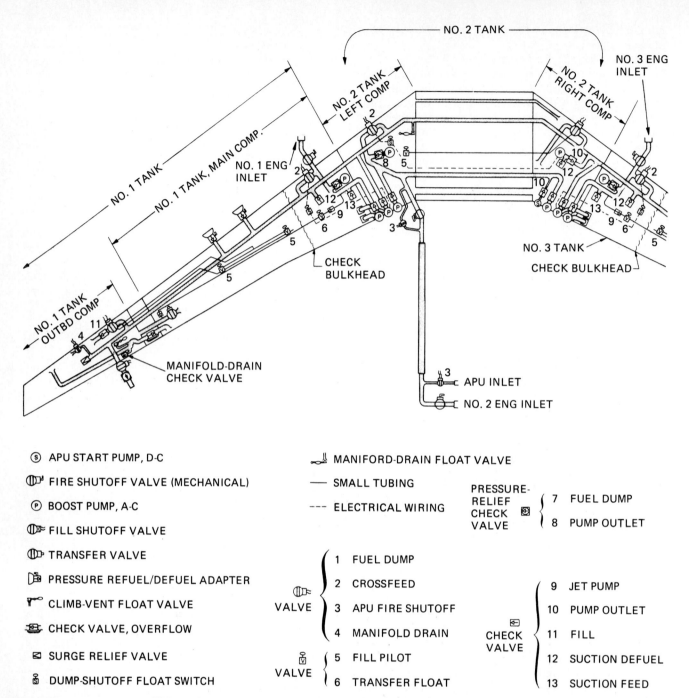

PRESSURE-RELIEF CHECK VALVE ⬚	7	FUEL DUMP
	8	PUMP OUTLET

VALVE ⬚		
	1	FUEL DUMP
	2	CROSSFEED
	3	APU FIRE SHUTOFF
	4	MANIFOLD DRAIN

VALVE ⬚		
	5	FILL PILOT
	6	TRANSFER FLOAT

CHECK VALVE ⬚		
	9	JET PUMP
	10	PUMP OUTLET
	11	FILL
	12	SUCTION DEFUEL
	13	SUCTION FEED

FIG. 11-32   Fuel system for the Douglas DC-10. *(McDonnell Douglas Corp.)*

that the APU supply line incorporates a fire shutoff valve which is actuated if a fire or overheat condition is indicated in the APU compartment.

Fuel jettisoning or dumping is accomplished by means of two dump outlets, one located inboard of each outboard aileron. The fuel is pumped by means of the tank boost-transfer pumps through the crossfeed manifold to the dump outlets. An automatic shutoff system is provided to prevent dumping of fuel below the minimum required dump level. Note that the location of the fuel dump outlets is such that the fuel is dumped clear of any part of the airplane.

The fuel quantity in the tanks is indicated by a capacitance-type indicating system. The capacitor-type of fuel-quantity indicator measures fuel by weight rather than by volume, thus giving the flight engineer or other member of the flight crew accurate information regarding the amount of fuel energy available. The changes in fuel volume due to temperature are compensated for by changes in fuel density and the dielectric constant of the fuel. In addition, the system is provided with temperature compensators to assure accurate measurement of fuel weight. Chapter 13 discusses the capacitance-type indicating system in detail.

Fuel scheduling is indicated by the **fuel-schedule**

light system on the flight engineer's panel. The lights indicate either proper or improper fuel scheduling in the No. 1 and No. 3 tanks.

The fuel pressure supplied by the tank boost pumps is monitored by a warning light system. If the pressure delivered by the boost pump falls below the required level, the **tank boost pump low-pressure lights** in the flight compartment will come on.

The fuel temperature is monitored by a fuel-temperature-indicating system having a sensor in the outboard section of the No. 3 tank. The indicator is located on the flight engineer's fuel-control panel. A knowledge of the fuel temperature enables the flight engineer to determine the viscosity of the fuel and to determine the possibility of fuel icing.

Helicopter Fuel Systems

Helicopter fuel systems cover the full spectrum of complexity. The first system that is discussed briefly is for a light reciprocating-engine-powered two-place helicopter and the second system is for a helicopter that can be considered the equal of a transport aircraft.

The small system shown in Fig. 11-33 consists of a fuel tank mounted in the area above the engine and behind the cabin. The tank is baffled to reduce sloshing and has all of the connections and components necessary for a basic fuel tank. Not shown in the illustration are the quantity indicator and the low-fuel sensor. The quantity indicator is of the variable-resistance type. The low-fuel sensor turns on an indicator light

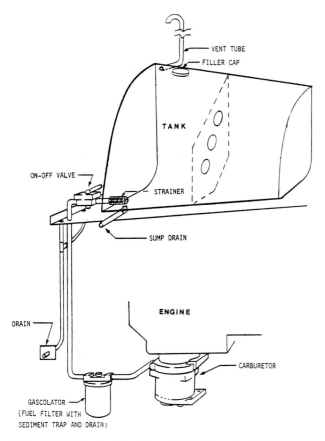

FIG. 11-33 Fuel system for a light helicopter. *(Robinson Helicopter Company, Inc.)*

on the instrument panel when the fuel quantity is less than 1.5 gal [5.68 L].

From the tank coarse finger screen, fuel flows through an on-off valve, then through a filter (gascolator), and then to the engine carburetor.

The fuel system shown in the drawing of Fig. 11-34 and in the schematic of Fig. 11-35 is described here briefly as an example of a fuel system for a turbine-engine-powered helicopter. Observe that the system includes many of the features of a jet transport airplane system as described previously.

The fuel system shown in these two figures is utilized on a model of the Sikorsky S-61N helicopter with a two-tank system. This system is an open-vent type consisting of two fuel tanks and associated pumps, filters, fuel lines, valves, and indicating components. The tanks are rubberized (synthetic) fabric fuel cells installed in tank compartments where they are adequately supported by the structure below the cabin floor panels. The forward tank supplies fuel to the No. 1 engine and the heating system, and the aft tank supplies fuel to the No. 2 engine. Separate filler caps on the left side of the helicopter permit gravity filling of the individual tanks if pressure fueling is not available. Each tank has three vents which terminate to the atmosphere of the left side of the fuselage.

A pressure fueling system allows the fuel tanks to be filled automatically by means of a pressure-fueling adapter on the left side of the helicopter. In conjunction with the pressure-fueling system, a fuel-level selector system, controlled from the cockpit, actuates the fueling shutoff valve in the pressure-fueling system to shut off fuel at a preselected level. Pressure fueling is controlled from the cockpit with the exception of the additional controls outside the fuselage that are used to precheck the pressure-fueling high-level shutoff valves, at the start of the pressure-fueling operations.

The fuel distribution system is such that each engine is provided with a specific fuel supply source as required by FAR. However, flexibility of operation is accomplished by means of the **cross-feed system** and valve. The cross-feed valve is controlled from the cockpit and offers the pilot the option of operating both engines from one tank if necessary. Fuel is pumped from each tank to its respective engine by two submerged motor-driven booster pumps. Each pair of pumps is installed in a **fuel collector can** installed in the forward part of each tank. During operation, a portion of the fuel from the booster pumps is routed back to a **fuel ejector** in the tank. The fuel ejector consists of a venturi through which fuel is pumped. The low pressure caused by the flow through the venturi draws additional fuel from the ejector location in the tank, and this fuel is delivered to the collector cans in the tank. This assures that there will always be an adequate amount of fuel in the boost pump area, regardless of aircraft attitude, to avoid fuel starvation of the engines.

Fuel flow from the tanks is to a lower fuselage fuel control which consists of a manual shutoff valve and a fuel filter. Fuel, piped from the filter to the engine through the upper fuselage, passes through a motor-

the line between the emergency shutoff valve and the engine-driven pump, and **fuel pressure** to the engine fuel nozzles.

Two fuel-quantity indicators are mounted in the upper left side of the instrument panel. They are calibrated in pounds × 100 and provide for a maximum of 1400 lb [635 kg] of fuel each. The transmitters (probes) are of the capacitance type as described previously and are located in the fuel cells. The transmitting probe installed in the rear tank is provided with a thermistor sensor which provides the signal for **low-level fuel,** indicated at the **master warning panel.**

Warning of insufficient pressure from the booster pumps is provided by pressure switches which activate warning lights on the **fuel-management panel** located in the cockpit. The **low-pressure warning lights,** which indicate low fuel pressure to the engine-driven pumps, are also located on the fuel-management panel.

Warning of clogged fuel filters is indicated by **fuel bypass** lights on the **master warning panel.** These lights are activated through pressure switches incorporated in the filter bypasses.

Warning of an overheat condition in the engine compartment is indicated by the illumination of lights in the **fire emergency shutoff selector handles** and by illumination of lights on the **fire warning panel.** Fuel piped through the upper fuselage en route to the engine passes through a motor-operated valve (**emergency shutoff valve**) which is an integral part of the emergency fuel-shutoff system. These valves are shown in the schematic drawing of Fig. 11-35.

● INSPECTION, MAINTENANCE, AND REPAIR OF FUEL SYSTEMS

The proper and regular inspection of aircraft fuel systems is critical to the safe operation of the aircraft. The failure of a component may result in an engine failure due to insufficient fuel being delivered or in a fire on the aircraft. While the following text provides general information concerning fuel systems, aircraft manufacturers provide specific guidelines as to the methods and frequency of maintenance actions for their aircraft.

Fuel Tank Inspections and Repairs

Fuel tank inspections involve visual inspection for any evidence of leaks. Gasoline has an identification dye added, and this dye concentrates around fuel leaks, making them easy to spot. Turbine fuel leaks are harder to spot when they are fresh, but the collection of dirt on the leak and discoloration make the leaks evident in a short period of time.

Fuel leaks are classified as a **stain,** a **seep,** a **heavy seep,** and a **running leak** as shown in Fig. 11-36. The general rules for these leaks is that any leak in an enclosed area is considered a fire hazard and the aircraft should not be flown. Stains, seeps, and heavy seeps are not flight hazards when on the outside of the aircraft and away from ignition sources. A running leak on the outside of the aircraft is considered a fire hazard. All leaks that are evident should be investi-

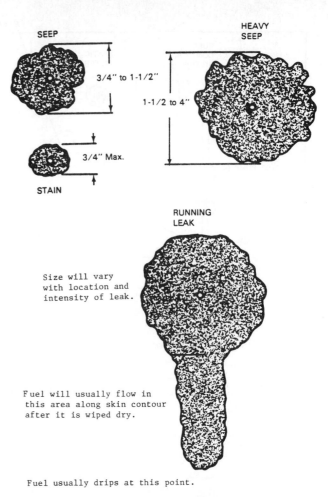

FIG. 11-36 Classification of fuel leaks. (*Cessna Aircraft Co.*)

gated to determine their cause, and if they are not a fire or flight hazard, they should be repaired during the next regular maintenance activity. All leaks should be considered a fire hazard until evaluated, and each situation should be evaluated based on the aircraft manufacturer's recommendations.

When inspecting rigid removable and bladder-type fuel tank installations, fuel leaks appearing on the skin of the aircraft are cause to inspect the fuel tank. First check all fittings for security and evidence of leaking. Also check the gasket where the fuel quantity sensor is mounted in the tank. Check the fuel filler neck and fuel cap for any evidence of leakage. If no cause can be found, it may be necessary to remove the fuel tank from the aircraft and check it for leaks. Leaks should show up with a visual inspection. On occasion the tank or bladder may have to be pressurized with air and brushed with soapy water to locate leaks. Perform this inspection in accordance with the manufacturer's instructions.

Integral fuel tank inspections are similar to those for other types of fuel tanks. These tanks often have access panels on the surfaces which can leak. The aircraft manufacturer will recommend a sealing compound to be used when installing these panels. If the seal is broken, the compound must be replaced with new material.

The interior surfaces and especially the bottoms of fuel tanks should be examined for the growth of microorganisms, that is, bacteria and fungi. If dark-colored, slimy growths are found, the tank should be cleaned thoroughly. Some manufacturers recommend the use of denatured ethyl alcohol as a cleaning agent. After the microbial growths are removed, the metal surfaces of the tank should be checked for corrosion. If corrosion has penetrated the metal surfaces beyond manufacturer-specified limits, the tank should be repaired.

Before actual repair procedures are described, it is important to consider certain safety precautions. The fuel vapor present in all empty fuel tanks is explosive; therefore caution should be observed in their repair. The following steps are recommended to eliminate fire and explosion hazards: The tank drain plug should be removed, and live steam circulated through the tank by placing the steam line in the filler neck opening. This steaming should continue for at least ½ h.

In another common procedure, hot water (150°F [65.56°C]) is allowed to flow through the tank from the bottom and out the top for 1 h. **Never apply heat to a tank when it is installed in an airplane.** This safety procedure applies only to welded or soldered metal tanks, not to riveted ones. The use of hot water in a riveted tank may loosen the sealing compound between joints and cause leaks. While heat is not required for rivet repairs, the tank should be purged with an inert gas, as described below, to prevent ignition of fuel vapors by any sparks such as from the use of tools.

The **purging of fuel tanks** with an inert gas is an acceptable procedure. This is accomplished by first filling the tank with water, then introducing CO_2, nitrogen, or some other inert gas into the tank as it is drained. An adapter plug is prepared to fit the filler opening of the tank, and a hose from the gas supply is connected to the adapter plug. The gas under controlled pressure flows into the tank as the fuel drains. When the tank is completely drained, it is filled with the gas, thus preventing any chance of combustion.

Metal fuel tanks are repaired by welding, soldering, or riveting. The repair method used, of course, depends on the construction of the tank. Tanks constructed of commercially pure aluminum 3003S, 5052SO, or similar metals may be repaired by welding. Heat-treated aluminum alloy tanks are generally put together by riveting. When it is necessary to repair a riveted tank with a riveted patch, a sealing compound that is insoluble in gasoline should be used to seal the patch. If the tank is to be used with aromatic fuels, the sealing compound must be of a type that is insoluble in aromatic fuel.

Leaks in tanks may be located by plugging all the outlets except one and admitting air pressure of about 2½ psi [17.24 kPa]. The application of soapy water on the seams of the tank will cause bubbles to form wherever a leak exists. The areas of leakage should then be marked and the repair made by using the proper method.

One type of solder repair used on stainless steel tanks is accomplished by applying a cover patch of

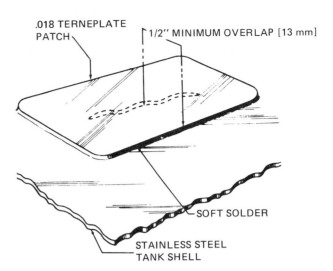

FIG. 11-37 Solder patch for a metal fuel tank.

0.018 terneplate over the crack and soldering it in place with soft solder. The patch is cut and formed so that it overlaps the damaged area by approximately ½ in [1.27 cm]. Figure 11-37 illustrates this method.

After a soldering repair is made, the tank must be flushed with warm water to remove all traces of the soldering flux and any solder beads that may have fallen into it. Similarly, after welding a fuel tank, it is necessary to remove all the welding flux to prevent corrosion. This is accomplished by immediately washing the inside and outside surfaces of the tank with hot water. After the water bath, the tank is drained and then filled with a 5 percent nitric or sulfuric acid solution. This solution should be allowed to remain in the tank for 1 h, after which the tank should be rinsed with clean fresh water. The outside weld also should be washed with the acid solution. To ensure that the water has removed all the corrosive elements, a small quantity of 5% silver nitrate should be placed in a sample of the rinse water. If a heavy white precipitate results, the rinsing operation should be repeated.

Minor seepage in a riveted tank can be repaired with a sealing compound, such as Thiokol B-18, applied externally. To do this, first clean the surface of all dirt, grease, and corrosion. The appropriate type of metal wool may be used for this purpose. After the surface is thoroughly cleaned, apply two coats of the compound, using a small brush. The first coat should be fairly thick, and after it has been allowed to dry for approximately 30 min, a second light coat should be applied and allowed to dry for 48 h.

Another often-used method for correcting minor seepage in a metal tank is **sloshing** the inside of the tank with an approved sloshing compound. The tank is thoroughly cleaned inside, then a specified amount of the compound is poured into the tank and sloshed until the interior surface is completely coated. The remaining compound is poured from the tank, and the tank is allowed to cure for the time specified by the manufacturer of the compound. If an integral tank is to have a sloshing compound applied, the compound will have to be applied by brushing or spraying.

Dripping or running leaks in a riveted tank must be

repaired by tightening the metal seam. This is done by drilling out all worn and damaged rivets near the leak and replacing them with new rivets. The new rivets should be headed by using a pneumatic squeeze riveter if such a tool is available and can be applied correctly to the rivet. It is good practice to dip the new rivets in Thiokol or similar compound before installation. This compound should also be applied to the seam in the same manner as for stopping seepage. If it is necessary to rivet a patch in place, a sealing compound that is insoluble in gasoline should be used. Bakelite varnish, Thiokol, neoprene, and zinc chromate compound are acceptable sealing cements for this purpose.

The repair of synthetic-rubber fuel bladders or cells is usually described in the manufacturer's overhaul manual. Typical of such instructions for an outside patch are the following:

1. Use a piece of synthetic-rubber-coated outside repair material (U.S. Rubber Company 5136) large enough to cover the damage at least 2 in [5.08 cm] from the cut in any direction. Buff this material lightly and thoroughly with fine sandpaper, and wash with methyl ethyl ketone (U.S. Rubber Company 3339 solution) to remove buffing dust.

2. Cement the buffed side of the patch with two coats of black rubber cement (3M Company EC678). Allow each coat to dry 10 to 15 min.

3. Buff the cell area to be patched lightly and thoroughly with fine sandpaper, and wash with methyl ethyl ketone to remove buffing dust.

4. Cement the buffed area with two coats of 3M Company EC678 cement. Allow to dry 10 to 15 min.

5. Freshen the cemented area of the patch and the cemented area of the cell with methyl ethyl ketone.

6. While still tacky, apply the edge of the patch to the edge of the cemented area and roll or press it down ½ to 1 in [1.27 to 2.54 cm] at a time to prevent air from being trapped between the patch and the cell.

7. Seal the patch and a ½-in [1.27-cm] strip of the cell around the patch with one coat of black rubber cement, and allow the patch to remain undisturbed for 6 h.

A damaged synthetic-rubber fuel cell must be patched inside as well as outside when the damage goes entirely through the cell wall. Typical instructions for the inside patching process are as follows:

1. After the damaged area has been patched on the outside of the cell and the repair allowed to stand a minimum of 6 h, the cell is ready to have the patch applied on the inside of the cell. The damaged area to which this patch is to be applied may be pulled through the filler-neck opening to make the repair simpler.

2. Lightly and thoroughly buff a piece of Buna nylon sandwich material (U.S. Rubber Company 5063).

3. Cement the patch opposite the red fabric side with two coats of the same cement used for the outside patch, allowing each coat to dry 10 to 15 min.

4. Buff the cell area to be patched lightly and thoroughly with fine sandpaper, then wash off the dust with methyl ethyl ketone.

5. Coat the buffed area of the cell with two coats of cement, allowing each coat to dry 10 to 15 min.

6. Freshen the cemented areas of the patch and cell with methyl ethyl ketone.

7. While the cemented areas are still tacky, apply the edge of the patch to the edge of the cemented area, centering the patch over the cut in the fuel cell. Hold part of the patch off the cemented area, and roll or press it down ½ in [1.27 cm] across at a time to avoid trapping air between the patch and the cell.

8. Remove the red fabric from the patch by moistening it with methyl ethyl ketone.

9. Seal-coat the patch and a ½-in [1.27-cm] strip of the cell around the patch with two coats of the black cement. Allow the first coat to dry 15 min and allow the second coat to dry 12 h or more, so that when the cell is in its original position, the patching area will not stick to other areas of the cell.

Thick-walled fuel cells such as those installed in transport aircraft can be repaired using methods and materials similar to those described above. In every case, however, the repair should be accomplished in accordance with manufacturer's instructions and by a person trained in the procedures.

In general, the reinstallation of fuel tanks or cells is accomplished by reversing the process of removal. When metal tanks are reinstalled, the felt padding should be examined for condition. If new felt is installed, it should be treated to make it nonabsorbent. Rawhide leather, which contains free alkalies, is unsuitable for padding an aluminum tank because excessive corrosion will take place where the pad comes in contact with the metal. The tanks must be anchored securely and vibration held to a minimum, especially where aluminum alloy tanks are used, since such tanks are subject to cracking.

Metal tanks are subject to both internal and external corrosion, and steps should be taken to prevent this. Zinc chromate or epoxy primers are satisfactory. Internal corrosion may be prevented by the use of dichromate crystals in a separate container located in the tank sump. This latter practice is not commonly employed in modern aircraft because most fuel tanks are designed so that it is possible to drain all water out of the tanks by means of the sump drains. Fuel tanks are often coated internally to prevent corrosion.

Synthetic-rubber bladders and cells are held in place by lacing cord, snaps, or other fasteners. The reinstallation procedure must follow the manufacturer's instructions to ensure that the cells are properly supported in the tank compartment. The area in which the cell is installed must be inspected to make sure that there are no sharp edges or protrusions to cause wear or other damage to the cells. Any portion of the structure that may cause damage must be covered with nonabsorbent padding.

Fuel tanks must be capable of withstanding certain pressure tests without failure or leakage. These pressures may be applied in a manner simulating the actual pressure distribution in service.

Conventional metal tanks with walls that are not supported by the aircraft structure must withstand a pressure of 3.5 psi [24.13 kPa]. If there is any doubt regarding the airworthiness of a particular fuel tank, it may be tested by applying air pressure through a pressure regulator set to 3.5 psi [24.13 kPa]. If this is done, great care must be taken to avoid excessive pressure.

The mechanic is not usually obliged to carry out all the tests for tanks required by Federal Air Regulations for original testing of tanks. Tests required at overhaul periods will be described in the manufacturer's overhaul manual.

Fuel System Inspections

The preflight inspection of a fuel system includes checking the fuel tanks visually for quantity of fuel. This requires the removal of tank caps and looking into fuel tanks. Sometimes a dipstick must be used in order to determine that the proper quantity of fuel is in the tanks. (Dipsticks should not be made of any material that will hold a charge of static electricity which could arc to the aircraft and ignite fuel vapors.) Another most important preflight inspection of the fuel system is the opening of fuel drains. All fuel drains should be opened for a few seconds to allow any accumulated water or sediment to drain out of the system. Other preflight inspections may be established by the owner or operator of the aircraft under particular circumstances, and, in each case, the required inspection should be carried out before the airplane is flown.

During engine runup, the fuel pressure and the proper operation of booster pumps should be checked. If any malfunction is found in the fuel system, the airplane should not be flown until the malfunction is corrected.

A 25-h routine inspection of the fuel system probably will not require more than a visual inspection for signs of fuel leakage and draining of the main fuel strainer. During the visual inspection, the security of all lines and fittings should be checked. Special inspections may be required after 25 h of operation for a new engine or a new airplane. These inspections are recommended because metal particles and other foreign matter may have accumulated during the first 25 h of flight. In such instances it is advisable to clean all fuel strainers, drains, and vent lines. All fittings, mountings, and attachments should be checked for security.

The 100-h and annual inspections require a complete examination of the fuel system. All fuel strainers should be removed and cleaned, all drains should be opened, and sumps should be drained to make sure that all sediment and water is removed from the system. The carburetor float chamber should be drained to remove water and sediment, and the carburetor fuel filter should be cleaned. All fuel lines and hoses should be examined carefully for condition, security, and wear due to rubbing on any portion of the structure. Any unsatisfactory condition must be corrected. The primer system and oil-dilution system should be checked for satisfactory operation.

Fuel tanks should be checked for leaks, corrosion, and microorganism growth as previously discussed.

Fuel tank caps should be examined for proper venting; that is, the vent opening should be checked for obstructions. If a cap is unserviceable, it should be replaced with one of the correct make and model for the installation. Substitution of the wrong type of cap can cause loss of fuel or fuel starvation. Fuel caps with special venting arrangements must be replaced with the same type.

Fuel tank vents and vent lines should be checked for obstructions. This can be accomplished by passing air through such vents. It is usually necessary to disconnect one end of a vent line for this inspection. Manufacturer's instructions should be followed. Fuel-system vent lines should be installed so there are no low points that are not drainable. Such points can collect water and cause the tubing to become corroded and possibly plugged. During inspection, the routing of the vent tubing should be examined to assure that it conforms to the requirements for fuel lines. Tubing that is plugged should be removed, thoroughly cleaned, and checked for corrosion damage.

Fuel-shutoff valves and tank selector valves should be checked for effectiveness and accuracy of valve handle position. Leakage can be checked by turning a valve off, disconnecting the line downstream of the valve, and turning on the booster pump briefly. If fuel flows with the valve turned off, the valve should be repaired or replaced. Fuel-selector valves should be rotated through their tank positions to see if a full flow of fuel flows from each tank when the valve is positioned at the detent indicating that tank.

Fuel-pressure, quantity, and temperature gauges should be given an operational check. If there is any indication of malfunction or inaccuracy, the gauge should be removed for bench checking. Fuel-quantity gauges are checked on the aircraft in accordance with manufacturer's instructions. Typical instructions for such a check are as follows:

1. Completely drain the fuel tank including unusable fuel.
2. Put the amount of fuel in the tank that is specified as unusable.
3. Check the quantity gauge to see that it reads zero.
4. Add fuel to the tank in increments of 10 gal [37.9 L] and check the quantity gauge at each increment to see that it accurately indicates the correct amount of fuel in the tank within acceptable limits.

During a test of the fuel-quantity gauge as described above, the airplane should be in a normal level flight attitude. Otherwise a false reading will be given by the quantity gauges.

The proper operation of a multitank fuel system can be checked by using the boost pumps to move fuel from one tank to another through the various combinations available. The cross-feed valve or valves are set as desired, and the appropriate fuel boost pumps turned on. The increase in fuel quantity in the tank being filled is noted on the fuel-quantity gauge. If the line to the tank being filled includes a flow indicator, this can be used to determine fuel flow.

Fuel-pressure and temperature warning systems are checked by artificially inducing the conditions in the systems which should produce the appropriate alarm. Fuel-pressure warning lights are easily checked by noting whether they come on as fuel pressure drops during shutdown.

The foregoing are examples of methods for making the indicated inspections and checks. In practice, the methods given in the manufacturer's or operator's instructions should be followed.

Required inspections are usually listed in the manufacturer's service manual, and all special inspections should be accomplished as specified.

Fuel Lines and Fittings

The maintenance and repair of fuel lines and fittings are the same as those practiced in the maintenance and repair of hydraulic systems and other systems requiring plumbing. Additional information is given in the associated text, *Aircraft Basic Science*.

The proper maintenance of fuel lines and fittings is particularly important because of the flammability of fuel. A small fuel leak in a confined area of an airplane can soon produce an explosive atmosphere which can be ignited by any kind of spark.

In the replacement of fittings which join sections of tubing or hose, the mechanic must make certain that the mating parts of a fitting are compatible. Parts of fittings may appear to mate properly and still not produce a dependable seal because of slight differences in threads or internal design.

Fuel lines must be routed and supported in such a manner that they will not be damaged by vibration, abrasion, or chafing. Fuel lines must be kept separate from electrical wiring except in cases where this is not possible. If fuel lines and electrical wiring must be routed together, the fuel line must be located below the electrical wiring and clamped securely to the aircraft structure. The electrical wiring must not be supported by the fuel line but must be separately attached to the airframe structure.

Tubing bends must be located accurately so that the tubing is aligned with all support clamps and end fittings and is not drawn, pulled, or otherwise forced into place by the fittings. A straight section of tubing must not be installed between two rigidly mounted fittings because expansion and contraction due to temperature changes will cause stresses which may cause the fittings to fail. Vibrational stresses are also a factor; hence at least one bend should be in a tube between fittings to absorb the stresses.

Metallic fuel lines must be bonded at each point where they are clamped to the structure. Clamps with integral metal bonding strips and cushioned line support are preferred over other clamp and bonding methods.

To prevent possible failure of lines and fittings, all fittings heavy enough to cause the line to sag should be supported by means other than the tubing. Support clamps for metallic lines should be spaced according to the following table:

Tube OD	Distance between Supports
1/8–1/16 in	9 in [22.86 cm]
1/4–5/16 in	12 in [30.49 cm]
3/8–1/2 in	16 in [40.64 cm]
5/8–3/4 in	22 in [55.88 cm]
1–1 1/4 in	30 in [76.20 cm]
1 1/4–2 in	40 in [101.6 cm]

Where bends occur in metal tubing, supporting clamps should be placed as close to the bends as possible to reduce **overhang**. Overhang is the distance that the bend extends outward from a line intersecting the inside points of clamp support at the two clamps on each side of the bend.

Before fuel lines and hoses are installed, they should be carefully inspected. Aluminum or aluminum alloy lines should not be annealed after forming because such materials are very sensitive to high temperatures and it is not possible to obtain a proper annealing of the material, except under carefully controlled conditions. On the other hand, copper tubing can be satisfactorily annealed merely by heating it to a cherry red and then quenching it in cold water.

Fuel lines should be inspected for scratches, abrasion, corrosion, kinks, dents, cuts, or any other damage that may cause them to be unairworthy. The end fittings should be examined for cracks, cross threads, flattening, and other damage. The lines should be checked for cleanliness inside so that there will be no danger of putting foreign material in the system.

Fuel hoses should be inspected, especially at the ends where the fittings are installed. Damaged fittings should be replaced. Hose assemblies that have worn surfaces, swelling, or leaks of any kind should be replaced. Many hose assemblies are equipped with reusable end fittings. When such fittings are damaged, they may be replaced as shown in Fig. 11-38. Undamaged fittings may also be removed from damaged tubing and used on new tubing. The steps for installation of the hose fittings are as follows:

1. Mount the end socket in a vise or other holding fixture, and screw the square end of the hose into the socket by turning the hose counterclockwise into the left-hand thread. The cover should not be removed from the hose.

2. Assemble the hose insert, tube nut, tube connector, and mandrel. Tighten the tube nut until the assembly is rigid. (Tube sizes 16 and over do not require a mandrel.)

3. Lubricate the hose ID and the insert of the subassembly with lubricating oil or light grease.

4. Screw the subassembly into the hose and socket. Leave 1/16-in [1.59-mm] clearance so that the nut is free to rotate.

During the assembly of fuel lines and hoses, it is important that certain standard practices be followed. These are as follows:

1. Tube and hose fittings should never be forced into place.

2. Fittings should be in accurate alignment before assembling. Alignment should be such that the fittings can be assembled and screwed together by hand.

3. No tube or hose should be under tension or other stress after fittings are tightened.

4. All fittings should be carefully checked for cleanliness before assembly.

5. Fittings should be tightened with the proper torque as specified by the manufacturer.

When tube fittings are assembled, no lubrication or joint compound should be used except for petroleum-type lubricating oil or petroleum jelly. In certain in-

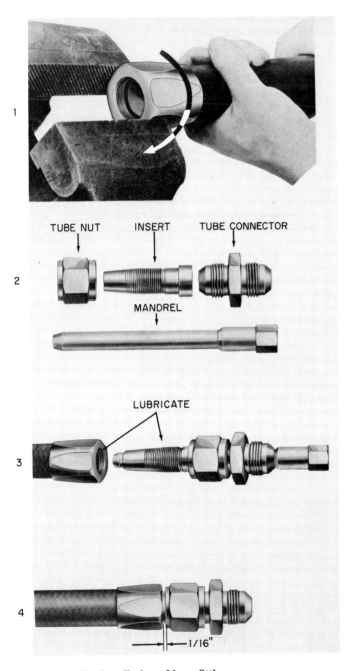

FIG. 11-38 **Installation of hose fittings.**

stances an approved-type thread compound may be used with pipe fittings, but the compound must not be of the hardening type. A small amount of the compound may be applied to the male threads of the assembly.

● TROUBLESHOOTING

Accurate and rapid troubleshooting on a fuel system necessitates a complete understanding of the operation and purpose of the entire system and its various units. Most aircraft mechanics are able to make quick and satisfactory repairs after a trouble has been located but may have problems when trying to trace the source of the difficulty. As in all troubleshooting, if the mechanic follows a definite plan, or procedure, in locating a defective unit, time is saved, and the long process of haphazardly removing unit after unit with the hope that eventually the trouble will be found is eliminated.

The first step in locating a fuel-system defect is to analyze the symptoms. This gives a clue as to the identity of the units or parts of the system that are defective or inoperative. In this way, by logical reasoning, the faulty unit can be ascertained and checked and the necessary servicing steps taken.

In checking for fuel-system troubles, a close observance of the action of the gauges, indicators, and various units of the system is important. Several typical examples of fuel-system troubleshooting procedures are as follows:

The daily line inspection shows an adequate fuel supply, and the check of the strainer indicates a normal flow of fuel through the strainer drain, but when the boost pump is turned on, the fuel-pressure-indicator needle fluctuates slightly and does not register the correct pressure.

Since the flow of fuel to the strainer is normal, the trouble could not be in the tank screen, the selector valve, or the lines to the strainer. The trouble must exist between the strainer and the carburetor. As the fuel-pressure connection is taken from the float-chamber side of the carburetor screen, improper fuel pressure at the gauge would indicate that the fuel is restricted at some point between the carburetor bowl and the strainer. This would call for the removal of the carburetor screen. If it is clear, hose fittings between the carburetor and the strainer are loosened and the hoses are disconnected in succession. After each hose is disconnected, the boost pump is operated to check for a free flow of fuel at this point. The restriction in the line is thus located systematically.

Another example of troubleshooting procedure is as follows: An engine is started on the primer charge but does not continue to run unless the boost pump is left turned on. The fuel-pressure indicator shows normal pressure as long as the pump is operated, but it becomes erratic and the reading drops when the boost pump is turned off.

The trouble should be approached logically. In the discussion earlier in the text, it was shown that the boost pump uses the same line as the engine-driven pump to force fuel to the carburetor. It was also shown that a bypass valve is incorporated in the engine-driven fuel pump to allow fuel under boost-pump pressure to flow around the engine-driven pump rotor and vanes. The lines and units of the system are not blocked since the engine will operate under boost-pump pressure. Thus it is obvious that the trouble is in the engine-driven pump.

In general, when a normally operating fuel pump suddenly ceases to function, it should be removed for dismantling and inspection. However, before doing this, the pressure-relief-valve setting should be readjusted while the boost pump is being operated. If this does not correct the trouble, the procedure for removing the pump should be followed.

Another example of troubleshooting procedure involves an airplane that is equipped with a gravity-feed fuel system and a float-type carburetor. The engine is started, runs normally for a few minutes, and then stops. After a short period of time, the engine is restarted; it runs for a few minutes and again stops.

Judging from the symptoms, it is apparent that for one reason or another the supply of fuel is restricted. When the engine is not running, the carburetor float chamber fills with fuel, but when the engine is started, the supply drops off sharply. An experienced mechanic would probably know immediately the cause of this trouble. The beginner, however, would get along better by adopting a fixed procedure. The first step in such a procedure in this particular case would be to isolate the part of the fuel system causing the trouble. The gascolator, or strainer drain, is opened and shows a restricted fuel supply. Thus, it is determined that the fault is located somewhere in the system between the tank and the strainer. The next step would be to isolate the trouble still further by disconnecting a line on the engine side of the shutoff cock. If this is done and it is seen that the flow of fuel is still restricted, the elimination procedure is continued; but before the tank screen is removed, the tank vent is checked. In this case it was found to be clogged. Other units, such as the carburetor, can cause the same symptoms to appear. Hence it is better to follow a definite procedure that isolates the trouble rather than to start checking the first unit that comes to mind.

Yet another example of troubleshooting procedure may be given: A pilot reports that the fuel pressure was normal on the ground but that it increased with altitude. Such a condition is obviously caused by the fuel-pump pressure-relief valve.

The relief-valve pressure setting itself cannot be at fault since the pressure was normal on the ground. Hence the fault must be due to the altitude-compensating part of the valve. An increase in fuel pressure with altitude is the result of improper balance on the diaphragm between carburetor-scoop pressure and atmospheric pressure on the fuel in the tanks. In other words, ground atmospheric pressure is trapped on the top of the fuel-pressure–relief-valve diaphragm. Therefore there must be a restriction in the fuel-pressure–relief-valve vent. The vent line, from the fuel-pump relief valve to the carburetor scoop, is disconnected, and the restrictor fitting is cleaned with the shank end of a twist drill of the proper size.

Still another example of troubleshooting concerns an engine that is started and "gallops" at idling speed. The tachometer shows the rpm at idle to be excessively low. As the throttle is opened, the fuel mixture becomes richer, a condition that is indicated by black smoke coming from the exhaust pipe.

This trouble may be due to the carburetor, but it is assumed that the carburetor is functioning normally. Some unit in the fuel system other than the carburetor is allowing fuel to enter the engine cylinders. The only unit that can do this is the primer. If a hand primer is used and the handle is not locked in the closed position, the engine will siphon fuel from the strainer through the primer and into the cylinders through the intake valves; or if a solenoid-operated primer valve sticks, the same trouble will result. Hence, when such indications appear, the priming system should be checked first.

Any malfunctioning of the fuel system that causes violent backfiring through the carburetor and induction system should be investigated immediately. If this malfunctioning is allowed to continue, serious engine damage may result, with the possible loss of the airplane. Backfiring can be caused by sticking intake valves, intake valve clearances that are too close, and fuel-system units that, through their failure, cause excessively lean mixtures. Lean mixtures are generally caused by a faulty carburetor, low fuel pressure, or allowing one fuel tank to run dry before switching to another.

Operating Data Helpful in Troubleshooting

In troubleshooting the fuel system, it is most helpful to have a good overall knowledge of the particular airplane in which the trouble is encountered. Just as the physician in diagnosing the illness of a patient tries to get a good knowledge of the patient's general health before prescribing a remedy for a particular ailment, so should mechanics learn to know the various operating weaknesses (if any) of the airplanes they customarily repair. This information is obtained by observation, from conversations with the pilots, or from the flight record forms. Generally, the engine operation temperatures and pressures are the most reliable clues to any fuel-system trouble that may be encountered.

Fuel-system troubles are rather elementary, but usually they occur more frequently than troubles encountered in the carburetor; and since they greatly affect the operation of the airplane, they should be corrected as quickly as possible. In their effect on the engine they can be said to be general in nature. An ignition-system trouble, such as a faulty spark plug, will affect only one cylinder of an engine in the first instance; fuel-system troubles may affect all cylinders and result in complete engine failure. For this reason, the fuel system requires the close attention of an expert and capable mechanic.

● FUELING AND DEFUELING AIRCRAFT

One of the little thought of, yet important, duties of the aircraft mechanic is servicing the airplane with fuel. In doing this work, care must always be exercised to avoid overlooking some detail of the task that might result in great damage being done to the airplane, not to mention the serious injury that may befall the pilot through some negligence. Fire is a hazard in any occupation, but it is particularly a great danger with regard to refueling the airplane.

Mechanics need to "keep their heads about them" in doing any of the maintenance required for an airplane, but in servicing it with fuel or in checking its fuel system, they **must keep their minds on their work** or great damage may result. Not only must the mechanic be conscious of every operation during the refueling task, but all personnel must be aware of the seriousness of the job and be properly warned when it is in progress. To this end, rules and restrictions have been set up by airlines to prevent any mistakes being made. In general, if cleanliness, carefulness, good judgment, exactness, and thoroughness are stressed in doing the job, it will be done efficiently and with little danger. Other workers in the area should be cautioned against doing any work on the airplane while it is being refueled.

Note that refueling a small, privately owned airplane is a vastly different operation from refueling a modern jet-transport airplane. Between these two extremes there is a wide variety of airplane characteristics to be considered.

There is much more to the refueling operation than meets the eye. The procedure is considerably more complex than merely unfastening a tank cap and putting in fuel as you would in an automobile. In the first place it is desirable to fill the tanks at the end of a flight rather than at the beginning. In this way the possibility of moisture collecting in the tank is greatly lessened. If the airplane has been flying at high altitudes, the remaining fuel in the tank will be cold, and at the warmer ground temperatures condensation from moisture in the air will form on the inner tank walls and settle into the tank.

Water condensation occurs under substantial changes in air temperature whether such changes occur during the day or between day and night. This is a particularly important consideration in areas of the country where high humidity is common and where large changes of temperature occur. Airplane operators in these areas must be diligent in carrying out regular drainage of points in the fuel system where water can collect.

When the fuel tank is filled at the end of a flight, there is only a small amount of air space in the tank in which water condensation can take place. The filling of fuel tanks at the end of a flight also reduces the volume of explosive vapors which can collect in fuel tanks, and this reduces fire danger to some extent. A filled fuel tank also assures an ample supply of fuel for the next takeoff, and since the refueling operation is, of necessity, a painstaking and time-consuming task, the advantage of doing the job at the end of a flight is obvious.

Refueling Procedure

Assuming that the refueling job is about to begin, the following procedure is recommended:

1. The person assigned to the task should first see to it that the airplane is in a safe place, the wheels carefully chocked, or the brakes set and all safety precautions observed. If fuel is to be taken from a truck, it should be driven up carefully and positioned parallel to the wings of the airplane at a reasonable distance from it.

2. Fire extinguishers should be placed within easy reach in case of fire.

3. Every piece of equipment used in doing the work should be absolutely clean. The refueling hoze nozzle should be wiped clean with a cloth free of lint and dirt. The hose nozzle should never be dragged over any part of the airplane or the ground.

4. The amount of fuel needed and the grade should be ascertained. It is very important that the airplane be refueled with gasoline or turbine fuel of the correct grade. Efficient performance of the engine depends upon this. Every aircraft engine requires fuel of a specific grade, and this information will be found marked on or near the fuel filler cap. Substitution of fuel may cause trouble that may very well prove serious.

5. If the person refueling the aircraft is required to stand or walk on any unprotected part of the airplane during the operation, the part or parts of the airplane involved should be protected with canvas covers.

6. It should be understood that gasoline flowing through a hose may build up a charge of static electricity. When the refueling hose nozzle is withdrawn from the tank, the charge of static will ignite the fuel. For this reason, before starting the refueling operation, the nozzle of the hose must be grounded.

Usually refueling hoses have ground wires attached, in which case all that needs to be done is to connect the wire (by means of the clip provided) to some metal part of the airplane. If a ground wire is not available, a short length of wire to which suitable clips have been soldered will serve the purpose. Two of these wires are needed. One end of one of the wires should be attached to the metal part of the nozzle; the other end should be clipped to the aircraft metal structure. The remaining wire is used similarly to "ground" the airplane to the earth in much the same manner that a fuel delivery truck is grounded by a ground wire and clip. The airplane grounding wire should be attached to some metal part permanently embedded in the earth.

Where fuel is drawn from a fuel pit, the same procedure of grounding the airplane is followed. In this case there should be an electrical connection between the fuel nozzle and the underground tank and the airplane also should be grounded to the earth.

7. Care must be exercised to avoid damaging the filler neck of the airplane fuel tank when the tank is being filled with gasoline. The fuel-hose nozzle should be carefully supported and the fuel introduced slowly so that there absolutely is no danger of splashing or overfilling the fuel tank.

Refueling Large Jet Aircraft

Modern jet or turboprop aircraft are usually equipped with single-point, underwing refueling systems. This means that a fuel hose can be connected at one point under the wing of the aircraft to refuel the entire system or that a fueling station is provided under each wing so that all the tanks in one wing can be fueled from one station.

The fueling operation of such a system consists essentially of coupling the fuel-hose nozzles to the receptacles, opening the fueling manual shutoff valves, and pumping fuel to the tanks. The fuel tanks may be filled completely by opening the fueling manual shutoff valves and allowing the fueling level-control valves to shut off the fuel flow. If it is desired to fill the tanks partially, the preset indicators may be employed to show when the desired quantity of fuel has entered a particular tank. At this time an indicator light will turn on and the fuel to the tank can be shut off by means of the manual valve or automatic mechanism.

The fueling of jet-transport aircraft is usually accomplished by trained refueling crews, and it is not necessary that the aircraft mechanic be concerned with the operation. It is well, however, for the mechanic to be familiar with the procedure and the mechanisms involved because malfunctions of the system must be corrected and it is the aircraft mechanic who must correct them.

The procedures for refueling a jet-transport airplane are established by the airline involved, and instructions are published for the guidance of fueling crews. These instructions must be followed to assure safe and effective refueling.

Defueling Aircraft

The **defueling** of aircraft is critical in that the danger of fire is increased owing to fuel tanks being filled with flammable vapors when empty and vapors being produced by spilled fuel, particularly gasoline. The mechanic involved with defueling should take every precaution to reduce the possibility of fire and should observe every rule and regulation established to prevent and combat fires. The **safety** of the procedure is the prime consideration.

Defueling procedures are usually given in manufacturer's aircraft maintenance manuals; however, these cannot always give consideration to conditions that may exist at the time and place of defueling. The mechanic or mechanics involved must, therefore, exercise great care in their preparations and performance to assure that all precautions have been observed.

When an airplane is to be defueled the following general rules should be followed unless other procedures which are just as effective have been established by the aircraft operator or operational organization:

1. Move the aircraft to be defueled to an open area at a distance from any other aircraft, structure, or vehicle such that a fire could not jump from the defueling aircraft to any other unit or structure.

2. Provide fire extinguishers of a type approved for oil fires (for example, dry chemical or CO_2 types) in sizes and numbers adequate for the size of the aircraft and volume of fuel involved. See that operators attend the fire extinguishers constantly while the defueling operation is taking place.

3. If possible, provide a supply of inert gas (nitrogen or CO_2) for purging the tank or tanks as they are being drained.

4. Ground the aircraft to the earth.

5. See that personnel in the area wear shoes with rubber or plastic soles which cannot cause sparks. Cigarette lighters, matches, and other sources of ignition should be removed from the area.

6. Disconnect or remove the aircraft battery.

7. Use no electrical equipment in the area except that which has been certified flameproof.

8. Provide for fuel disposal in a fuel truck or in clean, closed containers. Metal fuel containers which could cause sparks in handling should be avoided.

9. Do not allow fuel to be spilled on the surface beneath the aircraft.

10. If tools are needed to open fuel drain valves, use tools which cannot cause sparks.

11. As soon as fuel containers have been filled, install the container covers or caps. If open containers are used, they should be emptied immediately into containers or tanks which can be closed.

● REVIEW QUESTIONS

1. What requirements have been established to assure *reliability* of fuel systems for aircraft?
2. What is meant by *fuel-system independence?*
3. What are the requirements for lightning protection in fuel systems for aircraft?
4. Give fuel flow rates needed for aircraft systems.
5. Define *unusable* fuel supply.
6. What are the requirements for *hot-weather performance* of fuel systems?
7. Describe an *integral fuel tank design.*
8. How is a *bladder fuel cell* attached to the airframe?
9. Of what materials are fuel tanks constructed?
10. What internal pressures must a fuel tank be able to withstand?
11. How is it possible to inspect the interior of integral wing tanks?
12. What inertial forces must the fuel tanks in a transport aircraft be required to withstand?
13. What is the required capacity of a *fuel-tank sump*?
14. What markings are required at the fuel-filler cap location?
15. What is the general requirement for fuel-tank capacity?
16. Give requirements for fuel-tank installation.
17. Why is a positive pressure required within the vapor space of bladder fuel cells, and how is this pressure maintained?
18. Give the requirements for fuel-cell compartments, including location in the aircraft.
19. Describe the arrangement required for the venting of fuel tanks and how the *vapor elimination systems* of carburetors are interconnected.
20. Give the requirements for fuel-tank outlets.
21. How does an *ejector* fuel pump work?
22. Give the fuel-pump requirements for a fuel system.

23. Describe a *vane-type* fuel pump.
24. Describe a *variable-volume* fuel pump.
25. Explain the need for a *bypass valve* in a fuel pump.
26. What provision is made in a fuel-pump relief valve to compensate for changes in atmospheric pressure?
27. How is fuel-pump pressure adjusted?
28. What is the purpose of a *fuel boost pump*?
29. Where are fuel boost pumps for large aircraft usually located?
30. Describe the requirements for fuel strainers and filters.
31. Explain the operation of a *filter bypass warning system*.
32. Give the requirements for the use of drains in a fuel system.
33. What is the requirement for the installation of fuel-shutoff valves and fuel-system controls with respect to the fuel lines connected to the valve or control?
34. Why are fuel-shutoff valves for large aircraft interconnected with the fire protection systems?
35. What type of engine equipment renders an engine-priming system unnecessary?
36. Why are fuel heaters necessary?
37. What are the purposes of a fuel vent system?
38. Explain the need for an *oil-dilution system* and describe the operation of such a system.
39. What becomes of the fuel mixed with the oil when oil dilution is employed?
40. What provision is made to prevent overfilling of fuel tanks when a *pressure fuel system* is employed?
41. What are the principal requirements for a *fuel jettisoning system*?
42. Discuss the installation of fuel lines and fittings.
43. At what position on a fuel-quantity indicator must a red arc be placed?
44. What markings are required for *fuel-tank selector controls*?
45. How are the fuel lines attached to the outlets of a fuel bladder in a light airplane?
46. What is the purpose of a *vapor-return line* in a fuel system?
47. Briefly describe the fuel system for a large transport-type aircraft.
48. Describe the *fuel-dump system*.
49. What four subsystems compose the fuel system for a DC-10 airplane?
50. What is the function of a *continuous-scavenging system*?
51. Explain the value of a *cross-feed system*.
52. Why does a capacitor-type fuel-indicating system show the quantity of fuel by weight rather than by volume?
53. What is the function of the *fuel-schedule-light system*?
54. What is the purpose of the *fuel-collector cans* in the fuel tanks of the Sikorsky S-61N helicopter?
55. What *fuel-warning indications* are provided in the fuel system for the S-61N helicopter?
56. What inspections should be made of a fuel system immediately before each flight?
57. Describe a 100-h or periodic inspection for a fuel system.
58. What must be done when growth of *microorganisms* is found in a fuel tank?
59. How are fuel-selector valves checked for effectiveness?
60. Describe the four classifications of fuel leaks.
61. What precaution must be observed before repairing a metal fuel tank by soldering or welding?
62. Describe the purging of a fuel tank with inert gas.
63. How may leaks in a fuel tank by discovered?
64. What process must be carried out after repairing a metal fuel tank by soldering or welding? Describe the procedure.
65. How can a seam in a riveted metal fuel tank be sealed?
66. Describe the repair of synthetic-rubber fuel cells by patching.
67. How are synthetic-rubber fuel cells held in place?
68. How may a repaired metal fuel tank be tested?
69. What precautions must be observed in the installation of fuel lines and fitting?
70. Describe a troubleshooting procedure for a fuel system when the engine will not start owing to fuel stoppage.
71. In the operation of a light-airplane engine, the engine starts, then stops in a few minutes. It can be restarted a little later, then stops again. What is the likely cause of trouble?
72. What symptoms are observed when a priming system is leaking into the engine?
73. What fuel-system malfunctions may cause backfiring of the engine?
74. Discuss the precautions which should be observed in the refueling of an airplane.
75. How is the danger of a static electrical spark eliminated when refueling an airplane?
76. What conditions of weather or climate increase the likelihood of water collecting in a fuel tank?
77. Why is it good practice to "top off" a fuel tank immediately after completing a flight?
78. How are large commercial aircraft usually refueled?
79. Describe a safe procedure for *defueling* an airplane.

12 ENVIRONMENTAL SYSTEMS

Environmental systems are those aircraft systems which are used to make the interior environment of the aircraft comfortable and/or habitable for human beings. Depending on the type of aircraft and altitude of operation, this may only involve supplying a flow of fresh air through the cabin by using air vents and scoops. If the temperature must be adjusted for crew and passenger comfort, some method of heating or cooling the cabin interior is required. If the aircraft is to be operated at high altitude, pressurization is necessary to make the environment acceptable to the occupants of the aircraft. Oxygen systems can eliminate the need for pressurization in some instances if the crew and passengers are willing to put up with wearing masks for a portion of the trip.

Emergency oxygen systems are required on pressurized aircraft. This emergency oxygen supply is necessary to prevent injury to passengers and crew if the cabin should lose pressurization and the cabin should go to a high-altitude environment.

● HEATING SYSTEMS

Aircraft **heating systems** range in size and complexity from simple heat exchangers for small single-engine aircraft, through combustion heaters used with larger aircraft, to the use of compressor bleed air systems for turbine-engine-powered aircraft. The system being used may be independent of other systems or integrated into a complete aircraft environmental control package.

Exhaust Heating Systems

The simplest type of heating system, often employed on light aircraft, consists of a heater muff around the engine exhaust stacks, an air scoop to draw ram air into the heater muff, ducting to carry the heated air into the cabin, and a valve to control the flow of heated air. Such a system is shown schematically in Fig. 12-1.

The exhaust heating system for a light airplane, the Piper Cherokee Six, is shown in Fig. 12-2. This drawing also shows the ventilating system for the airplane.

The heating system consists of the muffler and heat shroud, ducting to the air box and windshield defroster outlets, and ducting to the heat outlets in the cabin. The amount of heat delivered to the cabin is controlled from the cockpit.

Exhaust heating systems must be given regular inspections to assure that exhaust fumes cannot enter the cabin of the airplane. This requires that the

shrouds or muffs around the exhaust pipes or mufflers be removed to inspect for cracks through which exhaust fumes can enter the heater ducts. Some manufacturers recommend that this be done every 100 h of operation. One method of checking for cracks is to pressurize the exhaust pipes with compressed air and apply soapy water to all areas where cracks may possibly occur. If there is a crack, the air will cause soap bubbles to form at the crack. When performing this pressure check of the exhaust system, be sure to follow the aircraft manufacturer's instructions so that the exhaust system is not damaged by the application of excessive pressure. Additional information on exhaust systems and exhaust heaters is given in the associated text, *Aircraft Powerplants*.

Combustion Heater Systems

In larger and more expensive aircraft, **combustion heaters,** also referred to as **surface combustion heaters,** are often employed to supply the heat needed for the cabin. This type of heater burns airplane fuel in a combustion chamber or tube to develop the required heat. Air flowing around the tube is heated and carried through ducting to the cabin. A typical South Wind combustion heater system installed in a light twin-engine airplane is shown in Fig. 12-3. The heater is mounted in the right side of the nose section. Fuel is routed from a tee in the fuel cross-feed line through a filter and a solenoid supply valve to the diaphragm-type heater fuel pump. The fuel pump is operated by the combustion air-blower motor which is mounted above the heater assembly. This pump provides the heater with sufficient fuel pressure, and no auxiliary boost pump assistance is necessary for proper operation of the heater.

The heater fuel pump and all external fittings on the

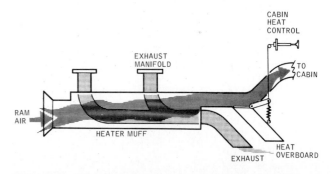

FIG. 12-1 Exhaust heating system for a light airplane.

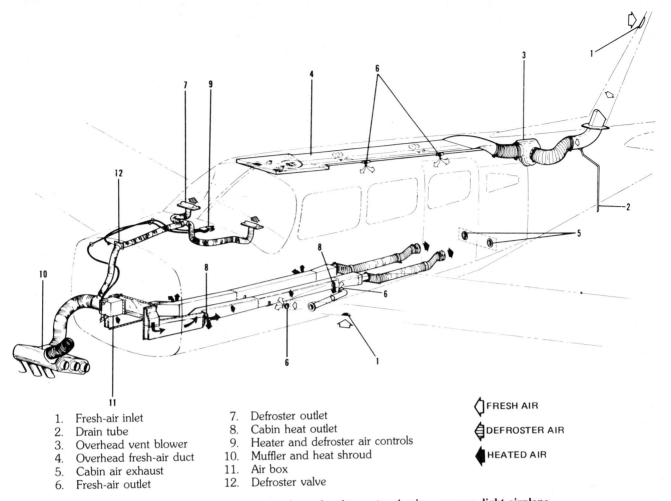

1. Fresh-air inlet
2. Drain tube
3. Overhead vent blower
4. Overhead fresh-air duct
5. Cabin air exhaust
6. Fresh-air outlet
7. Defroster outlet
8. Cabin heat outlet
9. Heater and defroster air controls
10. Muffler and heat shroud
11. Air box
12. Defroster valve

FRESH AIR
DEFROSTER AIR
HEATED AIR

FIG. 12-2   Arrangement of an exhaust heating system in six-passenger, light airplane. *(Piper Aircraft Co.)*

heater are enclosed in metal housings which are vented and drained as a precaution against fire in the event of leaky fittings. Fuel passes from the heater fuel pump through a solenoid valve to the combustion-chamber spray nozzle. When the cabin heater switch is placed in the HEAT position, current is supplied to the combustion air blower and to the ventilating fan. The fan actuates the cam-operated breaker points which start the spark plug firing. As the combustion air-blower air increases, the vane-type valve at the inlet of the combustion chamber opens. This actuates a microswitch, which in turn operates the solenoid valve, thus allowing fuel to spray into the heater where the spark plug ignites the fuel. When the heated air flowing from the heater to the cabin exceeds the temperature for which the thermostat is set. This causes the thermostat to close the solenoid valve and stop fuel flow to the heater. The heater thermostat cools, and the solenoid valve opens again to allow fuel to flow to the heater. Heated air flows from the heater, and the thermostat again causes the solenoid valve to close. This cycling on and off continues, and the heater thereby maintains an even temperature in the cabin.

The heater combustion chamber is completely separate from the ventilating system to prevent any exhaust gases from contaminating the cabin air. All exhaust gases are vented overboard through an exhaust tube directly beneath the heater.

Another combustion-type heater is shown in Fig. 12-4. This is the Janitrol heater which is also used in twin-engine airplanes. A cutaway view, showing the combustion action of the heater, is provided in Fig. 12-5. The heater incorporates a spray nozzle and a spark plug to initiate combustion. Aviation gasoline is injected into the combustion chamber through the spray nozzle, and this results in a cone-shaped fuel spray which mixes with combustion air and is ignited by the spark plug. Electrical energy for the spark plug is produced by a high-tension ignition coil which is supplied from the airplane dc power system. Combustion air enters the combustion chamber tangent to the inner surface. This angle imparts a whirling action to the air, in turn producing a whirling flame that is stable and sustains combustion under the most adverse conditions. The burning gases travel the length of the combustion tube, flow around the inside of the inner tube, pass through crossover passages into an outer radiating area, then travel the length of this surface and out the exhaust. Fresh air passes through spaces between the walls of the heated tubes to pick up heat that is delivered to the cabin as required.

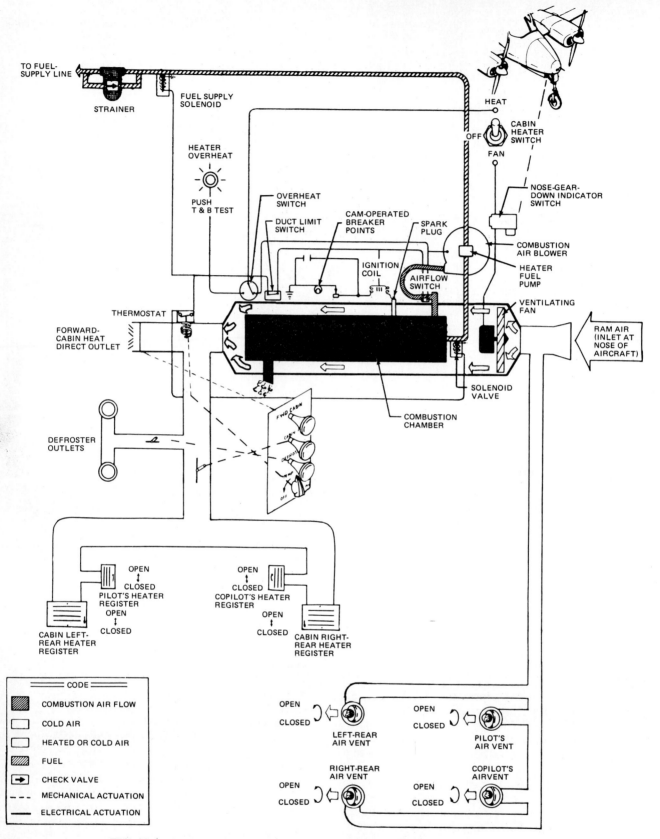

FIG. 12-3 Combustion heater system for a light twin airplane. *(Cessna Aircraft Co.)*

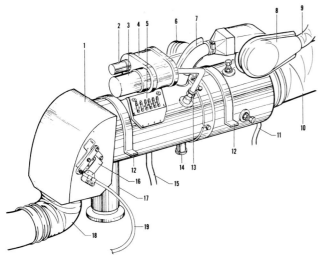

1. Heater output duct
2. Ignition vibrator
3. Ignition coil
4. Ignition unit
5. Terminal strip
6. Pressure switch
7. Elbow adapter
8. Combustion air blower and motor
9. Air inlet tube
10. Air duct hose
11. Water drain tube
12. Heater clamp
13. Spark plug
14. Heater fuel drain tube (hot fuel)
15. Heater fuel drain tube (cold fuel)
16. Adjustable duct switch
17. Exhaust shroud
18. Heat outlet duct
19. Duct switch control cable

FIG. 12-4 A combustion heater assembly for a light airplane. *(Piper Aircraft Co.)*

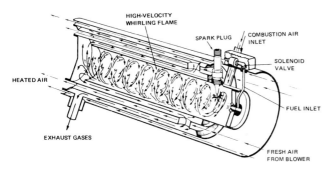

FIG. 12-5 Burning action in a surface combustion heater. *(Piper Aircraft Co.)*

The electrical control circuit for the heater is shown in Fig. 12-6. A study of this circuit will reveal that when the heater switch is turned to HEAT, electrical current will flow through the switch to the air-valve microswitches, overheat switch, combustion air pressure switch, duct switch, cycling switch, and to the fuel-cycle valve. At the same time, current will flow to the ignition unit. If any of the switches are open, the unit cannot operate.

The duct switch can be adjusted for the desired temperature. When the heater temperature reaches a predetermined level, the duct switch will open, closing the fuel-cycle valve and turning off the ignition. When the temperature drops to a given level, the duct switch will close, thus turning the heater on again.

When the heater switch is turned to the FAN position, the fan only will operate. This position is used on the ground when a flow of air without heat is desired.

Typical inspections of a combustion heater system include a visual inspection of the ducting and chamber for obstructions and conditions; inspection of the igniter plug for condition, gap, and operation; a check for any leakage in the airflow or fuel system; an operational check of individual system components (i.e., blower, fuel solenoids, temperature sensors); and an operational check of the complete system. Refer to the aircraft maintenance manual for specific inspection requirements for a particular model aircraft and heater.

Electric Heating Systems

Electrically operated heaters are used on some aircraft to provide heat in the cabin area when the aircraft is on the ground with the engines not running. Aircraft which typically incorporate this type of system include the smaller turboprop-powered aircraft.

The auxiliary electric heat system draws air from the inside of the aircraft cabin by the use of a recirculation fan. The air then passes over electrically heated coils and flows back into the cabin through the aircraft heat supply ducting.

The system incorporates safety features in the system design. For example, an airflow switch must sense that the recirculation fan is moving air through the heater before the heater can operate. Also, an over-temperature of the system turns off the heater and illuminates an annunciator light. After an overheat, the heater does not return to operation until the pilot has cycled the control switch.

Heating with Bleed Air

Unpressurized turbine aircraft normally make use of compressed air from the turbine engine to provide the hot air for cabin heating. When a turbine engine compresses air prior to directing it to the engine combustion chamber, the air temperature of this air is increased by several hundred degrees Fahrenheit by the compressing action. Some of this hot compressed air, called "bleed air," can be diverted to a cabin heating system.

The cabin heating system consists of ducting to contain the flow of air, a chamber where the bleed air is mixed with ambient or recirculated air, valves to control the flow of air in the system, and temperature sensors to prevent excessive heat from entering the cabin. Additional components which are used in a bleed-air heating system include check valves to prevent a loss of compressor bleed air when starting the engine and when full power is required of the engine, recirculation fans to move the air through the ducts and provide a flow of ambient or cabin air to the mixing chamber, and engine sensors to eliminate the bleed system if one engine of a multiengine aircraft becomes inoperative. The bleed-air heating system of a single-engine turbine aircraft is shown in Fig. 12-7.

The basic flow of air from the system is as follows: bleed air from the engine compressor flows through

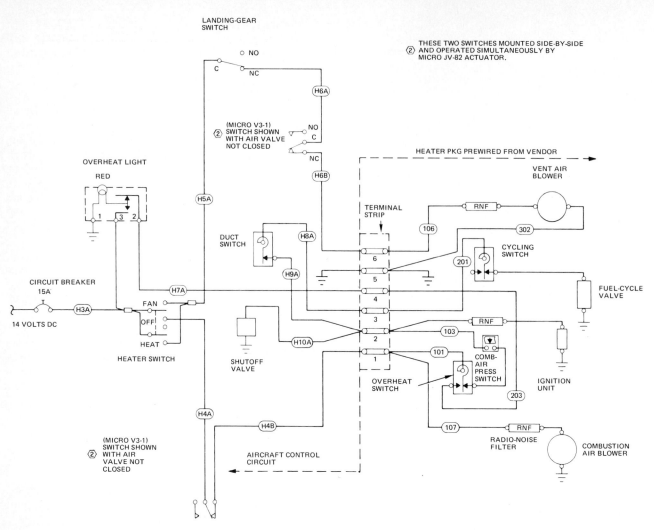

FIG. 12-6 Electrical control circuit for a combustion heater system. (*Piper Aircraft Co.*)

check valves to the mixing chamber through a temperature control valve; recirculation or ambient air is directed to the mixing chamber through a control valve; the mixed air is directed past a temperature sensor to cabin flow control valves; and the heated air flows into the cabin air from the distribution ductwork.

If any of the temperature sensors in the system senses an overtemperature, the system is shut down and crew action is required to restore operation to the system.

Heating Pressurized Aircraft

Heating pressurized aircraft is commonly achieved by regulating the temperature of the air used to pressurize the cabin. For this reason, heating pressurized aircraft is covered in the section of this chapter dealing with pressurization.

● CABIN COOLING SYSTEMS

Aircraft **cooling systems,** also called **air-conditioning systems,** are used to reduce the temperature inside an aircraft for crew and passenger comfort. The two basic methods of reducing the temperature of aircraft are the freon vapor-cycle machine and the air-cycle machine.

The vapor-cycle machine is a closed system using the evaporation and condensation of freon to remove heat from the cabin interior. The air-cycle machine uses the compression and expansion of air to lower the temperature of the cabin air.

Vapor-Cycle Cooling Systems

The vapor-cycle air-conditioning system is used in reciprocating-engine-powered aircraft and in smaller turboprop aircraft which do not make use of air-cycle machines to reduce the cabin interior temperature. The operation of vapor-cycle machines is controlled by the pilot and may incorporate automatic cutout or interrupt systems. These cutout and interrupt systems are used to disengage the refrigerant compressor during demand for high engine power output such as during takeoff operations or when one engine of a multiengine aircraft has failed. This interruption in compressor operation allows all available power to be used to maintain controllable flight.

The airflow for the condenser coils of the vapor-cycle system may rely on airflow entering through

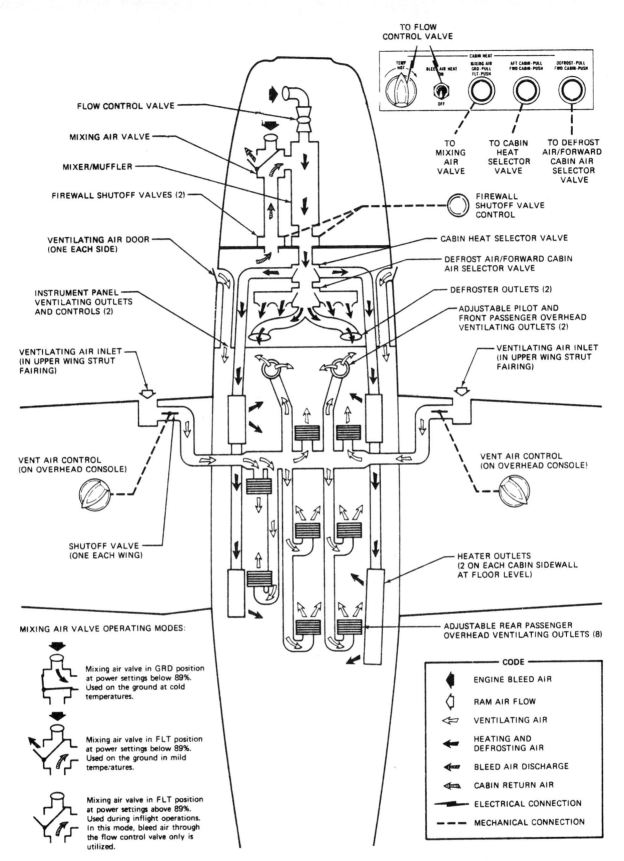

FLOW CONTROL VALVE

MIXING AIR VALVE

MIXER/MUFFLER

FIREWALL SHUTOFF VALVES (2)

VENTILATING AIR DOOR (ONE EACH SIDE)

INSTRUMENT PANEL VENTILATING OUTLETS AND CONTROLS (2)

VENTILATING AIR INLET (IN UPPER WING STRUT FAIRING)

VENT AIR CONTROL (ON OVERHEAD CONSOLE)

SHUTOFF VALVE (ONE EACH WING)

TO FLOW CONTROL VALVE

CABIN HEAT

TEMP HOT

BLEED AIR HEAT ON OFF

MIXING AIR GRD-PULL FLT-PUSH

AFT CABIN-PULL FWD CABIN-PUSH

DEFROST-PULL FWD CABIN-PUSH

TO MIXING AIR VALVE

TO CABIN HEAT SELECTOR VALVE

TO DEFROST AIR/FORWARD CABIN AIR SELECTOR VALVE

FIREWALL SHUTOFF VALVE CONTROL

CABIN HEAT SELECTOR VALVE

DEFROST AIR/FORWARD CABIN AIR SELECTOR VALVE

DEFROSTER OUTLETS (2)

ADJUSTABLE PILOT AND FRONT PASSENGER OVERHEAD VENTILATING OUTLETS (2)

VENTILATING AIR INLET (IN UPPER WING STRUT FAIRING)

VENT AIR CONTROL (ON OVERHEAD CONSOLE)

HEATER OUTLETS (2 ON EACH CABIN SIDEWALL AT FLOOR LEVEL)

ADJUSTABLE REAR PASSENGER OVERHEAD VENTILATING OUTLETS (8)

MIXING AIR VALVE OPERATING MODES:

Mixing air valve in GRD position at power settings below 89%. Used on the ground at cold temperatures.

Mixing air valve in FLT position at power settings below 89%. Used on the ground in mild temperatures.

Mixing air valve in FLT position at power settings above 89%. Used during inflight operations. In this mode, bleed air through the flow control valve only is utilized.

CODE

ENGINE BLEED AIR

RAM AIR FLOW

VENTILATING AIR

HEATING AND DEFROSTING AIR

BLEED AIR DISCHARGE

CABIN RETURN AIR

ELECTRICAL CONNECTION

MECHANICAL CONNECTION

FIG. 12-7 Heating and ventilation system for a single-engine turboprop aircraft. (*Cessna Aircraft Co.*)

inlets in the wings or fuselage, or the coils may be mounted on a structure which is lowered into the airstream during flight.

A vapor-cycle cooling (refrigeration) system utilizes basic laws of thermodynamics and physics. In simple terms, some of these laws may be stated as follows:

1. When a liquid is changed to a gas (vaporized), it absorbs heat. This heat is called the **latent heat of vaporization.**

2. When a given quantity of gas is condensed to a liquid, it emits heat in the same amount that it absorbs when being changed from a liquid to a gas.

3. Heat transfers only from a material having a given temperature to a material having a lower temperature.

4. When a gas is compressed, its temperature increases, and when the pressure on a gas is decreased, its temperature decreases.

A basic vapor-cycle system requires a compressor, an expansion valve, a condenser, and an evaporator (cooling coil). An actual system includes controlling devices to provide for changes in cooling demand and changes in operating conditions. A schematic diagram of a typical system is shown in Fig. 12-8. A system of

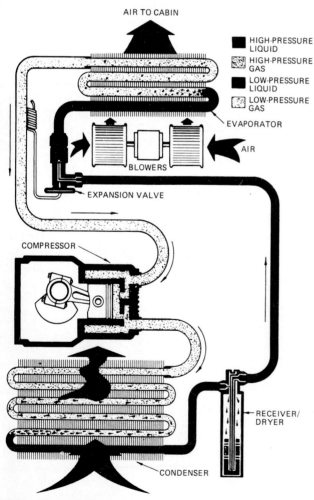

FIG. 12-8 Diagram of a vapor-cycle cooling system. *(A R A Manufacturing Co.)*

this type usually employs Refrigerant 12, also known as Freon 12, as the refrigerant. It is a gas at standard pressures and temperatures but becomes a liquid when pressure on it is increased sufficiently or when the temperature is reduced to the required level. The range of pressures and temperatures at which Refrigerant 12 liquefies or becomes a gas is such as to make it an ideal medium for producing the temperatures desirable for an automobile or aircraft cabin. Table 12-1 gives typical temperature-pressure values for Refrigerant 12 in the evaporator of a refrigeration system.

Note in Table 12-1 that the pressure reading in pounds per square inch gauge (psig) is very close numerically to the temperature reading in degrees Fahrenheit. This provides a handy reference for determining the temperature in the evaporator. This temperature is normally kept between 33 and 35°F [0.5 and 1.7°C] to avoid icing of the evaporator.

Freon is the trade name given to Refrigerant 12 by the E. I. Du Pont de Nemours Company. The same refrigerant is produced by other manufacturers under different names.

The refrigeration cycle, beginning with the **compressor,** involves the compression of the refrigerant gas which is comparatively cold and at a low pressure as it leaves the evaporator and flows to the compressor. The compressor is the source of energy required for the operation of the system. The gas leaving the compressor is at a high temperature and pressure. In a typical range of operation, the pressure of the gas leaving the compressor may be as high as 180 psig [1241 kPa] or more. From the compressor the hot, high-pressure gas (vapor) flows into the **condenser,** which is a heat radiator through which cool air is passed to remove heat from the vapor. On an airplane in flight the air through the condenser is supplied from a ram air duct. On the ground, the air must be caused to flow through the condenser by means of a blower or some type of an ejector. As the refrigerant vapor is cooled in the condenser, it becomes a liquid and flows to the **receiver-dryer-filter.** The receiver-dryer-filter is essentially a reservoir containing a filter and a desiccant. A **sight glass** is usually located on top of the receiver to allow observation of the fluid flow through the unit. If bubbles are seen in the fluid, the system refrigerant is known to be low and requires replenishment. A cutaway drawing of a typical receiver-dryer-

TABLE 12-1 Refrigerant 12 Pressure Values

Evaporator Pressure		Evaporator Temperature	
psig	kPa	°F	°C
0	0	−21	−29.45
10.1	69.64	−10	−23.33
21	144.80	20	−6.67
30	206.85	32	0.0
41.7	287.52	45	7.22
60	413.70	62	16.67
79.2	546.08	77	25.0
101.3	698.46	91	32.78
116.9	806.03	100	37.78

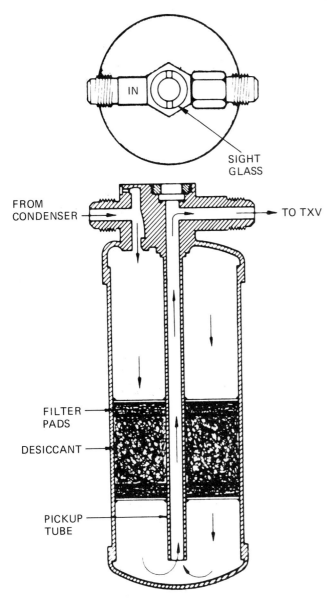

FIG. 12-9 Cutaway drawing of a receiver-filter. *(A R A Manufacturing Co.)*

The subcooler, in adding heat to the vapor from the vaporizer to the compressor, further superheats the vapor, thus reducing the possibility of condensation taking place in the vapor and prevents liquid from reaching the compressor. Liquid entering the compressor would interfere with its performance and is likely to cause damage to the compressor. When liquid refrigerant appears between the vaporizer (evaporator) and the compressor, the condition is called "slugging." Its presence indicates that the controls for the system are not functioning correctly and the system will not perform efficiently.

The high-pressure liquid refrigerant, after leaving the receiver-dryer, passes through the **thermal expansion valve.** This valve consists of a variable orifice through which the high-pressure liquid is forced. Low pressure exists at the outlet side of the expansion valve, through the evaporator, and to the inlet of the compressor. As the liquid refrigerant passes through the expansion valve into the low-pressure area, it begins to break up into droplets, and by the time it leaves the evaporator, it is a gas. When the liquid refrigerant becomes a gas, it absorbs heat, thus producing the cooling effect desired. The cabin air to be cooled is carried by ducting into one side of the evaporator and out the other side to the cabin.

The thermal expansion valve orifice is adjusted automatically by the pressure from a thermal sensor which senses the temperature of the gas leaving the evaporator. If the gas is warmer than it should be, the expansion valve provides greater restriction and, hence, greater cooling. If the gas is too cool, the expansion valve provides less restriction. A drawing of an expansion valve is shown in Fig. 12-10.

After the gas leaves the evaporator, it flows to the compressor and the cycle begins again. The evaporator provides the cooling for cabin air, and the condenser dissipates the heat developed when the gas is compressed.

filter is shown in Fig. 12-9. In some systems, the dryer-filter is separate from the receiver.

Refrigerant liquid flowing from the receiver is under high pressure and has been cooled by the condenser. In some systems, the liquid refrigerant at this point is passed through a **subcooler.** The subcooler is a heat exchanger through which the refrigerant liquid flowing to the **expansion valve** and the cold vapor flowing from the **evaporator** are passed through separate coils in the subcooler. Since the fluid is warmer than the vapor, heat from the fluid passes to the vapor. The effect is to subcool the fluid and superheat the vapor.

Subcooling is the process of reducing the temperature of a liquid below the temperature at which it was condensed, the pressure being held constant. If the liquid is subcooled 20 to 30°F [11 to 17°C] below the condensing temperature, this condition assures that there will be no premature vaporization ("flash-off") before the liquid reaches the expansion valve.

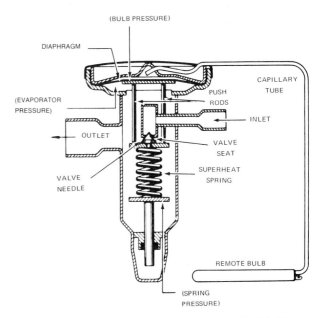

FIG. 12-10 Drawing of an expansion valve. *(A R A Manufacturing Co.)*

As will be noted from the foregoing discussions, the vapor-cycle refrigeration system has a high-pressure section from the compressor to the thermal expansion valve and a low-pressure section from the thermal expansion valve to the inlet side of the compressor. The high-pressure section is commonly referred to as the **high side,** and the low-pressure section is referred to as the **low side.** It is important for the mechanic to remember these terms because they are used in the service instructions for refrigeration systems of the vapor-cycle type.

An operational check involves running the engine of the aircraft, turning on the refrigeration system, and checking the temperature at the evaporator. The sight glass on the top of the evaporator-dryer should be checked for bubbles or foam which would indicate lack of refrigerant. If a refrigeration system operates satisfactorily for a few minutes and then stops cooling, it is an indication of water in the system. The water has frozen at the expansion valve and stopped the flow of refrigerant. Systems are provided with pressure sensors which control an electric circuit that disengages the compressor clutch when the pressures in the high side become too great.

Servicing of a vapor-cycle refrigeration system requires the use of a **service manifold** which makes it possible to "plug in" to the system as required to test pressures, add refrigerant, and purge, evacuate, and recharge the system. The service manifold usually has a high-pressure gauge which should have a capacity of as high as 500 psig [3447.5 kPa] and a compound low-pressure gauge which can provide readings of −30 inHg (inches of mercury) [−101.59 kPa] below atmospheric pressure (0 inHg absolute) up to 60 or more inHg [203.3 or more kPa]. The manifold also includes three fittings, one for the low side, one for the high side, and one by which refrigerant may be added or removed, or through which the system can be purged and evacuated. A drawing to illustrate the service manifold is shown in Fig. 12-11. Note that the manual valves in the manifold are arranged in such a manner that the gauges will give indications of pressures in the system even though the valves are closed. The purpose of the valves is to allow connection of either the high or low side, or both sides, of the system with the center service connection.

Vapor-cycle systems are provided with **service valves** to which the service manifold can be connected. These valves may be of the Schrader type (similar to a shock-strut or hydraulic accumulator valve) or some other type. In any case, the mechanic must know what type of valve is employed in the system and must be sure to have the correct type of fitting on the service manifold hose so it will properly connect to the service valve. The service valves in the system provide for connection to the low side and to the high side. The valves are often on top of the compressor, but they may be at other points in the system. The mechanic must be sure to connect the low-pressure side of the service manifold to the service valve for the low side of the system and the high-pressure side of service manifold to the high-side service valve.

When it becomes necessary to change a unit in a

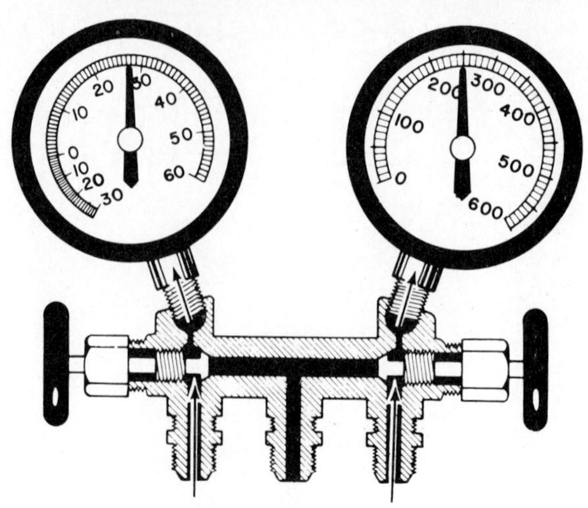

LOW SIDE   HIGH SIDE

BOTH VALVES CLOSED—GAUGES SHOW
HIGH-SIDE AND LOW-SIDE PRESSURE

FIG. 12-11   Service manifold for a vapor-cycle cooling system. (*A R A Manufacturing Co.*)

vapor-cycle refrigeration system, the refrigerant must be released. This is called **purging** the system.

The recommended procedure for purging the refrigeration system is first to connect the service manifold to the low-side and high-side service valves. As mentioned previously, the mechanic must assure that the valve fittings are correct for the type of valves involved. The service instructions provide this information. The manual valves on the service manifold must be *closed* before connecting the manifold to the system. After the service manifold is connected to the system, either one or both of the service valves are "cracked" (opened slightly) to allow a slow escape of the refrigerant. The escaping gas exits through the center connection of the manifold. It is suggested that the hose from the center connection be discharged into a cloth so the escape of oil can be detected. If oil is discharging with the gas, the discharge is too rapid and the manual valves should be closed slightly.

The R-12 refrigerant is odorless and nontoxic at normal temperatures. It does, however, displace air in a confined area and converts to a toxic gas at high temperatures. For these reasons, purging of the refrigeration system should always be done in an open area where there is adequate ventilation and no chance of exposure to high temperatures. When both pressure gauges on the service manifold indicate zero pressure, the system is purged and can be disassembled.

When one or more units are removed from the system, all fittings should be capped immediately to prevent the entrance of any detrimental material. Anything except pure, dry refrigerant and refrigerating system oil can cause malfunction of the system. Hoses which may become contaminated should be replaced with new hoses.

After a system has been reassembled and is once again a closed, sealed system, it must be evacuated (pumped down) with a suitable vacuum pump. The vacuum pump is connected to the center fitting of the

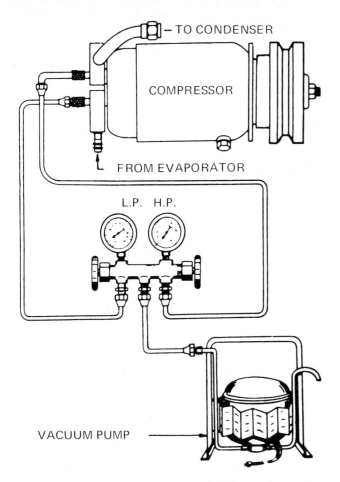

TO CONDENSER

COMPRESSOR

FROM EVAPORATOR

L.P. H.P.

VACUUM PUMP

FIG. 12-12 Vacuum pump connected to the service manifold. *(A R A Manufacturing Co.)*

service manifold as shown in Fig. 12-12. The manual valves on the manifold are opened and the pump started. The reason for evacuation of the system is that all air and attendant moisture must be removed from the system. As pressure decreases below atmospheric, the boiling point of water decreases. It is recommended that the pressure of the system be reduced to -29.0 inHg [-98.2 kPa], that is, below sea level standard pressure. This applies when the service is being performed at sea level pressure. At this pressure all water in the air is completely vaporized, and an extremely small amount of air or water exists in the system. Usually about 30 min with a good vacuum pump is required to pump down the system to the desired level.

After the system is evacuated as described above, the manual valves on the service manifold are closed. The low-pressure gauge on the manifold will register the vacuum pressure in the system.

Following the evacuation (pump down) of the system, the system must be recharged with the required amount of R-12 refrigerant. First, however, the drying agent in the receiver-dryer must be replaced. As explained previously, this drying agent will absorb any traces of moisture remaining in the system.

Refrigerant is sold in 15-oz [425-g] sealed containers with fittings to which appropriate valves can be at-

tached. It is also sold in larger containers and cylinders. For a small-capacity system, the 15-oz can (also known as a 1-lb can) is used because it is convenient and lets one determine the amount of refrigerant placed in the system.

CAUTION: Refrigerant in a liquid state can cause eye and skin damage due to the low temperature created as the refrigerant evaporates. Use a face shield and appropriate clothing to prevent injury.

Recharging the system is accomplished by connecting the container of refrigerant to the center fitting of the service manifold as shown in Fig. 12-13. First the appropriate hose is connected to the center fitting of the manifold. Then the other end of the hose is connected to the valve which is connected to the container of refrigerant. Remember, at this time, the system is in the evacuated condition and both manual valves on the service manifold are closed. After all connections are secure, the valve on the refrigerant container is turned in the assigned direction. This pierces the container and permits the gaseous refrigerant from the top of the container to flow into the service hose. The refrigerant container should be held in an upright position to assure that only gas flows into the system. If the container is inverted, liquid refrigerant will flow, and this must not be permitted in the low side of the system.

After the container valve is opened, the fitting of the hose from the container should be slightly loosened at the service manifold. Air and gas should be permitted to escape for a few seconds to drive the air out of the service hose. Remember that air and moisture, which air contains, are both detrimental to the proper operation of the system. The service connection at the manifold is then retightened, and the manual valve on the high side of the system is opened. The container can now be inverted to allow liquid refrigerant to flow into the high side of the system. Very quickly the gauge on the low side of the system should move out of the vacuum indication, showing

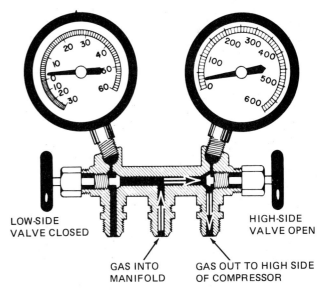

LOW-SIDE
VALVE CLOSED

HIGH-SIDE
VALVE OPEN

GAS INTO
MANIFOLD

GAS OUT TO HIGH SIDE
OF COMPRESSOR

FIG. 12-13 Arrangement of the service manifold for recharging the system. *(A R A Manufacturing Co.)*

that gaseous refrigerant is flowing through the evaporator to the low side of the compressor. If this does not occur, the system is blocked and must be corrected before the procedure is continued.

After the prescribed amount of refrigerant has been placed in the system, the service manifold should be removed and the service fittings capped. The system may then be given an operational test.

It is emphasized here that the procedures described in the foregoing are general in nature and are provided so the student will have an understanding of the principal considerations in the service and operation of vapor-cycle refrigeration systems. In servicing a particular system, the appropriate service instructions should be followed.

Air-Cycle Cooling

Modern large turbine-powered aircraft make use of air-cycle machines to adjust the temperature of the air directed into the passenger and crew compartments of these large aircraft. While this portion of the discussion of air-cycle machines is directed as the ability to provide cabin-cooling air, it should be noted that the cabin can also be heated and pressurized by the use of an air-cycle machine. These operations are discussed in a later portion of this chapter.

These large aircraft utilize air-cycle cooling because of its simplicity, freedom from troubles, and economy. In these systems, the refrigerant is air. Air-cycle cooling systems utilize the same principles of thermodynamics and the same laws of gases involved in vapor-cycle systems. One principal difference is that the air is not reduced to a liquid as the refrigerant is in a vapor-cycle system.

The principle of cooling by means of a gas is rather simple. When a gas (air) is compressed, it becomes heated, and when the pressure is reduced, the gas becomes cooled. If a pressure cylinder is connected to an air compressor and compressed air is forced into the cylinder, one can observe that the cylinder becomes warm or even hot, depending upon the level of compression and the rate at which the air was compressed. If the cylinder filled with highly compressed air is then allowed to cool to ambient temperature, the pressure in the cylinder will be reduced to a certain degree as the air temperature is reduced. Now, if a valve is opened and the air is allowed to escape from the cylinder, it will be noted that the temperature of the escaping air is much lower than the ambient temperature due to the air expanding as its pressure returns to the ambient value. This cold air could then be used as a cooling agent.

In an air-cycle system, the air is continuously compressed, then cooled by means of heat exchangers through which ram air is passed; then the pressure is reduced by passing the air through an expansion turbine. The air leaving the expansion turbine is now at low pressure and low temperature. The cooled air is directed through ducting with control valves to regulate the amount of cooling air needed to produce the desired cabin temperature.

The turbine-compressor unit by which air is cooled is called an **air-cycle machine** (ACM). A drawing to illustrate how the ACM is connected into a "cooling pack" is shown in Fig. 12-14. Hot compressed air from the compressor of one of the turbine engines flows through the **primary heat exchanger.** The heat exchanger is exposed to ram air which removes heat from the air. The cooled but still compressed air is then ducted to the compressor inlet of the ACM. The compressor further compresses the air and causes it to rise in temperature. This air is directed to the **secondary heat exchanger** which, being exposed to ram air, removes heat from the compressed air. The compressed air is then directed to the **expansion turbine.** The expansion turbine absorbs energy from the air and utilizes this energy to drive the compressor. As the air exits the expansion turbine, it enters a large chamber which allows the air to expand and causes a further reduction in the air temperature. Thus the air leaving the turbine is cooled by the loss of heat energy and by the expansion that takes place. The great reduction in temperature causes the moisture in the air to condense, and this moisture is removed by means of a **water separator.** The dried, cold air is then routed to ducting to be utilized as required to provide the desired temperature in the cabin. In the drawing of Fig. 12-14, note that a bypass duct with the cabin-temperature control valve will bypass air around the cooling system when cooling is not required.

● CABIN PRESSURIZATION SYSTEMS

The purpose of aircraft cabin pressurization is to maintain a comfortable environment for the aircraft occupants while allowing the aircraft to operate efficiently at high altitudes. At high altitudes the aircraft can fly above most of the weather conditions which contain turbulence and make flight uncomfortable for passengers and crew members. Additionally, the fuel efficiency of the aircraft is increased at high altitudes, resulting in less fuel being burned for any given cruising airspeed.

In order to make the cabin environment comfortable for the aircraft occupants, the cabin must normally be pressurized to maintain the cabin air pressure at the level reached at no higher than 8000 ft [2438 m]. This enables the crew and passengers to function without the use of supplemental oxygen and, with adjustments to the cabin air temperature, allows them to be in a "shirt sleeve" environment.

Along with allowing the aircraft and occupants to function in efficient environments, pressurization also permits the occupants to be insulated from the rapid changes in altitude associated with modern transport aircraft. For example, the aircraft normally climbs to cruising altitude as quickly as possible for maximum fuel efficiency, but the pressurized cabin gradually climbs to a selected lower pressure altitude. A similar situation can take place during descents for landing, where the aircraft might descend very rapidly, but the pressure in the cabin increases slowly until both the cabin pressure and the ambient pressure are the same when the aircraft lands. Example of the aircraft and cabin altitudes and relative rates of change are shown

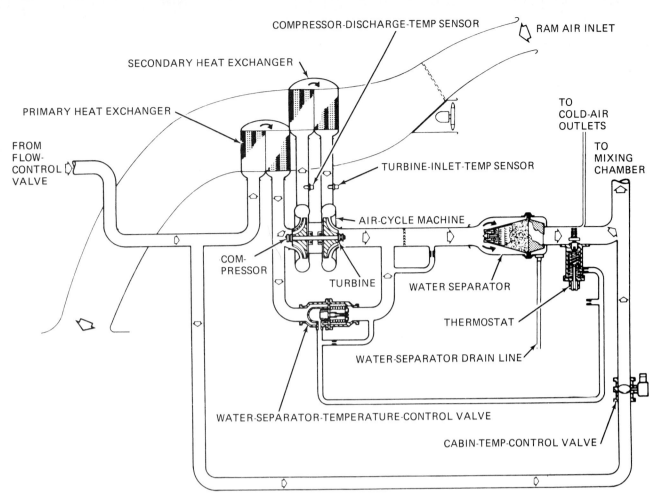

FIG. 12-14 Air-cycle machine in a cooling system. *(AiResearch Mfg. Co.)*

in the flight profile in Fig. 12-15. By being able to control the cabin rate of climb and descent pressure independent of the aircraft climb and descent pressure, the aircraft occupants are spared any discomfort from rapid pressure changes.

While the use of pressurization is normally associated with turbine-powered transport aircraft, pressurization may be found in aircraft ranging in size from light single-engine aircraft through light twins, turbo-prop-powered aircraft and reciprocating-engine-powered transports. While the basic controlling mechanisms for each of these types of aircraft are the same, the sources of pressure and the capabilities vary depending on the purpose and complexity of the aircraft.

Aircraft Structures

In order for an aircraft to be pressurized, it must have enough structural strength in the pressurized section, called the "pressure vessel," to withstand the operational stresses. The normal limiting factor as to how high the aircraft can operate is often the maximum allowed cabin differential pressure. Cabin differential pressure is the difference in pressure between the ambient outside air pressure and the pressure inside the aircraft. The higher the allowed differential pressure, the stronger the airframe structure must be.

Light aircraft are generally designed to operate with a maximum cabin differential pressure of about 3 to 5 psi [20.7 to 34.5 kPa]. Large reciprocating-engine-powered aircraft operate with a maximum differential of about 5.5 psi [37.9 kPa]. Turbine-powered transports are designed for a maximum differential pressure on the order of 9 psi [62.06 kPa].

Sources of Pressurization

The source of pressure for an aircraft varies depending on the type of engine being used and the design requirements of the aircraft manufacturer. In all cases, the engine provides the power to pressurize the aircraft, but the means of pressurization varies.

Reciprocating engines can supply pressure from a supercharger, a turbocharger, or an engine-driven compressor. A **supercharger** is an engine-driven air pump, mechanically driven from the engine drive train, which compresses air for use by the engine in the combustion process. A portion of this supercharger air can be directed into the cabin pressurization system, provided that the supercharger is positioned in the induction system before fuel is introduced into the airflow.

A **turbocharger** is used in a similar manner as a supercharger except that the turbocharger is driven

431

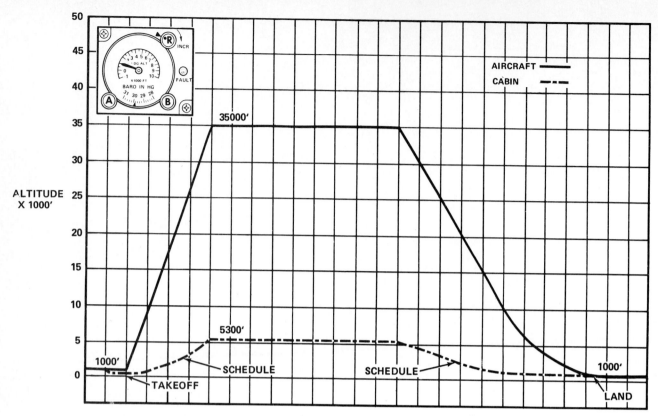

FIG. 12-15 Comparison of aircraft and cabin altitudes during a flight in a pressurized aircraft. (*Canadair Inc.*)

by exhaust gases from the engine, which drives an air compressor to supply an air charge to the engine.

Superchargers and turbochargers have disadvantages in that fumes and oil can be introduced into the pressurized air and foul the cabin air. Additionally, the use of either of these pressure sources may substantially reduce engine power output, especially at higher altitudes where the pressure output of the pump is minimal.

Aircraft using turbine engines usually make use of engine bleed air to pressurize the cabin. Bleed air is pressurized air which is "bled" from the compressor section of the turbine engine. The loss of this compressor air causes some reduction in total engine power output.

Independent cabin compressors are used in some aircraft to eliminate the problem associated with air contamination. These pumps are driven from the engine accessory section or by turbine engine bleed air. Two types of pumps used are the **Roots-type positive-displacement pump,** shown in Fig. 12-16, and the **centrifugal cabin compressor,** shown in Fig. 12-17.

Pressurization System Components

The complexity of a particular pressurization system depends on the various functions that it is designed to serve. In addition to supplying pressure to maintain the desired cabin altitude, a pressurization system may also incorporate components to heat and to cool the air prior to its entering the cabin. This is normally the case with transport aircraft. Smaller aircraft often incorporate vapor-cycle air conditioners

and heaters in the system to provide the proper temperature adjustment for the aircraft cabin. Typical systems for different types of aircraft are presented in the following sections.

When the pressurized air exits the pressure source, it is usually at a high temperature and must be cooled to a usable temperature. The unit used to cool the air is a **heat exchanger.** The heat exchanger typically uses ambient air flowing over the radiator-like structure to remove heat from the pressurized air moving through the unit. In flight the ambient airflow occurs by ram air. When the aircraft is on the ground, fans or ejectors may be used to cause air to flow across the heat exchanger.

Since all of the air from the compressor must flow through the heat exchanger, the air may be cooled too much. To adjust the air temperature, a heat source may be used to bring the air back up to the desired value. This heat source may be an electric heater, heated air that has been used to cool equipment such as from the avionics bay, bleed air from the engine, or air from an engine exhaust heat muff or augmentor tube. The amount of heated air mixed with the cooled air may be automatically or manually controlled by a mixing valve.

After the air temperature is adjusted, the airflow is directed in to the pressure vessel.

Several different valves are used to regulate the pressure in the pressure vessel. The **outflow valve,** shown in Fig. 12-18, is used as the primary means of controlling the cabin pressure. This valve controls the amount of air allowed to escape from the cabin. The

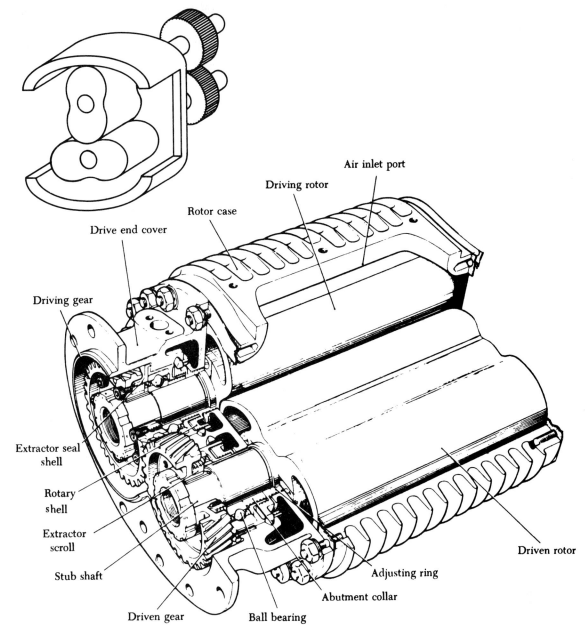

FIG. 12-16 A Roots-type cabin supercharger.

Labels in figure:
Air inlet port
Driving rotor
Rotor case
Drive end cover
Driving gear
Extractor seal shell
Rotary shell
Extractor scroll
Stub shaft
Driven gear
Ball bearing
Abutment collar
Adjusting ring
Driven rotor

outflow valve is controlled by the flight crew through the aircraft environmentals control panel. The outflow valve opens and closes to maintain the desired cabin pressure and, in many systems, operates to maintain a preset maximum cabin altitude value if the cabin pressure goes above that value. Outflow valves may be operated directly by pneumatic pressure, or their operation may be by electric motors whose operation is controlled by pneumatic pressure.

The **safety valve**, also called a **positive pressure-relief valve**, opens automatically and starts releasing cabin pressurization when its preset value is reached. This preset value is about 0.5 psi [3.4 kPa] higher than the maximum setting of the outflow valve. The safety valve prevents the cabin from being overpressurized, which could result in aircraft structural failure. In some aircraft the safety valve and the outflow valve are identical in design with the only differences being

the maximum pressure setting and the pneumatic connections for operation.

The **negative pressure-relief valve** prevents the cabin from being at a higher altitude (lower air pressure) than the ambient air. The operation of this valve is automatic. It opens to equalize the cabin and ambient pressure if the ambient pressure exceeds cabin pressure by more than about 0.3 psi [2.3 kPa]. While this is called a "valve," the actual operation may be performed by door seals or other fuselage components. Figure 12-19 shows the location of the negative pressure-relief valves on a jet transport.

A **dump valve** is used to release all cabin pressurization when the aircraft lands. This valve is commonly controlled by a landing-gear squat switch. When the landing-gear oleo is compressed, the squat switch causes the dump valve to open and equalizes the cabin and ambient atmospheric pressures. This prevents the

FIG. 12-17 A centrifugal compressor.

cabin from being pressurized after landing. If the cabin were pressurized on the ground, it might not be possible to open the aircraft cabin doors.

Note that one pressurization control valve may serve more than one function in a specific aircraft design. For example, the outflow valve or the safety valve may be configured to also act as the dump valve, and the outflow valve may be designed to serve as a negative pressure-relief valve.

Pressurization Control Operation

The control of the cabin pressurization is through various valves as has already been mentioned. These valves are operated by differences in air pressure in order to achieve the desired level of pressurization or to prevent overstressing the aircraft structure. To understand the basic principles of pressurization control operation, we will start by looking at a safety valve and then move on to an outflow valve and the controller. The components presented and described are intended to help the mechanic in understanding the basics of system operation. Before working on a specific system, the mechanic should be acquainted with that system's specific design.

The safety valve for a transport aircraft is shown in Fig. 12-20. This valve is designed to release cabin pressurization above a preset value. This function is

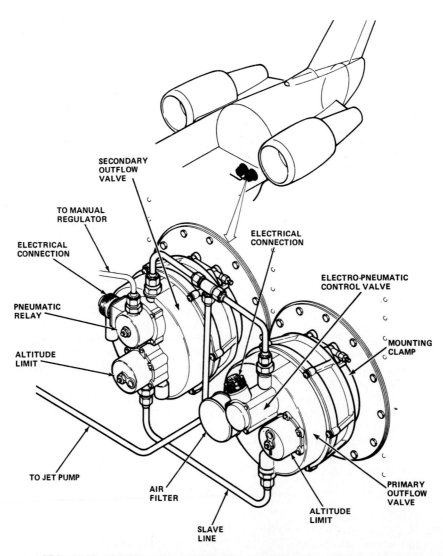

FIG. 12-18 Outflow valves installed in a corporate jet. *(Canadair Inc.)*

434

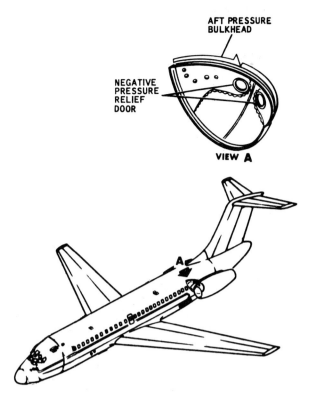

AFT PRESSURE
BULKHEAD

NEGATIVE
PRESSURE
RELIEF
DOOR

VIEW A

A

FIG. 12-19   The location of negative pressure-relief valves in a transport aircraft.

automatic and does not require the use of a separate controller. The small chamber (A) to the right of the differential diaphragm assembly is vented to cabin air pressure through a filter. The left side of this diaphragm assembly (B) is vented to atmospheric pressure. If cabin pressure exceeds the combined force of atmospheric pressure and the spring, the metering valve is lifted off of its seat. When the round head of the metering valve is moved to the left, air from the reference chamber (C) on the left side of the outflow valve poppet assembly begins to flow out to atmospheric pressure through the hollow center of the outflow valve pilot. The reduced pressure in the reference chamber allows the large spring to the right of the poppet assembly to move the assembly to the left. When the poppet is moved to the left, cabin air flows out around the base of the poppet valve, shown at the right of Fig. 12-20.

The outflow valve for a corporate jet aircraft is shown in Fig. 12-21. This valve is designed to serve as the outflow valve, altitude limiter, and positive pressure-relief valve for the aircraft. The outflow operation is controlled by the **reference air pressure** in the **reference chamber** (termed **actuator chamber** by the manufacturer) and is controlled through the electropneumatic control valve from the pilot's controller and the vacuum line. Air from the cabin air enters this chamber through the filter and flows out through the control valve to the controller. This keeps the reference chamber pressure below cabin pressure.

When the controller is set to pressurize the cabin, the control valve is closed or only slightly open so that the pressure in the reference chamber is great

enough to hold the poppet valve on its seat. Since no air can escape, the cabin pressure increases. Once the cabin has reached the desired amount of pressurization, the controller commands the control valve to open and reduces the reference chamber pressure. With the reduced reference pressure, cabin air pressure in the chamber between the poppet valve and the baffle plate overcomes the reference pressure and spring pressure on the poppet valve. This opens the valve enough to release air from the cabin. The rate of this exhaust air is the same as the air flowing into the cabin and maintains the cabin at a certain pressure.

While the system just discussed uses an electropneumatic control, many aircraft have the reference pressure established in the pilot's controller and lines are used to provide the outflow valve with the reference pressure.

To prevent the cabin differential pressure from becoming too great, a positive pressure-relief control system is included in the valve design. This consists of the differential pressure control diaphragm and spring and the metering pin. Cabin air pressure between the baffle plate and the poppet valve is applied to one side of the differential pressure diaphragm. If the force of this pressure exceeds that of the combined force of atmospheric pressure and the spring to the right of the diaphragm, the diaphragm moves to the right and allows the metering pin to move off of its seat (as shown). This allows air pressure in the reference chamber to escape through the passage now opened and causes the poppet valve to open. This lowers the cabin air pressure. The operation of this safety device is automatic.

The cabin altitude is prevented from exceeding approximately 13 000 ft [3962.4 m] by the altitude-limit components of the valve. The altitude-limit chamber on the upper left of Fig. 12-21 is vented to cabin air pressure. As cabin air pressure decreases, the sealed bellows expands. If the cabin altitude exceeds the preset limit, the bellows expands enough to press on the small poppet just to the right of the bellows. This opens the reference chamber to cabin air pressure and causes the outflow valve to close. The valve remains closed as long as the cabin altitude is above the setting of the bellows. This operation can be overridden by the positive pressure-relief control system.

The **controller** that operates the outflow valve is located on the flight deck and is used by the pilot to select the desired rate of cabin altitude change and the cabin pressure altitude. The controller requires pressure inputs from the cabin air pressure and a venturi system, and generates a reference pressure. The vacuum pressure is usually a value generated by the Bernoulli effect as cabin air pressure escapes from the cabin to the outside air through a venturi. The vacuum line opens into the venturi chamber at the throat to create a low pressure. The value of the vacuum is determined by the difference in pressure between the cabin and the atmosphere.

The principle of operation of a controller can best be understood by studying the operation of a manual controller of the type shown in Fig. 12-22. When it is desired to decrease the cabin altitude, the manual con-

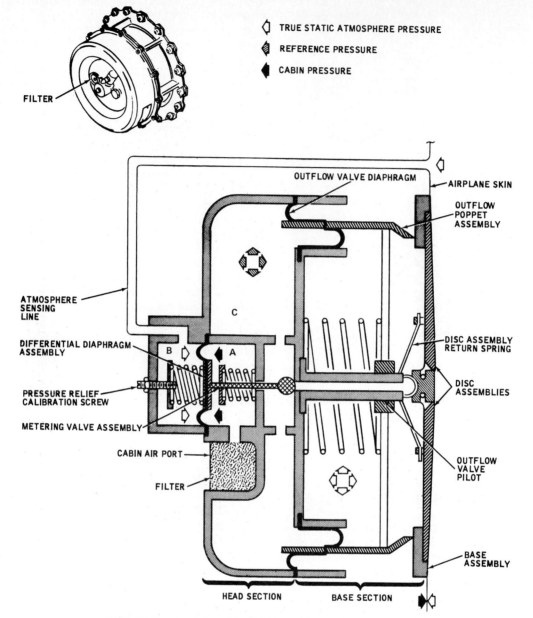

FIG. 12-20 A safety valve. *(McDonnell Douglas Aircraft Co.)*

trol lever is moved down. This opens the cabin pressure port and allows cabin pressure to be applied to the reference chamber in the outflow valve. This pressure in combination with the spring in the outflow valve holds the outflow valve closed, causing the cabin pressure to increase. The rate of airflow to the outflow valve is controlled by the manual rate control needle valve. If the pilot wishes to decrease the cabin pressure (increase cabin altitude), the control lever is moved upward and the vacuum port is opened to the line leading to the reference chamber. Pressure in the chamber is decreased, and this causes the outflow valve poppet to open and release cabin pressure.

The automatic controller performs the same basic operation as the manual controller just described. In the automatic controller, the pilot sets a rate control knob, if the manufacturer has not established a preset valve, and then he or she selects the desired cabin altitude. A spring and bellows arrangement then directs cabin pressure or vacuum to the outflow valve reference chamber. Once the preset altitude is reached, the controller maintains a reference chamber pressure to keep a constant cabin altitude.

● CABIN ENVIRONMENTAL SYSTEM FOR A JET AIRLINER

A typical **air-conditioning system** for a jet airliner is represented by the system employed for one model of the Boeing 727 airplane. This system provides conditioned, pressurized air to the crew cabin, passenger cabin, lower nose compartment, forward cargo compartment, air-conditioning distribution bay, and aft cargo compartment.

The air supply is furnished by engine bleed air when in flight and from engine bleed air, a ground pneumatic

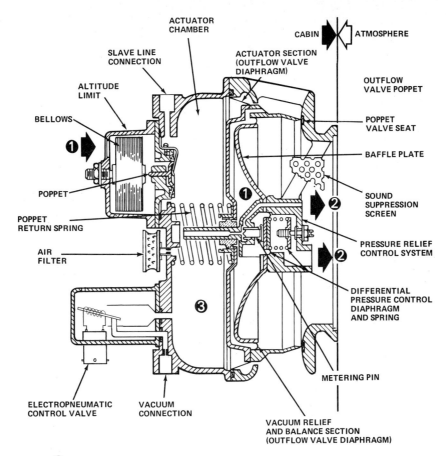

FIG. 12-21   An outflow valve. *(Canadair Inc.)*

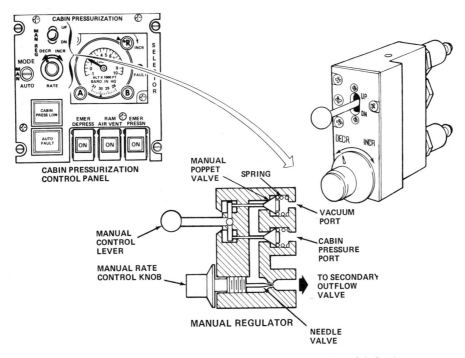

FIG. 12-22   A manual pressurization controller. *(Canadair Inc.)*

supply cart, or a ground conditioned-air supply cart during ground operation. Part of the warm-air supply from the engines (or pneumatic cart, if on the ground) is passed through the **air-conditioning packs** to be cooled. The cold air is then mixed with the remainder of the warm air as required to obtain the temperature of air called for by the temperature control system. This conditioned air then passes into conditioned areas through the distribution system. After the air has passed through the cabins, it is exhausted through a number of outlets. The combined air from all outlets other than the pressurization outflow valves, however, is limited to a value less than that which enters the cabin from the air-conditioning system. The **outflow valves** are regulated to exhaust only that additional quantity of air required to maintain the desired pressure in the cabin.

Other air outlets include the galley vent, lavatory vents, equipment-cooling outlets, the ground conditioned-air condensate drain, water-separator drains, the pressurization controllers cabin-to-ambient venturis, and the cargo-heat outflow valves. The cargo-heat outflow valves normally remain open to provide warmth around the cargo compartments, but they may be closed by a switch on the third crew member's panel.

Engines No. 1 and 3 furnish eighth- or thirteenth-stage compressor bleed air, depending upon engine power setting and air-conditioning demand. Eighth-stage bleed air from Engine No. 2 is also available as an alternate source. Bleed air from engines No. 1 and 3 passes through a heat exchanger (precooler) to reduce the air temperature to approximately 370°F [187.8°C]. A **precooler controller and modulating valve** combine to maintain the correct temperature. If difficulties occur in the controller, a thermoswitch prevents excessively hot air from entering the air-conditioning system by closing the bleed-air shutoff valve. Airflow to each air-conditioning system is regulated by a **flow-regulating servo and modulating valve.**

The air-conditioning system for the airplane described here consists, by function, of four subsystems. These are for cooling, temperature control, distribution, and pressurization control. (Cooling and temperature control are performed by the Cooling Packs.) These subsystems are shown schematically in Fig. 12-23. Another schematic-type drawing which provides a more realistic illustration of the system is shown in Fig. 12-24. This drawing gives the relative position of the various components of the system and can be studied in connection with further descriptions given in this section.

Cooling Packs

The cooling of air for this model of the Boeing 727 airplane is provided by means of two **cooling packs.** These packs also remove excess moisture from the air. With the exception of the water separator, which is located in the distribution bay, all cooling-pack equipment is contained inside the center fuselage fairing.

The cooling devices used in the cooling packs consist of a primary heat exchanger, a secondary heat exchanger, and an air-cycle machine (ACM). The heat exchangers are of the air-to-air type with heat being transferred from the air going through the packs to air going through the ram air system. The ACM consists of a turbine and a compressor. Air expanding through the turbine drops in temperature as the energy is extracted for the major cooling in the pack as explained previously. An air-cooling pack is shown in Fig. 12-25. In the drawing it can be seen that engine bleed air passes through the primary heat exchanger for initial cooling, then through the air-cycle-machine compressor, through the secondary heat exchanger, and then through the expansion turbine of the air-cycle machine. At this point the air is at its lowest temperature since the heat energy has been extracted by means of the heat exchangers and the expansion turbine.

Protection from overheat and overspeed of the air-cycle machine is provided by two thermal switches. One thermal switch senses compressor discharge temperature to close the pack valves when an overheat condition exists. The other thermal switch, located in the turbine inlet duct, closes the pack valves to prevent overspeed.

As the air cools, its moisture content condenses. The moisture is atomized so finely, however, that it will stay in suspension unless a special moisture-removing device is employed. This is the function of the **water separator.** Moisture entering the water separator is prevented from freezing by an anti-icing system. An anti-icing thermostat in the water separator actuates a 35°F [1.67°C] control valve in a duct between the primary heat-exchanger exit and the water-separator inlet. The valve opens to add warm air if the turbine discharge temperature approaches the freezing temperature of water.

The **primary heat exchanger** is the first unit of the cooling packs through which engine bleed air passes to be cooled. The unit is rectangular and is located between two sections of the ram air duct. Two plenum chambers in the heat exchanger are connected by a bank of tubes so as to allow maximum surface exposure of each tube to ram air passing across the outside of the tubes. Hot air enters one plenum chamber from the pneumatic duct at the aft inboard side of the exchanger. It is cooled as it passes through the tubes to a header and returns through tubes to the other plenum chamber, then leaves by way of the ACM duct connected to the forward inboard side of the heat exchanger. There is one primary heat exchanger for each cooling pack.

The ACM is a cooling unit consisting of an expansion turbine on a common shaft with a compressor. The shaft is bearing-mounted in a housing to support the rotating turbine and compressor. A wick extends from the shaft to the bottom of the oil sump formed by the housing for lubrication of the moving parts. A filler neck and filler cap with a dipstick are provided on each side of the housing.

The ACM unit is located in the midbody fairing between the duct leading from the primary heat exchanger and the duct to the water separator. A duct

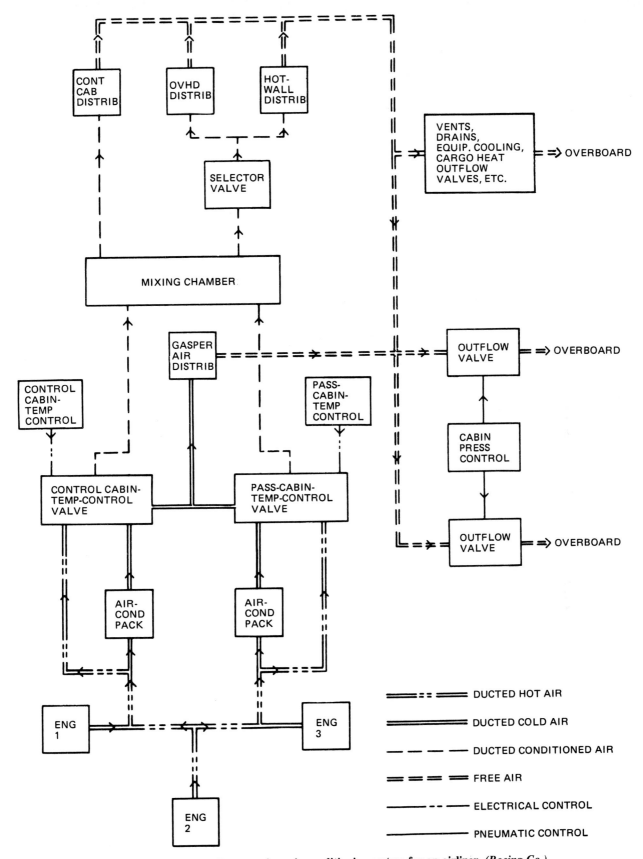

FIG. 12-23 Block diagram of an air-conditioning system for an airliner. *(Boeing Co.)*

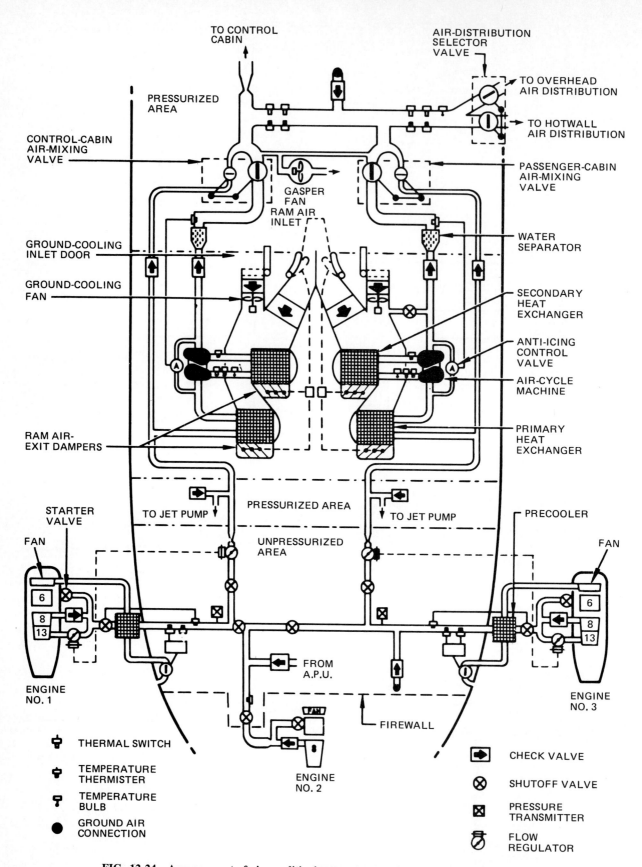

FIG. 12-24 Arrangement of air-conditioning components for an airliner. *(Boeing Co.)*

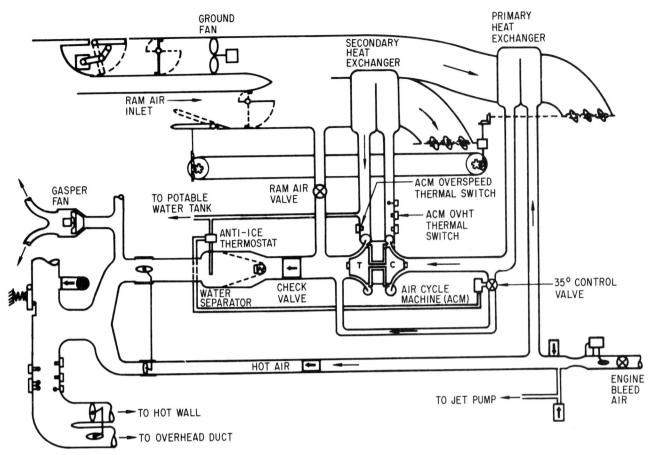

FIG. 12-25 Schematic diagram of a cooling pack. *(Boeing Co.)*

from the compressor and another to the turbine connect to the secondary heat exchanger. The turbine mounts are connected to the airplane structure through serrated plates to provide location adjustment. There is one air-cycle machine for each cooling pack.

As explained previously, the ACM cools compressed air by expansion. When the air is originally compressed by the engine compressor, its temperature rises in approximate proportion to the rise in air pressure. The heated compressed air is passed through the primary heat exchanger, where some of the heat energy is removed. It is then directed to the compressor section of the ACM.

In the compressor section the air is further compressed and heated. This additional heat is reduced in the **secondary heat exchanger,** which is located between the compressor and turbine of the air-cycle machine. The secondary heat exchanger is identical to the primary heat exchanger and is located between two sections of the inboard branch of the ram air duct. Air from the ACM compressor outlet enters the forward inboard connection to the secondary heat exchanger, passes through the cooling tubes, then returns to the turbine section of the ACM. As the air expands across the turbine, heat energy is expended in driving the turbine and through the expansion process. Thus the air leaving the turbine is at its lowest temperature.

Distribution

Air-conditioning **distribution** utilizes two entirely independent systems. The **individual air distribution system,** also called the **gasper system,** routes only the cold air from the air-conditioning packs to individually regulated outlets in the control and passenger cabins. The **conditioned-air distribution** system routes the mixture of hot and cold air to the passenger and control cabins.

The gasper system provides each crew member and each passenger with a method for cooling the local area to a value different from that provided by the normal air-conditioning automatic control. Air is received from the cold side of the **temperature control valve** and is ducted to each individual station. An adjustable nozzle at each station allows the individual a choice anywhere between no supplementary cold air and full-system-capacity cold air.

The conditioned-air distribution system dispenses temperature-controlled air evenly throughout the passenger and crew cabins. One duct system supplies the crew cabin, and another system supplies the passenger cabin. The passenger-cabin air is divided into two systems. The **overhead system** releases air into the cabin from holes in a duct running fore and aft in the passenger cabin ceiling. The **hot-wall duct system** takes air through ducts between the side-wall and interior lining and releases it through the cove light grills. A

441

selector valve at the main distribution manifold controlled from the control cabin permits using all overhead, all hot-wall, or any combination of the two distribution methods.

All the distribution systems originate in the **air-conditioning distribution bay.** The gasper distribution system originates at the cold ports of both air-mixing valves, and the conditioned-air distribution systems originate at the main distribution manifold. A drawing of the air-conditioning distribution bay is shown in Fig. 12-26.

Duct sections throughout both cabins are joined with clamps or tape. Means of equalizing the pressure in the ducts and headers and of balancing the flow from the outlets have been designed into each system. The distribution system ducts are protected against excessive pressure by a relief valve on the main distribution manifold.

The main distribution manifold is common to all the conditioned-air distribution systems. It is installed immediately downstream from the mixing chambers in the air-conditioning distribution bay. Protection against excessive pressure is afforded by means of a relief valve located as shown in Fig. 12-26. The relief valve is a spring-loaded flapper valve with a tension of 68.5 lb [304.8 N] on each of two springs. The valve is designed to limit the distribution pressure to a maximum of 18 in [45.7 cm] of water.

Approximately 10 percent of the conditioned air is directed to the airplane crew cabin. This is accomplished by the **control-cabin flow-limiting venturi.**

A dual selector valve divides the total passenger-cabin conditioned-air flow between the overhead distribution system and the sidewall distribution system. The selector valve consists of two butterfly valves installed in the main distribution manifold. One controls airflow to the overhead duct riser and the other controls airflow to the passenger-cabin sidewall air-distribution manifold. The valves are designed so that when one is fully closed, the other is fully open and vice versa. The selector valve is controlled by a lever mounted in the crew cabin. The lever can be operated by the third crewman from his seat.

Air is exhausted from the passenger cabin through air-exit grills and outflow holes in the sidewall just above the floor. It then flows around the cargo-compartment walls, where it assists in compartment temperature control. Some air then flows to the cargo-heat-distribution duct under the compartment floor and is discharged overboard through the cargo-heat outflow valves.

Part of the cabin air flows overboard through the two pressure-system **outflow valves** located in the rear of the aft cargo compartment. These valves regulate cabin air pressure.

Below each hole in the floor where air is exhausted

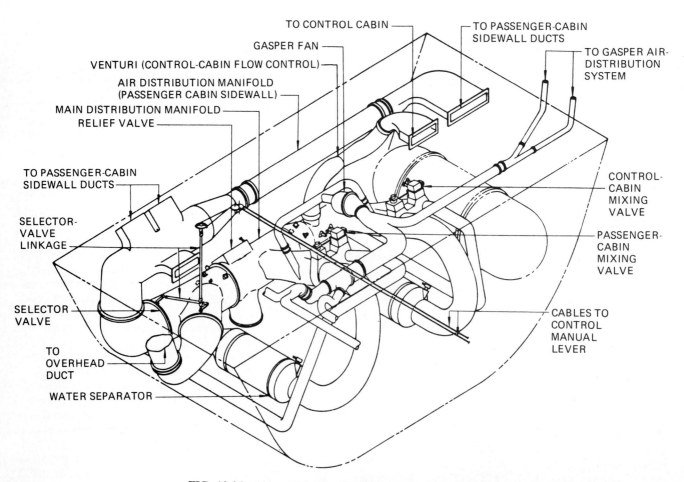

FIG. 12-26 Air-conditioning distribution bay. *(Boeing Co.)*

from the passenger cabin to the cargo compartment is a **flotation check valve.** This valve consists of a plastic ball retained by a cage. If the cargo compartment should become flooded, the ball will float up in its cage and block the hole to prevent flooding of the passenger cabin from the cargo compartment.

Pressurization Control System

The **pressurization control system** is a pneumatically operated system which meters the exhaust of cabin ventilating air to provide controlled pressurization of the crew and passenger cabins, the electronic compartment, both cargo compartments, and the lower nose compartment. Safety features of the system override selected control settings to prevent a pressure condition harmful to passengers or airplane structure.

The pressurization control system maintains constant low-altitude cabin pressure during airplane flight at high altitudes and controls the rate of pressure change in the cabin. Positive pressure relief at 9.42 ($\pm$0.15) psi [64.95 $\pm$ 1 kPa] pressure differential is provided to protect the airplane structure in the event of a pressure control system failure.

A negative pressure-relief mechanism lets air into the cabin when outside pressure exceeds cabin pressure and limits the negative pressure differential to 10 in [25.4 cm] of water. A barometric-correction selector helps choose proper landing-field altitude so the pressure differential at landing may approach 0 psi.

A **cabin-altitude limit control** will maintain a maximum of 13 000 ($\pm$1500) ft [3962 $\pm$ 457 m] cabin altitude if other control components fail and as long as the pneumatic system provides sufficient air for pressurization.

A **mode selector switch,** when placed in the GROUND VENTURI position, moves the outflow valves full open for ground operation of the air-conditioning system.

The pressurization control system consists of one automatic controller, one manual controller, two outflow valves, one test valve, one mode selector switch, two cabin-to-ambient venturis, and one fan venturi. The schematic drawing of Fig. 12-27 shows the relative position of these units in the system.

The indicating system includes a rate-of-climb indicator to show rate of pressure change in the cabin, an altitude warning horn to indicate low cabin pressure, and a dual altimeter and differential-pressure indicator.

During normal operation of the airplane, pressurized air is delivered from the pneumatic system, through the air-conditioning-and-distribution system to the pressurized compartments of the airplane. The desired

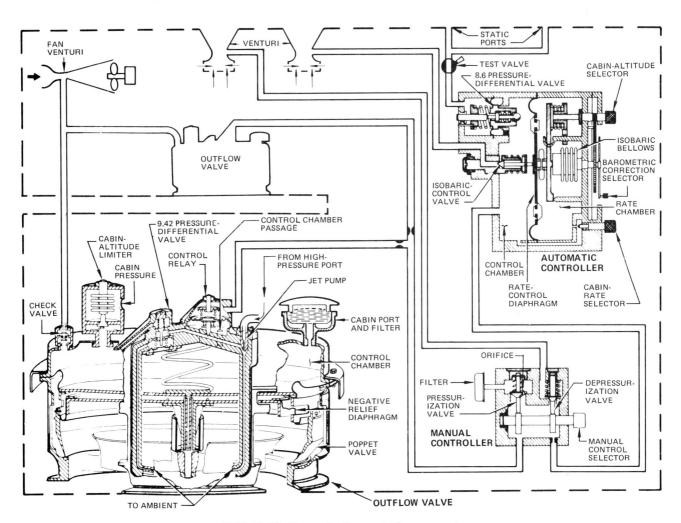

FIG. 12-27 Pressurization control components.

443

cabin pressure and rate of pressure change are selected on either the **automatic controller** or the **manual controller.** These controllers pneumatically signal the outflow valves so that the valve openings to the outside increase or decrease to vary air outflow in order to maintain the desired pressure. The automatic controller also regulates the rate of pressure change in the cabin and limits pressure differential between the interior of the cabin and the outside to 8.6 psi [59.3 kPa].

The pressurization control system components are shown in Fig. 12-27. The device at the lower left of the illustration is the **outflow valve,** that at the upper right is the **automatic controller,** and the unit at the lower right is the **manual controller.**

The **cabin-altitude selector** controls isobaric (constant-pressure) operation and can be set for cabin altitudes from 1000 ft [304.8 m] below sea level to 10 000 ft [3048 m] altitude. The selector dial also shows maximum airplane altitude (isobaric operation) for the selected cabin altitude and barometric correction. The selector setting affects the outflow valves through the controller components and the control lines to the outflow-valve pneumatic relays. The control line from the automatic controller connects to the manual controller, and another line from the manual controller connects to the outflow-valve pneumatic relays. A small orifice in the manual controller pressurization valve provides a high-pressure reference for the automatic controller. A line from the isobaric control valve port to the throat of a cabin-to-ambient (**ambient pressure** means the pressure surrounding the outside of the airplane) venturi provides the low-pressure reference for the automatic controller.

The cabin **rate-of-change selector** controls the rate of change of cabin pressure and can be set for rates from 50 to 2000 ft [15.24 to 609.6 m] per minute, though it is not calibrated. The rate-selector setting affects an orifice which regulates the rate of airflow between control chamber and rate chamber. Cabin pressure follows control-chamber pressure via the outflow valves; therefore, the rate of cabin-pressure change will follow the rate of control-chamber change.

The 8.6-psi [59.30-kPa] pressure-differential valve maintains a maximum pressure differential of 8.6 psi between cabin and ambient pressures, overriding cabin-altitude selections that would require more than 8.6 psi differential.

The cabin **barometric correction selector** corrects landing-field altitude for the barometric condition at the landing field, thus contributing toward an unpressurized cabin at landing. The **cabin-pressure manual controller** permits regulation of cabin pressure in case the automatic controller malfunctions or becomes inoperable. Having an independent low-pressure (cabin-to-ambient pressure venturi) and high-pressure (cabin-pressure) source, the manual controller will override any pneumatic signal from the automatic controller to the outflow valves. By adjusting the manual control, pressure in the outflow valve relays may be regulated to adjust outflow valve exhaust opening for desired pressurization. The controller consists of a chamber with a pressurization valve and a depressurization valve adjusted by a camshaft which is moved by a manual control selector. The manual controller is on the third crew member's panel.

The cabin-pressure manual control selector consists of a dial, an indicator, and a control knob. The knob moves a camshaft which adjusts the pressurization and depressurization valves so that when the knob indicator points to the right, pressure increases; when the indicator points to the left, the pressure decreases. Either operation overrides the automatic controller. When the knob indicator points to AUTO, the valves in the manual controller are closed, and only the automatic controller remains effective.

Two cabin-pressure outflow valves, mentioned previously, provide cabin-pressure regulation, cabin-altitude limiting, vacuum relief, and positive pressure relief. These valves are located to the right and left of the bottom centerline of the airplane, to the rear of the aft bulkhead of the aft cargo compartment. Each valve assembly includes a pneumatically balanced poppet valve with a vacuum-relief diaphragm, a control chamber, a cabin air port and filter, a positive pressure-relief valve, a pneumatic relay, a jet pump, an atmosphere port, a cabin-altitude limit control, and a ground venturi port.

The poppet valve assembly moves to regulate air passing from the cabin as pneumatic signals are received from the automatic or manual control through the pneumatic relay to the control chamber. The safety valves' positive pressure relief and cabin-altitude limiter also move the poppet valve by changing control-chamber pressure. Thus, the poppet valve either maintains a selected pressure or effects a change at a selected rate.

A vacuum-relief diaphragm lifts to contact and raise the poppet valve assembly to admit ambient air when ambient air pressure becomes higher than cabin pressure. The vacuum-relief system overrides automatic or manual control signals.

The **positive pressure-relief valve** causes the outflow valve to open and exhaust air when the differential between cabin and ambient pressure exceeds 9.42 (± 0.15) psi [65 kPa]. This function overrides automatic or manual control signals. The positive pressure-relief valve is built into the outflow valve and consists of two chambers divided by a spring-loaded diaphragm.

● SUMMARY OF PRESSURIZATION AND AIR-CONDITIONING SYSTEMS

In the foregoing section we have given a brief description of the principal functions and components of a typical air-conditioning system for a jet airliner. Numerous details have been omitted because space does not permit their description. The mechanic is reminded to consult the manufacturer's maintenance manual for service instructions and for information on the finer details.

As explained previously, air conditioning may include heating, ventilating, cooling, and pressurization. The methods and devices involved have been described but will be reviewed briefly in this summary.

Heating for an aircraft may be accomplished by

drawing air across a heated exhaust manifold (heat exchanger), drawing air through a combustion heater, or utilizing heated air from the compressor of one or more turbine engines. The use of exhaust heat from a piston engine involves the danger of a crack in the exhaust manifold, allowing exhaust fumes to enter the heating ducts. Frequent inspections and tests are required to assure that leaks do not occur.

Combustion heaters may become inoperable because of fuel-system failure, ignition-system failure, or overheating. If such a heater overheats, an overheat sensor will cause the fuel to be shut off to prevent damage due to excess heat. Regular inspection and testing of the heater system components are necessary to assure dependable operation.

Heating large commercial aircraft is accomplished through the use of heated air produced by the compressors of gas-turbine engines. The heated air is distributed to the cabin, flight compartment, cargo compartment, and other areas to provide the temperatures desired. When a particular temperature has been selected by a member of the flight crew, the temperature is maintained by automatic controls which sense the temperature and adjust valves in the ducting to increase or decrease hot or cold airflow and mix the air to provide the correct temperature. The valve controlling the cold-hot air mixture is called a **mixing valve,** and its function is to direct the correct proportions of cold and hot air to a **mixing chamber** or other mixing device to produce the temperatures desired. In some systems, **trim heat** is employed to raise the temperature in a particular area. A trim-heat manifold carries hot air which can be released through outlets in any one of several areas. Thus it is possible to have a higher temperature in one area than in other areas. As explained previously, the heating, cooling, ventilation, and pressurization systems are all interconnected to provide the air-conditioning or cabin atmosphere system. Thus we may say that the air-conditioning system consists of four subsystems.

Cooling in an air-conditioning system is usually provided by means of either a vapor-cycle refrigeration system or an ACM which utilizes air as a cooling medium. Cool air from the cooling unit or units is mixed with warm air to provide the desired temperature. The amount of cooling produced and utilized is also controlled by bypassing air around the cooling unit. The amount of bypassed air is controlled through a **cabin temperature control valve.** Commercial passenger aircraft incorporate a **gasper** system which enables each passenger to control cooled airflow to his or her location. An adjustable gasper valve is located overhead at each location or in the back of the seat ahead. The gasper system draws cold air directly from the cooling unit output before it is mixed with warmer air.

Pressurization and ventilation sysems are closely related. The flow of air which provides pressurization also provides ventilation.

Pressurization of small aircraft designed for high-altitude operation is usually accomplished by bleeding air from the engine turbocharger(s) or super charger(s) and ducting it into the cabin. Manual and automatic controllers are employed to adjust the outflow valve for desired cabin pressure. Pressurization for large aircraft is usually accomplished through the use of bleed air from the gas-turbine engines.

The pressure in the cabin of an airplane is usually designated as **cabin altitude** rather than in terms of pounds per square inch gauge or kilopascals. The **differential pressure** between the inside and the outside of the aircraft is given as pounds per square inch or kilopascals. The differential pressure must be limited to the value established by engineers as safe for the structural strength of the fuselage, thus the slang term "an aluminum balloon." The automatic pressure controller incorporates a valve which limits the value of the differential pressure to a given level. If this pressure-differential valve should not operate, a **differential pressure-relief valve** will open at a slightly higher pressure and release cabin air.

The cabin altitude is selected by a member of the flight crew by means of the cabin altitude selector on the automatic cabin pressure controller. The **isobaric** control system in the controller maintains a constant cabin altitude until the altitude of the aircraft produces a differential pressure above that which is safe for the aircraft. At this time, the pressure-differential valve opens and reduces the pressure in the control chamber of the controller. This causes the controller to send a pneumatic signal to the outflow valve(s), requiring an increased opening and a greater outflow of air from the cabin.

In addition to a differential pressure-relief valve in the fuselage of a pressurized aircraft, a **negative pressure-relief valve** is installed. The purpose of this valve is to allow outside air to enter the fuselage at any time outside pressure is greater than the pressure in the airplane.

As shown in the drawing of Fig. 12-28, an air-conditioning system includes a large number of flow-control valves, regulating valves, and check valves. This drawing shows how the cooling packs are incorporated in the air-conditioning system. The control valves are operated manually or automatically, either from the flight station or from points in the aircraft where special conditions are required. The check valves assure that the air can flow in one direction only. This prevents properly conditioned air from backflowing into inactive parts of the system or escaping overboard through ground service connections.

As explained previously, the cabin pressure is designated as cabin altitude. A particular cabin altitude is usually selected for the main part of the flight, and this cabin altitude is usually much greater (lower pressure) than the point of takeoff. It is, therefore, necessary for the cabin altitude to change gradually from the altitude at the point of takeoff to the cabin altitude selected for the flight. This change is made by the **cabin altitude rate selector,** which adjusts the rate system built into the automatic cabin pressure controller. The rate system is also called the **automatic cabin rate-of-climb control system.**

Because of the complexity of air-conditioning systems in large aircraft, it is sometimes necessary to provide for augmentation of airflow in some areas. This is true of the galley and toilet areas in order to

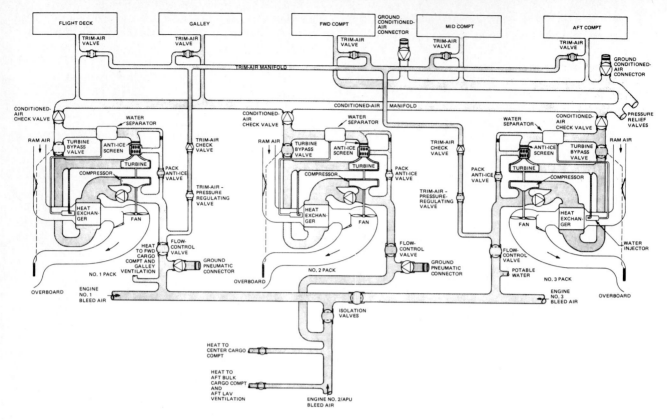

FIG. 12-28   Air-conditioning system for a wide-bodied airliner. *(McDonnell Douglas Aircraft Co.)*

eliminate fumes and odors. To accomplish this purpose, **jet pumps** are employed in some systems. A jet pump, sometimes called an **ejector,** consists of a high-velocity jet or air injected by means of a nozzle through a venturi or cylinder as shown in the schematic drawing of Fig. 12-29. The stream of high-ve-

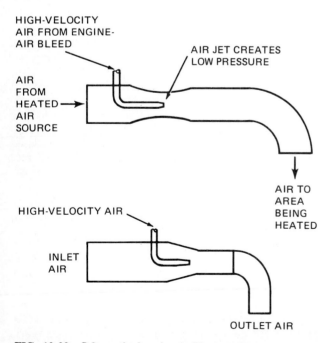

FIG. 12-29   Schematic drawing to illustrate jet pumps.

locity air from the jet nozzle creates a low-pressure area which draws air into the venturi or cylinder and causes it to flow to the discharge duct. Jet pumps are used in some systems to increase the temperature in areas where the basic system does not provide the desired temperature. For example, jet pumps are used in the DC-10 airplane to heat the cargo compartment as shown in Fig. 12-30. In this case, the jet pump is a cylindrically shaped device open at one end and connected to the distribution duct at the other end. A pneumatic supply line carrying pressurized hot air connects to the jet pump nozzle which is located on the center line of the cylinder and is pointed toward the distribution duct. High-pressure air from the pneumatic manifold is ejected from the nozzle, creating a negative pressure in the cylinder. Utility tunnel air flows into the open end of the cylinder, mixes with the hot air from the nozzle, and then is distributed by the ducting to the diffusers. A similar system is used to heat the lower galley floor area.

When an airplane is not in flight and air-conditioning is required, the air is supplied by the auxiliary power unit (APU) on board the aircraft or by a ground service unit. Both the APU and the ground service unit are small gas-turbine engines designed to produce a high volume of compressed air. The units also drive alternators which supply necessary electrical power. The air supply from the APU or the ground service unit is also used to operate the pneumatic turbine starters for some aircraft engines.

In recent years, highly efficient screw-type compressors have been developed for ground air supplies.

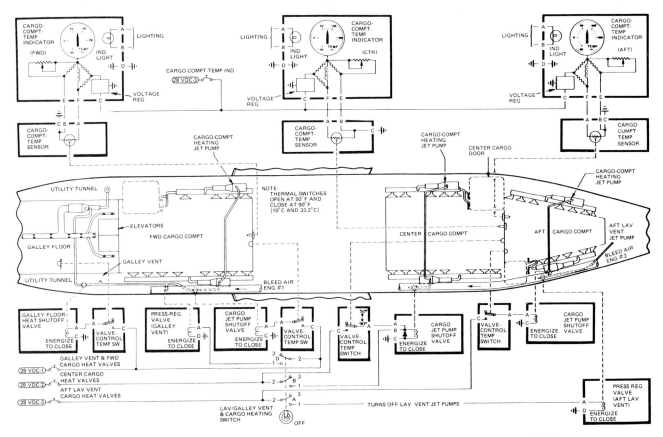

FIG. 12-30 Jet pumps used to heat cargo compartment. *(McDonnell Douglas Aircraft Co.)*

These are driven by diesel engines or electric motors and are mounted in mobile service units. Some airports have been equipped with fixed air supplies where the air is compressed at a central location and then it is delivered to individual aircraft stations through air ducts.

Inspection, service, and maintenance for the APU are similar to those prescribed for other gas-turbine engines. Instructions are provided in the maintenance manual for the aircraft.

● OXYGEN SYSTEMS

Oxygen systems are required on airplanes which fly for extended periods at altitudes substantially above 10 000 ft [3048 m]. Although the normal human body can survive without a special supply of oxygen at altitudes of over 15 000 ft [4573 m], the mental and physical capacities of the human being are reduced when the usual supply of oxygen is not available in the air. It is particularly important that the pilot and crew of an airplane have an adequate supply of oxygen when operating an unpressurized airplane at altitudes in excess of 10 000 ft [3048 m].

A lack of oxygen causes a person to experience a condition called **hypoxia.** This condition results in "lightheadedness," headaches, dizziness, nausea, unconsciousness, or death, depending upon the duration and degree of hypoxia. When permanent physical damage results from lack of oxygen, the condition is defined as **anoxia.**

The importance of oxygen, especially when flying at higher altitudes, is not appreciated by many persons who fly, including pilots. It is generally known that the human body requires oxygen to sustain life, but the effects of a lack of sufficient oxygen on various functions of the body are not understood by a large percentage of the flying public.

Studies have shown that the effects of hypoxia become apparent at approximately 5000 ft [1500 m] altitude in the form of reduced night vision. It is recommended, therefore, that a pilot flying above 5000 ft altitude at night use oxygen. As stated before, pilots flying above 10 000 ft [3048 m] altitude should use oxygen. Requirements for oxygen in aircraft are set forth in FAR Parts 23, 25, and 91.

Two principal factors affect the amount of oxygen that a person will absorb. These are (1) the amount of oxygen in the air the person is breathing and (2) the pressure of the air and oxygen mixture. Normal air contains approximately 21% oxygen, and this provides adequate oxygen for the human body at lower altitudes. At 34 000 ft [10 363 m] altitude, a person must be breathing 100% oxygen to absorb the same amount of oxygen as when breathing air at sea level. It is, therefore, apparent that the percentage of oxygen in the air which a person is breathing must be increased in keeping with altitude if a person is to receive an adequate supply of oxygen for optimum functioning of physical and mental faculties and functions. To adjust for variations in cabin altitude, oxygen systems are often equipped with barometric regulators which

447

increase the flow of oxygen as cabin altitude increases. In a nonpressurized aircraft, the cabin altitude is the same as the aircraft altitude, and the oxygen flow is adjusted for aircraft altitude.

Types of Oxygen Systems

Oxygen systems, classified according to source of oxygen supply, may be described as **stored-gas, chemical or solid-state,** and **liquid oxygen** (LOX) systems. Systems for private and commercial aircraft are of the stored-gas or chemical type. LOX systems are limited to military aircraft and will not be discussed in this text.

Oxygen systems may be **portable** or **fixed.** The fixed system is permanently installed in an airplane where a need for oxygen may exist at any time during flight at high altitudes. Commercial airplanes are always equipped with fixed systems augmented by a few portable units for crew members who must be mobile and for emergency situations where only one or two persons may require oxygen for unusual physical reasons.

A typical portable unit or system is shown in Fig. 12-31. The simplest type of portable oxygen system includes a Department of Transportation (DOT)–approved oxygen cylinder of either 11 ft^3 [311.5 L] capacity or 22 ft^3 [623 L] capacity, a regulator assembly, a pressure gauge, an ON-OFF valve, hose couplings, flow indicator, and one or two oronasal masks. This system is charged to 1800 psi [12 411 kPa] and is suitable for altitudes up to 28 000 ft [8536 m].

Portable oxygen systems are available with automatic flow-control regulators which adjust oxygen flow in accordance with altitude.

Oxygen systems are also classified according to the type of regulator which controls the flow of oxygen. The mask employed must be compatible with the type of regulator. The majority of oxygen systems for both private and commercial aircraft are of the **continuous-flow** type. The regulator on the oxygen supply provides a continuous flow of oxygen to the mask. The mask valving provides for mixing of ambient air with the oxygen during the breathing process. As mentioned previously, some continuous-flow systems adjust flow rate in accordance with altitude.

Demand and diluter-demand regulators used with demand masks supply oxygen to the user during inhalation. When the individual using the equipment

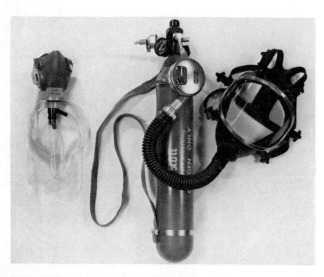

FIG. 12-31 A portable oxygen system with two regulators and masks. *(Scott Aviation)*

FIG. 12-32 A composite oxygen bottle *(left)* **and a steel bottle** *(right)*. *(Scott Aviation)*

inhales, he or she causes a reduction of pressure in a chamber in the regulator. This reduction in pressure activates the oxygen valve and supplies oxygen to the mask. A flow indicator shows when oxygen flow is taking place. The diluter-demand regulator automatically adjusts the percentage of oxygen and air supplied to the mask in accordance with altitude. The demand masks cover most of the user's face and create an airtight seal. This is why a low pressure is created when the user inhales. These masks are used primarily by aircrew members because they use the oxygen more efficiently and have higher altitude capabilities.

Pressure-demand regulators contain an aneroid mechanism which automatically increases the flow of oxygen into the mask under positive pressure. This enables the user to absorb more oxygen under the conditions at very high altitudes. This type of equipment is normally used at altitudes above 40 000 ft [13 632 m]. The additional pressure is needed to enable the user to absorb oxygen at a greater rate than it would be absorbed at ambient pressure. A **pressure-demand** mask must be worn with a pressure-demand regulator. By action of special pressure-compensating valves, the mask provides for a buildup of oxygen pressure from the regulator and creates the required input of oxygen into the lungs.

Oxygen Bottles

Oxygen cylinders, also called **oxygen bottles,** are the containers used to hold the aircraft gaseous oxygen supply. The cylinders may be designed to carry oxygen at a high or low pressure.

High-pressure cylinders are designed to contain oxygen at a pressure of approximately 1800 psi [12 411 kPa]. These cylinders can be identified by their green color and by the words "Aviators' Breathing Oxygen" on the side of the cylinder. Because of the high pressure in the cylinders they must be very strong to withstand the operational stress without shattering. Three types of construction are used: a high-strength, heat-treated, steel-alloy cylinder; a wire-wrapped metal cylinder; and a Kevlar-wrapped aluminum cylinder. Figure 12-32 shows typical oxygen cylinders.

High-pressure cylinders are manufactured in several sizes and shapes. The cylinders are designed for a maximum operating pressure of about 2000 psi [13 740 kPa] but are normally serviced to a pressure of be-

tween 1800 and 1850 psi [12 411 and 12 755.8 kPa]. To obtain the proper pressure for the ambient air temperature, aircraft manufacturers often supply charts similar to that shown in Fig. 12-33. When using one of these charts, make sure that it is the correct one for the system you are servicing.

Low-pressure cylinders are made either of stainless steel with stainless steel bands seam-welded to the body of the cylinder or of low-alloy steel. These cylinders are painted yellow to distinguish them from the high-pressure cylinders. The low-pressure cylinders are designed to store oxygen at a maximum of 450 psi [3100.5 kPa], although they are not normally filled above 425 psi [2928 kPa].

There are several types of cylinder valves in use. The hand-wheel type has a wheel on the top of the valve and operates like a water faucet. The valve opens as the wheel is turned counterclockwise. If the cylinder does not incorporate a hand-wheel design with a slow-opening feature, a surge of pressure can be sent into the oxygen system and cause damage.

Another type of valve is of the self-opening design. When the valve is attached to the oxygen system, a check valve is moved off of its seat, allowing the cylinder to charge the system.

A third type of valve uses a cabin-operated push-pull control to operate a control lever on the top of the valve. This eliminates the necessity of always having the oxygen system charged but allows the pilot to activate the system whenever needed. This valve also can incorporate a pressure regulator so that there is no damage from a pressure surge in the system when the valve is opened.

Oxygen cylinders are often fitted with safety disks which rupture if the pressure in the cylinder becomes too great. (The pressure can rise significantly due to high ambient air temperatures heating the cylinder.) The released oxygen is vented overboard through a discharge line. The discharge line should exit the aircraft through a discharge indicator, shown in Fig. 12-34, so that the discharge can be readily detected during preflight and maintenance inspections.

Regulators

Regulators for the pressure and flow of oxygen are incorporated in stored-gas systems because the oxygen is stored in high-pressure cylinders under pres-

Ambient Temperature, °F	Filling Pressure, psig	Ambient Temperature, °F	Filling Pressure, psig
0	1650	50	1875
10	1700	60	1925
20	1725	70	1975
30	1775	80	2000
40	1825	90	2050

FIG. 12-33 Oxygen bottle filling chart. (*Cessna Aircraft Co.*)

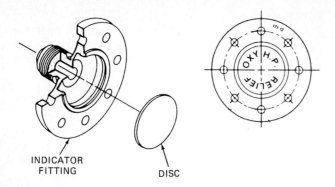

FIG. 12-34 Oxygen overboard discharge indicator. *(Scott Aviation)*

sures of 1800 psig [12 411 kPa] or more. The high pressure must be reduced to a value suitable for application directly to a mask or to a breathing regulator. This lower pressure is usually in the range of 40 to 75 psig [279 to 517 kPa], depending upon the system. One type of pressure regulator is illustrated in Fig. 12-35.

This pressure regulator is similar in design to many other gas- or air-pressure regulators in that it utilizes a diaphragm balanced against a spring to control the flow of gas. This regulator consists of a **housing, diaphragm, regulator spring, link actuator assembly, relief valve,** and an **inlet valve.** With no inlet pressure on the regulator, spring tension on the diaphragm through the link actuator assembly forces the inlet valve to the open position. When oxygen is flowing, regulated pressure in the lower diaphragm chamber acts against the diaphragm, causing it to move upward, compressing the regulator spring. The link actuator assembly then mechanically causes the regulator valve to move toward the closed position, thus reducing the flow of oxygen. When the pressure in the lower chamber of the diaphragm is equal to the regulator spring force, the diaphragm ceases to move and positions the inlet valve to maintain the proper oxygen flow.

Regulators for demand systems include both pressure regulators and demand or diluter-demand regulators. The demand regulator is sometimes built into the demand mask. Regulated oxygen pressure from

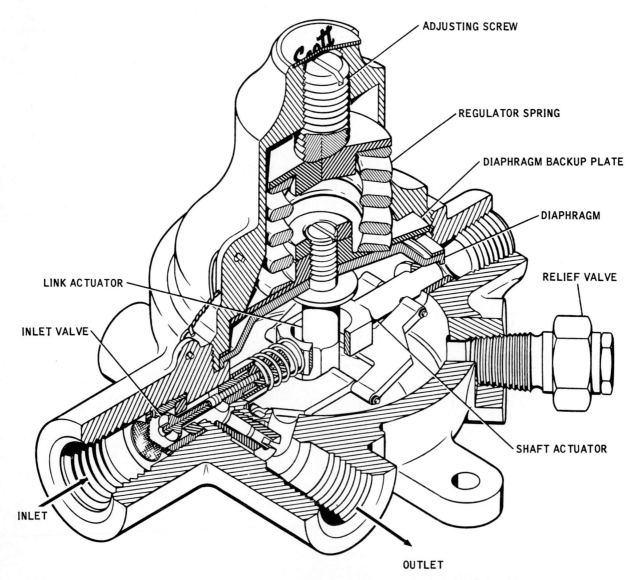

FIG. 12-35 Crew oxygen-supply regulator for an airliner.

the pressure regulator is applied to the demand regulator which, in turn, delivers it to the user while inhaling through the demand mask. As explained previously, the diluter-demand regulator "dilutes" the pure oxygen with air in accordance with the cabin altitude.

A diluter-demand regulator is shown in Fig. 12-36. When the user inhales, a slight negative pressure is created in the chamber to the right of the demand diaphragm. This pressure reduction causes the diaphragm to move to the right and opens the demand valve. This causes a negative pressure to be applied to the chamber under the reducing valve diaphragm, moving the diaphragm to the left. When the diaphragm moves to the left, the pressure-reducing valve is lifted off of its seat, allowing oxygen to enter the regulator and flow toward the mask.

The mixing of air with oxygen is caused by the **aneroid** in the mixing chamber. The aneroid is a sealed metal bellows. At sea level the aneroid is compressed by atmospheric pressure so that the oxygen-metering port is closed and the air-metering port is open. As atmospheric pressure is decreased, the aneroid expands, opening the oxygen-metering port and reducing the air-metering port. At an altitude of approximately 34 000 ft [10 363.2 m], the air-metering port is completely closed and the user is receiving only oxygen.

The diluter control closing mechanism can be used to override the diluter control operation of the system by mechanically closing off the air-metering port and

fully opening the oxygen-metering port. Additionally, if the mechanism should malfunction, the user can open the emergency metering control and bypass the diluter mechanism and be supplied with pure oxygen.

The pressure regulator for the continuous-flow passenger oxygen system installed in an airliner is shown in Fig. 12-37. This regulator is attached to the high-pressure oxygen storage cylinder hand shutoff valve. It is an altitude-compensating type which varies supply-line pressure in accordance with cabin altitude. The regulator is actuated automatically by sensing a rise in cabin-pressure altitude, or manually by controls located on the body of the regulator. A relief valve in the regulator will open to prevent outlet pressure from exceeding approximately 150 psig [1034 kPa].

At 10 500- to 12 000-ft [3200- to 3656-m] cabin pressure altitude, the **automatic-opening aneroid** expands, thus causing the valve to open and supply pressure to the **pressure surge unit.** Increased pressure through the surge unit actuates the **door-release check valve,** unlatches the mask container doors, and pressurizes the dispensing manifolds. On descent, at a cabin pressure altitude of 6000 to 10 000 ft [1829 to 3048 m], the automatic-opening aneroid contracts, causing the valve to close and shutting off the oxygen supply. It is then necessary to place the manual control in the ON position to supply supplemental oxygen to passengers as necessary. If the automatic-opening valve fails to function properly, the system is pressurized by placing the regulator manual control in the ON position

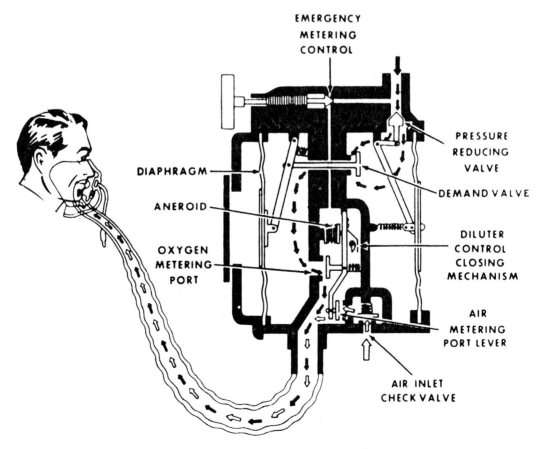

FIG. 12-36 Diluter-demand oxygen regulator.

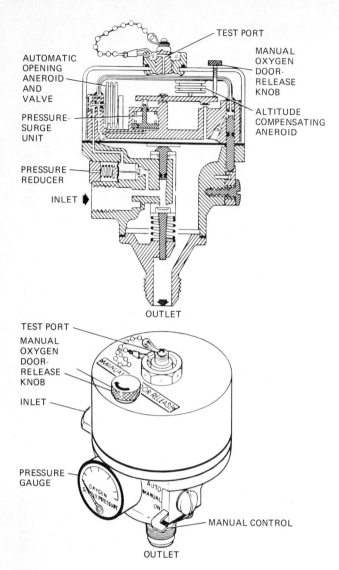

FIG. 12-37 Passenger oxygen-pressure regulator.

closely, enclosing both the mouth and nose, and must form an airtight seal with the face. Inhalation by the user will then cause a low pressure in the demand regulator which results in opening of an oxygen valve and a flow of oxygen to the mask. When the user exhales, the flow of oxygen is cut off.

An oxygen mask for a constant-flow system is designed so that some ambient air is mixed with the oxygen. The complete mask usually includes an oronasal face piece, a reservoir bag, valves, a supply hose, and a coupling fitting. Some models include a **flow indicator** in the supply hose.

When the oxygen is turned on to a constant-flow mask, it fills the reservoir through a valve. When inhaling, the user draws oxygen directly from the reservoir bag. When the oxygen in the reservoir bag is depleted, the user breathes cabin air. When the user exhales, the reservoir bag refills with oxygen. The oxygen from the supply line flows continuously into the mask, sometimes filling the reservoir bag and at other times being breathed by the user. Exhaled oxygen and air are discharged from the mask into the cabin. Typical examples of continuous-flow oxygen masks are shown in Fig. 12-38. Masks of these types are usually provided with space for the installation of a microphone.

Passenger oxygen masks for airliners are of the constant-flow type and the face piece is oronasal in design; that is, it is designed to cover both the nose and the mouth. They are referred to as **phase-dilution** masks because of the characteristics of their operation.

When oxygen is turned on to the passenger mask, it enters the bottom of the reservoir bag and causes it to inflate. When inhaling, the user draws oxygen from the reservoir bag until it is deflated. At that time, the user begins to breathe cabin air plus a small amount of oxygen which is flowing through the reservoir. Thus, there are two phases of oxygen consumption during inhalation. The first and largest part of the inhalation draws almost pure oxygen into the lungs. When the reservoir bag has deflated, the user continues to inhale but is breathing cabin air, primarily. The first part of the inhalation provides a very rich oxygen mixture which goes deep into the lungs. The last part of the inhalation, in which cabin air is being breathed, affects only the upper part of the lungs, the bronchial tubes, and the windpipe (trachea). Since these parts of the respiratory system do not contribute to the absorption of oxygen by the blood, the low oxygen content of the cabin air breathed during the last part of inhalation is of little consequence.

When the user of the mask exhales, the air is discharged through an exit valve in the mask to the cabin atmosphere. At this time, the reservoir bag refills with oxygen; however, the bag does not always fill completely, particularly if the user is breathing rapidly. If the flow rate of oxygen is only 1 L/min, which is normal for a cabin altitude of 15 000 ft [4573 m], the reservoir bag does not have time to fill between each inhalation by the passenger. This has caused concern among some passengers because they have thought they were not receiving an adequate flow of oxygen.

A passenger wearing an oxygen mask on a DC-10

and turning the manual oxygen-door release knob to the full-rotated position.

Oxygen entering the regulator passes through the **pressure reducer** and the **automatic-opening valve** and then enters the **altitude-compensating aneroid chamber.** As the aneroid expands and contracts owing to the changes in cabin pressure altitude, the outlet flow and pressure vary. When the cylinder is fully charged to approximately 1850 psig [12 756 kPa], the maximum outlet flow at the regulator is 430 L/min, and the maximum pressure is approximately 80 psig [552 kPa] at 35 000 ft [10 668 m].

First-aid oxygen can be made available during normal operation of the pressurized airplane if necessary. This is accomplished by a crew member placing the regulator manual control in the ON position.

Oxygen Masks

Oxygen masks vary considerably in size, shape, and design; however, each is designed for either a **demand** system or a **continuous-flow (constant-flow)** system. An oxygen mask for a demand system must fit the face

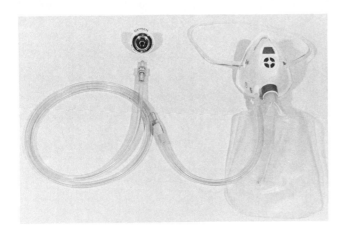

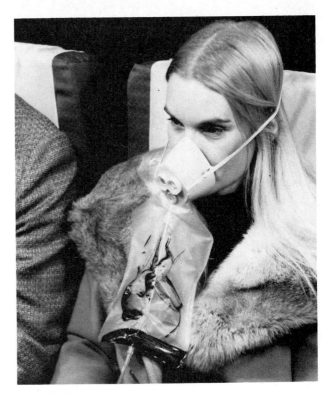

FIG. 12-39 A passenger wearing a continuous-flow oxygen mask on an airliner. *(Scott Aviation)*

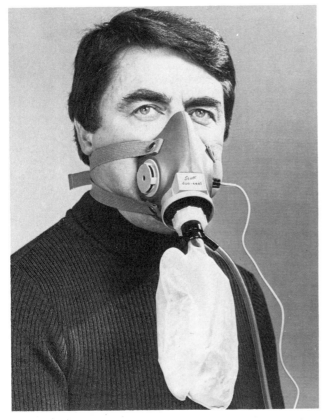

FIG. 12-38 Two types of continuous-flow oxygen masks. *(Scott Aviation)*

airliner is shown in Fig. 12-39. This particular mask has a built-in flow indicator at the bottom of the reservoir bag. A small section of the bag has been partially sealed off so it will inflate immediately when even a small amount of oxygen is flowing. The indicator is colored a bright green so the passenger can see at once whether oxygen is flowing into the mask.

Oxygen masks on airliners are stowed in overhead compartments or in a compartment at the top of the seat back. If the cabin should depressurize, the compartments open automatically and present oxygen masks to the passengers. If the automatic system fails to work, a backup electrical system can be activated by a member of the crew to open the oxygen compartments.

Pressurized aircraft are normally equipped with diluter-demand oxygen systems for use by the flight deck crew. The masks used by the crew are of an oronasal design and contain microphones and a strap or harness arrangement that will hold the mask securely in position. For some aircraft which operate at very high altitudes, quick-donning masks are used. These masks can be put on in 5 s or less. Figure 12-40 shows the pneumatic harness type of diluter-demand masks.

Gaseous Oxygen Systems for Unpressurized Aircraft

Unpressurized aircraft which are capable of flying at altitudes requiring the use of oxygen by crew and passengers may be equipped with portable or fixed gaseous oxygen systems. The system includes a high-pressure oxygen tank, a pressure regulator, pressure gauge, manifold, and various types of outlets (fittings) to which tubing connected to masks may be attached. The regulators may be of the demand type or the constant-flow type. It is preferred that the regulators and masks for the pilot and copilot be of the demand type. In most cases, however, constant-flow regulators and masks are used for both crew and passengers.

A permanently installed (fixed), stored-gas oxygen system for a light twin airplane is shown in Fig. 12-41. This system consists of a high-pressure oxygen cylinder with a regulator, an altitude-compensating regulator, a filler valve, an overboard discharge indicator, a control cable and knob, a cylinder pressure gauge, outlets, oxygen masks, and required plumbing. The supply regulator attached to the oxygen cylinder reduces the high cylinder pressure to a lower constant

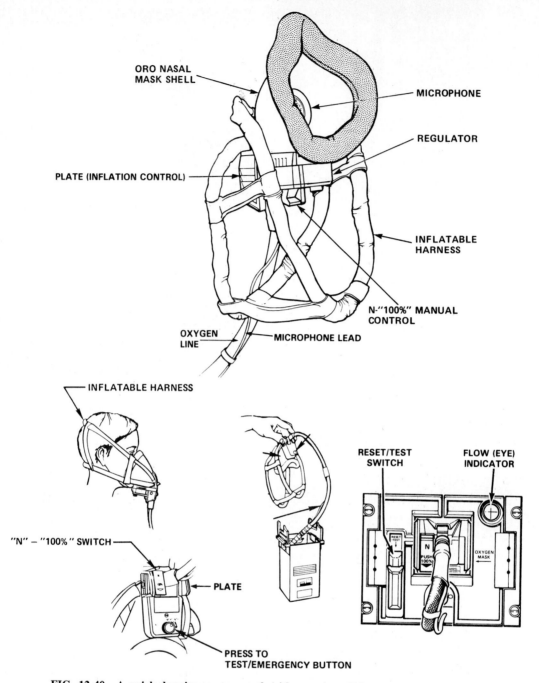

ORO NASAL
MASK SHELL

MICROPHONE

REGULATOR

PLATE (INFLATION CONTROL)

INFLATABLE
HARNESS

N-"100%" MANUAL
CONTROL

OXYGEN
LINE

MICROPHONE LEAD

INFLATABLE HARNESS

"N" – "100%" SWITCH

PLATE

PRESS TO
TEST/EMERGENCY BUTTON

RESET/TEST
SWITCH

FLOW (EYE)
INDICATOR

FIG. 12-40 A quick-donning oxygen mask with a pneumatic harness. *(Canadair Inc.)*

pressure. The altitude-compensating regulator reduces oxygen expenditure at lower altitudes, thus increasing oxygen supply duration. The pressure gauge shows actual cylinder pressure.

The control knob on the instrument panel is used to open a valve and allow controlled oxygen pressure to flow to the mask outlets. When a mask fitting is plugged into an outlet, a continuous flow of oxygen is available at the mask. The masks include flow indicators for visual verification of oxygen flow. The masks, hoses, and flow indicators are stored in plastic bags where they are readily available to crew and passengers.

The oxygen outlets are installed in the overhead

console and above the passenger seats. Each outlet contains a spring-loaded valve which prevents oxygen flow until the mask hose is engaged with the outlet.

The oxygen filler valve is usually located under an access panel on the outside of the fuselage and near the oxygen cylinder. The filler valve consists of the valve incorporating a filter and valve cap. A check valve is installed in the high-pressure line at the regulator to prevent the escape of oxygen from the cylinder at the filler line port. A typical service panel is shown in Fig. 12-42.

The overboard discharge indicator is located on the bottom or side of the aircraft near the oxygen bottle. A low-pressure (60 ± 20 psi [413.7 ± 137.9 kPa])

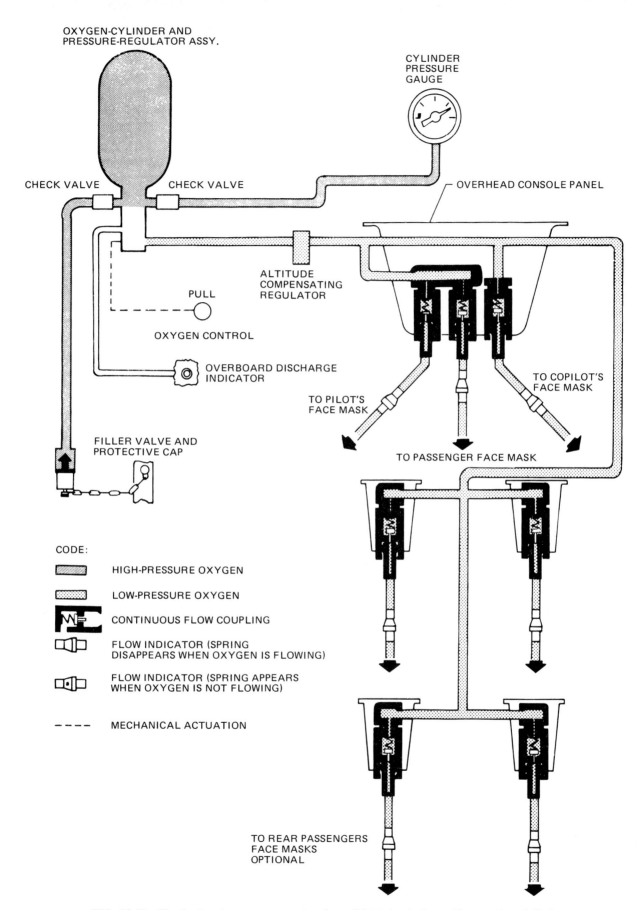

OXYGEN-CYLINDER AND
PRESSURE-REGULATOR ASSY.

CYLINDER
PRESSURE
GAUGE

CHECK VALVE   CHECK VALVE

OVERHEAD CONSOLE PANEL

ALTITUDE
COMPENSATING
REGULATOR

PULL

OXYGEN CONTROL

OVERBOARD DISCHARGE
INDICATOR

TO COPILOT'S
FACE MASK

TO PILOT'S
FACE MASK

TO PASSENGER FACE MASK

FILLER VALVE AND
PROTECTIVE CAP

CODE:

HIGH-PRESSURE OXYGEN

LOW-PRESSURE OXYGEN

CONTINUOUS FLOW COUPLING

FLOW INDICATOR (SPRING
DISAPPEARS WHEN OXYGEN IS FLOWING)

FLOW INDICATOR (SPRING APPEARS
WHEN OXYGEN IS NOT FLOWING)

---- MECHANICAL ACTUATION

TO REAR PASSENGERS
FACE MASKS
OPTIONAL

FIG. 12-41   Fixed, stored-gas oxygen system for a light twin airplane. *(Cessna Aircraft Co.)*

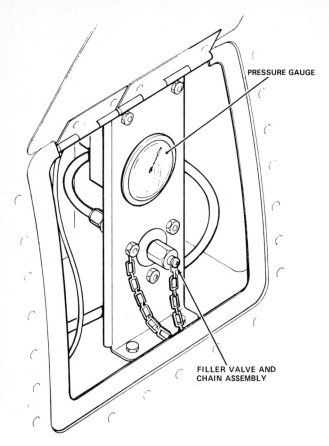

PRESSURE GAUGE

FILLER VALVE AND
CHAIN ASSEMBLY

FIG. 12-42 Oxygen ground servicing panel. *(Canadair Inc.)*

green disk is provided to prevent dust and contamination from entering the line. The indicator line is connected to the high-pressure rupture fitting of the regulator. A disk disappearance in the indicator indicates that oxygen cylinder overpressure existed and oxygen has been routed overboard.

Gaseous Oxygen Systems for Pressurized Aircraft

Oxygen systems for pressurized aircraft are primarily installed for emergency use in case of cabin pressurization failure or cabin decompression. The oxygen supply is sufficient to take care of all passengers and crew until the airplane is at a low altitude where oxygen is no longer necessary.

On one model of the Douglas DC-9, two independent gaseous systems are installed, one in the flight compartment for the crew and one in the passenger compartment for the passengers and cabin attendants. Thus, failure in one system will not affect the operation of the other system. In addition, a portable oxygen cylinder is located in the flight compartment to assure an emergency supply of oxygen for the flight crew. The portable cylinder is mounted on a bracket and secured by a quick-disconnect clamp.

A portable oxygen cylinder is also installed at each cabin attendant's station to enable the attendant to be mobile in the event of cabin decompression. The cylinder with a mask attached is mounted on a bracket and secured by quick-disconnect clamps.

Both the passenger and crew oxygen systems have

thermal-expansion safety discharge features and use a common discharge indicator. Discharge occurs if cylinder pressure exceeds about 2650 psig [18 272 kPa]. The indicator is mounted in the fuselage skin below the first officer's side window and contains a green plastic disk. Absence of this disk requires an inspection of both the passenger and crew oxygen cylinders.

A drawing showing the layout of the oxygen system for the airplane is shown in Fig. 12-43. Note that the passenger oxygen manifolds extend the full length of the cabin on each side. Only one passenger overhead oxygen installation is shown; however, such an installation is provided for each passenger.

The **crew oxygen system** shown in the schematic diagram of Fig. 12-44 consists of a high-pressure **supply cylinder**, a **shutoff valve** with a **cylinder pressure gauge**, a **pressure regulator, automatic pressure breathing-demand regulators, oronasal masks,** and a quick-disconnect test fitting.

The capacity of the crew oxygen supply cylinder is 48 ft^3 [1359 L] of oxygen at standard atmosphere and pressure. The pressure gauge, installed in the body of the shutoff valve, indicates cylinder pressure with the valve in either the open or closed position. The **pressure-reducing regulator,** attached by means of a union fitting to the cylinder shutoff valve, reduces the high cylinder pressure of 1850 psig [12 756 kPa] to a constant supply pressure of approximately 65 psig [448 kPa].

The **diluter-demand pressure breathing regulator** installed at each flight-crew station automatically controls the mixture ratio of air to oxygen, the ratio varying with cabin pressure. As explained previously, this type of regulator supplies the mixture of oxygen and air as it is "demanded" by the breathing of the person wearing the mask. It is possible to select 100% oxygen if desired. A light for panel illumination is installed in the regulator. The supply-line pressure is indicated by a pressure gauge on each regulator.

An **oxygen mask** is provided for each crew member and for each passenger. As explained previously, the **crew oxygen masks** are of the oronasal type and fit over the mouth and nose. The mask housing is plastic with a rubber seal between the housing and the user's face.

A breathing tube extends from the mask housing. The tube is equipped with a quick-disconnect fitting which connects into the crew oxygen supply connector or the portable cylinder.

A microphone and oxygen valve are inside the mask housing. A cable and jack extends from the microphone and is plugged into the radio system jack located adjacent to the oxygen connector. The oxygen valve opens and closes as the wearer inhales and exhales. The mask is ready for immediate use when removed from stowage and placed on the user's face.

A portion of the **passenger oxygen system** is illustrated schematically in Fig. 12-45. This drawing shows the high-pressure oxygen cylinder, pressure regulator, shutoff valve, manifold, passenger outlets, and associated parts. The cylinder has a capacity of 64 ft^3 [1812 L], weighs approximately 28 lb [12.7 kg], and is charged to a pressure of 1850 psig [12 756 kPa] under

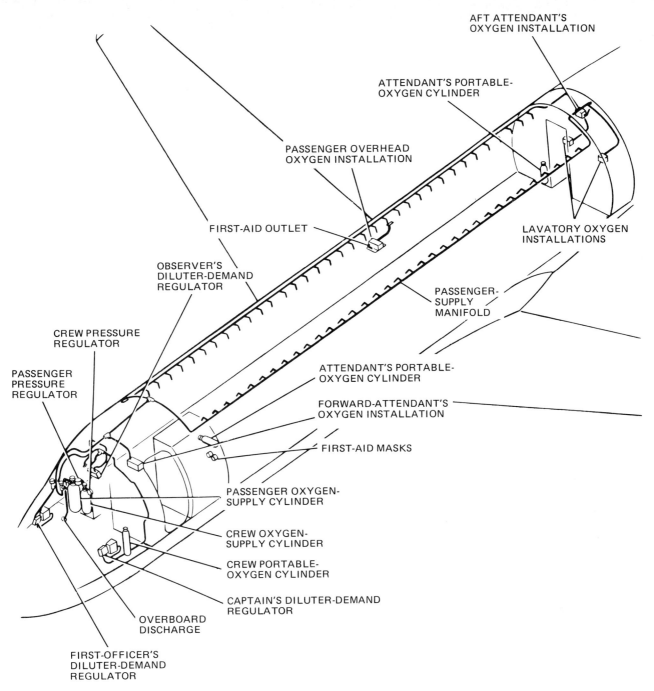

AFT ATTENDANT'S OXYGEN INSTALLATION

ATTENDANT'S PORTABLE-OXYGEN CYLINDER

PASSENGER OVERHEAD OXYGEN INSTALLATION

FIRST-AID OUTLET

LAVATORY OXYGEN INSTALLATIONS

OBSERVER'S DILUTER-DEMAND REGULATOR

PASSENGER-SUPPLY MANIFOLD

CREW PRESSURE REGULATOR

ATTENDANT'S PORTABLE-OXYGEN CYLINDER

PASSENGER PRESSURE REGULATOR

FORWARD-ATTENDANT'S OXYGEN INSTALLATION

FIRST-AID MASKS

PASSENGER OXYGEN-SUPPLY CYLINDER

CREW OXYGEN-SUPPLY CYLINDER

CREW PORTABLE-OXYGEN CYLINDER

CAPTAIN'S DILUTER-DEMAND REGULATOR

OVERBOARD DISCHARGE

FIRST-OFFICER'S DILUTER-DEMAND REGULATOR

FIG. 12-43 Oxygen system arrangement in an airliner. *(Douglas Aircraft Co.)*

normal atmospheric conditions. The cylinder is secured with strap clamps in an upright position in the aft right-hand corner of the flight compartment.

A direct-reading **pressure gauge** is installed in the shutoff valve body between the valve and the cylinder. The pressure gauge indicates cylinder pressure with the valve in either the OPEN or CLOSED position. An adapter containing a frangible ("burstible") blowout disk is connected to the shutoff valve body. The blowout disk will rupture and allow oxygen to escape overboard in the event that cylinder pressure should exceed approximately 2650 psig [18 272 kPa].

The **pressure regulator** for the passenger oxygen system is a constant-flow, altitude-compensating type

as described previously and illustrated in Fig. 12-37. This is one of several different types which are employed in stored-gas oxygen systems.

The **passenger oxygen masks** are of the oronasal type and are made of a plastic-type rubber which forms around the mouth and nose area. The mask consists of a face piece, three valves, a reservoir bag, a length of plastic tubing, a pull cord, and a head strap to secure the mask to the wearer's head. The masks are connected to outlet valves by a plastic tube. The mask is connected to an outlet-valve pull pin by a pull cord to initiate the flow of oxygen.

The passenger masks are stowed in oxygen stowage boxes above each seat row in the overhead stowage-

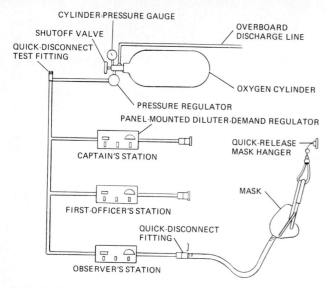

FIG. 12-44 Crew oxygen system.

Chemical Oxygen Generators

Chemical oxygen generators, also termed "solid-state" **generators** because the chemicals involved are solid, have proved to be effective, lower in cost than stored gaseous oxygen, safe, and comparatively maintenance free. The chemical oxygen generator burns a mixture of sodium chlorate ($NaClO_3$) and iron (Fe) to produce pure oxygen suitable for human use. Sodium chlorate, when heated to 478°C [892°F], decomposes into ordinary salt and oxygen. The fuel to produce the heat for the decomposition of the sodium chlorate is iron. When sufficient heat is applied to the mixture to start the burning of the iron with a portion of the released oxygen, the burning continues until the chemical process is completed. The burned iron becomes iron oxide (FeO).

The construction of a chemical oxygen generator is shown in Fig. 12-46. The fuel unit is sometimes called a "candle" as it burns somewhat like a candle, starting at the ignited end and burning slowly from one end to the other. The term "candle" is disappearing from usage, however. Ignition of the generator is accomplished by means of an electrical squib (detonator) or a mechanically fired detonator as is used to fire a rifle cartridge. The mixture of the material at the end of the generator where ignition takes place is "enriched" to make it start burning easily.

It will be noted in the drawing of Fig. 12-46 that the

rack utility panel, in each lavatory washstand, and at each attendant's station. All masks, except those installed at the attendant's forward station, are held in position on the stowage box door by a plastic holder and must be manually removed. The attendant's forward-station masks will fall free when the door is opened.

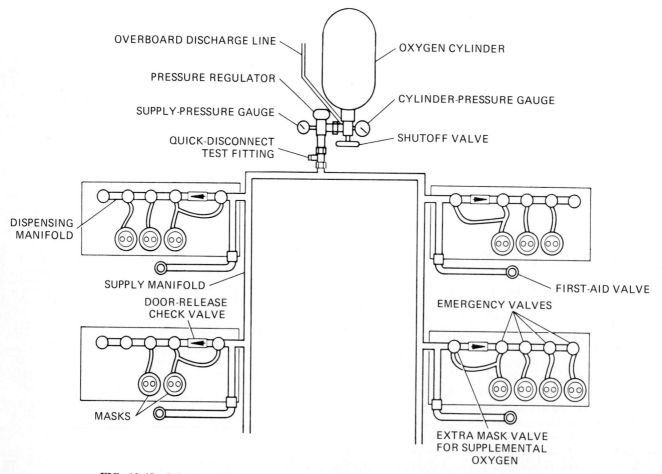

FIG. 12-45 Schematic diagram of a portion of the passenger oxygen system for the DC-9 airliner. *(Douglas Aircraft Co.)*

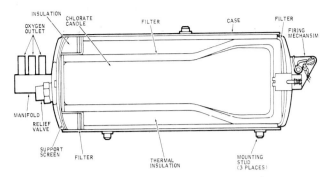

FIG. 12-46　Construction of a chemical oxygen generator. (*Douglas Aircraft Co.*)

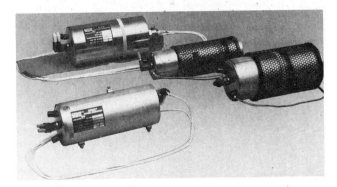

FIG. 12-48　Various chemical generators used in airliners. (*Scott Aviation*)

generator is larger at the starting end than it is farther along. The purpose of this shape is to provide an increased flow of oxygen at the beginning of operation to assure that the user will receive an adequate supply as soon as possible after ignition. Thereafter, the size of the generator is such that it provides oxygen sufficient for the number of people served from the generator. If more oxygen is produced than is required, the unneeded amount is vented through the relief valve to the cabin. The generator is surrounded by a filter and thermal insulation. The filter is to assure that only pure oxygen and no particulate matter is delivered to the user's mask. The thermal insulation is to prevent the heat of the burning generator from damaging the surrounding area. The exterior surface of the generator may reach a temperature as high as 500°F [260°C], and so it is provided with a heat shield to prevent a user from touching it. A warning placard is mounted on the heat shield.

Generators come in several sizes and configurations. The generator shown in Fig. 12-47 is designed

FIG. 12-47　Chemical generator for a portable system. (*Scott Aviation*)

for use in portable units. The generators shown in Fig. 12-48 are designed for use in fixed installations of transport aircraft. These fixed generators come in sizes designed to accommodate two, three, or four people.

Chemical Oxygen Systems

Chemical oxygen systems are used for the passenger oxygen system in many of the more modern transport

aircraft such as the McDonnell Douglas DC-10 and MD-80, Lockheed L-1011, and Boeing 757 and 767. Advantages of the chemical system over the gaseous system include low maintenance, reduced fire hazard, and reliability. Maintenance activity is decreased because of the elimination of cylinders, valves, regulators, and distribution lines and their associated periodic maintenance tests and inspections. The fire hazard has been reduced by the elimination of possible ruptured oxygen lines adding to a fire and the very low pressure at which oxygen flows from the generators. Additionally, no oxygen is generated to contribute to combustion without the generator being activated. Reliability is improved by the elimination of the possibility of thermal discharge, the independent nature of each unit, and the indefinite life of the generators.

The installation of a chemical oxygen generator in the DC-10 airplane is shown in the drawing of Fig. 12-49. The installation shown is the compartment located in the back of a seat.

Activation of the chemical oxygen generator shown in Fig. 12-49 is accomplished when the passenger pulls the mask from the compartment door and moves it to his or her face. A lanyard is attached to the mask and to a pin in the firing mechanism of the generator. Pulling on the lanyard withdraws the holding pin, and

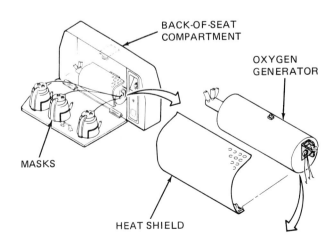

FIG. 12-49　Installation of a chemical oxygen generator in an airliner.

FIG. 12-50 Portable chemical oxygen generators. *(Scott Aviation)*

the firing mechanism snaps down against the firing pin and causes the percussion cap to fire.

As mentioned previously, some chemical oxygen generators are fired electrically. Those installed in the Lockheed L-1011 are connected to a common electrical circuit, and all generators are fired automatically when a cabin decompression occurs.

Portable chemical oxygen generators are available for emergency use and for use on private and business aircraft. Typical of these units are those shown in Fig. 12-50.

Service and Maintenance of Oxygen Systems

The service and maintenance of oxygen systems should be performed only by mechanics who are qualified through training and experience. Oxygen is not an explosive and is not flammable in its pure state, but it supports combustion, sometimes violently, when in contact or mixed with other materials. It is, therefore, important that certain precautions be exercised when working with oxygen systems. The following are essential:

1. Smoking, open flames, or items which may cause sparks must not be permitted near aircraft when maintenance is being performed on the oxygen system.

2. All electrical power must be off and the airplane must be grounded.

3. Oxygen must not be permitted to come in contact with oils, greases, or solvents. Such contacts can cause spontaneous explosions.

Typical instructions for the maintenance and service of a fixed system in a light twin airplane are as follows:

1. Use extreme caution to assure that every port in the oxygen system is kept thoroughly clean and free of water, oil, grease, and solvent contamination.

2. Cap all openings immediately upon removal of any component. Do not use masking or electrical tape or caps which will attract moisture.

3. Lines and fittings must be clean and dry. Manufacturers specify various methods which may be used to clean oxygen lines. One method is to use a vapor degreasing solution of stabilized perchlorethylene conforming to MIL-T-7003, then to blow the tubing clean and dry with a jet of nitrogen gas (BB-N411), Type 1, Class 1, Grade A, or technical argon (MIL-A-18455). Lines can also be cleaned with naphtha, Spec. TT-N-95, after which they are blown clean and dry as described above, or with dry, clean, filtered air. Air from a standard compressed-air supply usually contains minute quantities of entrained oil, so it is not suitable for blowing out oxygen lines.

Oxygen lines may be flushed with hot inhibited alkaline cleaner, washed with clean, hot water, and dried as previously explained. Lines should be capped as soon as they are cleaned and dried.

4. Fabrication of replacement oxygen lines is not recommended. New factory parts identified by part number should be used.

5. Thin Teflon fluorocarbon resin tape conforming to MIL-T-27730 may be used to aid in sealing tapered pipe threads. No compounds shall be used on aluminum-alloy flared fittings. No compound is used on the coupling sleeves or on the outside flares. Sealant tape is not applied to the first three threads of a coupling.

6. Mechanics must be sure that their hands are free of dirt or grease before they handle oxygen tubing, fittings, or other components.

7. Tools used for the installation of oxygen lines and fittings must be sparkless and free of all dirt, grease, or oil.

8. In all cases, instructions provided for the system by the manufacturer must be followed.

High-pressure oxygen cylinders must be inspected and checked for conformity with regulations. Each cylinder must have a Department of Transportation (DOT) designation number. **Standard-weight cylinders** are marked DOT-3AA-1800 or ICC-3AA-1800. These cylinders have no total life limitations and may be used until they fail hydrostatic testing at five-thirds of their operating pressure. The hydrostatic test must be made every 5 years. **Light-weight cylinders** are designated DOT-3HT-1850 and must be hydrostatically tested every 3 years to five-thirds of their operating pressure. These cylinders must be retired from service after 24 years or 4380 filling cycles, whichever occurs first. Composite cylinders (aluminum shell wrapped with Kevlar) must conform to DOT-E-8162. These cylinders are rated for 1850 psi [12 746.5 kPa] and have a life of 15 years or 10 000 filling cycles, whichever occurs first. Each filling of an oxygen cylinder requires an entry in the aircraft logbook.

Oxygen cylinders are inspected for damage such as nicks, dents, corroded fittings, hydrostatic test date, DOT designation, and leakage. Cylinders which do not meet requirements must be completely disassembled and inspected in an approved facility. DOT numbers, serial numbers, and dates of hydrostatic testing are stamped on the shoulder or neck of each cylinder.

Whenever a component of a high-pressure oxygen system has been removed and replaced or whenever the system has been disassembled in any way, the system must be leak tested and purged. **Leak testing** is accomplished by applying an approved **leak detector** conforming to MIL-L-25567A, Type 1, to all fittings as instructed. The leak detector solution is completely removed after each test. Where leaks are found, fittings must be repaired or replaced.

Purging the oxygen system involves fully charging the system in accordance with service instructions, then releasing oxygen from the system. The airplane should be outdoors if possible; otherwise it should be isolated in a well-ventilated building with no smoking or open flame permitted in the area. No grease or other lubricants should be near enough to come in contact with the oxygen. The doors and windows of the air-

plane must be open.

After the system is fully charged with oxygen, all oxygen masks are plugged into their outlets and the oxygen is allowed to flow for about 10 min. When the oxygen flowing from the masks is odorless, the purging is complete and the oxygen is shut off. The masks are removed from their outlets and the system is re-charged. Recharging is usually accomplished through a filling valve and fitting mounted conveniently on the lower part of the airplane or accessible through the baggage area. The cap is removed from the fitting and the refill hose is connected. Oxygen is allowed to flow into the system until automatically or manually shut off when the required pressure is registered on the high-pressure oxygen gauge. **Only aviator's breathing oxygen conforming to MIL-O-27210 can be used.** Do *not* assume that because a cylinder is colored green it

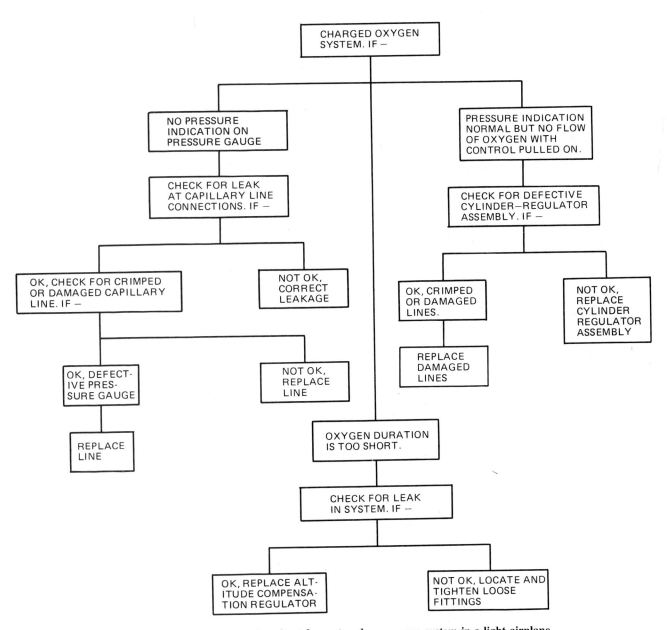

FIG. 12-51 **Troubleshooting chart for a stored-gas oxygen system in a light airplane.**

contains breathing oxygen. Cylinders containing other gases are sometimes colored green.

The foregoing information applies in general to stored-gas oxygen systems. It must be emphasized that for any specific system, the appropriate manufacturer's instructions must be followed. This is particularly true for the large, complex systems installed in commercial transport airplanes.

Troubleshooting oxygen systems is similar to the procedures for other systems. The need is to identify the malfunction, then isolate the cause. A typical troubleshooting chart for a small, fixed, stored-gas system is shown in Fig. 12-51. A logical sequence is employed to identify and repair the fault or faults which cause the malfunction.

Chemical oxygen systems require little or no maintenance and much less in the area of inspections than stored-gas systems. Replacement of expended generators and resetting firing mechanisms are the usual services required. Expended generators are identified by a heat-sensitive paint mark on the generator. This mark is white before the generator is used and black afterward. Procedures for replacement of generators are provided with the equipment. In fixed installations such as those on the DC-10 and the L-1011, manufacturer's service instructions should be followed.

● REVIEW QUESTIONS

1. What are the sources of heat for heating systems?
2. Describe a simple exhaust heating system.
3. Explain the need for regular and careful inspections of exhaust heating systems.
4. Describe a *combustion heater.*
5. What fuel is used in a combustion heater?
6. Describe a typical inspection for a combustion heater system.
7. Explain the *vapor-cycle* cooling system principle.
8. What are the principal units required in a *vapor-cycle cooling system?*
9. What refrigerant is commonly employed in a vapor-cycle cooling system?
10. Describe the use of each vapor-cycle-system unit.
11. How would a mechanic determine that the refrigerant supply is low?
12. Why is a *dryer* essential in a vapor-cycle system?
13. What is meant by *subcooling?*
14. What controls the size of the orifice in a *thermal expansion valve?*
15. What is meant by the *high side* and the *low side* in a vapor-cycle system?
16. List the precautions which must be taken when servicing a vapor-cycle refrigeration system.
17. During inspection of a vapor-cycle system, what is the indication of leaking refrigerant?
18. If a vapor-cycle refrigeration system operates satisfactorily for a short time and then stops cooling, what is the likely cause?
19. What is the purpose of the *service manifold* and how is it connected into a refrigeration system?
20. What is the purpose of the *service valves* in a vapor-cycle system?
21. What precaution should be observed when connecting a fitting to a service valve prior to servicing?
22. Explain *purging* of a refrigeration system and the procedure for doing this.
23. What precaution should be taken with regard to ventilation when purging a vapor-cycle system?
24. What should be done when any unit of a refrigeration system is disconnected?
25. How is a refrigeration system evacuated (pumped down)?
26. How is a vapor-cycle system recharged?
27. Why is aircraft pressurization necessary?
28. What are the sources of aircraft pressurization air pressure?
29. Describe the principle of *air-cycle* cooling.
30. Describe an *air-cycle machine* (ACM).
31. What is the function of the *heat exchangers* in an air-cycle cooling system?
32. What is the function of the *water separator* in an air-cycle cooling system?
33. Describe a *cooling pack.*
34. What is the *gasper* system and what is its air source?
35. What device limits the maximum cabin altitude in an airliner pressurization system?
36. Explain the need for limiting the pressure differential between the inside of the cabin and the outside.
37. What is the purpose of a *negative pressure-relief valve?*
38. Describe the operation of an *outflow valve.*
39. What are the functions of the *automatic* and *manual controllers* in the pressurization system?
40. What is the purpose of the *barometric correction selector?*
41. Explain the purpose of the *positive pressure-relief valve.*
42. Describe the operation and purpose of a *jet pump.*
43. How is air conditioning on an airliner accomplished when the airplane is on the ground and the engines are not running?
44. At what altitudes may a person begin to feel the effects of *hypoxia* in an unpressurized airplane?
45. What factors affect the amount of oxygen a person will absorb from the air he or she breathes?
46. Name three types of oxygen system with respect to the method by which oxygen is stored on the aircraft.
47. Describe a typical portable oxygen system.
48. Explain the difference between a *continuous-flow* oxygen system and a *demand-diluter* system.
49. Describe an oxygen *pressure regulator.*
50. Explain the operation of a *diluter-demand regulator.*
51. Describe the automatic opening provision of the pressure regulator for a typical airliner oxygen system.
52. How can an oxygen system bottle be distinguished from other gas bottles?
53. What advantages are associated with a chemical oxygen system when compared to a gaseous oxygen system?
54. Explain the difference between an oxygen mask

for a demand system and a mask for a continuous-flow system.

55. Describe the operation of a continuous-flow oxygen mask.
56. Explain the production of oxygen in a chemical oxygen system.
57. What are the advantages of a chemical oxygen system?
58. What precaution must be observed after a chemical oxygen generator has been fired?
59. Why is the chemical candle for an oxygen generator made larger at the starting end than it is farther along?
60. Describe a fixed oxygen system for a light airplane.
61. What indicator is used to show the escape of oxygen overboard in the system for a light airplane?
62. What are the range markings of the oxygen pressure gauge?
63. What are the two oxygen systems installed in some models of the DC-9 airliner?
64. What is the function of the *thermal-expansion safety discharge* valve?
65. How can a crew member determine that a safety valve has discharged oxygen from a cylinder?
66. Describe a crew oxygen system.
67. How many oxygen outlets are available to the passengers in an airliner?
68. Why are portable oxygen units required?
69. To what pressure is a stored oxygen system tank usually charged?
70. Give the precautions to be observed when working with oxygen systems.
71. List typical maintenance practices for an oxygen system.
72. Why is specially dried and filtered compressed air required for blowing out oxygen lines?
73. What sealing compound may be used on oxygen fittings?
74. How are oxygen cylinders marked for approval?
75. How often should oxygen cylinders be hydrostatically tested? To what pressure?
76. For what defects are oxygen cylinders inspected?
77. How is *leak testing* accomplished in an oxygen system? What material must be used.
78. Describe the *purging* of an oxygen system.
79. Explain the importance of capping all open oxygen lines and fittings.
80. How can the mechanic tell that the candle in a chemical oxygen generator has been expended?

13 AIRCRAFT INSTRUMENTS AND INSTRUMENT SYSTEMS

From the time that human beings began to fly, the need for instruments of various types has been apparent. It was soon determined that certain instruments were needed to determine whether the engine was operating satisfactorily. Engine revolutions per minute (rpm), oil pressure, and oil temperature were found to be vital signs in engine operation. If any of these were abnormal, the pilot could tell that something was wrong and could land before an engine failure occurred. It was also apparent that the pilot needed some indication of the airspeed of the airplane even though many old-time pilots swore that they could tell the airspeed by the sound of the air flowing past the rigging wires.

Eventually, instruments to indicate attitude and direction of flight also became desirable to help the pilot fly more knowledgeably and effectively. The continued increase in the number of instruments required or desired led to the large number of instruments found on aircraft today. The illustration of Fig. 13-1 is the instrument panel for a single-engine light airplane. All the instruments shown are not required by regulation, but each contributes to the safety and convenience of the pilot and passengers. Instruments required for aircraft are listed in FAR Part 91, Sec. 91.33.

In the early days of flying, pilots could tell approximately how high they were flying by looking at the horizon or the ground or by comparing the airplane height with the height of other objects, such as mountains, trees, buildings, etc. They could do this because they were unable to get very far off the ground. When airplanes began flying at higher altitudes, in overcast weather, and at greater distances from the home airport, the need for instruments increased. Pilots needed to know exactly how high they were, how fast the airplane was traveling, in what direction the airplane was headed, how fast they were climbing or descending, the attitude of the airplane, how the engine was performing, and numerous other factors. These demands have led to the development of instruments, the prime requisites of which have been sensitivity and dependability plus lightweight construction. The aircraft instruments of today are masterpieces of the designer's art. Even with the extreme conditions of pressure, temperature, velocity, and altitude, modern aircraft instruments continue to function accurately and dependably.

Instruments on an airplane may be classified according to function in three principal categories: **powerplant instruments, flight and navigational instruments,** and **systems instruments.** The powerplant instruments provide information concerning the operation of the engines and the powerplant systems. The flight and navigational instruments give the pilot information concerning flight speed, altitude, airplane attitude, heading, rate of ascent or descent, and other indications pertaining to the airplane and its flight path. The systems instruments provide information concerning the hydraulic system and its pressures, the air-conditioning system, the electric system, and other special systems that may be installed in the aircraft.

There are two particularly important reasons why the principles of operation and the art of interpreting the readings of instruments used in the modern aircraft should be thoroughly understood by the aircraft mechanic. First, the safety of the aircraft, the crew, and the passengers depends on the proper installation and correct operation of the instruments. The powerplant instruments can forewarn the pilot or flight engineer of impending engine failure, and the flight instruments indicate any irregularity of flight attitude or direction. It is the duty of the mechanic to check the instruments regularly.

The second reason why the mechanic must understand the operating principles of instruments is that they provide many indications of powerplant or system condition. Just as the physician diagnoses an illness by means of instruments, the aircraft mechanic can diagnose possible troubles in an aircraft powerplant or system by an understanding of instrument indications. Through a complete analysis of instrument readings that were recorded during flight, the mechanic can determine what units or systems are not functioning correctly. When a pilot returns from a flight and reports engine trouble, it is the duty of the aircraft mechanic to determine the cause of the trouble. The mechanic can eliminate several possible causes by determining such factors as the altitude at which the airplane has been flying, the temperature of the powerplant concerned, the rpm and the manifold pressure of the powerplant, and the recorded fuel and oil pressure. From an understanding of the instruments and their function, the mechanic can often determine where the trouble lies. Instruments are useful for troubleshooting regardless of whether the airplane concerned is a small private airplane or a large jet airliner. It is therefore the responsibility of the mechanic to ensure, as far as possible, continuous and accurate operation of all instruments.

Instruments are often classified according to the means by which they give their indication. In this type of classification we find four main categories: **pressure-**

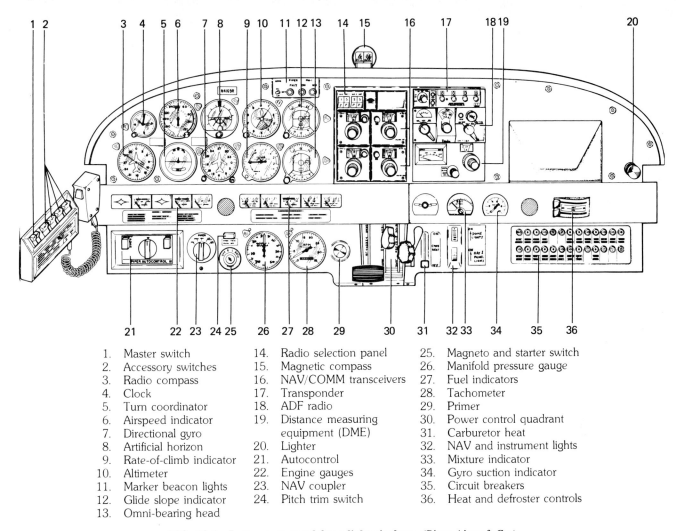

1. Master switch	14. Radio selection panel
2. Accessory switches	15. Magnetic compass
3. Radio compass	16. NAV/COMM transceivers
4. Clock	17. Transponder
5. Turn coordinator	18. ADF radio
6. Airspeed indicator	19. Distance measuring
7. Directional gyro	equipment (DME)
8. Artificial horizon	20. Lighter
9. Rate-of-climb indicator	21. Autocontrol
10. Altimeter	22. Engine gauges
11. Marker beacon lights	23. NAV coupler
12. Glide slope indicator	24. Pitch trim switch
13. Omni-bearing head	

25. Magneto and starter switch
26. Manifold pressure gauge
27. Fuel indicators
28. Tachometer
29. Primer
30. Power control quadrant
31. Carburetor heat
32. NAV and instrument lights
33. Mixture indicator
34. Gyro suction indicator
35. Circuit breakers
36. Heat and defroster controls

FIG. 13-1   Instrument panel for a light airplane. *(Piper Aircraft Co.)*

type instruments, **mechanical instruments, gyro instruments,** and **electrical and electronic instruments.** The basic principles of operation of each of these types of instruments are covered in this chapter. This chapter also describes the various instruments using these basic mechanisms for their operation, along with the installation, marking, and basic troubleshooting of the more common systems.

● **PRINCIPLES OF INSTRUMENT OPERATIONS**

Aircraft instruments are required to monitor a wide variety of aircraft conditions. To do this, many different methods are used to collect information and display the information for the flight crew. It is important that the mechanic have a basic understanding of the principles of operation of the common aircraft instruments so that he or she may efficiently maintain the systems in proper operating condition.

This section deals with the basic operational principles of pressure instruments, gyro instruments, electrically powered resistance indicators, and temperature indicators. These principles of operation are applied to many different types of instrument sytems

in later sections of this chapter. Mechanical instruments will be discussed individually later in this chapter.

Pressure Instruments

Pressure instruments are used to monitor many aircraft flight situations, such as altitude and airspeed, as well as the condition of systems such as hydraulic pressure and engine oil pressure. There are two basic types of mechanical pressure measuring instruments: bourdon tubes and diaphragms/bellows.

Instruments that measure pressures in relatively high pressure fluid sytems are usually operated through a mechanism known as a **bourdon tube.** Among the indications requiring this type of instrument are hydraulic pressure, engine oil pressure, oxygen pressure, and any other indication of comparatively high pressures. The bourdon tube is constructed of metal and is oval or flattened in cross-sectional shape, with the tube itself formed into a crescent or part circle.

Figure 13-2 indicates the general construction of a bourdon tube. One of the ends of the tube is open, and the other end is closed. The open end is attached to a casting that is anchored to the case of the instru-

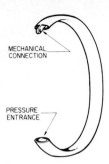

FIG. 13-2   A bourdon tube.

FIG. 13-4   Instrument diaphragm cross section.

ment, thus making the open end of the tube stationary. The closed end of the tube is free to move and is attached to a series of linkages such as levers and gears. When fluid under pressure enters the open end of the bourdon tube, it causes a pressure against the closed end and this tends to straighten the tube. The principle involved here is well illustrated by the familiar party novelty—the rolled-up paper tube that uncoils when you blow into it. The pressure on the closed end of the paper causes it to uncoil, and the springs inside cause it to coil up again when the pressure is released. The bourdon tube is constructed of a metal such as spring-tempered brass, bronze, or beryllium copper. These metals have a strong spring effect that causes the bourdon tube to return to its original position when pressure is released.

In Fig. 13-3 a simplified diagram of a bourdon-tube-

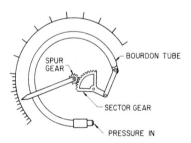

FIG. 13-3   Bourdon-tube instrument mechanism.

instrument mechanism is shown. When pressure enters the bourdon tube, the tube tends to straighten out, and, as it does so, it moves the linkage connected to the sector gear. The movement of the sector gear causes the spur gear to rotate, and this, in turn, moves the indicating needle along the scale to give a reading of the pressure. The indicating needle is mounted on the hand staff, which is rotated by the spur gear. Instruments such as this one are ruggedly constructed, with little maintenance required.

Pressure gauges designed to provide readings of comparatively low pressures are usually of the **diaphragm** or **bellows** type. In some cases, both a diaphragm and a bellows are used in the same instrument. A drawing of the cross section of a typical instrument diaphragm is shown in Fig. 13-4. The diaphragm consists of two disks of thin metal corrugated concentri-

cally and sealed together at the edges to form a cavity or capsule. The diaphragm in Fig. 13-4 is designed with an opening through one of the disks to admit the pressure to be measured. The opposite side is provided with a bridge that may bear against a rocking shaft lever through which the movement is transmitted to the indicating needle.

In some instruments, such as a simple barometer, the diaphragm is sealed with dry air or an inert gas inside at sea-level atmospheric pressure. Changes in the pressure of the air outside the diaphragm cause it to expand or contract, thus producing a movement that is converted to a dial reading through the instrument mechanism.

A bellows capsule is illustrated in Fig 13-5. The bellows is made of thin metal with corrugated sides and formed into a cylindrical capsule as shown. This unit operates in much the same manner as the diaphragm, but it provides a greater range of movement.

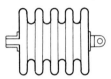

FIG. 13-5   Bellows capsule.

Examples of the types of instruments that typically use a diaphragm or bellows mechanism include altimeters, airspeed indicators, and manifold pressure gauges.

Pressure instruments may be designed to indicate pressure as a value referenced to the ambient (surrounding atmospheric) air pressure [pounds per square inch gauge (psig)], to absolute zero [pounds per square inch absolute (psia)], or to some other reference value [pounds per square inch differential (psid)]. If a value on a pressure gauge is identified as indicating pressure in psig, then the pressure indicated is a gauge pressure, that is, the pressure above or below ambient pressure. Instruments such as hydraulic system pressure and vacuum system values are psig values.

Instruments such as manifold pressure gauges are referenced to absolute zero and indicate the actual pressure in the engine intake manifold. That is why the manifold pressure gauge at sea level indicates about 30 inHg (inches of mercury) [762 mmHg] when the engine is not running. Standard day conditions at sea level give an atmospheric pressure of 29.92 inHg [760 mmHg]. The absolute pressure thus indicated is valued psia.

Other instruments such as the engine pressure ratio indicator for a turbine engine compare the ram air pressure at the inlet of the engine to the ram air pressure of the exhaust gases at the engine outlet to give a differential pressure indication (psid).

Gyroscopic Instruments

One of the most essential devices for the navigation of aircraft is the **gyroscope**. The gyroscope is defined as **a device consisting of a wheel having much of its mass concentrated around the rim, mounted on a spinning axis that is free to rotate about one or both of two axes perpendicular to each other and to the spinning axis.** The characteristic of a gyroscope that makes it valuable as a navigation device is its ability to remain rigid in space, thus providing a directional reference.

Everybody is familiar with the spinning tops used as toys for children. These toys are made in many shapes and sizes, but they all operate on the principle of the gyroscope; that is, a spinning mass tends to stabilize with its axis fixed in space and will continue to spin in the same plane unless outside forces are applied to it.

A gyroscope mounted in rings so that the mounting can be rotated in any direction without disturbing the gyro is called a **free gyro**. The rings in which the gyro is mounted and which permit it to move are called **gimbal rings**. Figure 13-6 is a drawing of a free gyro showing the three axes of rotation. The spinning axis of the gyro is the X axis and is horizontal in the illustration. The Y axis is also horizontal but is perpendicular to the spinning axis. The Z axis is vertical and is therefore perpendicular to the two other axis.

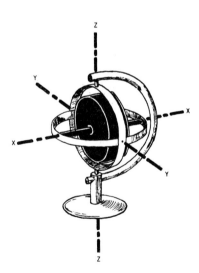

FIG. 13-6   A free gyroscope.

The **rigidity** of a gyro is the force of the gyro that opposes any other force that tends to change its plane of rotation in space. The rigidity is increased as the mass at the rim of the gyro wheel is increased and as the speed of rotation is increased. A gyro built in the form of a heavy-rimmed wheel will have much more rigidity than a gyro shaped like a sphere or cylinder.

If a free gyro without friction or other outside influences were started running in a horizontal plane (vertical axis) at 12:00 noon at a particular point on the equator and then were observed for 24 h, the plane of

rotation would shift with respect to the earth's surface. At 3:00 PM the plane of rotation would have tilted up 45° toward the east and 6:00 PM it would be vertical. At 12:00 midnight, the plane of rotation would be horizontal again, but it would appear to be inverted. As time continued for a total of 24 h, the gyro would return to the original position. The foregoing action is the result of the rigidity of the gyro, and it is this characteristic that makes the device effective as a navigation reference.

Another important characteristic of the gyro is its tendency to **precess** if external forces are applied to it. **Precession** can be described briefly as the tendency of a gyro to shift its plane of rotation in a direction that is at an angle of 90° to the force applied to cause the shift. This is illustrated in Fig. 13-7. If a gyro is

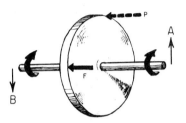

FIG. 13-7   Principle of precession.

mounted on a shaft and spinning in the direction shown by the arrows and a force F is applied at the side of the wheel as shown, the precession force P will act at a point 90° in the direction of rotation from the applied force. This will tend to shift the axis of rotation as shown by the arrows A and B.

An analysis of the cause of precession is beyond the scope of this discussion. However, the precession force can be determined by the vector addition of two angular velocities, one being the angular velocity of the applied force. When we consider further the nature of precession, we observe the effect of an applied force when the gyro is **not** spinning.

In Fig. 13-8 a gyro is mounted with a spinning axis

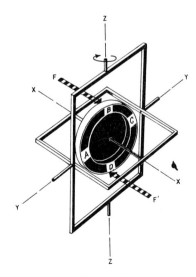

FIG. 13-8   Explanation of precession.

X. The axis of the inner gimbal is Y, and the axis of the outer gimbal is Z. When the rotor is not spinning, gyroscopic precession does not take place and the force F will cause the rotor to turn about the Y axis. We can say that the force F acting upon the nonspinning rotor causes each point on the upper half of the rotor to be accelerated in the direction of the applied force F. In the same way, because of the gimbal arrangement, every point on the lower half of the rotor is accelerated in the direction F'.

When the rotor is spinning, the force F must impart the same acceleration as before, but now each point on the rim is also moving about the spin axis. It is this spinning motion that contributes to the precessional motion. As each point moves around the spin axis from A to C, it is being accelerated in the direction F; and when it moves from C through D to A, it is accelerated in the direction F'. Since each point is continuously accelerated in the direction F during its travel through the upper portion of the circle, it must attain its maximum velocity in the F direction as it reaches position C. In the same way, as the point travels through the bottom portion of the circle, the acceleration in the F' direction results in the point attaining a maximum velocity in the F' direction at the end of this period of acceleration (at point A). Because of the gimbal system and the resulting velocity at A in the F' direction and at C in the F direction, the only compatible resulting motion of the rotor is a turning about the Z axis. Thus we see that applying an accelerating force to a spinning gyroscope results in a motion in the direction of the applied force at a point on the rotor 90° along the rim in the direction of spin.

The rate at which the gyroscope precesses about the Z axis is directly proportional to the magnitude of the applied force and inversely proportional to the speed of the rotor. Rotors of different sizes, weights, and shapes will precess at different rates. A large, heavy rotor will precess much more slowly than a small one as the result of the same applied force.

Bearing friction is another factor that affects gyro operation. In order to discuss the effect of bearing friction on the performance of a gyroscope, it is necessary to identify the axes of rotation as we have done previously. The spin axis of the rotor is axis X, and the rotor bearings will be called X bearings. The axis of rotation of the inner gimbal, which is horizontal, is the Y axis, and the axis of the outer gimbal is the Z axis. These are illustrated in Fig. 13-6. The Z axis is fixed to the case of the instrument, but the Y axis can move horizontally, and the X axis can turn in azimuth with the Y axis and also can rotate vertically. Thus, it is said that the X axis of the gyroscope rotor has two degrees of freedom. [During this discussion, any motion of the spin axis (the gyro rotor axle) as a result of an applied torque while the rotor is spinning will be called **precession.**]

The effect of friction in the X, Y, or Z axis makes it necessary to balance the gyroscope gimbals dynamically. If we balance the inner gimbal with the wheel stopped, there will be an unbalance remaining that is insufficient to overcome the static friction of the Y bearings. When the rotor is turning, there is a smaller

amount of friction present in the bearings and the unbalance will be evident. The effects of unbalance are discussed later. In any event, final balancing tests must be performed with the rotor spinning.

Friction in the Z bearings can be detected by hanging a weight on the inner gimbal at one end of the X axis while the gyroscope is running. Theoretically this should cause only a precession of the spin axis in azimuth, but the motion in azimuth about the Z axis is retarded by the friction in the Z bearings. This friction is the equivalent of a torque about the Z axis that causes precession about the Y axis. As a result of the Z-axis friction, not only will the gyroscope be precessed in azimuth by the weight, but also its spin axis will drop on the end where the weight is hung. If the Z-axis friction is made extremely great, the weight causes the gyroscope rotor axis to fall rapidly. Actually the drop is the result of extreme stress within the Z-axis bearings. If, on the other hand, the frame were made to follow the motion of the outer gimbal perfectly, there would be no friction and no drop at all in the end of the X axis.

If the Z-bearing friction is very slight, another interesting gyroscopic action can be observed when the weight is placed on the inner gimbal. If the weight is placed on the gimbal suddenly, the X-axis drops suddenly and then rises and oscillates until it settles out to a steady precessional motion in azimuth. The dip cannot now be caused by Z-axis friction since we have assumed that it is negligible. The dip is caused by the inertia of the outer gimbal, which prevents it from moving instantly. This inertia is equivalent to Z-axis friction at first, and the dip occurs; but once the outer gimbal is moving, the X axis will cease to drop.

During the transient movement, the weight is decelerating in a downward direction and thus exerting a precessional torque in excess of that which exists when the weight has no downward movement. The outer gimbal, during the transient movement, achieves a precessional rate in excess of that called for from the static weight. When the weight ceases its downward motion, the outer gimbal is moving faster than it would otherwise. This excess of outer gimbal velocity will (through its inertia) exert a torque on the gyroscope spin axis, causing the weighted end to rise. This action slows the outer gimbal down. A continuation of the foregoing action occurs, and the outer gimbal slows down too much, thus permitting the weighted end of the spin axis to dip again. This oscillation, up and down, continues until the outer gimbal is moving exactly at the precession rate. The oscillation is called **nutation.** Nutation requires no external torque to sustain it since energy is transferred back and forth from one element of the gimbal system to another. Nutation caused by the weight of the gimbals can be reduced by making the gimbal as light as possible in comparison with the mass of the rotor.

Friction in the X bearing, in addition to slowing down the rotor, is also apparent when the spin axis is precessed to the vertical so that the X and Z axes coincide. This friction then causes the inner and outer gimbals to be dragged around in the direction of spin.

If the gyroscope is driven electrically, the X-axis

FIG. 13-9 Gyro rotor of an air-driven turn-and-bank indicator.

friction is overcome by the motor. The motor, running at synchronous speed, presses back on the inner gimbal with a force equal to that of the friction trying to drag the gimbal around. However, when the motor is accelerating, the force pressing back on the inner gimbal is appreciably greater than is necessary to overcome bearing friction. This force, although opposite in direction to the X-axis frictional torque, has an effect similar to that just described. If the inner and outer gimbals are not perpendicular, this force pushes not only on the Y bearings but also against the outer gimbal. This causes the gyro rotor to be precessed about the Y axis, and the gyro rotor axis become horizontal. Since the deceleration present when the unit is turned off is similar to an acceleration, the rotor axis is precessed toward the vertical. Thus it is desirable to provide braking action of some kind when an electrically driven gyro is turned off.

Gyroscope rotors are designed to be operated either pneumatically or electrically. Pneumatically operated gyro rotors are made from a heavy material such as brass. They are disk-shaped with the majority of their mass located on the outer edge of the disk with a thin web of material between the rim and the central shaft of the disk. The outer edge of the disk has notches or "buckets" cut into the surface so that a flow of air can strike the buckets and cause the rotor to spin. The speed of a pneumatic rotor is on the order of 8000 rpm.

Electrically operated gyro rotors are actually the rotors of electric motors. The rotor is normally of a laminated soft-iron material using a squirrel-cage design inside of a steel motor shell. The rotor can be operated by 12 or 24 V dc or 115 V ac, 400-Hz power sources. The speed of an electrically operated gyro can be in the area of 24 000 rpm. With this high rpm, the electric gyros can be smaller than the pneumatic gyros and still provide equal performance.

The central shaft of a gyro rotor is supported on fine bearing surfaces, with the materials and shape selected to keep friction to a minimum. Some bearing designs incorporate a spring mechanism to maintain the proper loading of the bearing against the shaft and compensate for wear and changes in temperature and the resulting variation in component size.

Electrically Powered Sensor Instruments

Many indicating systems rely on variations in electrical resistance to denote variations in fluid levels and temperatures. These types of instruments can be direct-indicating or can rely on Wheatstone bridge or ratiometer circuits to indicate changes in the condition of a system.

Resistance Circuits. Direct-indicating electrical **resistance systems** are often used in fuel quantity transmitters. An example of such a system is shown in Fig. 13-10. Note that because the float level decreases as

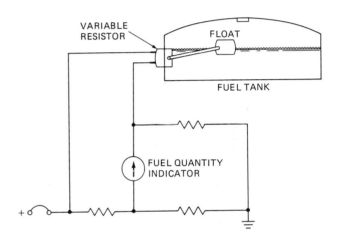

FIG. 13-10 Float-type fuel level indicator with variable resistor.

the fuel is used, the position of the wiper arm changes on the resistance wire. As the wiper moves up the resistance wire, the resistance in the circuit decreases and the quantity gauge indicates a lower value. (Some systems are designed to have an increase in the circuit resistance as the quantity decreases.)

A similar type of position sensor can be used to monitor the position of aircraft components such as secondary flight controls and cowl flaps.

Wheatstone Bridge Circuit. A **Wheatstone bridge circuit** is a type often used to monitor operating temperatures that do not exceed 300° F [149°C]. This includes measurement of coolant temperatures, free air temperatures, and carburetor air temperatures. The use of a bridge circuit gives a more accurate reading than is possible with other direct-reading electrical measurement circuits.

The circuit for a Wheatstone bride instrument is shown in Fig. 13-11. In this figure the bridge consists of three fixed resistors of 100 Ω each and one variable resistor whose resistance is 100 Ω at a fixed point such as 0°C, or 32°F. With the bridge circuit connected to a battery power source as shown, it can be seen that if all four resistances are equal, current flow through

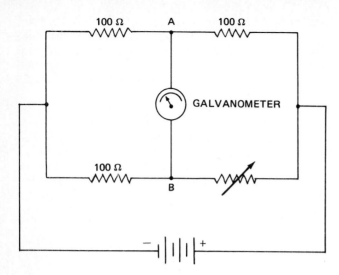

FIG. 13-11 Wheatstone bridge circuit.

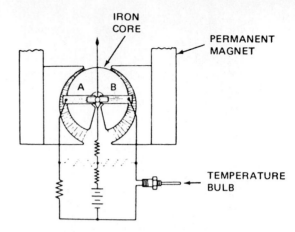

FIG. 13-12 Circuit for a ratiometer-type instrument.

each side of the bridge will be equal and there will be no differential in voltage between points *A* and *B*. When the variable resistor which is in the temperature-sensing bulb is exposed to heat, the resistance increases. When this happens it can be seen that more current flow through the top portion of the bridge than will flow through the bottom portion. This will cause a voltage differential between points *A* and *B* and current will then flow through the galvanometer indicator. Likewise, if the bulb is exposed to a low temperature, its resistance will decrease and current will increase through the bottom portion of the circuit and through the indicator in the opposite direction. The instrument is calibrated to give a correct reading of the temperature sensed by the variable resistor in the sensing bulb. If any one segment of the bridge circuit should be broken, the indicator needle would move to one end of the scale, depending on which circuit was broken.

Ratiometers. Ratiometers are used where the variations in electrical voltage in the aircraft electrical system cause the bridge circuit to give inaccurate readings beyond acceptable limits. The ratiometer eliminates the voltage-induced error by using the aircraft electrical system to power two electromagnetic fields. Since both fields have the same power source, their comparative accuracy is not affected by variations in voltage.

The circuit for a ratiometer instrument is shown in Fig. 13-12. This circuit has two sections, each supplied with current from the same source. As shown in the drawing, a circular iron core is located between the poles of a magnet in such a manner that the gap between the poles and the cores varies in width. The magnetic flux density in the narrower parts of the gap is much greater than the flux density in the wider portions of the gap. Two coils are mounted opposite each other on the iron core and both coils are fixed to a common shaft on which the indicating needle is mounted. The coils are wound to produce magnetic forces which oppose each other. When equal currents are flowing through the two coils, their opposing

forces will balance each other and they will be in the center position as shown. If the current flowing in coil *A* is greater than that flowing in coil *B*, the force produced by coil *A* will be greater than the force of coil *B*, and coil *A* will move toward the wider portion of the gap where a lower flux density exists. This moves coil *B* into an area of higher flux density a distance sufficient to create a force which will balance the force of coil *A*. At this point the position of the indicating needle gives the appropriate temperature reading.

Like the sensing bulb for the Wheatstone bridge instrument, the bulb for the ratiometer instrument contains a coil of fine resistance wire which increases in resistance as the temperature rises. The resistance wire is sealed in a metal tube and is connected to pin connectors for the electrical contacts.

● FLIGHT INSTRUMENTS

Flight instruments are those instruments which are used by the pilot to determine the attitude, heading, altitude, and rate of changes in attitude, altitude, and heading of the aircraft. This portion of the chapter discusses the various flight instruments and their method of operation.

Altimeter

The **altimeter** is used to indicate the height of the aircraft above sea level. The instrument also provides information for determining the true airspeed of the aircraft, proper engine power settings, proper clearance above the terrain, and proper flight altitude to avoid the flight path of other aircraft.

In general there are two types of altimeters which operate on the barometric principle: the non-sensitive or simple altimeter, and the sensitive altimeter. The nonsensitive altimeter is rarely used in aircraft because of the very compressed altitude scale. This altimeter usually indicates a change of 10 000 ft for each revolution of the pointer as shown in Fig. 13-13.

The **sensitive altimeter,** so named because of its sensitivity, is the commonly used type of altimeter for aircraft. The dial of a sensitive altimeter is shown in

FIG. 13-13 A nonsensitive altimeter. *(U.M.A., Inc.)*

Fig. 13-14. The longest hand, which has the appearance of the minute hand on a clock, registers 1000 ft [304.8m] for a complete revolution. The dial is indexed so this hand can easily show differences of 10 ft [3.05m] in altitude. Furthermore, as an average-sized person reads this altimeter at eye level and then places it on the floor and takes another reading, the person will note that the large needle has moved approximately one-half space, which indicates a difference of about 5 ft [1.52 m] in altitude. The shorter, wider pointer rotates one-tenth the distance of the long hand; hence it registers 10 000 ft [3048 m] for a complete revolution around the dial. Each numbered increment of the dial represents thousands of feet when read from this hand. The small hand and the center dial are arranged to read in increments of 10 000 or 40 000 ft [3048 or 12 192 m] for a complete revolution.

The dial shown in the illustration registers an altitude of about 1770 ft [540 m]. If the altimeter were

FIG. 13-14 Dial of a sensitive altimeter. *(Kollsman)*

showing 15 770 ft [4806.7 m], the small hand in the center would be slightly past the midpoint between the 1 and the 2 on the outer scale; the short, wide hand would be pointing about three-fourths the distance from the 5 to the 6; and the long hand would point to the same position shown.

The pressure element of the sensitive altimeter consists of two or three diaphragm capsules in series, and there may be either two or three dial pointers. The pointers register hundreds, thousands, or tens of thousands, as explained in the preceding paragraphs.

A cutaway view of the interior of a Kollsman sensitive altimeter is shown in Fig. 13-15. This instrument utilizes three diaphragm capsules to impart movement to the rocking shaft as changes in altitude occur. The rocking shaft is linked to a sector gear, which drives the multiplying mechanism. Note that the rotation of the rocking shaft must be multiplied many times since the large hand must rotate 50 times to indicate an altitude of 50 000 ft [15 240 m].

An altimeter must be compensated for atmospheric pressure changes if it is to give true indications under all conditions. This compensation must be done by mechanical means by the pilot or another member of the flight crew with the **barometric-pressure-setting** mechanism in the instrument. The setting device rotates the entire indicator drive mechanism within the case of the instrument and at the same time drives a barometric indicating dial that is visible through a window in the face of the instrument. When the adjusting knob is turned, the altitude dial remains stationary but the drive mechanism and pointers change position.

The reason for changing the barometric setting on an altimeter can be understood when the effect of barometric pressure on the altitude indication is considered. Assume that a certain airport is known to be at sea level with **standard** atmospheric pressure existing on a particular day. Before taking off in an airplane, the pilot sets the barometric scale to 29.92 in Hg [101.33 kPa] (standard sea-level atmospheric pressure). Then all altimeter pointers point to the zero mark on the altimeter scale. During this time the airplane has been in the air for, perhaps, 2 h, the barometric pressure at the airport has dropped rapidly and is only 29.38 inHg [99.49 kPa]. The pilot is ready to come in for a landing. If the pilot does not contact the field to obtain the corrected barometric pressure and leaves the altimeter at the setting made before taking off, the wheels of the airplane will hit the ground when the altimeter registers an altitude of approximately 500 ft [152 m].

The correct procedure, therefore, is to contact the field for the corrected existing barometric pressure before coming in for a landing. Upon receipt of the information in the foregoing case, the pilot sets the barometric scale at 29.38 inHg, [99.49 kPa] and can now expect the wheels to touch the ground when the altimeter indicates 0 ft altitude.

Temperature compensation is automatically accomplished in the altimeter mechanism. Although the amount of error due to temperature change would normally be small because of the materials used in the construction of the mechanism, this small error is off-

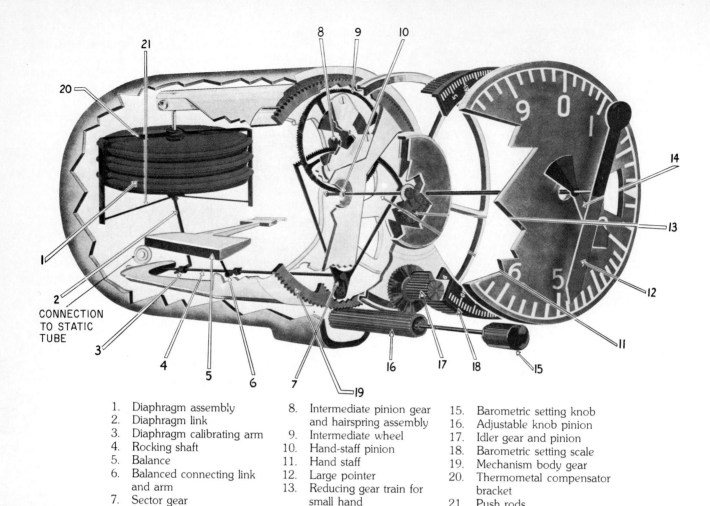

1. Diaphragm assembly	8. Intermediate pinion gear and hairspring assembly	15. Barometric setting knob
2. Diaphragm link		16. Adjustable knob pinion
3. Diaphragm calibrating arm	9. Intermediate wheel	17. Idler gear and pinion
4. Rocking shaft	10. Hand-staff pinion	18. Barometric setting scale
5. Balance	11. Hand staff	19. Mechanism body gear
6. Balanced connecting link and arm	12. Large pointer	20. Thermometal compensator bracket
7. Sector gear	13. Reducing gear train for small hand	21. Push rods
	14. Small hand	

FIG. 13-15 Cutaway view of a sensitive altimeter.

set by a bimetallic strip that neutralizes any expansion or contraction of the parts.

In a standard instrument-panel configuration the altimeter is mounted at the top right corner of the flight group. Static pressure is supplied to the altimeter from the static-pressure port through tubing. This tubing must be of sufficient strength to withstand the pressurization of the cabin in any pressurized airplane.

Compensated Altimeter. Because of the high speeds and altitudes at which many aircraft fly, the altimeters employed in such aircraft must be much more accurate than those used on aircraft designed to operate at more moderate altitudes. To provide an altimeter that will be sufficiently accurate for all conditions of operation, certain corrections and compensations must be made.

First, an accurate altimeter must be corrected for installation or position error. This error applies to a particular airplane. Second, the instrument must have automatic compensation for temperature changes. Third, the changes in static pressure due to changes in Mach number must be compensated. An altimeter designed to make the necessary adjustments for accuracy is the mechanically compensated, pneumatically operated altimeter.

The mechanically compensated altimeter operates from the aircraft pilot-static pressure system and consists of a combination of altimeter and machmeter mechanisms [see Fig. 13-16 (a)]. The indicated pressure altitude is sensed by an aneroid, and the Mach number is obtained from the combined motion of the **altitude-sensing aneroids** and a **differential-pressure-diaphragm capsule.** Aircraft-position-error information is applied to a two-dimensional cam and is algebraically added to the indicated pressure altitude by means of a mechanical differential. Thus, correction in feet of altitude is made to the altimeter indication for a given Mach number. This is required because of the change in static pressure at a given altitude for a change in Mach number. True altitude is computed by means of a mechanism actuated by the altitude- and Mach-sensing elements as shown in Fig. 13-16.

As the aircraft changes altitude, the two aneroid capsules sense the change in static pressure. Deflection of these capsules is transmitted through the **bi-metal units** to the rocking shaft. Hence, as altitude changes, the rocking shaft is caused to rotate.

When the aircraft changes velocity, the ram air pressure on the pitot tube changes, and this pressure differential ΔP is sensed by the **differential-capsule.** The

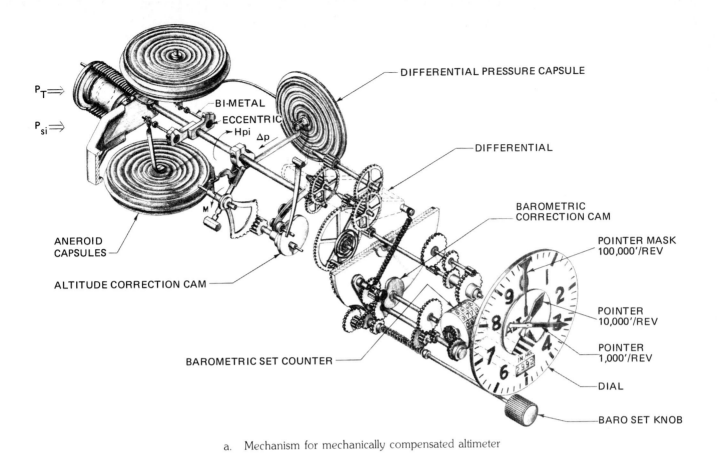

a. Mechanism for mechanically compensated altimeter

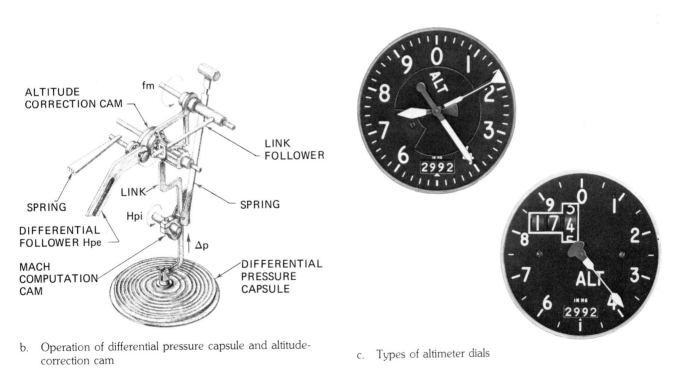

b. Operation of differential pressure capsule and altitude-correction cam

c. Types of altimeter dials

FIG. 13-16 Bendix compensated altimeter.

deflection of the capsule is transmitted through a **link** to the **link follower,** which rotates a rocking shaft and a sector gear. This gear changes the position of the **altitude-correction cam.** This mechanism is shown in Fig. 13-16 (b). The correction applied by the mechanism is proportional to altitude error caused by changes in Mach number and is the input to the **altitude-correction differential.** The differential output is geared to the dials and pointers to read directly in corrected altitude.

Temperature compensation for the altimeter is provided through the operation of the bimetal elements in the linkage between the aneroid capsules and the main rocking shaft. Calibration of the instrument is accomplished by making adjustments of the eccentric attachments between the bimetal units and the rocking-shaft lever arms. The lever arms can also be rotated on the shaft to cause a change in the linkage starting angle.

The **barometric-set** mechanism, shown in Fig. 13-16 (a), consists of an adjusting knob, gear train, cam, and rotating mechanism assembly. The range of ground-level pressure indications is 28.1 to 31.0 inHg [713.7 to 787.4 mmHg] with stops incorporated to limit the travel of the barometric counter to the range of desired operation.

Adjustment of the zero setting system is accomplished by unlocking the knob shaft from the front of the instrument by a single screwdriver lock. This allows the pinion to disengage the counter gear train while still engaging the rotating frame assembly. The adjusting knob will then rotate the pointers to the corrected setting.

The three-pointer dial display shown in Fig. 13-16 (c) consists of two pointers and a disk with a pointer extension indicating 1000, 10 000, and 100 000 ft [304.8, 3048, and 30 480 m] of altitude, respectively, for 1 revolution. An opening in the disk exposes a cross-hatched area, warning that the indication is below 15 000 ft.

If a counter-type readout is more desirable from the human engineering standpoint, it can be provided as an alternative to the three-pointer presentation. This dial is also shown in Fig. 13-16 (c) and consists of a three-digit counter and a rotating pointer. The two large digits indicate thousands of feet altitude, while the smaller third digit and the pointer indicate hundreds of feet. The small digit rotates continuously with pointer rotation, while the two larger digits index with an intermittent motion. One complete revolution of the pointer indicates 1000 ft of altitude, thereby providing a sensitive indication of altitude change to the pilot. The dial presentation in the illustration indicates an altitude of 17 390 ft [5300.5 m].

Encoding Altimeter. Because of the need to determine accurately the position and altitude of aircraft in high-density traffic areas, the **encoding altimeter** has been developed to provide a signal for Air Traffic Control (ATC) that shows up on the ATC radar screen. The encoding altimeter includes electronic circuitry which operates in conjunction with the aircraft transponder. When the transponder is interrogated by ATC, the identification and altitude of the aircraft are shown on the radar screen.

Encoding altimeters are required on aircraft which fly in controlled airspace above 12 500 ft (3810 m) altitude, aircraft which are equipped with Category II and Category III landing systems, and aircraft operating in Group I and Group II Terminal Controlled Areas.

Encoding altimeters are available as **indicating instruments** and as **blind instruments.** Indicating instruments display the altitude indication on the face of the instrument and also contain the electronic circuitry necessary to provide the altitude signal for the transponder. Blind encoders may be located in any area of the aircraft where electrical power and a static pressure line are available. The blind encoder has no external display (hence the term "blind") and functions only as an electronic sensor of static air pressure and a signal transmitter to provide the transponder with altitude information.

Airspeed Indicator

An **airspeed indicator** is required on all certificated aircraft except free balloons. The purpose of the airspeed indicator is to show the speed of the aircraft thorugh the air. The airspeed indicator is located in the upper left corner of a standard flight instrument grouping and is operated by a combination of pitot and static air pressure.

Some of the uses of the airspeed indicator are as follows:

1. It gives the pilot a definite indication of the attitude of the airplane with reference to the horizontal flight path. There will always be an increase in airspeed if the nose is down and a decrease in airspeed if the nose is high provided that there is no change in throttle setting.

2. It assists the pilot in determining the best throttle setting for most efficient flying speeds.

3. Indications of airspeed are necessary in estimating or calculating ground speed (speed of the airplane with reference to positions on the ground).

4. Every airplane has certain maximum speeds recommended by the manufacturer, and without the airspeed indicator these limits of design might be exceeded without the pilot's being aware of it. This is particularly true with respect to flap and landing-gear extension speeds.

5. The airspeed indicator shows the correct takeoff and landing speeds, and it warns when the airplane is approaching stalling speed. It also indicates angle of attack because higher speed generally means lower angle of attack.

The mechanism of an airspeed indicator is shown in Fig. 13-17. It consists of an airtight diaphragm enclosed in an airtight case, with linkages and gears designed to multiply the movement of the diaphragm and provide an indication on the dial of the instrument. The rear portion of the diaphgram is attached to the instrument case, and the forward portion is free to move. Unlike the diaphragm in an aneroid barometer,

TABLE 13-1

Airspeed, mph [km/h]	Ram Air Pressure			
	inHg	inH₂O	psi	kPa
20 [32.2]	0.0146	0.1985	0.007	0.048
40 [64.4]	0.0582	0.7912	0.028	0.193
60 [96.6]	0.1309	1.7796	0.064	0.441
80 [128.8]	0.2330	3.1676	0.114	0.786
100 [161]	0.3646	4.9567	0.180	1.241
120 [193.2]	0.5263	7.1550	0.258	1.779
140 [225.4]	0.7178	9.7585	0.352	2.427
160 [257.6]	0.940	12.7793	0.462	3.185
180 [289.8]	1.193	16.2188	0.586	4.040
200 [322]	1.477	20.0798	0.725	4.999
250 [402.5]	2.331	31.6899	1.145	7.895
300 [483]	3.397	46.1822	1.673	11.535
350 [563.5]	4.67	63.4887	2.29	15.79
400 [644]	6.19	84.153	3.04	20.96
500 [805]	9.97	135.542	4.89	33.72
600 [966]	15.02	204.197	7.38	50.89

a. Pitot pressure connection
b. Diaphragm
c. Rocking-shaft arm
d. Rocking shaft
e. Hairspring
f. Sector gear

FIG. 13-17 Mechanism of an airspeed indicator.

this one is provided with a connection for dynamic pressure from the pitot tube. Impact pressure from the pitot tube entering the diaphragm causes expansion that is transmitted through the multiplying mechanism to the indicating needle. Tubing connects the static side of the pitot head or other static ports to the instrument case, allowing static pressure to enter the case and surround the diaphragm. Thus the instruments actually measure **differential pressure** between the inside of the diaphragm and the inside of the instrument case. Table 13-1 shows the relationship between airspeed and impact pressure on the pitot head under standard conditions at sea level.

In level flight, as the speed of the airplane increases, the impact pressure becomes greater but the static pressure remains the same. This causes the diaphragm to expand more and more as the pressure increases inside. When the diaphragm expands, the rocking shaft picks up the motion and transmits it to the sector. The sector turns the pinion which is fastened to the tapered shaft (hand-staff). The pointer is pressed onto this tapered shaft and moves around a calibrated dial. The hairspring keeps the linkage taut and causes it to follow the movement of the diaphragm as the airspeed increases or decreases. The dial on the face of the instrument is calibrated in **knots,** miles per hour, or both.

There are three types of airspeed of which the mechanic should be aware: **indicated, calibrated,** and **true.**

Indicated airspeed is the airspeed indicated on the instrument.

Calibrated airspeed is indicated airspeed corrected for instrument and sensor position error. This correction is a result of the location of the pitot tube and static ports and the changing airflow around these sensors with different aircraft flight attitudes, various flap positions, and door, window, and vent positions as shown in Fig. 13-18. Each model aircraft and possibly each individual aircraft has a different set of calibrated airspeed values for specific indicated airspeed values.

Since the indicated and calibrated airspeeds are based on static and impact (pitot) air pressure, they only indicate the true aircraft speed through the air under standard day conditions at sea level. As the air density changes, the true airspeed of the aircraft changes. To find the true airspeed, the pilot must perform calculations with a flight computer or make use of a "true" airspeed indicator.

A true airspeed indicator is equipped with a rotating airspeed scale next to the standard airspeed scale. The movable scale can be positioned by the pilot to align the altitude value on the scale with an index mark. The pilot can then read the "true" airspeed of the aircraft directly from the scale. While this indicator does not take into account nonstandard air temperatures, it is considered accurate enough for most applications. A true airspeed indicator is shown in Fig. 13-19.

The dial or cover glass of an airspeed indicator is required to be marked with color arcs and radial lines to indicate various operating speeds.

A red radial line is applied at the never-exceed speed (V_{ne}).

A yellow arc is applied through the caution range of speeds. This arc extends from the red radial line just mentioned to the green arc described in the next paragraph.

A green arc is placed to indicate the normal operating range of speeds with the lower limit at the stalling speed with maximum weight and with landing gear and wing flaps retracted (V_{sl}), and the upper limit at the maximum structural cruising speed (V_{no}).

AIRSPEED CALIBRATION
NORMAL STATIC SOURCE

CONDITION:
Power required for level flight or maximum rated RPM dive.

FLAPS UP													
KIAS	40	50	60	70	80	90	100	110	120	130	140	150	160
KCAS	50	56	63	71	80	89	99	109	119	129	139	149	160
FLAPS 10°													
KIAS	40	50	60	70	80	90	100	110	---	---	---	---	---
KCAS	49	55	62	71	80	90	99	108	---	---	---	---	---
FLAPS 40°													
KIAS	40	50	60	70	80	85	---	---	---	---	---	---	---
KCAS	48	55	63	72	82	87	---	---	---	---	---	---	---

AIRSPEED CALIBRATION
ALTERNATE STATIC SOURCE

HEATER/VENTS AND WINDOWS CLOSED

FLAPS UP											
NORMAL KIAS	40	50	60	70	80	90	100	110	120	130	140
ALTERNATE KIAS	39	51	61	71	82	91	101	111	121	131	141
FLAPS 10°											
NORMAL KIAS	40	50	60	70	80	90	100	110	---	---	---
ALTERNATE KIAS	40	51	61	71	81	90	99	108	---	---	---
FLAPS 40°											
NORMAL KIAS	40	50	60	70	80	85	---	---	---	---	---
ALTERNATE KIAS	38	50	60	70	79	83	---	---	---	---	---

HEATER/VENTS OPEN AND WINDOWS CLOSED

FLAPS UP											
NORMAL KIAS	40	50	60	70	80	90	100	110	120	130	140
ALTERNATE KIAS	36	48	59	70	80	89	99	108	118	128	139
FLAPS 10°											
NORMAL KIAS	40	50	60	70	80	90	100	110	---	---	---
ALTERNATE KIAS	38	49	59	69	79	88	97	106	---	---	---
FLAPS 40°											
NORMAL KIAS	40	50	60	70	80	85	---	---	---	---	---
ALTERNATE KIAS	34	47	57	67	77	81	---	---	---	---	---

WINDOWS OPEN

FLAPS UP											
NORMAL KIAS	40	50	60	70	80	90	100	110	120	130	140
ALTERNATE KIAS	26	43	57	70	82	93	103	113	123	133	143
FLAPS 10°											
NORMAL KIAS	40	50	60	70	80	90	100	110	---	---	---
ALTERNATE KIAS	25	43	57	69	80	91	101	111	---	---	---
FLAPS 40°											
NORMAL KIAS	40	50	60	70	80	85	---	---	---	---	---
ALTERNATE KIAS	25	41	54	67	78	84	---	---	---	---	---

FIG. 13-18   An airspeed calibration chart. (*Cessna Aircraft Co.*)

A white arc is used for the flap operating range with the lower limit at the stalling speed at maximum weight with the landing gear and flaps fully extended (V_{s0}) and the upper limit at the flaps extended speed (V_{fe}).

For multiengine aircraft a blue radial line is used for the one-engine-inoperative best-rate-of-climb speed (V_{yse}), and a red radial line indicates the one-engine-inoperative minimum control speed (V_{mc}).

These markings are normally placed on the face card of the instrument. Where the required markings are placed on the instrument cover glass, an indicator line must be painted or otherwise applied from the glass to the case so that any slippage of the glass is apparent.

FIG. 13-19   A true speed airspeed indicator.

FIG. 13-20   Typical airspeed indicator markings.

Figure 13-20 shows the markings on the face of an airspeed indicator.

Airspeed-Angle-of-Attack Indicator

The instrument whose dial is shown in Fig. 13-21 is called an **airspeed-angle-of-attack** indicator. Its function is to indicate airspeed, maximum allowable indicated airspeed, and angle of attack. **Indicated airspeed** (IAS) is shown on the dial by means of a pointer driven by a conventional pressure diaphragm. This diaphragm is labeled "Airspeed diaphragm" in the schematic drawing of Fig. 13-22.

Angle-of-attack information is obtained by reading the indicated airspeed pointer against a segment rotating about the periphery of the instrument's dial. This movable segment is positioned relative to the IAS pointer by the servomechanism, which responds to

FIG. 13-21 Airspeed-angle-of-attack indicator. (Kollsman)

a signal from the **angle-of-attack** sensor. The IAS pointer, therefore, shows both indicated airspeed and angle of attack, the latter either in degrees or by markers showing best glide speed, best cruise, approach, over-the-fence, and stall angles. The angle-of-attack sensor provides electric signals that control the servomechanism driving the angle-of-attack sector on the dial.

The **maximum allowable** pointer shows "maximum allowable" and/or "never exceed" indicated airspeed. It is actuated by a static pressure diaphragm and mechanism with a special calibration, so that the pointer reads **maximum allowable indicated airspeed** as a function of absolute pressure only. Maximum allowable indicated airspeed increases as altitutde increases to about 25 000 ft and then decreases because it must not be allowed to approach Mach 1 (the speed of sound); that is, the airspeed is **Mach limited** at altitudes above 25 000 ft.

Machmeter

Because many of the modern jet aircraft fly near the speed of sound and some fly faster than the speed of sound, it is essential that such aircraft be equipped with an instrument that will compare the speed of the aircraft with the speed of sound. The flight characteristics of these high-speed aircraft change substantially as the speed of sound is approached or passed. These changes are associated with the occurrence of locally supersonic flow and shock waves. The result is that the pilot must substantially change the handling of the aircraft controls and retrim the airplane to meet the new conditions.

If an airplane is not designed to withstand the violent stresses that are sometimes imposed as a result of shock-wave formation during transonic flight, it may be severely damaged or may even disintegrate. In flying such an airplane the pilot must know when the craft is approaching the speed of sound.

Since the speed of sound varies according to temperature and altitude, it is obvious that an airspeed indicator will not give the pilot an accurate indication of the airplane speed relative to the speed of sound. It has, therefore, become necessary to use an instru-

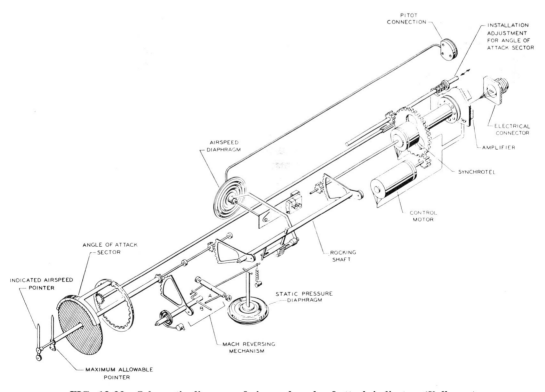

FIG. 13-22 Schematic diagram of airspeed-angle-of-attack indicator. (Kollsman)

ment that gives the airplane speed in proportion to the speed of sound under the atmospheric conditions in which the airplane is flying. The instrument designed to accomplish this is the **Machmeter,** or Mach indicator, and it measures the ratio of true airspeed to the speed of sound. This ratio is called the **Mach number,** named for the Austrian philosopher of science Ernst Mach (pronounced "mock"), who made the first studies of fast-moving projectiles.

The Machmeter, illustrated in Fig. 13-23 (a), shows the Mach number directly on its dial. For example, the number .7 is read as "Mach point seven," and it means that the airplane is flying at seven-tenths the speed of sound. The number 1.0 is read "Mach one" and means that the speed is equal to the speed of sound.

The Machmeter is similar in construction to an airspeed indicator; however, it includes an additional expanding diaphragm that modifies the magnifying ratio of the mechanism in proportion to altitude. As the altitude of the airplane increases, the altitude dia-

phragm expands and moves the floating rocking shaft. This movement changes the position of the rocking-shaft lever in relation to the sector lever, thus modifying the movement of the indicating needle to account for the effect of altitude. The arrangement of the diaphragm with respect to the rocking shaft is clearly shown in Fig. 13-23 (b). Observe that expansion of the diaphragm will decrease the proportional movement of the indicating needle.

The ram air pressure is registered through a diaphragm that rotates the rocking shaft as it expands or contracts. Temperature correction is applied through a thermometal fork mounted on the altitude diaphragm.

Vertical-Speed Indicator

Also referred to as a **rate-of-climb indicator,** a **vertical-speed indicator** is illustrated in Fig. 13-24. This instrument is valuable during instrument flight because it indicates the rate at which the airplane is climbing or descending. Level flight can be maintained by keeping the pointer of the instrument on zero, and any change in altitude is indicated on the dial in **feet per minute.** In this manner it assists the pilot in establishing a rate of climb that is within the prescribed limits of the engine. Likewise when the pilot is coming in for a landing or descending to a lower altitude, the rate of descent can be controlled.

Like the airspeed indicator, the climb indicator is a differential-pressure instrument. It operates from the differential between atmospheric pressure and the pressure of a chamber that is vented to the atmosphere through a small, calibrated capillary restriction. Modern rate-of-climb indicators are "self-contained," with all the necessary mechanisms enclosed in the instrument case. However, some of the outside-cell or bottle types are still being used on older aircraft.

The rate-of-climb (vertical-speed) indicator illustrated in Fig. 13-24 shows the internal mechanism of the instrument. Changes in pressure due to changes in altitude are transmitted quickly through a large tube to the inside of a diaphragm A and slowly through an orifice assembly B and capillary C to the inside of the case. This creates a pressure differential that causes the diaphragm to expand or contract according to the rate of change of altitude. Adjustable restraining springs D are provided, which control the diaphragm deflection and permit accurate calibration.

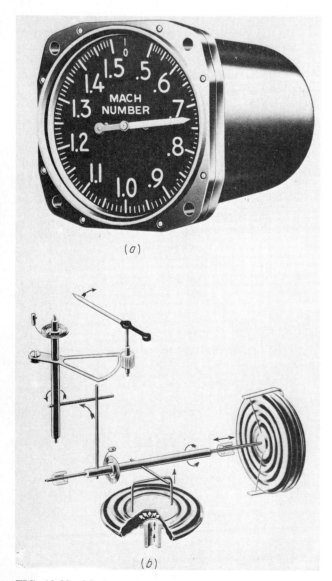

FIG. 13-23 Machmeter.

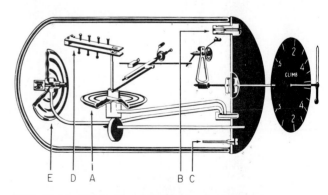

FIG. 13-24 Vertical-speed indicator mechanism.

478

The action of the diaphragm is transmitted through a lever-and-gear system to the pointer. As the plane assumes level flight, the pressures equalize and the pointer returns to zero. An overpressure diaphragm and valve E prevent excessive rates of climb or descent from damaging the mechanism.

It is characteristic of the rate-of-climb indicator to lag in its readings; that is, it does not respond instantaneously to changes in rate of climb. This is because it takes a few seconds for the differential pressures to develop after a change in rate of climb takes place. The more modern instruments used in recently manufactured aircraft have little or no lag.

Temperature changes have a tendency to cause variations in the flow of air through the capillary restrictors in the rate-of-climb instrument. Therefore, manufacturers have devised various methods of compensating the instrument for temperature. Likewise, altitude changes must be compensated for owing to a tendency toward a greater lag when flying at higher altitudes.

Although the rate-of-climb indicator is one of the most sensitive differential-pressure instruments, it is not easily damaged during steep dives or violent maneuvers because of mechanical stops that have been incorporated in the instrument. Vertical-speed indicators are made with ranges up to 2000 ft/min [609.6 m/min] for aircraft that operate at slow rates of climb or descent and at more than 10 000 ft/min [3048 m/min] for higher performance aircraft.

Variometers and **total-energy variometers** are sensitive vertical-speed indicators usually associated with gliders and sailplane operations. A variometer contains a sealed chamber with a balanced air vane inside as shown in Fig. 13-25. One side of the chamber is connected to the static system of the aircraft. The other side is connected to an insulated air chamber, referred to as a "thermos bottle." When the aircraft increases in altitude, the air in the thermos bottle is at a higher pressure than the static air pressure, so the air flows out of the bottle. To get out of the bottle, the air must push the variometer vane out of the way. This works against the balance spring used to center

the vane. The faster the aircraft is climbing, the greater the pressure differential and the higher the rate of flow out of the bottle. As the rate of flow varies, the amount of vane deflection varies. The vane drives an indicator needle on the instrument face and the rate of vertical speed is indicated in feet per minute or knots. If the aircraft descends, the static pressure is increasing. This causes the vane to deflect in the opposite direction and give an indication of a descent.

A total-energy variometer can be an electronic or mechanical device. It is designed to indicate the change in aircraft total energy (combination of potential and kinetic energy) by indicating a rate of climb or descent. This system is based on a variometer, but includes connections to the pitot system. If the aircraft is at some fixed airspeed and altitude, it has some amount of total energy based on speed and distance above the ground. If the aircraft enters a rising current of air and maintains the same airspeed, the potential energy of the aircraft is increased by its increase in altitude. In this case the total energy system would indicate a climb. On the other hand, if the air were smooth with no vertical movement and the pilot pulled back on the control stick to use excess airspeed to increase altitude, the total energy of the aircraft would not change. The aircraft would only have exchanged kinetic energy for potential energy. The total-energy instrument would not indicate a climb.

Accelerometer

The **accelerometer** is frequently used on new airplanes during test flights to measure the acceleration loads on the aircraft structure. It serves as a basis for stress analysis because it gives an accurate indication of stresses imposed on the airplane during flight. Its function is to measure in gravity units the accelerations of gravity being exerted on the airplane. It is also used as a service instrument on many aerobatic airplanes to indicate any excessive stress that might have occurred during flight. If an airplane is designed to withstand loads of 6 g (six times gravity) and it is found after a particular flight that 8 g has been imposed on the airplane, it is necessary to subject the airplane to a very careful inspection to determine whether damage has been done as a result of the excessive loading. The most likely cause of excessive loads during flight is rough weather. Severe updrafts or downdrafts can cause very high loads on the aircraft, and the accelerometer gives indication of the extent of the loads.

The accelerometer does not indicate any changes in velocity that take place in a line coinciding with the longitudinal axis of the aircraft. It only indicates changes along the aircraft vertical axis.

The accelerometer is usually graduated in gravity units up to plus 12 g, with minus 5 g as the lowest reading. Occasionally the instrument has a range from −1 to +8 g. Minus readings occur when the airplane is being nosed over into a dive or in level flight when a downward air current is encountered.

Vertical acceleration can be illustrated by carrying a heavy parcel in an elevator. When the elevator starts its downward motion, the parcel seems to lose weight. When the elevator assumes a steady rate of descent,

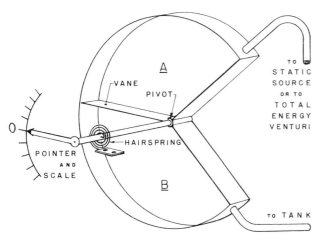

FIG. 13-25 Diagram illustrating the operation of a variometer. (Soaring Society of America)

the parcel again feels normal in weight. When the elevator slows down and just before it stops, the parcel seems to be excessively heavy. If these apparent changes in weight could actually be measured, the result would be the vertical acceleration of the parcel.

Some accelerometer instruments have two hands, but the more modern types are equipped with three hands. One hand measures the continuous acceleration, another measures the maximum acceleration reached at any time during the flight, and the third hand measures the minimum acceleration, or the largest minus reading, during the flight. The instrument is calibrated to read 1 g when the airplane is in normal flight or on the ground. This is the actual weight, or the vertical acceleration, of the airplane itself. This means that a load of 1 g is imposed upon the airplane as a result of its normal weight.

The principle of the accelerometer is illustrated in Fig. 13-26 where the mass weight is free to slide up and down on two mass shafts. As it moves up and down, it pulls on the cord that passes around three pulleys. The main pulley is attached to the shaft that carries the indicating needle. Thus, when the mass moves, it turns the main pulley and causes movement of the indicating needle. The mass is held in the 1-g position by the balance spring, which is of the flat-coiled type such as a clock spring. The inside of this spring is attached to the shaft on which the main pulley and indicating needle are mounted, and the outer end is attached to a stationary part of the case.

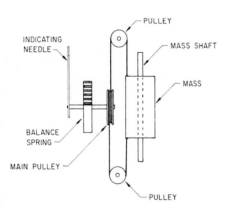

FIG. 13-26   Diagram illustrating the principle of an accelerometer.

A cutaway view of an accelerometer is shown in Fig. 13-27. In this instrument the main shaft is enclosed in a hollow shaft that is somewhat shorter than the main shaft. Attached to this hollow shaft is the maximum-reading hand. Also fixed to the hollow shaft is a ratchet. As the main shaft rotates, a driver arm pushes a small tab that is a part of the ratchet, thus turning the hollow shaft along with the main shaft. This means that both the continuous-reading hand and the maximum-reading hand move simultaneously up to the point where the vertical acceleration on the weight is counterbalanced by the calibrating spring. The maximum-reading hand is stopped on the high point by means of the pawl, which engages one of the ratchet teeth. Obviously the ratchet and hand will stay

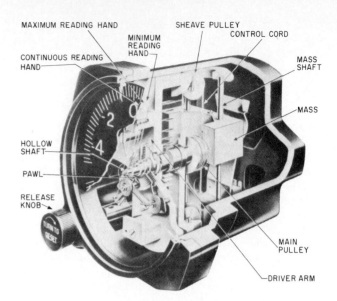

FIG. 13-27   Cutaway view of an accelerometer.

in this position until such a time as a greater vertical acceleration is produced to move it farther around the scale. When the knob in front of the instrument is turned, the pawl is disengaged and the maximum-reading hand can return to its normal position.

The mechanism described in the foregoing section is only one of the many types of accelerometers, but in all cases the weight or pendulum weight works against a calibrated spring that determines the degree of travel of the mass weight. In inertial guidance systems for missiles and spacecraft and aircraft inertial reference systems, accelerometers are used to develop signals indicating what degree of acceleration is taking place. In a stable platform for an inertial guidance and reference systems, there are usually three accelerometers: one for vertical acceleration, one for longitudinal acceleration, and one for lateral acceleration. These are arranged so that the mass can move up and down, fore and aft, and from side to side, respectively. The accelerometer signals are sent to the computer section of the system, where correction signals are developed.

Magnetic Compass

The magnetic compass is an independently operating instrument described here as mechanical because it requires no power from any aircraft source. A magnetic compass is illustrated in Fig. 13-28.

The magnetic compass is a comparatively simple device designed to indicate the direction in which an aircraft is headed. This is accomplished by one or more bar magnets mounted on a pivot with a circular **compass card** that is usually marked in increments of 5°. The movable assembly is contained in a compass bowl filled with a light petroleum oil which damps out oscillations and lubricates the pivot bearing.

The construction of a magnetic compass is shown in Fig. 13-29. The compass card assembly is mounted on a jewelled pivot bearing on the jewel post assembly. Immediately below the card can be seen the ends of the two parallel, permanent bar magnets which pro-

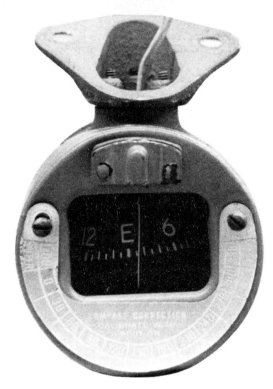

FIG. 13-28   A magnetic compass.

vide the magnetic direction indication. An expansion chamber is built into the compass to provide for the expansion and contraction of the liquid which results from changes in temperature and altitude. The flexible diaphragm moves as required to provide more or less space for the liquid. Between the aneroid back and the diaphragm is the air chamber which permits the expansion and contraction. The liquid in the compass bowl (case) damps the oscillations of the card, thus preventing the card from turning violently and vibrating. Compensating magnets are in the compensator assembly at the bottom of the case.

The compass provides an indication of *magnetic* direction rather than *true* direction. The bar magnet (or magnets) in the compass aligns itself (or themselves) with the magnetic lines of force in the earth's magnetic field. Since the magnetic poles of the earth are not located at the geographical poles, the magnetic compass reading is subject to **variation,** depending upon its location on the earth's surface. This variation must be taken into account by the pilot who is navigating the aircraft. For example, in the extreme western portion of the United States, the variation may be from 15 to 20° east of true north. If the variation is 15°E and the compass reading is 280°, the pilot must substract 15° from 280° to find the true heading.

Magnetic compasses are subject to **deviation.** This is an inaccuracy caused by magnetic influences in the airplane. These are caused primarily by the proximity of magnetic materials such as iron and steel and by current flowing in nearby electrical circuits. Deviation is corrected as much as possible by the use of small **compensating magnets** mounted in the case. These magnets are adjustable to correct for north-south deviation and east-west deviation. The process of com-

pass compensating is done by "swinging" the compass on a **compass rose.** The compass rose is a circle on which are marked magnetic directions in degrees, the 0° mark showing the magnetic North direction. A typical compass rose is illustrated in Fig. 13-30.

Instructions for compensating a compass vary to some extent, depending uopn the airplane involved and the equipment installed. Typical instructions are as follows:

Before attempting to compensate the compass, every effort should be made to place the aircraft in simulated level flight conditions. Check to see that the doors are closed, flaps in the retraced position, engines running, throttles set at cruise position, and aircraft in level flight attitude. All electrical switches, alternators, and radios should be on.

1. Set adjustment screws of compensator on zero. The adjustment screws are in zero position when the dot of the screw is lined up with the dot of the frame.

2. Head the aircraft in a magnetic north direction. Adjust the N-S adjustment screw until the compass reads exactly north (0°). Use only a nonmagnetic screwdriver.

3. Head the aircraft in a magnetic east direction and adjust the E-W screw until the compass reads exactly East.

4. Head the aircraft in a magnetic south direction and note the resulting south error. Adjust the N-S screw until one-half of the error has been removed.

5. Head the aircraft in a magnetic west direction and adjust the E-W screw to remove one-half the E-W error.

6. Head the aircraft in successive magnetic 30° headings and record the compass readings on the appropriate **deviation card.** Deviations must not exceed ±10° on any heading.

The compass on an airplane should be checked (swung) whenever there is an installation or removal of any radio equipment or any other equipment which could have an effect on the compass. In addition, the compass and correction card should be checked for deviation at least once a year at the annual inspection.

The compass is usually installed on the centerline of the fuselage. It is normally mounted on the top of the instrument panel or suspended from a mount on the windshield or near the top of the windshield. These mounting locations are chosen so that the compass is as far away from items which might affect its operation, such as the radios and electrical circuits, but still in easy view of the pilot. Only rarely is the compass mounted in the instrument panel with the other instruments.

Vertical-Dial Compass

The vertical-dial direction indicator is actually a direct-reading magnetic compass; instead of the direction's being read from the swinging compass card, however, the reading is taken from a vertical dial as shown in Fig. 13-31.

The reference index on the vertical dial can be set

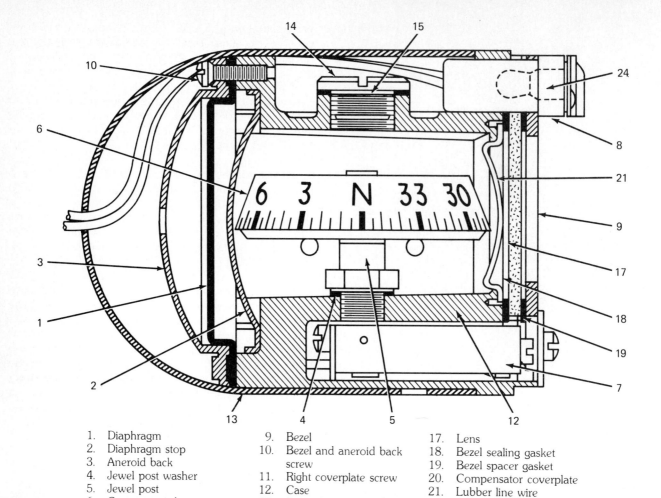

1.	Diaphragm	9.	Bezel	17.	Lens
2.	Diaphragm stop	10.	Bezel and aneroid back	18.	Bezel sealing gasket
3.	Aneroid back		screw	19.	Bezel spacer gasket
4.	Jewel post washer	11.	Right coverplate screw	20.	Compensator coverplate
5.	Jewel post	12.	Case	21.	Lubber line wire
6.	Compass card	13.	Streamline housing	22.	Light screw
7.	Compensator assembly	14.	Filler plug	23.	Left coverplate screw
8.	Light	15.	Filler plug washer	24.	Lamp
		16.	Insert nut		

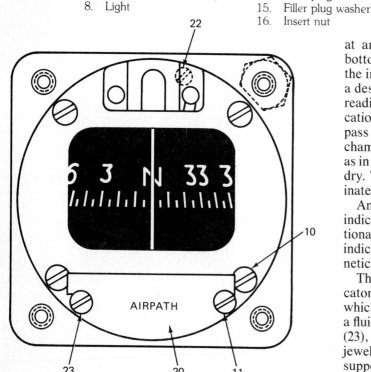

FIG. 13-29 **Construction of a magnetic compass.** (*Airpath Instrument Co.*)

at any desired heading by turning the knob at the bottom of the dial, and it is necessary only to match the indicator needle with the reference pointer to hold a desired course. The design of the dial provides easy reading of direction and also quick and positive indication of deviation from a selected heading. The compass liquid in the instrument is contained in a separate chamber, and the dial, instead of floating in the liquid as in other types of magnetic compasses, is completely dry. This makes the indicator easier to read and eliminates fluid leakage around the dial.

An important feature of the vertical-dial direction indicator is its stability in comparision to the conventional compass. Both the period and the swing of this indicator are less than half that of the ordinary magnetic compass.

The construction of the vertical-dial direction indicator is shown in Fig. 13-32. The float assembly (20), which contains the directive magnet (27), is located in a fluid-filled bowl. This assembly rides on a steel pivot (23), which in turn rests on a stud containing a cup jewel (24). The jewel stud rides in a guide and is supported on a spring (26) which absorbs external vibration. A change in the position of the instrument in relation to the directional magnet transmits this motion to the indicator needle (8) through the follower

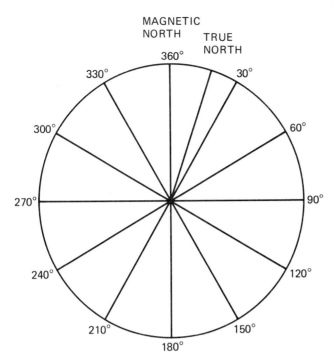

FIG. 13-30   A typical compass rose.

FIG. 13-31   Dial of a magnetic direction indicator.

magnets (18), the bevel gears (16), and the horizontal bevel-gear shaft (11) onto which the indicator needle is pressed. The follower magnets and bevel gears are all contained in the housing (17). Both bevel-gear shafts are carefully balanced and ride on steel pivots in jeweled bearings.

A compensation system [polycompensator (13)] is mounted directly over the bevel-gear housing. The compensation-magnet gear assemblies are turned through gear trains to two slotted adjustment stem pinions (2 and 3). The reference lines (7) are set through a gear train by means of the adjustment knob (1).

As temperature varies, expansion of the compass liquid surrounding the float assembly takes place through a small hole in the baffle plate, and the level of the liquid in the expansion chamber above the baffle plate will rise and fall with changes in temperature. The normal level of the liquid is about even with the hole, which is used to fill the chamber.

The indicator is equipped with rim lighting which utilizes a special diffusing lens at the lamp socket to distribute the light evenly over the entire dial. Three-volt lamps are used and are accessible from the front to facilitate replacement.

Flux-Gate Compass System

The Gyro Flux Gate compass system is one type of remote-indicating earth-inductor compass system. Its advantage is that it is comparatively free of the disadvantages of the standard magnetic compass. It consists of a flux gate (flux valve) transmitter, master direction indicator, amplifier, junction box, caging switch, and one or more compass repeaters. See Fig. 13-33.

The **flux gate** is a special three-section transformer which develops a signal whose characteristics are determined by the position of the unit with respect to the earth's magnetic field. The flux gate element consists of three highly permeable cores arranged in the form of an equilateral triangle with a primary and secondary winding on each core. The primary winding of the flux gate is energized by a single-phase 487.5-Hz 1.5-V power supply from an oscillator. This current saturates the three sections of the core twice each cycle. During the time that the core is not saturated, the earth's magnetic flux can enter the core and affect the induction of a voltage in the secondary. The effect of the primary excitation is to *gate* the earth's magnetic flux into and out of the core. This cycle occurs twice during each cycle of the excitation current; hence, the voltage induced in the secondary windings of the flux gate has twice the frequency of the primary current, because the core is saturated twice each cycle and has no excitation flux twice each cycle. The resulting voltage in the secondary windings has a frequency of 975 Hz.

The 975-Hz secondary signal is developed in the flux gate as illustrated in Fig. 13-34. At point 1 in the time cycle, the excitation voltage is zero, the earth's magnetic flux in the core of the flux gate is maximum, and the induced signal in the secondary is zero. There is no induced secondary signal because there is no flux change in the core at this instant. Between points 1 and 2, excitation voltage in the primary increases from zero to maximum. This saturates the core and causes the earth flux in the core to change from maximum to minimum, thus inducing a voltage in the secondary which rises to a maximum (A) in one direction and decreases to zero when there is no further change at point 2.

From point 2 to 3 the earth flux increases to maximum; hence, the secondary voltage at B is in a direction opposite that developed at A. Thus we see that there are two cycles of induced voltage in the secondary for each one cycle of primary excitation voltage.

The ratios of the output voltages in the three secondary coils are determined by the position of the flux gate element with respect to the earth's magnetic field, with only one possible position for any combination of voltages.

In the **transmitter,** shown in Fig. 13-35, the flux gate is held in a horizontal position by means of a gyro. This is necessary to provide a uniform signal from the flux gate element. If the gyro should be *tumbled,* that

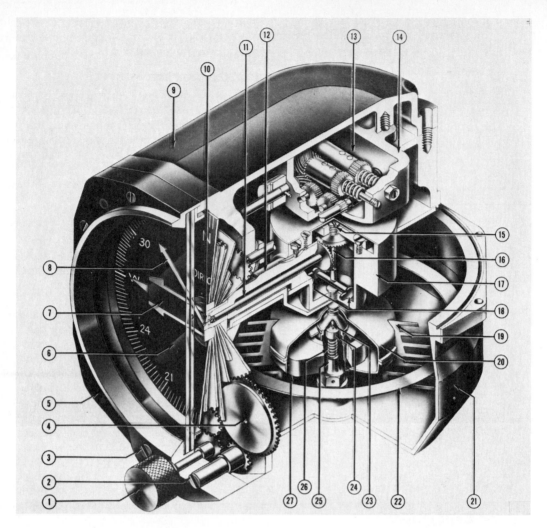

FIG. 13-32   Construction of a vertical-dial, magnetic direction indicator.

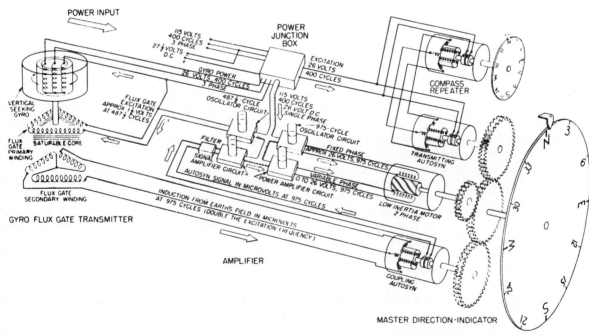

FIG. 13-33   Diagram of the Gyro Flux Gate system. (*Bendix Corp.*)

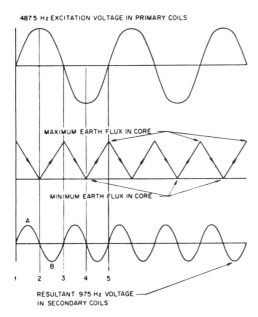

FIG. 13-34 Development of the signal in a flux gate. (Bendix Corp.)

FIG. 13-35 Flux gate transmitter. (Bendix Corp.)

is, moved out of the horizontal position, it can be erected by means of the **caging switch.**

The 975-Hz output of the secondary windings of the flux gate is connected by three leads to the stator of a **coupling Autosyn** in the **master direction indicator.** The currents in these leads set up a magnetic field in the stator of the coupling Autosyn similar in direction and strength to that appearing in the flux gate element. This field shifts its position whenever any change occurs in the stator voltages as a result of a change in the heading of the aircraft.

The rotor of the coupling Autosyn normally lies in a null (neutral) position; in this position no signal is induced in it by the stator field. When the stator field shifts is a result of a change in aircraft heading, the rotor will no longer be in the null position, and a signal will be induced in the rotor winding. This signal is fed to the amplifier and then to the variable phase of a low-inertia two-phase motor in the master direction indicator. This causes a torque to be produced, and the motor turns in a direction determined by the phase of the current in the variable-phase winding. The motor shaft turns the indicator dial to provide a visual

indication of the magnetic heading of the aircraft, and at the same time, it drives the rotor of the coupling Autosyn to a new null position. This reduces the rotor signal to zero, and the low-inertia motor stops turning until another change in the heading of the aircraft causes a new signal to be induced in the rotor of the coupling Autosyn.

The **master direction indicator,** shown in Fig. 13-36, is the indicating unit for the Gyro Flux Gate system. It contains the coupling Autosyn, the low-inertia two-phase motor, a transmitting Autosyn, and a course Autosyn synchro to supply a signal for the operation of the automatic pilot.

FIG. 13-36 Master direction indicator. (Bendix Corp.)

The **compass repeater** (Fig. 13-37) contains a single Autosyn which receives its signal from the transmitting Autosyn in the master direction indicator. The dial of the repeater shows the four cardinal headings as well as intermediate headings marked every 5° and numbered every 30°.

When it is desired to provide direction information at more than one location, the compass repeater is used. The repeater is a single Autosyn receiver having an indicating dial attached to the rotor shaft. As stated above, the repeater receives signals from the Autosyn transmitter in the master direction indicator and responds by reproducing the heading information on its dial.

FIG. 13-37 Compass repeater. (Bendix Corp.)

The **amplifier** serves to increase the power of the magnetic direction signal from the coupling Autosyn in the master direction indicator. It also furnishes a 487.5-Hz power supply for the excitation of the primary windings of the flux gate transmitter and a 975-Hz power supply for the excitation of the fixed phase of the master-direction-indicator motor.

The caging switch is used to control the cage-uncage cycle of the gyro in the flux gate transmitter. The gyro is said to be *caged* when it is held in a fixed position by mechanical means; it is *uncaged* when it is allowed complete freedom of motion.

The need for caging a gyro may be easily understood. The gyro in the flux gate transmitter must spin on an axis perpendicular to the earth's surface to keep the flux gate in the correct position with respect to the earth's flux. Since the gyro is free to move away from the vertical axis with respect to the airplane in which it is installed, there are many times when it is not in the correct position for operation. At these times it is necessary to erect the gyro by means of the caging switch.

To erect the gyro, the MOMENTARY-CONTACT-SWITCH button on the switch box is depressed and released. This starts the cage-uncage cycle, which then continues automatically until the cycle is complete. An indicator light on the switch box comes on when the gyro is caged.

Directional Gyro

The **directional gyro** is a gyro-operated directional reference instrument designed to eliminate some of the problems associated with the magnetic compass. The gyro does not seek the north pole; however, it will continue to tell the pilot of an aircraft whether the aircraft is holding a particular heading. The directional gyro must be reset by the pilot to the magnetic compass indication from time to time to correct for precession or drift after a period of operation, usually after every 15 min.

The airborne directional gyro consists of a gyro rotor mounted in a set of gimbals so that the position of its spin axis can be maintained independent of the case of the instrument. The spin axis is normally horizontal. The axis of the inner gimbal is also horizontal and is perpendicular to the spin axis. The outer gimbal is pivoted on a vertical axis, so that all three axes are mutually perpendicular. It is the relative angle between the outer gimbal and a reference point on the case that is measured by the instrument and presented on the dial. Since the spin axis is horizontal and the case can be considered aligned with the directional axis of the aircraft, the angle presented on the dial is also the angle between the heading of the aircraft and the direction of the spin axis of the gyro. Any change in the heading of the aircraft is indicated on the dial since the position of the gyro is rigid in space and is not affected by the motion of the aircraft.

The principal parts of a directional gyro are illustrated in Fig. 13-38. Observe the gyro with the *X* axis, the inner gimbal with the *Y* axis, and the outer gimbal with the *Z* axis. When the gyro is spinning, it will maintain its rigid position in space even though the

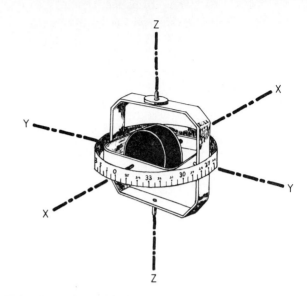

FIG. 13-38   Simplified drawing of a directional gyro.

case of the instrument is rotated about it in any direction. When the instrument is mounted in an aircraft and in operation, it is easy to understand that as the aircraft turns to the right or left, there will be a relative movement between the dial mounted on the outer gimbal and the instrument case. The amount of this movement will indicate to the pilot the angular degrees through which the airplane has turned.

The designs of the dial faces for directional gyros vary widely, but they all indicate a value in degrees from 0 to 360°. A knob is provided on the instrument that permits the reading to be changed by the pilot. The reading is usually made to coincide with the average reading of a magnetic compass. The directional-gyro instrument is used as a reference during flight instead of the magnetic compass since the magnetic

FIG. 13-39   A modern heading indicator. *(Edo Corp.)*

compass fluctuates and oscillates considerably during maneuvers. The directional gyro is a stable reference: hence the readings will be comparatively stable for normal flight maneuvers.

A **heading indicator** is a refined version of the directional gyro. Its principles of operation are the same as for the directional gyro, but the display presentation is a compass card, as shown in Fig. 13-39. This compass card display allows the pilot to visualize the heading of the aircraft in relation to heading changes that may be required. With this visualization, the mental workload of the pilot is reduced and flying by reference to the instruments is made easier. A simplified cutaway of a heading indicator is shown in Fig. 13-40.

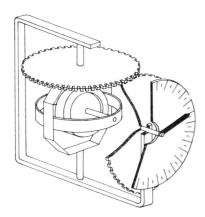

FIG. 13-40 Internal components of a heading indicator.

As mentioned previously, the gyros used in various instruments can be driven by air or by means of an electric current. If the gyro is electrically driven, the gyro itself is a part of the electric motor. Figure 13-41 is a photograph of the rotor mechanism in an air-driven directional gyro. To drive this gyro, the case of the instrument is connected to a vacuum or pressure

FIG. 13-41 Rotor mechanism in a directional gyro.

source. The resulting airflow through the instrument is directed onto the "buckets" machined on the rim of the rotor. Within a short time after the airflow is started, the rotor is turning at a high rate of speed.

Gyro instruments must necessarily be limited in the degree of movement through which the gimbals can travel, except in the case of the directional gyro where the Z axis can turn through a complete circle. If the degree of permitted movement is exceeded because of violent maneuvers of the airplane, the gyro rotor will be moved out of its normal position of rigidity, and it is then said to be **tumbled.** In order to restore the gyro to its correct alignment, a **caging** mechanism is installed. When the gyro is caged, it is locked into its correct position mechanically. The caging mechanism must then be released to permit the gyro to function normally.

To be most effective as an indicator of azimuthal direction, a directional gyro should have its spin axis horizontal. In more complex equipment this would be accomplished by slaving the gyro gimbals to a gravity-detecting device. However, in order to keep the construction as simple as possible, most directional gyros are leveled so that the inner gimbal is perpendicular to the outer gimbal. This is usually satisfactory since the instrument is installed in the aircraft with its outer gimbal approximately vertical. This means that in straight and level flight the spin axis is about horizontal. Furthermore, we have seen that gimbal error and X-axis frictional effects are at a minimum when the gimbals are perpendicular.

In the past, several devices have been used to obtain perpendicularity, or **level** position of the gyro. When a gyro is air-driven, the jets of air that spin the rotor are used to keep it level. In one model, there are two-parallel jets that are directed at the buckets on the gyro. If one of the spin axes rises, the buckets move out of the jet stream until one of the jets is directing its stream of air at the side of the gyro. This jet then applies force about the vertical axis, thus causing the gyro to precess back to the horizontal position. One of the faults of this system is that the jet also tends to apply a force about the horizontal axis. This causes the gyro to precess in azimuth and causes an erroneous heading indication.

In a later design for an air-driven gyro, the airstream flows over the top of the rotor and around in the direction of spin toward the lower portion of the vertical gimbal. On this gimbal there is a **plow** in the form of a wedge, which splits the airstream into two sections. This method is shown in Fig. 13-42. If the gyroscope is level, the force on each face of the plow is equal; but if the gyro is tilted, then the airstream strikes only one side of the plow. The resulting unbalanced force attempts to rotate the outer gimbal about its vertical axis, but instead the gyroscope is precessed back to its level position.

Another air-driven gyro instrument employs **pendulous vanes,** which act as air valves to direct air for correction of position. As long as the gyro is level, the airstreams are balanced. If the gyro shifts position, the vanes move by gravity to a position that changes the airflow and applies a corrective force.

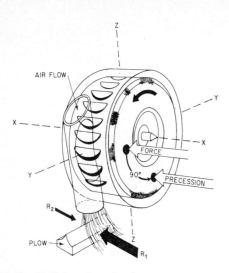

FIG. 13-42 Utilizing air to level a gyro.

Electrically driven directional gyros are leveled by means of a torque motor located above the outer gimbal. This motor, by applying torque to the gimbal about its vertical axis, causes the gyro to be precessed to a level position. The motor is usually energized by a switch located between the inner and outer gimbals.

The directional gyro is usually mounted at the bottom center position of the flight instrument group.

Horizontal Situation Indicator

A **horizontal situation indicator,** or HSI, is an instrument that combines the information supplied by a heading indicator with radio navigation information. This provides more flight information for the pilot on one instrument and reduces the eye motion required when flying by reference to instruments. This type of instrument also reduces both the number of instru-

ments that must be installed and the demand on panel space since one instrument can replace two or more old displays.

The simplest HSI has an electrically or pneumatically driven gyro for the heading indicator portion of the display. Information from the lateral navigation radio is displayed through a deviation bar and a selected-course pointer as shown in Fig. 13-43. Information from the glideslope radio receiver is displayed on the left side of the unit. "Flags," such as NAV, HDG, and GS, are displayed whenever that function is inoperative. For example, if the HOG flag is visible, the gyro is not operating properly. When the gyro is operating properly, this flag is retracted out of sight.

The more sophisticated HSI displays incorporate lateral navigation and glideslope information, distance measuring equipment information, and bearing pointers to indicate the location of other navigation ground stations in relation to the aircraft. An example of this type of display is given in Fig. 13-44.

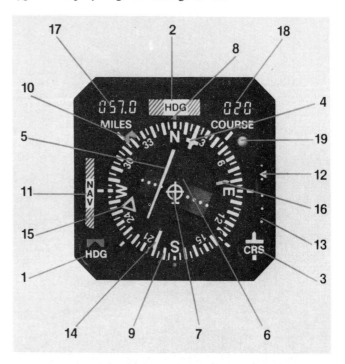

FIG. 13-44 Components of a horizontal situation indicator. *(Aeronetics)*
  1. Heading select knob.
  2. Heading warning flag.
  3. Course select knob.
  4. Selected course pointer.
  5. NAV lateral deviation bar.
  6. To-From indicator.
  7. Symbolic aircraft.
  8. Lubber line.
  9. Compass card.
 10. Heading select marker.
 11. NAV warning flag.
 12. VERT deviation indicator.
 13. VERT warning flag.
 14. Reciprocal course pointer.
 15. RMI bearing pointer.
 16. RMI bearing reciprocal pointer.
 17. Digital DME display.
 18. Digital course display.
 19. Synchronizing annunciator.

FIG. 13-43 A horizontal situation indicator. *(Edo Corp.)*

Artificial Horizon

The **gyro horizon indicator,** also called the **artificial horizon, attitude indicator,** or **attitude gyro,** is designed to provide a visual reference horizon for an airplane that is flying "blind," that is, with no visible reference outside the airplane. This instrument provides a horizontal reference similar to the natural horizon, thus making it possible for the pilot of an aircraft to see the position of the aircraft with respect to the horizon. A white bar across the face of the instrument represents the horizon, and a small figure of an airplane in the center of the dial represents the aircraft. The position of the airplane symbol relative to the horizon bar indicates the actual position of the aircraft with respect to the natural horizon. The face of an old-style artificial horizon is shown in Fig. 13-45. A more modern display is shown in Fig. 13-46.

A properly installed gimbaled gyroscope can measure motion about any axis except its spin axis. For example, the directional gyro has its spin axis maintained in a horizontal position, so that any change in the heading of the aircraft (motion about the Z axis) can be detected, but this instrument cannot measure roll motion about the X axis. In order to detect pitch-and-roll motion of an aircraft, we use a gyro with a vertical spin axis and horizontal gimbal axis. The gyro horizon indicator is one of several instruments with such a vertical gyroscope. With the spin axis of the gyro maintained in a vertical direction, roll motion is detected by motion of the case about the outer gimbal (Z axis) and pitch motion is detected between the inner and outer gimbals (Y axis).

A gyro erection mechanism is incorporated into the design of an artificial horizon. The purpose of this mechanism is to correct for any force such as precession, which might cause the gyroscope to tilt out of its vertical plane. Two methods commonly used for

FIG. 13-46   A modern artificial horizon. *(Edo Corp.)*

this purpose are the **ball erector** and the **pendulous vane** mechanisms.

The ball erector uses a concave plate attached to the bottom of the gyro support. When the gyro tilts out of the vertical, metal balls on the plate move to the low side of the plate. The movement of the balls causes a force to be exerted on the gyro axis which causes the gyro to return to the vertical position. The location of the ball erector is shown in Fig. 13-47 along with a simplified view of an artificial horizon.

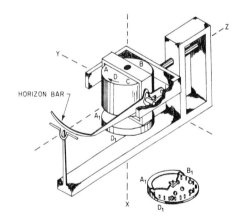

FIG. 13-47   Gyro horizon indicator with ball erector.

A pendulous vane mechanism can be used with pneumatically operated gyroscopes. A pendulous cover plate partially blocks the escape of the operating airflow from the gyro. As the axis of the gyro tilts out of the vertical, the plates either cover more of the opening or less of the opening, depending on the direction of gyro tilt. The resulting difference in airflow causes the gyro to return to the vertical position. The

FIG. 13-45   Face of a gyro horizon indicator.

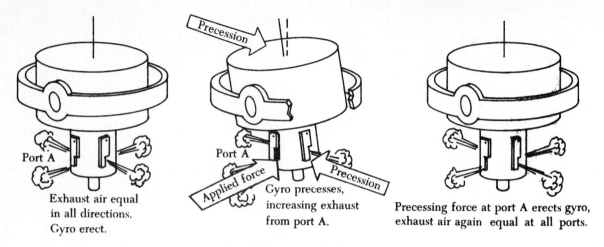

Exhaust air equal in all directions. Gyro erect.

Gyro precesses, increasing exhaust from port A.

Precessing force at port A erects gyro, exhaust air again equal at all ports.

FIG. 13-48   Erecting mechanism of a vacuum-driven attitude indicator.

operation of a pendulous vane mechanism is shown in Fig. 13-48.

The artificial horizon can be operated electrically or pneumatically. The instrument is usually mounted in the top center of the flight instrument group. Sophisticated versions of the artificial horizon, such as the one shown in Fig. 13-49, may include more than just pitch and bank attitude information. Additional information may include localizer and glideslope deviation needles, radar altimeter information, steering bars, and an inclinometer. Instruments with all of those features are called **flight directors.**

Turn-and-Bank Indicator

The **turn-and-bank indicator,** sometimes called the "needle and ball," actually consists of two instruments. The "needle" part of the instrument is a gyro instrument which indicates to the pilot the rate at which the aircraft is turning. The "ball" part of the instrument is an inclinometer, which denotes the quality of the turn by indicating whether or not the turn is coordinated.

The turn-indicating section of the turn-and-bank indicator is actually a **rate gyro,** and it produces an indication in proportion to the **rate of turn.** The face of the instrument normally includes marks, or "dog houses," on each side of the centered needle position. When the needle is pointing at one of these marks, the aircraft is in a standard-rate turn of 3°/s. Some rate indicators are designed to indicate a turn at one-half of standard rate when the needle points at a dog house. These instruments can be identified by the words "4 MINUTE TURN" at the bottom of the instrument, meaning that a 360° change in direction will take 4 min rather than the standard 2 min. These 4-min indicators are normally found in highspeed aircraft. If there are no dog houses on the instrument face, one needle width deflection is the standard-rate position.

Figure 13-50 shows how a gyro serves to indicate a rate of turn. This figure does not show the actual arrangement of a turn-and-bank-indicator gyro, but it does demonstrate the principle of operation. The gyro is set up to measure the rate at which its base is being turned about the Z axis. If the base is not turning, there is no force exerted on the gyro since the springs attached to the X axis are adjusted so that under these conditions they are in balance.

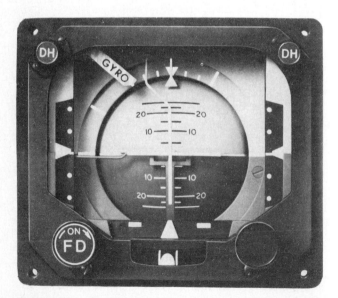

FIG. 13-49   An artificial horizon with flight director capabilities. *(Edo Corp.)*

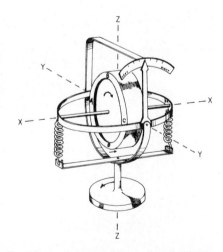

FIG. 13-50   How a gyro provides a turn indication.

If we turn the gyro assembly to the left as shown by the arrow on the base, a force will be applied to the left at A and to the right at C. As we remember the rule for precession, we find that the point B on the gyro will move to the left and the point D will move to the right, thus precessing the gyro about the Y axis and causing the indicating needle to show a left turn. The rate of turn indicated will depend upon how rapidly the base of the unit is turned.

As the gyro precesses around the Y axis, the spring on the right end of the spin axle will be extended. The stretched spring will then apply a downward force on the end of the axle and, in effect, will be applying a force at B and D. Thus force at B and D results in a precessional motion about the Z axis in the direction in which the base is turning. When the gyro is precessing about the Z axis at the same rate of speed as the base is being turned externally, there is no longer any force being exerted at points C and A. This means that the gyro will stop precessing about the Y axis and will hold its position. If, however, the rate at which the base is being turned is increased, once again there will be a force applied at C and D and the gyro will precess farther about the Y axis. Of course, the spring being stretched farther will cause a more rapid precession about the Z axis, and this will again match the external turning. Thus we see that, whenever the base is being turned, one of the springs is displaced enough to precess the gyro at a rate equal to the rate of turn. Whenever the base is stopped, the springs restore the gyro rotor to the neutral position.

A standard bank-and-turn indicator is shown in Fig. 13-51. This instrument is gyro-operated and functions on a principle similar to that described in the previous paragraphs. During a turn, the precession of the gyro causes the "needle" to swing to the right or left depending upon the direction of the turn. The amount of deflection will be proportional to the rate of turn. This enables the pilot to determine the rate of turn by the instrument.

Turn Coordinator

A **turn coordinator** is similar to a turn-and-bank indicator in that the pilot uses it to determine the rate of turn. The external difference between the two instruments is that the turn coordinator uses the outline of an airplane to indicate the rate of turn instead of a needle as shown in Fig. 13-51. The turn coordinator has replaced the turn-and-bank indicator as the standard turn-rate-indicating instrument on many aircraft.

Internally, the gimbal which holds the gyroscope in the turn coordinated is tilted back at about a 30° angle rather than being vertical, as in the turn-and-bank instrument. This tilting allows the gyro to indicate both yaw about the vertical axis and roll about the longitudinal axis of the aircraft.

Both types of turn indicators can be powered electrically or pneumatically. The position of the turn-rate-indicating instrument in the standard flight instrument group is in the lower left corner, below the airspeed indicator and to the left of the directional gyro.

Suction Gauges

Suction or **vacuum gauges** are used in airplanes for the purpose of indicating a reduction of pressure. In other words, they indicate the amount of vacuum being created by the vacuum pumps or venturi tube and assist in the proper setting of the relief valve in the vacuum system. A typical suction gauge is illustrated in Fig. 13-52. The suction gauge gives pilots warning of impending failures of the system and warns them not to rely on the instruments that are operated by vacuum. It will be learned later that gyroscopes will operate for a short period of time even after the source of vacuum has been shut off or partially cut off, but the indications may be erroneous. Some aircrafts have an alternate source of vacuum available

FIG. 13-51   A turn-and-bank indicator.

FIG. 13-52   Suction gauge.

in the event of failure of the vacuum source being used. The suction gauge indicates any fluctuation or impending failure of the system, thus giving the pilot warning to switch over to the alternative vacuum source. For example, if the engine-driven vacuum pump on one engine of a multi-engine aircraft is being used, the alternate pump may be located on the opposite engine. On the other hand, if the airplane has but one engine, the alternate source may be a **venturi tube,** discussed later in this chapter.

The suction gauge is vented to the atmosphere or to the air filter if one is used in the system. The tube leading from the pressure-sensitive diaphragm in the instrument tees into the vacuum line as close to the instrument as possible. It is recommended by many manufacturers that it tee into the line leading directly to the gyro horizon in aircraft that include this instrument in the instrument panel. Theoretically, if sufficient vacuum is being created to operate the gyro horizon, all other instruments in the system will function satisfactorily. Whatever reduction of pressure is caused by the vacuum pump or venturi tube tends to collapse the diaphragm in the gauge. This movement is transferred through the rocking shaft, sector, and pinion to give a continuous indication on the dial. The range of the dial is usually from 0 to 10 and represents inches of mercury below the surrounding atmospheric pressure.

If the suction gauge is mounted on a shockproof panel and connected to another instrument on the same panel, it is not necessary to use rubber tubing for the connection. However, when the connecting tube is fastened to a rigid part of the aircraft structure, flexible tubing must be used. The amount of vacuum that should be registered on the suction gauge is dependent on the instruments which operate on that particular system and on the manufacturer's specifications. In instances where one instrument should have less vacuum than another but both operate from the same source of vacuum, a small restriction is placed in the line leading directly to the instrument requiring the least vacuum.

The relief valve is set to furnish the maximum amount of vacuum required for any one instrument. The suction gauge is set to show 4 inHg [13.55 kPa] for artificial horizon and the direction gyro. The bank-and-turn instrument is set to 2 inHg [6.77 kPa] by a suction gauge connected temporarily to a fitting screwed into the bank-and-turn needle valve that is in the back of the indicator.

It must be pointed out that many aircraft are now equipped with electrically operated gyros, and it is not necessary for such aircraft to be equipped with vacuum systems.

● FLIGHT INSTRUMENT SYSTEMS

Some flight instruments must be provided with electrical or pneumatic power to allow them to operate. Other instruments must be provided information from remote sensors so that they may provide the pilot with the proper indications. When we discuss **flight instru-**

ment systems, we mean these power sources and sensor mechanisms.

Pitot-Static Systems

The purpose of a **pitot-static system** is to provide the pressures necessary to operate such instruments as the altimeter, airspeed indicator, and vertical-speed indicator. Static pressure is also required for such control units as air data transducers and automatic pilots.

Figure 13-53 illustrates a pitot head for a standard

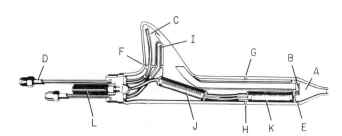

FIG. 13-53   Typical pitot head.

system on some older airplanes. The purpose of the head is to pick up indications of dynamic (ram) air pressure and static (ambient) air pressure to be transmitted through tubing to the instruments requiring these presures for operation. The dynamic pressure caused by the movement of the airplane through the air is picked up through port A (in Fig. 13-53). This pressure is carried through the head and out tube D to the airspeed indicator and Mach number sensing units. The baffle plate B helps keep water from entering the system. Water that goes by the baffle plate is stopped by the water trap C. Water is drained from the head through drain holes E and F.

Static pressure is picked up through the holes at G and H and is carried through the tube I to instruments such as the altimeter, vertical-speed indicator, and others requiring static pressure.

The pitot head shown is provided with heaters to prevent the formation of ice. These heaters are shown at J and K and the electrical connecting plug is indicated by L in the illustration. On many aircraft the dynamic pressure only is picked up by the pitot heads. The heads are mounted on the aircraft where they will provide the most accurate indications of dynamic pressure. The static pressure is obtained through one or more ports on the fuselage.

A pitot-static system as installed in a light, twin-engine airplane is illustrated in Figure 13-54. In this system, the pitot head mounted under the wing supplies ram air pressure only. The static pressure is supplied through the perforated static buttons (ports) mounted flush with the fuselage skin toward the rear of the airplane.

An important feature of the pitot pressure system is that it have provision for removing all water before it can reach the instruments. Baffles in the pitot head and drains in the pressure line are used to remove the water.

Pitot-static systems are often provided with an al-

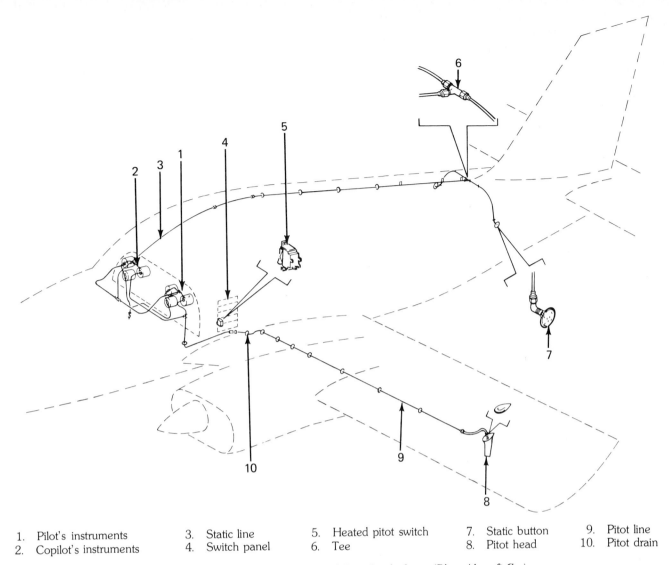

1.	Pilot's instruments	3.	Static line	5.	Heated pitot switch	7.	Static button	9.	Pitot line
2.	Copilot's instruments	4.	Switch panel	6.	Tee	8.	Pitot head	10.	Pitot drain

FIG. 13-54 Pitot-static system in a light twin airplane. *(Piper Aircraft Co.)*

ternate static pressure source in the cabin or cockpit. These are usually satisfactory except for pressurized aircraft. The pressure supplied to the static system must be that which exists outside the airplane. If the airplane is pressurized, the pressure inside the airplane will be substantially greater than that which exists outside, and the instruments will read at a lower value than normal if the static pressure is picked up inside the airplane. If there is a leak in the static line inside a pressurized airplane, pressure from the cabin will leak into the static line, and the instruments will register false readings. The altimeter will show an altitude below the actual altitude, the vertical-speed indicator will not give the correct rate of climb or descent, and the airspeed indicator will show the airplane speed below the actual speed.

Maintenance and testing practices for pitot-static systems are described later in this chapter.

Gyro Electrical Power Sources

All three of the basic gyro instruments are available in designs that rely on electrical power for operation. These instruments normally require one of four types of power sources: 14 or 28 V dc or 120 or 208 V ac.

Many of the electrically powered instruments have the word "electric" on the face, and all electrically operated instruments should have a flag visible when electrical power is not being supplied to the instrument, as shown in Fig. 13-55.

Gyro Pneumatic Power Sources

Many of the older and most of the lower-priced gyro instruments are operated by a flow of air moving over the buckets on the rotor disk. This flow of air can be caused by drawing air through the instrument with a venturi or vacuum pump or by forcing air through the instrument from a pressure source. Regardless of the type pump used, the air inlet to the instruments should be filtered to keep contaminants out of the instruments and out of the pump.

A **venturi,** shown in operation in Fig. 13-56, generates a vacuum by moving air through a restricted passage. As the air accelerates through the passage, the sidewall pressure is reduced, and air can be drawn

FIG. 13-55 The "OFF" flag indicates that the instrument is not receiving electrical power. *(Aeronetics)*

Venturis come in two sizes designated by the amount of suction they can generate, a 2-in [5.08-cm] size and an 8-in [20.32-cm] size. The 2-in size is suitable for operating one turn-and-bank–turn coordinator. The 8-in venturi can handle an artificial horizon and a directional gyro. A suction gauge is normally connected to the line between the venturi and the instruments so that the pilot can monitor the suction on the system. The desired value for the artificial horizon and the directional gyro is about 4 inHg [10.16 cmHg] of vacuum. If a turn-and-bank–turn coordinator is used with the large venturi, a pressure regulator is often required to drop the vacuum down to 2 inHg for these instruments to operate properly.

Aircraft to be used for instrument flying and those with operational speeds much above 100 mph usually rely on engine-driven vacuum or pressure pumps to power the pneumatically operated instruments. A cutaway view of an engine-driven vacuum pump is shown in Fig. 13-57.

Vacuum pumps can be either the **wet-pump** or **dry-pump** design. A wet pump relies on engine oil to lubricate the operating mechanism. The oil that is introduced into the air must be separated from the oil before the air is vented overboard or directed into other aircraft systems. This reclaimed oil is returned to the engine oil reservoir. The primary drawback associated with a wet pump is the oil contamination of pressure systems and oil appearing on the airframe as a result of inefficient oil separators.

A dry pump relies on the proper selection of construction materials to provide lubrication. The materials selected for the vanes are normally carbon-based, which provide low friction and proper sealing against the metal case walls. Dry pumps have become very popular because of the elimination of oil contamination of the system and the need for an oil separator. Figure 13-58 shows a schematic representation of a typical light-aircraft vacuum system.

into the venturi core through a hole placed on the side of the tube at the restriction. If a hole in the side of the venturi throat is connected to a pneumatically operated gyro instrument, air is drawn through the instrument, spins the gyro, and causes the instrument to operate.

A venturi is the simplest type of vacuum "pump" and is normally found on aircraft not intended for instrument flight. Its primary advantages are simple installation, no operation expense, and reliability. The drawbacks include requiring 100 mph of airspeed to operate the instrument properly, no means of powering the instruments before flight, and the possibility of being closed by ice.

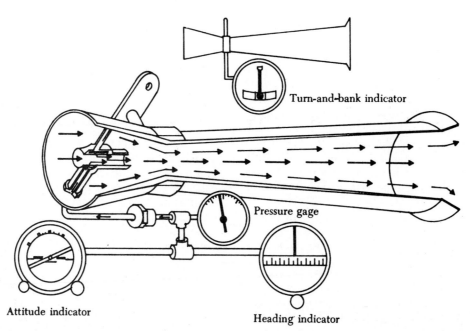

FIG. 13-56 Venturi vacuum system.

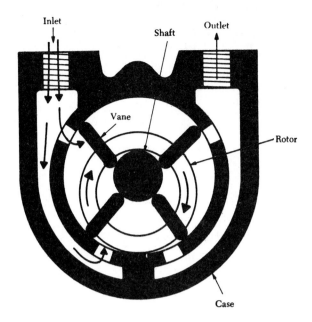

FIG. 13-57 Cross section of a vacuum pump.

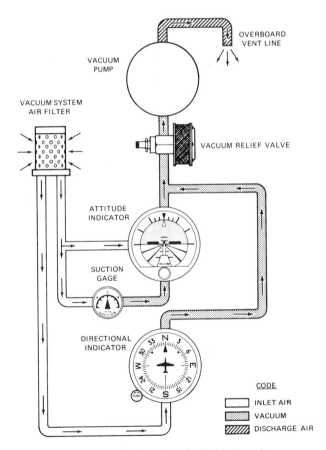

CODE

☐	INLET AIR
▦	VACUUM
▨	DISCHARGE AIR

FIG. 13-58 Schematic drawing of a light-aircraft vacuum system. *(Cessna Aircraft Co.)*

Aircraft intended for high-altitude flight often have the pneumatically operated instruments powered by air pressure rather than vacuum. This is because of the inability of vacuum pumps to draw the approximate 4 in [10.16 cm] of vacuum required when the air is already at a relatively low pressure. A pressure source may be as simple as connecting to the pressure side of the vacuum pump and connecting the pressure line to the inlet to the gyro instruments rather than to the outlet of the instrument as is done with a vacuum line.

Air Data Computer

An **air data computer** is used on most turbine-powered airplanes to power indication and control systems needing information about the ambient air and aircraft speed. The inputs to the system are pitot pressure, static pressure, and ambient air temperature. This information is processed by a computer and signals are sent to various systems so that the aircraft performs properly.

Systems which typically use data from the air data computer on transport aircraft are the flight instruments such as the true airspeed indicator, machmeter, and altimeter; navigation systems such as the inertial navigation systems, autopilots, and flight directors; warning units such as mach limit warning and altitude alert. The schematic drawing for the air data computer for an airliner is shown in Fig. 13-59.

The type of system shown in Fig. 13-59 allows compensation for compressibility at high airspeeds and the friction heating of probes. The system also allows the information collected to be changed to electrical and electronic signals for use by various flight computer systems.

⬤ ENGINE INSTRUMENTS

Engine instruments are necessary in order that the flight crew can properly adjust and monitor engine system operations. These instruments are also useful to the mechanic when evaluating and troubleshooting engine systems. The principles of operation of most engine instruments are the same as have been discussed for many other aircraft instruments. These include the use of electrical temperature sensors and bourdon tubes or bellows to measure pressures.

Tachometers

Tachometers are used to measure engine rpm. When discussing reciprocating engines, the crankshaft rpm is measured and indicated with the unit's rpm indicator. For helicopters and free-turbine propellers, the rpm of the rotor or propeller is indicated in rpm. For turbine engines, the engine rpm is indicated in *percent of rated rpm*.

Tachometers may be mechanically or electrically operated. Mechanically operated tachometers may be driven directly by the use of a flyweight mechanism, as shown in Fig. 13-60, or by a magnetic drag cup, as shown in Fig. 13-61. The magnetic tachometer is the most popular type in use in general aviation. This tachometer is operated by a flexible shaft that is rotated by a drive on the rear of the engine. As the shaft turns, it rotates a magnet inside of an aluminum drag cup in the instrument. The rotation of the magnet creates eddy currents in the drag cup and causes it to move in the same direction as the magnets. A light coil spring opposes this rotation. The faster the speed of rotation, the greater the deflection of the drag cup

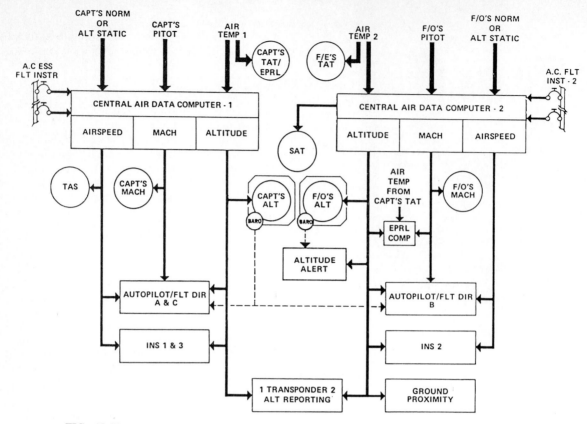

FIG. 13-59 Schematic drawing of a typical system incorporating an air data computer. *(Boeing Commercial Aircraft Co.)*

and the higher the indication of the needle attached to the drag cup.

Drag-cup tachometer cables should be routed so as to avoid kinks. If the tachometer oscillates or "bounces," the cable should be inspected for binding, damage, or lack of lubrication.

Electric tachometers are used on large aircraft where the distance from the engine to the instrument panel makes mechanical tachometers impractical. A common type of this tachometer, shown in Fig. 13-62, uses a three-phase ac alternator to generate a signal. This signal drives a synchronous motor inside the instrument which synchronizes its speed with that of the alternator. This motor turns a drag cup, and the drag cup positions the needle on the face of the instrument.

Oil Pressure Indicators

Oil pressure indicators can be mechanically operated or electrically powered. A mechanically operated gauge uses an oil pressure line from the engine to the instrument to operate a bourdon tube and gear segment to position the indicator needle. The oil line should have a restrictor at the engine to prevent rapid oil loss if the line should break. Some aircraft use a light oil in the line between the gauge and the engine so that there will be no delay in oil pressure indication due to cold engine oil being in the line.

Electric oil pressure sensors use a pressure sensor on the engine which varies in resistance as the pressure changes. As this pressure signal is generated, the pressure is indicated by one of the electrical indicating methods previously discussed.

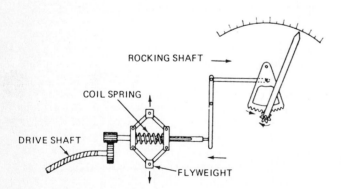

FIG. 13-60 A mechanically operated tachometer.

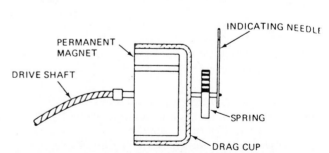

FIG. 13-61 Illustration of magnetic tachometer principle.

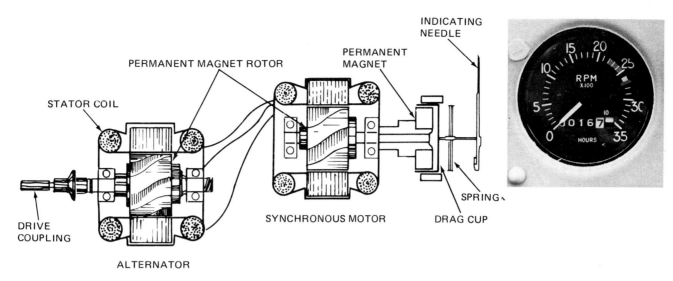

FIG. 13-62 Electric tachometer system. *(AC)*

Oil Temperature Indicators

Oil temperature indicators can be electrical or mechanical. To operate electrically, a resistance probe is placed in the oil line where the oil enters the engine. By one of the methods discussed at the beginning of this chapter, the oil temperature is derived by the change in probe resistance due to the temperature change.

Another method used to measure oil temperature is with a volatile liquid in a sealed sensor bulb and capillary tube. In this system a sensor bulb is placed in the oil line at the inlet to the engine. The temperature of the oil causes the volatile liquid to vaporize and increase the pressure in the capillary tube. The instrument is permanently attached to the other end of the tube, and the change in gas pressure causes a bourdon tube to move and indicate the oil temperature on the face of the instrument.

Exhaust Gas Temperature

Reciprocating-engine and turbine-engine exhaust gas temperature systems are used to monitor the performance of the engines and make flight and maintenance adjustments. These systems operate by placing thermocouples in the stream of exhaust gases exiting the engine. The thermocouples generate a current which drives the indicator. The amount of current is usually very low and is amplified or adjusted in order to drive the indicator display.

For a reciprocating engine, one probe may be used for the engine or a probe may be mounted near the exhaust of each cylinder. If multiple probes are used, a selector switch on the instrument is used to allow selection of the cylinder being monitored. In some displays all cylinder temperatures are displayed at the same time in the form of a vertical light bar with the length of each bar corresponding to the exhaust temperature of one cylinder.

In turbine-engine installations, the system uses several probes in parallel, as shown in Fig. 13-63. This assures an average reading of the temperature, and the indication does not change substantially if one probe should fail. The exhaust gas temperature is a primary instrument for monitoring turbine engine operation.

Engine Pressure Ratio

Engine pressure ratio (EPR) is used to indicate the amount of thrust being generated by a turbine engine. EPR is determined by measuring the total pressure at the engine inlet and comparing it to the total pressure of the engine exhaust. These pressures are measured by pitot tube-like probes pointing into the airflow. The total pressure of the exhaust stream divided by the total pressure of the inlet stream gives the EPR. These pressures are normally transmitted electrically to the indicating system, where they are compared electronically and the proper value is displayed on the instrument.

Manifold Pressure Indicator

The **manifold pressure gauge** measures the sidewall pressure in a reciprocating-engine intake manifold downstream of the carburetor throttle. This pressure is a measure of the engine power output. Most smaller aircraft use direct-indicating instruments for the manifold pressure gauge. The gauge uses a bellows, which expands and contracts with changes in the manifold pressure. This drives an indicator needle on the face of the instrument.

The manifold pressure gauge is an important instrument for reciprocating engines when determining proper power settings. Without this gauge, the pilot of a turbocharged or supercharged engine would not be able to tell if he or she were exceeding the allowed maximum manifold pressure. Pilots flying aircraft with constant-speed propellers rely on this gauge in conjunction with the tachometer to establish the proper powerplant control settings.

Cylinder Head Temperature Indicators

A **cylinder head temperature gauge** is used to determine if the engine is operating at the proper temper-

497

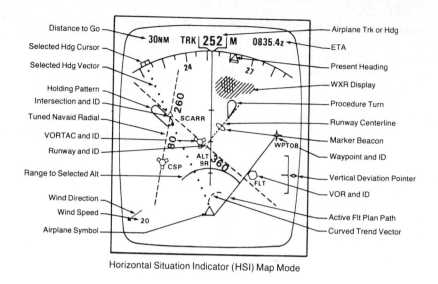

Horizontal Situation Indicator (HSI) Map Mode

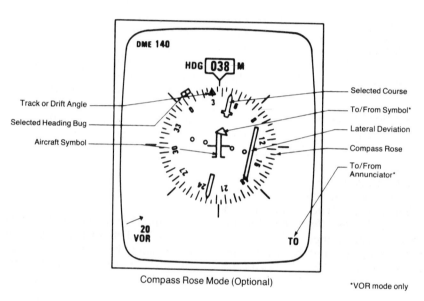

Compass Rose Mode (Optional)

*VOR mode only

Standard compass rose
DME and ILS information provided

FIG. 13-75 Two of the several displays available on an electronic horizontal situation indicator. *(Boeing Commercial Aircraft Co.)*

The grouping of powerplant instruments is not as standardized among the aircraft manufacturers as are the flight instruments. However, all engine instruments which are directing affected by the operation of cockpit controls (i.e., tachometer, manifold pressure, and fuel flow) should be located as close to the controls as is practical so that the pilot will be able to monitor the instrument as he or she adjusts the control. Other powerplant and system instruments should be grouped according to the system being monitored, i.e., oil temperature and oil pressure located together, or by type of value being measured if only one instrument is used for each system, i.e., hydraulic pressure and pneumatic pressure.

Installation and Handling

The installation of instruments requires that they be mounted to a metal instrument panel or subpanel. The mounting can be achieved by the use of two or more mounting screws, circumferential clamps, or brackets, depending on the instrument design. Regardless of the type of mount, the installation should allow the pilot or crew member to clearly view the instrument from a normal flight position, and the installation should cause a minimum of operational interference with control systems and other instruments.

Because of the large variety of installations, it is beyond the scope of this text to deal with all installations, and therefore we address the more common types of installations.

While some instruments require panel openings as small as 1-in [2.45-cm] in diameter and others require 4-in [10.16-cm] openings, the majority of instruments require panel openings 3 1/8 or 2 1/4 inches in diameter. Openings in the panel should be laid out so that the installation of the instrument will not interfere with

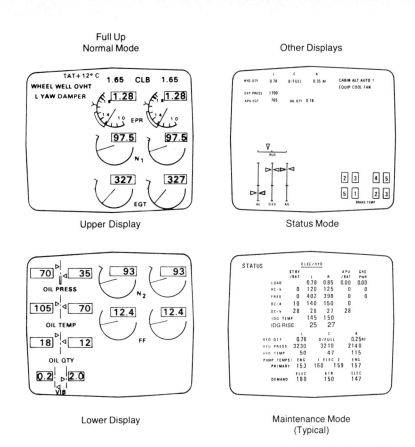

FIG. 13-76 Typical displays on a Boeing 767 system monitoring EICAS. *(Boeing Commercial Aircraft Co.)*

any other instrument or any of the aircraft control systems. The location of electrically operated instruments should take into account any effects on other equipment such as the magnetic compass. Another consideration when determining the exact position of instruments is allowing sufficient clearance around the instrument so that the installation hardware will be accessible.

Mounting instruments by the use of screws will usually involve positioning the instrument from behind the panel through the opening in the panel. Screw holes will have to be drilled at appropriate positions around the opening. Nonmagnetic screws, usually 4-40 size brass screws, are then used to attach the instrument to the panel. The mounting holes in the instrument may be threaded by the instrument manufacturer, or one may use a Tinnerman-type nut plate to accept the screw. If a separate fastener is required, brass nuts or special instrument mounting nuts can be used.

The use of a mounting bracket is common for some system-monitoring instruments such as engine oil pressure and oil temperature. These instruments are passed through the front of the panel until the flange of the instrument bears against the panel. The mounting bracket is then attached to the rear of the instrument and clamps the instrument to the panel.

Circumferential clamps are used in many modern instrument installations to allow ease of installation, positioning, and removal. The clamping mechanism is mounted to the instrument panel, and the instrument is then inserted into the clamp through the front of the instrument panel. The instrument can be rotated in the clamp until it is properly positioned, and the clamp is then tightened around the instrument by a screw on the front of the panel. Caution should be exercised when tightening the clamp as excessive tightening may bind the instrument case against the instrument operating mechanism. This may cause incorrect instrument indications or damage to the instrument.

Some aircraft manufacturers have mounted the instrument subpanel on sliding or hinged mounts so that the rear of the instrument panel is accessible without the mechanic having to work in the cramped and cuttered space behind the instrument panel. An example of this type of installation is shown in Fig. 13-77.

When handling instruments, they must be treated as delicate mechanisms. Avoid hitting or dropping the instrument, and avoid sudden movements of the instrument as this may cause internal components to contact internal stops with some force. Never apply air pressure, suction, or electrical power to instruments unless directed to by the manufacturer's instructions or other competent references. When installing the instruments, never force them into position. If they do not fit properly in position, correct the fault with the mounting panel and then install the instrument.

When instruments are removed from an aircraft, all lines and openings should be covered with protective caps or plugs and all electrical connections should be properly protected. If the instrument is not going to be immediately reinstalled, it should be tagged with appropriate information as to time in service, when

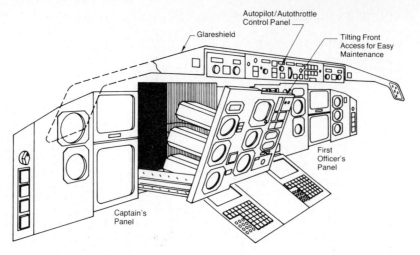

FIG. 13-77 Some instrument panels slide out for easy maintenance. *(Boeing Commercial Aircraft Co.)*

removed, and reason for removal. The instrument should then be placed in a plastic bag sealed against dirt and dust, and stored in a safe place.

If the instrument is to be shipped, it should be placed in a well-padded container. The container should be marked with words such as "delicate instrument" or "fragile."

Marking Instruments

Many instruments require that marks be placed on the face of the instrument or on the cover glass to indicate operational ranges and limits. An aircraft mechanic is not normally permitted to remove the cover glass from an instrument and must mark ranges and values on the cover glass of the instrument. Instrument repair stations normally are involved in placing marking directly on the face of instruments.

Operational ranges and limitations can be obtained from the aircraft operations manual, maintenance manual, and type certificate data sheet/aircraft specification.

Minimum and maximum operational limitations are indicated by a red radial line on the instrument. A green arc is used to indicate a normal operating range. A yellow arc on the instrument indicates a caution range. This caution range may require the use of a placard next to the instrument to describe the nature of the caution. This range may limit operation for specific periods of time or only under certain flight conditions.

The airspeed indicator has several types of markings which are not normally found on other instruments. These markings include a white arc to indicate the airspeed range through which full flaps can be used. A blue radial line is used on the airspeed indicators of multiengine aircraft to indicate the best single-engine rate-of-climb speed. Sailplanes often use a yellow triangle to indicate the minimum landing approach speed or best gliding speed.

A tachometer may incorporate a red arc to indicate a critical vibration range. This range should not be used for continuous operation.

When marking instructions by placing markings on the cover glass, a slippage mark should be placed on the glass and onto the case next to the glass. This mark will show if the glass has rotated from its original position, indicating that the markings no longer show the correct values.

Testing Instruments and Systems

Certain tests and adjustments can be made on some instruments by a qualified mechanic in the field. In this case, a qualified mechanic is one who is familiar with the particular instrument and the way the tests and adjustments should be made. The adjustments which can be made do not involve opening the case of the instrument. Whatever the instruments, the mechanic should consult the manufacturer's manual and FAA AC-43.13-1A.

Airspeed indicators are tested by applying controlled pressure to the pressure port of the instrument. A chart such as that shown in Table 13-1 of this chapter is used as a guide. The pressure can be obtained from a properly regulated instrument test unit or by using a bulb-type hand pump. The pressure source and an accurate pressure gauge (or manometer) are connected to the pressure port of the airspeed indicator as shown in Fig. 13-78. When a pressure of 0.1309 inHg [3.32 mmHg], 1.78 inH$_2$O [45.2 mmH$_2$O

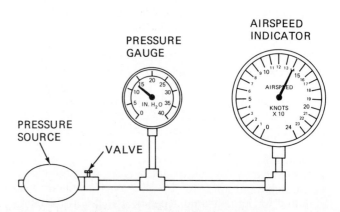

FIG. 13-78 Test system for an airspeed indicator.

or 0.441 kPa] is applied to the instrument, the airspeed indication should be 60 mph [52.1 kn]. When the chart is followed, additional checks should be made at airspeed increments specified. This method of testing can be used on the airplane by applying the test pressure to the pitot pressure line.

An altimeter is tested by comparing the altitude reading on the instrument with the actual altitude at the point of testing when the local barometric pressure is adjusted into the instrument. For example, if the barometric setting of the altimeter is placed at 29.92 inHg and the actual barometric pressure at the test location is 29.92 inHg [76 cmHg], then the altimeter should show an altitude of 0. If suction is applied to the suction port of the altimeter to a level of 28.86 inHg [73.3 cmHg], then the altimeter reading should be 1000 ft [305 m]. Additional tests should be made at specified intervals of altitude. *Positive pressure must not be applied to an altimeter* except in the small amount which may be specified by the manufacturer.

If it is found that the barometric setting and the altitude reading of an altimeter do not correlate, the instrument can be adjusted. A recommended procedure is as follows:

1. Rotate the barometric setting knob until the altimeter indicates the known altitude, exactly, of the test location.

2. Following the manufacturer's instructions, release the locking mechanism of the barometric setting device. Pull the barometric setting knob out until it is disengaged from the internal gearing. Be careful not to rotate the knob during this process.

3. Rotate the knob to the current correct barometric setting, then gently press the knob back until the internal gearing is meshed and engage the locking mechanism.

4. Check the operation of the barometric setting mechanism by rotating the knob. The movement should be smooth, and no grinding or sticking should be apparent.

If an adjustment of more than 40 ft [12.2 m] altitude is required to correlate the altimeter reading and the barometric scale, the instrument should be tested for scale error. This should be accomplished in an instrument shop. Adjustments to altimeters should be recorded in the aircraft permanent maintenance record.

Pitot-static systems on aircraft should be tested on a regular schedule in accordance with the manufacturer's instructions. The pitot system may be tested by sealing the drain holes and connecting the system to a regulated pressure source with a manometer, pressure gauge, or reliable airspeed indicator. A pressure that would produce a reading of 150 kn is applied to the system by means of a bulb pump or instrument pressure source. This pressure is 1.1 inHg [2.79 cmHg] or 14.9 inH$_2$O [37.85 cmH$_2$O]. The pressure source is clamped off, and the pressure gauge or altimeter observed after 1 min. The decrease in pressure should not exceed 10 kn [0.15 inHg or 2.04 inH$_2$O].

The static system should be tested in accordance with FAR 43 and flight regulations for aircraft flying under Instrument Flight Rules (IFR). The basic procedure is as follows:

1. Connect the test equipment (vacuum source and vacuum gauge) directly to the static ports, if practicable. Otherwise, connect to a static system drain or a tee connection and seal off the static ports. If the test equipment is connected to the static system at any point other than the static ports, it should be made at a point where the connection may be readily inspected for system integrity.

2. Apply a vacuum equivalent to 1000 ft [305 m] altitude (differential pressure of approximately 1.07 inHg [3.62 kPa] or 14.5 inH$_2$O) and hold.

3. After 1 min, check to see that the leakage has not exceeded the equivalent of 100 ft [30.5 m] of altitude. This is approximately 0.105 inHg [0.36 kPa] or 1.43 inH$_2$O.

During the testing of pitot-static systems, care must be taken to see that positive pressure is not applied to the altimeter or negative pressure (vacuum) applied to the airspeed indicator. Positive pressure should not be applied to the static system, and negative pressure should not be applied to the pitot system when instruments are connected. Pressure in the pitot system must always be equal or greater than that in the static system.

When positive pressure is applied to the pitot system or negative pressure to the static system, the rate of change of pressure applied should not exceed the design limits of the instruments connected to the system.

Upon completion of testing, the pitot and static systems must be restored to flight configuration. Static ports and drain holes should be unsealed, and drain plugs should be replaced. System inspection, instrument replacement, and required repairs are completed *before* the leak tests are made.

Inspection and Maintenance of Instruments and Systems

Instruments should be checked for proper operation, condition of the glass faces, condition and placement of range markings, condition of cases, cleanliness of case vent filters, security of mounting, and tightness of tube and electrical connections. The shock mounts by which panels or instruments are attached should be checked for looseness.

Gyro instruments should be checked for gyro erection time and unusual noise during operation. After operation, the run-down time provides an indication of condition. If the run-down time is shorter than normal, bearing wear or damage is indicated, or foreign matter has accumulated inside the instrument.

Instrument systems should be checked for condition of tubing, hose, hose clamps, and fittings. Bulkhead fittings should be checked for tightness in the bulkhead. When tubing fittings at bulkhead fittings are removed or replaced, the bulkhead fitting should be held with a wrench to prevent turning while the tubing fitting is being tightened.

Vacuum fittings should be checked carefully at all

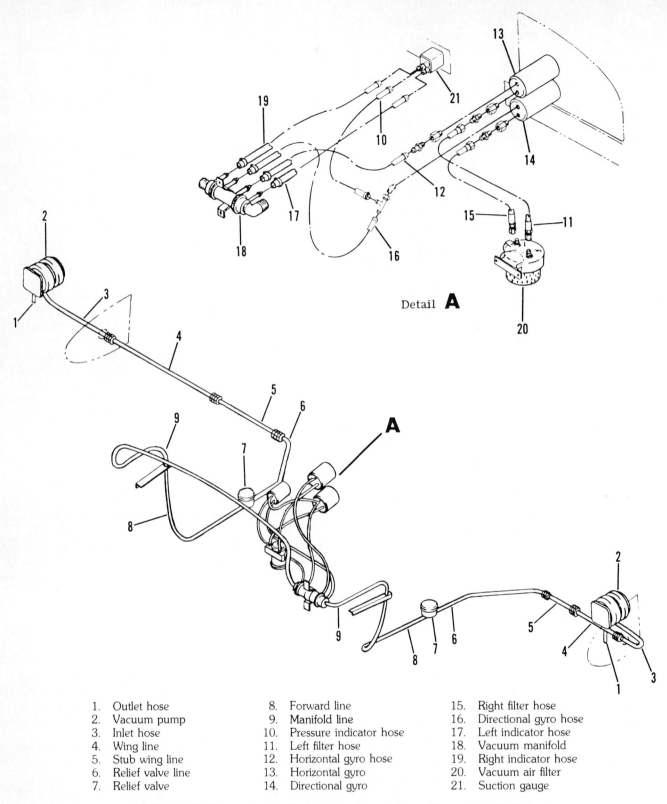

1.	Outlet hose	8.	Forward line	15.	Right filter hose
2.	Vacuum pump	9.	Manifold line	16.	Directional gyro hose
3.	Inlet hose	10.	Pressure indicator hose	17.	Left indicator hose
4.	Wing line	11.	Left filter hose	18.	Vacuum manifold
5.	Stub wing line	12.	Horizontal gyro hose	19.	Right indicator hose
6.	Relief valve line	13.	Horizontal gyro	20.	Vacuum air filter
7.	Relief valve	14.	Directional gyro	21.	Suction gauge

FIG. 13-79   Vacuum system for a twin-engine airplane. *(Cessna Aircraft Co.)*

hose and fitting connections. If the hose is starting to deteriorate, particles can be drawn into the system and cause damage to the instruments and pumps in the system. When connecting fittings in a vacuum system, standard thread lubricant or thread sealers should not be employed. Particles of the material

could be drawn into the system and cause damage. Material such as silicone spray may be employed.

A vacuum system may be checked for operation by running the engine which drives the vacuum pump at a medium speed. The suction gauge should indicate the correct suction pressure (vacuum), about 5 ±0.1

inHg [16.93 kPa]. If the amount of suction is not correct, the engine should be stopped and the caused determined. The vacuum regulator valve may have to be adjusted. The adjustment is made with a screw which is normally covered with a protective cap or secured with a locknut.

The routing of tubing and hoses for instrument systems should be checked for correct position. Tubing and hoses should be clear of any structure which could cause damage due to vibration. Tubing should be secured to the aircraft structure with approved clamps having rubber or plastic liners.

During complete inspections of instrument systems, it is usually advisable to blow air under pressure through the lines to remove water and dirt. *Before blowing air through a pitot or static system, all instruments connected to the system must be disconnected.* Air is then blown from the instrument end of the lines outward toward the static vents or pitot head. After the lines are blown clear, the instruments are reconnected and the system is pressure tested for leakage.

During the operation of vacuum systems, the filters in the associated instrument cases or the air inlet lines become clogged with dust and dirt particles. When this occurs, the reading of the vacuum gauge increases. When the vacuum reaches the allowable limit, the filters in the instruments or in the inlet line must be removed and cleaned. In some cases, the filter element can be cleaned according to manufacturer's directions; in others, the filter element is replaced.

A typical vacuum system for a twin-engine airplane is shown in Fig. 13-79. A schematic drawing of the system is shown in Fig. 13-80. This system utilizes dry vacuum pumps which require no lubrication. These are mounted on the accessory mount pads of each engine. The pump outlets are exhausted into the engine nacelles. The vacuum line plumbing is routed from the vacuum pumps through the nacelles and wings into the cabin and forward to the relief valves. The adjustable relief valves are provided to give the desired vacuum system pressure. From the relief valves, the lines are routed to the vacuum manifold

located on the left side of the forward cabin bulkhead. The manifold has check valves included to prevent reverse flow in the event of failure of either vacuum pump. Hoses are routed from the manifold to the directional gyro, horizontal gyro, and suction gauge. Other hoses connect the gyros to the central vacuum air filter and suction gauge. The suction gauge indicates the amount of vacuum present in the system. The system is provided with in-operation indicator buttons for each pump. The vacuum air filter is provided to remove dust particles, vapor, and other contaminants such as tobacco smoke from the air. Experience has shown that the tars from tobacco smoke rapidly clog the filters and render them ineffective. Such filter elements should be discarded rather than cleaned.

● REVIEW QUESTIONS

1. In what ways is the knowledge and understanding of aircraft instruments and instrument systems important for the aircraft mechanic?
2. What type of mechanism is generally used for instruments that measure high pressures?
3. Describe the operation of a *bourdon tube*.
4. Explain the operation of a *vapor-pressure temperature gauge*.
5. Explain the significance of *psia* and *psig*.
6. Describe a diaphragm-type pressure instrument.
7. Which pressure-sensing instruments are referenced to absolute zero?
8. List uses of an *airspeed indicator* in flight.
9. Explain the operation of an airspeed indicator.
10. What correction should be applied to the airspeed indication as altitude increases to obtain *true airspeed*?
11. Compare a *Machmeter* with an airspeed indicator.
12. Explain the operation of an *altimeter*.
13. Why is the barometric setting important in the use of an altimeter?
14. What is the purpose of an *encoding altimeter*?
15. What are the two basic types of altimeters and how do their displays differ?
16. How does a blind encoding altimeter differ from an encoding altimeter?
17. What is the difference between indicated, calibrated, and true airspeed?
18. Describe the operation of a *vertical-speed indicator*.
19. How does a *variometer* work?
20. Describe the purpose of a *total-energy variometer*.
21. What is the value of a *suction gauge* in an instrument system?
22. What methods may be used to power gyro instruments?
23. What is the purpose of a *venturi tube* in an instrument system?
24. Explain the function of a *pitot-static* system.
25. What is the purpose of a pitot system?
26. How is water removed from a pitot system?
27. Explain the alternate static system.
28. What would be the effect of a leaking or disconnected static line inside a pressurized airplane?

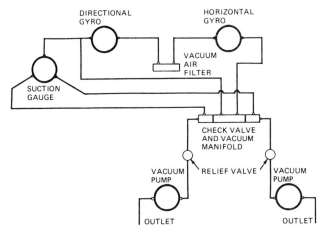

FIG. 13-80 Schematic drawing of a vacuum system. *(Cessna Aircraft Co.)*

29. Describe the construction of a magnetic compass.
30. What is meant by *variation* in a magnetic compass?
31. What are causes of *deviation* in compass readings?
32. Describe the procedure for *swinging* a magnetic compass.
33. Explain the operation of a *flux gate compass*.
34. Explain the operation of aa *bimetallic temperature gauge*.
35. What is the purpose of an *accelerometer?*
36. Describe the operation of an accelerometer.
37. How does a *horizontal situation indicator* differ from a *heading indicator?*
38. What are two types of gyro erection mechanisms and what is their purpose?
39. Explain the features of a spinning gyroscope which make it useful in some types of instruments.
40. Explain *precession*.
41. What is the effect of bearing friction in a gyro instrument?
43. Explain the operation of a *directional gyro*.
44. Describe the operation of a *turn-and-bank indicator*.
45. How does the gyro indicate a rate of turn?
46. How does a turn-and-bank indicator differ from a turn coordinator?
47. Which instrument is used to indicate a proper bank?
48. Describe a gyro-horizon indicator.
49. Discuss the handling of instruments to avoid damage.
50. How should instruments be prepared for storage?
51. How is foreign material prevented from entering instruments?
52. Explain the importance of shock mountings.
53. What is the purpose of an *air data computer?*
54. What are three types of *tachometers* and how does each operate?
55. Explain the basic operation of an *engine pressure ratio gauge*.

56. How does a *resistance-type fuel quantity indicator* operate?
57. What are the advantages of a *capacitance fuel quantity indicating system* when compared to a resistance-type system?
58. Explain the operation of one type of *fuel flowmeter*.
59. Describe three types of mechanical fuel quantity gauges.
60. What is a *symbol generator?*
61. What are the two flight displays in an electronic flight instrument system?
62. Draw the conventional flight instrument group arrangement.
63. Describe the different types of instrument mounting methods.
64. Describe the different types of instrument range and limit markings.
65. What type of hardware is used to attach instruments to panels?
66. Explain how an airspeed indicator may be tested.
67. How is an altimeter tested and adjusted?
68. Describe the testing of a pitot system.
69. Describe the testing of a static system.
70. What precautions must be observed in applying pressures to pitot and static systems?
71. During the inspection of instruments, what conditions are examined?
72. What checks should be made during the operational tests of gyro instruments?
73. What general conditions are observed in the inspection of the tubing, hoses, and fittings in instrument systems?
74. What special conditions are important in a vacuum system?
75. How may a vacuum system be checked for operation?
75. What precautions must be taken in blowing air through pitot-static lines to clear out dirt and water?
77. Discuss the importance of cleaning filters in a vacuum system.

14 AUXILIARY SYSTEMS

The majority of modern aircraft, primarily the large transport type, are equipped with certain systems which are not necessary for the actual operation and flight of the airplane but which are needed for the comfort and convenience of the crew and passengers and may be required by Federal Aviation Regulations (FARs). Some of these systems are important for the safe operation of the aircraft under a variety of conditions, and some are designed to provide for emergencies.

Systems not essential to the actual operation of the aircraft are commonly called **auxiliary systems.** Among such systems are ice and rain protection, fire-warning and -extinguishing systems, water and waste systems, and position and warning systems.

● FIRE PROTECTION SYSTEMS

Fire protection systems on aircraft usually consist of two separate operating systems with associated controls and indicators. One system is for fire or overheat **detection,** and the other is for fire suppression or extinguishment. In some cases, the systems can be interconnected so extinguishing takes place automatically when a fire is detected.

Requirements for Overheat and Fire Protection Systems

The requirements for fire protection in aircraft are set forth in FAR Part 25. These regulations specify the types of detecting and suppression devices and systems required in accordance with the classification of areas of the aircraft and the conditions existing in these areas.

Certain general features and operational capabilities for fire warning and protection systems must be met or exceeded if such systems are to be used in certificated aircraft. These are as follows:

1. The fire warning system must provide an immediate warning of fire or overheat by means of a red light and an audible signal in the cockpit or flight compartment.
2. The system must accurately indicate that a fire has been extinguished and indicate if a fire reignites.
3. The system must be durable and resistant to damage from all the environmental factors which may exist in the location where it is installed.
4. The system must include an accurate and effective method for testing to assure the integrity of the system.

5. The system must be easily inspected, removed, and installed.
6. The system and its components must be designed so the possibility of false indications is unlikely.
7. The system must require a minimum of electrical power and must operate from the aircraft electrical system without inverters or other special equipment.

Types of Fire or Overheat Detectors

High temperatures caused by fires or other conditions may be detected by a variety of devices. Among these are thermal switches, thermocouples, and tubular detectors. Tubular detectors are commonly employed in large aircraft for fire and heat detection wherever fire protection must be provided.

A thermal-switch fire detection system is simply a circuit in which one or more thermal switches are connected in an electrical circuit with a warning light and an aural alarm unit to warn the pilot or flight crew that an overheat condition exists in a particular area. If more than one thermal switch is in the circuit, the switches will be connected in parallel so the closing of any one switch will provide a warning. A thermal switch is shown in Fig. 14-1, and the circuit for a thermal-switch fire and overheat warning system is shown in Fig. 14-2. Note that a test circuit is included so the system may be tested for operation.

The thermal switch, called a spot detector, works by the expansion of the outer case of the unit. When the detector is exposed to heat, the case becomes longer and causes the two contacts inside the case to be drawn together. When the contacts meet, the electrical circuit is complete and the alarm will activate.

The thermocouple detection system, also called a "rate of rise" detection system, utilizes one or more thermocouples connected in series to activate an alarm system when there is a sufficiently high rate of temperature increase at the sensor. The thermocouple is made of two dissimilar metals, such as Chromel and constantan, which are twisted together and located inside an open frame as shown in Fig. 14-3. The frame protects the sensing wires from damage while allowing a free flow of air over the wires. The exposed wires make up the hot junction. A cold junction is located behind insulating material in the sensor unit. When there is a difference in temperature between the hot junction and the cold junction, a current is created. When sufficient current is being generated (about 4 mA), a sensitive relay in a relay box closes, activating a slave relay and causing the alarm to activate. The

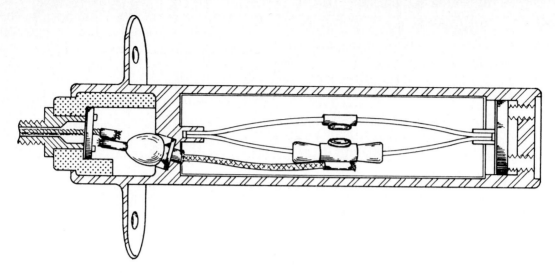

FIG. 14-1   Fenwal spot detector.

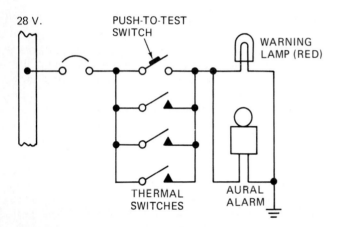

FIG. 14-2   Circuit for a thermal-switch fire and overheat warning system.

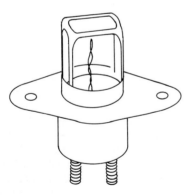

FIG. 14-3   A thermocouple heat dectector.

basic circuit for this system is shown in Fig. 14-4. If the rate of temperature increase is slow enough so that the temperature of the cold junction increases along with the hot junction, the sensitive relay will not close and the alarm will not activate.

A test circuit is provided for the system through the use of a heater next to a thermocouple. When the heater is energized, the thermocouple will generate sufficient current to activate the system.

There are three types of tubular sensing devices, called "continuous-loop" systems, commonly employed in modern aircraft for detecting overheat or fire. These tubular sensors are manufactured in lengths from 18 in [0.46 m] to more than 15 ft [4 to 5 m]. The diameters of these sensing elements may be from less than 0.060 in [1.5 mm] to more than 0.090 in [2.3 mm].

Cross-sectional drawings to illustrate the operating principles of the three most commonly employed sensors are shown in Fig. 14-5. These are the sensors manufactured by the Fenwal Company, the Walter Kidde Company, and the Systron-Donner Company.

The Fenwal sensor consists of a small (0.089-in OD [2.3-mm]), lightweight, flexible Inconel tube with a pure nickel wire center conductor. The space between the nickel conductor and the tubing wall is filled with a porous aluminum-oxide, ceramic insulating material. The voids and clearances between the tubing and the ceramic material are saturated with a eutectic salt mixture which has a low melting point.

The nickel wire in the center of the tube is insulated from the tube wall by the ceramic and eutectic salt materials. The tube is hermetically sealed at both ends with insulating material, and threaded fittings are located at each end of the tube.

When heated sufficiently, current can flow between the center wire and the tube wall because the eutectic salt melts and its resistance drops rapidly when the termperature reaches a given level. The elevated temperature will cause a response at any point along the entire length of the sensing element. The increased current flow between the nickel center wire and the tubing wall provides the signal which is utilized in the electronic **control unit** to produce the output signal which actuates the alarm system.

When the fire is extinguished or the overheat condition is corrected, the eutectic salt in the sensing element increases in resistance and the system returns to the stand-by condition. If the fire should reignite, the sensor would again produce a signal for an alarm.

The sensing element of the Kidde system consists of an Inconel tube filled with a thermistor material.

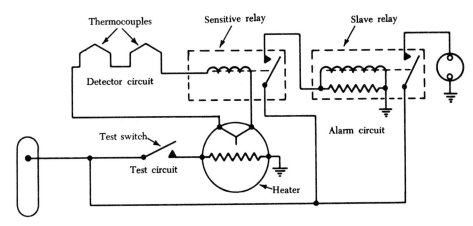

FIG. 14-4 Thermocouple fire warning circuit.

Two electrical conductors are embedded in this material, and one of the conductors is grounded to the outer shell of the connector at the end of the tube. Electrical connectors are provided at both ends of the tube.

In the Kidde sensing element the resistance of the thermistor material decreases rapidly when a high temperature is applied. This change in resistance is sensed by the electronic control circuit monitoring the system, and the control provides the warning signal to illuminate the fire warning light and activate the aural warning device. This sensor returns to a normal (stand-by) condition when the fire or overheat condition is corrected.

The **sensing element assembly** utilized in the Kidde fire and overheat warning system consists of a pair of sensing elements mounted on a preshaped, rigid support tube. The sensing elements are held in place by dual clamps riveted to the tube assembly approximately every 6 in [15 cm]. Asbestos grommets are provided to cushion the sensor tubing in the clamps. Four nuts per assembly are used to secure the sensing element end connectors to the bracket assemblies at

either end of the support tube assembly. The nuts are secured with safety wire.

The two sensing elements mounted on the support tube assembly provide separate sensing circuits, and each is connected to its own electronic control circuit mounted on a separate circuit card. This arrangement provides for complete redundancy, thus assuring operation of the system even though one side may fail.

A Kidde sensor assembly for a small area is shown in Fig. 14-6. Units for large areas are constructed in the same manner; however, they are several times as long and are preshaped to fit the contours of the area in which they are installed.

A drawing of the control unit for the Kidde system is shown in Fig. 14-7. Signals from the sensing units are processed in the control unit to provide visual and audible warnings in the flight compartment. The control unit is basically a transistorized electronic device consisting of two component board assemblies, a test switch, test jacks, wiring harness, and an electrical receptacle, all enclosed in a metal case.

There are two identical circuits in the control unit, one monitoring sensing element loop *A* and the other monitoring sensing element loop *B*. Each circuit is contained on its own component board assembly. Remember that in the Kidde system, two sensing elements are mounted on a preformed support tube assembly. If one circuit should fail, the other circuit will provide the overheat or fire warning signal.

The sensing element produced by the Systron-Donner Company, shown in Fig. 14-8, is pneumatic in operation. The pressure of the gas inside the element is increased by heat, and the increased pressure actuates a diaphragm switch inside the responder which closes the circuit and provides the warning signal.

The sensing element consists of a stainless steel tube containing two separate gases plus a gas absorption material in the form of a wire inside the tube. Under normal conditions, the tube is filled with helium gas under pressure. The titanium center wire, which is the gas absorption material, contains hydrogen gas. The wire is wrapped in a helical fashion with an inert metal tape for stabilization and protection. Gaps between the turns of the tape allow for rapid release of the hydrogen gas from the wire when the temperature reaches the required level.

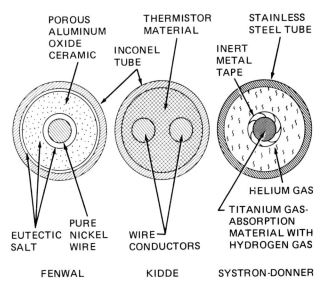

FIG. 14-5 Drawings to illustrate the operation of overheat and fire sensors.

515

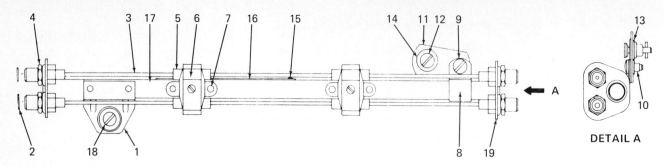

FIG. 14-6 A Kidde sensor assembly. (*Walter Kidde & Co.*)

1. Mounting plate	6. Clamp
2. Gasket	7. Blind rivet
3. Sensing element	8. Loop clamp
4. Nut	9. Machine screw
5. Grommet	10. Clinch nut

11. Mounting plate	16. Identification plate
12. Fastener stud	17. Support tube
13. Snap ring	18. Fastener stud
14. Grommet	19. End bracket
15. Rivet	

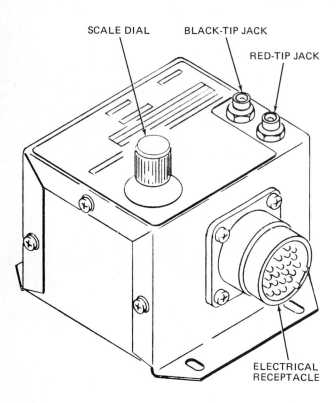

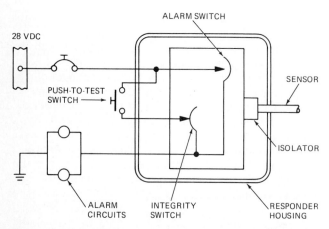

FIG. 14-7 Control unit for Kidde system. (*Walter Kidde & Co.*)

The sensor responds in accordance with the law of gases. If the volume of gas is held constant, its pressure will increase as temperature increases. The helium gas in the tube exerts a pressure proportional to the average temperature along the entire length of the tube. This is the **averaging** or **overheat function** of the sensor. If the average temperature exceeds a specified level, the helium gas pressure will be such that it closes the pneumatic switch in the responder and signals an overheat condition. If there is a very high temperature, as a fire would cause, anywhere along the sensing element, the center wire in the tube will release a large quantity of hydrogen gas. This will increase the total gas pressure in the tube to a level which will close the pneumatic switch. This is called the **discrete function** of the sensor. These operations are shown in Fig. 14-9.

When a fire is extinguished and the temperature begins to drop, the specially processed titanium wire in the tube will reabsorb the hydrogen gas and reduce the pressure in the tube. This will cause the pneumatic switch to open, and the system will be back to normal and ready to provide another signal in case of reignition.

The responder contains two identical diaphragm switches. One of the switches is normally open and closes only when gas pressure in the sensor tube increases owing to high temperature or fire in the area where the sensor is installed. The other switch is held

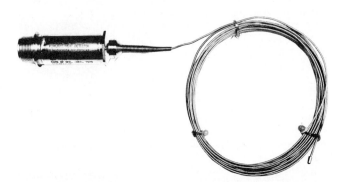

FIG. 14-8 A Systron-Donner pneumatic fire detection unit. (*Systron-Donner Corp.*)

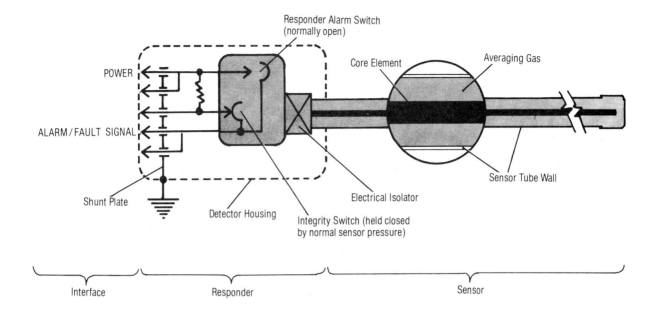

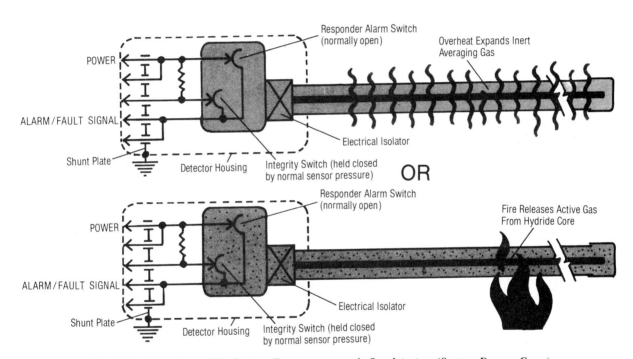

FIG. 14-9 Operation of the Systron-Donner pneumatic fire detector. *(Systron-Donner Corp.)*

closed by the normal helium pressure in the sensor tube. If the helium pressure should be lost, the switch opens the test circuit. When the test switch is closed by a member of the crew to check the circuit, the alarm will not respond and the loss of helium will be revealed.

The continuous-loop (Kidde and Fenwal) and continuous-length (Systron-Donner) types of fire detection mechanisms are considered superior to the spot and thermocouple systems where large areas must be covered such as around a jet engine. The continuous-loop systems do have a disadvantage in that damage to the tubing wall, which will cause it to be closer to the center elements, may cause false fire signals to be generated.

The continuous-length sensor is not as sensitive to damage as are the continuous-loop sensors. The outer tubing of these units can be bent, dented, kinked, and otherwise distorted without their effectiveness being affected. The wire inside the tube prevents complete collapse so there is always room for gas to flow. The only cause of failure is loss of the helium gas because the tube is worn or cut sufficiently to allow the gas to escape.

Each of the different sensor mechanisms can be selected for various operating temperatures. For example, the normal temperatures surrounding the turbine-engine combustion chamber will be much higher than the normal temperatures in the area of the engine inlet. A sensor selected for the inlet area of the engine

517

should actuate the alarm system at a lower temperature than the sensor used near the engine combustion chamber. Different temperature rating detectors may be included in a common alarm system such as the one shown in Fig. 14-10. The section from point 1 to point 2 uses a detector which will activate the alarm at 425°F [218°C], the area from 2 to 3 will activate the system at about 640°F [338°C], and the section between 3 and 4 will indicate a fire or overheat when the temperature exceeds 450°F [232°C]. For this reason, when installing or inspecting sensor units always be sure that the proper heat rating is being used.

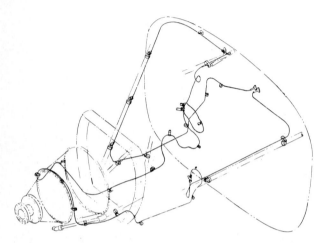

FIG. 14-10 The routing of a continuous-loop fire detection assembly in an engine compartment. *(Cessna Aircraft Co.)*

Installation and Routing of Sensing Units

The installation of overheat and fire warning sensing units must be done strictly in accordance with the instructions provided by the manufacturer. The routing of the sensors has been designed by engineers to provide the most effective performance and the detection of overheat or fire in the most likely areas. Routing must also be done in consideration of possible damage to the sensors. For example, in a baggage or cargo compartment, the sensors must be placed where there is no chance that cargo or luggage should strike them and cause damage.

Sensors must be supported with specially designed clamps in which the small tubing is held in rubber or soft plastic grommets. These prevent damage due to vibration and wear. The clamps with grommets must be spaced as specified in the appropriate instructions.

A typical method for installing the sensing element in an airplane is shown in Fig. 14-11. Electrical connector fittings are employed to connect the sensor into the circuit. The tubing of the sensor is held in place by means of mounting clips. The grommet placed around the tubing in the clip is essential to prevent damage due to chafing and vibration. The sensing element must be routed as described in the aircraft maintenance manual. A Systron-Donner system would be mounted in a similar manner except that connections are only made at the responder.

Typical installations for continuous systems are shown in Figs. 14-12 and 14-13.

Smoke and Toxic-Gas Detection Systems

Smoke detection systems are usually installed to monitor the condition of the air in cargo and baggage compartments where considerable smoke may be generated before the heat level reaches a point to set off the overheat and fire warning system. Detectors (sensors) are placed in locations where they will most likely provide the earliest possible warning.

Toxic-gas (carbon monoxide) detectors are usually installed in cockpits and cabins where the presence of the gas would affect the flight crew and passengers. Carbon monoxide (CO) is a clear gas and is not detectable by the type of smoke detectors which rely on a change in the transmission of light through a sample of air.

Smoke and flame detectors operate according to several different principles. Among these are light detection, light refraction, ionization, and the change in resistance of a solid-state semiconductor material.

In a light detection system, a photoelectric cell like the one in Fig. 14-14 is placed in a location where it can "see" the surrounding area and produce a change of current flow when there is a change in the visible light or infrared radiation striking the cell. (Units are designed to detect either visible light or infrared radiation.) This change in current flow is used to activate an amplifier circuit which produces the visual and aural alarm signals. This type of system is activated only by an open flame.

In a light refraction detector, shown in Fig. 14-15, a light beam is passed through the detection chamber, and a photoelectric cell is placed in the chamber where it is shielded from the direct light of the light source. Air from the area being monitored for smoke and fire is passed through the detector unit by normal airflow or by means of a fan or other device. When smoke is introduced into the chamber, the light from the particles of smoke is reflected into the photoelectric cell. This changes the resistance (conductivity) of the photoelectric cell and changes the flow of current through the cell. This change in the flow of current activates the amplifier and produces the visual and aural warning signals. A schematic drawing of the chamber is shown in Fig. 14-16, and a typical system wiring diagram is shown in Fig. 14-17.

In an ionization type of smoke detector, a small amount of radioactive material is used to bombard the oxygen and nitrogen molecules in the air within the detection chamber. The ionization that takes place permits a small current to flow through the chamber and in the external circuit. Air from the area being checked for smoke is passed through the chamber as shown in Fig. 14-18. If smoke is in the air, small particles of the smoke attach themselves to the oxygen and nitrogen ions and reduce the flow of current. When the current level is reduced by a predetermined amount, the alarm circuit will be triggered to produce the visual and aural alarm.

The solid-state type of smoke or toxic-gas detection utilizes two heated, solid-state detecting elements.

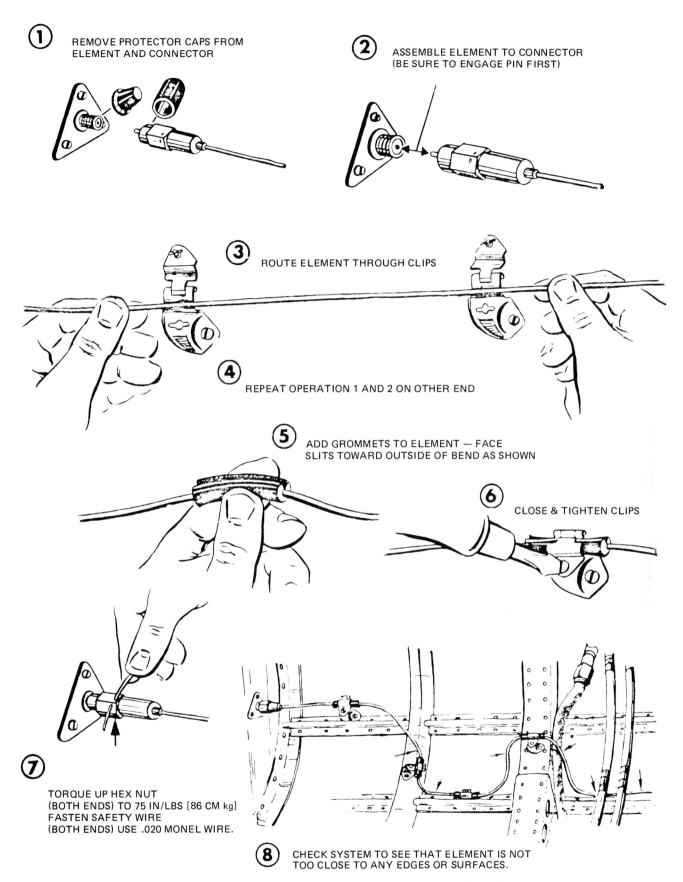

① REMOVE PROTECTOR CAPS FROM ELEMENT AND CONNECTOR

② ASSEMBLE ELEMENT TO CONNECTOR (BE SURE TO ENGAGE PIN FIRST)

③ ROUTE ELEMENT THROUGH CLIPS

④ REPEAT OPERATION 1 AND 2 ON OTHER END

⑤ ADD GROMMETS TO ELEMENT — FACE SLITS TOWARD OUTSIDE OF BEND AS SHOWN

⑥ CLOSE & TIGHTEN CLIPS

⑦ TORQUE UP HEX NUT (BOTH ENDS) TO 75 IN/LBS [86 CM kg] FASTEN SAFETY WIRE (BOTH ENDS) USE .020 MONEL WIRE.

⑧ CHECK SYSTEM TO SEE THAT ELEMENT IS NOT TOO CLOSE TO ANY EDGES OR SURFACES.

FIG. 14-11   Installation procedure for a tubular sensing unit. *(Fenwal, Inc.)*

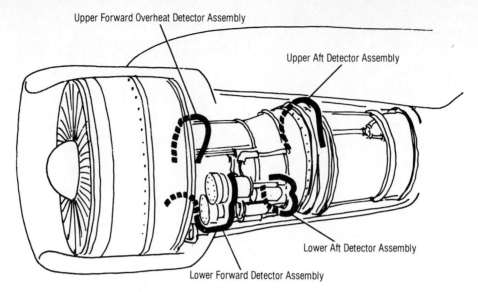

FIG. 14-12   Pneumatic sensor locations around a jet engine. *(Systron-Donner Corp.)*

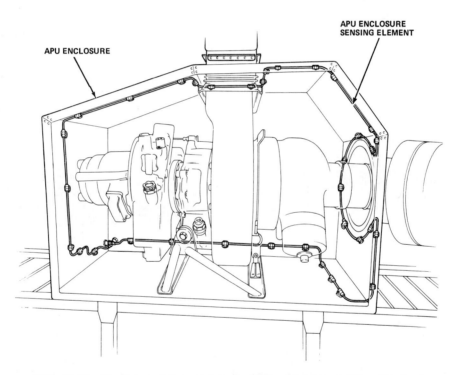

FIG. 14-13   Continuous-loop sensor in an APU compartment. *(Canadair Inc.)*

Each element is approximately 1 mm [0.0394 in] in diameter and consists of a heating coil encases in a coating (substrate) of the solid-state (semiconductor) material. The composition of the sensors is such that ions of carbon monoxide or nitrous oxide will be absorbed into the solid-state coating of the sensing element and change its current-carrying ability.

The system operates by comparing the electrical output of the two sensors, one of which is exposed to outside air and the other to cabin air. The sensors are connected in separate legs of a modified bridge circuit. When both are conducting equally, there will be no output and no signal. If the sensor sampling cabin air absorbs toxic gases from the cabin air inlet, the bridge circuit will be unbalanced, and this will produce the current flow which activates the warning system. The warning is provided by an illuminated annunciator unit. An aural signal can also be produced.

A circuit to illustrate how electrical-type sensors are connected to develop a warning signal is shown in Fig. 14-19. The bridge part of the circuit is designed to be in balance when the two sensing elements are conducting the same current. If one of the sensors changes its resistance or conductivity because of exposure to light or smoke, the bridge is unbalanced and a small current flow will occur through the sensitive

FIG. 14-14 A flame detector. *(Pyrotector)*

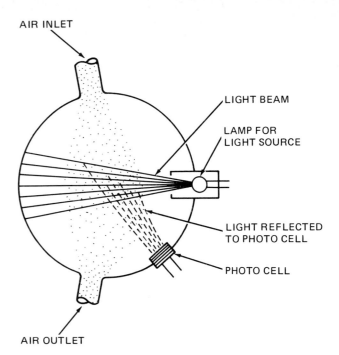

FIG. 14-16 Detector utilizing light refraction with a photoelectric cell.

Typical Wiring Diagram

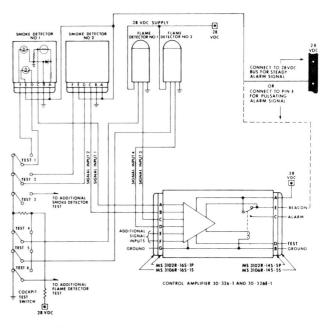

FIG. 14-17 Typical wiring diagram for a smoke and flame fire detector system. *(Pyrotector)*

FIG. 14-15 A smoke detector. *(Pyrotector)*

relay. When this current reaches the predetermined alarm level, the relay will close and send current to the main signal relay. This relay closes the circuit to the alarm elements (light and aural warning unit) to provide the warning.

Fire-Extinguishing Agents

Fire-extinguishing agents are those chemicals which are injected into a compartment or area to extinguish a fire. These agents work by either displacing the oxygen or chemically combining with the oxygen to prevent combustion. Some additional extinguishing effect can occur by the low temperature at which the agents are discharged.

The commonly used agents are carbon dioxide (CO_2), Freon (a chlorinated hydrocarbon), and Halon 1301 (monobromotrifluoromethane—CF_3Br). Nitrogen (N_2) is also an extinguishing agent but is primarily

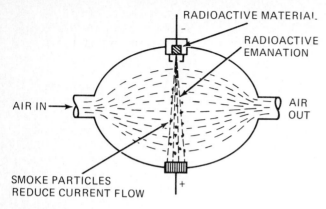

FIG. 14-18   An ionization-type detector cell.

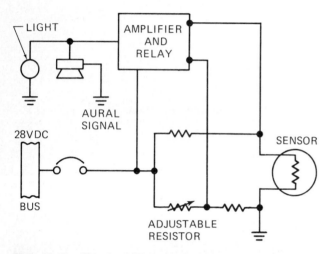

FIG. 14-19   Circuit to illustrate the use of a resistance bridge to compare sensor resistance with that of a reference resistor.

used in current systems as a propellant for one of the other chemicals. The Freon and Halon are in a liquid state when under sufficient pressure but become gaseous when released to atmospheric pressure. Liquid Freon and Halon must not be allowed to come into contact with the skin because they will cause frostbite due to extremely low temperatures attained when the liquid evaporates.

Most modern aircraft extinguishing systems make use of Halon 1301 as the extinguishing agent, while some manufacturers specify Freon. The use of CO_2 is usually limited to older reciprocating-engine-powered transports.

Dry chemical extinguishing agents are not used for aircraft fire-extinguishing systems and their use for handheld extinguishers has decreased greatly. Dry chemical agents are toxic and corrosive, while other agents, being gaseous, do not cause corrosive action to occur. Some of the gaseous agents may be considered toxic while they are present in an area in large quantities because of the displacement of free oxygen.

Fire-Suppression Systems

Fire-suppression or -extinguishing systems usually consist of a fire-extinguishing agent stored in pressur-

ized containers, tubing to carry the extinguishing agent to areas which require protection, control valves, indicators, control circuitry, and associated components. Systems vary considerably on different aircraft; however, the basic elements are similar.

Extinguishing-agent containers for modern aircraft are usually spherical or cylindrical in shape. Typical containers are shown in Fig. 14-20. The containers

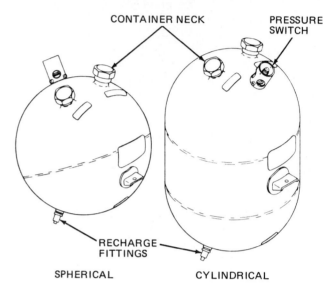

FIG. 14-20   Typical extinguishing-agent containers. (Walter Kidde & Co.)

shown are pressure tested hydrostatically at 1500 psi [10 342 kPa]. When charged, the spherical container holds 60 lb [27.22 kg] of Halon, and the cylindrical container holds 105 lb [47.63 kg] of Halon. An additional 300 psi [2068 kPa] nitrogen charge is placed in the containers to expel the agent. A discharge head containing an explosive cartridge is installed on one or both of the container necks to discharge the container by rupturing the disk when the cartridge is activated. One type of cartridge is shown in Fig. 14-21. The squib is the explosive charge which drives the slug through the disk. A screen in the discharge head prevents particles of the disk from entering the deployment lines.

A thermal pressure relief fitting is located on each bottle. If the bottle pressure exceeds approximately

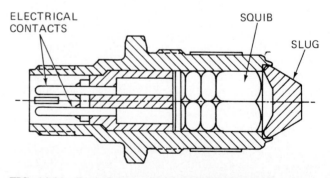

FIG. 14-21   Explosive cartridge. (Walter Kidde & Co.)

522

1400 psi [9653 kPa], the fitting will discharge the bottle contents either overboard or into the compartment containing the bottles.

Older aircraft still using CO_2 as the extinguishing agent use one or more gas cylinders equipped with quick-acting flood valves. When activated, the flood valves rapidly discharge the bottles into the distribution lines. The bottles have a thermal relief mechanism which will automatically discharge the bottles when the internal pressure exceeds 2650 psi [19 271.75 kPa].

Two methods are used to allow the pilot or mechanic to determine if the bottle has discharged thermally: the use of a pressure gauge or the use of a "blow-out" disk. Some aircraft have a gauge for the fire bottles visible from the outside of the aircraft or through access panels. If the gauge does not indicate a charge, then the bottle has been discharged. Other aircraft have a discharge line running from the bottle to the outside of the aircraft or to an open area such as a wheel well. The discharge line opening is covered with a red disk. If the bottle has discharged, the disk will be blown out of the discharge fitting. The absence of the red disk indicates a thermal discharge.

A similar system is used to indicate if the system has been discharged by actuation of the extinguishing system. In this case a small line from the system distribution line leads to a disk actuator line. This line is covered with a yellow disk. When the extinguishing system is activated, the yellow disk is pushed out by a plunger.

There are two classifications of fire-extinguishing systems. These are called the **conventional system** and the **high-rate-of-discharge system** (HRD system).

The conventional system is normally found on older reciprocating-engine-powered aircraft and is based on the design concept of the systems first used on aircraft. While this type of system is adequate, it is not as efficient as the HRD systems. The conventional system usually uses CO_2 as the extinguishing agent and makes use of a perforated ring and distributor-nozzle discharge arrangement. When the system is activated, the CO_2 bottles are opened and the gas flows through the lines to the selected engine. At the engine the gas flows out of the perforated ring and distributor nozzles to smother the fire.

The HRD system uses Freon or Halon 1301 and the spherical bottles actuated by explosive cartridges. The discharge tubes are configured to allow a rapid release of agent into the fire area and flood the compartment to eliminate the fire quickly. The advantage of this system over the conventional system lies in the ability to flood a compartment much more quickly.

Both conventional and HRD systems may be designed to allow only one extinguishing agent to discharge into a fire area, or they may be designed to allow several discharges into an area in an attempt to extinguish the fire. In most aircraft only two discharges are possible for any one location. The exact configuration of a system is determined by the aircraft manufacturer.

A schematic diagram of a typical fire-suppression system for an airliner is shown in Fig. 14-22. The system consists of two steel containers charged with Freon and nitrogen gas to a pressure of 600 psi [4136 kPa], connecting deployment lines to the control valves, and control circuitry. The system is activated when a member of the crew closes the fire switch to direct extinguishing agent to the area where a fire is indicated.

When the fire-extinguishing switch is closed, an explosive charge at the neck of the selected agent container is detonated and a cutter is driven through the sealing disk in the neck of the container. This releases the extinguishing agent from the container instantly and permits it to flow to the area selected. The pilot or other crew member will have selected the appropriate area by operating a switch on the fire control panel. This will direct the agent through the correct deployment line.

Figure 14-23 shows the extinguisher system used on a modern turboprop aircraft. Each engine system is independent and only one discharge is available to extinguish the fire.

Figure 14-24 shows the system for a twin-engine helicopter. One or both bottles can be used to extinguish a fire in either engine area. By moving the engine toggle switch from NORM to ARM, fuel is shut off to the engine and the system is armed. When the spring-loaded-to-center toggle marked AGENT RLSE is moved to the right or the left, the appropriate bottle will discharge into the armed engine area.

Portable Fire Extinguishers

Portable or hand-held fire extinguishers must be available as specified for the aircraft. The fire extinguishers must be of approved types and must be appropriate for the kinds of fires that are likely to occur in the areas concerned. For example, if electrical fires are most likely, the fire extinguisher must be of the dry-chemical type, a dry-gas type (CO_2), or a Halon 1301 type. Extinguishing agents containing water must not be used because water increases electrical conductivity and may cause more damage than good. Oil or fuel fires should be smothered with a foam-type agent or a dry-chemical agent.

Each extinguisher for use in a personnel compartment must be designed to minimize the hazard of toxic gas concentrations.

Readily accessible hand-held fire extinguishers must be available for use in each Class A or Class B cargo compartment. Class A and Class B cargo compartments are those which are accessible to members of the flight crew while the aircraft is in flight.

Inspection and Servicing of Fire Protection Systems

Inspections for fire warning and suppression systems follow the general procedures for the inspections of other systems. Mechanical parts of systems are examined for damage, wear, security of mounting, and compliance with technical and regulatory requirements. Electrical control systems are inspected in accordance with approved practices for electrical systems and the special instructions given in the manufacturer's instructions. Certain elements must be electrically tested with voltmeters, ohmmeters, meg-

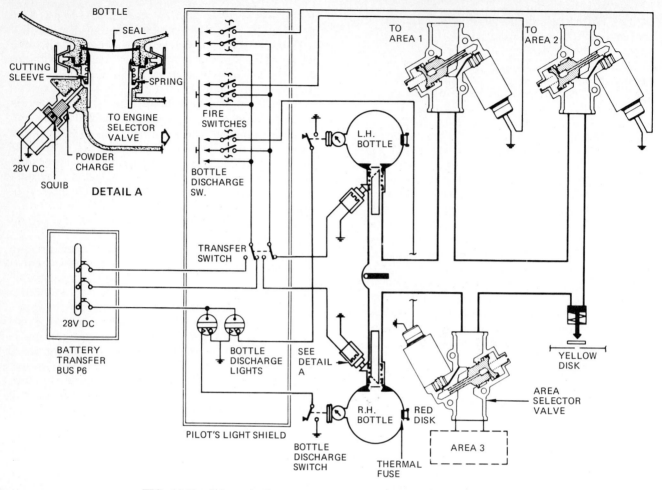

FIG. 14-22 Schematic diagram of a fire-suppression system. *(Boeing Co.)*

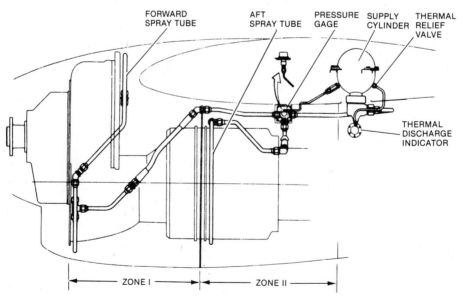

FIG. 14-23 Fire-extinguishing system configuration for a twin-engine turboprop airplane. *(Flight Safety International)*

gers, and otherwise as specified in the maintenance instructions. Continuity of electrical circuits may be tested with ohmmeters or continuity test lights.

For additional information on the maintenance and service of fire protection systems, refer to the associated text, *Aircraft Powerplants.*

For service of particular fire-warning and suppression systems, the mechanic must follow carefully the

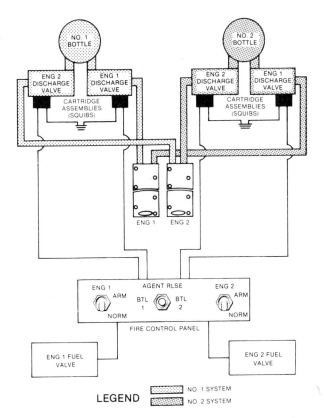

FIG. 14-24 Fire-extinguishing system schematic for a twin-engine helicopter. *(Flight Safety International)*

appropriate manufacturer's instructions. This is to assure that the correct materials are employed and the proper procedures followed.

● ICE-PROTECTION SYSTEMS

All aircraft which operate in weather conditions where ice is likely to form must be provided with ice protection. This protection may be in the form of anti-icing systems or deicing systems. An **anti-icing system** prevents the formation of ice on the airplane, and a **deicing system** removes ice which has already formed.

Among the parts of the airplane where ice prevention or removal is essential are the windshield, wing leading edges, tail airfoil leading edges, propellers, engine air inlets, pitot tubes, water drains, and any other part where the formation of ice can interfere with the operation of the airplane or its systems.

On piston-engine airplanes, especially those equipped with float-type carburetors, carburetor anti-icing is necessary, even in clear weather when the temperature and humidity are conducive to the formation of ice in the throat of the carburetor.

Ice Detection Systems

Some method of ice detection is desirable for aircraft so that the ice control systems are operated only when necessary. If ice control systems were operated continuously, there would be a significant increase in operational expense due to increased wear and tear on equipment and the consumption of fluids and power

unnecessarily. There are two basic methods used for ice detection: visual and electronic.

Visual detection is achieved by the flight crew monitoring the aircraft structures that first start to accumulate ice on their particular aircraft. This may involve no more than looking at the wing leading edge or checking the windshield wiper for ice buildup. At night this visual checking is aided by the use of lights designed to shine on the surface that accumulate ice. Many aircraft have ice lights mounted on the side of the fuselage or the side of the engine nacelle. These lights are usually aimed to shine on the wing surface.

Electronic instruments can be used to detect ice accumulation when there is no surface easily seen by the flight crew. One such system is used on the Canadair Challenger 601 and is shown in Fig. 14-25. The ice detector consists of a microprocessor circuit with an aerodynamic strut and probe extending into the slipstream. The probe vibrates at a frequency of 40 kHz. When ice starts to build on the probe, the frequency will decrease. When the frequency has decreased to a preset value, the microprocessor will turn on a red annunciator light to advise the flight crew that the aircraft is in icing conditions. If the flight crew then turns on the ice control systems, the red ICE light will go out and a white ICE light will illuminate. Once the probe detects ice, the microprocessor will energize a heating element in the probe to remove all ice so that the probe can recheck for icing conditions. As long as the probe continues to detect icing at each check, the ICE annunciator will remain on. When ice is no longer detected, the light will go out. The 601 has two of these detectors, one on each side of the forward fuselage section.

Pneumatic-Mechanical Deicing Systems

For many years, various airplanes have utilized mechanical deicing systems consisting of inflatable rubber "boots" formed to the leading edge of wings, struts, and stabilizers. The deicing boots are attached to the leading edge of the airfoils by means of cement and fasteners such as rivnuts, also called "bootnuts." Rivnuts are described in the section of this text covering structural repairs. Some aircraft use cement only for attaching the deicer boots to leading-edge surfaces.

The inflatable boots are usually constructed with several separate air passages or chambers such that some can be inflated while alternate chambers are deflated. The inflation of the boot is accomplished by utilizing the output pressure from a vacuum pump for inflation and the inlet side of the pump for deflation. The control of the pressure and suction is accomplished by means of a distributor valve which rotates and periodically changes the flow of air to or from the different section of the boots or by flow control valves. This results in alternate raising and lowering of sections of the boots, and this action cracks off any ice which has formed on the boots.

The pneumatic deicing system installed on one model of a twin-engine airplane provides a good example of the application of a pneumatic system. The system as installed in the airplane is illustrated in Fig. 14-26.

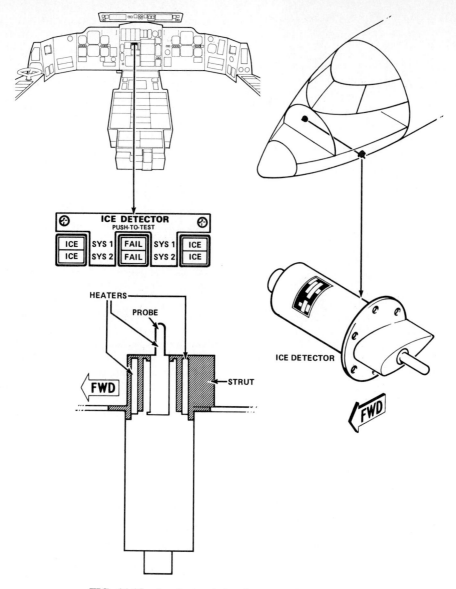

FIG. 14-25   An electronic ice detector. (*Canadair Inc.*)

The **deicer boots,** also referred to as **deicers,** consist of fabric-reinforced rubber sheet containing built-in inflation tubes. The operation and design of these deicer boots are shown in Fig. 14-27. The type used in this installation have spanwise inflation tubes. The deicers are attached by cement to the leading edges of the surfaces being protected. Either aluminum or flexible rubber air connections called **air-connection stems** are provided on the back side of each deicer. Each stem projects from the underside of the boot into the leading edge through a round hole provided in the metal skin. These provide for connection to the deicer pneumatic system.

Through the engine-driven vacuum pumps, the system normally applies vacuum to the deicer boots at all times except when the boots are being inflated. When it is desired to inflate the deicer boots, the pilot or copilot uses the deicer system control switch. This is a momentary ON type switch which returns to OFF when released. When the control switch is turned ON,

the **time module** (timer) energizes the pneumatic pressure control valve for 6 s. The boot solenoid valves are energized, and air pressure from the engine-driven pumps is supplied to the inflatable tubes in the boots. The inflation sequence is controlled by the time module (timer) and solenoid-operated valves located near the deicer air inlets. Upon automatic deenergization of the control valves by the timer, the deicer solenoid valves permit the deicer pressurizing air to return to the solenoid valves and be exhausted overboard. Deicer pressure is normally about 18 psig [124 kPa]. After the boots have been inflated and the pressure released as described, vacuum is again applied to the boots.

The deicing system for a large aircraft is shown in Fig. 14-28. In this system the inflation tubes in the boots alternate (as shown in Fig. 14-29) so that ice can be cleared from the large leading edge area without requiring a large volume of air from the engine pumps. Unlike the previous system, this system cycles continuously when turned on by a crew member. During

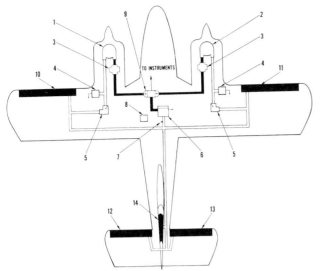

1. Vacuum pump, left engine
2. Vacuum pump, right engine
3. Vacuum regulator valve
4. Pressure-control valve
5. Flow check valve
6. Exhaust valve
7. Pressure switch
8. Time module
9. Vacuum manifold
10. Deicer boot, left wing
11. Deicer boot, right wing
12. Deicer boot, left stabilator
13. Deicer boot, right stabilator
14. Deicer boot, fin

FIG. 14-26 Pneumatic-mechanical deicing system on a twin-engine airplane. (Piper Aircraft Co.)

FIG. 14-27 Construction and operation of deicer boots. (Piper Aircraft Co.)

operation the distributor valve is rotated by the motor at a speed that will cause one cycle to last 40 s. During the cycling the center tube on both outboard wing sections are inflated, followed by the upper and lower tubes on these wing sections. A similar sequence is followed for the inboard wing boots. The fifth step in the sequence inflates all of the tubes in the stabilizer surfaces at the same time. The system then returns to the outboard wing boots and starts the sequence over. Each step in the operation requires 8 s.

Another mechanical system used for smaller aircraft utilizes a boot with a pressure bottle for the air supply. When ice forms on the leading edge of the wing, the pilot or copilot operates a valve to allow air pressure to enter the boot. This inflates the boot and cracks off the ice. This is not a continuously operating system and is used as sparingly as necessary to remove ice. The air-supply bottle contains sufficient air to operate the boots through several cycles, thus giving the pilot time to fly out of the icing area.

Inspection and Maintenance of Pneumatic-Mechanical Deicer Systems

The inspection of pneumatic-mechanical deicer systems requires an examination of the deicer boots for condition, adherence to the protected surface, and condition of the surface of the boots. If cuts, abrasion, or other damage is found, repairs should be made as specified by the manufacturer. Grease or oil found on the boots should be removed with an approved solvent, after which the boots should be scrubbed with soap and water, then rinsed with clean water.

Deicer boots are provided with a conductive neoprene coating to prevent the buildup of static charges on the boots. If this were not done, static charges would build up and then discharge to the metal surface of the airplane causing radio interference. During inspection and maintenance, the mechanic should determine whether the conductive coating is intact and effective.

Removal and replacement of deicer boots depends upon the type of attachment involved. If the boots are attached with screws and rivnuts, removal of the screws permits removal of the boots. If the boots are cemented, the mechanic must consult the manufacturer's instructions regarding the type of solvent to be used for dissolving the cement and the procedure for applying the solvent.

Operational tests are performed as specified in appropriate instructions. Usually, the test can be made by running one or more engines and turning the system on in the normal manner. The inflation of the tubes in the boots can easily be observed. If any of the tubes should fail to inflate in sequence or at the proper time, the air supply to that tube should be checked for obstruction or damage.

Thermal Anti-icing

Thermal anti-icing uses heated air flowing through passages in the leading edge of wings, stabilizers, and engine cowlings to prevent the formation of ice. The heat source for this operation normally comes from combustion heaters in reciprocating-engine-powered aircraft and from engine bleed air in turbine-powered aircraft. From the heat source the hot air is distributed along the leading edge of the item being anti-iced by the use of a perforated air duct called a "piccolo" or "spray" tube. When the air exits the piccolo tube, it is in contact with the leading-edge skin of the surface as shown in Fig. 14-30. The skin is heated and ice is prevented from forming. The air then flows out of the wing through openings in the end of the wing or on the bottom of the wing.

Figure 14-31 is a drawing of the layout of the thermal anti-icing system on one model of the Douglas DC-9 together with enlarged drawings of control components. The airfoil ice-protection system provides for the control of engine bleed air distributed to the leading edges of the wings and horizontal stabilizer. The ice-protection-system air temperature is maintained between 450 and 490°F [232 and 254°C] by controls placed in the pneumatic system. When either or both airfoil ice-protection switches are placed in the ON

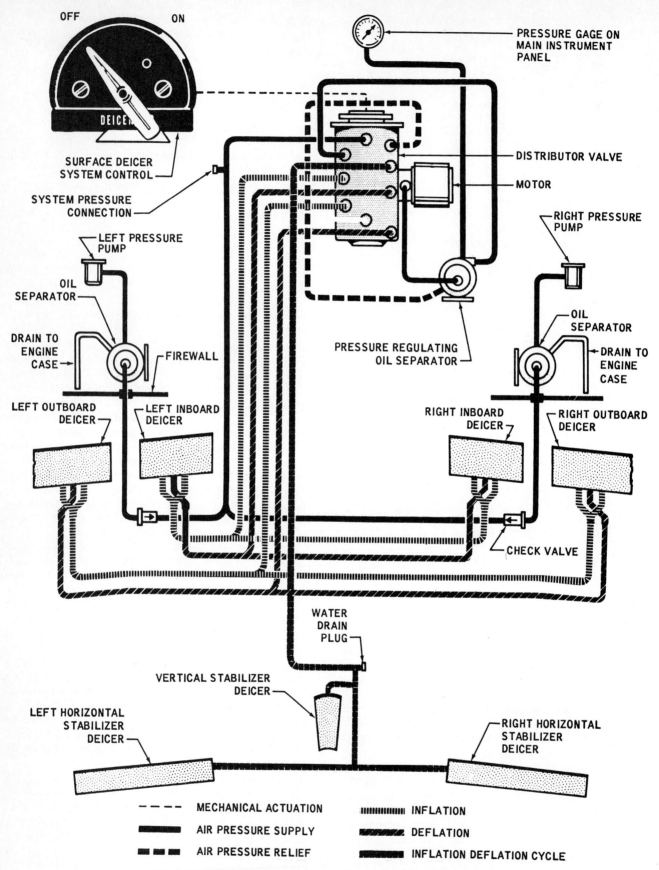

FIG. 14-28 Pneumatic deicing system for a large aircraft.

OFF

ON

DEICER

SURFACE DEICER
SYSTEM CONTROL

SYSTEM PRESSURE
CONNECTION

LEFT PRESSURE
PUMP

OIL
SEPARATOR

DRAIN TO
ENGINE
CASE

FIREWALL

LEFT OUTBOARD
DEICER

LEFT INBOARD
DEICER

PRESSURE GAGE ON
MAIN INSTRUMENT
PANEL

DISTRIBUTOR VALVE

MOTOR

RIGHT PRESSURE
PUMP

OIL
SEPARATOR

DRAIN TO
ENGINE
CASE

PRESSURE REGULATING
OIL SEPARATOR

RIGHT INBOARD
DEICER

RIGHT OUTBOARD
DEICER

CHECK VALVE

WATER
DRAIN
PLUG

VERTICAL STABILIZER
DEICER

LEFT HORIZONTAL
STABILIZER
DEICER

RIGHT HORIZONTAL
STABILIZER
DEICER

MECHANICAL ACTUATION

AIR PRESSURE SUPPLY

AIR PRESSURE RELIEF

INFLATION

DEFLATION

INFLATION DEFLATION CYCLE

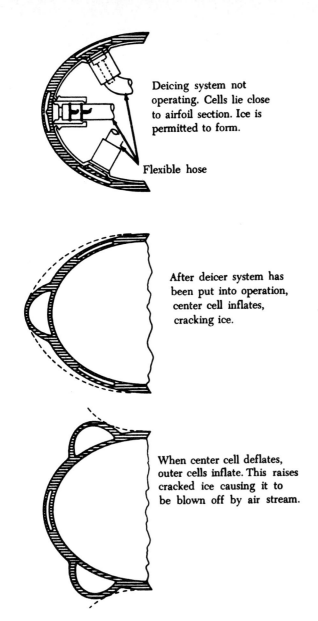

Deicing system not operating. Cells lie close to airfoil section. Ice is permitted to form.

Flexible hose

After deicer system has been put into operation, center cell inflates, cracking ice.

When center cell deflates, outer cells inflate. This raises cracked ice causing it to be blown off by air stream.

FIG. 14-29 Sequence of operation of pneumatic deicing boots.

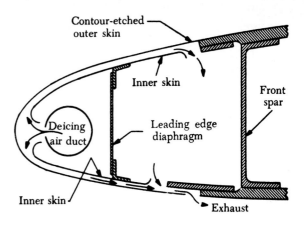

FIG. 14-30 A typical heated leading edge.

position, the ice-protection pressure-regulator and shutoff valve will open and allow engine bleed air to flow into the system. The same switches will cause the right, left, or both pneumatic system-augmentation valves to open and admit the amount of thirteenth-stage engine bleed air necessary to raise the temperature of the air to 450°F [232°C] or above. The ice-protection pressure regulator and shutoff valve regulates the pressure of the air passing into the ice-protection system at 18.5 psig [128 kPa]. With the airfoil ice-protection switches in the ON position, the flow of engine bleed air is normally directed to the wing leading edge and the ram air scoop. However, by pushing the switch marked TAIL, the **wing-protection shutoff valve** will close, the **tail ice-protection shutoff valve** will open, and air will flow to the horizontal stabilizer for a period of 2 to 2 1/2 min. After this interval the air is automatically redirected to the wing until the tail switch is pushed again. Thus, it can be seen that the

tail ice protection is deicing while the wing ice protection is anti-icing.

The ice-protection air is supplied to the wing- and horizontal-stabilizer leading edges through drilled ducting within the leading-edge "D" duct. Chemmilled skins form the chordwise double-skin passages in the leading edges.

The wing ice-protection valve on the Douglas DC-9 is installed on the inboard side of the left-hand wheel well in the wing ice-protection supply duct. It is an electrically controlled, pneumatically actuated, butterfly-type valve. The valve is normally open when the solenoid valve is deenergized. The valve consists of a solenoid and selector valve assembly, actuator assembly, and butterfly housing. The valve has a V-band-type clamp-mounting flange at each end. A mechanically operated indicator located on the actuator housing indicates the butterfly position.

The wing ice-protection shutoff valve works in conjunction with the tail ice-protection shutoff valve. When the ice-protection system is turned on, the wing shutoff valve is spring-loaded open. The shutoff will remain open until the tail deicing timer relay is actuated. At this time the solenoid on the wing shutoff valve is energized to open a valve and permit air to close the shutoff valve butterfly. At the same time, the tail ice-protection shutoff valve opens and now air is diverted to deice the horizontal stabilizer. Approximately 2 1/2 min later the timer relay automatically releases and shuts off the current to both valves. This causes the wing shutoff valve to open and the tail shutoff valve to close. A light on the annunciator panel comes on when the airfoil ice-protection switches are turned on, indicating that the wing leading edge is being anti-iced. When the tail deicing timer relay is pressed, the wing deicing light goes out and the tail deice light comes on, indicating that the horizontal stabilizer leading edge is being deiced. A drawing of the tail ice-protection shutoff valve is illustrated in Fig. 14-32.

Probe Anti-Icing

Aircraft are equipped with several sensors and devices which are exposed to the slipstream. These de-

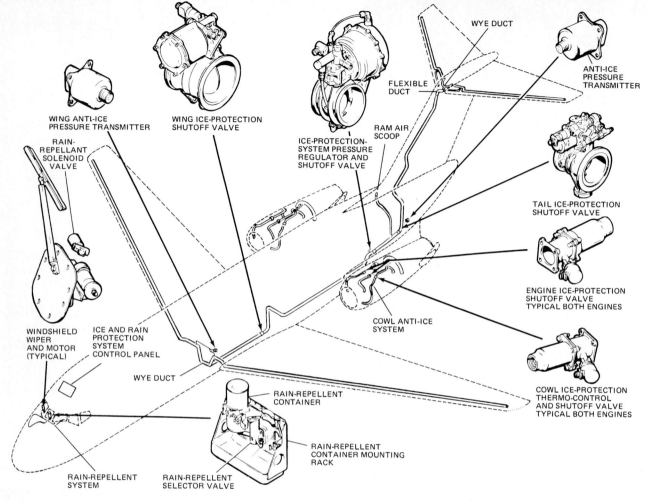

FIG. 14-31 Thermal anti-icing system for an airliner. *(Douglas Aircraft Co.)*

vices are required for safe operation of the aircraft and must be kept free of ice. Starting with the smaller aircraft, the items that need protection from ice buildup include the pitot mast and the stall warning indicator. Larger aircraft require that additional items such as static ports be kept clear along with total air temperature probes and angle of attack indicators.

These probes are normally kept free of ice by the use of electric heaters. These heaters are controlled by switches at the pilot's station. The heater elements may be operated by either ac or dc electrical power.

When inspecting these devices, the mechanic should be aware that even the units on small aircraft are capable of generating sufficient heat to cause painful burns on the skin. Never touch one of these devices if its heater element is operating.

Windshield Ice Control

The control of ice buildup on windshields may be accomplished by one of two basic methods: by heating the windshield or by spraying a fluid on the windshield to remove ice and prevent the formation of any more ice. The heating of windshields is the more common method and may involve the use of a heated panel over the windshield surface, electric heater elements inside the windshield structure, or the use of a flow of heated air between windshield surfaces.

Light aircraft can make use of an electrically heated panel to clear ice from the portion of the windshield immediately in front of the pilot. The panel provides a clear area of approximately 12 in [30.5 cm] high by 6 in [15.2 cm] wide, with the size of different units providing different clear areas. This system can be used on aircraft which are not available with internal windshield heater elements such as most aircraft with plastic windshields.

The system must be placed into operation by the pilot prior to any large ice buildup as the unit is designed for anti-icing rather than deicing. Once in operation the panel will maintain a surface temperature of approximately 100°F [37.8°C], with the temperature being regulated by a temperature sensing circuit which cycles the heater elements on and off to maintain the designed operating temperature range.

The panel is mounted on a fixture in front of the windshield and can be removed when the aircraft is not going to be operated in icing conditions. The panel used on the Cessna Caravan is shown in Fig. 14-33. This unit includes a restraining strap (not shown) which prevents the panel from pivoting forward on its mount when reverse thrust is used during landing.

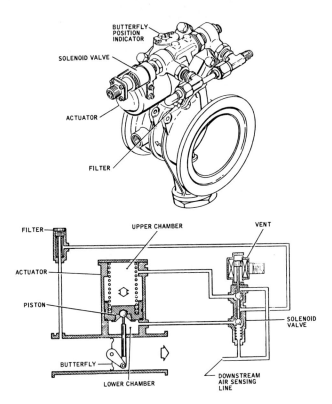

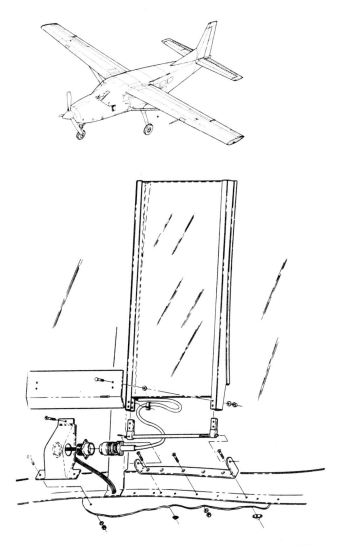

FIG. 14-32 Ice-protection shutoff valve.

Aircraft with integral windshield heaters are normally equipped with glass or hardened acrylic outer layers reinforced internally with shatter-resistant materials such as acrylic and polycarbonate materials and a polyvinyl butyral interlayer as shown in Fig. 14-34. A conductive coating is placed beneath the glass layer in the area of the windshield to be anti-iced, such as the area shown in Fig. 14-35. When in operation, current flows through the coating and generates heat due to the resistance of the coating. A portion of the windshield or complete panels can be kept ice-free by this method. This method of windshield ice control is commonly used on turbine-powered corporate and airline type aircraft.

Some older transport aircraft have windshields that consist of an inner and outer panel separated by an air passage. When windshield anti-icing is turned on, heated air from the cabin heating system is ducted through this passage, heating both panels of glass. The heated air exits the windshield area and flows into the flight deck area.

The following items should be checked when inspecting heated windshields:

Check for any delamination (separation of the layers) in the windshield panels.

Look for any scratching of the windshield and determine its cause. Scratching is often caused by dirty windshield wipers moving across the panel. For this reason, always keep windshield wipers clean and in good condition.

Any arcing that occurs during operation indicates that the conductive coating may be breaking down. This situation can lead to overheating of the panel where the arcing is occurring. Correct the problem

FIG. 14-33 Heated panel mounted in front of a windshield. *(Cessna Aircraft Co.)*

immediately in accordance with the manufacturer's maintenance instructions.

Discoloration of the windshield is not normally a problem unless the optical quality of the windshield is affected. Heated windshields are clear when looking directly through them, but they may have a gold, blue, or pink tint to them when viewed with light reflecting off of them.

When evaluating any of these types of damage to a windshield, follow the recommendations of the aircraft manufacturer. The basic guidelines are that the damage should not decrease the strength of the windshield, change the optical quality of the windshield, or affect the normal operation of the system.

Alcohol is used on some aircraft to provide for windshield deicing. This system sprays isopropyl alcohol on the outside of the windshield. The alcohol can be used to remove ice, but the supply is not normally great enough to be used throughout the flight. This system is normally used to clear the windshield prior to landing. Operation of the system requires that a crew member turn on the fluid pump and adjust the rate of flow according to the amount of ice that has accumulated. Care should be taken when inspecting

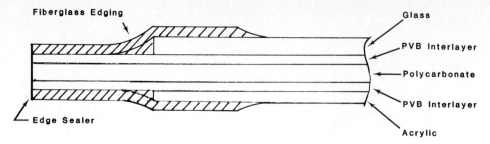

FIG. 14-34   Cross section of a heated windshield. *(Bell Helicopter Textron)*

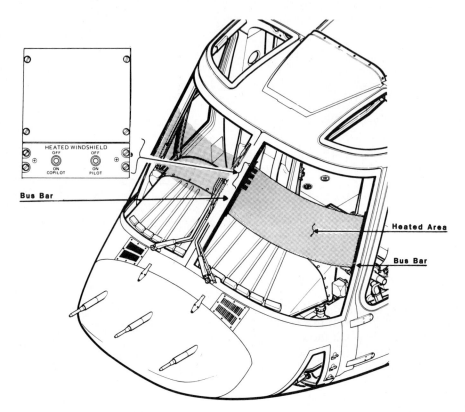

FIG. 14-35   A heated windshield installation. *(Bell Helicopter Textron)*

this system to be sure that all lines and fittings are in good condition. Inflight fires have resulted from the alcohol line rupturing and spraying onto electrical equipment.

● RAIN REMOVAL SYSTEMS

Rain removal systems are designed to allow the pilot to have a clear view of the airport when taxiing and to allow him or her to see the approach and departure paths and runway environment when taking off and landing during rain. The systems are not commonly used during flight at altitude.

Rain may be removed by the use of windshield wipers, chemical repellants in combination with windshield wipers, or by a flow of air.

Windshield-Wiper Systems

Windshield-wiper systems may be operated electrically, hydraulically, or pneumatically.

A typical electrically operated **windshield-wiper system** is illustrated in Fig. 14-36. This drawing shows the components of the wipers installed on an airliner. Each wiper on the airplane is operated by a separate system to ensure that clear vision through one of the windows will be maintained in the event of a system failure. The wiper blades clear a path 15 in [38.1 cm] wide through an arc of 40°.

Both wiper systems are electrically operated and controlled by a common gang switch located on the pilot's overhead panel. The switch provides a selection of four wiper-action speeds ranging from 190 to 275 strokes per minute and controls the stowing of the wiper blades in a PARK position when the system is not in use.

Each windshield-wiper system consists of a drive motor, a control switch, a resistor box, a flexible drive shaft, a torque converter, and a windshield-wiper assembly.

Speed control for the windshield wipers is accomplished by changing the voltage applied to the windshield-wiper motor by means of resistances arranged

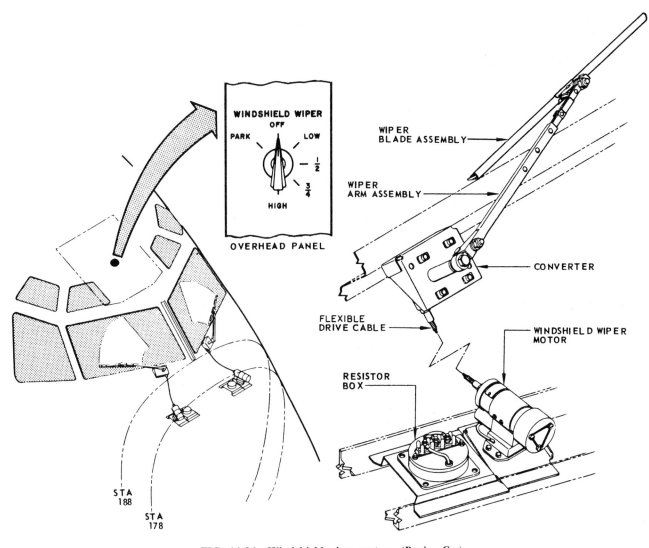

FIG. 14-36 Windshield-wiper system. *(Boeing Co.)*

in the resistor box. The required resistance is connected into the motor circuit by turning the windshield-wiper switch to a selected speed. The rotary motion of the windshield-wiper motor is transmitted by the flexible shaft to the converter. The converter reduces the shaft speed and changes the rotary motion to an oscillating motion of the windshield-wiper arm. The electrical circuit for the windshield wipers is shown schematically in Fig. 14-37.

Hydraulically and pneumatically operated wiper systems are similar in that each requires a pressure supply to be directed to an actuator. A typical system arrangement is shown in Fig. 14-38. A control unit alternately connects a pressure or return line to opposite sides of the actuator causing the piston to move back and forth. The actuator piston incorporates a rack which operates a pinion gear at the base of the wiper and causes the side-to-side motion of the wiper. A speed control valve allows the pilot to select the speed at which the wipers will operate.

Rain-Repellant Systems

To help maintain the clarity of vision through the windshield during rain conditions, a rain-repellant sys-

tem is provided for the windshields of many modern aircraft. This system consists of pressurized fluid containers, a selector valve, solenoid-actuated valves, spray nozzles, pushbutton switches, a control switch, a time-delay relay, and necessary plumbing. The rain-repellant system and windshield wipers for an airliner are shown in Fig. 14-39. During rain conditions, the windshield wipers are turned on, and the repellant is sprayed on the windshield. The repellant is spread evenly by the wiper blades. The rain repellant should not be sprayed on the windshield unless the windshield is wet and the wipers are operated; neither should the windshield wipers be operated on a dry windshield.

The effect of the rain repellant is to cause the water to form small globules which are quickly blown away by the rush of air over the windshield in flight.

Pneumatic Rain Removal System

Some turbine-powered aircraft use engine bleed air to prevent rain from striking the windshield. When the pilot turns on the rain removal system, bleed air at a high temperature and pressure is directed to an outlet at the base of the windshield as shown in Fig. 14-40. This flow of air over the windshield carries away the

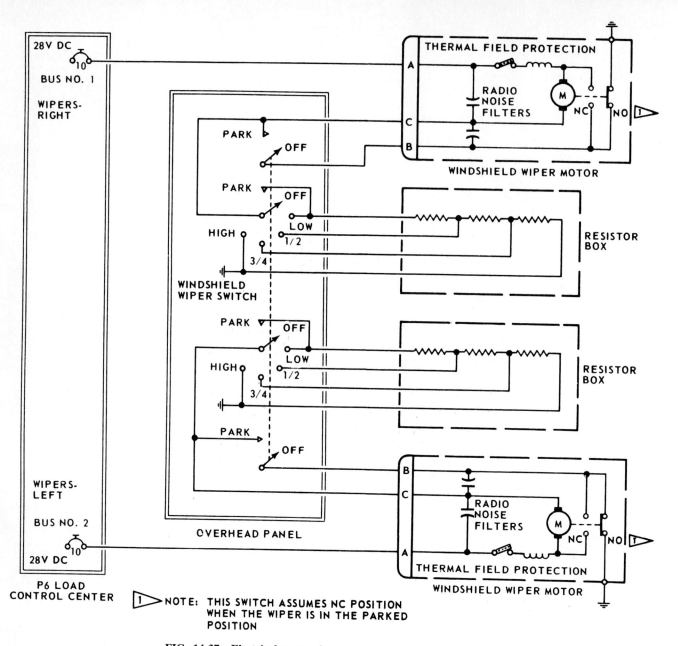

FIG. 14-37 Electrical system for windshield wipers. *(Boeing Co.)*

rain drops before they can strike the windshield. Any raindrops on the windshield when the system is turned on are also blown away.

● WATER AND WASTE SYSTEMS

All modern airliners are required to incorporate water systems to supply the needs and comforts of the passengers and crew. Such systems include potable (drinkable) water for the galley and drinking fountains, water for the lavatories, and water for the toilet systems. Systems may include one or more tanks of water with connections to the various units which require a water supply. The passenger water system for one model of the Boeing 727 airplane is illustrated in Fig. 14-41.

Potable Water Supply

The water for drinking fountains or faucets is usually drawn from main pressurized water tanks, passed through filters to remove any impurities and solids, cooled by dry ice or other means of cooling, and delivered to the faucets and/or drinking fountains. Disposable drinking cups are supplied at each location in the forward and rear parts of the passenger cabin.

Lavatory Water

Water for the lavatories is also drawn from the main water tanks and passed directly through suitable plumbing and valves to the lavatories. Hot water for washing is provided by means of electric water heaters located beneath the lavatory bowls. A typical hot-water supply is contained in a 2-qt [1.89-L] tank which

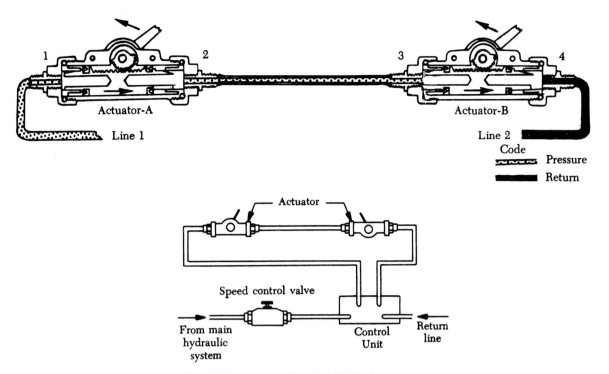

FIG. 14-38 A hydraulic windshield wiper system.

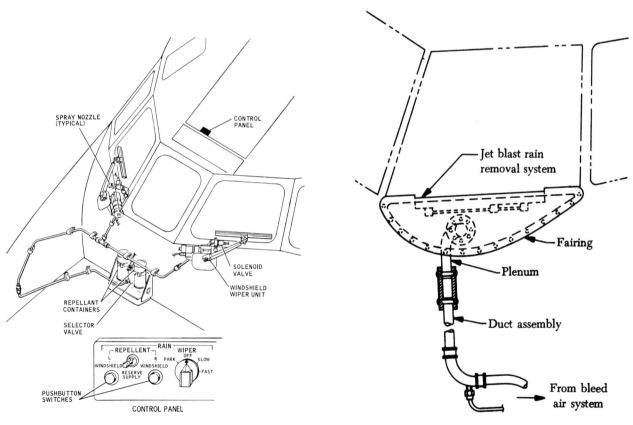

FIG. 14-39 Rain repellant system. *(Douglas Aircraft Co.)*

FIG. 14-40 Pneumatic rain repellant system.

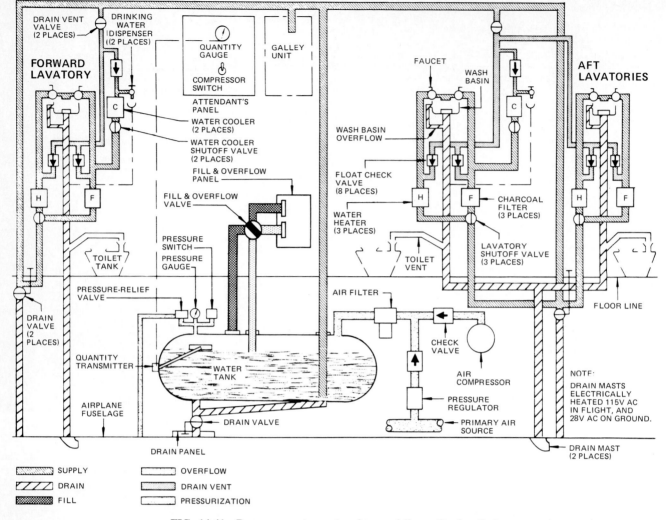

FIG. 14-41 Passenger water system for an airliner. *(Boeing Co.)*

includes the thermostatically controlled heating unit to maintain the water at a temperature of 110 to 120°F [43.3 to 48.9°C]. Drain water from the lavatories can be drained overboard through drain masts or can be drained into the toilet waste tanks.

Toilet System

The **toilet system** is designed so there is no possible contamination of the passenger water supply from the system. In the airplane discussed here, separate, independent toilet systems are provided in the forward and aft passenger cabins. Toilets in each lavatory compartment are electrically powered flushing units which collect the waste material in a waste tank and combine it with the flushing agent by chemical and mechanical treatment. The units are primed initially with 3 gal [11.37 L] of a concentrated solution of disinfectant, deodorant, and dye. The toilet units are installed in each lavatory compartment entirely above the lavatory compartment floor. Each unit consists of a toilet shroud assembly, flushing components, and a waste tank. The components of a toilet system are shown in Fig. 14-42.

Toilet flushing action is initiated by turning the toilet flush handle. This begins a cycle in which flushing liquid is drawn into a rotating filter and pumped through the toilet-bowl flush ring into the bowl with a swirling action. Waste material and flushing liquid flow out the bottom of the bowl into the waste tank. Servicing components in the forward and aft systems allow ground draining and cleansing of the toilet units.

The toilet shroud assembly consists of a standard commercial seat and cover attached to a shroud which covers the flushing components mounted on the tank top. The shroud is attached to the upper and lower ends of the shroud support angles.

The flushing components include a flush handle, timer, motor-and-pump assembly, filter assembly, and the required tubing. All the components, with the exception of the flush handle and timer, are mounted on the tank top. The flush handle and timer are located on the cabinet aft of the toilet unit. The stainless-steel toilet bowl with a flexible restrictor in the bottom is also mounted in the tank-top.

The toilet waste tank assembly includes a glass-fiber tank of 17 gal [64.4 L] capacity fitted with a bulb-type spring-loaded drain valve and a tank top. The drain valve is operated by a cable from the toilet service

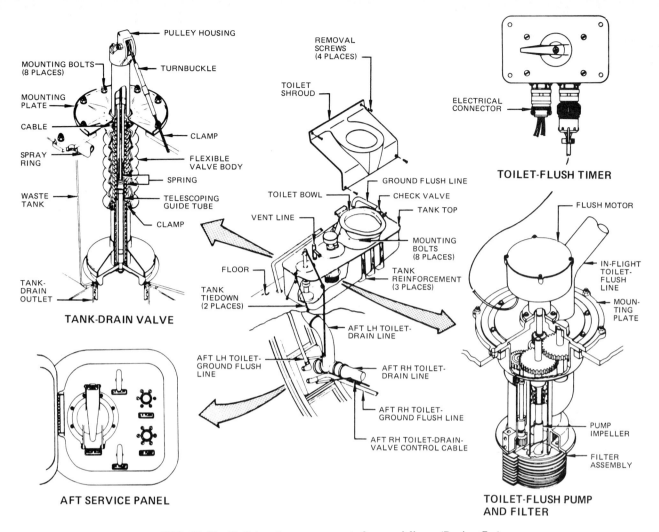

FIG. 14-42   Toilet system components for an airliner. *(Boeing Co.)*

panel. A rubber gasket is placed along the top edge of the tank to form a watertight seal when the tank top is installed. Access into the tank for maintenance purposes is obtained by removing the toilet bowl and base plate.

The drain valve, when fully open, permits unrestricted passage of waste from the tank to a service cart. In the closed position, it forms a positive seal. The valve is spring-loaded and self-closing and does not require lubrication. It is opened by pulling a handle on its related exterior service panel. When the handle is in the extended position, it can be rotated to latch it. A safety valve which is operated by a control on the service attachment is installed in the drain tube.

● POSITION AND WARNING SYSTEMS

Each aircraft system may incorporate a warning system to indicate when that particular system is not functioning properly. The purpose of this section is to discuss systems that do nothing but indicate the position of components and warn of unsafe conditions. These systems include control-surface indicator systems, takeoff warning systems, and stall warning systems.

Control-Surface Indicating Systems

The purpose of control-surface indicating systems is to allow the flight crew to determine if a control surface is in the correct position for some phase of flight and to determine if a flight control is moving properly.

The most common type of control-surface indicating system is that used for the elevator trim tab, and this will serve as an example for other mechanical indicating systems. This type of mechanism is found in most fixed-wing aircraft and is used by the pilot to indicate if the trim tab is properly positioned for some phase of flight, such as takeoff or landing, before that phase of flight is initiated. If the trim tab is out of position, the pilot may have to use large forces on the flight controls to achieve the desired action. If the trim tab is properly positioned, then it will provide most of the force necessary to hold a specific attitude and the pilot need only make small adjustments about the trimmed setting of the control surface.

These types of systems often use a mechanical indicator to show the control position. In some systems, a cable is attached to the control horn of the trim tab and as the tab moves the cable pulls against a spring

537

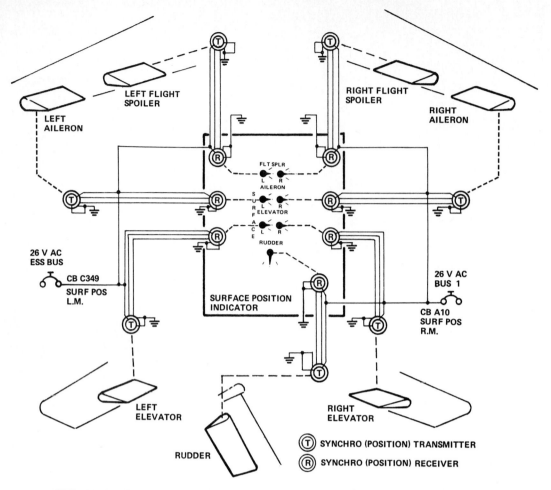

FIG. 14-43 Flight control position indicating system for a jet aircraft. *(Canadair Inc.)*

at the pilot's position. As the spring is stretched or released by the movement of the trim tab, a pointer located where the cable connects to the springs moves along a scale, indicating the trim tab position. In other systems a spiral groove in the trim tab control wheel causes a pointer to move, indicating the position of the trim tab.

Either of these systems or similar system designs can be used to monitor the position of any flight control surface. When inspecting these mechanical indicating systems, the mechanic should verify that the indicator agrees with the position of the surface being monitored.

Large aircraft may make use of electric control surface indicating systems such as the one shown in Fig. 14-43. In this system, synchro transmitters are located at each of the control surfaces. The voltage inducted into the armatures by their exciter windings are used at the synchro receivers to position the indicator pointers.

Takeoff Warning Indicator Systems

A takeoff warning indicator system is used to advise the pilot that one or more items is not properly positioned for takeoff. When a takeoff warning system

actuates, an intermittent horn is sounded until the incorrect situtation is corrected or until the takeoff is aborted.

The simplified takeoff warning system schematic for a large jet transport is shown in Fig. 14-44. Note that if anyone of the several items is not in the correct position for takeoff and the throttle for No. 3 engine is advanced beyond a certain position when the aircraft weight is on the landing gear, the horn will sound. The items that are checked by this system are the elevator trim in the takeoff range, the speedbrake (spoilers) handle in the zero degree position, the steerable fuselage landing gear is centered, the wing flaps are at 10°, and the leading-edge wing flaps are extended. The exact aircraft configuration monitored by a takeoff warning system will vary, but the intent of each system is to prevent a takeoff with the aircraft in an unsafe configuration.

Stall Warning Indicators

A stall warning indicator is designed to indicate to the pilot when the aircraft is a close to the stalling angle of attack. When the stall warning system is activated, the pilot will be given one or more of the following indications: a horn will sound, a light will

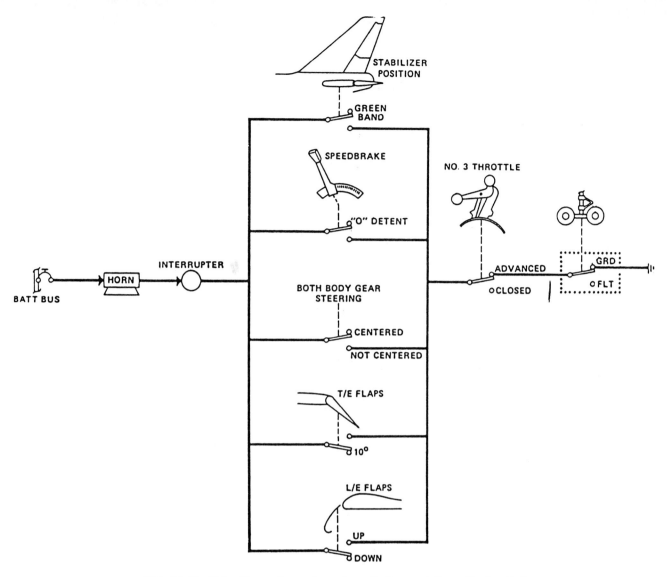

FIG. 14-44 Takeoff warning system schematic for an airliner. *(Boeing Co.)*

illuminate, and/or a "stick-shaker" will start vibrating the control wheel column. The specific warning method varies with the aircraft design.

While some light aircraft do not have stall warning indicator systems, most have a system using a sensor vane on the leading edge of the wing similar to that shown in Fig. 14-45. When the angle of attack of the wing causes the airflow to be from below the vane on the sensor, the vane moves up and completes a circuit to activate the stall warning indicator.

A pneumatic stall warning indication system is used by some light aircraft. A slot in the leading edge of the wing is connected to tubing routed to the cabin area. A horn reed is positioned in the end of the tubing. When the wing angle of attack increases to the point where a negative pressure exists on the slot, air flows through the reed, out the slot, and creates an audible stall warning indication.

Modern transport aircraft use stall warning computer circuits to activate the stall warning system. Inputs to the computer include angle of attack infor-

mation, flap and slat position information, and weight on landing gear information. When the computer determines that a stall is imminent, a stick shaker will start moving the control columns back and forth, an aural warning may be sounded, and an indicator may illuminate, depending on the specific system design.

● REVIEW QUESTIONS

1. Which type of fire-detection system is termed a "rate-of-rise" detection system?
2. Describe the theory of operation of a spot detector and a thermocouple system.
3. Describe the different types of operation of a Systron-Donner pneumatic fire detection system.
4. Which fire extinguishing agent is used on most modern aircraft?
5. What devices are used as *overheat* or *fire* detectors?
6. Describe three types of tubular fire detectors or sensors.

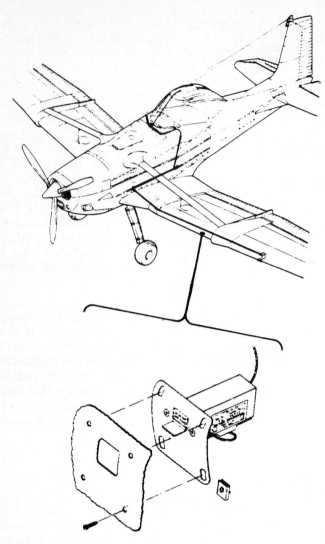

FIG. 14-45 Stall warning indicator installation. *(Cessna Aircraft Co.)*

7. List the general features and capabilities of overheat and fire warning systems for aircraft.
8. How are overheat and fire warning systems tested for operational capability?
9. How can a crew member tell when the helium gas in a pneumatic sensor has been lost?
10. Describe the operation of the *integrity monitoring circuit.*
11. Explain the importance of correct routing for overheat and fire warning sensors.
12. How are sensors protected from vibration, wear, and damage?
13. Describe a *toxic-gas detector.*
14. What is the importance of a toxic-gas detector and what is a likely source of toxic gas in a light airplane?

15. In what areas of an airplane are *smoke detectors* most likely to be used?
16. Name three types of extinguishing agents used in aircraft fire-suppression systems.
17. Describe extinguishing-agent containers.
18. What gas is usually employed to expel the extinguishing agent from a container?
19. To what pressure is a container usually charged?
20. Describe the method by which the *discharge head* attached to a container releases the extinguishing agent.
21. What is used to indicate that a fire-extinguishing agent bottle has discharged thermally?
22. What are two classifications of fire-extinguishing systems?
23. What indicators are required to show the discharge of extinguishing agent?
24. What type of extinguishing agent should be used for electrical fires?
25. Discuss the need for portable fire extinguishers.
26. What parts of an airplane are subject to ice collection during icing conditions?
27. Describe a pneumatic-mechanical deicing system.
28. How are *deicing boots* attached to leading edge surfaces?
29. How is air supplied to deicer boots?
30. Why is a conductive coating required for deicer boots?
31. For what conditions are deicer boots inspected?
32. Discuss the removal and replacement of deicer boots.
33. How is an operational test of a deicer system performed?
34. Describe the operation of a *thermal anti-icing system* on a large airplane.
35. What is the ususal source of heat for thermal anti-icing?
36. What units are usually electrically anti-iced?
37. What methods may be used to keep a windshield free of ice?
38. Describe a *rain-repellant system.*
39. What is the purpose of a *converter* in a windshield-wiper system?
40. What may be used to power a windshield wiper system?
41. What methods, other than wipers, may be used to remove rain from a windshield?
42. Describe the water system for an airliner.
43. By what method is water for the lavatory heated?
44. How is drinking water cooled?
45. Describe the operation of the toilet system.
46. By what method is flushing liquid forced through the system?
47. What is the purpose of a takeoff warning system?

15 ASSEMBLY AND RIGGING

● AIRCRAFT ASSEMBLY

The **assembly** of an aircraft refers to the joining of parts or subassemblies by various means until the entire aircraft is in condition for operation. **Rigging** is the alignment of aircraft parts or sections for proper flight characteristics. A certain amount of rigging is necessary during the assembly of an aircraft, but even after final assembly, certain rigging adjustments must be made. Thus there is some overlap between the assembly operation and rigging operation.

Throughout the other chapters of this text and the related texts, there are many detailed explanations of the installation, adjustment, inspection, and operation of aircraft units, subassemblies, assemblies, etc. All these explanations pertain to aircraft assembly, at least to some degree in each case. The purpose of this discussion of assembly is to tie together what the student has already learned in previous chapters and to provide examples of rigging instructions.

Equipment for Assembly and Rigging

To properly handle aircraft components to be assembled, a combination of stands, hoists, and alignment devices is required.

When assembling a light aircraft, the equipment necessary may only include a few sawhorses to support the structure, some sand bags for counterbalancing purposes, and a hoist to install an engine. This type of equipment is commonly available in a shop. For rigging the aircraft, a straightedge, measuring tape, plumb bobs, roll of twine, long and short spirit levels, cable tensiometer, and a protractor, along with common hand tools and power tools, are required.

When assembling larger aircraft, additional items such as a lifting bridle with spreader bars, slings, a heavy duty hoist, and floor jacks may also be required. These large items may only be occasional-use items, depending on the type of work normally performed by an operator.

The uses of each of these items is discussed throughout this chapter.

Assembly Procedures

Major assemblies, such as the fuselage, wings, engine nacelles, and landing gear, are normally constructed as complete subunits. These subunits are inspected for workmanship and for conformance to applicable specifications. During the manufacture of an airplane, the inspected and approved subunits are brought into the final assembly line at certain stations where they can be joined to the main structure most effectively.

The actual assembly of the aircraft obviously varies greatly according to the type, make, and model, but a few general principles apply. In a factory all operations can be planned for the greatest efficiency, but in a repair shop where the jobs vary to a great extent, this type of planning cannot be done so easily.

If the aircraft had been disassembled for repair or shipment, it should have been cleaned after disassembly and all of the attaching hardware checked for condition and replaced as necessary. When the structure was disassembled, all of the attaching hardware in airworthy condition should have been installed in the fittings on one of the separated structures. This avoids the problem of trying to locate the correct bolt, washer, or screw from a pile of hardware removed from the aircraft.

An assortment of tapered drifts is useful for lining up bolt holes. If a drift of the correct size is not available, an undersized bolt can be used for this purpose. During assembly operations, the mechanic must not distort or overstress any part in order to make the bolt holes line up. If parts will not fit together properly, the cause of the misfit must be determined and corrected.

The disassembly and assembly of complex parts and subunits of an aircraft are usually clearly described in the manufacturer's maintenance manual. In every case where manufacturer's instructions are available, the mechanic should follow them in detail.

The final assembly of an aircraft usually starts with the fuselage subassembly and progresses through various subassemblies until the entire aircraft is ready for test. In some cases the fuselage is assembled in sections. For example, the center portion of the fuselage will·be placed on a fixture or jig for support, while the other subassemblies are attached to it. Then, depending upon the particular design and type of aircraft, the nose section, tail section, wings, landing gear, and other parts are joined to the main assembly.

A fuselage is provided with fittings or attachments for the purpose of hoisting or jacking. These fittings may be a permanent part of the aircraft or they may be separate attachments which can be installed when it is necessary to lift the aircraft. When it is necessary to hoist or jack the aircraft, the mechanic must make sure that the correct procedure is used and that the proper fittings are available. The manufacturer's manual gives detailed instructions for handling the aircraft.

In some cases, the aircraft fuselage may be hoisted

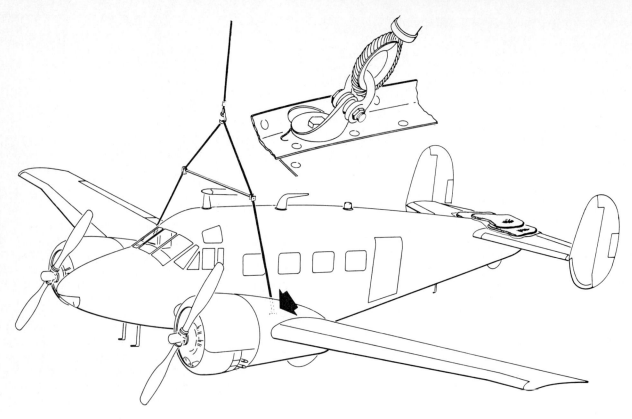

FIG. 15-1 Hoisting an airplane with the use of a spreader bar.

by means of a **sling.** The sling may attach to fittings on the upper portion of the fuselage, or it may be constructed of webbing which passes under the fuselage at specified points and is connected to the hoisting fittings at the top. It if often necessary that a **spreader bar** be used to provide a minimum clearance of 2 in [5 cm] between the fuselage and the hoisting cable. The use of the spreader bar is illustrated in Fig. 15-1.

If the aircraft is to be lifted by a lifting strap placed around the fuselage, the strap should be well padded to avoid surface damage. The strap should be placed at a reinforced position such as at a bulkhead or former so that undue stress will not be placed on unreinforced skin areas, causing structural damage.

The **landing gear** of an aircraft includes floats or pontoons, skis, skids, and wheels, together with their shock absorbers and devices necessary for the attachment of the gear to the wings or fuselage. To assemble the main landing gear to a fuselage, the fuselage is raised high enough so that the gear can be attached. The best way to do this for a particular aircraft is given in the manufacturer's instruction. In some cases a hoist will be used; in others the fuselage will be jacked up or placed in a suitable jig or cradle. If a chain hoist is used, the hoist should be placed above the forward portion of the fuselage. The hoist will be suspended from rafters or crossbeams of the shop, but these must be strong enough to hold the hoist and the aircraft without failure, and without damaging the building. A weak rafter may break and drop the aircraft on the floor, thus causing great damage. If there is any doubt about the security of the support, the rafters or crossbeams should be reinforced with temporary staging or props. The hoist is attached with a strong chain or cable. If the chain has no hooks, a clevis is fastened through the two end links.

After the hoist is attached to the chain or rope, the hook should be "moused." This is accomplished by closing the open throat of the hook by wrapping soft wire or twine around the tip and shank of the hook as shown in Fig. 15-2.

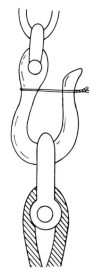

FIG. 15-2 Using a "mouse" to safety a shackle on lifting hook.

At the beginning of a major assembly job, the work crew should be properly organized so members will know their responsibilities and from whom they should take directions. One person should be in charge of the operation, but others can be assigned charge of subdivisions of the job.

In fastening a "bridle" or lifting sling to a fuselage, the attachments must be correctly located. The "station points" on either the fuselage or the engine mount are often used as lifting points; however, the lifting points designed by the manufacturer should be used when available.

When the hoisting gear is in place and securely attached, the fuselage is ready for lifting. The hoist should be operated slowly and smoothly until the fuselage clears the forward support. Members of the assembly crew should be alert to detect any rocking or swinging of the fuselage which could cause the fuselage to strike any object and cause damage. The fuselage should be raised just enough to permit installation of the gear shock-strut assemblies, and a support structure should be kept under the fuselage to keep it from falling on crew members in case of hoisting-gear failure. After the landing-gear struts are properly attached to the aircraft, all fittings are tightened and safetied. If bonding connections are necessary, these are secured. Hydraulic lines for the brakes and electrical wiring for safety switches are connected and secured. Other attachments are installed as required. When the gear is completely installed with wheels in place and tires properly inflated, the airplane weight can be supported on the gear.

Following assembly of the landing gear to the aircraft, the subsequent assembly operations can vary considerably. The manufacturer's manual may specify the sequence of assembly events or the choice may be up to the mechanic. In some cases it may be preferable to install the empennage before installing the wings; for other aircraft, the reverse may be better.

Although the assembly of different aircraft requires many varying procedures, some basic guidelines should be followed:

1. Always use the correct type and size of hardware. For example, standard bolts should not be used where high-strength bolts are required. A low-strength bolt could result in component separation in flight. Do not use a stack of washers to make up for a bolt being too long. Either get a bolt the proper length or determine what other fitting should be installed on that bolt.

2. Insert bolts and clevis pins in the proper direction, especially in the area of moving structures. If a bolt is installed backward, the threaded end and the nut may interfere with the operation of a control surface.

3. Use only the correct type of hardware safety mechanism. Unless specified by the manufacturer, fiber locknuts should not be used were the bolt will be subject to rotation such as when used as a control surface hinge. This can cause the nut to back off the bolt. Use the recommended safety mechanism, usually a cotter pin and occasionally safety wire.

4. If no direction for bolts to be inserted is specified or indicated by component configuration, they should be installed with the bolt head up or forward. This will reduce the chance of the bolt falling out of a fitting if the nut should come off.

5. Never force components together without checking to determine why the force is necessary. Some components are a push-fit, but exercise caution when performing this type of assembly to avoid damage to components.

6. Check the location and routing of all cables, hoses, tubing, etc., before assembling components. This will help prevent crossed control cables and the mixing of various fluid and gaseous lines.

7. Follow all recommended safety precautions when working with aircraft on jacks, hoists, and assembly supports. Do not allow anyone to be in a position where they can be injured if a support or lifting mechanism should fail.

● AIRCRAFT RIGGING

Aircraft rigging involves two principal types of operations. First, the aircraft structure must be rigged for correct alignment of all fixed components. The fuselage is aligned at the time of manufacture in the assembly jigs. All parts are correctly positioned in the assembly jig and then they are riveted, bolted, or welded into a complete assembly. Some types of fuselages require realignment at major overhaul periods or after damage. Wings and other large structures are aligned and assembled in jigs and fixtures to assure correct shape and positioning of attachment fittings. When the major components are assembled, they are aligned with each other.

The second type of rigging is the alignment of control surfaces and the controls which move the surfaces. These operations require the adjustment of cable length, cable tension, push-pull rods, bell cranks, cable drums, and various other parts. Angular deflection of control surfaces must be measured with protractors or other measuring devices to assure that the movements comply with the appropriate specifications.

Effects of Rigging on Flight

The purpose of rigging an aircraft correctly is to attain the most efficient flight characteristics possible. A properly rigged and trimmed airplane will fly straight and level "hands off" at its normal cruising speed. If air currents should disturb the stable flight attitude, it will correct itself and resume straight and level flight.

When an aircraft is flying straight and level at a constant cruising speed, the thrust produced by the engine is exactly equal to the total drag (induced drag plus parasite drag) of the aircraft. The weight of the aircraft is exactly equal to the total lift produced by the lifting surfaces.

If the aircraft is out of rig, meaning that components are not properly aligned, then the total drag of the aircraft will be increased or the amount of control movement available will not provide the correct response. For example, if the wing chord line is not properly aligned in relation to the fuselage longitudinal axis, the drag of the aircraft will be increased, resulting in a higher power setting being required to overcome the drag, or if the power setting is not increased, the airspeed will be lower. If flight controls do not have enough range of motion, the pilot may not be able to control the motion of the aircraft properly. If the range of control surface travel is too great, the pilot may be able to deflect the control surface enough to place excessive stresses on the structure resulting in failure of the structure.

The correct rigging of the wings and control surfaces on an aircraft is essential to the stability of the aircraft in flight. Stability around the longitudinal axis is provided by rigging the wings and ailerons correctly. The wings on a monoplane are rigged for **dihedral,** angle of incidence, and **washin** or **washout.** Dihedral is the angle between the lateral plane of a wing and the horizontal plane. It is adjusted by raising or lowering the outer end of the wing. On an aircraft with cantilevered wings, the dihedral is built into the wing and is not usually adjustable. Dihedral produces stability around the longitudinal axis because of the difference in vertical wing lift when the aircraft rolls slightly off of level flight. When a wing with dihedral lowers in flight, the wing angle with the horizontal plane decreases and the vertical wing lift increases. At the same time, the wing on the opposite side of the aircraft is increasing its angle with the horizontal, and its vertical lift decreases. Thus the low wing will rise and the high wing will lower.

The angle of incidence must be correct if the aircraft is to fly most efficiently. An aircraft is designed with an angle of incidence which will produce maximum lift and minimum drag at normal cruising speed. If the angle of incidence is not correct, the drag increases. The fuselage will not be in perfect alignment with the flight path but will be slightly nose up or nose down, depending upon whether the angle of incidence is too small or too great.

Washin is an increase in the angle of incidence of the wing from the root to the tip. If a wing has an angle of incidence of 2° at the root and an angle of incidence of 3° at the outer end, it has a washin of 1°. **Washout** is a decreasing angle of incidence from the root to the tip of a wing. Washin and washout are employed to give the wings on each side of an aircraft a slightly different amount of lift in order to aid in counteracting the effect of engine and propeller torque. Washout is also used to provide improved stall characteristics. If the angle of incidence is greatest at the wing roots, the root sections of the wings will stall before the tips. This characteristic gives the pilot warning of a stall before the complete stall occurs; the pilot will still have control of the aircraft with the ailerons and be able to make any desired corrections.

The control surfaces at the tail of an aircraft must be rigged correctly to provide for stability around the lateral and vertical axes. On a propeller-driven aircraft, the airflow from the propeller does not flow straight back but follows a helical course. This causes the ''prop wash'' to strike the vertical stabilizer and rudder at an angle. For this reason, the vertical sta-

bilizer and rudder are rigged off center so the chords of these surfaces will be parallel to the airflow at the cruising speed of the aircraft. If this were not done, the airflow would continuously apply a side load to the tail of the aircraft, and this would have to be continuously counteracted by the pilot using the rudder.

Wing flaps on an aircraft are designed in a number of configurations as explained in the first chapter of this text. The purpose of the flaps is to increase the lift of the wings, thus making it possible to descend at a greater glide angle and to land at a slower speed. Flaps on large aircraft are designed to produce a great amount of additional lift without producing a corresponding increase in drag. Flap control systems must be designed so that the flaps on one side of the aircraft cannot lower independently of the flaps on the opposite side. The flaps must lower together and at the same rate on each side of the aircraft.

Leveling the Aircraft

When rigging an aircraft, it may be necessary to establish the aircraft in a level attitude prior to checking and adjusting wings and control surfaces. The various aircraft manufacturers have devised several methods by which the mechanic can establish the level attitude of the aircraft. Keep in mind that the level attitude of the aircraft includes both a longitudinal level and a lateral level position. Once the aircraft is level longitudinally and laterally, the components can be rigged.

One method used on many light aircraft is to set a spirit level on a longitudinal structural member to establish the longitudinal level position and another level across specific structural members to establish the lateral level position, as shown in Fig. 15-3. This same basic procedure is accomplished in some aircraft by the installation of two nut plates on the side of the fuselage. Screws can be placed in these nut plates, and longitudinal level is determined when a spirit level

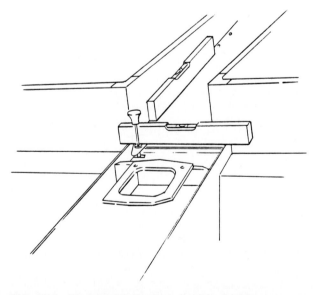

FIG. 15-3 Use of spirit levels on fuselage members to establish the aircraft level. *(Robinson Helicopter Co.)*

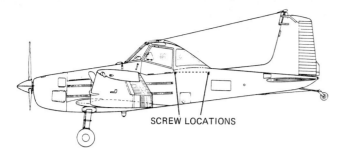

SCREW LOCATIONS

FIG. 15-4 Special nut plates and screw locations may be used to establish the aircraft level. *(Cessna Aircraft Co.)*

placed on the extended screws is level. This arrangement is shown in Fig. 15-4.

Some aircraft make use of a plumb bob and a target to establish the aircraft level on both axis. This is done, as shown in Figs. 15-5 and 15-6, by suspending a plumb bob from a specified structural member and adjusting the aircraft until the plumb bob is centered on the target.

Another method used is to attach a permanent spirit level to the aircraft for each of the two axes. These levels are normally located in an equipment compartment or a wheel well and may have an accuracy as great as 1/8°.

If an aircraft is not level, the aircraft may be leveled by the use of supports under the aircraft, such as under a tailwheel. The inflation of tires and struts can be adjusted as can the fuel loads in wings and fuselage

tanks. Sometimes jacks are used to level the aircraft. Regardless of the leveling means used, care must be taken not to place a support or jack at a structurally weak area, such as on a skin panel between bulkheads. Additionally, if the air pressure is reduced in tire or struts to establish the level attitude or if fuel is transferred for this purpose, be sure the aircraft is properly serviced before returning it to operation.

● **FIXED-SURFACE ALIGNMENT**

The fixed surfaces of an aircraft includes wings, stabilizers, and tailbooms. These components must be checked for alignment with the fuselage and with each other to determine if the aircraft is properly rigged. This involves a symmetry check longitudinally and laterally, and angular adjustments such as incidence and dihedral.

Symmetry Check

From time to time, it is necessary or advisable to check the alignment of a fully assembled aircraft. If a pilot reports poor flight characteristics that cannot be corrected by rerigging of controls, it is possible that the fuselage and wings are out of alignment or that a fixed surface is out of alignment with the aircraft. A **symmetry check** is used to verify this alignment.

Aircraft symmetry is determined by first leveling the aircraft and then measuring the distances from reference points on the aircraft central axis to reference points on the adjustable components. Figure

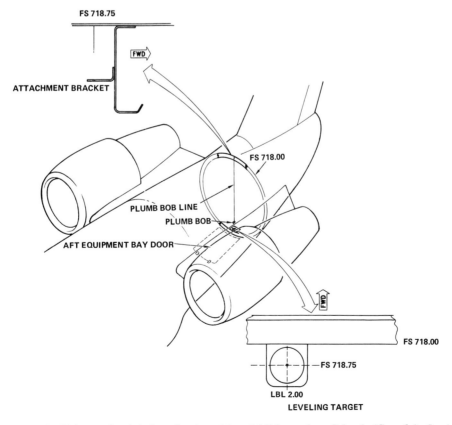

FIG. 15-5 Using a plumb bob and a target to establish an aircraft level. *(Canadair, Inc.)*

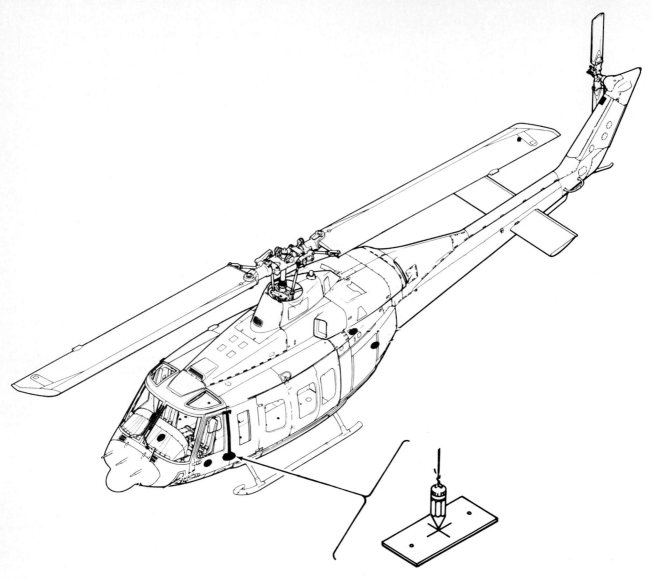

FIG. 15-6 Helicopters may be leveled by the use of a plumb bob. *(Bell Helicopter-Textron)*

15-7 shows the symmetry lines used for a particular airplane. Alignment points are numbered 1 to 6, left and right. As can be seen from the drawing, measurements are made from points 1, left and right, to point 3, left and right; from points 2, left and right, to points 5, left and right, and point *A*. Other measurements are made as shown. If all measurements are within the tolerances given in the maintenance manual, the aircraft is in correct alignment. If any of the measurements are not within tolerance, the alignment must be adjusted as specified.

The vertical symmetry of an aircraft can be checked in a like manner by the use of a measuring tape to check the distance between the tip of the vertical stabilizer and the horizontal stabilizers as shown in Fig. 15-8.

When checking an aircraft's symmetry, a drawing of the aircraft is helpful so that the values measured can be recorded and the lines of measurement indicated. Some mechanics prefer to lay out the reference points on the floor of the hanger. A plumb bob is

suspended from the reference point and the position is marked with chalk. The measurements are then taken from these floor markings. This method is especially useful for large aircraft. As adjustments are made, a plumb bob suspended from the reference point immediately indicates the amount of adjustment.

Checking Dihedral and Incidence

To check the dihedral angle of a wing, the fuselage should be leveled. A dihedral board can then be used at a specified location to check the amount of dihedral in a wing. The use of a dihedral board is shown in Fig. 15-9.

Some light aircraft use a vertical measurement to determine dihedral. In one high-wing aircraft, a string is stretched from one wing tip to the other wing tip, centered on the front spar. When the string is drawn tight, the distance from the string to the top of the fuselage is measured to determine if the dihedral is correct.

To determine if the angle of incidence for the wing

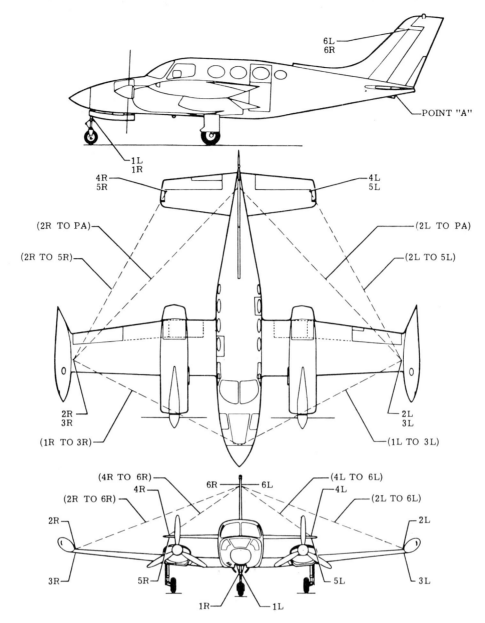

FIG. 15-7 Alignment measurements for a light twin-engine airplane. *(Cessna Aircraft Co.)*

or horizontal stabilizer is correct, the fuselage is leveled and an incidence board, as shown in Fig. 15-10, is used or a universal protractor of the type shown in Fig. 15-11 is placed on a designated surface of the wing or stabilizer and the angle of incidence measured.

In some instances it is not necessary to level the aircraft in order to measure incidence or dihedral if a

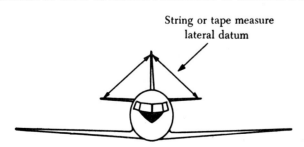

FIG. 15-8 Checking vertical symmetry.

universal protractor is used. The protractor can be zeroed in reference to the fuselage and then the angles are measured.

Cantilever Wing and Fuselage Alignment

Some aircraft with cantilever wings have the wings manufactured without any provision for adjustment of the dihedral or angle of incidence. This is accomplished by the use of manufacturing jigs which assure that all wing and fuselage joints will be identical. Other wing and fuselage fittings allow for some change in the angle of incidence of the wing during installation by the use of eccentric bushings in the mounting bolts.

Semicantilever Wing and Fuselage Alignment

Semicantilever wings have external braces, either wires or struts. As struts are the most common arrangement, they will be addressed here and the ad-

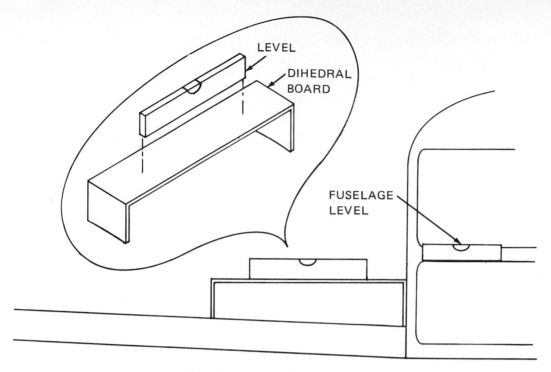

FIG. 15-9   Use of a dihedral board.

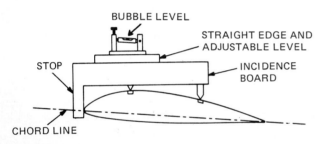

FIG. 15-10   An incidence board.

justment of wires will be addressed on the section dealing with biplanes.

Many struts have fittings threaded into the end of the strut which allow the length of the strut to be changed. This allows the dihedral to be adjusted by increasing or decreasing the length of the strut. The washin and washout of the wing can also be adjusted by changing the length of a strut if a strut is used for the rear spar and a strut is used for the front spar. By changing the length of only one of these struts through the adjustment fitting, the twist in the wing will change.

If a single strut of a fixed length is used on an aircraft, the amount of dihedral cannot be changed, but the angle of incidence of the wing may be adjusted through a mechanism as shown in Fig. 15-12. This uses an eccentric bushing fitted into the rear spar fuselage attachment fitting. By rotating the bushing, the rear spar is raised or lowered slightly, changing the angle of incidence of the wing. Once the wing is adjusted, the attachment bolt is fitted through the bushing and the bushing will no longer rotate.

Biplane Wing and Fuselage Alignment

Although the biplane is considered by many to be an obsolete type of aircraft, there are hundreds of these airplanes still in operation for pleasure, sport, and agricultural work. It is therefore deemed important that the well-qualified aircraft mechanic be familiar with the procedures required for this operation. A typical biplane is shown in Fig. 15-13.

The information the mechanic must have for rigging the biplane includes **stagger, angle of incidence, dihedral angle,** and **decalage.**

Stagger is the longitudinal difference in the positions of the leading edges of the wings of a biplane. If the leading edge of the upper wing is ahead of the leading edge of the lower wing, the stagger is **positive.**

Decalage is the difference between the angles of incidence of the upper and lower wings. If the upper wing has a greater angle of incidence than the lower wing, the decalage is said to be positive.

The first step in rigging a biplane is to level the fuselage, both laterally and longitudinally, in a location free from wind. The front of the fuselage should be supported in a cradle or by means of jacks. If the fuselage is supported by means of the landing gear, the flexibility of the shock struts and tires will permit movement which is not desirable.

The second step in rigging the biplane is to install the **center section** of the wing on the fuselage. The center section is lifted into position above the fuselage, either by means of a suitable hoist or by hand. Depending upon the size of the center section, either two or four persons will be required to lift the center section into position safely. While the center section is being held in position, the **cabane struts** and **stagger struts** are attached, either with temporary bolts or the

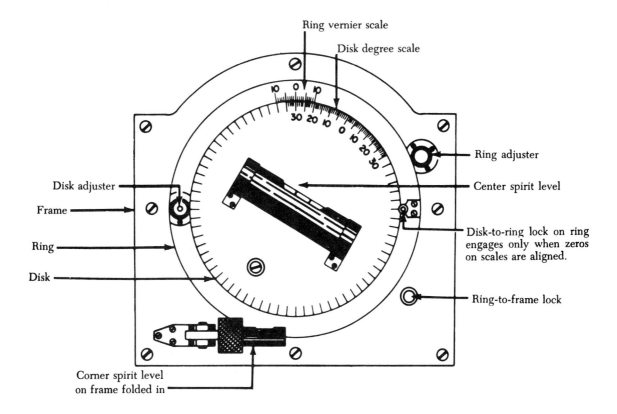

Ring vernier scale

Disk degree scale

Ring adjuster

Center spirit level

Disk-to-ring lock on **ring** engages only when **zeros** on scales are aligned.

Ring-to-frame lock

Disk adjuster

Frame

Ring

Disk

Corner spirit level on frame folded in

1 With disk-to-ring lock in the deep slot, turn disk adjuster to lock disk to ring.

2 Move control surface to neutral.   Place protractor on control surface and turn ring adjuster to center bubble in center spirit level (ring must be unlocked from frame).

3 Lock ring to frame with ring-to-frame lock.

4 Move control surface to extreme limit of movement

5 Unlock disk from ring with disk-to-ring lock.

6 Turn disk adjuster to center bubble in center spirit level.

7 Read surface travel in degrees on disk and tenths of a degree on vernier scale.

FIG. 15-11   A universal protractor may be used to measure alignment and movement angles.

regular assembly bolts. The **cross-brace** wires should also be installed at this time in order to support the center section laterally.

The next step is to adjust and secure the center section. It must be adjusted for lateral position, stagger, and angle of incidence. These adjustments must be made in an orderly sequence, and secondary adjustments may have to be made because of the effect of one adjustment upon another. The first operation is to adjust the cross-brace wires until the center section is aligned with the center line of the fuselage. The symmetry of the center section with the fuselage is checked with a plumb line, a straightedge, a spirit level, and a steel measuring tape or scale. When the spirit level is placed laterally across the top of the center section, a level reading should be obtained. Plumb bobs dropped from identical points on each end

of the center section should indicate that the center section is centered laterally. Measuring from the plumb line to reference points on the fuselage will show whether the center section is centered.

The stagger of the center section may or may not be adjustable. If fixed-length stagger struts are used on the airplane, no adjustment can be made. On the other hand, if the stagger struts are adjustable or if the airplane has **stagger** and **drift wires** between the cabane struts, adjustment must be made. Adjustment of the stagger struts or wires will move the center section forward or aft. The position is checked by dropping a plumb line from the leading edge of the center section on each side of the fuselage and measuring the distance from the plumb line to a fixed reference point such as the front fitting for the lower wing.

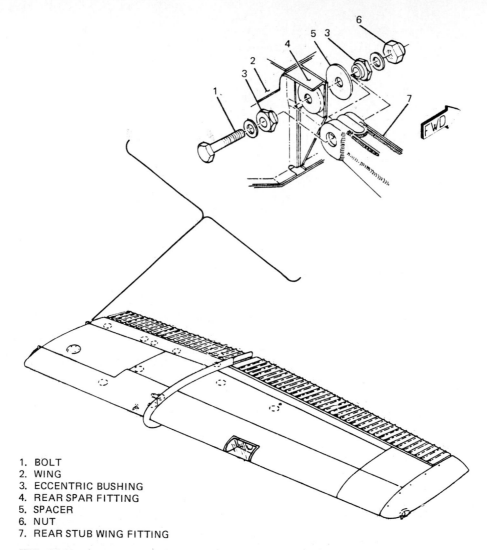

1. BOLT
2. WING
3. ECCENTRIC BUSHING
4. REAR SPAR FITTING
5. SPACER
6. NUT
7. REAR STUB WING FITTING

FIG. 15-12 An eccentric bushing is used to adjust the wing angle of incidence. *(Cessna Aircraft Co.)*

The final check on the rigging of the center section is to see that all wires have the correct tension, all lock nuts are properly tightened, and the correct bolts are installed in all fittings. Safetying of nuts and bolts must be checked.

FIG. 15-13 A typical biplane.

The next step in the rigging of the biplane is the attachment of the lower wings. A padded support is placed where it can support the outer end of the lower wing, and then the wing is lifted into place and attached at the fuselage fittings. The wing attachment bolts are inserted with the heads forward as a standard practice.

The **interplane struts** are attached to fittings on the top of each lower wing near the outer end. The struts must be held in an almost vertical position until the upper-wing panels are attached to the fittings on the ends of the center section. The upper ends of the struts are then attached to the fittings on the lower side of each upper wing. When this is done, both the upper and lower wings are supported by the stand or other support under the lower wing. The upper wing is supported through the interplane struts.

After the wing panels are in place, the **landing wires,** sometimes called **ground wires,** are installed between the fittings at the tops of the cabane struts and the fittings at the lower ends of the interplane struts. These wires are tightened to support the weight of both wing panels on each side of the fuselage. After the landing wires are tightened, the supports can be removed from under the lower wing.

The **flying wires,** which carry the wing load in flight, are installed between the fittings at the butt end of the lower wing and the fittings at the upper ends of the interplane struts. These wires are tightened just enough to take up the slack at this time.

The dihedral angle of the wings is established by adjusting the landing wires. A bubble protractor or a dihedral board with the correct angle is used for checking the dihedral angle. When the dihedral angle is correct, the flying wires are tightened. The wires are of the streamline design and are manufactured with right-hand threads at one end and left-hand threads at the other end. Thus, by turning the wire in one direction, it is tightened and by turning it in the opposite direction it is loosened. Tightening the landing wires increases the dihedral angle. After the wires are all tightened to the correct tension, the dihedral angle should be rechecked to see that it is correct.

When adjusting flying and landing wires, a nonmetallic wire wrench, as shown in Fig. 15-14, should be used. Do not use pliers or any metal tool to adjust the wires as these will damage the wire surface and can cause wire failure.

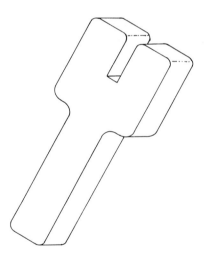

FIG. 15-14 A wire wrench.

The tension of a flying or landing wire can be checked by the use of a datum board as shown in Fig. 15-15. A support at each end of the datum board rests against the wire and a spring scale is used to deflect the wire. The amount of force required to deflect the wire a specific distance is measured. For each size wire the distance between the supports will vary. The amount of deflection will vary, depending on the desired tension.

The stagger at the outer ends of the wings should be checked to determine that it is correct. Some biplanes use a fixed N-strut arrangement such that no adjustment of stagger is required. If the airplane has incidence wires between the interplane struts, it is necessary to adjust these wires by means of turnbuck-

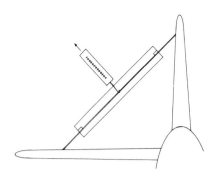

FIG. 15-15 Using a datum board to check wire tension. (*Schweizer Aircraft Co.*)

les or other means to set the correct stagger at these points.

After the wings and empennage are adjusted and set according to specifications, the airplane must be flown to determine whether the rigging is exactly as it should be. It is necessary to **wash in** and **wash out** the wings to compensate for propeller torque. Since the propeller of a conventional biplane turns to the right, the airplane will tend to rotate to the left about the longitudinal axis. For this reason it is necessary to rig the wings so the left wings will have more lift than the right. To increase the lift, the left-wing angle of incidence is increased slightly and the right-wing angle of incidence is decreased slightly. Decreasing the angle of incidence at the tip of a wing is called **washing out,** and increasing the angle of incidence is called **washing in.** From experience it is known approximately how much washout and washin is required for a particular airplane at cruising speed and this amount is rigged in at first. The airplane is then test flown and if a tendency to roll is found during the flight, the pilot makes his report and the rigging is corrected. The washin and washout are adjusted by shortening or lengthening the rear landing wires and adjusting the other wires to provide a reasonable balance in tension. If an airplane uses incidence wires between the interplane struts, these are adjusted.

The washin of the left wing will increase the drag of that wing because of the greater lift. This will cause the airplane to yaw to the left; however, the tendency to yaw can be corrected by the use of an adjustable **trim tab** on the rudder. The tab is adjusted to deflect the rudder slightly to the right, thus providing a balancing force to overcome the yaw.

To make the adjustments as small as possible for the correction of engine and propeller torque, it is common practice to divide the amount of correction equally between the right and left wings. Thus, if the left wing is given 1° of washin, the right wing is given 1° of washout.

Stabilizer Alignment

Some aircraft use strut or wire bracing for the horizontal and vertical stabilizers. These braces are adjusted in a manner similar to the wing flying and landing wires. The vertical surface is nearly always set perpendicular to the aircraft lateral axis and the horizontal surfaces are normally parallel to the lateral axis. These surfaces do not normally incorporate any twist, such as washin or washout. Figure 15-16 shows a tail section being checked for proper alignment and the location of the tail brace wires.

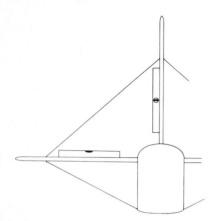

FIG. 15-16   Using a spirit level to check tail surface rigging.

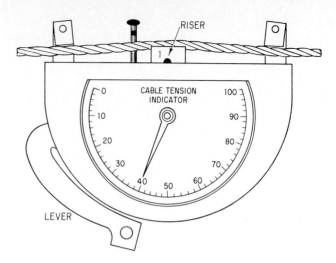

FIG. 15-17   Use of a tensiometer.

CONTROL SURFACE RIGGING

Although the actual rigging of controls for any particular airplane should be accomplished according to the instructions of the manufacturer, there are certain operations common to almost all systems and by which rigging of the majority of small airplanes can be accomplished. The control systems for very large aircraft are so complex that adjustment and rigging can be accomplished only in the operator's overhaul shops or similar large shops, and according to manufacturer's directions.

Among the objectives to be accomplished during the rigging procedure are (1) correct cable tensions, (2) balance or synchronization between dual controls, (3) synchronization of the cockpit control with the control surfaces to which it is linked, and (4) setting the range of control-surface movement.

Cable tensions must be set at the same time the control units are positioned because any change in control cable tension will likely produce a change in control-surface position. Cable tension is measured by means of a **tensiometer** or cable-tension indicator as shown in Fig. 15-17. The correct riser for the cable size is installed on the indicator, and then the indicator is hooked over the cable. The control lever is moved up against the case, and the reading on the dial is noted. This reading is located on the conversion chart supplied with the instrument, and the cable tension is shown opposite the indicator reading in the column for the size of cable being checked.

The objective in rigging a control system is to have the cockpit control in neutral at the same time that the control surface involved is in neutral. Usually the cockpit control (stick or control column and wheels) is locked in the neutral position by means of the **control lock** in the airplane if this lock position is neutral or by an installed locking arrangement such as a bar, block, or rod with clamps which will hold the control in neutral. Be aware that some control locks hold the

elevator in a nose-down position and cannot be used for rigging purposes. The control cables are then adjusted and tensioned so the control surface affected is in neutral. All adjusting elements, such as turnbuckles and rod ends, must be checked after rigging to see that they are within limits. Rod ends must be screwed into or onto the rod a distance sufficient to prevent the insertion of safety wire through the inspection hole. Turnbuckles must not have more than three threads showing outside the barrel.

Another point to remember in the final inspection of a control rigging job is to see that no cable splice or fitting can come within 2 in [5.08 cm] of a fairlead, pulley, guide, cable guard, or other unit which could cause the control to jam. The control should be moved to its extreme position both ways in making this inspection.

The range of control-surface movement is given in the manufacturer's instructions, in the Aircraft Specifications, or the Type Certificate Data Sheet. The control surface may have fixed or adjustable stops; this should be determined by inspection. If the stops are fixed and the control surface moves beyond its proper range, a repair must be made to set the stop correctly. This may involve welding a new stop in place or repairing the part of the surface which strikes the stop. The nature of the correction will be determined by examination. Adjustable stops are merely adjusted to bring the control surface into the correct range.

After all adjustments are completed, appropriate safeties (safety wire, cotter pins, jam nuts, etc.) should be installed.

Control System Components

We have already discussed some of the control system components such as cables, pulleys, and turnbuckles; however, there are other units involved which require description. Among these are **push-pull rods, bellcranks, quadrants, torque tubes, cable guards,** and **fairleads.**

The **push-pull rod** is used between bell cranks and from bell cranks to **torque arms** ("horns") to transmit the force and motion from one to the other. A push-pull rod connected to a bellcrank is shown in Fig. 15-18. Push-pull rods are also called **control rods** because they are often used in control systems.

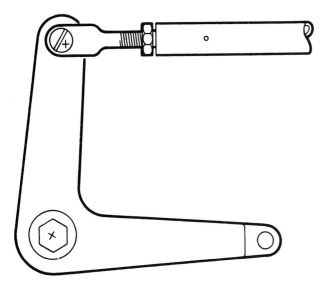

FIG. 15-18 A push-pull rod connected to a bellcrank.

A **bellcrank** is used to transmit force and permit a change in the direction of the force. In the illustration of 15-18 the effect of the bell crank operation can be seen.

A **quadrant** serves the same purpose as a wheel; however, the quadrant moves through a relatively small arc, perhaps as much as 100°. A quadrant, shown in Fig. 15-19, is often employed at the base of a control column or control stick to impart force and motion to a cable system.

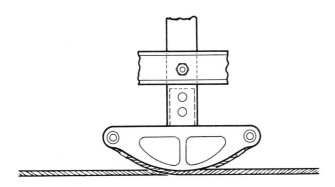

FIG. 15-19 A quadrant used for movement of control cables.

A **torque tube** is a hollow shaft by which the linear motion of a cable or push-pull tube is changed to rotary motion. A torque arm or "horn" is attached to the tube by welding or bolting and imparts a twisting motion to the tube as the arm is moved back and forth. This is illustrated in Fig. 15-20.

Cable guards or **guard pins** are installed in the flanges of pulley brackets to prevent the cable from

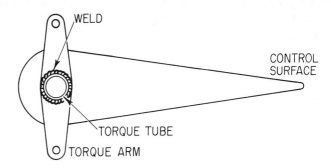

FIG. 15-20 A torque arm or horn.

jumping out of the pulley, as shown in Fig. 15-21. The guard must be located so it does not interfere with the rotation of the pulley. A guard pin can be either a bolt, a cotter pin, or a clevis pin.

A **fairlead** serves as a guide to prevent wear and vibration of a cable. The fairlead is made of phenolic

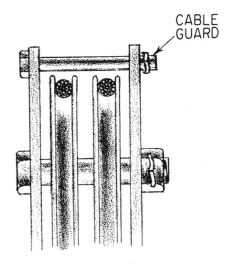

FIG. 15-21 A cable guard pin.

material, plastic, or soft aluminum and is either split or slotted to permit the installation of the cable. These units must be installed in such a manner that there is no contact between the cable and the aircraft structure. The principal functions or fairleads are to dampen vibration, maintain cable alignment, and to seal openings in bulkheads. In no case should the fairlead be permitted to deflect a cable more than 3°, and it is good practice to install fairleads so cable deflection is as small as possible. Since cables are tightened to the extent that from 25 lb [111.25 N] to more than 160 lb [712 N] is exerted on the cable, any appreciable deflection at a fairlead will cause excessive wear of the cable and the fairlead. A fairlead is shown in Fig. 15-22.

In a pressurized jet airplane, cables leading from a pressurized section of the airplane to a nonpressurized section must have **air-pressure seals** installed where the cable passes through the bulkhead. A seal of this type is shown in Fig. 15-23. The air-pressure seals are made of ozone-resistant rubber and are installed ac-

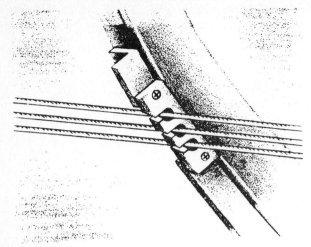

FIG. 15-22   A fairlead.

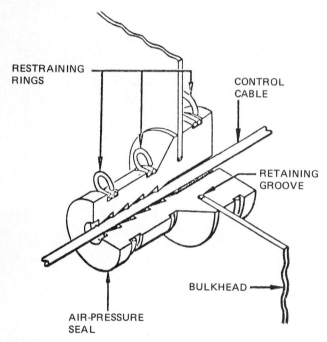

FIG. 15-23   An air-pressure seal for cable installations in pressurized airplanes. *(Boeing Co.)*

cording to the manufacturer's instructions. Typical instructions are as follows:

Fill the seal with graphite grease MIL-G-7187.

Lubricate the cable with graphite grease for the length of travel within the seal.

Bend the seal open and place it on the cable on the unpressurized side of the bulkhead, with the small end of the seal toward the bulkhead.

Insert the seal in the bulkhead so that the bulkhead web is entirely within the retainer groove of the seal and the small end of the seal is in the pressurized section.

Install two restraining rings on the seal on the pressurized side and one restraining ring on the unpressurized side of the bulkhead.

Controls and Control Systems

The three primary controls for an airplane are the ailerons, elevators or stabilators, and rudder or rudders. On small aircraft these are operated manually through cockpit controls.

The ailerons are mounted on the rear portions (trailing edges) of the wings, usually near the outer end of each wing, and are operated by moving the control stick sideways or by rotating the control wheel. The movement of the control to the right causes a right rolling effect and vice versa.

In some aircraft the operation of ailerons causes the aircraft to yaw against the direction of the control movement; that is, a movement of the control for a left roll would cause the airplane to yaw to the right. This is because the aileron which moves downward creates lift and drag, whereas the aileron which moves upward reduces lift and causes much less drag. This drag causes the condition which is called **adverse yaw.** To overcome this adverse yaw a number of modifications have been made in the design and operation of some aileron systems.

One method of combating adverse yaw was to design the aileron so that a substantial section extends foward of the hinge line. This forward section moves down into the airstream when the aileron is moved up and creates drag to balance the increased drag of the down aileron. The top portion of the forward section of the aileron is rounded off in order that it will not extend upward on the down aileron. This type of aileron is called a Friese aileron.

Another, more common, method for controlling adverse yaw through the operation of the ailerons is to design the control systems so there is differential movement between the ailerons. The aileron moving upward moves approximately twice as far as the aileron moving downward. In this way the drag on the up aileron tends to balance the drag on the down aileron. The difference in the amount of aileron travel between the upward and downward movement is caused by a **differential control.** This can be accomplished by several methods, one being the placement of the control-rod connections on the drive wheels. An example of differential control movement is illustrated in Fig. 15-24. In this illustration, it can be seen that the movement of the control stick in one direction will cause an aileron to move up a greater distance than the other aileron moves down. When the control stick is moved in the opposite direction, the opposite effect must occur.

The elevator or stabilator is used to control the aircraft pitching motion about the lateral axis. It is quite common for this control surface to have more travel above the neutral position than below the neutral position. (The neutral position is in alignment with the horizontal stabilizer if an elevator is used or at some reference angle to the aircraft longitudinal axis if a stabilator is used.) This is to permit the pilot to have sufficient control authority during low speed operations, such as when landing, so that the nose of the aircraft can be raised sufficiently to allow the aircraft to touch down on the runway at the slowest possible speed with the main landing gear contacting the runway first. The exact degree of control movement can be found in the aircraft maintenance manuals.

The rudder is used to correct for adverse aileron yaw and to control any yawing tendency of the aircraft during maneuvers and during flight through turbulent air. The most common control movement configuration is to provide the rudder with equal amount of movement on either side of the neutral position, which aligns with the aircraft longitudinal axis.

Typical Control System

A typical control system for a light airplane is shown in Fig. 15-25. This system consists of control wheels mounted on a yoke with sprocket chains interconnected between the two wheels to a cable drive pulley. Rotation of the control wheels is changed to angular movement of the ailerons through the cables, bellcranks, and aileron control tube assembly.

To rig and adjust the aileron system, the control wheels are placed in the neutral postion laterally with the lower surfaces of the wheels horizontal. The control wheels are secured in the neutral position by means of a bar or beam clamped to the wheels. The cables are rigged by means of the turnbuckles so that the aileron bellcrank assemblies [(20) in Fig. 15-25] are in the neutral position and the cable tension is between 28 and 42 lb [124.6 and 186.9 N] on a tensiometer. A fabricated special tool is inserted to determine aileron bellcrank neutral position.

The tension of control cables must be within the range specified by the manufacturer. Excessive tension places undue stress on the cables, pulleys, pulley brackets, and all other parts associated with the support of the control system. During operation, these stresses can lead to failure of the system. Excessive

tension also increases the wear on cables, pulleys, bearings, and other parts. In addition, excessive tension increases the difficulty of moving the controls, thus reducing the pilot's ability to control the aircraft smoothly and accurately.

The aileron control tubes [(2) in Fig. 15-25] are adjusted so that the ailerons are in neutral position. The aileron travel is set by adjusting the aileron stop bolts in the bellcranks. The travel is measured by means of a bubble protractor.

An elevator control system which utilizes push-pull control rods (control tubes) is illustrated in Fig. 15-26. When the control wheels are moved forward and rear-forward, the control arm at the lower end of the control column assembly is moved. This motion is transmitted through the push-pull rods to the bellcrank at the rear of the airplane which, in turn, transmits the motion to the rear elevator control tube assembly, thus moving the elevator up and down. Adjustments of the elevator movement and travel is made by means of adjustable rod ends on the control tubes.

Various types of control surface stops for mechanical flight control systems may be used. Three methods are shown in Figs. 15-27, 15-28, and 15-29. In Fig. 15-27, travel stop bolts are installed in nut plates that are mounted on a bulkhead. The stop is adjusted in or out as necessary to obtain the proper control travel. The flat plates on the bellcrank allow the control to move until the plate contacts the stop bolt. In Fig. 15-28, a stop bolt is mounted in the control stick. The bolt length protruding from the fork is adjusted to achieve the proper control movement. In Fig. 15-29, one of four positions can be selected on the bellcrank stops. The hole in the bellcrank is off center, which gives a different stop value for each side of the stop.

The manufacturers of some aircraft provide rigging

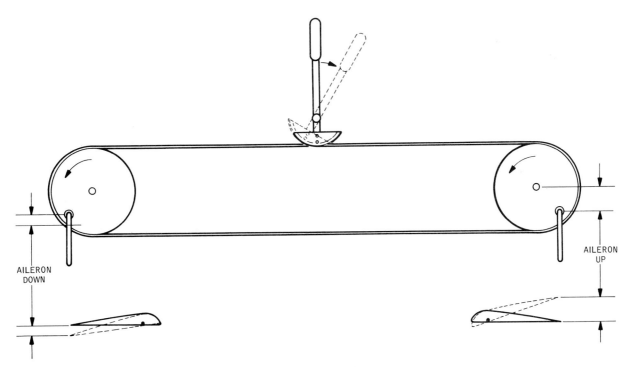

FIG. 15-24   Aileron differential control system.

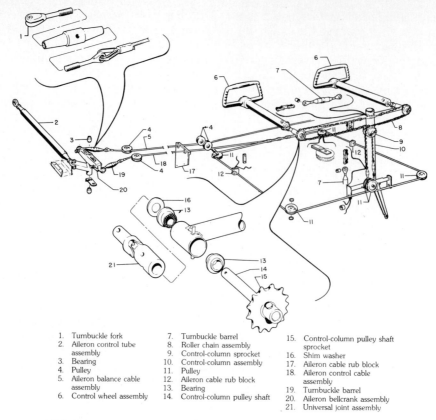

1.	Turnbuckle fork	7.	Turnbuckle barrel	15.	Control-column pulley shaft
2.	Aileron control tube	8.	Roller chain assembly		sprocket
	assembly	9.	Control-column sprocket	16.	Shim washer
3.	Bearing	10.	Control-column assembly	17.	Aileron cable rub block
4.	Pulley	11.	Pulley	18.	Aileron control cable
5.	Aileron balance cable	12.	Aileron cable rub block		assembly
	assembly	13.	Bearing	19.	Turnbuckle barrel
6.	Control wheel assembly	14.	Control-column pulley shaft	20.	Aileron bellcrank assembly
				21.	Universal joint assembly

FIG. 15-25   Aileron system for a light airplane. *(Piper Aircraft Co.)*

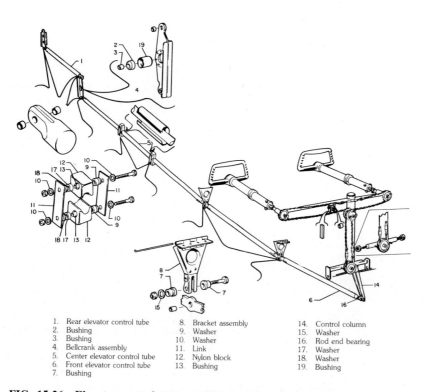

1.	Rear elevator control tube	8.	Bracket assembly	14.	Control column
2.	Bushing	9.	Washer	15.	Washer
3.	Bushing	10.	Washer	16.	Rod end bearing
4.	Bellcrank assembly	11.	Link	17.	Washer
5.	Center elevator control tube	12.	Nylon block	18.	Washer
6.	Front elevator control tube	13.	Bushing	19.	Bushing
7.	Bushing				

FIG. 15-26   Elevator control system utilizing push-pull rods. *(Piper Aircraft Co.)*

holes for the rigging of flight controls, as shown in Fig. 15-30. The hole in the bellcrank is lined up with the hole in the rigging fitting. A pin is placed through the two holes to prevent the bellcrank from moving.

The mechanism is then rigged to achieve a neutral control surface setting and a neutral cabin control position.

Another way of achieving a neutral control surface

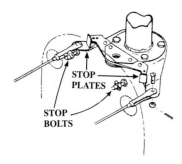

FIG. 15-27 Bolt stops located in a bulkhead. *(Cessna Aircraft Co.)*

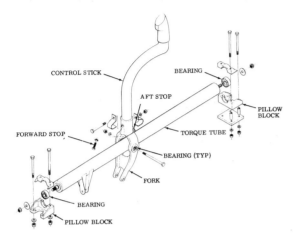

FIG. 15-28 Bolt stops located on a control stick. *(Ayres Corp.)*

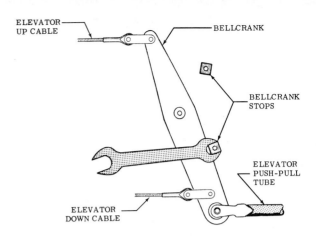

FIG. 15-29 The use of square bell-crank stops. *(Cessna Aircraft Co.)*

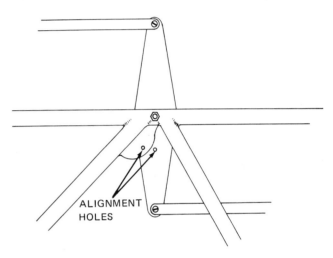

FIG. 15-30 An alignment hole used for control surface rigging.

position is to clamp the surface in a neutral position as shown in Fig. 15-31.

Rigging a Stabilator

A stabilator control system for a light airplane is shown in Fig. 15-32. A study of the drawing reveals clearly how the system operates. As the control column is moved fore and aft, it moves the cable to cause the stabilator balance arm to move up and down. This, in turn, rotates the stabilator about its support points.

The rigging of a stabilator system is similar in many respects to the rigging of any other cable control system. As explained previously, the stabilator combines the function of a horizontal stabilizer and an elevator. Its rigging, therefore, must be accurate if the airplane is to fly easily and comfortably. Typical instructions for the rigging of a stabilator system are as follows:

1. Level the airplane in accordance with instructions in the maintenance manual.

2. Check the stabilator travel by placing a rigging tool on the upper surface of the stabilator as shown in Fig. 15-33.

3. Set on a bubble protractor the number of degrees of up travel as given in the rigging data and place it on the rigging tool. Raise the trailing edge of the stabilator and determine that when the stabilator contacts its stops, the bubble of the protractor is centered.

4. Set on the protractor the number of degrees of down travel as given in rigging data and again place

the protractor on the rigging tool. Lower the trailing edge of the stabilator and determine that when it contacts its stops, the bubble of the protractor is centered.

5. Should the stabilator travel be incorrect in either the up or down position, remove the tail cone of the airplane. With the use of the bubble protractor and the rigging tool, obtain the correct degree of travel by turning the stops located at each stabilator hinge in or out.

6. Secure the stop screws with the lock nuts and reinstall the tail cone.

To check and set the stabilator control cable tension, the following procedure may be followed:

1. Check the stabilator travel and adjust it, if necessary.

2. Remove the access panel to the aft section of the fuselage.

3. Secure the control column in the near forward position. Allow 1/4 in [6.35 mm] between the column and the stop bumper.

4. Using a tensiometer, check the control cable tension and compare with rigging data.

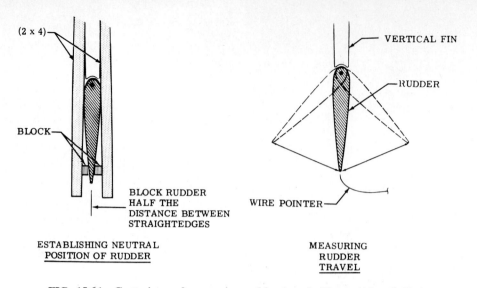

ESTABLISHING NEUTRAL
POSITION OF RUDDER

MEASURING
RUDDER
TRAVEL

FIG. 15-31 Centering and measuring rudder travel. *(Cessna Aircraft Co.)*

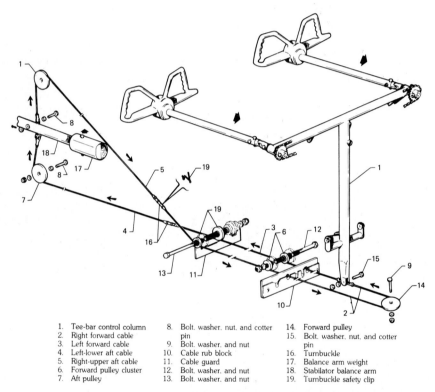

1. Tee-bar control column	8. Bolt, washer, nut, and cotter pin	14. Forward pulley
2. Right forward cable		15. Bolt, washer, nut, and cotter pin
3. Left forward cable	9. Bolt, washer, and nut	16. Turnbuckle
4. Left-lower aft cable	10. Cable rub block	17. Balance arm weight
5. Right-upper aft cable	11. Cable guard	18. Stabilator balance arm
6. Forward pulley cluster	12. Bolt, washer, and nut	19. Turnbuckle safety clip
7. Aft pulley	13. Bolt, washer, and nut	

FIG. 15-32 Stabilator control system. *(Piper Aircraft Co.)*

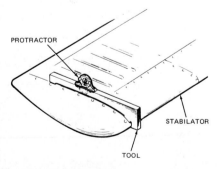

FIG. 15-33 Use of rigging tool.

5. Should the tension be incorrect, loosen the turnbuckle of the lower cable in the aft section of the fuselage and adjust the upper cable to obtain correct tension. Cable tension should be obtained with the control wheel at 1/4 in [6.35 mm] from the stop and with the stabilator contacting its stop.

6. See that all turnbuckles and bolts are safetied.

7. With the tension of the upper cable correct and the control wheel still forward, adjust the turnbuckle of the lower cable for the correct value of tension.

8. Check the full travel of the control wheel with relation to the full travel of the stabilator to determine

that the stabilator contacts its stops before the control column contacts its stops. With the control column in the fore and aft positions, the travel distance from the point where the stabilator contacts its stops and the control column contacts its stops should be approximately equal. Readjust the turnbuckles if the travel distances are not correct.

Unconventional Systems

Some aircraft are equipped with special types of controls which involve interconnections between aileron and rudder systems so the airplane can be turned by means of the control wheel only. This is usually a spring-type interconnection, such that the controls can be operated independently without difficulty. Adjustment of these systems must be exact and in accordance with specifications.

A **two-control airplane** does not have rudder controls. A rudder which has a very small range of travel is interconnected with the aileron system through the control wheel such that reasonably well-coordinated turns can be made by means of the wheel only.

A few aircraft are equipped with tail control surfaces called **ruddervators** arranged in a V configuration. These surfaces provide both rudder and elevator action. When the control wheel is pulled back, both surfaces raise. When the right rudder pedal is pressed, the left surface moves upward and to the right and the right surface moves downward and to the right. This action is accomplished by means of a mechanism which combines the action of the rudder pedals and the elevator control.

Tabs and Tab Systems

Various types of **tab systems** are employed on aircraft control surfaces to "trim" the aircraft so the pilot can fly straight and level without having to exert continuous pressure on the controls.

A **fixed trim tab** is one that can be adjusted on the ground but cannot be adjusted in flight. This type of tab is usually a sheet-metal plate attached to the rear of the control surface and extending aft of the trailing edge. If the pilot reports that the airplane will not fly straight and level at cruising speed, the appropriate tab is adjusted on the ground by bending.

When a rudder tab is moved or bent to the right, it causes deflection of the rudder to the left, thus causing the airplane to turn to the left. If an elevator tab is bent or moved upward, the elevator will be deflected downward and the nose of the aircraft will tend to move downward. If an aileron tab is bent down, the aileron moves up and the lift on the wing is decreased. This causes the aircraft to roll to the side with the lowered tab.

Modern aircraft employ adjustable trim tabs such that the pilot can make adjustments in flight. The tabs are operated through cable systems, utilizing cable smaller than the required for the primary controls. The mechanisms employed for the operation of the aileron trim control on a typical airplane are shown in Fig. 15-34. Note that the trim is adjusted by a control wheel located in the cockpit. The wheel is turned to the right to lower the right wing and vice versa. The control

wheel turns a sprocket and drives a sprocket chain. The chain turns another sprocket wheel connected through a shaft to a miter gear. Through the pair of gears, the axis of rotation is changed 90° and the motion is delivered to another sprocket. This sprocket wheel drives a chain which is connected to cable fittings. The cable is connected by means of conventional turnbuckles and routed through pulleys to the chain which drives the aileron trim-tab actuator. A similar mechanism can be used to trim the elevator and rudder.

The foregoing description provides a sample of a typical trim-tab system, although many systems on large aircraft are driven by means of electric actuators.

Control tabs are similar in effect to trim tabs; however, they are used on large aircraft to produce primary control forces. An example of the action of a control tab is shown in Fig. 15-35.

The control tab provides aerodynamic force to raise or lower the control surface in response to the operation of the control column. When the tab is moved in one direction, the control surface moves in the oposite direction. The effect of the tab may be assisted by the static balance weight and by the air pressure on the control surface balance panel shown in Fig. 15-35.

In addition to the control tab, the stabilizer of an aircraft may be equipped with a stabilizer-actuated elevator tab. This tab helps streamline the elevator with the horizontal stabilizer when the stabilizer is raised or lowered. It also provides an approximately constant force gradient in the elevator control system.

A **balance tab** is similar in function to the control tab in that it is designed to assist the pilot in moving the control surface. The action of a balance tab is illustrated in Fig. 15-36. As the control surface begins to move in a certain direction, the balance tab moves in the opposite direction. This produces an aerodynamic force to help move the control surface. In some designs, the balance tab is combined in function so it can be actuated in flight. In these cases it also serves as a controllable trim tab.

Auxiliary Control Surfaces

In addition to the primary control surfaces mentioned, modern airplanes are often equipped with other surfaces which help to provide safe operation of the airplane. These surfaces are usually found on larger aircraft and those which fly at high speeds.

Among the most common types of auxiliary control surfaces are the **flaps.** An extended flap often adds to the lifting area of the wing and provides additional drag which assists in slowing the speed of the airplane. Flaps are made in various designs including the **plain flap,** the **split flap,** the **Fowler flap,** and the **slotted flap.**

The construction and operation of flaps and slats has been discussed in Chap. 1 of this text and in the associated text, *Aircraft Basic Science.*

Control systems for flaps are subject to the same principles as described in this section for other control surfaces. Rigging is adjusted to provide for the correct range of operation and to assure accurate positioning of flaps in the partially extended conditions. Flap po-

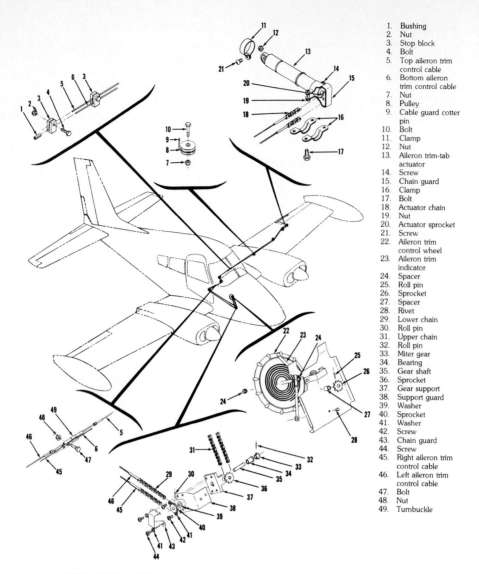

1.	Bushing
2.	Nut
3.	Stop block
4.	Bolt
5.	Top aileron trim control cable
6.	Bottom aileron trim control cable
7.	Nut
8.	Pulley
9.	Cable guard cotter pin
10.	Bolt
11.	Clamp
12.	Nut
13.	Aileron trim-tab actuator
14.	Screw
15.	Chain guard
16.	Clamp
17.	Bolt
18.	Actuator chain
19.	Nut
20.	Actuator sprocket
21.	Screw
22.	Aileron trim control wheel
23.	Aileron trim indicator
24.	Spacer
25.	Roll pin
26.	Sprocket
27.	Spacer
28.	Rivet
29.	Lower chain
30.	Roll pin
31.	Upper chain
32.	Roll pin
33.	Miter gear
34.	Bearing
35.	Gear shaft
36.	Sprocket
37.	Gear support
38.	Support guard
39.	Washer
40.	Sprocket
41.	Washer
42.	Screw
43.	Chain guard
44.	Screw
45.	Right aileron trim control cable
46.	Left aileron trim control cable
47.	Bolt
48.	Nut
49.	Turnbuckle

FIG. 15-34 Aileron trim-tab control system. (*Cessna Aircraft Co.*)

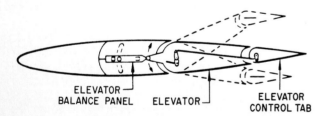

FIG. 15-35 Elevator control tab. (*Boeing Co.*)

sition indicators are included to show the pilot the degree of extension.

Flaps on large aircraft are operated electrically or hydraulically. The operation of a switch or valve control in the cockpit controls the power necessary to provide for extension and retraction.

● INSPECTION AND MAINTENANCE

The following inspections are typical of those which should be made for control systems; however, the inspections for a particular type of aircraft should fol-

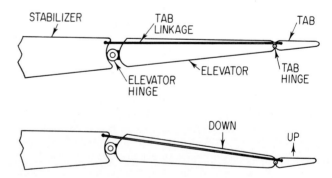

FIG. 15-36 Action of a balance tab.

low the instructions given in the manufacturer's service or maintenance manual.

1. Examine all cables for wear or corrosion. Wear will be most apparent at or near pulleys, the ends of cable fittings, fairleads, and other points where the cable may come into contact with another part of the system. Broken strands of cable can be detected by wrapping a rag around the cable and moving the rag back and forth. Cables which are badly worn, have broken strands, or are appreciably corroded should be replaced.

2. Examine all pulleys for wear, cracks, and alignment. If a pulley is worn to an appreciable extent or cracked, it should be replaced. The pulleys should turn freely when the control cables are moved. If a pulley is out of line, it will cause wear to both the pulley and the cable. The mountings for such pulleys should be corrected and the cable carefully examined for wear.

3. Where cables pass through fairleads or guides, the deflection of the cable should be noted. If it is more than 3°, a correction must be made. The wear of the cable and the fairlead should be checked.

4. Wear of pulley bearings, bearing bolts, bushings, clevis pins, and all other moving parts should be checked. Replacement must be made of all parts worn beyond specified limits.

5. Cable tension should be checked by means of a tensiometer; however, an experienced mechanic can often determine whether the tension on a small airplane system is correct by "feel." The cable tension is adjusted by means of turnbuckles. It may be necessary to check and adjust cable tensions with seasonal changes during the year as the ambient air temperatures change. This change in temperature can cause the airframe structure to expand or contract an amount different from that of the control cables due to the difference in coefficients of expansion of the airframe and cable materials. These changes may cause the cable tension to be too great or too small resulting in excessive system wear or loss of control effectiveness. Some large aircrafts incorporate cable tension regulators in their design to automatically correct for these variations.

6. The system should be checked to see that no cable fitting comes within 2 in [5.08 cm] of a pulley, fairlead, or guide when the control is moved to its limits.

7. Control-surface travel should be checked by means of a bubble protractor or a template. Travel can be adjusted by means of the stop bolts and/or rod ends. The control-surface stops should be set to make contact before the cockpit control has reached the end of its travel. The cockpit-control stops should be adjusted so they will make contact if the control-surface stop does not stop the movement of the control at the limit of its prescribed travel.

8. After all adjustments are made, all safetying of turnbuckles, clevis pins, nuts, etc., must be examined for correct application and effectiveness. Defective safetying must be corrected.

9. Upon completion of inspection, adjustment, and service, the control system should be given an operational check. The controls should move smoothly and easily through their full range of travel and should not exhibit any looseness or play. The systems must be checked for direction of control movement because it is often possible to cross cables and cause reverse movement. This is particularly true of aileron systems. When the right rudder pedal is pressed, the rudder should move to the right; when the control is pulled back, the elevator should move upward; and when the stick or wheel is moved to the right, the left aileron should move down and the right aileron should move up.

● ALIGNMENT OF STRUCTURES

When an aircraft has suffered major structural damage to the fuselage, wings, or control surfaces, it is necessary to partially disassemble the structure in order to make repairs. In such cases, it is common practice to mount the structure in a rigid steel frame (jig) to keep it in alignment while reassembling it.

One of the first steps in preparing to mount a structure in a jig is to establish an undamaged mounting point or points on the structure which can be used as a reference for locating the structure accurately and in proper alignment. Such mounting points could be the landing gear attachement points, the wing attachment points, or some other points strong enough to support the structure. When the primary reference point has been established, other points are established from reference to blueprints or the manufacturer's dimensional specifications.

On a fuselage, a variety of locations can be established by reference to a manufacturer's drawing. Both horizontal and vertical stations can be accurately located. Starting from the basic reference point, vertical and horizontal reference lines are established.

The level line to be used as a reference can be established with a spirit level, sight level, or transit. The fuselage can then be secured in the jig in a level position. When a sight level or a transit is used, the instrument must first be accurately set up. Small spirit levels are mounted on the instrument, and these are used to adjust the telescope portion of the instrument so its plane of rotation on the base will be perfectly level. The operator then knows that any point viewed at the intersection of the cross hairs in the telescope will have the same vertical distance from a level reference line as any other point viewed at the intersection of the cross hairs.

Lateral and longitudinal distances from reference points can be established by means of plumb bobs and steel tapes. In these cases, the plumb bob cord must be accurately centered at the point from or to which a measurement is to be made. Plumb bob reference points can be marked with cross lines on the shop floor.

When a fuselage or any other structure is secured in the jig with all attachment points accurately located, assembly can begin. During the process of replacing damaged parts such as skins, formers, and stringers, the structure should be checked from time to time for alignment. This will assure that when the assembly is completed, the structure will be in alignment.

The alignment of an internally braced wing is checked with trammel points on a trammel bar. Points are marked at the intersections of the center lines of the wing spars and the compression ribs. With the trammel bar, the diagonal distances between the marked points are compared. If the diagonal distances are not equal, the bay is not square (rectangular). Correction is made by adjusting the drag and antidrag wires.

● BALANCING CONTROL SURFACES

The control surfaces for new airplanes are properly balanced, both statically and aerodynamically, at the factory. After the airplane undergoes overhaul, painting, or repair of the control surfaces, the static balance may be altered to the extent that **flutter** will occur in flight. Flutter can lead to excessive stresses in flight with the result that the control surface, its attachments, and the structure near the attachments can suffer damage such as cracks or complete failure. It is, therefore, necessary that the control surface balance be checked whenever any operation is performed on a control surface which can change the static balance.

A control surface balance is checked by placing the surface on suitable bearings at the hinge line and measuring the moment forward or aft of the hinge line. At this time the control surface should be complete with all parts as it would be in flight. A new, unpainted surface should be painted before balancing. Trim tabs, pushrods, and all other parts should be included.

A diagram to illustrate the balance-checking procedure for a light airplane is shown in Fig. 15-37. In this drawing, the control surface is supported at the hinge line on a knife-edge support. A scale and screw jack are placed under the trailing edge of the surface. The screw jack is adjusted up or down to provide the correct angular reading on the bubble protractor which is placed on the top of the surface. After the correct angle is established, the protractor is removed and the reading of the scale is taken. The weight of the screw jack is subtracted from the scale reading to give the weight of the surface. The weight of the control surface at the scale support point is multiplied by the distance D to give the value of the moment. If the moment is too great, additional weight will have to be installed on the surface foward of the hinge line. Balance weights for a stabilator and an aileron are shown in the drawings of Fig. 15-38.

In some cases, balance weights consists of lead plates attached to the leading edge of the control surface. This type of installation is shown in Fig. 15-39.

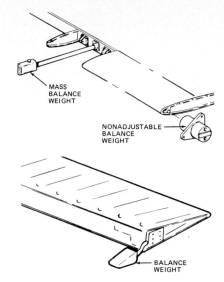

FIG. 15-38 Balance weights for stabilator and aileron. *(Piper Aircraft Co.)*

FIG. 15-39 Balance weight on an aileron.

● RIGGING OF HELICOPTERS

Controls for helicopters in some characteristics are similar to those for airplanes; however, the differences are greater than the similarities. Controls for a helicopter cause the aircraft to rise; move forward, sideways, or backwards; and change heading or turn. The main rotor provides lift and thrust while the tail rotor counteracts the torque of the main rotor and provides directional control.

The main rotor is controlled by two principal systems. These are the **collective-pitch control** and the **cyclic-pitch control.** The collective pitch control changes pitch on all blades of the main rotor simultaneously. Collective pitch is adjusted by raising or lowering the collective-pitch lever (stick).

Collective pitch and engine power control the ver-

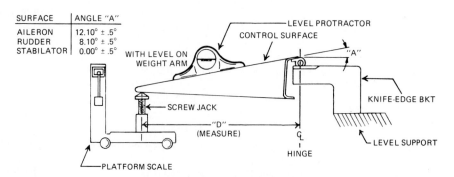

FIG. 15-37 Balance-checking procedure.

tical flight of a helicopter. To cause the helicopter to lift from the ground, the pilot raises the collective stick and at the same time increases the engine power by means of the motorcycle-type throttle control on the stick. The pilot ensures that the rotor speed is maintained constant, typically about 400 rpm, as the lift increases and the helicopter raises.

The collective-pitch control mechanism for the Bell Model 206L helicopter is shown in Fig. 15-40. The collective control utilizes the center servo and control tubes to raise and lower the swash plate to which the pitch-change link rods are attached. Adjustments are made on the control tube and link as shown to provide the correct pitch range for the rotor blades.

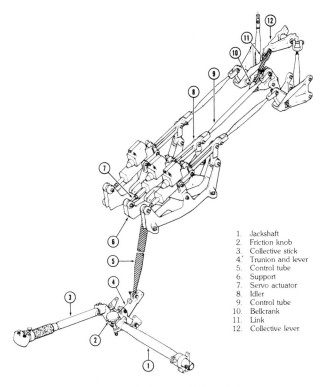

1.	Jackshaft
2.	Friction knob
3.	Collective stick
4.	Trunion and lever
5.	Control tube
6.	Support
7.	Servo actuator
8.	Idler
9.	Control tube
10.	Bellcrank
11.	Link
12.	Collective lever

FIG. 15-40 Collective-pitch control for a helicopter. (Bell Helicopter-Textron)

The **cyclic-pitch control** system is employed to change the pitch or angle of the plane or disk through which the main rotor blades rotate. The flying helicopter will move in the direction in which the rotor disk is tilted. The disk is caused to tilt because the cyclic control changes the blades pitch angles to different values as the blades rotate through their paths of travel around the disk. An upward force caused by increase of pitch on a blade at a point 90° after the blade has passed the forward point of the helicopter will cause the rotor disk to tilt forward due to gyroscopic precession. Thus when the cyclic control stick is moved forward, the up force on the rotor is applied at one side, and the rear of the disk rises.

A cyclic-pitch control system is shown in Fig. 15-41. Adjustments for the proper range of cyclic control are made by means of the control tubes indicated in the drawing.

The direction in which a helicopter is pointed is controlled by the **antitorque rotor** (tail rotor). The control system for the tail rotor is shown in the drawing of Fig. 15-42. The purpose of the system is to change the pitch of the rotor blades, thus changing the sideward thrust exerted by the rotor. The rotor speed remains essentially constant when the helicopter is in flight.

Note from the drawing that the tail rotor pitch is changed through the operation of control rods, walking beams, and bellcranks. To establish the correct range of pitch for the rotor blades, adjustments are made in the push-pull control rod ends. The system should be rigged so the foot pedals in the cockpit are in the neutral position when the tail rotor thrust balances the torque of the main rotor in normal operating conditions.

Helicopter Vibrations

The design and operating characteristics of helicopters are such that a variety of vibrations occur as a natural result of the forces generated by engines, rotors, transmissions, and other moving parts. Some types of vibrations below specified levels of intensity are expected and are acceptable. Vibrations which are abnormal or above a certain intensity cause discomfort to the crew and passengers and are likely to be damaging to the structure of the aircraft. These vibrations must be controlled or eliminated by adjusting, balancing, or repairing the areas affected.

Vibration frequencies in a helicopter are designated as **extremely low, low, medium,** and **high.** Extremely low frequency vibrations are less than one vibration cycle per revolution of the main rotor. One vibration per revolution is abbreviated 1/rev or 1:1. The extremely low vibration is limited to pylon rock and is controlled, primarily, by the design and shock mounting of the transmission.

Low-frequency vibrations, 1/rev or 2/rev, are associated with the main rotor. The 1/rev vibrations are of two basic types, vertical or lateral. In a vertical vibration, the entire helicopter tends to move up and down and in a lateral vibration one side of the helicopter moves up while the opposite side moves down, the movements occurring alternately in time with the vibration frequency.

A 1/rev vertical vibration is caused by one blade developing more lift at a given point than the other blade develops at the same point. This is due to incorrect pitch and track.

Lateral vibrations due to an unbalance in the rotor are of two types: spanwise and chordwise. Spanwise unbalance is caused by one blade and hub being heavier than the other. A chordwise unbalance occurs when there is more weight toward the trailing edge of one blade than the other.

Rigidly controlled manufacturing processes and techniques eliminate all but minor differences between blades, resulting in blades that are virtually identical. The minor differences that remain will affect flight but are compensated for by adjustments of trim tabs and pitch settings.

Medium frequencies of 4/rev or 6/rev are inherent

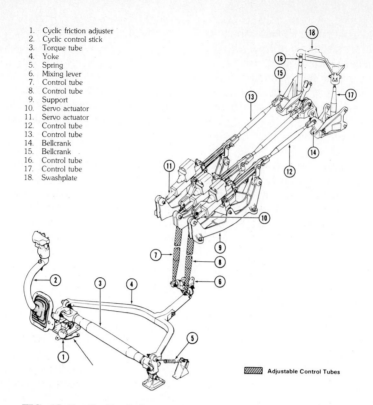

1. Cyclic friction adjuster
2. Cyclic control stick
3. Torque tube
4. Yoke
5. Spring
6. Mixing lever
7. Control tube
8. Control tube
9. Support
10. Servo actuator
11. Servo actuator
12. Control tube
13. Control tube
14. Bellcrank
15. Bellcrank
16. Control tube
17. Control tube
18. Swashplate

///// Adjustable Control Tubes

FIG. 15-41   Cyclic-pitch control system. *(Bell Helicopter-Textron)*

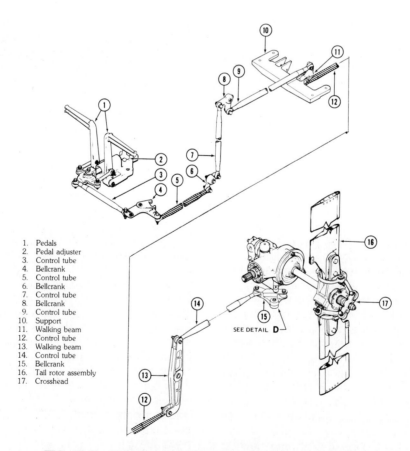

1. Pedals
2. Pedal adjuster
3. Control tube
4. Bellcrank
5. Control tube
6. Bellcrank
7. Control tube
8. Bellcrank
9. Control tube
10. Support
11. Walking beam
12. Control tube
13. Walking beam
14. Control tube
15. Bellcrank
16. Tail rotor assembly
17. Crosshead

SEE DETAIL **D**

FIG. 15-42   Tail rotor control system. *(Bell Helicopter-Textron)*

vibrations associated with most rotors. An increase in the level of these vibrations is caused by a change in the capability of the fuselage to absorb vibration, or a loose component such as the skids or landing gear vibrating at that frequency. Changes in the fuselage vibration absorption can be caused by such conditions as fuel level, external stores, structural damage, structural repairs, internal loading, or gross weight. Abnormal vibrations in the medium-frequency range are nearly always caused by something loose.

High-frequency vibrations can be caused by anything in the helicopter that vibrates or rotates at a speed equal to or greater than that of the tail rotor. Generally, determining the cause of a high-frequency vibration should begin with an examination of the tail rotor and a check of the rotor track. If these are satisfactory, the next step is to remove the rotor and balance it on a suitable stand. If tail rotor balance is satisfactory, then an inspection of the complete drive system should be made. By observing the drive shafting with the cover removed during operation, the mechanic can detect a bent drive shaft, misalignment of the drive shafting, and other possible defects.

The vibrations associated with a helicopter will be affected by the number of blades on the rotor. It is, therefore, necessary that mechanics examine the maintenance manual and vibration analysis for the type of helicopter they are troubleshooting. The general considerations discussed in this section apply, primarily, to a two-bladed rotor system.

Tracking and Balancing the Main Rotor

Tracking of a helicopter rotor simply means determining if one blade follows the path or track of the other blade or blades as they rotate during operation. The two principal methods for rotor tracking are flag tracking and stroboscopic light tracking.

Typical instructions for tracking the main rotor blades of a turbine-powered helicopter with a two-blade rotor are given below and illustrated in Fig. 15-43.

1. Construct a tracking flag from aluminum or steel tubing. The flag portion should be made of strong, lightweight fabric tape. Reinforcing tape as used in aircraft fabric work is a suitable material.

2. Color the main rotor blade tips with grease pencils. Use a different color on each tip.

3. Position trim tabs on both main rotor blades to 0° position using the tab bending tool and tab gauge.

4. Position the helicopter into the wind and on a

FIG. 15-43 Checking main rotor track with a flag. *(Bell Helicopter-Textron)*

level, hard surface. Place extra weight in the helicopter to permit application of higher power settings without hovering during tracking.

5. Mark a spot on the ground at approximately the 2 o'clock position relative to the nose of the helicopter and about 12 in [30.48 cm] outside the rotating disk area of the rotor blades. Position the base of the tracking flag on the marked spot.

6. Operate the helicopter at 100 percent N2 engine rpm. Apply sufficient collective pitch control to make the helicopter light on the ground. Maintain collective pitch setting (use collective pitch friction adjustment) and roll throttle off to reduce rpm to 70 to 75 percent N2. Remember or record torque readings when at 100 percent N2 and light on the ground, and at 70 to 75 percent N2 rpm. These same torque readings should be used during each subsequent low-speed track.

7. Position the base of the tracking flag on the previously marked spot with the tracking flag extending outward away from the rotor tip plane. The mechanic holding the tracking flag should stand with the flag in front and the advancing main rotor blades behind. The mechanic should be able to see the pilot in order to receive preplanned signals to obtain a track.

8. The mechanic, upon receiving a signal from the pilot to raise the tracking flag, will slowly raise it until it approaches the vertical position and remains outside the tip path plane.

9. At this point, the pilot should observe the relative position of the tip path plane to the center portion of the flag. The pilot will move the cyclic stick to position the tip path plane to the center portion of the tracking flag. When the tip path plane is in the desired position for tracking, the pilot will normally give a nod of the head, indicating that a track is to be taken. If the desired position is not obtained, the pilot will give a wave off until ready for tracking.

10. The mechanic, upon receiving a nod from the pilot to track the main rotor blades, will slowly rotate the tracking flag into the tip path plane. When the main rotor blades tips have touched the flag, the flag is immediately tipped away from the rotor plane.

11. The relative vertical position of the main rotor blade tips will be indicated by transfer of the colored marks from the blade tips to the flag. There should be only one mark for each main rotor blade. It is recommended that two tracks be taken prior to making any adjustments. A gust of wind or a slight movement of the controls or helicopter may cause erroneous indications. Identify original marks on the flag with a grease pencil before making the second track.

12. Inspect the tracking marks on the flag for an indication of any out-of-track condition. Identify the high main rotor blade by color marks and approximate distance between marks. Record the high main rotor blade color and dimension between track marks.

13. Shorten the pitch link assembly attached to the pitch horn of the high main rotor blade. This is accomplished by cutting and removing the lockwire and loosening the jam nuts. Align the flats on the jam nuts with the flats on the barrel. Rotate the barrel to shorten the pitch link assembly of the high main rotor blade one flat for each 1/2 in [12.7 mm] out of track. Hold the barrel stationary and torque the jam nuts 150 to 200 lb in [16.95 to 22.6 Nm] and install lockwire.

High-speed tracking is accomplished in essentially the same manner as described above except that the engine speed is set at 100 percent N2.

Balancing of rotor blades may be accomplished by a trial-and-error method or with the use of an electronic balancing system discussed later. When a 1/rev lateral vibration occurs, unbalance is known to exist in the main rotor assembly. One method for correcting the unbalance is as follows:

1. Wrap a strip of 2-in [5.08-cm] wide masking tape around one rotor blade a specified distance from the tip. This is usually only a few inches.

2. Fly the helicopter and note whether the vibration has increased or decreased in intensity.

3. If the vibration has increased in intensity, remove the tape from the first blade and place it on the other.

4. If the vibration intensity decreases when in flight, add one-quarter turn of tape to the blade and fly the helicopter again.

5. Add or remove sections of tape until the vibration has been reduced to a minimum.

6. Remove and weigh the tape.

Some helicopter blades have provision for adding or removing balance weight near the tip of the blade. In balancing this type of blade, the tape should be applied at the location where the balance weights are installed. Then the amount of balance weight required to balance the rotor will be equal to the weight of the tape required to bring the rotor in balance. Other rotors have balance weights installed near the hub. In this case, the ratio of the balance weight distance from the center of the rotor hub to the tape distance from the center of the hub will have to be applied to the tape weight to obtain the correct balance weight to be added. For example, if the balance weight location on a rotor is 50 cm from the center of the hub and the tape location during the balance check is 500 cm from the center of the hub, the ratio to be applied is 500/50 or 10. If the weight of the tape needed to correct the balance is 20 g, then 10 × 20 or 200 g will have to be added to the balance location to correct the rotor balance. The maintenance manual for the helicopter specifies the type of balances used and how they are to be installed. The mechanic must be certain to follow the instructions for the make and model of helicopter being serviced.

Electronic equipment has been developed which greatly aids in the accurate tracking and balancing of helicopter rotors. Equipment of this type is manufactured by the Chadwick-Helmuth Company and is recommended by many manufacturers and operators. This electronic equipment is designated by the trade name Vibrex Track and Balance System and is illustrated in Fig. 15-44.

The Vibrex Track and Balance System is used to correct track and balance by developing data in flight through the use of accelerometers and stroboscopic lights. The signals from these devices are referenced

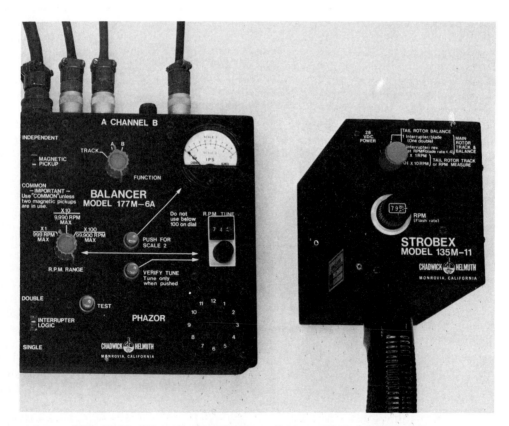

FIG. 15-44 Vibrex Track and Balance System. *(Chadwick-Helmuth Co.)*

to rotor position by means of a magnetic pickup and interrupter system. The data obtained are applied to circular charts which serve as computing devices through which the adjustments required and the amount of balance correction needed are determined.

The items required for analyzing the operation of a main rotor are a **magnetic pickup** on the fixed swashplate, **interrupters** on the rotating swashplate, **retroreflective targets** on the rotor blade tips, **accelerometers** on the airframe, a **Strobex light,** and the **electronic balancer** which includes the **Phazor.**

The magnetic pickup consists of a coil of wire wound on a permanent magnet. The center post of the magnet, on which the coil is wound, is one pole of the magnet. The cylindrical shell of the pickup is the other pole. The magnetic pickup is secured to the fixed swashplate of the main rotor and generates an electrical pulse when its magnetic flux lines are interrupted by the interrupter which is secured to the rotating swashplate and passes in proximity to the pickup gap. Interrupters must be magnetic material but must not be magnets.

Electrical pulses from the magnetic pickup are used to trigger the Strobex light each time an interrupter passes to provide light for viewing tip targets and observing the track and lead or lag of the blades. The pulses also provide an azimuth reference for the Phazor section of the balancer against which the accelerometer signal is measured to determine **clock angle.**

An accelerometer is a piezoelectric crystal device. A piezoelectric crystal produces electric current when subjected to stress. When it is attached to a vibrating part, it generates an electrical signal representative of the physical motion of the point to which it is attached. The voltage varies from plus to minus as the point vibrates back and forth, and the amplitude of the signal is proportional to the amplitude of the vibration.

Retroreflective target material is self-adhesive tape with a coating that reflects light back to its source. The balancer is the electronic circuitry which receives the signals from the accelerometers and magnetic pickup, then converts these inputs to readings that are transferred to the charts from which corrective information is obtained.

● REVIEW QUESTIONS

1. Define *aircraft rigging.*
2. What precautions must be taken in the hoisting of an aircraft?
3. What is the function of a spreader bar in a hoist?
4. What precaution must be taken if a hoist is attached to the rafters or overhead beams in a hangar?
5. What methods may be used to determine when an aircraft is level?
6. What device may be used to check aircraft dihedral?
7. What methods might be used to adjust an aircraft angle of incidence?
8. What is the purpose of a wire wrench?
9. Give a brief description of the rigging of a biplane when wings and tail surfaces are being installed.
10. Define *stagger* and *decalage* in a biplane.
11. How is the level position of an aircraft determined?
12. What is the effect of shortening the landing wires on a biplane?
13. How are washin and washout accomplished on a biplane?
14. Give the basic requirements for control-system rigging.
15. How is the cockpit control for a control system held in the neutral position while rigging?
16. How are cable tensions measured?
17. How is the travel of a control surface measured?
18. What precautions must be observed in the installation of a cable-guard pin?
19. Describe a *fairlead* and give the limit of cable deflection permitted at a fairlead.
20. What devices are used to prevent escape of air around cables passing through a bulkhead in a pressurized aircraft?
21. What design features of an aileron system are employed to overcome adverse yaw?
22. What are the effects of overtightening control cables?
23. Describe a stabilator system and how it is rigged.
24. Explain the importance of control-surface stops.
25. How are control-surface stops checked for adjustment?
26. Describe the function of *ruddervators.*
27. Discuss the use of fixed trim tabs.
28. Explain the operation of adjustable trim tabs.
29. How does an adjustable trim tab differ from a *control tab?*
30. If the trim tab on a rudder is moved to the right, what effect does it have on the flight of the aircraft?
31. Explain the operation of a *balance tab.*
32. What are the important considerations in the rigging of flaps?
33. How can a pilot tell how far the wing flaps are extended?
34. How may broken strands in a control cable be detected?
35. Describe the inspection of pulleys in a control system.
36. How close to a pulley, fairlead, or guide in a control system may a cable fitting or splice be allowed to approach?
37. What conditions are checked during the inspection of a control system?
38. What is the final inspection required for control systems?
39. What precaution must be taken in connecting control cables in a control system and how is correct connection determined?
40. What would be the effect of crossed control cables in an aileron system?
41. Give a brief description of the procedure for aligning an aircraft structure.
42. What is the purpose of a *jig?*
43. What is the purpose of a *slight level* or *transit?*

44. How is the alignment of an internally braced wing checked?
45. Briefly describe the alignment check for a complete aircraft.
46. Why is it necessary to balance control surfaces?
47. Describe how the balance of a control surface is accomplished.
48. Where are the functions of the main and tail rotors on a helicopter?
49. What systems control the operation of the main rotor of a helicopter?
50. What type of control movement induces forward flight in a helicopter?
51. How is vertical flight controlled in a helicopter?
52. How is directional control maintained in a helicopter?
53. What part of the helicopter is associated with low-frequency vibrations?
54. What are the causes of vertical and lateral vibrations in a helicopter?
55. What is the cause of a helicopter spanwise, low-frequency vibration?
56. What is the cause of an increase in medium-frequency vibrations in a helicopter?
57. What are the likely causes of high-frequency vibrations in a helicopter?
58. Describe the flag method for tracking main rotor blades.
59. How is the pitch of main rotor blades adjusted?
60. Describe a method for balancing main rotor blades.
61. Briefly discuss dynamic balancing of the main rotor blades using electronic equipment.
62. Describe the accelerometer used in dynamic rotor-blade balancing.

INDEX